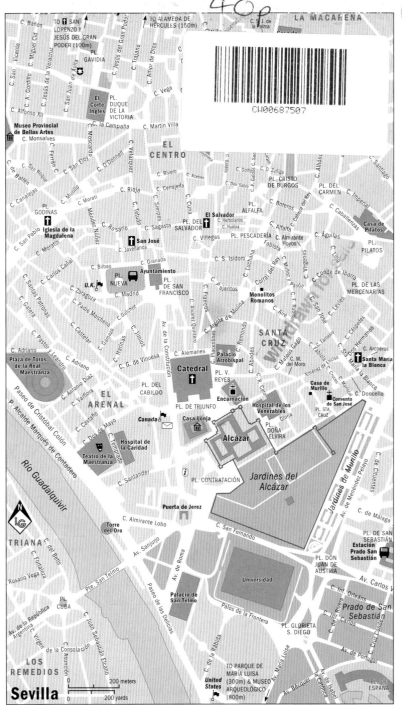

Sevilla

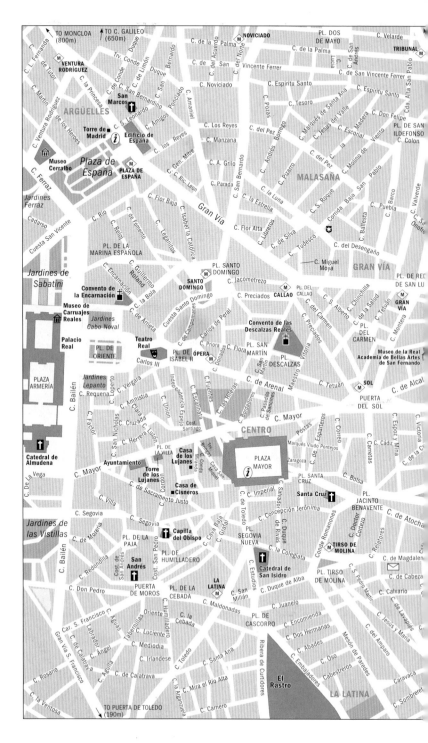

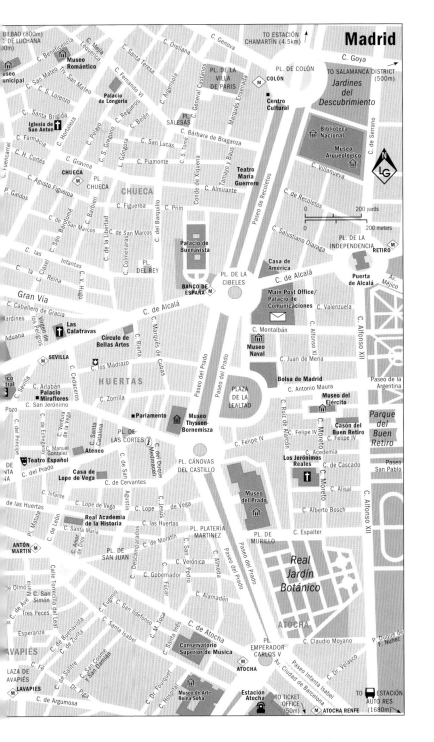

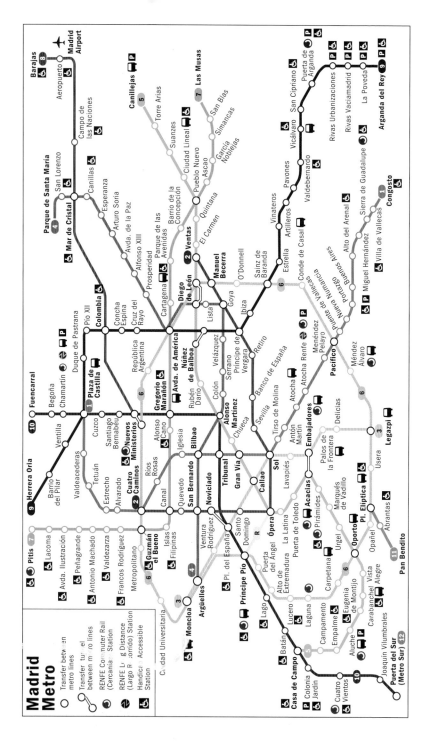

Madrid Metro

Transfer between metro lines

Transfer tunnel between metro lines

RENFE Commuter Rail (Cercanía) Station

RENFE Long Distance (Largo Recorrido) Station

Handicap Accessible Station

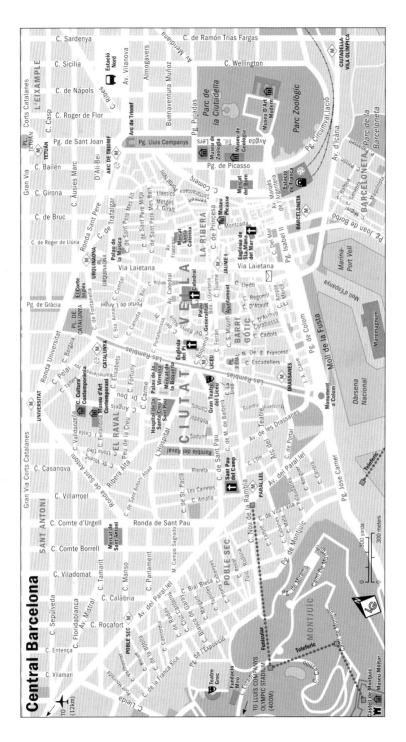

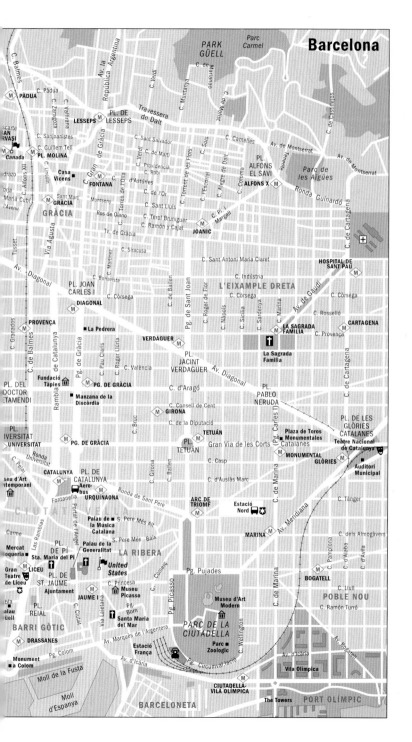

Barcelona Metro

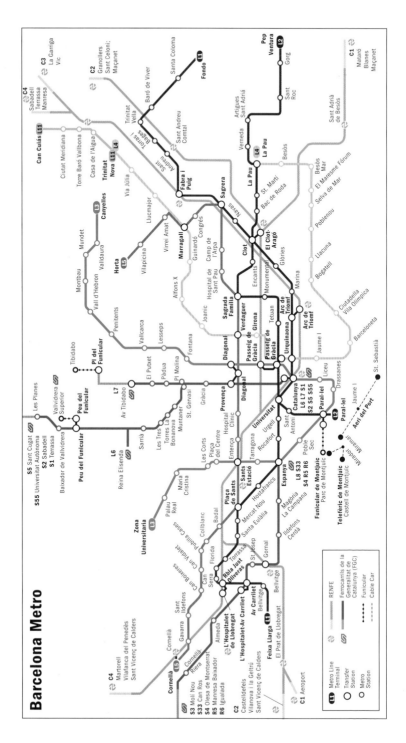

LET'S GO

■ THE RESOURCE FOR THE INDEPENDENT TRAVELER

"The guides are aimed not only at young budget travelers but at the indepedent traveler; a sort of streetwise cookbook for traveling alone."

—*The New York Times*

"Unbeatable; good sight-seeing advice; up-to-date info on restaurants, hotels, and inns; a commitment to money-saving travel; and a wry style that brightens nearly every page."

—*The Washington Post*

"Lighthearted and sophisticated, informative and fun to read. [Let's Go] helps the novice traveler navigate like a knowledgeable old hand."

—*Atlanta Journal-Constitution*

"A world-wise traveling companion—always ready with friendly advice and helpful hints, all sprinkled with a bit of wit."

—*The Philadelphia Inquirer*

■ THE BEST TRAVEL BARGAINS IN YOUR PRICE RANGE

"All the dirt, dirt cheap."

—*People*

"Anything you need to know about budget traveling is detailed in this book."

—*The Chicago Sun-Times*

"Let's Go follows the creed that you don't have to toss your life's savings to the wind to travel—unless you want to."

—*The Salt Lake Tribune*

■ REAL ADVICE FOR REAL EXPERIENCES

"The writers seem to have experienced every rooster-packed bus and lunar-surfaced mattress about which they write."

—*The New York Times*

"Value-packed, unbeatable, accurate, and comprehensive."

—*The Los Angeles Times*

"[Let's Go's] devoted updaters really walk the walk (and thumb the ride, and trek the trail). Learn how to fish, haggle, find work—anywhere."

—*Food & Wine*

LET'S GO PUBLICATIONS

TRAVEL GUIDES

Australia 8th Edition
Austria & Switzerland 12th edition
Brazil 1st edition
Britain & Ireland 2005
California 10th edition
Central America 9th edition
Chile 2nd edition
China 5th edition
Costa Rica 2nd edition
Eastern Europe 2005
Ecuador 1st edition **NEW TITLE**
Egypt 2nd edition
Europe 2005
France 2005
Germany 12th Edition
Greece 2005
Hawaii 3rd edition
India & Nepal 8th edition
Ireland 2005
Israel 4th edition
Italy 2005
Japan 1st edition
Mexico 20th edition
Middle East 4th edition
Peru 1st edition **NEW TITLE**
Puerto Rico 1st edition
South Africa 5th edition
Southeast Asia 9th edition
Spain & Portugal 2005
Thailand 2nd edition
Turkey 5th edition
USA 2005
Vietnam 1st edition **NEW TITLE**
Western Europe 2005

ROADTRIP GUIDE

Roadtripping USA **NEW TITLE**

ADVENTURE GUIDES

Alaska 1st edition
New Zealand **NEW TITLE**
Pacific Northwest **NEW TITLE**
Southwest USA 3rd edition

CITY GUIDES

Amsterdam 3rd edition
Barcelona 3rd edition
Boston 4th edition
London 2005
New York City 15th Edition
Paris 13th Edition
Rome 12th edition
San Francisco 4th edition
Washington, D.C. 13th edition

POCKET CITY GUIDES

Amsterdam
Berlin
Boston
Chicago
London
New York City
Paris
San Francisco
Venice
Washington, D.C.

LET'S GO

SPAIN AND PORTUGAL 2005

ALEXANDRA MOSS EDITOR
TIM CAITO ASSOCIATE EDITOR
DOMINIQUE ELIE ASSOCIATE EDITOR

RESEARCHER-WRITERS
PATRICK BAUR
JACOB KRAMER
DEFNE OZGEDIZ
SAM PERWIN
FERNANDO RODRIGO
OLIVIA SHABB
FELIPE A. TEWES

CLIFFORD EMMANUEL MAP EDITOR
LEIGH PASCAVAGE MANAGING EDITOR

ST. MARTIN'S PRESS ❧ NEW YORK

HELPING LET'S GO. If you want to share your discoveries, suggestions, or corrections, please drop us a line. We read every piece of correspondence, whether a postcard, a 10-page email, or a coconut. **Address mail to:**

Let's Go: Spain and Portugal
67 Mount Auburn Street
Cambridge, MA 02138
USA

Visit Let's Go at **http://www.letsgo.com,** or send email to:

feedback@letsgo.com
Subject: "Let's Go: Spain and Portugal"

In addition to the invaluable travel advice our readers share with us, many are kind enough to offer their services as researchers or editors. Unfortunately, our charter enables us to employ only currently enrolled Harvard students.

ABOUT LET'S GO

GUIDES FOR THE INDEPENDENT TRAVELER

At Let's Go, we see every trip as the chance of a lifetime. If your dream is to grab a machete and forge through the jungles of Brazil, we can take you there. If you'd rather bask in the Riviera sun at a beachside cafe, we'll set you a table. We write for readers who know that there's more to travel than sharing double deckers with tourists and who believe that travel can change both themselves and the world—whether they plan to spend six days in London or six months in Latin America. We'll show you just how far your money can go, and prove that the greatest limitation on your adventures is not your wallet, but your imagination. After all, traveling close to the ground lets you interact more directly with the places and people you've gone to see, making for the most authentic experience.

BEYOND THE TOURIST EXPERIENCE

To help you gain a deeper connection with the places you travel, our researchers give you the heads-up on both world-renowned and off-the-beaten-track attractions, sights, and destinations. They engage with the local culture, writing features on regional cuisine, local festivals, and hot political issues. We've also opened our pages to respected writers and scholars to hear their takes on the countries and regions we cover, and asked travelers who have worked, studied, or volunteered abroad to contribute first-person accounts of their experiences. We've also increased our coverage of responsible travel and expanded each guide's Alternatives to Tourism chapter to share more ideas about how to give back to local communities and learn about the places you travel.

FORTY-FIVE YEARS OF WISDOM

Let's Go got its start in 1960, when a group of creative and well-traveled students compiled their experience and advice into a 20-page mimeographed pamphlet, which they gave to travelers on charter flights to Europe. Four and a half decades later, we've expanded to cover six continents and all kinds of travel—while retaining our founders' adventurous attitude toward the world. Our guides are still researched and written entirely by students on shoestring budgets, experienced travelers who know that train strikes, stolen luggage, food poisoning, and marriage proposals are all part of a day's work. This year, we're expanding our coverage of South America and Southeast Asia, with brand-new *Let's Go: Ecuador*, *Let's Go: Peru*, and *Let's Go: Vietnam*. Our adventure guide series is growing, too, with the addition of *Let's Go: Pacific Northwest Adventure* and *Let's Go: New Zealand Adventure*. And we're immensely excited about our new *Let's Go: Roadtripping USA*—two years, eight routes, and sixteen researchers and editors have put together a travel guide like none other.

THE LET'S GO COMMUNITY

More than just a travel guide company, Let's Go is a community. Our small staff comes together because of our shared passion for travel and our desire to help other travelers see the world. We love it when our readers become part of the Let's Go community as well—when you travel, drop us a postcard (67 Mt. Auburn St., Cambridge, MA 02138, USA) or send us an e-mail (feedback@letsgo.com) to tell us about your adventures and discoveries.

For more information, visit us online: www.letsgo.com.

CONTENTS

DISCOVER SPAIN AND PORTUGAL 1
When to Go 1
What to Do 2
Suggested Itineraries 5

ESSENTIALS **8**
Planning Your Trip 8
Safety and Health 15
Getting to Spain or Portugal 21
Getting Around 30
Keeping in Touch 34
Accommodations 39
Specific Concerns 46
Other Resources 50

ALTERNATIVES TO TOURISM...... 53
A Philosophy for Travelers 53
Volunteering 53
Studying 55
Working 59

SPAIN **63**
History 63
Current Events 68
People and Culture 69
Spain Essentials 78

MADRID **85**
El Centro: Sol, Ópera, and Plaza Mayor 111
Huertas 119
Gran Vía 127
Malasaña and Chueca 129
Argüelles and Moncloa 133
Bilbao 136
San Lorenzo de El Escorial 141

COMUNIDAD DE MADRID 144
Alcalá de Henares 144
Aranjuez 146

SIERRA DE GUADARRAMA 147
Cercedilla 147
Puerto de Navacerrada and Los Cotos 149

CASTILLA Y LEÓN **150**
Segovia 150
Ávila 156
Salamanca 160
Zamora 169
León 170

Valladolid 175
Burgos 181
Palencia 186
Soria 188

**CASTILLA LA MANCHA AND
EXTREMADURA** **193**
CASTILLA LA MANCHA 193
Toledo 194
Almagro 200
Cuenca 202
Sigüenza 206

EXTREMADURA 207
Cáceres 207
Trujillo 211
Mérida 213
Badajoz 217

SEVILLA **221**
Santa Cruz 230
El Centro 235
La Macarena 238
El Arenal and Triana 240
Outer Neighborhoods 241

ANDALUCÍA **245**
Córdoba 245

COSTA DE LA LUZ 256
Huelva 256
Jerez de la Frontera 257
Sanlúcar de Barrameda 262
Arcos de la Frontera 263
Cádiz 265
Vejer de la Frontera 270
Tarifa 271
Algeciras 273
Gibraltar 275

COSTA DEL SOL 278
Málaga 279
Marbella 284
Almería 288
Mojácar 290
Ronda 293
Antequera 298
Granada 300

LAS ALPUJARRAS 312

Jaén 315
Baeza 317

VALENCIA AND MURCIA 318
VALENCIA 320
Valencia 320
Castellón (Castelló) 330
Morella 332

COSTA BLANCA 333
Alicante (Alacant) 334
Benidorm 341
Dénia 345

MURCIA 349
Murcia 349
Cartagena 353

LAS ISLAS BALEARES 355
MALLORCA (MAJORCA) 357
Palma 357
Western Mallorca 364
Northern Mallorca 366
Southeastern Mallorca 370

MENORCA 371
Mahón (Maó) 371
Ciutadella (Ciudadela) 376
Beaches 378

IBIZA (EIVISSA) 380
Ibiza City (Eivissa) 380
San Antonio de Portmany (Sant Antoni) 387

FORMENTERA 389

BARCELONA 390
Barri Gòtic and Las Ramblas 408
La Ribera 414
El Raval 417
L'Eixample 420
Montjuïc 425
The Waterfront 427
Zona Alta: Gràcia and Outer Barris 429
Montserrat 432

CATALUÑA (CATALUNYA) 434
COSTA DORADA 435
Sitges 435
Tarragona 440
Reus 445

COSTA BRAVA 448
Tossa de Mar 448

Palafrugell 453
Gerona (Girona) 456
Figueras (Figueres) 462
Cadaqués and Port Lligat 465

INLAND CATALUNYA 467
Lérida (Lleida) 467

THE PYRENEES 471
CATALAN PYRENEES 471
Ripoll 471
Puigcerdà 476
Parc Nacional d'Aigüestortes i Estany de
  Sant Maurici 478
Val d'Aran 482
Vielha 483
La Seu d'Urgell 485

ANDORRA 486
Andorra la Vella 487

ARAGONESE PYRENEES 491
Jaca 491
Valle de Hecho 494
Valle de Ansó 495
Parque Nacional de Ordesa 497
Valle de Benasque: Benasque 501

NAVARRAN PYRENEES 502
Roncesvalles 502
Valle de Roncal 505

ARAGÓN, LA RIOJA, AND NAVARRA (NAVARRE) 507
ARAGÓN 508
Zaragoza 508
Teruel 518

LA RIOJA 521
Logroño 521

NAVARRA (NAVARRE) 525
Pamplona (Iruña) 526
Estella 540

PAÍS VASCO (EUSKADI) 543
San Sebastián (Donostia) 544
Bilbao (Bilbo) 553
Guernica (Gernika) 559
Vitoria-Gasteiz 562

ASTURIAS AND CANTABRIA 567
ASTURIAS 568
Oviedo 568

Gijón 573
Llanes 577
Cangas de Onís 579
Arenas de Cabrales 581

PARQUE NACIONAL PICOS DE EUROPA 583

CANTABRIA 592
Santander 592

GALICIA (GALIZA) **601**
Santiago de Compostela 602

RÍAS BAJAS (RÍAS BAIXAS) 611
Vigo 611
Pontevedra 617

RÍAS ALTAS 622
La Coruña (A Coruña) 622
The Northern Coast 627

LAS ISLAS CANARIAS **630**

GRAN CANARIA 634
Las Palmas 634

TENERIFE 640
Santa Cruz de Tenerife 640
Los Cristianos and Playa de las Américas 644
Puerto de la Cruz 645

FUERTEVENTURA 649
Puerto del Rosario 649
Corralejo 650
Morro Jable 651

LANZAROTE 653

LA GOMERA 657
San Sebastián de la Gomera 657
Valle Gran Rey 660

PORTUGAL **662**
History 662
Current Events 666
People and Culture 666
Portugal Essentials 672

LISBOA **677**
Baixa 690
Bairro Alto 693
São Sebastião 699
Alfama 699
Graça 702
Belém 704
Sintra 710

Setúbal 715

ALGARVE AND ALENTEJO **719**

ALGARVE 719
Lagos 719
Sagres 725
Albufeira 727
Faro 729
Olhão 732

ALENTEJO 734
Évora 734
Elvas 738
Beja 740
Sines 743

RIBATEJO AND ESTREMADURA 745
Santarém 746
Peniche 750
Nazaré 753
Leiria 758
Batalha 760
Fátima 761
Tomar 764

THE NORTH **768**

DOURO AND MINHO 769
Porto (Oporto) 769
Braga 776
Parque Nacional de Peneda-Gerês 782
Viana do Castelo 784

THE THREE BEIRAS 787
Coimbra 787
Figueira da Foz 794
Aveiro 796
Guarda 799

TRÁS-OS-MONTES 802
Bragança 802
Miranda do Douro 806
Vila Real 807

APPENDIX **810**
Morocco Essentials 817
Tangier 818
Ceuta (Sebta) 818

INDEX **819**

MAP INDEX **830**

IX

ASTURIAS AND CANTABRIA
pp. 567-600

Gijón

La Coruña

ASTURIAS

Oviedo

Santander

Bilbao

Santiago de
Compostela

Cangas de Onís

CANTABRIA

GALICIA
pp. 601-629

León

Burgos

Viana do
Castelo

Bragança

Valladolid

DOURO AND
MINHO

TRÁS-OS MONTES

CASTILLA Y LEÓN
pp. 150-192

Porto

THE NORTH
pp. 768-809

Aveiro

Salamanca

THE THREE BEIRAS

Segovia

Coimbra

MADRID
pp. 85-149

PORTUGAL

Madrid

RIBATEJO AND
ESTREMADURA
pp. 745-767

Toledo

Cáceres

CASTILLA LA MANCHA
AND EXTREMADURA
p. 193-220

CASTILLA

LISBOA
pp. 677-718

Lisboa

EXTREMADURA

Setúbal

Mérida

ALENTEJO

Évora

Badajoz

Ciudad Real

Beja

ALGARVE AND
ALENTEJO
pp. 719-744

Córdoba

ANDALUCÍA
p. 245-317

Lagos

ALGARVE

Faro

SEVILLA
pp. 221-244

Granada

Málaga

ATLANTIC
OCEAN

Gibraltar

Algeciras

LAS ISLAS CANARIAS
pp. 630-661

MOROCCO

X

Spain and Portugal Chapters

AÍS VASCO
p. 543-566

itoria

FRANCE

• Pamplona

NAVARRA

THE PYRENEES
pp. 471-506

ANDORRA

ogroño
LA RIOJA

• Girona

• Zaragoza

CATALUNYA
pp. 434-470

BARCELONA
pp. 390-433

ARAGÓN, LA RIOJA,
AND NAVARRA
pp. 507-542

Tarragona

igüenza

ARAGÓN

S P A I N

Teruel •

TO
MENORCA →

Cuenca •

Mallorca
• Palma

A MANCHA

Valencia •

VALENCIA

LAS ISLAS BALEARES
pp. 355-389

Ibiza

• Eivissa/Ibiza City

Formentera

Menorca

Ciudadela •

• Mahón

Alicante •

VALENCIA AND MURCIA
pp. 318-354

Murcia •

MURCIA

MEDITERRANEAN SEA

ALGERIA

N

0   75 miles

0   75 kilometers

XI

Spain and Portugal Transportation

RESEARCHER-WRITERS

Patrick Baur   *Asturias, Cantabria, País Vasco, and the Pyrenees*

An eco-conscious researcher extraordinaire, Patrick spends his time in the States canoeing, fishing, and hiking (when he's not busy studying Environmental Science and Public Policy). His pioneer leanings were a perfect fit for the wild Picos de Europa and the Pyrenees, and he conquered them all, even if he had to hike from town to town. Always the eager budget traveler, Patrick subsisted on one granola bar for three days in the Parque Nacional de Ordesa.

Jacob Kramer   *Madrid, Castilla La Mancha, and Las Islas Canarias*

Notebook at his side and adventurous spirit dying to be tested, Jacob conquered everything from the clubs of Chueca to the volcanoes and sweet, sweet waves of the Canaries. Although the women of Spain's tourist offices broke his heart on a daily basis, he still managed to get what he needed from them. This intrepid filmmaker has a great eye for all things hip, can spot an El Greco from miles away, and is prepared to face down any old bull that charges him.

Defne Ozgediz   *Galicia, Castilla y León, and Trás-Os-Montes*

The title "Super RW" does not do justice to Defne. Always on top of her game, she sent back impeccable copy week after week. If it weren't for her dedication she might have stayed forever in Santiago, her newfound love, but this *Let's Go* veteran and world traveler pressed on, battling illness, injury, and the Spanish incomprehension of the word *"vegetariano."* She took the northwest by storm, only to prove that this underappreciated region is really where it's at.

Sam Perwin   *Valencia, Murcia, and Las Islas Baleares*

An opera singer and fluent Spanish speaker, Sam wrote his thesis on *Don Juan* and then took on the title role himself while researching the Mediterranean coast. A Miami native, he was more than qualified to evaluate its seemingly endless beaches, and his nightlife write-ups are unrivaled anywhere in the series. With an intuitive understanding of the *Let's Go* style, Sam completely revamped our coverage of Valencia and found great new spots to chill all along his route.

Fernando Rodrigo   *Portugal*

This macho man from Peru went to Portugal in search of three things: *futebol*, beer, and bulls. Hitting Lisboa at the same time as the Eurocup 2004 and its hordes of fans, he drank his way up the coast to Porto, leaving a swath of opinionated coverage in his path. Quick to debate philosophy or politics with anyone from the most grandmotherly of hostel owners to the most quizzical Englishman, he perfected his Portuguese while updating *Let's Go* with inimitable style.

Olivia Shabb   *Andalucía, Extremadura, and the Algarve*

Olivia left her editors speechless. This wild child from Lebanon cheered us on in spirit—and in the form of a giant self-portrait she left behind in the office. Never slow to invent a word to express exactly what she meant, she covered all of the Moorish south with more enthusiasm than *Let's Go* has seen in years. Olivia subsisted almost entirely on tomatoes and cheese while trekking across Andalucía, and, as she would say herself, the experience "transperced" her.

Felipe A. Tewes   *Barcelona, Catalunya, Aragón, and La Rioja*

Let's Go map in hand, Felipe scoured the streets of Barcelona to "chillax" at its hippest cafes and restaurants. This trooper from Venezuela and Florida set out on a self-proclaimed "gelato tour" of Spain's northeastern coast, letting nothing from cliffs to quarrelsome nightclub owners get in the way of his meticulous research. An expert in all things Latin American, Felipe was a quick study of the unique Catalan culture, and sent it home in his leviathan dispatches.

CONTRIBUTING WRITERS

Dr. Gloria Totoricagüena Egurrola received her Ph.D. from the London School of Economics and Political Science and is currently an Assistant Professor at the University of Nevada, Reno Center for Basque Studies.

Peter Brown was a researcher in Portugal for *Let's Go: Spain and Portugal 2004*.

HOW TO USE THIS BOOK

THE LAY OF THE LAND. Coverage of Spain spirals out counter-clockwise from Madrid, ending in Las Islas Canarias. Coverage of Portugal starts in Lisboa and then runs from the south to the north.

GETTING AROUND. Transportation information is listed in the departure city for most destinations. The information for some daytrips and smaller towns may appear only in the listings for those destinations. Parentheticals usually list the duration, schedule, and price of a one-way trip. For help planning a trip by rail, check out the **Spain and Portugal Transportation** map, on p. xii.

PRICE DIVERSITY. Our researchers list establishments in order of value from best to worst, with favorites denoted by the *Let's Go* thumbs-up (🖰). Since the best value does not always mean the cheapest price, we have incorporated a system of price ranges for food and accommodations. For price ranges, see p. xviii.

PHONE CODES AND TELEPHONE NUMBERS. City codes appear opposite the name of the city next to the ☎ icon and are always listed as part of local numbers. Phone numbers in text are also preceded by the ☎ icon.

LANGUAGE. Translations of words and phrases in foreign languages appear in parentheses directly following them. City and provincial names in this guide are listed in Castilian first, followed by the regional language in parentheses where appropriate. Information within cities is listed in the regional language. For details on Spanish, Portuguese, and regional languages, see the **Language** sections for each country (p. 69 and p. 666, respectively), or the **Appendix** (p. 810).

WHEN TO USE IT

TWO MONTHS BEFORE. The first chapter, **Discover Spain and Portugal** (p. 1), lists highlights of the region, including **Suggested Itineraries** (p. 5) that may help you plan your trip. The **Essentials** section (p. 8) has practical info on setting a budget, getting a passport, buying tickets, etc., and has lots of useful travel tips.

ONE MONTH BEFORE. Make a list of **packing** essentials (p. 14) and shop for anything you're missing. Read through the coverage and make sure you understand the logistics of your itinerary. Make any necessary reservations.

2 WEEKS BEFORE. Leave an itinerary and copies of important documents with someone at home. Peruse the introductory chapters for **Spain** (p. 63) and **Portugal** (p. 662), which have info on history, culture, current events, and more.

ON THE ROAD. The **Appendix** contains a **glossary, phrasebooks, distance** and **climate charts,** a **time zone map,** and other info for the road, including essentials for daytripping to **Morocco** (p. 817). The **Inside Back Cover** is also a handy reference tool.

A NOTE TO OUR READERS. The information for this book was gathered by *Let's Go* researchers from May through August of 2004. Each listing is based on one researcher's opinion, formed during his or her visit at a particular time. Those traveling at other times may have different experiences since prices, dates, hours, and conditions are always subject to change. You are urged to check the facts presented in this book beforehand to avoid inconvenience and surprises.

ACKNOWLEDGMENTS

LET'S GO

THE TEAM THANKS: Julie, Leanna, and Brie for putting up with us and tantalizing us with talk of Greece; Leigh for turning ideas and words into a book; our RWs for making our lives and jobs easy; our faithful iguanas, the town of Puigcerdà, and , , and .

ALI THANKS: Domi, for your questions, your enthusiasm, your unceasing ability to make yourself (and me) laugh, and your willingness to learn. Tim, for being more on top of things than I was half the time, helping out without being asked, and knowing what I'm going to say. I'm proud of both of you guys. Cliff, for putting up with minutiae. Leigh, for giving me freedom and responsibility. The good folks at the ▨OED. The Dane St. extended family, for a fantastic summer, great food, and parties. Matt, for text message mantras. Jay, for spreading the love. Mom, for always being there when I just needed to talk. Dad, for getting me hooked on Spain (and the world) to begin with.

TIM THANKS: Ali, for your encyclopedic knowledge of all things Spanish and the long hours you spent at the office bringing your vision for this book to life. Domi, for the cool tunes and your ability to stay level-headed no matter what came our way. Clay, for lunchtime transatlantic phone calls. My family, for your unending belief and encouragement. All of my friends for the emails and support, even if we've been scattered to all corners of the globe—which of you will I see first in a Norwegian ice chapel?

DOMI THANKS: Ali, for long nights that kept us ahead of schedule, always having the right answer, sharing your love of Spain, and making me more excited than I could ever be. Tim, for making the trek to the other side of the pod every time I had a question and easing my anxious first-timer worries with your wise words. Thank you guys for laughing with me, listening to stories of trips-to-be, and most of all guiding me through this. Thanks to my friends, Mami, Daddy, and Fabi for all your support.

CLIFF THANKS: RWs for your hard work and intra-tearsheet surprises, Ali for your minutiae, Elizabeth for helping me scale my enormous pile of edits.

Editor
Alexandra Moss
Associate Editors
Tim Caito, Dominique Elie
Managing Editor
Leigh Pascavage
Map Editor
Clifford Shawn Emmanuel
Typesetter
Amelia Aos Showalter

Publishing Director
Emma Nothmann
Editor-in-Chief
Teresa Elsey
Production Manager
Adam R. Perlman
Cartography Manager
Elizabeth Halbert Peterson
Design Manager
Amelia Aos Showalter
Editorial Managers
Briana Cummings, Charlotte Douglas, Ella M. Steim, Joel August Steinhaus, Lauren Truesdell, Christina Zaroulis
Financial Manager
R. Kirkie Maswoswe
Marketing and Publicity Managers
Stef Levner, Leigh Pascavage
Personnel Manager
Jeremy Todd
Low-Season Manager
Clay H. Kaminsky
Production Associate
Victoria Esquivel-Korsiak
IT Director
Matthew DePetro
Web Manager
Rob Dubbin
Associate Web Manager
Patrick Swieskowski
Web Content Manager
Tor Krever
Research and Development Consultant
Jennifer O'Brien
Office Coordinators
Stephanie Brown, Elizabeth Peterson

Director of Advertising Sales
Elizabeth S. Sabin
Senior Advertising Associates
Jesse R. Loffler, Francisco A. Robles, Zoe M. Savitsky
Advertising Graphic Designer
Christa Lee-Chuvala

President
Ryan M. Geraghty
General Manager
Robert B. Rombauer
Assistant General Manager
Anne E. Chisholm

①②③④⑤

PRICE RANGES>>SPAIN AND PORTUGAL

Our researchers list establishments in order of value from best to worst; our favorites are denoted by the Let's Go thumbs-up (🖐). Since the best value is not always the cheapest price, however, we have also incorporated a system of price ranges, based on a rough expectation of what you will spend. For **accommodations,** we base our range on the cheapest price for which a single traveler can stay for one night. For **restaurants** and other dining establishments, we estimate the average amount a traveler will spend. The table below tells you what you will *typically* find in Spain and Portugal at the corresponding price range; keep in mind that no system can allow for every individual establishment's quirks.

ACCOMMODATIONS	RANGE	WHAT YOU'RE *LIKELY* TO FIND
❶	under €15	Campsites or dorm rooms. Expect bunk beds and a communal bath; you may have to provide or rent towels and sheets.
❷	€15-25	Upper-end hostels or small hotels. You may have a private bathroom, or there may be a sink in your room and communal shower in the hall. Breakfast of toast and coffee may be included.
❸	€26-35	A small room with a private bath. Breakfast may be included in the price of the room.
❹	€36-45	Similar to 3, but may have more amenities, such as phone and TV or be in a more touristed area.
❺	over €45	Upscale hotels or unique inns. If it's a 5 and it doesn't have what you want, you're paying too much.
FOOD	RANGE	WHAT YOU'RE *LIKELY* TO FIND
❶	under €6	Mostly street-corner stands, cafeterias, and *kebap* or fast-food joints. Rarely ever a sit-down meal.
❷	€6-10	Some sandwiches and *menús*, but also options outside of urban centers like Madrid and Barcelona.
❸	€11-15	Entrees are more expensive, but chances are you're paying for decor and ambience. Tip will add a couple euros, since you'll probably have a waiter or waitress.
❹	€16-25	As in 3, the higher prices are probably related to better service, but in these restaurants, the food will tend to be a fancier, more elaborate, or exotic to Iberian palates.
❺	over €25	Expect delicious food with great service in a well-appointed space; otherwise you're paying for nothing more than hype.

DISCOVER SPAIN AND PORTUGAL

SPAIN

Spain is colorful and playful, cultured and refined. It is a country offering equally generous portions of art, architecture, beaches, and nightlife. Its people have a joyful, social lifestyle that they are eager to share, and the wildly diverse regions assure something for everyone. Art lovers flock to northeastern Spain to see trend-setting Barcelona, the rugged coastline that inspired Dalí, and Bilbao's shining Guggenheim Museum. Adventure-seekers trek through the dizzying Pyrenees and Picos de Europa, while architectural enthusiasts explore the Baroque cathedrals of Galicia, Antoni Gaudí's Modernista conjurings in Catalunya, and the Arab intricacies of Andalucía. Flamenco, bullfighting, and tapas, Spain's most familiar cultural expressions, also hail from Andalucía, while Madrid, Barcelona, and Ibiza do enough insane, all-night partying to make up for every early-to-bed grandmother the world over. Spain is the perfect destination for first-time travelers, seasoned adventurers, families with children, or college students in search of fast, easy fun. Once you're there, you'll wonder why you never came before.

PORTUGAL

Sandwiched between Spain and the Atlantic Ocean, Portugal is often unjustly overshadowed by its Western European neighbors. Most people know it only as the inventor of sugary-sweet port wine and the former home of intrepid, globe-trotting explorers. Travelers who come to Portugal today will discover one of Europe's newest hotspots. Lisboa, the capital and largest city, has the country's most impressive imperial monuments, while the southern Algarve boasts spectacular beaches and wild nightlife, drawing backpackers in droves. Northern Coimbra crackles with the energy of a university town, and Porto surpasses even Lisboa in sophisticated elegance. Portugal's small inland towns retain a timeless feel, with medieval castles overlooking rushing rivers and peaceful town squares. The wild northern hinterlands, where some villages have not changed in nearly a millennium, are perhaps the country's most unique region; the land in Trás-Os-Montes is among the most pristine in all of Europe.

WHEN TO GO

Summer is **high season** *(temporada alta)* for coastal and interior regions in Spain and Portugal; winter is high season for ski resorts and the Canary Islands. In many parts of Spain and Portugal, high season begins during **Semana Santa** (Holy Week; Mar. 21-27 in 2005) and includes festival days. Tourism on the Iberian Peninsula reaches its height in August; the coastal regions overflow while inland cities empty out, leaving closed offices, restaurants, and lodgings. As a general rule, always make **reservations** if you plan to travel in June, July, or August.

Traveling in the **low season** *(temporada baja)* has many advantages, most noticeably lighter crowds and lower prices. Many hostels cut their prices by at least 30%, and reservations are seldom necessary. While major cities and university towns may exude energy during these months, many smaller seaside spots are ghost towns, and tourist offices and sights cut their hours nearly everywhere. For a temperature table, see **Climate**, p. 810. For a chart of **National Holidays** in Spain, see p. 77; and in Portugal, p. 671.

1

TOP 10 WILD PARTIES

We know why you really want to go to Spain and Portugal, and it's not for the food, the art, or the history. You've heard about the wild parties—the over-the-top nightlife and exuberant festivals—and you can't wait to join the fun. Get your party started here:

1. Spain's most famous fiesta takes place in **Pamplona** (p. 526) from July 5-13, when they honor San Fermín by running after bulls and drinking for a week.

2. Ibiza (p. 380) is indisputably the clubbing capital of the world, with loud discos, renowned DJs, and lots of beautiful people.

3. Lisboa's **Bairro Alto** (p. 693) is the hipster hangout of Portugal, crammed with bars, clubs, and trendy 20-somethings.

4. Sitges (p. 435) is where party people from Barcelona head for raucous beachside revelry.

5. The Algarve heats up in **Lagos** (p. 719), a world-famous backpacker party town.

6. Hit up the themed discos of **Salamanca** (p. 160), home to 50,000 party-hungry students.

7. Cruise the oceanfront clubs of **Benidorm** (p. 334), with the best gay nightlife west of Ibiza.

8. Fall for Valencia during **Las Fallas** (p. 328), a festival that rocks the city March 11-18.

9. Wave a flag at Gay Pride, which takes over the Madrid neighborhood of **Chueca** (p. 129) in June.

10. Alicante (p. 334) is wild all year, but it's best June 20-29, during the **Festival de Sant Joan.**

WHAT TO DO

There are as many ways to see Spain and Portugal as there are places to go. One could search out every Baroque chapel, spend weeks trekking on some of Europe's best trails, or hop from city to city indulging cosmopolitan fantasies.

IT'S IN THE BLOOD

Spain and Portugal are *alive*. Two millennia of invaders have swept over these countries, resulting in a vibrant and eclectic culture filled with custom, religion, history, and an irrepressible energy. You can see it in Madrid's famous nightlife (p. 109), in the sidewalk cafes of Lisboa (p. 677), and above all in the spectacular festivals. During **Queima das Fitas** in Coimbra (p. 792), **Las Fallas** in Valencia (p. 328), the **Feria de Abril** in Sevilla (p. 230), and the infamous **San Fermín** in Pamplona (p. 532), there is no denying Iberia's overwhelming cultural exuberance.

Still, like all passions, it's not entirely manic—the poignant expressions of heartbreak are often as blood-quickening as the celebrations. The ritually tragic emotions of flamenco and *fado* bring tears to the eyes of even the most macho bullfighters, who in turn create their own tragedies on the bullring sand. Actual tragedy on a national scale scarred Spain during a good part of this century—Picasso's powerfully symbolic **Guernica** (p. 124) and the propagandistic **Valle de los Caídos** (p. 143) give travelers a taste of the pain of fascism, while **Madrid** recovers from the terrorist attacks of March 2004 (p. 82). All of this emotional heritage demands a break now and then. There is ample opportunity for peace and quiet here as well: the thin-aired reverence of **Montserrat** (p. 432), the serenity of a rowboat in **El Retiro** (p. 137), or the surreal calm of **Parc Güell** (p. 431).

ARCHITECTURE

From traditionally conservative to unconventionally decadent, the buildings and monuments of Iberia form a collage of architectural styles. The remains of ancient civilizations are everywhere—from the Celtiberian tower of **O Castro de Baroña** (p. 610) and the Punic walls of **Cartagena** (p. 353) to Roman ruins like the aqueduct in **Segovia** (p. 154) and the amphitheater in **Mérida** (p. 216). Hundreds of years of Moorish rule left breathtaking monuments all over Iberia, including Granada's spectacular **Alhambra** (p. 306), Córdoba's **Mezquita** (p. 251), and Sintra's **Castelo dos Mouros** (p. 713). The Catholic church has spent immense sums of money to build some of the world's most ornate religious complexes, ranging from the pastiche of the **Convento de Cristo** (p. 766) to the imposing **El Escorial** (p. 142), from which the Inquisition was conducted. Spain's magnificent cathedrals are Gothic, Plateresque, or just plain bizarre, as with Gaudí's magnificent, still-unfinished **Sagrada Família** in Barcelona (p. 423), a brilliant climax of the Modernista style. Modern additions to Iberia's rich architectural landscape include Lisboa's expansive **Parque das Nações** (p. 703), Bilbao's shining **Guggenheim Museum** (p. 557), and Valencia's huge **Ciudad de las Artes y las Ciencias** (p. 325).

NATURE

Iberia's best-kept secrets are its sprawling national parks and soaring, snowy mountain ranges. **Andorra,** in the heart of the Pyrenees, has easily accessible glacial valleys, rolling forests, and wild meadows (p. 486). In northern Spain, the **Parque Nacional de Ordesa** (p. 497) offers well-kept trails along jagged rock faces, rushing rivers, and thundering waterfalls, and the **Parc Nacional d'Aigüestortes** (p. 478) hides 50 ice-cold mountain lakes in its 24,700 acres of rugged peaks and valleys. The **Picos de Europa** (p. 583) offer some of Europe's best mountaineering. Northern Portugal's **Parque Natural de Montesinho** (p. 805) is probably the most isolated, untouched land in all of Europe. Farther south, greenery-starved *madrileños* hike through the **Sierra de Guadarrama** (p. 147), and nature-lovers are drawn to Andalucía's huge **Parque Nacional Coto de Doñana** (p. 262), which protects nearly 60,000 acres of land for threatened wildlife. **Las Alpujarras** (p. 312), the southern slopes of the Sierra Nevada, are perfect for hiking among Spain's famous *pueblos blancos* (white towns), while trails in **Mallorca** (p. 357) and the **Canary Islands** (p. 630) juxtapose mountain peaks with ocean horizons.

BEACHES

It would be a shame to spend your *entire* time in Spain and Portugal beach-hopping, but if you were to insist, the options are virtually endless. Marc Chagall deemed the red-cliffed shores of **Tossa de Mar** (p. 448) "Blue Paradise." **San Sebastián's** (p. 544) calm, voluptuous Playa de la Concha attracts young travelers from around the world, while **Santander** (p. 592) caters to an elite, refined clientele. The beaches of **Galicia** (p. 601) curve around crystal-green, misty inlets. On the **Islas Baleares** (p. 355) and **Canarias** (p. 630), glistening bodies crowd

TOP 10 PLACES TO LIVE LIKE A KING

On a peninsula that's played host to so many civilizations, it makes sense that many rulers have left behind their lodgings. Explore the homes of royalty past and imagine yourself in charge—or at least in the lap of luxury. Put on a crown and head here:

1. The **Palácio Nacional de Sintra** (p. 714) housed Moors, Christians, and tiles galore.

2. Eat strawberries and cream like the Queen did at the **Palacio Real** in Aranjuez (p. 116).

3. Wander through the wonder that is the **Alhambra** (p. 306), home to the Nasrid dynasty.

4. Hit the slopes with Prince Felipe and Letizia in **Val d'Aran** (p. 482), today's royal retreat.

5. Sevilla's **Alcázar** (p. 252) is the oldest European palace that's still used as a royal residence.

6. Relive the succession of power at the **Castelo de São Jorge** (p. 701) in Lisboa, home to Visigoths, Moors, and Portuguese.

7. Relax at **La Granja** (p. 156), the most extravagant of Spain's four royal retreats.

8. Wonder at the size of the **Palácio Nacional de Mafra** (p. 708), which took 50,000 workers and 30 years to build.

9. Revel in the majesty of the facade of the **Paszo de Raxoi** (p. 607), a former royal palace in Santiago de Compostela.

10. The **Parque del Buen Retiro** (p. 137) in Madrid is the garden of a destroyed palace—and the perfect place to exhale.

the chic beaches, and southern Spain's infamous **Costa del Sol** (p. 278) brings tourists to its scorched Mediterranean bays by the plane-load. The eastern **Costa Blanca** (p. 333) mixes small-town charm with ocean expanses, and the looming cliffs and turquoise waters of Portugal's southern **Algarve** (p. 719) adorn hundreds of postcards.

NIGHTLIFE

Nightlife in Spain and Portugal can be relaxing—whether sipping a cold beer in a local bar or people-watching in the town square. But who really wants that? Just setting foot outdoors is likely to lead to events of unabashed hedonism unlike anything you've ever experienced. With countless bars and clubs and an incredible, intoxicating energy, **Madrid** (p. 85) has earned international renown as one of the greatest party cities in the world. **Barcelona's** (p. 390) wild, edgy nightlife reflects the city's outrageous sense of style. Residents of **Sevilla** (p. 221) pack discos floating on the Río Guadalquivir to drink and dance the night away, and only on **Ibiza** (p. 380), the jetset's favorite party island, will you find the world's largest club filled with 10,000 decadent partiers. Student-packed **Salamanca** (p. 160) is a crazed, international game of "find-your-fling," and **Lagos,** Portugal (p. 719), has more bars and backpackers per square meter than any town in the world.

■ **LET'S GO PICKS**

BEST PLACE TO STUPIDLY ENDANGER YOUR LIFE: Pamplona (S), during the infamous Running of the Bulls (p. 526).

BEST UNFINISHED BUILDING: La Sagrada Família, Gaudí's masterpiece in Barcelona (S). 120 years under construction, and counting (p. 423).

BEST PLACE TO LOSE YOUR WOMAN: Mallorca (S), where Frédéric Chopin and George Sand spent a winter of passion and discontent (p. 355).

BEST PRESERVED BODY PARTS: San Vicente's hand (p. 326), a treasure of the Catedral de Valencia (S), rivals **Santa Teresa's finger** (p. 160), stored in her convent in Ávila (S).

BEST PLACE TO SEE A BURNING BUSH: Parque Nacional de Timanfaya, in the Islas Canarias (S), where volcanic fires burn just below ground (p. 654).

BEST PLACE TO SEE STONE PANCAKES: Sierra de Torcal, outside Antequera (S), the closest thing Spain has to Mars (p. 300).

BEST PLACE TO ATTACK OTHER TOURISTS: Festa de São João, in Braga (P), where for one evening in June, the entire town beats each other over the head with hammers (p. 780).

BEST PLACE TO SPOON A STRANGER: Refugio L'Atalaya, in the Parque Nacional de Ordesa (S), where tight quarters make for fast friends (p. 497).

BEST EXAMPLE OF MEDIEVAL RECYCLING: 5000 unwitting skeletons went into the making of Évora's (P) macabre **Capela dos Ossos** (p. 731).

BEST PLACE TO SLEEP SOUNDLY: The **hanging houses** of Cuenca (S) will give you acrophobic dreams (p. 204).

BEST SINFULLY DELICIOUS DESSERTS: The heavenly **pastries** made by the cloistered nuns of Sevilla's (S) Convento de Santa Inés (p. 237).

BEST PLACE TO SIT ON THE THRONE: In Sintra's **Palácio de Pena** (P), the Queen had a gold-tiled toilet (p. 714).

SUGGESTED ITINERARIES

THE BEST OF SPAIN AND PORTUGAL (6 WEEKS) Start the party off in **Madrid** (4 days, p. 85), with a daytrip to the twisting, medieval streets of **Toledo** (p. 194). Visit the ancient college town of **Salamanca** (2 days, p. 160) before traversing north to the mystical city of **Santiago de Compostela** (2 days, p. 602), with a foray to **Cabo Finisterre** (p. 609). Hop the border into **Portugal,** heading down to unpretentious **Porto** (2 days, p. 769), and then to **Aveiro** (1 day, p. 796), the beachside "Venice of Portugal." Continue to the vibrant university town of **Coimbra** (1 day, p. 787). Immerse yourself in the sights, sounds, and cafes of **Lisboa** (3 days, p. 677) with a day on the beach at **Cascais** (p. 706), followed by the castle-filled town of **Sintra** (1 day, p. 710). To the south lie the beaches and cliffs of the Algarve; stop in **Lagos** (1 day, p. 719) to dance the night away. Catch your shut-eye on the 7hr. bus from Lagos to **Sevilla** (2 days, p. 221) and prepare for a romantic stroll along the Río Guadalquivir. Next, head up to **Córdoba** (2 days, p. 257), once the largest city in the world but now just one of the prettiest, with

its gargantuan Mezquita, and **Granada** (2 days, p. 300), home of the world-famous Alhambra. Enjoy the beaches and vibrant nightlife in **Alicante** (1 day, p. 334), before heading up the Mediterranean Coast to **Valencia** (2 days, p. 320), where the food—paella and oranges—rivals the new planetarium as the top attraction. Hop over to **Ibiza** (2 days, p. 380) in the Islas Baleares for decadence, discos, and debauchery. Return to the mainland at **Barcelona** (4 days, p. 390), one of Europe's most vibrant cities, full of Modernista architecture and fierce nightlife, with a night-trip to **Sitges** (p. 435) for even more revelry. Visit Spain's second most popular museum, the Teatre-Museu Dalí in **Figueres** (1 day, p. 462) before heading on to **San Sebastián** (2 days, p. 544), where the city meets the beach, and **Bilbao** (1 day, p. 553), home to the Guggenheim. Enjoy the beaches and boardwalks of **Santander** (2 day, p. 592) for some relaxation before daring to try the *morcilla* (blood sausage) of **Burgos** (1 day, p. 181) and marvel at its Gothic cathedral. Wrap it all up in the magical Alcázar of **Segovia** (1 day, p. 150).

DISCOVER

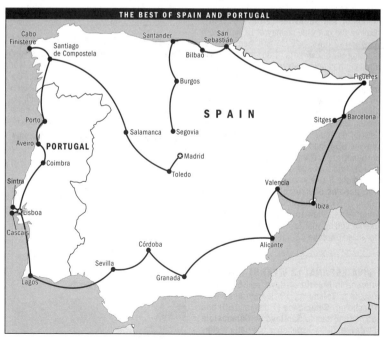

THE BEST OF SPAIN AND PORTUGAL

OFF THE BEATEN CAMINO (4 WEEKS)

Start in Malasaña and Argüelles, the neighborhoods where locals hang out in **Madrid** (3 days, p. 85) before heading out to **Burgos** (2 days, p. 181), the untouched heart of Castilla y León. Next, check out the Galician mystery that is **Santiago de Compostela** (3 days, p. 602), making time for daytrips to idyllic **Túy** (p. 616) and eerie **Cabo Finisterre** (p. 609). Gaze out to sea from the lighthouse in **A Coruña** (1 day, p. 622) before trekking through the rugged wilderness of the **Picos de Europa** (3 days, p. 583). Unwind on the low-key beaches of **Llanes** (1 day, p. 577) and on the city-front sands of **San Sebastián** (2 days, p. 544). Explore the rich wine country of La Rioja from **Logroño** (2 days, p. 521) and then the arid, bustling city of **Zaragoza** (1 day, p. 508). Take the long bus ride to **Morella** (1 day, p. 332), an undisturbed medieval town where truffles reign supreme, and continue south along the coast to **Valencia** (2 days, p. 320) to experience one of Spain's most unique big cities. Inland **Murcia** (1 day, p. 349) sees few tourists for no good reason, while **Cartagena** (1 day, p. 353) has more visitors, drawn by its intriguing ruins. **Granada** (1 day, p. 300) isn't exactly undiscovered, but the Alhambra (and the unique Sacromonte quarter) is a must-see. The *pueblos blancos* of **Las Alpujarras** (2 days, p. 312), which dot the Sierra Nevada mountains, allow for great hiking or biking before ending your journey in flower- and history-filled **Córdoba** (2 days, p. 257).

¡VIVA ESPAÑA! (3 WEEKS)

Begin *la marcha* in **Madrid** (4 days, p. 85), with a daytrip to **Toledo** (p. 194). Then head west to scholarly **Salamanca** (1 day, p. 160) and up north to sacred **Santiago de Compostela** (1 day, p. 602). Experience the natural glory of the **Picos de Europa** (2 days, p. 583) before enjoying some topless tanning in **San Sebastián** (1 day, p. 544). Venture to Spain's coastal jewel, **Barcelona** (3 days, p. 390), a pleasure for art, food, and clubbing lovers alike, and head over to **Sitges** (p. 435) for a night of fabulous partying. Then say hello to Dalí in **Figueres** (1 day, p. 462) before cruising down the coast to open-hearted **Valencia** (2 days, p. 320) and vibrant **Alicante** (1 day, p. 334). Head next to **Córdoba** (2 days, p. 257), the "city of three cultures," before ending in **Sevilla** (2 days, p. 221), where flamenco was born.

SEE YA IN ANDALUCÍA (2 WEEKS)

Whisk away from Madrid on the high-speed AVE train to **Córdoba** (2 days, p. 257) to tour the Mezquita mosque-turned-cathedral. Zip back on the AVE to **Sevilla** (3 days, p. 221) to inspect the three towers dedicated to gold, silver, and God. A quick trip down to Costa de la Luz yields the soft sand of **Cádiz's** beaches (2

days, p. 265). Move into the heart of Andalucía and the classic *pueblo blanco* **Arcos de la Frontera** (1 day, p. 263). Marvel at the *gorgeous* sights in **Ronda** (1 day, p. 293) before partying in the Costa del Sol resort town of **Marbella** (2 days, p. 284). Continue inland to **Granada** (2 days, p. 300), where the Alhambra and Albaicín impress with Spain's Moorish past. Mountain air awaits hiking from town to town in **Las Alpujarras** (1 day, p. 312).

EXPLORE THE NORTH (2 WEEKS) Set out from intriguing **Santiago de Compostela** (3 days, p. 602), with a day spent on the Atlantic coast in **Túy** (p. 616) or the **Illas Cíes** (p. 615). Head up to **A Coruña** (1 day, p. 622), in the fjord-like Rías Altas, before moving east to **Llanes** (1 day, p. 577) and the beach or the **Cuevas de Altamira** (1 day, p. 599) to gaze at prehistoric art. For more contemporary aesthetics, visit the Guggenheim Museum in **Bilbao** (1 day, p. 553). From there, choose a route depending on the season. In **summer,** lay out on the beach at **San Sebastián** (2 days, p. 544) before exploring the golden city of **Zaragoza** (1 day, p. 508). Move on to **Sitges** (2 days, p. 435), Barcelona's party-minded beach resort and then to **Barcelona** (2 days, p. 390) itself for Modernista madness. Spend your last day at **Palafrugell** (1 day, p. 453) on the Costa Brava, from where picturesque **Calella** (p. 455) is easily reached. In **winter,** go straight to **Zaragoza** (1 day, p. 508) from Bilbao and then to **Barcelona** (2 days, p. 390). From there, head to the Pyrenees for terrific skiing at **Puigcerdà** (2 days, p. 476), **Vielha** (2 days, p. 483), and **Boí** (1 day, p. 481).

THE BEST OF PORTUGAL (2 WEEKS)
Begin in busy **Lisboa** (4 days, p. 677) and daytrip to fairy tale **Sintra** (p. 710). Head down to the infamous beach-and-bar town **Lagos** (3 days, p. 719) and spend an afternoon in **Sagres** (p. 725), once considered the end of the world. Check out the creepy bone chapel in **Évora** (1 day, p. 734) before slamming shut those dusty books in the university town of **Coimbra** (2 days, p. 787) and taking in the youthful fun. Relax beside the ocean in **Aveiro** (1 day, p. 796), and finish in **Porto** (2 days, p. 769), home of fine artwork and port wine.

ESSENTIALS

PLANNING YOUR TRIP

ENTRANCE REQUIREMENTS
Passport (p. 9). Required of all foreign travelers.
Visa (p. 11). Required of anyone staying more than 90 days, except EU citizens.
Work Permit (p. 10). Required of all foreigners planning to work.
International Driving Permit (p. 32). Suggested for those planning to drive.

EMBASSIES AND CONSULATES

CONSULAR SERVICES ABROAD

The following listings are for Spanish and Portuguese embassies and consulates in selected foreign countries. For listings of foreign embassies and consulates in Spain or Portugal, consult the country-specific **Essentials,** (p. 78 and p. 672).

SPANISH

Australia: 15 Arkana St., Yarralumla, ACT 2600; mailing address: P.O. Box 9076, Deakin ACT 2600 (☎2 6273 3555; www.embaspain.com). **Consulates:** Level 24, St. Martin's Tower, 31 Market St., Sydney, NSW 2000 (☎2 9261 2433); 146 Elgin St., Carlton, VIC 3053 Melbourne (☎3 9347 1966).

Canada: 74 Stanley Ave., Ottawa, ON K1M 1P4 (☎613-747-2252; www.embaspain.ca). **Consulates:** 1 Westmount Sq., Suite 1456, Ave. Wood, Montreal, Quebec H3Z 2P9 (☎514-935-5235); 200 Front St., Suite 2401 Toronto, Ontario M5V 3K2 (☎416-977-1661).

Ireland: 17a Merlyn Park, Ballsbridge, Dublin 4 (☎269 1640; www.mae.es/embajadas/dublin).

New Zealand: See Australian embassy. **Consulates:** 345 Great South Road, Takanini Auckland (☎9 299 6019; fax 9 298 9986).

United Kingdom: 39 Chesham Pl., London SW1X 8SB (☎0207 235 5555; fax 259 5392). **Consulates:** 20 Draycott Pl., London SW3 2RZ (☎0207 589 8989; www.conspalon.org); Suite 1A, Brookhouse, 70, Spring Gardens, Manchester M2 2BQ (☎161 236 1262; fax 228 7467); 63 North Castle Street, Edinburgh EH2 3LJ(☎220 18 43 or 14 39; fax 226 45 68).

United States: 2375 Pennsylvania Ave. NW, Washington, D.C. 20037 (☎202-452-0100; www.spainemb.org). **Consulates:** 150 E. 58th St., 30th fl., New York, NY 10155 (☎212-355-4080; fax 644-3751); branches in Boston, Chicago, Houston, Los Angeles, Miami, New Orleans, San Francisco, and San Juan (PR).

PORTUGUESE

Australia: 23 Culgoa Circuit, O'Malley, ACT 2606; mailing address: P.O. Box 9092, Deakin, ACT 2600 (☎2 6290 1733; fax 6290 1957). **Consulate:** Level 9, 30 Clarence St., Sydney, NSW 2000; P.O. Box 3309, Sydney, NSW 2001 (☎2 9262 2199; www.consulportugalsydney.org.au).

Canada: 645 Island Park Dr., Ottawa, ON K1Y 0B8 (☎613-729-0883; fax 729-4236). **Consulates:** 438 University Ave., Suite 1400, Toronto, ON M5G 2K8 (☎416-217-0966; www.cgportugaltoronto.com); 904-700 W. Pender St., Vancouver, BC V6C 3S3 (☎604-688-6514; fax 685-7042).

Ireland: Knocksinna House, Knocksinna Road, Foxrock, Dublin 18 (☎289 4416; fax 289 2849).

New Zealand: See Australian embassy. **Consulates:** 33 Grafield St., Parnnall; P.O. Box 105, Auckland (☎9 309 1454; fax 308 9061); 21 Marion St.; P.O. Box 1024, Wellington (☎644 385 9639; fax 384 2534).

United Kingdom: 11 Belgrave Sq., London SWIX 8PP (☎0207 235 5331; www.portembassy.gla.ac.uk/info/embassy.html). **Consulate:** Silver City House 62, Brompton Rd., London SW3 1BJ (☎020 7581 8722; fax 7581 3085).

United States: 2125 Kalorama Rd. NW, Washington, D.C. 20008 (☎202-328-8610; fax 462-3726). **Consulates:** 630 5th Ave., Suite 801, New York, NY 10111 (☎212-221-3165; fax 459-0190); branches in Boston, Chicago, Coral Gables (FL), Honolulu, Houston, Los Angeles, Newark, New Bedford (MA), Philadelphia, Providence, Río Piedras (PR), San Francisco, and Waterbury (CT).

TOURIST OFFICES

SPANISH

Spain's official tourist board operates an extensive website at www.tourspain.es.

Canada: Tourist Office of Spain, 2 Bloor West, Suite 3402, Toronto, ON M4W 3E2 (☎416-961-3131; www.tourspain.toronto.on.ca).

United Kingdom: Spanish National Tourist Office, 22-23 Manchester Sq., London W1U 3PX (☎0207 486 8077; fax 486 8034).

United States: Tourist Office of Spain, 666 5th Ave., 35th fl., New York, NY 10103 (☎212-265-8822; fax 265-8864). Additional offices in Chicago, IL (☎312-642-1992), Beverly Hills, CA (☎323-658-7188), and Miami, FL (☎305-358-1992).

PORTUGUESE

The official Portuguese tourism website is located at www.portugalinsite.com.

Canada: Portuguese Trade and Tourism Commission, 60 Bloor West, Suite 1005, Toronto, ON M4W 3B8 (☎416-921-7376; fax 921-1353).

United Kingdom: Portuguese Trade and Tourism Office, 11 Belgrave Sq., London SWIX 8PP (☎0207 201 6666; fax 201 6633).

United States: Portuguese National Tourist Office, 590 5th Ave., 4th fl., New York, NY 10036 (☎800-767-8842 or 212-354-4403; www.portugal.org). Additional office in Washington, D.C. (☎202-331-8222).

DOCUMENTS AND FORMALITIES

PASSPORTS

REQUIREMENTS

Citizens of Australia, Canada, Ireland, New Zealand, the UK, and the US need valid passports to enter Spain or Portugal and to re-enter their home countries. Citizens of some countries will be denied entry to Spain or Portugal if their passports expire in less than six months; returning home with an expired passport is illegal, and may result in a fine.

NEW PASSPORTS

Citizens of Australia, Canada, Ireland, New Zealand, the UK, and the US can apply for a passport at any passport office and many post offices and courts of law. Any new passport or renewal applications must be filed well in advance of the departure date, although most passport offices offer rush services for a very steep fee.

ESSENTIALS

PASSPORT MAINTENANCE

Photocopy the page of your passport with your photo, as well as your visas, traveler's check serial numbers, and any other important documents. Carry one set of copies in a safe place, apart from the originals, and leave another set at home. Consulates also recommend that you carry an expired passport or an official copy of your birth certificate in a part of your baggage separate from other documents.

If you lose your passport, immediately notify the local police and the nearest embassy or consulate of your home government. To expedite its replacement, you will need to know all information previously recorded and show ID and proof of citizenship. In some cases, a replacement may take weeks to process, and it may be valid only for a limited time. Any visas stamped in your old passport will be irretrievably lost. In an emergency, ask for immediate temporary traveling papers that will permit you to re-enter your home country.

ONE EUROPE. European unity has come a long way since 1958, when the European Economic Community (EEC) was created to promote European solidarity and cooperation. Since then, the EEC has become the European Union (EU), a mighty political, legal, and economic institution. On May 1, 2004, ten Southern, Central, and Eastern European countries—Cyprus, the Czech Republic, Estonia, Hungary, Latvia, Lithuania, Malta, Poland, the Slovak Republic, and Slovenia—were admitted to the EU, joining fifteen other member states: Austria, Belgium, Denmark, Finland, France, Germany, Greece, Ireland, Italy, Luxembourg, the Netherlands, Portugal, Spain, Sweden, and the UK.

What does this have to do with the average non-EU tourist? The EU's policy of **freedom of movement** means that border controls between the first fifteen member states (minus Ireland and the UK, but plus Norway and Iceland) have been abolished, and visa policies harmonized. While you're still required to carry a passport (or government-issued ID card for EU citizens) when crossing an internal border, once you've been admitted into one country, you're free to travel to other participating states. Britain and Ireland have also formed a **common travel area,** abolishing passport controls between them.

For more important consequences of the EU for travelers, see **The Euro** (p. 12) and **Customs in the EU** (p. 11).

VISAS AND WORK PERMITS

VISAS

As of August 2004, citizens of Australia, Canada, Ireland, New Zealand, the UK, and the US do not need visas to visit Spain or Portugal for fewer than 90 days. Visas vary in cost based on the length of stay and can only be obtained with extensive documentation on your planned activity in the country. Applications are available at the nearest consulate or embassy for the country to which you are traveling. Generally speaking, visa applications must be filed in your home country. US citizens can take advantage of the **Center for International Business and Travel** (**CIBT;** ☎ 800-929-2428; www.cibt.com), which secures visas for travel to almost all countries for a variable service charge.

Double-check entrance requirements at the nearest embassy or consulate (see **Consular Services Abroad,** p. 8) for up-to-date info before departure. US citizens can also consult www.pueblo.gsa.gov/cic_text/travel/foreign/foreignentryreqs.html.

WORK PERMITS

Admission as a visitor does not include the right to work, which is authorized only by a work permit. For more information, see **Alternatives to Tourism** (p. 55).

IDENTIFICATION

When you travel, always carry at least two forms of identification on your person, including a photo ID; a passport and a driver's license or birth certificate is usually adequate. Never carry all of your IDs together; split them up in case of theft or loss, and keep photocopies of all of them in your luggage and at home.

STUDENT, TEACHER, AND YOUTH IDENTIFICATION

The **International Student Identity Card (ISIC)**, the most widely accepted form of student ID, provides discounts on some sights, accommodations, food, and transport; access to a 24hr. emergency helpline; and insurance benefits for US cardholders (see **Insurance,** p. 18). Significant discounts in Spain include 50% off at National Museums, including the Prado and the Reina Sofía, and up to 20% off car rentals with Avis; in Portugal cardholders receive 50% off at the Museu de Arte Contemporânea in Porto, along with other benefits. Applicants must be full-time secondary or post-secondary school students at least 12 years of age. Because of the proliferation of fake ISICs, some services (particularly airlines) require additional proof of student status.

The **International Teacher Identity Card (ITIC)** offers teachers the same insurance coverage as the ISIC and similar but limited discounts. For travelers who are 25 years old or under but are not students, the **International Youth Travel Card (IYTC)** also offers many of the same benefits as the ISIC.

Each of these identity cards costs US$22 or equivalent. ISIC and ITIC cards are valid for roughly one calendar year; IYTC cards are valid for one year from the date of issue. Many student travel agencies (p. 22) issue the cards; for a list of issuing agencies or more information, see the **International Student Travel Confederation (ISTC)** website (www.istc.org).

The **International Student Exchange Card (ISE)** is a similar card available to students, faculty, and youth ages 12 to 26. It provides discounts, medical benefits, access to a 24hr. emergency helpline, and the ability to purchase student airfares. The card costs US$25; call US ☎ 800-255-8000 or visit www.isecard.com.

CUSTOMS

Upon entering Spain or Portugal, you must declare certain items from abroad and pay a duty on the value of those articles that exceed the allowance established by the country's customs service. Duty-free allowances were abolished for travel between EU member states on July 1, 1999, but still exist for those arriving from outside the EU. Upon returning home, you must likewise declare all articles acquired abroad and pay a duty on the value of articles in excess of your home country's allowance. In order to expedite your return, make a list of any valuables brought from home and register them with customs before traveling abroad, and be sure to keep receipts for all goods acquired abroad, including duty-free items.

CUSTOMS IN THE EU. As well as freedom of movement of people within the EU (p. 10), travelers in the fifteen original EU member countries (Austria, Belgium, Denmark, Finland, France, Germany, Greece, Ireland, Italy, Luxembourg, the Netherlands, Portugal, Spain, Sweden, and the UK) can also take advantage of the freedom of movement of goods. This means that there are no customs controls at internal EU borders (i.e., you can take the blue customs channel at the airport), and travelers are free to transport whatever legal substances they like as long as it is for their own personal (non-commercial) use—up to 800 cigarettes, 10L of spirits, 90L of wine (60L of sparkling wine), and 110L of beer. You should also be aware that duty-free allowances were abolished on June 30, 1999 for travel between EU member states; however, travelers between the EU and the rest of the world still get a duty-free allowance when passing through customs.

MONEY

CURRENCY AND EXCHANGE

The chart below is based on August 2004 exchange rates between European Union euros (€) and Australian dollars (AUS$), Canadian dollars (CDN$), New Zealand dollars (NZ$), British pounds (UK£), and US dollars (US$). Check the currency converter on websites like www.xe.com or a newspaper for the latest rates.

ESSENTIALS

CURRENCY

1 AUS$ = €0.579	€1 = 1.726 AUS$
1 CDN$ = €0.618	€1 = 1.619 CDN$
1 NZ$ = €0.539	€1 = 1.856 NZ$
1 UK£ = €1.489	€1 = 0.671 UK£
1 US$ = €0.808	€1 = 1.237 US$

As a general rule, it's cheaper to convert money abroad than at home. While currency exchange is likely available at the airport, it's wise to bring enough to last the first 24 to 72 hours of your trip. When changing money, try to go only to banks that have at most a 5% margin between buy and sell prices. You lose money with each transaction, so **convert large sums, but no more than you'll need.** If you use traveler's checks or bills, carry some in small denominations for when you are forced to exchange at poor rates, but bring a range of denominations since charges may be levied per check cashed. Store your money in a variety of forms; ideally, at any given time you will have some cash and an ATM and/or credit card.

THE EURO. The official currency of 12 members of the European Union—Austria, Belgium, Finland, France, Germany, Greece, Ireland, Italy, Luxembourg, the Netherlands, Portugal, and Spain—is now the euro.

The currency has some important—and positive—consequences for travelers hitting more than one euro-zone country. For one thing, money-changers across the euro-zone are obliged to exchange money at the official, fixed rate and at no commission. Second, euro-denominated traveler's checks allow you to pay for goods and services across the euro-zone, again at the official rate and commission-free.

TRAVELER'S CHECKS

Traveler's checks are one of the safest and least troublesome means of carrying funds. American Express and Visa are the most recognized brands. Many banks and agencies sell them for a small commission. Issuers give refunds if the checks are lost or stolen, and many provide additional services like stolen credit card assistance. Ask about toll-free refund hotlines, and always carry emergency cash.

American Express: Cheques available with commission at select banks, at all AmEx offices, and online (www.americanexpress.com; US residents only). AmEx cardholders can purchase cheques by phone (☎800-721-9768). Cheques available in Australian, Canadian, Euro, UK, and US currencies. For more information contact AmEx's service centers: in Australia ☎800 68 80 22; in New Zealand 0508 555 358; in the UK 0800 587 6023; in the US and Canada 800-221-7282; in Spain 900 810 029; in Portugal 800 205 598. American Express offices will cash cheques commission-free.

Visa: Checks available with commission at banks worldwide. For location of the nearest office, call Visa's service centers: in the UK ☎0 800 89 5078; in the US 800-227-6811; elsewhere, call the UK collect at +44 173 331 8949. AAA (p. 32) offers commission-free checks to members. Checks available in Canadian, Euro, UK, and US currencies.

Travelex/Thomas Cook: In the US and Canada call ☎800-287-7362; in the UK call 0800 62 21 01; elsewhere call the UK collect at 44 1733 31 89 50. Checks available at 2% commission. Accepted only at certain banks in Spain and Portugal.

CREDIT, DEBIT, AND ATM CARDS

Where they are accepted, credit cards often offer superior exchange rates—up to 5% better than the retail rate used by banks and currency exchanges. Credit cards may also offer services like insurance or emergency help, and are sometimes required to reserve hotel rooms or rental cars. **MasterCard** (a.k.a. EuroCard or Access) and **Visa** (a.k.a. Carte Bleue or Barclaycard) are the most welcomed; **American Express** cards work at some ATMs and at AmEx offices and major airports.

ATMs are easy to find throughout Spain and Portugal. Depending on the system your home bank uses, you can most likely access your bank account from abroad with an ATM (cash) card. ATMs get the same wholesale exchange rate as credit cards, but there is often a limit on the amount you can withdraw per day (usually around US$500). There is typically also a surcharge of US$1-5 per withdrawal.

Debit cards are a relatively new form of purchasing power that are as convenient as credit cards but have a more immediate impact on your funds. A debit card can be used wherever its associated credit card company is accepted, but the money is withdrawn directly from the holder's checking account. Debit cards often also function as ATM cards and can be used to withdraw cash from associated banks and ATMs in Spain and Portugal. Ask your local bank about obtaining one.

The two major international money networks are **Cirrus** (US ☎800-424-7787; www.mastercard.com) and **Visa/PLUS** (US ☎800-843-7587; www.visa.com). The associated network is posted on the ATM; most accept both kinds of cards.

ATMS AND PINS. To use a cash or credit card to withdraw money from a cash machine (ATM) in Europe, you must have a four-digit **Personal Identification Number (PIN).** If your PIN is longer than four digits, ask your bank whether you can just use the first four, or whether you'll need a new one. **Credit cards** don't usually come with PINs, so if you intend to hit up ATMs with a credit card to get cash advances, call your credit card company before leaving to request one.

Travelers with alphabetic PINs may be thrown off by the lack of letters. The following are the corresponding numbers to use: 1=QZ; 2=ABC; 3=DEF; 4=GHI; 5=JKL; 6=MNO; 7=PRS; 8=TUV; and 9=WXY. Note that if you punch the wrong code into the machine three times, it will swallow your card for good.

GETTING MONEY FROM HOME

If you run out of money while traveling, the easiest and cheapest solution is to have someone back home make a deposit to your bank account, which you can access with your ATM card. Failing that, consider one of the following options. The online **International Money Transfer Consumer Guide** (http://international-money-transfer-consumer-guide.info) may also be helpful.

WIRING MONEY

It is possible to arrange a **bank money transfer,** which means asking a bank back home to wire money to a bank in Spain or Portugal. This is the cheapest way to transfer cash, but it's also the slowest, usually taking several days or more. Note that some banks may only release your funds in local currency, potentially sticking you with a poor exchange rate; inquire about this in advance. Wiring money is often easiest between two branches of an international bank. **Citibank** has branches throughout Spain and **Barclays** has branches in Spain and Portugal.

Money transfer services like **Western Union** are faster than bank transfers—but also much pricier. Western Union has many locations worldwide. To find one, visit www.westernunion.com, or call in Australia ☎800 501 500, in Canada 800-235-0000, in the UK 0800 83 38 33, in the US 800-325-6000, in Spain 952 05 02 19. You can also wire money from the website with a credit or debit card or your checking account. Money transfer is also available at **American Express** offices.

US STATE DEPARTMENT (US CITIZENS ONLY)

In serious emergencies, the US State Department will forward money within hours to the nearest consular office, which will disburse it according to instructions for US$30. If you wish to use this service, contact the Overseas Citizens Service division (☎317-472-2328; nights, Sundays, and holidays 202-647-4000).

COSTS

The cost of your trip will vary considerably, depending on where you go, how you travel, and where you stay. The most significant expense will be your round-trip (return) **airfare** to Spain or Portugal (for country-specific info, see **By Plane**, p. 79 and p. 673). Before you leave, spend time calculating a reasonable daily **budget.**

STAYING ON A BUDGET

To give you a general idea, a bare-bones day (camping or sleeping in hostels/guesthouses, buying food at supermarkets) in Spain would cost about US$50 (€41), in Portugal about US$45 (€37); a slightly more comfortable day (sleeping in hostels or guesthouses and the occasional budget hotel, eating one meal per day at a restaurant, going out at night) in Spain would cost US$85 (€70), in Portugal about US$73 (€60); and for a luxurious day, the sky's the limit. Don't forget to factor in emergency funds (at least US$300) when planning how much money you'll need.

TIPS FOR SAVING MONEY

Some simpler ways to budget include finding free entertainment, splitting accommodation and food costs with fellow travelers, and buying groceries rather than eating out. Bring a sleepsack (p. 15) to save on charges in hostels, and do your **laundry** in the sink (unless it's prohibited). Still, though staying within your budget is important, don't do so at the expense of your health or a great experience.

TIPPING, BARGAINING, AND TAXES

See the **Money** sections for Spain (p. 81) and Portugal (p. 674) for specifics on tipping, bargaining, and taxes in each country.

PACKING

Pack lightly: Lay out only what you absolutely need, then take half the clothes and twice the money. The **Travelite FAQ** (www.travelite.org) is a good resource for tips on traveling light. The online **Universal Packing List** (http://upl.codeq.info) will generate a customized list of suggested items based on your trip length, the expected climate, your planned activities, and other factors. If you plan to do a lot of hiking, also consult **Camping and the Outdoors**, p. 43.

> **Luggage:** If you plan to cover most of your itinerary by foot, a sturdy **frame backpack** is unbeatable. (For the basics on buying a pack, see p. 45.) Toting a **suitcase** or **trunk** is fine if you plan to stay put in a few cities, but not a great idea if you move around a lot. Besides your main piece of luggage, a **daypack** (a small backpack or courier bag) is useful.

> **Clothing:** It's a good idea to bring a warm jacket or sweater, a rain jacket, sturdy shoes or hiking boots, and thick socks; however, when traveling in southern Spain or Portugal in summer, the rain jacket may not be necessary. Flip-flops are must-haves for hostel showers. You may also want an outfit for going out, and a nice pair of shoes. If you plan to visit religious sites, remember to bring modest and respectful dress.

Sleepsack: Some hostels require that you either provide your own linen or rent sheets from them. Save cash by making your own sleepsack: fold a full-size sheet in half the long way, then sew it closed along the long side and one of the short sides.

Converters and Adapters: In Spain and Portugal, electricity is 220 volts AC. Americans and Canadians should buy an adapter (which changes the shape of the plug; US$5) and a converter (which changes the voltage; US$30). Don't make the mistake of using only an adapter (unless appliance instructions explicitly state otherwise; some laptops, hair dryers and the like have built-in converters). New Zealanders, Australians, and Brits won't need a converter, but will need a set of adapters to use anything electrical. For more on all things adaptable, check out http://kropla.com/electric.htm.

Toiletries: If you are dependent on particular brands of deodorant, razors, tampons, or condoms, bring extras, as you may not find them easily, especially outside of cities. **Contact lenses** are likely to be expensive and difficult to find, so bring enough extra pairs and solution for your entire trip. Also bring your glasses and a copy of your prescription in case you need emergency replacements.

First-Aid Kit: For a basic first-aid kit, pack bandages, a pain reliever, antibiotic cream, a thermometer, a Swiss Army knife, tweezers, moleskin, decongestant, motion-sickness remedy, diarrhea or upset-stomach medication (Pepto Bismol or Imodium), an antihistamine, sunscreen, insect repellent, and burn ointment.

Film: Film and developing in Spain and Portugal are expensive, so consider bringing along enough film for your entire trip and developing it at home. Despite disclaimers, airport security X-rays can fog film, so buy a lead-lined pouch. Always pack film in your carry-on luggage, since higher-intensity X-rays are used on checked luggage.

Other Useful Items: For safety purposes, you should bring a **money belt** and small **padlock.** Basic **outdoors equipment** (plastic water bottle, pocketknife, sunglasses, sunscreen, hat) may also prove useful. **Quick repairs** of garments can be done with a needle and thread; also consider bringing electrical tape for patching tears. If you want to do laundry by hand, bring detergent, a small rubber ball to stop up the sink, and string for a clothes line. Other things you're liable to forget are an umbrella; **plastic bags** (for damp clothes, soap, food, and other spillables); an **alarm clock;** safety pins; rubber bands; a flashlight; earplugs; garbage bags; and a **calculator.** A **cell phone** can be a lifesaver on the road; see p. 36 for how to find one that will work at your destination.

Important Documents: Don't forget your passport, traveler's checks, ATM and/or credit cards, adequate ID, and photocopies of all of the aforementioned in case these documents are lost or stolen (p. 11). Also check that you have any of the following that might apply to you: a hosteling membership card (p. 39); driver's license (p. 11); travel insurance forms (p. 18); ISIC card (p. 11), and/or rail or bus pass (p. 25).

SAFETY AND HEALTH

GENERAL ADVICE

The following section is intended as a general guide; refer to the **Health** sections of Spain (p. 82) and Portugal (p. 674) for more detailed info.

In any type of crisis situation, the most important thing to do is **stay calm.** Your country's embassy abroad (p. 78 and p. 672) is usually your best resource when things go wrong; registering with that embassy upon arrival in the country is often a good idea if you will be staying for any length of time. The government offices listed in the **Travel Advisories** box below can provide information on the services they offer their citizens in case of emergencies abroad.

LOCAL LAWS AND POLICE

Travelers are not likely to break major laws unintentionally while visiting Spain or Portugal. You can contact your embassy if arrested, although they can't do much to assist you. Police are generally helpful in Spain and Portugal; you should feel comfortable approaching them, although few officers speak English. National numbers for contacting police are in the **Essentials** sections of Spain (p. 78) and Portugal (p. 672). Local information is listed at the beginning of each city or town.

DRUGS AND ALCOHOL

Recreational drugs are illegal in Spain and Portugal. While locals may take these laws lightly, the police do not. *Let's Go* recommends playing it safe. Any attempt to possess, buy, or sell marijuana may land you in jail or with a heavy fine.

SPECIFIC CONCERNS

TERRORISM

On **March 11, 2004,** Madrid suffered the worst attack in Spain's recent history when a group of terrorists bombed four commuter trains as they entered the city. The attack caused almost 200 deaths and over 1400 injuries. Referred to by Spaniards as **11-M** (*el once eme*), the day became a signal of the growing threat of terrorism on a global scale. Many European countries reacted with heightened security on rail lines and at airports. Although Spanish authorities initially speculated that **ETA**, or Euskadi Ta Askatasuna (Basque Homeland and Freedom), was responsible for the attacks, their focus quickly shifted to **al-Qaeda,** who remain at the center of the ongoing investigation. Travelers should be aware that terrorism by Islamic groups is a threat throughout Western Europe.

Basque terrorism concerns all travelers in Spain and is a highly controversial issue both domestically and internationally. ETA is the militant wing of the Basque separatist movement. It was founded in 1959 to fight for Basque self-determination, concentrating on establishing the Basque region as its own independent country. ETA attacks, historically aimed at Spanish government targets, have resulted in more than 800 deaths since 1968. In March 2001, however, ETA issued a communiqué announcing its intention to target Spanish **tourist areas.** In June 2002, the ETA carried out a series of bombings in resort towns along the **Costa del Sol** and in northern Spain during an EU summit in Sevilla. These attacks were followed up by the **July 2003** bombings of a hotel in Benidorm and another in Alicante. In March 2004, Spanish police discovered large amounts of explosives on suspected ETA terrorists en route to Madrid. While there may be some risk to travelers, the attacks are targeted and are not considered random acts of terrorism. Since the events of **11-M,** however, the government has made a concerted effort to end ETA's operations once and for all. However, **August 2004** saw another slate of ETA bombings on the Cantabrian and Galician coasts, in cities like Santander and Llanes, but there were no injuries; ETA warned of the attacks in advance.

The box on **travel advisories** lists offices to contact and webpages to visit to get your home country's government's most recently updated advisories about travel.

PERSONAL SAFETY

EXPLORING AND TRAVELING

To avoid unwanted attention, try to blend in. Respecting local customs (in many cases, dressing more conservatively than normal) may quiet would-be hecklers. Familiarize yourself with the area before setting out, and carry yourself with con-

TRAVEL ADVISORIES. The following government offices provide travel information and advisories by telephone, by fax, or via the web:

Australian Department of Foreign Affairs and Trade: ☎13 00 555135; faxback service 02 6261 1299; www.dfat.gov.au.

Canadian Department of Foreign Affairs and International Trade (DFAIT): In Canada and the US call ☎800-267-8376, elsewhere call ☎+1 613-944-4000; www.dfait-maeci.gc.ca. Call for their free booklet, *Bon Voyage...But.*

New Zealand Ministry of Foreign Affairs: ☎04 439 8000; fax 494 8506; www.mft.govt.nz/travel/index.html.

United Kingdom Foreign and Commonwealth Office: ☎020 7008 0232; fax 7008 0155; www.fco.gov.uk.

US Department of State: ☎202-647-5225, faxback service 202-647-3000; http://travel.state.gov. For *A Safe Trip Abroad,* call ☎202-512-1800.

ESSENTIALS

fidence. Check maps in shops rather than on the street. If traveling alone, be sure someone at home knows your itinerary, and **never admit that you're by yourself.** When walking at night, stick to busy, well-lit streets and avoid dark alleyways. If you ever feel uncomfortable, leave the area as quickly and directly as you can.

There is no sure-fire way to avoid all the threatening situations you might encounter while traveling, but a good **self-defense course** will give you concrete ways to react to unwanted advances. **Impact, Prepare, and Model Mugging** can refer you to local self-defense courses in the US (☎800-345-5425). Visit the website at www.impactsafety.org for a list of nearby chapters. Workshops (1½-3hr.) start at US$75; full courses (20-25hr.) run US$350-400.

If you are **driving**, learn local signals and wear a seatbelt. Children under 40 lbs. should ride only in carseats, available for a small fee from most car rental agencies. Study maps before you hit the road, and if you plan on spending a lot of time driving, consider bringing spare parts. If your car breaks down, wait for the police to assist you. For drives in desolate areas, invest in a cellular phone and a roadside assistance program (p. 32). Park in a garage or well traveled area, and use a steering wheel lock in cities. **Sleeping in your car** is one of the most dangerous (and often illegal) ways to get your rest. For info on the perils of **hitchhiking**, see p. 33.

POSSESSIONS AND VALUABLES

Never leave your belongings unattended; crime occurs in even the most demure-looking hostel or hotel. Spain and parts of Portugal are heavily touristed, encouraging a thriving pickpocket trade. To minimize the risk, bring a **padlock** for hostel lockers, and don't ever store valuables in any locker. Be particularly careful on **buses** and **trains;** horror stories abound about determined thieves who wait for travelers to fall asleep. Carry your backpack in front where you can see it. When traveling with others, take turns sleeping. When alone, use good judgment in selecting a train compartment: never stay in an empty one, and use a lock to secure your pack to the luggage rack. Sleep on top bunks and store luggage above you (or in bed with you), and keep documents and valuables on your person.

There are a few steps you can take to minimize the financial risk associated with traveling. First, **bring as little with you as possible.** Second, buy a few combination **padlocks** to secure your belongings either in your pack or in a hostel or train station locker. Third, **carry as little cash as possible.** Keep your traveler's checks and ATM/credit cards in a **money belt**—not a "fanny pack"—along with your passport and ID cards. Fourth, **keep some cash separate from your primary stash**—about €50 sewn into your pack, along with traveler's check numbers and photocopies.

In large cities **con artists** often work in groups and may involve children. Beware of certain classics: sob stories that require money, rolls of bills "found" on the street, mustard spilled (or saliva spit) onto your shoulder to distract you while they snatch your bag. **Never let your passport or bags out of your sight.** Beware of **pickpockets** in city crowds, especially on public transportation. Also, be alert in public telephone booths: If you must say your calling card number, do so very quietly; if you punch it in, make sure no one can look over your shoulder.

If you will be traveling with electronic devices, such as a laptop or a PDA, check whether your homeowner's insurance covers loss, theft, or damage when you travel. If not, consider purchasing a low-cost separate insurance policy. **Safeware** (☎ US 800-800-1492; www.safeware.com) specializes in covering computers and charges $90 for 90-day comprehensive international travel coverage up to $4000.

PRE-DEPARTURE HEALTH

In your **passport,** write the names of any people you wish to be contacted in case of a medical emergency, and list any allergies or medical conditions. Matching a prescription to a foreign equivalent is not always easy, safe, or possible, so if you take prescription drugs, consider carrying up-to-date, legible prescriptions or a statement from your doctor with the trade name, manufacturer, chemical name, and dosage. While traveling, be sure to keep all medication with you in carry-on luggage. For tips on packing a basic **first-aid kit** and other health essentials, see p. 15.

IMMUNIZATIONS AND PRECAUTIONS

Travelers over two years old should make sure that the following vaccines are up to date: MMR (for measles, mumps, and rubella); DTaP or Td (for diphtheria, tetanus, and pertussis); IPV (for polio); Hib (for haemophilus influenza B); and HepB (for Hepatitis B). While yellow fever is only endemic to parts of South America and sub-Saharan Africa, Portugal requires proof of yellow fever vaccination for travelers older than one arriving from infected areas and destined for the Azores and Madeira. For immunization recommendations, consult the CDC in the US (p. 19) or your home country's equivalent, and check with a doctor for guidance.

INSURANCE

Travel insurance covers four basic areas: medical/health problems, property loss, trip cancellation/interruption, and emergency evacuation. Though regular insurance policies may well extend to travel-related accidents, you may consider purchasing supplemental travel insurance if the cost of potential trip cancellation, interruption, or emergency medical evacuation is greater than you can absorb. Prices for travel insurance purchased separately generally run about US$50 per week for full coverage, while trip cancellation/interruption may be purchased separately at a rate of US$3-5 per day depending on length of stay.

Medical insurance (especially university policies) often covers costs incurred abroad; check with your provider. **US Medicare** does not cover foreign travel. **Canadian** provincial health insurance plans increasingly do not either; check with the provincial Ministry of Health or Health Plan Headquarters for details. **Homeowners' insurance** (or your family's coverage) often covers theft during travel and loss of travel documents (passport, plane ticket, railpass, etc.) up to US$500.

ISIC and **ITIC** (p. 11) provide basic insurance benefits to US cardholders, including US$100 per day of in-hospital sickness for up to 60 days and US$5000 of accident-related medical reimbursement (see www.isicus.com for details). Cardholders have access to a toll-free 24hr. helpline for medical, legal, and financial emergencies overseas. **American Express** (US ☎ 800-528-4800) grants most card-holders automatic collision and theft car rental insurance and ground travel accident coverage of US$100,000 on car rental purchases made with the card.

INSURANCE PROVIDERS

STA (p. 22) offers a range of plans that can supplement your basic coverage. Other private insurance providers in the US and Canada include: Access America (☎ 800-284-8300; www.accessamerica.com); Berkely Group (☎ 800-797-4514; www.berkely.com); Globalcare Travel Insurance (☎ 800-821-2488; www.globalcare-cocco.com); Travel Assistance International (☎ 800-821-2828; www.europ-assistance.com); and Travel Guard (☎ 800-826-4919; www.travelguard.com). Columbus Direct (☎ 020 7375 0011; www.columbusdirect.co.uk) operates in the UK and AFTA (☎ 02 9264 3299; www.afta.com.au) in Australia.

USEFUL ORGANIZATIONS AND PUBLICATIONS

The US **Centers for Disease Control and Prevention** (**CDC;** ☎ 877-FYI-TRIP; fax 888-232-3299; www.cdc.gov/travel) maintains an international travelers' hotline and an informative website. The CDC's comprehensive booklet *Health Information for International Travel* (The Yellow Book), an annual rundown of disease, immunization, and general health advice, is free online or US$29-40 via the Public Health Foundation (☎ 877-252-1200; http://bookstore.phf.org). Consult the appropriate government agency of your home country for consular information on health, entry requirements, and other issues for various countries (see the box on **Travel Advisories,** p. 17). For information on health and other travel warnings, call the **Overseas Citizens Services** (☎ 888-407-4747 M-F 8am-8pm; after-hours 202-647-4000; from overseas 317-472-2328), or contact a passport agency, embassy, or consulate. For information on medical evacuation services and travel insurance firms, see the US government's website at http://travel.state.gov/medical.html or the **British Foreign and Commonwealth Office** (www.fco.gov.uk). For general health info, contact the **American Red Cross** (☎ 800-564-1234; www.redcross.org).

STAYING HEALTHY

Common sense is the simplest prescription for good health while you travel. Drink lots of fluids to prevent dehydration and constipation, and wear sturdy, broken-in shoes and clean socks.

ONCE IN SPAIN OR PORTUGAL

ENVIRONMENTAL HAZARDS

Heat exhaustion and dehydration: Heat exhaustion leads to nausea, excessive thirst, headaches, and dizziness. Avoid it by drinking plenty of fluids, eating salty foods (e.g. crackers), avoiding dehydrating beverages (e.g. alcohol and caffeinated beverages), and always wearing sunscreen. Continuous heat stress can eventually lead to heatstroke, characterized by a rising temperature, severe headache, delirium and cessation of sweating. Victims should be cooled off with wet towels and taken to a doctor.

Sunburn: Always wear sunscreen (SPF 30 is good) when spending excessive amounts of time outdoors. If you are planning on spending time near water, in the desert, or in the snow, you are at a higher risk of getting burned, even through clouds. If you get sunburned, drink more fluids than usual and apply an aloe-based lotion. Severe sunburns can lead to sun poisoning, a condition that affects the entire body, causing fever, chills, nausea, and vomiting. Sun poisoning should always be treated by a doctor.

Hypothermia and frostbite: A rapid drop in body temperature is the clearest sign of overexposure to cold. Victims may also shiver, feel exhausted, have poor coordination or slurred speech, hallucinate, or suffer amnesia. *Do not let hypothermia victims fall asleep.* To avoid hypothermia, keep dry, wear layers, and stay out of the wind. If skin turns white or blue, waxy, and cold, do not rub it. Drink warm beverages, stay dry, and slowly warm the area with dry fabric or steady body contact until a doctor can be found.

INSECT-BORNE DISEASES

Many diseases are transmitted by insects—mainly mosquitoes, fleas, ticks, and lice. Be aware of insects in wet or forested areas, especially while hiking and camping; wear long pants and sleeves, tuck your pants into your socks, and use a mosquito net. Use insect repellents such as DEET and spray your gear with permethrin (licensed in the US only for use on clothing). **Ticks** can be dangerous in rural and forested regions of Spain and Portugal. If you find a tick on you, grasp the head with tweezers as close to your skin as possible and apply slow, steady traction. Removing a tick within 24 hours greatly reduces the risk of infection. Do not use petroleum jelly, nail polish remover, or a lit match to remove them.

Tick-borne encephalitis: A viral infection of the central nervous system transmitted during the summer by tick bites or consumption of unpasteurized dairy products. The risk of contracting it is relatively low, especially if precautions are taken against tick bites.

Lyme disease: A bacterial infection carried by ticks and marked by a circular bull's-eye rash of 2 in. or more. Later symptoms include fever, headache, fatigue, and aches and pains. Antibiotics are effective if administered early. Left untreated, Lyme can cause problems in joints, the heart, and the nervous system.

FOOD- AND WATER-BORNE DISEASES

Prevention is the best cure: be sure that your food is properly cooked and the water you drink is clean. Other culprits are raw shellfish, unpasteurized milk, and sauces containing raw eggs. **Traveler's diarrhea** results from drinking water contaminated with fecal matter or eating uncooked and contaminated foods. Symptoms include nausea, bloating, and urgency. Try quick-energy, non-sugary foods with protein and carbohydrates to keep your strength up. Over-the-counter anti-diarrheals (e.g. Imodium) may counteract the problems. The most dangerous side effect is dehydration; drink 8 oz. of water with ½ tsp. of sugar and a pinch of salt, try uncaffeinated soft drinks, or eat salted crackers. If you develop a fever or symptoms don't subside after 4-5 days, consult a doctor. Consult a doctor immediately for treatment of diarrhea in children.

OTHER INFECTIOUS DISEASES

Hepatitis B: A viral infection of the liver transmitted via blood or other bodily fluids. Symptoms, which may not surface until years after infection, include jaundice, loss of appetite, fever, and joint pain. It is transmitted through activities such as unprotected sex, injections of illegal drugs, and unprotected health work. A 3-shot vaccination sequence is recommended for health-care workers, sexually active travelers, and anyone planning to seek medical treatment abroad; it must begin 6 mo. before traveling.

AIDS and HIV: For detailed information on Acquired Immune Deficiency Syndrome (AIDS) in Spain and Portugal, call the US CDC's 24hr. hotline at ☎800-342-2437, or contact the Joint United Nations Programme on HIV/AIDS (UNAIDS), 20, ave. Appia, CH-1211 Geneva 27, Switzerland (☎+41 22 791 3666; fax 22 791 4187).

Sexually transmitted diseases (STDs): Gonorrhea, chlamydia, genital warts, syphilis, herpes, and other STDs are more common than HIV and can cause serious complications. Hepatitis B and C can also be transmitted sexually. Though condoms may protect you from some STDs, oral or even tactile contact can lead to transmission. If you think you may have contracted an STD, see a doctor immediately.

OTHER HEALTH CONCERNS

MEDICAL CARE ON THE ROAD

For information on the quality and availability of medical care in Spain and Portugal, see the country-specific **Health** sections (p. 82 and p. 674).

If you are concerned about obtaining medical assistance while traveling, you may wish to employ special support services. The *MedPass* from **GlobalCare, Inc.,** 6875 Shiloh Rd. East, Alpharetta, GA 30005, USA (☎ 800-860-1111; fax 678-341-1800; www.globalcare.net), provides 24hr. international medical assistance, support, and medical evacuation resources. The **International Association for Medical Assistance to Travelers** (**IAMAT;** US ☎ 716-754-4883, Canada 519-836-0102; www.cybermall.co.nz/NZ/IAMAT) has free membership, lists English-speaking doctors worldwide, and offers info on immunization requirements and sanitation.

WOMEN'S HEALTH

Women traveling in unsanitary conditions are vulnerable to **urinary tract infections.** Over-the-counter medicines may alleviate symptoms, but if they persist, see a doctor. **Vaginal yeast infections** may flare up in hot and humid climates. Wearing loose trousers or a skirt and cotton underwear will help, as will over-the-counter remedies like Monistat or Gyne-Lotrimin. **Tampons, pads,** and **contraceptive devices** are widely available in Spain and Portugal, though some brands may not be stocked—bring extras of anything you can't live without. **Abortion** is illegal in Spain and Portugal, except in the first trimester for health reasons or in the case of rape. Women considering an abortion while traveling can contact the **International Planned Parenthood Federation** (**IPPF;** ☎ 0207 487 7900; www.ippf.org) for guidance.

GETTING TO SPAIN OR PORTUGAL

For country-specific information on traveling, travel organizations, and travel discounts, see the **Transportation** sections for Spain (p. 79) and Portugal (p. 672).

BY PLANE

When it comes to airfare, a little effort can save you a bundle. If your plans are flexible enough to deal with the restrictions, courier fares are the cheapest. Tickets bought from consolidators and standby seating are also good deals, but last-minute specials, airfare wars, and charter flights often beat these fares. The key is to hunt around, to be flexible, and to ask persistently about discounts. Students, seniors, and those under 26 should never pay full price for a ticket.

AIRFARES

Airfares to Spain and Portugal peak between mid-June and early September; holidays are also expensive. The cheapest time to travel is between December and February. Midweek (M-Th morning) round-trip flights run US$40-50 cheaper than weekend flights, but they are more crowded and less likely to permit frequent-flier upgrades. Not fixing a return date ("open return") or arriving in and departing from different cities ("open-jaw") can be pricier than round-trip flights. Patching one-way flights together is even more expensive. Flights between capitals or regional hubs—Madrid, Barcelona, Málaga, and Lisboa—tend to be cheaper.

If Spain or Portugal is only one stop on a more extensive globe-hop, consider a round-the-world (RTW) ticket. Tickets usually include at least five stops and are valid for about a year; prices range US$3400-5000. Try **Northwest Airlines/KLM** (US ☎ 800-447-4747; www.nwa.com) or **Star Alliance,** a consortium of 22 airlines including United Airlines (US ☎ 800-241-6522; www.staralliance.com).

BUDGET AND STUDENT TRAVEL AGENCIES

While knowledgeable agents specializing in flights to Spain or Portugal can make your life easy and help you save, they may not spend the time to find you the lowest possible fare—they get paid on commission. Travelers holding **ISIC** and **IYTC cards** (p. 11) qualify for big discounts from student travel agencies. Most flights from budget agencies are on major airlines, but in peak season some may sell seats on less-reliable chartered aircraft.

CTS Travel, 30 Rathbone Pl., London W1T 1GQ, UK (☎0207 209 0630; www.ctstravel.co.uk). A British student travel agent with offices in 39 countries including the US, Empire State Building, 350 Fifth Ave., Suite 7813, New York, NY 10118 (☎877-287-6665; www.ctstravelusa.com).

STA Travel, 5900 Wilshire Blvd., Ste. 900, Los Angeles, CA 90036, USA (☎800-781-4040; www.sta-travel.com). A student and youth travel organization with over 150 offices worldwide (check website for a list), including US offices in Boston, Chicago, L.A., New York, San Francisco, Seattle, and Washington, D.C. Ticket booking, travel insurance, railpasses, and more. Walk-in offices are located throughout Australia (☎03 9349 4344), New Zealand (☎09 309 9723), and the UK (☎0870 1 600 599).

Travel CUTS (Canadian Universities Travel Services Limited), 187 College St., Toronto, ON M5T 1P7 (☎416-979-2406; www.travelcuts.com). Offices across Canada and the US including Los Angeles, New York, San Francisco, and Seattle.

USIT, 19-21 Aston Quay, Dublin 2 (☎01 602 1777; www.usitworld.com), Ireland's leading budget travel agency has 22 offices in Northern Ireland and the Republic of Ireland.

Wasteels, Skoubogade 6, 1158 Copenhagen, Denmark. (☎3314 4633; www.wasteels.com). A huge chain with 180 locations across Europe. Sells BIJ (Billets Internationals de Jeunesse) tickets discounted 30-45% off regular fare, 2nd-class international point-to-point train tickets with unlimited stopovers for those under 26. Locations in Iberia are: Pl. Catalunya, Barcelona (☎933 01 18 81); C. Blasco de Garay, 13, Madrid (☎915 43 12 03); R. dos Caminhos de Ferro, 90, Lisboa (☎218 86 97 93).

COMMERCIAL AIRLINES

The commercial airlines' lowest regular offer is the **APEX** (Advance Purchase Excursion) fare, which provides confirmed reservations and allows "open-jaw" tickets. Generally, reservations must be made seven to 21 days ahead of departure, with seven- to 14-day minimum-stay and up to 90-day maximum-stay restrictions. These fares carry hefty cancellation and change penalties (fees rise in summer). Book peak-season APEX fares early. Use **Expedia** (www.expedia.com) or **Travelocity** (www.travelocity.com) to get an idea of the lowest published fares, then use the resources here to try and beat them. Low-season fares should be much cheaper than high-season (mid-June to Aug., Christmas and Easter) ones.

TRAVELING FROM NORTH AMERICA

Standard commercial carriers like American and United will probably offer the most convenient flights, but they may not be the cheapest, unless you manage to grab a special promotion or airfare war ticket. You will probably find flying with "discount" airlines a better deal, if any of their limited departure points is convenient for you. **Icelandair** (☎800-223-5500; www.icelandair.com) includes stopovers in Iceland at no extra cost on most transatlantic flights. For last-minute offers, subscribe to their Lucky Fares email. **Finnair** (☎800-950-5000; www.us.finnair.com) sells cheap round-trip tickets from San Francisco, New York, and Toronto to Madrid, Málaga, and Lisboa with connections throughout Europe.

TRAVELING FROM THE UK AND EUROPE

The recent emergence of no-frills airlines has made hopscotching around Europe by air increasingly affordable and convenient. Though these flights often feature inconvenient hours or serve less-popular regional airports, with one-way flights averaging about US$50, it's never been faster or easier to jet set across the Continent. Because of the myriad carriers flying from the British Isles to the continent, we only include discount airlines or those with cheap specials here. The **Air Travel Advisory Bureau** in London (☎ 020 763 11136; www.atab.co.uk) provides referrals to travel agencies and consolidators that offer discounted airfares out of the UK.

AirEuropa: Spain ☎ 902 401 501, UK 870 777 7709; www.aireuropa.com. Flights within Spain and throughout Europe, including Portugal, from 23 Spanish cities.

Aer Lingus: Ireland ☎ 0818 365 000; www.aerlingus.ie. Return tickets from Dublin, Cork, Galway, Kerry, and Shannon to Madrid (€102-244).

bmibaby: UK ☎ 0870 264 22 29; www.bmibaby.com. Departures from throughout the UK to Alicante, Barcelona, Ibiza, Málaga, Murcia, and Palma.

British Midland Airways: UK ☎ 087 0607 0555; www.flybmi.com. Departures from throughout the UK. London to Alicante, Madrid, and Palma (UK£60-110).

easyJet: UK ☎ 0871 750 01 00; www.easyjet.com. Serves 44 destinations in the UK and throughout Europe, including Spain and Portugal.

Ryanair: Ireland ☎ 0818 303 030, UK 087 246 00 00; www.ryanair.com. Serves 84 destinations in the UK and throughout Europe, including Spain and Portugal.

Spanair: Spain ☎ 902 13 14 15; www.spanair.es. Serves 19 destinations in Spain and 42 in Europe, mostly in Scandinavia.

The **Star Alliance European Airpass** offers economy class fares as low as US$65 for travel within Europe to more than 43 countries. The pass is available to transatlantic passengers on Star Alliance carriers. See www.staralliance.com for more information. In addition, a number of European airlines offer discount coupon packets. Most are only available as tack-ons for transatlantic passengers, but some are stand-alone. Most must be purchased before departure, so research in advance. The **Europe by Air FlightPass** (☎ 888-387-2479; www.europebyair.com) allows you to country-hop to over 150 European cities. US$99 per flight. **Iberia's Europass** (☎ 800-772-4642; www.iberia.com) allows Iberia passengers flying from the US to Spain to tack on a minimum of 2 additional destinations in Europe (US$133 each).

TRAVELING FROM AUSTRALIA AND NEW ZEALAND

Air New Zealand: New Zealand ☎ 0800 73 70 00; www.airnz.co.nz. Auckland to London and Frankfurt.

Qantas Air: Australia ☎ 13 11 31, New Zealand 0800 101 500; www.qantas.com.au. Flights from Australia and New Zealand to London for around AUS$2000.

Singapore Air: Australia ☎ 13 10 11; in New Zealand 0800 808 909; www.singaporeair.com. Flies from Auckland, Sydney, Melbourne, and Perth to Madrid.

Thai Airways: Australia ☎ 1300 65 19 60, New Zealand 09 377 38 86; www.thaiair.com. Auckland, Sydney, and Melbourne to London and Frankfurt.

AIR COURIER FLIGHTS

Those who travel light should consider courier flights. Couriers help transport cargo on international flights by using their checked luggage space for freight. Generally, couriers must travel with carry-ons only and deal with complex flight restrictions. Most flights are round-trip only, with short fixed-length stays (usually one week) and a limit of a one ticket per issue. Most of these flights also operate only out of major gateway cities, mostly in North America. In summer, the most popular destinations usually require an advance reservation of about two weeks (you can usually book up to two months ahead). Super-discounted fares are common for "last-minute" flights (three to 14 days ahead).

FROM NORTH AMERICA

Round-trip courier fares from North America to Madrid run about US$200-500. Most flights leave from New York, Los Angeles, San Francisco, or Miami in the US; and from Montreal, Toronto, or Vancouver in Canada. Generally, you must be over 21 (in some cases 18). The organizations below provide members with lists of opportunities and courier brokers for an annual fee. For more information, contact one of the following organizations: **International Association of Air Travel Couriers (IAATC)**, PO Box 847, Scottsbluff, NE 69363 (☎308-632-3273; www.courier.org); **Global Courier Travel**, PO Box 3051, Nederland, CO 80466 (www.globalcouriertravel.com); **Air Courier Association**, 1767 A Denver West Blvd., Golden, CO 80401 (☎800-280-5973; www.aircourier.org).

FROM THE UK, IRELAND, AUSTRALIA, AND NEW ZEALAND

The minimum age for couriers from the **UK** is usually 18. **Brave New World Enterprises**, P.O. Box 22212, London SE5 8WB (info@courierflights.com; www.courierflights.com) publishes a directory of all the companies offering courier flights in the UK (UK£10, in electronic form UK£8). **Global Courier Travel** (see above) also offers flights from London and Dublin to continental Europe. From **Australia**, they often have listings from Sydney to London. From **New Zealand**, the **IAATC** (see above) lists flights from Auckland to London.

STANDBY FLIGHTS

Traveling standby requires considerable flexibility in arrival and departure dates and cities. Companies dealing in standby flights sell vouchers rather than tickets, along with the promise to get you to or near your destination within a certain window of time (typically 1-5 days). You call in before your window of time to hear flight options and the probability that you will be able to board each flight. You then decide which flights you want to make, show up at the airport at the right time, present your voucher, and board if space is available. You may receive a refund only if every available flight within your date range is full; if you opt not to take an available flight, you can only get credit toward future travel. Read agreements with any company offering standby flights carefully. To check on a company's service record in the US, call the Better Business Bureau (☎703-276-0100).

TICKET CONSOLIDATORS

Ticket consolidators, or **"bucket shops,"** buy unsold tickets in bulk from commercial airlines and sell them at discounted rates. The best place to look is in the Sunday travel section of any major newspaper (such as the *New York Times*), where many bucket shops place tiny ads. Call quickly, as availability is typically extremely limited. Not all bucket shops are reliable, so insist on a receipt that gives full details of restrictions, refunds, and tickets, and pay by credit card (in spite of the 2-5% fee) so you can stop payment if you never receive your tickets. For more info, see www.travel-library.com/air-travel/consolidators.html.

Travel Avenue (☎800-333-3335; www.travelavenue.com) searches for best available published fares and then uses several consolidators to attempt to beat that fare. **NOW Voyager,** 315 W. 49th St. Plaza Arcade, New York, NY 10019 (☎212-459-1616; www.nowvoyagertravel.com) arranges discounted flights, mostly from New York, to Barcelona, Madrid, and London (from where many cheap flights to Spain and Portugal are available). Other consolidators worth trying are **Rebel** (☎ 800-732-3588; www.rebeltours.com) and **Cheap Tickets** (☎ 800-652-4327; www.cheaptickets.com). Other consolidators on the web include **Flights.com** (www.flights.com) and **TravelHUB** (www.travelhub.com). Keep in mind that these are just suggestions to get you started in your research; *Let's Go* does not endorse any of these agencies. As always, be cautious, and research companies before you hand over your credit card number.

CHARTER FLIGHTS

Charters are flights a tour operator contracts with an airline to fly extra loads of passengers during peak season. Charter flights fly less frequently than major airlines, make refunds particularly difficult, and are almost always fully booked. Schedules and itineraries may also change or be cancelled at the last moment (as late as 48 hours before the trip, and without a full refund), and check-in, boarding, and baggage claim are often much slower. However, they can also be cheaper.

Discount clubs and fare brokers offer members savings on last-minute charters. Study contracts closely; you don't want to end up with an unwanted overnight layover. Travelers Advantage, 7 Cambridge Dr., Trumbull, CT 06611, USA (☎ 877-259-2691; www.travelersadvantage.com; US$90 annual fee includes discounts and cheap flight directories) specializes in European travel and tour packages.

BY TRAIN

Rail travel is common and inexpensive throughout Spain and Portugal, although you may find bus schedules and routes more convenient. For more information on railway systems, refer to the country-specific **By Train** sections (p. 79 and p. 673).

SHOULD YOU BUY A RAILPASS? Railpasses were conceived to allow you to jump on any train in Europe, go wherever you want whenever you want, and change your plans at will. In practice, it's not so simple. You still must stand in line to validate your pass, pay for supplements, and fork over cash for seat and couchette reservations. More importantly, railpasses don't always pay off. Consult a **railplanner** to estimate the point-to-point cost of each leg of your journey; add them up and compare the total with the cost of a railpass. If you are planning to spend extensive time on trains, hopping between big cities and traveling to many countries, a railpass will probably be worth it. But in many cases, especially if you are under 26, point-to-point tickets may prove a cheaper option.

 JUST SAY NO. If you are planning on traveling in just Spain and Portugal, do not buy a Eurailpass. Train travel in these countries is less expensive than the rest of Europe, where passes can save you from paying for expensive train fares. A Eurailpass makes sense only for those planning to travel in other European countries as well. However, a Eurail Select Pass may still be a good bet.

MULTINATIONAL RAILPASSES

EURAILPASS. Eurail is **valid** in most of Western Europe: Austria, Belgium, Denmark, Finland, France, Germany, Greece, Hungary, Italy, Luxembourg, the Netherlands, Norway, Portugal, the Republic of Ireland, Romania, Spain, Sweden, and Switzerland. It is **not valid** in the UK or Morocco. Standard **Eurailpasses,** valid for a consecutive given number of days, are best for those planning on spending extensive time on trains every few days. **Flexipasses,** valid for any 10 or 15 (not necessarily consecutive) days within a two-month period, are more cost-effective for those traveling longer distances less frequently. **Saverpasses** provide first-class travel for travelers in groups of two to five (prices are per person). **Youthpasses** and **Youth Flexipasses** provide parallel second-class perks for those under 26.

EURAILPASSES	15 DAYS	21 DAYS	1 MONTH	2 MONTHS	3 MONTHS
1st class Eurailpass	US$588	US$762	US$946	US$1338	US$1654
Eurail Saverpass	US$498	US$648	US$804	US$1138	US$1408
Eurail Youthpass	US$414	US$534	US$664	US$938	US$1160

EURAIL FLEXIPASSES	10 DAYS IN 2 MONTHS	15 DAYS IN 2 MONTHS
1st class Eurail Flexipass	US$694	US$914
Eurail Saver Flexipass	US$592	US$778
Eurail Youth Flexipass	US$488	US$642

Passholders receive a timetable for major routes and a map with details on possible ferry, steamer, bus, car rental, hotel, and Eurostar discounts. Passholders often also receive reduced fares or free passage on many bus and boat lines.

EURAIL SELECT PASS. The Eurail Select Pass is a slimmed-down version of the Eurailpass: it allows five to 15 days of unlimited travel in any two-month period within three, four, or five bordering countries of the 18 Eurail network countries. **First-Class passes** (for individuals) and **Saverpasses** (for people traveling in groups of 2-5) range from US$356/304 per person (5 days) to US$794/674 (15 days). **Second-Class Youthpasses** for those aged 12-25 cost US$249-556. For a fee, you can add **additional zones** such as Portugal, which is not included in any of the zones available. You are entitled to the same **freebies** afforded by the Eurailpass, but only when they are within or between countries that you have purchased.

SHOPPING AROUND FOR A EURAIL. Eurailpasses are designed by the EU itself, and can be bought only by non-Europeans almost exclusively from non-European distributors. Some travel agents tack on a US$10 handling fee, and others offer certain bonuses with purchase, so shop around. Also, keep in mind that pass prices usually go up each year, so if you're planning to travel early in the year, you can save cash by purchasing before January 1. It is best to buy your Eurail before leaving; only a few places in major European cities sell them, and at a marked-up price. They will replace a lost pass only if you have purchased insurance on it under the Pass Protection Plan (US$14-17). Eurailpasses are available through travel agents, student travel agencies like STA (p. 22) and **Rail Europe** (Canada ☎ 800-361-7245; UK 08 705 848 848; US 877-257-2887; www.raileurope.com).

INTERRAIL PASSES. If you have lived for at least six months in one of the countries where **InterRail Passes** are valid, or in Algeria, Belarus, Estonia, Latvia, Lithuania, Moldova, Russia, Tunisia, or Ukraine, you are eligible to purchase them; they often prove an economical option. There are eight InterRail **zones**, one of which includes Spain and Portugal. The **Under 26 InterRail Card** allows either 21 consecutive days or one month of unlimited travel within one, two, three or all of the eight zones; the cost is determined by the number of zones the pass covers (UK£119-249). A card can also be purchased for 12 days of travel in one zone (£119). The **Over 26 InterRail Card** provides the same services as the Under 26 InterRail Card, but at higher prices: UK£169-355. The new **Child Pass** (ages 4-11) offers the same services (UK£85-178). Passholders receive **discounts** on rail travel, Eurostar journeys, and most ferries to Ireland, Scandinavia, and the rest of Europe. Most exclude **supplements** for high-speed trains. For info and ticket sales in Europe contact **Student Travel Centre**, 24 Rupert St., 1st fl., London W1D 6DQ (☎ 020 74 37 81 01; www.student-travel-centre.com). Tickets are also available from travel agents, at major train stations, or through on-line vendors (www.railpassdirect.co.uk).

DOMESTIC RAILPASSES

If you are planning to spend a significant amount of time within Spain or Portugal, a national pass—valid on all rail lines of a country's rail company—may be more cost-effective than a multinational pass, but not more so than point-to-point tickets unless you're taking many long-distance or high-speed trains. Many of them are limited and don't provide the free or discounted travel on private railways and ferries that Eurail does. Some of these passes can be bought only in Europe, some only outside of Europe; check with a railpass agent or with national tourist offices.

NATIONAL RAILPASSES. The domestic cousins of the Eurailpass, national railpasses are valid for a specific number of days within a given time period. Usually, they must be purchased before you leave. Three-day Iberic railpasses run US$219, a three-day Flexipass for Spain is US$175-225, and a four-day Flexipass for Portugal is US$105. Travelers can purchase additional days individually. For more information, check out www.raileurope.com/us/rail/passes/single_country_index.htm or the Spain (p. 79) and Portugal (p. 673) **By Train** sections.

EURO DOMINO. Like the Interrail Pass, the Euro Domino pass is available to anyone who has lived in a participating country for at least six months; however, it is only valid in one country (which you designate when buying the pass). It is available for 29 European countries plus Morocco. Reservations must still be paid for separately. **Supplements** are included for many high-speed trains. The pass must be bought within your country of residence; each country has its own price for the pass. Inquire with your national rail company for more info.

RAIL-AND-DRIVE PASSES. In addition to simple railpasses, Spain (as well as Eurail) offers rail-and-drive passes, which combine car rental with rail travel—a good option for travelers who want to visit cities accessible by rail and to make side trips into the surrounding areas (see **By Car**, p. 81).

DISCOUNTED TICKETS

For travelers under 26, **BIJ** tickets (Billets Internationals de Jeunesse; issued by **Wasteels**) are a great alternative to railpasses. Available for international trips within Europe as well as most ferry services, they knock 20-40% off 1st- and 2nd-class fares. Tickets are good for two months after purchase and allow stopovers along the normal direct route of the train journey. Issued for a specific international route between two points, they must be used in the direction and order of the designated route and must be bought in Europe. The equivalent for those over 26, **BIGT** tickets provide a 20-30% discount on 1st- and 2nd-class international tickets. Both types of tickets are available from European travel agents, at Wasteels offices (usually in or near train stations), or directly at the ticket counter in some nations. For more info, contact **Wasteels** (p. 22).

BY BUS

Though European trains and railpasses are extremely popular, in some cases buses prove a better option, especially once you've arrived in Spain or Portugal (see **Getting Around: By Bus**, p. 31). Amsterdam and London are centers for lines that offer long-distance rides across Europe. Often cheaper than railpasses, **international bus passes** allow unlimited travel on a hop-on, hop-off basis between major European cities. The prices below are based on high-season travel.

Busabout, 258 Vauxhall Bridge Rd., London SW1V 1BS (☎207 950 1661; www.busabout.com). Offers 5 interconnecting bus circuits covering 60 cities and towns including Barcelona, Lisboa, London, and Madrid. Consecutive Day Passes, Flexi Passes, and

Add On Passes are available. Consecutive Day Standard/student passes are valid for 2 weeks (UK£239/219), 4 weeks (UK£389/339), 6 weeks (UK£479/429), 8 weeks (UK£569/499), 12 weeks (UK£699/619), or the season (UK£819/729).

Eurolines, 4 Vicarage Rd., Edgbaston, Birmingham, B15 3ES (☎87 0514 3219; www.eurolines.com). The largest operator of Europe-wide coach services with offices in **Madrid** (Estación Sur de Autobuses, C. Méndez Álvaro, 83 (☎915 06 33 60) and **Barcelona** (Ronda Universitat, 5; ☎933 176 209). Unlimited 15-day (high season UK£174, under 26 and over 60 UK£145; low season UK£135/113); 30-day (high season UK£259/209; low season UK£189/153); or 60-day (high season UK£299/229; low season UK£239/189) travel passes that offer unlimited transit between 31 major European cities.

BY BOAT FROM THE UK

Sample fares are **one-way** for **adult foot passengers** unless otherwise noted. Though standard return fares are usually just twice the one-way fare, **fixed-period returns** are almost invariably cheaper. Ferries run **year-round** unless otherwise noted. **Bikes** are usually free, though you may have to pay up to UK£10 in high season. **Brittany Ferries** (UK ☎08703 665 333; France ☎08 25 82 88 28; www.brittany-ferries.com) run from Plymouth to Santander, Spain (18hr., 1-2 per week, round-trip £80-145). **P&O European Ferries** (UK ☎087 0242 4999; www.poportsmouth.com) sail from Portsmouth to Bilbao, Spain (35hr., 2 per week, from £150).

GETTING AROUND

BY PLANE

Many national airlines offer multi-stop tickets for travel within Spain and Portugal. These tickets are particularly useful for travel between the Spanish mainland and the Islas Baleares and Canarias. For more information on intra-country plane travel in Spain and Portugal, see **By Plane,** p. 79 and p. 673.

BY TRAIN

Trains in Spain and Portugal are generally comfortable, convenient, and swift. Second-class travel is pleasant, and compartments are great places to meet fellow travelers. However, they are not always safe; for safety tips, see p. 17. For long trips, make sure you're in the correct car, as trains sometimes split at crossroads.

RESERVATIONS. While seat reservations are required only for selected trains (usually on major lines), you are not guaranteed a seat without advance booking. Reservations are available on major trains up to two months in advance, and Europeans often reserve far ahead of time; you should strongly consider reserving during peak holiday and tourist seasons (at the very latest a few hours ahead). It will be necessary to purchase a **supplement** (US$10-50) or special fare for high speed or quality trains such as Spain's AVE.

OVERNIGHT TRAINS. Night trains have their advantages—you won't waste valuable daylight hours traveling, and you will be able to forego the hassle and considerable expense of securing a night's accommodation. However, night travel has its drawbacks as well: discomfort and sleepless nights are the most obvious. **Sleeping accommodations** on trains differ from country to country, but typically you can either sleep upright in your seat (for free) or pay for a separate space. **Couchettes** (berths) typically have four to six bunks per compartment (about US$20 per person); **sleepers** (beds) in private sleeping cars offer more privacy and comfort, but are considerably more expensive (US$40-150). If you are using a railpass valid only for a restricted number of days, inspect train schedules to maximize the use of your pass: an overnight train or boat journey uses only one of your travel days if it departs after 7pm (you need only write in the next day's date on your pass).

BY BUS

Though trains are quite popular in the rest of Europe, buses are often a better option in Spain and Portugal. In Spain, the bus and train systems are on par; in Portugal, bus networks are more extensive, more efficient, and often more comfortable. See the **By Bus** sections of Spain (p. 80) and Portugal (p. 673) for country-specific details on bus travel.

BY BOAT

It is possible to travel both to and among the **Islas Canarias** (p. 630) and the **Islas Baleares** (p. 355) by ferry. It is also the least expensive way of traveling between Spain and **Tangier** (p. 818) or the Spanish enclave of **Ceuta** in Morocco (p. 818). For specific information, see the section for your destination.

BY CAR

See the **By Car** sections for Spain (p. 81) and Portugal (p. 673) for specifics on driving in each country. Before setting off, learn the countries' traffic laws. The **Association for Safe International Road Travel (ASIRT)** can provide more information about road conditions in Spain and Portugal. ASIRT is located at 11769 Gainsborough Rd, Potomac, MD 20854 USA (☎301-983-5252; www.asirt.org).

 DRIVING PRECAUTIONS. When traveling in the summer, bring substantial amounts of water (a suggested 5 liters of **water** per person per day) for drinking and for the radiator. For long drives to unpopulated areas, register with police before beginning the trek, and again upon arrival at the destination. Check with the local automobile club for details. When traveling for long distances, make sure tires are in good repair and have enough air, and get good maps. A **compass** and a **car manual** can also be very useful. You should always carry a **spare tire** and **jack, jumper cables, extra oil, flares, a flashlight (torch),** and **heavy blankets** (in case your car breaks down at night or in the winter). If you don't know how to **change a tire,** learn before heading out, especially if you are planning on traveling in deserted areas. Blowouts on dirt roads are exceedingly common. If you do have a breakdown, **stay with your car;** if you wander off, there's less likelihood trackers will find you.

RENTING

Cars offer speed, freedom, access to countryside, and an escape from the town-to-town mentality of trains. Unfortunately, they also insulate you from the *esprit de corps* of rail traveling, and driving in major cities can be hair-raising. Although a single traveler won't save by renting a car, a group of four usually will. If you can't decide between train and car travel, you may benefit from a combination of the two; Rail Europe and other railpass vendors offer rail-and-drive packages.

Cheaper cars tend to be less reliable and harder to handle on difficult terrain. Less expensive 4WD vehicles in particular tend to be more top-heavy, and are more dangerous when navigating bumpy roads.

ESSENTIALS

RENTAL AGENCIES

You can generally make reservations before you leave by calling major international offices in your home country. However, occasionally the price and availability information they give doesn't jive with what the local offices in your country will tell you. Try checking with both numbers to make sure you get the best price and accurate information. Local desk numbers are included in town listings; for home-country numbers, call your toll-free directory.

The **minimum age** to rent in Spain and Portugal is usually 25 at larger agencies (Hertz, Avis) and 21 at local businesses. Usually, all you need is a US license and proof that you've had it for a year, although in Spain some agencies may require an International Driving Permit (p. 32). Rental agencies in Iberia include:

Alamo (☎ 800-GO-ALAMO; www.alamo.com). Alamo has 160 offices in Spain and 10 in Portugal, including the airports of Barcelona, Lisboa, Madrid, and Sevilla. Frequent flyer deals available when flying on most major US airlines.

Auto Europe (US ☎ 888-223-5555; www.autoeurope.com). Offers car rentals in Spain and Portugal, as well flight and hotel bookings. Also rents cell phones to US citizens traveling in Europe.

Budget (☎ 800-472-3325; www.budget.com). Rentals in Spain and Portugal.

Europcar (in the US and Canada ☎ 877-940-6900, in the UK ☎ 087 0607 5000; www.europcar.com, www.europcar.co.uk). Rentals in Spain and Portugal. One of the few services that will rent to those ages 21-24 in most locations.

Europe by Car (☎ 800-223-1516; www.europebycar.com). 5% student discount.

Hertz (in Australia ☎ 03 9698 2555, in the UK 087 0844 8844, in the US 800-654-3001; www.hertz.com). Rentals in Spain and Portugal.

Check the **By Car** sections for detailed information on average rental prices in Spain (p. 81) and Portugal (p. 673). When renting, return the car with a full tank of petrol to avoid high fuel charges at the end. Be sure to ask whether the price includes **insurance** against theft and collision. Remember that if you are driving a conventional rented vehicle on an **unpaved road** you are almost never covered by insurance; ask about this before leaving the rental agency. Beware that cars rented on an **American Express** or **Visa/MasterCard Gold or Platinum** credit cards in Spain or Portugal might *not* carry the automatic insurance that they would in some other countries; check with your credit card company. National chains often allow one-way rentals, picking up in one city and dropping off in another. There is usually a minimum hire period and sometimes a drop-off charge of several hundred dollars.

DRIVING PERMITS AND CAR INSURANCE

INTERNATIONAL DRIVING PERMIT (IDP)

If you plan to drive a car while in Spain or Portugal you must be over 18 and have had a driver's license for at least one year. An **International Driving Permit** is usually not required, but it may be a good idea to get one anyway, in case you're in a situation where the police do not know English; information on the IDP is printed in ten languages, including Spanish and Portuguese.

Your IDP, valid for one year, must be issued in your own country before you depart. An application for an IDP usually requires one or two photos, a current local license, an additional form of identification, and a fee. To apply, contact the national or local branch of your home country's automobile association, like the **American Automobile Association** (AAA) in the US or the **Automobile Association** (AA) in the UK. Be careful purchasing an IDP anywhere other than an automobile association. Many vendors sell permits of questionable legitimacy for higher prices.

CAR INSURANCE

Most credit cards cover standard insurance. If you rent, lease, or borrow a car, you will need a **green card**, or **International Insurance Certificate,** to certify that you have liability insurance and that it applies abroad. Green cards can be obtained at rental agencies, car dealers (for those leasing cars), travel agents, and border crossings.

BY BICYCLE

Today, biking is one of the key elements of the budget European adventure. With the proliferation of mountain bikes, you can do some serious natural sightseeing. If you're nervous about striking out alone, **Blue Marble Travel** (in Canada ☎519-624 2494, in the UK 0871 733 3148, in the US 215-923-3788; www.bluemarble.org) offers bike tours in Galicia and País Vasco designed for adults ages 20 to 50.

Few airlines will count your bike as your second piece of luggage, and most charge extra. The additional fee runs about US$50-75 each way. Airlines sell bike boxes at the airport (US$20-25), although it is easier and cheaper to get one from a local bike store. Most ferries let you take your bike for free or for a nominal fee. You can almost always ship your bike on trains, though the cost varies.

Renting a bike beats bringing your own if your touring will be confined to one or two regions. *Let's Go* lists bike rental shops for larger cities and towns, when they exist. Some youth hostels rent bicycles for low prices. Some train stations rent bikes and often allow you to drop them off elsewhere.

BY MOPED AND MOTORCYCLE

Motorized bikes don't use much gas, can be put on trains and ferries, and are a good compromise between the high cost of car travel and the limited range of bicycles. In Spain, they are an extremely popular method of transportation for locals, and they can be a fun alternative for tourist daytrips. However, they're uncomfortable for long distances, dangerous in the rain, and unpredictable on rough roads and gravel. Always wear a helmet, and never ride with a backpack. If you've never been on a moped, the windy roads of the Pyrenees and the congested streets of Madrid are not the place to start.

Before renting, ask if the quoted price includes tax and insurance, or you may be hit with an unexpected additional fee. Avoid handing your passport over as a deposit; if you have an accident or mechanical failure you may not get it back until you cover all repairs. Pay ahead of time instead.

BY THUMB

 Let's Go never recommends hitchhiking as a safe means of transportation, and none of the information presented here is intended to do so.

Let's Go strongly urges you to consider the risks before you choose to hitchhike. Hitching means entrusting your life to whatever stranger happens to stop beside you on the road, risking theft, assault, sexual harassment, and unsafe driving. Some travelers find that hitching allows them to meet locals and get where they want to go, especially in areas where public transportation is sparse or unreliable. The choice, however, remains yours.

Experienced hitchers pick a spot outside of built-up areas, where drivers can stop, return to the road without causing an accident, and have time to look over potential passengers as they approach. Hitching (or even standing) on super-high-

ESSENTIALS

ways is usually illegal: one may only thumb at rest stops or at the entrance ramps to highways. Finally, success will depend on what one looks like. Successful hitchers travel light and stack their belongings in a compact but visible cluster. Most Europeans signal with an open hand, rather than a thumb; many write their destination on a sign in large, bold letters and draw a smiley-face under it.

Safety issues are always imperative, even for those who are not hitching alone. Safety-minded hitchers never let go of their backpacks or get into a car that they can't get out of again in a hurry. If they ever feel threatened, they insist on being let off, regardless of where they are. Acting as if they are going to vomit or open the car door will usually get a driver to stop. Hitchhiking at night can be particularly dangerous; experienced hitchers stand in well-lit places. Women traveling alone or even in pairs should never hitchhike.

KEEPING IN TOUCH

BY MAIL

See the **Keeping in Touch** sections for Spain (p. 84) and Portugal (p. 675) for more detailed information about mailing from abroad.

SENDING MAIL HOME

Airmail is the best way to send mail home from Spain and Portugal. **Aerogrammes,** printed sheets that fold into envelopes and travel via airmail, are available at post offices. Write "airmail" or "par avion" on the front. Most post offices will charge exorbitant fees or simply refuse to send aerogrammes with enclosures. **Surface mail** is by far the cheapest and slowest way to send mail. It takes one to two months to cross the Atlantic and two to three to cross the Pacific—good for heavy items you won't need for a while, such as souvenirs or other articles you've acquired along the way that are weighing down your pack. To the United States, postcards and letters generally cost about €0.80, and may take weeks to arrive. For details on mailing to your country from Spain, see www.correos.es; from Portugal, see www.ctt.pt.

SENDING MAIL ABROAD

To ensure timely delivery, mark envelopes "airmail" or "par avion." In addition to the standard postage system whose rates are listed below, **Federal Express** (Australia ☎ 13 26 10; Canada and US 800-463-3339; Ireland 1800 535 800; New Zealand 0800 733 339; UK 0800 123 800; www.fedex.com) handles express mail services from most countries to Spain and Portugal; for example, they can get a letter from New York to Madrid in 2 days for US$40, and from London to Madrid in 1 day for UK£20.

RECEIVING MAIL ABROAD

There are several ways to arrange pick-up of letters sent to you by friends and relatives while you are abroad. Mail can be sent via **Poste Restante** (General Delivery; **Lista de Correos** in Spanish, **Posta Restante** in Portuguese) to almost any city or town in Spain or Portugal with a post office, and is fairly reliable. Address *Poste Restante* letters like so:

> **Spain:** ELIE, Dominique; Lista de Correos; Post Office Street Address; City; Postal Code; SPAIN; PAR AVION.

> **Portugal:** CAITO, Tim; Posta Restante; Post Office Street Address; City; Postal Code; POR-TUGAL; PAR AVION.

The mail will go to a special desk in the central post office, unless you specify a post office by street address. It's best to use the largest post office, since mail may be sent there regardless. Bring your passport for pick-up. There is generally no surcharge; if there is one, it should not exceed the cost of postage. If the clerks insist that there is nothing for you, have them check under your first name as well. *Let's Go* lists post offices in the **Practical Information** section for each city.

OTHER OPTIONS. DHL (in the US ☎ 800-225-5345, Spain 915 86 77 66, Portugal 918 10 00 80; www.dhl.com) can get a document from New York to Madrid in 1-2 days for US$40.

BY TELEPHONE

CALLING HOME

A **calling card** is probably your cheapest bet. Calls are billed collect or to your account. You can call collect without a calling card just by calling any access number and following the instructions. **To obtain a calling card** from your phone company before leaving home, contact them at the number listed below in the first column. To **call home with a calling card,** contact the operator for your service provider in Spain or Portugal by dialing the appropriate toll-free access number.

COMPANY	TO OBTAIN A CARD, DIAL:	TO CALL ABROAD, DIAL:
AT&T (US)	800-364-9292	**Spain:** 900 99 011 **Portugal:** 800 800 128
Canada Direct	800-561-8868	**Spain:** 900 99 0015 **Portugal:** 800 800 122
MCI (US)	800-777-5000	**Spain:** 800 09 9357 **Portugal:** 800 800 123
Telstra Australia	13 22 00	**Spain:** 900 99 6138 **Portugal:** 800 861 799

You can usually also make direct international calls from pay phones, but if you aren't using a calling card, you may need to drop your coins as quickly as your words. Prepaid phone cards and occasionally major credit cards can be used for direct international calls, but they are expensive. Calling collect through an international operator is even more expensive, but may be necessary in an emergency. Before settling on a calling card plan, be sure to research your options in order to pick the one that best fits both your needs and your destination.

 PLACING INTERNATIONAL CALLS. To call Spain or Portugal from home or to call home from abroad, dial:
1. The international dialing prefix. From **Australia,** dial 0011; **Canada** or the **US,** 011; **Ireland, New Zealand, Portugal, Spain,** or the **UK,** 00.
2. The **country code** of the country you want to call. For **Australia,** dial 61; **Canada** or the **US,** 1; **Ireland,** 353; **New Zealand,** 64; **Portugal,** 351; **Spain,** 34; the **UK,** 44.
3. The **city/area code.** *Let's Go* lists the city/area codes for cities and towns in Spain and Portugal opposite the city or town name, next to a ☎.
4. The **local number.**

CALLING WITHIN SPAIN AND PORTUGAL

The simplest way to call within Spain and Portugal is with **prepaid phone cards** (available at kiosks and tobacco stores), which carry a certain amount of time depending on the card's denomination and usually save time and money in the long

ESSENTIALS

run. The phone will tell you how much time remains. Another kind of prepaid phone card comes with a PIN and toll-free access number. Instead of inserting the card into the phone, you call the number and follow the directions. These can be used to make international as well as domestic calls. Phone rates are typically highest in the morning, lower in the evening, and lowest on Sunday and late at night.

CELLULAR PHONES

The international standard for cell phones is **GSM,** a system that began in Europe and has spread to much of the rest of the world. To make and receive calls in Spain or Portugal, you will need a **GSM-compatible phone** and a **SIM (subscriber identity module) card,** a country-specific, thumbnail-sized chip that gives you a local phone number and plugs you into the local network. Many SIM cards are **prepaid,** meaning that they come with calling time included and you don't need to sign up for a monthly service plan. Incoming calls are often free. When you use up the prepaid time, you can buy additional cards or vouchers (usually available at convenience stores) to get more. For more information on GSM phones, check out www.telestial.com, www.vodafone.com, www.telefonica.com, www.amena.com, or www.planetomni.com. Companies like **Cellular Abroad** (www.cellularabroad.com) rent cell phones that work in a variety of destinations around the world, providing a simpler but much more expensive option than picking up a phone in-country.

 GSM PHONES. Just having a GSM phone doesn't mean you're necessarily good to go when you travel abroad. The majority of GSM phones sold in the United States operate on a different frequency (1900) than international phones (900/1800) and will not work abroad. **Tri-band phones** work on all three frequencies (900/1800/1900) and will operate through most of the world. As well, some GSM phones are **SIM-locked** and will only accept SIM cards from a single carrier. You'll need a **SIM-unlocked** phone to use a SIM card from a local carrier when you travel.

Cell phones are extremely common throughout Spain and Portugal. Having one will make your life much easier, whether you use it to make plans with fellow travelers, call ahead for reservations, or keep in touch with people back home. If you own a tri-band GSM phone, all you will need to purchase is a SIM card, which will provide you with a local number in Spain or Portugal. If you need to buy a phone there because yours is not GSM, it will most likely not function in the US, but could be used for future travel in many other countries. A SIM card alone costs about €20, and it can be charged with however much money you desire. A SIM card and phone package usually runs about €80-100 and includes up to €60 of funds. International calls cost about €0.75-1.50 per min. from a cell phone in either country, but it's free to receive calls from anywhere in the world as long as you remain in the country where the phone was purchased. Local calls run between €0.05-0.40 per min. depending on the type of call, time of day, and service plan.

BY EMAIL AND INTERNET

Email is quite easy to access in Spain and Portugal. Though in some places it's possible to forge a remote link with your home server, in most cases this is a much slower (and thus more expensive) option than taking advantage of free **web-based email accounts** (e.g., www.hotmail.com and www.yahoo.com). **Internet cafes** and the occasional free Internet terminal at a public library or university are listed in the **Practical Information** sections of major cities. For lists of additional cybercafes in Spain and Portugal, check out www.globaltrekk.com or www.about.com.

Increasingly, travelers find that taking their **laptop computers** on the road can be a convenient way to stay connected. Laptop users can call an Internet service provider via a modem using long-distance phone cards. They may also find Internet cafes that allow them to connect their laptops to the Internet. Travelers with wireless-enabled computers may be able to take advantage of an increasing number of Internet "hotspots," where they can get online for free or for a small fee. Newer computers can detect these hotspots automatically; otherwise, websites like www.jiwire.com, www.wi-fihotspotlist.com, and www.locfinder.net can help you find them. For information on insuring your laptop while traveling, see p. 18.

ACCOMMODATIONS

For more specific information on accommodations, see the **Accommodations** sections for Spain (p. 83) and Portugal (p. 674).

HOSTELS

Many hostels are laid out dorm-style, with single-sex rooms and bunk beds, although private rooms have become more common. They sometimes have kitchens, bike or moped rentals, storage areas, airport shuttles, breakfast, laundry facilities, and Internet access. There can be drawbacks: some hostels close during certain daytime "lockout" hours, have a curfew, don't accept reservations, impose a maximum stay, or, less frequently, require that you do chores. In Spain, a bed in a hostel costs around €13-25 per night, while one in Portugal will be €12-20.

 A HOSTELER'S BILL OF RIGHTS. There are certain standard features that we do not include in our hostel listings. Unless we state otherwise, you can expect that every hostel has no lockout, no curfew, free hot showers, some system of secure luggage storage, and no key deposit.

HOSTELLING INTERNATIONAL

Joining the youth hostel association in your own country (listed below) automatically grants you membership privileges in **Hostelling International (HI),** a federation of national hosteling associations. Non-HI members may be allowed to stay in some hostels, but will have to pay extra to do so. HI hostels are scattered throughout Spain and Portugal and are typically less expensive than private hostels. HI's umbrella organization's web page (www.hihostels.com), which lists the web addresses and phone numbers of all national associations, can be a great place to begin researching hosteling in a specific region. Other comprehensive hosteling websites include www.hostels.com and www.hostelplanet.com.

Most HI hostels also honor **guest memberships**—you'll get a blank card with space for six validation stamps. Each night you'll pay a nonmember supplement (one-sixth the membership fee) and earn one guest stamp; get six stamps, and you're a member. This system works well in most of Western Europe, but in some countries you may need to remind the hostel reception. A new membership benefit is the FreeNites program, which allows hostelers to gain points toward free rooms. Most student travel agencies (p. 22) sell HI cards, as do all of the national hosteling organizations listed below. All prices listed below are valid for **one-year memberships** unless otherwise noted.

Australian Youth Hostels Association (AYHA), 422 Kent St., Sydney, NSW 200 (☎02 9261 1111; www.yha.com.au). AUS$52, under 18 AUS$19.

Hostelling International-Canada (HI-C), 205 Catherine St. #400, Ottawa, ON K2P 1C3 (☎613-237-7884; www.hihostels.ca). CDN$35, under 18 free.

An Óige (Irish Youth Hostel Association), 61 Mountjoy St., Dublin 7 (☎830 4555; www.irelandyha.org). €20, under 18 €10.

Hostelling International Northern Ireland (HINI), 22 Donegal Rd., Belfast BT12 5JN (☎02890 31 54 35; www.hini.org.uk). UK£13, under 18 UK£6.

Youth Hostels Association of New Zealand (YHANZ), Level 1, Moorhouse City, 166 Moorhouse Ave., P.O. Box 436, Christchurch (☎0800 278 299 (NZ only) or 03 379 9970; www.yha.org.nz). NZ$40, under 18 free.

Scottish Youth Hostels Association (SYHA), 7 Glebe Cres., Stirling FK8 2JA (☎01786 89 14 00; www.syha.org.uk). UK£6, under 17 £2.50.

Youth Hostels Association (England and Wales), Trevelyan House, Dimple Rd., Matlock, Derbyshire DE4 3YH (☎0870 770 8868; www.yha.org.uk). UK£13.50, under 18 UK£7.

Hostelling International-USA, 8401 Colesville Rd., Ste. 600, Silver Spring, MD 20910 (☎301-495-1240; www.hiayh.org). US$28, under 18 free.

BOOKING HOSTELS ONLINE. One of the easiest ways to ensure you've got a bed for the night is by reserving online. Click to the **Hostelworld** booking engine through **www.letsgo.com,** and you'll have access to bargain accommodations from Argentina to Zimbabwe with no added commission.

OTHER TYPES OF ACCOMMODATIONS

HOTELS, GUESTHOUSES, AND PENSIONES

Hotel singles in Spain cost about €17-25 per night, doubles €28-33. In Portugal rates run €16-25/€26-30. You'll typically share a hall bathroom; a private bathroom will cost extra, as may hot showers. Smaller **guesthouses** and **pensiones** are often cheaper than hotels. If you make **reservations** in writing, indicate your night of arrival and the number of nights you plan to stay. The hotel will send you a confirmation and may request payment for the first night.

BED & BREAKFASTS (B&BS)

For a cozy alternative to impersonal hotel rooms, B&Bs (private homes with rooms available to travelers) range from the acceptable to the sublime. Rooms in B&Bs generally cost €30-50 per person in Spain and €40-60 in Portugal. Any number of websites provide listings for B&Bs. For more information, check out Bed & Breakfast Inns Online (www.bbonline.com), InnFinder (www.inncrawler.com), InnSite (www.innsite.com), BedandBreakfast.com (www.bedandbreakfast.com), or Pamela Lanier's Bed & Breakfast Guide Online (www.lanierbb.com).

UNIVERSITY DORMS

Many **colleges and universities** open their residence halls to travelers when school is not in session; some do so even during term-time. Getting a room may take a couple of phone calls and require advanced planning, but rates tend to be low, and many offer free local calls and Internet access.

HOME EXCHANGES AND HOSPITALITY CLUBS

Home exchange offers the traveler various types of homes (houses, apartments, condominiums, villas, even castles in some cases), plus the opportunity to live like a native and to cut down on accommodations fees. For more information, contact HomeExchange.Com, P.O. Box 787, Hermosa Beach, CA 90254 USA (☎800-877-8723; fax 310-798-3865; www.homeexchange.com), or Intervac International Home Exchange (in Spain ☎934 53 31 71; www.intervac.com).

Hospitality clubs link their members with individuals or families abroad who are willing to host travelers for free or for a small fee to promote cultural exchange and general good karma. In exchange, members usually must be willing to host travelers in their own homes; a small membership fee may also be required. GlobalFreeloaders.com (www.globalfreeloaders.com) and The Hospitality Club (www.hospitalityclub.org) are good places to start. Servas (www.servas.org) is an established, more formal, peace-based organization that requires a fee and an interview to join. An Internet search will find many similar organizations, some of which cater to special interests (e.g., women, gay and lesbian travelers, or members of certain professions). As always, use common sense when planning to stay with or host someone you do not know.

LONG-TERM ACCOMMODATIONS

Travelers planning to stay in Spain or Portugal for extended periods of time may find it most cost-effective to rent an **apartment.** A basic one-bedroom (or studio) apartment in Madrid, Barcelona, or Lisboa will range €250-500 per month. Besides rent, prospective tenants usually are also required to front a security deposit (frequently one month's rent) and the last month's rent. Expatriates.com (www.expatriates.com) has a bulletin board with apartments for rent across Europe.

CAMPING AND THE OUTDOORS

Campgrounds exist throughout Spain and Portugal, although their popularity with travelers varies by region. Frequently, they are located way on the outskirts of cities, and towns making for long, inconvenient, or expensive commutes—so much so that it may work out cheaper for travelers to stay in hostels right in the heart of things, especially for people traveling alone or with one other person.

 LEAVE NO TRACE. Let's Go encourages travelers to embrace the "Leave No Trace" ethic, minimizing their impact on natural environments and protecting them for future generations. Trekkers and wilderness enthusiasts should set up camp on durable surfaces, use cookstoves instead of campfires, bury human waste away from water supplies, bag trash and carry it out with them, and respect wildlife and natural objects. For more detailed information, contact the **Leave No Trace Center for Outdoor Ethics,** PO Box 997, Boulder, CO 80306, USA (☎800-332-4100 or 303-442-8222; www.lnt.org).

USEFUL PUBLICATIONS AND RESOURCES

A variety of publishing companies offer hiking guidebooks to meet the educational needs of novice or expert. For information about camping, hiking, and biking, write or call the publishers listed below to receive a free catalog. Campers heading to Spain or Portugal should consider buying an **International Camping Carnet.** Similar to a hostel membership card, it's required at a few campgrounds and provides discounts at others. It is available in North America from the **Family Campers and RVers Association** and in the UK from **The Caravan Club** (see below).

Automobile Association, Contact Centre, Carr Ellison House, William Armstrong Drive, Newcastle-upon-Tyne NE4 7YA, UK. (☎0870 600 0371; www.theaa.com). Publishes *Caravan and Camping Europe* and *Britain* (both UK£8) as well as Big Road Atlases for Europe and Spain.

The Caravan Club, East Grinstead House, East Grinstead, West Sussex, RH19 1UA, UK (☎44 01342 326 944; www.caravanclub.co.uk). For UK£30, members receive travel equipment discounts, maps, and a monthly magazine.

ESSENTIALS

The Mountaineers Books, 1001 SW Klickitat Way, Ste. 201, Seattle, WA 98134, USA (☎206-223-6303; www.mountaineersbooks.org). Boasts over 600 titles on hiking, biking, mountaineering, natural history, and conservation.

Sierra Club Books, 85 Second St., 2nd fl., San Francisco, CA 94105, USA (☎415-977-5500; www.sierraclub.org). Publishes general resource books on hiking and camping.

NATIONAL PARKS

Spain and Portugal have extensive national park systems, which offer numerous opportunities for hiking, mountaineering, and generally avoiding the cities. Camping within national park boundaries is usually illegal, but campgrounds can be found in most nearby towns. The general procedure is to stock up on equipment and supplies, stop by the visitors' information center to pick up free maps, and head into the park. More detailed maps, with specific hiking or adventure information, can be purchased both at the visitors' centers and in nearby towns. The Spanish government website **La Red de Parques Nacionales** (The National Parks System; www.mma.es/parques/lared) provides information in Spanish about national parks, including trip-planning tools. **Portugal inSite** (www.portugalinsite.com), the official Portuguese tourist office website, offers some information in English and links to details about the parks, usually in Portuguese.

WILDERNESS SAFETY

THE GREAT OUTDOORS

Staying **warm, dry, and well-hydrated** is key to a happy and safe wilderness experience. For any hike, prepare yourself for an emergency by packing a first-aid kit, a reflector, a whistle, high energy food, extra water, raingear, a hat, and mittens. For warmth, wear wool or insulating synthetic materials designed for the outdoors. Cotton is a bad choice since it is useless when wet.

Check **weather forecasts** often and pay attention to the skies when hiking, as weather patterns can change suddenly. Always let someone, either a friend, your hostel, a park ranger, or a local hiking organization, know when and where you are going hiking. Know your limits and do not attempt a hike beyond your ability. See **Staying Healthy,** p. 19, for info on outdoor ailments and medical concerns.

CAMPING AND HIKING EQUIPMENT

WHAT TO BUY

Good camping equipment is both sturdy and light. North American suppliers tend to offer the most competitive prices.

Sleeping Bags: Most sleeping bags are rated by season; "summer" means 30-40°F (around 0°C) at night; "four-season" or "winter" often means below 0°F (-17°C). Bags are made of **down** (warm and light, but expensive, and miserable when wet) or of **synthetic** material (heavy, durable, and warm when wet). Prices range US$50-250 for a summer synthetic to US$200-300 for a good down winter bag. **Sleeping bag pads** include foam pads (US$10-30), air mattresses (US$15-50), and self-inflating mats (US$30-120). Bring a **stuff sack** to store your bag and keep it dry.

Tents: The best tents are free-standing (with their own frames and suspension systems), set up quickly, and only require staking in high winds. Low-profile dome tents are the best all-around. Worthy 2-person tents start at US$100, 4-person at US$160. Make sure your tent has a rain fly and seal its seams with waterproofer. Other useful accessories include a **battery-operated lantern,** a plastic **groundcloth,** and a nylon **tarp.**

Backpacks: Internal-frame packs mold well to your back, keep a lower center of gravity, and flex adequately to allow you to hike difficult trails, while **external-frame packs** are more comfortable for long hikes over even terrain, as they carry weight higher and distribute it more evenly. Make sure your pack has a strong, padded hip-belt to transfer weight to your legs. There are models designed specifically for women. Sturdy backpacks cost anywhere from US$125 to 420—your pack is an area where it doesn't pay to economize. To find the perfect pack, fill up prospective models with something heavy, strap it on, and walk around the store to get a sense of how it distributes weight. Either buy a **rain cover** (US$10-20) or store your belongings in plastic bags inside your pack.

Boots: Be sure to wear hiking boots with good **ankle support.** They should fit snugly and comfortably over 1-2 pairs of **wool socks** and a pair of thin **liner socks.** Break in boots over several weeks before you go to spare yourself blisters.

Other Necessities: Synthetic layers, like those made of polypropylene or polyester, and a pile jacket will keep you warm even when wet. A **space blanket** (US$5-15) will help you to retain body heat and doubles as a groundcloth. Plastic **water bottles** are vital. Carry **water-purification tablets** for when you can't boil water. Since most campgrounds forbid fires, you'll need a **camp stove** (the classic Coleman starts at US$50) and a propane-filled **fuel bottle** to operate it. Also bring a **first-aid kit, pocketknife, insect repellent,** and **waterproof matches** or a **lighter.**

WHERE TO BUY IT

The mail-order/online companies listed below offer lower prices than many retail stores. A visit to a local camping or outdoors store will give you a good sense of the look and weight of certain items.

Campmor, 28 Parkway, P.O. Box 700, Upper Saddle River, NJ 07458, USA (US ☎888-226-7667; www.campmor.com).

Discount Camping, 880 Main North Rd., Pooraka, South Australia 5095, Australia (☎08 8262 3399; www.discountcamping.com.au).

Eastern Mountain Sports (EMS), 1 Vose Farm Rd., Peterborough, NH 03458, USA (☎888-463-6367; www.ems.com).

L.L. Bean, Freeport, ME 04033 (US and Canada ☎800-441-5713; UK 0800 891 297; www.llbean.com).

Mountain Designs, 51 Bishop St., Kelvin Grove, Queensland 4059, Australia (☎07 3856 2344; www.mountaindesigns.com).

Recreational Equipment, Inc. (REI), Sumner, WA 98352, USA (US and Canada ☎800-426-4840, elsewhere 253-891-2500; www.rei.com).

YHA Adventure Shop, 19 High St., Staines, Middlesex, TW18 4QY, UK (☎1784 458625; www.yhaadventure.com).

ORGANIZED ADVENTURE TRIPS

Organized adventure tours offer another way of exploring the wild. Activities include hiking, biking, skiing, canoeing, kayaking, rafting, climbing, and archaeological digs. Tourism bureaus often can suggest parks, trails, and outfitters. Organizations that specialize in camping and outdoor equipment like REI and EMS (see above) are also good sources of info. The **Specialty Travel Index** (US ☎800-442-4922, elsewhere 415-459-4900; www.specialtytravel.com) is a great resource.

SPECIFIC CONCERNS

SUSTAINABLE TRAVEL

As the number of travelers on the road continues to rise, the detrimental effect they can have on natural environments is an increasing concern. With this in mind, *Let's Go* promotes the philosophy of **sustainable travel.** Through a sensitivity to issues of ecology and sustainability, today's travelers can be a powerful force in preserving and restoring the places they visit. **Ecotourism,** a rising trend, focuses on conserving natural habitats and using them to build up the economy without exploitation or overdevelopment. Travelers can make a difference by doing research and supporting organizations and establishments that pay attention to their impact on nature and strive to be environmentally friendly.

ECOTOURISM RESOURCES. For more information on environmentally responsible tourism, contact one of the organizations below:

The Centre for Environmentally Responsible Tourism (www.c-e-r-t.org).

Earthwatch, 3 Clock Tower Place, Ste. 100, Box 75, Maynard, MA 01754, USA (☎800-776-0188 or 978-461-0081; www.earthwatch.org).

Global Eco and Spiritual Tours (www.globalecospiritualtours.org).

International Ecotourism Society, 733 15th St. NW, Washington, D.C. 20005, USA (☎202-347-9203; www.ecotourism.org).

TRAVELING ALONE

There are many benefits to traveling alone, including independence and greater interaction with locals. On the other hand, any solo traveler is more vulnerable to harassment and street theft. As a lone traveler, try not to stand out as a tourist, look confident, and be especially careful in deserted or crowded areas. If questioned, never admit that you are alone. Maintain contact with someone at home who knows your itinerary. For more tips, pick up *Traveling Solo* by Eleanor Berman (Globe Pequot Press, US$18), visit www.travelaloneandloveit.com, or subscribe to **Connecting: Solo Travel Network,** 689 Park Rd., Unit 6, Gibsons, BC V0N 1V7, Canada (☎ 604-886-9099; www.cstn.org; membership US$28-45).

WOMEN TRAVELERS

Women exploring on their own inevitably face some additional safety concerns, but it's easy to be adventurous without taking undue risks. If you are concerned, consider staying in hostels which offer single rooms that lock from the inside or in religious organizations with rooms for women only. Stick to centrally located accommodations and avoid solitary late-night treks or metro rides.

Always carry extra money for a phone call, bus, or taxi. **Hitchhiking** is never safe for lone women, or even for two women traveling together. Look as if you know where you're going and approach older women or couples for directions.

Generally, the less you look like a tourist, the better off you'll be. Dress conservatively, especially in rural areas. Wearing a conspicuous **wedding band** sometimes helps to prevent unwanted overtures.

Your best answer to verbal harassment is no answer at all; feigning deafness, sitting motionless, and staring straight ahead at nothing in particular will do a world of good that reactions usually don't achieve. The extremely persistent can sometimes be dissuaded by a firm, loud, and very public "Go away!" in the appropriate language (in Spanish "vete," in Portuguese "vá-se embora"). Don't hesitate to seek out a police officer or a passerby if you are being harassed. Memorize the emergency numbers in places you visit, and consider carrying a whistle on your keychain. A self-defense course (p. 17) will both prepare you for a potential attack and raise your level of awareness of your surroundings to help you avoid them. Also be sure you are aware of the health concerns that women face when traveling (p. 21).

GLBT TRAVELERS

Attitudes toward gay, lesbian, bisexual, and transgendered (GLBT) people in Spain and Portugal vary by region. GLBT travelers may feel out of place in the smaller, rural areas of Spain and Portugal, given the countries' strong Catholic religious heritage, but overt homophobia is rare. Larger cities, especially Barcelona (see **l'Eixample,** p. 420), and Lisboa (see **Bairro Alto,** p. 693) have well-developed gay men's scenes, and lesbian scenes are growing rapidly. In Spain, **Sitges** (p. 435), **Benidorm** (p. 341), and **Ibiza** (p. 380) are internationally renowned as gay party destinations, and Madrid (see **Chueca,** p. 129), has one of the liveliest gay scenes in Europe, including the epic parties of *Orgullo Gay* (Gay Pride) in June. The website www.guiagay.com has info about gay Spain. The Portuguese website www.portugalgay.pt offers similar listings in Portuguese and English.

To avoid hassles at airports and border crossings, transgendered travelers should make sure that all of their travel documents consistently report the same gender. Many countries (including the US, the UK, Canada, Ireland, Australia, and

New Zealand) will amend the passports of post-operative transsexuals to reflect their true gender, although governments are generally less willing to amend documents for pre-operative transsexuals and other transgendered individuals.

Listed below are organizations, mail-order bookstores, and publishers that offer materials addressing some specific concerns. **Out and About** (www.outand-about.com) offers a bi-weekly newsletter addressing travel concerns and a comprehensive site addressing gay travel concerns. The online newspaper **365gay.com** also has a travel section (www.365gay.com/travel/travelchannel.htm).

Gay's the Word, 66 Marchmont St., London WC1N 1AB, UK (☎44 20 7278 7654; www.gaystheword.co.uk). The largest gay and lesbian bookshop in the UK, with both fiction and non-fiction titles. Mail-order service available.

Giovanni's Room, 1145 Pine St., Philadelphia, PA 19107, USA (☎215-923-2960; www.queerbooks.com). An international lesbian/feminist and gay bookstore with mail-order service (carries many of the publications listed below).

International Lesbian and Gay Association (ILGA), 81 rue Marché-au-Charbon, B-1000 Brussels, Belgium (☎32 2 502 2471; www.ilga.org). Provides political information, such as homosexuality laws of individual countries.

TRAVELERS WITH DISABILITIES

Wheelchair accessibility varies widely in Iberia but is generally inferior to that in the US. In Spain and Portugal, handicapped access is common in modern and big city museums. Some Spanish tourist offices abroad can provide useful listings of accessible (but often expensive) accommodations and sights.

FURTHER READING: GLBT TRAVEL.

Spartacus 2003-2004: International Gay Guide. Bruno Gmunder Verlag (US$33).

Damron Men's Travel Guide, Damron Accommodations Guide, Damron City Guide, and *Damron Women's Traveller.* Damron Travel Guides (US$11-19). For info, call ☎ 800-462-6654 or visit www.damron.com.

Ferrari Guides' Gay Travel A to Z, Ferrari Guides' Men's Travel in Your Pocket, Ferrari Guides' Women's Travel in Your Pocket, and *Ferrari Guides' Inn Places.* Ferrari Publications (US$16-20).

The Gay Vacation Guide: The Best Trips and How to Plan Them, Mark Chesnut. Kensington Books (US$15).

Those with disabilities should inform airlines and hotels of their disabilities when making reservations; some time may be needed to prepare special accommodations. Call ahead to restaurants, museums, and other facilities to find out if they are wheelchair-accessible. **Guide dog owners** should inquire as to the quarantine policies of each destination country.

Rail is probably the most convenient form of travel for disabled travelers in Europe: many stations have ramps, and some trains have wheelchair lifts, special seating areas, and specially equipped toilets. All Eurostar, some InterCity (IC) and some EuroCity (EC) trains are wheelchair-accessible and CityNightLine trains feature special compartments. Spain and Portugal's rail systems have limited resources for wheelchair accessibility, especially in smaller stations. For those who wish to rent cars, some major **car rental** agencies (Hertz, Avis, and National) offer hand-controlled vehicles.

USEFUL ORGANIZATIONS

Access Abroad, www.umabroad.umn.edu/access. A website devoted to making study abroad available to students with disabilities. The site is maintained by Disability Services Research and Training, University of Minnesota, University Gateway, Ste. 180, 200 Oak St. SE, Minneapolis, MN 55455, USA (☎ 612-624-6884).

Accessible Journeys, 35 West Sellers Ave., Ridley Park, PA 19078, USA (☎ 800-846-4537; www.disabilitytravel.com). Designs tours for wheelchair users and slow walkers. The site has tips and forums for all travelers.

Directions Unlimited, 123 Green Ln., Bedford Hills, NY 10507, USA (☎ 800-533-5343). Books individual vacations for the physically disabled; not an info service.

Mobility International USA (MIUSA), PO Box 10767, Eugene, OR 97440, USA (☎ 541-343-1284; www.miusa.org). Provides a variety of books and other publications containing information for travelers with disabilities.

Society for Accessible Travel & Hospitality (SATH), 347 Fifth Ave., #610, New York, NY 10016, USA (☎ 212-447-7284; www.sath.org). An advocacy group that publishes free online travel information and the travel magazine *OPEN WORLD* (annual subscription US$13, free for members). Annual membership US$45, students and seniors US$30.

MINORITY TRAVELERS

Because of demographic homogeneity, Spanish people experience little interaction with other races. The infrequent incidents of racism are rarely violent or threatening, just a little awkward. They occur out of naiveté, ignorance, or curiosity rather than insensitivity. However, after the arrest of Moroccans for the terrorist attack of **11-M,** travelers who appear Middle Eastern or wear clearly Muslim garb may face some harassment. Portugal, with its rich ethnic composition, is actively anti-racist, and minority travelers have little to fear.

DIETARY CONCERNS

Spain and Portugal can be difficult places to visit as a strict vegetarian; in Spain meat or fish is featured in the majority of popular dishes. Most restaurants serve salads, however, and there are also many egg-, rice- and bean-based dishes that can be requested without meat. Be careful, though, as many servers may interpret a "vegetarian" order to mean "with tuna instead of ham." The travel section of the The Vegetarian Resource Group's website, at www.vrg.org/travel, has a comprehensive list of organizations and websites that are geared toward helping vegetarians and vegans traveling abroad. For more information, visit your local bookstore or health food store, and consult *The Vegetarian Traveler: Where to Stay if You're Vegetarian, Vegan, Environmentally Sensitive,* by Jed and Susan Civic (Larson Publications; US$16) or *Vegetarian Europe* by Alex Bourke (Vegetarian Guides; US$16.95). Vegetarians will also find numerous resources on the web; try www.vegetariansabroad.com for restaurant listings in Spain. The **North American Vegetarian Society** (☎518-568-7970; www.vegdining.com), also has an excellent database of vegetarian and vegan restaurants worldwide.

Keeping kosher is difficult in Spain and Portugal. If you are strict in your observance, you may have to prepare your own food. Travelers who keep kosher should contact synagogues in larger cities for info on kosher restaurants. Good resources include the website www.shamash.org/kosher and the Jewish Travel Guide, by Michael Zaidner (Vallentine Mitchell; US$17). Your synagogue or college Hillel should have access to lists of Jewish institutions across the nation. Travelers looking for halal restaurants may find www.zabihah.com a useful resource.

OTHER RESOURCES

Let's Go tries to cover all aspects of budget travel, but we can't put *everything* in our guides. Listed below are books and websites that can serve as jumping-off points for your own research.

USEFUL PUBLICATIONS

The Broadsheet, monthly magazine for English speakers in Spain. Features current cultural and social events, as well as news. Web edition at www.tbs.com.es.

Contemporary Spain: A Handbook, Christopher Ross. Broad and informative discussion of Spanish politics, culture, society, and travel (US$25/£13).

Culture Shock! Spain, Marie Louise Graff. With a comprehensive coverage of Spain's history, beliefs, festivals, and working conditions, this book navigates the visitor through local customs, bureaucracy, and eating and entertaining habits (US$14/£10).

Culture Shock! Portugal, Volker Poelzl. Provides information along the same line as Culture Shock! Spain, especially regarding customs and etiquette (US$14/£10).

Focus Magazine (www.focusmm.com), monthly online magazine about the Mediterranean world, with information on Spain.

A Traveller's History of Spain, Juan Lalaguna. Helpful for those seeking more background historical and cultural background information about Spain (US$15).

Worst Case Survival Handbook: Travel, Joshua Piven and David Borgenicht. Finally someone has filled the void: 2 experts offer advice on such things as how to stop a runaway camel and how to navigate a minefield (US$15).

WORLD WIDE WEB

Almost every aspect of budget travel is accessible via the web. In 10min. at the keyboard, you can make a hostel reservation, get advice on travel hotspots from other travelers, or find out how much a train from Madrid to Barcelona costs.

Listed here are some regional and travel-related sites to start off your surfing; other relevant web sites are listed throughout the book. Because website turnover is high, use search engines (such as ☛**www.google.com**) to strike out on your own.

 WWW.LETSGO.COM. Our freshly redesigned website features extensive content from our guides; community forums where travelers can connect with each other and ask questions or advice—as well as share stories and tips; and expanded resources to help you plan your trip. Visit us soon to browse by destination, find information about ordering our titles, and sign up for our e-newsletter!

THE ART OF TRAVEL

Adventure Travel: www.adventuretravelabroad.com. Listings of adventure travel trips around the world.

Backpacker's Ultimate Guide: www.bugeurope.com. Tips on packing, transportation, and where to go. Also tons of country-specific travel information.

BootsnAll.com: www.bootsnall.com. Numerous resources for independent travelers, from planning your trip to reporting on it when you get back.

How to See the World: www.artoftravel.com. A compendium of great travel tips, from cheap flights to self defense to interacting with local culture.

Travel Intelligence: www.travelintelligence.net. A large collection of travel writing by distinguished travel writers.

Travel Library: www.travel-library.com. A fantastic set of links for general information and personal travelogues.

World Hum: www.worldhum.com. An independently produced collection of "travel dispatches from a shrinking planet."

INFORMATION ON SPAIN AND PORTUGAL

All About Spain: www.red2000.com/spain/index.html. Has an excellent photo tour of Spain, traveler's yellow pages, and information on major regions and cities.

Atevo Travel: www.atevo.com/guides/destinations. Detailed introductions, travel tips, and suggested itineraries.

CIA World Factbook: www.odci.gov/cia/publications/factbook/index.html. Statistics on Spanish and Portuguese geography, government, economy, and people.

CyberSpain: www.cyberspain.com. Has a wide variety of tourist and cultural info as well as links to other good sites inside and outside of Spain.

Geographia: www.geographia.com. Highlights and culture of Spain and Portugal.

MadridMan: www.madridman.com. A site devoted entirely to the city of Madrid, with tons of useful info for visitors as well as history, culture, and current events sections.

MyTravelGuide: www.mytravelguide.com. Country overviews, with everything from history to transportation to live web-cam coverage.

ESSENTIALS

PlanetRider: www.planetrider.com. A subjective list of links to the "best" websites covering the culture and tourist attractions of Spain and Portugal.

Portugal-info: www.portugal-info.net. An excellent source for all types of information, from photos to wine descriptions to Portuguese personals.

Sí, Spain: www.sispain.org. Run by the Spanish Ministry of Foreign affairs, this site offers cultural and historical info, tourist info, and another great set of links.

Spain Tourism: www.tourspain.es. The **official** Spanish tourism site. Offers national and city-specific info, an information request service, helpful links on all aspects of travel, cultural and practical info including stats on national parks and museums, and links to the biggest Spanish newspapers. In French, English, Spanish, and German.

TravelPage: www.travelpage.com. Links to tourist office sites in Spain and Portugal.

World Travel Guide: www.travel-guides.com. Helpful practical info.

ALTERNATIVES TO TOURISM

A PHILOSOPHY FOR TRAVELERS

Let's Go believes that travelers can have an important impact on their destinations. We know that many travelers care passionately about the communities and environments they explore—but also that even conscientious tourists can inadvertently damage natural wonders and harm cultural environments. With this "Alternatives to Tourism" chapter, *Let's Go* hopes to promote a better understanding of Spain and Portugal and afford travelers the opportunity to enhance their experience there.

There are several different options for those who seek an alternative to tourism. Opportunities for **volunteering** abound, both with local and international organizations. **Studying** can also be enriching, either in the form of direct enrollment in a local university or in an independent research project. **Working** is a way to both immerse yourself in the local culture and finance your travels.

As a **volunteer** in Spain or Portugal, you can participate in projects from researching ways to prevent desertification in Almería or protecting dolphins on the Costa del Sol to fighting for immigrants' rights in La Coruña. It is possible to volunteer either on a short-term basis or as the main component of your trip. Later in this section, we recommend organizations that can help you find opportunities that suit your interests, whether you're looking to pitch in for a day or a year.

Studying at a college or language program is another option. You can enroll directly in most Spanish and Portuguese universities or study with American programs that guide you through the experience. Study abroad or language programs will often also organize cultural activities that allow you to travel and meet other students. From an art history class at the Prado to a homestay with a Portuguese family, studying abroad turns the country into your classroom.

Many travelers also structure their trips by the **work** that they can do along the way—either odd jobs as they go, or full-time stints in cities where they plan to stay for some time. Those staying in a city, particularly one with a university, will find positions teaching English readily available in most of Spain and Portugal. In both countries, make sure you have met the **legal requirements** for short- or long-term work (see **Working,** p. 59, for more information).

VOLUNTEERING

Volunteering can be one of the most fulfilling experiences you have in life, especially if you combine it with the thrill of traveling in a new place. Throughout Spain and Portugal, you will find ample opportunities to help out, whether by working to conserve diverse habitats or unique creatures, reaching out to immigrants, AIDS victims, or children in need, or fighting for a cause you're passionate about.

Most people who volunteer in Spain or Portugal do so on a short-term basis, at organizations that make use of drop-in or once-a-week volunteers. More intensive volunteer experiences may charge you a fee to participate. These costs can be surprisingly hefty (although they frequently cover airfare and most living expenses). Most people choose to go through a parent organization that takes care of logistical details and often provides a group environment and support system. Going it solo will be exceedingly difficult unless you are proficient in the language of the country in which you want to volunteer.

ENVIRONMENTAL CONSERVATION

As an oil spill off the coast of Galicia made frighteningly apparent in 2003, the environment is vulnerable even in places of great natural beauty, and often more so. Spain and Portugal are lucky to house vast tracts of unspoiled terrain and water; however, every day these regions come under threats from development, business concerns, the abuse of natural resources—and tourism. One way to give back to the countries you visit is to help preserve them for future travelers and future generations. An added bonus of working with the following organizations (or any environmental conservation group in Spain and Portugal) is the chance to revel in the immense beauty of the landscapes you'll be protecting.

Earthwatch, 3 Clocktower Pl. Suite 100, Box 75, Maynard, MA 01754, USA (☎800-776-0188 or 978-461-0081; www.earthwatch.org). Arranges 1- to 3-week programs in Spain to assist archaeologists or conservationists conducting field research. Fees vary based on program location and duration; costs average $2000 plus airfare.

Grupo de Acção e Intervenção Ambiental (GAIA), Faculdade de Ciências e Tecnologia, 2829-516 Caparica, Portugal (☎212 94 96 50; www.gaia.org.pt). Works to educate the Portuguese public about environmental issues and campaigns against the production and sale of genetically modified food.

Sunseed, APDO 9, Sorbas, Almería, Spain (☎950 52 57 70; www.sunseed.org.uk). Researches methods of preventing desertification in the driest part of Spain. Volunteers can stay from 1 week to 1 year at costs varying from €137 per week in high season to none for a year-long residency. Student discount available.

IMMIGRATION ISSUES

Immigration to Spain has been on the rise ever since the *"destapeo"* ("uncovering") that followed the fall of fascism. The greatest number of immigrants come from North Africa (particularly from Morocco), while most of the rest are from Latin America. Portugal is home to many immigrants from Brazil and its former African colonies. An immigrant's life can be difficult, and legal structures often fail to provide equal rights for non-citizens. Portugal is much more tolerant of other cultures than Spain, however, and its attitude toward immigration is less hostile. There are many organizations working to alleviate the burdens placed on immigrants and eliminate the inequality they face; listed below are just a few of them.

ARSIS, C. General Weyler, 257, 08912 Badalona (Barcelona), Spain (☎933 83 67 43; www.arsis.org). Volunteer in their tutoring program for underprivileged children and women's center, or work on food and clothing drives for recent immigrants.

Comisión Española de Ayuda al Refugio (CEAR), Pl. de la Constitución, 2, Madrid, Spain (☎91 804 54 54; www.cear.es). The fundamental aim of this non-profit non-governmental organization is to protect the right to asylum, especially in Spain. Volunteer opportunities in outreach, legal assistance, translation, and human rights research.

Ecos do Sur, C. Ángel Senra, 25, A Coruña, Spain (☎985 15 01 18; www.ecosdosur.org). Works to ease the transition into Galician society for recent immigrants. Opportunities exist to teach English, Spanish, or *gallego* language classes (if you're fluent), conduct tests for tuberculosis, and do outreach work in the community.

Federació Catalana de Voluntariat Social, C. Père Verges, 1, 08020 Barcelona, Spain (☎933 14 11 08; www.federacio.net). Assist with their projects to achieve equality and better standards of living for immigrants to the region.

SOS Racism, Bou de St. Pere, 3, 08003 Barcelona, Spain (☎933 01 05 97; www.sos-racisme.org) and Quinta da Torrinha, Lote 11A, 1750 Lisboa Ameixoeira, Portugal (☎217 55 27 00; www.sosracismo.pt). Offices throughout Spain and Portugal. Combats racism and strives to achieve equal rights for non-citizens and migratory workers.

POLITICAL ACTIVISM

Opportunities to help your pet cause abound in Spain, from organizations working to combat *la SIDA* (AIDS; a growing problem in Spanish cities and among young people) to those trying to ban bullfighting. Since activists are likely to befriend those who share the same concerns, working for a cause that interests you in Spain or Portugal may not only give you insight into the global implications of your interests but also help you get to know some natives.

Alternativa para la Liberación Animal (ALA), C. Montera, 34, 28013 Madrid, Spain (☎/fax 915 32 84 95; www.liberacionanimal.org). Works for animal rights, including ending bullfighting. Participate in street theater and educational efforts.

Fundación Triángulo, C. Eloy Gonzalo, 25, 28010 Madrid, Spain (☎915 93 05 40; www.fundaciontriangulo.es). Fights discrimination and promotes equality for gay, lesbian, bisexual and transgendered people in Spain and around the world. Also sponsors a GLBT film festival in Madrid (see **Film,** p. 106). Volunteer on outreach or legal efforts.

Stop SIDA, C. Finlandià, 45, 08014 Barcelona, Spain (☎900 06 01 60; www.stop-sida.org). Helps combat the spread of AIDS by providing info on AIDS prevention, offering support services, and promoting understanding.

SOCIAL WELFARE

One of the most meaningful ways to volunteer in Spain and Portugal is through working directly with people in need. In order to devote as much of your time as possible to actually interacting with the people you'll be helping, it is often easier to arrange such opportunities through established programs.

Service Civil International Voluntary Service (SCI-IVS), 5474 Walnut Level Rd., Crozet, VA, USA (☎/fax 206-350-6585; www.sci-ivs.org). Arranges placement in work camps in Spain and Portugal (both 18+). Registration fee US$65-200.

Volunteers for Peace, 1034 Tiffany Rd., Belmont, VT, USA (☎802-259-2759; www.vfp.org). Arranges 3-week placements in work camps (cooler than they sound) in both countries. Membership ($20) required for registration (usually $200).

STUDYING

Study abroad programs range from basic language and culture courses to college-level classes, often for credit. In order to choose a program that best fits your needs, research as much as you can before making your decision—determine costs and duration, as well as what kind of students participate in the program and what sort of accommodations are provided.

Spain is one of the most popular destinations in the world for study-abroad students. To find out more, contact US university programs and youth organizations that send students to Spanish universities and language centers. Many programs cluster around Madrid, Sevilla, and Salamanca. While not many students think of studying abroad in **Portugal,** most Portuguese universities open their gates to foreign students.

ALTERNATIVES TO TOURISM

VISA INFORMATION

Foreigners planning to study in Spain or Portugal must obtain a student visa. However, those studying for less than three months in Spain only need a passport. Visa applications for study in Spain and Portugal can be completed in your destination country's consulate in your home country. Obtaining a visa can be an arduous process; the consulate will often require you to apply in person and demand loads of paperwork (letter verifying enrollment, medical certificate, proof of health insurance, etc.) before they process your application. They are also likely to charge a processing fee of around US$100. If studying for more than six months, you must obtain a student residency card from local authorities once in Spain which is valid for as long as you are enrolled in the university. Make sure to contact the consulate for requirements at least three months before your departure.

In programs that have large groups of students who speak the same language, there is a trade-off: you may feel more comfortable in the community, but you will not have the same opportunity to practice a foreign language or to befriend other international students. For accommodations, dorm life provides a better opportunity to mingle with fellow students, but there is less of a chance to experience the local scene. If you live with a family, there is a potential to build lifelong friendships with natives and to experience day-to-day life in more depth, but conditions can vary greatly from family to family.

UNIVERSITIES

Most university-level study-abroad programs are conducted in the language of the country, although many programs offer classes in English as well as beginner- and lower-level language courses. Those relatively fluent in Spanish or Portuguese may find it cheaper to enroll directly in a university abroad, although getting college credit may be more difficult. You can search **www.studyabroad.com** for various semester-abroad programs that meet your criteria, including your desired location and focus of study. The following is a list of organizations that can help place students in programs abroad or have their own branch in Spain or Portugal.

AMERICAN PROGRAMS

Academic Programs International (API), 107 E. Hopkins, San Marcos, TX 78666 (☎800-844-4124; www.academicintl.com). Programs available in Barcelona, Cádiz, Granada, Madrid, Salamanca, and Sevilla. Classes include international business, Spanish literature, and Spanish studies.

American Institute for Foreign Study, College Division, River Plaza, 9 West Broad St., Stamford, CT 06902 (☎800-727-2437, ext. 5163; www.aifsabroad.com). Organizes programs for high school and college study in Spanish universities.

Central College Abroad, Office of International Education, 812 University, Pella, IA 50219 (☎800-831-3629; www.central.edu/abroad). Offers internships, summer-, semester-, and year-long programs in Granada, as well as a Basque Ethnographic research summer program in San Sebastián.

College Consortium for International Study, 2000 P St. NW Suite 503, Washington, DC 20036 (☎800-453-6956 or 202-223-0330; www.ccisabroad.org). Offers a variety of study abroad programs in Spain and Portugal.

Council on International Educational Exchange (CIEE), 7 Custom House St., 3rd floor, Portland, ME 04101 (☎800-407-8839; www.ciee.org). Sponsors study abroad and volunteer programs in Spain.

Institute for the International Education of Students (IES), 33 N. LaSalle St., 15th fl., Chicago, IL 60602, USA (☎800-995-2300; www.IESabroad.org). Offers year-long, semester, and summer programs for college study in Barcelona, Madrid, and Salamanca. Internship opportunities. US$50 application fee. Scholarships available.

International Academic Programs, Study Abroad Resource Room, 250 Basom Hall, 500 Lincoln Dr., Madison, WI 53706 (☎608-265-6329; www.studyabroad.wisc.edu). Program affiliated with the University of Wisconsin-Madison offering semester and year-long study at the University of Coimbra in Portugal.

School for International Training, Admissions, Kipling Rd., P.O. Box 676, Brattleboro, VT 05302 (☎802-257-7751; www.sit.edu). Semester- and year-long programs in Spain. Also runs the **Experiment in International Living** (☎800-345-2929; www.usexperiment.org), 3- to 5-week summer programs that offer high school students homestays, community service, ecological adventures, and language training in Spain; programs cost US$1900-5000.

Two Worlds United Educational Foundation, 207 W. Los Angeles Ave. Suite 213, Moorpark, CA 93021 (☎800-696-8808 or 805-581-9191; www.twoworldsunited.com). Provides cultural exchange programs for summer, semester and year-long sessions by placing teenagers in high schools abroad in Spain and Portugal.

FOREIGN PROGRAMS

Universities in major cities like Madrid and Lisboa generally have options available for foreign students who wish to study abroad, but many other universities in smaller cities like Salamanca, Granada, and Coimbra also have active study abroad programs and host thousands of foreign students every year. Check with the individual school for specific requirements and enrollment procedures.

Agencia Nacional Erasmus, Consejo de Coordinación Universitaria, Ciudad Universitaria, 28040 Madrid, Spain (☎914 53 98 00; fax 914 53 98 85). Spanish branch of the European Union's Erasmus program which offers EU members the opportunity to study within Europe.

Agencia Nacional para os Programas Comunitários Sócrates e Leonardo da Vinci, Ave. D. João II, Edificio Administrativo da Parque Expo, Lote 1.07.2.1- Piso 1- Ala B, 1990-096 Lisboa (☎21 891 99 33; www.socleo.pt). National branch in Portugal of the European Union's study abroad program, which offers the citizens of EU member states the opportunity to study within Europe.

Universidad Complutense de Madrid, Vicerectorado de Relaciones Internacionales, C. Isaac Peral, 28040 Madrid, Spain (☎913 94 69 20; www.ucm.es/info/vicrint). Largest university in Spain. Hosts 3500 foreign students annually. Opportunities for study in a variety of fields with or without a specific study abroad program.

Universidade de Lisboa, Rectorate Al. da Universidade, Cidade Universitária, 1649-004 Lisboa, Portugal (☎217 96 76 24; www.ul.pt). Allows foreign students to enroll directly.

LANGUAGE SCHOOLS

Language schools can be independently run international or local organizations or divisions of foreign universities. They rarely offer college credit. They are a good alternative to university study if you are looking for a deeper focus on the language or a slightly less rigorous course load. These programs are also good for younger high school students who might not feel comfortable with students in a university setting. Some good programs include:

Amerispan, P.O. Box 58129, Philadelphia, PA 19102-8129 (☎800-879-6640 or 215-751-1100; www.amerispan.com). Offers language immersion programs in Spain and Portugal with homestays and organized activities.

Center for Cross-Cultural Study, C. Harinas, 16 y 18, 41001 Sevilla, Spain (☎954 22 41 07). Coordinates a variety of study abroad programs in Sevilla and throughout Spain. Students take classes at either the center or the University of Sevilla. US office at 446 Main Street, Amherst, MA 01002, USA (☎413-256-0011; www.cccs.com).

CIAL Centro de Linguas, Av. de República, 41-2° Esq., 1050-191, Lisboa, Portugal (☎217 940 448; www.cial.pt). Portuguese courses in Lisboa and Faro.

Don Quijote, C. Conde de Ibarra, 2, 41080 Sevilla, Spain (☎923 27 72 00; www.donquijote.org). A huge language school chain in Spain and Latin America. Offers Spanish courses for all levels in Barcelona, Granada, Madrid, Málaga, Salamanca, Sevilla, Tenerife, and Valencia. Very social atmosphere. 2-week intensive courses (20hr. language plus 5hr. "culture") start at €375. €33 enrollment fee. Discounts for longer sessions.

Languages Abroad, 413 Ontario St., Toronto, ON M5A2V9 (☎800-219-9924 or 416-925-2112; www.languagesabroad.com). Language immersion programs and opportunities to live in the home of your own private tutor in Spain and Portugal.

OTHER STUDY ABROAD

For those who are looking for something less traditional, these are only a few of the many exciting opportunities available.

Associació per a Defensa i L'Estudí de la Natura (ADENC), Ca l'Estruch, C. Sant Isidre, 08208 Sabadell, Spain (☎937 17 18 87; www.adenc.org). Catalan conservation group offers short summer courses on bird-watching, landscape photography, biology, and other eco-tourism related topics.

Escuela de Cocina Luis Irizar, C. Mari, 5, 20003 San Sebastián, Spain (☎943 43 15 40; www.escuelairizar.com). Learn how to cook Basque cuisine at this culinary institute. Programs range from week-long summer courses to the comprehensive 2-year apprenticeship. Some of the summer courses may be taught in English.

Taller Flamenco School, C. Peral, 49, E-41002 Sevilla, Spain (☎954 56 42 34; www.tallerflamenco.com). Offers courses in flamenco dance (€180-240 per week) and guitar (€204 per week) with substantial discounts for longer commitments.

WORKING

VISA INFORMATION
Travelers from within the European Union can work in any EU member country, but those from outside the EU need a work permit. Obtaining a work permit requires extensive documentation, often including a passport, police background check, and medical records, and the cost varies. Contact your nearest consulate (p. 8) for a complete list of requirements.

As with volunteering, work opportunities tend to fall into two categories. Some travelers want long-term jobs that allow them to get to know another part of the world as a member of the community, while other travelers seek out short-term jobs to finance the next leg of their travels. In Spain and Portugal, those seeking long-term work should consider teaching English. Short-term jobs are widely available in the restaurant, hotel, and tourism industries.

In Spain, the national employment service *(Oficinas de Empleo)* has a monopoly on the job market; begin your search here. Many seasoned travelers, however, go straight to a particular town's Yellow Pages *(Páginas Amarillas)* or even go door-to-door. In Portugal, the English-language weekly newspaper *Anglo-Portuguese News* carries job listings.

LONG-TERM WORK

If you're planning on spending a substantial amount of time (more than three months) working in Spain or Portugal, search for a job well in advance. International placement agencies are often the easiest way to find employment abroad, especially for teaching English. **Internships,** usually for college students, are a good way to segue into working abroad, although they are often unpaid or poorly paid (many say the experience, however, is well worth it). Be wary of advertisements or companies that claim they can get you a job abroad for a fee—often the same listings are available online or in newspapers, or are even out-of-date. Some reputable organizations include:

Career Journal (www.careerjournaleurope.com). The *Wall Street Journal* publishes this online journal listing thousands of jobs throughout Europe. There are both short- and long-term jobs as well as part- and full-time jobs.

Escape Artist (www.escapeartist.com/jobs/overseas1). Provides information on living abroad, including job listings for Spain and Portugal.

Expat Exchange (www.expatexchange.com). Provides message boards where individuals seeking employment in Spain and Portugal can advertise.

Go Jobsite (www.gojobsite.com). Lists jobs for European countries, including Spain.

PAYAway (www.payaway.co.uk). Features an extensive index of employers in Spain and Portugal.

Resort Jobs (www.resortjobs.com). Self-explanatory and ridiculously cool. Short- and long-term jobs in some of the most beautiful places on the planet. Jobs include camp counseling, bartending, waiting tables, and working on a cruise ship.

Trabajos (www.trabajos.com). Provides job listings for all regions of Spain.

TEACHING ENGLISH

Teaching English is one of the most popular jobs in Spain and Portugal for those craving a more long-term experience. For non-EU citizens, teaching English is likely one of the few options available that avoid the long and bureaucratic process of obtaining a work permit through a sponsoring company. However, even though the teaching job market in Spain has become one of the world's largest, it has recently begun to slow down. Non-EU citizens in particular may have difficulty immediately landing a job; it might be easier to find work in Portugal, especially in the north. Before making a commitment to any school, it is a good idea to ask others about their experience there. Dave's ESL Cafe (listed below) has country forums where former teachers can post advice about particular schools.

Teaching jobs abroad are rarely well-paid, although some elite private American schools offer somewhat competitive salaries. Volunteering as a teacher is also a popular option; even in those cases, teachers often get some sort of daily stipend to help with expenses. Do not be deterred by the seemingly low salaries. The cost of living is often lower as well, making such jobs more profitable. In almost all cases, you must have at least a bachelor's degree to be a full-fledged teacher, although undergraduates can often get summer positions teaching or tutoring.

Many schools require teachers to have a **Teaching English as a Foreign Language (TEFL)** certificate. Not having this certification does not necessarily exclude you from finding a teaching job, but certified teachers often find higher-paying jobs. Native English speakers working in private schools are most often hired for English-immersion classrooms where no local languages are spoken. Those volunteering or teaching in public schools are more likely to be working in both English and Spanish or Portuguese. Placement agencies or university fellowship programs are the best resources for finding teaching jobs. The alternative is to make contact directly with schools or just to try your luck once you get there. If you are going for the latter, the best time to look is several weeks before the start of the school year. The following organizations are extremely helpful in placing teachers in Spain and Portugal.

Dave's ESL Cafe (www.eslcafe.com). Site dedicated to teaching English as a second language worldwide. Job listings and advice offered.

International Schools Services (ISS), 15 Roszel Rd., P.O. Box 5910, Princeton, NJ 08543, USA (☎609-452-0990; www.iss.edu). Hires teachers for more than 200 overseas schools, several in Spain; candidates should have experience teaching or with international affairs. 2-year commitment expected.

Teach Abroad (www.teach.studyabroad.com). Sponsored by Study Abroad, brings you to listings around the world for paid or stipended positions to teach English.

TeachAbroad.com (www.teachabroad.com). Features worldwide job listings including some in Spain and Portugal.

TESOL-Spain (www.tesol-spain.org). Non-profit association of English teachers in Spain. Site features a jobs board among its many resources.

AU PAIR WORK

Au pairs are typically women (although sometimes men), aged 18-27, who work as live-in nannies, caring for children and doing light housework in foreign countries in exchange for room, board, and a small spending allowance or stipend. Most former au pairs speak favorably of their experience. One perk of the job is that allows you to really get to know the country without the high expenses of traveling. Drawbacks, however, often include long hours of constantly being on duty and somewhat mediocre pay (€55-60 per week). Much of the au pair experience really does depend on the family with whom you're placed. The agencies below are a good starting point for your search.

Accord Cultural Exchange, 3145 Geary Blvd., San Francisco, CA 94118, USA (☎415-386-6203; www.aupairsaccord.com).

Au Pair Homestay, World Learning, Inc., 1015 15th St. NW, Suite 750, Washington, DC 20005, USA (☎800-287-2477; fax 202-408-5397).

Au Pair in Europe, P.O. Box 68056, Blakely Postal Outlet, Hamilton, Ontario, Canada L8M 3M7 (☎905-545-6305; www.princeent.com).

Childcare International, Ltd., Trafalgar House, Grenville Pl., London NW7 3SA (☎44 020 8906-3116; www.childint.co.uk).

InterExchange, 161 Sixth Ave., New York, NY 10013, USA (☎212-924-0446; www.interexchange.org).

SHORT-TERM WORK

Traveling for long periods of time can get expensive; therefore, many travelers try their hand at odd jobs for a few weeks at a time to help finance another month or two of touring around. Because the process for obtaining a work permit is often long, complicated, bureaucratic, and requires a prior job contract, few travelers seeking short-term work have one. For non-EU citizens, working without a permit is illegal in Spain and Portugal, but many establishments hire travelers anyway, particularly in highly seasonal resort areas. These jobs often include bartending, waiting tables, or promoting bars and clubs. Another popular option is to work several hours a day at a hostel in exchange for free or discounted room and/or board. *Let's Go* does not recommend working illegally. Most often, short-term jobs are found by word of mouth, or simply by talking to the owner of an establishment. Due to the high turnover in the tourism industry, many places are eager for help, even temporarily. *Let's Go* tries to list jobs like these whenever possible; check out the list below for some of the available short-term jobs in popular destinations.

EcoForest, Apdo. Correos, 29, 29100 Coin, Málaga, Spain (☎661 07 99 50; www.ecoforest.org). Exchanges free camping space for 3hr. of work per day with a €20 initial fee.

Bodega Tour Guide, in Jerez de la Frontera, Spain (p. 257). Many of Jerez's famed sherry *bodegas* hire summer guides. Call the *bodegas* directly for more information.

Intern Jobs (www.internjobs.com). Not only lists internships, but also includes many ideal short-term jobs like camp counseling and bartending.

Summer Jobs (www.summerjobs.com). A website mostly for those 25 and under (students) who are looking for summer jobs. The website also has listings for resources where students can find the most up-to-date job listings.

Transitions Abroad (www.transitionsabroad.com). Lists organizations in Spain and Portugal that hire short-term workers. Also provides links to informational articles about working abroad.

FURTHER READING ON ALTERNATIVES TO TOURISM

Alternatives to the Peace Corps: A Directory of Third World and U.S. Volunteer Opportunities, by Joan Powell. Food First Books, 2000 (US$10).

How to Get a Job in Europe, by Sanborn and Matherly. Surrey Books, 1999 (US$22).

How to Live Your Dream of Volunteering Overseas, by Collins, DeZerega, and Heckscher. Penguin Books, 2002 (US$17).

International Directory of Voluntary Work, by Whetter and Pybus. Peterson's Guides and Vacation Work, 2000 (US$16).

International Jobs, by Kocher and Segal. Perseus Books, 1999 (US$18).

Invest Yourself: The Catalogue of Volunteer Opportunities, published by the Commission on Voluntary Service and Action (☎ 718-638-8487).

Overseas Summer Jobs 2002, by Collier and Woodworth. Peterson's Guides and Vacation Work, 2002 (US$18).

Work Abroad: The Complete Guide to Finding a Job Overseas, by Hubbs, Griffith, and Nolting. Transitions Abroad Publishing, 2000 ($16).

Work Your Way Around the World, by Susan Griffith. Worldview Publishing Services, 2001 (US$18).

DISCOVER

SPAIN

Imagine a parched central plateau surrounded by lush rolling hills, craggy snow-covered peaks, and glistening white sand beaches, a land where tradition and modern life collide with spectacular results, one whose glorious past is overshadowed only by its people's passion for living. This is Spain. Though travelers are drawn here by visions of flamenco dancers and bullfighting, these are but two of the country's multiple personalities. At a banquet of civilizations and empires, attended over a millennium by foreign invaders, artistic and literary geniuses, architectural masterminds, and religious crusaders, Spain gorged itself, resulting in a cultural cocktail spiked with an enviable array of treasures and an unmistakable flair for the celebratory. Modern Spain is a constellation of autonomous regions, each with its own character and often its own language. Speaking of the country as a whole is difficult, but there is a certain indefinable yet irrepressible spirit that binds it together. Travelers who come here find breathtaking landscapes and priceless cultural riches along with some of the world's best nightlife and wildest festivals. Easily accessible and relatively inexpensive, Spain mesmerizes visitors with its vibrant energy and unforgettable hospitality.

HISTORY

With a history that spans over 50 constitutions and an endless array of amorphous kingdoms controlled by Iberians, Celts, Romans, Visigoths, Arabs, and Frenchmen, and an empire that once spread to the Americas, Spain has emerged economically scarred but culturally enriched from its encounters as both colony and colonizer. In 1588, Spain began a long and arduous descent from world-class empire to Pyrenean pauper, during which its military defeats were matched only by its artistic and literary achievements.

RULE HISPANIA (PREHISTORY-AD 711). Spain played host to a succession of civilizations—**Basque, Celtiberian,** and **Greek**—each of which left its mark before the **Romans** came for a visit in the 3rd century BC. Over the next seven centuries, the Romans drastically altered the face and character of Spain, introducing their language, architecture, roads, and the cultivation of grapes, olives, and wheat. A slew of Germanic tribes swept over Iberia, but the **Visigoths,** newly converted Christians, emerged victorious. The Visigoths established their court at Barcelona in AD 419 and effectively ruled Spain for the next three hundred years.

PLEASE, SIR, MAY I HAVE SOME MOORS? (711-1492). Following Muslim unification, a small force of **Arabs, Berbers,** and **Syrians** invaded Spain in 711. The Moors encountered little resistance from the divided Visigoths, and the peninsula soon fell under the dominion of the caliphate of Damascus. Christian hero Roland blew his horn at **Roncesvalles** (p. 502) in 778, but to no avail; the Moors made their Iberian capital at **Córdoba** (p. 257), which by the 10th century was the largest city in Europe, with over 500,000 inhabitants. During **Abderramán III's** rule at that time, many considered Spain the wealthiest and most cultivated country in the world. His successor, **Al Mansur,** snuffed out all opposition within his court and undertook a series of military campaigns that climaxed with the destruction of **Santiago de Compostela** (p. 602) in 997 and the kidnapping of its bells. It took the Christians 240 years—until Fernando III took Córdoba in 1236—to get them back.

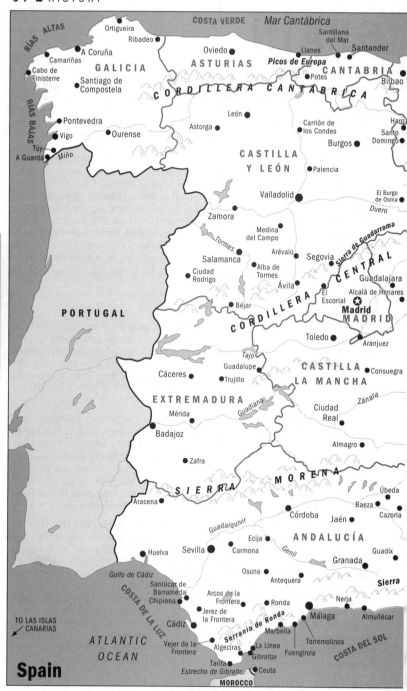

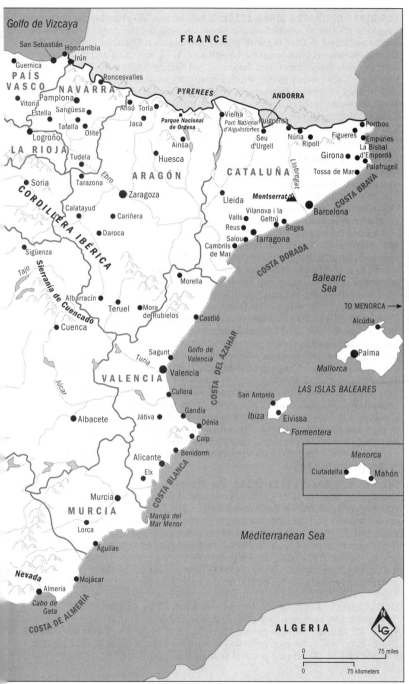

LOS REYES CATÓLICOS (1469-1516). It took almost 750 years for the Christian kingdoms to "retake" Spain from the Moors. In 1469, the marriage of **Fernando de Aragón** and **Isabel de Castilla** joined Iberia's two mightiest Christian kingdoms. The Catholic Monarchs introduced the **Inquisition** in 1478, executing and then burning heretics, principally Jews (even those who had already converted). Jews and Muslims were forced either to convert to Christianity or to leave Spain. In 1492, the power couple captured Granada (p. 300) and swallowed **Columbus's** pack of lies about the world being round. During their approximately fifty years of rule, these Catholic Monarchs ensconced Spain as not only the prime European exponent of Catholicism, but also as an international economic, political, and cultural power— power made even more enduring by lucrative conquests in the Americas.

ENTER THE HABSBURGS (1516-1713). The daughter of Fernando and Isabel, **Juana la Loca** (the Mad), married **Felipe el Hermoso** (the Fair) of the powerful Habsburg family. When pretty boy died playing *jai alai*, *La Loca* refused to believe that he was gone and dragged his corpse through the streets screaming. Juana and Felipe secured their genetic legacy with the birth of the half-Habsburg **Carlos I**, better known as Holy Roman Emperor Charles V (1516-1556).

When Carlos retired to a monastery, **Felipe II** (1556-1598) inherited a handful of rebellious territories in the Protestant Netherlands. In 1581, a year after he annexed Portugal, the Dutch declared their independence from Spain, starting a war and spurring an embroilment with England's Elizabeth I. It ground to a halt when Sir Francis Drake totaled Spain's "invincible" **Armada** in 1588. With much of his European empire lost and wealth from the Americas sapped, Felipe retreated to **El Escorial** (p. 142) and, like his father, sulked in its monastery until his death.

Felipe III (1598-1621) expelled nearly 300,000 of Spain's remaining Moors in 1609. **Felipe IV** (1621-1665) painstakingly held the country together through his long, tumultuous reign while patronizing the arts (painter Diego Velázquez and playwright Lope de Vega graced his court) and architecture (he commissioned the Parque del Buen Retiro in Madrid; p. 137). Then the **Thirty Years' War** (1618-1648) broke out in Europe, and defending Catholicism drained Spain's resources. It ended with the marriage of Felipe IV's daughter María Teresa to Louis XIV of France. Felipe's successor **Carlos II el Hechizado** (the bewitched; 1665-1700), the product of generations of inbreeding, was known to fly into fits of rage and epileptic seizures. From then on, little went right: Carlos II left no heirs because of his "problem," Spain fell into a depression, and cultural bankruptcy ensued. Rulers from all over battled for the crown; the **War of the Spanish Succession** had begun.

THE REIGN IN SPAIN (1713-1931). The 1713 Peace of Utrecht ended the ordeal (and Spain's possession of Gibraltar) and landed **Felipe V** (1713-1746), a Bourbon grandson of **Louis XIV**, on the Spanish throne. The king cultivated a flamboyant, debaucherous court but administered the Empire competently, at last beginning to regain control of the Spanish-American trade. As part of his bid for world domination, **Napoleon** invaded Spain in 1808, inaugurating an occupation as short as the general himself that ended, ironically enough, when the Protestant Brits beat up the Corsican's troops at Waterloo (1814). This victory led to the restoration of reactionary **Fernando VII** (1814-1833), who sought to revoke the progressive constitution of 1812. Galvanized by Fernando's ineptitude and inspired by liberal ideas, most of Spain's Latin American empire soon threw off the colonial yoke.

Domestically, parliamentary liberalism was restored in 1833 upon Fernando VII's death and survived the conservative challenge of the first **Carlist War** (1833-1840), during which the monarchy was so weakened that the first **Spanish republic** was proclaimed. Despite the political anarchy that ensued until the 1920s, the last two decades of the 19th-century were marked by rapid industrialization. However, Spain's 1898 loss to the US in the **Spanish-American War** cost it the Philippines, Puerto Rico, Cuba, and any remaining dreams of colonial wealth.

Closer to home, Moroccan tribesmen rebelled against Spanish troops in northern Africa beginning in 1917, resulting in a series of embarrassing military defeats that further weakened Spaniards' morale and culminated with the **massacre** of 14,000 Spanish troops in 1921, an event that threatened the very survival of the monarchy. The search for those "responsible" for the disaster occupied aristocrats, bureaucrats, and generals for the next decade, throwing the country into political and social chaos. In 1923, **General Miguel Primo de Rivera** brought order to the situation in the form of Spain's first dictatorship.

REPUBLIC AND REBELLION (1931-1939). In April 1931, **King Alfonso XIII** (1902-1931) abdicated, disgraced by his support for the Primo de Rivera dictatorship and afraid of his own military, giving rise to the **Second Republic** (1931-1936). Republican Liberals and Socialists established safeguards for farmers and industrial workers, granted women's suffrage, assured religious tolerance, and chipped away at traditional military dominance. National euphoria, however, faded fast. The 1933 elections split the Republican-Socialist coalition, increasing the power of right wing and Catholic parties in parliament. Military dissatisfaction led to a heightened profile of the **Fascist Falange** (founded by Primo de Rivera's son José Antonio), which further polarized national politics. By 1936, radicals, anarchists, Socialists, and Republicans had formed a **Popular Front** coalition to win the February elections, though the victory was short-lived. Once **Generalísimo Francisco Franco** snatched control of the Spanish army, militarist uprisings ensued, and the nation plunged into war. The **Spanish Civil War** (1936-1939) ignited worldwide ideological passions. Germany and Italy dropped troops, supplies, and munitions into Franco's lap, while the US and liberal European states hid behind the Non-Intervention Treaty. The Soviet Union organized the International Brigades—an amalgamation of Communists and other leftist volunteers from all over Europe and the US—to battle Franco's fascism. But soon after, aid waned as Stalin began to see the benefits of an alliance with Hitler. All told, bombings, executions, combat, starvation, and disease took nearly 600,000 lives and forced nearly a million to emigrate. In April 1939, Franco marched into Madrid and ended the war.

FRANCO AND THE NATIONAL TRAGEDY (1939-1975). As scientists, artists, intellectuals, and sympathizers emigrated or faced imprisonment and execution, dissatisfied workers and students took to the streets, encouraging regional discontent and international isolation. Groups like the **Basque ETA** resisted the dictatorship throughout Franco's reign, often via terrorist acts. In his old age, Franco tried to smooth international relations by joining NATO, courting the Pope, and encouraging tourism, but the **national tragedy** (as it was later called) did not officially end until Franco died in 1975. King Juan Carlos I (1975-), grandson of Alfonso XIII and nominally a Franco protégé, carefully set out to undo Franco's damage.

TRANSITION TO DEMOCRACY (1975-2000). In 1978, under centrist prime minister Adolfo Suárez, Spain adopted a new constitution and restored parliamentary government and regional autonomy. The post-Franco years have been marked by progressive social change. Although some women still choose to fill more traditional roles, others have begun to chip away at the glass ceiling in the public sector, and Spain has one of the most active trade union cultures in Europe. Suárez's resignation in early 1981 left the country ripe for an attempted **coup** on February 23 of that year, when a group of rebels took over parliament in an effort to impose a military-backed government. King Juan Carlos I used his personal influence to convince the rebels to stand down, and order was restored, paving the way for the

SPAIN

charismatic **Felipe González** to lead the PSOE (Spanish Socialist Worker's Party) to victory in the 1982 elections. González opened the Spanish economy and championed consensus policies, overseeing Spain's integration into the European Community (now the EU) four years later. Despite unpopular economic stands, González was reelected in 1986 and continued a program of massive public investment that rejuvenated the nation's economy. By the end of 1993, however, recession and revelations of large-scale corruption led to a resounding Socialist defeat at the hands of the Partido Popular (PP) in the 1994 European parliamentary elections. The PP's leader was **José María Aznar,** who managed to maintain a fragile coalition with the support of the Catalan and Canary Islands regional parties. Though it won an absolute majority in 2000, Aznar's chosen successor lost to **José Luis Rodríguez Zapatero** of the PSOE in the March 2004 elections, partially because voters lost faith in Aznar and his party after attempts to shirk responsibility for the terrorist attacks (see below) that had occurred in Madrid days before the vote.

CURRENT EVENTS

Most recently, Spain suffered what is thought to be one in a string of worldwide terrorist attacks perpetrated by terrorists linked to al-Qaeda. On **March 11, 2004,** often referred to as **11-3** *(el once eme),* ten bombs exploded on four trains heading to Madrid from the suburbs just before they reached the city. 191 passengers were killed and more than 1800 were injured. The assault was the most deadly terrorist attack in Europe since the Lockerbie bombing in 1988 and by far the worst in modern Spanish history. Spain was rattled to its core in much the same way the US was by September 11, exactly two and a half years before the Madrid bombings. Spain had faced terrorists in the past, what with the ongoing operations of **Euskadi Ta Askatasuna** (ETA; Basque Homeland and Freedom; see below), but the deadliest of their attacks had killed only 21 people in a Hipercor supermarket in Barcelona in 1987. Then-president Aznar and his government tried at first to place the blame for 11-3 on ETA, but it soon became clear that al-Qaeda supporters were most likely responsible, and they remain at the center of investigations.

Basque separatists in northwestern Spain have pressed on in their effort to establish an autonomous state, despite a government crackdown on their movement as well after the events of 11-3. The movement's militant wing, ETA, is known for its terrorist activities; over 800 people have been killed since 1968, though their trademark car bombings commonly target specific politicians rather than innocent bystanders. In June 2002, authorities seized 288 pounds of dynamite near Valencia, charging ETA with planning to strike tourist spots along the Mediterranean coast. Additionally, during a 2002 EU summit in Sevilla, ETA planted several car bombs in resort towns along the Costa del Sol and northern Spain, injuring several. In the fall of 2002, controversy ensued when the Spanish parliament banned **Herri Batasuna,** a pro-independence Basque political party that prime minister Aznar and others allege to be allied with ETA. The bombings in touristed Santander and Llanes in August 2004 and Alicante and Benidorm in July 2003 are only the most recent attempts to intimidate the Spanish government. Thankfully, ETA notified the locations prior to the attacks, so injuries were minimized.

For the past three hundred years, Spain has fought an uphill battle to regain control of **Gibraltar** (p. 275), a strategic 6km territory in the south currently under British rule. Despite considerable resistance from the Rock, which is overwhelmingly loyal to the crown, Britain's desire to improve relations with Spain has paved the way for some concessions. Spain and Britain vowed to resolve the issue by summer 2002, considering proposals such as joint Anglo-Spanish sovereignty and self-government. But residents continue to delay agreements, registering disapproval through massive pro-British marches and media campaigns against Spanish rule.

In July 2002, a handful of Moroccan soldiers "occupied" the goat-infested island of **Perejil** in Spanish territorial waters off Morocco, sparking a minor international event; Spain removed the soldiers and their Moroccan flag amid much fanfare and grandstanding. Its sovereignty and military prowess secured, Spain could once again direct its attention to pressing internal affairs, including increased **immigration** from northern Africa and environmental protection issues.

PEOPLE AND CULTURE

LANGUAGE

Castellano (Castilian), spoken almost everywhere, is Spain's official language. **Català** (Catalan) is spoken throughout Catalunya in the northeast and is the official language of Andorra. It has given rise through permutations to **valencià** (Valencian), the regional tongue of Valencia, and **mallorquí,** the principal dialect of the Islas Baleares. The once-Celtic northwest corner of Iberia gabs in **gallego** (Galician), which is closely related to Portuguese. Although more prevalent in the countryside than cities, *gallego* is now spreading among the young, as is **euskera** (Basque), spoken in País Vasco and northern Navarra. Even tiny Asturias has its own dialect, **bable,** spoken mostly among older generations.

City and provincial names in this guide are listed in Castilian first, followed by the regional language in parentheses where appropriate. Information within cities (i.e. street and plaza names) is listed in the regional language. For a **phrasebook, glossary,** and **pronunciation guide,** see p. 811.

RELIGION

The **Roman Catholic Church** has dominated everyday life in Spain since 1492, but there are still remnants of a strong **Jewish** and **Muslim** heritage. **Protestant** denominations enjoy begrudging tolerance, but the Catholic Church still reigns supreme even though congregations are increasingly gray-headed. Many towns still celebrate their patron saint's feast day as they have for hundreds of years. Treat churches, cathedrals, and **soccer** stadiums with respect, as most Spaniards are deeply religious and expect you to behave properly in places of worship.

FOOD AND DRINK

Traditionally, Spanish food's taste ranks above appearance, preparation is rarely complicated, and many of the best meals are served not in expensive restaurants, but rather in private homes or street-side bars. However, these days Spanish food is becoming increasingly sophisticated and cosmopolitan. Fresh local ingredients are still an integral part of the cuisine, varying according to each region's climate, geography, and history. Still, it's clear that the old Spanish saying holds true: "Que comer es muy importante, porque de la panza, nace la danza!" (Eating is very important, because from the belly, the dance is born!)

LOCAL FARE

ANDALUCÍA. Andalusian cuisine is the oldest in Spain, flavored with spices and prepared according to traditional methods brought by Islamic tribes during the first millennium. Centuries later, it was through Sevilla (p. 221) that New World products like corn, peppers, tomatoes, and potatoes first entered Europe. Andalusians have since mastered the art of gazpacho, a cool, tomato-based soup perfectly suited to the hot southern climate. The area is also known for its *pescadito frito* (fried fish), *rabo de toro* (bull's tail), egg yolk desserts, sherry wines, and tasty tapas. Spain's best cured ham, *jamón ibérico*, comes from the town of Jabugo, where black-footed pigs are pampered with daily oak acorn feasts.

CENTRAL SPAIN. Sheep share space with more of these prized pigs in nearby **Extremadura** (p. 207), where the pastoral life has inspired *cocidos* (hearty stews), cheeses, and unique meals based on *migas* (bread crumbs). This type of dry-land "shepherd's cuisine" dominates central Spain. **Castilla La Mancha** (p. 193) is famous for its sheep's milk *queso manchego*, the most widely eaten cheese in Spain, and the deliciously vegetarian *pisto manchego*, a mix of zucchini, tomatoes, and eggplant; still, lamb and roasted game are essential parts of menus both here and in **Castilla y Léon** (p. 150). *Escabeche*, an Arab tradition of sautéing with vinegar, has become a specialty, as has *tortilla española* (potato omelette) and *menestra de verduras*, a succulent vegetable mix. **Madrid** (p. 85) rivals Andalucía with its tapas and renowned *cocido*, a heavy stew of meat, cabbage, carrots, and potatoes.

CANTABRIAN COAST. Farther north, the 800 miles of coastline in **Galicia** (p. 601) provide fresh ingredients for local shellfish dishes. Octopus, spider crab, and mussels are popular here, as is *empanada gallega*, the Galician pastry filled with anything from pork to chicken to fish. In **Asturias** (p. 567), dried beans rule the kitchen; *fabada asturiana*, a bean and sausage stew, is the best-known way to regain strength after a long work day. Apples, *sidra* (cider), and cow's milk are also especially good here. **Cantabrian** (p. 592) sardines and tuna are among the best in Spain. Food in the **País Vasco** (p. 543) rivals that of Catalunya in national prominence. Popular dishes include *bacalao* (salt cod), *angulas* (baby eels), and squid *en su tinta* (in its own ink). Spain's first gastronomic society was founded here on January 1, 1900; these all-male cooking groups now number over 1,000.

NORTH CENTRAL. **Navarra** (p. 525) boasts the best red peppers in Spain, as well as the famous Roncal cheese; cooked game, sausages, and caldron stews are popular here. Neighboring **La Rioja** (p. 521) is known for its pork, vegetables, and above all *vino* (wine). **Aragón's** (p. 508) hearty cuisine reflects the region's varied character. *Migas de pastor* (bread crumbs fried with ham) and lamb are ubiquitous; more surprising treats include *melocotones al vino* (native peaches steeped in wine).

MEDITERRANEAN. In **Catalunya** (p. 434), the Roman trilogy of olives, grapes, and wheat dominates. Seafood, grilling, and unique sauces are key elements of many meals. Catalunya houses the avant-garde movement, led by innovative chef Ferran Adrià of El Bulli. **Valencia** (p. 320), on the Mediterranean coast, has been the home of paella and oranges ever since Arab short-grain rice and American oranges were introduced to the area. Less than 200 years old, paella has evolved from a simple dish to an increasingly elaborate mix of rice, vegetables, seafood, and meat.

MEALS AND DINING HOURS

Spaniards start their day with a continental breakfast, *el desayuno*, of coffee or thick, liquid chocolate combined with *bollos* (rolls) and *churros* or *porros* (dough fritters). Mid-morning they often have another coffee with a *tapa* to tide them over to the main meal of the day, *la comida*, which is eaten around 2 or 3pm. *La comida* consists of several courses: soup or salad; meat, fish, or, on special occasions, paella; and a dessert of fruit, cheese, or sweets. Supper at home, *la cena*, tends to be light, usually a sandwich or tortilla around 8pm. Eating out starts anywhere between 9pm and midnight. Going out for tapas is an integral part of the Spanish lifestyle; groups of friends will often spend several hours bar-hopping.

S P A I N

EATING OUT

While some restaurants are open from 8am to 1 or 2am, most serve meals from 1 or 2 to 4pm only and in the evening from 8pm until midnight. Some hints: eating at the bar is cheaper than at tables or on a terrace, and the check won't be brought to your table unless you request it. Service in Spain is notoriously slow and frustrating. Spaniards commonly choose the **menú del día**—two or three dishes, bread, wine/beer/water, and dessert—for the *comida*, a good deal at roughly €5-9. Large tapas, often comparable in size to entrees, are called *raciones*.

DRINKING

When in doubt among your choices, the *vino de la casa* (house wine) is an economical, often delectable choice. Also good are *vino tinto* (red wine), *vino blanco* (white wine), or *rosado* (rosé). Castilla y León's **Ribera del Dueros** are smooth and full-bodied reds. Catalunya's whites and **cavas** (champagnes) and Galicia's **Albariños** pack a refreshing punch, while the reds and whites of **La Rioja** are justifiably famous. **Sidra** (cider) from Asturias and **sangria** (red-wine punch with fruit, seltzer, and sugar) are delicious alcoholic options. A popular drink is *tinto de verano*, a mix of red wine and carbonated water. **Jerez** (sherry), Spain's most famous wine, hails from Jerez de la Frontera (p. 257) in Andalucía. Try the dry *fino* and *amontillado* as aperitifs, or finish off a rich supper with the sweet *dulce*.

Wash down your tapas with a *caña de cerveza*, a normal-sized draft-beer. A *tubo* is a little bigger, and small beers go by different names—*corto* in Castellano, *zurito* in Basque. Pros refer to **mixed drinks** as *copas*. Beer and Schweppes Limón make a **clara**. A **calimocho,** popular with young crowds, is a mix of Coca-Cola and red wine. Spain whips up numerous non-alcoholic quenchers as well, notably **horchata de chufa** (made by blending almonds and ice) and the flavored crushed-ice **granizados**. *Café solo* means black coffee; add a touch of milk for a *nube;* a little more and it's a *café cortado;* half milk, half coffee and you have *café con leche*.

CUSTOMS AND ETIQUETTE

Although Spaniards are stereotyped as proud, they are generally polite and courteous to foreigners. Attempts to be culturally correct will not go unnoticed; you'll be treated with cooperative friendliness if you make the extra effort.

TABOOS. As is to be expected, Spaniards take offense to critical comments about their country or customs. Foreigners should be careful when approaching Spanish women; overly *macho* fathers, husbands, or boyfriends can be unusually aggressive. Though dress in Spain is more casual in summer than in winter, be aware that shorts and flip-flops may be seen as disrespectful in some establishments.

PUBLIC BEHAVIOR. Spaniards are formally polite in mannerisms and social behavior. To blend in, it's a good idea to be as formal as possible upon a first meeting. Introduce yourself in detail, giving more than just your *nombre* (name). You'll be welcomed openly and made to feel at home if you mention who you are, where you're from, and what you are doing in Spain. Be sure to address Spaniards as *Señor* (Mr.), *Señora* (Mrs.), or *Señorita* (Ms.), and don't be surprised if you get kissed on both cheeks instead of receiving a handshake.

TABLE MANNERS. Having a meal, whether at home or at a restaurant, is one of the most popular forms of socializing in Spain. The key to acceptance at a Spanish *mesa* is not imitating *how* Spaniards eat, but rather *when* they do. You'll encounter odd looks if you demand an evening meal at six o'clock. As for Spanish table manners, be sure to keep both hands visible during the meal.

THE ARTS

From the dark solemnity of El Greco's paintings to the playful exuberance of Gaudí's buildings, Spanish art and architecture ranges from the austere to the ostentatious. While the tradition has been shaped by foreign influences, Spain's dazzling architecture, paintings, and literature are distinctly Spanish.

ARCHITECTURE

Spanish architecture is as impressive and varied as the civilizations that have ruled over it. Remnants of Spain's glorious past dot the landscape, hinting at the wealth and power that once flowed through the land. Bold postmodern projects promise to maintain Spain's proud architectural tradition for years to come.

ANCIENT AND EARLY MODERN. Scattered **Roman ruins** testify to six centuries of colonization. Highlights include some of the finest Roman ruins in existence: the aqueduct in Segovia (p. 154), the amphitheater in Mérida (p. 216), and the town of Tarragona (p. 442). Other vestiges of Spain's Roman past include the ruined towns of Itálica (near Sevilla; p. 243) and Sagunt (near Valencia; p. 329).

After their 711 invasion, the **Moors** constructed mosques and palaces throughout southern Spain. Because the Qur'an forbids human and animal representation, Moorish architects instead adorned their buildings with stylized geometric designs, red-and-white horseshoe arches, and ornate tiles. Intricate and elegant decorative work combined with courtyards, pools, and fountains created buildings destined to delight the senses. The spectacular 14th-century **Alhambra** in Granada (p. 306), said to be one of the most beautiful buildings in the world, and the **Mezquita** in Córdoba (p. 251) epitomize the Moorish style. Long periods of peaceful coexistence between Islam and Christianity inspired the unique *mudéjar* architectural movement, created by Moors living under Christian rule in the years between the Christian resurgence (11th century) and the Reconquista (1492). Sevilla's **Alcázar** (p. 233) is an exquisite example of *mudéjar*.

The **Spanish Gothic** style experimented with pointed arches, flying buttresses, slender walls, airy spaces, and stained-glass windows. The first Gothic cathedral in Spain was that of Burgos (begun in 1221; p. 181). Along with those in Toledo (p. 194) and León (p. 170), the cathedral of Burgos is one of the finest examples of the Spanish Gothic style. Sevilla boasts the largest Gothic cathedral (p. 232) in world. Maestro Mateo's **Pórtico de la Gloria,** completed in 1188 in Santiago de Compostela (p. 602), is considered one of the best examples of Spanish **Romanesque** sculpture.

RENAISSANCE AND BAROQUE. New World riches inspired the **Plateresque** ("silversmith") style, a flashy extreme of Gothic that transformed wealthier parts of Spain. Intricate stonework and extravagant use of gold and silver made 15th- and 16th-century buildings shine, most notably in Salamanca, where the university (p. 164) practically drips with ornamentation. In the late 16th century, Italian innovations in perspective and symmetry arrived in Spain to sober up the Plateresque style and influence **Juan de Herrera** in his design for **El Escorial** (p. 142), Felipe II's immense palace-cum-monastery. Opulence took center stage in 17th- and 18th-century **Baroque** Spain. The Churriguera brothers pioneered the new **Churrigueresque** style, which reflected the wealth and ostentation of the era. Wildly elaborate ornamentation with extensive sculptural detail gave buildings of this period a rich exuberance, most resonant in Salamanca's Plaza Mayor (p. 165).

MODERN AND POSTMODERN. In the late 19th and early 20th centuries, Catalunya's **Modernistes** burst on the scene in Barcelona, led by the eccentric genius of **Antoni Gaudí, Lluís Domènech i Montaner,** and **Josep Puig y Cadafalch.** *Modernista* structures defied any and all previous standards with their voluptuous curves and unusual textures. The new style was inspired in part by *mudéjar*, but far more so by organic forms and unbridled imagination. Gaudí's **La Sagrada Família** (p. 423) and **Casa Milà** (p. 424), stand as the best examples of Catalan *Modernisme*.

In the mid-20th century, Catalan architect **Josep Lluís Sert** helped introduce European Modernism with his stark concrete buildings. Spain's outstanding architectural tradition continues today with current stars like **Rafael Moneo** and **Santiago Calatrava**, who has become the most recent sensation with his elegant steel-and-crystal buildings in Valencia (p. 325), and unmistakable bridges in Sevilla, Mérida, and Bilbao. Spain has also acquired new landmarks from foreign architects, including the stunning **Guggenheim Museum** in Bilbao (p. 557) by Frank Gehry.

PAINTING

Ever since ancient Spaniards created the cave art at **Altamira** (p. 599), Spanish painting has been enlightened by luminaries. Flemish and Italian influences often dominated the Spanish scene, but such heavy hitters as El Greco, Velázquez, Goya, and Picasso have forged a distinctive and hugely influential body of work.

MEDIEVAL AND RENAISSANCE. In the 11th and 12th centuries, fresco painters and manuscript illuminators adorned churches and their libraries along the Camino de Santiago and in León and Toledo. Not until after Spain's imperial ascendance in the 16th century did painting reach its **Siglo de Oro** (Golden Age; roughly 1492-1650). Felipe II imported foreign art and artists in order to jump-start native production and embellish his palace, El Escorial. Although he supposedly came to Spain seeking a royal commission, Crete-born Doménikos Theotokópoulos, known as **El Greco** (1541-1614), was rejected by Felipe II because of his intensely personal style. Misunderstood by his contemporaries, El Greco has received newfound appreciation for his haunting, elongated figures and dramatic use of light and color. One of his most famous canvases, *El entierro del Conde de Orgaz* (*The Burial of Count Orgaz*, 1586) graces the Iglesia de Santo Tomé in Toledo (p. 198), the city whose landscape he so vividly painted beginning in 1597.

Felipe IV's foremost court painter, **Diego Velázquez** (1599-1660), is generally considered one of the world's greatest artists. Whether depicting Felipe IV's family or lowly court jesters and dwarves, Velázquez painted with naturalistic precision; working slowly and meticulously, he captured light with a virtually photographic quality. Nearly half of this Sevilla-born artist's works reside in the Prado, notably his famous *Las Meninas* (1656; p. 123). Other distinguished Golden Age painters include **Francisco de Zurbarán** (1598-1664) and **Bartoloméo Murillo** (1617-1682).

FROM MODERN TO AVANT-GARDE. While Spain's political power declined, its cultural capital flourished. **Francisco de Goya** (1746-1828) ushered European painting into the modern age. Hailing from provincial Aragón, Goya rose to the position of official court painter under the degenerate Carlos IV. Dispensing with flattery, Goya's depictions of the royal family come closer to caricature, as Queen María Luisa's haughty, cruel jaw line in Goya's famous *The Family of Charles IV* (1800) attests. His series of etchings *The Disasters of War* (1810-1814), which includes the landmark *El 2 de mayo* and *Fusilamientos del 3 de mayo*, records the horrific Napoleonic invasion of 1808. Deaf and alone in his later years, Goya painted nightmarishly fantastic visions, inspiring expressionist and surrealist artists of the next century. His chilling *Black Paintings* (1820-1823) fill a room in the Prado.

It is hard to imagine an artist who has affected 20th-century painting as profoundly as Málaga-born **Pablo Picasso** (1881-1973). Alternating between Barcelona and Paris, Picasso inaugurated his Blue Period in 1900, characterized by somber depictions of society's outcasts. His permanent move to Paris in 1904 initiated his Rose Period as he probed into the engrossing lives of clowns and acrobats. With

SPAIN

his French colleague Georges Braque, he founded **Cubism,** a method of painting objects simultaneously from multiple perspectives. His huge 1937 painting *Guernica* portrays the bombing of that Basque city (p. 559) by Nazi planes in cahoots with Franco during the Spanish Civil War. A protest against violence, *Guernica* now resides in the Museo Nacional Centro de Arte Reina Sofía in Madrid (p. 124).

Catalan painter and sculptor **Joan Miró** (1893-1983) created simple shapes in bright primary colors. His haphazard, undefined squiggles rebelled against the authoritarian society of the post-Civil War years. By contrast, fellow Catalan **Salvador Dalí** (1904-1989) scandalized society and leftist intellectuals in France and Spain by claiming to support the Fascists. Dalí's name is now synonymous with **Surrealism.** A self-congratulatory fellow, Dalí founded the **Teatro-Museu Dalí** in Figueres (p. 464), the second-most visited museum in Spain after the Prado.

Since Franco's death in 1975, a younger generation of artists has thrived. With new museums in Madrid, Barcelona, Valencia, Sevilla, and Bilbao, Spanish painters and sculptors once again have a national forum for their work. **Antonio Tápies** constructs unorthodox collages and is a founding member of the self-proclaimed "Abstract Generation," while **Antonio López García** paints hyperrealist works.

LITERATURE

Spanish poets, playwrights, and authors have given the world some of its most iconic literary figures, from the idealistic Don Quixote to the unenviable Don Juan.

FROM THE MIDDLE AGES TO THE GOLDEN AGE. Spain's rich literary tradition blossomed in the late Middle Ages (1000-1500). The 12th-century *El Cantar del Mío Cid (Song of My Cid)*, Spain's most important epic poem, chronicles national hero Rodrigo Díaz de Vivar's life and military triumphs, from his exile to his eventual return to grace in the king's court. No less integral to the national identity is **Fernando de Rojas's** *La Celestina* (1499), a tragicomedy beloved for the strong, witch-like female character who serves as a go-between for star-crossed lovers Calixto and Melibea. *La Celestina* can be said to mark the start of Spain's **Siglo de Oro** (Golden Age), which spanned the 16th and 17th centuries. Poetry thrived in this era; some consider the sonnets of **Garcilaso de la Vega** the most perfect ever written in *castellano*. The Golden Age also bred outstanding dramatists, including **Pedro Calderón de la Barca** (1600-1681) and **Lope de Vega** (1562-1635), who collectively wrote over 2,300 plays. **Tirso de Molina's** (1584-1648) famed *El Burlador de Sevilla* (1630) introduced the character of Don Juan into the national psyche. **Miguel de Cervantes's** *Don Quixote de la Mancha* (1605-1615)—often considered the world's first novel—is the most famous work of Spanish literature. Cervantes relates the hilarious parable of the hapless Don and his servant Sancho Panza, who fancy themselves bold knights out to save the world.

ROMANTICS AND INNOVATORS. The 18th century brought a period of economic and political decline accompanied by a belated Enlightenment, while the 19th century inspired contrasting variety, including **Rosalía del Castro's** innovative lyrical verse and the naturalistic novels of **Leopoldo Alas ("Clarín").** Essayist and philosopher **Miguel de Unamuno** and critic **José Ortega y Gasset** led the **Generación de 1898,** along with novelist **Pío Baroja,** playwright **Ramón del Valle Inclán,** and poets **Antonio Machado** and **Juan Ramón Jiménez.** Reacting to Spain's defeat in the Spanish-American War (1898), these nationalistic authors argued that each individual must spiritually and ideologically attain peace before society can do the same. These men influenced the **Generación de 1927,** a group of experimental lyric poets like **Federico García Lorca** and **Rafael Alberti** who wrote Surrealist and avant-garde poetry.

MODERN MARVELS. Spanish Nobel Prize recipients include playwright and essayist **Jacinto Benavente y Martínez** (1922), poet **Vicente Aleixandre** (1977), and novelist **Camilo José Cela** (1989). Female writers, like **Mercè Rodoreda, Carmen Martín Gaite,** and **Almudena Grandes** have likewise earned international critical acclaim. As Spanish artists are again migrating to Madrid, just as they did in the early part of the century, an avant-garde spirit—known as *La Movida*—has been reborn in the capital. **Ana Rossetti** and **Juana Castro** led a new generation of erotic poets into the 80s, placing women at the forefront of Spanish literature for the first time.

MUSIC

Flamenco, one of Spain's most famous and clichéd cultural attributes, combines melodramatic song, guitar, and dance. It originated among Andalusian gypsies and remains an extremely popular tradition that hypnotizes audiences around the world even today. While it is possible to buy flamenco recordings, nothing compares to seeing a live performance. **Andrés Segovia** (1893-1987) was instrumental in endowing the flamenco guitar with the same renown as the violin and the cello.

Pau (Pablo) Casals (1876-1973), Catalan cellist, conductor, composer, pianist, and humanitarian, was one of the most influential classical musicians of the 20th century. To promote world peace, Casals composed the oratorio *The Manger* (1960) and conducted it throughout the world. Hailing from Lleida, **Enrique Granados** (1867-1916) contributed the opera *Goyescas*, based on (oddly enough) paintings by Goya, and his own personal takes on the **zarzuela,** a form of light opera particular to Madrid. Arguably the greatest Spanish composer of this century, Cádiz native **Manuel de Falla** (1876-1946) wrote the popular opera *El sombrero de tres picos* (*The Three-Cornered Hat*), which premiered in London in 1919 with stage design by Picasso. Another favorite de Falla work is the frequently performed *Noches en los jardines de España* (*Nights in the Gardens of Spain;* 1914). Barcelona-born **José Carreras** and **Plácido Domingo** are recognized as two of the world's finest operatic tenors.

While youth throughout Spain covet American rock, there is considerable national pride in the Spanish version, which is plentiful and widespread. **Jarabe de Palo** enthralls audiences around the world, and Barcelona band **El Último de la Fila** and big-forum **Héroes del Silencio** are well worth a listen. Their former member **Bunbury** now tops the best-selling charts, and other popular groups and soloists are **Alejandro Sanz, Estopa,** and **David Bisbal.** We can't forget **Julio Iglesias,** beloved the world over, and of course, his handsome offspring **Enrique.**

FILM

Spain's first film, *Riña en un Café* (directed by Fructuoso Gelabert), dates back to 1897, and director **Segundo de Chomón** is recognized worldwide as a pioneer of early cinema. Surrealist **Luis Buñuel,** close friend and collaborator of **Salvador Dalí,** produced several early classics, most notably *L'Âge d'or* (1930). Later, in exile from fascist Spain, he produced a number of brilliantly sardonic films including *Viridiana* (1961), denounced by the Church as heretical. Meanwhile, Franco's censors stifled most creative tendencies and left the public with nothing to watch but cheap westerns and bland spy flicks. As censorship waned in the early 1970s, Spanish cinema showed signs of life, led by **Carlos Saura's** dark, subversive hits such as *El jardín de las delicias* (1970) and *Cría cuervos* (1976).

In 1977, in the wake of Franco's death, domestic censorship laws were completely revoked, bringing artistic freedom (and financial hardship) for Spanish filmmakers, who found their films shunned domestically in favor of newly permitted foreign films. Depictions of the exuberant excesses of a super-liberated Spain found increasing attention and respect elsewhere. **Pedro Almodóvar's** *La ley del*

SPAIN

deseo (1987), featuring **Antonio Banderas** as a gay man, and Basque director **Eloy de la Iglesia's** *El diputado* (1979), exploring the intersections of class, ethnicity, and sexuality, capture the risqué themes that contemporary Spanish cinema often focuses on. **Penelope Cruz's** role as a pregnant nun in Almodóvar's Oscar-winning 1999 film *Todo sobre mi madre* garnered her almost as much attention as her recent fling with Tom Cruise. Other directors to look for in Spain include **Bigas Luna**, director of the controversial *Jamón, jamón* (1992); **Fernando Trueba**, whose *Belle époque* won the Best Foreign Film Oscar in 1993; woman director **Icíar Bollaín**, noted for her powerful film *Te doy mis ojos* (2003); and **Vicente Aranda**, director of *El amante bilingüe* (1993) and *Carmen* (2003).

BULLFIGHTING

The national spectacle that is bullfighting *("la corrida")* dates in its modern form to about 1726, although it derives from both Roman and Moorish practices. Bullfighting's growing popularity meant that Roman amphitheaters like those in Sevilla and Córdoba were restored, and bulls were bred for aggressive instincts. The techniques of the modern *matador* (bullfighter) were refined around 1914 by **Juan Belmonte,** considered one of the greatest matadors of all time (others include **Joselito, Manolete,** and **Cristina,** the first female matador).

A bullfight is divided into three principal stages: in the first, *picadores* (lancers on horseback) pierce the bull's neck muscles to lower his head for the kill; next, assistants on foot thrust *banderillas* (decorated darts) into his back to enliven the tiring animal for the final stage; finally, the matador has ten minutes to kill his opponent with a sword between the shoulder blades. He can be granted up to five extra minutes if necessary, but after that the bull is taken out alive, much to the matador's disgrace. On the other hand, if the matador has shown special skill and daring, the audience waves white *pañuelos* (handkerchiefs), imploring the bullfight's president to award him the coveted ears (and, very rarely, the tail).

Bullfighting has always had its **critics**—in the 17th century the Church felt that the risks made it tantamount to suicide. More recently, the argument comes from animal rights activists who object to the slaughter of the bull. Whatever its faults, bullfighting is an essential element of the Spanish national consciousness. ¡Olé!

THE MEDIA

NEWSPAPERS AND MAGAZINES. *ABC*, tangibly conservative and pro-monarchist, is the oldest national daily paper. It jockeys with the more liberal *El País* for Spain's largest readership. *El Mundo* is a younger left-wing daily renowned for its investigative reporting. *Cambio 16* is a popular newsweekly whose main competitor is *Tiempo*. *Hola*, the original *revista del corazón* (magazine of the heart), caters to Spain's love affair with aristocratic titles, Julio Iglesias, and "beautiful" people, as does the tabloid *Semana*.

TELEVISION. Tune in to news at 3 and 8:30pm on most stations. Programming includes dubbed American movies, sports, melodramatic Latin American *telenovelas* (soaps), game shows, jazzed-up documentaries, and cheesy variety extravaganzas. If all else fails, try *fútbol* games or bullfights.

SPORTS

Fútbol is a nationally unifying and locally divisive passion for Spaniards. You have not lived until you have shared a national victory (or defeat) with a bar full of unnervingly interactive Spaniards. Spanish teams—including decorated clubs Real Madrid, Barcelona, and Valencia—consistently appear in European championship series, often upsetting the competition. Real Madrid signed former Manchester United Spice Boy David Beckham in summer 2003, the latest jewel in a crown already studded with Brazilian icons Ronaldo and Roberto Carlos, Luis Figo from Portugal, and French darling Zinedine Zidane. Spanish La Liga competition starts up every September. If it's age-old rivalries you've come for, don't miss a game between Real Madrid and Barcelona or Atlético de Madrid.

Spanish sports prowess doesn't stop with *fútbol*. The retired 5-time consecutive Tour de France champion **Miguel Indurain**, a Navarran hero and Spain's most decorated athlete, is remembered fondly by his fans. Old favorites like **Arantxa Sánchez-Vicario** (also retired) and **Conchita Martínez** and up-and-comers like **Carlos Moya** and **Alex Corretja** have made their names in tennis. Regional specialties spice up the sports scene, including *cesta punta* (a.k.a. *jai alai*) from the País Vasco, windsurfing along the southern coast, and skiing in the Sierra Nevada and the Pyrenees.

NATIONAL HOLIDAYS

The following table lists the national holidays for 2005.

DATE	HOLIDAYS
January 1	New Year's Day
January 6	Epiphany
February 8	Carneval (Carnival)
March 1	*Día de la Victoria* (Victory Day)
March 20-27	*Semana Santa* (Holy Week)
March 24	Maundy Thursday
March 25	Good Friday
March 27	Easter
May 1	*Fiesta del Trabajo* (Labor Day)
May 2	Autonomous Community Day
July 6-14	*Fiesta de San Fermín* (Feast of San Fermín in Pamplona)
July 25	*Día de Santiago* (St. James's Day)
August 15	*La Asunción* (Feast of the Assumption)
October 12	*Fiesta Nacional de España* (National Day)
November 1	*Día de Todos los Santos* (All Saints' Day)
November 9	*Virgen de la Almudena* (Feast of the Virgin of the Almudena)
December 6	*Día de la Constitución* (Constitution Day)
December 8	*La Inmaculada Concepción* (Feast of the Immaculate Conception)
December 25	*Navidad* (Christmas)
December 31	New Year's Eve

SPAIN

RECOMMENDED READING

English-speaking scribes have penned several first-class Spanish travel narratives, ranging from the patronizing to the sublime. Most time-honored classics are region-specific, including Washington Irving's *Tales of the Alhambra* and Bloomsbury Circle-expat Gerald Brenan's *South from Granada*. If you read Spanish, there's nothing better than picking up a book in the original language to enrich your travels, but Spanish works in translation are the next best thing.

FICTION, SPANISH, AND FOREIGN. Start with the epic medieval poem *El Cantar del Mío Cid*. Alternatively, if you like reading about how a Spanish hunk steals the virtue of all the ladies in one medieval Spanish town, enjoy Tirso de Molina's

El burlador de Sevilla. Dream the impossible dream and actually finish Cervantes's two-part über-classic *Don Quixote de la Mancha*. To get a taste of Spain during the Franco regime, read Ana María Matute's wondrous memoir, *Primera Memoria*. Spain has also inspired a number of American and British authors. Ernest Hemingway immortalized bullfighting, machismo, and Spain itself in *The Sun Also Rises* and *For Whom the Bell Tolls*.

ART AND ARCHITECTURE. The definitive work is Bradley Smith's *Spain: A History in Art*. For late 20th-century art, check out William Dyckes's *Contemporary Spanish Art*. If you want to splurge, go for Fred Licht's *Goya* (2001), a must-read for fans of the artist. Biographies of Pablo Picasso, Salvador Dalí, and Antoni Gaudí can be found with minimal fuss. Bernard Bevan wrote the standard text on Spanish architecture: *History of Spanish Architecture*.

HISTORY AND CULTURE. James Michener's best-seller *Iberia* (1968) continues to captivate audiences with its thoroughness and style. *Barcelona*, by Robert Hughes, delves into Catalan culture. George Orwell's *Homage to Catalonia*, a personal account of the Civil War, rivals *Iberia* and *Barcelona* in quality. Finally, don't miss María Rosa Menocal's *The Ornament of the World* (2003), about the peaceful interaction of Moorish, Christian, and Jewish cultures in Toledo.

SPAIN ESSENTIALS

This section is designed to help travelers get their bearings once in Spain. For info about general **travel preparations** (including passports (p. 9), money (p. 12), health (p. 15), packing (p. 14), and more), consult **Essentials** (p. 8). Essentials also has important information for those with specific concerns. See **Alternatives to Tourism** (p. 53) for opportunities to study and work in Spain.

EMBASSIES AND CONSULATES

Embassies and consulates are usually open Monday through Friday, punctuated by *siestas*. Many consulates are only open mornings. Call ahead for exact hours.

Australia: Embassy: Pl. Descubridor Diego de Ordás, 3, Madrid 28003 (☎914 41 60 25; www.spain.embassy.gov.au). **Consulates:** Gran Vía de Carlos III, 98, 9th fl., Barcelona 08028 (☎934 90 90 13); Federico Rubio, 14, Sevilla 41004 (☎954 22 09 71).

Canada: Embassy: C. Núñez de Balboa, 35, Madrid 28001 (☎914 23 32 50; www.canada-es.org). **Consulates:** Elisenda de Pinós, 10 Barcelona 08034 (☎932 04 27 00); Pl. de la Malagueta, 2, 1st fl., Málaga 29016 (☎952 22 33 46).

Ireland: Embassy: Po. de la Castellana, 46, 4th fl., Madrid, 28046 (☎914 36 40 93; fax 35 16 77). **Consulate:** Gran Vía de Carlos III, 94, 10th fl., Barcelona 08028 (☎934 91 50 21; fax 11 29 21).

New Zealand: Embassy: Pl. de la Lealtad, 2, 3rd fl., Madrid 28014 (☎915 23 02 26; fax 23 01 71). **Consulate:** Pg. de Gràcia, 64, 4th fl., Barcelona 08006 (☎932 09 03 99; fax 02 08 90).

United Kingdom: Embassy: C. Fernando el Santo, 16, Madrid 28010 (☎917 00 82 00; www.ukinspain.com). **Consulate-General:** Edificio Torre de Barcelona, Av. Diagonal, 477, 13th fl., Barcelona 08036 (☎933 66 62 00). **Consulates** in Alicante, Bilbao, Ibiza, Las Palmas, Madrid, Málaga, and Palma.

United States: Embassy: C. Serrano, 75, Madrid 28006 (☎915 87 22 00; www.embusa.es). **Consulate General:** Po. Reina Elisenda, 23-25, Barcelona 08034 (☎932 80 22 27). **Consulates** in La Coruña, Las Palmas, Palma, Sevilla, and Valencia.

TRANSPORTATION

Transportation to and within Spain is generally efficient and reliable. The easiest, quickest method of entering Spain is by plane, although Barcelona is well-connected to Europe by rail. Despite the romanticized view of train travel, buses offer the best coverage and are ideal for short trips. Spain's islands are accessible by plane and ferry. For specifics on island travel, see **Las Islas Baleares** (p. 355) and **Las Islas Canarias** (p. 630). For general info, see **Getting to Spain or Portugal**, p. 21.

BY PLANE

All major international airlines offer service to Madrid and Barcelona, most serve the Islas Baleares and Canarias, and many serve Spain's smaller cities. **Iberia** (in Ireland ☎ 1 407 30 17, Spain 902 40 05 00, UK 45 850 90 00, US and Canada 800-772-4642; www.iberia.com) serves all domestic locations and all major international cities. Iberia's two less-established domestic competitors often offer cheaper fares and are worth looking into. **Air Europa** (in US ☎ 888-238-7672, Spain 902 40 15 01; www.aireuropa.com) flies out of New York City and most European cities to Madrid, Málaga, Santiago de Compostela, and Tenerife. Discounts available for youth and senior citizens. No service Wednesdays or Sundays during the summer. **SpanAir** (US ☎ 888-545-5757, Spain 902 13 14 15, elsewhere 34 971 74 50 20; www.spanair.com) offers international and domestic flights.

SpanAir and Iberia offer the following special flight packages for travel throughout Spain, and especially between the islands and the mainland; it may only be possible to add them on to tickets from international destinations.

Iberia Spain Pass: One-way coupons good for all mainland airports and the Canary and Balearic Islands. Reservations must be made five days prior to departure for Spain, and you must purchase your international return ticket before starting your trip. Minimum purchase 3 coupons. Mainland and Balearics: 3 coupons €228, 4 coupons €292. Mainland and Canary Islands: 3 coupons €396, 4 coupons €463.

SpanAir Spain Pass A: Good for flying to any airport within Spain, including Ibiza, Mallorca, or Menorca. No minimum stay; maximum stay 6 months. Reservations must be made before arriving in Spain. Valid for 1 year. Under 12 65% discount. Minimum purchase of 3 tickets €158; additional tickets €53. **SpanAir Spain Pass B** is the same as Spain Pass A, but also includes Lanzarote, Gran Canaria, or Tenerife. Three tickets €280; additional tickets €63.

BY TRAIN

Spanish trains are clean, relatively punctual, and reasonably priced, but tend to bypass many small towns. Spain's national railway is **RENFE** (www.renfe.es). Avoid *transvía*, *semidirecto*, or *correo* trains—they are very slow. The following list includes many types of trains you will find in Spain and their relative speed. Check the website to find out if reservations are required for a particular train.

AVE (Alta Velocidad Española): High-speed trains dart between Madrid and Sevilla, Ciudad Real, Puertollano, Lleida, Zaragoza, and Córdoba. AVE trains soar above others in comfort, price, and speed. The 10am and noon trains are cheapest; student discounts available.

Talgo 200: Sleek trains zip passengers in air-conditioned compartments from Madrid to Málaga, Cádiz/Huelva, or Algeciras. It's more comfortable, possibly faster, and twice as pricey as Cercanías-Regionales trains. Changing a Talgo 200 ticket carries a 10% fine.

Grandes Líneas: RENFE's business unit for long distance travel. A wide range of lines including Euromed, Alaris, Arco, Talgo, and Trenhotel meet every traveler's needs.

Intercity: Cheaper than Talgo, but fewer stops. A/C and comfy. Five lines: Madrid-Valencia, Madrid-Zaragoza-Barcelona, Madrid-Alicante, Madrid-Zaragoza-Logroño-Pamplona, and Madrid-Murcia-Cartagena.

Estrella: A pretty slow night train that has *literas* (bunks).

Cercanías: Commuter trains from large cities to suburbs and towns, with frequent stops.

Regional: Like cercanías but older; multi-stop, cheap rides to small towns and cities.

There is absolutely no reason to buy a Eurail pass if you plan to travel only within Spain and Portugal. Trains are cheap, so a pass saves little money. For the most part, buses are an easier and more efficient means of traveling around Spain. Visit www.raileurope.com for more specific information on the passes below.

Spain Flexipass offers 3 days of unlimited travel in a 2mo. period. 1st-class US$225; 2nd-class US$175. Each additional rail-day (up to 7) US$35 for 1st-class, US$30 for 2nd-class.

Iberic Railpass is good for 3 days of unlimited 1st-class travel in Spain and Portugal in a 2mo. period for €217. Each additional rail-day (up to 7) €48.

Spain Rail 'n' Drive Pass is good for 3 days of unlimited 1st-class train travel and 2 days of unlimited mileage in a rental car within a 2mo. period. Prices €289-578, depending on how many travelers and type of car. Up to 2 additional rail-days and extra car days are also available, and a 3rd and 4th person can join in the car using only a Flexipass.

BY BUS

Bus routes, far more comprehensive than the rail network, provide the only public transportation to many isolated areas and almost always cost less than trains. They are generally quite comfortable, though leg room may be limited. For those traveling primarily within one region, **buses are the best method of transport.**

Spain has numerous private companies; the lack of a centralized bus company may make itinerary planning an ordeal. Companies' routes rarely overlap; it's unlikely that more than one will serve your intended destination. We list below the major national companies, along with the phone number of the Madrid office; you will likely use other companies for travel within any given region; for more information, see the section for your destination.

ALSA/Enatcar (☎902 42 22 42; www.alsa.es). Serves Madrid, Galicia, Asturias, and Castilla y León. Also to France, Italy, Morocco, Poland, and Portugal.

Alosa (☎934 90 40 00; www.alosa.es). Operating primarily in northeastern Spain, Alosa serves Barcelona, Huesca, Jaca, Lleida, and Pamplona.

Alsina Graells (☎932 65 65 92; www.alsinagraells.es). Primarily serves southern Spain, including Granada, Jaén, Sevilla, and Córdoba.

Auto-Res/Cunisa, S.A. (☎902 02 00 52; www.auto-res.net). From Madrid to Castilla y León, Extremadura, Galicia, and Valencia.

Busabout (www.busabout.com, see p. 29). Serves: Barcelona, Bilbao, Granada, Madrid, Pamplona, Salamanca, San Sebastián, Sevilla, Tarifa, Toledo, Valencia, and Zaragoza.

Daibus (☎902 27 79 99; www.daibus.es). To Algeciras, Madrid, Málaga, and Marbella.

Juliá Tours (☎917 79 18 60; www.juliatours.es). Iberia, Western Europe, and Morocco.

Linebús (☎902 33 55 33). Runs to Italy, France, Morocco, the Netherlands, and the UK.

Samar, SA (☎914 68 48 39; www.samar.es). To Andorra, Aragón, Portugal, and Toulouse (France).

BY BOAT

Ferries leave from **Algeciras** for **Tangier** (p. 818) and the Spanish enclave of **Ceuta** (p. 818) in **Morocco** and from **Valencia** and **Barcelona** for the **Islas Baleares** (p. 355). Ferries are also the cheapest, if longest and slowest, way to travel between the mainland and the **Islas Canarias** (p. 630).

BY CAR

Spain's highway system connects major cities by four-lane *autopistas* with plenty of service stations. Traffic moves quickly and drivers can get annoyed if you don't—study your map before you leave. **Speeders beware:** police can "photograph" the speed and license plate of your car and issue a ticket without pulling you over. Purchase **gas** in super (97-octane), normal (92-octane), diesel, and unleaded. Prices are astronomical by North American standards, about €1.50-1.60 per liter.

Renting a car in Spain is considerably cheaper than in many other European countries; prices start at around €50 a day from national companies, €25 from local agencies. Expect to pay more for larger cars and for 4WD. Cars with **automatic transmission** can cost up to €30 a day more than standard manuals (stick shift), and in some places, automatic transmission is hard to find in the first place. It is virtually impossible, no matter where you are, to find an automatic 4WD. Rental agencies are listed in the **Practical Information** at the start of each city.

The Spanish automobile association is **Real Automóvil Club de España (RACE),** C. José Abascal, 10, Madrid (☎915 94 74 75; fax 94 73 29).

BY THUMB

Hitchers report that Castilla and Andalucía are long, hot waits; hitchhiking out of Madrid is virtually impossible. The Mediterranean Coast and the islands are much more promising. Approaching people for rides at gas stations near highways and rest stops purportedly gets results. *Let's Go* does not recommend hitchhiking.

MONEY

Banking hours in Spain from June through September are generally Monday through Friday 9am to 2pm; from October to May, banks are also open Saturday 9am to 1pm. Some banks may be open in the afternoon. **Banco Santander Central Hispano** often provides good exchange rates. For more info on money, see p. 12.

Tipping is not very common in Spain. In restaurants, all prices include service charge. Satisfied customers occasionally toss in some spare change—usually no more than 5%—but this is purely optional. Many people give train, airport, and hotel porters €1 per bag while taxi drivers sometimes get 5-10%. **Bargaining** is really only common at flea markets and with street vendors.

Spain has a 7% **Value Added Tax,** known as IVA, on all meals and accommodations. The prices listed in *Let's Go* include IVA unless otherwise mentioned. Retail goods bear a much higher 16% IVA, although listed prices are usually inclusive. Non-EU citizens who have stayed in the EU fewer than 180 days can claim back the tax paid on purchases at the airport. Ask the shop where you have made the purchase to supply you with a tax return form, though stores will often provide them only for purchases of more than €50-100.

SAFETY AND SECURITY

EMERGENCY	**LOCAL POLICE: ☎092. NATIONAL POLICE: ☎091.** **MEDICAL EMERGENCY ☎112 GUARDIA CIVIL: ☎061.**

PERSONAL SAFETY

Spain has a low **crime** rate, but visitors can always fall victim to tourist-related crimes. Tourists should take particular care in Madrid, especially in El Centro, and in Barcelona around Las Ramblas. If visiting the Costa del Sol in a car, be aware of the fact that this area has seen increased **car theft** in recent years. If you happen to experience car problems, be wary of people posing as Good Samaritans. Drivers should be extremely careful about accepting help from anyone other than a uniformed Spanish police officer or *Guardia Civil* (Civil Guard.) Travelers who accept unofficial assistance should keep their valuables in sight and at hand. For those travelers using public transportation, it is essential to be aware at all times of your belongings and those around you. For more **general safety tips,** see p. 15.

TERRORISM

On **March 11, 2004**, Madrid suffered one of the worst attacks in Spain's recent history when a group of terrorists bombed four commuter trains as they entered the city. The attack caused almost 200 deaths and over 1800 injuries. Referred to by Spaniards as 11-M (*el once eme*), the day became a signal of the growing threat of terrorism on a global scale. Many European countries reacted with heightened security on rail lines and at airports. Although Spanish authorities initially speculated that **ETA**, or Euskadi Ta Askatasuna (Basque Homeland and Freedom), was responsible for the attacks, their focus quickly shifted to **al-Qaeda**, and this group remains at the center of the ongoing investigation. Travelers should be aware that terrorism by Islamic groups remains a threat throughout Western Europe.

Basque terrorism concerns all travelers in Spain and is a highly controversial issue both domestically and internationally. ETA is the militant wing of the Basque separatist movement. It was founded in 1959 to fight for Basque self-determination, concentrating on establishing the Basque region as its own independent country. ETA attacks have resulted in more than 800 deaths since 1968. In 1998, the Spanish government issued the **Declaración Lazarra,** which called for an open dialogue between all involved parties, and ETA publicly declared a truce eight days later. However, ETA ended the cease-fire after 14 months. It is blamed for 39 deaths since November 1999, and 26 car bombings since January 2001. ETA has historically aimed its attacks at the police, military, and other Spanish government targets, but in March 2001, ETA issued a communiqué announcing its intention to target Spanish **tourist areas**. In June 2002, the ETA carried out a series of bombings in resort towns along the **Costa del Sol** and in northern Spain during an EU summit in Sevilla. These attacks were followed up in the **July 2003** bombings of a hotel in Benidorm and another in Alicante. In March 2004, Spanish police discovered large amounts of explosives possessed by suspected ETA terrorists on their way to Madrid. While there may be some risk to travelers, the attacks are very targeted and are not considered random acts of terrorism. Since the events of **11-M**, however, the Spanish government has made a concerted effort to end ETA's operations once and for all.

HEALTH

The public health care system in Spain is very reliable; in an emergency, seek out the *urgencias* (emergency) section of the nearest hospital. For smaller concerns, it is probably best to go to a private clinic to avoid the frustration of long lines. Expect to pay cash up front (though most travel insurance will pick up the tab later; request a receipt) and bring your passport and other forms of identification. A visit to a clinic in Spain can cost anywhere from €70-180, depending on the service. Visit the following site for the most recent updates on travel-related health concerns in Spain: www.mdtravelhealth.com/destinations/europe/spain.html.

Farmacias in Spain are also very helpful. A duty system has been set up so that at least one farmacia is open at all times in each town; look for a flashing green cross. Spanish pharmacies are not the place to find your cheap summer flip-flops or greeting cards, but they sell contraceptives, common drugs, and many prescription drugs; they can answer simple medical questions and help you find a doctor. For more general info on travel-related health concerns, see **Health,** p. 15.

ACCOMMODATIONS

PENSIONES, HOSTALES, AND HOTELES

Spanish accommodations have many aliases, distinguished by the different grades of rooms. The cheapest and barest options are **casas de huéspedes** and **hospedajes.** While **pensiones** and **fondas** tend to be a bit nicer, all are essentially just boarding houses. Higher up the ladder, **hostales** generally have sinks in bedrooms and provide sheets and lockers, while **hostal-residencias** are similar to hotels in overall quality. The government rates *hostales* on a two-star system; even establishments receiving one star are typically quite comfortable. The system also fixes each *hostal*'s prices, posted in the lounge or main entrance. *Hostal* owners invariably dip below the official rates in the off season (Sept.-May), so bargain away.

The highest-priced accommodations are **hoteles**, which have a bathroom in each room but are usually on the pricey side for the budget traveler. The top-notch hotels are the handsome **Paradores Nacionales**—castles, palaces, convents, and historic buildings that have been converted into luxurious hotels and often are interesting sights in their own right. For a *parador*, €75 per night is a bargain. If you have trouble with rates or service, ask for the **libro de reclamaciones** (complaint book), which by law must be produced on demand. The argument will usually end immediately, since all complaints must be forwarded to the authorities within 48 hours. Report any problems to tourist offices, who may help you resolve disputes.

YOUTH HOSTELS

Red Española de Albergues Juveniles (REAJ), C. Galera, 1a, Sevilla 41001 (☎954 21 68 03; www.reaj.com), the Spanish Hostelling International (HI) affiliate, runs 165 youth hostels year-round. Prices depend on location (typically some distance away from town center) and services offered, but are generally €9-15 for guests under 26 and higher for those 26 and over. Breakfast is usually included; lunch and dinner are occasionally offered at an additional charge. Hostels usually lockout around 11:30am and have curfews between midnight and 3am. As a rule, don't expect much privacy—rooms typically are dorm-style with four to 20 beds in one room. Call in advance to reserve a bed in high season (July-Aug. and during fiestas). A national **Youth Hostel Card** is usually required (see **Hostels,** p. 39). HI cards are available from Spain's youth travel company, **TIVE.** Occasionally, guests can stay in a hostel without one and pay extra for six nights to become a member.

ALTERNATIVE ACCOMMODATIONS

In less-touristed areas, **casas particulares** (private residences) may sometimes be the only option. Look for signs in windows if you're not accosted by owners in the bus or train station. **Casas rurales** (rural cottages) and **casas rústicas** (farmhouses), referred to as *agroturismo*, have overnight rates from €6-21. In the Pyrenees and Picos de Europa, there are several **refugios,** rustic mountain huts for hikers.

CAMPING

In Spain, **campgrounds** are generally the cheapest choice for three or more people. Most charge separate fees per person, per tent, and per car; others charge for a *parcela*—a small plot of land—plus per-person fees. Although it may seem like an inexpensive option, prices can get high for lone travelers and even for pairs. Campgrounds are categorized on a three-class system, with rating and prices based on amenity quality. Like hostels, they must post fees within view of the entrance. They must also provide sinks, showers, and toilets. Most tourist offices provide information on official areas, including the hefty *Guía de campings*.

KEEPING IN TOUCH

Some useful **communication information** (including international access codes, calling card numbers, country codes, operator and directory assistance, and emergency numbers) is listed on the **inside back cover.**

TELEPHONES AND FAX

The central Spanish phone company is *Telefónica*. Most bars have pay phones, though they are often only coin-operated. The best way to make local calls is with a phone card, issued in denominations of €6 and €12 and sold at kiosks, tobacconists (*estancos* or *tabacos*, identifiable by brown signs with yellow lettering and tobacco leaf icons), and most post offices. Ask tobacconists for calling cards known as *Phonepass*: €6 gives you 62min. to the US; €12 gets 150min. Calling internationally with a Spanish phone card is inexpensive and easy; however, you may prefer to use a calling card issued by your phone company. Numbers for obtaining calling cards from home are in the **Essentials** section (p. 35).

Most Spanish post offices have **fax** services. Some photocopy shops and telephone offices (*Telefónica, locutorios*) also offer fax service, but they tend to charge more than post offices, and faxes can only be sent, not received. Cybercafes are also becoming increasingly popular places to send faxes at cheap rates.

MAIL

Air mail (*por avión*) takes five to eight business days to reach the US or Canada. Standard postage is €0.80 to North America. Surface mail (*por barco*), while considerably less expensive than air mail, can take over a month, and packages will take two to three months. Express mail (*certificado*), is the most reliable way to send a letter or parcel, and takes four to seven business days. Spain's overnight mail is not worth the expense, since it isn't exactly "overnight." For better service, try companies like DHL, UPS, or SEUR; look under *mensajerías* in the yellow pages. Their reliability, however, comes at a high cost. Stamps are sold at post offices and tobacconists (*estancos* or *tabacos*). Mail letters and postcards from yellow mailboxes scattered through cities, or from the post office in small towns.

EMAIL

Email is easily accessible within Spain and much quicker and more reliable than the regular mail system. An increasing number of bars offer Internet access for a fee of €1-3 per hour. Cybercafes are listed in most towns and all cities. In small towns, if Internet access is not listed, check the library or the tourist office (where occasionally travelers may get access for a small fee).

MADRID

The relentless summer sun parches sidewalks and side streets, blazing across a city filled with tremendous history and life. In this city of restless energy, the morning rush hour coincides with the move to after-hours clubs, and fervent activity seems to pause only for an afternoon siesta. *Madrileños* leave straight from work for the city's many plazas, tapas bars, and romantic parks, surviving on minimal sleep and living each day to its fullest. While tourists inundate the city, spending their days absorbed in its Old World monuments, world-renowned museums, and raging nightlife, Madrid's population of 5 million roams the labyrinthine neighborhoods with a simple and energetic joy.

Madrid's history does not read like that of rival European capitals. Although the city witnessed the coronation of Fernando and Isabel, Madrid did not gain importance until Habsburg monarch Felipe II moved the court here in 1561. Despite its considerable distance from vital ports and rivers, it immediately became a seat of wealth, culture, and imperial glory, serving as the center of Spain's 16th- and 17th-century Golden Age of literature, art, and architecture. In the 18th century, Madrid witnessed a Neoclassical rebirth as Carlos III embellished the city with wide, tree-lined boulevards and scores of imposing buildings. However, the 19th-century Peninsular Wars against Napoleon scarred Madrid and provided the bloody inspiration for some of Francisco de Goya's most famous canvases. In 1939, Madrid was the next to last city to fall in the Civil War. Though hostile to Franco's nationalism, it served as the seat of his government. This time, its location—smack in the country's center—was its greatest strength. Franco's death nearly 40 years later brought an explosion known as *la movida* ("shift" or "movement") or *el destapeo* ("uncovering"). After decades of totalitarian repression, Madrid exploded in a breathtaking, city-wide release of inhibition. A 200,000-strong student population took to the streets and stayed there—they haven't stopped moving yet.

Today Madrid continues to serve as Spain's political, intellectual, and cultural center. It is neither as cosmopolitan as Barcelona nor as charming as Sevilla, but it is undeniably the *capital*—the wild, pulsing heart of Spain. Students, families, artists, and immigrants flock here in pursuit of their dreams, and Madrid continues to grow as a city of opportunity. Its very architecture—with modern skyscrapers and shining industrial spaces rising from narrow alleys and ancient plazas—epitomizes the mix of galvanizing history and passion for life that so defines Spain.

HIGHLIGHTS OF MADRID

SCOPE OUT other travelers in the **Parque del Buen Retiro** (p. 137).

FEAST on suckling pig at **Sobrino del Botín,** the world's oldest restaurant (p. 113).

STROLL down the three **paseos** in leisurely, high-bourgeois style (p. 138).

RIDE out to **Aranjuez** for strawberries and cream (p. 146).

DANCE until dawn at killer club **Kapital** (p. 127).

◼ INTERCITY TRANSPORTATION

BY PLANE

All flights land at **Aeropuerto Internacional de Barajas** (general info ☎913 05 83 43, 44, 45, or 46), 13km and 20min. northeast of Madrid. A branch of the **regional tourist office** in the international arrivals area has maps and info. (☎913

MADRID

Madrid Overview

1/2 mile
1/2 kilometer

TO AEROPUERTO
DE BARAJAS

Parque
Breogán

PARQUE
DE LAS
AVENIDAS

Av. San Luis

C. de Arturo Soria

M30

Av. Aster

Alfonso

XIII

C. Cartagena

AVENIDA
DE LA PAZ

F. Núñez

Av. Ramón y Cajal

C. Clara del Rey

CARTAGENA

AV. DE
AMÉRICA

Av. de América

Av. Pío XII

C. Marqués
de Toroja

PÍO XII

C. Alfonso XIII

C. Costa Rica

C. Colombia

ALFONSO XIII

C. López de Hoyos

C. Pradillo

PROSPERIDAD

Parque
de Berlín

CONCHA
ESPIÑA

Auditorio
Nacional

CRUZ DEL
RAYO

C. Francisco

Av. Pío XII

D. PASTRANA

Estación
Chamartín

M CHAMARTÍN

CASTILLA

C. Mateo Inurria

C. Agustín Foxá

Po. de la Castellana

C. Felix Boix

Fray B. Sahagún

Av. Alberto Alcocer

C. potosi

COLOMBIA

C. Príncipe de Vergara

C. Diego de León

C. Emilio
Castelar

GLORIETA
DE EMILIO
CASTELAR

VENTANILLA

CASTILLA

CUZCO

C. Padre Damián

PL. DE
CUZCO

Po. de la Habana

PL. REP.
EL SALVADOR

Habana

Av. Concha Espina

Av. Dr. Arce

Po. de la Castellana

C. Serrano

Av. de Vitruvio

REPÚBLICA
ARGENTINA

Residencia de
Estudiantes

GREGORIO MARAÑÓN

C. de Joaquín Costa

C. de María de Molina

PL. SAN JUAN
DE LA CRUZ

Museo
Sorolla

Po. General
Martínez Campos

SANTIAGO
BERNABÉU

LIMA

Australia

PL. DE
LIMA

NUEVOS
MINISTERIOS

Nuevos
Ministerios

VALDEACEDERAS

TETUÁN

C. de Bravo Murillo

C. Capitán Blanco Argibay

C. Sinesio Delgado

PEÑAGRANDE

ANTONIO
MACHADO

C. Antonio Machado

C. de Orense

C. Infanta Mercedes

Av. del General Perón

C. Cmndte. Zofita

C. de Ponzano

ALONSO
CANO

C. de Alonso Cano

C. José Abascal

C. de Ríos Rosas

RÍOS
ROSAS

C. Santa Engracia

IGLESIA

Eloy Gonzalo

CANAL

ALVARADO

CUATRO
CAMINOS

C. Raimundo
Fernández Villaverde

ESTRECHO

GUZMÁN EL BUENO

Reina Victoria

Av. Juan Montalvo

Av. de Pablo Iglesias

FRANCOS
RODRÍGUEZ

C. de Francos Rodríguez

C. de Ofelia Nieto

Dehesa
de la
Villa

XXIII

Po. de Juan

METROPOLITANO

C. del Valle

C. Guzmán

Parque
Santander

Av. Filipinas

Cea Bermúdez

el Bueno

ISLAS
FILIPINAS

Po. S. Francisco de Sales

C. de
Isaac Peral

PL. DE
CRISTO
REY

Museo de
América

Hospital Clínico
San Carlos

CIUDAD
UNIVERSITARIA

CIUDAD UNIVERSITARIA

Av. de la Complutense

Av. de la Puerta de Hierro

C. de Arco de
la Victoria

EL CARMEN

ESTRELLA

VENTAS

PUENTE DE VALLECAS

PL. DE TOROS MONUMENTAL (PL DE LAS VENTAS)

(M30)

Parque Fuente del Berro

Parque de Roma

Jardines Sancho Dávila

Parque Eva Perón

PL. DE ROMA

Av. de Baraja

Estación Auto Res

MANUEL BECERRA

C. del Doctor Esquerdo

SAINZ DE BARANDA

CONDE DE CASAL

(M30)

C. del Dr. Esquerdo

Silvella

LISTA

Gregorio Marañón

O'DONNELL

C. Alcalde Sainz

C. de Ibiza

Av. Nazaret

Po. del Mediterráneo

Estación Sur de Autobuses

DIEGO DE LEÓN

NÚÑEZ DE BALBOA

C. Conde de Peñalver

GOYA

O'DONNELL

IBIZA

MÉNDEZ ÁLVARO

MÉNDEZ PELAYO

C. Juan Bravo

C. de Padilla

C. José Ortega y Gasset

C. Príncipe de Vergara

VELÁZQUEZ

PRÍNCIPE DE VERGARA

RETIRO

Av. Menéndez y

Av. de la Ciudad de Barcelona

PACÍFICO

C. Méndez Álvaro

Po. de Pelayo

C. Reina Cristina

C. Ancora

Av. del Mediterráneo

C. Velázquez

SERRANO

C. de Serrano

Canadá

Parque del Buen Retiro

Palacio de Velázquez

Palacio de Cristal

Po. del Ecuador

Po. de Fernán Núñez

C. Duque de Fernán Núñez

C. Menorca

Po. de Santa Isabel

TO PARQUE TIERNO GALVÁN

Museo del Ferrocarril

PL. DE LA INDEPENDENCIA

C. Alfonso XII

ATOCHA

Estación Atocha

PO. DE LA FRONTERA

C. Canarias

C. Ramírez Prado

Po. de la Castellana

RUBÉN DARÍO

UK

COLÓN

Biblioteca Nacional

Museo Arqueológico

Museo del Prado

PL. DEL EMPERADOR CARLOS V

Real Jardín Botánico

Delicias

DELICIAS

EMBAJADORES

Po. de la Cabeza

Po. de las Acacias

Po. Santa María de la Cabeza

Po. Eduardo Dato

PL. DE COLÓN

CHUECA

BANCO DE ESPAÑA

Museo Thyssen-Bornemisza

CÁNOVAS DEL CASTILLO

Po. del Prado

Museo de Arte Reina Sofía

C. Sta. María de la Cabeza

C. la Frontera

Po. Sta. María de la Cabeza

C. Santa Engracia

Po. de Recoletos

Museo Romántico

PL. DE LA CIBELES

SEVILLA

PL. DE LA CIBELES

C. de las Huertas

C. de Atocha

C. de Santa Isabel

ANTÓN MARTÍN

LAVAPIÉS

EMBAJADORES

Río Valencia Regla

PL. DE OLAVIDE

Museo Municipal

ALONSO MARTÍNEZ

GRAN VÍA

Gran Vía

C. de Alcalá

C. San Jerónimo

C. del Prado

C. Argumosa

Av. de la Esperanza

C. Lucientes

BILBAO

C. Sagasta

C. de Fuencarral

C. de Hortaleza

SOL

PUERTA DEL SOL

TIRSO DE MOLINA

LA LATINA

C. del Amparo

EL RASTRO

MADRID, see p. 88-89

Po. de la Esperanza

GLORIETA DE QUEVEDO

QUEVEDO

San Bernardo

SAN BERNARDO

TRIBUNAL

NOVICIADO

CALLAO

Car Rental

Gran Vía Car Rental

OPERA

C. Mayor

C. del Arenal

PL. MAYOR

PL. DE CASCORRO

C. Toledo

PTA. DE TOLEDO

EMBAJADORES

ACACIAS

C. de las Acacias

PIRÁMIDES

GLORIETA DE BILBAO

PL. DE ESPAÑA

SANTO DOMINGO

PLAZA DE ESPAÑA

PL. DE ORIENTE

Palacio Real

Jardines de Sabatini

PL. DE ESPAÑA

San Francisco

GLORIETA PTA. DE TOLEDO

PTA. DE TOLEDO

C. Toledo

Po. Imperial

Ronda de Toledo

C. de Toledo

Puente de Toledo

MARTÍN DE VADILLO

C. Santa Virtudes

C. Alberto Aguilera

VENTURA RODRÍGUEZ

Museo Cerralbo

C. Bailén

Catedral de la Almudena

C. Segovia

Ronda de Segovia

Po. de los Pontones

Po. de la Virgen del Puerto

Po. de Segovia

Puente de Segovia

Po. 15 de Mayo

ARGÜELLES

Viajes TIVE

MONCLOA

C. de Princesa

C. Martín de Vargas

C. Quintana

C. de Ferraz

PRÍNCIPE PÍO

Estación del Norte

Campo del Moro

Puente del Rey

Ermita del Santo

Po. de la

C. Aniceto Marinas

Av. Valladolid

Río Manzanares

Casa de Campo

Parque del Oeste

C. de Ruperto

Po. del Rey

Capilla de San Antonio

Templo de Debod

Parque de la Montaña

Po. de la Florida

EL LAGO

Av. Portugal

Av. Extremadura

C. Sepúlveda

MADRID

MADRID

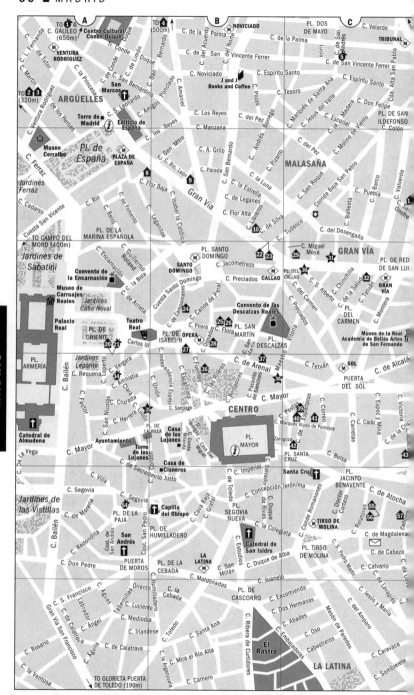

Madrid
see key p. 90

BILBAO & 800m)
C. DE LUCHANA
(00m)

Museo
Municipal

Museo
Romántico

C. Beneficencia
C. Mejia Lequerica
C. Santa Teresa
C. Orellana
C. Genova

PL. DE LA
VILLA
DE PARIS

PL. DE COLÓN
COLÓN

Jardines del
Descubrimiento

C. Goya

Palacio
de Longoria

Centro
Cultural

Biblioteca
Nacional

Museo
Arqueológico

Iglesia de
San Anton

PL.
SALESAS

C. Bárbara de Braganza

C. San Lucas

C. Piamonte

Teatro
Maria
Guerrero

C. de Serrano

C. Villanueva

CHUECA

CHUECA

C. Figueroa

C. Prim

C. de Recoletos

C. Salustiano Olazaga

0   200 yards

0   200 meters

PL. DE LA
INDEPENDENCIA
RETIRO

Palacio de
Buenavista

PL.
DEL REY

Casa de
América

C. de Alcalá

PL. DE LA
CIBELES

Puerta
de Alcalá

Al
Méjico

Gran Via

BANCO DE
ESPAÑA

Main Post Office/
Palacio de
Comunicaciones

C. Valenzuela

C. Alfonso XI

C. Alfonso XII

Las
Calatravas

Círculo de
Bellas Artes

C. Montalbán

Museo
Naval

C. Juan de Mena

SEVILLA

HUERTAS

Bolsa de Madrid

C. Antonio Maura

Po. de la
Argentina

Palacio
Miraflores

C. Zorrilla

PL.
DE LA
LEALTAD

Museo del
Ejército

Parque
del
Buen
Retiro

Parlamento

Museo
Thyssen-
Bornemisza

Casón del
Buen Retiro

Teatro Español

PL. DE
LAS CORTES

C. Felipe IV

C. Academia

Los Jerónimos
Reales

Po.
San Pablo

Casa de
Lope de Vega

PL. CÁNOVAS
DEL CASTILLO

C. de Cascado

C. Alisal

ANTÓN
MARTÍN

Real Academia
de la Historia

Museo
del Prado

C. Alberto Bosch

C. Alfonso XII

PL. PLATERÍA
MARTINEZ

PL. DE
SAN JUAN

PL. DE
MURILLO

C. Espalter

Real
Jardín
Botánico

LAVAPIÉS

ATOCHA

Conservatorio
Superior de Música

PL.
EMPERADOR
CARLOS V

C. Claudio Moyano

P. Duque de
F. Nuñez

ATOCHA

Estación
Atocha

Museo de Arte
Reina Sofía

TO TICKET
OFFICE
(50m)

ATOCHA RENFE

TO ESTACIÓN
AUTO RES
(1680m)

Madrid
see map p. 88-89

⌂ ACCOMMODATIONS

Albergue Juvenil Santa Cruz de Marcenado (HI), **4**	B1
Los Amigos Backpackers' Hostel, **24**	B3
Barbieri International Youth Hostel, **16**	D2
Cat's Hostel, **57**	C5
Hispa Domus, **15**	D2
Hostal A. Nebrija, **8**	A2
Hostal Abril, **13**	D2
Hostal Aguilar, **45**	D4
Hostal Alicante, **37**	B4
Hostal Los Arcos, **41**	C4
Hostal Armesto, **53**	D4
Hostal Betanzos, **55**	C5
Hostal Cantábrico, **46**	D4
Hostal Chelo, **20**	D2
Hostal Esparteros, **40**	C4
Hostal Gonzalo, **62**	E5
Hostal Internacional, **48**	D4
Hostal Lauria, **22**	B3
Hostal Madrid, **39**	C4
Hostal Margarita, **23**	B3
Hostal Medieval, **12**	D2
Hostal Oriente, **27**	B3
Hostal Palacios/Hostal Ribadavia, **11**	C2
Hostal Paz, **26**	B3
Hostal Pérez, **3**	A1
Hostal Portugal, **25**	B3
Hostal R. Rodríguez, **43**	C4
Hostal Santillan, **9**	B2
Hostal Triana, **32**	C3
Hostal Valencia, **20**	A3
Hostal Villar, **52**	D4
Hostal-Residencia Alibel, **29**	C3
Hostal-Residencia Carreras, **51**	D4
Hostal-Residencia Cruz-Sol, **42**	C4
Hostal-Residencia Domínguez, **7**	D1
Hostal-Residencia Lamalonga, **10**	B2
Hostal-Residencia Lido, **49**	D4
Hostal-Residencia Luz, **36**	B4
Hostal-Residencia Ríos, **2**	A1
Hostal-Residencia Rober, **28**	B3
Hostal-Residencia Sud-Americana, **63**	E5
Hotel Mónaco, **17**	D2
Hotel San Lorenzo, **33**	D3
Huéspedaje Yolanda, **56**	C5

🍎 BEST OF FOOD

Al-Jaima, **18**	D2
Ananias, **1**	A1
Arrocería Gala, **65**	E5
Café-Botillería Manuela, **5**	C1
Café de Oriente, **21**	A3
Casa Alberto, **59**	D5
El Estragón Vegetariano, **54**	A5
La Finca de Susana, **44**	D4
Inshala, **34**	A4
Osteria Il Regno di Napoli, **6**	D1
Ricci Gelateria & Yogurteria Artiginale, **58**	D5
La Sanabresa, **60**	D5
Taberna Macieras, **64**	E5

🌟 BEST OF NIGHTLIFE

Acuarela, **14**	D2
El Café de Sheherezade, **61**	D5
Cardamomo, **50**	D4
Cuevas de Sesamo, **47**	D4
Kapital, **66**	E6
Kathmandú, **35**	A4
Ocho y Medio Club, **31**	C3
Palacio Gaviria, **38**	B4
Pasapoga, **30**	C3

HOW TO USE THIS CHAPTER. Madrid is divided into several neighborhoods. We have grouped together all of each area's accommodations, food, sights, museums, and nightlife listings. General information on these aspects of Madrid, as well as shopping and specific listings for camping and entertainment (including sports, theater, concerts, and film), appears after the practical information.

05 86 56. Open M-F 8am-8pm, Sa 9am-1pm.) **Luggage storage** *(consigna)* is available. (☎913 93 68 05. 1 day €2.60, 2-15 days €3.40 per day. 15 day max. Open 24hr.)

The **Barajas metro stop** connects the airport to all of Madrid (€1.20). From the airport arrivals area, follow signs to the metro (10min.). Take Line 8 (pink) to Nuevos Ministerios and switch to Line 10 (dark blue, dir.: Puerta del Sur). At Tribunal, change to Line 1 (light blue, dir.: Congosto), and two stops later you'll find yourself at Sol, smack in the middle of Madrid's best accommodations and sights. The blue **Bus-Aeropuerto #89** leaves from the national and international terminals and runs to the city center. (☎914 31 61 92. Look for "EMT" signs just outside the airport doors. Daily 4:45, 5:15, 6:15am; every 10min. 6am-11pm; every 15min. 11pm-1:30am; last bus 1:50am. €2.50.) The bus stops underground beneath the Jardines del Descubrimiento in **Plaza de Colón** (M: Colón). After surfacing in Pl. de Colón, walk toward the neo-Gothic statue that overlooks the

Paseo de Recoletos. The Colón metro station is across the street. Fleets of **taxis** swarm the airport. Taxi fare to central Madrid should cost €16-27, including the €4.20 airport surcharge, depending on traffic and time of day.

AIRLINES

Over 65 airlines fly in and out of Aeropuerto Internacional de Barajas. Below are the numbers for the most relevant airlines in Madrid.

Air Europa: 24hr. ☎902 40 15 01, in airport 913 93 70 31; www.aireuropa.com. Airport booth open 5am-10pm.

Air France: Pl. de España, 18, 5th fl. (☎901 11 22 66, in airport 913 05 43 41; www.airfrance.com). M: Pl. de España. Open M-F 9am-5pm, airport booth open 5:15am-8pm.

American Airlines: ☎902 11 55 70, in airport 913 05 81 74; www.aa.com. Open M-F 9am-6pm.

British Airways: ☎902 11 13 33, in airport 913 05 42 43; www.ba.com. Open M-F 9am-7pm, Sa 9am-2pm.

Continental: C. Leganitos, 47, 9th fl. (☎915 59 27 10). M: Pl. de España. Open M-F 9am-6pm.

Delta Airlines: C. Goya, 8 (☎915 77 06 50, reservations 917 49 66 30). M: Serrano.

Iberia: C. Velázquez, 130 (☎915 87 47 47, 24hr. reservations and info 902 40 05 00). M: Av. de las Américas. Open M-F 9:30am-1pm and 4-6:30pm.

Lufthansa: ☎902 22 01 01, in airport 913 054 240. Open daily 6am-8pm.

Portugalia: C. Leganitos, 47, 6th fl. (☎915 42 21 61, in airport 913 93 64 26). M: Pl. de España. Open M-F 9:30am-2:30pm and 3:30-6:30pm.

SpanAir: ☎913 93 67 40, info and reservations 902 13 14 15, in airport 913 93 70 55; www.spanair.com.

TAP Air Portugal: Pl. de los Mostenses, 13, 6th fl. (☎915 42 12 03, in airport 913 93 82 53; www.tap-airportugal.pt). M: Pl. de España. Open M-F 9am-6pm.

USAirways: C. Alberto Aguilera, 38, 2nd fl. (☎901 11 70 73, in airport 913 93 71 46; www.usairways.com). M: Argüelles. Open daily 9am-3:15pm.

BY TRAIN

Two *largo recorrido* (long-distance) **RENFE** stations, **Chamartín** and **Atocha**, connect Madrid to surrounding areas and the rest of Europe. Both stations are easily accessible by metro. (For Atocha, avoid lost tourist syndrome and get off the metro at Atocha Renfe, *not* Atocha.) Call RENFE (☎902 24 02 02; www.renfe.es) for reservations and info. Buy tickets at the stations or at the **RENFE Main Office,** C. Alcalá, 44, at Gran Vía. (M: Banco de España. Open M-F 9:30am-8pm.) Schedules for are available at the stations and online.

Estación Atocha (☎915 06 61 37). M: Atocha Renfe. The cast-iron atrium of the original station has been turned into a rainforest with lush plants and turtles. Galleries, boutiques, and restaurants provide additional diversions. **RENFE information office** in the main terminal (☎902 24 02 02). Open daily 6:30am-10:30pm. **Luggage storage** (*consignas automáticas;* €2.40-4.50), at the back right corner of the atrium. Open daily 6:30am-10:30pm. Ticket windows open 6:30am-10:30pm, advance purchases 7am-11:30pm. No international service. **AVE** (☎902 24 02 02) offers high-speed service to southern Spain, including **Málaga** (3hr., 6 per day 7:10am-8:10pm, €49-54) and **Sevilla** (2½hr., 20 per day 7am-11pm, €59-65) via **Córdoba** (1¾hr., €43-48). Daytime *Grandes Líneas* for **Barcelona** leave from Atocha (4½-5hr., 5 per day 7:45am-7pm, €35-59); overnight trains leave from **Chamartín.**

THE LOCAL STORY

OF BEARS AND BERRIES

Strolling around Madrid, you may notice the city's remarkably cute heraldic crest, a bear, or *oso*, standing on its hind paws to eat fruit out of a *madroño* tree *(Arbutus unedo)*. Though the sculpture of the bear in Pl. del Sol is the backdrop for modern family photo-ops and a perfect place to meet your friends, its origin is far more ancient.

In the 13th century, the local government and the Church struggled for dominion over lands. After 20 years of dispute, they finally came to an agreement: the Church would own the pastures, and the Municipality would own the fruits of the trees. Thereafter, the Church used a bear on four paws on its banners, and the city adopted the more adventurous forager. The crest is surrounded by five stars, which appropriately represent the stars in the constellation known to Americans as the Big Dipper—*Ursa Major*, the Great Bear.

Though featured in Hieronymous Bosch's triptych in the Prado, *The Garden of Earthly Delights*, the *madroño* is rarely eaten fresh. The Latin name, "*unedo*," means "I eat one (only)." For a taste of the bear's favorite, try it in jam form or distilled into a sweet liqueur. The latter can be found for €2 at **El Oso y el Madroño**, C. Bolsa, 4 (☎915 22 77 96), a bar just off Pl. Benavente near Pl. del Sol.

Estación Chamartín (☎913 00 69 69). M: Chamartín. Bus #5 runs to and from Puerta del Sol (45min.); the stop is just beyond the lockers. Alternatively, get off at M: Atocha Renfe and take a *Cercanías* train (15min., every 5-10min., €1) to Chamartín. Chamartín is a mini-mall of useful services, including a **tourist office** (Vestíbulo, Puerta 14; ☎913 15 99 76; open M-Sa 8am-8pm, Su 8am-2pm), **currency exchange, accommodations service, post office, car rental, police,** and **luggage storage** (*consignas;* €2.40-4.50; open daily 7am-11pm). For international destinations, call RENFE or ☎902 24 34 02; for domestic destinations call RENFE (☎902 24 02 02; Spanish only). Ticket windows open 6:35am-10:55pm, advance sales 8am-9pm. Chamartín serves both international and domestic destinations to the northeast and south. Most *Cercanías* (local) trains stop at both Chamartín and Atocha. Major destinations include: **Barcelona** (9hr., 10 and 11pm, €35-42); **Bilbao** (6hr., 7:30am and 9:13pm, €30-38); **Lisboa,** Portugal (9½hr., 10:45pm, €53-70); **Paris,** France (13½hr.; 7pm; €112-135, students with ISIC and seniors €90-108).

BY BUS

Numerous private companies serve Madrid, each with its own station and set of destinations. Most buses pass through **Estación Sur de Autobuses** and **Estación Auto-Res,** both easily accessible by metro. The Pl. Mayor tourist office has information on the most relevant intercity buses. For more general info, see **Bus,** p. 95.

ALSA (☎902 42 22 42) international destinations include: **Czech Republic, France, Germany, Holland, Italy, Poland, Portugal, Romania,** and **Switzerland,** but flying can actually be cheaper. Contact **Eurolines** for more information (reservations ☎902 40 50 40). Madrid office in **Estación Sur** bus station (☎915 06 33 60; www.eurolines.es). M: Méndez Álvaro. Open daily 8:30am-10pm.

Estación Empresa Alacuber: Po. de Moret (☎913 76 01 04). M: Moncloa. To **El Pardo** (20min., every 15min. 6am-1:30am, €1.10).

Estación Auto-Res: C. Fernández Shaw, 1 (☎902 02 09 99; www.auto-res.net). M: Conde de Casal. **Luggage storage** €1.20 per bag per day. Info booth open daily 6:30am-1am. Tickets sold daily 6am-1am. To: **Badajoz** (5¼hr., 9-10 per day 8am-1am, €22.40; express 4½hr., 10am-9pm, €26.50); **Cáceres** (4¾hr., 7-9 per day 8am-1am, €16.70; express 3½hr., €20); **Cuenca** (2½hr.; M-F 8-10 per day 6:45am-10pm, Sa-Su 5-6 per day 8am-8pm, Su last bus 10pm; €9.10; express 2hr.; M-F and Su 10am and 6:30pm, Sa 10am; €11.80); **Mérida** (4¼hr.; M-Sa 9 per day 8am-1am, Su 8 per day 8am-9pm; €19; express 4hr., €22.20); **Salamanca** (3-

3¼hr., 9 per day 8:30am-10:30pm, €10.20; express 2½hr.; M-Sa 15-16 per day 7am-10pm, Su 8am-11pm; €15); **Trujillo** (3¼hr., 11-12 per day 8am-1am, €14; express 2¾hr., €17.30); **Valencia** (5hr., 4 per day 1am-2pm, €19.80; express 4hr., 10-11 per day M-Sa 7am-1am, Su 8am-1am, €24).

Estación Empresa Continental Auto: Av. de América, 9 (☎917 45 63 00). M: Av. de América. To: **Alcalá de Henares** (40min.; M-Sa every 15min. 6:15am-11pm, Su every 20min. 7-11pm; €1.90); **Guadalajara** (1hr.; M-F every 30min. 7am-10:30pm, Sa-Su every hr. 9am-10pm; €3.40); **Toledo** (1½hr.; M-Sa every 30min. 6:30am-10pm, Su every 30min. 8:30am-midnight; €4).

Estación Autocares Herranz: C. del Rey, 27 (☎918 96 90 28), in the Intercambio de Moncloa. M: Moncloa. To **Valle de los Caídos** (20min.; departs El Escorial 3:15pm, returns 5:30pm; round-trip plus admission €7.90) via **El Escorial** (50min.; every 30min. M-F 7am-10:30pm, Sa 8:30am-10:15pm, Su 9am-11pm; €2.90).

Empresa Larrea: Est. Sur de Autobuses (☎915 30 48 00). To **Ávila** (1½hr.; M-F 8 per day 7:15am-8pm, Sa-Su 3 per day 10am-8pm; €6.45).

Estación La Sepulvedana: Po. de la Florida, 11 (☎915 30 48 00). M: Príncipe Pío (via extension from M: Ópera). To **Segovia** (1½hr., every 30min. 6:30am-10:15pm, €5.60).

Estación Sur de Autobuses: C. Méndez Álvaro (☎914 68 42 00). M: Méndez Álvaro; metro stop inside station. Info booth open daily 6:30am-1am. **ATMs,** food, and **luggage storage** (€1.25 per bag per day). National destinations include: **Algeciras, Alicante, Aranjuez, Benidorm, Cartagena, La Coruña, Gijón, Lugo, Murcia, Oviedo, Santiago de Compostela,** and **Toledo.** Check at the station or call for specific info on routes and schedules. **ALSA** (☎915 27 12 94) is the best option to get to **Aranjuez** (45min.; M-F every 15-30min. 6:30am-11:30pm, Sa-Su every hr. 8am-11pm; €3.10).

✠ ORIENTATION

The "Kilómetro 0" sign in front of the police station in **Puerta del Sol** marks the intersection of eight of Madrid's most celebrated streets and the starting point of the country's major highways. To make Madrid's infinite plazas and serpentine streets more navigable, coverage of the city is broken down into six major neighborhoods: **El Centro, Huertas, Gran Vía, Malasaña and Chueca, Argüelles and Moncloa,** and **Bilbao,** all within walking distance or a short metro ride of one another.

Most of Madrid's prominent sights, including the **Ópera** and **Plaza Mayor,** surround Sol in El Centro. Just west of Sol off C. Mayor, Pl. Mayor is the hub of activity for tourists and *madrileños* alike; the plaza houses both contemporary cafes and the churches and historical buildings of **Habsburg Madrid,** also known as **Madrid de los Austrias.** Farther west of Sol, by way of C. del Arenal, lies the reigning monument of **Bourbon Madrid,** the Palacio Real. This section of Madrid, also known as Ópera, contains fantastic gardens and churches.

To the southeast of Sol lies **Huertas,** once the literary district and now the place to find the city's three great museums (see **Museums,** p. 122) and the lush **Parque del Buen Retiro** (p. 137). Bordered by C. Alcalá to the north, Po. del Prado to the east, and C. Atocha to the south, the neighborhood is the home of traditional cafes, lively theaters, and intoxicating nightlife. Centered around **Plaza de Santa Ana,** Huertas is crowded with some of the best budget accommodations in the city, as well as some of the best traditional tapas bars.

Also south of Sol and west of Huertas is the area around the metro stop **La Latina,** which has less prestige and fewer tourists than the rest of Old Madrid. Small markets line winding streets, perfect for an evening of gourmet treats. **El Rastro,** a gargantuan ancient flea market, is staged here every Sunday morning. Farther south is **Lavapiés,** a working-class neighborhood undergoing gentrification.

North of Sol, busy **Gran Vía** is the commercial center of Madrid, littered with fast-food joints and a handful of skyscrapers. Linked to C. Fuencarral, it acts as the southern border of **Malasaña** and **Chueca,** both full of trendy restaurants and shops. Beyond Gran Vía and east of Malasaña and Chueca lies modern Madrid. Running the length of Madrid from **Atocha** in the south to **Plaza de Castilla** in the north, **Paseo del Prado, Paseo de Recoletos,** and **Paseo de la Castellana** pass the Prado, the fountains at **Plaza de Cibeles** and **Plaza de Colón,** and the elaborate skyscrapers beyond Pl. de Colón, including the leaning towers of the **Puerta de Europa.**

The area northwest of Sol holds the **Plaza de España** and the soaring **Torre de Madrid,** the pride of 1950s Spain. Still farther northwest of Sol are the energetic neighborhoods of **Bilbao** and **Argüelles,** which spill over into **Moncloa,** all student districts filled with cheap eateries and neon nightclubs.

Madrid is much safer than most major European cities, but Puerta del Sol, Pl. de España, Pl. Chueca, and Malasaña's Pl. 2 de Mayo can be intimidating late at night. As a general rule, avoid parks and quiet residential streets after dark, and always watch out for thieves and pickpockets in crowds.

MAPS

The free *Plano de Madrid* (street map) and *Plano de Transportes* (public transportation map) are fantastic. Pick them up at any tourist office. Public transportation info is also available by phone (☎012) or on the web (www.ctm-madrid.es). **El Corte Inglés** (p. 97) offers a one-page map of Madrid. For a comprehensive map with street index, pick up the *Almax* map (€4.50) at any newsstand.

▐▔ LOCAL TRANSPORTATION

METRO

Safe, speedy, and spotless, Madrid's metro puts most major subway systems to shame. Trains run frequently; green timers above most platforms show increments of five minutes or less between trains. The free *Plano del Metro* (available at any ticket booth) and the wall maps of surrounding neighborhoods are clear and helpful. Fare and schedule info is posted in every station; trains run daily 6am-2am.

Twelve lines, totaling 220.5km, connect Madrid's 190 stations, making the city incredibly easy to get around. Line 12, Puerta del Sur, now extends coverage to the Casa de Campo, Móstoles, and Getafe regions south of the city. Lines are distinguished by color and number. An individual metro ticket costs €1.15, but frequent riders opt for the ▉**bonotransporte** (ticket of 10 rides valid for both the metro and bus system; €5.40). Buy them at machines in metro stops, *estancos* (tobacco shops), or newsstands. Remember to keep your ticket until you leave the metro—riding without one can subject you to outrageous fines. For more detail, call **metro info** (☎902 44 44 03). For a comprehensive guide, visit www.metromadrid.es.

Violent crime in metro stations is almost unheard of, and women usually feel safe traveling alone. Pickpockets tend to do their best work in crowded cars, though. If you feel uncomfortable, avoid empty cars and ride in sight of the conductor. At night, avoid the stations to the north, which tend to be less frequented. Metro stations Tirso de Molina, La Latina, Lavapiés, Gran Vía, Pl. de España, Chueca, and Sol can be intimidating after midnight if alone. These areas are usually busy all through the night with bar- and club-hoppers, but many crimes are reported in the area; use caution and common sense.

BUS

While the metro makes the most sense for trips across Madrid, buses cover areas inaccessible by metro and are a great way to see the city. Like the metro, the bus system is exceptionally well organized. Most stops are clearly marked, but if you want extra guidance in finding routes and stops, try the handy *Plano de Transportes*, free at the tourist office, or *Madrid en Autobús*, free at bus kiosks.

Bus fares are the same as those for the metro, and tickets are interchangeable. Buses run from 6am to 11:30pm. From midnight until 3am, the night bus, the **Búho** (owl), travels from Pl. de Cibeles (and other marked routes) to the outskirts every 20min.; from 3-6am, they run every hour. Night buses (N1-N20), the cheapest form of transportation for late-night revelers, are listed in a section of the *Plano*. For info, call **Empresa Municipal de Transportes.** (☎914 06 88 10. Open M-F 8am-2pm.)

TAXI

Taxis stream through Madrid around the clock. If one does not appear when you need it, or if you want to summon one to your door, call **Radio Taxi** (☎914 47 51 80), **Radio-Taxi Independiente** (☎914 05 12 13), or **Teletaxi** (☎913 71 37 11). A *"libre"* sign in the window or a green light indicates availability. Base fare is €1.60, plus €0.70-0.90 per kilometer from 6am-10pm and €0.90-1 from 10pm-6am. **Teletaxi** charges a flat rate of €1 per km. Fare supplements include: airport (€4.20); bus and train stations (€2.20); luggage (€0.50 per bag). Official taxis are white with a red stripe on the door; avoid impostors.

Check that the driver starts the meter. If you have a complaint or think you've been overcharged, demand a *recibo oficial* (official receipt) and an *hoja de reclamaciones* (complaint form), which the driver is required to supply. Take down the license number, route taken, and fare charged. Drop off the forms and information at the **Oficina Municipal del Taxi,** C. Vallehermoso, 1, 2nd fl. (☎915 88 96 32; fax 88 96 35; M: Islas Filipinas) or the **Ayuntamiento** (City Hall), Pl. de la Villa, 4 (info ☎010; 915 88 10 00; M: Ópera) to request a refund. To request **taxi service for the disabled,** call ☎915 47 85 00 or 47 86 00. Rates are the same as other taxis. If you leave belongings in a taxi, visit or call the **Negociado de Objetos Perdidos,** Pl. Legazpi, 7. (☎915 88 43 46. M: Legazpi. Open M-F 9am-2pm.)

CAR RENTAL

There is no reason to rent a car in Madrid. If congested traffic and nightmarish parking don't drive you into hysterics, aggressive drivers, annoying mopeds, and sky-high gasoline prices will. If you do choose to drive, parking permits are available on the street from column-like machines with "P" signs. If you plan to drive to destinations outside of Madrid, a larger car rental chain is the best bet.

Atesa: Reservations: in Spain ☎902 10 01 01, elsewhere 10 05 15; www.atesa.com. Offices: Gran Vía, 80 (☎915 42 50 15; fax 41 80 89; M: Pl. de España); airport (☎913 93 72 32; fax 93 72 34).

Avis: Reservations: ☎902 13 55 31; www.avis.com. Offices: Estación de Atocha (☎915 30 01 68); Gran Vía, 60 (☎915 48 42 04; M: Gran Vía); airport (☎913 93 72 22).

Budget: Reservations: ☎913 93 72 16; www.budget.com. Booth at airport.

Europcar: Reservations: ☎902 10 50 30; www.europcar.com. Offices: Estación de Atocha (☎915 30 01 94); airport (☎913 93 72 35).

MADRID

Hertz: Reservations: ☎902 40 24 05; www.hertz.com. Offices: Estación de Atocha (☎915 06 04 97); Estación de Chamartín (☎917 33 04 00); Gran Vía, 88, #12 (☎915 42 58 05; M: Gran Vía); airport (☎913 93 72 28).

MOPED AND BIKE RENTAL

Fortunately for pedestrians, Madrid is not scarred by the moped mayhem that has taken over Europe. Though mopeds are swift, Madrid's stellar public transport system is more than sufficient for getting around. If you choose to ride, you'll need a lock and helmet. **Motocicletas Antonio Castro,** C. Conde Duque, 13, rents mopeds from €26 per day or €120 per week, including unlimited mileage and insurance. (☎915 42 06 57. M: San Bernardo. 21+ with **International Driver's Permit** only. €120 deposit required for 1-day rentals, €390 for 1-week rentals. Open M-F 8am-1:30pm and 5-8pm.) For **bike rental,** try **Karacol Sport,** C. Tortosa, 8. (☎915 39 96 33; www.karacol.com. M: Atocha. Rental €15 per day; €40 deposit and passport required. Open Su-W and F 10:30am-8pm, Th 10:30am-10pm, Sa 10:30am-2pm.)

◪ PRACTICAL INFORMATION

TOURIST AND FINANCIAL SERVICES

Tourist Offices: English is spoken at most tourist offices. Those planning trips outside the Comunidad de Madrid can visit region-specific offices within Madrid; ask at any tourist office for their addresses. **Regional Office of the Comunidad de Madrid,** C. Duque de Medinaceli, 2 (☎914 29 49 51, info 902 10 00 07; www.comadrid.es/turismo). M: Banco de España. Brochures, transportation info, and maps for the Comunidad. Extremely helpful; make this your first stop. Open M-Sa 9am-7pm, Su 9am-3pm. **Municipal Office,** Pl. Mayor, 3 (☎913 66 54 77). M: Sol. Hands out indispensable city and transportation maps and a complete guide to accommodations, as well as *In Madrid* and *Enjoy Madrid,* monthly activity and information guides in English. In 2005, it will expand and move across the plaza. Open M-Sa 10am-8pm, Su 10am-3pm. **Branch** at Mercado Pta. de Toledo, Ronda de Toledo, 1, stand #3134 (☎913 64 18 75). M: Pta. de Toledo. In a gallery with large banners on a plaza across from the metro station. Open M-Sa 9am-7pm, Su 9am-3pm. **Branches** at Estación Chamartín (p. 92) and the airport (p. 85). **El Corte Inglés** (p. 97) offers **free maps** and information.

▨ **General Info Line:** ☎901 30 06 00 or 010. Run by the Ayuntamiento. They'll tell you anything about Madrid, from police locations to zoo hours. Ask for *inglés* for an English-speaking operator.

Websites: www.munimadrid.es; www.tourspain.es; www.cronicamadrid.com; www.guiadelocio.com; www.madridman.com; www.red2000.com/spain/madrid. For the history of practically any building or monument, check www.madridhistorico.com.

Tours: Tours can be informative but pricey. Read the fine print before signing on. The **Ayuntamiento** (☎915 88 16 36, advance tickets 902 22 16 22) offers various **walking tours** in English and Spanish, some of which include historical reenactments; call or pick up more info at the municipal tourist office. €3.20, reenactment tour €7; students, children, and seniors €2.60/€6. **Madrid Vision** (☎917 79 18 88) offers tours on double-decker buses. A great option for those with limited time. There are 3 routes (*Madrid Histórico, Moderno,* and *Monumental*) each of which makes 15-20 key stops around the city. Get off and on the bus as you please. Adults €10.60, ages 7-16 and seniors €5.30; 2-day ticket €13.60/€6.80. **Juliá Tours,** Gran Vía, 65 (☎915 59 96 05; www.juliatours.com). M: Pl. de España. Tours of Andalucía and Portugal. Open daily 9am-8:30pm.

Budget Travel:

Viajes TIVE, C. Fernando el Católico, 88 (☎915 43 74 12; fax 44 00 62). M: Moncloa. Walk straight down C. Arcipreste de Hita and turn left on C. Fernando el Católico. A great resource for long-term visitors. ISIC €6; HI card €5, over 30 €11, non-Spaniards €18.10. Organizes group excursions and language classes. Lodging and student residence info. Some English spoken. Open M-F 9am-2pm. Arrive early to avoid lines.

Comunidad de Madrid, Dirección General de Juventud, Gran Vía, 10 (☎901 51 06 10; www.madrid.org/inforjoven). M: Banco de España. Open Sept.-July M-F 9am-2pm and 5-8pm.

ASATEJ Group, C. San Jerónimo, 18, 1st fl. (☎915 22 96 93; www.asatej.com). M: Sol or Sevilla. Sells student airfares, tours, car rental, bus passes, and ISICs. Open M-F 10:30am-7:30pm, Sa 10:30am-1:30pm.

Viajes Barceló, C. Princesa, 3 (☎915 59 18 19; www.barceloviajes.com). M: Pl. de España. Student travel. Open daily 10am-7pm.

Currency Exchange: Banco Santander Central Hispano does not charge commission on AmEx traveler's cheques, but will charge a minimum of €9 commission on all others. Maximum exchange €300. **Main branch,** Pl. Canalejas, 1 (☎915 58 11 11). M: Sol. Follow C. San Jerónimo to Pl. Canalejas. Open Apr.-Sept. M-F 8:30am-2pm; Oct.-Mar. M-F 8:30am-2pm, Sa 8:30am-1pm. **Banks** usually charge 1-2% commission (minimum charge €3). Booths in Sol and Gran Vía, open as late as midnight and on weekends, have poor rates and are not a good deal. **ServiRed, ServiCaixa,** and **Telebanco** machines accept bank cards with the Cirrus, PLUS, EuroCard, or NYCE logos.

American Express: Pl. de las Cortes, 2 (traveler services ☎917 43 77 40, currency exchange 43 77 55). Entrance on C. Marqués de Cubas. M: Banco de España. **Exchanges currency** (€3 on cash exchange; 3% commission for non-AmEx travelers checks), will hold mail for 30 days, and can help send and receive wired money. Traveler services open M-F 9am-7:30pm, Sa 10am-2pm; currency exchange open M-F 9am-7:30pm, Sa 9am-2pm. 24hr. Express Cash machine outside. **Branch** at airport (☎913 93 82 22 or 93 82 15). To report lost travelers checks, call toll free ☎900 81 00 29.

Lost or stolen credit cards: American Express (☎917 43 70 00); Visa (☎915 19 21 00); MasterCard (☎915 19 21 00).

LOCAL SERVICES

Luggage Storage: Available at the airport and bus and train stations.

El Corte Inglés: C. Preciados, 3 (☎913 79 80 00). M: Sol. C. Goya, 76 (☎914 32 93 00). M: Goya. C. Princesa, 56 (☎914 54 60 00). M: Argüelles. *La mama grande* of department stores, its official motto is: "A place to shop. A place to dream." No matter what you need, from groceries to train tickets, you can find it here. Currency exchange with no commission but mediocre rates. Open M-Sa 10am-10pm, first Su of the month 11am-9pm. AmEx/MC/V.

English-Language Periodicals: International edition dailies and weeklies available at kiosks everywhere, especially on Gran Vía, Paseos del Prado, Recoletos, Castellana, and around Pta. del Sol. If you're dying for the *New York Times,* try one of the **VIPS** restaurants (see **Red-Eye Establishments,** p. 103).

Language Service: Forocio, C. San Jerónimo, 18, 1st fl. (☎902 36 36 33; www.forocio.com). M: Sol. An organization dedicated to bringing foreigners and natives together to share languages and good times. Sponsors weekly parties. Open M-F 10am-8pm.

Libraries: The municipal tourist office has a comprehensive list of *bibliotecas* around the city. These include **Bibliotecas Municipales Especializadas,** numerous branches of the **Bibliotecas Públicas Municipales por Distritos** (22 locations), and **Bibliotecas Populares** (18 locations). Large branch (☎913 66 54 07) at M: Pta. de Toledo, with English-language periodicals. Open M-F 8:30am-9pm, Sa 9am-2pm.

MADRID

Religious Services: Our Lady of Mercy, C. Alfonso XIII, 165 (☎917 73 98 29; www.our-ladyofmercy.info), at Pl. Habana. M: Colombia. Sunday mass in English 11am, followed by coffee and doughnuts. **Immanuel Baptist Church,** C. Hernández de Tejada, 4 (☎914 07 43 47). M: Canillas. English services Su 11am. **Community Church of Madrid,** C. Viña, 3 (☎655 93 18 57), Suffolk University Building. M: Metropolitano. Interdenominational Protestant services in English Su 11am. **British Embassy Church of St. George,** C. Núñez de Balboa, 43 (☎915 76 51 09). M: Velázquez. Services Su 8:30, 10, and 11:15am. **Sinagoga Beth Yaacov,** C. Balmes, 3 (☎915 91 31 31). M: Iglesia. Services F 8:30pm and Sa 9:15am. Kosher restaurant (☎914 457 380) can be reserved. ID required; Spanish only. **Centro Islámico,** C. Alonso Cano, 3 (☎914 48 05 54). M: Iglesia. Services and language classes. Open M-F 10:45am-2pm.

Women's Services: For general information on women's services in Spain or to report an incident, call **Instituto de la Mujer** (☎900 19 10 10). For literature concerning women's issues, try the **Librería de Mujeres,** C. San Cristóbal, 17 (☎915 21 70 43; www.unapa-labraotra.org/libreriamujeres.html), near Pl. Mayor. M: Sol. From Sol, C. San Cristóbal is the 2nd left off C. Mayor. The shop's motto is *"Los libros no muerden, el feminismo tampoco."* (Books don't bite; neither does feminism.) Books and gifts, but more useful for Spanish speakers. Resource for finding local support and discussion groups. Open M-F 10am-2pm and 5-8pm; Oct.-May also Sa 10am-2pm.

Gay and Lesbian Services: Most establishments in Chueca carry a free guide to gay nightlife in Spain called **Shanguide.** If you can't find one right away, ask someone in a store near Pl. Chueca where to find one. This guide book offers detailed listings and maps of the many gay bars, clubs, cafes, restaurants, bookstores, shops, and associations in and around Madrid. Alternatively, you can purchase **Zero** (€4) at any kiosk. The magazine includes a small pull-out guide to nightlife and gay activities. These listings are often more up-to-date than the **Spartacus International Gay Guide,** sold at almost any newsstand or bookstore. Support groups and associations: **Colectivo de Gais y Lesbianas de Madrid (COGAM),** C. Fuencarral, 37 (☎915 22 45 17; www.cogam.org). M: Gran Vía. Relocating within the same neighborhood in 2005. Provides a wide range of services and activities of interest to gays, lesbians, and bisexuals. English usually spoken. Free screenings of gay-interest movies, COGAM youth group (25 and under, meets Sa at 7:30pm for dinner and nighttime activities), HIV-positive support group (M 8-10:30pm, first-timers welcomed M-F 7-8pm), and sport get-togethers. Reception daily M-Sa 5-10pm. Free counseling M-Th 7-9pm, AIDS-specific counseling M-F 10am-2pm, phone hotline 5-9pm (☎915 23 00 70). Library open daily; call ahead for hours at new location. **Berkana Librería Gay y Lesbiana,** C. Hortaleza, 64 (☎915 22 55 99; www.libreriaberkana.com), has guidebooks and listings of gay establishments. (see **Books,** p. 109). Most entertainment guides list gay and lesbian clubs. **GAY-INFORM,** a gay info line (☎915 23 00 70), provides information in Spanish (and sometimes French and English) about gay associations, leisure activities, health issues, sports, workshops in French and English, dinners, and **Brujulai,** COGAM's weekend excursion group. Open daily 5-9pm.

Laundromat: Lavandería Ondablu, C. León, 3 (☎913 69 50 71). M: Antón Martín, Sol, or Sevilla. Wash €3.50, dry €3.50. Open daily 9am-10:30pm. Also at C. Hortaleza, 84 (☎915 31 28 73), next to Pizzaiolo. M: Chueca. Same hours and prices. Just up the street is **Lavandería Cervantes,** C. León, 6. Wash €2, dry €1. Open daily 9am-9pm.

EMERGENCY AND COMMUNICATIONS

Police: C. Madrazos, 9 (☎915 41 71 60). M: Sevilla. English forms available. To report crimes in the **metro,** go to the office in the Sol station. Open daily 8am-11pm. **Guardia Civil** (☎062 or 915 34 02 00). **Protección Civil** (☎915 37 31 00).

Crisis Lines: Poison Control (24hr. ☎915 62 04 20). **Rape Hotline** (☎915 74 01 10). Open M-F 10am-2pm and 4-7pm (at other times, machine-recorded instructions).

Help Lines: Alcoholics Anonymous, C. Juan Bravo, 40, 2nd fl. (English ☎913 09 19 47, Spanish 913 41 82 82). M: Núñez de Balboa.

Late-Night Pharmacy: Dial ☎098 for locations. One at C. Mayor, 13 (☎913 66 46 16), off Pta. del Sol; another at C. Mayor, 59 (☎915 48 00 14), closer to M: Ópera.

First Aid Stations: Scattered about the city, all open 24hr. Ask for *primeros auxilios.* One at C. de Navas de Tolosa (☎915 21 00 25). M: Callao.

Hospitals: Prompt appointments are hard to obtain, but public hospitals don't require advance payment. Emergency rooms are the best option for immediate attention. US insurance is not accepted, but get a receipt, and your insurance may pick up the tab when you get home. General emergency exam runs €150, but may be as low as €80. For non-emergency concerns, **Anglo-American Medical Unit,** C. del Conde de Aranda, 1, 1st fl. (☎914 35 18 23), is quick and friendly. M: Serrano or Retiro. Doctors, dentists, and optometrists. Regular personnel on duty 9am-8pm. Not an emergency clinic. Initial visit €70 for students, €100 for non-students. AmEx/MC/V. Embassies and consulates keep lists of English-speaking doctors in private practice. **Hospital Clínico San Carlos** (☎913 30 30 00), on Pl. Cristo Rey. M: Islas Filipinas or Moncloa. **Equipo Quirúrgico Municipal No. 1,** C. Montesa, 22 (☎915 88 51 00). M: Manuel Becerra.

Emergency Clinics: In a **medical emergency,** dial ☎061 or 112. **Hospital de Madrid,** Pl. del Conde del Valle Suchil, 16 (☎914 47 66 00; www.hospitaldemadrid.com). **Hospital Ramón y Cajal,** Ctra. Colmenar Viejo, km 9100 (☎913 36 80 00). Bus #135 from Pl. de Castilla. **Red Cross** (☎915 22 22 22, info 902 22 22 92). **Centro de Salud Santobal,** C. Santobal, 7 (☎914 45 23 28). M: Bilbao. Free, confidential government clinic specializing in treating HIV/AIDS and other STDs. Open M-F 9am-2pm.

Telephones: Information ☎1003. No English spoken. (For further information, see **Keeping in Touch,** p. 34.)

Internet Access: Hundreds of Internet cafes are spread across the city. The rates are generally consistent (roughly €0.80-1.50 per 30min., €1.30-2.50 per hr.). The cheapest spots are in Lavapiés, where mom-and-pop places charge less than €0.02 per min.

▨ **Interpublic,** Ctra. de San Jerónimo, 16. Shares a floor with Asatej travel agency. Fast connections, good music, printing, fax, disks, CDs, and a *locutorio.* €1.60 per hr., and you are not obligated to use all of your time at once. (☎/fax 915 32 09 70. Open daily 10am-midnight.)

Easy Everything, C. Montera, 10 (www.easyeverything.com). M: Sol. Lots of computers, fast connections, and cheap rates. Great for quick email checks, as you don't have to use all your time at once. Rates fluctuate based on the number of computers in use. Open daily 8am-1am.

Oficina13, C. Mayor, 1, 4th fl., office 13 (☎915 23 20 89). M: Sol. Take the elevator up and buzz the office. Friendly service and good music. Free coffee. €1 per hr. Open daily 10am-10pm.

Post Office: Palacio de Comunicaciones, C. Alcalá, 51, on Pl. de Cibeles (☎902 19 71 97). M: Banco de España. Enormous, ornate palace on the far side of the plaza from the metro. Info (main vestibule) open M-Sa 8:30am-9:30pm. Windows open M-Sa 8:30am-9:30pm, Su 9am-2pm for stamp purchases. Receive **Lista de Correos** (Poste Restante) at windows 80-82; passport required. For **certified mail, fax,** and the information booth, enter main door. Send packages at windows marked *"Admisión Polivalente"* behind the main info counter or through door N (enter from C. Montalbán); cash only. Postal Express is also located at door N. **Postal Code:** 28080.

▟ ACCOMMODATIONS

The demand for rooms in Madrid is always high and increases dramatically in summer. Though the city is filled with hostels, good quality at good prices can be hard to find. Prices range from €15 to €50 per person, depending on location, amenities, and season. Don't be deceived; higher prices do not necessarily translate into nicer accommodations. Try negotiating the price if you plan on staying a while. Those staying in Madrid for long periods may want to check out **The Broadsheet** (€3), a no-frills listing of English-language classifieds, or the weekly **Segundamano**, with listings of apartments and roommate seekers, on sale at kiosks.

Because there are so many reasonably priced hostels *(hostales)* in Madrid, the listings here focus almost exclusively on them. Be aware that there are other accommodations options in Madrid, including hotels and *pensiones*. In Madrid, the difference between a one-star *hostal* and a *pensión* is often minimal. A room in a one- or two-star *hostal* has at least the basics: bed, closet space, desk with chair, sink and towel, window, light fixture, fake flowers, a lock on the door, and the occasional religious icon. Winter heating is standard; air-conditioning is not. Unless otherwise noted, communal bathrooms (toilet and shower) are the norm. Most places accept reservations, but few require them. Still, reservations are recommended in summer and on weekends, especially in the Pta. del Sol area and at the first few places *Let's Go* lists in each neighborhood. Owners are usually accustomed to opening the doors, albeit groggily, at all hours, or providing keys for guests, but ask before club-hopping into the wee hours; late-night lockouts and confrontations with irate owners are never fun. *Pensiones* are like boarding houses: they are inexpensive, sometimes have curfews, and often host guests staying for longer periods of time. Good deals can usually be found outside central locations, and stellar public transportation makes virtually any place central.

Budget lodgings are rarer near the **Chamartín** train station and in most of the residential districts located away from the city center. There are a handful of hostels near the **Atocha** train station, the closest of which are down Po. de Santa María de la Cabeza. Be aware that this neighborhood is not as safe as those that are more central. The tourist office in Pl. Mayor has a full list of lodgings.

CAMPING

Tourist offices provide info about the 13 campsites within 50km of Madrid. Similar info can be found in the *Guía Oficial de Campings* (official camping guide), available at most bookstores and on reserve at tourist offices. The *Mapa de Campings* shows the location of every official campsite in Spain. Also ask for the brochure *Hoteles, Campings, Apartamentos*, which lists hotels, campsites, and apartments in and around Madrid. For further camping info, contact the *Consejería de Educación* (☎901 51 06 10).

> **Camping Alpha** (☎916 95 80 69), on a tree-lined site 12.4km down Ctra. de Andalucía in Getafe. M: Legazpi. From the metro station take bus #447, which stops next to the Nissan dealership (10min., every 20min. 6am-10pm, €1.20). Ask to get off at the pedestrian overpass. Cross the bridge and walk 1.5km back toward Madrid along the busy highway; signs lead the way. Pool, showers, and laundry. €5 per person, €5.80 per tent, €5.40 per car. ❶

> **Camping Osuna** (☎917 41 05 10), on Av. Logroño. M: Canillejas. From the metro, cross the pedestrian overpass, walk through the parking lot, and turn right along the freeway. Pass under a freeway and an arch and look for campground signs. Or grab the #101

bus from the metro toward Barajas and ask for the campsite. Closer than Alpha, but not as nice. Showers, laundromat, supermarket, and restaurant-bar. Reception daily 8am-10pm. €6 per person, per tent, and per car. Electricity €4.50. ●

ACCOMMODATIONS BY PRICE

A Argüelles and Moncloa **E** Elsewhere **EC** El Centro: Sol, Ópera, and Plaza Mayor **GV** Gran Vía **H** Huertas **M** Malasaña and Chueca

UNDER €15 (●)	
Albergue Juvenil Santa Cruz (133)	A
Barbieri International Youth Hostel (130)	M
Camping Alpha (100)	E
Camping Osuna (100)	E
Cat's Hostel (120)	H
Hostal Betanzos (120)	H
Hostal Pérez (134)	A
▣ Hostal-Residencia Luz (111)	EC
Hostal-Residencia Ríos (134)	A

€15-25 (●)	
Hostal Abril (130)	M
Hostal Alicante (112)	EC
Hostal Esparteros (111)	EC
Hostal Los Arcos (111)	EC
▣ Hostal Medieval (129)	M
Hostal Palacios/Hostal Ribadavia (129)	M
▣ Hostal Paz (111)	EC
Hostal Portugal (112)	EC
▣ Hostal Villar (119)	H
Hostal-Residencia Carreras (120)	H
▣ Hostal-Residencia Domínguez (129)	M
Hostal-Residencia Lido (120)	H
Hostal-Residencia Sud-Americana (120)	H
Huéspede Yolanda (120)	H
Los Amigos Backpackers' Hostel (112)	EC

€26-35 (●)	
Hostal A. Nebrija (127)	GV
Hostal Aguilar (120)	H
Hostal Cantábrico (111)	EC
Hostal Chelo (130)	M
Hostal Internacional (120)	H
Hostal Lauria (127)	GV
Hostal Margarita (127)	GV
Hostal Oriente (111)	EC
Hostal R. Rodríguez (120)	H
Hostal Santillan (127)	GV
Hostal Triana (128)	GV
Hostal-Residencia Rober (111)	EC

€36-45 (●)	
Hispa Domus (129)	M
Hostal Armesto (120)	H
▣ Hostal Gonzalo (119)	H
Hotel Mónaco (130)	M
Hotel San Lorenzo (130)	M
Hostal Valencia (111)	EC
Hostal-Residencia Alibel (127)	GV
Hostal-Residencia Cruz-Sol (112)	EC
Hostal-Residencia Lamalonga (128)	GV

OVER €45 (●)	
Hostal Madrid (111)	EC

◖ FOOD

In Madrid, it's easy to eat without emptying your wallet. You can't walk a block without tripping over at least five *cafeterías*, where a sandwich, coffee, and dessert go for €3.60. Vegetarians should check out the *Guía del Ocio* (€1), which has a complete listing of Madrid's vegetarian havens under the section *Otras Cocinas*. Also check out www.mundovegetariano.com. Even carnivores may appreciate a veggie meal, given Madrid's indulgence in fatty meats and fried food.

Expect to spend at least €7 for a full meal at a *restaurante*, one step up from the typical *cafetería*. Most restaurants offer a *menú del día*, which includes bread, one drink, and a choice from the day's selections for appetizers, main courses, and desserts. For €6.75-9, it's a fantastic way to fill up. Keep the following buzz words in mind for quicker, cheaper *madrileño* fare: *bocadillo* (a sandwich on a long, hard roll; €2-2.75); *sandwich* (on sliced bread, ask for it *a la plancha* if you want it grilled; €2.25); *croissant* (with ham and cheese; €1.50); *ración* (a large tapa served with bread; €1.85-12); and *empanada* (a puff pastry with meat filling; €1.25-1.85). See the **Glossary,** p. 813, for additional translations.

FOOD BY TYPE

> **A** Argüelles and Moncloa **B** Bilbao **E** Elsewhere **EC** El Centro: Ópera, Sol, and Plaza Mayor **GV** Gran Vía **H** Huertas **L** Lavapiés and La Latina **M** Malasaña and Chueca

CAFES	
Café Comercial (104)	B ❶
Café Gijón (105)	E ❶
☒ Café de Oriente (104)	EC ❶
Café del Real (105)	EC ❶
☒ Café-Botillería Manuela (104)	M ❶
Eucalipto (104)	L ❶
La Botillería del Café de Oriente (105)	EC ❶

ITALIAN	
☒ Osteria Il Regno di Napoli (136)	B ❷
Pizzaiolo (131)	M ❷
Pizzeria Cervantes (121)	H ❷
Pizzeria Mastropiero (131)	M ❷
Pizzeria Vesuvio (131)	M ❶

LATIN AMERICAN	
El Cuchi (113)	EC ❸
El Novillo Carioca (128)	GV ❸
El Rey del Barrio (131)	M ❸
La Farfalla (121)	H ❷
La Vaca Argentina (134)	A ❹

MIDDLE EASTERN	
☒ Al-Jaima, Cocina del Desierto (130)	M ❷
Bar Samara (136)	B ❸
Bósforos (113)	EC ❶
☒ Inshala (112)	EC ❸
La Granja de Said (131)	M ❷

SPANISH	
Ananias (134)	A ❸
☒ Arrocería Gala (120)	H ❸
El Carabinero (136)	B ❹
El Oso y el Madroño (113)	EC ❷
Gula Gula (121)	H ❹
☒ La Finca de Susana (128)	GV ❷

La Sacristía (131)	M ❹
☒ La Sanabresa (120)	H ❷
Lhardy Restaurante (113)	EC ❺
Museo del Jamón (113)	EC ❶
Museo Chicote (128)	GV ❷
Sobrino del Botín (113)	EC ❹
☒ Taberna Macieras (120)	H ❸

SWEETS	
Horno La Santiagüesa (103)	EC ❶
Horno San Onofre (103)	M ❶
La Crêperie (134)	A ❶
La Mallorquina (103)	EC ❶
☒ Ricci Gelateria & Yogurteria (121)	H ❶

TAPAS	
Almendro 13 (104)	L ❷
☒ Casa Alberto (103)	H ❷
Casa Amadeo (104)	L ❷
Cáscaras (134)	A ❷
El Encinar del Bierzo (104)	L ❷
La Toscana (104)	EC ❷
La Trucha (104)	EC ❸
☒ Los Gabrieles (104)	H ❶
Stop Madrid (131)	M ❸
Taberna del Alabarder (104)	EC ❸

VEGETARIAN	
Achuri (112)	L ❶
Al Natural (121)	H ❸
Chez Pomme (131)	M ❷
Collage (136)	B ❸
☒ El Estragón Vegetariano (112)	L ❸
El Granero de Lavapiés (112)	L ❷
Restaurante Integral Artemisa (121)	H ❷
Vegaviana (131)	M ❷

FOOD SHOPPING

In general, groceries get cheaper the farther you get from the center. Specialty items may require a visit to a pricey store in the center, but for daily fare, slipping into any corner store will reward you with an inexpensive selection of standards at drastically lower prices than would be found in a major chain.

Groceries: Champion and **%Dia** are the cheapest city-wide supermarket chains, though their locations tend to be a bit far from the city center. There is, however, a **Champion** in Pl. Lavapiés, next to the metro. To satisfy grocery needs near El Centro, try the numerous *alimentaciones* (food marts) on side streets that sell soft drinks, candy, ice cream, and some basics. The *supermercado* in the basement of **El Corte Inglés** near Pta. del Sol (p. 97) is somewhat pricier but über-convenient. Other more upscale options are **Mantequerías Leonesas, Expreso,** and **Jumbo.**

Markets: Mercado de San Miguel, a covered market on Pl. de San Miguel, off the northwest corner of Pl. Mayor, sells the finest seafood and produce in the city at high prices. A wide selection of tourists can be found on display between the *bacalao* and the tuna.

Open M-F 9am-2:30pm and 5:15-8:15pm, Sa 9am-3pm. **Mercado de la Cebada,** at the corner of C. Toledo and C. San Francisco, is larger, less expensive, and caters to many more locals. M: La Latina. Open M-F 9am-2pm and 5:30-8pm, Sa 9am-2pm.

Pastry Shops: These are everywhere. **La Mallorquina,** C. Mayor, 2 (☎915 21 12 01) is the most famous in all Madrid, and for good reason. Open Sept.-July daily 9am-9:15pm. The sublime **Horno La Santiagüesa,** C. Mayor, 73 (☎915 59 62 14) sells everything from *roscones de reyes* (sweet bread for the Feast of the Epiphany) to *empanadas* and pastries doused in rich chocolate. Don't pass through without trying the *tarta de santiago* (almond bread). Open M-Sa 8am-9pm, Su 8am-8pm. **Horno San Onofre,** C. San Onofre, 4 (☎915 32 90 60), off C. Fuencarral, serves sumptuous fruit tarts and *suspiros de modistilla* (seamstress's sighs), a *madrileño* specialty. Open M-Sa 9am-9pm, Su 9am-8pm.

Red-Eye Establishments: *Guía del Ocio* lists late-night eateries under *Cenar a última hora*. **VIPS,** Gran Vía, 43 (☎915 42 15 78; M: Callao); C. Serrano, 41 (M: Serrano); C. Princesa, 5 (M: Ventura Rodríguez); C. Fuencarral, 101 (M: Tribunal); and other locations is a standard late-night option. An American-style diner with cushioned booths, average service, and overpriced burgers, VIPS also carries English books and magazines, records, and canned food. Open daily 9am-3am. **Hot & Cool,** C. Gaztambide in Argüelles, serves fresh *bocadillos* until 3am on weekends. Street vendors sell Chinese food to hungry clubbers until late. *Cervecerías* open until 2am aren't hard to find.

TAPAS

Not so long ago, bartenders in Andalucía used to cover *(tapar)* drinks with saucers to keep out flies. Later, servers began putting little sandwiches on the saucers, and there you have it: tapas. Hopping from bar to bar gobbling tapas is an active alternative to a full sit-down meal and a fun way to sample food you might never otherwise dream of trying. Most tapas bars *(tascas* or *tabernas)* are open noon-4pm and 8pm-midnight or later. Some, like **Museo del Jamón** (p. 113), double as restaurants, and many cluster around **Plaza Santa Ana** and **Plaza Mayor** (beware the tourist traps!). Authentic bars pack **Calle Cuchilleros** and **Calle de la Cruz.**

🖺 **Casa Alberto,** C. Huertas, 18 (☎914 29 93 56; www.casaalberto.es). M: Antón Martín. A classic tapas bar founded in 1827. Dining room decorated with bullfighting and Cervantes memorabilia. Sweet vermouth (€1.30) is served with original house tapas. Try the delicious *gambas al ajillo* (shrimp with garlic; €9.10) or the *canapés* (€2.25-€3). Sit-down dinner is pricey. Open Tu-Sa noon-5:30pm and 8pm-1:30am. AmEx/MC/V. ❷

TAPAS FROM A TO Z

Tapas—the tasty little dishes that are Spain's answer to *hors d'oeuvres,* with more taste and less pretension. To experience the *madrileño* lifestyle, you have to give them a try. The only problem is: What are you going to order?

To the untrained reader, tapas menus are often undecipherable—if the bar has even bothered to print any. To make sure you don't end up eating the stewed parts of the ox you rode in on, keep the following words in mind before you *tapear.* Servings come in three sizes: *pincho* (normally eaten with toothpicks between sips of beer), *tapa* (small plate), or *ración* (meal portion). *Aceitunas* (olives), *albóndigas* (meatballs), *anchoas* (anchovies), *callos* (tripe), *chorizo* (sausage), *croquetas* (croquettes), *gambas* (shrimp), *jamón* (ham), *patatas bravas* (fried potatoes with spicy sauce), *pimientos* (peppers), *pulpo* (octopus), and *tortilla española* (onion and potato omelette) comprise any basic menu. Many are served with a thick mayonnaise; ask for them *"sin mayonesa"* if you're not a fan. More adventurous tasters should try *morcilla* (blood sausage), or *sesos* (cow's brains).

Often, bartenders will offer tastes of tapas with your drink and strike up a conversation. If you're not given some with your drink, be sure to ask for them. To ensure the full treatment and local respect, the house *cerveza* is always a good choice.

■ **Los Gabrieles,** C. Echegaray, 17 (☎914 29 62 61). M: Sol. The tiled mural at the back depicts artists—from Velázquez to Goya—as drunks. Serves tapas in afternoon and drinks at night. Flamenco Tu. Open Su-W 1pm-2:30am, Th-Sa 1pm-3:30am. ❶

Casa Amadeo, Pl. de Cascorro, 18 (☎913 65 94 39). M: La Latina. The jovial owner of 62 years supervises the making of house specialty *caracoles* (snails; tapas €4.50, *ración* €11) and *chorizo* with snails (€4.80). Eat them on checked tablecloths or at the bar. Other *raciones* €4-6. Open Tu-Su 10:30am-4pm and 7-10:30pm. ❷

La Trucha, C. Manuel Fernández González, 3 (☎914 29 58 33). M: Sol. Also at C. Núñez de Arce, 6 (☎915 32 08 90), without terrace. Impressive selection of seasonal veggies (€5-9) and daily specials. Grab the *rabo de toro* (bull's tail; €9.30). Entrees €12-15. Open M-Sa 12:30-4pm and 7:30pm-midnight. AmEx/MC/V. ❸

Almendro 13, C. Almendro, 13 (☎913 65 42 52). M: La Latina. Locals dive into huge plates of *huevos rotos* (eggs and ham over fried potatoes; €7.80) and the lighter tomato salad (€5). Not exactly tapas, but a great lunch or a filling accompaniment to the beer (€2). Open daily M-F 1-4pm and 8pm-1am, Sa-Su 1-3pm and 8pm-1am. ❷

La Toscana, C. Manuel Fernández González, 10-12 (☎914 29 60 31). M: Sol or Sevilla. A local crowd hangs out over tapas of *morcilla asado* (blood sausage; €9.60). Despite the antique lettering and wrought iron, the range of dishes is anything but medieval. Spacious bar jam-packed on weekends. Open Tu-Sa 1-4pm and 8pm-midnight. ❷

Taberna del Alabarder, C. Felipe V, 6 (☎915 47 25 77), just off Pl. del Oriente. M: Ópera. Overlooking the glorious Palacio Real, try the nationally famous *patatas al pobre* (potatoes with garlic; €4.10) or *tigres unidad* (fried mussels; €1.30). Tapas €1.30-7.70, *raciones* €4.10-21. Open M-Sa 1-4pm and 8:45pm-midnight. AmEx/MC/V. ❸

El Encinar del Bierzo, C. Toledo, 82 (☎913 66 23 89). M: La Latina. Neighborhood landmark loaded with locals. Try the specialty *gambas a la plancha* (grilled shrimp; €13). *Menú* M-Sa €8, Su €10. Open daily 1-4:30pm and 9-11:30pm. MC/V. ❷

CAFES

Madrid's cafes offer ambience as well as caffeine, allowing contemplative coffee drinkers to lose themselves in atmosphere and history. Marvel at the scenery, reflect, and linger for an hour or two in these historic cafes—an economical way to soak up a little of Madrid's culture and finally write those postcards you bought a few days ago. You won't be bothered with the check until you ask.

■ **Café-Botillería Manuela,** C. San Vicente Ferrer, 29 (☎915 31 70 37). M: Tribunal. Upbeat music and occasional impromptu piano playing add to Manuela's inviting atmosphere. Contemporary artwork contrasts with *fin de siecle* decor. Specialty cocktails (€3-5), coffees (€3.50-4.50), fruit shakes *(batidos),* and juices, as well as a traditional tapas menu (€2-8). Story-telling, literature reviews, live music (Sa 9:30pm), and poetry nights are highlights. Open July-Aug. Tu-Su 6pm-2:30am; Sept.-June daily 4pm-2am. ❶

■ **Café de Oriente,** Pl. del Oriente, 2 (☎915 47 15 64). M: Ópera. An old-fashioned cafe catering to a ritzy, older crowd. Spectacular view of the Palacio Real from the terraza, especially at night when floodlights illuminate the facade. Specialty coffees (€2.50-6.50) live up to their price. Open Su-Th 8:30am-1:30am, F-Sa 8:30am-12:30am. ❶

Café Comercial, Glorieta de Bilbao, 7 (☎915 21 56 55). M: Bilbao. Founded in 1887, Madrid's oldest cafe boasts high ceilings, cushioned chairs, and huge mirrors perfect for people-watching. Frequented by artists and Republican aviators alike, Comercial saw the first anti-Franco protests take place. Coffee at the bar €1.20, at a table €1.90. Open M-Th 8am-1am, F-Sa 8am-2am, Su 10am-1am. ❶

Eucalipto, C. Argumosa, 4. M: Lavapiés. Take a break from normal coffee fare and head for refreshing *zumos tropicales* (fresh juice; €2.60-3.50). The *batidos* (shakes; €3.50) are delicious. Spike up the night with a *daiquiri* (€4.50-4.80), or enjoy a fantastic, huge fruit salad (€7). Lively sidewalk seating. Open M-Sa 5pm-2am, Su noon-2am. ❶

Café Gijón, Po. de Recoletos, 21 (☎915 21 54 25). M: Colón. Enjoy thought-provoking conversation and good coffee in this historic landmark, popular with intellectuals for its *tertulias* (get-togethers). A perfect stop during your walking tour of the *paseos*. Coffee from €2.80. Open M-Th and Su 7am-1:30am, F-Sa 7am-2am. AmEx/MC/V. ❶

Café del Real, Pl. de Isabel II, 2 (☎915 47 21 24). M: Ópera. Hang out upstairs, where tables are surrounded by theatrical pictures on burgundy and gold walls, or go down to the pizzeria for a quick bite. Coffee at the bar €1.40, at a table €2. Famous chocolate cake €3.40-4.30. Open M-Th 9am-1am, F-Sa 10am-3pm, Su 10am-midnight. ❶

La Botillería del Café de Oriente, Pl. del Oriente, 4 (☎915 48 46 20). M: Ópera. Yet another gorgeous cafe on Pl. del Oriente with views of the garden and the Palacio Real. Coffees (€2.70), teas (€2.70), wines (€2-4.50), and a variety of tapas (€2.80-3.50). Open Su-Th 12:30pm-1:30am, F-Sa 12:30pm-2am. ❶

◎ SIGHTS

Madrid, large as it may seem, is a walker's city. Its fantastic public transportation system should only be used for longer distances, or between the day's starting and ending points. Although the word *paseo* refers to a major avenue (such as Paseo de la Castellana or Paseo del Prado), it literally means "a stroll." Do just that, from Sol to Cibeles and Plaza Mayor to the Palacio Real—sights will appear everywhere. The city's art, architecture, culture, and atmosphere will convince wide-eyed visitors that it was once the capital of the world's greatest empire. While Madrid is perfect for walking, it also offers some fantastic places to relax. Whether soothing tired feet or seeking shelter from the summer's sweltering heat, there's nothing better than a shaded sidewalk cafe or a romantic park.

For hardcore visitors with a checklist of destinations, the municipal tourist office's *Plano de Transportes* map, which marks monuments as well as bus and metro lines, is indispensable. In this chapter, sights are arranged by neighborhood. Each section has a designated center from which all directions are given. If you are trying to design a walking tour of the entire city, it is best to begin in El Centro, the self-evident nucleus of Madrid. The neighborhoods fall naturally in geographical order from there; a good day of sightseeing might move from historic Madrid, to the cafes of Huertas, to the celebrated *paseos*, to a stroll through El Retiro (see **The Paseos: A Walking Tour,** p. 138). El Pardo is best visited last as a daytrip.

◪ ENTERTAINMENT

Anyone interested in the latest on live entertainment—from music to dance to theater—should stop by the **Círculo de Bellas Artes,** C. Marqués de Casa Riera, 2 (☎913 60 54 00; fax 915 23 28 12) at M: Sevilla or Banco de España. The six-floor building houses not only performance venues and art exhibits, but also an organizing center for events throughout Madrid; it has current information on virtually all performances. Their monthly magazine, **Minerva,** free at the front desk, is indispensable.

MUSIC

In summer, Madrid sponsors free concerts, ranging from classical and jazz to bolero and salsa, at Pl. Mayor, Lavapiés, Oriente, and Villa de París; check the *Guía del Ocio* for the current schedule. Many night spots also have live music.

The **Auditorio Nacional,** C. Príncipe de Vergara, 146, home to the National Orchestra, features Madrid's best classical performances. (☎913 37 01 00, box office 913 37 03 07, tickets through ServiCaixa 902 33 22 11; www.auditorionacional.mcu.es. M: Cruz del Rayo. Tickets €5-36. Box office open M 4-6pm, Tu-F 10am-5pm, Sa 11am-1pm.) **Fundación Joan March,** C. Castelló, 77, hosts summer cultural activities such as a lecture series (usually Tu and Th 7:30pm) and poetry readings, and sponsors free concerts. (☎914 35 42 40; www.march.es. M: Núñez de Balboa. Concerts M, W, and Sa; call ahead for details.) **Teatro Monumental,** C. Atocha, 65, is home to Madrid's Symphonic Orchestra. Reinforced concrete—a Spanish invention—was first used in its construction in the 1920s, so be prepared for unusual acoustics. (☎914 29 81 19, tickets 29 21 81. M: Antón Martín. No concerts mid-Apr. to mid-Oct.) For opera and *zarzuela* (light opera native to Madrid), head for the ornate **Teatro de la Zarzuela,** C. Jovellanos, 4. Built in 1856, it was modeled on Milan's La Scala. (☎915 24 54 00; http://teatrodelazarzuela.mcu.es. M: Sevilla or Banco de España. No performances late July to Aug.) The city's principal performance venue is the prestigious **Teatro Real,** Pl. de Isabel II, featuring the city's best ballet and opera. (☎915 16 06 06. M: Ópera. Tickets sold M-Sa 10am-1:30pm, and 4:30-7pm.) The grand 19th-century **Teatro de la Ópera** is the city's principal venue for classical ballet. Most theaters close in July and August, but many participate in **Veranos en la Villa,** hosting summer events or productions.

FLAMENCO

Flamenco in Madrid is tourist-oriented and expensive. A few nightlife spots are authentic (see ■Cardamomo, p. 126), but can be pricey. **Las Tablas,** Pl. de España, on the corner of C. Bailén and Cuesta San Vicente, has lower prices than most other flamenco clubs (entrance €15). Shows start every night at 10:30pm. (☎915 420 52; www.lastablasmadrid.com. M: Pl. de España.) **Casa Patas,** C. Cañizares, 10, offers excellent quality for a bit less than usual (*espectáculo* €25), and teaches intensive summer courses in flamenco dance and song; 20 hours of instruction cost €154. (☎913 69 04 96; www.casapatas.com. M: Antón Martín. Call for prices and reservations.) **Café de Chinitas,** C. Torija, 7, is as overstated as they come. Shows start at 10:30pm and midnight, but the memories last forever—or at least they should, given the price. (☎915 47 15 02. M: Santo Domingo. Cover from €31.60.) At **Corral de la Morería,** C. Morería, 17, by the viaduct on C. Bailén, shows start at 10:30pm and last until 2am. (☎913 65 84 46. M: La Latina. Cover €32.) **Teatro Albéniz,** C. de la Paz, 11, hosts an annual *Certamen de Coreografía de Danza Española y Flamenco* (Choreography Competition; 3-4 days during the first 2 weeks of June) that features original music and extraordinary flamenco. (☎915 31 83 11. M: Sol.)

FILM

In summer, the city sponsors free movies and plays, all listed in the *Guía del Ocio* and the entertainment supplements of Friday newspapers. In July, watch for the **Fescinal,** a film festival at the Parque de la Bombilla. Selections are mostly mainstream, but some art cinema is thrown in the mix. From M: Príncipe Pío, turn right and follow the river down Po. de la Florida, off C. de la Florida. Most cinemas show three films per day at around 4:30, 7:30, and 10:30pm; tickets cost €2.40-5.40. In mid-November, look for the two-week long **Festival Internacional de Cine Lésbico y Gay de Madrid,** held at venues throughout central Madrid (www.lesgaicinemad.com). Some cinemas offer weekday-only matinee student discounts for €3.70. Wednesday (or sometimes Monday) is *día del espectador,* when tickets cost around €3—show up early. Check the *versión original (V.O. subtitulada)* listings in the *Guía del Ocio* for English movies subtitled in Spanish. Three excellent movie theaters cluster near M: Ventura Rodríguez, between Pl. de España and Argüelles. **Princesa,** C. Princesa, 3 (☎915 41 41 00), shows mainstream Spanish films and subtitled foreign films. The theater-bar **Alphaville,** C. Martín de los Héroes, 14 (☎915 59 38 36), behind Princesa and underneath the patio, shows current alternative foreign and Spanish titles. **Renoir,** C. Raimundo Fernández Villaverde, 10 (☎915 41 41 00), shows highly acclaimed films, many foreign and subtitled. Check the *Guía del Ocio* for other cineplexes in and around the city.

The **Filmoteca Española,** C. Santa Isabela, 3, is a cinephile's dream, housing over 70,000 prints of 35,000 titles, and a library with more than 25,000 books and periodicals. A small museum displays stills from old movies and photos from their sets. (☎914 67 26 00; www.cultura.mecd.es/cine/film/filmoteca.jsp. M: Antón Martín. Library open M-F 9:30am-2pm; museum open Tu-Sa 10am-2pm.) The Filmoteca sponsors cheap (€1.35) nightly screenings of historic films, rare prints, and art cinema at the nearby **Cine Doré,** C. Santa Isabel, 3. (☎ 913 69 11 25. M: Antón Martín. Screenings usually at 6, 8, 10:15, and 10:30pm.)

THEATER

Huertas, east of Sol, is Madrid's theater district. In July and August, Pl. Mayor, Lavapiés, and Villa de París frequently host outdoor performances. For a complete list of theaters and shows, consult the *Guía del Ocio.* Seeing a play in Madrid is an entertaining way to participate in traditional culture and to practice your Spanish. Tickets start around €24, but specials for as low as €12 are not rare. Student and senior discounts are also often available. Theatergoers should consult the magazines published by state-sponsored theaters, such as **Teatro Español,** C. del Príncipe, 25, in Pl. de Santa Ana (☎913 60 14 80; M: Sol or Sevilla), **Teatro Infanta Isabel,** C. Barquillo, 24 (☎915 21 02 12; M: Banco de España), and the superb **Teatro María Guerrero,** C. Tamayo y Baus, 4 (☎913 10 15 00; M: Colón). Tickets can be purchased at theater box offices or at ticket agencies. (**El Corte Inglés** ☎902 40 02 22; **FNAC** 915 95 62 00; **Crisol** 902 11 83 12; **TelEntrada** 902 10 12 12; **Entradas.com** 902 48 84 88.)

FÚTBOL

Spaniards obsess over *fútbol* (soccer). The festivities start hours before matches as fans congregate in the streets, headphones and radio in one hand and *cerveza* in the other, listening to pre-game commentary and discussing it with other diehards. If either **Real Madrid** (in all white) or **Atlético de Madrid** (in red and white stripes) wins a match, count on streets clogged with honking cars. Every Sunday and some Saturdays between September and June, one of these two teams plays at home. Real Madrid plays at **Estadio Santiago Bernabéu,** Po. de la Castellana, 104. (☎914 57 11 12. M: Santiago Bernabéu.) Atlético de Madrid plays at **Estadio Vicente Calderón,** C. Virgen del Puerto, 67. (☎913 66 47 07. M: Pirámides or Marqués de Vadillos.) Tickets cost €18-42 and sell out quickly.

RECREATIONAL SPORTS

Madrid's swimming pools provide the perfect solution to summertime heat and land-locked shortcomings. Gawkers be warned: most women go topless. (Pool info ☎915 40 39 00; www.imd.es. Municipal tourist office offers a comprehensive list of the 25 pools in and around Madrid. All pools have same hours and prices.) Swimmers splash in the outdoor pools at **Lago/Casa de Campo,** on C. del Ángel. The Lago pools are yet another one of Madrid's social meccas, with several pools and sunbathing areas. Lots of kids, ice cream stands, and fun, but watch your valuables. (☎914 63 00 50. M: Lago. Open 10:30am-8pm. €3.80.) Other cooling relief includes the pool at **Peñuelas,** on C. Arganda. (☎914 74 28 08. M: Acacias, Pirámides, or Embajadores; or bus #18.)

Call the **Oficina de Información Deportiva** (☎914 63 55 63) for more info on sports in Madrid. The tourist office's *Plano de las Instalaciones Deportivas Municipales* lists public facilities. For **cycling info** and bicycle repair, pedal over to **Calmera Bicicletas,** C. Atocha, 98. (☎915 27 75 74; www.calmera.net. M: Antón Martín.)

MADRID

BULLFIGHTS

Bullfighters are either loved or loathed. So, too, are the bullfights themselves. Nevertheless, bullfights are a Spanish tradition, and locals joke that they are the only things in Spain to ever start on time. Hemingway-obsessed Americans and true fans of this contorted struggle between man and nature descend on Pl. de las Ventas for the heart-pounding, albeit gruesome, events.

From May 15-22 every year, the **Fiestas de San Isidro** provide a daily *corrida* (bullfight) with top *matadores* and the fiercest bulls. The fights are nationally televised; those without tickets crowd into bars. There are also bullfights every Sunday from March to October and less frequently throughout the rest of the year. Look for posters in bars and cafes for upcoming *corridas* (especially on C. Victoria, off C. San Jerónimo). **Plaza de las Ventas,** C. Alcalá, 237, is the biggest ring in Spain. (☎913 56 22 00; www.las-ventas.com. M: Ventas.) A seat costs €3-92, depending on its location in the *sol* (sun) or *sombra* (shade); shade is more expensive but offers comfort and the best view. Tickets are available, in person only, the Friday and Saturday before and Sunday of a bullfight. **Plaza de Toros Palacio de Vista Alegre** also hosts bullfights and cultural events. (☎914 22 07 80. M: Vista Alegre. Call ahead for schedule and prices.) To watch amateurs, head to the **bullfighting school,** which has its own *corridas* on Saturdays at 7:30pm. (☎914 70 19 90. M: Batán. Tickets €7, children €3.50.)

▛ SHOPPING

For upscale shopping, sashay down swanky **Calle Serrano** and **Calle Velázquez** in the famous **Salamanca** district (near Pl. de Colón), where fine boutiques and specialty stores line the streets next to Gucci, Prada, Calvin Klein, and the like. Most major department stores can be found between Puerta del Sol and Callao, with smaller clothing stores scattered along Gran Vía. **El Cortes Inglés,** Spain's unavoidable all-in-one store, sports over 10 locations throughout the city. Countless boutiques in **Chueca** specialize in hot clubwear, tight jeans, and sexy street clothes. **Mercado Fuencarral,** C. Fuencarral, 42, specializes in funky attire and tattoo and piercing parlors. (☎915 21 59 85; www.mdf.es. Open M-Sa 11am-9pm.) Most stores in Madrid are open 10am-2pm and 5-8pm. Some stay open on Saturday afternoon and during *siesta*. By law, *grandes almacenes* (department stores) may open only the first Sunday of every month to allow smaller business to compete. Many boutiques close in August, when almost everyone flees to the coast. Non-EU residents can shop tax-free at major stores, as long as they remember to ask for their VAT return form and spend more than €100 (☎900 43 54 82 for more info).

MALLS

Mallrats may go through a bit of withdrawal in Madrid, since smaller, scattered stores are the norm. **La Vaguada** (M: Barrio del Pilar; bus #132 from Moncloa), in the northern neighborhood of **Madrid-2,** is Madrid's first experiment in super-malls. It offers everything the homesick Anglophone could want: 350 shops, including The Body Shop, Burberry's, a trusty McDonald's, multi-cinemas, and a bowling alley. (Open daily 10am-10pm.) **ABC,** C. Serrano, 61, in the old ABC newspaper headquarters, has food courts and Spanish clothing chains from Mango to Zara. (M: Castellano. Open M-Sa 10am-9:30pm.) Madrid's outlet mall is **Las Rozas,** C. Juan Ramón Jiménez, a 30min. drive from the center, with up to 60% off favorite brands. (☎916 40 49 08; www.lasrosasvellaje.com.) By far the poshest spot is the **Galería del Prado,** Pl. de las Cortes, located beneath the Hotel Palace and across Po. de la Castellana from the Ritz. (M: Banco de España. Open M-Sa 10am-9pm.)

▨ EL RASTRO (FLEA MARKET)

For hundreds of years, *El Rastro* has been a Sunday morning tradition in Madrid. The market begins in La Latina at Pl. Cascorro off C. Toledo and ends at the bottom of C. Ribera de Co+rtidores. Get lost in the insanity and excitement as your senses are overwhelmed with sights, sounds, and smells from every direction. Seek out that souvenir you've been dying for since your first day in Madrid and haggle for it until you're blue in the face. At *El Rastro* you can find anything, from zebra hides to jeans to antique tools to pet birds. As crazy as the market seems, it is actually thematically organized. The main street is a labyrinth of cheap jewelry, leather goods, incense, and sunglasses, branching out into side streets, each with its own concert of vendors and wares. Antique-sellers contribute their peculiar mustiness to C. del Prado, and in their own shops in small plazas off C. Ribera de Cortidores. Fantastic collections of old books and LPs are sold in Pl. del Campillo del Mundo at the bottom of C. Carlos Arnides. Tapas bars and small restaurants line the streets and provide a cool respite for market-weary bargain hunters. The flea market is a pickpocket's paradise, so leave your camera behind, bust out the money belt, and turn that backpack into a frontpack. Police are everywhere if you have any problems. El Rastro is open Sundays and holidays from 9am to 2pm.

BOOKS

Books in English tend to be outrageously expensive in Spain. If you read Spanish, however, it's worthwhile to buy books here and ship or carry them home. You'll save a good deal of money and the selection is obviously better.

Altair, C. Gaztambide, 31 (☎915 43 53 00). M: Moncloa or Argüelles. Comprehensive travel bookstore, with the world's best travel guides and others. Knowledgeable staff. Open M-F 10am-2pm and 4:30-8:30pm, Sa 10:30am-2:30pm and 4:30-8pm.

Berkana Librería Gay y Lesbiana, C. Hortaleza, 64 (☎/fax 915 22 55 99). M: Chueca. Gay and lesbian bookstore with loads of contact info for foreigners and a free map of gay Madrid. Open M-F 10:30am-2pm and 5-8:30pm, Sa noon-2pm and 5-8:30pm.

Booksellers, C. José Abascal, 48 (☎914 42 79 59). M: Gregorio Marañón. A vast array of books, videos, magazines, and children's literature in English. Open M-F 9:30am-2pm and 5-8pm, Sa 10am-2pm.

Casa del Libro, Gran Vía, 29 (☎915 22 66 57; www.casadelibro.com). M: Callao. Madrid's largest and most comprehensive bookstore. Open M-Sa 9:30am-9:30pm, Su 11am-9pm. **Branch** at C. del Maestro Victoria.

FNAC, C. Preciados, 28 (☎915 95 62 00; www.fnac.es). M: Callao. Best music and book selection. English books on 3rd fl. Periodicals in basement cafeteria. Open M-Sa 10am-9:30pm, Su noon-9:30pm.

J and J Books and Coffee, C. Espíritu Santo, 47 (☎915 21 85 76), right around the corner from M: Noviciado. A friendly haven for English-speaking bookworms. Travelers can exchange used books for a third of the selling price and pick fresh titles from an ever-changing selection. Free coffee for first-timers. Open Sept.-June M-Th 10am-10pm, F-Sa 10am-1am, Su 2-10pm; July-Aug. M-F noon-8pm, F-Sa noon-10pm, Su 2-8pm.

▨ NIGHTLIFE

Madrid offers some of the greatest nightlife in the world. As the sun sets, the streets and plazas begin to radiate a frenetic energy, an intoxicating mixture of excitement and alcohol. Partying in Madrid is a celebration of life and a denial of the necessity of sleep—why go to bed when the party rages until 7am? Undeterred by occasional spells of bad weather, traffic jams on small streets, and shady characters that always seem to appear in dark plazas, partygoers in Madrid have only one goal for the night: fun. Both gay and straight bar- and club-hoppers will be overwhelmed by the countless ways to spend a single evening. Proud of their nocturnal offerings—*madrileños* will tell you with a straight face that they were bored in Paris or New York—they insist that no one goes to bed until they've "killed the night" and, in most cases, a good part of the following morning.

An average successful night involves several neighborhoods and countless venues; half the party is the in-between. A typical evening might start in the tapas bars of Huertas, move to a disco in Malasaña, and then crash the wild parties of Chueca. Some clubs don't even bother opening until 4 or 5am; the only (relatively) quiet nights of the week are Monday and Tuesday. For clubs and discos, life begins around 2am. The *entrada* (cover) often includes a drink and can be as high as €15; men may be charged up to €3 more than women, who may not be charged at all. Venues often change prices depending on the night, with Saturdays the most expensive. Keep an eye out for *invitaciones* and *oferta* cards—in stores, restaurants, tourist publications, and on the street—that offer discounts on admission.

For the most up-to-date info on what's going on, scan Madrid's entertainment guides. The **Guía del Ocio,** available behind the counter of any news kiosk, should be your first purchase in Madrid (€1). It has concert, theater, sports, cinema, and TV schedules, and lists exhibits, restaurants, bars, and clubs. Although it's in Spanish, alphabetical listings of clubs and restaurants are invaluable even to non-speakers. The Guía comes out on Thursday, so be sure you're buying the latest issue. For an English magazine with articles on new finds in and around the city, pick up **In Madrid,** free at tourist offices and many restaurants. For articles as well as listings, do what the cool *madrileños* do and check out **Salir Salir Madrid** at any kiosk. Gay travelers will want to pick up the free magazine **Shanguide,** which lists activities and nightspots, or buy **Zero** magazine at any kiosk (€4).

Walking home alone is never a good plan. Check a bus map for the best *Búho* (night bus) home from Pl. de Cibeles. Alternatively, taxis are a safe ride home.

▒ FESTIVALS

The city bursts with dancing, and processions during **Carnaval** in February, culminating on Ash Wednesday with the beginning of Lent and the *Entierro de la Sardina* (Burial of the Sardine) procession in the Casa de Campo. A haunting painting by Goya of these ancient rites hangs in the **Real Academia de Bellas Artes.** In March, the city bubbles with the renowned **International Theater Festival.** The Comunidad de Madrid celebrates its struggle against the French invasion of 1808 during the **Fiestas del 2 de Mayo** with bullfights and concerts. Starting May 15, the week-long **Fiestas de San Isidro** honor Madrid's patron saint with a pilgrimage to his meadow, concerts and parades, and Spain's best bullfights. The last week of June, Madrid goes mad with ◙**Orgullo Gay** (Gay Pride). Outrageous floats filled with drag queens, muscle boys, and rallying lesbians shut down traffic between El Retiro and Puerta del Sol that Saturday. The weekend sees free concerts in Pl. Chueca and bar crawls among the congested streets of Chueca. Throughout the summer, the city sponsors the **Veranos de la Villa** (see **Among the Stars,** p. 135). Movies play nightly at 10:30pm in **Parque de la Bombilla,** Av. de Valladolid, M: Príncipe Pío (€4.50, students €3.50; schedule at tourist office). The **Festivales de Otoño** (Autumn Festivals), from September to November, offer more refined music, theater, and film events. On November 1, an **International Jazz Festival** entices great musicians to Madrid. On New Year's Eve, **El Fin del Año,** crowds gather at Puerta del Sol to countdown to the new year and eat 12 *uvas* (grapes), one by one, as the clock strikes midnight. The brochure *Las Fiestas de España*, available at tourist offices and bigger hotels, contains comprehensive details on Spain's festivals.

EL CENTRO: SOL, ÓPERA, AND PLAZA MAYOR

Puerta del Sol is the center of the city in the center of the country. All roads converge here (it's Spain's *kilómetro 0*) and most visitors pass through at least once. Signs indicating *hostales* and *pensiones* stick out from flower-potted balconies and decaying facades on narrow, sloping streets. For better deals in quieter spots, stray several blocks from Sol. Don't be afraid to climb that extra flight of dusty stairs to find a good deal. The following listings fall in the area between the Sol and Ópera metro stops. Price and location in El Centro are as good as they get, especially if you are planning to brave the legendary nightlife. Buses #3, 25, 39, and 500 serve Ópera; buses #3, 5, 15, 20, 50, 51, 52, 53, and 150 serve Sol.

ACCOMMODATIONS

Hostal-Residencia Luz, C. Fuentes, 10, 3rd fl. (☎915 42 07 59; fax 42 07 59). M: Ópera. 12 sunny, newly redecorated rooms exude comfort: all have hardwood floors, elegant furniture, and beautiful curtains and bedspreads. Friendly owner, satellite TV, and A/C complete the deal to make this the best value in town. Laundry €5. Singles €15; doubles €33.50-39; triples €39-45. Discounts for longer stays. ❶

Hostal Paz, C. Flora, 4, 1st and 4th fl. (☎915 47 30 47). M: Ópera. Unbeatable hospitality from wonderful owners. Peaceful, secure, and spotless rooms with large windows, satellite TV, and A/C. Reservations advised. Laundry €9. Singles €20; doubles €32-38; triples €45. Monthly rentals available but must be arranged far in advance. MC/V. ❷

Hostal Esparteros, C. Esparteros, 12, 4th fl. (☎/fax 915 21 09 03). M: Sol. The 4-flight hike (a free workout) is worth it for sparkling rooms with balconies or large windows; some have private bath and TV (no fans or A/C). Public phone and small common room with couches. Jovial, English-speaking owner ensures a terrific stay. Laundry €7. Singles €20-25; doubles €35; triples €42. 10% discount after 1 week. ❷

Hostal-Residencia Rober, C. Arenal, 26, 5th fl. (☎915 41 91 75). M: Ópera. Quiet *hostal* with brilliant balcony views down C. de Arenal. Smoking strictly prohibited. All 14 spartan but pristine soundproof rooms have their own tiny TVs and fans. Singles with double bed and shower €31, with bath €34; doubles €37, with bath €45; triples with bath €60. Discounts for longer stays. MC/V. ❸

Hostal Valencia, Pl. del Oriente, 2, 3rd fl. (☎915 59 84 50). M: Ópera. Narrow glass elevator lifts you to 7 elegant rooms, each uniquely decorated, some overlooking the gorgeous Pl. del Oriente and Palacio Real. All rooms have TV. Reservations advised. Interior singles €42; doubles €72; master suite €92. ❹

Hostal Oriente, C. Arenal, 23, 1st fl. (☎915 48 03 14; www.hostaloriente.com). M: Ópera. Classy, newly renovated hostel with friendly owners and lounge. 17 squeaky-clean rooms have TV, phone, A/C, and bath. Singles €35; doubles €55; triples €70. ❸

Hostal Los Arcos, C. Marqués Viudo de Pontejos, 3, 2nd fl. (☎915 22 59 76; fax 32 78 96). Spare rooms strive for luxury with shiny, satiny bedspreads. High ceilings and baths, but no fans or A/C. Lounge with couches. Doubles €40; triples €50. ❷

Hostal Madrid, C. Esparteros, 6, 2nd fl. (☎915 22 00 60; www.hostal-madrid.info), off C. Mayor. M: Sol. Rooms with TV, phone, safe, A/C, free wireless Internet, and new bathrooms. 7 furnished apartments on nightly (2 people €100, up to 5 €125), weekly, or monthly basis; big discounts for longer stays. English spoken. Reservations advised. Singles €50-58; doubles €70; triple with balcony €88. MC/V. ❺

Hostal Cantábrico, C. de la Cruz, 5 (☎915 31 01 30). M: Sol. Welcoming reception leads to rooms with complete bath, some with nice balcony views. Over 100 years in operation. Singles €34; doubles €50; triples €66. ❸

Hostal Alicante, C. Arenal, 16, 2nd fl. (☎915 31 51 78). M: Ópera or Sol. Clean rooms with TV, some with fans. Singles €23-26; doubles €42, with bath €48; triples with bath €60. MC/V. ❷

Hostal-Residencia Cruz-Sol, Pl. Santa Cruz, 6, 3rd fl. (☎915 32 71 97). M: Sol. Clean and comfy hostel boasts modern rooms with all the amenities: double-paned windows, safes, phones, A/C, and baths. Vending machines slake late-night thirst. Laundry €6. Singles €38; doubles €48; triples €66; quads €75. MC/V. ❹

Hostal Portugal, C. Flora, 4, 1st fl. (☎915 59 40 14). M: Ópera. Old rooms with sagging beds, TV, bath, and high prices, but a great location, especially if other places are full and you're tired of searching. Singles €30; doubles €38; triples €48; quads €64. ❷

Los Amigos Backpackers' Hostel, C. Campomanes, 6, 4th fl. (☎915 47 17 07). M: Ópera. Just over 2 years old, Los Amigos offers bright and clean dorm-style accommodations (rooms with 4, 6, or 8 beds) with common baths. Amenities include a kitchen, festive common room with bar and occasional parties, and Internet (€2 per hr.). English spoken. Breakfast (bread with jam) included. €5 sheet deposit, lockers in room, lock rental (€1). Dorms €16. MC/V. ❷

🍴 FOOD

Flooded with tourists looking for "traditional" fare, this area is packed with over-priced mediocre food. A little sifting, however, can lead to some amazing restaurants at decent prices. Streets near M: Ópera teem with crowded cafes, markets, and restaurants. Side streets off Puerta del Sol offer international cuisine. Places with menus in several different languages tend to be tourist traps; avoid them like green *gambas*. Cruise to nearby Pl. Santa Ana for better deals. The surrounding streets, especially through Arco de los Cuchilleros in the southwest corner of Pl. Mayor, house specialty shops and renowned *mesones*. Head here for garlicky tapas and pitchers of sangria in a festive, albeit touristy, atmosphere.

Lavapiés and La Latina, the neighborhoods south of Sol bounded by C. de Atocha and C. de Toledo, are generally residential and working class. No caviar or champagne here, but you'll find plenty of *menús* for around €6.50. Grab some chow in a funky outdoor eatery on **Calle de Argumosa,** or head up the hill toward Huertas for more tasty options.

🏆 **El Estragón Vegetariano,** Pl. de la Paja, 10 (☎913 65 89 82; www.guiadelocio.com/estragonvegetariano), on the far side of the plaza. M: La Latina. Perhaps the best medium-priced restaurant—of any kind—in Madrid, with vegetarian food to convince even the most die-hard carnivores to switch teams. Treat yourself to *crêpes à la Muselino* (€13), their specialty, or try the delicious and creative *menús* (M-F €9.50, Sa-Su and evenings €25). Open daily 1:30-4:30pm and 8pm-1am. AmEx/MC/V. ❸

🏆 **Inshala,** C. Amnistía, 10 (☎915 48 26 32). M: Ópera. Eclectic menu filled with delicious Spanish, Mexican, Japanese, Italian, and Moroccan dishes. Weekday lunch *menú* €9. Dinner €8-15. The couscous (€12) is both tasty and filling. Reservations strongly recommended. Open M-Th noon-2am, F-Sa noon-3am. ❸

Achuri, C. Argumosa, 2 (☎914 68 78 56). M: Lavapiés. The coolest left-wingers gather here for great music, cheap food, and wine. Mostly vegetarian, but some meat options. Patio chatters with evening conversations. Large portions of *berenjenas napolitana* are delicious and filling. Salads €4.50, main dishes €4.80, *bocadillos* €2.70, wine €0.80-2.20 per glass. Open daily July-Aug. 6pm-12:30am; Sept.-June 3:30pm-12:30am. ❶

El Granero de Lavapiés, C. Argumosa, 10 (☎914 67 76 11). M: Lavapiés. For 17 years, rotating art exhibitions and inventive specials have kept this hideaway packed with locals. Vegetarian *menú* allows diners to order from the full range of first courses and fantastic deserts, with a daily special as the main dish (M-F €8.50, Sa €9.50, Su no *menú*). Open Su-Th and Sa 1-4pm, F 1-4pm and 8:30-11pm. MC/V. ❷

Sobrino del Botín, C. Cuchilleros, 17 (☎913 66 42 17), off Pl. Mayor. According to the *Guinness Book of World Records,* Botín is the oldest continually operating restaurant in the world (founded 1725). Chow down on a variety of simple but filling Spanish dishes (€7.40-26.70; *menú* of roast suckling pig or lamb €30.70). Ask to sit in the cave-like cellar *(sótano).* Lunch daily 1-4pm, dinner 8pm-midnight. AmEx/MC/V. ❹

El Oso y el Madroño, C. Bolsa, 4 (☎925 22 77 96; www.eoyem.com). From M: Sol, go uphill on C. Carretas to Pl. Benavente and turn right onto C. Bolsa. This restaurant is as local as its mascot (the foraging bear) and home to hearty cuisine. A rich *cocido de garbanzos* (chickpea and meat stew) is their special (€11). Calm your stomach with *licor de madroño,* a sweet liquor distilled from the fruit of the "strawberry tree," found growing along C. Mayor. Open Su-Th 11am-midnight, F-Sa 11am-2am. ❷

Bósforos, C. de la Cruz, 10. M: Sol. One of the many Turkish restaurants in Madrid. Serves succulent *Doner kebap* (chicken or lamb gyro sandwich). Probably the most delicious and least expensive lunch in Madrid. *Tavuk kebap* with trimmings €3. Entrees €2.40-5.50. *Menú* includes fries and a drink (€4.80). Open daily noon-1:30am. ❶

Museo del Jamón, C. San Jerónimo, 6 (☎915 21 03 46). M: Sol. 5 other locations in Madrid, including C. Mayor, 7 (☎915 31 45 50). A vegetarian's nightmare and pork lover's dream. Dodge hooves and shanks at the bar or head upstairs for the chef's specialties (€3.75-7). *Menús* €7.30. Generous plates €4-6. Cafeteria and store open daily 7am-12:30am, restaurant 1-11:30pm. *Menús* served 1-5pm and 8-11pm. ❶

El Cuchi, C. Cuchilleros, 3 (☎913 66 44 24). Right outside Pl. Mayor, but better and cheaper than other spots. Delicious Mexican food in a festive setting. Unlike Botín, which prides itself on celebrity diners, El Cuchi advertises, "Hemingway never ate here." Entrees €6.70-18.90. Lunch *menú* €9.70. Open daily 1pm-midnight. AmEx/MC/V. ❸

Lhardy Restaurante, C. San Jerónimo, 8 (☎915 21 33 85), at C. Victoria. M: Sol. Get slicked up (men must wear ties) and bring an overstuffed wallet for an expensive feast. This gorgeous 165-year-old restaurant boasts original wallpaper and woodwork. Their specialty, *cocido de garbanzos* (chickpea stew; €27.50), has won deserved fame as a *madrileño* classic. Expect to spend upwards of €55 per person, including wine. Open M-Sa 1-3:30pm and 8:30-11:30pm, Su 1-3:30pm. AmEx/MC/V. ❺

◎ SIGHTS

The area known as El Centro, spreading out from Puerta del Sol ("Gate of the Sun"), is the gateway to the history and spirit of Madrid. Although several rulers carved the winding streets, the Habsburg and Bourbon families left El Centro's most celebrated monuments. As a result, the area is divided into two major sections: Madrid de los Habsburgos and Madrid de los Borbones. Most Habsburg directions are given from Puerta del Sol and Bourbon directions from Ópera. The sights are easily accessible by metro and foot, and the neighborhood itself is quite simple to navigate. All of El Centro can be conquered in a single day, but take more time to enjoy the sights leisurely and marvel at their beauty.

PUERTA DEL SOL

Kilómetro 0—the origin of six highways fanning out to the rest of Spain—marks the country's physical center in the most chaotic of Madrid's numerous plazas, Puerta del Sol. Sol bustles day and night with taxis, performers, and countless locals trying to evade the tourists. A web of pedestrian-only streets originating at Gran Vía leads a rush of consumers down a gallery of stores, funneling them into Sol. Named for the actual *Puerta del Sol* (Gate of the Sun) that stood here in the 1500s, Sol today is dominated by government buildings, stores, and restaurants. Spaniards and tourists alike converge upon *El oso y el*

ONCE UPON A TIME...

There was a handsome young Spanish prince, educated at Georgetown, with a soft spot for the environment. He was well-loved by his people, but had yet to find that special someone. He had spent five years dating Eva Sannum, a Norwegian model, but ended things because the relationship had failed to "thrive," according to the prince. Other girlfriends had included the American co-ed Giselle Howard and the German royal Carolina de Waldburg. As he rounded 35, however, international gossips were driven to a frenzy—who would end up as the lucky lady?

When Felipe de Borbón y Grecia, the Prince of Asturias, finally announced his engagement to Letizia Ortiz Rocasolano, Spain both sighed with relief and bubbled with controversy. The beautiful news anchor was a smart dresser and a familiar face, but she was a commoner, and a divorcée at that. The shock soon passed; Felipe was following both his heart and a trend in courtly couplings; in recent years the Princes of Denmark and Japan had also taken "common" brides, with varying degrees of public support.

The two met under less-than-romantic circumstances. In November of 2002, Letizia was reporting on the worst Spanish environmental catastrophe ever, the sinking of the *Prestige* oil tanker, which dumped over 10

madroño, a bronze statue of the bear and "strawberry tree" from the city's heraldic coat of arms. On New Year's Eve, citizens congregate here to gobble one grape per chime at midnight.

HABSBURG MADRID

"Old Madrid," the city's central neighborhood, is the most densely packed with both monuments and tourists. In the 16th century, the Habsburgs funded the construction of **Plaza Mayor** and the **Catedral de San Isidro.** Many of Old Madrid's buildings, however, date from much earlier, some as far back as the Moorish empire. When Felipe II moved the seat of Castilla from Toledo to Madrid (then only a town of 20,000) in 1561, he and his descendants commissioned the court architects (including Juan de Herrera, master behind the austere El Escorial) to update many of Madrid's buildings to the latest styles. Another Juan, Juan de Villanueva, added his architectural flavor to the mix under Carlos III, designing the Prado. After only a century of development and expansion, Madrid's population more than doubled.

PLAZA MAYOR. In 1620, Pl. Mayor was completed for Felipe III; his statue, installed in 1847, graces the plaza's center. Though also designed by Juan de Herrera, Pl. Mayor is much softer in style than his stolid El Escorial. Its elegant arcades, spindly towers, and pleasant verandas are defining elements of the "Madrid style," which inspired architects across the city and throughout the country. Seventeenth-century nobles on horseback spent Sunday afternoons chasing bulls in the plaza. They had such a jolly time that eventually everyone joined in the fun. Citizens, on foot and armed with sticks, also began running after those pesky bulls. The tradition came to be known as a *corrida*, from the verb *correr* (to run). Later, Carlos II (the Bewitched) sanctioned chasing heretics as well, generously offering Pl. Mayor as the site of a grand *auto-da-fé* during the Inquisition. Thankfully, that tradition faded.

Toward evening, Pl. Mayor awakens as *madrileños* resurface, tourists multiply, and cafe tables fill with lively patrons. Live performances of flamenco and music are a common treat. While the cafes are a nice spot for a drink, food is overpriced; have dinner elsewhere. On Sunday mornings, the plaza holds a rare coin and stamp sale, marking the start of **El Rastro** (p. 109). During the annual **Fiesta de San Isidro** (p. 108), held the Friday before May 15 through the following Sunday, the plaza explodes with celebration and dancing in traditional costume. *(From Pta. del Sol, walk down C. Mayor. M: Sol.)*

CATEDRAL DE SAN ISIDRO. Though Isidro, patron saint of crops, farmers, and Madrid, was humble, his final resting place is anything but. The elaborate wood altar, covered in gold, glows in the afternoon light. The church was designed in the Jesuit Baroque style at the beginning of the 17th century, before San Isidro's remains were disinterred from San Andrés and brought here in 1769 at Carlos II's command. During the Civil War, rioting workers burned the exterior—all that survived were the main Capilla, a 17th century banner, and the mummified remains of San Isidro and his wife, María de la Cabeza. The cathedral, which has since been restored, reigned as the cathedral of Madrid from the late-19th century until the Catedral de la Almudena (p. 117) was consecrated in 1993. *(From Pta. del Sol, take C. Mayor to Pl. Mayor, cross the plaza, and exit onto C. Toledo. Cathedral is at the intersection of C. Toledo and C. Sacramento. M: Latina. Open daily summer 7:30am-1:30pm and 5:30-9pm; winter 7:30am-1pm and 5:30-8:30pm. Free.)*

PLAZA DE LA VILLA. When Felipe II made Madrid the capital of his empire in 1561, most of the town existed between Pl. Mayor and the Palacio Real; Pl. de la Villa marks the heart of what was once Old Madrid. Though only a handful of medieval buildings remain, the plaza still features a nice courtyard, a statue of Don Álvaro de Bazán, beautiful tile work, and eclectic architecture. The horseshoe-shaped door on C. Codo is one of the few examples of the Gothic-*mudéjar* style left in Madrid, and the 15th-century *Torre de los Lujanes* was once the prison for Francisco I, King of France. Across the plaza is the 17th-century Ayuntamiento, designed in 1640 by Juan Gómez de Mora as both the mayor's home and the city jail. Inside is Goya's *Allegory of the City of Madrid* (1819). The neighboring Casa de Cisneros, a 16th-century Plateresque house, has served as a government building since 1907. *(From Pta. del Sol, go down C. Mayor and past Pl. Mayor. M: Sol.)*

CONVENTO DE LAS DESCALZAS REALES. In 1559, Juana of Austria, Felipe II's sister, converted the former royal palace into a convent; today it is home to 26 Franciscan nuns who watch over Juana's tomb. Claudio Coello's magnificent 17th-century frescoes line the staircase. The **Salón de Tapices** contains 10 renowned tapestries based on cartoons by Rubens, along with Santa Úrsula's jewel-encrusted bones. The highlights of the tour are in the final three rooms, which include a portrait of Carlos II "The Bewitched" (the last, most terribly inbred Habsburg monarch), an allegorical Flemish painting of demons assaulting society, a dark portrait of San Francisco by Zurbarán, and Titian's *Tributo de la Moneda al César*. Lines

million gallons of crude oil into Galicia's richest fisheries. Felipe came to assess the damage, and the two hit it off.

The wedding day, March 22, 2004, came at an even more horrific time—just 11 days after the March 11 terrorist attacks. Over 1500 VIP guests crowded the Catedral de Nuestra Señora de la Almudena (p. 117), while nearly 18,000 police officers patrolled the rainy streets. Nobody wanted a repetition of Alfonso XIII's wedding day, when an anarchist tossed a bomb into the crowd, killing 23 people. Fortunately, they were hitched without a hitch, and everyone retired to El Pardo (p. 138) to feast on a 2m high wedding cake, washed down with over 1000 bottles of bubbly. There was, however, a vocal minority of malcontents; the extravagant celebration was a painful reminder that Spain is *not* a republic, and hasn't been one since Franco won the civil war in 1939. Foreigners frequently have trouble remembering this; Jeb Bush pulled a George in 2003 when he called then-Prime Minister José María Aznar the "President of the Republic of Spain."

are long in the summer; arrive early. *(Pl. las Descalzas, between Pl. de Callao and Pta. de Sol. ☎915 454 88 00. M: Callao, Ópera, or Sol. Open Tu-Th and Sa 10:30am-12:45pm and 4-5:45pm, F 10:30am-12:45pm, Su 11am-1:45pm. €5, students €2.50. EU citizens free W.)*

CONVENTO DE LA ENCARNACIÓN. Designed by Juan de Herrera's disciple Juan Gómez de Mora, the monastery is an oasis in the middle of Madrid's bustle; Spain's finest reliquary is housed there, with more than 1500 saintly relics, including a vial of San Pantaleón's blood believed to liquefy every year on July 27. According to legend, if the blood does not liquefy, disaster will strike Madrid. Rumor has it that the blood didn't change before the Civil War broke out, but the Church insists it has never once remained crystalline. Artistic highlights include a dramatic *San Juan Bautista* by José Ribera, an exquisitely contorted wooden Christ by Pedro de Mano, and a dark *Last Supper* by Vicente Carducho. *(Pl. de la Encarnación. From the metro stop, facing the Ópera building, bear diagonally right up C. Arrieta. M: Ópera. ☎915 47 53 50. Open M-Th and Sa 10:30am-12:45pm and 4-5:45pm, F 10:30am-12:45pm, Su 11am-1:45pm. €3.60; students, under 18, and over 65 €2. EU citizens free W.)*

ALONG THE RÍO MANZANARES. Madrid's notoriously puny river snakes its way around the city past the **Puerta de Toledo.** The triumphal arch was commissioned by Joseph Bonaparte to celebrate his brother Napoleon, but was completed in honor of Fernando VII, the "exterminator of the French usurpers." The Baroque **Puente de Toledo** makes up for the river's inadequacies. Sandstone carvings by Juan Ron on both sides depict the martyrdom of San Isidro and his family. The **Puente de Segovia,** which spans the river along C. Segovia, was conceived by Juan de Herrera and constructed in the late 16th century, making it the oldest bridge in Madrid. Both offer gorgeous views and are popular with young couples. *(To reach Puente de Toledo from Pta. del Sol take C. Mayor through the Pl. Mayor and onto C. Toledo; follow C. Toledo to the bridge; approx. 15min. M: Puerta de Toledo or Ópera.)*

OTHER SIGHTS. As the legend goes, **Iglesia de San Pedro,** C. de Nuncio, 14, began as a *mudéjar* mosque. A 17th-century overhaul commissioned by Felipe IV infused the original structure with Baroque intricacies. *(Facing the Palacio, go left on C. de Bailén and right onto C. de Segovia. The church will be on your right when you reach Cost. San Pedro. Open for mass only.)* Next to Iglesia de San Pedro is the **Museo de San Isidro,** where the saint is said to have lived; his sarcophagus rests here now, in the **Capilla de San Isidro,** but his body is in the nearby Catedral. The museum has exhibits on the history of Madrid, archaeological finds, paintings, and a beautiful courtyard. *(Cost. San Andrés. M: La Latina. Open Tu-F 9:30am-8pm, Sa-Su 10am-2pm. Free.)*

BOURBON MADRID

Weakened by plagues and political losses, the Habsburg era in Spain ended with the death of Carlos II in 1700. Felipe V, the first of Spain's Bourbon monarchs, ascended the throne in 1714 after the 12-year War of the Spanish Succession. Bankruptcy, industrial stagnation, and widespread moral disillusionment compelled Felipe V to embark on a crusade of urban renewal. His successors, Fernando VI and Carlos III, fervently pursued the same ends, with astounding results. Today, the lavish palaces, churches, and parks that they left are the most touristed in Madrid; a walk around them requires planning and patience.

PALACIO REAL. The impossibly luxurious Palacio Real overlooks the Río Manzanares at the western tip of central Madrid. Felipe V commissioned Giovanni Sachetti to replace the Alcázar, which burned down in 1734, with a palace that would dwarf all others—he succeeded. When Sachetti died, Filippo Juvara took over, basing his new facade on Bernini's rejected designs for the Louvre. The shell took 26 years to build, and the decoration of its 2000 rooms with a vast collection of porcelain, tapestries, furniture, and art dragged on for over a century. Today, the palace is used by the royal couple only on official occasions, but it continues to stand as one of Europe's most grandiose residences.

The palace's most impressive rooms are decorated in the Rococo style. The **Salón de Gasparini**, site of the king's ceremonial dressing before the court, houses Goya's portrait of Carlos IV and a Mengs ceiling fresco. The **Salón del Trono** (Throne Room) also contains a ceiling fresco, painted by Tiepolo, outlining the qualities of the ideal ruler. Perhaps the most beautiful is the **Chinese Room,** whose walls swirl with verdant tendril patterns. The **Real Oficina de Farmacia** (Royal Pharmacy) features crystal and china receptacles used to hold royal medicine. Also open to the public is the **Real Armería** (Armory), which displays the most finely wrought armor that belonged to Carlos V and Felipe II, 13th-century broadswords, nine foot-long *espingada* guns, and Toledo's best dueling *espadrillos* (shoes). *(From Pl. de Isabel II, head toward the Teatro Real. M: Ópera. ☎914 54 88 00. Open Apr.-Sept. M-Sa 9am-6pm, Su 9am-3pm; Oct.-Mar. M-Sa 9:30am-5pm, Su 9am-2pm. Arrive early to avoid lines. €8, with tour €9; students €3.50/€8. EU citizens free W.)*

CATEDRAL DE NUESTRA SEÑORA DE LA ALMUDENA. Take a break from the cherub-filled frescoes of most Spanish cathedrals for refreshingly modern decor. Begun in 1879 and finished a century later, this cathedral is a stark contrast to the gilded Palacio Real. After a 30-year hibernation, the building, dedicated to Madrid's other patron saint, received a controversial face-lift. The reasons for the controversy are apparent, as the cathedral's frescoes and stained glass windows sport a discordant mix of traditional and abstract styles: gray stone walls clash with the ceiling panels of brilliant colors and sharp geometric shapes. *(Left of the Palacio Real on C. Bailén. M: Ópera. Closed during mass. Open daily 9am-9pm. Free.)*

MUSEO DE LA REAL ACADEMÍA DE BELLAS ARTES DE SAN FERNANDO. Following the examples of Italy and France, Spain's Old Masters convinced Ferdinand VI to establish a royal academy in 1752 to train the country's most talented artists—the collection of Old Masters in this beautiful museum represents their legacy. Ribera's *Martirio de San Bartolomé* and Velázquez's portrait of Felipe IV are masterpieces; the Raphael and Titian collections are also excellent. The two rooms dedicated to Goya (a former academy director) display his range, juxtaposing the satirical *Casa de Locos* and macabre *El Entierro de la Sardinera* with portraits of nobility. Other highlights include 17th-century canvases by Ribera, Murillo, Zurbarán, and Rubens. The top floor houses 20th-century works, including Picasso sketches. The **Calcografía Real** (Royal Print and Drawing Collection) holds Goya's studio and organizes exhibitions. Guides to all collections are available at the front desk. *(C. Alcalá, 13. ☎915 24 08 64. M: Sol or Sevilla. Open July-Aug. M-F 9:30am-9pm, Sa 9:30am-2pm and 5:30-9pm, Su 9:30am-2pm; Sept.-June Tu-F 9am-7pm, Sa-M 9am-2:30pm. €2.40, students €1.20. W free. Top 2 floors often closed; call for details.)*

PLAZA DEL ORIENTE. An architectural miscalculation resulted in this sculpture park. Its statues were designed for the palace roof, but because the queen had a nightmare about the roof collapsing, they were instead placed in this symmetrical plaza. An equestrian statue of Felipe IV, sculpted by Pietro Tacca, dominates the center; other structures include the **Teatro Real,** inaugurated by Isabel II (see **Music,** p. 105). Treat yourself to coffee at one of the elegant terraces on the plaza. *(From Pl. Isabel II, walk past Teatro Real. Across the street from the Palacio Real. M: Ópera.)*

OTHER SIGHTS. The **Campo de Moro** lies below the palace; with its wide, gentle slope of grass, and lush, leafy trees, it is a park fit for kings. Walking trails wind through the woods to shady resting places. *(From the Palace, turn left onto C. Bailén, left again down Cuesta San Vicente, and at the bottom of the hill turn left onto C. del Puerto. From M: Príncipe Pío, cross the plaza to the entrance on C. del Puerto. Open summer 10am-*

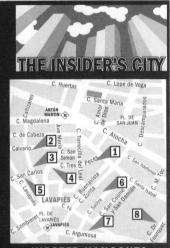

THE INSIDER'S CITY

HIPSTER HANGOUTS

The *barrio* of Lavapiés, around the metro stop of the same name, is home to a diverse mix of North African, Middle Eastern, and Chinese families, but the most recent wave of immigrants is a colony of hip Spanish 20-somethings who've carved out great spots for shopping, drinking, dancing, and chilling. If you're around, check out the Fiestas de San Lorenzo y San Cayetano (Aug. 4-9), which celebrate the neighborhood's patron saints with music and beer.

1 **La Lechería,** C. Tres Peces, 36 (☎914 67 07 59). The young owners of this shop make all the cute T-shirts, bags, and sculptures by hand. You can take home a Vicky Monforte original for under €18. Open Tu-Sa 5-10pm.

2 **Candela,** C. Olmo, 2 (☎914 67 33 82). Dance to flamenco until dawn; the crowd gets going around 2am. Open daily 10:30pm-5:30am.

3 **Africultor,** C. Olivar, 35 (☎654 25 25 41). The ideal place to pick up a *djembe*

8pm; winter 10am-6pm; last entrance 30min. before closing.) The **Jardines de Sabatini,** just to the right when facing the palace, is the romantic's park of choice. Wade in the fountain and lie among topiaries. A pine grove on the right offers much-needed shade. Be sure to catch the ◙**sunset** from the garden walls. *(Open daily 9am-10pm.)*

🔲 NIGHTLIFE

In the middle of Madrid and at the heart of the action are the grandiose and spectacular clubs of El Centro. With multiple floors, swinging lights, cages, and disco balls, they meet even the wildest clubber's expectations. The mainstream clubs found on these streets are often tourist hotspots; as a result, a night of fun here is the most expensive in the city. El Centro includes more territory than Madrid's other neighborhoods, so make a plan for the night and bring a map.

◙ **Kathmandú,** C. Señores de Luzón, 3 (☎635 873 896), a right off C. Mayor from Puerta del Sol, after Pl. Mayor and facing the Ayuntamiento. M: Ópera. Jammed with locals dancing to funk, soul, and hip-hop until the early morning. Low couches downstairs are perfect for chilling. Cover €7, includes 1 drink. Open Th midnight-5am, F-Sa 1-6am.

◙ **Palacio Gaviria,** C. Arenal, 9 (☎915 26 60 69; www.palaciogaviria.com). M: Sol or Ópera. A red carpet leads to 3 ballrooms-turned-club spaces, complete with dancers and blazing light shows. Cover Su-Th €9, F-Sa €15; includes 1 drink, additional drinks €9. Open M-W 11pm-4am, Th 10:30pm-6am, F-Sa 11pm-6am, Su 9pm-2:30am.

Suite, C. Virgen de los Peligros, 4 (☎915 21 40 31). M: Sevilla. Classy restaurant, bar, and club boasts a lunch *menú* (€10) by day and sleek drinks (€5-6) by night. Upstairs dance floor rolls with house while the mixed crowd downstairs at the bar and terrace makes its own music. No cover. Open daily 1-5pm and 8pm-3:30am.

La Casa de los Jacintos, C. Arganzuela, 11 (www.frado.net/lacasadelosjacintos). M: La Latina or Puerta de Toledo. From M: La Latina, walk downhill on C. Toledo and turn left onto C. Arganzuela. From M: Puerta de Toledo, go uphill, turn right onto C. Salazar, then left onto C. Arganzuela. A cross between an arts society, a gallery, and a cafe, this intimate venue hosts flamenco performances (Th 10:30pm-midnight) and art-house cinema F and Sa. It's a very local scene, but *extranjeros* are more than welcome. Performances, movies, and *mojitos* €3. Open W-Sa 9pm-3am, Su 9pm-midnight.

El Barbu, C. Santiago, 3 (☎915 42 56 98). M: Ópera. From the metro, go uphill on C. del Espejo to C. Santiago. Chill to lounge music upstairs and dance to house in the caves below. Cover Th-Sa €6, includes 1 drink. Mixed drinks €5, F-Sa €7. Open June-Aug. M-Th 10:30pm-4am, F-Sa 10:30pm-5:30am; Sept.-May Tu-Sa 8pm-4am.

Joy Madrid, C. Arenal, 11 (☎913 66 37 33). M: Sol or Ópera. A well-dressed crowd parties the night away to disco, techno, and R&B on a 3-tiered dance floor (all 3 floors only open Sa). Drinks €9.60. Cover Su-Th €12, F-Sa €15. Open daily 11:30pm-6am.

Sweet Club Dance, C. Dr. Cortezo, 1 (☎918 69 40 38). M: Tirso de Molina. Steel doors covered in vines lead to an outrageous scene. Cages and disco-ball dance floor get packed after 3am. Cover €7, includes 1 drink. Open Th-Sa 1-6:30am.

HUERTAS

Although *madrileños* have never settled on a nickname for this neighborhood, the area between C. San Jerónimo and C. Huertas is generally referred to as Huertas. Once a seedy area, Huertas has grown into a hotbed of food and drink. Though quieter than El Centro, **Plaza Santa Ana, Calle del Príncipe,** and **Calle de Echegaray** offer some of the best bars in Madrid, and **Calle de Ventura de la Vega** some of the best restaurants. Sol, Pl. Mayor, *el triángulo del arte,* and Estación Atocha are all nearby. Sol-bound buses stop near accommodations on C. del Príncipe, C. Núñez de Arce, and C. San Jerónimo; buses #10, 14, 27, 34, 37, and 45 run along Po. del Prado. Buses # 6, 26, and 32 run up C. Atocha; get off at C. San Sebastián for Pl. Santa Ana. The closest metro stops are Sol, Sevilla, and Antón Martín.

▚ ACCOMMODATIONS

▨ **Hostal Villar,** C. del Príncipe, 18 (☎915 31 66 00; www.arrakis.es/~h-villar). M: Sol or Sevilla. Perfect location and low prices make this a winner. The 1970s stormed through here, leaving unintentionally retro rooms with TV and phone, some with A/C. Big lounge. Singles €23, with bath €26; doubles €31/€42; triples €43/€57. MC/V. ❷

▨ **Hostal Gonzalo,** C. Cervantes, 34, 3rd fl. (☎914 29 27 14; fax 20 20 07), off C. de León. M: Antón Martín. A budget traveler's dream. The friendly staff welcomes you to this lively *hostal* with newly renovated rooms, pristine baths, firm beds, TVs, and fans in summer. Leather-plush lounge. Singles €40; doubles €50; triples €60. AmEx/MC/V. ❹

(African drum; €50-100) for the Sunday afternoon jam sessions in the Parque del Buen Retiro (p. 137). Open M-F 10am-2:30pm and 5-8:30pm.

4 **Taberna la Aguja,** C. Ave María, 25. A sweet, cozy hole-in-the-wall bar that spins vinyl rock n' roll to the in-crowd. Beer €1, *copas* €3.50. Open daily 8:30pm-12:30am.

5 **El Tío Vinagre,** C. San Carlos, 5. A smooth little bar with drinks under €3. Open M-F 7pm-2am, Su 7pm-1am.

6 **Badulake,** C. Salitre, 30 (☎609 51 24 78). Hipsters hang out on the worn velvet sofa or dance to live rock, jazz (W and Su), or DJs (F-Sa). Open summer W-Th 10pm-2:30am, F-Su 10pm-3am; winter 8:30pm-late.

7 **La Boca del Lobo,** C. Argumosa, 11 (☎914 67 61 51). The restaurant-bar fills with locals and tourists. Even if you're not eating (entrees €7-18), check out the art gallery next door. Open daily noon-12:30pm; gallery 7pm-midnight with monthly shows.

8 **Pepita is Dead,** C. Dr. Fourquet, 10 (☎915 28 87 88). The vintage clothes (shirts €15-30) here are almost as cool as the name. Open M-Sa 11am-2pm and 5-8:30pm.

Cat's Hostel, C. Cañizares, 6 (☎ 902 88 91 92; www.catshostel.com). M: Antón Martín. Join over 200 other travelers at this brand-new hostel for an international experience. In a renovated 18th-century palace, it has clean dorms (2-16 beds), as well as small rooms with private baths, a fantastic *mudéjar* patio area, a bar, and a cafe. Breakfast, luggage storage, and Internet included. English spoken. Dorms €15. ❶

Hostal Betanzos, C. Luis de Guevera, 8, 3rd fl. (☎913 691 440). M: Antón Martín. Climb up the fantastic double staircase to classic rooms with high ceilings and wooden furniture. Singles €15; doubles €25. ❶ Across the hall, **Huéspede Yolanda** (☎913 691 315) offers nice rooms and baths. Singles €16; doubles €30; triples €45. ❷

Hostal Armesto, C. San Agustín, 6, 1st fl. (☎/fax 914 29 90 31), in front of Pl. Cortés. M: Banco de España or Antón Martín. This small hostel offers a quiet night's sleep for an older crowd and has a very hospitable owner. Some rooms have garden view; all have private bath, TV, and fan. Singles €35; doubles €45; triples €50. AmEx/MC/V. ❹

Hostal R. Rodríguez, C. Núñez de Arce, 9, 3rd fl. (☎915 22 44 31). M: Sol. Spacious rooms. English spoken. Singles €30; doubles €46, with bath €53. AmEx/MC/V. ❸

Hostal-Residencia Carreras, C. del Príncipe, 18, 3rd fl. (☎/fax 915 22 00 36), off C. San Jerónimo. M: Antón Martín, Sol, or Sevilla. Request a room with a balcony—they're larger. Rooms have TV, fan, and safe. Singles €24, with shower €27, with bath €33; doubles €36/€42/€48; triples with shower €54, with bath €60. AmEx/MC/V. ❷

Hostal-Residencia Sud-Americana, Po. del Prado, 12, 6th fl. (☎914 29 25 64), across from the Prado. M: Banco de España or Atocha. Airy doubles facing the Prado. Simple rooms. Often occupied by long term lodgers. Singles €18; doubles €35; triples €45. ❷

Hostal Internacional, C. Echegaray, 5, 2nd fl. (☎914 29 62 09). M: Sol. With extensive renovations completed 2 years ago, the rooms here are new and crisp, all with TV, A/C, safe, and shower. Nice common room. Singles €25-30; doubles €40. ❸

Hostal-Residencia Lido, C. Echegaray, 5, 2nd fl. (☎914 29 62 07). M: Sol or Sevilla. Across the hall from Internacional, Lido also has new rooms with comfy beds, TV, refrigerator, fans, and full bath. Singles €22-25, with bath €30; doubles €38. ❷

Hostal Aguilar, C. San Jerónimo, 32, 2nd fl. (☎914 29 59 26; www.hostalaguilar.com). M: Sol or Sevilla. Clean, large, modern rooms with vast baths, phones, safes, A/C, and TVs. Singles €35; doubles €47; triples €63; quads €76. MC/V. ❸

◖ FOOD

A popular place with locals, Pl. de Santa Ana is perfect for killing some time with a drink and snack. **Calles de Echegaray, Ventura de la Vega,** and **Manuel Fernández González** offer the best options; quality is high and prices are low. As the evening grows and wine flows, these streets become the first stop for a night out in Madrid.

▨ **Arrocería Gala,** C. Moratín, 22 (☎914 29 25 62; www.paellas-gala.com). M: Antón Martín. The paella buck stops here, with decor as colorful as its specialty. *Menú* (€13) offers paella with salad, bread, wine, and dessert. Excellent sangria. Enjoy the vine-covered interior garden. Reserve on weekends. Open daily 1:30-3:45pm and 9-11pm. ❸

▨ **Taberna Macieras,** C. Jesús, 7 (☎914 29 15 84), also C. Huertas, 66 (☎914 29 58 18). M: Antón Martín. The green walls, horseshoes, and bagpipes may recall Ireland, but the food is the best Galician seafood served up in a local atmosphere for great prices. Try the *pulpo gallego* (octopus; €9) or the *mejillones con tomate* (mussels in tomato broth; €10). 2 people can feast for under €25, including a bottle of wine. Open M 8pm-12:45am, Tu-F 1-4:30pm and 8pm-12:45am, Sa-Su 1-4:45pm and 8:30pm-1:30am. ❸

▨ **La Sanabresa,** C. Amor de Dios, 9 (☎914 29 03 38). M: Antón Martín. Incredibly popular with locals, La Sanabresa's plastic tablecloths are always covered with great Spanish food that costs next to nothing. Menus offer many delicious options (€7.40-8). The fried fresh anchovies are excellent. Open daily 1-4pm and 8:30-11pm. MC/V. ❷

▓ **Ricci Gelateria & Yogurteria Artiginale,** C. Huertas, 9 (☎687 98 96 12). M: Antón Martín. Forget tapas and *jamón;* here's the best ice cream in Madrid, available for all meals. Try the *horchata* or *granizados.* Weekends they make vegan-soy ice cream. Small cones €2, but you'll want a €3 large. Open Su-Th 9am-12:30am, F-Sa 9am-1:30am. ❶

Restaurante Integral Artemisa, C. Ventura de la Vega, 4 (☎914 29 50 92). M: Sol. 2nd location in Pl. del Carmen (☎915 21 87 21). Elegant vegetarian fare in mellow ambience. Veggie *menú* €9. Open daily 1:30-4pm and 9pm-midnight. AmEx/MC/V. ❷

La Farfalla, C. Santa María, 17 (☎913 69 46 91). M: Antón Martín. 1 block from the metro along C. Huertas; look for the butterfly. This intimate restaurant's specialty is Argentine-style grilled meat (*parrilla,* €10.50), but don't miss the thin-crust pizzas (€5.30). Open for dinner Su-Th 9:30pm-3am, F-Sa 9:30pm-4am. AmEx/MC/V. ❷

Al Natural, C. Zorrilla, 11 (☎913 69 47 09; www.alnatural.biz). M: Sevilla. From the metro, a left off C. de Cedaceros. A unique and creative offering of vegetarian Mediterranean dishes (€8.70-12) served in a lively, candlelit atmosphere. Try a salad with wheat rolls. Open M-Sa 1-4pm and 9pm-midnight, Su 1-4pm. MC/V. ❸

Gula Gula, C. Infante, 5 (☎914 20 29 19; www.gulagula.net), off C. Echegaray near C. las Huertas. M: Antón Martín. New location at Gran Vía, 1 (☎915 22 87 64). Outrageous drag shows and all-you-can-eat buffet (lunch €9; dinner €20). Reserve 1 week ahead for weekend dinner. Open daily 1-5pm and 9pm-3am. AmEx/MC/V. ❹

Pizzeria Cervantes, C. León, 8 (☎914 20 12 98), off C. del Prado. Hands down one of the best cheap lunch *menús* in the area (€8; served M-F), offering much more than pizza and including a selection of exquisite desserts. Most entrees €6. Open Su-M and W-Th 1-4:30pm and 8:30pm-12:15am, Tu 7pm-12:15am, F-Sa 1-4:30pm and 8:30pm-1:30am. AmEx/MC/V. ❷

◔ SIGHTS

The area east of Sol is a wedge bordered by C. de Alcalá to the north, C. de Atocha to the south, and Po. del Prado to the east. Off C. San Jerónimo, streets slope downward, outward, and eastward toward various points along Po. del Prado and Pl. Cánovas de Castillo. **Plaza de Santa Ana** and its *terrazas* are the center of this old literary neighborhood. Huertas's sights, from authors' houses to famous cafes, reflect its artistic past. Home to Cervantes, Quevedo, and Calderón de la Barca during its *Siglo de Oro* heyday (see **Literature,** p. 74), Huertas enjoyed a fleeting return to literary prominence when Hemingway dropped by to drink in the 1920s.

CASA DE LOPE DE VEGA. Golden Age authors Lope de Vega and Miguel de Cervantes were bitter rivals, but Lope de Vega's 17th-century home is ironically located on C. Cervantes (and of course, Cervantes is buried on C. Lope de Vega). A prolific playwright and poet, Lope de Vega spent the last 25 years of his life writing plays in this house. None of the objects here belonged to him, but they are all period pieces painstakingly collected using a catalog that he left behind. Although historians were able to reconstruct nearly exactly what his house looked like, they are not as familiar with his amorous exploits; his exact number of children is unknown; estimates range from 12 to 15. (*C. Cervantes, 11. With your back to Pl. de Santa Ana, turn left onto C. del Prado, right onto C. León, and left onto C. Cervantes.* ☎914 29 92 16. *Open Th-F 9:30am-2pm, Sa 10am-2pm. Entrance and tour €2, students €1.*)

CÍRCULO DE BELLAS ARTES. Designed by Antonio Palacios, this building houses two stages and several studios for lectures and workshops run by prominent artists. The Círculo is the hub of much of Madrid's art scene, sponsoring and organizing performances and shows around the city. Pick up their free monthly magazine, *Minerva,* at the entrance. Many facilities are for *socios* (members) only, but the galleries are open to the public. Exhibitions range from

ALL SAINTS

While touring Spain's cathedrals and museums, you may become familiar with some of the recurring characters of Catholic art. Here is a brief introduction to some of the iconography you will encounter. If you see:

• A beautiful young man with flowing hair, tied to a tree and shot through with arrows, it is San Sebastián. Sebastián was the son of a wealthy Roman family, and a favorite of Emperor Diocletian. In 288, he visited Christians in prison to comfort them and was punished for his kindness. The Romans tied him to a tree and shot him many times, but he survived to try to convert Diocletian. The emperor was not pleased, and Sebastián was beaten to death. He was most popular in the 14th century, when the Black Death swept through Europe. The plague's random devastation was likened to stray arrows shot by "Nature's archers," and Sebastián was impervious to arrows. He is the patron of archers, the moribund, and gardeners.

• An old man with a bible, a skull, and a lion, it is San Jerónimo. One of the first "doctors of the Church," he spent 30 years as a hermit, translating the scriptures. Said to have befriended a lion by removing a thorn from its paw, he's the patron of archaeologists, school children, librarians, and travel writers.

photography to video art to abstract sculpture. It also sponsors **Radio Círculo,** 100.4 FM, which plays jazz, folk music, and whatever guest DJs feel like spinning. *(C. Alcalá, 42. From Pl. de Santa Ana, go up C. del Príncipe, cross C. San Jerónimo, and turn right onto C. Alcalá. ☎ 913 60 54 00. Open Tu-F 5-9pm, Sa 11am-2pm and 5-9pm, Su 11am-2pm. €1. Cafe open daily 10am-1am.)*

FACADES. Juan de Villanueva's simple **Real Academia de la Historia** houses an old library and exemplifies *madrileño* architecture. *(At the C. de León and C. de las Huertas intersection. From Pl. de Santa Ana, take C. del Príncipe; turn left onto C. de las Huertas. Library access for researchers only.)* Eighteenth-century architect Pedro de Ribera designed the impressive facades of the **Palacios de Miraflores** and **del Marqués de Ugena.** *(Palacio de Miraflores, C. San Jerónimo, 15. Palacio de Marqués de Ugena, Pl. de Canalejas, 3.)*

🏛 MUSEUMS

Madrid's great museums need no introduction. If you're not a student and plan on visiting the big three, your best bet is the **Paseo del Arte** ticket (€7.70), which grants admission to the Museo del Prado, Museo Nacional Centro de Arte Reina Sofía, and Museo Thyssen-Bornemisza. The pass is available at all three museums.

🖼 MUSEO DEL PRADO

Po. del Prado at Pl. Cánovas del Castillo. M: Banco de España or Atocha. ☎/fax 913 30 28 00; www.museoprado.es. Open Tu-Su 9am-7pm. €3, students €1.50, under 18 and over 65 free. Su free.

The Prado is Spain's most prestigious museum, as well as one of Europe's finest centers for 12th- to 17th-century art. In 1785, architect **Juan de Villanueva** began construction of the Neoclassical building, following Carlos III's order for a museum of natural history and sciences. In 1819 Fernando VII transformed it into the royal painting archive; the museum's 7000 pieces are the result of hundreds of years of Bourbon art collecting. The walls are filled with Spanish and foreign masterpieces, including a comprehensive selection from the Flemish and Venetian schools. The museum is well-organized: each room is numbered and described in the museum's free guide. The sheer quantity of paintings means you'll have to be selective—walk past the rooms of imitation Rubens and Rococo cherubs and into the groves of the masters. The ground floor houses Spanish painting from the 12th through 16th centuries and 15th- to 16th-century Flemish, German, and Italian works. The first floor contains 17th-century pieces, and 18th-century paintings are located on the second floor. In addition to the free, indispensable floorplan you receive upon entry, the museum's guidebooks can help you sift through the floors and offer extensive art history and criticism (€0.60-18).

DIEGO VELÁZQUEZ. The first floor houses Spanish, Flemish, French, Dutch, and Italian works from the 16th and 17th centuries. The most notable of these are an unparalleled collection of works by Diego Velázquez (1599-1660), court painter and majordomo to Felipe IV (portraits of the foppish monarch abound). Velázquez's unforgiving realism and transcendent use of light resonates even in the 21st century. Several of his most famous paintings are here, including *Las hilanderas (The Weavers)*, *Marzo (Mars)*, and *La fragua de Vúlcano (Vulcan's Forge)*. In *Las lanzas (The Lances)*, Velázquez experimented with perspective, developing a technique to imply continuous movement. Smoke from a recent battle clears in the background as an anxious horse dominates the front. This method climaxed in his magnum opus, ☒**Las Meninas** *(The Maids of Honor)*, dubbed an "encounter" rather than a painting. The snapshot quality of the figures transformed painting in the 17th century.

FRANCISCO DE GOYA. In 1785, Francisco de Goya y Lucientes (1746-1828) became the court portraitist. Perhaps the most intriguing aspect of his works is how he depicted the royal family so unflatteringly without being expelled from court. Some suggest that he manipulated light and shadow to focus the viewer's gaze on the figure of the queen (rather than the king) in *La familia de Carlos IV*—a discreet way of supporting contemporary popular opinion about the power behind the monarchy. Goya's range of subjects and moods is unparalleled; one room has pastoral hunting scenes and peasant dances, while the other bristles with much darker scenes. The stark *2 de Mayo* and *Fusilamientos de 3 de Mayo*, which depict the terrors of the 1808 Napoleonic invasion, may be Goya's most recognized works, along with the expressionless woman in *La maja vestida* and *La maja desnuda*, thought to be his mistress the Dutchess of Alba. However, the *Pinturas Negras (Black Paintings)* are the most evocative. These paintings were aptly named for the darkness of both the colors and the subject matter—Goya painted them at the end of his life, when he was deaf and alone. *Saturno devorando a su hijo (Saturn Devouring His Son)* stands out, a reminder that time destroys its creations. Goya captures Saturn eating his children after hearing a prophesy that one would overthrow him. Another black painting, *El perro semihundido (The Half-drowned Dog)*, mystifies and disturbs viewers.

• A man in a simple brown robe, surrounded by animals, with Christ's wounds (stigmata)—it's San Francisco de Asissi. Once a street brawler and soldier, San Francisco became a monk later in life. Two years before he died, in 1224, he received the stigmata, which bled periodically until his death. He is the patron saint of environmentalists, animals, and those who fear dying alone.

• A very large man carrying a child, often with palm trees in the background, you're looking at San Cristóbal. His name means "Christ bearer." As the legend goes, he was a sort of gigantic ferryman, who would carry travelers across his stream. One day, a young boy came to the stream and Cristóbal struggled mightily to transport him. The boy was Christ, and he was so heavy because he bore the weight of the entire world on his shoulders. A fantastic, huge painting of Cristóbal can be viewed in the Catedral de Toledo.

• A young girl accompanied by oxen, holding a plate with eyes on it, you're looking at Santa Lucía. Lucía was martyred in 283 BC when she refused to marry a pagan suitor. The Romans tried to force her into prostitution, but they couldn't move her even with a team of oxen. They tore out her eyes and tried to burn her, but the wood would not light. At the end, she regained her sight, but was then stabbed in the throat. Lucía is the patron saint of the blind—and of ophthalmologists.

ITALIAN, FLEMISH, AND OTHER SPANISH ARTISTS. The ground floor of the Prado displays many of **El Greco's** (Doménikos Theotokópoulos, 1541-1614) religious paintings. *La Trinidad (The Trinity)* and *San Andrés y San Francisco (St. Andrew and St. Francis)* are characterized by El Greco's luminous colors, elongated figures, and mystical subjects. On the second floor are other works by Spanish artists like **Bartoloméo Murillo, José de Ribera,** and **Francisco Zurbarán.**

The collection of **Italian** works is formidable, including **Titian's** portraits of Carlos I and Felipe II and his mythologically inspired *Danäe Receiving the Shower of Gold* and **Raphael's** *El cardenal desconocido (The Unknown Cardinal)*. **Tintoretto's** rendition of the homicidal seductress Judith and her hapless victim Holofernes, as well as his awesome *Washing of the Feet*, are also here. Some minor **Botticellis** and a slew of imitations are on display. Among the works by **Rubens,** *The Adoration of the Magi* and *The Three Graces* best show his voluptuous style. Still, **Fra Angelico's** *Annunciation* is the most resplendent of all the Italian works.

As a result of the Spanish Habsburgs' control of the Netherlands, the **Flemish** holdings are also top-notch. **Van Dyck's** *Marquesa de Legunes* is here, as well as landscapes by **Joachim Patinir.** Especially amazing is room **56A** which houses a collection of phantasmagorical Flemish paintings, like **Peter Brueghel the Elder's** terrifying *The Triumph of Death.* **Hieronymus Bosch's** moralistic ▓**The Garden of Earthly Delights** is a favorite, with pink crystal fountains, composite creatures, hedonistic pleasure-seekers, the Hell that awaits them, and the Heaven that doesn't.

CASÓN DEL BUEN RETIRO. Three minutes from the Prado is the Casón del Buen Retiro, which, though closed for renovations, is still worth a peek. Once part of Felipe IV's Palacio del Buen Retiro, the Casón was destroyed in the Napoleonic wars. The rebuilt version normally houses the Prado's 19th- and 20th-century works, currently on loan to the Museo Nacional Centro de Arte Reina Sofía. *(C. Alfonso XII, 28.* ☎ *913 30 28 60.)*

▓ MUSEO NACIONAL CENTRO DE ARTE REINA SOFÍA

C. Santa Isabel, 52. ☎ *914 67 50 62; http://museoreinasofia.mcu.es. M: Atocha. Open M and W-Sa 10am-9pm, Su 10am-2:30pm. €3, students €1.50. Sa after 2:30pm, Su, and holidays free.*

Since Juan Carlos I decreed this renovated hospital a national museum in 1988 and named it for his wife, the Reina Sofía's collection of **20th-century art** has grown steadily. A massive new addition is nearing completion, set to open up over 26,000 square meters of new space for visitors to enjoy. A ride up the soaring glass elevators adds to the mystique and character of the museum. The second and fourth floors are mazes of permanent exhibits charting the Spanish avant-garde and contemporary movements. Rooms dedicated to Juan Gris, Joan Miró, and Salvador Dalí display Spain's vital contributions to the Surrealist movement. Miró's works show a spare, colorful abstraction, while Dalí's paintings, including *El gran masturbador (The Great Masturbator)* and *El enigma sin fin (Enigma Without End)*, portray the artist's Freudian nightmares and sexual fantasies.

Picasso's masterpiece, ▓**Guernica,** is the highlight of the Reina Sofía's permanent collection. Now freed from its restrictive glass cover and exile in New York, it depicts the Basque town bombed by the Germans during the Spanish Civil War (see **The Tragedy of Guernica,** p. 560). Picasso denounced the bloodshed in a huge, colorless work of contorted, agonized figures. While many have attempted to explain the allegory behind this work and its components, Picasso himself refused to acknowledge its symbolism; still, most critics insist that the screaming horse represents war and the twisted bull represents Spain. Picasso loaned the canvas to the Museum of Modern Art in New York on the condition that it be returned to Spain when democracy was restored. In 1981, six years after Franco's death, *Guernica* was delivered to the Prado. The subsequent move to the Reina Sofía sparked an international controversy—Picasso's other stipulation had been that the painting hang only in the Prado, to affirm his equivalent status to artists like El Greco and Velázquez. Basques want it relocated to the Guggenheim in Bilbao, but Madrid officials declare it too delicate to move. Preliminary sketches and other Picasso paintings surround *Guernica*, testimony to the breadth of his talent.

▨ MUSEO THYSSEN-BORNEMISZA

On the corner of Po. del Prado and C. Manuel González. M: Banco de España or Atocha. Buses #1, 2, 5, 9, 10, 14, 15, 20, 27, 34, 37, 45, 51, 52, 53, 74, 146, and 150. ☎913 69 01 51; www.museothyssen.org. Open Tu-F 10am-7pm, Su 3-7pm. Last entrance 6:30pm. €6, students with ISIC and seniors €3, under 12 free.

Unlike the Prado and the Reina Sofía, the Thyssen-Bornemisza covers many periods and diverse media; exhibits range from 14th-century canvases to 20th-century sculptures. The museum is housed in the 18th-century **Palacio de Villahermosa** and contains the former collection of the late Baron Heinrich Thyssen-Bornemisza. The baron donated his collection in 1993, and today the museum is the world's most extensive private showcase. In June 2004, a new wing was opened to house the collection of his wife, Baroness Carmen.

The top floor is dedicated to the **Old Masters,** with stars like Hans Holbein's austere *Portrait of Henry VIII* and El Greco's *Annunciation*. The organization of the Thyssen-Bornemisza provokes natural chronological comparisons — note how the representation of the body evolves from Lucas Cranach's *The Nymph of the Spring* to Titian's *Saint Jerome in the Desert* to Anthony van Dyck's *Portrait of Jacques Le Roy.* The Thyssen-Bornemisza's **Baroque** collection, with pieces by Caravaggio, Ribera, and Claude Lorraine, rivals the Prado's.

The movement from the dark canvases of the top floor to the vibrant ones below reflects the revolutionary command of light and arbitrary use of color that became popular in the 17th century. During this period, Dutch works, like Frans Hals's *Family Group in a Landscape,* began to display a mastery of natural light. The **Impressionist** and **Post-Impressionist** collections explode with texture and color— look for works by Renoir, Manet, Degas, Monet, van Gogh, Cézanne, and Matisse. The museum is also home to Europe's only collection of 19th-century American paintings, including Winslow Homer's *The Signal of Distress.*

The highlight of the tour is the museum's **20th-century** collection, which reflects a diversity of styles and philosophies. You can trace the deconstruction of figurative painting, starting with Picasso, Georges Braque, and Juan Gris. From there, observe a split: the vibrant colors and action of Frantisek Kupka *(The Machine Drill)* contrast with the sterility of Piet Mondrian and the Constructivists. Room 45 features great pieces by Picasso (*Corrida de Toros* and *Harlequin with a Mirror*), Marc Chagall, and Wassily Kandinsky. Room 46 ushers in **American Abstract Expressionism** (Pollack, Mark Rothko, Morris Louis, and Willem de Kooning) with its bold enthusiasm. **German Expressionist** artists are also well-represented, with *Summer Clouds* by Emile Nolde, brooding portraits by Max Beckmann, and *The Dream* by Franz Marc. Of the same era is Egon Schiele's *The Old Town,* in which huddled houses peer out over a frozen river. The final room chills with an evocative Lucien Freud portrait and *Hotel Room* by Edward Hopper. A peek across the room, however, is cheering—Henri Magritte's games with broken glass in *La Clef de Champs, Dream Caused by the Flight of a Bumblebee around a Pomegranate* by Dalí, and Joseph Cornell's poetic boxes are sure to please.

MADRID

▶ NIGHTLIFE

Plaza de Santa Ana, the pulsing heart of Huertas, brims with *terrazas*, bars, and live street music. Many bars convert to clubs as night unfolds, spinning house and techno on intimate dance floors. With its variety of styles, Huertas is one of the best places to party. Calle del Príncipe is lined with smaller spots, but check out the *discotecas* on Calle de Atocha. Most locals begin their nights in Huertas and end them, slightly worn out and more than slightly later, in El Centro or Chueca.

BARS

▓ **Cuevas de Sesamo,** C. del Príncipe, 7 (☎913 429 0542). M: Antón Martín. "Descend into these caves like Dante!" (Antonio Machado) is the first of many choice literary tidbits that welcome you to this gem of the Huertas underground. Cheap pitchers of sangria (small €5, large €8.50) and live jazz piano draw cool kids of all ages. The atmosphere is fantastic, but very smoky. Open Su-Th 6pm-2am, F-Sa 6pm-2:30am.

▓ **El Café de Sheherezade,** C. Santa María, 18 (☎913 69 24 74), a block from C. de las Huertas. M: Antón Martín. Recline on opulent pillows while sipping cinnamon tea (€3). Amidst Middle Eastern music and decor, groups cluster around *pipas* (€7-10) that filter sweet tobacco smoke through water. Late nights sometimes end with belly dancing. Open summer Su-Th 6pm-2:30am, F-Sa 6pm-3:30am; winter Su-Th 5pm-2am, F-Sa 5pm-3am.

Trocha, C. Huertas, 55 (☎914 29 78 61; www.trochabar.com). M: Antón Martín or Sol. Come here for *caipirinhas* (€5). The tasty, potent drinks are served in a chill setting with jazz and cushioned wicker couches. Open Su-Th 4:30pm-3am, F-Sa 4:30pm-4am.

El Parnaso, C. de Moratín, 25 (☎686 62 67 53). Off the beaten path, this dadaist bar is packed with eclectic sculptures; an ideal place for a small gathering. Specialty concoctions and Moroccan sweets (€5-7) served in a plush red-upholstered lounge. Groups should call ahead to reserve space. Open Tu-Su 8pm-3am.

La Creación, C. Núñez de Arce, 14. M: Antón Martín, Sevilla, or Sol. Drink hard cider (€4 per bottle), watch passersby, and listen to classic jazz in this hip little bar just off Pl. de Santa Ana. Fresh fruit tapas in summer. Bartenders are experts at pouring cider from great heights. Open Su-Th 7pm-2am, F-Sa 7pm-2:30am.

Mauna Loa, Pl. de Santa Ana, 13 (☎914 29 70 62). M: Sevilla. Feels like Hawaii—birds fly freely and scantily clad patrons get down. Sip on a *fuerte volcano* (€5.80-11.50) at this crowded pre-party destination. Open Su-Th 7pm-2am, F-Sa 7pm-3am.

Viva Madrid, C. Manuel Fernández González, 7 (☎914 29 36 40), off C. Echegaray. M: Sol or Sevilla. *"Lo mejor del mundo"* (the best in the world) is the humble motto of this daytime cafe/nighttime foray. A local favorite for a romantic evening among 20-somethings. Cocktails €7. Open daily 1pm-2am.

BARES MUSICALES

▓ **Cardamomo,** C. Echegaray, 15 (☎913 69 07 57). M: Sevilla. Flamenco and Latin music spins all night. A joyful crowd dances to live music on W nights. Those who prefer to relax retreat to the lounge area. Mixed drinks €7, shots €3. Open daily 9pm-4am.

Café Jazz Populart, C. Huertas, 22 (☎914 29 84 07; www.populart.es). M: Sevilla or Antón Martín. This intimate, smoke-filled scene hosts local and foreign talent. Live jazz, blues, and reggae. Shows daily 11pm-2am. Open daily 6pm-3am.

Café Central, Pl. de Ángel, 10 (☎913 69 41 43), off Pl. de Santa Ana. M: Antón Martín or Sol. Art Deco meets old-world cafe in one of Europe's top jazz venues. Shows nightly. Beer €2.30. Cover €8-15. Open daily 1:30pm-2:30am, F-Sa 1:30pm-3:30am.

La Boca del Lobo, C. Echegaray, 11 (☎914 29 70 13). M: Sevilla. Funk, blues, and rock bands hit this 2-story joint, drawing a varied crowd. Waterfall mirrors in the bathrooms may drench you. Shows W-Th 10:30pm. Cover €6. Open daily 10pm-3:30am.

La Comedia, C. del Príncipe, 16 (☎915 21 51 64). M: Sevilla. Americans feel at home in a crowd dancing to hip-hop, R&B, and reggae. Hit up the DJ with requests; he spins to please. Beer €4.50, mixed drinks €6. Open daily 10pm-4am.

DISCOTECAS

☒ **Kapital,** C. Atocha, 125 (☎914 20 29 06). M: Atocha. 7 floors of *discoteca* insanity. From hip-hop to house, open *terrazas* to cinemas, lose yourself in the madness. Hot, stylish outfits encouraged. Drinks €10. Cover (€12-16) includes 1 drink. *Kapital Love* Su draws a mostly gay crowd and gets going around 2am. Open Th-Su midnight-7am.

Ananda, Estación Atocha, 2. To find this massive garden party, walk down the stairs behind the rotunda at the station. Large *terraza* with multiple bars and a *pijo* (posh) 20-something crowd. Dance in the white room. W and Su transforms into a wild party that rivals weekends. Cover €10, may include 1 drink. Drinks €8. Open daily 11pm-dawn.

No Se Lo Digas a Nadie, C. Ventura de la Vega, 7 (☎913 69 12 27; www.noselodigasa-nadie.foro.st), next to Pl. de Santa Ana. M: Sevilla. Head through the garage doors onto the packed dance floor and squeeze in some dancing along your bar crawl, or play a game of pool upstairs. Cover €7 includes 1 drink. Open Tu-W midnight-3am, Th-Sa until 6am.

Villa Rosa, Pl. de Santa Ana. M: Sol or Sevilla. 21st-century pop meets 15th-century Moorish architecture, with 4 bars. Gyrating bottoms compete with flat-screen TVs for attention. Drinks €7. F-Sa after 2am cover €7. Open M-Sa 11pm-6am.

GRAN VÍA

The neon lights of Broadway and the Champs-Élysées have met their match on Gran Vía. The massive avenue pulsates with the sharp lights of sex shops, McDonald's, and hotels in a 24hr. parade of flashing cars, swishing skirts, and stack-heeled shoes. *Hostal* signs line the horizon, but accommodations are pricier and less comfortable than in other areas, and you'll need your wits about you late at night.

MADRID

ACCOMMODATIONS

Hostal A. Nebrija, Gran Vía, 67, 8th fl., elevator A (☎915 47 73 19). M: Pl. de España. A grandson continues a family tradition with pleasant rooms offering magnificent views of the city. Tidy building generously furnished in classic style. All rooms have TV and fan, but shared baths. Singles €26; doubles €36; triples €49. AmEx/MC/V. ❸

Hostal-Residencia Alibel, Gran Vía, 44, 8th fl. (☎915 21 00 51). M: Callao. Well-lit, spacious rooms with great views, high ceilings, and a cool blue color scheme show off Alibel's recent face-lift. All have private bath, TV, fan, and balcony. Perks include lounge area and free wireless Internet. Doubles €40; triples €50. ❹

Hostal Santillan, Gran Vía, 64, 8th fl. (☎/fax 915 48 23 28; www.hostalsantillan.com). M: Pl. de España. Take the glass elevator to the top of this gorgeous building. Friendly management, the Beatles, and gifts from travelers past welcome you. Simple rooms with shower, sink, TV, and fan. Singles €30; doubles €45; triples €60. MC/V. ❸

Hostal Lauria, Gran Vía, 50, 4th fl. (☎/fax 915 41 91 82; www.geocities.com/hostal lauria). M: Callao. Spotless rooms with large beds, baths, phones, fans, and TVs. Lounge with TV. English spoken. Singles €35; doubles €45; triples €64. MC/V. ❸

Hostal Margarita, Gran Vía, 50, 5th fl. (☎/fax 915 47 35 49). M: Callao. Warm and inviting family offers simple rooms with large windows, TV, and telephone, most with street views. TV lounge and big kitchen. Laundry €10. Singles €25; doubles with shower €36, with bath €38; triples with bath €48. MC/V. ❸

Hostal Triana, C. de la Salud, 13, 1st fl. (☎915 32 68 12; www.hostaltriana.com). M: Callao or Gran Vía. With white walls, soothing environment, and attentive receptionists, Hostal Triana feels like the spa of the hostel world. All rooms have TV, fan, and bath. Reserve 2 weeks ahead. Singles €35; doubles €45, with A/C €47; triples €60. ❸

Hostal-Residencia Lamalonga, Gran Vía, 56, 2nd fl. (☎915 47 26 31). M: Santo Domingo. Rooms with views, A/C, TV, bath, and phone. Singles €40; doubles €48; triples €65. 10% discount for stays over 5 days. IVA not included. MC/V. ❹

🍴 FOOD

Tourists and locals alike battle their love/hate relationship with the golden arches, KFC, and Burger King under the shimmering lights of Gran Vía. Long lines at fast-food joints demonstrate that convenience and time often beat out fine dining. Fear not—there are still some culinary diamonds hidden in the rough. Small markets can be found in Chueca, a couple streets north of Gran Vía.

🏅 La Finca de Susana, C. Arlabán, 4 (☎913 69 35 57). M: Sevilla. Probably the most popular lunch eatery in all of Madrid, where delicious fine dining and swanky surroundings come at an extremely low price. *Menú* M-F €7.30. Be prepared to wait in line. Open daily 1-3:45pm and 8:30-11:45pm. AmEx/MC/V. ❷

Museo Chicote, C. Gran Vía, 12 (☎915 32 97 80). M: Gran Vía. Lose yourself in green leather booths amidst pictures of the stars, from Ava Gardner and John Wayne to Lola Flores and Luis Buñuel. Throw back a cocktail with Madrid's socialites after 11pm. Lunchtime *menú* €10. Lunch served 1-4pm. Open M-Sa 8am-3am. ❷

El Novillo Carioca, C. Legitanos, 3 (☎915 47 10 62). M: Pl de España or Santo Domingo. Cheesy decor, but relaxed atmosphere and delicious food. €15 buys a fresh salad bar with cold dishes and choice of 2 kinds of succulent barbecue. Desserts €3-4.50, *caipirinhas* €4.50. Open Tu-Sa 1:30-4pm and 8pm-midnight, Su 8pm-midnight. ❸

👁 SIGHTS

Urban planners paved Gran Vía in 1910 to link C. Princesa with Pl. de Cibeles, creating a cosmopolitan center of life in the city. After Madrid gained wealth as a neutral supplier during WWI, the city funneled much of its earnings into making Gran Vía one of the world's great thoroughfares. In its heyday, Hemmingway described it as a cross between Broadway and Fifth Avenue. To see it today, just throw yourself in among the throngs on the sidewalk and keep up the pace.

Sol's shopping streets converge at Gran Vía's highest elevation in **Plaza de Callao** (M: Callao). C. Postigo San Martín splits off southward, where you'll find the famed **Convento de las Descalzas Reales** (p. 115). Westward from Pl. de Callao (left when facing the conspicuous sex shop), Gran Vía descends toward **Plaza de España** (M: Pl. de España), where a statue commemorates Spain's most prized fictional duo: Don Quixote and Sancho Panza. Locals relax on the shady grass, but you're better off going to the bottom of the park (with their backs to Quixote) and turning left toward the Royal Gardens, or right to **El Templo de Debod.** Next to Pl. de España are two of Madrid's tallest skyscrapers, the **Telefónica building** (1929) and the **Edificio de España** (1953), which line up symmetrically with the fountains. Lewis S. Weeks of the Chicago School designed the Telefónica building, the tallest concrete building at the time (81m), which was used as a lookout by Republican forces during the Civil War. The Edificio de España, designed by Franco's architect, represents the other side of the struggle. Tucked between them on C. San Leonardo is the small **Iglesia de San Marcos,** a Neoclassical church composed of five intersecting ellipses—this Euclidean dream of a building doesn't have a straight line.

NIGHTLIFE

The deepest drum and bass pounds in the boisterous landmark clubs on the side streets of Gran Vía well into the early morning. Subtlety has never been a strong suit of this area, nor is it known for its safety; a mix of sketchy tourists and sketchier locals makes Gran Vía less than ideal for late-night wandering.

Ocho y Medio Club, C. Mesonero Romanos, 13 (☎915 413 500; www.tripfamily.com). Where the cool kids go for their late-night *discoteca* fix. F local hipsters dance to electronica remixes of their favorite tunes—DJs reach back to the Beastie Boys and Blur and segue into the latest sub-chart hits. Th is **Pink Flamingo,** a gay disco; Sa is **Dark Hole,** a goth-themed party. Drinks €7. Cover €8, includes 1 drink. Open Th-F 1-6am.

Pasapoga, Gran Vía, 37 (☎915 47 57 11; www.pasapoga.com), around the corner from Pl. de Callao. M: Callao. Gay nightlife explodes on weekends, especially Sa. Strut down the staircase like the *reina que tú eres*. Spectacular chandelier. Beautiful people dance to pumping music. Disco F and Sa. Cover €15. Open Tu-Su 6pm-dawn.

Cool, C. Isabel la Católica, 6 (☎917 333 505). M: Santo Domingo. Though expensive, this club has earned its name. Mesmerizing video projections set the mood as a mix of locals, Brits, and Americans dance the night away. Drinks €9. Cover €15. Open Th midnight-6am, F-Sa midnight-7am.

MALASAÑA AND CHUECA

Split down the middle by C. Fuencarral, Malasaña and Chueca are two of Madrid's best hard-core party pits. Beyond outrageous nightlife and numerous watering holes, the area offers a wide range of excellent restaurants, great shopping, and charming plazas. Chueca is hip, fun, funky, and wild. While it's clearly the pleasure dome of Madrid's gay population, it offers something for everyone.

ACCOMMODATIONS

Hostales and *pensiones* in Malasaña and Chueca are usually located on the upper floors of older buildings, and accommodations can be a bit pricier here than in other areas. Newly renovated rooms are chock full of amenities but lack authentic flavor. Buses #3, 40, and 149 run along C. de Fuencarral and C. Hortaleza. Metro stops Chueca, Gran Vía, and Tribunal service the area.

Hostal Medieval, C. Fuencarral, 46, 2nd fl. (☎915 22 25 49). M: Tribunal. Wonderful, older-feeling, pink rooms with high ceilings, big windows, showers, and sinks. Central location and kind owners make this a great base from which to explore Chueca. TV lounge honors the royal family. Singles €22; doubles €30, with bath €36; triples €44. ❷

Hostal-Residencia Domínguez, C. Santa Brígida, 1, 1st fl. (☎/fax 915 32 15 47). M: Tribunal. Offers a modern feel at low prices. The doubles on the 2nd and 3rd fl. are immaculate and brand new. Hospitable young owner is ready with tips on local nightlife. English spoken. Singles €22, with bath €29.50; doubles with bath and A/C €40. ❷

Hostal Palacios/Hostal Ribadavia, C. Fuencarral, 25, 1st-3rd fl. (☎915 31 10 58). M: Gran Vía. Both run by the same cheerful family. Palacio offers tiled rooms with modern furniture; Ribadavia's are comfortable and have TVs. All have fans. Singles €20, with bath €32; doubles €30/€38; triples €48/€54; quads with bath €60. MC/V. ❷

Hispa Domus, C. San Bartolomé, 4, 2nd fl. (☎915 23 81 27; www.hispadomus.com). M: Chueca. Gay-friendly. Rooms with A/C, bath, satellite TV, free Internet, and postmodern decor. Reservations required. Singles €42; doubles €59. MC/V. ❹

THE RIGHT TO PARTY

After 40 years of Franco-imposed repression, Madrid was a cultural explosion waiting to happen. Franco's death in 1975 served as a catalyst for change—not one day passed before every newspaper printed a controversial photo on its front page. *El Destapeo* ("the uncorking" or "uncovering" that followed Franco's demise) and *La Movida* ("the Movement," which took place a few years later) exploded in Madrid, inspiring political diversity, apolitical revelry, and eccentricity of all kinds. Filmmaker Pedro Almodóvar became a reflection of the heady times and their most famous participant, creating farcical films about loony grandmothers, outgoing young women, unapologetic homosexuals, and troubled students. Gradually, *La Movida* became too much for the city. Artists and club-rats were forced to give up their favorite pastimes for practical jobs—no one could afford to keep up the careless and eccentric lifestyle that *La Movida* represented. Remnants of *La Movida* are still visible, however, in today's outrageous clubs, ambitious bars, and avant garde art centers, as well as in the excitement of young *madrileños* planning to *ir de marcha* ("to party," literally "to go on the march"). Madrid is one of the hardest-working and hardest-partying cities in the world.

Hotel Mónaco, C. Barbieri, 5 (☎915 22 46 30; fax 21 16 01). M: Chueca. In the 1900s a brothel catering to high society, it still encourages naughtiness. Frescoes of Eve-like temptresses excite the imagination while hundreds of mirrors and lush, satin beds help make it reality. Green-lit lounge and a lively bar-cafeteria area. Adventurous older crowd. Simple singles €75; triples €105. AmEx/MC/V. ❹

Hostal Chelo, C. Hortaleza, 17, 3rd fl. (☎915 32 70 33; www.chelo.com). M: Gran Vía. In addition to its great location, the biggest draw of this *hostal* is the helpful staff, educated on everything about Madrid. Rooms are clean and spacious with TV, fan, and bath. English spoken. Singles €20, with bath €27; doubles €40; triples €51. ❸

Hostal Abril, C. Fuencarral, 39, 4th fl. (☎915 31 53 38). M: Tribunal or Gran Vía. Rooms like college dorms, but cleaner and cozier; ones with balconies surprisingly tranquil. Singles €20, with shower €22; doubles with bath €38; triples with bath €48. ❷

Barbieri International Youth Hostel, C. Barbieri, 15. (☎915 31 92 58; www.barbierihostel.com). Shared rooms with bunks are cramped but cheap. Lively English-speaking crew meets in kitchen and common room, then heads out. Expect to pay for services; Internet €0.50 per 15min., luggage storage €1, towels €1. Quiet time 11pm and check-out 10am strictly enforced. 8-bed dorms €14.50; 4-bed dorms €15; 2-bed dorms €16. ❶

Hotel San Lorenzo, C. Clavel, 8 (☎915 21 30 57). M: Gran Vía. A former hostel, San Lorenzo has renovated 3 floors. Quiet rooms with new furniture, baths, A/C, TV, and phone. Also has a lounge, coffee bar, room service, and laundry. Reservations recommended. Singles €50; doubles €75-85. IVA not included. AmEx/MC/V. ❹

◧ FOOD

Before the nighttime insanity, Malasaña and Chueca offer the best dining options in all of Madrid. The area has exceptional vegetarian, Middle Eastern, and Italian eateries. Most are small and intimate, with high quality and low prices.

▧ **Al-Jaima, Cocina del Desierto,** C. Barbieri, 1 (☎915 23 11 42). M: Gran Vía or Chueca. Lebanese, Moroccan, and Egyptian food transports you to North Africa. Specialties include *pastela*, couscous, *kebaps*, and *tajine* (1st courses €4, main courses €8). Try *pollo con higos y miel* (chicken with figs and honey). Open daily 1:30-4pm and 9pm-midnight. Dinner reservations highly recommended, sometimes required. ❷

Pizzeria Mastropiero, C. San Vicente Ferrer, 34. M: Tribunal or Bilbao. Revolutionary politics meet gustatory pleasure every night in this cozy all-natural pizzeria. Friendly owner bakes pizza of all kinds (small €8-9, large €16-18) and serves up huge slices of spinach pie (€3, enough for 2). If you're lucky, you may get a free *postre,* but it's worth paying for (€2.50). Open Su-Th 9pm-1am, F-Sa 9pm-1:30am. ❷

La Granja de Said, C. San Andrés, 11 (☎915 32 87 93). M: Tribunal or Bilbao. Dim yellow lights glow above tiled walls in this Arab-themed restaurant. Youthful crowd, friendly owner, and big portions. Lunch *menú* €8.50. Open daily noon-midnight. MC/V. ❷

El Rey del Barrio, C. Hernán Cortés, 19 (☎915 32 97 01). M: Chueca. Authentic yet creative Mexican restaurant. Try the fruit-infused tequila. Lunch *menú* €8. Tacos and enchiladas €9-10; 2-person *menús* €12-25; desserts €5. 2-for-1 happy hour 8:30-10pm. Open Tu-Th 1:30-4pm and 8pm-1am, F-Sa 1:30-4pm and 8pm-2am, Su 2-5pm. ❸

Pizzeria Vesuvio, C. Hortaleza, 4 (☎915 21 51 71). M: Gran Vía. Mix and match pasta and sauce or try the 30+ varieties of personal pizzas. Fresh food and fast service. Meals €3.30-5. Open M-Th 1-4pm and 8pm-midnight, F-Sa 1-4pm and 8pm-1am. ❶

Chez Pomme, C. Pelayo, 4 (☎915 32 16 46). M: Chueca. Quiet, artsy spot that serves filling portions of French-fusion vegetarian (and non-veggie) cuisine. Try the *berenjenas al horno* (baked eggplant), one of the many tofu dishes, or a creative salad (€5-8.50). *Menú* €8.50-9, dinner *menú* €14. Open M-Th 1:30-4:30pm and 9pm-midnight, F-Sa 2-4:30pm and 9pm-12:30am. MC/V. ❷

Pizzaiolo, C. Hortaleza, 84 (☎913 19 29 64). M: Chueca. Authentic thin-crust Italian pizzas made with fresh ingredients. Friendly staff and bright, casual atmosphere. Pies €8-9. Open M-F 1-5pm and 8:30pm-1am, Sa-Su 8pm-2am. ❷

Vegaviana, C. Pelayo, 35 (☎913 08 03 81). M: Chueca. Wholesome vegetarian cuisine. Very popular with locals and tourists. Lunch *menú* €7.90, meals €7.50-8. Pizzas €6.50. Open Tu-Sa 1:30-4pm and 9pm-midnight. No smoking. MC/V. ❷

La Sacristía, C. las Infantas, 28 (☎915 22 09 45). M: Gran Vía or Chueca. Creative Spanish cuisine, including 60 types of *bacalao* (cod, €16). Lunch *menú* €10. Choose the more casual bar seating for a shorter menu and a cheaper meal (lunch and dinner only). Open M-F 8am-midnight, F-Sa 8am-2am. AmEx/MC/V. ❹

Stop Madrid, C. Hortaleza, 11 (☎915 21 88 87). Classic tapas and *canapés* (€2-3.50) served in a marbled former *jamonería* (ham shop). Extensive wine list for under €2 per glass. Open M-Tu noon-1am, W-Sa noon-2am, Su 1:30-4pm and 7:30pm-12:30am. ❸

🔘 SIGHTS

Devoid of the numerous historic monuments and palaces that characterize most of Madrid, the labyrinthine streets of Malasaña and Chueca house countless undocumented "sights," from platform shoe stores to spontaneous street performers. These streets are an ultra-modern, funkified relief for travelers weary of crucifixes and brushstrokes. Chueca, in particular, remains the ideal area for people-watching and boutique shopping. By night, both of these districts bristle with Madrid's alternative scene. Overall, most of the scenery is the people, though the region between **Calle de Fuencarral** and **Calle de San Bernardo** contains some of Madrid's most avant-garde architecture and current art exhibitions.

IGLESIA DE LAS SALESAS REALES. Bourbon King Fernando VI commissioned this church in 1758 at the request of his wife, Doña Bárbara. The Baroque-Neoclassical domed church is clad in granite, with sculptures by Alfonso Vergaza and a dome painting by the brothers González Velázquez. The church's ostentatious facade and interior prompted critics to pun on the queen's name: "Barbaric queen, barbaric tastes, barbaric building, barbarous expense," they said, giving rise to the expression *"¡qué bárbaro!"* Today, the phrase refers to absurdity, extravagance, or just plain craziness. *(C. Bárbara de Braganza, 1. M: Colón. From Pl. Colón, go down Po. de Recoletos and take a right onto C. de Bárbara de Braganza. ☎913 19 48 11. Open M-F 8:30am-1pm and 5:30-9pm. Not open to tourists during mass.)*

MUSEO MUNICIPAL. An intricate facade welcomes visitors to explore Madrid's history through its art. Exhibits feature paintings, prints, and photographs that document the changes and consistencies of this dynamic city over the past four centuries. Though much of the museum is under renovation until 2007, a small, well-curated exhibit is open to the public. Highlights include lithographs of the 1837 revolution and paintings of chivalric festivities in the Pl. Mayor. *(C. de Fuencarral, 78, right outside M: Tribunal. ☎915 88 86 72. Open Tu-F 9:30am-8pm, Sa-Su 10am-2pm. Free.)*

MUSEO ROMÁNTICO. Housed in a 19th-century mansion, this museum is a time capsule of the Romantic period's decorative arts. However, it is closed for renovations until some point in 2006. *(C. San Mateo, 13. M: Alonso Martínez. ☎914 48 10 45; www.mcu.es/nmuseos/romantico.)*

🎆 NIGHTLIFE

Chueca and Malasaña come to life in the early evening, especially in **Plaza Chueca** and **Plaza Dos de Mayo**. By sunset, these plazas are social meccas—places to hang out, meet your friends, and get drunk. A more economical evening might start out with a *"mini"* of sangria (1 liter; €4.50), *calimocho* (€3), or beer (€3.50) from **Bar Nike**, C. Augusto Figueroa, one street below Pl. Chueca. (☎915 21 16 84. Open 7am-2:30am.) Bar-filled streets radiate from the plazas; though many people eventually migrate away, this area remains busy with activity well into *la madrugada* (dawn). The alcoholic circus that is Chueca at night guarantees entertainment. Beyond the plazas, most nightlife consists of classy cafes, cruisy bars, and shady clubs. Much of the dance music is saccharine techno-pop, but rock 'n rollers and jazz mavens can find their niches too. Though Chueca is largely gay, most of its establishments are quite mixed. The area is ideal for bar-hopping until 2 or 3am, when it's time to hit the clubs near Sol, El Centro, and Gran Vía.

🎆 **Acuarela,** C. Gravina, 10 (☎915 22 21 43). M: Chueca. A welcome alternative to the club scene. Buddhas and candles surround cushy antique furniture, inspiring good conversation, and a nice buzz. Coffees and teas €1.80-4.50. Liquor €3.20-5. Open daily summer 3pm-3am; winter 11pm-3am.

El Clandestino, C. del Barquillo, 34 (☎915 21 55 63). M: Chueca. A chill 20-something crowd drinks and debates at the bar upstairs, then heads down to the caves to nod and dance to the DJ's acid jazz, fusion, and funk selections. Mixed drinks €6, beer €3. Live music most Th-Sa at 11 or 11:30pm. Open M-Sa 6pm-3am.

Tupperware, Corredera Alta de San Pablo, 20 (☎915 94 21 09; www.planx.tk). M: Tribunal. Where latte sippers go for liquor. The mural of über-cool hipsters on the wall is a mirror of the locals; soul patches, Buddy Holly glasses, and horizontal stripes galore. DJ plays a great mix of rock and pop favorites from all ages, so feel free to dance, even if the locals are too cool. Mixed drinks €4.50-5. Open daily 9pm-3:20am.

Vía Láctea, C. Velarde, 18. M: Tribunal. Dive into the Brit underground scene nightly 9-11pm, when soft drinks and beer on tap are €2-3.50 each. After midnight, a late 20s crowd gets groovy between the pink walls. The loudspeakers can be deafening. Th offers funk and *afrodisia*. Open daily 7:30pm-3am.

Nueva Visión, C. Velarde, 13. M: Tribunal. Hey! Ho! Let's Go! This hole-in-the-wall rocks out to punky music from the 70s and 80s (Ramones, Dead Kennedys, The Clash), and sells drinks for a song (8pm-midnight 3 *"minis"* (liters) of beer or *calimocho* for €7, shots €1). Open Th-Sa 8pm-3:30am.

Mama Inés, C. Hortaleza, 22 (☎915 23 23 33; www.mamaines.com). M: Chueca. Chic cafe-bar with perfect diva lighting. Great for drinks and conversation. Good desserts (€3-4), light meals (€5-8), and teas (€1.60.) Food is more expensive at night. Open Su-Th 10am-2am, F-Sa 10am-3am.

Café la Palma, C. de la Palma, 62 (☎915 22 50 31). M: San Bernardo or Noviciado. Slip back into the comfy pillows of this decadent venue for live music and late-night whispering. Beer €2.20. Mixed drinks €5. Shows Th-Sa at 10pm range from jazz to rock to folk. No concerts Jul-Aug. Open daily 4pm-3:30am.

Why Not?, C. San Bartolomé, 7. M: Chueca. When in doubt around 2am, people flock to Why Not? Small, well-air-conditioned downstairs bar packed almost every night of the week with a wild, mixed crowd. Mixed drinks €8, beer €4. Open daily 11pm-6am. The same owners manage **Polana,** C. Barbieri, 8-10 (☎915 32 33 05), which gets going around 2:30am, blasting campy Spanish pop music for a mixed crowd. Open M-Th and Su 11pm-4am, F-Sa 11pm-8am.

Star's Café Dance, C. Marqués de Valdeiglesias, 5 (☎915 22 27 12). M: Chueca. A stylish cafe during the week turned vivacious dance club downstairs on weekends. Music varies; afternoons more jazzy, nights are techno. Mixed drinks €7, beer €5. Come well-dressed. Open M-Tu 1pm-2am, W 1pm-3am, Th 1pm-3:30am, F-Sa 1pm-4am.

El Truco, C. de Gravina, 10 (☎915 32 89 21). M: Chueca. Watch the smoky windows from Pl. Chueca to see shadows of people dancing inside. This lesbian-friendly bar features local artists' works and pop artists' hits. Outdoor seating in Pl. Chueca is a welcome alternative to the packed, noisy interior. Open Su-Th 8pm-2:30am, F-Sa 9pm-4am. Same owners run **Escape,** also on the plaza. Open F-Sa midnight-6am.

ARGÜELLES AND MONCLOA

The 19th century witnessed the growth of several neighborhoods around the core of the city north and northwest of the Palacio Real. Today, the area known as Argüelles and the zone around **Calle San Bernardo** form a cluttered mixture of middle-class homes, student apartments, and bohemian hangouts, all brimming with cultural activity. Heavily bombarded during the Spanish Civil War, Argüelles inspired Chilean poet Pablo Neruda to write *España en el corazón*.

High-schoolers dominate Moncloa's streets. Unless you're Lolita, or looking for one, the only reason to leave Madrid's better nighttime areas for Moncloa is **Los Bajos,** a concrete megaplex of diminutive bars serving incredibly **cheap drinks.** The bars tend to be slightly grimy, the dance floors small, and the crowd pubescent, but at €1 each, the *chupitos* (shots) are hard to turn down. Bars are usually only open F-Sa and close around 2-3am. From M: Moncloa, align yourself with the center of the imposing Ejército del Aire building on C. Princesa and cross the street under the double archway. Walk one block up C. Hilarion Eslava and turn left onto C. Fernando el Católico. Los Bajos is a few blocks down on the left.

⚐ ACCOMMODATIONS

Albergue Juvenil Santa Cruz de Marcenado (HI), C. Santa Cruz de Marcenado, 28 (☎915 47 45 32; fax 48 11 96). M: Argüelles. From the metro, walk 1 block down C. Alberto Aguilera away from C. Princesa, turn right onto C. Serrano Jóver, then left onto C. Santa Cruz de Marcenado. Lounge is great for mingling and late-night card playing. The 72 beds fill quickly, even in winter. Separate floors for men and women. Some English spoken. Rooms have cubbies, but use the hall lockers (€2 extra). Breakfast and sheets included. Laundry €3.50. 3-day max. stay. Quiet hours after midnight. Reception daily 9am-10pm. 1:30am curfew. Reserve in advance by mail, fax, or in person, or arrive early and pray. Closed Christmas and New Year's. €3.50 extra per night without HI card. Dorms €7.80, 26 and over €11.60. ●

Hostal-Residencia Ríos, C. Juan Álvarez Mendizabal, 44, 4th fl. (☎915 59 51 56). M: Ventura Rodríguez or Argüelles. From M: Argüelles, face the shrubbery, walk 3 blocks left (south) down C. Princesa to C. Rey Francisco, go 3 blocks to C. Juan Álvarez Mendizabal, and turn left again. Nothing fancy: just clean, cheap, comfortable rooms close to the park, some with A/C (€5 extra). Singles €15; doubles with shower €30; triples €45. **Hostal Pérez,** in the same building, 3rd fl. (☎915 41 92 90), offers similarly simple, clean rooms with firm beds. Singles €13; doubles with shower €28. ❶

FOOD

Argüelles is a middle-class neighborhood near the Ciudad Universitaria. It's geared toward locals rather than tourists and is therefore full of inexpensive markets, moderately priced restaurants, and informal neighborhood bars. Check out the *terrazas* on Po. del Pintor Rosales overlooking the park.

Ananias, C. Galileo, 9 (☎914 48 68 01). M: Argüelles, a left off C. Alberto Aguilera. *Torero* paraphernalia covers the walls in the front room, while regulars enjoy *castellano* cuisine in the elegance of the back room. Entrees €7.40-15. Open Su 1-4pm, M-Tu and Th-Sa 1-4pm and 9pm-midnight. AmEx/MC/V. ❸

La Crêperie, Po. del Pintor Rosales, 28 (☎915 48 23 58). M: Ventura Rodríguez. The cherub decorations are almost as sweet as the dessert crepes (€2.70-4.70). Eat lunch and dinner crepes (€3.85-6.50) on the chic Po. del Pintor Rosales *terraza*. Open Su-Th 1:30-4:15pm and 8pm-1am, F-Sa 1:30-4:15pm and 8pm-1:15am. ❶

Cáscaras, C. Ventura Rodríguez, 7 (☎915 42 83 36). M: Ventura Rodríguez. Sleek interior enhances the dining experience. Popular for tapas, *pinchos*, and ice-cold Mahou beer in the early afternoon and evening. Exotic vegetarian entrees €6-8. Open M-Th 7am-1am, F 7am-2am, Sa 10am-2am, Su 10am-1am. AmEx/MC/V. ❷

La Vaca Argentina, Po. del Pintor Rosales, 52 (☎915 59 66 05). M: Moncloa or Argüelles. Follow C. Marqués de Urquijo downhill, then take a left on Po. del Pintor Rosales. One of 10 in Madrid, this restaurant is famous for its steak (€7-27) and cowhide wallpaper. Salads €5-7. Open daily 1-5pm and 9pm-midnight. AmEx/MC/V. ❹

⦿ SIGHTS

▧ **MUSEO DE AMÉRICA.** This under-appreciated museum reopened after painstaking renovations and is now a must-see. It documents the cultures of the Americas' pre-Columbian civilizations and the legacy of Spanish conquest with detail and insight. The wealth of Pre-Columbian artifacts include tools, pottery, codices, ceremonial and daily dress, funeral shrouds, and shrunken heads. Colonial accounts and artwork provide insight into the conquistadors' perspectives on the peoples they encountered. Especially fascinating are instructional paintings depicting mixed families and the various ethnic identities assigned to their offspring. To fully appreciate the museum's offerings, visitors should set aside an entire morning or afternoon for all the exhibits. Reading knowledge of Spanish is helpful for detailed understanding, although the English brochure provides a solid overview. (*Av. de los Reyes Católicos, 6, next to the Faro de Moncloa. ☎915 49 26 41. M: Moncloa. Open Tu-Su 9:30am-3pm. €3, students €1.50, under 18 and over 65 free. Su free.*)

TEMPLO DE DEBOD. Built by King Adijalamani of Meröe in the 2nd century BC, it's the only Egyptian temple in Spain. The Egyptian government shipped the temple stone by stone to Spain in appreciation of Spanish archaeologists who helped rescue the Abu Simbel temples from the floods of the Aswan dam. The temple was originally built to honor Isis and Ammon, and was elaborated by Egyptian monarchs and later, Roman emperors Augustus and Tiberius. The **Parque de la Montaña** is home to the temple and two of its three original gateways and provides a peaceful haven with beautiful views. At ▓**sunset,** marvel at the landscape from the look-out points. *(M: Pl. de España or Ventura Rodríguez. Buses #1 and 74. From the metro, walk down C. Ventura Rodríguez to Parque de la Montaña; the temple is on the left. ☎917 65 10 08; www.munimadrid.es/templodebod. Open Apr.-Sept. Tu-F 10am-2pm and 4-8pm, Sa-Su 10am-2pm; Oct.-Mar. Tu-F 9:45am-1:45pm and 4:15-5:15pm, Sa-Su 10am-2pm. Closed M. Free. Park open daily year-round, free.)*

ERMITA DE SAN ANTONIO DE LA FLORIDA.

Although out of the way, the Ermita is worth the trouble. It contains Goya's pantheon—a frescoed dome that arches above his buried corpse. Goya's skull, apparently stolen by a phrenologist, was missing when the corpse arrived from Bordeaux. On June 13th, single *madrileñas* offer their faith (and blood) to San Antonio in exchange for his help in the husband-hunt. The women line the baptismal font with thirty pins and then press their hands into them; the number of resulting pin-pricks represents how many *novios* (boyfriends) they'll have in the coming year. *(M: Príncipe Pío. From the metro go right onto Po. de la Florida and walk to the first traffic circle. The Ermita is on the right side of the street. ☎915 42 07 22. Open Tu-F 10am-2pm and 4-8pm, Sa-Su 10am-2pm. Free.)*

CASA DEL CAMPO. Take the **Teleférico** *(☎915 41 74 50; one way €2.90, round-trip €4.20; open M-F noon-9:30pm, Sa-Su noon-10pm)* from Po. del Pintor Rosales into Madrid's largest park. Shaded by pines, oaks, and cypresses, families, joggers, and walkers roam the grounds by day. Early morning reveals evidence of questionable nighttime activities; it's wise to stay away after dark. Inside the amusement park, **Parque de Atracciones,** relive your childhood on the roller coaster. One of Madrid's largest pools is in the corner of the park, next to M: Lago. *(Take bus #33 or M: Batán. Walk up the main street away from the lake. ☎914 63 29 00; www.parquedeatracciones.es. Entrance with 2 rides €9.60, additional rides €1.50. Open Su-F noon-11pm, Sa noon-midnight.)* The **Zoo/Aquarium,** 5min. away, features gorillas, leopards, and a dolphin show. *(☎915 12 37 70. Open M-F 10:30am-8pm, Sa-Su 10:30am-9:30pm. Mid-summer M-W 10:30am-9pm, Th-Sa 10:30am-midnight. €13.10, under 7 €10.60.)*

MUSEO CERRALBO. Ah, the Belle Epoch! This museum displays the collections of the Marqués de Cerralbo in all their ornate, eclectic, 19th-century *fin de siecle* glory. Highlights include El Greco's *Ecstasy of St. Francis* in the chapel, collections

AMONG THE STARS

During Madrid's *Veranos de la Villa,* the Centro Cultural Conde Duque draws *madrileños* and visitors for an open-air music festival loaded with international stars. The past two years have seen artists like Caetano Veloso, Cesaria Evora, Bonnie Raitt, Ibrahim Ferrer, Dido, Wynton Marsalis, and a host of jazz, rock, and flamenco artists. August and September feature dance and opera. Take a break from sightseeing to attend this festival in the cultural center of Madrid.

The festival also breaks loose in the Casa de America, in the Jardines de Sabatini (near the Palacio Real), and in the streets, with free performances in various plazas around the city center. Particularly moving was last July's concert in the Pl. Mayor, commemorating the victims of the March 11 terrorist attacks.

This is also an opportune time to experience one of Spain's oldest and most traditional types of performance—*zarzuela.* This is Spain's very own breed of opera, which is really more of a cross between opera and musical comedy. These performances are often amusing as they portray the more patriarchal gender roles of *fin de siècle* Spain.

Centro Cultural Conde Duque, C. Conde Duque, 9-11. ☎915 88 58 61 or 88 59 28; www.munimadrid.es/condeduque. M: San Bernardo or Ventura Rodríguez. Concerts run late June to July. Free to €30. Contact Caixa Catalunya for tickets ☎902 10 12 12.

of battle-scarred European and Japanese arms, the perfect bathtub, and a golden ballroom lined with mirrors and capped by a ceiling fresco of tumbling revelers. *(C. Ventura Rodríguez, 17. ☎915 47 36 46; www.museocerralbo.mcu.es. M: Ventura Rodríguez or Pl. de España. Open Tu-Sa 9:30am-3pm, Su 10am-3pm. €2.40, students €1.20, under 18 and over 65 free. W and Su free.)*

OTHER SIGHTS. The **Parque del Oeste** is a large, sloping park known for the **Rosaleda** (rose garden) at its bottom. A yearly competition determines which rose will be added to the permanent collection. The garden is best viewed in late-spring to early summer, when the flowers are most voluptuous. *(M: Moncloa. From the metro, take C. Princesa. Garden open daily 10am-8pm.)* A prime example of Fascist Neoclassicism, the arcaded **Cuartel General del Aire** (*Ejército del Aire;* Air Force Headquarters) commands the view on the other side of the Arco de la Victoria (by the Moncloa metro station). The renovation of Felipe V's soldiers' barracks has produced one of Madrid's finest cultural centers, the **Centro Cultural Conde Duque,** which hosts traveling exhibitions and is home to the **Museo Municipal de Arte Contemporáneo.** *(C. Conde Duque, 11. Centro ☎915 88 58 34, Museo 88 59 28; www.munimadrid.es/museoartecontemporaneo. M: San Bernardo. Open Tu-Sa 10am-4pm and 5:30-9pm, Su 10:30am-2:30pm. Free.)* The **Faro de Moncloa** is a 92m high metal observation tower near the Museo de América that offers views of the city. On a clear day, you can see El Escorial. *(Av. Arco de la Victoria. ☎915 44 81 04. Open Tu-Su 10am-2pm and 5-8pm. €1, over 65 and under 10 €0.50.)*

BILBAO

The area north of Glorieta de Bilbao (M: Bilbao), in the "V" formed by C. Fuencarral and C. Luchana including Pl. de Olavide, is the ethnic food nexus of Madrid; it overflows with bars, clubs, cafes, and restaurants of all nationalities. **Calle Hartzenbusch** and **Calle Cisneros** present endless options for cheap tapas to the youthful crowd that swarms the area at night. In the student-filled streets radiating from **Glorieta de Bilbao,** it's easy to find a cheap drink. Although discos are plentiful, no one comes here to dance; it's the *terrazas* that are packed until late with lively customers sipping Mahou beer on Pl. de Olavide, C. Fuencarral, and C. Luchana.

🍴 FOOD

▨ Osteria Il Regno de Napoli, C. San Andrés, 21 (☎914 45 63 00). From Gl. de Bilbao, head 1 block down C. Carranza; turn left onto C. San Andres. Delicious Italian food in an understatedly hip setting. Lunch *menú* €10, dinner entrees €9-12. Try the penne Napoli, with shrimp in a white wine and fresh tomato sauce. Reserve on weekends. Open M-F 2-4pm and 9pm-midnight, Sa 9pm-midnight, Su 2-4pm. AmEx/MC/V. ❷

El Carabinero, C. Cardenal Cisneros, 33 (☎914 47 68 28). A well-loved local spot specializing in seafood and rice dishes; expect to pay €15-18 per person. Don't worry if you can't get a table right away: pass the time at the bar with sangria and some tapas. *Raciones* €4.50-18, lunch *menú* M-F €7.50. Open M-Sa 1-5pm and 8pm-1am. ❹

Collage, C. Olid, 6 (☎914 48 45 62), 3rd street on the right off C. Fuencarral. M: Bilbao. A group of Swedish chefs mix and match in style. Entrees €11-17.50. *Menú* €7.80. Open M-F 1:30-4pm, Th-Sa 9pm-midnight. AmEx/MC/V. ❸

Bar Samara, C. Cardenal Cisneros, 13 (☎914 48 80 56). From M: Bilbao, walk up C. Luchana and take a quick left. Bills itself as Egyptian. Middle Eastern staples. *Kebaps* and other entrees €11-15, small meat and falafel pockets at bar €4-5. Open Tu-Th 2-4pm and 8:30pm-midnight, F-Su 2-4pm and 8:30pm-1am. ❸

◉ SIGHTS

▨ **MUSEO SOROLLA.** The former residence and studio of the Valencian painter displays his art and that of other late-19th-century painters. Sorolla's charming house and garden are as captivating as his work, which includes *Trata de Blancas* and *Clotilde con Traje de Noche.* The highlights of the collection are *Mis Hijos*, a portrait of his children, and *La Siesta*, a relaxed depiction of the very best part of the day. *(Po. General Martínez Campos, 37. M: Iglesia or Rubén Darío. ☎913 10 15 84. Open Tu-Sa 9:30am-3pm, Su 10am-3pm. €2.40, students €1.20. Su Free.)*

MUSEO LÁZARO GALDIANO. This small palace, once owned by 19th-century financier Lázaro Galdiano, displays a private collection of Italian Renaissance bronzes and Celtic and Visigoth brasses. Paintings include Leonardo da Vinci's *The Savior* and Hieronymus Bosch's *Ecce Homo*, as well as works by the Spanish trifecta: El Greco, Velázquez, and Goya. *(C. Serrano, 122. Turn right off Po. de la Castellana onto C. María de Molina. M: Rubén Darío or Núñez de Balboa. ☎915 61 60 84; www.flg.es. Open Su-M and W-Sa 10am-4:30pm. €4, students €3. W free.)*

◪ NIGHTLIFE

Clamores Jazz Club, C. Albuquerque, 14 (☎914 45 79 38), off C. Cardenal Cisneros. M: Bilbao. Swanky, neon setting and interesting jazz. The cover (€3-12) is added to the bill if you're there for the music (Tu-Su starting around 10pm). Check posters outside and arrive early for a seat. Open M-Th and Su 6:30pm-3am, F-Sa 6pm-4am.

De Bote en Bote, C. Cardenal Cisneros, 21 (☎655 81 34 11). M: Bilbao. This bright red *bar de copas* plays an eclectic mix that jives with the mirrors and pop-art on its walls. Mid-20s crowd sips on €5 cocktails over *tostas* (€2.50) and cake (€3.50). Open Th-Sa 7:30pm-3am.

El Alivio, C. Manuela Malasaña, 16 (☎626 85 22 82). M: Bilbao. Remarkably chill atmosphere for chatting and drinking. Friendly owner serves up generous, cheap drinks (*copas* €4), and plays relaxed music. A great place to start the night before working your way south into Malasaña and Chueca. Open Tu-Sa 10:30pm-2:30am.

Morgenstern, C. Manuela Malasaña, 31 (☎649 76 76 76). Down the street from El Alivio, this "pseudo-pub" plays power-pop and rock for the hip kids. Late-night dancing to Elvis Costello. Drinks €6-7. Open M-Th 9:30pm-2:30am, F-Sa 9:30pm-3am.

PARQUE DEL BUEN RETIRO

With the construction of the 300-acre Parque del Buen Retiro, Felipe IV intended to transform the former hunting grounds into a personal retreat, *un buen retiro.* Today, the magnificent park and its accompanying gardens are filled with palmreaders, sunbathers, young couples, soccer players, reflective students, and occasional drug pushers (just ignore them and they should leave you alone). The northeast corner of the park enchants with medieval monastic ruins and waterfalls. The park also houses the spectacular Palacio de Cristal and Estanque Grande. On weekends, the promenades fill with musicians, families, and young lovers; on summer nights (when only the north gate remains open), the lively bars and cafes scattered around the park become quite active. The park is easily accessible from the Retiro metro stop. There are four entrances: C. Alfonso XII, C. Alcalá, Pl. de la Independencia, and Av. Menéndez y Pelayo. Avoid venturing in alone after dark.

ESTANQUE GRANDE. Overlooked by Alfonso XII's mausoleum, rowers crowd the rectangular lake in the middle of the park, the Estanque Grande. The lake has been the social center of El Retiro ever since aspiring caricaturists, fortune-tellers, and sunflower-seed *(pipas)* vendors first parked their goods along its marble shores. The colonnaded monument is the perfect spot for late afternoon relaxation and people-watching. Rowboats can be rented for €4 per 45min. Sundays from 5pm to midnight, over 100 percussionists gather for an immense ◨**drum circle** by the monument on the Estanque; synchronistic rhythms and hash smoke fill the air. *(The Pl. de la Independencia entrance leads to Av. de Méjico, the path to the lake.)*

PALACIO DE VELÁZQUEZ. This Ricardo Velázquez creation has billowing ceilings, marble floors, and tile work by Daniel Zuloaga. The Palacio exhibits frequently changing works in conjunction with the Museo Nacional Centro de Arte Reina Sofía (p. 124). *(From the Estanque, walk straight to Pl. de Honduras and turn left onto Po. Venezuela. The palace will be on your right. ☎915 73 62 45. Open May.-Sept. M and W-Sa 11am-8pm, Su 11am-6pm; Oct.-Apr. M and W-Sa 10am-6pm, Su 10am-4pm. Free.)*

PALACIO DE CRISTAL. Built by Ricardo Velázquez to exhibit flowers from the Philippines in 1887, this exquisite steel-and-glass structure hosts a variety of art shows and exhibits, with subjects ranging from Bugs Bunny to Spanish portraiture to vocal recognition of bird calls. *(From Palacio de Velázquez, head out the main door until you reach the lake and the palace. ☎915 74 66 14. Open May.-Sept. M and W-Sa 11am-8pm; Su 11am-6pm; Oct.-Apr. M and W-Sa 10am-6pm, Su 10am-4pm. Free.)*

OTHER SIGHTS. Bullets from the 1921 assassination of prime minister Eduardo Dato permanently scarred the eastern face of the Puerta de Alcalá (1778), outside El Retiro's Puerta de la Independencia. To the south, the Casón del Buen Retiro (p. 124) faces the park; behind it sits the **Museo del Ejército.** In this stately fragment of the Casón is a vast collection of over 27,000 artifacts tracing the history of the Spanish military. Each room is dedicated to a different period or conquest; the most famous contains the *Tizona* sword of El Cid Campeador and a fragment of the cross Columbus was wearing when he arrived in the New World. The two buildings are remnants of Felipe IV's palace, which burned down in 1764. *(C. Méndez Núñez, 1. M: Retiro or Banco de España. ☎915 22 89 77. Open Tu-Su 10am-2pm. €1, students €0.50, under 18 and over 65 free. Sa free.)*

EL PARDO

Built as a hunting lodge for Carlos I in 1547, El Pardo was enlarged by generations of Habsburgs and Bourbons. Though Spain's growing capital eventually engulfed it, El Pardo still stands as one of Spain's greatest country palaces. It gained attention again in 1940 when Franco decided to make it his home; he resided here until his death in 1975. Although politics have changed, the palace is still the official reception site for distinguished foreign visitors. Renowned for its collection of vivid pastoral **tapestries**—several of which were designed by Goya—the palace also holds a Velázquez painting and Ribera's *Techo de los Hombres Ilustres* (Ceiling of the Illustrious Men). You can also see Franco's bathroom, and the bedroom cabinet in which he kept Santa Teresa's silver-encrusted arm. Entrance to the palace's **capilla** and the nearby **Casita del Príncipe,** created by Juan de Villanueva of Museo del Prado fame, is free. *(Take bus #601 from the stop in front of the Ejército del Aire building above M: Moncloa; every 15min., €1.10. ☎913 76 15 00. Palace open Apr.-Sept. M-Sa 10:30am-5:45pm, Su 9:30am-1:30pm; Oct.-Mar. M-Sa 10:30am-4:45pm, Su 9:55am-1:30pm. Compulsory 45min. guided tour in Spanish. €5, over 65 and students with ID €2.50. W free for EU citizens. The Casita del Príncipe may be undergoing restorations; call ahead.)*

◨ THE PASEOS: A WALKING TOUR

Madrid's thoroughfare *paseos* connect the city through three contiguous segments, **Paseo del Prado, Paseo de Recoletos,** and **Paseo de la Castellana,** running from Atocha in the south to Chamartín in the north. The *paseos* are a great starting point for walking tours, since most major sights branch out from these main avenues. Plants, gardens, and cafes separate traffic in pleasant median oases along your stroll. A walking tour could last several hours, an entire day, or even several days, depending on how much time you want to spend at the various sights and how far you stray from the main *paseo* paths. You may be tempted to head to El Retiro after the Museo del Prado, or venture to Puerta del Sol once you have reached Pl. de Cibeles. Regardless of the path chosen, the *paseos* are a simple way to acquaint yourself with the city and organize a daily itinerary.

The Paseo del Prado connects Atocha to Pl. de Cibeles, passing the **Museo del Prado** (p. 122), the **Museo Thyssen-Bornemisza** (p. 125), and the Ritz Hotel. Along the Paseo de Recoletos, extending from Pl. de Cibeles to Pl. de Colón, the *nouveaux riche* congregate at luxuriously shaded *terrazas*. Contemporary Madrid stretches farther north along Po. de la Castellana (lined with bank buildings from the 1970s and 80s) to Pl. de Castilla's *Puerta de Europa* (leaning twin towers).

PASEO DEL PRADO

Modeled after the Piazza Navona in Rome, Po. del Prado is the center of Madrid's art district. Virtually every major museum is in the vicinity of this museum mile, known as the *triángulo de arte*. Directly across from Estación Atocha, the **Museo Nacional Centro de Arte Reina Sofía** (p. 124), home of Picasso's *Guernica*, presides over Pl. del Emperador Carlos V. Its innovative glass elevators and outdoor sculptures hint at the impressive collection of modern art within.

Walking up Po. del Prado, you'll pass the **Real Jardín Botánico** on the right. Opened during Carlos III's reign, the garden showcases over 30,000 species of plants, ranging from traditional roses to medicinal herbs. The garden's vast collection of imported trees, bushes, and flowers has a universal appeal. *(Pl. de Murillo, 2, next to the Prado. ☎914 20 30 17; www.rjb.csic.es. Open daily summer 10am-9pm; spring and fall 10am-7pm; winter 10am-6pm. €2, students €1.)* Next to the garden is the world-renowned **Museo del Prado** (p. 122) and behind it, on C. Ruiz de Alarcón, stands the **Iglesia de San Jerónimo**, Madrid's royal church. Built by Hieronymite monks and re-endowed by *los Reyes Católicos*, the church has witnessed a few joyous milestones, including the coronation of Fernando and Isabel and the marriage of King Alfonso XIII. These days, only the highest of high-society weddings are held in the church. *(Open daily 8am-1:30pm and 5-8:30pm. Closed for renovations through summer.)* Back on Po. del Prado, to the north in Pl. de la Lealtad, stands the **Obelisco a los Mártires del 2 de Mayo**, filled with the ashes of those who died in the 1808 uprising against Napoleon. Its four statues represent Constancy, Virtue, Valor, and Patriotism, and the flame burns continuously in honor of the patriots. Behind the memorial sits the colonnaded classical **Bolsa de Madrid** (Stock Exchange), designed by Enrique Repullés. Ventura Rodríguez's **Fuente de Neptuno**, in Pl. Cánovas de Castillo, is one of three aquatic masterpieces along the avenue, good enough to have earned him a metro stop. Crossing the plaza brings you to another great museum, the **Museo Thyssen-Bornemisza** (p. 125).

The arts of the Po. del Prado meld into the Po. de Recoletos at the tulip-encircled **Plaza de Cibeles.** With its infamous marble fountain, the Pl. de Cibeles has been Madrid's spiritual center since its construction in 1781. Depicting the fertility goddess's triumph over the emblematic Castilian lions, the fountain's image of Cybele has long captivated citizens. Legend has it that the fleet-footed Atalanta, one of Cybele's maids, would take as her lover only the man who could outrun her. No man was up to the challenge until one cunning suitor instructed his cohorts to scatter golden apples (as distractions) in Atalanta's path. The goddess Cybele, watching the prank, was overcome with rage at men's evil ways. After punishing the plotters by turning them into lions, she hitched them to her own carriage. This assertion of power and sexuality charmed Madrid, resulting in the proverb *"más popular que Cibeles"* (more popular than Cibeles). *Madrileños* protected this emblem of their city during Franco's bomb raids by covering it with a pyramid of sandbags. From the plaza, the small **Museo Naval** is to the right. *(Entrance at Po. del Prado, 5.* ☎ *913 79 52 99; www.armada.mde.es. Open Tu-Su 10am-2pm. Closed Aug. Free.)* In the southeast corner of the plaza sits the spectacular **Palacio de Comunicaciones** (p. 99), designed by Antonio Palacios and Julián Otamendi of Otto Wagner's Vienna School in 1920.

Looking to the right up C. Alcalá from the Palacio de Comunicaciones is Sabatini's **Puerta de Alcalá,** the 18th-century emblematic gateway and court symbol. On the northeastern corner of the plaza roundabout (behind black gates) is the former **Palacio de Linares,** a 19th-century townhouse built for Madrid nobility. Proven by a team of "scientists" to be inhabited by ghosts, it was transformed into the **Casa de América** with a library and lecture halls for the study of Latin American culture and politics. It also sponsors art exhibits and guest lectures. *(Po. de Recoletos, 2. M: Banco de España.* ☎ *915 95 48 00. Open Tu-Sa 11am-2pm and 5-8pm, Su 11am-2pm.)*

PASEO DE RECOLETOS

Continuing north toward the brown **Torres de Colón** (Towers of Columbus), you'll pass the **Biblioteca Nacional** (National Library), where the sleek **Museo del Libro** displays treasures from the monarchy's collection, including a first edition copy of *Don Quixote. (Entrance at #20.* ☎ *915 80 78 00. Open Tu-Sa 10am-9pm, Su 10am-2pm. Free.)* Behind the library is the massive **Museo Arqueológico Nacional.** After countless moves, Madrid's display of the history of the Western world settled in this huge museum in 1895. Founded by a decree of Isabel II, the museum houses an astounding collection of items from Spain's past, including the country's most famous archaeological find, *Dama de Elche,* a 4th-century funerary urn, Felipe II's astrolabe, and a 16th-century porcelain clock belonging to Lady Baza. Outside stands a replica of the Cuevas de Altamira (p. 599) and their Paleolithic paintings. *(C. Serrano, 13. M: Serrano.* ☎ *915 77 79 12; www.man.es. Open summer Tu-Sa 9:30am-8:30pm, Su 9:30am-2:30pm; winter daily 9:30am-2pm.* €*3. Sa after 2:30pm and Su free.)* The museum entrance is on C. Serrano, an avenue lined with pricey boutiques in the posh **Barrio de Salamanca.** The museum and library huddle just beyond the modern **Plaza de Colón** (M: Colón) and the adjoining **Jardines del Descubrimiento** (Gardens of Discovery). At one side loom huge clay boulders, inscribed with trivia about the New World, including Seneca's prediction of its discovery, the names of the mariners onboard the caravels, and passages from Columbus's diary. A neo-Gothic spire honoring Columbus rises from a thundering fountain in the center of the plaza. An inlaid map detailing Columbus's journey covers the wall behind the waterfall. Concerts, lectures, ballets, and plays are held in the **Centro Cultural de la Villa** (☎ 914 80 03 00), the municipal art center beneath the statue and waterfall.

PASEO DE LA CASTELLANA

Nineteenth- and early 20th-century aristocrats dislodged themselves from Old Madrid to settle along Po. de la Castellana. During the Spanish Civil War, Republican forces used the mansions as barracks. Most were torn down in the 1960s when banks and insurance companies commissioned new, more innovative structures. Competition promoted architectural excellence, offering the lowly pedestrian a rich man's spectacle of architecture and fashion. Some notables include: Rafael Moneo's **Bankinter,** #29, the first to integrate rather than demolish a townhouse; **Banco Urquijo,** known as "the coffeepot;" the Sevillian-tiled **Edificio ABC,** #34, formerly the office of the conservative, pro-monarchy newspaper and now a shopping center; the pink **Edificio Bankunion,** #46; **Banca Catalana Occidente,** #50, which looks like an ice cube on a cracker; and the famous **Edificio La Caixa,** #61.

Just south of the American Embassy, between Pl. de Colón and Glorieta de Emilio Castelar, is an **open-air sculpture museum** displaying works by Joan Miró and Eduardo Chillida. Look up—works also hang from the bridge. Intimate, private museums, including the **Museo Lázaro Galdiano** (p. 137), are just off the Paseo. At **Plaza de Lima** is the 110,000-seat **Estadio Santiago Bernabéu** (M: Lima), home to the beloved **Real Madrid** soccer club, which won its 9th European Championship in 2002 and its 29th Spanish La Liga Championship in 2003. Farther north, the **Puerta de Europa,** with its two 27-story leaning towers connected by a tunnel, dominates Pl. de Castilla (M: Pl. de Castilla). They were designed as a doorway to the city.

▶ DAYTRIP FROM MADRID

SAN LORENZO DE EL ESCORIAL ☎918

El Escorial—half monastery and half mausoleum—is the most popular daytrip from Madrid. Although Felipe II constructed El Escorial primarily for himself and God, the complex, with its magnificent library, palaces, and works of art, seems made for tourists. Visits are popular during the *Fiestas de San Lorenzo* (Aug. 10-20), when parades line the streets and fireworks fill the sky, and on *Romería a la Ermita de la Virgen de Gracia*, the second Sunday in September, when folk dancing contests fill the forests. The whole town shuts down on Mondays.

▣▶ **TRANSPORTATION AND PRACTICAL INFORMATION.** El Escorial's **train station** (☎918 90 00 15), on Ctra. Estación, is 2km outside of town. Trains run to **Atocha** and **Chamartín** stations in **Madrid** (1hr.; 7-9 per day M-F 6:32am-9:26pm, Sa-Su 10:15am-9:26pm; €2.70). **Autocares Herranz buses** (☎918 96 90 28) run from Madrid's **Moncloa metro station** (50min.; every 15min. M-F 6:55am-11:30pm, Sa 8:30am-10:15pm, Su 9am-11pm; €2.90) and back (every 15min. M-F 6am-10:30pm, Sa 7:30am-9pm, Su 7:45am-10pm; €2.90). Shuttles go between the stations (M-F every 15-20min. 7:23am-10:38pm, Sa-Su every 20-60min. 9:44am-10:38pm; €0.90).

The **tourist office** is located beneath a huge arch near the monastery at C. Grimaldi, 2. (☎ 918 90 53 13; www.sanlorenzodeelescorial.org. Open daily 10am-6pm.) With your back to the bus station, turn right down C. Juan de Toledo, then make a right onto C. Floridablanca. Follow C. Floridablanca until the first archway on the left. From the train station, take the shuttle to the bus station or exit the train station, walk straight ahead, and follow the signs uphill (25min.). For a more peaceful walk, exit the train station and enter the Casita del Príncipe main entrance straight ahead. Start walking uphill and take the C. de los Tilos path, which leads to the monastery (25min.). The **police** are at Pl. de la Constitución, 1 (☎918 90 52 23).

▶▣ **ACCOMMODATIONS AND FOOD.** Because of its proximity to Madrid, El Escorial makes an easy daytrip. For those wishing to stay, **Hostal Cristina ❸,** C. Juan de Toledo, 6, on the same street as the bus station, fits the bill with private baths, TVs, and phones. With your back to the station, turn right and walk 100m. (☎918 90 19 61; www.lanzadera.com/hcristina. July-Aug. doubles €46.50, Sept.-June €44.50. MC/V.) To reach **Residencia Juvenil El Escorial (HI) ❶,** C. Residencia, 14, from C. del Rey, turn right onto C. Tozas, left onto C. Claudio Coello, left again onto Po. Unamuno, then right onto C. Residencia. It's an uphill climb the whole way, but the price is unbeatable. All dorm rooms have attached bath; towels not provided. (☎918 90 59 24; fax 90 06 20. HI card required. Laundry €2.

Closed Sept. Dorms €7.80, with dinner €10.60, with lunch and dinner €12.70; over 26 €10.80/€14/€16.80. MC/V.) **Mercado San Lorenzo,** C. del Rey, 7, is just off the central plaza. (Open M-Sa 9:30am-1:30pm and 5-8pm.)

🔆 SIGHTS

EL ESCORIAL

☎918 90 59 03. *Complex open Tu-Su Apr.-Sept. 10am-8pm; Oct.-Mar. 10am-6pm. Last admission to palaces, pantheons, and museums 1hr. before closing. Complete visit takes 2hr. Guided tour €9. Spanish tours every 15min.; English tour times vary. Monastery €7, students and seniors €3.50. Complete admission to tombs and library €8/€4. W free for EU citizens. Joint admission ticket for both El Escorial and El Valle de los Caídos with guide €10, without guide €8.50; students €5.)*

MONASTERIO. "El Escorial" translates loosely to "The Slag Heap," but don't let the name sour you—the gargantuan monastery is fantastic and entirely un-slaggy. Felipe II built the **Monasterio de San Lorenzo del Escorial** as a gift to God, his people, and himself to commemorate his victory over the French at the battle of San Quintín in 1557. He commissioned Juan Bautista de Toledo to design the monastery-mausoleum complex, but Juan de Herrera inherited the job when Toledo died just four years into the project. With the exception of the Panteón Real and minor additions, the monastery was completed in just 21 years. Felipe oversaw much of the work from a chair-shaped rock, the **Silla de Felipe II,** 7km from the site.

Considering the resources Felipe II commanded, the building is noteworthy for its symmetry and simplicity; the monastery is made of granite hewn from nearby quarries. The entire structure is built in a gridiron pattern: four massive towers pin the corners, and a great dome surmounts the towers of the central basilica. Felipe himself described it as "majesty without ostentation."

GALLERIES AND LIVING QUARTERS. To avoid the worst of the crowds, enter El Escorial through the gateway on C. Floridablanca, where you'll find a collection of Flemish art. Though much of the work is standard religious fare, keep an eye out for some exceptions. In the first room hang lovingly woven replicas of Hieronymus Bosch's paintings; El Greco's *Martirios de San Mauricio* is nearby. Though these masterpieces and others by Durer, Tintoretto, Titian, Van Dyck, and Zurbarán still adorn the walls, most of the collection is now housed in Madrid's Museo del Prado. The adjacent **Museo de Arquitectura and Pintura** has an exhibition comparing El Escorial's construction to that of other related structures, featuring wooden models of 16th-century machinery and gigantic iron clamps.

Azulejos (tiles) from Toledo line the **Palacio Real,** which includes the **Salón del Trono** (Throne Room) and two dwellings: Felipe II's spartan 16th-century apartments and the more luxurious 18th-century rooms of Carlos III and Carlos IV. The *Puertas de Marquetería,* German doors inlaid with 18 species of wood, show incredible craftsmanship. The **Sala de Batallas** (Battle Room) links the two parts of the palace with frescoes by Italian artists Grabelo and Castello. The walls and ceiling trumpet first Castilla's and then united Spain's greatest victories—including Juan II's 1431 triumph over the Muslims at Higueruela, Felipe II's successful expeditions in the Azores, and the Battle of San Quintín. Look closer to find comic details of the everyday; crossbowmen share a laugh during the battle, while two peasants look on, passing a wineskin. Maps line the **Salon de Paseo;** the last one on the right portrays the world as (mis)understood by 16th-century Europeans.

LIBRARY. The *biblioteca* on the second floor holds over 4000 priceless folios and manuscripts. Though several fires have reduced the collection, the extant volumes—some bound as early as 1500—are in remarkably good condition; the bindings, made of scraped hide, can last hundreds of years. Alfonso X's *Cantigas de Santa María*, Santa Teresa's manuscripts and diary, the gold-scrolled Aureus Codex of 1039 (by German Emperor Conrad III), and an 11th-century *Commentary on the Apocalypse* by Beato de Liébana are just a sampling of the documents displayed here. Clever allegorical frescoes of the seven fields of knowledge grace the ceiling; note the shriveled hindquarters of the lion that flanks "Rhetoric."

BASILICA. Under the gigantic central dome is the basilica, which for years served as a direct link between the kings and God. Marble steps arrive at an altar adorned by golden sculptures of the royal family, who kneel in perpetual prayer to saints, popes, and Jesus. The *Coro Alto* (High Choir) has a magnificent ceiling fresco of heaven. The cloister shines under Titian's fresco of the martyrdom of San Lorenzo.

PANTHEONS. Lit by an immense chandelier, the nearby Panteón Real displays the green marble tombs of past monarchs. The connecting **Pudrería** is where royal bodies are cured over 25 to 30 years in a solution of water and *cal* (limestone). The Pudrería is currently home to three corpses who are attended to regularly by monks. Unfortunately, out of respect for the dead, tourists are not allowed in. Two centuries later, the **Panteón de los Infantes** was built to have space for over 50 children. It is rumored that many illegitimate royal offspring lie within the crypts.

CASITAS. Commissioned by the Prince of Asturias, later to become Carlos IV, the Casita del Príncipe displays a collection of ornaments, including chandeliers, lamps, rugs, furniture, clocks, tapestries, china, and engraved oranges. Though the French roughed up the *casita* during the Napoleonic invasions, Fernando VII later redecorated many rooms in the then-popular Empire style. *(Approx. 1km from the monastery on the way to Madrid. Call ahead for reservations ☎918 90 59 03 weekdays, 90 04 21 weekends. Open Sa-Su 10am-1pm and 4-6:30pm. Visitors may enter only with a guided tour (every 30min.); 10-person max.; €3.60 per person, students and seniors €2.)* The Casita del Infante, commissioned as a retreat in the mid-16th century by Carlos's brother, was meant to entertain guests with stunning views and performances. *(Open Semana Santa and July-Sept. Tu-Su 10am-7pm; final entrance 30min. before closing. €3.40)*

VALLE DE LOS CAÍDOS

The Valle de los Caídos is accessible only via El Escorial. Autocares Herranz runs 1 bus to the monument from C. Juan de Toledo. (☎918 90 41 25 or 96 90 28. 20min.; Tu-Su 3:15pm, returns 5:30pm; round-trip plus admission €7.70.) Mass M-Sa 11am; Su 11am, 12:30, 1, and 5:30pm. Entrance gate open Tu-Su 10am-6pm. €5, seniors and students €2.50. W free for EU citizens. Funicular to the cross €2.50.

In a once untouched valley 8km north of El Escorial, General Franco forced Republican prisoners to build the overpowering monument of Santa Cruz del Valle de los Caídos (Holy Cross of the Valley of the Fallen) as a memorial to those who gave their lives in the Spanish Civil War. Although ostensibly a monument to both sides, the massive granite cross (150m tall and 46m wide) honors only those who died "serving *Dios* and *España*" (i.e. the Fascist Nationalists). Many who worked on the monument also died under the grueling conditions of its construction. To climb to the base of the cross, follow the paved road up to the trailhead just past the monastery on the right, or take the **funicular.** Apocalyptic tapestries line the cave-like **basilica,** where the ghost of Fascist architecture rests. Muscular warrior monks watch the pews, while gigantic death-angels guard the crucified Jesus. 40,000 dead Nationalists are buried behind the chapel walls, and beside the high altar, underneath the mammoth cross with its giant statues, rest **José Antonio Primo de Rivera** (founder of the Fascist Falange party) and General Franco himself.

COMUNIDAD DE MADRID

The Comunidad de Madrid is an autonomous administrative region smack in the middle of Spain, bordered by Castilla y León to the north and west and Castilla La Mancha to the south and east. Beyond Madrid proper, the Comunidad offers travelers a variety of daytrips to exquisite cultural landscapes and small town serenity.

ALCALÁ DE HENARES

Alcalá de Henares (pop. 191,000) draws intellectuals looking to follow in the footsteps of the city's distinguished scions, including Golden Age authors Miguel de Cervantes, Francisco de Quevedo, and Lope de Vega. Alcalá's history and exceptional Renaissance architecture make the city a worthwhile stop.

F.Z TRANSPORTATION AND PRACTICAL INFORMATION. The **train station** is on Po. de la Estación (☎902 24 02 02). **Cercanías** trains run to Estación Atocha in **Madrid** (50min., every 10min. 6:30am-9:16pm, €2.10). **Continental Auto,** Av. Guadalajara, 5 (☎918 88 16 22), runs buses between Alcalá and **Madrid** (45min.; M-Sa every 15min. 6:10am-11pm, Su every 30min. 7-9am and every 20min. 9am-11pm; €1.90). To reach the city center from the bus station, turn right onto Av. Guadalajara and continue as it turns into C. de Libreros. To find the **tourist office,** Callejón de Santa María, 1, walk the length of Pl. Cervantes toward the bell tower and turn left down the small street. The office offers a list of local cultural events and has maps and suggestions for accommodations and restaurants. (☎918 89 26 94; www.alcalatourismo.com. Open June and Sept. daily 10am-2pm and 5-7:30pm; July-Aug. Tu-Sa 10am-2pm and 5-7:30pm; Oct.-May daily 10am-2pm and 4-6:30pm.) **ATMs** line C. de Libreros, and **Banco Santander Central Hispano** is at C. de Libreros, 19. (Open M-F 8:30am-2pm, Sa 8:30am-1pm.) Local services include: **ambulance** ☎061; **police** ☎918 81 92 63; **Internet access** at **ADES,** C. Santa Úrsula, 5 (from the bell tower end of Pl. Cervantes, turn right down C. Santa Úrsula and walk about a block (☎918 87 11 25; free, limit 1hr.; open M-Sa 9am-7pm). The **post office** is at Pl. de Cervantes, 5. (☎918 89 23 34. Open M-F 8:30am-8:30pm, Sa 9:30am-1pm.) **Postal Code:** 28801.

F.C ACCOMMODATIONS AND FOOD. Some of the least expensive rooms are at **Hostal Jacinto ❷,** Po. de la Estación, 2, 2nd staircase, 1-D. The pleasant, tiled rooms all have sink and TV. (☎/fax 918 89 14 32. Singles with shower €25; doubles €34, with bath €37; triples €40.) Alternately, try **Hostal El Torero ❷,** Av. de Madrid, 14, past Pl. de los Santos Niños. (☎918 89 03 73. Singles €19; doubles with bath €37.) Alcalá's famed *almendras garrapiñadas* (honey- and sugar-coated almonds) beg to be sampled. For fantastically cheap *menús* (€5-7.50), take C. Mayor from Pl. de Cervantes and check out the restaurants on the right side of the street. **El Gringo Viejo ❸,** C. Ramón y Cajal, 8, offers great Mexican entrees (€6-17) and burgers from €5-6. (☎918 78 89 01. Open M-Th 8:30am-midnight, F 8:30am-1am, Sa 10:30am-1am, Su 11am-midnight. MC/V.) **El Ruedo ❶,** C. de Libreros, 38, through the arch on the left side of the street walking toward Pl. de Cervantes, offers a welcome break from heavy *comida típica* with a vegetarian-friendly menu full of delicious crepes and desserts. (☎918 80 69 19. Crêpes €4.50-12, pitas and pastas €5.50-7, lunch *menú* €7. Open M-F 8:30am-midnight, Sa-Su noon-1am.) For groceries, the gigantic **Champion** is behind the bus station on Vía Complutense. From the train station, take a left at the traffic circle. (☎918 89 36 37. Open June 15-Sept. 15 M-Sa 9am-10pm; Sept. 16-June 14 M-Sa 9:15am-9:15pm. MC/V.)

Comunidad de Madrid

◉ ❀ **SIGHTS AND FESTIVALS. Plaza de Cervantes,** filled with cafes, rose bushes, and a statue of its namesake, bursts with color in the summertime. At the end of the plaza opposite C. de Libreros lie the **ruinas de Santa María,** the remains of a 16th-century church destroyed during the Spanish Civil War. In the surviving **Capilla del Oidor,** rotating art exhibits surround the fountain where Cervantes was christened. (Open June-Sept. Tu-Su noon-2pm and 5-9pm; Oct.-May Tu-Su noon-2pm and 6-9pm. Free.) Just before Pl. de Cervantes in Pl. de San Diego, take a left off C. de Libreros onto C. Bedel to see the **Colegio Mayor de San Ildefonso** (☎918 85 40 00). In the **paraninfo,** where doctorates were once awarded, the king now presents the Premio Cervantes, Spain's most prestigious literary award, during the weeklong **Festival de Cervantes.** The *paraninfo* and **Capilla de San Ildefonso** both have spectacular *mudéjar* ceilings. (Mandatory tours summer M-F 6 per day 11am-7pm, Sa-Su every 30min. 11am-2pm and 5-9:30pm. Winter tour schedule starts and ends 1hr. earlier. €2.50.) The town's **Catedral Magistral,** at the end of C. Mayor in Pl. de los Santos Niños, is one of only two in the world with this title (the other is in Lovaina, Belgium). To be so named, each priest must also be a university professor. (Open M-Sa 9-11:30am and 6:30-8:30pm, Su 9am-12:45pm and 6:30-9pm. Free.) Down C. Mayor from Pl. de Cervantes is the **Casa de Cervantes,** the reconstructed house where the author was born in 1547. The house displays a variety of period furniture and editions of *Don Quixote* in languages Cervantes never knew. (☎918 89 96 54. Open summer M-Sa 10-6pm; winter Tu-Su 10am-1:30pm and 4-6:30pm. Free.) The **Convento de San Bernardo** hides a gorgeous 17th-century interior behind a simple facade. (Mandatory tour leaves from the courtyard; 6 per day 11:30am-7pm, €2.50.) Love is in the air every November 1, when the town puts on an epic version of **Don Juan Tenorio** with a cast of 300 for an audience of 10,000.

ARANJUEZ

History and natural beauty converge at the heart of green Aranjuez (pop. 48,000). Once a getaway for generations of Habsburg and Bourbon royalty, Aranjuez still maintains a pastoral elegance thanks to its dazzling gardens and palaces. UNESCO recently declared this small city, famed for its strawberries, asparagus, and formal gardens, a World Heritage Cultural Landscape. Aranjuez is an easy daytrip from Madrid or Toledo, but consider staying longer during the festivals. The last weekend in May, Aranjuez holds parades, concerts, and bullfights. In September the town celebrates the Feria del Motín with a battle reenactment on the river Tajo.

 TRANSPORTATION. RENFE trains, C. de la Estación (☎902 24 00 42), go to: **Cuenca** (2hr.; M-F 4-5 per day 6:10am-8:14pm, Sa-Su 9:23am-8:14pm; €6.70); **Madrid** (45min.; to Estación Atocha every 15-30min. M-F 5:30am-11:30pm, Sa-Su 6am-11:30pm; to Estación Chamartín M-F 8-10 per day 6:57am-9:27pm, Sa-Su 8:57am-9:27pm; €3); **Toledo** (30min.; M-F 7-10 per day 7:20am-9:12pm, Sa-Su 9:17am-9:12pm; €3). **AISA** runs from the **bus station,** C. de las Infantas, 16 (☎918 91 01 83), to Estación Sur in **Madrid** (45min.; M-F every 15-30min. 6am-1am, Sa every 20min. 7am-11pm, Su every hr. 7am-11pm, also 10:30am, 12:30, 1:30, 2:30, 2:45pm; €3.10).

 ORIENTATION AND PRACTICAL INFORMATION. To get to the city by foot, exit the train station parking lot, go right, and follow the signs to the Palacio Real. With your back to the bus station, head left onto C. de las Infantas toward the main fountain. Orienting yourself from the palace is easy, and friendly locals can point you toward your destination or the tourist office. Alternatively, on the corner outside the palace, climb aboard the **Chiquitren de Aranjuez** to catch all the major sights. (☎918 92 93 92. €5, not including admission to museums and sights.)

The **tourist office** is in Pl. San Antonio, 9. (☎918 91 04 27; www.aranjuez.net. Open daily summer 10am-7:30pm; winter 10am-6:30pm.) Local services include: **police,** C. de las Infantas, 36 (☎918 09 09 80); **pharmacy,** on the corner of C. del Capitán Angosto Gómez Castrillón and C. Real. (Open M-F 9:30am-1:45pm and 5:30-8:30pm, Sa 10am-1:45pm. MC/V.) For **Internet access,** head to the **Mercado de Abostos.** In the left-central part of the market is an **Internet** center. (Free. Open summer M-Sa 10am-2pm and 6-9pm; winter 10am-2pm and 5-8pm.) The **post office** is on C. Peñarredonda, 3, off C. del Capitán Angosto Gómez Castrillón. (☎918 91 11 32. Open M-F 8:30am-2:30pm, Sa 9:30am-1pm.) **Postal Code:** 28300.

 ACCOMMODATIONS AND FOOD. Aranjuez has a wide variety of choices for accommodations and food, especially for a city its size. **Hostal Rusiñol ❷,** on C. de San Antonio, has bright, open doubles with TV. (☎918 91 01 55. €24, with shower €35, with bath €39.) **Hostal Infantas ❶,** C. de las Infantas, 4-6, is on the left with your back to the bus station. All the rooms have sink, TV, and phone; doubles with shower or bath have A/C. (☎918 91 13 41; fax 91 66 43. Singles €17, with shower €25; doubles €25, with shower €44, with bath €46. MC/V.) The rooms at **Hostal Castilla ❸,** Ctra. de Andalucía, 98, face an ivy-shaded garden terrace; all have TV, A/C, phone, and bath. (☎918 91 26 27; fax 91 61 33. Breakfast €3. Singles €35; doubles €45.) **Camping Soto del Castillo ❶,** across the Río Tajo and off the highway to the right, sits amid lush fields and has a restaurant, supermarket, and swimming pool. (☎918 91 13 95. Open year-round. €4.20 per person, €3.70-4.50 per tent, €3.50 per car. MC/V.) For groceries or a quick meal, try the indoor **Mercado de Abastos** on Ctra. de Andalucía. With your back to the tourist office, go left through the arch; the market is on the left. (Open M-F 9am-2pm and 6-9pm, Sa 9am-2pm.) Be sure to grab some delicious ▨**fresas con nata** (strawberries and cream) from the vendors just over the small bridge near the main fountain in front of the palace gardens. For some savory asparagus specialties and typical Spanish entrees, head to **El Rana Verde ❸**, C. de la Reina, 1 (☎918 01 15 71; open daily 9am-midnight), or **La Alegría de la Huerta ❸**, Ctra. de Madrid, 4. (☎918 91 29 38. Dinner €15-20. Open daily 9am-4pm and 9pm-midnight.)

🗿 **SIGHTS.** Juan de Herrera, chief architect of gloomy El Escorial, designed the resplendent white **Palacio Real** under the direction of Felipe II. When not busy conquering, the Spanish kings dedicated themselves to the more peaceful art of interior decorating. Felipe V, Fernando VI, and Carlos III enlarged and embellished the palace, but it was Isabel II who left her mark with over-the-top draperies and decor in the mid-19th century. Particularly remarkable are the Asian **porcelain room,** with hand-tooled and painted three-dimensional ceramic Rococo walls, and the Mozárabe **smoking room,** which bears a striking resemblance to rooms in the Alhambra. On your way out, take note of the last room of the **Museo de la Vida en Palacio,** which contains toys of the royal children. (☎918 91 07 40. Open Tu-Sa Apr.-Sept. 10am-6:15pm; Oct.-Mar. 10am-5:15pm. Mandatory 30min. tours in English or Spanish every 15min. €3, students €1.50. EU citizens free W.) Just outside the palace is a labyrinth of river walkways, freshly trimmed hedges, and mythological statues. The gardens continue a short walk from the palace on C. de la Reina with the **Jardín del Príncipe,** built for the amusement of Carlos IV. (Open daily Apr.-Sept. 8am-6:30pm; Oct.-Mar. 8am-8:30pm. Free.) A 30min. stroll through the park leads to the **Casa del Labrador,** a cottage full of decorative arts, including an impressive collection of timepieces. (3km down C. de la Reina from the Palacio Real. ☎918 91 03 05. Reserve ahead. Open daily 10am-sunset. €3, students and under 16 €1.50.) The **Falúas Museum,** once home to the Tajo's sailing squad, stores royal gondolas. (Open Tu-Su June-Aug. 10am-6:15pm; Sept.-May 10am-5:15pm. €3.40, students and under 16 €1.70. EU citizens free W.) **Aranjuez, Una Gran Fiesta,** has exhibits on the history of bullfighting. (Pl. de Toros, all the way up Ctra. de Andalucía from the tourist office. ☎918 92 16 43. Open Tu-Su 10am-6pm. €3; students, seniors, and under 16 €1.20.)

SIERRA DE GUADARRAMA

If Madrid's pollution, traffic, and general hipness are getting to you, consider spending an afternoon (or a few days) in the Sierra de Guadarrama, a pine-covered mountain range halfway between Madrid and Segovia. With *La Mujer Muerta* (The Dead Woman) to the west, the *Sierra de la Maliciosa* (Mountains of the Evil Woman) to the east, and the less imaginatively named *Siete Picos* (Seven Peaks), the Sierra draws visitors in all seasons to hike and ski.

CERCEDILLA   ☎918

A picturesque chalet town blessed with great weather, Cercedilla is the ideal base for venturing into the Sierra. In summer, cooler temperatures and a relaxed pace lure sweltering city dwellers; in the winter, skiers enjoy the nearby resorts. For those weary of Madrid's sights, great day hikes provide an escape from the city.

F R **TRANSPORTATION AND PRACTICAL INFORMATION.** Cercedilla makes an easy daytrip from Madrid. Camping is not allowed in the area, so pack for a day hike or reserve a hostel in advance. The **train station** (☎918 52 00 57), at the base of the hill on C. Emilio Serrano, sends trains to: **El Escorial** (1hr.; Su-F 23 per day 6:07am-10:35pm, Sa 19 per day 6:37am-10:35pm; €1.10) via **Villalba; Los Cotos** (45min.; Su-F 4 per day 9:35am-6:35pm, Sa every hr. 9:35am-6:35pm; €3.40) via **Puerto de Navacerrada; Atocha** or **Chamartín** station **(Madrid)** (1½hr.; over 20 per day Su-F 6:07am-10:35pm, Sa 6:37am-9:35pm; €3.20) via **Villalba** (30min., €1.60); **Segovia** (45min., 8-9 per day 7:26am-9:22pm, €2.10). The **bus station,** Av. José Antonio, 2 (☎918 52 02 39), sends buses to **Madrid** (1-1½hr., M-F 29 per day 6am-8:45pm, Sa 15-17 per day 6:20am-8:45pm, Su 17 per day 8:30am-9:30pm; €2.90).

Upon arrival in Cercedilla, proceed to the **Consejería de Medio Ambiente,** the starting point for several hikes (see **Hiking,** p. 148), to pick up **tourist info** and great hiking maps (some in English). To get there from either station, you may want to call a **taxi** (try Manolo ☎619 806 452, Francisco 650 363 043, or Juan 619 226 272; about €6.50 but negotiable) or wait for one, though they do not come often. The Consejería is roughly 3km from the train station on **Carretera de las Dehesas,** km 2. By foot (a 40min. hike), go straight uphill and stay left at the fork. Local services include: **police** (☎918 53 15 53); **Centro de Salud** (☎918 52 30 31, urgent 52 04 79).

F C **ACCOMMODATIONS AND FOOD.** Many of the youth hostels in Cercedilla are booked during the summer by camp groups and other organizations. For most *albergues* and *hostales,* reservations should be made more than 15 days in advance. Conveniently located near the trails is **Albergue Juvenil "Las Dehesas" (HI) ❶,** Ctra. de las Dehesas, a beautiful government-subsidized hostel at the foot of the mountains. Rooms (for 2-6 people) are bright and clean with shared bath. Guests mingle in the large common spaces and basketball court. (☎918 52 01 35; www.madrid.org/inforjoven. Blankets provided, but not sheets or towels. HI card required. With breakfast €7.80, with 2 meals €10.60, with 3 €12.60; over 26 €10.80/€14/€16.80.) **Hostal Longinos "El Aribel" ❷,** right across the street from the train station, has spacious rooms with TVs and a simple, mountain lodge feel. (☎918 52 15 11 or 52 06 86. Singles €18; doubles with bath €40.) For cheaper accommodations, try **Villa Castora (HI) ❶,** about 1km up Ctra. de las Dehesas on the left. (☎918 52 03 34; fax 52 24 11. All rooms with private bath. Reception 8am-10pm. Reservations strongly recommended. With breakfast €7.80, with 2 meals €10.60, with 3 €12.60; over 26 €10.80/€14/€16.80.) Camping is strictly controlled throughout the Sierra de Guadarrama and is prohibited throughout the area surrounding Cercedilla. Since you'll be staying in town, ask the Consejería for a list of Cercedilla's restaurants. For groceries, **Supermarket Gigante,** C. Doctor Cañados, 2, is in the town center off Av. del Generalísimo. (☎918 52 23 19. Open M-Sa 9:30am-2pm and 5-9pm, Su 9:30am-2pm.) Convenience stores outside the bus and train stations sell all the essentials. Near the train station, the **bar** at Hostal Longino serves up large *bocadillos* (€3), which can be wrapped for picnics.

N **HIKING.** The **Consejería de Medio Ambiente** functions as a **tourist office** and offers hiking information. (☎/fax 918 52 22 13. Open daily 10am-6pm. Some English spoken.) The Consejería provides detailed maps of six trails and day hikes ranging from the challenging 14.3km (5-6hr.) **El GR-10** to the more relaxed 4km (1½hr.) ◼**Camino Puricelli.** Set aside an afternoon for the orange trail, **Los Miradores,** a 9.3km (3hr.) hike with fantastic views of the valley. Most of the hiking around Cercedilla begins up **Carretera las Dehesas,** near the Consejería. At the top of the Carretera, the **Calzada Romana** (about 1.5km from the Consejería) offers hiking along a Roman road that connected Madrid to Segovia (1½hr.). Springs marked with a blue dot on the trail map should have potable water, but double check at the Consejería. Weather is unpredictable, so bring a rain jacket and sweater. Those who prefer wheels over heels should check out the bike trails. Rentals are rare, but try **Cercedilla Aventura** (☎ 629 60 25 22; www.cercedillaaventura.com). Someone else can even do the walking for you—horses are available at **Hípica La Vaqueriza,** next to Albergue Juvenil "Las Dehesas," uphill from the Consejería. (Fernando ☎ 637 80 90 37, Gustavo 679 44 59 59. €10 per hr. for guide and lesson.)

PUERTO DE NAVACERRADA AND LOS COTOS

A year-round magnet for nature lovers, **Puerto de Navacerrada** offers **skiing** in the winter (late December to early April) and beautiful **hiking** in the summer. Expert skiers will enjoy the challenging bowl trails off **Guarramillas** ski slope, but there are only two easy trails for beginners. Snowboarders are allowed on five out of eight lifts. (M-F skiers €17, snowboarders €15, 3-day pass €34, 5-day pass €51; Sa-Su skiers €26, snowboarders €23.) Those in search of challenging hikes often take the popular **Camino Schmid,** a 7km trail from Navacerrada to **Pradera de los Corralillos;** from there it is another 3km to the Consejería in Cercedilla. Most hikers go in that direction, as it offers a net loss of elevation (trail info ☎ 918 853 14 35).

Deporte y Montaña, 1.5km from the train station, offers info on many outdoor activities. (Madrid ☎ 91 594 30 34, Navacerrada 918 52 33 02; www.puertonavacerrada.com.) More details can be found at the **Asociación Turística de Estaciones de Esquí y Montaña** (☎ 913 50 20 20) in Madrid. To head for the trails, exit the train station, turn left at the highway, and left again at the large intersection marking the pass. The dirt path leads uphill to several trails through the pine forests. For budget accommodations in Navacerrada, try **Residencia Navacerrada,** a mountainside hotel featuring an unmistakable bell tower on its roof. (☎ 918 52 39 84; fax 52 03 68. July-Sept. 15 €19; Sept 16-Nov. €16.30; Dec.-Apr. €24.50; May-June €20.50.)

MADRID

CASTILLA Y LEÓN

The aqueduct of Segovia, the Gothic cathedrals of Burgos and León, the Romanesque belfries along the Camino de Santiago, the sandstone of Salamanca, and the city walls of Ávila: these images all belong to Castilla y León. Well before Castilla's famous 1469 union with Aragón, when Fernando of Aragón and Isabel of Castilla were joined in world-shaking matrimony, it was clear that Castilla had its act together. During the High Middle Ages, the region emerged from obscurity to lead the Christian charge against Islam. Its nobles, sanguine from the spoils of combat, introduced the concept of "Spain" (under Castilian command, of course), and *castellano* became the dominant language throughout the nation. Castilla's comrade in arms, imperious León, though chagrined to be lumped with Castilla in a 1970s provincial reorganization, shares a great deal with its famous co-province.

HIGHLIGHTS OF CASTILLA Y LEÓN

REJOICE in the sun through the stained-glass windows of **León's** cathedral (p. 173).

FIND the frog on the facade of the **Universidad de Salamanca** (p. 164).

REDEFINE obsession with Santa Teresa in the walled city of **Ávila** (p. 156).

GORGE on chocolate in medieval **Astorga** (p. 175).

EXPLORE the streets of **Valladolid** in the steps of Columbus and Magellan (p. 175).

BAA-GAIN for sheep at the market in **Medina del Campo** (p. 179).

SEGOVIA
☎ 921

Segovia (pop. 56,000) is immersed in legend. The history that surrounds each monument in the "Stone Ship"—so named because of the prow-shaped profile of the city's Alcázar, its cathedral's mast-like tower, and the world-famous aqueduct that comprises the ship's helm—is told and retold. Legend has it that the devil constructed the aqueduct in one night in a failed effort to win the soul of a Segovian water-seller named Juanilla. Devil or not, Segovia's attractions and winding alleyways draw their share of Spanish and international tourists as well as students looking for language practice. Such old-town charm comes at a price, though; food and accommodations are even more expensive here than in cosmopolitan Madrid.

▐▀ TRANSPORTATION

Trains: Po. Obispo Quesada (☎903 24 02 02). To **Madrid** (2hr.; 7-9 per day M-F 5:55am-8:55pm, Sa-Su 8:55am-8:55pm; €5.10) and **Villalba** (1hr., 7-9 per day M-F 5:55am-8:55pm, €3.30). Transfers to **Ávila, El Escorial, León,** and **Salamanca.**

Buses: Estación Municipal de Autobuses, Po. Ezequiel González, 12 (☎921 42 77 07). **Linecar** (☎921 42 77 06) to **Salamanca** (3hr.; M-Sa 3 per day 8:50am-5:30pm, Su 5:45pm; €8.90) and **Valladolid** (2hr.; M-F 12 per day and Sa 8 per day 6:45am-9pm, Su 6 per day 9am-9pm; €6.20). **La Sepulvedana** (☎921 42 77 07) to: **Ávila** (1hr.; M-F 5 per day, Sa 7 per day 7:45am-7pm; €3.70); **La Granja** (20min.; 9-15 per day M-Sa 7:40am-9:30pm, Su 10:30am-10:30pm; round-trip €1.70); **Madrid** (1½hr.; every 30min. M-F 6am-9:30pm, Sa 7:30am-9:30pm, Su 8:30am-10:30pm; €5.80).

Public Transportation: Transportes Urbanos de Segovia, Pl. Mayor, 8 (☎921 46 27 27). €0.70; discounted refillable electronic passes available at the office.

Taxis: Radio Taxi (24hr. ☎921 44 50 00). Taxis pull up by the train and bus stations.

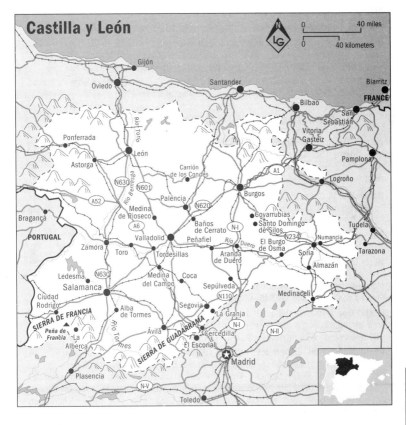

Castilla y León

0   40 miles
0   40 kilometers

Gijón
Oviedo   Santander   Biarritz
                                     FRANCE
                          Bilbao
                                  San
                                  Sebastián
                          Vitoria-
Ponferrada   Gasteiz
                                        Pamplona
León
Astorga   Carrión
             de los Condes   A1
    N630 N601   Logroño
         Palència   Burgos
A52   N620
Bragança   Medina   Covarrubias
                de Rioseco   Baños   Santo Domingo
PORTUGAL   A6   de Cerrato N-I de Silos   Tudela
        Zamora Valladolid Peñafiel Río Duero N234 Numancia
              Toro Tordesillas Aranda El Burgo Soria   Tarazona
Ledesma N630   Medina Coca de Duero de Osma   Almazán
Salamanca   del Campo   Sepúlveda
Ciudad   N110   Medinaceli
Rodrigo Alba   Segovia
SIERRA DE FRANCIA de Tormes   La Granja
Peña de   Ávila   SIERRA DE GUADARRAMA N-I   N-II
Francia La   Cercedilla
Alberca   El Escorial
                              Madrid
Plasencia
         N-V
              Toledo

ORIENTATION AND PRACTICAL INFORMATION

Take any bus from the train station to **Plaza Mayor**, the city's historic center, or **Plaza del Azoguejo**, just downhill from Pl. Mayor. The **Paseo del Salón** bus (M-F every 30min. 7:45am-10:15pm) runs directly to the steps of **Puerta del Sol**. The Pl. del Azoguejo bus (every 30min. M-F 7:30am-10pm, Sa-Su 7:45am-10:15pm) goes to the **aqueduct** and **municipal tourist office.** On foot from the **train station** (20min.), turn right, cross the street, and walk toward town along Po. Obispo Quesada, which becomes Av. Conde de Sepúlveda and then Po. Ezequiel González, before coming to the bus station. From the **bus station** (15min.), cross Po. Ezequiel González and follow Av. de Fernández Ladreda to Pl. del Azoguejo.

Tourist Office: Regional office, Pl. Mayor, 10 (☎921 46 03 34). Some English spoken. Open daily July-Sept. 15 9am-8pm; Sept. 16-June 9am-2pm and 5-8pm. **Municipal office,** Pl. del Azoguejo, 1 (☎921 46 29 06 or 46 29 14). Open daily 10am-8pm.

Currency Exchange: Banco Santander Central Hispano, Av. de Fernández Ladreda, 17. Open Apr.-Sept. M-F 8:30am-2pm; Oct.-Mar. M-F 8:30am-2pm, Sa 8:30am-1pm. **ATMs** line Av. de Fernández Ladreda.

Luggage Storage: Lockers at the **train station** €3 per day. Open daily 6am-10:30pm.

Police: C. Guadarrama, 26 (☎921 43 12 12).

Hospital: Policlínico San Agustín, C. San Agustín, 13 (☎921 41 92 75).

Internet Access: Biblioteca Pública, C. Juan Bravo, 11 (☎ 921 46 35 33). Free and fast. Limit 30min. Open M-F 9am-9pm, Sa 9am-2pm. **Locutorio Mundo 2000,** Pl. del Azoguejo, 4 (☎921 44 17 09). €0.90 per 30min. Open daily 11am-11pm.

Post Office: Pl. Dr. Laguna, 5 (☎921 46 16 16), up C. Cronista Lecea from Pl. Mayor. Open M-F 8:30am-8:30pm, Sa 9:30am-2pm. **Postal Code:** 40001.

■ ■ ACCOMMODATIONS AND CAMPING

Segovia's numerous sights and proximity to Madrid and La Granja make rooms scarce during the summer. Reservations are a must for any of the hotels, especially those in or around major plazas. *Pensiones* are significantly cheaper, but expect basic rooms and shared bathrooms.

Hospedaje El Gato, Pl. del Salvador, 10 (☎921 42 32 44; fax 43 80 47). Follow the aqueduct uphill to comfortable pine rooms. All rooms have A/C, satellite TV, and private bath. Doubles €35; triples €49. MC/V. ❸

Pensión Ferri, C. Escuderos, 10 (☎921 46 09 57), off Pl. Mayor. Rustic rooms, some with garden views. Central location. Showers €2. Singles €13; doubles €23. ❶

Hotel Las Sirenas, C. Juan Bravo, 30 (☎921 46 26 63; fax 46 26 57), down C. Cervantes. High ceilings in rooms with TV, shower, telephone, and A/C. Ask for a room overlooking the valley. Reservations encouraged. July-Sept. singles €48-53; doubles €70; triples €90. Oct.-June €40-45/€50/€80. AmEx/MC/V. ❹

Hostal Don Jaime, C. Ochoa Ondategui, 8 (☎921 44 47 87), around the corner from the aqueduct. Bright rooms with TV, phone, and large mirrors. Breakfast €3. Singles €22, with bath €30; doubles with bath €40; triples with bath €50. MC/V. ❷

Residencia Juvenil Emperador Teodosio (HI), Av. Conde de Sepúlveda, 4 (☎921 44 11 11). From the train station, turn right down Po. Obispo Quesada, which becomes Av. Conde de Sepúlveda (10min.). From the bus station, turn right onto Po. Ezequiel González, which turns into Av. Conde de Sepúlveda (10min.). Look for a red fire escape in front. 3 beds per room with bath. Breakfast €1. 3-night max. stay. Curfew 2am. Open July-Sept. 15. Dorms €7, with 3 meals €14; over 26 €10/€18. ❶

Camping: Camping Acueducto, C. Borbón, 49/Highway CN-601, km112 (☎921 42 50 00), 2km toward La Granja. Take the AutoBus Urbano #3 (€0.70) from Pl. del Azoguejo to Nueva Segovia. Restaurant, supermarket, hot showers, pool, and laundry. Open *Semana Santa*-Sept. €4 per person, per tent, and per car. ❶

◪ FOOD

To avoid tourist traps, steer clear of Pl. Mayor, Pl. del Azoguejo, and any menus posted on worn "medieval" parchment. *Sopa castellana* (soup with eggs, and garlic), *cochinillo asado* (roast suckling pig), *ponche* (egg-yolk pastry), and lamb are all regional specialties. Segovia's many sights and steps are ideal for ▓ **picnics.** A **market** comes to Pl. Mayor every Thursday and next to Av. de la Constitución every Saturday (9am-2:30pm). Buy **groceries** at **%Dia,** C. Gobernador Fernández Jiménez, 3, off Av. de Fernández Ladreda. (Open M-Th 9:30am-8:30pm, F-Sa 9am-9pm.)

▓ **Bar-Mesón Cueva de San Esteban,** C. Valdeláguila, 15 (☎921 46 09 82). The owner knows his wines (he won the 2002 "nose of gold" trophy) and his food. Attentive and friendly service in both the entrance room and the 600-year-old cave-turned-*comedor*. This *cueva* makes anyone feel like a connoisseur. Lunch *menú* M-F €8, Sa-Su €10. Entrees €7-14. Wines €1-3. Open daily 10am-midnight. MC/V. ❸

CASTILLA Y LEÓN

Segovia

▲ ACCOMMODATIONS
Hospedaje El Gato, **10**
Hostal Don Jaime, **9**
Hotel Las Sirenas, **7**
Pensión Ferri, **2**
Residencia Juvenil
  Emperador Teodosio (HI), **11**

● FOOD
Bar-Mesón Cueva de San
  Esteban, **3**
Pizzeria Avanti
Restaurante, **8**
Restaurante La Almuzara, **1**
Las Tres BBB, **4**

★ NIGHTLIFE
La Luna, **6**
Bar Santana, **5**

TO (2km); TO LA GRANJA (9km);
TO MADRID (88km)

Santa Isabel

PL. DEL SALVADOR

Soldado Español

C. de los Vargas
C. de Santa Catalina
Vía Roma
C. de Antonio Coronel
C. de San Lorenzo
San Lorenzo
C. de Echarquedra
C. Cardenal Zúñiga
C. del Pozo
C. de Gascos
Av. Padre Claret
C. de Fuencidueña
C. San Justo
Iglesia del Salvador
C. Santa
C. Alfonso Rodríguez
PL. DE Romano
DÍAZ SANZ
C. Ochoa Ondátegui
C. de Almira
C. Las Morenas

Monasterio de
Santa Cruz la Real
C. de los Molinos

San Juan de
los Caballeros
& Museo Zuloaga
PL. DE
COLMENARES
C. L. de Peñalosa
C. San Juan
Acueducto
Acedosio El Grande
C. San Francisco

San Sebastián
C. San Agustín
i
PL. DEL AZOGUEJO
%Dia
C. Gobr.
F. Jiménez
Av. de Fernández Ladreda
$

C. Taray
Hospital Policlínico
PL. DE LOS CAÍDOS
Seminario Conciliar
C. Santa Engracia
C. A. Marinas
San Millán
Grabador Espinosa
Casa de los Picos
Torreón de Lozoya

San Nicolás
La Trinidad
Museo de Arte Contemporáneo
E. Vicente
Biblioteca Pública
Palacio del Conde Alpuente

PL. MAYOR
i
Museo de Antonio Machado
Convento Corpus Cristi
Puente Sancti Spíritus
TO (300m)
TO (500m); TO (100m)

Catedral
Puerta del Sol
Casa-Museo de Antonio Machado
C. San Valentín

Puerta de Santiago
Casa de la Moneda
San Andrés
Museo de Segovia
PL. DE LA MERCED

Iglesia de la Vera Cruz
Alcázar
Río Eresma
Po. de la Alameda del Parral
Po. de Santo Domingo de Guzmán
Arroyo Clamores
Cuesta de Los Hoyos

200 yards
200 meters

N

■ **Restaurante La Almuzara,** C. Marqués del Arco, 3 (☎921 46 06 22), past the cathedral. Serves up ample vegetarian cuisine in a bright setting. Big salads €3.60-9. Lunch *menú* €9. Open Tu 8pm-midnight, W-Su 12:45-4pm and 8pm-midnight. MC/V. ❷

Las Tres BBB, Pl. Mayor, 13 (☎921 46 21 25). Follow locals here for cheap eats. Specializes in seafood (€2.40-8.40), but offers all the basics, including simple *bocadillos* (€1.80-2.70). Open daily 8am-1:30am. MC/V. ❶

Pizzeria Avanti Restaurante, C. Santa Columba, 5 (☎921 46 60 22), up the steps to the right of the tourist office. Cheap pizzas (€7), burgers (€3.10), and Spanish fare provide respite from the inflated prices of nearby restaurants. Pay an extra €1 to sit on the patio with a view of the aqueduct. Open daily 12:30-4pm and 7:30pm-midnight. ❶

◎ SIGHTS

Segovia rewards the wanderer. Its picturesque museums, palaces, churches, and streets beg you to put aside your map and just explore. Often overlooked by visitors are Segovia's northern regions, outside the walls and away from the Alcázar. For a relaxing walk, tour the monasteries and churches along the Río Eresma.

■ **AQUEDUCT.** The ever-engineering Romans built Segovia's aqueduct around 50 BC to pipe in water from the Río Frío, 18km away. Today, *segovianos* use it to pipe tourists into the old city. The two tiers of 163 arches supported by 128 pillars span 813m and reach a height of 29m near Pl. del Azoguejo. Some 20,000 blocks of granite were used in the construction—without a drop of mortar. This spectacular feat of engineering, restored by the monarchy in the 1400s, transported 30L of water per second and was used until 60 years ago. The water didn't stop at the visible end of the structure; from there it flowed underground to the **Alcázar.**

■ **ALCÁZAR.** From afar, Segovia's Alcázar looks strangely familiar, but fear not: Disneyworld's Magic Kingdom palace is thousands of miles away. Of classic late-medieval design, it dominates the far northern end of the old quarter and provides astounding views of Queen Victoria Eugenia's gardens and the surrounding countryside. Fortifications have occupied this site since the time of the Celts due to its strategic location at the confluence of two rivers. Alfonso X, who supposedly believed he was God, took the original 11th-century fortress and beautified it. Successive monarchs increased the Alcázar's grandeur, and the final touches were added for the coronation of Isabel I in 1474. The black spots that stain the outer walls of the castle are slag, a by-product of coal-burning stoves. The walls of the **Sala de Reyes** (Room of Kings) are adorned with wood- and gold-inlaid friezes. In the **Sala de Solio** (Throne Room), the inscription above the throne reads: *"tanto monta, monta tanto"* (she mounts, as does he). Get your mind out of the gutter—it means that Fernando and Isabel had equal authority. The **Museo Real Colegio de Artillería** commemorates the period during which the Alcázar was used as an artillery school (1764-1862). Cannons, charts, and models abound. For a great ■ **view** (and workout), climb the seemingly endless spiral staircase that begins in the gift shop to stand atop the castle. (*Pl. de la Reina Victoria Eugenia. ☎921 46 07 59. Open Apr.-Sept. daily 10am-7pm; Oct. M-F 10am-6pm, Sa-Su 10am-7pm; Nov.-Mar. daily 10am-6pm. Tower closed Tu. €3.30, seniors and students €2.50. Tower only €1. Audio guides in English, €3.)*

CATHEDRAL. In 1525, Charles V commissioned the construction of a cathedral to replace the 12th-century edifice destroyed in the *Revuelta de las Comunidades.* The new one, he hoped, would tower over Pl. Mayor. When it was finished 200 years later, with 23 chapels, it earned the nickname "The Lady of All Cathedrals." The **Sala Capitular,** hung with 17th-century tapestries, displays an ornate silver-and-gold chariot. Off the cloister (moved from the Alcázar) is the **Capilla de Santa**

Catalina, filled with incredible crosses, chalices, and candelabras. (☎921 46 22 05. *Open daily Apr.-Oct. 9am-6:30pm; Nov.-Mar. 9:30am-6pm; final entrance 30min. before closing. Mass M-Sa 10am, Su 11am and 12:30pm. €2, under 14 free. Su until 2:30pm free.)*

🏛 MUSEUMS

🖎**CASA-MUSEO DE ANTONIO MACHADO.** Antonio Machado (1875-1939)—literature professor, playwright, and, above all, author of love poems and melancholic verse—never made much money. The poet rented this small *pensión*-turned-museum from 1919 to 1932 for three pesetas per day. A short, informative tour details major influences on Machado's poetry, including the 1909 death of his first wife and an affair with a married woman he called "Guiomar" in his writings. The poet's room has been left untouched, filled with manuscripts and portraits (including a Picasso). Of his room Machado once wrote *"Blanca Hospedería, Celda de Viajero, ¡Con la Sombra Mi!"* (Modest and clean lodging, traveler's cell, alone with my shadow!). Though significantly more humble than the Alcázar, this museum holds its own among Segovia's treasures. *(C. des Desamparados, 5. ☎921 46 03 77. Open W-Su 11am-2pm and 4:30-7:30pm. Guided Spanish tour required. €1.50, W free.)*

MUSEO DE ARTE CONTEMPORÁNEO ESTEBAN VICENTE. This elegant museum holds well-curated exhibitions of 20th-century art. Highlights include a permanent collection of native Segovian Esteban Vicente's works. *(Pl. de las Bellas Artes, just above Pl. de San Martín, off C. de Cervantes. ☎921 46 20 10. Open Tu-F 11am-2pm and 4-7pm, Sa 11am-7pm, Su and festivals 11am-2pm. €2.40, students and seniors €1.20. Th free.)*

MUSEO ZULOAGA. Ceramics fans, head here first. This former church and palace was the home and workshop of Daniel Zuloaga, a 20th-century artist who worked closely with Gaudí and whose tile murals grace many walls in Madrid. The museum now showcases his paintings and tile work. *(Pl. Colmenares. ☎921 46 33 48. Open Tu-Sa 10am-2pm and 4-7pm, Su 10am-2pm. €1.20, students and seniors free.)*

🎭 🌺 NIGHTLIFE AND FESTIVALS

Though the city isn't known for its sleepless nights, when it comes to nightlife, *segovianos* (and their visitors) go all out. Packed with bars and cafes, Pl. Mayor is the center of it all. Specifically, head for **Calle Infanta Isabel** (creatively nicknamed *"calle de los barres"* by the locals) and follow the crowd to find the evening's hotspot. The bars filling Pl. del Azoguejo and C. Carmen, near the aqueduct, are frequented by the high school set. For a casual older crowd try **Bar Santana,** C. Infanta Isabel, 18. Tasty tapas and rock music draw locals. (☎921 46 35 64. *Bocadillos* €2-3. Live music Tu and Th nights. Open daily 9am-midnight.) Club headquarters are C. Ruiz de Alda, off Pl. del Azoguejo. You can count on a party every night of the week at **La Luna,** C. Pta. de la Luna, 8. From Pl. Mayor, head down C. Isabel la Católica onto C. Juan Bravo and take the second right. A young local and international crowd mixes it up in this popular disco-pub, downing cheap shots and Heineken. (☎921 46 26 51. Shots €1, beer €1.50. Open daily 4:30pm-4am.)

From June 24 to 29, Segovia holds a **fiesta** in honor of San Juan and San Pedro, featuring free open-air concerts on Pl. del Azoguejo, as well as dances and fireworks on June 29. **Zamarramala,** 3km northwest of Segovia, hosts the **Fiestas de Santa Águeda** (Feb. 4-6). Women take over the town's administration for a day, dress in period costumes, and parade through the streets to commemorate a sneak attack on the Alcázar in which women distracted the castle guards with wine and song (and maybe something else). The all-female local council takes advantage of its authority to ridicule men and, at the festival's end, burn a male effigy.

🖅 DAYTRIP FROM SEGOVIA

🖅 LA GRANJA DE SAN ILDEFONSO

La Sepulvedana buses (☎921 42 77 07) run from Segovia to La Granja (20min.; 9-12 per day M-Sa 7:40am-9:30pm, Su 10:30am-10:30pm; return M-Sa 7:20am-9pm, Su 11am-10pm; round-trip €1.50). From the bus stop, walk uphill through the ornate gates and watch for signs. ☎921 47 00 19. Open Apr.-Sept. daily 10am-6pm; Oct.-Mar. M-Sa 10am-1:30pm and 3-5pm, Su 10am-2pm. Tours in Spanish depart every 15min. €4, with guide €5; students, under 16, and EU seniors €2.50; under 5 free. EU citizens free W.

A must-see for any visitor to Segovia, the royal palace of La Granja, 9km southeast of the city, is the most extravagant of Spain's four royal summer retreats (the others being El Pardo, El Escorial, and Aranjuez). Felipe V, the first Bourbon King of Spain and grandson of Louis XIV, detested the Habsburgs' austere El Escorial. Nostalgic for Versailles, he commissioned La Granja in the early 18th century, choosing the site based on its hunting and gardening potential. A fire destroyed the living quarters in 1918, but the structure was rebuilt in 1932 to house one of the world's finest collections of Flemish tapestries. The highlight of the collection is the tapestry series by Pierre van Aelst entitled *The Honors;* it was said to be an allegory of Charles I's moral development. Be sure not to miss the floor below either, with its four Goya tapestries and the 16th-century "Triumphs of Petrarch" and 17th-century "History of Venus" series. René Carlier designed the **gardens** surrounding the palace. Carefully manicured hedges surround impressive flowerbeds, but even those are no match for the decadent 🖅**Cascadas Nuevas,** an ensemble of illuminated fountains and pools representing the continents and seasons. The **Andromeda** fountain is also a worthwhile stop. (Fountains run W and Sa-Su at 5:30pm; ask at the Segovia tourist office. Open daily June 17-Aug. 10am-9pm; May-June 16 and Sept. 10am-8pm; Apr. 10am-7pm; Mar. and Oct. 10am-6:30pm; Nov.-Feb. 10am-6pm. W and Sa-Su €3.40; students €1.70. M-Tu and Th-F free.)

ÁVILA ☎920

Ávila (pop. 50,000) has two main attractions: an impressive set of restored 12th-century stone walls and the abode of Santa Teresa de Jesús. Museums and monuments welcome outsiders to learn about Santa Teresa, depicting her divine visitations and daily life in exhaustive detail; the celebration of her feast day (Oct. 15) lasts a full week. Within its walls, Ávila is untouched by pollution, advertisements, or traffic, and well-worth a daytrip from Madrid, Segovia, or Salamanca.

🚃 TRANSPORTATION

Trains: Av. de la Estación, 40 (☎902 24 02 02). Info open daily 7:30am-1:30pm and 3:30-9:30pm. To: **El Escorial** (1hr.; M-F 9 per day 5:30am-8:37pm, Sa-Su 6 per day 9:15am-8:37pm; €3.30); **Madrid** (1½-2hr.; 15-23 per day M-F 5:30am-10:13pm, Sa-Su 7:05am-10:15pm; €6); **Salamanca** (1¾hr., 5-7 per day 7:10am-10:49pm, €7.20); €6.40); **Segovia** (1hr., 12 per day 7:05am-7:35pm, €7.70) via **Villalba** (1hr., €4.40); **Valladolid** (1½hr.; 10-13 per day M-F and Su 9:53am-9:53pm, Sa 9:53am-7:52pm.

Buses: Av. de Madrid, 2 (☎920 22 01 54). To **Madrid's** Estación Sur de Autobuses (1½hr.; M-F 8 per day 6am-7pm, Sa-Su 4 per day 10am-7pm; €6.50) and **Segovia** (1hr.; M-F 5 per day 5:30am-8pm; Sa-Su 10am and 7pm; €3.80).

Taxis: Radio Taxis (☎920 35 35 45), in Pl. Sta. Teresa and at the train station.

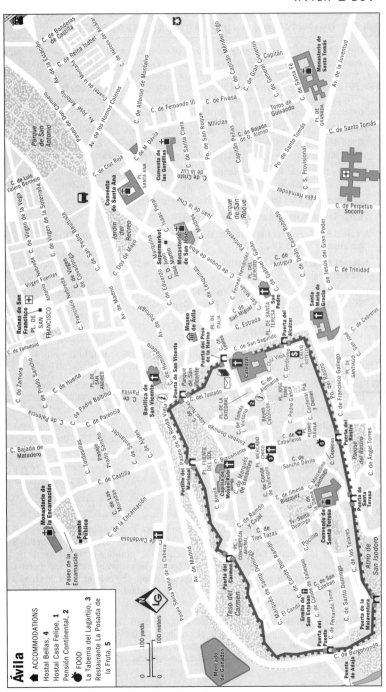

Ávila

▲ ACCOMMODATIONS
Hostal Bellas, **4**
Hostal Casa Felipe, **1**
Pensión Continental, **2**

🍴 FOOD
La Taberna La Lagartijo, **3**
Restaurante La Posada de la Fruta, **5**

CASTILLA Y LEÓN

⚡🛈 ORIENTATION AND PRACTICAL INFORMATION

All the worthwhile tourist sights lie within or around the city walls. The winding streets of the old city meet in two main squares: **Plaza del Mercado Chico** inside the city walls and the recently revamped **Plaza de Santa Teresa** just outside. Bus #1 (€0.60) runs to Pl. del Mercado Chico from the stop one block from the train station. To get from the bus station to Pl. Sta. Teresa, cross the intersection in front, follow the length of the park, and turn left onto C. Duque de Alba.

Tourist Office: Pl. de la Catedral, 4 (☎920 21 13 87; www.avila.net). English spoken. Open daily 9am-8pm. Branch office, Av. de Madrid, 29 (☎920 22 59 69), across the street from the northwest corner tower of the wall. Open daily 9am-7pm.

Currency Exchange: Banco Santander Central Hispano, C. Don Jerónimo, 8 (☎920 21 11 39). Open Apr.-Sept. M-F 8:30am-2pm, Oct.-May also Sa 8:30am-1pm.

Luggage storage: At the bus station. €1-2. Open daily 9am-7pm.

Police: Av. de la Inmaculada, 11 (☎092 or 920 35 24 24).

Medical Services: Hospital Provincial, Jesús del Gran Poder, 42 (☎920 35 72 00). **Ambulance:** ☎920 22 22 22.

Internet Access: Access in the public library, across the street from the main entrance to the cathedral.

Post Office: Pl. de la Catedral, 2 (☎920 35 31 06). **Fax** service available. Open M-F 8:30am-8:30pm, Sa 9:30am-2pm. **Postal Code:** 05001.

⌂ ACCOMMODATIONS

Comfortable and affordable accommodations can be found within the city walls. Those near the cathedral and Pl. de Sta. Teresa fill up in summer, so call early.

Pensión Continental, Pl. de la Catedral, 6 (☎920 21 15 02; fax 21 15 63). Beautiful, bright rooms with high ceilings and phone overlook the plaza; those without bath have sink. Singles €15.10; doubles €25.90, with bath €33.10; triples €39. AmEx/MC/V. ❶

Hostal Bellas, C. de Caballeros, 19 (☎920 21 29 10). Clean rooms with bath are tasteful but come at tourist prices. 3 meals €16.20. July-Sept. singles €30; doubles €40; triples (extra bed in a double) €55. Oct.-June €24/€33/€47. MC/V. ❸

Hostal Casa Felipe, Pl. Mercado Chico, 12 (☎920 21 39 24). Tiny rooms with TV and sink over the square. Singles €20; doubles €32, with bath €38; triples €54. MC/V. ❷

◖ FOOD

Budget sandwich shops surround Pl. Mercado Chico. The most affordable restaurant area is C. de San Segundo, off Pl. de Sta. Teresa, while cafes in the plaza itself peddle more expensive fare. Renowned local food includes *ternera de Ávila* (veal), *mollejas* (sweetbreads), *judías del barco* (beans with pork), and *yemas de Santa Teresa* (egg yolk and sugar). Every Friday, the **market** in Pl. Mercado Chico sells produce from 10am to 2pm. The **supermarket,** C. Juan José Martín, 6, stocks all the basics (open M-Sa 9:45am-2pm and 5-8pm).

La Taberna del Lagartijo, C. Martín Carramolino, 4 (☎920 22 88 25), just behind Iglesia de San Juan. Autographed bullfight photos decorate the walls. Delicious food and a casual atmosphere inside and out make this a favorite of *abulenses* (Ávila residents). Entrees €12-15. Open M-Th 1:30-4pm and 8pm-midnight. MC/V. ❸

Restaurante La Posada de la Fruta, Pl. Pedro Dávila, 8 (☎920 25 47 02). 4 different seating locations at different prices—the *terraza* is the nicest and cheapest. *Menú* €9-12. Sandwiches and a less expensive *menú* on the terrace €7.90-10. Open daily 1-4pm and 8:30-11:30pm; bar open 9am-11:30pm. ❷

👁 SIGHTS

■ **LAS MURALLAS.** Though originally built to deter foreigners from invading Ávila, these gigantic city walls now welcome thousands of tourists year-round. The walls are impressive on their own, but the real attraction is walking around them, viewing the city from above. Research has placed construction of the 2500 battlements, 88 towers, and nine gates in the 12th century, though legend holds that they are the oldest in Spain, dating back to 1090. **Cimorro,** the most imposing tower, doubles as the cathedral's apse. To walk along the 2.5km of walls, start from Puerta del Alcázar. *(Walk straight ahead with your back to Pl. de Sta. Teresa. €3.50; students, groups, over 65, and under 8 €2.)* The best view of the walls and of Ávila itself is from the **Cuatro Postes,** past the Río Adaja, 1.5km along the highway to Salamanca. *(From Pl. de Sta. Teresa, walk through the inner city and out the Puerta del Puente. Cross the bridge and follow the road to the right for about 1km. Total walk 25min.)*

CATEDRAL. Begun in the late 12th century, Ávila's is the oldest Spanish cathedral in the transitional style between Romanesque and Gothic—a stunning architectural experience. Look for the **Altar de La Virgen de la Caridad,** where 12-year-old Santa Teresa prostrated herself after the death of her mother. Behind the main altar is the alabaster **tomb** of Cardinal Alonso de Madrigal, a bishop of Ávila and prolific writer whose dark complexion won him the title "El Tostado" (The Swarthy, or "Toasted"). The nickname spread, and during the Golden Age, it became popular to call an aspiring author *un tostado.* The **museum** displays an El Greco portrait, enormous *libros de canti* (hymnals), and Juan de Arfe's silver, six-leveled **Custodia del Corpus,** complete with swiveling bells. Upon exiting the side of the church, look on either side above the doors; the sculptures of bearded men with clubs and scaly skin are actually "noble savages," a 15th-century artist's version of Inca warriors wearing feathered ceremonial armor. *(Pl. de la Catedral. ☎920 21 16 41. Open June-Oct. 10am-7:15pm; Apr.-May M-F 10am-6pm, Sa 10am-7pm, Su noon-6pm; Nov.-Mar. M-F 10am-5pm, Sa 10am-6pm, Su noon-6pm. Last entrance 45min. before closing. Cathedral free; museum €2.50.)*

THE LOCAL STORY

AVES OF ÁVILA

Though the largest migratory species in Spanish cathedral towns may be *touristicus americanus,* there are other seasonal guests that seem to enjoy the churches even more. The enormous basket-like nests balanced on bell towers and ramparts are built by *cigüeñas* (storks), who fly all the way from Africa to perch atop spires in central Spain. As in America and England, Spanish storks are considered avian obstetricians; the old folktale probably comes from their arrival in springtime, the season of fecundity. These territorial birds fill the still summer air with the loud clacking of their beaks.

In contrast to these raucous storks are the thousands of *vencejos* (tree swifts) that swoop and swarm in random clouds and circular formations. But no bird is more common in Ávila than the notorious *paloma* (dove) that hovers over Santa Teresa's shoulder, representing the Holy Ghost. The symbolism of the dove is drawn from Luke 3:22, in which the Ghost descends upon Jesus in the form of a dove at his baptism. If, by chance, a bird happens to "baptize" you from above, regard it as good luck—the Spaniards do.

For more information on Spanish animalia, see http://faunaiberica.org, an organization devoted to the study and conservation of native species.

MONASTERIO DE LA ENCARNACIÓN. The monastery museum shows the contrast between Santa Teresa's two lifestyles. Coming from a wealthy family, she had many expensive possessions, some of which are on display in the **museum.** Later, she renounced these for a life of asceticism and sandal-wearing. Among the most interesting relics is a wooden log she used as her pillow. The mandatory guided tour visits Santa Teresa's tiny cell and the **main staircase** where she had a mystical encounter with the child Jesus. Upstairs from the cloister, the museum features a collection of personal effects given to the convent by wealthier nuns as bribes to procure entrance. *(Po. de la Encarnación.* ☎*920 21 12 12. Museum open daily M-F 9:30am-1:30pm and 3:30-6pm, Sa-Su 10am-1:30pm and 3:30-6pm. Admission and tour €1.50.)*

MONASTERIO DE SANTO TOMÁS. About a 20min. walk from the Puerta del Alcázar is another enormous church and monastery. Fernando and Isabel used it as a summer refuge and a seat of the Inquisition. Inside the church, in front of the *retablo*, is the tomb of Prince Don Juan, Fernando and Isabel's only son, who died in 1497 at age 19. There are also three cloisters with contrasting architectural styles: the Tuscan Claustro del Noviciado (Cloister of the Noviciate) is simplest, the Gothic Claustro del Silencio (Cloister of Silence) more elaborate, and the Renaissance-Transition Claustro de los Reyes is fit for kings. *(Pl. Granada, 1.* ☎*920 22 04 00. Monastery and cloisters open daily 10am-1pm and 4-8pm. Last entrance to cloisters 30min. before closing. Monastery free. Cloisters €3, groups €2.)*

OTHER SIGHTS. Santa Teresa's admirers built the 17th-century **Convento de Santa Teresa** at the site of her birth. *(Inside the city walls, near Puerta de Sta. Teresa. Open daily 9:30am-1:30pm and 3:30-7:30pm.)* If you only see one site related to Santa Teresa, visit **Sala de Reliquías,** a small building near the convent, where you will find a small scrapbook of Santa Teresa relics, including her right ring finger, the sole of her sandal, and the cord she used to flagellate herself. *(Open daily Apr.-Oct. 9:30am-1:30pm and 3:30-7:30pm; Nov.-Mar. Tu-Su 10am-1:30pm and 3:30-7pm. Free.)* For a larger collection of items that Santa Teresa may have touched, looked at, or lived among, visit the **Museo de Santa Teresa,** built into the convent's crypt, around the corner and to the left of the entrance. *(*☎*920 22 07 08. Open Apr.-Oct. daily 10am-2pm and 4-7pm; Nov.-Mar. Tu-Su 10am-1:30pm and 3:30-5:30pm. Last entrance 30min. before closing. €2.)*

SALAMANCA ☎923

Salamanca, city of scholars, saints, royals, and rogues, showcases the best examples of Spanish Plateresque architecture by day, and a vivacious club scene that contends with Barcelona and Madrid by night. Fantastic facades glow in the afternoon sunshine, shadowed only by immense towers that loom overhead. Look closely: Salamanca has many hidden architectural surprises that reward the diligent visitor, from modern interpretations of cathedral iconography to a mythological calendar near the Plaza Mayor. If the architecture is not enough, the prestigious Universidad de Salamanca, grouped in medieval times with Bologna, Paris, and Oxford as one of the "four leading lights of the world," continues to add the energy of its thousands of students to the well-touristed city—an explosive mix that provides what locals claim to be Spain's best nightlife.

▐ TRANSPORTATION

Trains: Po. de la Estación (☎923 12 02 02). To: **Ávila** (1½hr., 6-7 per day 6am-7:55pm, €7.20); **Lisboa** (6hr., 4:51am, €45.40); **Madrid** (2½hr., 5-6 per day 6am-7:53pm, €14.20); **Palencia** (2hr., 1:55pm and 7:50pm, €8.40 or €19); **Valladolid** (2hr., 8-12 per day 12:05am-8:05pm, €5.60-12.50).

Buses: Av. Filiberto Villalobos, 71-85 (☎923 23 67 17). Take C. Ramón y Cajal to Po. de San Vicente. Cross this avenue, and C. Ramón y Cajal becomes Av. Filiberto Villalobos. Open M-F 8am-8:30pm, Sa 9am-2:30pm and 4:30-6:30pm, Su 10am-2pm and 4-7:30pm. To: **Ávila** (1½hr.; M-F 4 per day 6:30am-8:30pm, Sa 4 per day 9am-8:30pm, Su 3:30 and 8:30pm; €4.90); **Barcelona** (11hr., 7:30am and noon, €43); **Ciudad Rodrigo** (1hr.; M-F 13 per day 7am-9:30pm, Sa 6 per day 8:30am-6pm, Su 4 per day 11am-10pm; €4.90); **León** (2½hr.; M-F 3 per day 11am-6:30pm, Sa 11am, Su 10pm; €10.90); **Madrid** (3hr.; M-Sa 16 per day 6am-9:30pm, Su 16 per day 8am-11pm; €10.20-15); **Segovia** (3hr.; M-F 7:30am and 1:30pm, Sa 7:30 and 9:30am, Su 1:30 and 8:45pm; €8.90); **Valladolid** (1½hr.; M-Sa 6 per day 8am-8pm, Su 4 per day 10:30am-10pm; €6.60); **Zamora** (1hr.; M-F 15 per day 6:40am-9:35pm, Sa 10 per day 7:45am-8:30pm, Su 7 per day 8:45am-10:15pm; €3.70).

Taxis: Auto-Taxi (24hr. ☎923 25 00 09) and **Radio Taxi** (24hr. ☎923 25 00 00).

Car Rental: Avis, Po. de Canalejas, 49 (☎923 26 97 53). Open M-F 9:30am-1:30pm and 4-7pm, Sa 9am-1:30pm. **Europcar,** Po. de Canalejas, 123 (☎923 26 90 41). Open M-F 9am-1:30pm and 4:30-7:30pm, Sa 9am-1:30pm.

■■ ORIENTATION AND PRACTICAL INFORMATION

The majestic **Plaza Mayor** is the social and geographic center of Salamanca. Most hostels are to the south on **Rúa Mayor** and **Plaza de Anaya,** as are the **university** and most sights. From the **train station,** catch bus #1 (€0.70) to Gran Vía and ask to be let off at Pl. San Julián (20min. from train station, 15min. from bus station).

Tourist Office: Municipal office, Pl. Mayor, 32 (☎923 21 83 42). Open June-Sept. M-F 9am-2pm and 4:30-8pm, Sa 10am-8pm, Su 10am-2pm; Oct.-May M-F 9am-2pm and 4:30-6:30pm, Sa 10am-2pm and 4:30-8pm, Su 10am-2pm. **Regional office,** R. Mayor (☎923 26 58 71), in the Casa de las Conchas. Open July-Aug. Su-Th 9am-8pm, F-Sa 9am-9pm; Sept.-June daily 9am-2pm and 5-8pm. Look out for **DGratis,** a free weekly listing of goings-on. Available at kiosks, tourist offices, and distributors in Pl. Mayor.

Currency exchange: EuroDivisas, R. Mayor, 2 (☎923 21 21 80). Open M-F 8:30am-10pm, Sa-Su 10am-7pm. **ATMs** can be found on every major street.

Luggage Storage: At the **train station** (24hr.; €3) and **bus station** (open daily 7am-7:45pm; €0.60).

Police: ☎092 or 923 27 91 38.

Pharmacy: Farmacia Amador Felipe, C. Toro, 25 (☎923 21 41 24). Friendly, English-speaking staff. Open daily 9:30am-10pm.

Hospital: Hospital Clínico Universitario, Po. de San Vicente, 108 (☎923 29 11 00).

Internet Access: Public Library, Casa de Las Conchas, C. Compañía, 2 (☎923 269 317). Free Internet (limit 30min.) and a cool reading room. Open M-F 9am-9pm, Sa 9am-2pm. **CiberPlaza,** Pl. Mayor, 10 (☎923 26 42 81). Open daily 10:30am-2am. €0.80-1.20 per hr. **Cyber Anuario,** C. La Latina, 8, has comfortable chairs, fast connections, and services including copying, printing, CD burning, fax, and long distance calls (€0.10 per min. to the US). Internet €1.50. Open daily 9am-1am.

Post Office: Gran Vía, 25-29 (☎923 263 011). **Lista de Correos.** Open M-F 8:30am-8:30pm, Sa 9:30am-2pm. **Postal Code:** 37080.

▐ ACCOMMODATIONS AND CAMPING

Thanks to floods of student visitors, reasonably priced *hostales* and *pensiones* pepper the streets of Salamanca, especially off Pl. Mayor and C. Meléndez. Try to make reservations a day or two in advance during July and August, when hostel-hungry students and tourists overrun the city.

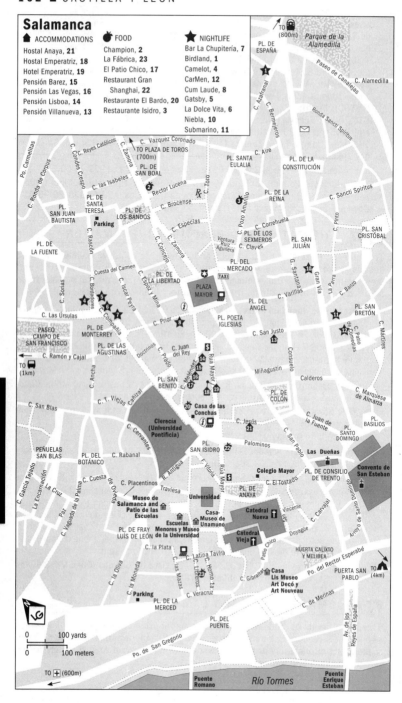

Salamanca

⌂ ACCOMMODATIONS

Hostal Anaya, **21**
Hostal Emperatriz, **18**
Hotel Emperatriz, **19**
Pensión Barez, **15**
Pensión Las Vegas, **16**
Pensión Lisboa, **14**
Pensión Villanueva, **13**

🍎 FOOD

Champion, **2**
La Fábrica, **23**
El Patio Chico, **17**
Restaurant Gran
  Shanghai, **22**
Restaurante El Bardo, **20**
Restaurante Isidro, **3**

★ NIGHTLIFE

Bar La Chupitería, **7**
Birdland, **1**
Camelot, **4**
CarMen, **12**
Cum Laude, **8**
Gatsby, **5**
La Dolce Vita, **6**
Niebla, **10**
Submarino, **11**

CASTILLA Y LEÓN

Pensión Las Vegas, C. Meléndez, 13, 1st fl. (☎923 21 87 49; www.lasvegascentro.com). Friendly owners, terraces, and TVs make this *pensión* a great deal. Singles with shower €18; doubles €24, with bath €30-36; triples with bath €45. MC/V. ❷

Pensión Barez, C. Meléndez, 19, 1st fl. (☎923 21 74 95). Rooms overlook the street; some without windows. Common room with terrace makes up for tiny spaces. Singles €12; doubles €22; triples €33. ❶

Pensión Villanueva, C. San Justo, 8, 1st fl. (☎923 26 88 33). Decent rooms with simple beds. Close to R. Mayor. Singles €13 (no window); doubles €23. Extra bed €13. ❶

Pensión Los Ángeles, Pl. Mayor, 10, 2nd-3rd fl. (☎923 21 81 66). Rooms with balconies over the stunning Pl. Mayor must be reserved far in advance. If you can't get a view, look around for better prices. Some rooms without windows. English spoken. Singles €15-16; doubles €28-30, with bath €30-32; triples and larger €15 per person. ❷

Pensión Lisboa, C. Meléndez, 1 (☎923 21 43 33). Rooms are small, clean, and pink. Most have sinks, some have rooftop city views. Singles €16; doubles €32. ❷

Hostal Emperatriz, R. Mayor, 16 (☎/fax 923 21 87 83). Operates out of hotel next door. Don't let the dark, creaky staircase deter you—spacious rooms have bath and phone. Rooms facing R. Mayor have a great view, but can be noisy. Breakfast €2.10. Singles €24; doubles €33; triples €44. ❷

Hotel Emperatriz, R. Mayor, 18 (☎923 21 91 56). Pricier, bright rooms with medieval charm: wooden, old-style beds and hand-carved drawers. Singles €36; doubles €51. ❹

Hostal Anaya, C. Jesús, 18 (☎923 27 17 73). Steps away from the Pl. Mayor and most historical sights, with clean rooms and service that will make you feel at home. Singles €24; doubles €36, with bath €42; triples €54; quads €72. ❷

Camping: Camping Regio (☎923 13 88 88), on Ctra. Salamanca, 4km toward Madrid. Albertur buses leave every 30min. from Gran Vía near Pl. de la Constitución. First-class sites with hot showers. Tennis courts and restaurants in a complex next door. €3 per person, per tent, and per car. MC/V. ❶

⬛ FOOD

Salamanca offers a variety of restaurants serving everything from *salmantino* dishes like *chanfaina* (a type of beef stew) and *tostón asado* (roasted baby pork) to cheeseburgers. Cafes and restaurants surrounding the Pl. Mayor, which lights up around 10pm, provide great views and excellent food; you can get a three-course meal for about €9. **Champion,** C. Toro, 64, is a central supermarket. (Open M-Sa 9am-9:30pm.) Another tactic is to go from bar to bar, ordering drinks and *pinchos*, the free tapas (some are quite filling) that come with them.

El Patio Chico, C. Meléndez, 13 (☎923 26 51 03). *Salmantinos* crowd this place at lunch and dinner, but hefty portions are worth the wait. If outdoor tables are filled, take a chance with the throng inside. Try the *morcilla picante* (spicy blood sausage). *Bocadillos* €2-3. Entrees €4-8. *Menú* €11. Open daily 1-4pm and 8pm-midnight. ❷

Restaurante Isidro, C. Pozo Amarillo, 19 (☎923 26 28 48), a block from Pl. Mayor. Don't let the fake roses fool you—this is a quality place. Prompt, courteous service and large portions. Numerous vegetable, egg, seafood (try *gambas en ajo*), and meat entrees (€3-9). *Menú* €8.40. Open daily 1-4pm and 8pm-midnight. MC/V. ❷

La Fábrica, C. Libreros, 47-49 (☎923 26 95 74). Students head straight for La Fábrica's 80s music after a night in the University library. It looks more like a hangout than a restaurant, and good, cheap food keeps the students coming. Breakfast (coffee and pastry) €1.50, *bocadillos* €3-6. *Menú* €9. *Litros* (liters) of beer €2.70. Open daily 9am until the last customer leaves—usually 2am, weekends 4am. ❶

Restaurant Gran Shanghai, R. Mayor, 35-37 (☎923 21 18 10). Delicious and supremely affordable Chinese food near Pl. de Anaya. Serving up soup (€2-3), rice (€2-4), and other entrees (€3-9) in a pleasant, quiet setting. Open 1-4pm and 8-11pm. ❶

Restaurante El Bardo, C. Compañía, 8 (☎923 21 90 89), between the Casa de las Conchas and the Clerecía. Traditional Spanish food at low prices. *Menú* €9. Paella €7.60 per person. Entrees €6-13. Open daily 1:30-4pm and 9-11:30pm. MC/V. ❷

◉ 🏛 SIGHTS AND MUSEUMS

🖾 LA UNIVERSIDAD DE SALAMANCA

From Pl. Mayor follow R. Mayor, veer right onto R. Antigua, then left onto C. Libreros; the university is on the left. University ☎923 29 44 00, museum 923 29 12 25. Open M-F 9:30am-1pm and 4-7pm, Sa 9:30am-1:30pm and 4-7pm, Su 10am-1:30pm. University and museum €2.40, students and seniors €1.20.

The renowned university, established in 1218, is *the* focal point of Salamanca. Though located next to the cathedrals on R. Mayor, it is best approached from C. Libreros. The university's entrance is one of the best examples of Spanish Plateresque, a style named after the work of *plateros* (silversmiths). The iron-rich sandstone unearthed in this region is pliable and easy to work with when new; Miguel de Unamuno wrote that it "cuts like cheese" when fresh from the quarry. The material, however, hardens and weathers like granite when old, creating the illusion of silver filigree-like work on hard stone. The central medallion depicts Fernando and Isabel, *los Reyes Católicos.* Sculpted into the facade is a tiny frog perched atop a skull; according to legend, those who can spot the frog without assistance will be blessed with good luck or marriage. Try to stand away from finger-pointing tourist groups if you actually want to accomplish this feat.

The old lecture halls inside the university are open to the public. Entering the cool stone foyer feels like stepping into another era; a cough echoes through the building, and outdoor noise disappears. The 15th-century classroom **Aula Fray Luis de León** has been left in more or less its original state; medieval students considered the hard benches luxurious, as most students then sat on the floor. On the 2nd floor, the **Biblioteca Antigua,** one of Europe's oldest libraries, is the most spectacular room of all, located atop a magnificent Plateresque staircase. The staircase itself is another famous case of ambiguous symbols with multiple interpretations, but it is generally considered to represent the ascent of the scholar through careless youth, love, and adventure on the perilous path to true knowledge.

Look closely at the walls of the university and cathedral and you'll see faded red scrawlings on the sandstone; this is not graffiti. 800 years ago, students at the university attended classes in the Old Cathedral. They would come to the church the night before their final exam to pray for success; the rigorous oral test was administered the next day in front of the chapel now known as *La Capilla del Estudiante.* Those fortunate enough to pass left the cathedral through the main entrance to shouts of congratulation from the throng of anxious *salmantinos* waiting outside. Later that evening, the town would host a bullfight in honor of the new graduates; the fresh blood of the bull was mixed with a flour paste and used to paint the names of the new doctors on the university and cathedral walls.

Don't miss the **University Museum.** Walk through the hall on the left corner of the patio; the museum is on the left. The reconstructed **Cielo de Salamanca,** the library's famous 15th-century ceiling fresco of the zodiac by the celebrated Fernando Gallego, is preserved here in all its splendor. Take a peek at the intricate strongbox with its many locks. *(Below Pl. San Isidro, off R. Mayor.)*

OTHER SIGHTS AND MUSEUMS

CATEDRAL NUEVA. This cathedral first stuns visitors with its sheer size and openness, and then with its opulent details. Walk in through the main door to admire the intricate Plateresque style and awesome forest of columns supporting vaulted ceilings of blue and gold. It took 220 years (1513-1733) to build this spectacular example of Spanish Gothic architecture. While several architects decided to retain the original late Gothic style, they could not resist adding touches from later periods, most notably to the Baroque tower. The church is best viewed first from the ground, but be sure to climb the tower to get a spectacular ▨ **view from above.** The route through the tower lets you compare the old and new cathedrals from their balconies. It also includes an exhibit contrasting their architecture. Modern renovators left their marks too: look for an astronaut and a dragon eating ice cream on the left side of the main door. *(Pl. de Anaya. Open daily Apr.-Sept. 9am-8pm; Oct.-Mar. 10am-2:30pm and 4-5:30pm. Free. Tower ☎923 28 11 23. Open daily 10am-7:30pm, last entrance 30min. before closing. €2.)*

CATEDRAL VIEJA. The smaller Catedral Vieja (1140) was built in Romanesque style. Its cupola is one of the most detailed in Spain and was assembled from many intricately carved miniature pieces. Gargoyles and expectant faces peer down from the columns' capitals, some funny, others strangely haunting; the faces in the **Capilla de Talavera** are also unnerving. Above the high altar, Jesus separates the damned from the saved. The oldest original part of the cathedral is the **Capilla de San Martín,** with brilliant frescoes dating from 1242. Look for the image of the Virgen de la Vega, Salamanca's patron saint. The **museum** features works by Fernando Gallego, a Renaissance painter who experimented with deep perspective. Pedro Bello's work is also of note; central figures in his religious paintings are often bored or asleep. Be sure to check out the famed **Patio Chico** behind the cathedral, where students congregate and tourists head for a splendid view of both cathedrals. *(Enter through the Catedral Nueva. Museum ☎923 21 74 76. Cathedral open daily Oct.-Mar. 10am-1:30pm and 4-7:30pm; Apr.-Sept. 10am-7:30pm. €3, students €2.30, children €1.50.)*

PLAZA MAYOR. Salamanca's Plaza Mayor, considered one of the most beautiful squares in Spain, is the people-watching site *par excellence.* Hundreds of tables border the colonnade, while in the center street performers and musicians entertain and couples stroll hand in hand. The sandstone plaza appears golden in the afternoon sun, and when the evening lights come on, the whole city comes out to party under them. Designed and built by Alberto Churriguera (see **Architecture,** p. 72) between 1729 and 1755, the plaza contains 88 towering arches, the Ayuntamiento, and three pavilions dedicated to historical figures. The Pabellón Real, to the right of the Ayuntamiento, honors the Spanish monarchy (and, quite controversially, the 20th-century dictator Francisco Franco, behind the blue tarpaulin); the Pabellón del Sur, in front of the Ayuntamiento, is dedicated to famous Spanish conquistadors; and the Pabellón del Oeste, to the left of the Ayuntamiento, pays homage to important *salmantinos* like San Juan de Sahagún and Miguel de Unamuno. Before the pavilions were built, the square served as the town bullring.

CONVENTO DE SAN ESTEBAN. Visit the Convento de San Esteban and the cathedrals, and you've seen the full spectrum of Salamanca's architectural and artistic styles. Here is Salamanca's most gold-encrusted altar, and a magnificent facade depicting the stoning of San Esteban. The beautiful **Claustro de los Reyes** (Kings' Cloister), with its Gothic interior and Plateresque exterior, is visibly the product of two different eras. Its capitals are decorated with fantastic creatures. José Churriguera's central painting, *The Triumph of the Catholic Church* (1693), is not as allegorical as one might hope; horses pulling a carriage full of saints and popes trample less holy figures. *(Off C. San Pablo and C. Palominos. ☎ 923 21 50 00. Open Tu-Su Apr.-Sept. 9am-1pm and 4-8pm; Oct.-Mar. 9am-1pm and 4-5:30pm. €1.20, free M mornings.)*

CASA LIS MUSEO ART NOUVEAU Y ART DECO. If religious art is getting a bit too heavy, step into the Casa Lis for an aesthetic lollipop. Underneath a stunning stained-glass ceiling is a patio full of early 20th-century art and kitsch. Decorative objects, including lamps and perfume bottles, are pretty, but not as pretty as the bronze and ivory statues of flappers. The best works here will make you laugh; *Allegory* by Godard A. presents a satirical perspective on the "modern woman," a collection of bottles depict curmudgeonly old men from Dickens, and two rooms of dolls may give you the willies. *(C. Gibraltar, 14, behind the cathedrals. ☎ 923 12 14 25. Open Apr.-Oct. 15 Tu-F 11am-2pm and 5-9pm, Sa-Su 11am-9pm; Oct. 16-Mar. Tu-F 11am-2pm and 4-7pm, Sa-Su 11am-8pm. €2.10, students €1.50, children and Th mornings free.)*

MUSEO DE SALAMANCA. Across from the university in the Patio de las Escuelas, the Museo de Salamanca occupies an astounding building that was once home to Álvarez Albarca, physician to Fernando and Isabel. Along with the Casa de las Conchas, this structure is among Spain's most important examples of 15th-century architecture. The museum has an intriguing collection of sculptures and paintings including *Mesa Alegre* (Happy Table) by Vincenzo Camp and *Viejo Bebedor* (Old Drunk) by Esteban March. Juan de Flandes's portrait of San Andrés and Luis de Morales's *Llanto por Cristo muerto* are more serious. *(Patio de las Escuelas, 2. ☎ 923 21 22 35. Open Tu-Sa 10am-2pm and 4-7pm, Su 10am-2pm. €1.20, students €0.60.)*

CASA DE LAS CONCHAS. Follow R. Mayor until you reach a plaza with an organ-pipe fountain. Take a right and look up at the face of the building on your right. The 15th-century Casa de las Conchas (House of Shells), with over 300 scallop halves, is one of Salamanca's most famous landmarks. Pilgrims who journeyed to Santiago de Compostela (p. 602) traditionally wore shells to commemorate their visit to the tomb of Santiago. The owner of the *casa* supposedly created this monument to honor either the renowned pilgrimage or his wife, whose family shield featured scallops. Legend has it that the Jesuits bought and leveled every house in the area to build their college—*except* the Casa de las Conchas, despite their offer of one gold coin for every shell. The building now hosts the public library and tourist office. *(C. Compañía, 39. Library ☎ 923 26 93 17. Open M-F 9am-9pm, Sa 9am-2pm. Casa open M-F 9am-9pm, Sa-Su 9am-2pm and 4-7pm. Su 10am-2pm and 4-7pm. Free.)* Directly across from the Casa de las Conchas is **La Clerecía** (Royal College of the Holy Spirit), the main building of La Universidad Pontificia de Salamanca. The building has a unique plan, allowing visitors to peer over the Cloister of Studies into the gallery and courtyard. *(☎ 923 26 46 60. Open for Mass M-Sa 1:15 and 7pm, Su noon. €1.50.)*

CASA MUSEO DE UNAMUNO. If you are a fan of Unamuno, this is the place for you. Miguel de Unamuno, rector of the university during the early 20th century, is revered as one of the founding figures of the Spanish literary phenomenon known as the *Generación de 98*. Unamuno passionately opposed dictatorship and encouraged his students to do so as well. His stand against General Miguel Primo de Rivera's 1923 coup led to his dismissal, though he was triumphantly reinstated some years later. Unamuno lived here while rector; his library and bedroom are the best and most intimate parts of the museum. Photographs, letters, and origami animals line the walls. *(To the right of the university's main entrance. Ring bell if house appears closed. ☎ 923 29 44 00, ext. 1196. Open July-Sept. Tu-F 9:30am-1:30pm, Sa-Su 10am-1:30pm; Oct.-June Tu-F 9:30am-1:30pm and 4-6pm, Sa-Su 10am-2pm. Research room open M-F 9am-2pm. Mandatory tour in Spanish every 30min. €1.80, students €0.90.)*

PUENTE ROMANO. A 2000-year-old Roman bridge spans the scenic Río Tormes at the southern edge of the city. It was once part of the *Camino de la Plata* (Silver Way), a Roman trade route running from Mérida in Extremadura to Astorga. In medieval times, that was the route most Andalusian and Castilian Christians took to complete their pilgrimage to Santiago de Compostela. A headless granite bull called the **Toro Ibérico** guards one end of the bridge. Though it dates to pre-Roman times, the bull gained fame in the 16th century when it appeared in *Lazarillo de Tormes*, the prototype of the picaresque novel and a predecessor of *Don Quixote*; in one karmic episode, Lazarillo gets his head slammed into the bull's ear after cheating his blind employer. *(To reach the bridge go downhill toward the river).*

🎵 NIGHTLIFE

Salmantinos claim Salamanca to be the best place in Spain *para ir de marcha* (to go out). It is said that there is one bar for every hundred people that live here. *Chupiterías* (bars selling mostly shots), *barres*, and *discotecas* line nearly every street, and when some close at 4am, others are just opening. *La marcha* starts in Pl. Mayor, where members of local college or graduate-school *tunas* (medieval-style student troubadour groups) finish their rounds. Dressed in traditional black capes, they strut around the plaza with mandolins and tambourines, serenading women while students start to hit the many bars and *mesones* in the area. Student nightlife spreads out to **Gran Vía, Calle Bordadores,** and side streets. Spacious disco-bars blast music until dawn. **Calle Prior** and **Rúa Mayor** are full of bars; **Plaza de San Juan Bautista** fills with university students kicking out their evening—date in one hand, infamous *litro* of beer in the other. Intense late-night drunken revelry occurs off **Calle Varillas** until dawn. Once your game is sufficiently prepped, wander from club to club on C. Prior and C. Compañía, where young Americans and clubby *salmantinos* mix at places like **Niebla, Gatsby, Camelot,** and **Cum Laude**—all hosts to the same tight pants and loose morals. All open around 10:30-11pm, and the party peaks at 2:30-3:30am, winding down around 4:30-5:30am. Dress to impress; though none of the clubs have cover charges, bouncers at **Cum Laude** and **Camelot** can be picky. Look for club promoters in the streets handing out cards for free drinks; if they don't approach to give you one, ask politely.

🍸 **Bar La Chupitería,** Pl. Monterrey. Unusually low prices have built La Chupitería's reputation among students as a premier pre-gaming establishment. Make your way through the crowds to order from *Los Exóticos,* the changing list of specialty shots (€0.90). *Chupitos* (slightly larger than shots) €1. Open daily 10pm-very late.

Birdland, C. Azafranal, 57 (☎923 60 05 25). Take five and drink to jazz. 30-somethings skip the clubs to chill. Beer €1.50-2.40. Mixed drinks €3-6. Open Su-Th 4pm-3am, F-Sa 4pm-4:30am; opens 6:30pm in summer. Jan.-May live music Tu and Th.

Submarino, C. San Justo, 17. Party in the stripped down body of a gutted submarine. Techno music draws a variety of students. Shots €2, Mixed drinks €4.50. Open weekends 10pm-5am, weeknights 9pm-4am.

CarMen Bar, C. Patio de Comedias, 2, across from the Teatro Breton. A slightly older gay crowd knows how to party in this intimate bar. Shots €2, beer €2.50, mixed drinks €4.50. Open daily summer 10pm-5am, winter 10pm-4:30am.

La Dolce Vita, Gran Vía, 48. Groove on Gran Vía to salsa and pop in a totally kitsch Hollywood-themed disco. Shots €1, beer €3, mixed drinks from €5. Unbeatable weeknight promotions; €3 gets you all the beer and sangria you can drink. Women drink free Tu. Open daily 10pm-4:30am.

🎵 🎭 ENTERTAINMENT AND FESTIVALS

Ocio, a free pamphlet distributed at the tourist office and at some bars, lists everything from movies and special events to bus schedules. Posters at the **Colegio Mayor** (in Pl. de Anaya) advertise university events, free films, and student theater. The city hosts many events and festivals during the summer. On June 12, in honor of San Juan de Sahagún, there is a bullfight for charity in the **Plaza de Toros.** (Seats in the sun from €35.) Take C. Zamora to Po. Dr. Torres Villarroel; the bullring is just beyond Pl. de la Glorieta. Parades and craft fairs grace Pl. de Anaya until June 15. During the week of September 8-15, Salamanca indulges in exhibitions, most honoring the bullfighting tradition that has made the region's *ganaderías* (bull farms) the best in all of Spain. Salamanca goes all out during *Semana Santa* with local traditions like *Lunes de Aguas*, celebrated the Monday after Easter. On this day locals take off from work and head for the countryside to picnic with their families and feast on *hornazo* (meat pie). The feast remembers the tradition of banishing local prostitutes across the river during the 40 days of Lent; they used to return triumphantly on *Lunes de Quasimodo*, when eager (male) *salmantinos* would picnic along the bridge to await their arrival—those were the days.

🎯 DAYTRIP FROM SALAMANCA

CIUDAD RODRIGO

Buses arrive from the Salamanca station (1hr.; M-F 13 per day 7am-9:30pm, Sa 6 per day 8:30am-6pm; Su 4 per day 11am-10pm; last return to Salamanca M-F 7:30pm, Sa 5:45pm, Su 8pm; €5.10). Buy tickets from El Pilar, windows 23 and 24.

The hushed, labyrinthine streets and 18th-century ramparts of Ciudad Rodrigo (pop. 15,000), a sleepy town just 27km from Portugal, harbor sandstone churches, Roman ruins, and medieval masonry. Although the town was originally a Roman outpost, today it is known for its namesake, Conde Rodrigo González Girón, the count who brought the site back to life in 1100 after destructive Moorish invasions. Fortified during the numerous border wars between Spain and Portugal, the walled city of Ciudad Rodrigo soon grew into a prominent outpost for the Spanish military. Now, in peacetime, the city has applied its history to the tourist industry, and welcomes travelers unsated by Salamanca.

The **cathedral** is the town's crowning glory. Originally a Romanesque church commissioned by Fernando II of León, it was later modified in the 16th-century Gothic style. Rodrigo Alemán worked on the **coro** (choir) from 1498 to 1504. Look for the sculptor's signature—a depiction of his head hidden among the rest of the carvings. The two 16th-century organs star in a series of concerts every August. The cathedral's **claustro** (cloister) is the highlight of a trip to Ciudad Rodrigo. The capitals of the ruined columns are covered with figures doing everything from making love to playing peek-a-boo to flirting with cannibalism. The cathedral's **museum** is filled with unique pieces, including an ancient clavichord, the cathedral's "ballot box," richly embroidered robes and slippers worn by bishops and priors, and Velázquez's *Llanto de Adán y Eva por Abel muerto*. (Cathedral open July-Sept. Tu-Su 10-11am, noon-2pm, and 4-7pm; Oct.-June daily 10am-1pm and 3:30-7pm. Free. Cloister and museum open M-Sa 10am-1pm and 3:30-7pm, Su 4-7pm. €2, W 3:30-7pm free; includes tour in Spanish.)

The **bus station** (☎923 46 10 09) is on Campo de Toledo, 3-25. From the bus station entrance, walk uphill on Av. Yurramendi and through the stone arch; the cathedral is just ahead to the right. The **tourist office**, Pl. de Amayuelas, 5, is immediately to the left through the arch. (☎923 46 05 61. French spoken. Open M-F 9am-2pm and 5-7pm, Sa-

Su 10am-2pm and 5-8pm.) To get to Pl. Mayor from the tourist office, continue straight on Pl. de Amayuelas into town, then turn left onto C. del Cardenal Pacheco just before Pl. de San Salvador and take a left again onto C. Julián Sánchez; Pl. Mayor is at the end of this street. Most **restaurants, bars,** and **cafes** in town cluster on Pl. Mayor and on the streets around it.

ZAMORA
☎ 980

Atop a cliff over the Río Duero, Zamora (pop. 70,000) is a beguiling mix of modern and medieval: 11th-century churches rub shoulders with the trendy fashions of Mango and Zara, 15th-century palaces house Internet cafes and luxury hotels, and the magnificent 12th-century cathedral overlooks modern subdivisions and steel bridges in the distance. While locals enjoy the town's modern conveniences, it is Zamora's history as one of the most powerful cities in medieval Castilla that continually lures Spanish tourists. Monuments in nearly every plaza venerate Zamora's infamous figures, including the fierce Roman warrior Viriato, who was born here, El Cid, who fled here, and Sancho II, who died here during an attempt to overthrow his sister and claim the House of Castilla as his own. Zamora is only a short bus ride from Salamanca, making it an easy—and worthwhile—trip.

⌨🔌 TRANSPORTATION AND PRACTICAL INFORMATION. The best way to reach Zamora is by **bus.** Buses leave from the station on Av. Alfonso Peña (☎980 52 12 81; open 24hr.; lockers €1-2) and travel to: **Madrid** (3½hr.; M-Sa 6 per day 7am-7:30pm, Su 6 per day 10:30am-9:30pm; €11.50-17); **Salamanca** (1hr.; M-F 15 per day 6:40am-9:35pm, Sa 10 per day 7:45am-8:30pm, Su 6 per day 10am-9pm; €3.80); **Valladolid** (1½hr.; M-F 7 per day 7am-6:30pm, Sa 5 per day 8am-5:30pm, Su 3 per day 10:30am-10pm; €5.90). **Trains** leave from C. de la Estación (☎980 52 11 10; open 24hr.) at the end of Av. Alfonso Peña and go to **Madrid** (3hr., 4am and 7pm, €23) and **Valladolid** (1½hr., 8:32am, €6.50). Both stations are a 15min. walk from the Pl. Mayor. The **tourist office** is at Pl. Arias Gonzalo, 6. From the bus station, exit the arrival platform and turn left onto Av. Alfonso Peña. Go several blocks, passing through the Pl. Mayor, until R. de los Francos. At Pl. los Ciento, take a left onto C. Magistral Erro; turn right at the end. (☎987 53 36 94; www.ayto-zamora.org. Open M-Sa Oct.-Mar. 10am-2pm and 4-7pm; Apr.-Sept. 10am-2pm and 5-8pm.) If you decide to stay the night, good accommodations can be found at **Hostal La Reina ❷,** C. Reina, 1, which features TV, A/C, and private baths. (☎980 53 39 39. Singles €18; doubles €30.) The Pl. Mayor also houses a number of inviting restaurants.

ON THE MENU

GARLIC LOVERS UNITE

Often neglected as a peripheral condiment or denounced as the harbinger of bad breath, garlic has finally found its well-deserved place in the spotlight in Zamora. The distinctive aroma and richness of Zamora's culinary specialties, from the signature *arroz zamoriano* (Zamora-style rice) and garbanzo beans, to roast leg of lamb and suckling pig, all depend on this not-so-secret key to success. Zamora annually pays its respect to the ubiquitous garlic clove during the *Feria de Ajo* (Garlic Fair), June 27-29, at the end of the *Festa de San Pedro*. For three days, unbridled odors infuse the city and visitors can eat their hearts out at garlic stands surrounding the Pl. Mayor.

For those who can't make it to the *Feria,* the countless cafeterias and restaurants of Zamora's historic district, especially those in the Pl. Mayor and the neighboring Pl. de Santa Eulalia, offer a year-round opportunity to enjoy its garlic-laden cuisine. For traditional dining, enthusiasts can head to the upscale **Casa Mariano,** Av. de Portugal, 28. The notorious *sopa de ajo* is a hearty, stew-like combination of red peppers, olive oil, and bread; vegetarians can request it without *jamón* (ham) and *huevo* (egg). Other redolent dishes include *mollejas lechadas al ajillo* (sweetbreads) and any entrees with *ternera* (veal) or *bacalao* (cod).

◘ **SIGHTS.** While Zamora owes its character to the medieval churches dotting its streets, the ◪**Museo de Semana Santa,** Pl. Santa María la Nueva, 9, is a rare find. Hooded mannequins guard elaborately sculpted floats, used during the *romería* processions of *Semana Santa,* which depict the stations of the cross. The crypt-like atmosphere and impressive collection, which includes pieces ranging from the 16th century to today, make this museum a unique, worthwhile stop in town. (☎980 53 22 95. Open M-Sa 10am-2pm and 5-8pm, Su 10am-2pm. €2.70.)

Twelve striking **Romanesque churches** remain within the walls of the old city, gleaming in the wake of recent restoration. Almost all were built in the 11th and 12th centuries, though their ornate altars were not added until the 15th and 16th centuries. Visitors can follow a self-guided tour of all of the churches available at the tourist office. They tend to blend together, but there are a few standouts. In Pl. Mayor, the **Iglesia San Juan** is notable for its marble-veined windows. **La Magdalena,** straight up C. Ramón Carrión from Pl. Mayor, features an intricately carved door and houses a revered Mary Magdalene icon. Finally, **Iglesia Santa María la Nueva** was the site of one of Zamora's most significant historical events, *El Motín de la Trucha;* in 1158 villagers set the church on fire (with the nobles inside) to protest a law giving the nobility priority over the people in buying trout. From the Pl. Mayor, walk up C. Sacramento and turn right onto C. Barandales; the church is in Pl. Santa María la Nueva. (All open Mar.-Sept. Tu-Sa 10am-1pm and 5-8pm. Free.)

Beyond its medieval heritage, Zamora also hosts the contemporary **Museo Etnográfico,** C. Corral Pintado, a five-story glass building just off the Pl. Mayor. Since opening in 2003 with a mere 18 pieces, the museum has expanded its collection to over one thousand eclectic works chronicling life in Castilla y León over the last few centuries. (☎980 53 15 27. Open Tu-Sa 10am-2pm and 5-8pm, Su 10am-2pm. €3, students €1). Zamora's foremost monument is its Romanesque **cathedral,** built in the 12th-15th centuries. Highlights include the intricately carved choir stalls and the main altar, an ornate marble and gold structure. In the cloister, the **Museo de la Catedral** features the priceless 15th-century **Black Tapestries,** which illustrate the story of the Trojan War. From the tourist office, walk one block up C. del Obispo. (☎980 53 06 44. Cathedral and museum open Tu-Su 10am-2pm and 5-8pm; mass daily at 10am, also Sa 6pm and Su 1pm. Cathedral free; museum €2.) The **Parque del Castillo,** behind the cathedral, is a great spot for a picnic.

◪ **HIKING.** For those looking to escape the city, the tourist office offers info on hikes about 25km west of the city. Two popular routes are those from **Muelas del Pan** and **Ricobayo de Alba,** both of which include great views and pass through undisturbed countryside. **Vivas** runs buses from the Zamora station (M-Th 1:30 and 5:45pm, F-Sa 1:30 and 6pm; return M-Sa 8:30am; €1.30). Trails are well-marked, and the hikes are 8-9km each. Going to either town requires an overnight stay, since buses only return early in the morning. **Pensión Tomasita ❸,** Ctra. Alcañices, has rooms in Muelas del Pan (☎980 55 30 07; doubles €36), and those traveling to Ricobayo can stay at **Hostal del Río ❷,** Ctra. Alcañices, 90 (☎980 55 32 45; €20).

LEÓN   ☎987

The residents of León (pop. 165,000) are proud of their riverside oasis. From the *barrio gótico* to the stunning cathedral, locals boast that their city is the best in Castilla, if not in Spain. It's fitting that the city's unofficial mascot is the oh-so-proud lion—images of lions are everywhere, and the term for its residents is *leonés.* Strangely enough, the name has nothing to do with lions; it actually comes from *legio,* a name that the Roman Legion gave the town in AD

León

ACCOMMODATIONS
Hostal Bayón, **10**
Hostal Orejas, **14**
Hostal Oviedo, **9**
Pensión Berta, **8**
La Posada Regia, **11**

FOOD
Café Europa, **3**
Café Gótico, **4**

Cafetería-Restaurante
Catedral, **6**
Restaurante La
Posada, **15**
Restaurant Bodega
Regia, **12**
Vivaldi Restaurant, **7**

NIGHTLIFE
Glam, **5**
Nodo, **13**
SOHO, **1**

68. During the Middle Ages, the city was an important stop on the pilgrim route to Santiago de Compostela, with gold shells marking the *camino*'s path through the city center. León was also an essential defense point against the Moors during the *Reconquista*. Today, it is best known for its cathedral, whose spectacular blue stained-glass windows have earned León the nickname *La Ciudad Azul*. But this Gothic masterpiece is only a starting point for exploration; from tranquil parks to bustling cafes and raucous nightlife, it's impossible not to appreciate the city's vibrancy.

TRANSPORTATION

Trains: RENFE, Av. de Astorga, 2 (☎902 24 02 02). Open 24hr. To: **Barcelona** (9½hr., 2-3 per day 1:21pm-12:25am, €39-50); **Bilbao** (5½hr., 3:16pm, €23); **Burgos** (2-3hr., 4 per day 1:21pm-12:25am, €15.50-21); **La Coruña** (7hr., express 4½hr.; 2-3 per day 2:07pm-4:35am; €26-33); **Gijón** (3hr.; M-F 6 per day 9:12am-7:40pm, Sa 5 per day 9:12am-7pm, Su 5 per day 11:52am-7:40pm; €9-17) via **Oviedo** (2hr., €6-15); **Madrid** (4½hr.; M-Sa 7 per day 7:10am-3:34am, Su 7 per day 7:10am-8:35pm; €22-29); **Valladolid** (2½hr.; M-Sa 10-11 per day 7:10am-3:34am, Su 10 per day 7:10am-8:35pm; €10-17). Schedules are printed daily in *Diario de León* (€0.65).

Buses: Estación de Autobuses, Po. del Ingeniero Sáenz de Miera (☎987 21 00 00). Open daily 7:30am-9pm. To: **Madrid** (4½hr.; M-F 12 per day 6am-2:30am, Sa 7 per day 6am-2:30pm, Su 9 per day 9:30am-2:30am; €20-30); **Salamanca** (2½hr., 5-6 per day 8am-6pm, €12); **Santander** (5hr.; M-Th and Sa 3:30pm, F and Su 9am and 3:30pm; €11); **Valladolid** (2hr.; M-Sa 8 per day 6am-2:30am, Su 7 per day 9:30am-2:30am; €8); **Zamora** (2½hr.; M-Th 7 per day 8am-6pm, F 8 per day 8am-6:30pm, Sa 6 per day 8am-5pm, Su 4 per day 10:15am-7pm; €8).

Taxis: Radio Taxi (☎987 24 24 51). 24hr. service.

Car Rental: Europcar, Av. de Astorga, next to the train station (☎987 23 02 51; fax 27 19 80). 21+ and must have had license for 1yr. From €65.30 per day with 350km limit. Open M-F 9am-1:30pm and 4-7:30pm, Sa 9am-1pm.

⚡🛈 ORIENTATION AND PRACTICAL INFORMATION

Most of León, including the old city *(León Gótico)* and modern commercial district, lies on the east side of the **Río Bernesga**. The bus and train stations are across the river on the west side. Av. de Palencia leads across the river to the fountain at **Glorieta de Guzmán el Bueno.** After the rotary, it becomes **Avenida de Ordoño II,** which bisects the new city. At Pl. de Santo Domingo, Av. de Ordoño II becomes **Calle Ancha,** which splits the old town in two and leads to the cathedral.

Tourist Office: Pl. Regla, 3 (☎987 23 70 82). Free city maps, regional brochures, and accommodations guide. Open M-F 9am-2pm and 5-7pm, Sa-Su 10am-2pm and 5-8pm.

Currency Exchange: ATMs and banks line Pl. de Santo Domingo. **Banco Santander Central Hispano,** Pl. de Santo Domingo (☎987 24 10 12). Open Apr.-Sept. M-F 8:30am-2:30pm; Oct.-Mar. also Sa 8:30am-1pm. **Citibank,** on Av. de la Independencia at C. Legión VII. Open M-F 8:30am-2pm.

Luggage Storage: At the **train station** (€3). Open 24hr. At the **bus station** (€3-4.50). Buy tokens M-F 7:30am-9pm, Sa 8am-1pm and 2:15-8:30pm, Su 3:30-8:30pm.

English-Language Bookstore: Librería Galatea, C. Sierra Pambley, 1 (☎987 27 26 52). Open M-F 10am-2pm and 5-8:30pm, Sa 10am-2pm.

Police: C. Villa de Benavente, 6 (☎092 or 987 21 89 00).

Medical Services: Complejo Hospitalario de León (☎987 23 74 00), off C. San Antonio. **Medical emergency:** ☎987 22 22 22.

Late-Night Pharmacy: Farmacia Mata Espeso, Av. de Ordoño II, 3, is open overnight. Open M-F 4:30-8pm and 10pm-2pm, Sa-Su 10pm-9:30am.

Internet Access: Cafetería Santo Domingo, Av. de Ordoño II (☎987 26 13 84). Fast computers. €0.75 per 45min. Open daily 8am-midnight. **NavegaWeb,** C. del Burgo Nuevo, 15, in the Telefónica store. €1.80 per hr. Open daily 10am-2pm and 5-10pm.

Post Office: Jardín de San Francisco (☎987 24 10 12). **Lista de Correos** (windows #12-13) and **fax.** Open M-F 8:30am-8:30pm, Sa 9:30am-2pm. **Postal Code:** 24004.

⌂ ACCOMMODATIONS

Moderately priced hostels are fairly easy to find here, thanks to the yearly influx of pilgrims on their way to Santiago, but they tend to fill during the June fiestas. Rooms cluster on **Avenida de Roma, Avenida de Ordoño II,** and **Avenida de la República Argentina,** which lead into the old town from Glorieta de Guzmán el Bueno.

⬛ Hostal Bayón, C. Alcázar de Toledo, 6, 2nd fl. (☎987 23 14 46). Wicker chairs, old photos of León, and sun-drenched rooms with hardwood floors and uplifting colors make this a great deal. Clean hall baths. Singles €12; doubles €20. ❶

Hostal Orejas, C. Villafranca, 6, 2nd fl. (☎987 25 29 09). Sparkling new rooms, complete with bath, shower, and cable TV. Free Internet access. Singles €28, with bath €38; doubles €41-51; triples €62. MC/V. ❸

Hostal Oviedo, Av. de Roma, 26, 2nd fl. (☎987 22 22 36). Comfy rooms with clean hall baths. Apr.-Sept. singles €18; doubles €30; triples €44. Oct.-Mar. €15/€25/€39. ❷

Pensión Berta, Pl. Mayor, 8, 2nd fl. (☎987 25 70 39). Caring owner maintains average-sized rooms accented by cheerful decor. Central location with all-night bars just steps away. Rooms overlooking Pl. Mayor are noisy at night. Singles €12; doubles €20. ❶

La Posada Regia, C. General Mola, 9-11 (☎987 21 30 31). Three-star hotel has handsome, uniquely shaped rooms with individualized decor and bold colors. In the heart of the old city. Breakfast buffet included. Singles €55; doubles €90. MC/V. ❺

FOOD

Inexpensive eateries fill the area near the cathedral and on the small streets off C. Ancha; also check **Plaza de San Martín** near Pl. Mayor. Meat-lovers will rejoice, as many variations of pork top the local menus. Fresh produce as well as bread, cheese, and milk are available at the **Mercado Municipal del Conde,** Pl. del Conde, off C. General Mola. (Open M-Sa 9am-3:30pm.)

Café Gótico, C. Varillas, 5 (☎987 08 49 56). Delicious, fresh, and carefully prepared food with pleasant outdoor seating close to the cathedral. The daily *menú* (€8) has a vegetarian option. Also a wide variety of salads (€4-6.75), *platos combinados* (€6-8), and coffee dessert drinks. Be sure to try the incredible *BonBon* (€2.50). Open M and W-Su noon-very late. AmEx/MC/V. ❷

Restaurant Bodega Regia, C. General Mola, 9 (☎987 21 31 73). Part of the hotel of the same name, Bodega Regia specializes in *cocina leonesa* and is popular with locals. Full *menú* with wine €17. Entrees €10-19. Open daily 1:30pm-late. MC/V. ❸

Cafetería-Restaurante Catedral, C. Mariano Domínguez Berrueta, 17 (☎987 21 59 18). Huge portions, garlicky trout, and fresh desserts (€2-6). *Menú* €9. Entrees €6-12. Open M and Th-Su 10am-6pm and 8pm-midnight, Tu-W 10am-6pm. AmEx/MC/V. ❷

Restaurante La Posada, C. La Rúa, 33 (☎987 25 82 66). Munch on delicious *raciones* (€3.60-13) in front of a stone hearth in this small, quiet family restaurant. *Menú* €7.50. Open Tu-Su 1-4pm and 9pm-midnight. MC/V. ❷

Café Europa, Pl. Regla, 9 (☎987 25 61 17). The spacious, sunny terrace offers great views of the cathedral to complement the delicious varieties of coffee (€2-3) and pastries. Also offers breakfast (€3) and ice cream (€1-2.50). Open daily 9am-11pm. ❶

Vivaldi Restaurant, C. Cardiles Platerías, 4 (☎987 26 07 60). A wide selection of meat (€19-22) and vegetables prepared with creative recipes and a variety of cheeses (€9-13). Spacious, breezy setting. *Menú* €35-50. Open July-Aug. M-Sa 1-3:30pm and 9-11:30pm; Sept.-June Tu-Su 1-3:30pm and 9-11:30pm. MC/V. ❺

SIGHTS

León has several worthwhile sights, crowned by its magnificent cathedral. The city still retains a small-town feel and has many attractive parks where weary travelers can sit and laze away the day.

IGLESIA CATEDRAL DE SANTA MARÍA. The 13th-century Gothic cathedral, *La Pulchra Leonina*, is arguably the most beautiful in Spain. It is also one of the country's best examples of Gothic architecture. The exceptional facade depicts smiling saints amidst bug-eyed monsters munching on the damned. But the real attractions are its stained-glass windows, which feature angels and brilliant flowers, and the elaborate altar painting of the stations of the cross. *(On Pl. Regla. ☎ 987 87 57 70; www.catedraldeleon.org. Open July-Sept. M-Sa 8:30am-1:30pm and 4-8pm, Su 8:30am-2:30pm and 5-8pm; Oct.-June M-Sa 8:30am-1:30pm and 4-7pm, Su 8:30am-2:30pm and 5-7pm. Free. Museum open June-Sept. M-F 9:30am-2pm and 4-7:30pm, Sa until 7pm; Oct.-May M-F 9:30am-1:30pm and 4-7pm, Sa 9:30am-1:30pm. Cathedral €3.50, cloisters €1.)*

BASÍLICA SAN ISIDORO. The Romanesque Basílica San Isidoro was dedicated in the 11th century to San Isidoro of Sevilla. After his death, his remains were brought from Muslim-controlled Andalucía to the Christian stronghold of León. The corpses of countless royals rest in the **Panteón Real,** whose ceilings are covered by vibrant 12th-century frescoes with the themes of infancy, passion, and the Apocalypse. Admission includes the library, which houses a 10th-century handwritten Bible, and the treasury, home of San Isidoro's reliquary depicting the story of Adam and Eve, as well the agate chalices of King Fernando I's daughter, Doña Urraca. *(On Pl. San Isidoro. www.sanisidorodeleon.org. Open July-Aug. M-Sa 9am-8pm, Su 9am-2pm; Sept.-June M-Sa 10am-1:30pm and 4-6:30pm, Su 10am-1:30pm. €3, Th afternoons free.)*

OTHER SIGHTS. The **Museo de León,** Pl. de San Marcos, displays an extensive archaeological collection of pieces dating from the Paleolithic era; particularly stunning are the 4th-century Roman mosaics. *(☎ 987 24 50 61. Open July-Sept. Tu-Sa 10am-2pm and 5-8pm, Su 10am-4pm; Oct.-June Tu-Sa 10am-2pm and 4-7pm, Su 10am-4pm. €1.20, students free Sa-Su.)* **Casa de los Botines,** on C. Ancha just off of Pl. Santo Domingo, is one of the few buildings outside Catalunya designed by Modernista architect Antoni Gaudí, the most famous member of the *Modernisme* movement in Spain. The relatively restrained structure holds hints of his later style in its turrets and windows. It now contains bank offices and is not open to the public. Some of León's most enjoyable attractions are its parks and promenades, where locals spend their evenings picnicking and exchanging *besos.* Two of the most peaceful are the **Jardines El Cid,** directly behind Casa de los Botines on C. Pilotos Regueral between C. El Cid and C. Ruiz de Salazar, and the **Jardines Papalaguinda,** running along the river from Pl. de San Marcos in the north to the Pl. de Toros in the south.

🅟 🌺 NIGHTLIFE AND FESTIVALS

For bars, discos, and techno music, head to the *barrio húmedo* (drinker's neighborhood) around **Plaza de San Martín** and **Plaza Mayor.** Walk up C. Ancha toward the cathedral and turn right onto C. Varillas (which becomes C. Cardiles Platerías). Walk to where the street hits C. Carnicerías; to reach Pl. de San Martín, go right; to reach Pl. Mayor, take a left onto C. Plegaría.

Unless otherwise noted, all bars are open Monday to Thursday until 2am and Friday to Sunday until 5-6am. **Nodo,** with entrances at C. Ramiro II, 1, and C. Matasiete, 7, attracts a young crowd with popular Spanish beats. For a club with funkier decor but similar crowds and music head to **SOHO,** C. Varillas, 4. (Beer €2.20, mixed drinks €4. Open daily 10:30pm-5am.) After 2am, the crowds weave to the many discos and bars of **Avenida de Lancia** and **Calle Conde de Guillén;** one of the most popular, **Glam,** C. Cardiles Platerías, 8, comes complete with raised platforms where you can try your hand at pole-dancing. (Open Th-Sa 11pm-5am.)

In the first week of June, León's 3500km of trout-filled streams host the **International Trout Festival,** with a well-attended *concurso gastronómica* on Tuesday. Festivals commemorating **San Juan** and **San Pedro** occur June 21-30. Highlights include a *corrida de torros* (bullfight) and the feast days of San Juan on June 23 and San Pedro on June 30. King Juan Carlos I and Queen Sofía sometimes attend the fiestas and the cathedral's **International Organ Festival** on October 5th.

▶ DAYTRIP FROM LEÓN

▧ ASTORGA

Astorga is most easily reached by bus from León (45min.; M-F 17 per day 6am-9:30pm, Sa-Su 6-8 per day 8:30am-8:30pm; €3, round-trip €5.40). RENFE trains run to Astorga from León (45min.; M-F 4 per day 7:10am-8:05pm, Sa-Su 3 per day 2:15-8:05pm; €3), but the station is a 15min. walk from the main sights.

For the rich and pious, there was no way to avoid Astorga in the 15th century; it was an important stop on both the Roman silver route and the *Camino de Santiago*. In the early 17th century it became one of the world's main chocolate-making centers; a few die-hards still produce bars of authentic *chocolate de Astorga*.

Today Astorga is perhaps most distinguished by the ▧**Palacio Episcopal,** designed in the late 19th century by Antoni Gaudí. The palace's turrets, main entryway, and beveled stone exterior are characteristic of Gaudí's style. Gaudí built the palace to replace the one that burned down in 1886, but no bishop has ever actually lived there. It now houses the **Museo de los Caminos,** dedicated to the various paths toward Santiago de Compostela that converge in 2000-year-old Astorga. The eclectic collection and unique design transforms the building from room to room from an archaeology museum to an art collection and finally a Gothic church. (☎ 987 61 88 82. Open July-Sept. Tu-Sa 10am-2pm and 4-8pm, Su 10am-2pm; Oct.-June Tu-Sa 11am-2pm and 4-6pm, Su 11am-2pm. €2.50.) The **Catedral,** directly to the left when facing the Palacio Episcopal, is definitely worth a quick visit. Although less opulent than León's, its emptiness—there are no pews, chapel gates, or candle tables—affords a rare opportunity to experience the immensity of its architecture, which combines Gothic, Baroque, and Neoclassical styles since its construction lasted 300 years. The cathedral's **museo** has 10 rooms filled with religious relics and a series of paintings depicting the temptations of St. Anthony—including several panels of him being gruesomely attacked by demons. (☎ 987 61 58 20. Cathedral open daily June-Sept. 9am-noon and 5-6:30pm; Oct.-May 9:30am-noon and 4:30-6pm. Free. Museum open June-Sept. Tu-Sa 10am-2pm and 4-8pm, Su 10am-2pm; Oct.-May Tu-Sa 11am-2pm and 4-6pm, Su 11am-2pm. €2.50; joint ticket with the Museo de los Caminos €4.) The sweet-toothed must stop by the **Museo de Chocolate,** C. José María Goy, 5. From the Palacio Episcopal, walk up C. los Sitios to Pl. Obispo Alcolea; veer to the right onto C. Lorenzo Segura and C. José María Goy is on the right. The tiny but impressive museum sells old advertisement reproductions and Astorga-made chocolate bars, pieces of which you can try for free. (Open Tu-Sa 10:30am-2pm and 4:30-8pm, Su 10:30am-2pm. €1.) Traditional *confiterías* infuse the streets with their sweet aromas; visiting Astorga without buying a box of *milagritos* or *hojaldres* pastries would be a sin.

The **bus station,** Av. las Murallas, 54 (☎ 987 61 93 51), faces the back of the Palacio Episcopal. To reach the center from the **train station,** Pl. de la Estación (☎ 987 84 21 22), cross the parking lot in front and follow C. Pedro de Castro until it crosses C. Puerta de Rey. A large building is on the right. Walk through the city wall onto C. Enfermas and turn right onto C. los Sitios, which leads to the palace. With your back to the palace, the **tourist office,** Glorieta Eduardo de Castro, 5, is across the plaza. (☎ 987 61 82 22. Open June-Sept. M 10am-1:30pm, Tu-Su 10am-1:30pm and 4-7:30pm; Oct.-May Tu-Sa 10am-1:30pm and 4-7pm, Su 10am-1:30pm.)

VALLADOLID   ☎ 983

For nearly 300 years, Valladolid was the most important town in Castilla; when Fernando and Isabel married here in 1469, it stood at the forefront of Spanish politics, finance, and culture. Explorers Fernão Magelhães (Ferdinand Magellan) and Juan Sebastián El Cano came to Valladolid to discuss their plans to circumnavigate the globe. Miguel de Cervantes, creator of the hero Don Quixote, lived here; in 1506, Christopher Columbus died here. Close to a century later, shady dealings by minister Conde Duque de Lerma brought the city's glory days to an end. In return for a whopping bribe, Lerma took Valladolid (then capital of Castilla) out of the running for capital of Spain. Although it is now the administrative capital and vibrant urban center of Castilla y León, the city maintains a serene calm amidst the busy roads and modern buildings that have appeared in recent decades.

⊏ TRANSPORTATION

Flights: Villanubla Airport, CN-601, km13 (☎983 41 55 00). Taxi to airport €20-21. Daily flights to **Barcelona** and **Paris.** June-Oct. service to the **Islas Baleares.** Info open daily 8am-8pm. **Iberia** (☎983 56 01 62). Open daily 8am-8pm.

Trains: Estación del Norte, C. Recondo (☎902 24 02 02), south of Parque del Campo Grande. Info open daily 7am-8pm. Trains to: **Barcelona** (9¾-11hr.; 9:18am, F and Su also 9:30pm; €38*); **Bilbao** (4hr.; M-Sa 2-3 per day 1:42am-11:47am, Su 11:47am; €20-26.50); **Burgos** (1¾-2½hr.; M-F 9 per day 1:42am-8:10pm, Sa-Su 6 per day noon-8:10pm; €6.10-16.50); **León** (2-3hr.; M-Sa 8 per day 1:42am-9:08pm, Su 7 per day 10:26am-5:25pm; €9.50-17.50); **Lisboa,** Portugal (7¾hr., 3:20am, €50.40); **Madrid** (3-3¾hr.; M-Sa 14-15 per day 4am-8:41pm, Su 13 per day 7am-9pm; €12.60-23.50); **Oviedo** (4-5½hr., 2-3 per day 1:42am-5:25pm, €24-27); **Paris,** France (11hr., 9:20pm, €112); **Salamanca** (1¾-2¾hr.; M-Sa 7 per day 7:15am-10:02pm, Su 6 per day 2-10:02pm; €5.60-13); **Santander** (3-6hr.; M-F 6 per day 9:35am-1:42am, Sa 7 per day 7:15am-1:42am, Su 5 per day 7:15am-6:40pm; €13-26); **San Sebastián** (5hr., 5 per day 1:40am-4pm, €20-31); **Zamora** (2hr., 5:30pm, €7).

Buses: C. de Puente Colgante, 2 (☎983 23 63 08). Info open daily 8am-10pm. **ALSA** to: **Barcelona** (10hr., 4 per day 10:45am-9:30pm, €37); **Bilbao** (5hr.; M-Th and Sa 1:30 and 5pm, F 3 per day 1:30-5pm, Su 5:30pm; €16; Eurobus service 3½hr., 11am, €21); **Burgos** (1¾-2¾hr., M-Th and Su 6 per day 10:45am-9:30pm, €8); **León** (2hr.; M-Sa 8 per day 2:45am-12:45am, Su 6 per day 2:45am-9:45pm; €8); **Madrid** (2¼hr.; M-Sa 18 per day 4:15am-12:30am, Su 16 per day 4:15am-9:30pm; €11); **Oviedo** (3¼-4¼hr., 4 per day 2:30am-7pm, €15); **Santander** (4hr.; M-Th and Sa 9:45am and 5:45pm, F and Su 3 per day 9:45am-8:30pm; €10). **La Regional** to **Palencia** (45min.; M-F every hr. 7am-9pm, Sa 5 per day 8am-8:15pm, Su 3 per day 10am-8pm; €3) and **Zamora** (1½hr.; M-Sa 5-7 per day 8:30am-6pm, Su 3 per day 8:30am-8pm; €6).

Taxis: Agrupación de Taxistas de Valladolid (☎983 20 77 55.) 24hr. About €4-5 from stations to Pl. Mayor.

✈🚪 ORIENTATION AND PRACTICAL INFORMATION

The bus and train stations are on the southern edge of town, near the Parque del Campo Grande. To get from the **bus station** to the **tourist office** (15min.), exit at the corner of Po. del Arco de Ladrillo and C. San José (do not exit onto the corner of Po. del Arco de Ladrillo and C. de Puente Colgante). Turn left onto Po. del Arco de Ladrillo and keep right onto C. Ladrillo at the rotary. Follow C. Ladrillo to Po. de Los Filipinos. Turn right, and walk along the park until Pl. de Colón. Turn left onto Av. Acera de Recoletos, keeping the park on your left, and continue to the glass-paneled tourist office on the edge of the park. From the front entrance of the **train station** (10min.), walk up the street perpendicular to the station, C. Estación del Norte, following it to Pl. de Colón. Follow the rotary to the right; Av. Acera de Recoletos will be the third street on the right. From the tourist office, continue up Av. Acera de Recoletos until you reach Pl. de Zorilla. **Calle Santiago,** the main pedestrian street, is the second to the right. **Plaza Mayor** is straight up C. Santiago from the tourist office; the **cathedral** and **sculpture museum** are 10min. to the north.

Tourist Office: Acera de Recoletos (☎983 34 40 13; www.asomateavalladolid.org). Open July-Aug. and *Semana Santa* Su-Th 9am-8pm, F-Sa 9am-9pm; Sept.-June daily 9am-2pm and 5-8pm.

Currency Exchange: Banco Santander Central Hispano, C. Perú, 6 (☎902 24 24 24), on the corner of Acera de Recoletos. Open M-F 8:30am-2:30pm. **Citibank,** C. Miguel Iscar, 7, off Pl. de Zorrilla. Open M-F 8am-2pm.

Luggage Storage: At the **train station.** Lockers €2.50. 24hr. At the **bus station.** €0.50 per bag. Open M-Sa 8am-10pm.

Local Police: In the Ayuntamiento (☎983 42 61 07).

Late-Night Pharmacy: Pharmacies line C. Santiago. **Licenciada López,** Po. de Zorrilla, 85, is the only night pharmacy. Open M-Th and Sa-Su 10pm-9:30am, F 10pm-10am.

Medical Services: Hospital Pío del Río Hortega, Rnda. de Sta. Teresa (☎983 42 04 00).

Internet Access: Ciberc@fé Segafredo, Po. de Zorrilla, 46 (☎983 33 80 63). From Pl. de Zorrilla, walk down Po. de Zorrilla alongside park; cafe is on right before Av. García Morato. Exact change needed for machines. €0.60 per 15min. Open daily 8am-11pm.

Post Office: Pl. Rinconada (☎983 33 02 31), near the Ayuntamiento. **Lista de Correos** and **fax.** Open M-Sa 8:30am-8:30pm, Su 8:30am-2pm. **Postal Code:** 47001.

ACCOMMODATIONS

Cheap lodgings with winter heat are easy to come by. The streets off Acera de Recoletos near the train station are packed with *pensiones*, as are those near the cathedral and behind Pl. Mayor at Pl. del Val.

Hostal los Arces, C. San Antonio de Padúa, 2, 1st fl. (☎983 35 38 53; benid-iopor@terra.es). Small, clean rooms and a lounge with TV in an unbeatable location, only 2 blocks from Pl. Mayor. Singles €15-17, with shower €21-24; doubles €24-27/ €30-33; triples €30-36, with bath €45-51. MC/V. ❷

Pensión Dani, C. Perú, 11, 1st fl. (☎983 30 02 49), off Acera de Recoletos near Parque del Campo Grande. Large, comfortable rooms. Singles €12; doubles €22. ❶

Hotel El Nogal, C. Conde Ansúrez, 10-12 (☎983 34 03 33; www.hotelelnogal.com). On Pl. del Val, 2 blocks from Pl. Mayor. With TV, A/C, and full bath, rooms offer a taste of luxury at excellent prices. Singles €42; doubles €65. IVA not included. AmEx/MC/V. ❹

Hotel Olid Meliá, Pl. San Miguel, 10 (☎983 35 72 00; fax 33 68 28). A huge 7-story building with conference rooms, bars, a nice restaurant, and comfortable, fully-equipped rooms. Singles €74-76; doubles €85-118. IVA not included. AmEx/MC/V. ❺

FOOD

The area between Pl. Mayor and Pl. del Val and near the cathedral is home to many eateries. If you're feeling adventurous, head to the Castilian restaurants around Pl. Marti y Monso, off Pl. Mayor, for a taste of Valladolid's gastronomic specialties like **lechazo** (roast lamb) and roast quail, pork, and partridge. **Mercado del Val,** in Pl. del Val, has fresh food. (Open M-Sa 6am-3pm.)

Cantina La Puñeta, C. Santa María, 19 (☎983 20 71 36). With a wooden bar, pastel-colored walls, and delicious burritos (€6-7), La Puñeta is a great place for Tex-Mex fanatics. Salads €5-6, entrees €5-8. Open daily 1-5pm and 9:30pm-midnight. ❷

Casa San Pedro Regalad, Pl. Ochavo, 1 (☎983 34 45 06), near the Pl. Mayor. Descend into the pleasant, cavernous depths of this 16th-century *bodega* to enjoy elegant dining. *Menú* €8, dinner *tabla variada* with your choice of shellfish, mushrooms, pork, and ham €12-13 per person. Open daily 1:30-4pm and 8-11:30pm. AmEx/MC/V. ❷

Restaurante Chino Gran Muralla, C. Santa María, 1 (☎983 34 23 07), off C. Santiago, north of Pl. de Zorrilla. Neon dragons greet patrons at this Spanish pagoda named for the Great Wall. Enjoy popular duck dishes (€3.70-4.70) or the 4-course *menú del día* (€4.80). Entrees €2.80-5.20. Open daily 11:30am-4:30pm and 7pm-midnight. ❶

🔍 SIGHTS

Valladolid is surrounded by churches, bridges, and picturesque pastures. Although the city's sights predictably revolve around the art, religion, and culture of centuries past, Valladolid has gracefully merged the medieval with the modern to provide a refreshing glimpse into its old days.

CATEDRAL METROPOLITANA. This cathedral was partly designed by Juan de Herrera, creator of El Escorial (p. 142). Despite the fact that other architects felt the need to ornament—gargoyles leer down at parishioners—the cathedral is still an excellent example of Herrera's *desornamentado* style of plain masonry. The extensive **Museo Diocesano,** in the cathedral's Gothic addition, houses the remains of the original 11th- to 13th-century structure as well as Herrera's model of the basilica. *(C. Arribas, 1. From Pl. Mayor, walk up C. Ferrari. After 2 blocks, veer left onto Bajada de la Libertad. At Pl. de la Libertad, turn right. ☎983 30 43 62. Cathedral and museum open M-F 10am-1:30pm and 4:30-7pm, Sa-Su 10am-2pm. Cathedral free. Museum €2.50.)*

CASA DE CERVANTES. The home in which Cervantes penned *Don Quixote* from 1603 to 1606, this *casa* houses an amusing collection of old books and furniture; the medieval bed-warmer is a unique highlight. *(C. Rastro. From Pl. de Zorrilla, walk up C. Miguel Iscar; C. Rastro will be 2 blocks up on the right. ☎983 33 88 10. Open Tu-Sa 9:30am-3pm, Su 10am-3pm. €2.40, students with ID €1.30, under 18 and over 65 free. Su free.)*

MUSEO NACIONAL DE ESCULTURA. The museum boasts a chronological collection of Spanish sculpture, from an international Gothic piet of the 16th century to more recent Baroque works. *(Palacio de Villena, C. San Gregorio, 1. ☎983 25 03 75; http://pymes.tsai.es/museocultura. Open Tu-Sa 10am-2pm and 4-6pm, Su 10am-2pm. €2.40, students €1.20, under 18 and over 65 free. Sa afternoon and Su free.)*

PLAYA DE LAS MORENAS. For a convenient escape from the *museos, palacios,* and churches dotting the city, look no further than this inland beach. Topless twenty-somethings sunbathe by day and mingle by night on the small, surprisingly pleasant stretch of sand minutes away from the city center. Be sure to bring your own towel, as none are available there. *(From Pl. Mayor, take C. Manzana, turn left on C. Cebadería, and continue until you reach Po. Isabel la Católica. Turn right and walk 5min. along the river, with the water on your left, until you hit the beach. Lifeguards on duty and signs indicating water conditions. Open Su-Th 11am-3am, F-Sa until 4am.)*

🎵 ENTERTAINMENT

Valladolid's cafes and bars are lively, though nothing to write home about. A student crowd fills the countless bars on **Calle Paraíso,** just beyond the cathedral. From Pl. de la Universidad at the cathedral, turn left onto C. Duque de Lerma, then right onto C. Marqués del Duero; C. Paraíso will be on the right. For pubs, try **Plaza San Miguel:** from Pl. Mayor, walk up Pl. Corrillo, turn left onto C. Val; after the plaza, continue onto C. Zapico, and at Pl. los Arces, turn left onto C. San Antonio de Padua, which brings you to Pl. San Miguel. Cafes on **Calle Vicente Moliner** draw an older crowd; from Pl. Mayor, walk up C. Ferrari, and at Pl. Fuente Dorada, C. Vicente Moliner is on the left. The area around **Plaza Martí Monsó,** however, is the most central nightlife spot in Valladolid. In addition to numerous late-night tapas bars like **El Corcho,** C. Correos, 2 (tapas €1.20-1.80, beer and wine €1.20; open M-

Th and Su 1-3:30pm and 8pm-midnight, F-Sa until 1am), and chic wine bars like **Vino Tinto,** C. Calixto Fernández de la Torre, 4 (wine €2-3.50; open M-Sa 7pm-4am), this neighborhood also houses Valladolid's best dance clubs. **TinTin,** C. Campanas, 12, is deservedly the most popular (open Tu-Sa 10pm-sunrise).

The renowned **Valladolid International Film Festival** (end of Oct.) features indie European films of all genres, from fiction and animation to documentaries and shorts. (Info ☎923 42 64 60; www.seminci.com.) **Fiesta Mayor** (Sept. 8-17) features bullfights, carnivals, and parades in honor of the Virgen de San Lorenzo.

▣ DAYTRIPS FROM VALLADOLID

MEDINA DEL CAMPO

Buses run to Medina del Campo from Valladolid (45min.-1hr.; M-F 16 per day 7:15am-8:30pm, Sa 10 per day 8:30am-8:15pm, €3). La Regional V.S.A. runs buses back to Valladolid from the bus stop at the Pl. de San Agustín (M-F 16 per day 7am-7:30pm, Sa 10 per day 8am-7:30pm; €3, round-trip €4.80). Tickets and information are available at the neighboring Bar Punto Rojo. (☎983 80 12 98. Open daily 6am-midnight.)

Medina del Campo was once *the* destination for wealthy medieval traders and moneylenders. At its peak, the town was world-famous for its banking business and sheep industry, drawing tens of thousands of visitors every year and serving as the gateway for art imports to the rest of the country. Today, Medina del Campo is free of the visiting hordes of years past, an untouristed oasis and pleasant daytrip from the bustle of Valladolid. An informative and well-kept collection of artifacts from more prosperous times is housed in **El Museo de las Ferias,** C. San Martín, 9. To get to the museum from the bus stop, cross the street keeping the statue of the two dogs on your right and veer left onto C. San Martín. The museum, located in the former church of San Martín, features first-rate examples of objects from wool, textile, and silver artisans as well as the weights and scales used for trading. (☎983 83 75 27. Open Tu-Sa 10am-1:30pm and 4-7pm, Su 11am-2pm. €1.50, large groups €1.) Medina del Campo's most impressive sight is the robust, 15th-century brick **Castillo de la Mota,** on a hilltop overlooking the town. To get there from the museum, continue down C. San Martín and turn right on C. Almirante, which leads to Pl. Mayor. Exit Pl. Mayor from the corner opposite the tourist office. Cross the river, walk underneath the highway, turn right, and go uphill onto Av. del Castillo. Queen Isabel and her daughter, Juana la Loca, once lived in the castle, and it has functioned as an arsenal and prison over the centuries. Today, the castle welcomes tourists, who come to see the art-laden chapel of Santa María del Castillo, as well as a mural-sized copy of a map of the world from 1500. (☎983 80 10 24. Open M-Sa 11am-2pm and 4-7pm, Su 11am-2pm. Free. Inquire at the tourist office about outdoor plays and concerts in the summer, especially in mid-August. €10-12.)

Isabel enthusiasts can head to the **Palacio Real Testamentario,** on the corner of the Pl. Mayor, which has exhibits on the queen's childhood, reign, and final days there, along with copies of her signed will. (☎983 81 00 63; www.palaciorealtestamentario.com. Open M-Sa 10am-1:30pm and 5-8pm, Su 11am-2pm. €2, seniors and students under 28 €1.50. English audio tours €1.50).

The town center is the Pl. Mayor, where restaurants and stores abound. From the bus stop, take C. San Martín past the museum. Go right onto C. Almirante until you reach the plaza and the **tourist office.** (☎983 81 13 57; www.ayto-medinadel-campo.es. Open M 8am-3pm, Tu-F 8am-3pm and 5-8pm, Sa 10am-2pm and 4-7pm, Su 10am-2pm.) **Monaco,** a bustling cafeteria with an upstairs restaurant across from the tourist office, offers *canapes* (€1.40), entrees (€5-9), and a *menú del día* (€9) with three courses. (Open Tu-Sa 8am-2am. MC/V.)

THE LOCAL STORY

MADLY IN LOVE

One of the most enigmatic figures in Spanish history, Queen Juana of Castilla earned the title la Loca (the Mad) for her bizarre obsession with her arranged husband, Felipe el Hermoso (the Fair). Born to Fernando and Isabel in 1479, Juana grew into an enviably influential position as heir to Isabel's throne. Although the men in her life deprived her of power after Isabel's death, Juana's worries were hardly political. Supposedly, she was so enamored of her husband that she stabbed a lady-in-waiting, ordered her hair cut off, and thereafter did not allow women to serve in her palace.

Felipe died later in 1506, and Juana had the corpse embalmed, organizing a massive funeral procession that would travel for three years on its way to Granada, where Felipe had requested to be buried. Although she is said to have lost her sanity by this point, documentation of her mental state is lacking and rumors abound; some even claim that she put Felipe's corpse on a throne every day as they traveled south. In 1509, upon returning home, the queen was supposedly lured into and locked inside the Convento de Santa Clara until her death in 1555. However, this is just a misconception, as Juana really spent her last 50 years in the Palacio Real. She was buried in the convent, though, and later moved south, where her body was laid alongside her husband's.

TORDESILLAS

Tordesillas is a 30min. bus ride from Valladolid (M-F 13 per day 7:30am-8:30pm, Sa 8 per day 8:30am-8:30pm, Su 5 per day 8:30am-10:30pm; €1.90, round-trip €3.30). To get back, go to the bus station on C. de Valdehuertos, 1 (☎ 983 77 00 72). La Regional V.S.A. runs buses to Valladolid (30min.; M-F 14 per day 7am-7:30pm, Sa 8 per day 7:45am-6:30pm, Su 5 per day 11:30am-11pm; €1.90) and Zamora (1hr.; M-F 7 per day 9am-8:45pm, Sa 5 per day 9am-6:30pm, Su 9am, 3:30, 8:30pm; €4).

A playing field and building ground for several Catholic kings and queens, Tordesillas (pop. 8190) is best known as the site of the signing of the 1494 treaty which divided the New World between Spain and Portugal. The walls of the old city prevent modern tastes and tempos from spoiling the town's precious monasteries, churches, and easygoing hospitality.

One of the town's most unique artistic sights is the ▓**Museo y Centro Didáctico del Encaje de Castilla y León,** C. Carnicerías, 4. This internationally recognized sewing museum and research center preserves the distinct historical designs of Castilla's regions and creates modern ones. (☎ 983 79 60 35; www.museoencaje.com. Open M-F 5-8pm. €2.) Another sight of interest is the **Real Monasterio de Santa Clara,** on C. Santa Clara. Construction of this former palace was completed in 1363 under Pedro I, who incorporated Moorish designs and dedicated the building to his Andalusian mistress, María de Padilla. The guided tour takes you through several impressive rooms, the most spectacular of which is the main chapel, its shimmering ceiling emblazoned with gold. (☎ 983 77 00 71. Open Tu-Sa 10am-1:30pm and 4-5:45pm, Su 10:30am-1:30pm and 3:30-5:30pm. €3.60 including tour, with ISIC card €2, W free for EU citizens.) For history buffs, the **Museo del Tratado,** on C. Tratado, has all you need to know—and more—about the Treaty of Tordesillas. The displays include replicas of 15th-century maps and models of the Niña, Pinta, and Santa María. (See tourist office for hours.)

The center of town and of the old district is the Pl. Mayor, a 10min. walk from the bus station. All major sights are within a few blocks of it. Standing with your back to the station platform, turn right onto C. Valdehuertos, which quickly merges with Av. Madrid Coruña. Continue until you reach the statue of a bull. Veer left, walk uphill, and continue on C. San Antolín until you reach the Pl. Mayor. Several sights stem off of C. Antolín, which also leads you to the medieval bridge over the Río Duero. The especially helpful **tourist office,** C. Tratado, shares its entrance with the Museo del Tratado. (☎ 983 77 10 67; www.tordesillas.net. Museum and tourist office open Apr.-Sept. Tu-Sa 10am-1:30pm and 5-7:30pm, Su 10am-2pm;

Oct.-Mar. Tu-Sa 10am-1:30pm and 4-6:30pm, Su 10am-2pm.) Restaurants crowd the Pl. Mayor. One of the best, **Mesón Antolín ❹**, C. San Antolín, 8, just off the plaza, serves a delicious cold tomato and garlic soup and Castilian-style roast lamb, veal, and fish. (☎983 79 67 71. Entrees €11-18. Open daily 1-4pm and 8-11pm. MC/V.) If you are planning on staying the night, the adjoining 🖾**Hostal San Antolín ❸** is an excellent choice. Its spotless and tasteful color-themed rooms with shining hardwood floors are the closest to the Pl. Mayor. Private bath, TV, A/C, towels, and toiletries are all included. (☎983 79 67 71; www.iespana.es/tordesillas_es/sanantolin. Singles €27; doubles €45.) Cheaper lodgings can be found at **Puerta de la Villa ❶**, Av. Valladolid, 54. Exit Pl. Mayor on C. de San Pedro, which will turn into C. Valverde, and continue until you reach Av. de Valladolid. The rooms are simple with soft sheets. (☎983 77 19 90. Singles €12, with bath €18; doubles €24/€26.)

BURGOS   ☎947

Travelers remember two things about Burgos (pop. 346,000): the church and the cheese. When entering the city, the traveler's first view is of the magnificent Gothic spires of Burgos's cathedral towering over even the most remote streets and plazas. While this architectural and religious landmark is the city's claim to fame, there is much more to the town than transepts and altars. Food connoisseurs will appreciate the delectable *queso de Burgos* and the *morcilla*, a blood sausage with rice and tripe, all washed down with a glass of Burgos's famous Ribera del Duero wine. From couples strolling along the Río Arlanzón to college kids out on the town, Burgos conveys an aura of vivacity, prosperity, and elegance, perhaps due to its 500-year stint as Castilla's capital. Even when filled with wide-eyed tourists, every street manages to cling to some historical legacy, particularly that of El Cid Campeador, the region's hero. Perhaps the kings of yore just knew a good thing when they saw it; with its debaucherous nightlife and unique cuisine, Burgos is a city fit for royalty and commoners alike.

▐▀ TRANSPORTATION

Trains: Pl. de la Estación (☎947 20 35 60). 10min. walk or €3 taxi ride to the city center. Info open daily 7am-11pm. To: **Barcelona** (9-14hr.; M-F and Su 4 per day 2:17am-11:43pm, Sa 3 per day 2:17am-3pm; €35); **Bilbao** (2½-4hr., 5 per day 3:17am-6:07pm, €16); **La Coruña** (6-9hr., 3 per day noon-2:38am, €31-38); **Lisboa** (8-10hr., 2am, €55); **Madrid** (3-5½hr.; M-Sa 6 per day 8:44am-2:20am, Su 5 per day 11:25am-2:20am; €24); **Palencia** (45min., 6-8 per day 2:38am-8:20pm, €4-12); **Valladolid** (1-2hr., 9-11 per day 7am-2:20am, €7-13).

Buses: C. Miranda, 4 (☎947 28 88 55). **ALSA** runs to: **Barcelona** (7½hr., 6 per day 11:40am-12:30am, €30); **Bilbao** (2-3hr., M-F 4 per day 8:30am-7pm, €9); **La Coruña** (7hr., 10am, €36) via **Santiago de Compostela; Oviedo** (4-5hr., 5:25am and 5:25pm, €16.20) via **León** (3½hr., €15); **Salamanca** (3-4hr.; M-Sa 3 per day 10:15am-6pm, Su 3 per day 12:45-7:45pm; €14-18); **Valladolid** (2-3hr.; M-Th and Sa 5 per day 6:05am-6pm, F 6 per day 6:05am-9:15pm, Su 5 per day 6:05am-7:45pm; €7.20-10). **Continental-Auto** runs to: **Madrid** (2¾hr.; M-Sa 12-15 per day 7:30am-3:45am, Su 17 per day 9:30am-3:45am; €14); **San Sebastián** (4-5hr.; M-Sa 7 per day 7:15am-3:15am, Su 7 per day 10:30am-3:15am; €13); **Santander** (3hr., 5-6 per day 8am-3:15am, €9.50); **Vitoria-Gasteiz** (2hr.; M-Sa 9-10 per day 7:15am-3:15am, Su 9 per day 10:30am-3:15am; €6.50).

Car Rental: Hertz, C. Progreso, 5 (☎947 20 16 75, reservations 902 40 24 05). 23+. Credit card in driver's name required for deposit. Small cars with unlimited mileage from €75 per day. Open M-F 9am-1pm and 4-7pm, Sa 9am-1pm. AmEx/MC/V.

Taxis: Abutaxi (☎947 27 77 77) or **Radio Taxi** (☎947 48 10 10). 24hr. service.

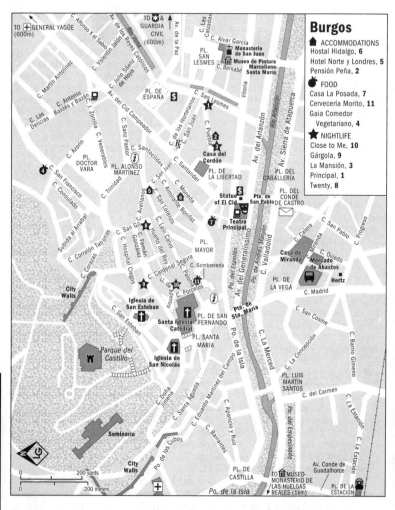

Burgos

⌂ ACCOMMODATIONS
Hostal Hidalgo, 6
Hotel Norte y Londres, 5
Pensión Peña, 2

🍎 FOOD
Casa La Posada, 7
Cervecería Morito, 11
Gaia Comedor
  Vegetariano, 4

★ NIGHTLIFE
Close to Me, 10
Gárgola, 9
La Mansión, 3
Principal, 1
Twenty, 8

🗺️ 🇮 ORIENTATION AND PRACTICAL INFORMATION

The Río Arlanzón splits Burgos into north and south. While the **train** and **bus stations** are to the south, the **Catedral Santa Iglesia** and most other sights of interest are in the north. Turning left from **Puente de Santa María** brings you to the cathedral, while a right on **Paseo del Espolón** leads to **Plaza Mayor** and **Plaza de la Libertad.**

Tourist Office: Regional Office, Pl. Alonso Martínez, 7 (☎947 20 31 25). Offers brochures and advice about Castilla y León. Open July-Sept. Su-Th 9am-8pm, F-Sa 9am-9pm; Oct.-June daily 9am-2pm and 5-8pm. **Municipal Office,** Pl. de San Fernando, 2 (☎947 28 88 74; fax 27 65 29). Open July-Sept. daily 10am-8pm; Oct.-June M-F 10am-2pm and 4:30-7:30pm, Sa-Su and holidays 10am-1:30pm and 4-7:30pm.

Currency Exchange: Banco Santander Central Hispano, Pl. del Mío Cid, 6 (☎947 26 13 93). Open Apr.-Sept. M-F 8:30am-2pm; Oct.-Mar. also Sa 8:30am-1pm.

Police: Av. Cantabria, 54 (☎947 28 88 39). **Guardia Civil,** Av. Cantabria, 87-95 (☎062 or 947 22 22 63).

Pharmacy: Farmacia Natividad Combarro Rodríguez, C. San Juan, 25 (☎947 20 12 89). Open M-F 9:45am-2pm and 5-8pm, Sa 10:15am-2pm. All pharmacies post a list of late-night and Su pharmacies in their windows.

Medical Services: Ambulance ☎ 112 or 947 23 22 22. **Hospital General Yagüe,** Av. del Cid Campeador, 96 (☎947 28 18 00). **Hospital de San Juan de Dios,** Po. de la Isla, 41 (☎947 25 77 30).

Internet Access: Net Gaming, C. Antonio Báldez y Bazán, 1 (☎947 25 03 67). Fast connections. €1.50 per hr. Open Su-Th 10am-10pm, F-Sa 10am-midnight. **Biblioteca del Teatro Principal,** Po. del Espolón (☎947 28 88 73), has free 30min. slots. ID required. Open July M-F 8:30am-2:30pm; Aug. M-F 8:30am-9pm, Sa 9:30am-2pm; Sept.-June M-F 9am-9pm, Sa 9:30am-2pm.

Post Office: Pl. del Conde de Castro (☎/fax 947 25 66 11). **Lista de Correos** and **fax.** Open M-F 8:30am-8:30pm, Sa 9:30am-2pm. **Postal Code:** 09070.

ACCOMMODATIONS AND CAMPING

Inexpensive *pensiones* line the streets near **Plaza Alonso Martínez.** The C. San Juan area is also dotted with reasonably priced hostels. Otherwise, the tourist office distributes a complete list of accommodations. Reservations are crucial on summer weekends, for the festivals in June and July, and throughout August.

Pensión Peña, C. Puebla, 18 (☎947 20 63 23). Immaculate, newly renovated rooms with hardwood floors and lots of sunlight, only steps away from all-night bars. Singles €12-14; doubles €19-21. ●

Hotel Norte y Londres, Pl. Alonso Martínez, 10 (☎947 26 41 25; www.hotelnorteylondres.com). Enormous rooms with bath, TV, and great views of the city. June-Sept. singles €50; doubles €74. Oct.-May €43/€61. IVA not included. AmEx/MC/V. ●

Hostal Hidalgo, C. Almirante Bonifaz, 14, 1st fl. (☎947 20 34 81). This old building's excellent location more than makes up for the austerity of the rooms; be sure to request one with a window. Clean hall bath. June-Aug. singles €13-15; doubles €25-29. ●

Camping: Fuentes Blancas, Pl. de la Vega, 6 (☎947 20 54 57). The "Fuentes Blancas" bus leaves from Pl. de España (Aug. every hr. 11am-2pm, 5-9pm, and 4:30pm; Sept.-July 4 per day 9:30am-7:15pm; €0.70). Pool, showers, and restaurant on site. Open Apr.-Sept. €3.50 per person, €3 per tent and per car. MC/V. ●

FOOD

Burgaleses take pride in their delicious *queso de Burgos,* a soft cheese usually served with honey or in a *tarta* as dessert, and their *morcilla* sausage. The area around **Plaza Alonso Martínez** is laden with restaurants serving these staples, while C. San Lorenzo is tapas heaven. **Mercado Municipal de Abastos (Sur),** on C. Miranda, sells fresh meat and bread. (Open M-Sa 7am-3pm, or until the vendors sell out.)

Gaia Comedor Vegetariano, C. San Francisco, 31 (☎947 23 76 45). Photos of smiling Indonesian villagers and colorful wooden chairs greet herbivores at this counterculture luncheonette. Rotating menu features international dishes, from *moussaka* to *dal,* that would make Mother Earth proud. 4-course *menú* €8. Open M-Sa 1:30-4pm. ●

CASTILLA Y LEÓN

Cervecería Morito, C. Sombrerería, 27 (☎947 26 75 55). Good food and great service make Morito a hit with the locals. Try the *tarta al whisky* (€3.50). *Raciones* €1-5.30, sandwiches €2.50-4.50, *revueltos* €3.60-4.50. Open daily 7pm-2am. ❶

Casa La Posada, Pl. Santo Domingo de Guzmán, 18 (☎947 20 45 78). The rotating *menú* (€11) features vegetarian-friendly fare prepared with local recipes. Fish and meat entrees €9.50-14. Open M-F 8am-midnight, Sa-Su 10am-midnight; serves meals daily 1-4pm and 8:30pm-midnight. AmEx/MC/V. ❸

🔎 SIGHTS

▓ SANTA IGLESIA CATEDRAL. Considered one of Spain's most beautiful cathedrals, the **Santa Iglesia Catedral** deserves its notoriety. Its magnificent spires, which find their way into every view of the city, are matched only by its Gothic interior. Originally a Romanesque church built by 13th-century *Reconquista* hero Fernando III (El Santo), the cathedral was transformed over the following three centuries into a Gothic marvel. Devout visitors can enter the Chapel of Christ, the cathedral's holiest and most infamous arch—the crucified Jesus is constructed of buffalo skin with human hair and nails. Fortunately, the cathedral has other wonders for those not attending services: the 16th-century stained glass dome of the Capilla Mayor; the eerily lifelike *papamoscas* (flycatcher), a strange creature high up near the main door in the central aisle that tolls the hours by opening its mouth and gulping; and, under the transept, marked by a small brick beneath a star-shaped lantern, the remains of El Cid. The cathedral's **museum** displays a Visigoth Bible and El Cid's nuptial documents, as well as countless chalices, paintings, and tapestries. *(☎947 20 47 12. Open July-Sept. M-Sa 9:30am-8pm, Su 9:30am-3pm and 3:30-8pm; Oct.-June M-Sa 9:30am-1pm and 4-7pm, Su 9:30-11:45am and 4-7pm. Audioguide in English €1. Chapel of Christ free. Cathedral and museum €3.60, students €2.40.)*

▓ MUSEO-MONASTERIO DE LAS HUELGAS REALES. Built by King Alfonso VIII in 1187, the austere Museo-Monasterio de las Huelgas Reales is slightly out of the way, but certainly worth the trip. Once a summer palace for Castilian kings and later an elite convent for Cistercian nuns, today's monastery-cum-museum allows visitors a glimpse of the austerity and glory of medieval Castilian royalty. The chapels of Santa Catarina and San Juan inside the expansive church house several elaborately carved tombs and religious paintings from the 16th and 17th centuries. Burial wardrobes can be viewed in the **Museo de Telas.** *(Take the "Barrio del Pilar" bus from Pl. de España to the Museo stop; €0.70. ☎947 20 16 30. Open Tu-Sa 10am-1:15pm and 3:45-5:45pm, Su 10:30am-2:15pm. Mandatory tours in Spanish every 30min. €5, students and under 14 €2.50, under 5 free. EU citizens free W.)*

CASA DE MIRANDA. This sprawling 16th-century mansion houses four floors of provincial *burgalese* art and archaeology. Included in the exhibits are a piece of the front facade of the monastery at Santo Domingo de Silos, the sepulchre of Don Juan de Padilla, and paintings from the 14th to 20th centuries. *(C. Miranda, 13. ☎947 26 58 75. Open Tu-F 10am-2pm and 4:30-7:30pm, Sa 10am-2pm and 5-8pm, Su 10am-2pm. €1.20; under 18, seniors, and students with ID free. Sa and Su free.)*

PARQUE DEL CASTILLO. Atop a hill high above the cathedral, the ruins of a medieval castle and a sprawling, tangled park preside over Burgos. Sections of the walls and building demolished by Napoleonic troops are still undergoing reconstruction. The bleached castle rocks offer astounding views of the red roofs of Burgos and the surrounding countryside. *(From the front entrance of Iglesia San Esteban, climb the 200 steps directly across the street. Free.)*

NIGHTLIFE AND FESTIVALS

Nightlife starts late in Burgos. By midnight, C. Avellanos (across from Pl. Alonso Martínez) fills with night owls migrating onto nearby **Calle Huerto del Rey**. On Sunday mornings, the crowds will still be dancing at *discotecas* along **Calle San Juan** and **Calle la Puebla** and in the complex on **Plaza San Lesmes**. Nightlife shifts into overdrive the last week of June, when Burgos honors its patron saints with concerts, parades, fireworks, and bullfights. On May 28, citizens parade through town with the *pendón de las Navas*, a banner captured from the Moors in the 1212 battle of Las Navas de Tolosa.

> **La Mansión,** C. Puebla, 10. This little bar-that-could has more CDs than bottles on its shelves. The owner and his bartenders are none-too-quietly waging war against the pop music that dominates the late-night scene, serving up a mix of rock, funk, and blues that goes well with any *cerveza* (€1.50). Open M-W 6pm-1am, Th-Sa 9pm-4am.

> **Twenty,** C. Huerto del Rey, 20 (☎947 26 46 92). Easily the most popular and crowded stop on the Huerto del Rey club-hopping route. Techno, pop, and house infuse the multi-level dance floor. Beer €2. Open M-Sa 7pm-5am, Su 7pm-midnight.

> **Close to Me,** C. Llanas de Afuera, 19 (☎947 26 18 62). Loud alternative music draws a grungy crowd. Beer €2.20. Open Su-W 6pm-3:30am, Th-Sa 6pm-5am.

> **Gárgola,** C. Llanas de Afuera, 3 (☎947 27 91 86). This sweaty, energetic club plays pop and Spanish fiesta music to a gyrating crowd, breaking out the tango music after 3:30am. Beer €2.40, mixed drinks €4.70. Open Th-Sa 10pm-5am.

> **Principal,** C. Puebla, 40 (☎947 27 88 97), at the corner of C. San Juan and C. San Lesmes. The sleek glass bar attracts an older, low-key crowd. Beer €1.50, mixed drinks €4.50. Open daily June-Aug. 1pm-3:30am; Sept-May 4pm-4am.

DAYTRIP FROM BURGOS

SANTO DOMINGO DE SILOS

Arcoredillo runs a bus to Santo Domingo from Burgos, C. Miranda, 4 (1½hr.; departs Burgos M-Th 5:30pm, F 6pm, Sa 2pm; departs Santo Domingo M-F 8:30am; €4.70). Since buses leave Santo Domingo only in the morning, visitors may have to stay a night. To get from Burgos to Santo Domingo de Silos (50km) by car, take N-234 toward Salas de los Infantes to Hortigüela. From there, C-110, which borders the Arlanza River, will pass the monastery of San Pedro de Arlanza before arriving at Covarrubias; it's only 17km farther.

Since 1993, the Benedictine monks of Santo Domingo de Silos (pop. 380) have sold five million recordings, including the Gregorian chant album that reached #1 on global charts. In the **Abadía de Santo Domingo de Silos,** listeners are transported back in time as black-cloaked monks chant along with the organ and the soothing echoes of their own voices. Sit in on morning song at high mass at 9am (Su noon), vespers at 7pm (summer Th 8pm), and compline at 9:40pm. The **museum** and **cloister** next door highlight an ancient pharmacy of 300-year-old chemicals, skulls, and preserved animal parts. (☎947 39 00 68. Museum and cloister open Su-M 4:30-6pm, Tu-Sa 10am-1pm and 4:30-6pm. €1.50.) The real attraction of Santo Domingo, however, is the town itself; the view from the hill behind the abbey is a miracle all its own. Rooms are easy to find in this friendly village—a good thing, since visitors without cars are almost forced to stay the night. Near the bus stop, **Hostal Santo Domingo ❷,** C. Santo Domingo, 14-16, has well-kept, air-conditioned rooms with full baths, phones, and TVs. (☎947 39 00 53; www.hostalsantodomingodesilos.com. Singles €22; doubles €34-50.) Just up the street is **Hostal Cruces ❷,** Pl.

Mayor, 20, offering clean, sunny rooms with baths. *Los señores* Cruces speak proficient English and French and a little German. (☎947 39 00 64. Singles €21; doubles €36. AmEx/MC/V.) Both feature **restaurants ❷** downstairs.

CARRIÓN DE LOS CONDES

Buses run to Carrión de los Condes from Burgos (1½hr., Su-F 5:30pm, €4.70) and Palencia (45min.; M-Sa 3 per day 8:55am-5:25pm, Su 3:05 and 5:05pm; €2.20).

Tourists might easily bypass this tiny riverside town, but many pilgrims consider Carrión de los Condes (pop. 2500) one of the most important stops on the Camino de Santiago. Blessed with well-preserved churches and welcoming residents, Carrión makes for a pleasantly quiet afternoon of church- and monastery-hopping. The **Iglesia de Santiago,** the town's most famous church, was built in the 12th century but underwent large-scale reconstruction after Castilian troops burned it down to prevent the French army from using it as a stronghold in the 1811 War of Independence. Today, it boasts a well-known Romanesque portal. On the way to this church from the bus stop, you'll pass by **Iglesia Santa María del Camino,** the oldest church in Carrión, built in 1130. Downhill and across the river is the 11th-century **Real Monasterio de San Zoilo,** with an expansive cloister and an elaborate facade. (☎979 88 09 02. All sights open daily 10:30am-1:30pm and 5-8pm.)

The few hostels in town offer comfortable accommodations. **Hostal Santiago ❷,** Pl. de los Regentes, 8, with an entrance on C. Santa María, has free Internet and modern, spotless rooms with TV and private bath. (☎979 88 10 52; fax 88 02 72. Reception 11am-2pm and 6-11pm. Singles €24; doubles €33-39; triples €39.) **Camping El Eden ❶** is in a shaded area right on the riverbank, in the Parque Municipal. (☎979 88 01 95. €2.40 per person, €2.10-2.40 per tent, €3.90 per car. Electricity €2.10.) Many **restaurants** along C. Santa María offer a hearty *menú del peregrino* for €7-8. The **tourist office** is right across the street from the bus stop. (☎979 88 09 32. Open July to mid-Oct. 10am-2pm and 4:30-8pm.)

PALENCIA   ☎979

Although Palencia (pop. 80,000) lacks the attractions and pizzazz of its fellow Castilian capitals, it is, of course, rich in history and religious monuments. After being catapulted to fame for fending off the Duke of Lancaster's attack in the 14th century, Palencia underwent a surge of construction. As a result, its historic center is riddled with 14th- to 16th-century churches. While not as well-known as the cathedrals in León or Burgos, many provide a worthwhile glimpse into the development of Romanesque and Gothic architecture. Most travelers can skip Palencia, but those with time to spare can explore its city center peppered with modern sculptures or join the locals in sunbathing in the riverside Parque Islas dos Aguas.

◧ **TRANSPORTATION. RENFE trains** depart from Parque Jardinillos de la Estación (☎902 24 02 02) to: **Barcelona** (8½-9hr.; M, W, F, Su 3 per day 1:30am-11pm; Tu, Th 1:30am and 2:19pm; Sa 1:30am; €35.50-45); **Bilbao** and **San Sebastián** (4hr., 4:19pm, €18); **Burgos** (1hr.; M-Sa 7-9 per day 7:45am-1:30am, Su 8 per day 11:38am-1:30am; €4); **La Coruña** (8hr., 3 per day 3:25am-4pm, €35); **León** (1¼hr.; M-Sa 8-9 per day 8:08am-3:19am, Su 7 per day 10:53am-9:08pm; €6.10-7); **Madrid** (3-5hr.; M-Sa 14 per day 2:24am-8:10pm, Su 11 per day 8:15am-8:25pm; €16-25.30); **Salamanca** (2½hr., 1:20pm, €8.30); **Santander** (3-3¾hr.; M-F 5-7 per day 10:20am-3:56am, Sa 7 per day 7:49am-3:56am, Su 6 per day 7:49am-7:24pm; €10.30-19.50); **Valladolid** (45min.; M-Sa 15-18 per day 6:40am-9:53pm, Su 13 per day 11:40am-9:53pm; €2.70-3.10). **Buses** depart from Jardinillos de la Estación (☎979 74 32 22). Info open M-F 8am-10:30pm, Sa-Su 8am-1:30pm and 5-10:30pm. To **Burgos** (1½hr., 3 per day 8:45am-6:45pm, €5.40) and **Valladolid** (45min.; M-F every hr. 7am-10pm, Sa 6 per day 8am-7:30pm, Su 3 per day 11am-9pm; €3).

⊞ ⊡ ORIENTATION AND PRACTICAL INFORMATION. Palencian life is centered along Calle Mayor, a broad pedestrian avenue. From the bus or train station, head past the Jardinillos de la Estación to Pl. León; from there you can see the foot traffic on C. Mayor. The tourist office, C. Mayor, 105, is a 15min. walk down C. Mayor from Pl. León. (☎979 74 00 68; fax 70 08 22. Open July to mid-Sept. daily 9am-8pm; mid-Sept to June daily 9am-2pm and 5-8pm.) Local services include: **Banco Santander Central Hispano**, on the corner of C. Mayor and C. Martínez de Azcotita (open Apr.-Sept. M-F 8:30am-2pm; Oct.-Mar. also Sa 8:30am-1pm); **police,** C. Ortega y Gasset (☎092 or 979 71 82 00); **Hospital Río Carrión**, C. Villamuriel (☎979 16 70 00); and **Internet access** at **Zon@virtual**, C. Estrada, 7 (€2 per hr.; open M-F 11am-3pm and 4:30pm-midnight, Sa until 10pm, Su until 11pm). Of the two **post offices,** the one at Pl. León, 2 (☎979 74 21 80; fax 74 22 60), has **fax** service. The office next to the train station (☎979 72 19 44) provides **Lista de Correos.** (Both open M-F 8:30am-8:30pm, Sa 9:30am-2pm.) **Postal Code:** 34001.

⊡ ⊡ ACCOMMODATIONS AND FOOD. Palencia has fewer tourists than many of its neighbors, so its hotels and hostels are less abundant and more expensive. Hostels can be found on the many side streets branching off C. Mayor. One of the best is **Tres de Noviembre ❷**, C. Mancornador, 18, just off C. Mayor across from the tourist office, at the end of C. Los Manteros, which has a TV and radio in every room. (☎979 70 30 42. Reception 7-11pm. Singles with shower €16, with full bath €19-21; doubles €35-40.) Located in the trendy *zona vieja* district, **Hostal Ávila ❸**, C. Conde de Vallellano, 5, has telephones, TVs, radios, a common room, a parking garage, and a cafeteria. From Pl. León on C. Mayor, turn left onto C. San Bernardo, which becomes C. Empedrada. (☎979 71 19 10. Singles €31; doubles €43-48; triples €60. MC/V.)

Cafeterias and restaurants also fill the *zona vieja* and the streets branching off of C. Mayor. For good *raciones* at reasonable prices, hungry travelers can head to the pleasant outdoor terrace at **Cervecería Gambrinus ❶**, C. Patio Castaño, 1, off C. Mayor from Pl. León. (☎979 75 08 28. *Raciones* €2.50-11. Open daily 7am-1am. AmEx/MC/V.) **Rincón de Istanbul**, C. San Bernardo, 4, has made a name for itself among locals serving delicious and cheap Turkish fare (€3-4.50) such as *doner kebap* and *kofte.* (☎979 74 75 33. Open daily 1-5pm and 7pm-1am.) If all else fails, there's always **El Árbol supermarket**, C. Mayor, 99. (Open M-Sa 9am-9pm.)

◪ SIGHTS. Palencia's biggest attraction is its Gothic cathedral, **Santa Iglesia de San Pedro**, also known as *La Bella Desconocida*, where 14-year-old Catherine of Lancaster married 10-year-old Enrique III in 1388—ahh, young love. Built between the 14th and 16th centuries with predominantly Gothic features, the cathedral has a sandstone and pastel interior. During the Spanish tour, guides illuminate the various altars and then lead visitors down a stone staircase to the spooky **Cripta de San Antolín**, a 7th-century sepulchre. The cathedral's **museum** houses El Greco's famed *San Sebastián* and some spectacular 16th-century Flemish tapestries—not to mention a tiny caricature of Carlos V. From Pl. León, walk down C. Eduardo Dato, and at Pl. Carmelitas turn left onto C. Santa Teresa de Jesús; the cathedral is at the end of this street in Pl. de la Inmaculada Concepción. (☎979 70 13 47. Open mid-May to Sept. M-Sa 8:45am-1:30pm and 4:30-7:30pm, Su 9am-1:30pm; Oct. to mid-May M-Sa 8:45am-1:30pm and 4-6:45pm, Su 8:45am-1:30pm. Tours in Spanish M-Sa every hr. 10:30am-1:30pm, 4:30, and 5:30pm; Su mornings only. Cathedral free, museum €3.) Of the other churches in town, the favorite of El Cid fans is **Iglesia de San Miguel.** According to legend, it was here that El Cid Campeador wed Doña Jimena. Its most notable feature is the 13th-century Gothic tower graced with tall openwork windows, which has been undergoing long-term construction to repair the damage done by the same 1755 earthquake that leveled Lisboa. To reach it from the cathedral, walk down C. San Pedro from Pl. de la Inmaculada Concepción and turn left at C. General Mola, which leads to San Miguel. (☎979 70 08 84. Open M-Sa 9:30am-1:30pm and 6-7:30pm, Su 9:30am-2pm and 6-8pm. Free.)

■■ **NIGHTLIFE AND FESTIVALS** Midweek nightlife is tame since establishments have to close by 2:30am, but on weekends plenty of *palentinos* roam the streets of the *zona vieja*, off of C. Mayor, in search of revelry until the wee hours. Palencia claims to be the birthplace of the university, and you'll certainly find the college crowd at **Merlin**, C. Conde de Vallellano, 4, where they serve up drinks and dancing dungeons-and-dragons style. (Beer €2, mixed drinks €4. Open Th-Sa 7pm-4:30am, Su until 2:30am.) **Disco-Bar Cendal**, another dark, pop-music infused favorite among young crowds, is right across the street. (Beer €1.20, mixed drinks €4. Open Su-Th 7:30pm-2:30am, F-Sa until 4:30am.) A few blocks away, on C. Estrada, 3, **Sábana's** cheap drinks and good service draw the thirstiest clients to its bar stools. (Beer €1.10, mixed drinks €3.70. Open Su-Th 1pm-2:30am, F-Sa until 4:30am.) The **Fiesta de San Antolín** (Sept. 2) celebrates Palencia's patron saint in the biggest party of the year.

SORIA ☎975

Though museums and surrounding archaeological sites are the city's biggest attractions, Soria (pop. 37,000) also claims the lush Parque Alameda de Cervantes, a lively city center, and, on its outskirts, the intriguing Monasterio de San Juan de Duero and Ermita de San Saturio. Though built as a fortress against invasions from neighboring Aragón, the city proper is idyllic and peaceful, and the area along the Río Ebro is a serenely beautiful setting for sunbathing, relaxation, and swimming.

⌐ TRANSPORTATION

Trains: Estación El Cañuelo (☎975 23 02 02), Ctra. de Madrid. Buses (€0.45) run from Pl. Mariano Granados to the station 20min. before each train departs and return immediately after new arrivals. Trains run to: **Madrid** (3hr.; M-F 7:40am and 5:40pm, Sa 8:45am, Su 8:45am and 6:25pm; €11.90) via **Alcalá de Henares** (2¾hr.; €10.10).

Buses: Av. de Valladolid (☎975 22 51 60). Info open daily 9am-7pm and 8-10pm. **Continental Auto** (☎975 22 44 01; www.continental-auto.es) to: **Logroño** (1½hr.; 4-7 per day M-Sa 11am-10:15pm, F and Su 11am-12:15am; €5.60); **Madrid** (2½hr.; 6-9 per day M-Th and Sa 9:15am-8:45pm, F and Su 9:15am-11:45pm; €11.50-12.00); **Pamplona** (2hr.; 4-7 per day M-Th and Sa 10:45am-10:15pm, F and Su 10:45am-12:15am; €10.70). **La Serrana** (☎975 22 20 60) to **Burgos** (2½hr.; 1-3 per day M-F 7am-6:30pm, Sa 1:45pm; €8.70). **Therpasa** (☎975 22 20 60) to **Zaragoza** (2¼hr.; 3-6 per day M-Sa 7:30am-8pm, Su noon-9pm; €8.70) via **Tarazona** (1hr., €4.20). **Linecar** (☎975 22 15 55) to **Valladolid** (3hr.; 3 per day M-Sa 9:45am-6:45pm, Su 11:15am-6:45pm; €11.30).

Car Rental: AVIS, Av. de Mariano Vicén, 1 (☎975 22 84 61), on the way to the train station. Open M-F 9am-1pm and 4-7pm, Sa 10am-1pm. AmEx/MC/V. **Europcar,** C. Ángel Terrel, 3-5 (☎975 22 05 05), off Av. San Benito. 21+. Open M-F 9:30am-1:30pm and 4:30-8pm, Sa 10:30am-1pm. AmEx/MC/V.

Taxis: Stands at Pl. Ramón y Cajal (☎975 21 30 34) and bus station (☎975 23 13 13).

◼◼ ◼ ORIENTATION AND PRACTICAL INFORMATION

The city center is about a 15min. walk from the **bus station.** From the traffic circle outside the station, **Avenida de Valladolid** runs downhill to the *centro ciudad.* Keep walking for five blocks and bear right at the fork onto Po. del Espolón, which borders the **Parque Alameda de Cervantes.** When the park ends, **Plaza Mariano Granados** will be directly in front of you. To reach the center from the **train station,** either take the shuttle or turn left onto **Calle Madrid** and follow the signs to *centro ciudad.* Continue on C. Almazán as it bears left and becomes Av. de Mariano Vicén, follow the road for six blocks, and keep left at the fork onto Av. Alfonso VIII until you reach Pl. Mariano Granados. Facing the plaza from the park, the street on the other side on the left, C. Marqués de Vadillo, leads to C. El Collado, the shopping street cutting through the old quarter to **Plaza Mayor.**

Tourist Office: C. Medinaceli, 2 (☎975 21 20 52; www.sorianitelaimaginas.com). From Pl. Mariano Granados, walk 1 block up Av. Alfonso VIII. English-speaking staff with useful **map** and brochures. Open July-Aug. Su-Th 9am-8pm, F-Sa 9am-9pm; Sept.-June daily 9am-2pm and 5-8pm.

Currency Exchange: Banco Santander Central Hispano, C. El Collado, 56 (☎975 22 02 25), 1 block from the plaza. Open Apr.-Sept. M-F 8:30am-2pm; Oct.-May M-F 8:30am-2pm, Sa 8:30am-1pm. **Second location** at Av. Navarra, 6, and several other banks around Pl. Mariano Granados.

Luggage Storage: At the **bus station.** 1st day €0.60, €0.30 each additional day. Open daily 9am-7pm and 8-10pm. At train station €3. Open until 7:30pm.

Guardia Civil: C. Eduardo Saavedra, 6 (☎062 or 975 22 03 50). **Municipal Police:** C. Obispo Agustín, 1 (☎092 or 975 21 18 62). **National Police:** C. Nicolás Rabal, 9 (☎091 or 975 23 93 23).

Hospital: Hospital General Santa Bárbara, Po. de Santa Bárbara (☎975 23 43 00).

Pharmacy: Many around Pl. Mariano Granados; check any for listing of *"en guardia"* location for that night. **Farmacia Martínez Borque,** C. El Collado, 3, by the plaza. Open 9am-2pm and 4:30-7:30pm. **Farmacia Sánchez Barreiro,** Av. de Mariano Vicén, 1. Open M-F 9am-1:30pm and 4:30-8pm.

Internet Access: Cyber Centro, Pje. Tejera, 16 (☎975 23 90 85), down the small tunnel between C. las Casas and C. Caro on Po. Tejera. €2.40 per 30min., €3.60 per hr., €8 per 3hr. Free soft drink every hr. Open M-F 10:30am-2pm and 5-9pm, Sa 10:30am-2:30pm. **Locutorio Nuevo Mundo,** C. Campo, 18 (☎975 23 92 34). Free Internet if you use phone or fax. Open 11am-2pm and 5-11pm.

Post Office: Po. del Espolón, 6 (☎975 22 13 99; fax 23 35 61). Open M-F 8:30am-8:30pm, Sa 9:30am-2pm. **Postal Code:** 42070.

ACCOMMODATIONS AND CAMPING

▨ **Solar de Tejada,** C. Claustrilla, 1 (☎/fax 975 23 00 54; http://perso.wanadoo.es/solardetejada), on the corner of C. El Collado, off Pl. Mariano Granados. Look for a blue sign with a moon. 17 fully equipped (TV, A/C, bath), beautiful rooms, most with balconies, each colorfully decorated with cast-iron flower bedposts, stained-glass lamps, and glass sinks. Singles €47; doubles €52; triples €61. IVA not included. MC/V. ❹

Hostal Residencia Alvi, C. Alberca, 2 (☎975 22 81 12; fax 22 81 40). 24 large rooms with simple decor, TVs, A/C, full baths, and big beds. Without all the bells and whistles of Solar, but half the price. Breakfast €2.50. Singles €26; doubles €46. MC/V. ❸

Residencia Juvenil Juan Antonio Gaya Nuño (HI), Po. San Francisco (☎975 22 14 66). With your back to Pl. Mariano Granados, take C. Nicolás Rabal, to the left along the park. Take the 2nd left onto C. Santa Luisa de Marillac and look for yellow dorms 1 block ahead. Spacious rooms (15 singles, 45 doubles) with large baths. TV room, laundry. Convenient location. Breakfast €0.90. Reception 10am-2pm and 4-8pm. Check-in before 8pm. Curfew midnight, but doors open hourly. Open July-Sept. 15. Doubles have private bath. Wheelchair-accessible. €6.61 per person, over 26 €9. ❶

Pension Ersogo, C. Alberca, 4 (☎975 21 35 08). Next to Hostal Residencia Alvi. 7 sunny 4th fl. rooms with 2 squeaky-clean common baths run by friendly owner. Large single beds and tiny TVs next to wide windows. Singles €15; doubles €22; triples €30. ❷

Casa Diocesana Pío XII, C. San Juan, 5 (☎975 21 21 76; fax 24 02 78). From Pl. Mariano Granados, go up C. El Collado and turn right on C. San Juan after Pl. San Blas y el Rosel; in the tall building on the left with the huge cross. Hide away in 54 somewhat monastic rooms. Breakfast €2.70. Laundry. Reception 8am-11pm. July-Aug. singles €17, with bath €25; doubles €26/€33. Sept.-June €13/€20/€22/€29. MC/V. ❷

Camping: Camping Fuente la Teja (☎975 22 29 67), 2km from town on Ctra. de Madrid. Only accessible by car or a long walk on the highway. Huge cafeteria, laundry, and playground. Pool open July-Aug. Wheelchair-accessible. Open *Semana Santa*-Sept. €3.60 per person, €3.30 per car, €4 per tent. IVA not included. AmEx/MC/V. ❶

🍴 FOOD

Savor the local specialties, roast lamb and *migas* (breadcrumbs fried in fat with garlic and paprika), at the bars and inexpensive restaurants peppering C. El Collado and Pl. Mayor. Buy Soria's famed butter at *mantequerías* throughout the town center, or less fatty fresh foods at the small **market** in Pl. Bernardo Robles on C. los Estudios, left off C. El Collado. (Open M-Sa 8:30am-2pm.) **SPAR supermarket** is at Av. de Mariano Vicén, 10, four blocks from Pl. Mariano Granados toward the train station. (Open M-Sa 9am-2pm and 5:30-8:30pm. MC/V.)

TriBeca New York, C. El Collado, 7 (☎975 21 43 95). On the corner with C. San Juan. This modern but casual bar-restaurant packs in the locals at all hours. Sandwiches on 3 types of bread €3.50-3.75. Large sides €2.50-6. Huge combination plates €7-10. *Menú* €8.50. Wide selection of desserts €2.50-3. Open Su-Th 8:30am-11:30pm, F-Sa 8:30am-midnight. AmEx/MC/V. ❶

El Fogón del Salvador, Pl. El Salvador, 1 (☎975 23 01 94; www.fogonsalvador.com). To the left at the end of Pl. Ramón Benito Aceña. Elegant yellow-toned restaurant complete with mounted bull's head serves traditional specialties. Fish €13.30-15.70; meat €12-30. *Menú* €15. Open daily 1-4pm and 9:30pm-midnight. AmEx/MC/V. ❹

Nuevo Siglo, C. Almazán, 9 (☎975 22 13 32). Good Chinese food in an attractive dining room with fine china and chandeliers at obscenely cheap prices. Entrees €3-8. Huge four-course *menú* €5.40. Open daily noon-4pm and 8pm-midnight. MC/V. ❶

Callado 58, C. El Callado, 58 (☎975 24 00 53). Large meals and even larger frozen desserts at this popular, laid-back bar-restaurant. Unique ice cream concoctions (€4.30-5.40), shakes (€3.50), and heaping banana splits (€4.30). Combo plates €8.60-12.80, burgers €4-5. Open daily 8am-11pm. ❸

🔾 SIGHTS

Aside from the lush **Parque Alameda de Cervantes** in the center of the city, Soria's other natural surroundings and the monuments hidden in them are its biggest draw. The great 20th-century poet Antonio Machado once likened the serene **Río Duero** to a drawn bow arching around Soria. To find the river from Pl. Mariano Granados, walk straight down past Callado 58 and take the middle road once you hit the Pl. San Blas y el Rosel, follow C. Zapatería until the end, and then take C. San Agustín to the bridge.

ERMITA DE SAN SATURIO. Soria's most popular sight is well worth the peaceful 1.5km ▨**trek downstream.** The 17th-century Ermita de San Saturio, dedicated to Soria's patron saint and built into the side of a cliff, is a heavenly retreat where light seeps into the caves through stained-glass windows. San Saturio himself keeps vigil over the upstairs chapel, every inch of which is covered by frescoes. It is believed that the son of a noble Visigoth, now commemorated in a black bust, renounced society and chose to live in a cave by the river. To get there by car, cross the bridge onto Ctra. de Ágreda, turning right with the road. On foot, take the shorter, cooler, more scenic route through the lush **Soto Playa**. Turn right just before the main bridge and cross the first red and green footbridge, then take the small wooden bridge at the end. Keeping the river to your left, walk off the small island, meandering across small footpaths and boardwalks until they end, and then continue for two blocks on the road until you reach the bridge; the hermitage will be across the river, perched on the mountain. *(Open July-Aug. Tu-Sa 10:30am-2pm and 4:30-8:30pm, Su 10:30am-2pm; Apr.-June and Sept.-Oct. Tu-Sa 10:30am-2pm and 4:30-7:30pm, Su 10:30am-2pm; Nov.-Mar. Tu-Sa 10:30am-2pm and 4:30-6:30pm, Su 10:30am-2pm. Free.)*

MONASTERIO DE SAN JUAN DE DUERO. The Monasterio San Juan de Duero sits quietly by the river amid fields of cottonwoods. The church, dating from the 12th century, is quite simple, but still one of the most visited in Castilla y León. Its graceful arches blend Romanesque, *mudéjar*, and Islamic styles and are all that remain of the 13th-century cloister. Inside, an annex to the Museo Numantino displays medieval artifacts. *(Turn left after crossing the bridge. Open Tu-Sa July-Sept. 10am-2pm and 5-8pm, Oct.-June 10am-2pm and 4-7pm; Su year-round 10am-2pm. €0.60; under 18, over 65, and students free. Sa-Su free.)*

MUSEO NUMANTINO. The museum exhibits an impressive collection of Celtiberian and Roman artifacts excavated from nearby Numancia. *(Po. del Espolón, 8. ☎975 22 13 97. Same hours as the Monasterio de San Juan de Duero. €1.20; under 18, over 65, and students free. Sa-Su free.)*

CONCATEDRAL DE SAN PEDRO. This impressive 16th-century Roman cathedral was built over the ruins of a 13th-century church. Its cloister, with wide stone arches and thick columns, is considered one of the most beautiful of its kind. *(Pl. de San Pedro, before the bridge on C. Obispo Agustín. ☎902 20 30 30. Open daily 11am-2pm and 5-8pm. Free.)*

🎭 🎆 NIGHTLIFE AND FESTIVALS

As the moon rises, revelers of all ages crowd the bars' outside seating in **Plaza Ramón Benito Aceña** and the adjacent **Plaza San Clemente**, off C. El Collado. At the dim and narrow **La Ventana de la Apolonia**, Pl. Ramón Benito Aceña, 8, you can crowd yourself in with the locals or go out to the even more crowded plaza and have a peek through the window display, which features the latest in local art. (☎975 23 02 43). Late-night disco-bars center on the intersection of **Rota de Calatañazor** and **Calle Cardenal Frías**, near Pl. de Toros. On weekends, young people convene in **Parque Alameda de Cervantes** with store-bought liquor. A few small clubs lie near **Calle Zapatería**. Spend a night out with the younger, hipper *sorianos* crowded around the intimate tables and quirky antique decor of **Bar Ogham**, C. Nicolás Rabal, 3, on the left border of the park. (☎975 22 57 71. Open daily noon-3am.) **Kavanagh's**, C. del Campo, 14, three blocks down C. Ferial from Pl. Mariano Granados, offers a friendly Irish bar setting with great deals on large quantities of alcohol. Tired of wine and beer? A *calimocho* or lemon- or orange-flavored *orgasmo* (€3.50 per L) should do the trick. (☎975 22 47 01. Open M-Sa noon-midnight.) For a more intimate and sophisticated ambience, head to hidden jewel **Chayofa**, C. Ramillete, 2, one block before Kavanagh's. With red armchairs and antique touches (except for the huge plasma TV showing 80s videos), this is the place for conversation. Try the "American Beauty" (€5), a divine mix of brandy, port wine, and mint, or any of the varied cocktails (€3.50-5)—from *mojitos* and *caipirinhas* to Manhattans and martinis. (Open Su-Th 6pm-3:30am, F-Sa 6pm-4:30am.)

Throughout the summer, Soria hosts a series of concerts and street theater. Pick up the free *Actividades Culturales* at the tourist office for specific dates. The end of July (around the 24th) brings Soria's biggest celebration, the **Fiestas de San Juan.** The bull is the star of the show, with a somewhat unbalanced mixture of religious ceremonies, *corridas*, and partying. **San Saturio** is celebrated on Oct. 12 with a more low-key festival.

🖪 DAYTRIP FROM SORIA

NUMANCIA

By car, take N-111 toward Logroño for 6km and look for the signs. Without a car, good luck. The bus from the station to Garray comes within 1½km of the ruins (15min.; in summer M-Sa 1:15 and 4:15pm, F also 6pm, Su 4:15pm; in winter M-F 2pm, F and Sa also 6pm; €1), but the return buses run only in summer (M-F 9:50am and 1:35pm, Su and holidays 2:20pm). A taxi costs €20 round-trip, plus waiting time. Ruins ☎975 18 07 12. Open June-Aug. Tu-Sa 10am-2pm and 5-9pm, Su 10am-2pm; Sept.-Oct. and Apr.-May Tu-Sa 10am-2pm and 4-7pm, Su 10am-2pm; Nov.-Mar. Tu-Sa 10am-2pm and 3:30-6pm, Su 10am-2pm. €0.60; under 18, over 65, and students free. Sa-Su free.

Archaeology fans will enjoy the ruins of Numancia, a smartly designed (to protect against the bitter winds) hilltop settlement 7km north of Soria that dates back more than 4000 years. The Celtiberians settled here by the 2nd century BC and fiercely resisted Roman conquest from 153 to 133 BC. It took 20 years of war and the leadership of Rome's most famous general, Scipio Africanus, to dislodge them. Scipio built seven campgrounds on nearby hills, blocked the water source, and encircled the town in a 9km system of thick walls in order to starve its residents. In the face of defeat in 133 BC, the majority of Numancia residents took their own lives. Scipio kept 50 survivors as trophies, sold the rest into slavery, burned the city, and divided its lands among its indigenous helpers. Numancia lived on as a metaphor for patriotic heroism in Golden Age and Neoclassical tragedies (it is the most cited Celtiberian city in ancient texts), and the ruins, though battered (two houses have been reconstructed for visitors), are worth a visit. The reception house has models of the original city. Call ahead for tours in Spanish.

In Garray, the **Aula Arqueológica "El Cerco de Numancia"** features exhibits about ancient Numancia and the surrounding area. From the ruins, turn left on Garray's main road back toward Soria; it is to the right. (☎975 25 20 01. Open Tu-Sa June-Aug. 10am-2pm and 5-9pm, Apr.-May and Sept.-Oct. 10am-2pm and 4-7pm, Nov.-Mar. 10am-2pm and 3:30-6pm; year-round Su 10am-2pm. €0.60, under 15 free.)

CASTILLA LA MANCHA AND EXTREMADURA

Castilla La Mancha and Extremadura are the Outback of Spain. This harsh, arid land is both empty compared to the rest of the country and populated with some of the greatest figures in the Spanish imagination, both fictional and historical. Cervantes chose to set Don Quixote's adventures in La Mancha to evoke a cultural and material backwater. Extremadura is the region that hardened New World *conquistadores* like Hernán Cortés and Francisco Pizarro. While much of Castilla La Mancha remains unexplored by tourists, Extremadura is undiscovered even by Spaniards themselves, despite the fact that its Roman ruins and traditional towns radiate a rare beauty.

HIGHLIGHTS OF CASTILLA LA MANCHA AND EXTREMADURA

EXPLORE the amazingly well-preserved Roman city at **Mérida** (p. 213).

REMINISCE about the days when everyone got along in **Toledo** (p. 194).

SUMMON the world of Don Quixote (and El Cid) in **Consuegra** (p. 199).

MARVEL at the hanging houses of **Cuenca** (p. 202).

CASTILLA LA MANCHA

While Castilla La Mancha (*manxa* means parched earth in Arabic, and *mancha* is Spanish for stain) is one of Spain's least-developed regions, this windswept plateau is both austere and beautiful. Its brooding medieval fortresses and cliffs evoke both melancholy and reverence. Long ago, it was the epicenter of conflict between Christians and Muslims, and so became the domain of military orders modeled after crusading institutions like the Knights Templar, a society of powerful warrior-monks. In the 14th and 15th centuries, the region

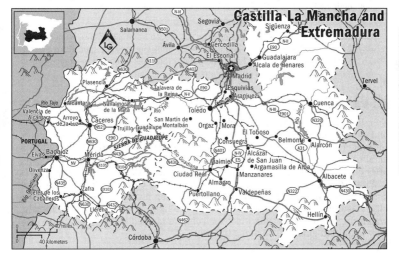

Castilla La Mancha and Extremadura

saw struggles between Castilla and Aragón before they were united in 1492. Castilla La Mancha is Spain's largest wine-producing region, if not its best (*Valdepeñas* is a popular table wine), and the abundant olive groves and wild game influence local recipes, including Toledo's famed partridge dish. Stews, roast meats, and game are all *manchego* staples, as is *queso manchego*, Spain's beloved national cheese.

TOLEDO ☎925

For Cervantes, Toledo was the "glory of Spain and light of her cities." Manuel Cossío called it "the most brilliant and evocative summary of Spain's history." Toledo holds a special mystique and charm, opening a page of history against a spectacular backdrop. Modern-day Toledo (pop. 66,000) may be marred by swarms of tourists and caravans of kitsch, but it remains a treasure trove of Spanish culture. The city's numerous churches, synagogues, and mosques share twisting alleyways, relics of a time when Spain's three religions coexisted peacefully. Visitors delight in Toledo's Damascene swords and knives, colorful pottery, and delicious marzipan. In June, Toledo comes alive with costumed processions during its renowned Corpus Cristi celebration.

█ TRANSPORTATION

Trains: Po. de la Rosa, 2 (RENFE Info ☎902 24 02 02), in an exquisite neo-*mudéjar* station just over Puente de Azarquiel. To **Atocha** and **Chamartín** station in **Madrid** (1¼-1½hr.; 6 per day M-F 6:15am-6:42pm, Sa-Su 8:10am-6:42pm; €5), usually via **Aranjuez** (45min.; 5 per day M-F 6:15am-6:42pm, Sa-Su 8:10am-6:42pm; €2.50).

Buses: Av. Castilla La Mancha (☎925 21 58 50), 5min. from Puerta de Bisagra. Open daily 7am-11pm. **Alsina Graells** (in Toledo ☎925 21 58 50, in Valencia 963 49 72 30) goes to **Valencia** (5½hr., M-F 3pm, €19; buy ticket on board). **Continental Auto** (in Toledo ☎925 22 36 41, in Madrid 915 27 29 61) runs to Estación Sur in **Madrid** (1½hr.; every 30min. M-F 5am-10pm, Sa 6:30am-10pm, Su 8:30am-11:30pm; €4).

Public Transportation: Buses #5 and 6 serve several city points, mainly the bus and train stations and the central Pl. de Zocodóver. Buses stop to the right of the train station, underneath and across the street from the bus station (€0.80).

Taxis: Radio Taxi and **Gruas de Toledo** (☎925 25 50 50).

Car Rental: Avis, C. Venancio González, 9 (☎925 21 45 35 or 21 57 94). From €80 per day. 23+. Open M-F 9:30am-1:30pm and 4:30-8pm, Sa 9:30am-2pm. **Hertz** (☎925 25 38 90), at the train station. From €58 per day (includes taxes and insurance). Open M-F 9am-1:30pm and 4:30-7pm, Sa 9am-1pm.

█ █ ORIENTATION AND PRACTICAL INFORMATION

Toledo is an almost unconquerable maze of narrow streets where pedestrians and cars battle for sovereignty. To get to **Plaza de Zocodóver** in the town center on foot from the train station, turn right and follow the left fork uphill to a smaller bridge, **Puente de Alcántara.** Cross the bridge to the stone staircase; after climbing it, turn left and go up, veering right at C. Cervantes, which leads to Pl. de Zocodóver. From the bus station, exit the cafeteria, head toward the traffic circle, and take the first right on the steep highway that surrounds the city. Despite well-labeled streets, visitors are likely to lose their way; luckily, wandering is the best way to discover Toledo's tangled beauty. Locals are also very helpful in guiding you along the way.

Toledo

▲ ACCOMMODATIONS
Hostal Centro, 11
Hostal Descalzos, 1
Pensión Castilla, 9
Pensión Nuncio Viejo, 3
Residencia Juvenil San
Servando (HI), 13

◆ FOOD
La Abadía, 7
Market, 5
Pastucci, 4
Restaurante-Mesón
Palacios, 2

★ NIGHTLIFE
Bar La Abadía, 6
Café Teatro Pícaro, 8
Enebro, 12
O'Brien's Irish Pub, 10

Tourist Office: Regional office, Puerta de Bisagra (☎925 22 08 43). From the train station, turn right and take the right-hand fork across the bridge (Puente de Azarquiel), following the walls until you reach the second traffic circle; the office is across the road, outside the walls. English-speaking staff offers handy maps. Open July-Sept. M-Sa 9am-7pm, Su 9am-3pm; Oct.-June M-F 9am-6pm, Sa 9am-7pm, Su 9am-3pm. **Municipal office,** Pl. del Ayuntamiento (☎925 25 40 30). Multilingual staff. Open Tu-Su 10am-2pm and 4-7pm. **Zococentro,** another information office, is just off Pl. de Zocodóver; look for the light green signs. Open daily summer 10:30am-7pm; winter 10:30am-6pm.

Currency Exchange: Banco Santander Central Hispano, C. del Comercio, 47 (☎925 22 98 00). No commission and 24hr. **ATM.** Open Apr.-Sept. M-F 8:30am-2pm; Oct.-Mar. M-F 8:30am-2pm, Sa 8:30am-1pm.

Luggage Storage: At the bus station (€1.80-3). Open daily 7am-11pm.

Local police: ☎092, at the intersection of Av. de la Reconquista and Av. de Carlos III.

Pharmacy: Pl. de Zocodóver (☎925 22 17 68). Some English spoken. Open daily 9:30am-2pm and 5-8pm.

Hospital: Hospital Virgen de la Salud Av. de Barber (☎925 26 92 00), outside the city walls. With your back to Puerta de Bisagra, go left until Glorieta de la Reconquista (200m). Take Av. de la Reconquista to Pl. de Colón; Av. de Barber is to the left.

Internet Access: Options are limited, but access is available at **Zococentro** (see above) and at the **Public Library,** in the Alcázar. Open M-Sa 9am-2pm and 5-9pm.

Post Office: C. de la Plata, 1 (☎925 22 36 11; fax 21 57 64). **Lista de Correos.** Open M-F 8:30am-8:30pm, Sa 9am-2pm. **Postal Code:** 45070.

⌘ ACCOMMODATIONS AND CAMPING

Toledo is full of accommodations, but finding a bed in summer can be a hassle, especially on weekends. Reservations are strongly recommended; try the tourist office if you run into trouble. There are several campgrounds around Toledo. Out-of-town sites bring quiet and shade; those in town trade convenience for noise.

▧ **Residencia Juvenil San Servando (HI),** Castillo de San Servando (☎925 22 45 54). Cross the street from the train station, turn left, then immediately right up Subida del Hospital. When the steps reach a road, turn right, then right again, following the signs to Hospital Provincial. The steep walk uphill past the hospital leads to the *hostal,* housed in a 14th-century castle. From the bus station, exit the restaurant, go toward the traffic circle, and continue uphill; cross the footbridge to the left and head up to the castle. Monumental building has 38 rooms, each with 2-4 bunk beds and bath, some with good views. Pool and TV room. Dorms €9, with breakfast €11; over 30 €11/€14. ❶

▧ **Pensión Castilla,** C. Recoletos, 6 (☎925 25 63 18). Go down C. des Armes from Pl. de Zocodóver. Turn left on C. Recoletos. The building is in the 1st corner; hostel is upstairs. Great prices, location, and atmosphere. Singles €15; doubles with bath €25. ❷

Hostal Descalzos, C. de los Descalzos, 30 (☎925 22 28 88; www.hostaldescalzos.com), down the steps off Po. del Tránsito. Modern rooms with TV, A/C, bath, and phone, some with balconies and stunning views. Pool and jacuzzi. Apr.-Oct. singles €31-42; doubles €49-53. Nov.-Mar. €26-36/€42-45. IVA not included. MC/V. ❸

Hostal Centro, C. Nueva, 13 (☎925 25 70 91; www.hostalcentro.com), toward C. del Comercio on Pl. de Zocodóver. Centrally located. Clean, spacious rooms with TV, bath, A/C, phone. New rooftop terrace for sunbathing or a view of the cathedral and plaza. Friendly staff. Singles €30; doubles €45; triples €60. MC/V. ❸

Pensión Nuncio Viejo, C. Nuncio Viejo, 19, 3rd fl. (☎925 22 81 78). These 7 rooms close to the cathedral are small, but they're bright and polished. Owner cooks great breakfast (€1.50), other meals (€7.50). Singles €19; doubles €30, with bath €34. ❷

Camping: Camping El Greco (☎925 22 00 90), 1.5km from town on Ctra. CM-4000, km 0.7. Take bus #7 from Pl. de Zocodóver. Shady site between river and an olive grove. Restaurant, bar, supermarket, and pool. €5 per person, per tent, and per car. MC/V. ❶

📄 FOOD

Pastelería windows on every corner in Toledo beckon with marzipan of every shape and size, from colorful fruity nuggets to half-moon cookies. Alternatively, grab the basics at **%Dia,** C. Las Nieves, 19. (Open M-Sa 9am-2pm and 5:30-8:30pm.) The **market** is in Pl. Mayor, behind the cathedral. (Open M-Sa 9am-8pm.)

La Abadía, Pl. de San Nicolás, 3 (☎925 25 11 40). From Pl. de Zocodóver bear left when C. de la Sillería splits; Pl. de San Nicolás is to the right. Dine on the delicious lunch *menú* (€10) in a maze of cave-like underground rooms. Open M-Th 8am-12:30am, F 8am-1:30am, Sa noon-1:30am. AmEx/MC/V. ❷

Pastucci, C. Sinagoga, 10 (☎925 25 77 42). From Pl. de Zocodóver take C. del Comercio; stay right below the underpass just past Rodier. Cheerful atmosphere. Pastas €5.70-7.50; try the excellent *spaghetti a la carbonara*. Small pizzas €6-8.50. 10% discount with *Let's Go* (cash only). Open Tu-Su noon-4pm and 7pm-midnight. MC/V. ❶

Restaurante-Mesón Palacios, C. Alfonso X el Sabio, 3 (☎925 21 59 72). Two extravagant *menús* (€6.60-11.90)—including Toledo's famous partridge dish—loaded with meat, fish, and egg dishes are good and simple. Entrees €5-12. Open M-Sa 1-4pm and 7-11pm, Su noon-4pm. Closed Su in Aug. AmEx/MC/V. ❷

📷 SIGHTS

Toledo's many excellent museums, churches, synagogues, and mosques merit more than one day for a thorough visit. Toledo's attractions form a belt around its middle within the fortified seventh-century walls. An east-west tour beginning in Pl. de Zocodóver is largely downhill. Most sights are closed on Mondays.

▧ **CATEDRAL.** Built between 1226 and 1498, Toledo's cathedral boasts five naves, delicate stained glass, and unapologetic ostentation. Noteworthy art and sculpture include the 14th-century Gothic *Virgen Blanca* by the entrance and Narciso Tomés's *Transparente,* a Spanish-Baroque whirlpool of architecture, sculpture, and painting. In the **Capilla Mayor,** the massive Gothic altarpiece stretches to the ceiling. The tomb of Cardinal Mendoza, an early leader of the Spanish Inquisition, lies to the left. Beneath the dome is the **Capilla Mozárabe,** the only place in the world where the ancient Visigoth Mass (in Mozarabic) is still held. The **treasury** flaunts the Church's wealth, with its replica of one of Columbus's ships and a 400lb., 16th-century gold monstrosity lugged through the streets during the annual Corpus Cristi procession on June 10th. The **sacristía** holds 18 El Grecos (including *El Espolio*), two Van Dycks, and a Caravaggio. Portraits of every archbishop of Toledo can be found in the **Sala Capitulla.** The red hats hanging from the ceiling mark their tombs. *(☎925 22 22 41. Open daily 10am-noon and 4-6pm. The cathedral is free, but it's worth the €5.50 to see the sacristía and capillas. Open June-Aug. M-Sa 10:30am-6:30pm, Su 2-6pm; Sept.-May M-Sa 10:30am-6pm, Su 2-6pm. Audio guide in English, French, and Italian; €3. Tickets sold at the store opposite the entrance. Modest dress required.)*

ALCÁZAR. Toledo's most formidable landmark, the Alcázar served as a military stronghold for the Romans, Visigoths, Moors, and Spaniards. It was reduced to rubble in the Civil War, when Fascist troops used it as a refuge. Don't miss the room detailing Colonel Moscardó's refusal to surrender the fort, even at the cost of his son's life. Over 500 civilians hid in the dark basement during the siege. The

CASTILLA LA MANCHA AND EXTREMADURA

rooms aboveground have been turned into a military museum complete with armor, swords, guns, and comparatively benign dried plants. *(Cuesta de Carlos V, 2, a block down from Pl. de Zocodóver. ☎ 925 22 16 73. Open Tu-Su 9:30am-2pm. €2. W free.)*

EL GRECO SIGHTS. Greek painter Doménikos Theotokópoulos, better known as El Greco, spent most of his life in Toledo. Many works are displayed throughout town, but the majority of his masterpieces have been carted off to the Prado and other big-name museums. The best place to start is the ◼**Casa Museo del Greco**, the master's former home, which contains 19 of his paintings, among them glowing portraits of a sad-eyed Christ, both Santiagos, and a San Bartolomé who is poised to kill a *diablito* with a large knife. *(C. Samuel Leví, 2. ☎ 925 22 40 46. Open Tu-Sa 10am-2pm and 4-9pm, Su 10am-2pm. €2.40; students, under 18, and over 65 free. Sa-Su afternoons free.)* Up the hill and to the right is the **Iglesia de Santo Tomé,** which still houses his famous *El Entierro del Conde de Orgaz* (The Burial of Count Orgaz). Both San Agustín and San Esteban are pictured descending from heaven to serve as pall-bearers at the funeral of Orgaz, a benefactor of the Church. The stark figure staring out from the back is El Greco himself, and the boy is his son, Jorge Manuel, architect of Toledo's city hall. *(Pl. del Conde, 1. ☎ 925 25 60 98; www.santotome.org. Open daily Mar.-Oct. 15 10am-6:45pm; Oct.16-Feb. 10am-5:45pm. €1.50.)* Outside handsome Puerta de Bisagra, the 16th-century **Hospital de Tavera** displays five El Grecos and several works by his mentor, Titian. *(C. Cardenal Tavera, 2, near the tourist office. ☎ 925 22 04 51. Open daily 10:30am-1:30pm and 3:30-6pm. €3.)*

SYNAGOGUES. Only two of the many synagogues once in Toledo's *judería* (Jewish quarter) have been preserved. Samuel Ha Leví, diplomat and treasurer to Pedro el Cruel, built the **Sinagoga del Tránsito** in 1366. Its exterior hides an ornate sanctuary with *mudéjar* plasterwork and a stunning *artesonado* (coffered) wood ceiling. The Hebrew inscriptions on the walls are taken mostly from the Psalter. Inside, the ◼**Museo Sefardí** documents early Jewish history in Spain. Highlights include a Torah (parts of which are over 400 years old) and a beautiful set of Sephardic wedding costumes. *(C. Samuel Leví. ☎ 925 22 36 65; www.museosefardi.net. Open M-Sa 10am-2pm and 4-9pm, Su 10am-2pm. €2.40, students and under 18 €1.20. Free Sa after 4pm and Su.)* **Sinagoga de Santa María la Blanca,** down the street to the right, is a testament to the peaceful and violent interactions of Christians, Jews, and Muslims. Built by Moorish craftsmen, it served as the city's principal synagogue before the Jews were expelled in 1492. After a period of neglect, it was converted into a church around 1550. Now secular, its Moorish arches and tranquil garden make for a pleasant retreat. *(C. de los Reyes Católicos, 2. ☎ 925 22 72 57. Open daily June-Aug. 10am-7pm; Sept.-May 10am-6pm. €1.50, students and over 65 €1.20.)*

MONASTERIO DE SAN JUAN DE LOS REYES. At the far western edge of the city stands this Franciscan monastery commissioned by Fernando and Isabel to commemorate their victory over the Portuguese in the Battle of Toro (1476). Over the church's entrance, a grinning skeleton awaits resurrection. The cloister is bright, with a pretty garden melding Gothic and *mudéjar* architecture. The Catholic monarchs planned to use the church as their crypt, but decided to be interred at Granada, the site of their 1492 victory over the Moorish kingdom.-*(☎ 925 22 38 02. Open daily Apr.-Sept. 10am-1:45pm and 3:30-6:45pm; Oct.-Mar. 10am-2pm and 3:30-6pm. €1.50.)*

MUSEUMS. Toledo was the seat of Visigoth rule and culture for three centuries prior to the Muslim invasion in 711. The exhibits at the **Museo de los Concilios y de la Cultura Visigótica** pale in comparison to their beautiful setting: a 13th-century *mudéjar* church. *(C. San Clemente, 4. ☎ 925 22 78 72. Open Tu-Sa 10am-2pm and 4-6:30pm, Su 10am-2pm. €0.60, students €0.30.)* The **Museo del Taller del Moro** features outstanding woodwork, plasterwork, and tiles. *(C. Taller del Moro, 3. Head through Pl. de San Antonio and down C. San Bernardo. ☎ 925 22 71 15. Closed for renovations through*

2006; check with the tourist office for updates.) The impressive and under-touristed **Museo de Santa Cruz** (1504) exhibits a handful of El Grecos in its eclectic art collection, including the haunting *Verónica.* The basement holds remains from local archaeological digs; most impressive is a mastodon skull with tusks intact. *(C. Miguel de Cervantes, 3. ☎ 925 22 10 36. Open Tu-Sa 10am-6:30pm, Su 10am-2pm. Free.)*

🔊 NIGHTLIFE

For nightlife, head through the arch and to the left from Pl. de Zocodóver to **Calle Santa Fé,** brimming with beer and local youth. **Enebro,** tucked away on small Pl. Santiago de los Caballeros off C. Miguel de Cervantes, lures in customers with free evening tapas. (Beer €1.20. Open daily 11am-4pm and 7pm-1:30am.) **Calle de la Sillería** and **Calle de los Alfileritos** host a few upscale bars and clubs, including **Bar La Abadía.** (☎ 925 25 11 40. For directions, see p. 197.) For funky non-mainstream dance music, check out **Café Teatro Pícaro,** C. Cadenas, 6, a hip club where its just as cool to be sipping on a milkshake *(batido;* €3) as a mixed drink. (☎ 925 221 301; www.picarocafeteatro.com. Exiting **Abadía** go left down C. Núñez de Arce. *Copas* €5, pints €3. Open daily 3pm-4am.) **O'Brien's Irish Pub,** C. Las Armas, 12, fills with young Anglophones in the evening and has live music on Thursdays at 11pm. (☎ 925 21 26 65. Guinness €4. Open Su-Th noon-2:30am, F-Sa noon-4am. MC/V.)

📐 DAYTRIP FROM TOLEDO

CONSUEGRA

Samar buses (☎ 925 22 39 15) depart from the Toledo bus station (1¼hr.; M-F 10 per day 9:15am-8:30pm, Sa 5 per day 9:15am-11pm, Su 3 per day 10:30am-11pm; €3.90) and return from C. Castilla de la Mancha (1¼hr.; M-F 9 per day 6:10am-5:55pm, Sa 5 per day 6:10am-5:55pm, Su 3 per day 6:55am-1:25pm). In Toledo, buy tickets at the office; when returning, get them on board. Plan around departure times to avoid spending the night.

Of all Manchegan villages, tiny Consuegra, replete with windmills, vast landscapes, and medieval charm, provides the most raw material for summoning Don Quixote's world. Though small, Consuegra is home to a palace, a Franciscan convent, a Carmelite monastery, an olive oil factory, and a winery. The village ▧ **castle,** called *cresteria manchega* by locals, was a Roman, then Arab, then Castilian fortress. From the 12th to 19th cen-

BULLBOARDS

Staring glassy-eyed out the window of your preferred mode of transportation, you may notice rather unusual monuments along the highway: massive, black paper cut-outs of solitary bulls. The bull was the brainchild of Manuel Preito, who designed it as an advertisement for Osborne Sherry. The first cut-out went up in 1956, and by 1964 there were over 500 of the metal monstrosities (each one is over 11m by 5m). In 1988, however, the Osborne bulls became an endangered species, as a law was passed banning all billboard advertising in Spain. A plan was drafted to take the bulls down, but Spaniards protested, since the lone bull towering along the roadside had become an important national symbol. After considerable clamoring and hoofing, the bulls were painted black and left to loom proudly against the horizon. In 1997, the bull finally got its due and was named a Symbol of Spain's National Heritage. The familiar shape now decorates t-shirts and pins in souvenir shops, but the real thing is still impressive. Keep your eyes peeled as you ride through the countryside.

turies, the castle was held by a powerful order of warrior monks. In the mid-19th century, they were forced to sell most of their riches to raise funds for the War of Independence against Napoleon. Their efforts were in vain; Napoleon's army conquered, sacked, and burned the fortress, causing much of the damage that makes it such a dramatic ruin today. (Open May 15-Sept. 9am-2pm and 4:30-7pm; Oct.-May 14 4:30-7pm.) El Cid's only son, Diego, died in the stable; you can visit a lavish monument in his honor near the Ayuntamiento. From August 14-15, the town holds a festival in his honor, including a reenactment of a medieval siege and a reconstruction of a battle using a human chess set with Castilians in white and Moors in black. The **tourist office,** located halfway up the road to the castle in a windmill with blue trim, will gladly provide more information on all these sights. (☎925 47 57 31. Open June-Sept. M-F 9:30am-2pm and 4:30-7pm, Sa-Su 10:30am-2pm and 4:30-7pm; Oct.-May daily 9:30am-2pm and 3:30-6pm.)

ALMAGRO   ☎926

Most of the year, sleepy Almagro, with its narrow cobblestone streets and endless rows of whitewashed and half-timbered houses, evokes the image of the quintessential, relaxed Spanish town. But for three weeks every July, all the world's a stage in Almagro, when a world-renowned classical theater festival swells the town with local and international visitors. Even if theater's not your thing, Almagro makes a pleasant stop on your way to Andalucía.

⌧ TRANSPORTATION. The **train station** is at Po. de la Estación (☎926 86 02 76), outside the city center, at the end of the pedestrian street. To get from the station to Pl. Mayor, walk down Po. de la Estación and turn left onto C. Rondo de Calatrava; turn right onto C. Madre de Dios (a sign points to Centro Urbano), which becomes C. Feria and leads to the plaza. Trains go to **Ciudad Real** (15min., 5 per day 8:40am-10:20pm, €1.70-2) and **Madrid** (2¾hr., 3 and 6:05pm, €11.70-14.60). Change at Ciudad Real for **Córdoba, Sevilla, Granada,** and **Valencia. Buses** (☎926 21 13 42) go to **Ciudad Real,** the connection point for most other cities. **ALSA** (☎926 21 13 42) buses go to **Ciudad Real,** the connection point for most other cities (30min.; M-F 8 per day 8am-6:15pm, Sa 9:15am and 3pm; €1:20), and **Madrid** (2¼hr.; 3 per day M-F 7am-4pm, Sa 9:40am-6:15pm; €10.40).

⌧ ⓘ ORIENTATION AND PRACTICAL INFORMATION. The center of Almagro is the long, arcaded Pl. Mayor. From the bus station, walk down C. Rondo de Calatrava, turn left on C. Madre de Dios, and follow it straight to the plaza. The **tourist office,** Pl. Mayor, 1, is located on the ground floor of the Ayuntamiento, directly beneath the clocktower. (☎926 86 07 17. Open July-Aug. Tu-Sa 10am-2pm and 6-9pm, Su 11am-2pm; Apr.-June and Sept. Tu-F 10am-2pm and 5-8pm, Sa 10am-2pm and 5-7pm, Su 11am-2pm; Oct.-Mar. Tu-F 10am-2pm and 4-7pm, Sa 10am-2pm and 4-6pm. All sights have coordinated their hours with the tourist office.) **Banks** and **ATMs** line C. Mayor de Carnicerías. Local services include: **police,** C. Mercado, 1 (☎609 01 41 36), adjacent to the Pl. Mayor; **Centro de Salud,** C. Mayor de Carnicerías, 11 (☎926 86 10 26); **Internet access** at the Biblioteca Pública (public library), C. San Agustín (☎926 882 090; limit 1hr.; open M-F 11am-1pm and 5-8pm, Sa 10:30am-1:30pm); **post office,** C. Mayor de Carnicerías, 16 (☎926 86 00 52; open M-F 8:30am-2:30pm, Sa 9:30am-1pm). **Postal Code:** 13270.

⌧ ⓒ ACCOMMODATIONS AND FOOD. Finding a place to sleep during the theater festival, from the first Thursday to the last Sunday of July, can be a drama in and of itself. Reserve as early as April, particularly at the **Hospedería de Almagro ❷,**

C. Ejido de Calatrava. The rooms overlook the courtyard and echo the austerity of the adjacent monastery. Clean baths, phones, and TVs provide for a comfortable stay. (☎926 88 20 87; fax 88 21 22. July singles with bath €25.50; doubles with shower €36, with bath €42. Aug.-June €22/€30/€36. MC/V.) Closer to Pl. Mayor is **La Posada de Almagro ❹**, C. Gran Maestre, 5. From the tourist office, head toward the opposite end of the Pl. Mayor, passing the small park and statue of Diego de Almagro on the left. Make an immediate right onto C. Gran Maestre. Inside the large wooden gate is a beautiful courtyard with hanging vines and potted flowers. Rooms are charming and rustic with colorfully tiled bathrooms. (☎/fax 926 26 12 01. July singles €52; doubles €75; triples €90. Aug.-June €36/€55/€67. To the right of the Hospedería is the more expensive **Hotel Don Diego ❸**, C. Bolaños, 1, which has bright hallways and equally clean and comfortable rooms, all complete with bath, shower, TV, and phone. (☎926 86 12 87; fax 86 05 74. July singles €49; doubles €67; triples €82. Aug.-June €31.50/€44; triples €59.) Outdoor restaurants crowd Pl. Mayor, offering some of the best (and most expensive) food in town. Inside the Hospedería de Almagro is the cozy dining hall of **Restaurante Dos Tenedores ❷**, which has an extensive selection of seafood, meat, poultry, and vegetable entrees (€7.80-13). The *menú* (€8) is a great deal, and the *pisto manchego*, a regional tomato and green pepper stew, is especially good. (Open daily July-Aug. 1:30-4pm and 9-11:30pm; Sept.-June 1:30-4pm and 8:30-11pm.) For groceries, stop at **%Dia,** C. San Agustín, across from public library. (Open M-Th 9:30am-2pm and 5:30-8:30pm, F-Sa 9am-2:30pm and 5:30-9pm.) The freshest fruits and veggies are sold at the outdoor **market.** From Pl. Mayor, walk down C. Mayor de Carnicerías for one block, then turn left onto Rastro de San Juan. (Open W 8am-3pm.)

⬛⬛ SIGHTS AND ENTERTAINMENT. Plaza Mayor is square one for cultural sights in Almagro. Here you can find the **Corral de Comedias,** an open-air multi-level theater resembling Shakespeare's Globe. This theater is the only one left intact from the Golden Age of Spanish drama, and its stage was home to the works of such literary masters as Cervantes and Lope de Vega. (☎926 86 15 39. Same hours as tourist office. €2, children and groups of 15 or more €1.50.) Directly across the plaza from the *corral* and through a few arches, the **Museo Nacional del Teatro,** C. Gran Maestre, 2, displays the history of Spanish drama. Ticket includes entrance to the museum's temporary exhibits on different aspects of Spanish theater, such as costumes and stage design, which are housed in the Iglesia de San Agustín, on the corner of C. San Agustín and C. Feria. (☎/fax 926 26 10 14. Same hours as tourist office. €1.20; under 18, Sa afternoon, and Su morning free.) The closing act of the theater tour is the **Teatro Municipal,** C. San Agustín, 20. Follow C. San Agustín out of Pl. Mayor and look for a crimson and white building on the right. Inside is a renovated theater and a small collection of elaborate costumes. (☎926 86 13 61. Same hours as tourist office.) Teatro Municipal hosts modern Spanish plays on weekends in September, October, and November. Contact the *teatro* for details.

▓ FESTIVALS. Every year, prestigious theater companies and players from around the world descend on the town for the **Festival Internacional de Teatro Clásico de Almagro** from the first Thursday to the last Sunday in July. Daily performances of Spanish and international classics take place throughout the city. The **box office** is in the Hospital de San Juan, C. San Agustín. (☎902 10 12 12; www.festivaldealmagro.com. Open May-June Th 11:30am-1:30pm; July daily 11:30am-2pm and 7:30-10:30pm. MC/V.) There are daily productions in July at 10:45pm. Look online or inquire at the tourist office for specific details. Tickets are €11-16 (Tu half-price) and should be purchased in May before the festival begins, as they tend to sell out very quickly. The festival also has an office in Madrid at C. del Príncipe,

14 (☎915 21 07 20), and the 2005 program is listed online. From Sept.-June, there are **classical theater** performances nearly every weekend at the Corral. (☎926 88 24 58; www.corraldecomedias.com. Performances at 7, 7:30, or 9pm, depending on the date. Programs available online and at the tourist office.)

CUENCA   ☎969

Cuenca (pop. 50,000) owes its fame to its location. Perched atop a hill, the city is flanked by two rivers and the stunning rock formations they have carved. These natural boundaries have served the city well; Muslims and then Christians settled in Cuenca because it was a nearly impenetrable natural fortress. Since the 19th century, the city has strained against these boundaries, spilling modern commercial life downhill into New Cuenca. The enchanting old city still safeguards most of Cuenca's treasures, including the *casas colgadas* (hanging houses) dangling high above the Río Huécar and the Plaza Mayor's magnificent cathedral.

▐▀ TRANSPORTATION

Trains: C. Mariano Catalina, 10 (☎902 24 02 02). To: **Aranjuez** (2hr., 5-6 per day 7:05am-6:55pm, €6.60); **Madrid** (2½-3hr., 5-6 per day 7:05am-6:55pm, €9.20); **Valencia** (3-4hr., 3-4 per day 7:35am-6:50pm, €10.10).

Buses: C. Fermín Caballero, 20 (☎969 22 70 87). Info open daily 7am-3:30pm and 4-9pm. **AutoRes** (☎969 22 11 84) to **Madrid** (2½hr.; 8-9 per day M-Sa 8am-8pm, Su 8am-10pm; €9-11). **Ciudad Directo** to **Toledo** (2¼hr.; M-F 6:30am and 4:30pm; €10). **SIAL** (☎969 22 27 51) to **Barcelona** (9hr.; M-Sa 9:30am, Su-2pm; €30.40).

Taxis: Radio Taxi (☎969 23 33 43). From the train station to Pl. Mayor €4.

✈❷ ORIENTATION AND PRACTICAL INFORMATION

Upon exiting the train station, the back of the bus station (a large brick building) will be directly in front of you; head up the steps to C. Fermín Caballero and turn right to enter the bus station. To reach **Plaza Mayor** in the old city from either station, take a left onto C. Fermín Caballero, following it as it becomes C. Cervantes, C. José Cobo, and finally, bearing left through Pl. de la Hispanidad, **Calle Carretería.** Street signs point the way. Alternately, take bus #1, 3, or 4 (every 20min., €0.60) to the last stop in the old city. From the stop on C. Carretería, head toward the river. The winding route up is more scenic; for a more car-filled route, turn right onto C. Fray Luis de León; it's a hike uphill to Pl. Mayor and the old city (20-25min.).

Tourist Office: Pl. Mayor (☎969 23 21 19; www.cuenca.org). Open July-Sept. M-Sa 9am-9pm, Su 9am-2pm; Oct.-June M-Sa 9am-2pm and 4-6:30pm, Su 9am-2pm.

Currency Exchange: Banco Santander Central Hispano, C. Sánchez Vera, 5 (☎969 21 17 26). Open Apr.-Sept. M-F 8:30am-2pm, Oct.-Mar. also Sa 8:30am-2pm.

Luggage Storage: At the **bus station** (€2 per day). Open daily 7am-2pm and 4-9pm).

Police: C. González Palencia (☎092).

Pharmacy: Farmacia Castellanos, C. Cervantes, 12 (☎969 21 23 37), at the corner of C. Alférez Rubianes. Open Apr.-Oct. M-F 9:30am-2pm and 5-8pm, Sa 10am-2pm; Nov.-Mar. M-F 9:30am-2pm and 4:30-7:30pm, Sa 10am-2pm.

Internet Access: Cyber Viajero, Av. de la República Argentina, 3 (☎969 523 66 96). €2 per hr., €6 for 4hr. Open M-Sa 10:30am-2pm and 5-11pm.

Post Office: Parque de San Julián, 16 (☎969 22 10 42). Open M-F 8:30am-8:30pm, Sa 9:30am-2pm. Smaller **branch** with fewer services right next to the train station. Open M-F 8:30am-2:30pm, Sa 8am-2pm. **Postal Code:** 16002.

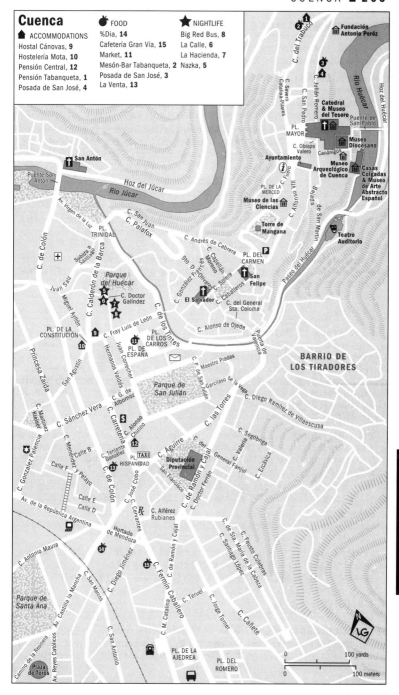

🛈 ACCOMMODATIONS

The dearth of cheap lodging in the old city may convince you to stay in the new city's less luxurious hostels. Rooms on the hill charge for their spectacular views.

Posada de San José, C. Julián Romero, 4 (☎ 969 21 13 00; fax 23 03 65). Cushy beds and gorgeous views. Some rooms with balcony, all with modern bath. Reservations recommended. Singles €22, with bath €43; doubles €32/€63; triples €43; quads with bath €100. *Semana Santa* higher; weeknights and low season lower. AmEx/MC/V. ❷

Pensión Tabanqueta, C. del Trabuco, 13 (☎969 21 12 90), up C. San Pedro from the cathedral past Pl. del Trabuco. Quite a hike from New Cuenca, but the view is worth the trip. Terrace bar shouldn't be missed. Singles €15; doubles €30; triples €45. ❷

Hostal Cánovas, C. Fray Luis de León, 38, 1st fl. (☎969 21 39 73; www.servinet.net/ canovas). Refurbished rooms are elegant and comfortable. Hardwood floors, balconies in all doubles, private baths, and rooftop terrace justify price. M-F doubles €40; triples €52. Sa-Su and holidays €45/€57. Singles on weekdays and in winter. MC/V. ❹

Pensión Central, C. Alonso Chirino, 7, 2nd fl. (☎969 21 15 11). Clean rooms with big windows and high ceilings. Balconies over street. 2 common baths. Cheap meals. July-Sept. singles €13; doubles €22; triples €29. Oct.-June €11.50/€19/€26. ❶

Hostelería Mota, Pl. de la Constitución, 6, 1st fl. (☎969 22 55 67). Marble floors, polished wooden walls, and A/C. Cheerful modern rooms have sink and TV. Singles occasionally available in winter. Doubles €28, with bath €37. ❸

🍴 FOOD

The area around Pl. Mayor is filled with mid- to high-priced restaurants, but side streets near the plaza yield cheaper alternatives. Budget spots line **Calle Cervantes** and **Avenida de la República Argentina;** the cafes off **Calle Fray Luis de León** are even cheaper. Area specialties *resoli* (a liqueur of coffee, sugar, orange peel, and *eau-de-vie*) and *alajú* (a nougat of honey, almonds, and figs) are a heavenly match. For fresh fruit, vegetables, meat, and cheese, hit the **market** on C. Fray Luis de León. (Open M-Sa 8:30am-2pm.) Grab **groceries** at **%Dia** on Av. Castilla La Mancha. (Open M-Th 9:30am-2pm and 5:30-8:30pm, F-Sa 9am-2:30pm and 5:30-9pm.)

Mesón-Bar Tabanqueta, C. del Trabuco, 13 (☎969 21 12 90). This little cafe bustles with patrons enjoying views of the gorge over cheap food and drinks. Several options including a *menú del día* (€10) and sandwiches (€2.40-5). Open Tu-Su noon-2am. ❶

Posada de San José, C. Julián Romero, 4 (☎969 21 13 00). Enjoy terrace views with their *pisto* (tomato, pepper, and onion stew; €3.50). *Bocadillos* and omelettes €2-3.80. Lamb and fried trout €5-9. Open Tu-Su 8-11am and 6-10:30pm. AmEx/MC/V. ❶

La Venta, C. Colón, 81 (☎969 212 911). Locals flock here for the delicious weeknight *menú*. Main courses include meat and fish dishes; appetizers offer vegetarian options. Open M-F 1-3pm and 9:30-11:45pm, Su 1-3pm. MC/V. ❸

Cafetería Gran Vía, C. Fermín Caballero, 4 (☎969 23 62 26). Well-dressed waiters attend the elegant wooden dining room and scurry among the people-watchers on the outdoor patio. Combo plates of eggs and pork €7-11. Open daily 7:30pm-1am. V. ❷

🔍 SIGHTS

CASAS COLGADAS. Cuenca draws its fame from the gravity-defying *casas colgadas* that have dangled over the riverbanks for six centuries. These "hanging houses," built precariously on the edges of Cuenca's high cliffs, are believed to have been the summer homes of 14th-century monarchs. A walk across Puente de San Pablo at sunset offers a spectacular ⬛ **view** of the *casas* and the surrounding cliffs. For fantastic views of Cuenca, stroll along two trails that flank Hoz del Júcar and Hoz del Huécar (the steep river gorges on either side of the old city).

MUSEO DE ARTE ABSTRACTO ESPAÑOL. Inside one of the *casas*, the award-winning Museo de Arte Abstracto Español exhibits works by the odd yet internationally renowned Abstract Generation of Spanish painters. All pieces, most by Canogar, Tápies, Chillida, and Fernando Zóbel, were chosen by Zóbel himself. The "White Room" and striking views of the gorge are added bonuses. *(Pl. Ciudad de Ronda; follow signs from Pl. Mayor. ☎ 969 21 29 83. Open Tu-F 11am-2pm and 4-6pm, Sa 11am-2pm and 4-8pm, Su 11am-2pm. €3, students and seniors €1.50.)*

CATEDRAL DE CUENCA. Constructed under Alfonso VIII six years after he conquered Castilla, the cathedral dominates Pl. Mayor. A perfect square, 25m on each side, it is the only Anglo-Norman Gothic cathedral in Spain and has been cursed by disasters through the ages. A Spanish Renaissance facade and tower were added in the 16th and 17th centuries, only to be torn down when deemed aesthetically inappropriate. A 1724 fire prevented a subsequent attempt to build a front, leaving the current exterior strangely reminiscent of a Hollywood set. Colorful stained glass windows illuminate the entrance to the **Museo del Tesoro,** which houses late medieval psalters and gold jewelry. More impressive is the **Sala Capitular** with its pink pastel ceiling. *(Pl. Mayor. Cathedral open daily 9am-2pm and 4-6pm; museum open Tu-Sa 11am-2pm and 4-6pm, Su 11am-2pm. Cathedral free, museum €1.)*

OTHER SIGHTS. The **Fundación Antonio Pérez,** C. Julian Romero, is near the top of the street. Antonio Pérez, a contemporary writer and critic, has opened his impressive, eclectic collection of 20th-century art to the public. Highlights include surrealist collages, Pérez's *"objetos encontrados"* (found objects), a couple of Warhols, and pieces dealing with the Michelin Man by Ximo Amigó. The downstairs gallery hosts exhibits. *(☎ 969 23 06 19. Open daily 9am-11pm.)* Down the hill on C. Julián Romero is the **Museo Diocesano,** whose exhibits include Juan de Borgoña's altarpiece from the local Convento de San Pablo, colossal Flemish tapestries, splendid rugs, and two El Grecos—*Oración del huerto* and *Cristo con la cruz.* *(☎ 969 22 42 10. Open Apr.-Sept. Tu-Sa 11am-2pm and 5-8pm, Su 11am-2pm; Oct.-Mar. Tu-Sa 11am-2pm and 4-7pm. €1.80, under 18 and over 65 free.)* Down C. Obispo Valero, the **Museo Arqueológico de Cuenca** is a treasure trove of Roman mosaics, coins, and Visigoth jewelry. *(☎ 969 21 30 69. Open June-Sept. Tu-Sa 10am-2pm and 5-7pm, Su 11am-2pm; Oct.-June Tu-Sa 10am-2pm and 4-7pm, Su and holidays 11am-2pm. €1.20, students €0.60. Sa afternoon and Su free.)*

⬛ NIGHTLIFE

Cuenca's nightlife scene extends into the wee hours of the morning from Thursday to Saturday. The older crowd stays near Pl. Mayor, while teens and twenty-somethings flock to the newer city. Numerous bars with young, well-dressed crowds line **Calle Doctor Galíndez,** off C. Fray Luis de León. It's a hot spot in the new city, but a long, dark walk down the hill from Old Cuenca; a taxi costs about €4. Locals drink in the Pl. de España before getting down at mirror-walled **Nazka,** at the end of the street. **La Hacienda,** down the street on the right, features stock ticker drink bargains and a strobing chandelier, and **Big Red Bus** attracts a slightly older crowd that boogies to radio hits. For a chiller vibe, check out **La Calle,** which has inside-out decor and nightly drink specials. Prices can be high, though they're pretty much standard at all these bars; mixed drinks cost €4-5 (€6 at **Nazka**), beer €2, and shots €1-2. If you're making a night of it, stock up at **%Dia** (open F and Sa to 9pm) and join the locals in the plaza. Most bars provide plastic cups for free.

SIGÜENZA ☎949

Peaceful and lovely Sigüenza (pop. 5000) is somewhat humdrum for any longer than a day. Its stone buildings and red-roofed houses surround a stunning Gothic cathedral and storybook castle. In the Civil War, Republicans seized the cathedral and Nationalists took the castle; the bloody standoff ended when Nationalists bombed the church and stormed it with tanks. Since then, Sigüenza's architecture has been restored, and a walk through the streets—from the medieval city to the 18th-century Baroque neighborhoods—makes an enjoyable escape from Madrid.

▐▛ TRANSPORTATION AND PRACTICAL INFORMATION. The **train station** (☎949 39 14 94) is at the end of Av. de Alfonso VI. Trains run to Estación Chamartín in **Madrid** (1½-2hr., 6-7 per day 6:52am-8:05pm, €7.30-8.40) and **Soria** (1½hr.; Su-Th and Sa 9:45am and 8:52pm, F 3 per day 9:45am-8:52pm; €5.10). **Buses** (☎949 34 72 77) run to **Guadalajara** (M-F 8am and 2:25pm, Sa 8am). For a **taxi** call ☎949 39 14 11. To get to the **tourist office,** follow Av. de Alfonso VI to the first intersection after the Parque de la Alameda (on the left). The office is around the corner in the restored Ermita. (☎949 34 70 07. Open M-F 10am-2pm and 4-6pm, Sa 9:30am-3pm and 4-7pm, Su 9:30am-3:30pm; Oct.-Apr. closed M.) Across the intersection **Banco Santander Hispano Central,** Av. Calvo Siteco, 9, has a 24hr. **ATM.** (☎949 39 01 50. Open M-F 8:30am-2pm.) Local services include: **luggage storage** at the train station (€1.80 per locker); **police,** Ctra. de Atienzo (☎949 39 01 95); **Red Cross,** Ctra. Madrid (☎949 39 13 33). Free **Internet** is available at the Biblioteca Pública, C. de Valencia, on the top floor of the Ayuntamiento, in the Torreón de la Muralla. Bear right going uphill on C. de la Humilidero; the building is on the left. (Open M-F noon-2pm and 4-8:30pm.) The **post office,** C. de Villaviciosa, 10, is off Pl. Hilario Yabén. (☎949 39 08 44. Open M-F 8:30am-2:30pm, Sa 9:30am-1pm.) **Postal Code:** 19250.

▐▛ ACCOMMODATIONS AND FOOD. Although you can do Sigüenza in a few hours, train schedules might force you to spend the night. The **Pensión Venancio ❶,** C. San Roque, 3, is old but charming. From the station, follow Av. de Alfonso VI and turn left at the first intersection onto Av. Pío XII. (☎949 39 03 47. Singles €15; doubles €28; triples €38.) Or, try the spacious, bright rooms at **Pension Pérez ❷,** C. de Comedias, 8. Travelers have access to a fridge. (☎949 39 12 69. Doubles €24.) Small places offering delicious *menús* for under €8 can be found everywhere.

◨ SIGHTS. The tourist office leads guided **city tours,** including entrance to all parts of the cathedral; prices vary with the number of people and are expensive (€40 for 1-4 people), but more economical for a larger group. Call ahead for reservations. From the bottom of the hill, two buildings jut out from Sigüenza's low skyline: the cathedral and the fortified 12th-century **castle,** now a *parador.* Restored in the 1970s, the castle merits an uphill stroll through the cobblestone streets, even just for a glance at the luxuriously decorated hotel and its marvelous view. To get to the ◨**cathedral,** follow Av. de Alfonso VI uphill (it changes to C. del Humillad-ero), then take a left onto C. del Cardenal Mendoza. Work on the cathedral began in the mid-12th century and continued until the 16th century; 400 years of construction made for a fantastic combination of Romanesque, *mudéjar,* Plater-esque, Gothic, Baroque, and Renaissance revival. Renowned for its naturalistic grace is the 15th-century **Tumba del Doncel** (Tomb of the Virginal Youth). The alabaster sarcophagi contain remains of the de Arce family, nobles loyal to the Spanish Crown. Martín Barque de Arce (reclining) died at 25 fighting the Moors in Granada. Centuries later, Miguel de Unamuno dubbed him "El Doncel," and the name stuck. De Arce's brother, the Archbishop of the Islas Canarias, bought the chapel for his family; they lay undisturbed until Napoleon's troops sacked the church and chiseled their faces. The sacristy's Renaissance ceiling, designed by Alonso de Covarrubias, boasts 304 stone portraits (3700 counting minor cherubim). The adjoining chapel houses El Greco's *Anunciación*. (☎619 36 27 15. Tour required to enter sacristy and chapel; Tu-Sa 4 per day 11am-5:30pm; Su tours available June-Nov. 12 noon and 4:30pm; Nov. 13-May noon, 1, 5:30pm. €3. Cathedral open daily 9am-1:30pm and 4:30-8pm. Free.) Opposite the cathedral, the **Museo de Arte Antiguo** (Museo Diocesano) houses medieval and early modern religious works, including a Ribera and Zurbarán's *La Inmaculada Niña*. (☎949 39 10 23. Call ahead, as it is undergoing restoration. Open Tu-Su 11am-2pm and 4-7pm. €2.)

EXTREMADURA

Extremadura doesn't seem to care much for the 21st century, and most of its charm comes from the medieval mood—the hardly tameable landscape of thirsty soil, scattered lakes, occasional sunflower fields, and gorgeous, unchanged stone towns with prominent church towers and castle remains. The aptly named Extremadura is a land of harsh beauty and cruel extremes. Mérida's Roman ruins and the hushed ancient beauty of Trujillo and Cáceres are only beginning to draw flocks of admirers looking for the "traditional" Spanish countryside. Beyond the region's rugged landscape, its hearty pastoral cuisine is particularly appealing; local specialties include rabbit, partridge, lizard with green sauce, wild pigeon with herbs, and *migas* (fried bread crumbs) with chocolate. Thick *cocido* (chick pea stew) warms *extremeños* in winter, while endless varieties of gazpacho (including an unusual white variation) cool them in summer.

CÁCERES   ☎927

Stepping into Cáceres's *barrio antiguo* is an immediate time warp. The bustle of the modern city is silenced, and the purely medieval takes over. Unlike many other Golden Age cities, Cáceres lacks the clichéd mix of old and new. Built between the 14th and 16th centuries by rival noble families vying for socio-political control, the old quarter remains frozen in that era's architecture, culture, and decor, each family having built a miniature palace demonstrating power and wealth. Stop by and wander the town's wonderful maze of palaces and mansions inhabited by storks. Although Cáceres's newer areas are less interesting, the Parque del Príncipe and healthy nightlife provide enough amusement for a short stay.

▐ TRANSPORTATION

Trains: RENFE (☎902 24 02 02), on Av. de Alemania, 3km from the old city. Across the highway from the bus station. Open daily 9am-9pm. To: **Badajoz** (2hr., 3 per day 11:45am-10pm, €7-15); **Lisboa,** Portugal (6hr., 3 and 8:13am, €35); **Madrid** (4hr., 6 per day 4:10am-6:51pm, €16-35); **Sevilla** (4hr., 8:33am, €15) via **Mérida** (1hr., €4).

Buses: (☎902 42 22 42), on Ctra. Sevilla. Info open M-Th 7:30am-7:30pm, Sa 8:30am-9pm, Su 8:30am-11:30pm. Buses to: **Badajoz** (1½hr.; M-F 3 per day 8:30am-7:30pm, Sa 8:30am and 2:30pm, Su 8pm; €5.90); **Madrid** (4-5hr., 7-9 per day 1:45am-6pm, €16.70); **Mérida** (1hr., 4 per day 6:30am-7:30pm, €4.30); **Salamanca** (4hr.; 3-6 per day M-F 7am-6pm, Sa 7am-2pm, Su 5am-7pm; €11.70); **Sevilla** (4hr., 6 per day 4:10am-9:45pm, €14.60); **Trujillo** (45min.; M-F 3 per day 1-5:30pm, Sa 1pm, Su 7:30pm; €2.70); **Valladolid** (5½hr., 12:30 and 5:30pm, €17.60).

Taxis: Radio Taxi (☎927 21 21 21). Stands at Pl. Mayor and bus and train stations.

Car Rental: Avis (☎689 84 90 18), in the bus station. 23+. 1-day rental from €72. Open summer M-F 9:30am-1pm and 5-8pm, Sa 9:30am-1pm; winter M-F 5-8pm.

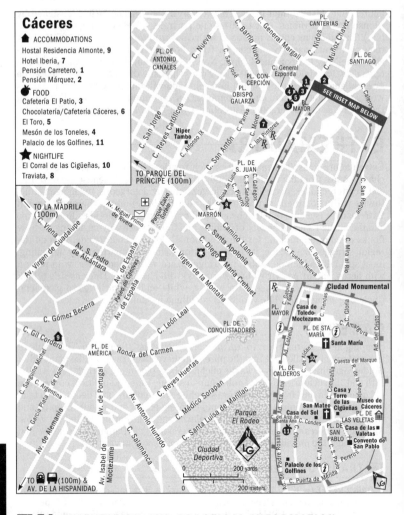

Cáceres

▲ ACCOMMODATIONS
Hostal Residencia Almonte, **9**
Hotel Iberia, **7**
Pensión Carretero, **1**
Pensión Márquez, **2**

🍴 FOOD
Cafetería El Patio, **3**
Chocolatería/Cafetería Cáceres, **6**
El Toro, **5**
Mesón de los Toneles, **4**
Palacio de los Golfines, **11**

★ NIGHTLIFE
El Corral de las Cigüeñas, **10**
Traviata, **8**

⚡ 🔢 ORIENTATION AND PRACTICAL INFORMATION

The **ciudad monumental** (also called the *barrio antiguo*) and the commercial **Avenida de España** flank the **Plaza Mayor.** The plaza is 3km from the **bus** and **train stations,** which face each other across the rotary intersection of Av. de la Hispanidad and Av. de Alemania. From the bus or train station, the best way to get to the center of town is via bus #1 (€0.65), which stops at the far end of Av. de Alemania across from the train station; however, this stop changes location, so check at the info window or with locals if it is not visible. Hop off at Pl. Obispo Galarza. Facing the bus stop, walk right and take the first left down the steps near the "Pl. Mayor 60m" sign. At the first intersection, turn right, then left to continue downhill and past the next street. When you reach the arches, Pl. Mayor will be on the left. Bus

#2 stops on Av. de la Hispanidad, around the corner to the right from the bus station, and runs to **Plaza de América,** hub of the new downtown. From there, signs point up tree-lined **Avenida de España (Paseo de Cánovas)** toward the Pl. Mayor.

Tourist Office: Pl. Mayor (☎927 01 08 34). Open July-Sept. M-F 9am-2pm and 5-7pm, Sa-Su 9:45am-2pm; Oct.-June M-F 9am-2pm and 4-6pm, Sa-Su 9:45am-2pm. The **Patronato de Turismo** (☎927 25 55 97), on C. Amargura in the Palacio de Carvajal, provides quality maps of the monuments and hosts a modern art museum. Open M-F 8am-8pm, Sa-Su 10am-2pm. **Branch** office with an excellent map at C. Ancha, 7 (☎927 24 71 72). Open M-Sa 10am-2pm and 5-8pm, Su 10am-2pm.

Currency Exchange: Banks line Av. de España and the streets leading to Pl. Mayor.

Luggage Storage: At the **train station** (€3 per day) and **bus station** (€0.60 per day).

Police: Municipal (☎927 24 84 24), on C. Diego María Crehuet.

Late-Night Pharmacies: Farmacia Castel, Pl. Mayor, 28A (☎927 24 50 87); **Farmacia Jiménez Rebolledo,** C. los Pintores, 23 (☎927 24 55 18); and **Farmacia Acedo,** C. los Pintores, 31 (☎927 24 55 26) post the list of 24hr. pharmacies.

Hospital: Hospital Provincial (☎927 25 68 00), on Av. de España.

Internet Access: Ciberjust, C. Diego María Crehuet, 7 (☎927 21 46 77). €2 per hr. Open M-Sa 10am-2:30pm and 4:30pm-midnight, Su 5pm-2am.

Post Office: Av. Miguel Primo de Rivera (☎927 62 66 81). Stamps and **Lista de Correos.** Open M-F 8:30am-8:30pm, Sa 9:30am-2pm. **Postal Code:** 10071

▚ ACCOMMODATIONS

Hostales are scattered throughout the new city and line Pl. Mayor in the old town. Prices rise during festivals, and advance reservations are recommended on summer weekends, especially for *pensiones* near Pl. Mayor.

Pensión Carretero, Pl. Mayor, 22 (☎927 24 74 82). Rooms are spacious and comfortable, and some have balconies overlooking the plaza. Warm, friendly staff. Curfew 2am. Singles €13-15; doubles €22; triples €30. V. ❶

Hostal Residencia Almonte, C. Gil Cordero, 6 (☎927 24 09 25; fax 24 86 02). Comfortable rooms with TV and bath. Some have A/C; others have fans. A bit of a hike from Pl. Mayor. Singles €22; doubles €35; triples €40. MC/V. ❷

Hotel Iberia, C. los Pintores, 2 (☎927 24 76 34). Decked out with 16th-century paintings and furniture. Excellent rooms with TV, bath, and A/C. Breakfast €3.50. Singles €35-40; doubles €48-50; triples €55-60. MC/V. ❹

Pensión Márquez, C. Gabriel y Galán, 2 (☎927 24 49 60), off Pl. Mayor. The friendly owner makes Márquez feel like home. Hall baths. Doubles €20; triples €30. ❷

▚ FOOD

Pl. Mayor overflows with restaurants and cafes serving up *bocadillos, raciones,* and *menús.* Side streets offer less-touristed local bars and pastry shops. **Hiper Tambo,** C. Alfonso IX, 25 (☎927 21 17 71; open M-Sa 9:30am-9pm) sells groceries.

Mesón de los Toneles, C. General Ezponda, 8 (☎927 21 61 70). Traditional *cocina extremeña* in a charming, romantically dim folkloric setting. Don't leave without trying the delicious *migas extremeñas* (stuffing-like dish; €5). Entrees €5-13. *Menú del día* €7.80-10. Restaurant open daily noon-5pm and 7pm-1am; bar open noon-1am. ❷

El Toro, C. General Ezponda, 2 (☎927 21 15 48). Yuppified Spanish cuisine in upscale setting. For a quicker meal, try the co-owned **Cafetería El Patio** in the Pl. Mayor. Entrees €6.60-15. *Menú* €9-12. Open Tu-Sa 11am-5pm and 8pm-1am. MC/V. ❸

Palacio de los Golfines, Ad. del Padre Rosalío, 2 (☎927 24 24 14). Dine like a nobleman in a gorgeous 15th-century palace in the old city. Golfines has received numerous awards for its exquisite Spanish cuisine. Appetizers €3.50-10. Entrees €11-25. *Menú* €25. Open Tu-Sa noon-5pm and 8pm-1am, Su noon-5pm. AmEx/D/MC/V. ❹

Chocolatería/Cafetería Cáceres, Pl. Mayor, 16 (☎927 24 97 63). Convenient restaurant on the plaza with terrace and quick service. Standard Iberian fare in *extremeño* style. Breakfast €5. Tapas €1-5. Entrees €6-12. *Menú* €7-9. Open 8am-12:30am. ❷

🔊 SIGHTS

The golden, stork-filled **ciudad monumental** is a melting pot of architectural ensembles: Roman, Arabic, Gothic, Renaissance, and even Incan influences (brought back by the *conquistadores*) can be detected throughout. The main attraction is the neighborhood itself, since most buildings don't open their doors to tourists. Turn off that internal compass and wander along the narrow streets. Though the area is small, a map will come in handy. From Pl. Mayor, take the stairs from the left of the tourist office to the Arco de la Estrella, the entrance to the walled old city.

MUSEO DE CÁCERES. Inside the Casa de los Caballos, the Museo de Cáceres is a must-see, housing a tiny but brilliant *Who's Who* of Spanish art. It features originals by El Greco, Picasso, Miró, and recent abstractionist stars, along with rotating exhibits. The neighboring **Casa de las Veletas** (House of Weathervanes) displays Celtiberian stone animals, Roman and Visigothic tombstones, and an astonishing 🏛 **Muslim cistern.** *(Pl. de las Veletas. ☎927 01 08 77. Open Apr. 14-Sept. Tu-Sa 9am-2:30pm and 5-8pm, Su 10:15am-2:30pm; Oct.-Apr. 13 Tu-Sa 9am-2:30pm and 4-7pm, Su 10:15am-2:30pm. €1.20; students, seniors, and EU citizens free.)*

IGLESIA CONCATEDRAL DE SANTA MARÍA. A statue of San Pedro de Alcántara, one of Extremadura's two patron saints, eyes Pl. de Sta. María from a corner pedestal raised outside the cathedral. His shiny toes are the result of years of good-luck foot rubs. The Gothic cathedral, built between 1229 and 1547, has a remarkable ceiling and an intricate, 16th-century carved wood altar. An audio guide (€1) on the history of the church is available inside. *(Pl. de Sta. María. ☎927 21 53 13. Open M-Sa 10am-2pm and 5-8pm, Su 9:30am-2pm and 5-7:30pm. Free.)*

CONVENTO DE SAN PABLO. The convent is late-Gothic eye candy for architecture addicts. Cloistered nuns sell delicious homemade pastries through a peculiar rotating window that protects them from the unholy gaze of customers. Have your pastry selection ready from the list on the wall and ask politely during opening hours, even if the door seems closed. *(Pl. de San Pablo. To the left of Casa y Torre de las Cigüeñas. Open M-Sa 9am-1pm and 5-8pm. Pastries €3-9.)*

CASA Y TORRE DE LAS CIGÜEÑAS. Cáceres's aristocracy was a war-like lot. The city's monarchs removed all battlements and spires from local lords' houses to punish them for their violent quarreling. Due to his loyalty to the ruling family, Don Golfín's Casa y Torre de las Cigüeñas (House and Tower of the Storks) was the lone estate allowed to keep its battlements, and the storks are still grateful. Though the interior is closed to the public, the stork nests are worth a peek. *(From Arco de la Estrella, take a right up the hill, a left onto Adarve de Sta. Ana, then a right and a quick left onto C. de los Condes. Cross Pl. de San Mateo to Pl. del Conde de Canilleros; it is on the left.)*

OTHER SIGHTS. Most *palacios* and *casas* in the *ciudad monumental* are still inhabited and closed to visitors. The 16th-century **Casa del Sol** is the most famous of Cáceres's numerous mansions; its crest is the city's emblem. The **Casa de Toledo-Moctezuma** was built by the grandson of the Aztec princess Isabel Moctezuma to represent the union of two worlds. *(On Pl. del Conde de Canilleros, to the left as you enter*

Arco de la Estrella.) On October 26, 1936, in the **Palacio de los Golfines de Arriba,** yet another Golfín family palace, Franco was proclaimed head of the Spanish state and general of its armies. *(Between C. Olmos and Adarve del Padre Rosalío.)*

NIGHTLIFE

Just follow the flock for a tipsy evening in Cáceres—the nobles never partied this good. Revelry starts in Pl. Mayor and along C. Pizarro, lined with bars showcasing live music. **Traviata,** C. Sergio Sánchez, 8, is a gorgeously colorful, artsy, and hip musical cafe blasting a mix of lounge, techno, and pop, and hosting one-man shows on Thursdays at 10:30pm. (☎ 927 21 13 74. Beer €2.50, mixed drinks €4-4.50. Open daily 4pm-3am.) For live jazz, poetry festivals, and tarot readings, head to **El Corral de las Cigüeñas,** Cuesta de Aldana, 6, in the old city. Enclosed by vine-covered walls but open to a star-filled sky and located in the middle of the otherwise sleepy *ciudad monumental,* El Corral offers fantastic music and occasional Friday night concerts for €3-8. (☎ 647 75 82 45. Beer €1.80-2.20, mixed drinks from €5. Open M and W-Su from 7pm until the last customer leaves.) Later, the party migrates to **La Madrila,** a club-filled area near Pl. del Albatros in the new city. From Pl. Mayor, take Av. de España, take a right onto Av. Miguel Primo de Rivera, and cross the intersection onto C. Dr. Fleming.

DAYTRIP FROM CÁCERES

GUADALUPE
Transportation to and from Guadalupe can be somewhat tricky; most visitors arrive via tour bus or in their own cars. Empresa Mirat (☎ 927 23 48 63) sends buses from Cáceres to Guadalupe (2½hr., M-Sa 1:30 and 5:30pm, €7.70) and back (M-Sa 6:45 and 7:30am).

Guadalupe rests on a mountainside in the Sierra de Guadalupe, two hours east of Trujillo and four hours southwest of Madrid. The **Real Monasterio de Santa María de Guadalupe,** with its eclectic history and decadent architecture, is a worthy daytrip, particularly for pilgrims and those with an interest in history, art, or architecture. The fairy-tale monastery has even been nicknamed "the Spanish Sistine Chapel." Its 25,000 square meters host an incredible collection of artwork, including many El Grecos and a *mudéjar*-style central courtyard: At the Battle of Salado in 1340, Alfonso XI, believed to have been aided by the Virgin Mary, defeated a much superior Muslim army. As a token of his gratitude, he commissioned the lavish Real Monasterio. Years later, it became customary to grant licenses for foreign expeditions on the premises; in fact, Columbus finalized his contract with Fernando and Isabel here. To pay homage to the city, he named one of the islands he discovered Guadalupe (now known as Turugueira). The most prominent object in the basilica is the **Icon of the Virgin,** carved out of wood, blackened with age, and cloaked in robes of silver and gold. (Monastery open daily 9:30am-1pm and 3:30-6:30pm. €3.)

The **tourist office** in Pl. Mayor posts information on the door; follow signs from the bus station. (☎ 927 15 41 28. Open June-Aug. Tu-F 10am-2pm and 5-7pm, Sa-Su 10am-2pm; Sept.-May Tu-F 10am-2pm and 4-6pm, Sa-Su 10am-2pm.) Travelers looking for food or beds (singles generally run €20) should head to Pl. Mayor.

TRUJILLO ☎ 927

The gem of Extremadura, hilltop Trujillo (pop. 9800) is an enchanting old-world town (even *Gladiator*'s Maximus had a home here). Often called the "Cradle of Conquistadors," Trujillo furnished history with over 600 explorers of the New World, including Peru's conqueror Francisco Pizarro and the Amazon's first European explorer, Francisco de Orellana. Scattered with medieval palaces, Roman ruins, Arabic fortresses, and churches of every era, Trujillo is a hodgepodge of histories and cultures. The pace of life today is slow and tranquil, and locals and visitors alike spend evenings sipping *café con leche* at the plaza's many cafes while relishing the beauty of this well-preserved city.

TRANSPORTATION. The **bus station** (☎927 32 18 22) is at the corner of C. de las Cruces and C. del M. de Albayada; look for the **AutoRes** sign. Since most buses stop only en route to larger destinations, there are not always seats available—reserve them in advance. Buses run to: **Badajoz** (2hr., 10 per day 1:15am-11:40pm, €8.40); **Cáceres** (45min., 5-7 per day 11:15am-10:30pm, €2.70); **Madrid** (2½hr., 14-16 per day 2:15am-10:30pm, €14); **Salamanca** (5hr., 10:30am, €15).

PRACTICAL INFORMATION. An English-speaking staff gives advice at the **tourist office** in Pl. Mayor, on the left when facing Pizarro's statue. Info is posted on the windows when it's closed. Guided tours (€6.80) leave from Pl. Mayor at 11:30am and 5pm. (☎927 32 26 77. Open June-Sept. 9:30am-2pm and 4:30-7:30pm; Oct.-May 9:30am-2pm and 4-7pm.) **Currency exchange** and an **ATM** are at **Banco Santander Central Hispano**, Pl. Mayor, 25. (☎927 24 24 24. Open Apr.-Sept. M-F 8:30am-2:30pm; Oct.-Mar. M-F 8:30am-2:30pm, Sa 8:30am-1pm.) The **police** are at C. Carnicería, 2 (☎927 32 01 08), just off Pl. Mayor. In a **medical emergency** call the **centro de salud** (☎927 32 20 16). Get your **Internet** fix at Ciberalia, C. Tiendas, 18, off Pl. Mayor. (☎927 65 90 89. €2 per hr. Open daily 10am-2am.) The **post office,** Po. Ruiz de Mendoza, 28, is on the way from the station to Pl. Mayor. (☎927 32 05 33. Open M-F 9am-2:30pm, Sa 9:30am-1pm.) **Postal Code:** 10200.

ACCOMMODATIONS AND FOOD. Get medieval at ⊠**Hostal Trujillo ❷**, C. Francisco Pizarro, 4-6. From the bus station, turn left onto C. de las Cruces, right onto C. de la Encarnación, then right again onto C. Francisco Pizarro. The armor, lance, and shield-bedecked halls of this renovated 15th-century hospital lead to classy colorful rooms with bath, A/C, and satellite TV. The only downside is the 10min. uphill walk to Pl. Mayor and all the sights. (☎/fax 927 32 22 74; www.hostaltrujillo.com. Singles €24; doubles €40.) The pleasant **Camas Boni ❶**, C. Domingo Ramos, 11, owned and run by a friendly German and Spanish couple, is off Pl. Mayor on the street directly across from the church. With comfortable, clean rooms, a TV lounge, and a location only steps from all the major sites, you can't go wrong here. (☎927 32 16 04. Singles €15; doubles €28, with bath €30-35. Extra bed €10.) **Posada Dos Orillas ❺**, C. Cambreras, 6, offers top notch rooms in Trujillo's historic center. The decor of Dos Orillas' seven exclusive rooms is inspired by the seven cities in Latin America named Trujillo, giving this 16th-century building and its beautiful garden an eclectic feel. (☎927 65 90 79; www.dosorillas.com. All rooms with bath, Internet, cable TV, and A/C. Breakfast buffet €9. Doubles €90 plus tax. Extra bed €30. MC/V.)

Meals in Trujillo are unfortunately overpriced. For something that won't break the bank, head to **La Tahona ❶**, C. Afueras, 2, for homemade pizzas (€3.10-8.80), pastas (€4-5.20), and other tasty meals. Exit Pl. Mayor by the church and walk four blocks. (☎927 32 18 49. Open M 7:30pm-midnight, Tu-Su 1-4pm and 7:30pm-midnight.) Enjoy glorious views of the plaza along with delectable coffees, hot chocolates, and snacks at the trendy **Que Arte! ❶**, Pl. Mayor, 7. (☎927 32 29 96. Drinks €1.40-2.75. Sandwiches €1.80-2.50. Tapas €1.50-2. Open Tu-Su 5pm-2am.) If all else fails, head to **Consum Supermarket**, Av. Monfragüe. (Open M-Sa 9:30am-10pm. MC/V.)

⬛ SIGHTS. An afternoon stroll through Trujillo's *barrio* may be the best in Extremadura. A *bono* ticket (€4), available at the tourist office, allows entrance to the **Casa-Museo de Pizarro,** the **Moorish castle,** and **Iglesia de Santiago,** and includes a guide book. The tourist office runs tours of the old city, including the Museo del Traje. (Except where otherwise indicated, sights are open daily June-Sept. 10am-2pm and 5-8:30pm; Oct.-May 9:30am-2pm and 4:30-8pm. Each €1.25-1.50.)

Trujillo's **Plaza Mayor** was the inspiration for the Plaza de Armas in Cuzco, Perú, constructed after Francisco Pizarro defeated the Incas. Palaces, arched corridors, and cafes surround the central fountain and figure of Pizarro. The gift of an American admirer of Pizarro, the bronze statue was erected in 1929 and has a twin in Lima, Perú. Festooned with stork nests, **Iglesia de San Martín** dominates the plaza's northeastern corner. The church has several historic tombs, but contrary to local lore, Francisco de Orellana does not rest here. (Open M-Sa 10am-2pm and 4:30-7:30pm; Su 10am-2pm and 4:30-7pm. €1.25. Mass summer M-Sa 8:30pm, Su 1 and 8:30pm; winter M-Sa 7:30pm, Su 1 and 7:30pm. Free.) Across the street, seven chimneys on the **Palacio de los Duques de San Carlos** symbolize the oppressed New World religions. (Open daily 9:30am-1pm and 4:30-6:30pm. €1.25.)

At the entrance to the *zona monumental*, the 13th-century **Puerta de Santiago** is connected to the **Iglesia de Santiago.** The tower is the oldest part of the church and served as a defensive structure. To reach the Gothic **Iglesia de Santa María la Mayor,** take C. de las Cambroneras from the plaza in front of the Iglesia de San Martín and turn right onto C. Santa María. According to legend, the giant soldier Diego García de Paredes picked up the fountain (now located next to the rear door) at age 11 and carried it to his mother. After a fatal fall from a horse, the giant was buried here. Commonly known as the "Extremaduran Samson," the giant is referenced in chapter 32 of Cervantes's *Don Quixote*. The church's 25-panel Gothic altarpiece was painted by master Fernando Gallego in 1480. The tiny steps leading to the top of the Romanesque church tower are a workout, but climb them to ⬛**let Extremaduran winds blow through your hair** as you take in the 360° panoramic view of the amazing landscape of brick rooftops, castle ruins, church towers, stretches of arid land, distant mountains, and scattered lakes. (Open May-Oct. 10am-2pm and 4:30-8pm; Nov.-Apr. 10am-2pm and 4-7pm. €1.25. Mass Su 11am.) To the left of the church is the restored **Museo de la Coria,** which explores the relationship between Extremadura and Latin America both during the Conquest and in the continent's later independence. (Open Sa-Su 11:30am-2pm. Free.) Up the stairs to the right of the church when facing it, inside a restored convent, is the **Museo del Traje,** exhibiting the spectacular evening gowns worn by royalty and famous actresses from the 17th century on. (Open 10am-2pm and 5-8:30pm. €1.50.) To get to the **Casa-Museo de Pizarro,** walk uphill on the stone road to the right of the Iglesia de Santa María. The bottom floor of the house is a reproduction of a 15th-century nobleman's living quarters, while the top floor is dedicated to the life and times of Francisco Pizarro. Crowning the hill are the ruins of a 10th-century **Moorish castle.** Pacing the battlements and ramparts is like playing in your best Lego creation. Enjoy a view of unspoiled landscape, with Trujillo on one side and fields scattered with ancient battlements on the other.

MÉRIDA ☎924

For quality of Roman ruins per square foot, it doesn't get better than Mérida (pop. 60,000). In 26 BC, as a reward for services rendered to the Roman Empire, Augustus Caesar granted a heroic group of veteran legionnaires a new city in Lusitania, a province comprised of Portugal and part of Spain. The veterans chose a lovely spot surrounded by hills on the banks of the Río Guadiana to found their new home, which they named Augusta Emerita. Not content to rest on their laurels and itching to gossip with fellow patricians in Sevilla and Salamanca, the soldiers built the largest bridge in Lusitania, the Puente Romano. The nostalgic crew adorned their "little Rome" with baths, aqueducts, a hippodrome, an arena, and a famous amphitheater. Modern Mérida has complemented the Roman buildings with walkways, small plazas, and the world-class Museo Nacional de Arte Romano. In July and August, the spectacular *Festival de Teatro Clásico* offers some of Europe's best classical and modern theater and dance, performed among the ruins.

▐ TRANSPORTATION

Trains: C. Carderos (☎902 24 02 02). Info open daily 7am-10pm. To: **Badajoz** (1hr.; M-Sa 7 per day 7:16am-10:10pm, Su 5 per day 2:18pm-10:10pm; €2.70-11); **Cáceres** (1hr., 3-4 per day 8:20am-9:15pm, €3.30-11.50); **Madrid** (4hr., 3-4 per day 8:20am-3:28pm, €19.20-28.50); **Sevilla** (4½hr., 9:45am, €11); **Zafra** (1hr., 9:45am, €3.30).

Buses: Av. de la Libertad (☎924 37 14 04). Info open M-F 7am-11pm, Sa-Su 7am-1pm and 3:15-11pm. **ALSA** (☎902 42 22 42) goes to **Salamanca** (5hr.; 4-5 per day M-Sa 9:15am-1:30am, Su 9:15am-12:10am; €14.20) and **Sevilla** (3hr., 6-7 per day 2:35am-10:45pm, €11). **AutoRes** (☎924 37 19 55) goes to **Madrid** (5½hr., 7-9 per day 1:15pm-7:15pm, €19-24). **LEDA** (☎924 37 14 03) runs to: **Badajoz** (1hr.; 4-9 per day M-F 8am-12:30am, Sa 8:45am-10:50pm, Su 11:40am-10:50pm; €4); **Cáceres** (1hr.; M-Sa 9:10am and 3:50pm, M and Th also at 9:15pm, Su 7:10pm; €4.30); **Sevilla** (3hr.; 7-9 per day M-F 7am-8:30pm, Sa 7am-9:50pm, Su 9am-11:05pm; €11).

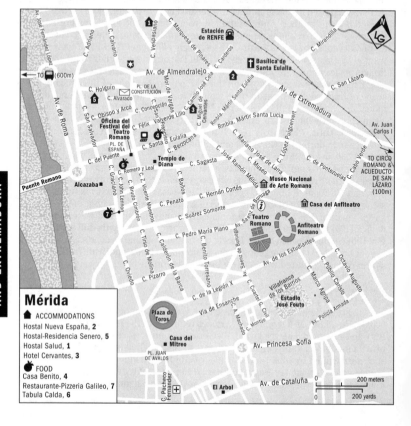

Mérida

⬆ ACCOMMODATIONS
Hostal Nueva España, **2**
Hostal-Residencia Senero, **5**
Hostal Salud, **1**
Hotel Cervantes, **3**

⬤ FOOD
Casa Benito, **4**
Restaurante-Pizzeria Galileo, **7**
Tabula Calda, **6**

Taxis: Teletaxi (☎924 31 57 56). 24hr.

Car Rental: Avis (☎924 37 33 11), at the bus station. 23+. From €48 per day plus taxes. Insurance included. Open M-F 9am-1pm and 5-8pm, Sa 9:30am-1pm.

■ 🔋 ORIENTATION AND PRACTICAL INFORMATION

Plaza de España, the town center, is two blocks up from the Puente Romano and easily accessible from the **Teatro Romano.** Walking outward from the center, cafes and shops around the plaza quickly transform into quiet residential neighborhoods, and streets often lose their signs. To reach Pl. de España from the bus station, cross the suspension bridge and turn right onto Av. de Roma. Continue along the river until you reach the Puente Romano, then turn left onto C. del Puente. From the **train station,** take C. Carderos and its continuation, C. Camilo José Cela; bear right onto C. Félix Valverde Lillo and follow it to Pl. de España (5-10min.).

Tourist Office: Av. J. Álvarez Sáenz de Buruaga (☎/fax 924 00 97 30). English spoken. Ask for anything, from info on the *Festival de Teatro Clásico* to a full-color guide to *extremeño* ecotourism in Dutch. Open summer M-F 9am-1:45pm and 5-7:15pm, Sa-Su 9:30am-1:45pm; winter M-F 9am-1:45pm and 4-6:15pm, Sa-Su 9:30am-1:45pm.

Police: Av. Almendralejo (☎092).

Hospital: Residencia Sanitaria de la Seguridad Social Centralita (☎924 38 10 00).

Medical Assistance: ☎924 38 10 18.

Internet Access: Escuela de Idiomas Santa Eulalia, C. Santa Eulalia, 19, 2nd fl. (☎924 31 19 60). 30min. minimum. €1 per 30min., €1.50 per hr. Open M-F July-Sept. 10am-2pm and 7-10pm; Oct.-June 10am-3pm and 5-10pm.

Post Office: Pl. de la Constitución (☎924 31 24 58; fax 30 24 56). Open July 15-Sept. 15 M-F 8:30am-2:30pm, Sa 9:30am-1pm; Sept. 16-July 14 M-F 8:30am-8:30pm, Sa 9:30am-1pm. **Postal Code:** 06800.

🏠 ACCOMMODATIONS

Despite the flocks of visor-sporting tourists, finding a reasonably priced room in Mérida won't leave you in ruins. Check the tourist office for complete listings.

Hostal-Residencia Senero, C. Holguín, 12 (☎924 31 72 07; www.hostalsenero.com). Lively, charming owners make you feel at home. Simple, generous, and clean rooms, some with a balcony facing the street. Apr.-Oct. and Dec. 22-31 singles €20, with bath €25; doubles with bath €35. Nov.-Dec. 21 and Jan.-Mar. €18/€20/€30. MC/V. ❷

Hostal Nueva España, Av. de Extremadura, 6 (☎924 31 33 56). Standard spacious rooms with bath. Singles €23, with A/C €25; doubles €35/€38. MC/V. ❷

Hostal Salud, C. Vespasiano, 41 (☎626 32 41 67; fax 924 31 22 59). Dark hallways open up to light and comfortable rooms with TV and private bath. Singles €15-18; doubles €26-36, depending on season and A/C. MC/V. ❷

Hotel Cervantes, C. Camilo José Cela, 8 (☎924 31 49 01). Centrally located, modern building with comfortable facilities. Bright rooms with large screen TV and great baths. Breakfast €3.90. Parking €6. Singles €40-50; doubles €60-70. AmEx/MC/V. ❹

🍴 FOOD

Plaza de España is filled with overpriced outdoor cafes. Buy fresh food at the **market** in Pl. Mercado de Calatrava. (Open M-Sa 8am-2pm.) A supermarket, **El Árbol,** is at C. Félix Valverde Lillo, 8. (☎924 30 13 56. Open M-Sa 9:30am-2pm and 6-9pm. MC/V.) A **branch** is closer to the train station on C. Marquesa de Pinares.

🟥 **Restaurante-Pizzeria Galileo,** C. John Lennon, 28 (☎924 31 55 05). A partially glass-floored dining room reveals the Roman ruins below. Fresh salads, pastas, and 34 creative varieties of pizza. Desserts freshly imported from Italy. Entrees €4-6. Open Th-Su 1:30pm-midnight. MC/V. ❶

   Tabula Calda, C. Romero y Leal, 11 (☎924 30 49 50; www.tabulacalda.com). The house special Sephardic-Jewish salad with orange, sugar, and olive oil is a good start to any meal. Eclectic art surrounds tables in an intimate interior garden. Entrees from €8, 3-course *menús* from €15. Open daily June-Sept. 1-4:30pm and 8pm-12:30am; Oct.-May 1-4:30pm and 7pm-midnight. AmEx/MC/V. ❸

   Casa Benito, C. San Francisco, 3 (☎924 31 55 00). The ivy-walled terrace is the perfect place for a beer; the hidden restaurant behind the bar has a fascinating carnivorous menu and is as much a bullfighting museum as it is an eatery. Bar open M-Sa 8:30am-midnight; restaurant open daily 1-4pm and 9pm-midnight. ❶

🔵 SIGHTS

From the **Puente Romano** to astrological mosaics, Mérida offers Spain's best view of Roman civilization in Iberia. A **combined ticket,** valid for all the listings below except the Museo Nacional de Arte Romano, can be purchased at any of the sights. (Valid for several days; includes a guide book to the ruins. €8, EU students €4. Ruins all open daily June-Sept. 9:30am-1:45pm and 5-7:15pm; Oct.-May 9:30am-1:45pm and 4-6:15pm.)

🟥 **MUSEO NACIONAL DE ARTE ROMANO.** Vast, elegant galleries below colossal brick arches house all the Roman memorabilia you could ask for: statues, dioramas, coins, and other relics. The giant mosaics are particularly stunning. Downstairs, the **cripta** displays parts of an ancient Augusta Emerita street found at the time of the museum's construction. Budget anywhere from 40 minutes to several hours to peruse the building's breathtaking architecture and intriguing content. *(C. José Ramón Mélida, 2. ☎924 31 16 90. Open Mar.-Nov. Tu-Sa 10am-2pm and 4-9pm, Su and holidays 10am-2pm; Dec.-Apr. Tu-Sa 10am-2pm and 4-6pm, Su and holidays 10am-2pm. €2.40, students €1.20. Sa afternoon and Su free.)*

🟥 **TEATRO ROMANO AND ANFITEATRO ROMANO.** The spectacular *teatro* was a gift from Agrippa, a Roman administrator, in 16 BC. Its 6000 seats face a *scaenae-frons*, an incredible marble colonnade built upstage. Today the stage features performances of Spanish classical theater during the popular **Festival de Teatro Clásico de Mérida** every July and August. *(Performances on alternate days July-Aug. 10:45pm. Info at the Oficina del Festival, C. Santa Eulalia, 4. ☎924 00 49 30; www.festivaldemerida.com. Tickets €10-40. Combined ticket for all performances €100-250. Consult tourist office Sept.-June for more info.)* Inaugurated in 8 BC, the *anfiteatro* was used for contests between any combination of animals and men. *(In the park across from the Museo Nacional; also accessible by tunnel from the cripta. €5.50, includes teatro.)*

CASA DEL ANFITEATRO AND CASA DEL MITREO. These ruins of Roman homes showcase some of the world's finest Roman mosaics. The Casa del Mitreo's **Mosaico Cosmológico** is world-famous among historians of Rome and depicts the Romans' conception of the world and forces of nature. Do not be deterred by the **Casa del Anfiteatro's** unimpressive entrance; venture a few steps farther downhill and you will find yourself walking on expanses of beautifully preserved mosaic floors in total amazement. The site also features foundations and arrangements of residential quarters in Roman Iberia. *(Casa del Anfiteatro is between the Anfiteatro Romano and the Museo de Arte Romano. Casa del Mitreo is on Vía Ensanche opposite the Pl. de Toros. Each €3.50.)*

OTHER RUINS. At the end of Rmbla. Mártir Santa Eulalia are the **Museo, Basílica,** and **Iglesia de Santa Eulalia,** all commemorating the child martyr. In 1990, in the midst of repairs to the 6th-century church, layers of previous construction were uncovered to reveal the ruins of Roman houses dating from the 3rd to 1st centuries BC, a 4th-century AD necropolis, and a basilica dedicated to Santa Eulalia. *(Same hours as ruins, but opens at 10am. Museum and basilica €2.80.)* Near the theater complex is the **Circo Romano,** the hippodrome or circus. Diocles, the most famous Lusitanian racer, had his start here; he ended his career with a whopping 1462 victories. The arena (capacity 30,000) is currently under excavation and closed to the public—though the view from outside is still worth the trip. Next to the *Circo* are the remains of the **Acueducto de San Lázaro.** *(From C. Cabo Verde, take the pedestrian walkway under the train tracks.)* The **Templo de Diana** is the only surviving Roman temple of worship, with an impressive colonnaded facade. *(C. Sagasta. Free.)* Built from materials discarded by the Visigoths, the **Alcazaba** was designed by the Moors to guard the Roman bridge. Today, only the walls and interior ruins remain. *(Near the Puente Romano. €2.80.)*

BADAJOZ   ☎924

Badajoz (pop. 120,000) is not a stop on most travel itineraries, and for good reason. Known mostly as a transportation hub on the way into Portugal, Badajoz has only recently refreshed its ruins, cleared up much of the industrial pollution that once plagued it, and added a tourist office—making forced layovers en route to or from Portugal a bit more pleasant. Three lively *zonas de pubs* and a contemporary art museum provide for an afternoon's distraction while waiting for the long ride to Lisboa. Nightlife here gets hot; parties erupt in the evening in Pl. de España and along the river, enticing jealous Portuguese neighbors to cross the border and join the fun.

▐◘ TRANSPORTATION

From Badajoz, buses to Portugal are faster and more convenient than trains.

Trains: Av. Carolina Coronado (☎924 27 11 70). Info open daily 9am-10pm. From the train station to Pl. de la Libertad, take bus #1. To: **Cáceres** (2½hr.; M-F and Su 7:35am and 2:40pm; Sa 7:35am; €13.50-15); **Madrid** (5hr.; M-F and Su 3 per day 8:15am-2:30pm, Sa 8:15am and 12:30pm; €28-32); **Mérida** (1½hr., 4-7 per day 6:40am-7:45pm, €2.70-11).

Buses: Central Station, C. José Rebollo López, 2 (☎924 25 86 61). Info booth open daily 7:45am-1am. Buses #3, 6a, 6b, and 9 run between the station and Pl. de la Libertad (€0.65). Schedules are unusually flexible; call ahead.

  ALSA to: **Cáceres** (1½hr.; M 3 per day 8am-4:30pm, Tu-Sa 9:30am and 4:30pm, Su 4:30pm; €7) via **Salamanca** (5hr., €15.30); **Lisboa** (3½hr., 3:45am and 4pm, €17).

  AutoRes (☎924 23 85 15) to: **Lisboa** (2½hr., 5pm and 2am, €14.30); **Madrid** (4hr., 9-10 per day 12:30am-4pm, €22-25.50); **Trujillo** (2hr.; M-Th and Sa 6 per day 8am-4pm, F 8am-6:30pm, Su 9am-6:30pm; €8.40).

  Caballero (☎924 25 57 56) to **Cáceres** (1½hr.; M-F 3 per day 8:30am-7:30pm, Sa 8:30am and 2:30pm, Su 6pm; €5.90).

  Damas to **Sevilla** (4½hr.; M-F 7 per day 6:45am-8pm, Sa-Su 3-4 per day 9am-8pm; €12.20).

  LEDA (☎924 23 34 78) to **Mérida** (1½hr.; M-F 8 per day 8:30am-9pm, Sa 4 per day 9:30am-9pm, Su 3 per day 3-9:30pm; €3.80).

Taxis: At bus and train stations and Pl. de España. **Radio Taxi** (24hr. ☎924 24 31 01).

❖ ⓘ ORIENTATION AND PRACTICAL INFORMATION

Across the Río Guadiana from the **train station** and home to the municipal tourist office, **Plaza de España** is the heart of Badajoz. From the plaza, C. Juan de Ribera and C. Pedro de Valdivia lead to Pl. Dragones Hernán Cortés; one block to the right is **Plaza de la Libertad** (5min.) and the regional tourist office. Between Pl. de España and Pl. de la Libertad is **Paseo de San Francisco.** From the **train station,** follow Av. Carolina Coronado straight to Puente de las Palmas, cross the bridge, then continue on C. Prim. Turn left onto C. Juan de Ribera at Pl. Minayo to get to Pl. de España, or right to Pl. de la Libertad (35min.). Bus #1 runs from the train station stops directly across from the regional tourist office. From the **bus station,** turn left, take a quick right, and then turn left onto C. Damián Téllez la Fuente. Pass straight through Pl. de la Constitución and Pl. Dragones Hernán Cortés to Pl. de España (20min.).

Tourist Office: Municipal Office, C. San Juan (☎924 22 49 81; www.turismoextremadura.com). Facing the Ayuntamiento from Pl. de España, take C. San Juan to its left. English spoken. Open M-F 10am-2pm and 5-7pm, Sa 10am-1:30pm. **Regional Office,** Pl. de la Libertad, 3 (☎924 01 36 59). Open M-F 9am-2pm and 5-7pm, Sa-Su 10am-2pm. **Juventud/Oficina de Información Juvenil,** Ronda de Pilar, 20 (☎924 22 44 49), has info on nightlife. Open June-Sept. M-F 9am-2pm and 5:30-7:30pm; Oct.-May 8am-3pm and 6:30-8:30pm.

Luggage Storage: In the bus station (€0.60) and train station (€3).

Police: Av. de Ramón y Cajal (☎091 or 924 21 00 72).

Hospital: Hospital Perpetual Socorro, Ctra. de Valverde (☎924 23 04 00).

Internet Access: HD Zone, C. Antonio Montero Moreno, 6A (☎924 24 86 16). €1.50 per hr. until 2pm, €2 per hr. thereafter. Open daily 8am-2am.

Post Office: Po. de San Francisco, 4 (☎924 22 25 48). **Lista de Correos.** Open M-F 8am-9pm, Sa 9am-2pm. **Postal Code:** 06001.

⌂ ACCOMMODATIONS

Hostales line streets radiating from Pl. de España.

Hostal Niza II, C. Arco Agüero, 35 (☎924 22 38 81). From Pl. de España, take C. San Blas downhill, then the 1st right onto C. Arco Agüero. Sturdy brown rooms with TV, private bath, and central A/C in most rooms at night. Owner eagerly provides maps and brochures. Singles €24; doubles €40; triples €49. ❷

Pensión Pintor, C. Arco Agüero, 26 (☎924 22 42 28). You may need to ring the bell across the street at #33. Simple but comfortable rooms make for a pleasant layover; doubles have bath, TV, and A/C. 1 single with bath €24; doubles €40. MC/V. ❷

Hotel Condedú, C. Muñoz Torrero, 27 (☎924 20 72 47). On one of the busiest side streets off Pl. de España. Luxurious, quiet rooms equipped with TV, bath, A/C, phone, and one of those irresistible mini-bars. Singles €38; doubles €55. ❹

⌂ FOOD

For **groceries,** head to **Consum,** next to the post office. (Open M-Sa 9am-9pm. MC/V.) Beyond Pl. de España, cafes and eateries crowd Po. de San Francisco.

La Ochava, C. Zurbarán, 15 (☎924 24 70 15). Calls itself the only vegetarian restaurant in Extremadura, which is quite possibly true. Creative recipes in a charming bar-like setting; a couple of meat dishes also served (€6-13). Starters and salads €3.50-6. Entrees €4-9. Open daily 9am-noon, 2-4pm, and 9pm-midnight. AmEx/MC/V. ❷

Cocina Portuguesa, C. Muñoz Torrero, 7 (☎924 22 41 50). Try traditional Portuguese food without crossing the nearby border; the menu here is sure to please carnivores. Portuguese specialties €4.80-15, other fish and meat dishes €5.50-9. Open daily noon-4:30pm and 9-11pm. AmEx/MC/V. ❶

Bar-Restaurante La Ría, Pl. de España (☎924 22 20 05). Behind the glitzy bar and fast food decor lie yummy *raciones* and traditional Spanish foods, setting your wallet back only €2.50-4. 3-course *menú del día* €7.50. Open daily 10am-midnight. ❷

◎ SIGHTS

In 1995, Badajoz renovated its high-security prison to make way for the **Museo Extremeño e Iberoamericano de Arte Contemporáneo.** Five floors exhibit recent works from Spain, Portugal, and Latin America. The permanent collection includes Marta María Pérez Bravo's photo of a woman's breasts as a communion offering. (From Pl. de España, head down C. Juan de Ribera, continuing as it turns into Av. de Europa; the museum is on the left after Pl. de la Constitución. ☎924 26 03 84. Open Tu-Sa 10am-1pm and 5-8pm, Su 10am-1pm. Free.) Badajoz's **old quarter,** including Pl. de España and Paseo de San Francisco, is rich with history. With one Renaissance, one Gothic, and one Plateresque window, the 13th-century **cathedral** (a converted mosque) in Pl. de España is an artistic timeline. (Open Tu-Sa 11am-1pm and 6-8pm. Free.) The ruins of the **Alcazaba,** a Moorish citadel, stand at the top of the hill. (Ruins and archaeological museum open Tu-Su 10am-3pm. Free.)

◎ NIGHTLIFE

Locals rave about Badajoz's weekend **nightlife** and **pub culture**—the only redeeming aspect of an overnight stay in this town. City maps proudly display three *zonas de pubs.* The largest and, according to some locals, best of the three is in the old quarter, where every street off Pl. de España has at least three bars. Though usually home to a more elderly crowd than the other two, Badajoz mainstays like **Mercantil,** C. Zurbarán, 10, populate this area. With live music every Thursday and Friday starting at 11pm and a large floor to groove on, Mercantil spins a mix of Spanish hip-hop, jazz, and pop on non-concert days to packed crowds late into the night. (Beer €2.50, mixed drinks from €4. Open daily June-Aug. 4pm-late; Sept.-May 8pm-late. Closing times vary from 2 to 5am.)

"I'LL HAVE MINE MINUS MEAT!"

"You're in the wrong country, my friend!" remarked a friendly bartender in Toledo when I declined his offer of free *chorizo* tapas with my drink. Seeking to allay further generous, yet still carnivorous, overtures with the statement *"Soy vegetariano"* only brought weird looks, followed by attempts to feed me some form of fish or poultry. Indeed, in a country tempting travelers with local delights such as omelettes with, among other things, bull's brains and testicles, asking for a *bocadillo de queso* does seem pretty lame. When every *sandwich vegetal* includes anchovies, how does an herbivore survive?

The vegetarian adventurer quickly learns. Beyond the obvious *tortilla española* and the *ensalada mixta,* waiters are often happy to prepare *paella verdura sin carne,* or any dish *sin pescados* or *pollo.* While a majority of Spanish cuisine will still rely on a base of ham or fish, a detailed explanation of dietary concerns along the lines of "without anything that moves" usually elicits chuckles and acquiescence, even though strange looks are not completely avoided. Soon enough those partial to plants will navigate fluently among *patatas a los pobres* and *gazpacho andaluz.* "Switch my *chorizo* for *patatas bravas,* please."

University students crowd the area around the intersection of Av. José María Alcaraz y Alenda and Av. de Sinforiano Madroñero. Walking downhill from Pl. de la Constitución on Av. Fernando Calzadilla Maestre, turn right onto Av. Juan Pereda Pila, left onto Av. de María Auxiliadora, and right again onto Av. de Sinforiano Madroñero. The *zona de pubs* is up two intersections straight ahead, a 30min. walk from Pl. de España. Ask directions to **Cinema Puerta Real** near Ctra. de la Granadilla, a movie theater converted into a student hangout by night, with free Internet access and locals chilling at the bar. (Open Th-Sa 10pm-2am.) The newest and perhaps most scenic *zona de pubs* is located across the river. A mix of young, old, tourist, local, and Portuguese revelers are attracted to this park-side bar zone packed on weekend evenings. Crossing Puente de Palmas en route to the train station, turn left onto Av. Adolfo Díaz Ambrona and pass by the Puente de la Universidad on the left. Happening pubs such as **C.K., Flydays,** and **Robinson** are located on the right. One caveat: Badajoz nightlife can be quite tame Monday to Wednesday, and the long walks may be unrewarding. Stick to Pl. de España and Po. de San Francisco if you're stuck here during the week.

SEVILLA

Sevilla (pop. 700,000) is arguably the most charming and romantic of Spain's great cities. Narrow, tangled streets unfold from the center, leading to an awe-inspiring cathedral, the third largest in the world, and city's world-class Alcázar, a great Moorish and Catholic palace and the official residence of the king and queen of Spain. Tourists, locals, students, history buffs, flamenco lovers, and partiers alike infuse Sevilla with an energy and vibrancy hard to match. The budget traveler's experience here can be one of the best in Spain—with so many students packed in during the academic year, the opportunities for things to do and see on a tight budget are truly overwhelming. Once the site of a Roman acropolis founded by Julius Caesar, Sevilla later became the capital of the Moorish empire and a focal point of the Spanish Renaissance. The city is now the guardian of traditional Andalusian culture: flamenco, tapas, and bullfighting. For a taste of Sevilla gone *really* wild, visit during its most prominent festivals—*Semana Santa* and *Feria de Abril* are among the most lavish celebrations in all of Europe.

HIGHLIGHTS OF SEVILLA

FIND OUT what the **flamenco** fuss is all about (p. 228).

SEE the dolls "good" sisters play with at the **Convento de la Encarnación** (p. 242).

EXULT in **Semana Santa** madness, and never party the same way again (p. 230).

SHOUT ¡OLE! and cover your eyes at a **bullfight** in the Plaza de Toros (p. 240).

 HOW TO USE THIS CHAPTER. Sevilla is divided into several neighborhoods. We have grouped together all of each area's accommodations, food, sights, museums, and nightlife listings. General information on these aspects of Sevilla, as well as shopping and specific listings for camping and entertainment (including sports, theater, concerts, and film), appears after the practical information.

INTERCITY TRANSPORTATION

BY PLANE

All flights arrive at **Aeropuerto San Pablo,** Ctra. de Madrid (☎954 44 90 00), 12km outside town. A taxi from the center costs approximately €15-18. **Los Amarillos** (☎954 98 91 84) runs a bus from outside Hotel Alfonso XIII at Pta. de Jerez (M-F every 30-45min., Sa-Su every hr. 6:15am-11pm; €2.40). **Iberia,** C. Guadaira, 8 (☎954 22 89 01, nationwide 902 40 05 00; open M-F 9am-1:30pm) books six flights daily to **Barcelona** (55min.) and **Madrid** (45min.). For student fares to national and international destinations, head to **Barceló Viajes** (see **Local Services,** p. 225).

BY TRAIN

Estación Santa Justa, Av. de Kansas City. (☎902 24 02 02. Info and reservations open daily 4:30am-12:30am.) Services include **luggage storage, car rental,** and **ATM.** In town, make international bookings at the **RENFE** office, C. Zaragoza, 29. (☎954 54 02 02. Open M-F 9am-1:15pm and 4-7pm.)

TO PUENTE DE LA BARQUETA (1km)

C. Baños

TO SAN LORENZO Y JESÚS DEL GRAN PODER (100m)

TO ALAMEDA DE HÉRCULES (150m)

TO HOSPITAL UNIVERSITARIO (1.3km)

LA

Casa de las Duer

C. Nueva Torneo

C. Ríos

C. Miguel Cid

C. Alfaqueque

C. Mendoza Ríos

C. Gracia

C. San Vicente

PL. GAVIDIA

C. Jesús del Gran Poder

C. Trajano

C. Amor de Dios

C. Atienza

C. S. J. de la Palma

C. Sor Ángela de la Cruz

C. Jerónimo Hernández

%Día

C. Nueva Torneo

TO ÍTALICA (9km)

C. Redes

C. San Juan de Veracruz

C. A. Gordito

C. Alfonso XII

El Corte Inglés

PL. DUQUE DE LA VICTORIA

PL. DE LA ENCARNACIÓN

COLEGA

Convento de Santa Inés

C. Laraña

C. Imagen

PL. SA PEDR

Women's Institute of Andalucía

C. Marqués de Paradas

C. Gravina

Museo Provincial de Bellas Artes

PL. DEL C. Monsalves MUSEO

C. la Campaña

C. Martín Villa

La Anunciación

C. Goleneta

EL CENTRO

C. Cuna

C. Zúñiga

C. Santillana

PL. CRIS DE BURG

Cines Warner Lusomundo

C. Pedro del Toro

Cine Avenida

C. San Roque

C. San Eloy

C. O'Donnell

C. Olaunde

C. Velázquez

C. las Sierpes

C. Puente Pellón

Golfo

C. Gallos

Super Sol

Estación Plaza de Armas

PL. DE LA LEGIÓN

C. S. Pedro Martín

C. de Bailén

C. Murillo

C. Rioja

PL. ALFALFA

C. Trastámara

C. Ajona

C. Canalejas

C. Julio César

C. San Pablo

C. Moratín

PL. GODINAS

Iglesia de la Magdalena

C. Méndez Núñez

C. Tetuán

C. Sagasta

Librería Beta

PL. DEL SALVADOR

Iglesia del Salvador

PL. C. Alfalfa PESCADERÍA

C. Almi Hoy

C. Albuera

C. de los Reyes Católicos

C. San José

C. Villegas

Cuesta del Rosario

C. S. Isidoro

C. Luchana

C. Fabiola

TO (200m) & EXPO '92 FAIRGROUNDS (2.5km)

C. El Barranco

Barceló Viajes

C. Almansa

C. Genil

C. Santas Patronas

C. Carlos Cañal

C. Bilbao

C. Granada

AmEx U.K.

PL. NUEVA

Ayuntamiento

C. Madrid

Templo Romano

C. Aire

RENFE

C. Zaragoza

C. Padre Marchena

PL. DE SAN FRANCISCO

Av. de la Constitución

C. Francos

C. Argote de Molina

C. Segovias

C. Guzmán El Bueno

SANTA CRUZ

TO (1.5km)

Pte. de Isabel II/Triana

Mercado del Arenal

C. Pastor y Leandro

C. Adriano

Plaza de Toros de la Real Maestranza

C. Castelar

C. Harinas

C. G. de Vinuesa

C. Alemanes

Catedral

Palacio Arzobispal

PL. V. REYES

C. Abades

C. R. Caro

Trueque

TO PL. SAN MARTÍN DE PORRES (900m)

C. del Betis

Po. de Cristóbal Colón

C. Adriano

Lavandería Auto-Servicio

PL. DEL CABILDO

EL ARENAL

C. Antonio Díaz

C. Varflora

Encarnación

PL. DE TRIUNFO

Hospital de los Venerables

PL. DOÑA ELVIRA

Capilla de los Marineros

Po. Alcalde Marqués de Contadero

Río Guadalquivir

El Patio Sevillano

C. Dos de Mayo

C. Almirantazgo

Casa Lonja & Archivo General de las Indias

Alcázar

Canadá

TO C. DE SAN JACINTO (200m); TO SANTA CECILIA (400m)

C. de la Pureza

Santa Ana

Hospital de la Caridad

C. Temprado

Teatro de la Maestranza

C. Santander

C. Almirante Lobo

Librería Beta

Puerta de Jerez

Jardines de Alcázar

SEE BARR

TRIANA

C. Luca de Tena

C. Pelay Correa

C. Pagés del Corro

C. Rodrigo de Triana

C. Pilar de Gracia

Torre del Oro

ATA Car Rental

Av. Sanjurjo

C. San Fernando

C. Fortaleza

Torre de la Plata

Po. San Telmo

Av. de Roma

Universidad

C. Luz Arriero

C. de la Andía

C. Rosario Vegara

C. Paraíso

Cines Corona Center

C. Genova

PL. CUBA

Pte. San Telmo

Palacio de San Telmo

Po. de las Delicias

C. Palos de la Frontera

C. F. Murillo Herrera

C. M. Champagnat

LOS REMEDIOS

VIPS

C. Salado

C. J. Mª Mª M. Sánchez Arjona

Av. de la República Argentina

C. Virgen Belén

C. Virgen del Valle

C. Virgen de la Asunción

de la Consolación

C. Juan Sebastián Elcano

Teatro Lope de Vega

C. de la Rábida

TO C. LÓPEZ DE GOMARA (600m)

C. de la Niebla

C. Turia

TO (50m), (700m) &

United States

TO MUSEO ARQUEOLÓGICO (800m)

C. María Luc

Parq Marí

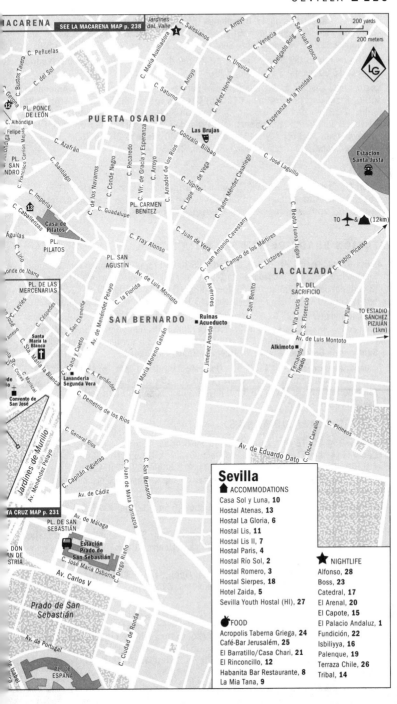

MACARENA   SEE LA MACARENA MAP p. 238

Jardines del Valle

C. Peñuelas

PUERTA OSARIO

Las Brujas

Estación Santa Justa

PL. PONCE DE LEÓN

PL. SAN NDRO

Casa de Pilatos

PL. PILATOS

PL. SAN AGUSTÍN

PL. DE LAS MERCENARIAS

SAN BERNARDO

Ruinas ■ Acueducto

Alkimoto ■

LA CALZADA

PL. DEL SACRIFICIO

TO ESTADIO SÁNCHEZ PIZJUÁN (1km)

Santa María la Blanca

Convento de San José

Lavandería Segunda Vera

Jardines de Murillo

TA CRUZ MAP p. 231

PL. DE SAN SEBASTIÁN

Estación Prado de San Sebastián

Prado de San Sebastián

PL. DE ESPAÑA

Av. de Eduardo Dato

TO ✈ & ▲ (12km)

0   200 yards
0   200 meters

Sevilla

▲ ACCOMMODATIONS

Casa Sol y Luna, **10**
Hostal Atenas, **13**
Hostal La Gloria, **6**
Hostal Lis, **11**
Hostal Lis II, **7**
Hostal Paris, **4**
Hostal Río Sol, **2**
Hostal Romero, **3**
Hostal Sierpes, **18**
Hotel Zaida, **5**
Sevilla Youth Hostal (HI), **27**

🍴 FOOD

Acropolis Taberna Griega, **24**
Café-Bar Jerusalém, **25**
El Barratillo/Casa Chari, **21**
El Rinconcillo, **12**
Habanita Bar Restaurante, **8**
La Mia Tana, **9**

★ NIGHTLIFE

Alfonso, **28**
Boss, **23**
Catedral, **17**
El Arenal, **20**
El Capote, **15**
El Palacio Andaluz, **1**
Fundición, **22**
Isbiliyya, **16**
Palenque, **19**
Terraza Chile, **26**
Tribal, **14**

S E V I L L A

Altaria and **Talgo** trains run to: **Barcelona** (10½-13hr., 3 per day 8am-10:20pm, €66); **Córdoba** (1hr., 4-6 per day 7:50am-7:55pm, €7); **Madrid** (3½hr., 9:44am and 6:15pm, €61.50); **Valencia** (9hr., 8am, €41.50); **Zaragoza** (7½hr., 9:43am, €58).

AVE trains run to **Córdoba** (45min., 16-20 per day 7am-10pm, €20) and **Madrid** (2½hr., 16-20 per day 7am-10pm, €65).

Regionales trains run to: **Almería** (5½hr., 4 per day 7am-5:40pm, €28.30); **Antequera** (2hr., 3 per day 7am-5:40pm, €10.20); **Cáceres** (5½hr., 4:15pm, €14.40); **Cádiz** (2hr.; 7-12 per day M-F 6:53am-9:35pm, Sa-Su 9am-9:35pm; €8.50); **Córdoba** (1½hr., 6 per day 7:50am-9:55pm, €7); **Granada** (3hr., 4 per day 7am-5:40pm, €18); **Huelva** (1½hr., 2-3 per day 9:10am-8:45pm, €6.40); **Jaén** (2-3hr., 6:46pm, €14.40); **Málaga** (2½hr., 4-6 per day 7:40am-8:10pm, €14.30).

BY BUS

Estación Prado de San Sebastián, C. Manuel Vázquez Sagastizabal (☎954 41 71 11), serves most of Andalucía. (Open daily 5:30am-1am.) **Estación Plaza de Armas,** Av. Cristo de la Expiración (☎954 90 80 40), primarily serves destinations outside of Andalucía.

ESTACIÓN PRADO DE SAN SEBASTIÁN

Alsina Graells (☎954 41 88 11). Open daily 6:30am-11pm. To: **Almería** (7hr., 3 per day 7am-midnight, €24.30); **Córdoba** (2hr., 12-15 per day 7:30am-10pm, €8.60); **Granada** (3hr., 8 per day 8am-7:30pm, €16); **Jaén** (4hr., 3-5 per day 7:30am-6pm, €13.90); **Málaga** (2½hr., 10-12 per day 7am-midnight, €13.10); **Murcia** (8hr., 8 and 11am, €31.20).

Los Amarillos (☎954 98 91 84). Open M-F 7:30am-2pm and 2:30-8pm, Sa-Su 7:30am-2pm and 2:30-9pm. To: **Arcos de la Frontera** (2hr., 8am and 4:30pm, €5.90); **Marbella** (3hr., 2-3 per day 8am-8pm, €14.10); **Ronda** (2½hr., 3-5 per day 7am-5pm, €8.40); **Sanlúcar de Barrameda** (2hr., 7-11 per day 7am-9pm, €6.40).

Transportes Comes (☎954 41 68 58). Open M-Sa 6:30am-10pm. To: **Algeciras** (3½hr., 4 per day 9am-8pm, €13.80); **Cádiz** (1½hr., 12-15 per day 7am-10pm, €9-13.30); **Jerez de la Frontera** (1½hr., 6-9 per day 10:30am-10pm, €5.70); **Tarifa** (3hr., 4 per day 9am-8pm, €13.10).

ESTACIÓN PLAZA DE ARMAS

ALSA (☎954 90 78 00). Open M-F and Su 5:45am-11pm, Sa 8am-10:45pm. To: **Cáceres** (4¼hr., 7 per day 6am-10:30pm, €14.20); **León** (11hr., 3 per day 6-9pm, €35.60); **Salamanca** (8hr., 5-6 per day 6am-10:30pm, €25.30); **Valencia** (9-11hr., 3 per day 9:30am-9:30pm, €39.90). Under 26 and seniors 10% discount, under 12 50% discount.

Autocares Aníbal (☎902 36 00 73). To **Lisboa** (6½hr., 1-2 per day M-F 9:30am-midnight, €29). 10% student discount.

Damas (☎954 90 80 40). Open M-F 6:30am-9:30pm, Sa-Su 7am-9pm. To **Badajoz** (3½hr., 3-5 per day 6:45am-8pm, €10.30) and **Huelva** (1¼hr., 21-23 per day 6am-9pm, €5.60).

Socibus (☎954 90 11 60; fax 90 16 92). Open daily 7:30-10am and 10:30am-12:45am. To **Madrid** (6hr., 14 per day 8am-1am, €16.90).

■ ORIENTATION

The **Río Guadalquivir** flows roughly north to south through the city, bordered by the busy Po. de Cristobal, which becomes Po. de las Delicias by the municipal tourist office. Most of the touristed areas of Sevilla, including **Santa Cruz** and **El Arenal,** are on the east bank. The historic *barrios* of **Triana, Santa Cecilia,** and **Los Remedios** and the **Expo '92 fairgrounds** occupy the western bank. **Avenida de la Constitución,** home of the tourist office, runs alongside the cathedral. **El Centro,** a busy commercial pedestrian zone, lies north of the cathedral, starting where Av. de la Constitución hits **Plaza Nueva,** site of the Ayuntamiento. **Calle Tetuán,** a popular street for shopping, takes off from Pl. Nueva and runs northward through El Centro.

To get to Santa Cruz from the train station, take bus C-2 and transfer to C-3 at the Jardines del Valle; it will drop you off at the **Jardines de Murillo.** Walk right one block past the gardens; C. Santa María la Blanca is on the left. Otherwise, it's a 15-20min. walk. To reach El Centro from the train station, catch bus #32 to **Plaza de la Encarnación,** several blocks north of the cathedral. Bus C-4 connects the bus station at **Plaza de Armas** to Prado de San Sebastián.

LOCAL TRANSPORTATION

Public Transportation: TUSSAM (☎900 71 01 71; www.tussam.es). Most bus lines run daily every 10min. 6am-11:15pm and converge in Pl. Nueva, Pl. de la Encarnación, and in front of the cathedral. **Night service** departs from Pl. Nueva (every hr. midnight-2am; F-Sa all night). C-3 and C-4 circle the center, and #34 hits the youth hostel, university, cathedral, and Pl. Nueva. €1, *bonobús* (10 rides) €4.50, 30-day pass €26.

Taxis: TeleTaxi (☎954 62 22 22). **Radio Taxi** (☎954 58 00 00). Base rate €1 plus €0.40 per km, Su 25% surcharge. Extra charge for luggage and night taxis.

Car Rental: Hertz, at the airport (☎954 25 42 98) and train station (☎954 53 39 14). General information and reservations (☎902 40 24 05). 21+. From €52.50 per day. Open daily 8am-midnight. AmEx/MC/V. **ATA,** C. Almirante Lobo, 2 (☎954 22 09 58). 21+. Manual shift only. From €36 per day plus tax. Open M-F 9am-2pm and 4:30-8:30pm, Sa 9am-2pm. MC/V.

Moped Rental: Alkimoto, C. Fernando Tirado, 5 (☎954 58 49 27). €23 per day. Open M-F 9am-1:30pm and 5-8pm.

PRACTICAL INFORMATION

TOURIST AND FINANCIAL SERVICES

Tourist Offices: Centro de Información de Sevilla, Po. de las Delicias, 9 (☎954 23 44 65; www.turismo.sevilla.org). English spoken. Open M-F 8am-7pm. **Turismo Andaluz,** Av. de la Constitución, 21B (☎954 22 14 04; fax 22 97 53). English spoken. Info on all of Andalucía. Open M-F 9am-7pm, Sa 10am-2pm and 3-7pm, Su 10am-2pm.

Currency Exchange: Banco Santander Central Hispano, C. la Campaña, 19 (☎902 24 24 24). Open M-F 8:30am-2pm, Sa 8:30am-1pm.

American Express: Pl. Nueva, 7 (☎954 21 16 17). Open M-F 9:30am-1:30pm and 4:30-7:30pm, Sa 10am-1pm.

LOCAL SERVICES

Luggage Storage: Estación Prado de San Sebastián (€0.90 per bag per day; open 6:30am-10pm); **Estación Plaza de Armas** (€3 per day); **train station** (€3 per day).

English-Language Bookstore: Librería Beta, C. Sagasta, 16 (☎954 22 84 95). Good selection of books and travel guides, including ▨**Let's Go. Branch,** Av. de la Constitución, 27 (☎954 56 07 03). Both open June-Aug. M-F 10am-2pm and 5:30-9pm, Sa 10am-2pm; Sept.-May M-F 10am-2pm and 5-8:30pm, Sa 10am-2pm. MC/V. **Trueque,** C. Pasaje de Vila, 2 (☎954 56 32 66). Used bookstore with English selections (paperback novels €1-5; hardcovers up to €20). Open M-Sa 10:30am-1:30pm.

SEVILLA

VIPS: Av. de la República Argentina, 25 (☎954 27 93 97). International newspapers, books, liquor, non-perishable groceries, and an American-style restaurant. Open Su-Th 8am-1:30am, F 8am-3:30am, Sa 9am-3am. MC/V.

El Corte Inglés: Pl. Duque de la Victoria (☎954 27 93 97). Huge department store with English-language books. Supermarket on ground floor. Open M-Sa 10am-10pm and first Su of the month. AmEx/MC/V.

Budget Travel Agency: Barceló Viajes, C. de los Reyes Católicos, 11 (☎954 22 61 31). An STA Travel affiliate. Open June-Sept. M-F 9:30am-1:30pm and 5-8pm, Sa 10am-1pm; Oct.-May M-F 9:30am-1:30pm and 4:30-7:30pm, Sa 10am-1pm. MC/V.

Women's Services: Women's Institute of Andalucía, C. Alfonso XII, 52 (24hr. toll-free hotline ☎900 20 09 99, office 954 03 49 53; www.iam.juntadeandalucia.es). Info on feminist and lesbian organizations, plus legal and psychological counseling for rape victims. Office open to public M-Tu and Th-Su 10am-1pm.

Gay and Lesbian Services: COLEGA (Colectiva de Lesbianas y Gays de Andalucía), Pl. de la Encarnación, 23, 2nd fl. (☎954 50 13 77; www.colegaweb.net). Look for the sign in the window; the door is not marked. Open M-F 10am-2pm.

Laundromats: Lavandería Auto-Servicio, C. Castelar, 2 (☎954 21 05 35). Wash and dry €6 per 5kg. Open M-Sa 9:30am-1:30pm and 5-8:30pm. **Lavandería Segunda Vera,** Av. Menéndez Pelayo, 11 (☎954 53 63 76). Wash and dry €7.80 per load. Open M-F 9:30am-1:30pm and 5-8pm.

Alternatives to Tourism: Sevilla is full of language schools; ask at the tourist office. All schools can arrange student accommodations and offer excursions for an additional fee. **CLIC** and **Don Quijote** come highly recommended (see **Language Schools,** p. 57).

EMERGENCY AND COMMUNICATIONS

Police: Po. Concordia (local ☎092, national 091).

Medical Assistance: Red Cross: (☎913 35 45 45). **Ambulatorio Esperanza Macarena** (☎954 42 01 05). **Hospital Universitario Virgen Macarena,** Av. Dr. Fedriani (☎954 24 81 81). English spoken.

Internet Access: It is substantially cheaper to use pre-paid minutes.

Sevilla Internet Center, C. Almirantazgo, 2, 2nd fl. (☎954 50 02 75). €3 per hr., with pre-paid cards €1.80 per hr. Open M-F 9am-10pm, Sa-Su 10am-10pm.

CiberBoston, C. San Fernando, 23 (☎954 21 94 49). €2 per hr.; Sa €1 per hr. Open June-Sept. M-F 10am-1am, Sa noon-midnight; Oct.-May also Su noon-midnight. Closed Aug. 1-17.

The Email Place, C. las Sierpes, 54 (☎954 21 85 92). €0.70 per 10min., €2.20 per hr. Open June-Sept. M-F 10am-10pm, Sa-Su noon-9pm; Oct.-May M-F 10am-11pm, Sa-Su noon-9pm.

WORKcenter, C. San Fernando, 1 (☎954 21 20 74; www.workcenter.es). An office center providing Internet access (€0.50 per 10min.; €3 per hr.). Fax, copying, and other services. Sells office supplies and film. Open 24hr. MC/V.

@DS Macarena, C. San Luis, 108 (☎954 38 06 13), in La Macarena. €1.50 per hr. Open daily June-Aug. 11am-11:30pm; Sept.-May 11am-midnight.

Post Office: Av. de la Constitución, 32 (☎954 21 64 76). **Lista de Correos** and **fax.** Open M-F 10am-8:30pm, Sa 8:30am-2pm. **Postal Code:** 41080.

⋔ ACCOMMODATIONS

The *Semana Santa* processions in Sevilla are the largest most acclaimed in Spain. During **Semana Santa** and **Feria de Abril,** vacant rooms vanish and prices double, at least; reserve several months in advance. The tourist office has lists of *casas particulares* (private residences) that open for visitors on special occasions. In general, you should reserve at least two weeks in advance.

ACCOMMODATIONS BY PRICE

EC El Centro **M** La Macarena **ON** Outer Neighborhoods **SC** Santa Cruz

UNDER €15 ❶		Hostal Río Sol (241)	ON
Camping Sevilla (242)	ON	Hostal Romero (241)	ON
Club de Campo (242)	ON	Hostal-Residencia Montreal (232)	SC
Sevilla Youth Hostel (242)	ON	🖾 Pensión Vergara (230)	SC
€15-25 ❷		**€26-35 ❸**	
🖾 Casa Sol y Luna (235)	EC	Hostal Atenas (231)	SC
Hostal Alameda (238)	M	Hostal Paris (241)	ON
Hostal Bienvenido (231)	SC	Hostal-Residencia Córdoba (232)	SC
Hostal Buen Dormir (231)	SC	Hostal Goya (232)	SC
Hostal Dulces-Sueños (231)	SC		
Hostal La Gloria (235)	EC	**€36-45 ❹**	
Hostal Lis (235)	EC	🖾 Airesevilla (231)	SC
Hostal Lis II (235)	EC	Hostal Sierpes (232)	SC
Hostal Macarena (238)	M	Hotel Zaida (235)	EC

◎ SIGHTS

While most visits tend to center around the amazing **Catedral** and **Alcázar,** there is much more to Sevilla than this clash of ideological architecture. The streets around these central icons are a winding wonderland, where tapas and *artesanía* dominate. The **Plaza de Toros de la Real Maestranza** is nestled along the riverbank and serves as an ideal place to begin a scenic tour along the Guadalquivir. Heading south toward the **Torre del Oro,** garden oases offer respite from the intense activity of the city center. The **Jardines** behind the Alcázar are flanked by the **Jardines de Murillo,** and from there it's a short jaunt to the stately **Plaza de España** and nearby **Parque de María Luisa.**

◘ FOOD

Sevilla is a city of tapas; locals spend their evenings relaxing and socializing over plates of *caracoles* (snails), *cocido andaluz* (thick chickpea soup), *pisto* (tomato and eggplant stew), *espinacas con garbanzos* (spinach with chick peas), and fresh seafood. The local favorite, *salmorejo* (a thicker version of gazpacho), is especially good. For those on a tighter budget, markets such as **Mercado del Arenal,** near the bullring on C. Pastor y Leandro, have fresh meat and produce (open M-Sa 9am-2pm). For a supermarket, try the mammoth one in the basement of **El Corte Inglés** (see p. 226), or head to any of the smaller ones like **%Día** and **Super Sol.**

FOOD BY TYPE

AT El Arenal and Triana **EC** El Centro **M** Macarena **SC** Santa Cruz

BREAKFAST		PIZZA/ITALIAN	
Café Cáceres (232)	SC ❶	La Mia Tana (236)	EC ❶
CUBAN		San Marco (232)	SC ❷
🖾 Habanita Bar Restaurante (236)	EC ❷	**SPANISH**	
		Ancha de la Feria (238)	M ❶
DESSERT		Café-Bar Campanario (232)	SC ❷
Histórico Horno, SA (240)	AT ❷	El Rinconcillo (236)	EC ❷
		Restaurante Coello (232)	SC ❸
GREEK AND MIDDLE EASTERN		🖾 El Baratillo/Casa Chari (240)	AT ❶
Acropolis Taberna Griega (240)	AT ❶		
Café-Bar Jerusalém (240)	AT ❶		

▣ NIGHTLIFE

Sevilla's reputation for partying is tried and true. A typical night of *la marcha* (going out) begins with visits to several bars for tapas and *copas*, continues with dancing at *discotecas*, and culminates with an early morning breakfast of *churros con chocolate*. Most clubs don't get crowded until well after midnight; the real fun often starts after 3am. Popular bars can be found around **Calle Mateos Gago** near the cathedral, **Calle Adriano** by the bullring, and **Calle del Betis** across the river in Triana; several popular summertime clubs lie along the river near **Puente de la Barqueta**. Many gay clubs cluster around Pl. de Armas, and some can be found on C. Azofaifo near Pl. Duque de la Victoria. Sevilla is also famous for the *botellón*, a (mostly student) tradition of getting drunk in massive crowds in plazas or at bars along the river to start the night. In the winter, the most popular places for *botellón* are in Pl. Alfalfa and Pl. del Salvador. In summer, the crowds sweep toward the river in hopes of a breeze, and even on "slow" nights most *terrazas* stay open until 4am. During the school year, bars and clubs are packed regardless of the night; in summer, it takes a bit more searching to find weeknight crowds.

▣ ENTERTAINMENT

The tourist office distributes *El Giraldillo*, a free monthly magazine with complete listings on music, art exhibits, theater, dance, fairs, and film. It can also be found online at www.elgiraldillo.es.

THEATERS

Sevilla is a haven for the performing arts. The venerable **Teatro Lope de Vega** (☎954 59 08 53), near Parque de María Luisa, has long been the city's leading stage. Ask about scheduled events at the tourist office or check the bulletin board in the university lobby on C. San Fernando. **Sala la Herrería** and **Sala la Imperdible** put on avant-garde productions in Pl. San Antonio de Padua. (Both ☎954 38 82 19.) **Teatro de la Maestranza**, on the river between the Torre del Oro and the bullring, is a splendid concert hall accommodating orchestral performances, opera, and dance. (☎954 22 65 73. Box office open M-F 10am-2pm and 6-9pm.) On spring and summer evenings, neighborhood fairs are often accompanied by free **open-air concerts** in Santa Cruz and Triana; inquire at the tourist office for specific schedules and locations. **Cine Avenida**, C. Marqués de las Paradas, 15 (☎954 29 30 25), and **Corona Center** (☎954 27 80 64), in the mall between C. Salado and C. Paraíso in Triana, screen original-language films subtitled in Spanish. **Cines Warner Lusomundo**, Co. Comercial Plaza de Armas, shows American films dubbed in Spanish (☎902 23 33 43). **Cines Corona Center,** in the mall between C. Salado and C. Paraíso, screens subtitled films, often in English. (☎954 27 80 64. M-F €3, Sa-Su €3.50.) For more, look under "Cinema" in *El Giraldillo* or any local newspaper.

FLAMENCO

Flamenco, originally brought to Spain by the *gitanos* (Roma people), is at its best in Sevilla. Traditionally consisting of dance, guitar, and song, it expresses the passion and soul of the region. Rhythmic clapping, intricate fretwork on the guitar, throaty wailing, and rapid foot-tapping form a mesmerizing backdrop to the swirling dancers. Flamenco can be seen either in *tablaos*, where skilled professional dancers perform, or in *tabernas*, bars where locals merrily dance *sevillanas*. Both have merit, but the *tabernas* tend to be free. The tourist office provides a complete list of both *tablaos* and *tabernas*; ask about student discounts.

TABLAOS

Small and intimate **Los Gallos,** Pl. de Santa Cruz, 11, is probably the best tourist show in Sevilla. Buy tickets in advance at hostels or stores in Santa Cruz and arrive early. (☎954 21 69 81. Shows nightly 9 and 11:30pm. Cover €27, includes 1 drink.) Less expensive alternatives are the impressive 1hr. shows at the cultural center ▨**Casa de la Memoria Al-Andalus,** C. Ximénez de Enciso, 28. Ask at the tourist office or swing by their ticket office for a schedule of different themed performances. (☎/fax 954 56 06 70. Shows nightly 9pm; very limited seating so buy tickets in advance. €11, students €9.) **El Arenal** is a *tablao-restaurante*, so you can eat a meal while watching, although dinner is often expensive. (Shows nightly 9 and 11pm. Cover €30.50, includes 1 drink.) **El Patio Sevillano,** Po. de Cristóbal Colón, 11, offers nightly performances at 7:30 and 10pm. (☎954 22 20 68. €29, includes 1 drink). **El Palacio Andaluz,** C. María Auxiliadora, 18, has a mixed flamenco and classical dance show. (☎954 53 47 20. Shows nightly 10pm. Advance reservation required. €27.50, includes 1 drink.) **Sol Café Cantante,** C. del Sol, 5, has 1½hr. shows of dancing and singing. (☎954 22 51 65. Shows W-Sa 9pm. €18, students €11; includes 1 drink.) Though farther afield in Puerta Osario, **Las Brujas,** C. Gonzalo Bilbao, 10, is worth the trek. (☎954 41 36 51. Shows daily 9:15 and 11:30pm. Buy tickets in advance. Cover €23, includes 1 drink.)

TABERNAS

El Tamboril, Pl. de Santa Cruz, hosts a primarily middle-aged tourist crowd for midnight *canciones* and dancing. (☎954 56 15 90. Open daily June-Sept. 5pm-3am; Oct.-May noon-3am.) **La Carbonería,** C. Levies, 18, is a large bar complex with a courtyard popular with backpackers. Bar-filled **Calle del Betis,** across the river, houses several other *tabernas:* **Lo Nuestro, El Rejoneo,** and **Taberna Flamenca Triana.**

FÚTBOL

Sevilla has two wildly popular pro teams that play at **Estadio Sánchez Pizjuán** (☎954 53 53 53) on Av. de Eduardo Dato. Buy tickets at the stadium; price and availability depend on the quality of the match-up. Even if you can't make it, the jerseyed crowds in the streets make the whole city feel like a stadium: **Real Betis** wears green and white, **Sevilla** white and red. Both teams struggle against the competitive Barcelona and Real Madrid clubs; over the last few years Real Betis has underachieved, but locals are optimistic for the coming years, particularly with 2002 World Cup star and Spanish national team member Joaquín on the field.

BULLFIGHTING

Sevilla's bullring, one of the most beautiful in Spain, hosts bullfights from *Semana Santa* through October. The cheapest place to buy tickets is at the ring on Po. Alcalde Marqués de Contadero. However, when there's a good *cartel* (line-up), the booths on C. las Sierpes, C. Velázquez, and Pl. de Toros might be the only source of advance tickets. Ticket prices can run from €18 for a *grada de sol* (nosebleed seat in the sun) to €75 for a *barrera de sombra* (front-row seat in the shade); scalpers usually add 20%. *Corridas de toros* (bullfights) and *novilladas* (fights with apprentice bullfighters and younger bulls) are held on the 13 days around the *Feria de Abril* and into May, every Sunday April-June and September-October, more often during *Corpus Cristi* in June and early July, and during the *Feria de San Miguel* near the end of September. During July and August, *corridas* occur on occasional Thursdays at 9pm; check posters around town. Some of the most popular *sevillano* bullfighters include **El Juli, Joselito,** and **José Tomás.** (For current info and **ticket sales,** call ☎954 50 13 82. For more on **bullfighting,** see p. 76.)

SEVILLA

SHOPPING

Sevilla is a great place to find Andalusian crafts such as hand-embroidered silk and lace shawls and traditional flamenco wear, albeit often at inflated tourist prices. The area including C. las Sierpes, C. San Eloy, C. Velázquez, and C. Francos offers a wide array of crafts, as well as modern clothing, shoe stores, and jewelry. In January, July, and August, all the stores hold huge ▨**rebajas** (sales), where everything is marked down 30-70%. A large, eclectic **flea market** is held Thursday 9am-2pm, extending along C. Feria in La Macarena.

▨ FESTIVALS

Sevilla swells with tourists during its *fiestas*, and with good reason: they are insanely fun. If you're in Spain during any of the major festivals, head straight to Sevilla—you won't regret it (if you remember it, that is). Reserve a room a few months in advance, and expect to pay at least twice what you would normally.

▨ **SEMANA SANTA.** Sevilla's world-famous *Semana Santa* lasts from Palm Sunday to Easter Sunday (March 20-27). In each neighborhood, thousands of penitents in hooded cassocks guide *pasos* (stunning, extravagant floats) through the streets, illuminated by hundreds of candles; Americans should be prepared, as the costumes bear more than a passing resemblance to those of the Ku Klux Klan. The climax is Good Friday, when the entire city turns out for the procession along the bridges and through the oldest neighborhoods. Book rooms well in advance and expect to pay triple the usual price. The tourist office has a helpful booklet on where to eat and sleep during the week's festivities.

▨ **FERIA DE ABRIL.** From April 12-17, the city rewards itself for its Lenten piety with the *Feria de Abril*. Begun as part of a 19th-century revolt against foreign influence, the *Feria* has grown into a massive celebration of all things Andalusian with circuses, bullfights, and flamenco shows. A spectacular array of flowers and lanterns decorates over 1000 kiosks, tents, and pavilions, collectively called *casetas*. Each *caseta* has a small kitchen, bar, and dance floor. Though there are a few large public ones, most are privately owned, and the only way to get invited is by making friends with the locals. Either way, people-watching from the sidelines can be almost as exciting—costumed girls dance *sevillanas* and men parade on horseback through the streets. The city holds bullfights daily during the festival; buy tickets in advance. *(The fairgrounds are on the southern end of Los Remedios.)*

SANTA CRUZ

In many ways, Santa Cruz is the heart of Sevilla: not only is it the middle of the city, but it also proudly claims the most breathtaking sights. This lively, cozy neighborhood manages to bring together excellent eateries, affordable lodging, wild flamenco shows, and dazzling architecture.

⌂ ACCOMMODATIONS

The narrow streets east of the cathedral around C. Santa María la Blanca are full of cheap hostels, most with virtually identical rooms. The neighborhood is highly touristed; reserve early. Santa Cruz's location makes it an excellent place to stay, but the budget lodging often does not live up to the charm of the neighborhood.

▨ **Pensión Vergara,** C. Ximénez de Enciso, 11, 2nd fl. (☎954 21 56 68). Breezy, pleasant rooms with fans and gorgeous common areas. Towels provided. €20 per person. ❷

SEVILLA

Airesevilla, C. Aire (☎954 500 905; www.airesevilla-gay.com). A gorgeous gay guest house merges Andalusian styles with modern art. Rooms, bathrooms, and lounges are bright and incredibly tasteful. Breakfast on the rooftop *terraza*. Singles €35-45; doubles €55-75. Price varies with time of year and bath availability. MC/V. ❹

Hostal Bienvenido, C. Archeros, 14 (☎954 41 36 55). Simple but comfortable and cheap rooms. 5 rooftop rooms surround a social patio; downstairs rooms overlook inner atrium. Singles €18-20; doubles €30-40; triples and quads €15-16 per person. ❷

Hostal Buen Dormir, C. Farnesio, 8 (☎954 21 74 92). Quilted bedspreads, tiled walls, and sunny rooms make *hostal* "Good Sleep" one of the best deals in town. Rooftop terrace. Singles have fans, all other rooms have A/C. Laundry €6. Singles €18; doubles €35; triples with shower €50, with bath €55. ❷

Hostal Dulces-Sueños, C. Puerta de la Carne, 21 (☎954 41 93 93). Rooms all have A/C except small singles, which have fans. Clean common baths. Rooftop terrace. Barest and smallest singles €20, larger with A/C and bath €35; doubles €40, with bath €50; 1 triple with bath €65. MC/V. ❷

Hostal Atenas, C. Caballerizas, 1 (☎954 21 80 47; fax 22 76 90). Pricier than other options, but with good reason—all these sunny, orange rooms come with private baths and A/C. Singles €30; doubles €50; triples €70. MC/V. ❸

Hostal-Residencia Córdoba, C. Farnesio, 12 (☎954 22 74 98). Simple yet delightfully clean and spacious rooms, with A/C in the evening and at night, are worth the extra euros. Curfew 3am. Singles €27, with bath €38; doubles €41/€50. ❸

Hostal-Residencia Montreal, C. Rodrigo Caro, 8 (☎954 21 41 66). Check out your room before taking it: some here are bright and pleasant, others are grimmer. Ask for one overlooking the plaza. The downstairs cafe caters to backpackers. Breakfast €2.50-4. Singles €20; doubles €40, with bath €60. MC/V. ❷

Hostal Goya, C. Mateos Gago, 31 (☎954 21 11 70). Hotel-like, but worth the splurge only if you get an outside-facing room; inner ones are dim. Spacious and sparkling-clean rooms have A/C and private bath. June-Mar. singles €30; doubles €60; triples €90; quads €110. Apr.-May and *Semana Santa* €45/€75/€105/€123. MC/V. ❸

Hostal Sierpes, C. Corral del Rey, 22 (☎954 22 49 48; www.hsierpes.com). Lace-canopied lobby, beautiful common spaces, and clean rooms with bath. Many with A/C. Breakfast €2.50. Parking €14. Mar.-Dec. singles €44; doubles €65; triples €85; quads €105. Jan.-Feb. €34/€47/€60/€74. MC/V. ❹

🍴 FOOD

Restaurants near the cathedral cater almost exclusively to tourists. Beware the unexceptional, omnipresent *menús* featuring gazpacho and paella for €7. Food quality and prices improve in the backstreet establishments between the cathedral and the river in El Arenal and along side streets in Santa Cruz.

San Marco, C. Mesón del Moro, 6 (☎954 21 43 90; www.san-marco.net). Pizzas, pastas, and Italian desserts in an amazing setting—an 18th-century house with old Arab baths. Surprisingly affordable, and highly recommended by locals, although tourists do come in swarms. Entrees €5-10. Open Tu-Su 1:15-4:30pm and 8:15pm-12:30am. **Other locations** in equally impressive settings at C. Betis, 68 (☎954 28 03 10), and at C. Santo Domingo de la Calzada, 5 (☎954 58 33 43). AmEx/D/MC/V. ❷

Café-Bar Campanario, C. Mateos Gago, 8 (☎954 56 41 89). Mixes the best (and strongest) jugs of sangria around (½-liter €7.30, liter €9.70). Tapas €1-2.40, *raciones* €6.40-9.60. Vegetarian-friendly. Open daily noon-midnight. AmEx/D/MC/V. ❷

Café Cáceres, C. San José, 24 (☎954 21 51 31). The closest thing to a buffet-style breakfast in Sevilla. Choose from a spread of cheeses, jams, yogurts, countless condiments, fresh orange juice, and omelettes. *Desayuno de la casa* (orange juice, coffee, ham, eggs, and toast) €4.50. Open M-F 7:30am-5:30pm, Sa-Su 8am-1:30pm. ❶

Restaurante Coello, C. Doncellas, 8 (☎658 38 69 18), on a tiny street off C. Santa María la Blanca. Cheap *menú* (€6) and delicately prepared meat and fish entrees (€10-15). Appetizers €4-11. Open daily noon-midnight. V. ❸

🔵 SIGHTS

▨ CATEDRAL. Legend has it that in 1401 the *reconquistadores* wanted to demonstrate their religious fervor by constructing a church so great, they said, that "those who come after us will take us for madmen." With 44 individual chapels, the cathedral of Sevilla is the third largest in the world, after St. Peter's Basilica in Rome and St. Paul's Cathedral in London, and the biggest Gothic edifice ever constructed. Not surprisingly, it took more than a century to build.

In 1401, a 12th-century Almohad mosque was destroyed to clear space for the massive cathedral. All that remains is the **Patio de Los Naranjos,** where the faithful washed before prayer, the Puerta del Perdón entryway from C. Alemanes, and the famed **La Giralda** minaret, built in 1198. The tower and its twins in Marrakesh and Rabat are the oldest and longest-surviving Almohad minarets in the world. The 35 ramps inside leading to the tower's top replaced the stairs that once stood there, allowing a disabled *muezzín* to climb up on his horse for the call to prayer; today they enable tourists to take pictures.

In the center of the cathedral, the Renaissance-style **Capilla Real** stands opposite **choir stalls** made of mahogany recycled from a 19th-century Austrian railway. The ▨**retablo mayor,** one of the largest in the world, is a golden wall of intricately wrought saints and disciples. Nearby, the **Sepulcro de Cristóbal Colón** (Columbus's tomb) supposedly holds the explorer's remains, brought back to Sevilla in 1902 after Cuba gained independence (the tomb had been located in Havana's cathedral). The black-and-gold pallbearers represent the eternally grateful monarchs of Castilla, León, Aragón, and Navarra.

Farther on and to the right stands the **Sacristía Mayor** (sacristy), which holds gilded panels of Alfonso X el Sabio by Juan de Arefe, works by Ribera and Murillo, and a glittering *Corpus Cristi* icon, **La Custodia Processional.** A small, disembodied head of John the Baptist eyes visitors who enter the gift shop. It overlooks keys presented to the city of Sevilla by Jewish leaders after Fernando III ousted the Muslims in 1248. In the northwest corner of the cathedral is the architecturally stunning **Sala de las Columnas.** Each year, restoration and maintenance expenses for the cathedral total over €3.8 million. *(Entrance by Pl. de la Virgen de los Reyes. ☎954 21 49 71. Open M-Sa 11am-5pm, Su 2:30-6pm. Last entrance 1hr. before closing. €6, seniors and students €1.50, under 12 free. Su free. Mass held in the Capilla Real M-Sa 8:30, 10am, and noon; Su 8:30, 10, 11am, noon, and 1pm.)*

▨**ALCÁZAR.** The oldest European palace still used as a private residence for royals, Sevilla's Alcázar is nothing short of magnificent. Like the Alhambra in Granada, the Alcázar has Moorish architecture and gardens, and although the Alhambra gets more press, the Alcázar is equally impressive. Constructed by the Moors in the 7th century, the palace was embellished during the 15th century and now displays an interesting mix of Moorish and Christian architecture, displayed most prominently in the *mudéjar* style of many of the arches, tiles, and ceilings. Fernando and Isabel are the palace's most well-known former residents; Carlos V also lived here, marrying his cousin Isabel of Portugal in the incestuous **Salón Techo Carlos V.**

Visitors enter through the **Patio de la Montería,** directly across from the intricate Almohad facade of the Moorish palace. Through the archway are the Arabic residences, including the **Patio del Yeso** used by Moorish governors before the palace itself was even built, and the exquisitely carved **Patio de las Muñecas** (Patio of the Dolls), so named because of miniature faces carved into the bottom of one of the room's pillars. Originally a courtyard, the Patio de las Muñecas served as a private area for Moorish kings with an escape path (no longer in existence) so that, in case of an attack, the king would not have to cross the open space. Of the Christian additions, the most notable is the **Patio de las Doncellas** (Patio of the Maids). Court life in the Alcázar revolved around this colonnaded quadrangle, which is encircled by archways adorned with glistening tilework. The golden-domed **Salón de los Embajadores** (Ambassadors' Room) is supposedly the site where Fernando and Isabel welcomed Columbus back from the New World. Several beautiful silk tapestries adorn the walls of the appropriately named **Sala de Tapices.** The son of Fernando and Isabel, Prince Juan, was born in the red-and-blue tiled **Cuarto del Príncipe;** the room was named for him after his untimely death of, according to legend, a broken heart.

The **private residences** upstairs, official home to the King and Queen and their lodging on visits to Sevilla, have been renovated and redecorated throughout the years; most of the furniture today dates from the 18th and 19th centuries. They are accessible only by 25min. guided tours. Peaceful **gardens** stretch from the residential quarters in all directions. *(Pl. del Triunfo, 7. ☎954 50 23 23. Open Tu-Sa 9:30am-7pm, Su 9:30am-5pm. €5; students, handicapped, residents, over 65, and under 16 free. Tours of the upper palace living quarters every 30min. Aug.-May 10am-1:30pm and 3:30-5:30pm; June-July 10am-1:30pm. 15 people max. per tour, so buy tickets in advance. €3. Worthwhile audio-guides offer anecdotes, historical info, and a clearly marked route through the complex; €3.)*

CASA LONJA. Between the cathedral and the Alcázar stands the 16th-century Casa Lonja, built by Felipe II as a *casa de contratación* (commercial exchange) for trade with the Americas. In 1785, Carlos III converted the building into the **Archivo General de las Índias.** Today it contains a collection of over 44,000 documents relating to the conquest of the New World. Among its books is Juan Bautista Muñoz's "definitive" history of the conquest, commissioned by Carlos III. Other highlights include Juan de la Costa's wildly inaccurate *Mapa Mundi* (map of the world), letters from Columbus to Fernando and Isabel, and a 1590 letter from Cervantes (pre-*Don Quixote*) requesting employment in America. *(☎954 21 12 34. Access to documents is limited to scholars. Currently closed for renovations, call ahead.)*

TEMPLO ROMANO. A few blocks southeast of Pl. del Salvador on C. Mármoles stand the ruins of a Roman temple. Its columns rise 15m from below street level and offer a glimpse of the literal depth of Sevilla's history; river sediment that accumulated after the construction of the temple caused the ground level to rise.

OTHER SIGHTS. Fernando III forced Jews exiled from Toledo during the Inquisition to live in Santa Cruz, and it thrived as a lively Jewish quarter. On **Calle Susona,** a ceramic tile with a skull rests above a door, evoking the tale of beautiful Susona, a Jewish girl who fell in love with a Christian knight. When Susona learned that her father and friends planned to kill several inquisitors, including the knight, she warned her lover. A bloody reprisal was unleashed on the Jewish ghetto, during which Susona's entire family was slaughtered. She requested that her skull be placed above the doorway in atonement for her betrayal, and it supposedly remained there until the 18th century. C. Susona leads to **Plaza Doña Elvira,** where *sevillano* Lope de Rueda's works, precursors to the dramas of Spain's Golden Age, were staged. A turn down C. Gloria leads to the 17th-century **Hospital de los Venerables,** a hospital-church adorned with art from the *Sevillana* School. *(☎954 56 26 96. Open daily for guided visits 10am-2pm and 4-8pm. €3.60, students and over 65 €1.80.)*

Calle Lope de Rueda, off C. Ximénez de Enciso, is graced with two noble mansions, beyond which lies the charming and fragrant **Plaza de Santa Cruz,** built on the former site of the neighborhood's main synagogue. South of the plaza are the **Jardines de Murillo,** a shady expanse of shrubbery and benches. The **Convento de San José** cherishes a cloak and portrait of Santa Teresa de Ávila. *(C. Santa Teresa, off Pl. de Santa Cruz. Open daily 9-11am. Free.)* The church in Pl. de Santa Cruz houses the grave of artist Bartoloméo Murillo, who died in what is now known as the **Casa Murillo** after being injured falling from a scaffold while painting frescoes in Cádiz's Iglesia de los Capuchinos. The house has information on Murillo's life and work. *(C. Santa Teresa, 8. ☎954 22 12 72. Open M-F 8am-3pm and 4-8pm. Free.)* **Iglesia de Santa María la Blanca** was built in 1391 on the foundation of a synagogue. It features red marble columns, Baroque plasterwork, and Murillo's *Last Supper*. *(C. Santa María la Blanca. Open M-Sa 10-11am and 6:30-8pm, Su 9:30am-2pm and 6:30-8pm. Free.)*

NIGHTLIFE

La Carbonería, C. Levies, 18 (☎954 21 44 60). Don't let the drab entrance deter you—beyond lies a gigantic bar where guests give spontaneous performances and free live flamenco shows are put on daily from 10:30pm-midnight. Live blues Sa 11pm. Tapas (€1.50-2) served until late. Beer €1.50, mixed drinks €5. Sangria pitchers €8. Open July-Aug. M-Sa 8pm-4am, Su 8pm-2:30am; Sept.-May M-Sa 8pm-4am, Su 7pm-3am.

Alfonso, Av. la Palmera (☎954 23 37 35), adjacent to Po. de las Delicias. Avoid the longer lines elsewhere and shake it to the DJ's crazy beats in this spacious outdoor club, among palm trees and mini-bars. Beer €1.50, mixed drinks €4.50-6. Open Su-Th 10pm-5am, F-Sa 10pm-7am. AmEx/D/MC/V.

Terraza Chile, Po. de las Delicias. A calm, peaceful *terraza* by day, Chile morphs into a packed dance club and bar by night with loud salsa and pop, bringing together young *sevillanos,* foreign students, and tourists. Beer €2, mixed drinks €5. Open June-Sept. daily 8am-5am; Oct.-May Th-Sa 8pm-5am. MC/V.

Antigüedades, C. Argote de Molina, 40. This mellow bar with small tables plays soul for a 20-something crowd. Creative redecorating every few months, with themes like "disembodiment." Beer €2, mixed drinks €4.50. Open Su-Th 9pm-3am, F-Sa 9pm-4am.

Flaherty's, C. Alemanes, 7 (☎954 21 04 51). Gigantic, sprawling Irish pub, the most popular bar in the city, attracts tourists, expats, and students. Friendly atmosphere for solo travelers. Serves food daily until 11:30pm (entrees and sandwiches €5-10). Beer €2, mixed drinks €4.60. Open daily 11am-3am. AmEx/MC/V.

EL CENTRO

El Centro, a mess of narrow streets radiating from Pl. de la Encarnación and Pl. Duque de la Victoria, is a bustling shopping district during the day, but mostly deserted at night. The area near Pl. Alfalfa, a prime tapas location, is more lively.

ACCOMMODATIONS

Casa Sol y Luna, C. Pérez Galdós, 1A (☎954 21 06 82). A friendly Spanish and British couple keep the most beautiful *hostal* in town. Rooms with high ceilings and tiled mirrors surround a huge, sunny living room. Laundry €7. Singles €22; doubles €35, with bath €42; triples €54; quads €72. Discounts for longer stays. ❷

Hostal Lis, C. Escarpín, 10 (☎954 21 30 88). Cozy rooms in a traditional *sevillana* house. All rooms have fans. Free Internet. Laundry €5 for 5kg. Singles with shower €24, with bath €30; doubles with bath €45; triples with bath €66. AmEx/D/MC/V. ❷

Hostal La Gloria, C. San Eloy, 58, 2nd fl. (☎954 22 26 73), at the end of a lively shopping street. Rooms are airy and reasonably sized. José, the owner, will make you feel at home (and insists you reserve at least 3 days in advance). Singles €20; doubles €30, with bath €36; triples €45. ❷

Hostal Lis II, C. Olavide, 5 (☎954 56 02 28). Smack in the middle of the main shopping zone, but pretty pricey for what you get. Pleasant but simple rooms have fans. Internet €1.20 per 30min., €1.80 per hr. Singles €25; doubles €35, with bath €45; triples €60; quads €75. AmEx/D/MC/V. ❷

Hotel Zaida, C. San Roque, 26 (☎954 21 11 38; www.ahsevilla.com). Hotel-sized lobby with wicker furniture disguises simple rooms with bath, TV, and A/C. Singles €36.50; doubles €55. *Semana Santa* and *Feria* €51.50/€109.50. MC/V. ❹

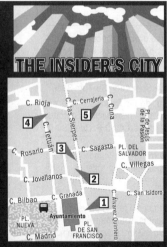

THE INSIDER'S CITY

THE BARGAINS OF SEVILLA

Sevilla is a city full of wonderful *artesanía* and plenty of people selling it. Avoid the overpriced tourist shops by the cathedral and head to specialty stores for high-quality, authentic merchandise. After dropping a few euros on authentic trappings, you can dress in flamenco fashion, bat your eyes at that handsome Don Juan from behind a hand-made fan, and wrap yourself in a luxurious silk shawl like a true *sevillana*.

1 Abanicos de Sevilla, Pl. de San Francisco, 7 (☎954 21 38 18). Large selection of hand-painted fans, from dirt cheap to outrageously expensive. Open June-Aug. M-F 9:30am-1:30pm and 5-8:30pm, Sa 9:30am-2pm; Sept.-May M-Sa 9:30am-1:30pm and 5-8:30pm. MC/V.

2 Martian Cerámica Sevillana, C. las Sierpes, 74 (☎954 21 34 13). Colorful hand-painted ceramics, all made in Sevilla. Tiny trays and vases start at

FOOD

Packed with shoppers by day and young people by night, the area around Pl. Alfalfa is full of unassuming tapas bars and restaurants serving *comida típica* and excellent international food.

◙ **Habanita Bar Restaurante,** C. Golfo, 3 (☎606 71 64 56; www.andalunet.com/habanita). Popular vegetarian/vegan-oriented cafe-restaurant serving tapas and *ración*-sized Cuban fare, pastas, salads, and tropical drinks in a breezy private *terraza*. Entrees €7-10. Open daily 12:30-4:30pm and 8pm-12:30am; closed Su night. MC/V. ❷

La Mia Tana, C. Pérez Galdós, 24 (☎954 22 68 97). The charm of this fine mini-Italy makes even pizza romantic. Affordable, vegetarian-friendly options. *Pizzeta* €3.70-4.90; large pizzas €9.60-11.90. Pastas €4.10-4.60. Non-Italian specialties like *empanadas* and *kebaps* €2.60-4.60. Open daily 1-4:30pm and 8pm-1am. D/MC/V. ❶

El Rinconcillo, C. Gerona, 40 (☎954 22 31 83). Founded in 1670 and among the oldest in town, this *bodega* is the epitome of local hangouts, teeming with gray-haired men deep in conversation. Sip *cerveza* and savor *aceitunas* on top of discarded Tío Pepe barrels. Tapas €1.25-2. *Raciones* €4-10. Open daily 1pm-2am. AmEx/MC/V. ❷

SIGHTS

◙ **MUSEO PROVINCIAL DE BELLAS ARTES.** Cobbled together from decommissioned convents in the mid-1800s, this museum contains Spain's finest collection of works by painters of the *Sevillana* School, most notably Murillo, Valdés Leal, and Zurbarán, as well as El Greco and Dutch master Peter Brueghel. Although the art (displayed more or less chronologically) is heavily biased toward religious themes, later works include some landscape paintings and portraits of Sevilla, its environs, and residents. The building itself, with many tiny courtyards, is as impressive as the art inside. *(Pl. del Museo, 9. ☎954 22 07 90. Open Tu 3-8pm, W-Sa 9am-8pm, Su 9am-2pm. €1.50, EU citizens free.)*

◙ **CASA DE PILATOS.** Inhabited continuously by Spanish aristocrats since the 15th century, this large private residence combines all the virtues of Andalusian architecture and art and has only recently been opened to the bourgeois public, although sections are still used as a private home. On the ground floor, Roman artifacts and tropical gardens coexist in *mudéjar* patios. The second floor features rooms decorated over the centuries with oil portraits, sculptures, painted ceilings, and tapestries. (*Pl. Pilatos, 1.* ☎ *954 22 52 98. Open daily 9am-7pm. Guided tours every 30min. 10am-6:30pm. Ground level only €5, with upper chambers €8.*)

IGLESIA DEL SALVADOR. Fronted by a Montañés sculpture, this 17th-century church was built on the foundations of the city's main mosque. The courtyard and the belfry's base are remnants of the old building. As grandiose as a cathedral, the church is adorned with exceptional Baroque *retablos*, sculptures, and paintings, including Montañés's *Jesús de la pasión.* (*Pl. del Salvador, 1 block from C. las Sierpes. Closed for renovations, check sign on door.*)

OTHER SIGHTS. Originating from Pl. San Francisco, **Calle las Sierpes** cuts through the Aristocratic Quarter. At the beginning of this pedestrian street, lined with shoe stores, fan shops, and chic boutiques, a plaque marks the spot where the royal prison once loomed. Some scholars believe Cervantes began writing *Don Quixote* here. Legend states that the founder of **Convento de Santa Inés**, C. María Coronel, was pursued so insistently by King Pedro the Cruel that she disfigured her face with boiling oil so he would leave her alone. Cooking liquids are used more positively today—the cloistered nuns sell puff pastries and coffee cakes through the courtyard's revolving window. (*Sweets €2.50-3.60, sold M-Sa 9am-1pm and 4-7pm.*) The **Ayuntamiento** has 16th-century Gothic and Renaissance interior halls, a richly decorated domed ceiling, and a Plateresque facade. Impressive artwork graces many of the walls, and art exhibitions take place frequently; check with the tourist office for information. (*Pl. San Francisco, enter from Pl. Nueva.* ☎ *954 59 01 01. Open Sept.-June Tu-Th 5:30-6:30pm. Passport or other official documentation required. Free.*) The **Iglesia de la Anunciación** features a pantheon honoring illustrious *sevillanos*, including Romantic poet Gustavo Adolfo Bécquer. (*Pl. de la Encarnación; enter on C. Laraña. Open daily 9am-1pm. Mass M-Sa noon, Su 12:30pm; Th and Su also 8:30pm. Free.*)

🎵 NIGHTLIFE

▧ **Isbiliyya,** Po. de Cristóbal Colón, 2 (☎954 21 04 60). Popular gay and lesbian bar with outdoor seating. Tu, Th, and Su they open up the dance floor and host drag performances after midnight. Beer €2-2.50. Mixed drinks €5. Open daily 8pm-5am.

El Capote, C. El Barranco, near Puente de Elizabeth II. A laid-back, jazzy outdoor bar with tables overlooking the river and a clientele of all ages and nationalities. Live music in summer. Open June-Sept. 15 daily noon-4am.

€3, larger ones run €20-30. Open M-Sa 10am-2pm and 5-8:30pm. MC/V.

3 **Artesanía Textil,** C. las Sierpes, 70 (☎954 56 28 40). Authentic, hand-sewn, silk shawls. Prices start at €56. Open June-Aug. M-F 10am-1:30pm and 5:15-8:15pm, Sa 10am-1:30pm; Sept.-May M-Sa 10am-1:30pm and 5:15-8:15pm. MC/V.

4 **Diza,** C. Tetuán, 5 (☎954 21 41 54). Lots of *abanicos* (fans), some dating back to the 19th-century. Hand-painted fans €3.75 and up. June-Aug. M-F 9:30am-1:30pm and 5-8:30pm, Sa 9:30am-2pm; Sept.-May M-Sa 9:30am-1:30pm and 5-8:30pm. MC/V.

5 **Trajes Sevillanos, Modas Muñoz,** C. Cerrajería, 5 (☎954 22 85 96). The real deal when it comes to traditional flamenco outfits. Very colorful, high-quality costumes, with equally high price tags (€120 and up). Also sells flamenco accessories (fans, flowers, etc.). Open M-F 10am-1:30pm and 5-8:30pm, Sa 10am-1:30pm. MC/V.

LA MACARENA

Nothing much happens in this area north of El Centro. Quiet and residential, it is the neighborhood least altered by tourist hype, and entertainment value is substantially compromised for authenticity. Its main and perhaps only attractions are the centuries-old churches that grace the neighborhood.

ACCOMMODATIONS AND FOOD

The homey, welcoming rooms of **Hostal Macarena ❷,** C. San Luis, 91, have curtains, tiles, wooden furniture, quilted bedspreads, and A/C. (☎954 37 01 41. Singles €20; doubles €30, with bath €36; triples €51. MC/V.) **Hostal Alameda ❷,** Alameda de Hércules, 31, has sterile, hotel-like rooms, all with A/C. (☎954 90 01 91; fax 90 22 48. Singles €20; doubles with bath €40. MC/V.) **Ancha de la Feria ❶,** C. Feria, 61, serves delicious homemade tapas (€1.50-2; *raciones* from €4) in a breezier version of the traditional taberna. Old sherry barrels line the walls and ceiling. A great *menú del día* (€5.80) is served afternoons only. (☎954 90 97 45. Open Tu-Sa 9am-4pm and 9pm-2am, Su 9am-4pm.)

🞇 SIGHTS

Though charming, La Macarena is certainly not the brightest gem in Sevilla. Its collection of ancient churches do not compare to the Catedral, but they may be worth a visit if time and interest allow.

CONVENTO DE SANTA PAULA. Convento de Santa Paula includes a church with Gothic, *mudéjar*, and Renaissance elements, a magnificent ceiling, and Montañés sculptures. The **museum** has religious art including Ribera's *San Jerónimo*. Nuns peddle scrumptious 🞠**homemade marmalade** and angel hair pastries. Knock if the door is closed. *(Pl. Santa Paula, 11. Open Tu-Su 10am-1pm. €2. Marmalade €2.70 for 300g.)*

CHURCHES. A stretch of **murallas** (walls) built in the 12th century runs between Pta. Macarena and Pta. Córdoba on Ronda de Capuchinos. Flanking the west end of the walls, the **Basílica Macarena** houses the venerated image of *La Virgen de la Macarena*, which is borne through the streets at the climax of the *Semana Santa* processions. A **treasury** glitters with the virgin's jewels and other finery. *(C. Bécquer, 1. ☎ 954 90 18 00. Basilica open M-Sa 9am-2pm and 5-9pm, Su 9:30am-2pm and 5-9pm. Free. Mass M-F 9, 11:30am, 8, and 8:30pm; Sa 9am and 8pm; Su 10:30am, 12:30, and 8pm. Treasury open daily 9:30am-2pm and 5-8pm. €3, students and over 65 €1.50. Sa free.)* Opposite the belfry of the Iglesia de San Marcos rises **Iglesia de Santa Isabel**, featuring an altarpiece by Montañés. Nearby stands the exuberantly Baroque **Iglesia de San Luis**, crowned by octagonal glazed-tile domes. The site of the church was the endpoint of a 12-step prayer route based on the ascent to Golgotha. *(C. San Luis. ☎ 954 55 02 07. Open Tu-Th 9am-2pm, F-Sa 9am-2pm and 5-8pm.)* Toward the river is **Iglesia de San Lorenzo y Jesús del Gran Poder,** with Montañés's remarkably lifelike sculpture, *El Cristo del gran poder;* worshippers kiss Jesus's ankle. *(Pl. San Lorenzo. ☎ 954 91 56 86. Open M-Th 8am-1:30pm and 6-9pm, F 7:30am-10pm, Sa-Su 8am-2pm and 6-9pm. Free.)*

OTHER SIGHTS. A large garden beyond the *murallas* and the Basílica leads to the **Hospital de las Cinco Llagas**, a spectacular Renaissance building recently renovated to host the Andalusian parliament. Thursday mornings from 9am to 2pm a large **flea market** is held along C. Feria.

🞇 NIGHTLIFE

The area near **Puente de la Barqueta** is *the* place to go dancing during summer. The near side of the river features several outdoor discos, while the far side hosts the more rowdy clubbing scene. From La Macarena, follow C. Resolana to C. Nueva Torneo, which runs by Pte. de la Barqueta. (The A2 night bus runs at midnight, 1, and 2am from Pl. Nueva; ask to be let off near Pte. de la Barqueta. Taxi from Pl. Nueva €5.)

🞠 **Palenque,** Av. Blas Pascal (☎ 954 46 74 08). Cross Puente. de la Barqueta, turn left, and follow C. Materático Rey Pastor to the intersection. Turn left again and look for the entrance on the right. Gigantic dance club, complete with 2 dance floors, 2 musical choices, and a small ice skating rink (€3, including skate rental). Dress to impress or you'll be turned away at the door. Mainly *sevillano* university crowd. Beer €3. Mixed drinks €5. F-Sa cover €7, Th free. Open June-Sept. Th-Sa midnight-7am.

Tribal, Av. de Los Descubrimientos, next to Pte. de la Barqueta. Hip, tropical, tent-like *discoteca* playing American hip-hop and Latin favorites. W hip-hop nights are especially popular with the international crowd. Drinks €5-10 depending on the size of the group (the larger, the cheaper). Open W-Sa midnight-6am.

SEVILLA

EL ARENAL AND TRIANA

Immortalized by *Siglo de Oro* writers Lope de Vega, Francisco de Quevedo, and Miguel de Cervantes, Triana was Sevilla's chaotic 16th- and 17th-century mariners' district. Today, it is home to many of Sevilla's best ethnic restaurants. Avoid overpriced C. del Betis and plunge down less expensive side streets. Tapas bars cluster around Pl. San Martín and along C. San Jacinto, the neighborhood's northern border. El Arenal was once a stretch of sand by the harbor on the opposite bank, exposed when the river was diverted to its present course.

FOOD

El Baratillo/Casa Chari, C. Pavía, 12 (☎954 22 96 51). Premium Spanish cuisine and hospitality. Ask 1hr. in advance for the tour-de-force: paella, homemade with love (vegetarian available), with a pitcher of wine, beer, or sangria (€18 for 2 people). *Menú* €4-9. Open M-F 10am-10pm, Sa 10am-5pm; later when busy. ❶

Acropolis Taberna Griega, C. Rosario Vega, 10 (☎954 28 46 85). This small restaurant, popular with foreign students and locals, serves delicious Greek specialties and vegetarian options. The personable owner has plans to move his Taberna to Madrid; call his mobile (☎615 53 86 42) to make sure he's still in town, and catch him while you can! Entrees and appetizers €3-4.50. Open M 8:30-11:30pm, Tu-Th 1:30-3:30pm and 8:30-11:30pm, F-Sa 1:30-3:30pm and 8:30-midnight. Closed Aug. AmEx/D/MC/V. ❶

Histórico Horno, SA, Av. de la Constitución, 16 (☎954 22 18 19). Though *bocadillos* are served here, this gourmet *"panadería, pastelería, y charcutería"* is renowned for its desserts: heavenly sweets, pastries, cookies, ice cream, and cakes will satisfy any sugar craving. Enjoy your delicacy in the sophisticated restaurant or have it *para llevar* (to go). Open M-Sa 7:30am-11pm, Su 9am-11pm. AmEx/D/MC/V. ❷

Café-Bar Jerusalém, C. Salado, 6. Neighborhood *kebap* bar with chicken, lamb, pork, and cheese Shawarma (€3-4.50). Open Su-Th 8pm-2am, F-Sa 8pm-3am. AmEx/V. ❶

SIGHTS

The inviting riverside esplanade Po. Alcalde Marqués de Contadero stretches along the banks of the Guadalquivir from the base of the Torre del Oro. **Boat tours** of Sevilla leave from in front of the tower (1hr., €4.50).

PLAZA DE TOROS DE LA REAL MAESTRANZA. Though ethically questionable, it's undeniable that bullfighting has for centuries been a staple of *Sevillano* culture, evidenced by the city's beautiful and world-renowned Plaza de Toros. Construction began in 1761 and took over 120 years. Home to one of the two great bullfighting schools (the other is in **Ronda,** see p. 293), the plaza fills to capacity (13,800) for the 13 *corridas* of the *Feria de Abril* as well as for weekly fights. Multilingual tours take visitors through a small but telling museum, as well as behind the ring to the chapel where *matadores* pray before fights, and the medical emergency room used when their prayers go unanswered, though only three matadors have died in the history of bullfighting in Sevilla. (☎954 22 45 77. Open nonfight days 9:30am-7pm; fight days 9:30am-3pm. Mandatory tours every 20min. in English and Spanish. €4. See **Bullfights,** p. 229, for ticket info.)

TORRE DEL ORO. The 12-sided Torre del Oro (Gold Tower), built by the Almohads in the early 13th century, overlooks the river from Po. de Cristóbal Colón. Today, a tiny yellow dome is all that remains of the glistening golden tiles that once covered the entire tower. Inside, however, is the small yet thought-provoking **Museo Náutico,** a storehouse of naval relics and other maritime antiquities. Museum officers enthusiastically tend to curious visitors. Look out for the whale jaw. (☎954 22 24 19. Open Sept.-July Tu-F 10am-2pm, Sa-Su 11am-2pm. €1. Tu free.)

OTHER SIGHTS. Related to and opposite the Torre del Oro across the river is the **Torre de la Plata** (Silver Tower); they used to be connected by underwater chains, designed to protect the city from river-borne trespassers. With old-fashioned piracy no longer a concern, the Torre de la Plata has since been put to a more modern use—it now hosts a bank. The **Hospital de la Caridad** on C. Temprado consists of arcaded yet plain courtyards lined with ceramic tableaux, and the Iglesia de San Jorge, a perplexing, incongruent mix of humility and boisterousness. (☎954 22 32 32. Open M-Sa 9am-1:30pm and 3:30-7:30pm, Su 9am-1pm. €4.) The **Capilla de los Marineros** (Sailors' Chapel) in Triana was constructed in the 18th century to worship the Esperanza de Triana, who, along with the Virgin Mary and La Macarena, is one of the most adored figures of Sevilla. (C. de la Pureza, 53. ☎954 33 26 45. Open M-Sa 9am-1pm and 5:30-9pm. Free.) One block farther inland, midway between Puente de Isabel II and Puente de San Telmo, is the **Iglesia de Santa Ana,** Sevilla's oldest church and the focal point of the exuberant *fiestas* that take over the area in July. (C. Pelay Correa. Open M and W 7:30-8:30pm.) The terraced riverside promenade **Calle del Betis** is an ideal spot from which to view Sevilla's skyline.

🎵 NIGHTLIFE

🎵 **Boss,** C. del Betis. In Sevilla the night is always young, and Boss is...boss. If you pierce its aura of exclusivity, it will show you who, indeed, knows how to get a crowd fired up. Sensual, irresistible beats and hazy blue lights make this a desirable nocturnal destination. Beer €3.50, mixed drinks €6. Open daily 9pm-5am. MC/V.

Fundición, C. del Betis, 49. Very popular among exchange students; packed during the school year, emptier in summer. American decor fills the huge interior; great music selection. Beer €1-2.50. Mixed drinks €4-5.50. Open Sept.-July 14 M-Sa 10pm-5am.

Catedral, Cuesta del Rosario, 12 (☎630 61 55 02). Underground disco with metal, stone, and wood decor. No cover for women and those with coupons (available in stores, restaurants, and hostels). Cover for men €6, includes 1 mixed drink or 2 beers. Open Sept.-June W-Sa midnight-6am.

OUTER NEIGHBORHOODS

NEAR ESTACIÓN PLAZA DE ARMAS

Several hostels line C. Gravina, parallel to C. Marqués de las Paradas two blocks from the station. Hostels here tend to be cheaper than those in other neighborhoods and are convenient for exploring El Centro (10min.) and C. del Betis and Triana on the west bank of the river (10-15min.). Be prepared to schlep at least 20-30min. to the cathedral and the sight-filled Santa Cruz neighborhood.

Hostal Paris, C. San Pedro Mártir, 14 (☎954 22 98 61; fax 21 96 45). Rooms here tend to be clean, refreshing, and spacious, with private bath, A/C, phone, and TV. Slightly pricier than other options in the area but clearly superior. Mar.-Oct. singles €36; doubles €50. Nov.-Feb. €32/€45. IVA not included. AmEx/D/MC/V. ❸

Hostal Romero, C. Gravina, 21 (☎954 21 13 53). Large rooms are mildly grim and colorless but clean. Singles €18; doubles €30, with bath €42; triples €60. ❷

Hostal Río Sol, C. Marqués de Paradas, 25 (☎954 22 90 38). Circular staircase leads to tidy rooms tighter than your budget. Singles €15, with bath €18; slightly more spacious doubles with bath, TV, and A/C €36. MC/V. ❷

Sevilla Youth Hostel (HI), C. Isaac Peral, 2 (☎954 61 31 50; reservas@inturjoven.junta-andalucia.es). Take bus #34 across from the tourist office near the cathedral; the 5th stop is behind the hostel. Taxi from the cathedral approx. €5. Isolated and difficult to find. A/C. Doubles, triples, and quads; many with private bath. Breakfast €1.40, other meals €5. Dorms Mar.-Oct. €13.75, over 26 €18.75; Nov.-Feb. €11.65/16.20. Non-members can pay €3 extra per night for 6 nights to become members. ❶

Camping Sevilla, Ctra. Madrid-Cádiz, km 534 (☎954 51 43 79), near the airport. Take bus #70 (stops 800m away at Parque Alcosa) from Prado de San Sebastián. Hot showers, supermarket, and pool. €6.50 per 1-person tent, €7 per car. ❶

Club de Campo, C. Libertad, 13 (☎954 72 02 50), Ctra. Sevilla-Dos Hermanas, 8km out of town. Los Amarillos buses leave from C. Infante Carlos de Borbón, at the back of Prado San Sebastián, to Dos Hermanas (every 45min., €0.75). Lots of grass and a pool. €3.65 per 1-person tent, €2.85 per child, €3.65 per car. ❶

PLAZA DE ESPAÑA

The twin spires of Plaza de España gracefully mark the ends of the over 200m long wonder of a building. Designed by Aníbal González, one of Sevilla's most prominent 20th-century architects, the aristocratic-looking structure hugs a large and beautiful plaza, featuring mosaic floors and a large marble fountain, within its semicircle. Horse-drawn carriages clatter around the plaza and rowboats can be rented to navigate its narrow moat. Mosaics depicting every province in Spain line the crumbling colonnade, and balconies offer a beautiful view of the surrounding gardens. The nearby **Parque de María Luisa** is a reminder of Sevilla's 1929 plans for an Ibero-American world fair. *(Adjacent to Pl. de España. Open daily 8am-10pm.)*

🔁 DAYTRIPS FROM SEVILLA

OSUNA

Trains (☎/fax 954 81 03 08; station open 7am-8pm) from Sevilla (1hr., 6 per day 7:30am-6:35pm, €6.50). Empresa Dipasa/Linesur (☎954 98 82 22) runs buses to and from Sevilla's Estación Prado de San Sebastián (1½hr., 5-11 per day 6:15am-7:40pm, round-trip with same day open return time €10.60) Bus station on Av. de la Constitución. (Ticket office open M-F 6:30-9am, 10am-2:30pm, 3:15-6pm and 7-8pm; Sa 7:30-9am and 10:30am-2pm; Su 3-4pm and 7-8pm.)

Julius Caesar founded Osuna (pop. 17,500), naming it after the *osos* (bears) that once lumbered about its hills. Visitors today come for its myriad churches and convents as well as the tranquil, intimate feel (though it has become increasingly touristed). Most sights are found on the hill that rises above town; the tourist office has good maps with highlighted walking tours. The **Colegiata de Santa María de la Asunción**, Callejón de las Descalzas, was commissioned by the Dukes of Osuna in the Renaissance style and now houses the **Museo de Arte Sacro Panteón Ducal**, which is unfortunately closed for renovation indefinitely. The refreshing overall whiteness and simplicity of the Colegiata highlight the intricacy of the imposing, organic, vine-like golden altar. It is most famous, however, for its five Riberas. From Pl. Mayor, walk to the adjacent Pl. Duquesa Osuna and then uphill to Pl. de la Encarnación; knock to enter. (☎954 81 04 44. Mandatory guided tours. Open Tu-SuMay-Sept. 10am-1:30pm and 4-7pm; Oct.-Apr. 10am-1:30pm and 3:30-6:30pm. €2.) On the right side of the church is the university and the ⬛**Convento de la Encarnación**, Pl. de la Encarnación, 2, a Baroque church founded by the Duke of Osuna in 1626 and lavishly decorated in the 18th century. A resident nun will show you room upon room of polychromed wooden sculptures, silver crucifixes, painted tiles, and handmade Christ-doll clothes. Make sure to knock and wait until the previous tour group finishes. (☎954 81 11 21. Open Tu-Su 10am-1:30pm and 4-7pm. €2. Mass daily 8:30am. Free.)

To reach Pl. Mayor from the train station, walk up Av. de la Estación, curving right on C. Mancilla. At Pl. Salitre, turn left on C. Carmen and then right on C. Sevilla, which leads into the plaza. From the bus station, exit right and walk downhill on C. Santa Ana past Pl. Santa Rita; continue on Av. Arjona until the plaza. The **tourist office** is in Pl. Mayor. (☎954 81 57 32. Open M-Sa 9am-2pm.)

ITÁLICA

Take the Empresa Casal bus (☎954 41 06 58) toward Santiponce from the Pl. de Armas bus station, platform 34. Get off at the last stop (30min.; M-Sa every 30min. 6:30am-midnight, Su every hr. 7:30am-midnight; €1). Pay onboard. The entrance to the ruins is next to the gas station where the bus stops. When returning to Sevilla, wait at the bus sign in front of the entrance to Itálica; the bus will turn around at the gas station.

Just 9km northwest of Sevilla and right outside the village of **Santiponce** (pop. 7000) lie the excavated ruins of Itálica, the first important Roman settlement in Iberia. The birthplace of emperors Trajan (AD 53) and Hadrian (AD 76), Itálica was founded in 206 BC as a settlement for soldiers wounded in the Battle of Illipa, and was later utilized as a strategic military outpost. During the 4th and 5th centuries AD, the city burgeoned into a cosmopolitan trading center, but by the early 500s, Sevilla had become the regional seat of power. Archaeological excavations began in the 18th century and continue today, although the oldest neighborhoods in Itálica are still buried under downtown Santiponce and may never be recovered. The **Casa del Planetario** (House of Planets) has intricate **mosaic floors** depicting the seven gods that represent planets; other nearby houses, such as the **Casa de Neptuno** and **Casa de Hylas,** also have unique floors. Reconstructed patios and a bakery depict life as it was during the city's decline. The amazingly well-preserved ▓**amphitheater,** among Spain's largest, at one time seated 25,000. It was used to stage fights between gladiators and lions. Today, visitors can wander the grounds and the curving hallways that circle the structure at the center of the site. Although there is plenty of grass and shade, the ruins themselves are in direct sunlight, so bring lots of water. (☎955 99 73 76. Open Apr.-Sept. Tu-Sa 8:30am-8:30pm, Su 9am-3pm; Oct.-Mar. Tu-Sa 9am-5:30pm, Su 10am-4pm. €1.50, EU citizens free.)

CARMONA

Empresa Casal buses to Carmona depart Sevilla from the Pr. de San Sebastián station, platform 25 (1hr.; 7-20 per day 7am-10pm; €2, pay on the bus). In Carmona, buses return to Sevilla from the main square along Av. Jorge Bonsor.

Thirty-three kilometers east of Sevilla, ancient Carmona (pop. 25,300) dominates a hill overlooking the countryside. Founded by the Carthaginians, it became an important trade city under Roman occupation in later centuries, and a Moorish stronghold thereafter. Moorish palaces mingle with Renaissance mansions in a network of streets partially enclosed by fortified walls. The **Puerta de Sevilla,** a horseshoe-shaped passageway with both Roman and Arab architectural elements, and the Baroque **Puerta de Córdoba,** on the opposite end of town, once linked Carmona to the east and west. From the bus stop, walk from the back of the bus onto C. San Pedro. On the right is the **Iglesia de San Pedro,** whose *mudéjar* tower is a scaled-down copy of Sevilla's Giralda. (☎954 14 12 77. Open M and Th-Su 11am-2pm; closed July. €1.20. Mass Sa-Su 8:30pm. Free.) Enter the **Alcázar de la Puerta Sevilla,** across the roundabout, through the tourist office on the right. Although some remains on the site date as far back as the 14th to 12th centuries BC, the fortress reached its heyday between the 3rd and 1st centuries BC as a key defensive structure, first for the Carthaginians and later the Romans. This relatively modest fortress is worth visiting if only for the ▓**Torre del Oro,** which affords a magnificent 360° bird's-eye view of the landscape. (☎954 19 09 55. Open M-Sa 10am-6pm, Su 10am-

3pm. €2; students, seniors, and under 12 €1.) From the Alcázar, take C. Prim and then C. Martín to find Pl. Marqués de las Torres, where the late-Gothic **Iglesia de Santa María** was built over an old mosque. The splendid **Patio de los Naranjos** remains from Moorish days. An even older Visigothic liturgical calendar graces one of the columns. (☎954 19 14 82. Open Tu-F 10am-2pm and 5:30-7:30pm, Sa 10am-2pm. €3.) The **Alcázar del Rey Don Pedro,** an old Almohad fortress and now a ritzy hotel, guards the eastern edge of town. In the opposite direction from the bus stop, along C. Enmedio, lie the ruins of the **Necrópolis Romana,** Av. de Jorge Bonsor, 9. Inside the Roman tombs here lie the noteworthy **Tumba de Servilia** and **Tumba del Elefante,** where depictions of Mother Nature and Eastern divinities were overshadowed by the presence of a giant stone elephant. Unfortunately, the tombs have been cleared of many of the interesting artifacts and statues they contained in order to fill the less-than-impressive **museo** that exhibits them in a plain room. (☎954 14 08 11. Both open June-Aug. Tu-F 8:30am-2pm, Sa 10am-2pm; Sept.-May Tu-F 9am-5pm, Sa-Su 10am-2pm. Free.) The **tourist office,** at the entrance to the Alcázar, is down C. San Pedro from the bus stop. (☎954 19 09 55; fax 19 00 80. Open M-Sa 10am-6pm, Su 10am-3pm.) The **police** (☎954 14 00 08) are on C. Carmen Llorca.

ANDALUCÍA

Andalucía is, without a doubt, Spain at its best. Many of the quintessential images of Spain—from bullfighting to flamenco, Moorish architecture to grandiose churches, glorious castles to Roman ruins, and sun-drenched beaches to expanses of olive groves—can all be found in this region. The intoxicating mix of cultures that helped make southern Spain what it is today can be seen both in the area's largest metropolises and in some of its tiniest towns.

The ancient kingdom of Tartessus—which some say is the same Tarshish mentioned in the Bible for its fabulous troves of silver—grew wealthy off the Sierra Nevada's rich ore deposits. The Greeks and Phoenicians established colonies here and traded up and down the coast, and the Romans later cultivated wheat, olive oil, and wine from the fertile soil watered by the Guadalquivir. In the 5th century AD, the Vandals passed through the region on their way to North Africa, leaving little more than a name—Vandalusia (House of the Vandals). The Moors provided a more enduring influence. Arriving in 711 and establishing an enduring link to Africa and the Islamic world, they endowed the region with far more than the flamenco music and gypsy ballads proverbially associated with southern Spain.

Moorish rule lasted until 1492, and during this time Sevilla and Granada reached the pinnacle of Islamic arts, while Córdoba matured into the most culturally and intellectually influential city in Islam. The Moors preserved and perfected Roman architecture, blending it with their own to create a style that became distinctively and uniquely Andalusian—patios, garden oases with fountains and ponds, and alternating red brick and white stone bands are its hallmarks. Two descendent peoples, the *mozárabes* (Christians of Muslim Spain) and later the *mudéjares* (Moors who remained in Spain after the *Reconquista*), had further architectural influence, the former with horseshoe arches and the latter with intricate wooden ceilings. The mingling of Roman and Moorish influences sparked the European Renaissance, merging Classical wisdom and science with that of the Arab world.

HIGHLIGHTS OF ANDALUCÍA

SAMPLE enough sherry to get sufficiently silly in **Jerez de la Frontera** (p. 260).

CLEAN UP like a sultan in the Arab baths of **Córdoba** (p. 257).

DISCOVER what happens when the **Costa del Sol** meets James Bond (p. 284).

SIGH like the last Moor when you too have to leave **Granada** (p. 300).

CÓRDOBA   ☎ 957

Abundant courtyards, flowers dripping from balconies, and narrow, winding streets make Córdoba (pop. 310,000) a captivating and unhurried city. Perched on the south bank of the Río Guadalquivir, it was once the largest city in Western Europe and for three centuries the hub of the Moorish Empire, capital of the mighty Ummayad Caliphate, and rivaled only by Baghdad and Cairo. Córdoba remembers that heyday with amazingly well-preserved monuments of Roman, Jewish, Islamic, and Christian origin in baffling proximity. Only in Toledo are the remnants of Spain's colorful heritage as visibly intermixed. The *judería* is one of Spain's oldest Jewish quarters, containing one of the few synagogues in the Iberian peninsula, and the 14th-century Palacio del Marqués de Viana anticipates Spain's Golden Age by two centuries. Spectacular scenery, perfected gastronomic specialties such as the irresistible *salmorejo* and *rabo de toro*, and refreshing fountains charm visitors with the grace of a Córdoban flamenco dancer.

ANDALUCÍA

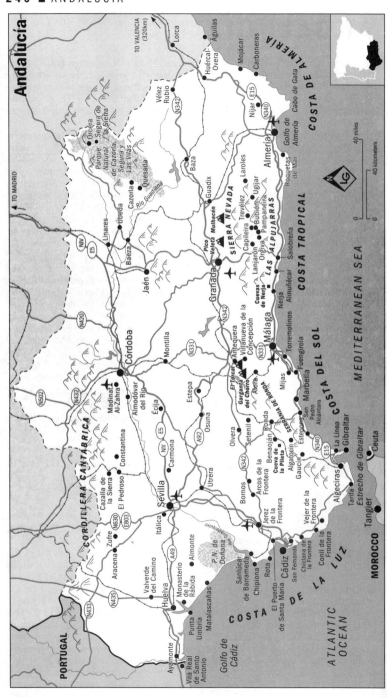

Andalucía

TRANSPORTATION

Trains: Pl. de las Tres Culturas (☎957 24 02 02), off Av. de América. To: **Algeciras** (5 per day 4:55am-4:37pm, €16.50-26.50); **Barcelona** (10-11hr., 4 per day 9:45am-11:24pm, €47-64.50); **Cádiz** (2½hr., 5 per day 6:55am-8:15pm, €15.80-32); **Madrid** (2-4hr., 21-31 per day 2:28am-11:44pm, €26-48); **Málaga** (2-3hr., 9-12 per day 6:41am-10:12pm, €11.25-19.50); **Sevilla** (45min., 20-30 per day 6:55am-12:44am, €7-23.50). For international tickets, visit the **RENFE** office, Ronda de los Tejares, 10.

Buses: Estación de Autobuses (☎957 40 40 40; fax 40 44 15), on Av. de América across from the train station.

Alsina Graells Sur (☎957 27 81 00) to: **Algeciras** (5hr., 8am and 3:15pm, €20.50); **Almería** (5hr., 8am, €20.10); **Antequera** (2½hr., 9am and 4pm, €7.70); **Cádiz** (4-5hr.; M-F 10am and 6pm, Sa-Su 10am; €18.40) via **Sevilla** (2hr., 10-13 per day 5:30am-10pm, €8.90); **Granada** (3hr., 8 per day 8am-7pm, €10.70); **Málaga** (3-3½hr., 5 per day 8am-7pm, €10.70).

Bacoma (☎957 45 65 14) goes to **Barcelona** (10hr., 3 per day 12:35am-7:15pm, €69) and **Baeza** and **Valencia.**

Secorbus (☎902 22 92 92) runs cheap buses to **Madrid** (4½hr., 3-6 per day 1am-5pm, €11.20).

Transportes Ureña (☎957 40 45 58) runs to **Jaén** (2hr., 6-8 per day 7:30am-8pm, €6.90). **Autocares Priego** (☎957 40 44 79), **Empresa Carrera** (☎957 40 44 14), and **Empresa Rafael Ramírez** (☎957 42 21 77) run buses to surrounding towns and campsites.

Local Transportation: 12 bus lines (☎957 25 57 00) cover the city, running from the wee hours until 11pm. Bus #3 makes a loop from the bus and train stations through Pl. de las Tendillas, up to the Santuario, and back along the river and up C. Dr. Fleming. Bus #10 runs from the train station to Barrio Brillante. Buy tickets on board. €0.90.

Taxis: Radio Taxi (☎957 76 44 44). From the bus and train stations to the *judería* €3-5.

Car Rental: Hertz (☎957 49 29 61; fax 40 20 60), in the train station. 25+. Compact car €61.40 per day, discounts for longer periods. Open M-F 8:30am-10pm, Sa 9am-7pm, Su 9am-2pm.

ORIENTATION

Córdoba is split into two parts: the old city and the new. The modern and commercial northern half extends from the train station on Av. de América down to **Plaza de las Tendillas**, the center of the city. The old section in the south is a medieval maze known as the **judería** (Jewish quarter). This tangle of beautiful and disorienting streets extends from Pl. de las Tendillas to the banks of the Río Guadalquivir, winding past the **Mezquita** and **Alcázar**. The easiest way to reach the old city from the train or bus station is to take bus #3 to **Plaza Campo Santo de los Mártires.** Alternatively, the walk is about 20min. From the train station, with your back to the platforms, exit left, cross the parking plaza, and make a right onto Av. de los Mozárabes. When you reach the Roman columns, turn left and cross Glorieta Sargentos Provisionales. Make a right onto Po. de la Victoria and veer toward the left until you reach Puerto de Almodóvar in the old city.

PRACTICAL INFORMATION

Tourist Office: Andalucía Regional Office, C. Torrijos, 10 (☎957 47 12 35). From the train station, take bus #3 along the river until the stone arch on the right. English-speaking staff distributes free maps of the monument section. Open May-Sept. M-F 9:30am-7pm, Sa 10am-7pm, Su 10am-2pm; Oct.-Apr. M-F 9:30am-6pm, Su 10am-2pm.

Tours: Córdoba Vision, Av. Dr. Fleming, 1 (☎957 76 02 41). Offers excellent guided tours in English, French, or Spanish, including a walking tour of Córdoba's monuments (€25) and of Madinat al-Zahra (€18).

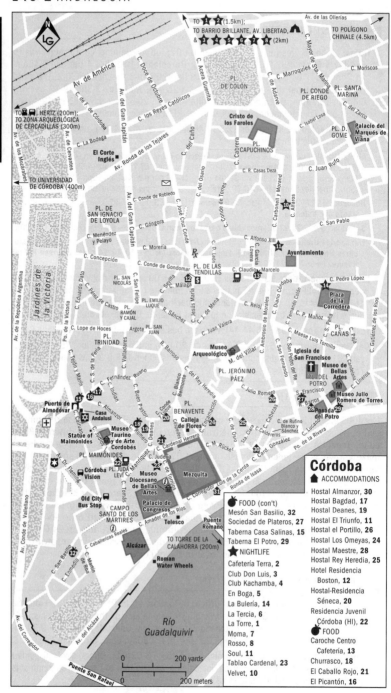

Córdoba

⬥ ACCOMMODATIONS

Hostal Almanzor, **30**
Hostal Bagdad, **17**
Hostal Deanes, **19**
Hostal El Triunfo, **11**
Hostal El Portillo, **26**
Hostal Los Omeyas, **24**
Hostal Maestre, **28**
Hostal Rey Heredia, **25**
Hotel Residencia
  Boston, **12**
Hostal-Residencia
  Séneca, **20**
Residencia Juvenil
  Córdoba (HI), **22**
🍴 FOOD
Caroche Centro
  Cafetería, **13**
Churrasco, **18**
El Caballo Rojo, **21**
El Picantón, **16**

🍴 FOOD (con't)
Mesón San Basilio, **32**
Sociedad de Plateros, **27**
Taberna Casa Salinas, **15**
Taberna El Potro, **29**
★ NIGHTLIFE
Cafetería Terra, **2**
Club Don Luis, **3**
Club Kachamba, **4**
En Boga, **5**
La Bulería, **14**
La Tercia, **6**
La Torre, **1**
Moma, **7**
Rosso, **8**
Soul, **11**
Tablao Cardenal, **23**
Velvet, **10**

Currency Exchange: Banco Santander Central Hispano, Pl. de las Tendillas, 5 (☎957 49 70 00). No commission. Open M-F 8:30am-2:30pm.

Luggage Storage: At the train and bus stations. €2 per day. Open 24hr.

Laundry: Teleseco, Ronda de Isasa, 10 (☎957 48 33 56), 1 block from La Mezquita, near the river. Coin service and dry cleaning. Washers €4.80, dryers €3.

Police: Av. Doctor Fleming, 2 (☎092).

Medical Assistance: Red Cross Hospital, Po. de la Victoria (☎957 42 06 66, urgent 22 22 22). English spoken. Open M-F 9am-1:30pm and 4:30-5:30pm.

Internet Access: In the old city, surf at **NavegaWeb**, Pl. Judá Levi (☎957 29 00 66). Enter through the HI youth hostel. Slick new machines, A/C, and a young crowd. €1.20 per hr. Open daily 10am-10pm. **Ch@t-is**, C. Claudio Marcelo, 15 (☎957 47 45 00). €1.80 per hr. Open M-F 10am-2pm and 5-9:30pm, Sa 10am-2pm.

Post Office: C. José Cruz Conde, 15 (☎957 47 97 96). **Lista de Correos.** Open M-F 8:30am-8:30pm, Sa-Su 9:30am-2pm. **Postal Code:** 14070.

ACCOMMODATIONS AND CAMPING

Hostels are clustered between La Mezquita and **Calle de San Fernando.** Córdoba is especially crowded during *Semana Santa* and May to September, but tourism dies down during the sweltering months of July and August. It is generally advisable to call well in advance for reservations. Prices are higher in summer.

IN AND AROUND THE JUDERÍA

The *judería*'s whitewashed walls, twisting streets, and proximity to sights make it a great place to stay. During the day, souvenir booths and cafes keep the streets lively, but the area feels desolate at night. Take bus #3 from the train station to Pl. Campo Santo de los Mártires, and go up C. Manríques to reach the neighborhood.

Residencia Juvenil Córdoba (HI), Pl. Judá Levi (☎957 29 01 66). A former mental asylum converted into a backpacker's paradise with large, spotless doubles, triples, and quads with bath and A/C. Pleasant courtyards, public phones, and a conveniently located Internet cafe. Wheelchair-accessible. Breakfast included, other meals €4.70. Storage available. Towels €1.10. Laundry €2.50, dry €1.50. Reservations recommended. Mar.-Oct. €13.80, over 26 €18.40; Nov.-Feb. €2.10 less. €3.50 extra per day for non-members. Private rooms with per-bed surcharge. MC/V. ❶

Hostal Bagdad, C. Fernández Ruano, 11 (☎957 20 28 54). This hostel's bright yet soothing colors, lush courtyard, comfy rooms, and very own teahouse make it a real favorite. Singles €20; doubles €36; triples €45. MC/V. ❸

Hostal El Triunfo, C. Corregidor Luis de la Cerda, 79 (☎957 49 84 84; www.htriunfo.com). Luxury at reasonable prices. All rooms boast A/C, phone, TV, bath, and safe. 3rd fl. terrace welcomes readers and tanners. Wheelchair-accessible. Parking €12 per day. Singles €28-34; doubles €48-60; triples available. AmEx/D/MC/V. ❸

Hostal-Residencia Séneca, C. Conde y Luque, 7 (☎/fax 957 47 32 34). A beautiful courtyard greets you as you enter this homey hostel. All rooms have fans or A/C. Breakfast included. Singles €22, with bath €34; doubles €39/€46; triples available. ❷

Hostal Deanes, C. Deanes, 6 (☎957 29 37 44). In a 16th-century building, 5 rooms with cavernous baths surround a courtyard cafe (*raciones* €5-9; open daily 9am-10:30pm). Check out the autographed pictures of famous matadors in the adjacent bar. Doubles €31. Extra bed €10. ❷

BETWEEN LA MEZQUITA AND CALLE DE SAN FERNANDO

Hostal Rey Heredia, C. del Rey Heredia, 26 (☎957 47 41 82). Warm and welcoming, this is a great deal for budget travelers: the spacious rooms and good service are surprisingly cheap. Singles €12, with bath €15; doubles €24. ❶

Hostal Maestre, C. Romero Barros, 6 (☎/fax 957 47 53 95), off C. de San Fernando. Immaculate rooms with windows overlooking the street or a courtyard. All with private bath, most with TV. 1st fl. rooms have fans, other floors A/C. Breakfast €2.50. Parking €6 per day. Singles €22; doubles €35. AmEx/D/MC/V. ❷

Hostal Almanzor, C. Cardenal González, 10 (☎/fax 957 48 54 00). Spotless rooms with balcony-like windows, TV, bath, and A/C. Singles have king-sized beds. Parking included. Singles €12; doubles €30-35. AmEx/MC/V. ❶

Hostal el Portillo, C. Cabezas, 2 (☎957 472 091). Simple but charming. Spacious rooms with bath and a pleasant staff. Singles €16; doubles €30. MC/V. ❷

Hostal Los Omeyas, C. Encarnación, 17 (☎957 49 22 67). Named for the Moorish dynasty, Los Omeyas offers Moorish-styled marble rooms with A/C, TV, phone, and bath. Breakfast €3.50. Parking €12 per day. Singles €34-40; doubles €52-64. V. ❹

ELSEWHERE

Hotel Residencia Boston, C. Málaga, 2 (☎957 47 41 76; fax 47 85 23). Simple but spacious rooms equipped with A/C, TV, phone, safe, and bath. Breakfast €3. Laundry service. Parking nearby. Singles €30-34; doubles €45-55. AmEx/D/MC/V. ❸

Camping Municipal, Av. del Brillante, 50 (☎957 40 38 36). From the train station, turn left onto Av. de América, left onto Av. del Brillante, and walk uphill (20min.). Bus #10 and 11 from Av. Cervantes stop across the street. Pool, supermarket, restaurant, free hot showers, and laundry (€3). Some English and French spoken. Very close to Córdoba's nightlife. Wheelchair-accessible. 1 person and tent €8; 2 people and tent €12; 2 people, car, and tent €16; 2 people and camper €17. IVA not included. ❶

🍴 FOOD

The Mezquita area falls flat with many hyper-touristed restaurants, but a 5min. walk in any direction yields local specialties at reasonable prices. In the evenings, locals converge at the outdoor *terrazas* between **Calle Severo Ochoa** and **Calle Dr. Jiménez Díaz** for drinks and tapas. Cheap eateries are clustered farther from the *judería* in **Barrio Cruz Conde** and around **Avenida Menéndez Pidal** and **Plaza de las Tendillas.** Regional specialties include *salmorejo* (a gazpacho-like cream soup topped with hard-boiled egg and pieces of ham) and *rabo de toro* (bull's tail simmered in tomato sauce). **El Corte Inglés,** Av. Ronda de los Tejares, 30, has a grocery store. (Open M-Sa 10am-10pm.)

El Picantón, C. Fernández Ruano, 19 (☎629 58 28 64). This unpretentious yet irresistable tiny restaurant is great for budget travelers; take ordinary tapas, put them in a roll, add on the homemade *salsa picante,* and *voilà:* a cheap, hearty meal. No seats. Sandwiches €1-3, beer €1. Open daily 10am-3:30pm and 8pm-midnight. ❶

Churrasco, C. Romero, 16 (☎957 29 08 19; www.elchurrasco.com). As if an extensive menu of delicious specialties isn't enough, they also have a varied selection of rooms to match your every mood. The *Patio Limonero,* upstairs, is especially gorgeous. Main dishes €9-20. Open daily 1-4pm and 8pm-midnight. Closed Aug. AmEx/D/MC/V. ❸

Taberna Casa Salinas, Puerto de Almodóvar (☎957 29 08 46). Pepe Salinas has been running this place for over 38 years. Eschew the jam-packed bar and enjoy the mellow dining room or, if the weather is right, request a table on the romantic outdoor patio. Starters €4-7.20. Entrees €4.80-10. Open M-Sa 11:30am-4:30pm and 8:30pm-12:30am, Su 11:30am-4:30pm. Closed Aug. ❷

Sociedad de Plateros, C. San Francisco, 6 (☎957 47 00 42). A mainstay since 1872, this breezy place is great for late-night tapas. *Media raciones* and *raciones* €4-7. Open M-F 8am-4pm and 7:30pm-midnight, Sa 9am-4pm and 7:30pm-midnight. MC/V. ❶

El Caballo Rojo Restaurante, C. Cardenal Herrero, 28 (☎957 47 53 75). Though tapas (somewhat over-priced at up to €15) are better enjoyed in a more authentic *taberna* setting, the gorgeous restaurant upstairs with traditional favorites is definitely recommended for those seeking a more sophisticated meal. Fish and vegetarian options (€10-18). Open daily 1-4:30pm and 8:30pm-2am. MC/V. ❸

Taberna El Potro, C. Lineros, 2 (☎957 47 34 95). With its charming *terraza* on a semi-private plaza, El Potro is especially nice at night, and its extensive menu is slightly more vegetarian-friendly than the usual. Entrees €4-10. AmEx/D/MC/V. ❷

Mesón San Basilio, C. San Basilio, 19 (☎957 29 70 07). 2 floors surround a breezy patio. *Menú* M-F €7.50, Sa-Su €15. Entrees €6.50-14. Open daily 1-4pm and 8pm-midnight. AmEx/MC/V. ❷

Caroche Centro Cafetería, C. García Lovera, 7 (☎957 49 25 71). Don't let the address fool you—Caroche Centro is on C. Claudio Marcelo across from C. García Lovera. Lively ambience, a casual and attractive setting, and pleasant A/C. Perfect for breakfast (full *desayuno* for under €2). Open daily 7:30am-4am. AmEx/MC/V. ❷

 SIGHTS

▧ LA MEZQUITA

☎957 47 05 12. *Open Apr.-June M-Sa 10am-7:30pm, Su and holidays 2-7:30pm; July-Oct. daily 10am-7pm; Nov.-Mar. daily 10am-6pm. €6.50, under 10 free. Wheelchair-accessible. Last ticket sold 30min. before closing. Opens M-Sa 8:30am for mass starting at 9:30am; Su mass 11am, noon, and 1pm. Take advantage of the free admission M-Sa during mass. Strict silence is enforced; no groups.*

Built in 784 on the site of a Visigoth basilica, this architectural masterpiece is considered the most important Islamic monument in the Western world. Over the course of two centuries, La Mezquita was enlarged to cover an area the size of several city blocks with more than 850 columns, making it the largest mosque in the Islamic world at the time of its completion. Visitors enter through the **Patio de los Naranjos,** an arcaded courtyard featuring carefully spaced orange trees, palm trees, and fountains, where the dutiful performed their ablutions before prayer. The **Torre del Alminar** encloses remains of the minaret from which the *muezzin* called the faithful to prayer.

HISTORICAL HYDROTHERAPY

Water was key in medieval Muslim culture. It purified worshippers before prayer, it gave life and serenity to royal courtyards, and it was, in the form of Arab baths (or *hammam*), a means of washing one's burdens away in a pleasant social atmosphere.

Though most Arab baths were unfortunately abandoned, destroyed, or left to ruin after the *Reconquista,* many around the country have been restored and opened for public usage. The *hammam* of Córdoba is one of these, and it is certain to charm you with its gorgeous and rich, yet cozy, Moorish decor and its gracious service.

Like all traditional Arab baths, the structure suggests that you proceed from the dressing room to the cold room, and from there to the warm room, which gives access to the hot ones. You are, of course, free to experiment with temperature as your body sees fit.

Though this alone is an infinitely rewarding experience, opt for the full-body, scented-oil massage, and allow professionals to work happiness into your body. A tea room with music, pastries, and belly dancing awaits for a few extra euros.

Baños Árabes, Hammam, Medin Caliphal. C. Corregidor Luis de la Cerda, 51. ☎957 48 47 46. *Open daily 10am-midnight. Bath €15; bath and massage €22, with student ID €18.50. Reservations required.*

The grand, multiple entrances to the mosque were closed during its conversion to a Gothic cathedral, and entrance today is through the right corner of the facade. Beginning in the oldest part of the mosque, built under Abd Al-Rahman I, the multiple pillars carved from granite and marble are capped by characteristically striped Moorish arches of different heights.

La Mezquita's most elaborate additions—the dazzling **mihrab** (prayer niche) and the triple **maksourah** (caliph's niche)—were created in the 10th century. Historians to this day are stumped as to why the *mihrab* does not face Mecca. Muslim architects had highly precise methods of calculation, and such a "mistake" was unlikely. One theory holds that it symbolized separation from Baghdad, ruled by the rival Abbasid dynasty. Nevertheless, prayers continue in the traditional direction. The *mihrab* formerly housed a gilt copy of the Qur'an and remains covered in Kufic inscriptions reciting the 99 names of Allah. Holy Roman Emperor Constantine VII gave the caliphs the nearly 35 tons of intricate gold, pink, and blue marble Byzantine mosaics shimmering across the arches of the *mihrab*. To its left and right, panels glorify the new caliph of the Muslim world.

At the far end of the Mezquita lies the **Capilla Villaviciosa**, where caliphal vaulting appeared for the first time. Completed in 1371, it was the first Christian chapel to be built in the mosque, thus beginning the transition of La Mezquita into a place of Christian worship. In 1523, Bishop Alonso Manrique, an ally of Carlos V, proposed the construction of a cathedral in the center of the mosque. The town rallied violently against the idea, promising painful death to any worker who helped tear down La Mezquita. Nevertheless, a towering **crucero** (transept) and **coro** (choir stall) were eventually erected, incongruously planting a richly adorned Baroque cathedral amidst far more austere environs. Constructed over 200 years, it is possible to see the stylistic progression from Gothic to Renaissance to early Baroque in the ceiling and walls of the cathedral. The townspeople were less than pleased, and even Carlos I regretted the changes to La Mezquita, lamenting, "You have destroyed something unique to create something commonplace." Indeed, though the result is far from commonplace, it is almost humorously odd, as the Christian reforms struggle without much success to assert a forced rather than natural presence in this magical—and still clearly Islamic—place of worship.

IN AND AROUND THE JUDERÍA

A combined ticket for the Alcázar, Museo Taurino y de Arte Cordobés, and Museo Julio Romero is available at all 3 locations. €7.10, students €3.60. F free.

■ **ALCÁZAR.** Along the river on the left side of La Mezquita lies the Alcázar, whose walls enclose a garden with terraced flower beds, ponds, palm trees, and fountains. Built in 1328 during the *Reconquista*, the building was both a fortress and a residence for Alfonso XI. Fernando and Isabel bade Columbus farewell here, and from 1490 to 1821 it served as a headquarters for the Inquisition. The museum displays first-century Roman mosaics and a 3rd-century marble sarcophagus. Don't miss the Arab bath turned Counter-Reformation interrogation chamber in the basement. *Cordobeses* come to cool down in the splendid gardens. (☎957 42 01 51. *Open Tu-Sa 10am-2pm and 4:30-6:30pm, Su and holidays 9:30am-2:30pm. Closed M. €2, students €1; F free. Gardens open June-Sept. 8pm-midnight.)*

SINAGOGA. Built in 1315, the synagogue, where famed philosopher Maimonides once prayed, is a hollow remnant of Córdoba's once vibrant Jewish community. Adorned with carved Mozárabe patterns and Hebrew inscriptions, the walls of the small temple have been restored to much of their original intricacy, although little else has been preserved. The only other synagogues to survive the 1492 expulsion of the Jews are both in Toledo. (*C. Judíos, 20, just past the statue of Maimonides.* ☎957 20 29 28. *Open M-Sa 9:30am-2pm and 3:30-5:30pm, Su 9:30am-1:30pm. €0.30, EU citizens free.)*

MUSEO TAURINO Y DE ARTE CORDOBÉS. Get ready for a lot of bull. Dedicated to the history and lore of the bullfight, rooms contain uniforms, posters, and artifacts from decades of bullfighting in Spain. The main exhibit includes a replica of the tomb of Spain's most famous matador, the dashing Manolete, and the hide of the bull that killed him. *(Pl. Maimónides. ☎957 20 10 56. Open Tu-Sa 10:30am-2pm and 5:30-7:30pm, Su 9:30am-2pm. Last entrance 15min. before closing. €3, students €1.50; F free.)*

MUSEO DIOCESANO DE BELLAS ARTES. Home to Córdoba's bishops while the Inquisition raged within the Alcázar, this 17th-century ecclesiastical palace houses a modest collection of Renaissance and Baroque religious art. *(C. Torrijos, 12, across from the Mezquita in the Palacio de Congresos. ☎957 49 60 85. Open M-F 9:30am-1:30pm and 4-6pm, Sa 9:30am-1:30pm. €1.50, under 12 free.)*

OTHER SIGHTS. Townspeople take great pride in their traditional **patios,** many of which date from Roman times. These open-air courtyards, tranquil havens with orange and lemon trees, flowers, and fountains, flourish in the old quarter. Among the streets of exceptional beauty are **Calleja del Indiano,** off C. Fernández Ruano at Pl. Ángel Torres, and the aptly named **Calleja de Flores,** off C. Blanco Belmonte, where lustrous geraniums in full bloom cluster along the white walls of the alley. In Pl. Tiberiades, rub the toes of the statue of Maimonides to gain the knowledge of this 12th-century Jewish thinker and religious rationalist. The statue was used as the model for the face of the New Israeli Shekel. Farther past the statue is **Casa Andalusí,** a house restored to its 12th-century state. The tranquil home features mosaic floors, fountains, old Arabic texts and coins, a replica of a paper factory, and, in the basement, an ancient well. *(C. Judíos, 12, between the Sinagoga and the Puerta de Almodóvar. Open M-Sa 10:30am-7pm. €2.50.)*

OUTSIDE THE JUDERÍA

MUSEO JULIO ROMERO DE TORRES. Romero mastered the complications and subtleties of mixing a dark yet varied palette and applied this talent to renditions of sensual *cordobés* women in static poses. Among the works exhibited here in the artist's former home is the lauded *Naranjas y Limones* that has made it on to postcards and numerous hotel lobbies. *(Pl. Potro, 5-10min. from La Mezquita. ☎957 49 19 09. Open Tu-Sa 10am-2pm and 4:30-6:30pm, Su and holidays 9:30am-2:30pm. Last entrance 30min. before closing. €3, students €1.50. F free.*

MUSEO DE BELLAS ARTES. Across the courtyard from Museo Julio Romero de Torres, this museum now occupies a building that served as a hospital during the reign of Fernando and Isabel. It hosts a mildly unsettling collection of Renaissance religious art as well as works by more modern *cordobés* artists. *(Pl. Potro, 5-10min. from La Mezquita. ☎957 47 33 45. Open Tu 2:30-10:30pm, W-Sa 9am-10:30pm, Su and holidays 9am-2:30pm. Last entrance 20min. before closing. €1.50, EU citizens free.)*

PALACIO DEL MARQUÉS DE VIANA. An elegant 14th-century mansion, the palace displays 12 typical patios complete with sprawling gardens, majestic fountains, tapestries, furniture, and porcelain. *(Pl. Don Gome, 2, a 20min. walk from La Mezquita. ☎957 49 67 41. Open M-F 10am-1pm and 4-6pm, Sa 10am-1pm. Closed June 1-16. Complete tour €6, garden and courtyards only €3.)*

OTHER SIGHTS. Spanning the river near La Mezquita is the pedestrian **Puente Romano,** a restored Roman bridge. The bridge passes through a natural bird sanctuary on its way to the **Torre de la Calahorra,** a Muslim military tower built in 1369 to protect the Roman bridge. The tower now houses a museum that documents an inspirational history of the coexistence of religions in medieval Córdoba. *(Open daily 10am-2pm and 4:30-8:30pm. €4.20, includes audio tour; students €2.50.)* Near the Palacio del Marqués de Viana in Pl. Capuchinos (also known as Pl. de los Dolores) and next to a monastery is the **Cristo de los Faroles** (Christ of the Lanterns), one of the most famous religious icons in Spain and the site of frequent all-night vigils. The eight lanterns that are lit at night symbolize the eight provinces of Andalucía. Facing the Museo de Bellas Artes and the Museo Julio Romero de Torres is the **Posada del Potro,** a 14th-century inn mentioned in *Don Quixote.* Remnants of 2nd-century **Roman water wheels** line the sides of the Río Guadalquivir. Believed to have been originally used by Romans as mills, they were later used to bring water to the caliph's palace. The mills continued to function until Isabel la Católica demanded they be shut down—they disturbed her sleep.

🅡 NIGHTLIFE

Nightlife is almost non-existent in the old city, and hip bars and clubs tend to cluster together. Nearest to the old city, **Calle Alfonso XIII** and the adjacent **Calle Alfaros** host a number of popular nightlife spots. Farther away, the **Barrio Brillante** is also a hot spot, though its bars and clubs tend to open only on weekends. Bus #10 goes to Brillante from the train station until about 11pm, but the bars there do not wake up until at least 1am and stay open until 4am. A taxi should cost €3-6. If you're walking, get ready for a 45min. uphill hike. Relatively close to the Brillante, a more chic (and costly) ambience awaits on **Avenida Libertad,** with its palette of very different, all gorgeous, modern-looking pubs. Serious **disco** action is not easily accessible, as the better dance clubs are a distance away from the rest of the nightlife, in the **Polígono Chinales** (what locals refer to as "the industrial part of town"), a good 4-5km from the city center. *Cordobeses* recommend **Silion** and **Kenia.**

In the winter, nightlife tends to center around the neighborhood where the Universidad de Córdoba used to be, especially in pubs on **Calle Los Alderetes** and **Calle Julio Pellicer,** and near the **Plaza de la Corredera.**

While *cordobeses* and tourists groove together every weekend until the sun rises, the Sunday to Wednesday nightlife can be quite tame, as bars and clubs shut down around midnight—if they open at all. An alternative to partying is a nighttime (after 10pm) stroll along the **walk-through fountains** and falling sheets of water that line Av. de América between Pl. de Colón and the train station, to cool off from the heat, meet locals, or simply people-watch.

NEAREST TO THE OLD CITY

🅢 **Soul,** C. Alfonso XIII, 3 (☎957 49 15 80; www.bar-soul.com). A hip, chill bar loved by both locals and foreign students. Bartenders mingle with the crowd below a couch suspended from the ceiling. Reggae, drum and bass, house, and jazz music, with occasional themed nights. Beer €1.50-2.10, mixed drinks €3.60-4.20. Try the delectable Honey Rum. Open daily 9pm-3am, later on weekends.

Velvet, C. Alfaros, 29 (☎957 48 60 92). Hip, hippie, and retro; enjoy a drink under the shiny disco balls. Beer €1.50-2.40, mixed drinks €3.60-4.80. Open summer 10pm-5am; winter 5pm-4am. **Club Pequiño,** across the street, is also a local favorite.

EL BRILLANTE

These trendy pubs open Th-Sa at midnight and start closing at 4am.

La Torre, C. Poeta Emilio Prados. An outdoor nightclub with a vibrant young crowd that plays a mix of well-known Latin music and Spanish pop. Beer €1.50. Mixed drinks around €4. Across the street is **Cafetería Terra,** where locals converge before hitting Brillante's bars and clubs.

Club Don Luis, Av. El Brillante. Draws a university crowd that dances to Spanish pop. Young crowd, cheap beer (€2).

Club Kachamba, Av. El Brillante. The friendly staff at Kachamba makes it another entertaining stop on a tour of Av. El Brillante's popular nightclubs.

AVENIDA LIBERTAD

■ **Moma,** Av. Libertad, 4 (☎957 76 84 77). This ethnic-chic bar has African-styled stools, fake mosaic lampshades, and more couches than most of the nightlife spots in this happening neighborhood. Beer €2-2.50, mixed drinks from €5. Open Su-W 9am-3am, Th-Sa 9am-5am. AmEx/MC/V.

Rosso, Av. Libertad, 2. An R&B-playing ultra-modern club, Rosso features a glass platform above a pond, transparent tables, and outdoor seating. Beer €1.80-2, mixed drinks €4-5.50. Open M-W 9am-2am, Th-Sa 2pm-5am, Su 2pm-2am. AmEx/D/MC/V.

En Boga, Av. Libertad, 2 (☎957 08 25 55). With metallic walls featuring elongated, diagonal windows and a flatscreen TV, En Boga has a trendy but calm, lounge-like atmosphere. Beer €1.50-2, mixed drinks €5. Open daily 5:30pm-3am. AmEx/D/MC/V.

La Tercia, C. Llanos del Pretorio (☎957 47 46 75), adjacent to Av. Libertad. A casual atmosphere that is less dressy and expensive than its neighbors. Beer €1.50-2.80, mixed drinks €4-4.50. Open Su-W 8pm-3am, Th-Sa 8pm-4am.

🎵 ENTERTAINMENT

For the latest cultural events, pick up a free copy of the *Guía del Ocio* at the tourist office. Though flamenco is not cheap in Córdoba, the shows are high-quality and worth a visit for those not heading to Sevilla. Prize-winning dancers perform *flamenco puro* at **Tablao Cardenal,** C. Torrijos, 10, facing La Mezquita. Reserve seats there or at your hostel. (☎957 48 33 20. Shows M-Sa 10:30pm. €18, includes one drink.) A cheaper but equally entertaining option is **La Bulería,** C. Pedro López, 3, with nightly shows also at 10:30pm. (☎957 48 38 39. €11, includes 1 drink.)

🏛 DAYTRIP FROM CÓRDOBA

MADINAT AL-ZAHRA

Madinat al-Zahra can be hard to reach. Bus #3 (€0.90) will drop you off or pick you up 2½km from the site; from there it's an uphill hike. Alternatively, the bus station tourist office sells tickets for the Autobús Turístico (€5) that drops you off at the site and picks you up 1½hr. later, which gives you plenty of time to visit. The bus returns near La Mezquita.

Legend has it that Abd al-Rahman III built the city of Madinat al-Zahra for his favorite concubine, Zahra. Since Zahra pined for the snow-capped peaks of her hometown in Granada, the thoughtful Abd al-Rahman planted white-blossoming almond groves to substitute for the snow of the Sierra Nevada. Historians, on the other hand, tend to believe that Madinat al-Zahra (literally, the prosperous city) was built to demonstrate Abd al-Rahman III's power as the new caliph in al-Andalus. If so, it must have been an effective project, for this 10th-century medina was considered one of the greatest cities of its time before it was abandoned by Al-Mansur, sacked by Berbers, vandalized by locals, and buried by mountain silt. Construction began in 940, and the city was built rapidly out of the world's best materials; 10,000 people worked day and night to complete it within 50 years. The city had an equally short but exciting life; between 940 and 1010, it served as the seat of the *cordobés* caliphate, receiving ambassadors from Byzantium and Germany. It was constructed in three terraces (one for the nobility, another for servants, and a third for an enclosed garden and almond grove), and included roads, bridges, and aqueducts. Today, Madinat al-Zahra is in ruins, but with the help of reconstructions one can still get a sense of its past. Amazingly, only 10% of this impressive city has been unearthed so far, but its lessons on Moorish royal life and its maze-like structure make it a worthwile excursion from Córdoba. Placards in English and Spanish and an accompanying color pamphlet explain the history and major sites within the ruins. Don't miss the (mostly) reconstructed throne room or the world's largest archaeological jigsaw puzzle: millions of fragments from the intricate wall waiting to be reassembled by scholars. A complete tour of the ruins can take anywhere from 20min. to 1hr., depending on one's pace. (☎957 32 91 30. Open May to mid-Sept. Tu-Sa 10am-8:30pm, Su and holidays 10am-2pm; mid-Sept. to Apr. Tu-Su and holidays 10am-2pm. €1.50, EU citizens free.)

COSTA DE LA LUZ

Whereas much of Andalucía is the domain of foreign tourists seeking Moorish relics, miles of beaches, or wild nightlife, the Costa de la Luz remains a destination primarily for Spanish vacationers, looking for some fun in the sun. Beyond the sherry *bodegas* of Jerez de la Frontera, the region offers picture-perfect *pueblos blancos* (white towns) and untold opportunities to catch some wind or waves.

HUELVA   ☎959

This capital city of the Costa de la Luz offers little more than an industrial port; not much is appealing about Huelva (pop. 140,000) other than its proximity to the towns from which Columbus mustered men. Nevertheless, it is often a necessary stop en route to some of the region's more beautiful beaches, or on the backpacker pilgrimage to Lagos, and spending a night here can be relaxing.

TRANSPORTATION. RENFE trains on Av. de Italia (info ☎902 24 02 02, station 959 24 56 14) run to: **Córdoba** (2¼hr., 4:50pm, €29); **Madrid** (4¼hr., 4:50pm, €55); **Sevilla** (1½hr., 4 per day 7:15am-7pm, €6.40-15.50). **Buses** (☎959 25 69 00) depart from Av. Dr. Rubio to: **Cádiz** (5hr., 9:30am, €16.20); **Faro, Portugal** (2½hr., 9am and 6pm, €7); **Lagos, Portugal** (5hr., 9am and 6pm, €9); **Madrid** (7hr., 4 per day 9:45am-11:15pm, €19.20); **Málaga** (8am, €23.10); **Sevilla** (1hr.; M-Sa nearly every 30min. 6am-9pm, Su 21 per day 7am-9pm; €6.30).

ORIENTATION AND PRACTICAL INFORMATION. The central axis of the city is **Avenida Martín Alonso Pinzón** (Gran Vía). To reach it from the train station, go out the front door, cross the street, and go straight down C. Alonso XII, the street in front of you. From the bus station, exit across Av. Alemania. Take C. Gravina, turn left onto C. M. Núñez, then right onto C. Concepción. Follow C. Concepción for three blocks, then turn left. Av. Martín Alonso Pinzón is one block over. The **Junta de Andalucía tourist office,** Av. de Alemania, 12, across from the bus station and half a block to the right, has info on and maps of regional beaches and excursions. (☎959 25 74 03. English spoken. Open M-F 9am-7pm, Sa-Su 10am-2pm.) For **Internet access,** try **Cybercafe Interpool,** C. Vázquez Limón, 9. (☎959 80 24 78. €1 per 30min. Open M-F 10am-1am, Sa-Su 6pm-1am.) **Banco Santander Central Hispano** is at C. Palacios, 10. (☎902 24 24 24. Open M-F 8:30am-2pm, Sa 8:30am-1pm.)

ACCOMMODATIONS AND FOOD. Unless you're stuck waiting overnight for a bus or train, there's really no reason to spend the night in Huelva. If you do need somewhere to crash, look for cheap *hostales* clustered between the train station and Av. Martín Alonso Pinzón. A decent option is the somewhat out-of-the-way **Albergue Juvenil Huelva ❶,** Av. Marchena Colombo, 14, a good base for daytrips to nearby beaches. (Take city bus #6 from the central bus station; €0.95. ☎959 25 37 93. Up to 4 people per room. Breakfast included. Some wheelchair-accessible rooms. July-Aug. €14, 26 and over €18.20. Sept.-June €11.80/€16. €3.50 extra per day for non-members. AmEx/MC/V.) **Mercado de Carmen,** the town's market, is at the intersection of C. Barcelona, C. Carmen, and C. Duque de la Victoria; it sells fresh fish and produce daily 8am-2pm. Look for inexpensive restaurants and cafeterias in the center of town on the pedestrian streets, such as C. Concepción, C. Palacios, and C. Arq. Carasca.

JEREZ DE LA FRONTERA ☎956

Jerez de la Frontera (pop. 200,000) is the cradle of three staples of Andalusian culture: flamenco, Carthusian horses, and, of course, *jerez* (sherry). It is the sheer quantity and quality of this third staple that draws in the tourists, most of whom are older, well-to-do Europeans. The city also makes a good departure point for the *ruta de los pueblos blancos*, but those not particularly interested in *bodega* tours or horse shows would be better off spending their time elsewhere.

⌐ TRANSPORTATION

Flights: Airport, Ctra. Jerez-Sevilla (☎956 15 00 00), 7km from town. Taxi to the airport approximately €12. **Iberia** (☎956 18 43 94) has an office at the terminal.

Trains: Pl. de la Estación (☎956 34 23 19). **RENFE,** C. Larga, 34 (☎902 24 02 02). To: **Barcelona** (12hr., 8:36am and 9pm, €73); **Cádiz** (45min., every 30min. 6:45am-10:15pm, €3.10); **Madrid** (4½hr., 8:36am, €53.50); **Sevilla** (1¼hr., 12 per day 6:34am-9:40pm, €6).

Buses: C. Cartuja (☎956 34 52 07), at the corner of C. Madre de Dios.

Transportes Los Amarillos (☎956 32 93 47) to **Arcos de la Frontera** (30min.; M-F 16 per day 7:15am-9pm, Sa 4 per day 9am-8:15pm, Su 3 per day 9am-7:30pm; €2.10) and **Córdoba** (2¾hr., M-F 5pm, €13.50).

Transportes Generales Comes (☎956 34 21 74) to: **Cádiz** (50min.; M-F 16 per day 7am-9pm, Sa-Su 4 per day 9am-4:30pm; €2.50); **Granada** (4½hr., 1pm, €22.50); **Ronda** (2½hr., 3 per day 7:45am-3:30pm, €9.20); **Sevilla** (1½hr.; M-F 6 per day 9am-9pm, Sa-Su 5 per day 11am-9pm; €6).

Linesur (☎956 34 10 63) to: **Algeciras** (1¾hr., 7 per day 7:15am-10pm, €7.60); **Sanlúcar** (45min.; M-F every hr. 7am-10pm, Sa-Su every 2hr.; €1.50); **Sevilla** (1¼hr., 11 per day 6:30am-11pm, €5.80).

Secorbus (☎902 22 92 92) to **Madrid** (7hr., 6 per day 8:10am-11:10pm, €21.60).

Local Transportation: Each of the 12 **bus** lines runs every 15min. (less frequently at night). Most pass through Pl. del Arenal or next to Pl. Romero Martínez. €0.90. **Info office** (☎956 34 34 46) in Pl. del Arenal.

Car Rental: Niza, Ctra. N-IV Madrid-Cádiz, km 634 (☎956 30 28 60). Take Av. Alcalde Álvaro Domecq to highway N-IV toward Sevilla. 21+ and must have had license for at least 1yr. From €58 per day. Open daily 8:30am-1pm and 4:30-8pm.

▓▐ ORIENTATION AND PRACTICAL INFORMATION

The labyrinthine streets of Jerez are difficult to navigate without a map. Get one free from the tourist office at Pl. del Arenal or buy one at any bookstore or newsstand (€2.60). **Plaza Romero Martínez** is the city's commercial center; from there, walk left on C. Cerrón to reach C. Santa María and C. Lancería, heading into **Plaza del Arenal** and the **tourist office. Calle Lancería/Calle Larga** is the main pedestrian thoroughfare in the center of the city.

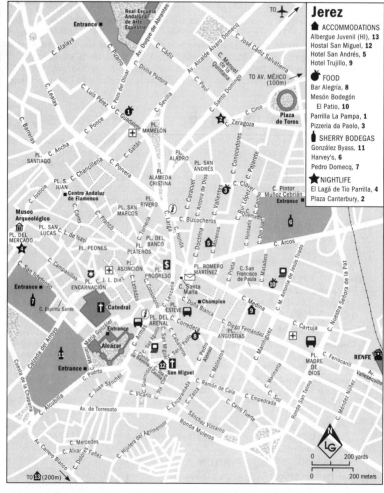

Jerez

▲ ACCOMMODATIONS
Albergue Juvenil (HI), **13**
Hostal San Miguel, **12**
Hotel San Andrés, **5**
Hotel Trujillo, **9**

🍴 FOOD
Bar Alegría, **8**
Mesón Bodegón
El Patio, **10**
Parrilla La Pampa, **1**
Pizzeria da Paolo, **3**

🍶 SHERRY BODEGAS
González Byass, **11**
Harvey's, **6**
Pedro Domecq, **7**

★ NIGHTLIFE
El Lagá de Tío Parrilla, **4**
Plaza Canterbury, **2**

Tourist Office: Pl. del Arenal (☎956 35 96 54). English-speaking staff has free maps and info on sherry production, *bodega* tours, and horse shows. Open June-Sept. M-F 10am-3pm and 5-7pm, Sa-Su 9:30am-2pm; Oct.-May M-F 9am-2:30pm and 4:30-6:30pm, Sa-Su 9am-2pm. This office may be closed due to construction work in Pl. del Arenal; consult the **municipal office** on Pl. Alameda Cristina (☎956 33 11 62). Open M-F 10am-3pm and 5-7pm, Sa-Su 9:30am-2:30pm.

Currency Exchange: Banco Santander Central Hispano, C. Larga, 11 (☎902 24 24 24). Open M-F 8:30am-1:30pm.

Police: ☎091 or 956 33 03 46.

Medical Assistance: Ambulatorio de la Seguridad Social, C. José Luis Díez (☎956 32 32 02).

Internet Access: Locutorio Jerez, C. San Agustín, 15. €1.60 per hr. Open M-Sa 11am-11pm, Su 4-11pm. **The Big Orange,** C. Antonia de Jesús Tirado (☎956 35 01 01), near the bus station. €1.80 per hr. Open Su-Th 11am-1am, F-Sa 11am-3am.

Post Office: C. Cerrón, 2 (☎956 34 22 95). Open M-F 8:30am-8:30pm, Sa 9am-2pm. **Lista de Correos** open M-Sa 9am-2pm. **Postal Code:** 11480.

ACCOMMODATIONS

Finding a place to crash in Jerez is as easy as finding a cork to sniff, though accommodations, like wine, don't come cheap. Prices increase during Jerez's festivals in September and October.

Hostal San Miguel, Pl. San Miguel, 4 (☎/fax 956 34 85 62). Elegant double doors open up to pleasant, spacious rooms, all with A/C and TV. Ask for one with a balcony for views of the church; others face inside. Singles €20, with bath €30; doubles €35/€40; triples €50/€55. AmEx/MC/V. ❷

Hotel/Hostal San Andrés, C. Morenos, 14 and 2 (☎956 34 09 83; fax 34 31 96). The *hostal* consists of simple, down-to-earth rooms surrounding 2 lively, leafy courtyards; more comfort for a minimal price difference can be found at the adjacent hotel, where rooms have private baths, A/C, and TV, but a less adventurous feel. *Hostal* singles €20; doubles €28. Hotel €24/€38. ❷

Hotel Trujillo, C. Medina, 38 (☎956 34 24 38). Definitely a step up from the usual pension or hostel—rooms have marble floors, mosaic-walled private baths, phones, and TVs; 2nd- and 3rd-floor rooms have A/C. Parking €6 per day. Singles €20-50; doubles €40-75. Prices depend on month and bathroom facilities; call ahead. MC/V. ❷

Albergue Juvenil (HI), Av. Carrero Blanco, 30 (☎956 14 39 01; fax 14 32 63), a 25min. walk or 10min. bus ride from downtown; 5min. cab ride from the bus and train stations. Bus #1 runs to Pl. del Arenal; #9 goes to the bus station. Clean, sunny doubles, a pool, tennis and basketball courts, small soccer field, TV room, and rooftop terrace. Breakfast €1.40, other meals €5. Towels €1.10. Laundry €2.40. Reservations strongly recommended. June-Sept. dorms €11.70, over 26 €16.20. Oct.-May €9.10/€12.30. ❶

FOOD

Tapas-hoppers bounce around Pl. del Arenal, C. Larga, and around Pl. del Banco in the old town; food in Jerez is rarely cheap. For groceries, head to **Champion,** C. Doña Blanca, a few blocks from Pl. Romero Martínez (open M-Sa 9am-10pm).

Parilla La Pampa, C. Guadalete, 24 (☎956 34 17 49), near Pl. Mamelón. Although you can get all kinds of meat from pork (€5.50-9) to chicken (€5.90-6.90), veal (€3.40-9.40), and ostrich (€16.20-17.70), the real specialty is authentic Argentine beef (€8.80-19.70), straight from the source. Soft rock and pictures of the *pampas* make the experience anything but plain. Open M-Sa 12:30-4:30pm and 7:30-11:30pm. ❹

Mesón Bodegón El Patio, C. San Francisco de Paula, 7 (☎956 34 07 36). Savor sumptuous traditional fare on tables made from barrels in a dining room filled with antiques, bear heads, and deer antlers. *Raciones* €4.30-18. Open M-Sa 11:30-4:30pm and 8pm-12:30am. MC/V. ❷

Bar Alegría, C. Corredera, 30 (☎956 33 80 70), 3 blocks from Pl. del Arenal. One of the more authentic bars, low on tourists and high on hospitality. Great *croquettas de pollo* (chicken croquettes; €2). Tapas €1.50, *raciones* €6. Open daily 7:30am-midnight. ❶

THE LOCAL STORY

LIQUOR FOR LINGUISTS

The Islamic prohibition against consumption of alcohol did not prevent Jerez's Moorish merchants from exporting wine to the infidel English in the 12th-century. "Sherry," an anglicization of Shir-az, the Arabic name for Jerez, is a legacy of this early commerce.

Today, only wines produced in Jerez, Sanlúcar de Barrameda, and Puerto de Santa María are considered sherries. There is no vintage sherry; wines from various years are continuously combined in what is known as the *solera* process. A different process—placing burnt distilled wine in old sherry casks—eventually results in cognac. Unable to use the term for the same reason that wineries in other regions cannot call their products sherry, Jerez's merchants have settled with "brandy," another English bastardization, this time of the Dutch word "brandewyn," meaning "burnt wine."

Impress your friends at dinner parties by knowing the major sherry types: *Fino:* A dry, light colored sherry served chilled and sipped with tapas popular in Andalucía. *Manzanilla,* a type of *fino* from Sanlúcar de Barrameda, is slightly salty. *Amontillado:* Somewhat sweeter and amber in color. Excellent with cheese. *Oloroso dulce:* A dessert wine, dark in color, with a raisin-like taste. Go ahead, be pretentious. You know you want to.

Pizzeria da Paolo, C. Clavel at C. Valientes. Like a semi-fancy Italian restaurant, only affordable. Great pizzas (€4.80-7.50) and pastas (€4.50-7.50). Plenty of vegetarian options. Open Tu-Su 1:15-4pm and 8:45pm-midnight. MC/V. ●

⚡ SHERRY BODEGAS

People come to Jerez for the *jerez*, and *bodegas* have a story and mood all their own. Multilingual tour guides proudly explain the city's trademark sherry-making process, leading you in and out of heavenly-smelling barrel storage rooms. Tours are topped off with (lots of) free samples. The best time to visit is early September during the harvest; the worst is August, when many *bodegas* close down (waiting for the grapes to ripen). Group reservations for tours must be made at least one week in advance; reservations for individuals are usually unnecessary. Call ahead for exact times. Looking for a job? Many *bodegas* hire and train English-speaking tour guides for as few as two or three months (even if you're not a wino), depending on need. Call to inquire—a summer of sherry could be in your future.

Pedro Domecq, C. San Ildefonso, 3 (☎956 15 15 00; www.domecq.es). Founded in 1730, Domecq is the oldest and most prestigious *bodega* in town. 1½hr. tours include an informative 20min. video followed by a guided stroll through the numerous rooms and gardens of the sprawling complex. Unlimited sampling of 3 sherries and 2 brandies. Tours every hr. M-F 10am-1pm. €5. AmEx/MC/V.

González Byass, C. Manuel María González, 12 (☎956 35 70 16; www.gonzalezbyass.es). The makers of the popular Tío Pepe brand seen all over the city. The Disneyworld of *bodegas:* uncomfortably commercial and definitely overblown, but worth visiting and very kid-friendly. Yellow trolleys whisk visitors past the world's largest weathervane and a storage room designed by Gustave Eiffel. At the end of the tour, a trained mouse climbs a miniature ladder to sip a glass of *oloroso.* Check out the rows upon rows of celebrity- and politician-autographed wine barrels—Steven Spielberg, Margaret Thatcher, and Orson Welles, among others. June-Sept. tours in English M-Sa every hr. 11:30am-1:30pm and 4:30-6:30pm; in Spanish M-Sa every hr. 11am-2pm and 5-7pm, Su 11am-1pm. Oct.-May tours in English M-Sa every hr. 11:30am-5:30pm, Su 11:30am-1:30pm; in Spanish M-Sa every hr. 11am-6pm, Su 11am-1pm. €8, 2pm tour with light tapas €11.50. AmEx/MC/V.

Harvey's, C. Arcos, 57 (☎956 34 60 04; www.jerezharveys.es). Makers of Harvey's Cream, the best-selling sherry in the world. Visit includes a video of the production process and a tour featuring peacocks, countless oak barrels, and a crocodile. 1½hr. tours M-F 10am and noon (€5), Sa noon (€7). MC/V.

☉ SIGHTS

▓**ALCÁZAR.** Seized by Christian knights under Alfonso X during the *Reconquista* in 1255, the Alcázar has changed slowly over the centuries. During the 1300s, the Moorish governor's private mosque was transformed into a chapel to commemorate the intercession of the Virgin Mary on behalf of Christian raids into the Kingdom of Granada. Later, in the 17th century, the neighboring Arab baths became servants' quarters for the Palacio de Villavicencio, where the Cámara Oscura resides today. Designed along a model by Leonardo Da Vinci, it uses reflective lenses to project panoramas of the city. *(☎956 31 97 98. Open May-Sept. 15 M-Sa 10am-8pm, Su 10am-3pm; Sept. 16-Apr. daily 10am-6pm. Alcázar only €1.40, students €0.65; Alcázar and Cámara Oscura €3.40, students €2.70.)*

REAL ESCUELA ANDALUZA DE ARTE EQUESTRE. Jerez's love for wine is almost matched by its passion for horses. During the first or second week of May, the Royal Andalusian School of Equestrian Art sponsors the Feria del Caballo—a horse fair with shows, carriage competitions, and races of Jerez-bred Carthusian horses. During the rest of the year, weekly shows feature a troupe of horses dancing in choreographed sequences. The training sessions are almost as impressive. The new, interactive **Museo del Enganche** (Harness Museum), on the school grounds, displays old-fashioned carriages led by specially trained horses. *(Av. Duque de Abrantes. ☎956 31 80 08; www.realescuela.org. Training sessions M and W 10am-12:30pm, July-Sept. also F. €6. Shows Th noon; Aug. also F noon. €13-21, depending on seat; children and seniors 40% off. Museum and training session €7, museum only €3. MC/V.)*

🎵 🎭 ENTERTAINMENT AND NIGHTLIFE

Rare footage of Spain's most highly regarded **flamenco** singers, dancers, and guitarists is available for viewing at the **Centro Andaluz de Flamenco,** in Palacio Pemartín, on Pl. San Juan. The library upstairs has lots of information on flamenco in the city and region. (☎956 34 92 65; www.caf.cica.es. Open M-F 9am-2pm. Videos every hr. 10am-2pm. Free.) Most *peñas* and *tablaos* (clubs and bars that host flamenco) are in the old town and host special performances in July and August. Ask for details in the tourist office or look for posters along the main streets; occasionally there are free evening performances in some plazas. For more frequent (and touristy) shows, make the trek to **El Lagá de Tío Parrilla,** Pl. del Mercado, which hosts some of Jerez's best flamenco. (☎/fax 956 33 83 34. Shows M-Sa 10:30pm and 12:30am. Reservations recommended. Cover €12, includes 1 drink.)

Visitors to Jerez tend to be on the older side, and nightlife in the city center caters directly to them—there are plenty of tapas bars where you can knock back a few glasses of sherry, but to get to the more lively, younger scene, head to the outskirts of the city. Although certainly not authentically Spanish (and more alive in winter) the Irish-themed bar and disco complex **Plaza Canterbury,** C. Nuño, is a hot spot for tourists and students alike, with two bars (**O'Donoghue's** and **Gambrinus,** the latter serving tapas), an outdoor patio, and a popular club. (Beer at bars €1.25-1.80, mixed drinks €3.50-5; at club €2.50/€5. Cover at club €8. Gambrinus Bar open M-Sa 9am-1:30pm, Su 4pm-1:30am. O'Donoghue's open daily 6pm-6am. Club open F-Sa 1:30-7am.) A slew of bars and clubs lines the well-lit **Avenida Méjico**

ANDALUCÍA

between C. Santo Domingo and C. Salvatierra, as well as some of the side streets (a 25min. walk from Pl. del Arenal). Bars and pubs also cluster on the lively **Avenida Lola Flores** (near the fútbol stadium).

Autumn, in addition to being grape harvest season, is festival season, when Jerez showcases its best equine and flamenco traditions. These festivals are collectively known as the **Fiestas de Otoño,** occurring from early September until the end of October. In September, the **Fiesta de la Bulería** and the **Festival de Teatro, Música, y Baile** celebrate flamenco. The largest **horse parade** in the world, with races in Pl. del Arenal, is the highlight of the final week. Check at the tourist office for details; schedules are available in September for the upcoming year.

SANLÚCAR DE BARRAMEDA ☎956

Sanlúcar de Barrameda (pop. 62,000), at the mouth of the Río Guadalquivir, borders both the Parque Nacional Coto de Doñana and a variety of relatively uncrowded beaches. Visitors come to Sanlúcar mostly to get a taste of southern Spain's sherry *bodegas*, fine sands, and *cascos antiguos* without all the tourists of nearby Jerez and Cádiz. This seaside corner of the illustrious "sherry triangle," along with Jerez and El Puerto de Santa María, makes for a good weekend getaway, but there's not enough to entertain visitors for much longer.

TRANSPORTATION. The bus station is on Av. de la Estación, one block from the main Calzada del Ejército. **Transportes Los Amarillos** (☎956 38 50 60) runs **buses** to **Cádiz** (1hr., 5-9 per day 6:15am-8.20pm, €2.80); **Sevilla** (2hr., 6-12 per day 6:45am-8:15pm, €6.50). **Linesur** (☎956 34 10 63) goes to **Jerez** (45min.; M-F every hr. 7:20am-10:20pm, Sa-Su every 2hr.; €1.50). Buy tickets on the bus. For **taxis,** call ☎956 36 11 02 or 36 00 04.

ORIENTATION AND PRACTICAL INFORMATION. The **tourist office** is in a Moorish-looking building on Calzada del Ejército, which runs perpendicular to the beach. English-speaking staff has info on the Parque Nacional Coto de Doñana. (☎956 36 61 10. Open daily June-Aug. 10am-2pm and 6-8pm; Sept.-May 10am-2pm and 4-6pm.) To hit the beach from the bus station, exit from the stairs facing the supermarket and turn left; turn left again at the intersection. For the historic center and tourist office, turn right at the intersection. Local services include: **Ambulatorio de la S.S.** on Calzada del Ejército (☎956 36 71 65); **police,** Av. de la Constitución (☎956 38 80 11); **Internet** access at **Cyber Guadalquivir,** C. Infanta Beatriz, 11 (€1.80 per hr.; open daily 10am-1am); **post office,** C. Correos and Av. Cerro Falcón, toward the beach from the tourist office (☎956 36 09 37; open M-F 8:30am-2:30pm, Sa 9am-1pm). **Postal Code:** 11540.

ACCOMMODATIONS AND FOOD. Few true bargains exist in Sanlúcar; it may be worthwhile to inquire at doorway signs reading *"se alquilan habitaciones"* (rooms for rent). **Hostal La Blanca Paloma ❷,** Pl. San Roque, 15, keeps clean rooms of varying sizes, a few with balconies. (☎956 36 36 44. Singles €15; doubles €27; triples €39.) Sanlúcar is famous for its *langostinos* (crawfish). For a sit-down meal, head for the side streets off C. San Juan or uphill into the *casco antiguo*. *Terrazas* fill Pl. San Roque and Pl. del Cabildo, its tree-lined neighbor. Find relief from the heat and make the summer even sweeter at **Helados Artesanos Toni ❶,** Pl. del Cabildo, 2, established in 1896, where women in flashy pink dresses scoop up endless varieties of the best ice cream in town. (☎956 36 22 13. Small cone €1, large €2. Banana split €4.20. Shakes €2. Open daily 11am-2am.)

⚙ ♫ SIGHTS AND ENTERTAINMENT. Two impressive palaces compete for the attention of sun-struck tourists with the enormous 14th-century **Iglesia de Nuestra Señora de la O,** Pl. de la Paz. (☎956 36 05 55. Open Tu-Sa 10am-1pm, Su 10am-noon. Free.) Sanlúcar has put its historic buildings to good use; most are still inhabited or have been transformed into offices. The **Palacio Medina Sidonia,** Pl. Condes de Niebla, is still the home of the Duque de Medina Sidonia. (☎956 36 01 61. Open Su 10:30am-1:30pm. Free.) The 19th-century **Palacio de Orleáns y Borbón,** C. Cuesta de Belén, now houses the Ayuntamiento. (☎956 38 80 00. Open M-F 10am-1:30pm. Free.) Sanlúcar's sandy **beaches** stretch for 6km from the mouth of the Río Guadalquivir toward the open Atlantic. At low tide, sandbars make it possible to walk halfway out into the river. Several **bodegas** tower over Sanlúcar's small streets; check at the tourist office for their schedules. (Tours M-Sa, call for exact times. €1.80-3.) Locals celebrate their sherry during the **Feria de la Manzanilla** (late May or early June). In August, the ⚑**Carreras de Caballos** (horse races) thunder along the beach, and the **Festival de la Exaltación del Río Guadalquivir** brings poetry readings, a flamenco competition, dancing, and bullfights.

ARCOS DE LA FRONTERA ☎956

Arcos de la Frontera has been described as one of the most perfect towns in Spain Its whitewashed houses sit on a narrow ridge overlooking a silent, murky river that courses through the outlying fields. One of several peaceful beauties in Spain's collection of *pueblos blancos,* Arcos (pop. 33,000) is an historical and romantic gem. The various plazas and churches, huddled in convoluted medieval streets flush with geraniums, make it an attractive, restful locale. As with other *pueblos blancos,* however, it is not meant for the restless, and a couple of days here will probably be more than enough.

▬ TRANSPORTATION

Buses: Station on C. Corregidores. **Los Amarillos** (☎956 70 49 77) runs buses to **Jerez** (30min.; M-F 19 per day 7:15am-8:15pm, Sa-Su 8 per day 8am-6:30pm; €2.20) and **Sevilla** (2hr., 7am and 5pm, €6.30). **Transportes Generales Comes** to: **Cádiz** (1½hr., 6 per day 7:20am-7:15pm, €4.80); **Costa del Sol** (3-4hr., 4pm, €10-12.80); **Ronda** (1¾hr., 3 per day 8:15am-3:45pm, €6).

Taxis: Cluster around C. Debajo del Corral. **Radio Taxi** (24hr. ☎956 70 13 55).

THE BIG SPLURGE

FINE-FEATHERED FRIENDS

Bust out your binoculars—the 60,000 acre **Parque Nacional Coto de Doñana** on the Río Guadalquivir delta is home to flamingos, vultures, mongeese, wild boars, and lynx. If ornithological delights don't entice you, the salt marshes, sand dunes, wooded areas, and beach might. Nature purists beware, though, lest you stumble upon the lair of the dreaded species *turgrupus touristicus*—the park borders Matalascañas, with a concrete shopping center and hotel complex.

Access to most of the park is restricted, and back-country hiking and camping are prohibited. The park can be visited only on a guided tour. Call the Visitor's Center ☎956 38 16 35. Open daily June-Aug. 9am-8pm; Sept.-May 9am-2:30pm and 4-7pm. 4hr. guided tours daily 8:30am and 5pm, €9.50.

The western end of the park is accessible from Huelva and Matalascañas. Boat tours on the S.S. Real Fernando depart from Sanlúcar. ☎956 36 38 13. 4hr.; daily June.-Sept. 10am and 5pm; Apr., May, and Oct. 10am and 4pm; Nov.-Mar. 10am; €14.64. Call or visit the office in the old ice factory by the dock on Av. Bajo de Guía. Those more interested in sand than life on the wild side can take the launch across the bay (8am-8pm, leaves when full, €3) to one of the few non-touristed beaches in Spain.

■ ☀ ❼ ORIENTATION AND PRACTICAL INFORMATION

To reach the town center from the bus station, exit left, follow the road, and turn left again. Continue uphill for two blocks on C. Josefa Moreno Seguro, taking a right onto C. Muñoz Vázquez. From there it's a 20min. walk uphill. Continue until reaching Pl. de España, then veer left onto C. Debajo del Coral, which quickly changes into C. Corredera; the old quarter is 500m ahead. Mini-buses run every 30min. from the bus station to C. Corredera (€0.90). A taxi costs around €3.

Tourist Office: Pl. del Cabildo (☎956 70 22 64). Runs **tours** of the old city M-F 10:30am and 5pm, Sa 10:30am. €5, children free. Open Mar. 15-Oct. 15 M-Sa 10am-2pm and 4-8pm; Oct. 16-Mar. 14 M-Sa 10am-2pm and 3:30-7:30pm.

Bank: Banco Santander Central Hispano, C. Corredera, 62 (☎902 24 24 24). Open M-F 8:30am-2pm, Sa 8:30am-1pm.

Police: Av. Miguel Mancheño (☎956 70 16 52).

Medical Emergency: ☎061 or 956 51 15 53. **Hospital: Centro de Salud,** C. Rafael Benat Rubio (☎956 70 0787), in the Barrio Bajo.

Pharmacy: Ldo. Ildefonso Guerrero Seijo, C. Corredera, 11 (☎956 70 02 13). Open Apr.-Sept. M-F 9:30am-1:30pm and 5-9pm; Oct.-Mar. M-F 9:30am-1:30pm and 4:30-8pm, Sa 9:30am-1:30pm.

Post Office: C. Murete, 24 (☎956 70 15 60), overlooking the cliffs and the river. Open M-F 8:30am-2:30pm, Sa 9:30am-1pm. **Postal Code:** 11630.

▐ ACCOMMODATIONS

Arcos has few budget hostels, although for a couple euros more, you can often get a room at one of the classier hotels in town. Call ahead during *Semana Santa* and in the summer to be safe.

Pensión Callejon de las Monjas, C. Deán Espinosa, 4 (☎956 70 23 02), shaded by the buttresses of Iglesia de Sta. María. Restaurant and barbershop on the ground floor. Spotless, cheerful rooms, some with TV, bath, and A/C. Singles €20, with bath €25; doubles €30/€35, with large terrace €40; 4-person suite €66. MC/V. ❷

Hostal San Marcos, C. Marqués de Torresoto, 6 (☎956 70 07 21), past C. Deán Espinosa and Pl. del Cabildo. Ascend the steep, tiled stairs to quiet and colorful rooms, all with large private baths, some with A/C and TV. Restaurant below serves one of the cheapest *menús* in town (€6). Prices depend on room and season. Singles €20-25; doubles €30-36; triples €45. AmEx/MC/V. ❷

Hotel La Fonda, C. Corredera, 83 (☎956 70 00 57; fax 70 36 61). Originally a 19th-century inn, La Fonda retains its old-time charm. Wide, plushly carpeted hallways lead to large rooms with balconies, some with terraces. Breakfast included. Singles €30; doubles €45. Prices lower in winter. AmEx/MC/V. ❸

▟ FOOD

Cheap cafes and restaurants huddle at the bottom end of C. Corredera, while tapas nirvana can be reached uphill in the old quarter.

Los Faraones, C. Debajo del Corral, 8 (☎956 70 06 12), downhill from C. Corredera. Replace bull's head trophies with Pharaoh busts for a break from *comida típica* with a taste of hearty Egyptian cuisine. Extensive vegetarian *menú* €11, regular meaty *menú* €9, *platos combinados* €6. Open Tu-Su 9am-5:30pm and 8pm-midnight. ❸

Restaurante El Convento, C. Marqués de Torresoto, 7 (☎956 70 41 28). Rabbit, partridge, duck, and deer served in a 17th-century setting. Appetizers €4-12, entrees €7-15. Open daily 1-4pm and 7:30-10:30pm. Closed first 2 weeks of July. AmEx/MC/V. ❸

Mesón Los Murales, Pl. Boticas, 1 (☎956 70 06 07). Enjoy delicious *comida típica* in the blue-and-white-decorated interior or on the peaceful plaza outside. Great homemade flan (€2.40). Entrees €4.80-8.40. *Menú* €7.50. Open daily 9am-11pm. ❷

ANDALUCÍA

📷 🌸 SIGHTS AND FESTIVALS

The most beautiful sights in Arcos are the winding white alleys, Roman ruins, and hanging flowers of the old quarter, combined with the view from the ◪**Plaza del Cabildo.** The balcony, overlooking the entire region, earned the nickname *Balcón de Coño* because the view is so startling that people often exclaim *¡Coño!* (an expletive) in disbelief. In this square is the **Basílica de Santa María de la Asunción,** a blend of Baroque, Renaissance, and Gothic styles built between the 15th and 18th centuries. A symbol of the Inquisition—a circular design within which exorcisms were once performed—is still etched into the ground on the church's left side. (Open M-F 10am-1pm and 3:30-6:30pm, Sa 10am-2pm. €1.50.) The late Gothic **Iglesia de San Pedro** stands on the site of an Arab fortress in the old quarter. A collection of religious paintings by Murillo, Zurbarán, and Ribera decorates the interior. (Open M-Su 10am-1:30pm. €1. Mass winter 11:30am. Free.) An artificial **lake** built in 1960 laps at Arcos's feet; although you can't swim in the lake itself, the beach, **Mesón de la Molinera,** is a pretty change of scenery and a popular spot for a *paseo.* Buses run there from Arcos (M-Sa 5 per day 9:15am-8:15pm, Su 2-4 per day 12:15-8:15pm; €0.85). **Festivals** are highly spirited and quite popular; book accommodations far in advance. A favorite is the **Toro de Aleluya,** on Easter: two bulls run rampant through the steep streets amidst flamenco, drinking, and general merriment.

CÁDIZ ☎956

Located on a peninsula, Cádiz (pop. 155,000) has a powerful ocean on one side and a placid bay on the other. Despite this, one can wander through the narrow streets of the old town, strolling from plaza to plaza between soaring churches and outdoor cafes, without realizing the city is surrounded by water. Cádiz is both a thriving metropolis and a touristed beach town. Founded by the Phoenicians in 1100 BC, Cádiz is thought to be the oldest inhabited city in Europe. From the 16th to the 18th century, the Spanish colonial shipping industry transformed the port into one of the wealthiest in Europe. The city is renowned for its extravagant *Carnaval,* the only festival of its size and kind not suppressed during the Franco regime. Perhaps Spain's most dazzling party, *Carnaval* makes Cádiz an essential stop on February itineraries. During the rest of the year, Cádiz offers visitors a little of everything—a thoroughly Spanish city trimmed by ribbons of golden sand.

▤ TRANSPORTATION

Trains: RENFE, Pl. de Sevilla (☎956 25 43 01). To: **Barcelona** (12hr., 8am and 8:25pm, €73); **Córdoba** (3hr., 4 per day 8am-8:25pm, €15.50); **Jerez** (40min., 15-21 per day 6:36am-10:06pm, €3.10); **Madrid** (5hr., 8am, €55-85); **Sevilla** (2hr., 12 per day 5:55am-7:57pm, €8.50-20).

Buses: Several private companies operate out of small stations in Cádiz.

Secorbus (☎902 22 92 92) depart from near Estadio Ramón de Carranza, past Glorieta Ingeniero La Cierva in New Cádiz. To **Madrid** (8hr., 6 per day 8:10am-11:10pm, €21.10).

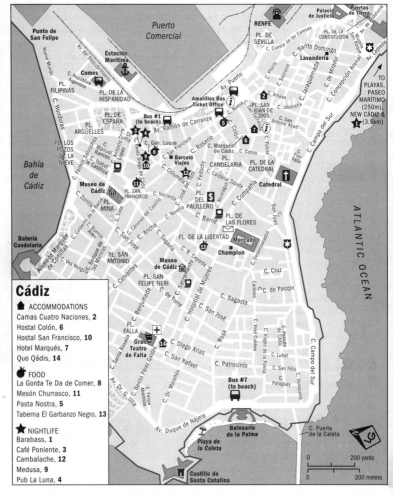

Cádiz

ACCOMMODATIONS
Camas Cuatro Naciones, **2**
Hostal Colón, **6**
Hostal San Francisco, **10**
Hotel Marqués, **7**
Quo Qádis, **14**

FOOD
La Gorda Te Da de Comer, **8**
Mesón Churrasco, **11**
Pasta Nostra, **5**
Taberna El Garbanzo Negro, **13**

NIGHTLIFE
Barabass, **1**
Café Poniente, **3**
Cambalache, **12**
Medusa, **9**
Pub La Luna, **4**

Transportes Generales Comes, Pl. de la Hispanidad, 1 (☎956 22 78 11). To: **Algeciras** (3hr., 10 per day 6:45am-8pm, €9); **Córdoba** (5hr., 7am and 3:45pm, €18); **Arcos de la Frontera** (1½hr., 6 per day 7am-6:30pm, €5); **Granada** (5hr., 4 per day 2:30am-11pm, €25); **Jerez de la Frontera** (45min., 24 per day 6am-9pm, €3); **La Línea** (3hr., 3 per day 11:30am-5pm, €10.40); **Málaga** (4hr., 6 per day 6:45am-8pm, €19); **Ronda** (3hr., 7am and 2:30pm, €12); **Sevilla** (2hr., 14 per day 7am-9pm, €10); **Vejer de la Frontera** (1½hr., 11 per day 9am-9:15pm, €4).

Transportes Los Amarillos (☎956 28 58 52) depart from beside the port in front of Po. de Canalejas. Purchase tickets on buses or at the Viajes Socialtur office on Av. Ramón de Carranza, 31 (open M-F 9:30am-1:30pm and 5-8:30pm). To **Arcos de la Frontera** (1hr., 2-5 per day 8:30am-7:15pm, €4) and **Sanlúcar** (1hr., 5-9 per day 7:15am-9:30pm, €2.70).

Ferry: El Vaporcito (☎956 87 02 70) departs from a dock behind the Estación Marítima near the Transportes Generales Comes station and runs to **Puerto de Santa María** (30-45min.; 4-6 per day 10am-8:30pm, return 9am-7:30pm; €3, round-trip €5, bikes €1).

Municipal Buses: (☎956 26 28 06). Pick up a map/schedule and *bonobus* (discount packet of 10 tickets for €6) at the kiosk across from the Transportes Generales Comes bus station. Most lines run through Pl. de España. Bus #1 (Cortadura), a favorite with beach bums, runs along the shore to new Cádiz (every 10min. 6:40am-1:10am, €0.80). Bus #7 runs the same route, leaving from **Playa de la Caleta.**

Taxis: ☎956 21 21 21.

ORIENTATION AND PRACTICAL INFORMATION

Cádiz's old town was built on the end of the peninsula, and the new town grew up behind it, farther inland. The old town hosts most of the cheap hostels and historic sights (not to mention the bus and train stations), while the new town is home to high-rise hotels, numerous bars and restaurants, and kilometers of lovely sand. When you take the bus into new Cádiz (down the main avenue), hop off at **Glorieta Ingeniero La Cierva;** the beach is directly behind it.

Tourist Office: Municipal, Pl. San Juan de Dios, 11 (☎956 24 10 01). Useful free map. English spoken. Open M-F 9am-2pm and 5-8pm. Kiosk in front of the main office open Sa-Su and holidays June-Sept. 10am-1pm and 5-7:30pm; Oct.-May 10am-1:30pm and 4-6pm. **Junta de Andalucía,** Av. Ramón de Carranza (☎956 25 86 46). Large selection of regional maps. Open M and Sa 9am-2pm, Tu-F 9am-7pm.

Currency Exchange: Banco Santander Central Hispano, C. Columela, 13 (☎902 24 24 24). Open M-F 8:30am-2pm, Sa 8:30am-1pm.

Luggage Storage: Lockers at train station (€3 per day). Open daily 8am-11pm.

Student Travel Agency: Barceló Viajes, C. San Francisco, 15 (☎956 21 22 23; www.barceloviajes.com). Open M-F 9:30am-1:30pm and 5-9pm, Sa 9:30am-1:30pm.

Laundromat: Lavandería Europa, C. Santo Domingo, 17 (☎956 25 73 98). €3 per kg. Open M-F 9am-1pm and 3-7pm, Sa 9am-1pm.

Municipal Police: C. Campo del Sur (☎092), in the new city. **National police:** Av. de Andalucía, 28 (☎091), in the new city.

Medical Assistance: Ambulatorio Vargas Ponce (☎062 or 956 28 38 55). **Hospital: Centro de Salud,** Av. Ana de Viya, 21 (☎956 24 21 00).

Internet Access: Enred@dos, C. Sacramento, 36 (☎956 80 81 81), and **Enred@dos 2,** C. Isabel la Católica. Both €2.40 per hr. Open M-Sa 11am-11pm. **Salon Columela,** C. Columela. Coin-operated. €0.50 per 15min. Open daily 9am-10:30pm.

Post Office: Pl. de las Flores (☎956 21 39 45). Open M-F 8:30am-8:30pm, Sa 9:30am-2pm. **Postal Code:** 11070.

ACCOMMODATIONS

Most hostels huddle around the harbor, in and around Pl. San Juan de Dios. Singles and private baths are scarce. Call months in advance to find a room during February's *Carnaval;* calling a few days ahead in summer should be fine. Many owners are willing to bargain a bit, except during the busiest times of the year.

Hostal San Francisco, C. San Francisco, 12 (☎956 22 18 42). Spacious rooms surround a Spanish patio with Japanese decor. Large communal baths. Fantastic self-taught multilingual receptionist is sure to keep you entertained. Singles €21-23; doubles €32-37, with bath €42-48; triples €46-51. AmEx/D/MC/V. ❷

Hostal Colón, C. Marqués de Cádiz, 6 (☎956 28 53 51). Spotless, comfortable sunny white rooms with sinks, colorful tiles, and balconies. Great rooftop terrace. Doubles €32, with bath €45. Prices lower in winter. ❸

ANDALUCÍA

Quo Qádis, C. Diego Arias, 1 (☎/fax 956 22 19 39). Rooms are poorly lit, but the atmosphere is social, active, and down-to-earth. The rooftop terrace sports mattresses, dinners (€3.50) are delicious and vegetarian, and bikes are available for rent (€6 per day). Breakfast included. Sheets €1.20. Laundry €4.80. Dorm lockout 11am-5pm. Dorms €9; doubles €36. 10% discount if you arrive by bike. ❶

Hotel Marqués, C. Marqués de Cádiz, 1 (☎956 28 58 54). Rooms are pleasant though stuffy, with clean common baths, all surrounding an interior courtyard. Singles €20; doubles €25, with bath €35; triples €35. ❷

Camas Cuatro Naciones, C. Plocia, 3 (☎956 25 55 39). Tiny, bare rooms with industrial-looking metal beds, but one of the cheapest places to stay in Cádiz. Some inner rooms only have windows onto the hallway. June-Sept. singles €12, with balcony €15; doubles €25. Oct.-May €11/€12/€22. ❶

🍴 FOOD

Once you leave Pl. San Juan de Dios, finding eateries can be a trying experience. Opt for cafes and *heladerías* (ice cream shops) in any of Cádiz's many plazas, or try the streets off C. San Francisco for local tapas bars and restaurants. To stock up on food for the beach, head to **Champion,** next to the market off Pl. de las Flores (open M-Sa 9am-10pm), or try the market behind the plaza.

Taberna El Garbanzo Negro, C. Sacramento, 18 (☎956 22 10 90). Extensive menu features delicious variations on traditional Spanish staples such as meat croquettes and squid and potato stew (tapas €1.20-1.50, *raciones* €4-7). Wooden tables, stools, and art deco posters. Great *tinto del verano* (red wine with Fanta; €1.20). Lunch *menú* €6.50. Open M 1:30-4pm, Tu-Sa 1:30-4pm and 8:30pm-midnight. MC/V. ❶

Pasta Nostra, C. Colón (☎625 50 43 13). Hidden away on a tiny side street with only a few tables. Mouthwatering ravioli, lasagna, salads, and crepes served up *con gusto* by the owner himself, sure to please anyone in a *"vegetariano italiano"* mood (as they describe it). Tapas-sized pasta portions €4. Entrees €6-8. Pizzas €5-8. Open June-Sept. M-Sa 12:30-4pm and 8pm-midnight; Oct.-May Tu-Su 12:30-4pm and 8pm-midnight. ❶

La Gorda Te Da de Comer, C. General Luque, 1. "The Fat Woman Gives You Food" is a trendy, new-age tapas bar that puts a 21st-century spin on age-old cuisine. Tapas €1.20-1.50. Open M 9pm-12:30am, Tu-Sa 1:30-5pm and 9pm-1:30am. ❶

Mesón Churrasco, C. San Francisco, 3 (☎956 22 03 73). Traditional *bodega* packed with locals and legs of ham (their specialty). Tapas €1.20-3. Entrees €6.60-11. Open daily 9am-4pm and 8pm-midnight. ❶

👁 SIGHTS

▩ CATEDRAL. This gold-domed 18th-century masterpiece is considered the last great cathedral financed by colonial riches. It took 116 years to build, resulting in a mix of Baroque and Neoclassical styles. The treasury bulges with valuables—the *Custodia del Millón* is said to be set with a million precious stones. Visit the nearby **museum** for all sorts of treasures and art. *(Pl. de la Catedral. ☎956 28 61 54. Mass W and F 7:30pm, Su noon. Open Tu-F 10am-1:30pm and 4:30-7:30pm, Sa 10am-1:30pm. Last entrance 30min. before close. Admission to cathedral and museum €3, children €2.)*

MUSEO DE CÁDIZ. You've been spared the trek to and from endless museums: due to a fusion of the Fine Arts and Provincial Archaeological Museums, Murillo, Rubens, and Zurbarán works reside here alongside Phoenician sarcophagi, ancient jewelry, blown glass, and pottery. The first floor displays archaeological exhibits; the second houses mostly religious, 17th- to 19th-century paintings; the third holds an impressive collection of modern art. *(Pl. Mina. ☎ 956 21 22 81. Wheelchair-accessible. Open for public Tu 2:30-8pm, W-Sa 9am-8pm, Su 9:30am-2:30pm; guided tours by appt. only Tu 9am-2:30pm. €1.50, EU citizens and students with ID free.)*

PASEO. Cádiz's seaside *paseo* runs around the old city and along the Atlantic; walking the path is a good way to get a feel for the layout of the city. Stupendous views of ships leaving the harbor recall Spain's golden age. Exotic trees, fanciful hedges, and a few chattering monkeys enliven the adjacent **Parque Genovés.** *(Paseo accessible via Pl. Argüelles or C. Fermín Salvochea, off Pl. de España.)*

BEACHES

Since Cádiz was built on a peninsula, the exhaust-spewing ships on one coast don't pollute the pristine beaches on the other. **Playa de la Caleta** is the most convenient beach to the old city, at the far tip of Cádiz. Better sand and more space can be found in the new city, serviced by bus #1 from Pl. de España (€0.80), or reached by walking along the *paseo* by the water (20-30min. from behind the cathedral). The first beach beyond the rocks is the unremarkable **Playa de Santa María del Mar.** Next to it is the endless and clean ⍰**Playa de la Victoria,** recognized by the EU for its excellence. Get off bus #1 at Glorieta Ingeniero La Cierva in front of McDonald's. A more natural landscape with fewer hotels belongs to **Playa de Cortadura.** Take bus #1 until just before the highway, where it turns around. The boardwalk ends here, and sunbather density falls steadily.

▮ ❀ NIGHTLIFE AND FESTIVALS

Cádiz's nightlife is a migratory animal; in winter the scene is situated primarily in the old city, while summer takes the party closer to the beach in the new city. In the old city, look for bars on the side streets off C. Columela and C. San Francisco. The popular jazz club **Cambalache,** C. José del Toro, 20, on the left after the intersection with C. Columela, gets packed Thursday nights when there's live jazz and usually fills with a vibrant intellectual crowd. (☎ 607 86 58 01. Beer €1.50, mixed drinks €5. Open daily 8:30pm-2:30am.) For a slightly younger scene, head to nearby hippie-style **Medusa,** C. General Luque, 8. The specialty here is *la musica:* DJs change daily, providing dance, funk, garage, rock, and retro nights. (Beer €1.50. Mixed drinks €5. W international night, with €1 beers. Dancing F-Sa. Open Su and Tu-Th 10pm-3:30am, F-Sa 10pm-4:30am.) Nearby **Pub La Luna,** on C. Dr. Zurita, hosts a mixed gay and lesbian scene with Friday night drag queen performances at midnight. Their self-declared specialty is *"la simpatia"* (attractiveness); the proprietress spends as much time on the dance floor as she does behind the bar. (Beer €2, mixed drinks €6. Open Tu-Su 11pm-4am.) **Café Poniente,** C. Beato Diego de Cádiz, 18, another gay club, starts picking up later in the early morning and attracts a mixed yet mostly male crowd. (☎ 956 21 26 92. Beer €2, mixed drinks €5.50. Th drag shows at midnight. Open daily 11pm-4am.)

In the new city, C. General Muñoz Arenillas, off Glorieta Ingeniero La Cierva, and **Paseo Marítimo,** the main drag along Playa Victoria, have some of Cádiz's best bars. Especially popular in summer are the numerous *chiringuitos* (beach bars). **Barabass,** C. General Muñoz Arenillas, 9, is one of the most popular disco-bars, reasonably full even on weeknights. It features an endless bar, sparkling lights, a dance floor, slick (if sparse) furniture, and creatively modernized retro decor. (☎ 856 07 90 26. Beer €2.50, mixed drinks €5. Open Su-Th 5pm-5am, F-Sa 5pm-6am. AmEx/MC/V.) Hardcore clubbers will prefer **Punto de**

San Felipe, a strip of numerous busy bars and clubs reached by walking north along the sea from Pl. de España (take a right before the tunnel); these spots don't get going until 4 or 5am, and some close on weekdays.

◙**Carnaval** insanity is legendary. The gray of winter gives way to dazzling color as the city hosts one of the most raucous *carnavales* in the world (late Feb. to early Mar.). Costumed dancers, street singers, ebullient residents, and spectators from around the world take to the streets in a week-long frenzy that makes New Orleans's Mardi Gras look like Thursday night bingo at the old folks' home.

VEJER DE LA FRONTERA ☎956

The most charming of the *pueblos blancos*, Vejer (pop. 20,000) is a true village; its pace is steady, and its nights are truly black; its cobblestone alleys are narrow, and it houses a collection of affectionately clustered white cubes. Perched atop a little mountain, it generously offers breathtaking views of the unspoiled surrounding landscape. The perfect place for an artistic retreat, Vejer attracts the appreciative, less-commercial tourist with its down-to-earth charm. If you define yourself as such, plan to spend a night, as the evenings have an unparalleled romantic flair. However, this is not the place for a few rushed hours, or for restless travelers.

■ TRANSPORTATION. While some buses stop at the end of **Avenida de Los Remedios,** which leads uphill into **La Plazuela** (10min.), many leave you by the highway at **La Barca de Vejer,** a small town at the base of the hill. Take one of the numerous taxis waiting by the bus stop (€5). The alternative, an arduous 20min. uphill climb, is extremely difficult with a backpack. If you do make the trek, go up the cobbled track to the left of the restaurant. When you reach the top, follow the road to the left to reach quiet **Plaza de España;** the road on the right leads uphill to smaller La Plazuela, a tiny intersection where Av. de Los Remedios and C. Juan Bueno meet.

For **bus** info and tickets, stop by the small **Transportes Generales Comes** office, La Plazuela, 2b. (☎956 44 71 46. Open M-F 9am-2:30pm and 6-11pm, Sa-Su 11am-2:30pm and 6-11pm. When the office is closed, buy tickets on the bus.) From the stop on Av. de Los Remedios near the tourist office, buses leave for **Cádiz** (1½hr., M-F 5 per day 7:15am-8pm, €4.80). For other destinations, descend the hill (1½km) to **La Barca de Vejer** or take the bus down (every 15min. 10:15am-10:15pm, €1). Service to: **Algeciras** (2hr., 11 per day 7:50am-10:25pm, €5); **Málaga** (4hr., 7:50am and 5:05pm, €14.50); **Sevilla** (3½hr., 5 per day 8:30am-5:45pm, €11); **Tarifa** (1hr., 11 per day 7:45am-10:45pm, €3.30). For a **taxi,** call ☎956 45 04 08.

⛢ PRACTICAL INFORMATION. The staff at the **tourist office,** Av. de Los Remedios, 2, speaks English. (☎956 45 17 36. Open June-Aug. M-F 9am-2:30pm and 6-8pm, Aug. also Sa 10:30am-2pm; Sept.-May call for hours.) Local services include: **Banco Santander Central Hispano,** C. Juan Bueno, 5 (☎902 24 24 24; open M-F 8:30am-2pm, Sa 8:30am-1pm); **Centro de Salud,** Av. de Andalucía (☎956 44 76 25); **police,** Av. de Andalucía, 9 (☎956 45 04 00); **Internet,** free at the Casa de la Juventud located on La Plazuela (open 8:30am-2pm); **post office** at C. Juan Bueno, 10 (☎956 45 02 38; open M-F 8:30am-2:30pm, Sa 9:30am-1pm). **Postal Code:** 11150.

⛶⛶ ACCOMMODATIONS AND FOOD. The most affordable places to stay in Vejer are *casas particulares* (private houses); the tourist office has an extensive list of *hostales* and *casas* if other options are full. Several options line C. San Filmo; to get there, follow C. Juan Relinque from La Plazuela, go right through the small Pl. del Mercado, and head left uphill. Each of the rooms at the gorgeous and tranquil *casa rural,* ◙**El Cobijo de Vejer ❺,** C. San Filmo, 7, is nothing short of a marvel. Uniquely and passionately decorated, some rooms have small kitchens, terraces, and lounges, among other amenities. All rooms are wired for Internet and have A/C, satellite TV, and a refrigerator. This, combined with magnificent views of the surrounding landscape and a most welcoming owner, make El Cobijo a worthwhile splurge (☎956 45 50 23; www.elcobijo.com. Elaborate breakfast included. Reserve well in advance. Doubles June-Sept. and *Semana Santa* €62-83; Oct.-May €52-69.) Certainly not as charming or unique, but spotless, roomy, convenient and with more rooms, is the pleasant **Hostal La Posada ❷**, Av. de Los Remedios, 21. (☎956 45 02 58. Oct.-Mar. singles €18; doubles €30. Apr.-Sept. €20/€38.) Friendly Sra. Rosa Romero owns **Casa Los Cántaros ❷**, C. San Filmo, 14, a restored Andalusian home with a grape-vined patio. Clean, affordable rooms with private baths are comfortable though somewhat dark. (☎956 44 75 92. Doubles June-Sept. €25; Oct.-May €23.)

The cheapest eats are tapas or *raciones* at the bars around La Plazuela; full-service restaurants are more expensive. At French-owned creperie **La Chozita ❷**, Pl. de España, 28, fresh ingredients make for delicious savory and sweet crepes (€3-8), some with a Caribbean flair. The Haitian chef also makes over a dozen different-flavored—and colored—🍹rums. (☎956 44 75 29. Live jazz and salsa some nights. Open daily noon-late.) Renowned for its *jamón ibérico*, family-run **Mesón Pepe Julián ❷**, C. Juan Relinque, 7, prepares the best tapas in town (€1-1.50) and serves reasonably priced entrees (€4.20-8) to locals. (Open daily 1:30-3:30pm and 8:30-11:30pm; Oct.-June closed W. MC/V.)

🅖 **SIGHTS.** The best way to enjoy Vejer is by wandering along the labyrinthine streets and cliffside *paseos*, as those are more interesting than the actual monuments. The 9th-century **Castillo Moro**, down C. Ramón y Cajal from the church, almost blends in with the surrounding scenery. (Open daily 11am-9pm. €3 includes entrance to the Iglesia.) **Iglesia del Divino Salvador**, 1, is a choice blend of Romanesque, *mudéjar*, and Gothic styles. (☎956 45 00 56. Open daily 11am-1:30pm and 5-8pm; closed Tu evenings.) Ten kilometers down the road to Los Caños is **El Palmar**, 7km of fine sand and clear waters accessible by car or bus (June-Aug. 4 per day 11:45am-8:45pm, €0.90). To reach it, catch the Cádiz-bound bus to **Conil de la Frontera** and walk southeast along the shore for 3-4km. For info on outdoor activities, consult **Discover Andalucía**, Av. de los Remedios, 45b, across from the bus stop. (☎956 44 75 75. Bicycles €12-15 per day. Surfboards from €6 per day. Open M-F 9am-2pm and 6-9pm, Sa 9am-2pm. AmEx/MC/V.)

🅕 **FESTIVALS.** Vejer throws brilliant *fiestas*. Soon after the **Corpus Cristi** revelry in June comes the **Candelas de San Juan** (June 23), climaxing with the midnight release of the 🐂**toro de fuego** (bull of fire). A local (obviously one with a death wish) dressed in an iron bull costume charges the crowd as the firecrackers attached to his body fly off in all directions. The town demonstrates its creativity again during the delirious **Semana Santa** celebrations, when a *toro embolao* (sheathed bull) with wooden balls affixed to the tips of his horns is set loose through the narrow streets of Vejer on Easter Sunday. The good-natured **Feria de Primavera** (2 weeks after *Semana Santa*) is a bit tamer, with people dancing *sevillanas* and downing cups of *vino* until sunrise.

TARIFA   ☎956

You know you've reached Tarifa (pop. 15,000) when the sky suddenly fills with happy swarms of kitesurfers. Newcomers are invariably pleasantly shocked by the unique love of life, activity, and of course, beaches, that the locals and countless visitors sport. When the breezes pick up in this southernmost city of continental

ANDALUCÍA

Europe, it becomes clear why it is known as the Hawaii of Spain. World-renowned winds combined with kilometers of empty, white, sandy beaches bring some of the best kite- and windsurfers from around the world, while the tropical, relaxed environment beckons to those a little less adventurous. Expect to see more board shorts and Quicksilver attire than you ever thought existed in Spain; in fact, everything about Tarifa defies expectations. Location-wise, it doesn't get much better than this—directly across the Strait of Gibraltar from Tangier, Tarifa boasts incomparable views of Morocco to the south, the Atlantic to the east, and the Mediterranean to the west—from few, if any, other places in the world can you see two continents and two wide open seas at once.

⨍ TRANSPORTATION. Transportes Generales Comes buses roll in on C. Batalla del Salado, 19. (☎ 956 67 57 55. Open M-F 7:30-11am and 2-6:30pm, Sa-Su 3-8pm. Schedule in window; if office is closed, buy tickets from driver.) **Buses** run to: **Algeciras** (30min., 10 per day 6:30am-8:15pm, €1.60); **Cádiz** (2¼hr., 9 per day 7:25am-8:55pm, €7.20); **La Línea** (1hr., 8 per day 11am-11:15pm, €3.30); **Sevilla** (3hr., 5 per day 7:55am-5:15pm, €14.50-23.50). **FRS ferries** (☎ 956 68 18 30; www.frs.com) leave from the port at the end of Po. de la Alameda for **Tangier** (35min.; 5 per day 9am-7:15pm, return 9:30am-7:30pm Morocco time; €24.50, round-trip €45; ages 3-12 €13.30/22.50; small car €73, motorcycle €23).

⚎ ⨍ ORIENTATION AND PRACTICAL INFORMATION. The small **bus station** is on C. Batalla del Salado. With your back to the station turn right and walk a short distance to the intersection with Av. de Andalucía. To reach the center of the old town, cross Av. de Andalucía and pass under the arch. To the left is C. Nuestra Señora de la Luz; follow this street to its end and you will be on C. Sancho IV el Bravo, the location of many cafes and restaurants. To reach the **tourist office**, turn right on Av. de Andalucía. The pedestrian thoroughfare Po. de la Alameda will be about one block ahead on the left; the tourist office is in the center. Ask at the tourist office for adventure sports information. (☎ 956 68 09 93. Open M-F 10am-12pm and 6-8pm, Sa-Su 9:30am-3pm.) Exchange currency at **Banco Santander Central Hispano,** C. Batalla del Salado, 17. (☎ 902 24 24 24. Open M-F 8:30am-2pm, Sa 8:30am-1pm; May-Sept. M-F 8:30am-2pm,). **Exchange books** at **Café Zumo,** C. Sancho IV el Bravo. (☎ 956 62 72 51. Books €2 with an exchange, €4 without. Open daily 9am-2:30pm and 5:30-9pm.) Local services include: **police,** Pl. Santa María, 3 (☎ 956 68 41 86); **Hospital de Caridad,** C. Guzmán el Bueno (☎ 956 68 21 56). **Internet** access is available at **Tarifa Diving,** Av. de la Constitución, near the tourist office (€2.50 per hr; open Tu-Sa 10:30am-2pm and 5:30-9pm) and **Ciber-Papelería Pandor@'s,** C. Sancho IV el Bravo, 5. (€3 per hr. Open June-Aug. daily 10am-1am; Sept.-May M-F 10am-2pm and 4-11pm, Sa-Su 10am-2pm and 5pm-midnight.) The **post office,** C. General Moscardó, 9, is near Pl. San Mateo. (☎ 956 68 42 37. Open M-F 8:30am-2:30pm, Sa 9:30am-1pm.) **Postal Code:** 11380.

⌂ ⌂ ACCOMMODATIONS AND FOOD. Affordable rooms line main C. Batalla del Salado and its side streets. Prices rise significantly in summer; those visiting in August and on weekends from June to September should call ahead and arrive early. **Hostal Facundo ❷,** C. Batalla del Saludo, 47, with its "Welcome backpackers" slogan, is a great option, with a fun social atmosphere and kitchen access (8am-10pm), as well as a small TV room and spacious common baths. (☎ 956 68 42 98. Dorms €12-22; singles €25; doubles €22-55.) Comfortable **Hostal Villanueva ❷,** Av. de Andalucía, 11, features a rooftop terrace with an ocean view and spotless rooms, all with bath. (☎ 956 68 41 49. Singles €20-25; doubles €35-45.) Truly hard-core windsurfers often stay at one of the several **campgrounds** along the beach several kilometers from town; all have full bath and shower facilities, bars, and mini-supermarkets. Guests must bring their own tent. Although Cádiz-bound buses will drop you off if you ask, flagging one down to get back to town is next to impossible; call for a taxi or befriend a fellow surfer with a car. Try **Camping Río Jara ❶**, 4km from town (☎956 68 05 70; €6 per person, €10 per site including tent, car, and electricity) or **Camping Tarifa ❶**, 6km from town (☎956 68 47 78; €5.60 per person, €9 per site including tent, car, and electricity), both on highway CN-340.

For cheap and varied sandwiches (€1.50-3), try any one of the many *bagueterías* lining C. Sancho IV el Bravo and the side streets nearby. Alternately, C. San Francisco offers a variety of appetizing and affordable options. **⊠Misiana ❷**, C. San Joaquín, 2, on the corner of C. Sancho IV el Bravo, serves delicious, healthy breakfasts until 1pm. Take your pick of beer or one of the exotic tea blends and enjoy the outdoor patio or the uplifting, colorful lounge. (☎956 62 70 83. Lots of veggie options. Wildly popular bar at night. Open daily 9am-2am.)

◨ ⤵ SIGHTS AND ENTERTAINMENT. Next to the port and just outside the old town are the ruins of the **Castillo de Guzmán el Bueno.** In the 13th century, the Moors kidnapped Guzmán's son and threatened his life if Guzmán didn't relinquish the castle. Surprisingly, the father didn't surrender, even after his son's throat was slashed before his eyes. (Open Apr.-Oct. Tu-Su 11am-2pm and 6-8pm; Oct.-Apr. Tu-Su 11am-2pm and 4-6pm. €1.80.) Those with something less historical in mind can head 200m south to **Playa de los Lances** for 5km of the finest white sand on the Atlantic coast. Bathers should be aware of the occasional high winds and strong undertow. Adjacent to Playa de los Lances is **Playa Chica,** which is tiny but more sheltered from the winds. **Tarifa Spin Out Surfbase,** 9km up the road toward Cádiz (ask the bus driver on the Cádiz route to stop, or take a taxi for €6), rents **windsurfing** and **kitesurfing** boards and instructs all levels. (☎956 23 63 52; www.tarifaspinout.com. Book in advance. Windsurf rental €24 per hr., €48 per day; 2hr. lesson including all equipment €48. Kite and board rental €28 per hr., €58 per day; 2hr. lesson with all equipment €68.) Many campgrounds and hotels along CN-340 between km 70 and km 80 provide instruction and gear for outdoor sports; ask at the tourist office for their list of kite- and windsurfing schools and rental places.

At night, sunburnt travelers mellow out in the old town's many bars, which range from jazz to psychedelic to Irish. People start migrating to the clubs around 1 or 2am. The *terrazas* on C. Sancho IV el Bravo fill at night with locals and windsurfers chatting over beer or coffee. Almost every place on C. San Francisco is a hotspot; the street hosts endless places for young backpackers and locals to meet, drink, and move to the music. **Moskito,** C. San Francisco, 11, is a combination bar-club with a Caribbean motif, great music, and delicious tropical cocktails. (Free salsa lessons W 10pm. Beer €2.50. Mixed drinks €4.50-6. Open summer daily 11pm-4:30am; winter Th-Sa 11pm-4:30am.) **La Tribu,** C. Nuestra Señora de la Luz, 7, makes some of the best and most creative cocktails in town, while trance and techno pump energy into the otherwise chill nightspot. (Beer €2-3. Shots €1.50. Mixed drinks €4-6. Open daily 8pm-2 or 3am.)

ALGECIRAS ☎956

Franco dreamed of transforming Algeciras into a burgeoning southern metropolis that would eclipse Gibraltar as the commercial center of the southwestern Mediterranean and force the Royal Army out of Iberia. Innumerable concrete wharfs and slapdash highrises remain, but so do the British. And, unfortunately, despite a peaceful and nicer old neighborhood set back from the port, Algeciras remains a somewhat dingy city—you'd be best off just passing through.

ANDALUCÍA

▤ TRANSPORTATION

Trains: RENFE, Ctra. a Cádiz (☎902 24 02 02), down C. San Bernardo. To **Granada** (4hr., 4 per day 7am-6:30pm, €16) and **Ronda** (1½hr., 4 per day 7am-6:25pm, €6). Also to **Bobadilla** (€10), with connections to: **Córdoba** (5hr., 6 per day 7am-9:45pm, €27); **Málaga** (3½hr., 7 per day 8:43am-9:39pm, €14); **Sevilla** (6hr., 3-4 per day 7am-3:35pm, €21).

Buses: There is no bus station. Buses depart from the office of the individual company.

Empresa Portillo, Av. Virgen del Carmen, 15 (☎956 65 43 04). To: **Córdoba** (6hr., 8:15am and 3pm, €20.50); **Granada** (4hr., 5 per day 8am-5:45pm, €17.60); **Málaga** (2hr., 20 per day 8am-10pm, €9.30); **Marbella** (1hr., 20 per day 8am-10pm, €5.50).

Daibus, C. San Bernardo, 1 (☎956 65 34 56) to **Madrid** (9hr., 4 per day 8:40am-9:45pm, €23.60) via **La Línea** (30min., 12:40-9:45pm).

Transportes Generales Comes, C. San Bernardo, 1 (☎956 65 34 56), by Hotel Octavio and across from the train station. To: **Cádiz** (2½hr., 10 per day 7am-10pm, €8.80).

Ferries: From the bus and train stations, follow C. San Bernardo to C. Juan de la Cierva, and turn left at its end; the port entrance is on the right. You can book at the train station, but tickets are overpriced; book at a travel agency or at the port. Only **Trasmediterránea**, at the entrance to the port, offers Eurail discounts. (☎902 45 46 45. Open daily 9am-7pm. MC/V.) All ferry companies sell tickets for all departures at the same price, regardless of whose boat it is. Allow 30min. to clear customs and board, 90min. with a car. Summer ferries to **Ceuta** (35min.; 16 per day 6am-9:45pm, return 7:30am-11pm Moroccan time; €22.80, under 12 €11, small car €60.70, motorcycle €19.60) and **Tangier** (2½hr.; every hr. 7am-11pm, return 6am-9pm Moroccan time; €25.30, with Eurail pass €20, under 12 €11.70, small car €71.90, motorcycle €22.20). Fast ferries also go to **Tangier** (1hr., 9am and 1:45pm, €25). Limited service in winter.

▣ ORIENTATION AND PRACTICAL INFORMATION

Lined with travel agencies, banks, and hotels, **Avenida de la Marina** runs along the coast, turning into Av. Virgen del Carmen north of the port. **Calle Juan de la Cierva** runs perpendicular to the coast from the port, becoming **Calle San Bernardo** as it nears the **train** and **bus stations**. The train station is directly across the street from the Comes Bus Station; the Portillo bus station is near the port. To reach the **tourist office** from the train station, follow C. San Bernardo along the abandoned tracks toward the port, passing a parking lot on the left. From the **port**, take a left onto Av. Virgen del Carmen, then a quick right onto C. Juan de la Cierva; the office is on the left. To get to the old center of town and its outdoor cafes and stores, walk past the port on Av. de la Marina and after 5min. take a left onto C. Trafalgar, which intersects C. Alfonso XI and later C. Regino Martínez, the main pedestrian thoroughfare. All services necessary for transit to Morocco cluster near the port, accessible by a single gate and driveway. Be wary of impostors peddling ferry tickets.

Tourist Office: C. Juan de la Cierva (☎956 57 26 36; fax 57 04 75). Provides maps (free for Algeciras, €0.60 for other cities). Some English spoken. Open M-F 9am-2pm.

Currency Exchange: Banco Santander Central Hispano, Av. Virgen del Carmen, 9-11. Open M-F 8:30am-2pm, Sa 8:30am-1pm. Other banks line Av. de la Marina and continue past the port. For a daytrip to Tangier, buying **dirham** may not be necessary; many places accept euros and it is not possible to convert dirham back upon return. For longer trips, change money in Morocco. For more info, see **Morocco Essentials,** p. 817.

Luggage Storage: At the **train station,** €3 per day. Open daily 5:30am-10:30pm. At the **port,** lockers €2.40; behind the counter €1.20-1.80 per item. Open daily 7am-9:30pm.

Police: C. Ruiz Zorrilla (☎092 or 956 66 01 55).

Medical Assistance: Ambulatorio Central, Pl. Menéndez Tolosa (☎956 66 19 56).

Internet Access: Travel agencies along Av. de la Marina offer Internet access for €2-3 per hr.; look for signs in windows.

Post Office: C. Ruiz Zorrilla, 42 (☎956 66 36 48). **Lista de Correos.** Open M-F 8:30am-2:30pm, Sa 9:30am-1pm. **Postal Code:** 11203.

ACCOMMODATIONS

Hostels line **Calle José Santacana,** parallel to the seafront along Av. de la Marina and about a 10min. walk from the bus and train stations. From either station, follow C. San Bernardo, turning left before the bush-lined median; take a right onto Av. Segismundo Moret and then take the third left, C. José Santacana. Women traveling alone, however, might not feel safe there after dark; it's worth the extra few euros for a better neighborhood.

Hostal Residencia Versailles, C. Montero Ríos, 12 (☎/fax 956 65 43 00), close to the bus station. Clean and inviting well-sized rooms, all with private bath. Singles €15; doubles €24, with TV €27. ❶

Hostal Nuestra Señora de la Palma, Pl. Nuestra Señora de la Palma, 12 (☎956 63 24 81), on the town's main square, right next to the market and close to the port. Dark hallways open up to brighter, clean, and spacious rooms, all with bath and TV. Singles €20; doubles €28; triples €42. ❷

Hotel Reina Cristina, Po. de la Conferencia (☎956 60 26 22; www.reinacristina.com), a 10min. walk down Av. de la Marina when facing the port. Spend your days in Morocco and your nights in luxury at this 4-star hotel. An oasis of tranquility and beauty within the hubbub of the city. Well-kept grounds, pool, and restaurant. All rooms have bath, safe, A/C, TV, and phone. Singles €48.40-67, doubles €62.30-98. AmEx/D/MC/V. ❺

FOOD

The options in Algeciras are far from gastronomic sophistication; outdoor cafes line C. Regino Martínez, Algeciras's main drag, while authentic Moroccan specialties are served in small restaurants all around. The **supermarket** is on the corner of C. José Santacana and C. Maroto. (Open daily 9am-2pm and 5-8pm.) The outdoor **market** at Pl. Nuestra Señora de la Palma is at the end of C. José Santacana. (Open M-Sa 8:30am-2pm.) **Montes Restaurante ❷,** C. Castellar, 36, is packed day and night with foreigners in transit. Montes boasts an extensive menu of *comida típica* with filling meat, fish, and seafood entrees (€6-12), as well as countless varieties of tapas. (☎956 65 69 05. Open daily 8am-midnight. MC/V.) For Moroccan fare with flair, swing by **La Alegría ❶,** C. José Santacana, 6. This menu-less restaurant dishes out huge portions of chicken, lamb, and vegetarian entrees (€5-6) from their glass display case. (Open daily 7am-1am.)

GIBRALTAR

Emerging from the morning mist, the Rock of Gibraltar's craggy face menaces those who pass by its shores. Ancient seafarers referred to the rock as one of the Pillars of Hercules, believing that it marked the end of the world. Today, it is known affectionately to locals as "Gib" and is home to more fish 'n' chips plates and pints of bitter per capita than anywhere in the Mediterranean. Though Gibraltar is officially a self-governing British colony, Spain continues to campaign for sovereignty. When a 1969 vote showed that Gibraltar's populace favored its colonial ties to Britain—a near-tie at 12,138 to 44—Franco sealed the border. After 16 years of isolation and a decade of negotiations, the border re-opened on February 4, 1985. Tourists and residents now cross with ease, but Gibraltar has a culture all its own, one that remains detached from Spain. While the peculiar mix of wild roaming primates (the only non-human ones in Europe) and a curious enclave of not-quite-British-definitely-not-Spanish culture make Gibraltar worth visiting, it is in many ways a tourist trap. Cross the border, explore the Rock, and stock up on duty-free liquor and tobacco, then scurry back to Spain before nightfall.

TRANSPORTATION

Flights: Airport (☎730 26). **British Airways** (☎793 00) flies to **London** (2½hr., 2 per day, £168/€233) for those scared to set foot back in Spain.

Buses: From **La Línea,** on the Spanish border, to: **Algeciras** (40min., every 30min. 7:45am-10:15pm, €1.60); **Cádiz** (3hr., 4 per day 6:30am-8pm, €10.20); **Granada** (5hr., 7:15am and 2:15pm, €17.60); **Madrid** (7hr., 1:10 and 10:15pm, €22.90); **Málaga** (3¼hr., 4 per day 7:15am-5:30pm, €9.40); **Marbella** (1¾hr., 4 per day 7:15am-5:30pm, €5.20); **Sevilla** (6hr., 3 per day 7am-4:15pm, €18.40); **Tarifa** (1hr., 7 per day 6:30am-8pm, €3.40).

Ferries: Turner & Co., 65/67 Irish Town St. (☎783 05; fax 720 06). To: **Tangier** (1¼hr.; F 6pm, return Sa 5:30pm Moroccan time; £18/€32, under 12 £9/€16.20).

Public Transport: Most bus lines run from one end of the Rock to the other. Buses #9 and 10 go between the border and the Rock for £0.60/€1. Unlimited day pass €2.

Taxis: Gibraltar Taxi Association ☎700 27.

EUROS OR POUNDS? Although euros are accepted almost everywhere (except in pay phones and post offices), the **pound sterling (£)** is the preferred method of payment in Gibraltar. ATMs dispense money in pounds. Merchants and sights sometimes charge a higher price in euros than in the pound's exchange equivalent. However, unless stated otherwise, assume an establishment will accept euros; change is often given in British currency. The exchange rate fluctuates around £1 to €1.50. As of press date, **1£ = €1.48.**

ORIENTATION AND PRACTICAL INFORMATION

Before you head to Gibraltar, make sure you have a valid passport; otherwise you'll be turned away at the border. If you need a visa, the UK embassy in Madrid takes roughly a day to process them. Buses from Spain terminate in the nearby town of **La Línea.** From the bus station, walk directly toward the Rock; the border is 5min. away. Once through customs and passport control, catch bus #9 or 10 or walk across the airport tarmac (look both ways and hold hands) into town (20min.); stay left on Av. Winston Churchill when the road forks with Corral Ln. Cars take longer to enter and exit Gibraltar—often an hour or more.

Tourist Office: Duke of Kent House, Cathedral Sq. (☎450 00). Open M-F 9am-5:30pm. **Branch,** Watergate House, Casemates Sq. (☎749 82). Open M-F 9am-5:30pm, Sa 10am-3pm, Su 10am-1pm. **Info booth** at Spanish border. Open daily 7am-10pm.

Luggage Storage: Bus station in La Línea. €4 per day. Open daily 7am-10pm.

Bookstore: Gibraltar Bookshop, 300 Main St. (☎718 94). Tons of paperbacks, including ⬛ *Let's Go.* Open M-F 10am-6:30pm. AmEx/MC/V.

Emergency: ☎199. **Police:** 120 Irish Town St. (☎725 00).

Hospital: St. Bernard's Hospital, on Hospital Hill (☎797 00).

Telephone Code: From Britain (00) 350. From the US (011) 350. From Spain 9567.

Gibraltar

🔺 ACCOMMODATIONS

Emile Youth Hostel
Gibraltar, **1**

🍎 FOOD

The Viceroy of India, **3**
Uncle Sam's, **2**

Internet Access: Café Cyberworld, Ocean Heights Gallery, Queensway Rd. (☎514 16) £4.50/€7.50 per hr. Open daily noon-midnight. **John McIntosh Hall Library,** 308 Main St., 2nd fl. £0.75 per 30min., but a slower connection. Open M-F 9:30am-7:30pm.

Post Office: 104 Main St. (☎756 62). **Poste Restante:** LAST NAME, First Name; Poste Restante, Gibraltar (Main Post Office). Open June to mid-Sept. M-F 9am-2:15pm, Sa 10am-1pm; mid-Sept. to May M-F 9am-4:30pm, Sa 10am-1pm. Pounds only.

🏠 ACCOMMODATIONS AND FOOD

Gibraltar is best done as a daytrip. The few accommodations in the area are pricey and often full, especially in the summer, and camping is illegal. At worst, you can crash across the border in La Línea. Back on the Rock, **🏠Emile Youth Hostel Gibraltar ❷,** on Montague Bastian, has bunkbeds in cheerfully painted rooms with clean communal baths. (☎511 06. Breakfast included. Lockout 10:30am-4:30pm. Dorms £15/€25; doubles £30/€50.) International restaurants are easy to find, but you may choke on the prices. Sample the tasty treats of Gibraltar's large, thriving Jewish community at **Uncle Sam's ❶,** 62 Irish Town St., a Kosher deli and grocer. The bagel sandwiches (£3) are especially good, as is the matzah ball soup (£3.50), and the chef-owner is delightfully hospitable. (☎512 36. Entrees, including *schnitzel*, £6. Take-out deli and market open M-F 9am-7pm; restaurant open Tu-Th 7pm-midnight.) Another option is **The Viceroy of India ,** with fabulous Indian food. (Vegetarian entrees £4-5; meat and seafood £6-10. Open M-F noon-3pm and 7-11pm, Sa 7-11pm. MC/V.) As a back-up, try the **Checkout** supermarket on Main St. next to Marks & Spencer. (Open M-F 8:30am-8pm, Sa 10am-6pm, Su 10am-3pm. MC/V.)

◎ SIGHTS

▧THE ROCK OF GIBRALTAR

Top of the Rock Nature Reserve is accessible by car or cable car, or for the truly adventurous and athletic, by foot. Cable cars (☎ 778 26) depart daily every 10min. 9:30am-5:15pm; last return 5:45pm. Tickets sold until 5:15pm. It's possible to buy a ticket for only the cable car (round-trip £7.50/€11, one-way £6/€9), but if you plan on visiting any of the sights highlighted below, it's better to buy a combined admittance ticket (they don't offer individual sight tickets), including one-way cable car ride, for £14.50/€21.50. The walk down takes 2-3hr., including stops at the sights. Tour operators offer van or taxi tours that take visitors to all attractions in about 1½hr.; these are only a good choice if you really want to see all the sights, but don't want to walk at all. If you drive, there is a £7/€10.50 per person entrance fee, including all sights, plus £2/€3 per car. The truly budget-savvy walk both ways. To walk up, take Library St. to Library Ramp from Main St., follow it uphill to the end, and turn right. At the next intersection there is a sign for the footpath to the Rock. Follow the footpath uphill for 20min. until you hit a road mid-rock, and turn left.

No visit to Gibraltar is complete without a stop at the legendary Rock. About halfway up the Rock (at the first cable car stop, or a 25min. walk down from the top stop) is the infamous **Apes' Den,** where a colony of **Barbary apes** cavorts on the sides of rocks, the tops of taxis, and tourists' heads. These disturbingly tailless apes have inhabited Gibraltar since the 18th century. When the ape population nearly went extinct in 1944, Churchill ordered reinforcements from North Africa; now they are procreating at such a rate that population control has become an issue. The apes are very tourist-friendly but have been known to steal food and other items from visitors; keep all food hidden and bags closed to avoid unwanted confrontations with the animals. At the northern tip of the Rock, facing Spain, are the **Great Siege Tunnels.** Originally used to fend off a combined Franco-Spanish siege at the end of the American Revolution, the tunnels were expanded during WWII to span 33 miles underground. Nearby, on the way back to town, is the old **Moorish castle,** rebuilt several times, most recently in 1333. Although the castle is currently under renovation, the exterior still merits a quick look if you're already on the Rock. Thousands of years of water erosion carved the eerie chambers of **St. Michael's Cave,** located 500m opposite the siege tunnels. Ask at the entrance about getting a guided tour to the lower caves, with an underground lake and dramatic stalagmites. At the southern tip of Gibraltar, guarded by three machine guns and a lighthouse, **Europa Point** commands a view of the straits; the lighthouse can be seen from 37km away at sea. Nearby, the **Ibrahim-Al-Ibrahim Mosque,** Europe's largest, and the **Shrine of Our Lady of Europe** face each other in pluralistic harmony. (Take bus #3 or 1B from Line Wall Rd., just off Main St., all the way to the end.)

COSTA DEL SOL

The coast has sold its soul to the devil, and now he's starting to collect. Artifice covers its once-natural charms as chic promenades, swanky hotels, and apartment buildings spring up between the small towns and the shoreline. The

Costa del Sol extends from Tarifa in the southwest to Cabo de Gata, east of Almería; post-industrial Málaga lies smack in the middle. To the northeast, hills dip straight into the ocean, and rocky beaches help preserve the shore's natural beauty. To the southwest, however, waves seem to wash up onto more concrete than sand. Still, nothing can detract from the coast's major attraction: eight months of spring and four months of summer. News of the fantastic weather has spread, and July and August bring swarms of pale northern Europeans. Reservations are essential in the summer anywhere on the coast, especially at hostels. It is best to visit in June, when summer has already hit the beach but tourists haven't. Private bus lines offer connections along the coast—trains go only as far as Málaga and Fuengirola.

MÁLAGA ☎952

Celebrated by the likes of Hans Christian Andersen, Málaga (pop. 550,000) is the busiest city on the coast, and while its beaches are known more for their bars than for their natural beauty, the city has much to offer. The Alcazaba, gorgeous and commanding on a hill to the west of the city, offers magnificent—and telling—views of Málaga: cranes and industrial ports in the distance contrast with the charming *casco antiguo* and verdant gardens. Picasso's hometown finally got its own museum dedicated to the prodigy in 2003, and the Santa Iglesia Cathedral, with its sculpted 75m high ceiling and gorgeous twin organs, inspires nothing short of absolute awe. Because it is a critical transportation hub, many see Málaga en route to other coastal stops, but it is well worth a day or two in its own right.

▐▀ TRANSPORTATION

Flights: (☎952 04 88 04). From the airport, bus #19 (every 30min. 6:30am-11:35pm, €1) runs from the "City Bus" sign, stopping at the bus station and at the corner of C. Molina Lario and Postigo de los Abades behind the cathedral. RENFE trains connect the city and the airport (12min., €1). **Iberia,** C. Molina Lario, 13 (☎952 13 61 66, 24hr. reservations 902 40 05 00), has numerous international flights daily.

Trains: Estación de Málaga, Explanada de la Estación (☎952 36 02 02). Take bus #3 at Po. del Parque or #4 at Pl. de la Marina to the station. **RENFE** office, C. Strachan, 4 (☎902 24 02 02). To: **Barcelona** (13hr., 7am and 9pm, €49.50); **Córdoba** (2hr., 12 per day 6:45am-9pm, €13); **Fuengirola** (30min., every 30min. 7:15am-10:30pm, €1.20); **Madrid** (5hr., 7 per day 6:45am-7:45pm, €53); **Sevilla** (3hr., 5 per day 7:45am-8pm, €13.60); **Torremolinos** (20min., every 30min. 5:45am-10:10pm, €1.10). Reservations for long-distance trains are highly recommended.

Buses: Po. de los Tilos (☎952 31 82 95, **ALSA** 902 42 22 42, **Alsina Graells Sur** 952 31 82 95, **Casado** 952 31 59 08, **Daibus** 952 31 52 47, **Portillo** 952 36 01 91), 1 block from the RENFE station along C. Roger de Flor. To: **Algeciras** (3hr., 16 per day 5am-9:45pm, €9); **Almería** (8 per day 7am-7pm, €13.20); **Antequera** (1hr., 9-12 per day 7am-10pm, €3.30); **Cádiz** (5hr., 5 per day 6:45am-8pm, €17.90); **Córdoba** (3hr., 5 per day 9am-6pm, €10.50); **Granada** (2hr., 17 per day 7am-9pm, €8.10); **Madrid** (7hr., 12 per day 8:30am-1am, €18); **Marbella** (1½hr., approx. every hr. 7am-8pm, €4.20); **Murcia** (6hr., 5 per day 8:30am-9:45pm, €26); **Ronda** (3hr., 4 per day 8:15am-4:30pm, €8.10); **Sevilla** (3hr., 11-12 per day 7am-3am, €13.10); **Torremolinos** (20min., every 15min. 6:15am-1am, €1).

Taxis: Radio Taxi (☎952 32 00 00). Town center to waterfront €6; to the airport €10.

ANDALUCÍA

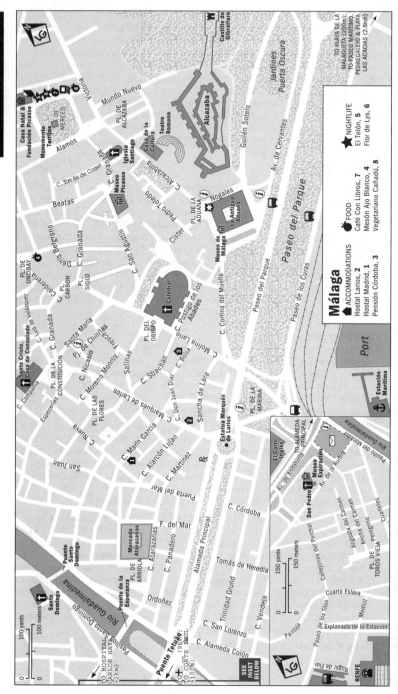

Málaga

▲ ACCOMMODATIONS
Hostal Larios, **2**
Hostal Madrid, **1**
Pensión Córdoba, **3**

◆ FOOD
Café Con Libros, **7**
Mesón Ajo Blanco, **4**
Vegetariano Cañadú, **8**

★ NIGHTLIFE
El Telón, **5**
Flor de Lys, **6**

■ ＊ ⑰ ORIENTATION AND PRACTICAL INFORMATION

The bus and train stations lie a block away from each other along C. Roger de Flor, on the other side of the Río Guadalmedina from the historical center and the majority of other sights. To get to the town center from the bus station, exit right onto Callejones del Perchel, walk straight through the big intersection with Av. de la Aurora, take a right onto Av. de Andalucía, and cross Puente de Tetuán. From here, **Alameda Principal** leads into **Plaza de la Marina** (20min.). Alternatively, take bus #4 or 21 along the same route (€0.90). From Pl. de la Marina, C. Molina Lario leads to the **cathedral** and the old town. C. Marqués de Larios, the main shopping and pedestrian street, connects Pl. de la Marina to **Plaza de la Constitución.** Behind the plaza, C. Granada leads to many good tapas bars and **Plaza de la Merced,** renowned for its nightlife. Av. Cánovas del Castillo leads to **Playa de la Malagueta** (20min. walk), Málaga's closest beach worth visiting. After dark, be wary of both the neighborhood of **Cruz del Molinillo** (near the market) and desolate beaches.

Tourist Offices: Municipal, Pl. de la Marina (☎952 12 20 20). Open M-F 9am-7pm. Branch: Av. de Cervantes, 1 (☎/fax 952 134 730). Open M-F 8:15am-2pm and 4:30-7pm, Sa-Su 9:30am-1:30pm. **Junta de Andalucía,** Pje. de Chinitas, 4 (☎952 21 34 45). Open M-F 8:30am-8:30pm, Sa-Su 10am-2pm.

Currency Exchange: Banks (and **ATMs**) line most major roads and cluster around the intersection of Alameda Principal and C. Marqués de Larios. Most open M-F 8:30am-2pm; some also open Sa mornings.

Luggage Storage: Lockers at the **train station** (open daily 7am-10:45pm) and **bus station** (open daily 6:30am-11pm). Both €2.40-4.50 per 24hr.

English-Language Bookstore: Rayuela Idiomas, Pl. de la Merced, 17 (☎952 22 48 10). Open M-F 9:45am-1:30pm and 5-8:30pm, Sa 10am-2pm.

El Corte Inglés: Av. de Andalucía, 4-6 (☎952 07 65 00). Department store with a supermarket downstairs; sells a street map of Málaga. Open M-Sa 10am-10pm. AmEx/MC/V.

Police: ☎092.

24hr. Pharmacy: Farmacia Caffarena, Alameda Principal, 2 (☎952 21 28 58), at the intersection with C. Marqués de Larios.

Medical Services: ☎952 39 04 00, urgent calls 952 30 30 34. **Medical Emergency:** ☎061. **Hospital Carlos Haya,** Av. Carlos Haya.

Internet Access: Internet Meeting Point, Pl. de la Merced, 14. Internet €1 per hr. Also has a pool table, video games, and a coffee and liquor bar. Open daily 10am-1:30am.

Post Office: Av. de Andalucía, 1 (☎902 19 71 97). **Lista de Correos.** Open M-F 8:30am-8:30pm, Sa 9:30am-2pm. **Postal Code:** 29080.

⌐ ACCOMMODATIONS

"Budget" accommodations in Málaga aren't exactly cheap—expect to pay at least €18-22 for a single, and more if you want a private bath. Most *hostales* are in the old town, between Pl. de la Marina and Pl. de la Constitución.

Hostal Larios, C. Marqués de Larios, 9, 3rd fl. (☎952 22 54 90). It's worth the mini-splurge for Larios's sparkling, brightly painted rooms and unbeatable location on the primary pedestrian thoroughfare. No need to pay for a room with a private bath; the common ones couldn't be cleaner or newer. All rooms with TV and A/C. Singles €27, with bath €35; doubles €37/€45; triples with bath €63. V. ❸

Pensión Córdoba, C. Bolsa, 11 (☎952 21 44 69). Delightfully unpretentious, the rooms beckon those who enjoy simplicity and authenticity. Spotless but dark common baths. Singles €19; doubles €36; triples €54. ❷

ANDALUCÍA

Hostal Madrid, C. Marín García, 4, 2nd fl. (☎952 22 45 92). About as cheap as it gets in the city, Hostal Madrid offers simple yet spacious rooms with private balconies and basic showers. Singles €15-20; doubles €25-40. ❷

🍴 FOOD

Beachfront restaurants specialize in fresh seafood; for anything else, stick to the restaurants and tapas bars hiding in the streets around C. Granada, Pl. de la Constitución, and Pl. de la Merced. Fresh produce fills the **market** on C. Ataranzas (open daily 8am-2pm).

🥗 **Vegetariano Cañadú,** Pl. de la Merced, 21 (☎952 22 90 56; www.cuidate.com/canadu). Let your mind enjoy the artistic, breezy, down-to-earth feel while your body heals itself with the 4-course vegetarian *menú* (€7). Order a ginger-infused fruit cocktail for an enhanced experience. Open Su-Th 1:30-4pm and 8-11pm, F-Sa 1:30-4pm and 8pm-midnight. Closed Tu evening. AmEx/MC/V. ❶

🥗 **Café Con Libros,** Pl. de la Merced, 19. Newly relocated and brilliantly painted by the personable, engaging owner, this cafe is sure to draw you back again and again, so discover it early! Their extensive menu of milkshakes, smoothies, teas, and coffees (€1.30-2.30), crepes and pastries (€1.20-2.80), and beer (€1.90) offers something special and affordable for any taste bud. Open M 4pm-1am, Tu-Su 11am-1am. ❶

Mesón Ajo Blanco, Pl. de Uncibay, 2 (☎952 21 29 35). Sample traditional Spanish cuisine served at the traditional pace. Popular with both locals and tourists, Ajo Blanco is a cross between a neighborhood bar and a full-fledged restaurant, featuring meat-heavy baguettes (€3) and tapas (€2-8). Wash it all down with a pitcher of sangria or a drink from the full bar. Open Su-Th noon-1am, F-Sa noon-2am. ❷

👁 SIGHTS

ALCAZABA. Towering high above the city, the Alcazaba is Málaga's most imposing sight, offering great views of the harbor and capturing a medieval tranquility within its brick and stone walls. Guarding the east end of Po. del Parque, this 11th-century structure was originally used as both a military fortress and royal palace for Moorish kings. *(Open June-Aug. Tu-Su 9:30am-8pm; Sept.-May Tu-Sa 8:30am-7pm. €1.80, students and seniors €0.60, under 7 free.)*

MUSEO PICASSO. C. San Agustín, 8 (☎902 44 33 77; www.museopicassomalaga.org). Start off on the ground floor and witness the emergence, through experimentation, of the prodigy's distinctive style; then, when you reach the 2nd floor, prepare for full-blown Picasso. The chronology of the exhibit highlights this artistic genius's transition from man to legend and his progression from tentative detail to ultimate self-confidence and boldness. *(Open Tu-Th, Su, and holidays 10am-8pm; F-Sa 10am-9pm. €6; students, ages 10-16, and large groups €3; under 10 free.)*

SANTA IGLESIA CATEDRAL DE MÁLAGA. Málaga's breathtaking cathedral blends a lot of Renaissance with a bit of Baroque. The incredibly intricate structure, complete with detailed columns, stained glass windows, and more than 15 side chapels, was built on the site of a former mosque, of which only the courtyard remains. Although work on the cathedral began in 1527 and continued for centuries thanks to a hefty harbor tax, the cathedral's second tower, under construction for over 300 years, was never completed—hence the cathedral's nickname *La Manquita* (One-Armed Lady). The small museum upstairs displays religious art, and is certainly worth a peek. *(C. Molina Lario, 4. ☎952 22 03 45. Open M-F 10am-6:45pm, Sa 10am-5:45pm. Mass daily 9am. €3, includes audio guide.)*

CASTILLO DE GIBRALFARO. An Arab lighthouse was built in this Phoenician castle, which offers sweeping views of Málaga and the Mediterranean. The grounds are relatively untouristed, so it can feel somewhat desolate; avoid exploring them alone. *(Bus #35 to the castle leaves every 20min. from the Alameda Principal; otherwise it's a steep uphill hike. Open daily Apr.-Oct. 9am-7:15pm; Nov.-Mar. 9am-5:45pm.)*

CASA NATAL Y FUNDACIÓN PICASSO. Picasso left Málaga when he was young, but according to local officials, he always "felt himself to be a true *malagueño*." The artist's birthplace now houses the Picasso Foundation, which organizes a series of exhibitions, concerts, and lectures. The first floor has been converted into an exhibition gallery; upstairs is a permanent collection of photographs, drawings, and correspondence. One room in the front of the house is decorated to look as it did when Picasso lived here; glass cases display his christening gown. *(Pl. de la Merced, 15. ☎952 06 02 15. Open M-Sa 10am-8pm, Su 10am-2pm. €1; seniors, under 17, and students free.)*

🞂 NIGHTLIFE

Málaga is not especially known for hard-core clubbing; the nightlife scene is of a slightly calmer nature, centering around crowded bars that are liveliest on weekends. Many nightlife spots are not open Sunday through Wednesday. Although you can find the occasional bar or club almost anywhere in the city, Pl. de la Merced hosts a cluster of bars with outside terraces and attracts a young, fun-seeking crowd. Some of these bars morph into dance floors as the morning hours approach. One of these diverse spots, the hip and gay-friendly **Flor de Lys**, is known for its excellent funky music mixes, especially on Wednesdays. (Beer €2, mixed drinks €4.50-6. Open Su-W 11:30pm-2:30am, Th-Sa 11:30pm-3:30am.) Neighboring **El Telón** has an appealing, laid-back ambience spiced with world music mixes and the house specialty *mojitos*, a Cuban rum-based delight. For a change in scenery, head to **Playa de la Malagueta,** where young locals party at beachfront bars and *chiringuitos*. (A 30min. walk, but quick and affordable taxi ride; buses don't run during late party hours.)

🞂 DAYTRIP FROM MÁLAGA

TORREMOLINOS

Trains (☎902 24 02 02) connect Málaga and Torremolinos (30min.; every 30min. 5:45am-10:30pm, return 6:52am-11:34pm; €1.10). Portillo buses (☎952 38 24 19) also make the trip (30min., every 20-30min., €1.10).

A 30min. ride from Málaga can get you to some of the best beaches in the area. Souvenir shops and beachfront restaurants specializing in fresh fish dot the waterfront, while throngs of tourists crowd the kilometers of soft sand. To get to the **beach** from the train station, exit the station, turn left, and then right onto C. San Miguel, a pedestrian street that winds down to the beach, changing names along the way. Get maps at the beachfront **tourist office** in Pl. de las Comunidades Autónomas. (☎952 81 78. Open M-F 9:30am-2:30pm.) Rent **bikes** and **scooters** at **Moto Mercado,** also in the plaza. (☎952 05 26 71; www.rent-abike.org. 16+ with valid drivers license for scooters and motorcycles. Check website for more info and fees. Open M-Sa 9:30am-7:30pm, Su 9am-2pm.)

What cheap accommodations there are lie on the other side of town from the beach. If you decide to spend the night, **Hostal Micaela ❷,** C. Bajondillo, 4, a continuation of C. San Miguel, is about as cheap as you'll get within a few minutes of the beach. (☎952 38 33 10. All rooms with bath and fan. Singles €25;

ANDALUCÍA

doubles €45; triples €55.) Although there are more restaurants and bars lining the waterfront than meals to be had there, **Restaurante Bananas ❶**, at the far end of the beach, is a peaceful alternative to other spots on the strip. Straw tables and chairs, a huge drink menu, and a beautiful porch with a sea view make Bananas almost tropical. (Full breakfast €3-6. Seafood entrees €4-9, meat entrees €3-7. Open June-Sept. daily 9am-3am; Oct.-May hours vary.)

MARBELLA ☎952

Marbella's seemingly endless beaches are a major highlight of the Costa del Sol, and the tan, tan, and tan some more attitude can be appealing. Due to the mountains nearby, Marbella's winter temperatures tend to be 5-8°F warmer than Málaga's, and swimsuit season lasts at least 10 months. In the midst of all this beach hype, however, the richest part of Marbella often goes unvisited: the *casco antiguo* (old city) is a nutshell of authenticity not yet consumed by the generic, making it unique among coastal towns. The city has a long history as an important merchant town occupied by the Phoenicians, Greeks, Romans, and Arabs, and the influence of these groups is still evident in the structure and architecture of the *casco antiguo*. So while Marbella serves primarily as a Mediterranean playground for international jet-setters, anyone interested in life beyond yachts and watersports shouldn't leave without experiencing the old city in depth. Gorgeous and vibrant, spotted with excellent restaurants, bars, clubs, and (unfortunately) a ton of trendy clothes shops, it is a center of activity as well as a historical masterpiece.

▮ TRANSPORTATION

Buses: Marbella, 56km south of Málaga, can be reached only by bus. Ctra. del Trapiche (☎952 76 44 00). To: **Algeciras** (1½hr., 9 per day 7:30am-11:35pm, €5.50); **Cádiz** (2¾hr., 3 per day 7:30am-10:45pm, €14.30); **Fuengirola** (1hr., approx. every 35min. 6:50am-10:25pm, €2.30); **Granada** (3½hr., 3 per day 9am-6:55pm, €12.50); **Málaga** (1½hr., 6 per day 8am-8pm, €4.20); **Ronda** (1½hr., 7 per day 9am-8:55pm, €4.60); **Sevilla** (4hr.; 9am and 4pm, F and Su also 8:30pm; €13.90).

Boats: To **Puerto Banús** from the port (30min.; every hr.; €5, round-trip €8).

Taxis: Taxi Sol (☎952 82 35 35) serves Marbella center (€5) and Puerto Banús (€10).

▮▮ ORIENTATION AND PRACTICAL INFORMATION

The **bus station** is at the top of Ctra. del Trapiche. To reach the city center, exit the station, walk left, make the first right onto Ctra. del Trapiche, and turn right at the end of the road onto C. Salvador Rueda. Continue downhill on Av. del Mercado and turn left onto C. Castillejos, which leads to the perpendicular **Avenida Ramón y Cajal,** the main street in the new town—this becomes Av. Ricardo Soriano on the way to the swanky harbor of **Puerto Banús** (7km away). C. Peral curves up from Av. Ramón y Cajal around the **casco antiguo.** C. de la Estación leads to **Plaza de los Naranjos,** the central hub of the old town.

Tourist Office: Pl. de los Naranjos (☎952 82 35 50). Sells detailed maps of the city (€0.60); smaller ones are free. Open M-F 9am-9pm, Sa 10am-2pm. **Municipal Office,** Glorieta de la Fontanilla (☎952 77 14 42), across from and several blocks to the right of the main beach when facing the water. English, German, French, Italian, and Dutch spoken. Open M-F 9:30am-9pm, Sa 10am-2pm.

Currency Exchange: Banco Santander Central Hispano, Av. Ramón y Cajal, 9 (☎902 24 24 24). Good exchange rates. Open M-F 8:30am-2pm, Sa 8:30am-1pm. **ATMs** abound, especially near the *casco antiguo* and along Av. Ramón y Cajal.

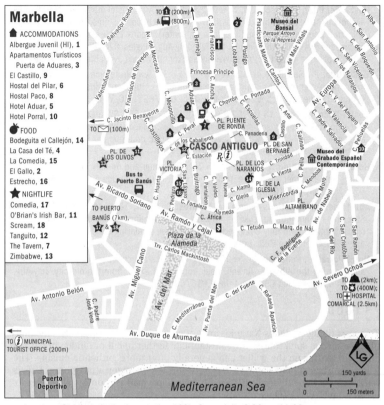

Marbella

🏠 ACCOMMODATIONS
Albergue Juvenil (HI), **1**
Apartamentos Turísticos
Puerta de Aduares, **3**
El Castillo, **9**
Hostal del Pilar, **6**
Hostal Paco, **8**
Hotel Aduar, **5**
Hotel Porral, **10**

🍴 FOOD
Bodeguita el Callejón, **14**
La Casa del Té, **4**
La Comedia, **15**
El Gallo, **2**
Estrecho, **16**

⭐ NIGHTLIFE
Comedia, **17**
O'Brian's Irish Bar, **11**
Scream, **18**
Tanguito, **12**
The Tavern, **7**
Zimbabwe, **13**

Luggage Storage: At the bus station (€3). Open daily 6:30am-11:30pm.

Police: Av. Juan de la Cierva (☎952 89 99 00).

Medical Emergency: ☎061. **Hospital: Comarcal,** CN-340, km187 (☎952 86 27 48).

Pharmacy: Farmacia Espejo, Pl. de los Naranjos, 4 (☎952 77 12 91). Open summer M-F 9:30am-2pm and 5:30-9:30pm; winter M-F 9:30am-2pm and 4-8:30pm.

Internet Access: Neotel Locutorios, Pl. Puente de Ronda, 6 (☎655 54 73 11). €2 per hr. Open daily 10am-2pm and 4pm-midnight. MC/V. **Sky Techno,** C. Sierra Blanca, 3. €2 per hr. Open daily 10am-2am.

Post Office: C. Jacinto Benavente, 26 (☎952 77 28 98), uphill from C. Ricardo Soriano. Open M-F 8:30am-8:30pm, Sa 9:30am-1pm. **Postal Code:** 29600.

🏠 ACCOMMODATIONS

If you have no reservations, especially from May to September, arrive early and pray for a miracle. Swing by the youth hostel first; it's the most likely to have beds.

Albergue Juvenil (HI), Ctra. del Trapiche, 2 (☎952 77 14 91; fax 86 32 27). A youthful spirit unites travelers, who enjoy its huge 🏊 swimming pool, basketball court, and pool table. Self-service laundry €5. 2- to 4-bed dorms, some with bath; common baths are spotless. Mid-June to mid-Sept. €18, under 26 €13; Apr. to mid-June and mid-Sept. to Oct. €16/€13; Nov.-Mar. €12/€9. €3 fee for non-HI members. ❶

Hostal del Pilar, C. Mesoncillo, 4 (☎952 82 99 36; www.hostel-marbella.com). Run by accommodating Scots, this 17th-century inn used to house pilgrims. Now, backpackers enjoy the pool table, bar, and fireplace (in winter). Hearty English breakfast €5. Roof mattresses available when rooms are full. July-Aug. singles €20; doubles €35; triples €45. Sept.-June €15/€25/€36. Weekly and monthly rates available during winter. ❷

El Castillo, Pl. San Bernabé, 2 (☎952 77 17 39; www.hotelelcastillo.com). Sunny rooms with high ceilings, fans, and spacious baths. July-Sept. singles €27; doubles €45. Mar.-June and Oct. €25/€40. Nov.-Feb. €22/€35. MC/V. ❷

Hostal Paco, C. Peral, 16 (☎952 77 12 00; fax 82 22 65). Situated near many nightclubs on one of the *casco antiguo*'s main arteries. Reasonably sized rooms with bath and small TV; ask for one with a view. July to mid-Oct. and *Semana Santa* singles €33; doubles €45. Mid-Oct. to June €30/€40. MC/V. ❸

Hotel Aduar, C. Aduar, 7 (☎952 77 35 78). This small and friendly hotel offers simple rooms and a calmer alternative to lodgings on C. Peral. June-Oct. singles €25; doubles €28. Nov.-May €20/€25. ❷

Apartamentos Turísticos Puerta de Aduares, C. Aduar, 18 (☎/fax 952 82 13 12). Stunningly beautiful studio-like apartments on a charming, narrow old city street. Spacious, spotless, and fully equipped, they guarantee a relaxing stay. Doubles only. July-Aug. €76; Sept.-June €62. Extra bed €20. MC/V. ❺

Hotel Porral, C. Peñuelas, 12 (☎952 77 26 69). It's the cheapest hostel in the *casco antiguo* after the Albergue Juvenil. Basic rooms just 2min. from the old city. July-Aug. singles €18; doubles €30. Sept.-June €15/€25. ❶

🍴 FOOD

Terrazas filling Pl. de los Naranjos are not particularly budget-friendly—the multilingual menus spell tourist trap. Restaurants farther uphill or hidden in narrow alleys are easier on the wallet and generally offer more authentic cuisine. The waterfront has similar eateries, but a livelier and younger atmosphere. Locals retreat to Av. Nabeul for cheap eats. The municipal **market** is on Av. del Mercado, uphill from C. Peral. (Open M-Sa 8am-2pm.)

🗺 **La Casa del Té,** C. Ancha, 7 (☎639 16 79 18). With beckoning incense and music, eclectic art, infinite teas, and delicate crepes (€2.50), La Casa del Té is sure to please all your senses. Open May-Sept. 10am-1:30pm and 5-10:30pm; Oct.-Apr. 4-10:30pm. ❶

Bodeguita el Callejón, C. Alamo, 5 (☎649 71 53 14). In sharp contrast to the plastictabled cafes that flood Marbella's plazas, this small restaurant offers a welcome taste of authenticity. Try the stellar specialties—*jamón ibérico* and regional wines and cheeses. Tapas €1.30-2.50. *Raciones* €3.50-15. Sangria €9 per pitcher. Open Su-Tu and Th-Sa 12:30-3pm and 8pm-12:30am. ❶

La Comedia, Pl. Victoria (☎952 77 64 78; www.lacomedia.net). La Comedia confirms that cuisine is an art from preparation to presentation. Enjoy a creative meal overlooking the beautiful Pl. Victoria. Vegetarian options. Entrees €9-23 with half-portions available. Open Tu-Su 7pm-1am. AmEx/MC/V. ❸

El Gallo, C. Lobatas, 44 (☎952 82 79 98). One of the few truly local restaurants in the area; ironically, a perennial favorite with backpackers as well. Huge portions and cheap, flavorful meals. Tapas from €1. Entrees including rabbit in garlic sauce, pork filet, or chicken, €5-12. Open M and W-Su 9am-4:30pm and 7-11:30pm. MC/V. ❶

Estrecho, C. San Lázaro, 12 (☎952 77 00 04). Praised by locals for its mastery of simple Spanish cuisine, Estrecho is your stomach's unpretentious home away from home. Tapas €2-8, *raciones* €5-14. Open daily 11:30am-4pm and 6:30-11pm. ❶

◎ SIGHTS

If you're not staying in the old city, at least relish a stroll through its maze of narrow cobbled streets and white-washed facades trimmed with wild roses. The dazzling **Museo del Grabado Español Contemporáneo,** C. Hospital Bazán, in a restored hospital for the poor, contains a captivatingly eclectic collection of artistic styles with works by Miró, Picasso, Dalí, Goya, and others. The temporary exhibits are also almost always worth visiting. (☎952 82 50 35. Open Tu-Sa 10am-2pm and 5:30-8:30pm. €2.50.) To the northeast is the **Museo del Bonsai,** Av. de Maiz Viñals, a zen experience brought to you by a large and varied collection of centuries-old miniature trees and the sound of trickling water. (☎952 86 29 26. Open daily 10:30am-1:30pm and 4-7pm. €3, under 12 €1.50.)

◙ NIGHTLIFE

Nightlife in Marbella begins and ends late and is very much scattered throughout town. Except for the busiest weeks of the summer, bars in the *casco antiguo* and along the waterfront only get packed on weekend nights; the expensive bars and clubs in Puerto Banús are busy all the time, though, again, livelier on weekends. The nightlife routine in Marbella means hitting up bars in the *casco antiguo* at midnight or 1am and proceeding to clubbing capital Puerto Banús in the early morning, around 3am. **Plaza de los Olivos** contains a handful of bars and clubs, the best of which is **O'Brian's Irish Bar**—popular, pulsing with life, and famous for its merging of traditional celtic music with funky new-age beats. It's particularly throbbing on Tuesdays. (☎952 76 46 95. Beer €2, mixed drinks €5. Open Su-Th 5pm-3am, F-Sa 5pm-4am.) **Zimbabwe,** also on the plaza, is more of an after-hours club than a bar; it's liveliest after 3am. An interesting contrast of blasting Spanish house and an African-inspired setting attracts mostly enthusiastic Spanish clubbers, though a substantial tourist clientele fits in nicely. (Beer €2.50-3, mixed drinks €5.50-6.50. Open Tu-Th midnight-4:30am, F-Sa midnight-6am.) **Tanguito,** C. Buitrago, 2, attracts mostly locals with its Spanish beats and gets full early on. (☎952 86 35 20. Beer €1.50-2, mixed drinks €5-6. Open M-Th 7:30pm-2am, F-Sa 7:30pm-4am.) For a mellower night out, **The Tavern,** C. Peral, 7, is a small sports bar where *fútbol* fans drink opponents' goals away on game nights. Owner Ken's mixing talents cater to a diverse crowd. (Beer €1.50, mixed drinks €5. Open M-Su 8pm-3am, occasionally opens midday.)

After-hours clubbing happens at Puerto Banús, a short drive by taxi (€10) from Marbella's old city. Though open relatively early, the clubs clustered there don't fill up until around 4am. One of many options is ◙**Comedia,** C. Ribera, which attracts a dancing crowd with an electrically artistic ambience and high energy techno, hip-hop, and house music. (☎952 81 40 04. Beer €5, mixed drinks €8. Open June-Oct. daily 11pm-5am; Nov.-May Th-Sa 11pm-5am.) On Pl. del Puerto, **Scream** keeps the crowd pumped on diverse music and green light beam showers. (Beer €7, mixed drinks €10. Open Su-Th 12:30am-6am, F-Sa 12:30am-7am.)

◤ BEACHES

If you like to walk, the 7km stroll from Marbella center to **Puerto Banús,** almost entirely along a boardwalk, is one of the most beautiful ways to spend an hour and a half; stop in the middle at one of many secluded beaches to cool off. If you prefer to sit back and enjoy the ride, city buses along Av. Ricardo Soriano, heading for San Pedro or Hipercor (€1), bring you to the chic port where brilliant beaches are buffered by imposing white yachts and row upon row of boutiques and restaurants. On exceptionally clear days, the Moroccan coast is just barely visible. Throngs of well-dressed Euro-chicks and -*chicos* mill about the marina in search of well-banked spouses—the port has been frequented by the likes of Sean Connery, King Fahd of Saudi Arabia, Antonio Banderas, and even the late Princess Diana. With 22km of beach, Marbella offers a variety of settings despite its homogenous facade. Shores to the east of the port are popular with British backpackers; those to the west attract a more posh crowd. **Funny Beach,** popular with families, is a 10min. bus ride (take the bus to Fuengirola and ask the driver to stop, €1), or a 2km walk east along the beach.

Water-skiing and jet skiing are especially popular along the strip between Marbella and Puerto Banús, although different companies offer a wide array of watersports. Try calling **Álvaro** (☎686 48 80 68), who coordinates watersports for several hotels and beaches; you will likely find what you're looking for. For sailing lessons try **Club Marítimo** (☎952 77 25 04) or **Club de Mar Puerto Banús** (☎952 81 77 50).

ALMERÍA ☎950

A small, bustling city on the Mediterranean coast, Almería has recently become an incredibly popular spot for wealthy weekend travelers and beach-hungry backpackers alike. As a result, construction is going on everywhere. Cranes and bulldozers fill the streets, refurbishing old buildings or constructing new underground parking garages. Beyond construction equipment, Almería offers beautiful plazas and promenades complete with fountains, sculptures, and rows of flowerbeds and palm trees. A huge Moorish fortress, the Alcazaba, presides over the city, but the best parts of Almería are the vibrant nightlife and the kilometers of sand stretching along the eastern edge of the Costa del Sol.

TRANSPORTATION. The **airport** (☎950 21 37 00), 9km outside town, has daily flights to **Barcelona** (1½ hr.; M-Sa 3 per day, Su 1 per day) and **Madrid** (1hr.; M-F 6 per day, Sa 5 per day, Su 3 per day). The **train station,** Pl. de la Estación (☎902 24 02 02) sends trains to: **Barcelona** (14hr.; W, F, Su 7:30am; €49.50); **Granada** (2hr., 4 per day 6am-6:10pm, €11.40); **Madrid** (7hr., 7:15am and 3:45pm, €31-48.50); **Sevilla** (6hr., 4 per day 6am-6pm, €27.20); **Valencia** (8hr.; W, F, Su 7:30am; €42). **Buses** (☎902 42 22 42) leave from Pl. de la Estación. **ALSA/Enatcar** goes to: **Barcelona** (14hr., 4 per day 8:30am-10:30pm, €52.90); 11hr. express daily 8:30am, €64.90); **Mojácar** (1hr., 4-5 per day 5:15am-8:05pm, €5.70); **Murcia** (3hr., 6 per day 9:30am-10:45pm, €14.70-17.40); **Valencia** (8hr., 4 per day 8:30am-9:30pm, €30.20; 6½hr. express daily 8:30am, €37.40). **Alsina Graells** sends buses to: **Córdoba** (6hr., 3:30pm, €20.10); **Granada** (2hr., 12 per day 7am-8pm, €9.40); **Málaga** (3½hr.; M-F 9 per day 6:30am-11pm, Sa-Su 8-9 per day 8am-11pm; €13.60); **Sevilla** (5-9hr., 3 per day 9:30am-11pm, €26.70). **Almeraya** goes to **Madrid** (8hr., 5 per day 9:30am-midnight, €21.10).

ORIENTATION AND PRACTICAL INFORMATION. The city revolves around **Puerta de Purchena,** a six-way intersection in the center of town. From either station, go out the front door and walk straight through the Pl. de la Estación to the Pl. de Barcelona (both are traffic circles; Pl. de Barcelona has a bronze sculpture in the middle). Take the second left off the circle onto Av. de la Estacíon, walk to Av. Federico García Lorca, and take a right. Go left onto Rmbla. Obispo Orberá. Pta. de Purchena is at the end of that street (15min.). **Paseo de Almería** runs out of Pta. de Purchena to the port—local services, including banks with ATMs, can be found on Po. de Almería or just off it. The **tourist office** is underneath the Mirador de la Rambla, a small building in the middle of pedestrian Av. Federico García Lorca, one block toward the port from the intersection with Av. de la Estación. (☎950 28 07 48; www.almeria-turismo.org. Open summer M-F 6-8pm, Sa 10am-noon; winter M-F 10am-1pm and 5:30-7:30pm, Sa 10am-noon.) Local services include: **police,** C. Santos Zarate (☎92); **Hospital Torre Cardenas,** Paraje Torre Cardenas (☎950 14 16 99); **Internet access** at **Ali Locutorio-Ciber,** C. Calzada de Castro, 14, near the train station (☎950 28 06 77; open daily 10am-10pm); **post office,** Pl. Juan Cassinello, down Po. de Almería. (☎950 28 15 12. Open M-F 8:30am-8:30pm, Sa 9:30am-2pm.) **Postal Code:** 04080.

ANDALUCÍA

▜ ACCOMMODATIONS. Almería has a wide variety of accommodations, from simple rooms in the center of town to luxurious suites that fill the hotels overlooking the beach. **Hostal Residencia Nixar ❷,** C. Antonio Vico, 24, off the Pta. de Puchena a few blocks up from Pl. del Carmen, has an air of tropical luxury downstairs with wicker chairs, potted palms, and hidden courtyards. All the rooms come with A/C, TV, and a half-bath. (☎950 23 72 55. Breakfast €2. July-Aug. singles €27; doubles €45.50; triples €53. Sept.-June €22.50/€37/€45. MC/V.) If you're looking to stay on the beach without emptying your wallet, **Hostal Delfin Verde ❸,** C. García Cañas, 2, on the corner of Po. Marítimo, offers clean, comfortable rooms with ocean views, TV, A/C, and private bath. (☎950 26 79 27. July-Aug. singles €30; doubles €60; triples €70. Sept.-June €26/€42/€50.) **Hostal Americano ❷,** Av. de la Estación, is one of the simpler hostels in town, with small, comfortable rooms and a great location convenient to both the train station and the Pta. de Puchena. (☎950 28 10 15. July-Aug. singles €20, with bath €26; doubles €36, with bath €42. Sept.-June €18.50/€23/€32/€38.)

▐ FOOD. Pricey and touristy cafes and restaurants line Po. de Almería and the Po. Marítimo, which runs along the beach. For the best and cheapest tapas in town, join the lively crowd of locals of all ages at ▨**Casa Puga ❶,** C. Jovellanos, 7, just off Calle Real in the old quarter. Try their fantastic *plancha de champiñones*, mushrooms sauteed in garlic, salt, and olive oil. (☎950 23 15 30. Open M-Sa 11:30am-4:30pm and 8pm-midnight.) For a break from Spanish food, try **Pizzeria-Ristorante Nello ❷,** Av. de la Estación, 26, one block down from Hostal Americano toward the bus station. Nello serves excellent pizza (€7.50-9.50) and pasta (€9.80) in a traditional Italian setting—bottles of wine and old photographs adorn a wooden trellis. (☎950 26 77 39. Open daily noon-4pm and 8pm-midnight.) A great, cheap lunch on the beach can be found at **Cafetería Antárdita ❶,** on the Po. Marítimo (sandwiches €3, tapas €1). Sample their wide selection of ice-cream concoctions (€1.80-6) on the covered terrace. (☎950 24 65 83. Open 8am-3am.) The supermarket is **Champion,** on Po. de Almería. (☎950 23 28 00. Open 9am-9:30pm.)

◩ SIGHTS. Built in 995 by order of Abderramán III of Córdoba, the ▨**Alcazaba,** a magnificent 14-acre Moorish fortress, spans two ridges overlooking the city and sea. Try to visit at sunset for a stunning view of the city after the short trek up to the fortress. The small museum at the site contains Moorish artifacts recovered from archaeological digs in the area. From Pta. de Purchena, go down C. de las Tiendas and follow the green and purple signs posted every 20ft. (☎950 27 16 17. Open Tu-Sa 9am-8:30pm. €1.50, EU citizens free.) The **cathedral,** in the old town, resembles a fortress; its design was intended to prevent raids by Berber pirates. Though bare and imposing on the outside, the inside is all Renaissance, with a touch of Baroque on the altar. (☎609 57 58 02. Open M-F 10am-4:30pm, Sa 10am-1pm, and during mass. €2.) The **Museo del Aceite,** C. Real, 15, will tell you everything you ever wanted to know about the history and preparation of olive oil. There's even a restaurant in the back where you can experience Spain's biggest export in its natural habitat, with tapas for €1-3. (☎950 62 00 02. Open M-F 11am-3pm and 6:30-10pm, Sa 11am-3pm. Free.) Almería is also home to the **Centro Andaluz de Fotografía,** located in the Escuela de Artes on C. Condefalia, one block off the Po. de Almería down C. General Tamayo. Photography exhibitions from all over Andalucía are shown here in a beautiful courtyard gallery. (☎950 00 27 00. Open M-F 9am-2pm and 4-9pm. Free.) For info on exhibitions, visit the office down the block at C. Martinez Campos, 20.

◪ NIGHTLIFE. Nightlife centers around four winding streets behind the post office, appropriately called **Cuatro Calles.** Dozens of bars, pubs, and discos filled with young and old alike dot every corner. Start your night (or your day) at ◪**Changó,** C. Eduardo Pérez, 13. This fun, modern cafe-bar, popular with the twenty-something mixed crowd, opens in the morning for breakfast and serves tapas all day and drinks all night. (Beer €2, mixed drinks €4-8, tapas €1-3. Open 8am-4am.) Beautiful people pack the bar at **Chambao,** C. San Pedro, 13, a new place in town with an enormous photo of Marilyn Monroe, Humphrey Bogart, and Grace Kelly on the wall. (Beer €3, mixed drinks €5-8. Open 11pm-late.) The largest and most popular, if not necessarily the best, disco is **Dolce Vita,** Po. de Almería. An enormous complex with multiple bars and dance floors, the club caters more to older tourists and younger neophytes. If the line is too long out front, use the back entrance at C. Marques de Comillas, 18. (Beer €2.50, mixed drinks €5. M-F no cover, Sa €7, Su €6; includes one drink. Open daily 11pm-6:30am.) For a smaller and much hipper crowd, check out **Underground,** C. Trajano, 23, to dance to the latest Spanish pop and house; it's also a cafe-bar in the afternoon. (☎687 58 73 87. Open daily 3:30pm-5am.) At **Chupiteria Dalia,** C. Dalia, 3, €8 gets you a huge cocktail shaker full of not-so-subtly named cocktail shooters like the sacrilegious *orgasmo de monja* (nun's orgasm). (☎950 26 25 84. Shots €2, mixed drinks €4. Open daily 10pm-5am.) A slightly older crowd gathers at the outdoor tables and by the bar at **The Irish Tavern,** C. Antonio González Egesa, 4. (www.theirishtavern.cjb.net. Beer €2-3, mixed drinks €4.50. Open daily 3pm-4:30am). Afterward, head over to the two huge dance floors at **Parrot's Café,** C. Trajana, 14, at the corner of C. San Pedro, which also has drag shows and salsa lessons; call for details. (☎950 08 40 51. Mixed drinks €3.50. Open Th-Sa 11pm-4am.)

◪ BEACHES. Almería's beaches offer relief from the stifling heat of the city. From the Pta. de Puchena, stroll down the Po. de Almería until you reach the Pl. Emilio Pérez at the end, then head toward the water. Alternatively, take a left from the train station and follow the Carreta de Ronda. First you'll find **Playa Almadravillas,** whose waters are often churned up by the traffic of private yachts motoring in and out of the nearby marina. Take a left and keep going down Po. Marítimo, well past the marina, where **Playa Ciudad Luminosa** and **Playa del Zapillo** offer the many beachgoers calmer waters flanked by numerous stone jetties and a beautiful path lined with benches, hotels, restaurants, and ice-cream stands. The beaches generally improve north of the city heading toward the protected coast of Cabo de Gata.

MOJÁCAR ☎950

Divided between a stunning, white-stoned, picture-perfect hilltop village and 17km of smooth coastline along the turquoise Mediterranean, Mojácar is the ideal European vacation spot. Scores of Spanish, British, German, French, and American tourists flock to oceanfront resorts in July and August to enjoy beautiful stretches of beach, relax in village cafes at sunset, and spend the night hopping from bar to bar along the boardwalk. Between the numerous expats who have made Mojácar their home and the hordes of foreign tourists, you're about equally as likely to hear English spoken as Spanish by visitors and residents alike.

⌶ TRANSPORTATION. Mojácar has no bus stations, but there are two main **bus stops: "Mojácar playa,"** in front of the shopping plaza near the beach, and **"Mojácar pueblo,"** just down the hill from the Plaza Nueva in town. **ALSA/Enatcar** buses (☎902 42 22 42) leave from both stops for: **Almería** (1hr.; M-F 4 per day, Sa-Su 3 per day 7:50am-8:40pm; €5.50); **Madrid** (8hr., 3 per day, €29.20); **Murcia** (2½ hr.; M-F 6 per day, Sa-Su 5 per day 6:50am-9:05pm; €8.80). For a **taxi** call ☎608 33 93 42 or ☎659 93 69 08, or wait at the Pl. Nueva stop in town. The tourist office has a list of nearly a dozen **car rental** agencies. **Indal-futur,** Po. del Mediterráneo, 293, rents **scooters.** (☎950 61 51 56. €35 per day, €99 for 3 days, €109 per week. Driver's license and €40 deposit required. Open M-F 10am-2pm and 5-8pm.)

If you get off at "Mojácar pueblo," it's still 5-10min. up the hill to Pl. Nueva and the main part of the village. Walk or wait for the yellow **Transportes Urbanos** buses, known as *"el Amarillo,"* which run to and from Pl. Nueva and the beachfront bus stop. (Daily 2 per hr. 9:30am-1:30pm and 5pm-midnight, 1 per hr. 1:30-5pm; €0.75.) *El Amarillo* also serves the beaches along the coast. Lines A and B both run in a continuous loop between the two ends of the beach and the town. The point where Av. Andalucía meets Po. del Mediterráneo is the main bus stop, called the *cruce* (crossing). Check the main bus stop or the tourist office for schedules. There's also a new **tourist train** which costs €4 and follows the same route as the bus up and down the **Paseo Mediterráneo,** but goes about twice as slowly; take the bus.

⌶⌶ ORIENTATION AND PRACTICAL INFORMATION. Mojácar is split into two parts: the beach, lined with pricey hotels, tourist-oriented restaurants, and beach-bars known as *"chiringuitos"* along Po. del Mediterráneo, and the pueblo, a charming hilltop village centered around **Plaza Nueva.** The town is connected to the beach by a long, steep, and winding road, **Avenida Andalucía.** Since most budget lodgings are in town, you're much better off staying in the village and commuting to the beach during the day.

The main **tourist office** is in the indoor arcade a few steps below Pl. Nueva. (☎950 61 50 25; www.mojacarviva.es. Open M-F 10am-2pm and 5-8pm, Sa 10:30am-1:30pm.) There is also a **branch** on Po. del Mediterráneo, across from the large shopping center (same hours as the main office). Local services include: **police** (☎950 47 20 00), in the arcade with the tourist office; **Bish's Lavandería,** Po. del Mediterráneo (☎950 47 80 11; washers €4.40-5.40; dryers €1.50 per 15min; open M-Sa 9am-5pm, last wash 4pm); **Internet** access at **Café Calima,** Plaza Arbollón, 1 (☎950 47 87 65. €3 per hr. Open 9am-2pm and 7pm-3am.) and on the beach at **Indal-Futur,** Po. Mediterráneo, 293 (☎950 61 51 56. €1 per 15min.); **post office,** in the arcade with the police (open M-F 12:30-2:30pm, Sa 10am-noon). **Postal Code:** 04638.

⌶⌶ ACCOMMODATIONS AND CAMPING. Finding a bed in Mojácar at the last minute can be difficult, especially in July and August when the city is taken over by partying tourists. Locations close to town have better amenities. The simple, airy, and pleasant accommodations at **Casa Justa ❷,** C. Morote, 5, are a great deal in a lovely building with tiled outdoor staircases and views of the hills. From Pl. Nueva, take a right onto C. Alcalde Jacinto, a left onto C. Estación Nueva, a right onto C. Esteve, a sharp right again onto C. Ruiz, and go down the hill to C. Morote. (☎950 47 83 72. June-Aug. singles €18; doubles €36-42; triples €50-63, some with A/C and private bath. Sept.-May €3 less.) For slightly smaller, cheaper rooms, try **Pensión La Esquinica ❶,** right around the corner on C. Esquinica. (☎950 47 50 09. Singles €12, with bath €15; doubles €25; one triple €36.) The five elegant

SON OF A BEACH

The beach is many things to many people: a dream for those who have never seen the ocean, a relaxing way to commune with nature, even a wild party. For me, the beach is a way of life. Raised in Miami Beach, I grew up with the ocean just a few blocks away. This, I suppose, is what made me a good candidate for the dirty job of tackling Spain's beaches.

When choosing where to lay my towel, I keep in mind exactly what I want out of the day. Do I want peace and quiet and a tan? Do I want to lay among the beautiful people and get a tan? Do I want to swim while getting a tan? You always have options, and the beaches of Spain provide more than most. Mojácar, for example, has over 17km of beach.

An adventurous spirit can even take you to the *"playas naturistas"* (nude beaches)—the perfect spots to make sure your tan goes all the way down. In Mojácar, these lie beyond the edge of the Po. Mediterráneo. Most of the good ones take a little searching to find; if it's a well-publicized nude beach, you probably don't want to go there.

My best advice is to know what you want from your experience. Don't be afraid to shop around; all beaches are not created equal. Especially in Spain, there's plenty of shoreline to explore—whether you want to relax, take a swim, brush up on your surfing skills, or, of course, just get a tan.
— *Sam Perwin*

bedrooms at **Pensión Torreón ❹**, C. Jazmín, 4, are surrounded by green and purple stained glass and an enormous terrace with the best view in town. From Pl. Nueva, follow C. Indalo and take the second right onto C. Enmedio, then take a left downhill along C. Unión, and a right at the end of the hill. (☎950 47 52 59. Call early to reserve a room. July-Aug. doubles with shared bath €50, one room with ocean view €60. Sept.-June €36/€42.) Several inexpensive options line Po. del Mediterráneo, all with similar accommodations and prices. **Hostal Flamenco ❸**, Po. del Mediterráneo, has simple rooms with bath, TV, and A/C along breezy courtyards. (☎950 47 82 27. June-Aug. singles €36, with terrace €42; doubles €60. Sept.-May €24/€30/€36.) On the beach, by far the cheapest place to stay is **Camping El Cantal Playa de Mojácar ❶**, an enclosed campground across the highway from Playa del Cantal. (☎950 47 82 04. €3.90 per person, €2.90 per child, €4.30 per car, €6.10 per camper. Electricity €2.60. Discounts Oct.-Mar.)

🍴 **FOOD.** As with accommodations, you're much better off spending the day at the beach and coming back to eat in town, where you'll find more variety on your plate and better value. **M&J's ❷**, C. Enmedio, 24, offers three separate menus: vegetarian (€8-11), regular (€9-15), and a *menú del día* (€8). There's also a rotating board of appetizers (€4-6). M&J stands for Mark & Jackie, a chatty, expat British couple who love to talk about their loyal clientele or just about anything. (☎600 62 58 08. Reservations suggested. Open daily 7:30pm-1am.) For authentic, cheap, and excellent Spanish cuisine, head to the terrace at **El Rincón del Embrujo ❶**, C. La Iglesia, and don't be put off by the bilingual menu—this place is as local as it gets. (Entrees €6-12. Open 11am-4pm and 7pm-midnight.) On the beach, the *"chiringuitos"* are usually the way to go for food, as most of the other restaurants are fairly overpriced. **El Cid ❶**, on the Playa del Cantal, is the spot to head for a great sandwich (€5) and an even better *mojito* (€5) in the afternoon. (☎950 47 20 63; www.elcidmojacar.com. Open daily 10am-10pm.) For dinner, head to **La Cantina ❷**, Po. del Mediterráneo, 2, in Tito's Beach complex, for what are quite possibly the most authentic tacos and quesadillas (€5-7) in southern Spain. (☎950 47 88 41. Reservations suggested on weekends. Open daily 7:30pm-midnight.)

🏖 **BEACHES.** The beaches are the main attraction in Mojácar. Buses run twice per hour between the town and beach and along the shore (see **Practical Information**, p. 291). There are many beaches to choose from, including the crowded **Playa del Cantal** and **Playa de la Cueva del Lobo,** as well as the more sedate **Playa Piedra Villazar. Playa de las Ventanicas** marks the start of a gorgeous palm-lined path that stretches several kilometers to the south (right at the bottom of the hill from town). The better, though more crowded, beaches, lined with *chiringuitos*, restaurants, beach chairs, and umbrellas, are in the same direction. Those to the left are rockier but quieter. For watersports head to **Samoa Surf** on the Playa del Cantal. (☎950 47 84 90; samoasurf@vodafone.es. Banana boats €10 per 15min. Sea kayaks for 1 person €5 per 30min., €7 per hr.; for 2 people €7/€9. Windsurfing €12 per hr., €50 for 5hr. Wakeboarding and waterskiing €35 per 20min.)

🎭 🎵 **NIGHTLIFE AND ENTERTAINMENT.** Mojácar pulses with nightlife. Tented beach bars sprawl out along the water by Po. del Mediterráneo and are the most popular places to begin (or end) a night. If you're staying on the beach, stick to the bars around your hotel; if you're in town, go by car or scooter if you can. Buses stop running at midnight, and taxis disappear at sundown—you can call one (see **Transportation,** above), but you'll have to wait, and it will set you back at least €7. Walking the poorly lit road, however, is a dangerous and exhausting alternative, as the Po. Mediterráneo is over 17km long.

Some of the best *chiringuitos* include **Tito's,** Po. del Mediterráneo, 2, on Playa de las Ventanicas, which serves excellent margaritas (€3.60-4.50) in a relaxed setting with local photography and white linen curtains. It also holds open-air jazz festivals every summer; call for schedules. (☎950 61 50 30. Open daily 10am-8pm, bar 7pm-3am.) **El Patio,** on Playa del Cantal, offers a similarly laid-back atmosphere amidst tropical trees and tiki torches. Local rock and salsa bands play in the afternoons and through the night on weekends. (Beer €2, mixed drinks €5. Open daily 10am-2am.) Nearby, palm trees grace the bar at **Pascha,** a popular discoteca. **Lua** is an upscale *chiringuito* on Playa de las Ventanicas, about a block from Tito's. (Beer €2.10, mixed drinks €4.50. Open daily noon-4am.)

Back in town, more relaxed bars make up the mini-scene on C. de la Estación Nueva. To get there, follow C. Indalo out of the plaza and take a right on C. Enmedio; C. de la Estación Nueva will be your first right. Locals recommend **El Loro Azúl,** C. Frontón, 1, right next to C. de la Estación, which also dubs itself "La Casa del Mojito." Try one for €5 while experiencing their laid-back atmosphere and outdoor seating. (www.loroazulbar.com. Open 10pm-4am.) Directly across is **Café Calima,** Pl. Arbollón, 1, where great music plays in a gold-trimmed bar decorated with candelabras dripping red wax. Try one of their delicious sandwiches (€3-5) in the afternoon. (☎950 47 87 65. Open 9am-2pm and 7pm-3am.) Because Mojácar has dozens of night spots, the "in" place changes constantly; pick up the free *Mojácar Viva* leaflet at the tourist office for more detailed info.

RONDA ☎952

Graced with rolling hills, valleys, and farms, picturesque Ronda (pop. 35,000) has all the charm of a small, medieval town but the amenities and culture of a thriving city. Centuries-old bridges and arches span the 100m El Tajo gorge, connecting the *casco antiguo*, where most of the sites lie, to the newer part of town, less picturesque but full of life. The old city remains from the Roman era, when Ronda was a pivotal commercial center. Fortunes dwindled under Moorish rule after Al Mutadid ibn Abbad drowned the ruling lord in his bath and annexed the city for Sevilla. More recently, Ronda—the birthplace of modern bullfighting—has attracted such forlorn artists as Rainer Maria Rilke, who wrote his *Spanish Elegies* here, and Orson Welles, whose ashes are buried on a bull farm outside of town. Brimming with sights and fertile ground for romance, you really don't want to miss out on Ronda; it also makes an excellent base for exploring the *pueblos blancos* and the nearby Cuevas de la Pileta.

ANDALUCÍA

⌐ TRANSPORTATION

The **train** and **bus stations** are in the new city three blocks away from each other on Av. de Andalucía.

Trains: Av. Alférez Provisional (☎902 24 02 02). Ticket booth at C. Infantes, 20 (☎952 87 16 62). Open M-F 10am-2pm and 6-8:30pm. To: **Algeciras** (2hr., 4 per day 7am-8:28pm, €5.80); **Granada** (3hr., 3 per day 8:48am-5:23pm, €10.30); **Madrid** (4½hr., 4:35 and 11:39pm, €40-48.50); **Málaga** (2hr., M-Sa 7:50am, €7.60); or take the train to **Bobadilla** (1hr., 4 per day 7:50am-5:23pm, €4-13) which has more frequent trains to **Málaga** (1hr., 14-16 per day 8:21am-10:52pm, €4.30-12).

Buses: Pl. Concepción García Redondo, 2 (☎952 18 70 61). To: **Cádiz** (4hr., 3 per day 9:30am-5:30pm, €11.80); **Málaga** (2½hr.; M-F 9 per day 6am-7:30pm, fewer Sa-Su; €7.80); **Marbella** (1½hr., 7 per day 6:30am-8pm, €4.60); **Sevilla** (2½hr., 3-5 per day 7am-7pm, €9.30).

Taxis: (☎952 87 23 16 or 670 20 74 38). From the train station to Pl. de España €4.

✳ 🛈 ORIENTATION AND PRACTICAL INFORMATION

The 18th-century **Puente Nuevo** connects Ronda's old and new sections. On the new side of the city, **Carrera Espinel** (the main street, which includes the pedestrian walkway known as **La Bola**) runs perpendicular to C. Virgen de la Paz. Carrera Espinel intersects C. Virgen de la Paz between the bullring and Pl. de España. To reach the tourist office and the town center from the train station, turn right onto Av. de Andalucía and follow it to Pl. Concepción García Redondo in front of the bus station. Turn left onto C. Naranja, then right four blocks up onto pedestrian Carrera Espinel, which leads to **Plaza de España.**

Tourist Office: Po. Blas Infante (☎952 18 71 19; www.turismoronda.es), across from the bullring. English spoken. Open June-Aug. M-F 9:30am-7:30pm, Sa-Su 10am-2pm and 3:30-6:30pm; Sept.-May M-F 9:30am-6:30pm, Sa-Su 10am-2pm and 3:30-6:30pm. **Regional office,** Pl. de España, 1 (☎952 87 12 72). English spoken. Open June-Aug. M-F 9am-8pm, Sa-Su 10am-2pm; Sept.-May M-F 9am-7pm, Sa-Su 10am-2pm.

Currency Exchange: Banco Santander Central Hispano, Carrera Espinel, 17 (☎902 24 24 24), near C. los Remedios.Open M-F 8:30am-2pm, Sa 8:30am-1pm.

Luggage Storage: At the **bus station** (€3 per day). Open daily 9am-8pm.

Police: Pl. Duquesa de Parcent, 3 (☎952 87 13 69).

Medical Emergency: ☎952 87 17 73. **Centro de Salud** (☎952 87 56 75), on the road to El Burgo.

Pharmacy: Farmacia Homeopatía, Pl. de España, 5 (☎952 87 52 49). Open M-F 9:30am-2pm and 5-8:30pm.

Internet Access: Planet Adventure, C. Molino, 6 (☎952 87 52 49). Speedy Internet access upstairs (9am-2pm €1.80 per hr., 2-10pm €2.40 per hr.); coffee, smoothies (€1.50), and pastries (€1) downstairs. Open M-Sa 9am-10pm.

Post Office: C. Virgen de la Paz, 20 (☎952 87 25 57), across from Pl. de Toros. **Lista de Correos.** Open M-F 8:30am-2:30pm, Sa 9:30am-1pm. **Postal Code:** 29400.

⌐ ACCOMMODATIONS

Most budget lodgings are concentrated in the new city near the bus station, along the streets perpendicular to C. Espinel—try C. Naranja and C. Lorenzo Borrego. Expect room shortages during the *Feria de Ronda* in September.

▨ **Pensión La Purísima,** C. Sevilla, 10 (☎952 87 10 50). Plant-filled hallways lead to bright rooms decorated with tasteful religious art. Some have private bath. Singles €15; doubles €28-30, with bath €30-33; triples with bath €45. ❶

Hostal Ronda Sol, C. Almendra, 11 (☎952 87 44 97), and **Hostal Biarritz,** C. Almendra, 7 (☎952 87 29 10). Both are run by the same owner, have the same prices, and feature similar spotless, spacious, but slightly dark rooms, most with shared bath. Biarritz is slightly older, but some rooms have private bath. Parking €10. Singles €11; doubles €17, with bath €25; triples €25. ❶

Hotel Morales, C. Sevilla, 51 (☎952 87 15 38; fax 18 70 02). With myriad framed maps, the lobby and hallways are a cartographer's dream. Renovated rooms are clean, pleasant, and have private baths. Singles €18-21; doubles €33-39. MC/V. ❷

Hotel Polo, C. Mariano Souviron, 8 (☎952 87 24 47; fax 87 24 49). Airy, sunny rooms all come with bath, A/C, and satellite TV, although such comfort comes at a price. Breakfast €5.30. Singles €34-42; doubles €53-72. AmEx/D/MC/V. ❸

▐ FOOD

Restaurants and cafes abound in Ronda, although many are geared to tourists and tend to be overpriced, especially those near Pl. de España. Rabbit and stewed bull's tail *(rabo de toro)* are local specialties.

▨ **Relax Bar and Restaurant,** C. los Remedios, 27 (☎952 87 72 07; www.relaxcafebar.com). Tourists and residents occupy the wooden tables and bar for vegetarian fare with an international flair. Many vegan options. Turns into a flea market Sa 5-7pm. Tapas €1.50, salads €4.50-5.50, sandwiches and open-faced "melts" €3.70-4. Try the delicious healthy milkshakes (€2.75-3). Open daily 1-4pm and 8pm-midnight. ❶

Albacara, C. Tenorio, 8 (☎952 16 11 84). Though the ambience here is chic and the food savory, this restaurant is recommended primarily for its ▨ **terraza,** which offers a dazzling view of the El Tajo Gorge and the Sierra in the distance, especially at sunset. The terraza is well worth the splurge; the rest of the restaurant may not be. Starters €7-10, entrees €15-20. Open daily 1-4pm and 8-11pm. AmEx/D/MC/V. ❸

La Gota de Vino 13, C. Sevilla, 13 (☎952 87 57 16). A self-proclaimed "creative tapas and wine bar," La Gota is a couple of steps up from the traditional tapas bar, serving trendy versions of *comida típica* (mostly combinations of Spanish hams and cheeses) to an equally trendy crowd of 20- and 30-something locals and tourists. Great selection of regional wines (€1.80-4.50 per glass). Some vegetarian options. *"Tapas Creativas"* €2-3.50. Open Tu-Sa 1-4pm and 8pm-12:30am. AmEx/D/MC/V. ❸

Pizzería Ristorante Italiano Nonno Peppe, C. Nueva, 18 (☎952 87 28 50). Fabulous pizzas (€3.50-8) and pastas (€3.50-6) with many ingredients imported from Italy. Wide array of Italian desserts (€1.60-3.50) tempt you from a rotating glass case. Open daily 11:30-5pm and 8pm-2am. MC/V. ❶

◎ SIGHTS

▨ **CASA DEL REY MORO.** The name of this sight, House of the Moorish King, is misleading in many ways. Despite its Moorish facade, the house dates from the 18th century and is not the main attraction; in fact, you only enter it to pay your admission. Descend the steep stairs 60m into a 14th-century mine, which, over the centuries, has housed more than its share of prisoners and slaves, forced to climb up and down the stairs to gather water. At the very bottom, a small balcony brings you out at water level right above the river, looking up at the ravine walls and the city. The other main attractions are Forestier's Gardens, high atop the cliffs and house, which were designed and constructed in the 1920s by the famous French landscape architect and boast views as impressive as those from the mine, but from the completely opposite perspective. *(Cuesta de Santo Domingo, 17. Take the first left after crossing the Puente Nuevo. ☎952 18 72 00. Open daily summer 10am-8pm; winter 10am-7pm. €4, children €2.)*

■ **PLAZA DE TOROS AND MUSEO TAURINO.** Bullfighting lies at the heart of Ronda's livelihood, evident in the stunning bullring, the oldest in Spain (est. 1785), and its small yet eclectic bullfighting museum located in a stretch of curving corridor beneath the stands. The recently remodeled museum traces the history of the sport, focusing largely on Ronda's native matadors. Original Goya prints of fights and bullfighters, authentic costumes, weapons, and the heads of the bravest bulls grace the walls and glass cases in the narrow museum hallways, while multilingual posters describe noteworthy fights and explain the exhibits. Ronda has had its share of famous bullfighters, including the Romero dynasty—three generations of fighters from the same family. Pedro, the most famous, killed his first bull at age 17 in 1771; over the course of his career, it is said he fought more than 5600 bulls without ever being injured. Of much greater interest than the museum, however, is the actual bullring and its annexes, such as the bullpens and stables, the architecture and mechanics of which shed some light on how the bulls and horses are dealt with outside the arena. In early September, the Plaza de Toros hosts *corridas goyescas* (bullfights in traditional costumes) as part of the **Feria de Ronda.** The town fills to capacity—book rooms months in advance. Aside from the *feria*, visitors must go elsewhere to see a live bullfight. *(☎952 87 15 39; www.rmcr.org. Open daily Apr. 16-Oct. 10am-8pm; Nov.-Feb. 10am-6pm; Mar.-Apr. 15 10am-7pm. €5.)*

BRIDGES. Carved by the Río Guadalquivir, Ronda's gorge extends 100m below the **Puente Nuevo,** across from Pl. de España. Arrested highwaymen were once held in a prison cell beneath the bridge's center; during the Civil War, political prisoners were thrown from the top. The view from the center is unparalleled—looking to the left with your back to Pl. de España you see the other bridges, while to the right the valley and hills stretch out to the countryside. Two other bridges span the gap and can be reached by walking on C. Santo Domingo past the Casa del Rey Moro: the innovative **Puente Viejo** was rebuilt in 1616 over an earlier Arab bridge, with the Arco de Felipe V, built in 1742, presiding over one end of it; farther down, the **Puente San Miguel** (or Puente Árabe) is an Andalusian hybrid of a Roman base and Arabic arches.

PALACIO DE MONDRAGÓN. Originally inhabited by Don Fernando Valenzuela, a prominent minister under Carlos III, this 17th-century palace has since been transformed into a carefully constructed anthropological museum. Exhibits on ancient life in the area fill former sitting rooms and libraries. *(2 blocks behind Pl. Duquesa de Parcent. ☎952 87 84 50. Open summer M-F 10am-7pm, Sa-Su 10am-3pm; winter M-F 10am-6pm, Sa-Su 10am-3pm. €2, students €1, under 12 and disabled free.)*

OTHER SIGHTS. Learn what life as a Spanish bandit was like at the tiny but informative **Museo del Bandolero,** C. Armiñán, 65, dedicated to presenting "pillage, theft, and rebellion in Spain since Roman times." *(C. Armiñán, 65. ☎952 87 77 85; www.museobandolero.com. Open daily summer 10am-7pm; winter 10am-6pm. €2.70, students and children €2.40.)* The **Museo Lara** will walk you through time, from Phoenician urns to Inquisition torture devices, tracing the development of microscopes and typewriters, and hosting limitless other collections that make for a wildly eclectic yet somehow logical exhibition. *(C. Armiñán, 29. ☎/fax 952 87 12 63; www.museolara.org. Open daily 10:30am-8pm. €2.50; students, children, and large groups €2.)* The **Museo de Caza** displays mounted hunting trophies from four continents. With mountains of taxidermy, it's definitely not a good place for vegetarians or those with weak stomachs. *(C. Armiñán, 59. ☎ 952 87 78 62. Open daily 10am-7pm. €1.50.)* Following the Christian reconquest of Ronda in 1485, the **Colegiata de Santa María la Mayor** was assembled slowly over the next two centuries on the grounds of a mosque and features both Gothic and Renaissance styles. A small arch near the entrance and a verse from the Qur'an engraved behind the sacristy are the last vestiges of the church's Moorish origins. *(Facing Pl. Duquesa de Parent in the old town. ☎ 952 87 22 46. Open daily high season 10am-8pm; low season 10am-6pm. €2, groups €1.50 per person.)*

ANDALUCÍA

⚑ NIGHTLIFE

Except for weekends, nightlife in Ronda is fairly low-key. Locals congregate in the pubs and *discotecas* along C. Jerez and the streets behind Pl. del Socorro. Popular with young Spaniards is **Bar Antonio**, C. San José, 1, with cheap drinks and tasty tapas. (Beer €0.90, mixed drinks €3. Tapas €0.80. Open M-Sa 7am-2am.) An eclectic crowd heads to **Huskies Sport Bar-Café**, C. Molino, 1, for beer, conversation, and the occasional sports game. (☎ 637 51 54 74; www.huskiesbar.com. Beer €1.80, mixed drinks €3.50. Open daily noon-3am.)

⚑ DAYTRIP FROM RONDA

▩ CUEVAS DE LA PILETA
By car, take highway C-339 north (Ctra. Sevilla from the new city). The turnoff to Benaoján and the caves is about 13km out, in front of an abandoned restaurant. Taxis will go round-trip from Ronda for €46. A cheaper alternative is the train to Benaoján (20min.; 3 per day 7am-4:33pm, return 3 per day 1:39pm-7:59pm; round-trip €3.50). From the train station, it's a tough but scenic 1-1½hr. climb to the caves. The hike is mostly uphill and there is little shade; bring water and sturdy shoes. With your back to the station, exit left and follow the road parallel to the tracks for 100m until you reach the sign for Hotel Molino del Santo. Walk 15m past the sign on the narrow path next to the tracks and take the first right; continue past the hotel until you see a sign on the left for the caves. Follow the wide path for 1km up to a dilapidated farm; just before the old farm turn right onto the goat track leading uphill. Near the summit is a narrow highway; turn left and go 500m to the cave parking lot. (☎ 952 16 73 43. Caves open daily 10am-1pm and 4-6pm. Mandatory 1hr. tours begin on the hour, but call beforehand to avoid surprises, especially if you don't have a car—there is nothing within reasonable walking distance here if you end up with extra time. €6.50, groups of 9 or more €6 per person.)

The **Cuevas de la Pileta,** 22km west of Ronda, are a dark expanse of stalactites and Paleolithic paintings stretching for over a kilometer underground, formed tens of thousands of years ago by an underground river. Despite their well-preserved paintings and impressive size, the caves have remained relatively untouristed. More than 22,000 years ago local inhabitants took refuge here, painting the walls with cryptic symbols and animal imagery. The highlights are the *yegua preñada* (pregnant mare; located in a cave accessible only to professional groups) and the beautifully preserved *pez* (fish). Its walls are darkened with soot, and small human bones have been discovered in a number of locations; it's believed that the caves held special significance during Neolithic times and were the site of child sacrifices. Gas-lantern tours are given in Spanish and English by the passionate grandson of the man who discovered the caves in 1906. Reservations are accepted only in winter. Wear comfortable, sturdy shoes and bring a light sweatshirt—the caves are slippery and cool.

ANDALUCÍA

ANTEQUERA ☎ 952

The Romans gave Antequera (pop. 42,000) its name, but older civilizations contributed to making the Antequera of today such an historical and cultural wonder. On the outskirts of town, the *dólmenes* (funerary chambers built from rock slabs) showcase primitive art, and the municipal museum's exhibit of religious art and artifacts tells southern Spain's history since the Moorish conquest. The abundance of beautiful churches in Antequera is owed to the fact that this was the first town to be "retaken" for Christianity. Wind has artfully eroded the boulders of Sierra de Torcal for centuries, but does not minimize the scorching heat of summer. Spared of the hype and commercialized identity problems that many of the coastal cities increasingly experience, Antequera is a true Andalusian gem.

▐ TRANSPORTATION

Trains: Av. de la Estación (☎902 24 02 02). To: **Algericas** (3hr., 3 per day 8:43am-7:10pm, €10.50) **Almería** (4hr., 3 per day 8:44am-7:28pm, €18), **Granada** (1½hr., 6 per day 10:21am-9pm, €6-7), **Ronda** (1¼hr., 3 per day 8:43am-7:10pm, €5), **Sevilla** (1¾hr., 4 per day 9:54am-10:38pm, €11).

Buses: Po. García Olmo (☎952 84 19 57 or 84 13 65). To: **Córdoba** (1¼-1½hr., 9:45 and 10am, €7.70); **Granada** (1-1½hr., 4 per day 7:15am-4:40pm, €6.40); **Málaga** (1hr., 10am, €4.80); **Murcia** (5hr., 9:45am, €22.60); **Sevilla** (1¼-1½hr., 4 per day 8:45am-6:45pm, €10.30).

Taxis: Taxi Radio Antequera (☎952 84 55 30) services Antequera and will go to Sierra de Torcal. Fare to town center approx. €4, but the walk is manageable.

◄▶ ⬛ ORIENTATION AND PRACTICAL INFORMATION

From the train station, it's a 10min. hike up a shadeless hill along Av. de la Estación to reach **Plaza de San Sebastián,** the town center. At the top, continue straight past the market, turn right onto C. de la Encarnación, and pass the Museo Municipal to reach the plaza. Alternatively, from the bus station it is just under a 15min. walk *down* a shadeless hill. Exit the station at the top, cross the street, and turn right on Ctra. del Albergue; when you reach Pl. de la Constitución, cross the street at the gas station and walk left along Alameda de Andalucía, which becomes C. Infante Don Fernando and leads to the tourist office and Pl. de San Sebastián.

Tourist Office: Pl. de San Sebastián, 7 (☎/fax 952 70 25 05). Open mid-June to mid-Sept. M-Sa 11am-2pm and 5-8pm, Su 11am-2pm; mid-Sept. to mid-June M-Sa 10:30am-1:30pm and 4-7pm, Su 11am-2pm.

Bank: Banco Santander Central Hispano, C. Infante Don Fernando, 51 (☎952 24 24 24). Open M-F 8:30am-2pm, Sa 8:30am-1pm.

Municipal Police: Av. de la Legión (☎952 70 81 04).

Pharmacy: Pl. de San Francisco. Open M-F 9am-1:30pm and 5-8:30pm, Sa 10:30am-1:30pm.

Medical Emergency: ☎952 84 19 66. **Hospital: Hospital Comarcal,** C. Polígono Industrial, 67 (☎952 84 62 63, urgent care 952 06 11 50).

Internet Access: Sala Ozono, C. Merecillas, 14 (☎952 84 10 84). €1.50 per hr. Open daily 11am-midnight.

Post Office: C. Nájera (☎952 84 20 83). Open M-F 8am-2pm, Sa 9:30am-1pm. **Postal Code:** 29200.

ACCOMMODATIONS

Relative to its size, Antequera offers many accommodation options from *pensiones* to fancier hotels, most of which are located toward the center of the city. Most hostels provide cheap, comfortable rooms; reserving in advance is advised.

■ **Pensión Toril,** C. Toril, 3-5 (☎/fax 952 84 31 84), off Pl. de San Francisco. Accommodating owner offers bright, clean rooms with fans and TV. Locals gather on the patio to play dominoes. Restaurant serves a filling *menú* complete with wine for €6. Breakfast €1.20. Parking included. Singles €10, with bath €15; doubles €20/€24. ❶

Hotel Plaza San Sebastián, Pl. San Sebastián, 4 (☎952 84 42 39; www.hotelplaza-sansebastian.com). Luxury for a fraction of big city prices. Read in the sun on the tiled terrace, watch TV on the leather sofas in the lounge, enjoy a delicious *menú* (€7) at the restaurant, then relax in your air-conditioned room with bath and TV. Internet €1.20 per hr. Singles €25; doubles €39. Prices slightly higher during *Semana Santa.* ❷

Hotel Residencia Colón, C. Infante Don Fernando, 29 (☎952 84 00 10; www.castelcolon.com). This maze-like hotel has large, surprisingly inexpensive—albeit slightly dark—rooms. Great location. Rooms with private bath have A/C. Free Internet. Singles €15, with bath €20; doubles €20/€35; triples with bath €52; quads with bath €65. ❶

FOOD AND NIGHTLIFE

Restaurant and nightlife options in Antequera are surprisingly limited. The restaurants at the hostels and hotels listed above are a good bet for an authentic *menú,* as are those lining C. Calzada. Get fresh produce, fish, and meat at the **market** in Pl. San Francisco. (Open M-Sa 8am-3pm.) **Mercadona,** C. Calzada, 18, and C. Infante Don Fernando, 17, has all the basics. (Open M-Sa 9am-9pm. MC/V.)

La Espuela, C. San Agustín, 1 (☎952 70 30 31). Excellent Andalusian and Italian cuisine; the menu generously accommodates most tastes and has a comprehensive vegetarian selection. Entrees €8-16. *Menú* €13.50. Open daily noon-midnight. MC/V. ❸

Manolo Bar, C. Calzada, 14 (☎952 84 10 15). Ever wonder where Spain and Marlboro country cross? Come find your answer at this unique bar. Ultra-cheap tapas €1, *raciones* €5-6, sangria €2. Open W-Th 5pm-1am, F-Sa 5pm-3am. ❶

Cafetería Florida, C. Lucena, 44 (☎952 70 10 14). This place is convenient for a very simple breakfast, especially if your hostel doesn't provide it. Lunch is more elaborate; although they have great tapas (try the stuffed artichokes), you can't beat the cheap, filling *menú* (€6). Open M-Th and Sa 7am-8pm, F 7am-midnight. V. ❶

La Madriguera, C. Calzedon (☎952 70 29 37). Let the blasting Spanish music lure you into this bar along with the locals and partake in the unique clubbing experience. Dancing begins at 8pm. Open M-Th 5pm-11pm and F-Su 4pm-5am.

SIGHTS

LOS DÓLMENES. Antequera's three ancient caves are some of the oldest in Europe. Once burial chambers with storerooms for the riches of the dead, they illustrate the fascinating process of human cultural evolution from the Stone Age on. Although they were looted long ago, the caves are still worth visiting. The 200-ton roof of the **Cueva de Menga** (2500 BC) was hauled five miles to its present location. Carved millennia ago, the four figures engraved on the chamber walls typify Mediterranean Stone Age art (look closely to decipher them). The **Cueva de Viera** (2000 BC), uncovered in 1905, begins with a narrow passageway leading deep into the darkness of the earth. Somewhat farther afield, **Cueva del Romeral** (1800 BC) consists of a long corridor leading to two round chambers; the second was used for funerary offerings. *(1km walk to reach the Cuevas de Menga and Viera; follow signs toward Granada from the town center (20min.) and watch for a small sign past the gas station. To reach Cueva del Romeral from the other caves, continue on the highway to Granada for another 3km. After the 4th rotary, across from Mercadona, a gravel road leads to a narrow path bordered by cyprus trees; take this across the tracks to reach the cave. Ask the guard to let you in if the gate is locked. All 3 caves open Tu 10am-2pm, W-Sa 9am-3pm, Su 9:30am-2pm. Free.)*

OTHER SIGHTS. Back in town, all that remains of the **Alcazaba** are its two towers, the wall between them, and some well-trimmed hedges. From the top, visitors get unparalleled views of the city and surrounding countryside; it's especially magnificent at dusk. *(Always open, although it's best to go during daylight hours. Free.)* Next door, the towering **Real Colegiata de Santa María la Mayor** was the first church in Andalucía to incorporate Renaissance style. *(Open July to mid-Sept. Tu-F 10:30am-2pm and 8-10pm, Sa 10:30am-2pm, Su 11:30am-2pm; mid-Sept. to June Tu-F 10:30am-2pm and 4:30-7:30pm, Sa 10:30am-2pm, Su 11:30am-2pm. Free.)* To the left of the church when facing it are the ruins of **Las Termas de Santa María.** The Roman thermal baths, excavated in 1988, feature mosaic tiles, although they're almost impossible to see from the church plaza. Downhill, one block from the tourist office in the Palacio de Nájera, the **Museo Municipal** displays a breathtaking collection of religious art that brings history to life, as well as avant-garde 1970s paintings by native son Cristóbal Toral alongside dozens of Roman artifacts, including the pride of the city: **Efebo,** a rare bronze statue of a Roman page. *(☎ 952 70 40 21. Open Tu-F 9am-2:30pm, Sa 10am-1:30pm, Su 11am-1:30pm. Mandatory tours leave from entrance every 30min. €3.)*

🔲 DAYTRIP FROM ANTEQUERA

EL TORCAL DE ANTEQUERA

Two-thirds of the 13km to the Sierra de Torcal can be covered by bus. Ask the driver to let you off at the turnoff for El Torcal; from there it's a 5km walk. Casado buses (☎ 952 84 19 57) leave from Antequera (M-F 1pm, €2); the return bus leaves from the turnoff (M-F 4:15pm). You can also take a taxi (have the tourist office call one for you or the fare may be higher) to the refugio (round-trip €25); the driver will wait for 1hr.

A garden of wind-sculpted boulders, the Sierra de Torcal glows like the surface of a barren and distant planet. The central peak, **El Torcal** (1369m), dominates the horizon, but the surrounding clumps of eroded rocks are even more extraordinary. Declared a natural park in 1978, the Sierra stretches for 11.7km. Several trails circle the summit. The well-traveled green arrow path (1½km) takes about 45min.; the red arrow path (4½km) takes over 2hr. All but the green path require a guided tour; call the **Centro de Información** for details. (☎ 952 03 13 89. Open daily 10am-5pm.) Each path begins and ends at the *refugio* (lodge) at the mountain base. Try to catch a spectacular sunset from the striking 🔲**Mirador de las Ventanillas.**

GRANADA ☎958

The splendors of the Alhambra, the magnificent palace which crowns the highest point of this city, have fascinated both prince and pauper for centuries. To this day, visitors are still captivated by the charm, the mystery, and the indescribable romance that emanates from the stones of the ancient and winding streets.

Conquered by invading Muslim armies in 711, Granada blossomed into one of Europe's wealthiest, most refined cities. As Christian armies turned back the tide of Moorish conquest in the 13th century, the city became the last Muslim outpost in Iberia, surrounded by a unified Christian kingdom. The relentless Christian onslaught and growing disputes and corruption within the ruling dynasty caused Moorish rule over Granada to wane by the end of the 15th century. Fernando and Isabel capitalized on the chaos, finally capturing Boabdil—Granada's last Moorish ruler—and the Alhambra on the momentous night of January 1, 1492. As Boabdil fled, his mother berated him for casting a longing look back at the Alhambra, saying, "You do well to weep as a woman for what you could not defend as a man."

Although the Christians torched all the mosques and the lower city, embers of Granada's Arab past still linger. The Albaicín, an enchanting maze of Moorish houses and twisting alleys, is Spain's best-preserved Arab quarter and the only part of the Muslim city to survive the *Reconquista* intact. Since then, Granada has grown into a university town, surrendering to throngs of international students, backpackers, and Andalusian youth. Spend a day or two discovering the history of Moorish Spain and experiencing the energetic local nightlife.

TRANSPORTATION

Flights: Airport (☎958 24 52 37), 17km west of the city. **Autocares J. Gonzales** (☎958 13 13 09) runs a bus from Gran Vía, in front of the cathedral, to the airport (25min., 5 per day 8am-7pm, €3). A **taxi** to the airport costs €15. **Iberia** (☎902 40 05 00), at the corner of Pl. Isabel la Católica and C. Pavaneras (open M-F 9am-1:45pm and 4-7pm), flies to **Barcelona** (1hr., 3 per day, €135) and **Madrid** (30min., 4 per day, €85).

Trains: RENFE Station, Av. Andaluces (☎902 24 02 02). Take bus #3-6, 9, or 11 from Gran Vía to the Constitución 3 stop and turn left onto Av. Andaluces. Call for exact train schedules, as they change frequently. To: **Algeciras** (5-7hr., 3 per day, €15.40); **Almería** (3hr., 4 per day, €11.40); **Antequera** (2hr., 3 per day, €6.40); **Barcelona** (12-13hr., 1-2 per day, €47.50-49); **Madrid** (5-6hr., 2 per day, €28-44); **Ronda** (3-4hr., 3 per day, €10.30); **Sevilla** (4-5hr., 4 per day, €17).

Buses: All major intercity bus routes originate from the **bus station** on the outskirts of Granada on Ctra. de Madrid, near C. Arzobispo Pedro de Castro.

ALSA (☎902 42 22 42) to: **Alicante** (6hr., 6 per day 7:50am-4:30pm, €24); **Barcelona** (14hr., 6 per day 12:15am-5:15pm, €58.20); **Valencia** (10hr., 6 per day 12:30am-7:30pm, €35.50).

Alsina Graells (☎958 18 54 80) to: **Algeciras** (5hr., 4 per day 9am-10pm, €17.60); **Almería** (2¼hr., 6 per day 8:30am-7:30pm, €9.40); **Antequera** (2hr., 3 per day 3am-2:30pm, €6.40); **Cádiz** (4hr., 4 per day 3am-6:30pm, €26); **Córdoba** (3hr., 7 per day 7:30am-7pm, €10.70); **Jaén** (1½hr., 12 per day 7am-9pm, €6.50); **Madrid** (5hr., 10 per day 12:30am-7pm, €13); **Málaga** (2hr., 16 per day 7am-9pm, €8.30); **Sevilla** (3hr., 7 per day 8am-10pm, €16.50).

Public Transportation: Local buses (☎900 71 09 00). Pick up the bus map at the tourist office. Important buses include: **"Bus Alhambra" #30** from Pl. Nueva to the Alhambra; **#31** from Pl. Nueva to the Albaicín; **#10** from the bus station to the youth hostel, C. de Ronda, C. Recogidas, and C. Acera de Darro; **#3** from the bus station to Av. de la Constitución, Gran Vía, and Pl. Isabel la Católica. €0.90, *bonobus* (10 tickets) €5.10.

Taxis: Teletaxi (24hr. ☎958 28 06 54), with service throughout Granada and its environs.

Car Rental: Atasa, Pl. Cuchilleros, 1 (☎958 22 40 04), on the right side of Pl. Nueva from Pl. Isabel la Católica. 21+ and must have had license for at least 1 yr. From €284 per wk. with unlimited mileage and insurance. Prices rise with shorter rentals.

ORIENTATION AND PRACTICAL INFORMATION

The geographic center of Granada is small **Plaza Isabel la Católica,** at the intersection of the city's two main arteries, **Calle de los Reyes Católicos** and **Gran Vía de Colón.** On Gran Vía, you'll find the **cathedral.** Two short blocks uphill on C. de los Reyes Católicos sits Pl. Nueva. The **Alhambra** commands the hill above Pl. Nueva. Downhill, also along C. de los Reyes Católicos, are **Plaza Carmen** and **Puerta Real.**

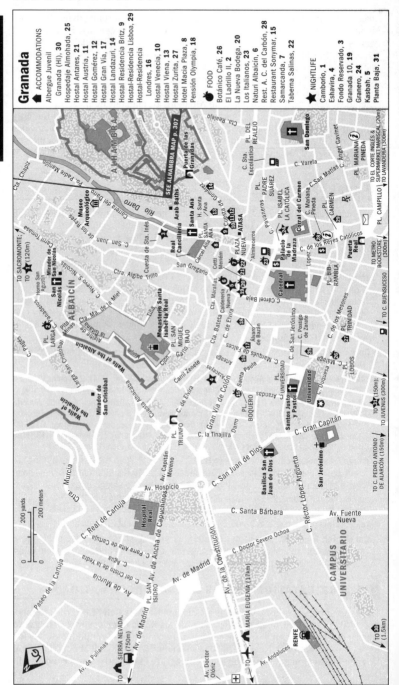

Granada

▲ ACCOMMODATIONS

Albergue Juvenil
Granada (HI), 30
Hospedaje Almohada, 25
Hostal Antares, 21
Hostal Austria, 11
Hostal Goméréz, 12
Hostal Gran Via, 17
Hostal Landazuri, 14
Hostal Residencia Britz, 9
Hostal-Residencia Lisboa, 29
Hostal-Residencia
Londres, 16
Hostal Venecia, 10
Hostal Viena, 13
Hostal Zurita, 27
Hotel Macia Plaza, 8
Pensión Olympia, 18

● FOOD

Botánico Café, 26
El Ladrillo II, 2
La Nueva Bodega, 20
Los Italianos, 23
Naturi Albaicín, 6
Rest. A. C. del Carbón, 28
Restaurant Sonymar, 15
Samarcanda, 7
Taberna Salinas, 22

★ NIGHTLIFE

Camborio, 1
Eshavira, 4
Fondo Reservado, 3
Granada 10, 19
Granero, 24
Kasbah, 5
Planta Baja, 31

Tourist Offices: Oficina Provincial, Pl. Mariana Pineda, 10 (☎958 24 71 28). English spoken. Open M-F 9am-8pm, Sa 10am-7pm, Su 10am-4pm. **Junta de Andalucía,** C. Mariana Pineda (☎958 22 59 90). Open M-Sa 9am-7pm, Su 10am-2pm.

Currency Exchange: Banco Santander Central Hispano, Gran Vía, 3 (☎958 21 73 00). Exchanges money and cashes AmEx Traveler's Cheques commission free. Open May-Sept. M-F 9am-2pm; Oct.-Apr. M-Sa 9am-2pm.

American Express: C. de los Reyes Católicos, 31 (☎958 22 45 12). Open M-F 9am-1:30pm and 2-9pm, Sa 10am-2pm.

Luggage Storage: 24hr. storage at the **train station** (€3).

El Corte Inglés: C. Genil, 20-22 (☎958 22 32 40). Follow Acera del Casino from Pta. Real to C. Genil. Open M-Sa 10am-10pm.

English-Language Bookstore: Metro, C. Gracia, 31 (☎958 26 15 65). Vast foreign language section. Open M-F 10am-2pm and 5-8:30pm, Sa 11am-2pm.

Gay and Lesbian Services: Juvenós, C. Lavadero de las Tablas, 15, organizes weekly activities for gay youth. **Información Homosexual Hotline** (☎958 20 06 02).

Laundromat: C. de la Paz, 19. Wash €5, dry €1 per 15min. Detergent, softener, and bleach available. Open M-F 10am-2pm and 5-8pm.

Police: C. Duquesa, 21 (☎958 80 80 00). English spoken.

Pharmacy: Farmacia Gran Vía, Gran Vía, 6 (☎958 22 29 90). Open M-F 9:30am-2pm and 5-8:30pm. Other pharmacies throughout the city.

Medical Assistance: Clínica de San Cecilio, C. Dr. Olóriz, 16 (☎958 28 02 00).

Internet Access: NavegaWeb, C. de los Reyes Católicos, 55 (navegagranada@terra.es). English spoken. €1.50 per hr., students €1. Open 10am-11pm. **Net** (☎958 22 69 19) has 2 locations: Pl. de los Girones, 3 (€1 per hr.) and C. Buensuceso, 22, 1 block from Pl. Trinidad (€0.80 per hr.). Both open M-F 9am-11pm, Sa-Su 10am-11pm.

Post Office: Pta. Real (☎958 22 48 35). **Lista de Correos** and **fax** service. Wires money M-F 8:30am-2:30pm. Open M-F 8am-9pm, Sa 9:30am-2pm. **Postal Code:** 18009.

ACCOMMODATIONS AND CAMPING

NEAR PLAZA NUEVA

Hostels line Cuesta de Gomérez, the street leading uphill to the Alhambra, to the right of Pl. Nueva. Crashing in this area is wise for those planning to spend serious time in the Alhambra complex, but these spots tend to fill up most quickly.

Hostal Venecia, Cuesta de Gomérez, 2, 3rd fl. (☎958 22 39 87). A hint of incense, cozy rooms, and attentive service with morning tea make Sergio and María del Carmen's small *hostal* the best bargain in town. Reserve early, especially in summer, since the secret is out. Singles €15; doubles €28; triples and quads €13 per person. ❶

Hostal Austria, Cuesta de Gomérez, 4 (☎958 22 70 75). Delightfully clean and spacious, rooms here make great temporary homes. Singles €25; doubles €45. MC/V. ❷

Hostal Viena, H. Santa Ana, 2 (☎958 22 18 59). Rooms all have A/C and are invariably pleasant. Singles €25; doubles €37, with bath €45; triples €50/€60. MC/V. ❷

Hostal Residencia Britz, Cuesta de Gomérez, 1 (☎/fax 958 22 36 52). Large, spotless rooms. Laundry €4. Singles €19; doubles €29, with bath €42. 6% discount if you show your copy of *Let's Go* and pay in cash. MC/V. ❷

Hostal Gomérez, Cuesta de Gomérez, 10 (☎958 22 44 37). Simple rooms with hall baths. Multilingual owner will assist guests planning longer stays. Laundry €6. Singles €15; doubles €28; triples €30. ❷

Hostal Landazuri, Cuesta de Gomérez, 24 (☎/fax 958 22 14 06). Plain hallways open into big, colorful rooms. Rooftop terrace with potted flowers and ivy has splendid views of the Alhambra and Sierra Nevada. English spoken. Curfew 1am. Singles €20, with bath €28; doubles €28/€36; suite €40. ❷

Hotel Macia Plaza, Pl. Nueva, 4 (☎958 22 75 36; fax 22 75 33). A modern, comfortable hotel located right on the plaza. All rooms are carpeted and have marble bath, TV, phone, and A/C. Singles €47; doubles €70; triples €90. ❹

NEAR THE CATHEDRAL/UNIVERSITY

Hostels surround Pl. Trinidad, at the end of C. de los Mesones when coming from Pta. Real. Many *pensiones* around C. de los Mesones cater to students during the academic year but free up during the summer, offering excellent deals to the diligent stair-climber. The ones listed below are open year-round.

■ **Hospedaje Almohada,** C. Postigo de Zárate, 4 (☎958 20 74 46; if Mercedes, the hip proprietress, isn't in, call her cell phone ☎627 47 25 53; www.hospedajealmohada.com). Lounge in the TV area, listen to the stereo, use the fridge, cook your own pasta, and appreciate the art hand-made by Mercedes and her husband. Laundry €3. Dorms €14; singles €16; doubles €30; triples €40. Negotiate for longer stays. ❶

Hostal Zurita, Pl. Trinidad, 7 (☎958 27 50 20). Standard rooms with A/C, TV, and sound-proof balcony doors allow you to take a break from the busy student neighborhood. Singles €18; doubles €30, with bath €36; triples €43/€54. ❷

Hostal-Residencia Lisboa, Pl. Carmen, 29 (☎958 22 14 14; www.lisboaweb.com). Singles €19, with bath €32; doubles €29/€44; triples €37/€54. MC/V. ❷

ALONG GRAN VÍA DE COLÓN AND ELSEWHERE

Hostels are sprinkled along the center of Gran Vía. In all cases, rooms with balconies on the street are much noisier than those that open onto an inner patio.

■ **Hostal Antares,** C. Cetti Meriém, 10 (☎958 22 83 13). Immaculate, large, and well-lit rooms and a Led Zepplin-worshiping owner make this a fun place to live for a few days. Rooms with A/C and TV available. Singles €18; doubles €28, with bath €36. ❷

Pensión Olympia, C. Álvaro de Bazán, 6 (☎958 27 82 38). Standard place with simple, spacious rooms. Singles €15; doubles €20, with shower €25, with bath €30. MC/V. ❶

Hostal-Residencia Londres, Gran Vía, 29, 6th fl. (☎958 27 80 34), perched atop a fin-de-siècle edifice with multiple patios. Great views of the Alhambra and the cathedral from most rooms. 1 large bath for every 2 bedrooms. English spoken. Singles €18; doubles €27, with bath €35. Extra person €10. ❷

Hostal Gran Vía, Gran Vía, 17 (☎958 27 92 12). Singles with shower €17; doubles with shower €25, with bath €33; triples €35/€45. ❷

Albergue Juvenil Granada (HI), C. Ramón y Cajal, 2 (☎958 00 29 00). From the bus station, take bus #10; from the train station, #11. Ask the driver to stop at "El Estadio de la Juventud." Across the field on the left. Towels €1.50. Dorms €10-12; over 26 €14-16. Non-HI guests can join for an extra €3.50 per night for 6 nights. ❶

CAMPING

Buses serve five campgrounds within 5km of Granada. Check the departure schedules at the tourist office, sit up front, and ask the driver to alert you at your stop.

Sierra Nevada, Av. de Madrid, 107 (☎958 15 00 62; fax 15 09 54). Take bus #3 or 10. Shady trees, modern facilities, a large outdoor pool, and free hot showers. If you arrive when the town fair is here, stay elsewhere—you'll have clown nightmares. Open Mar.-Oct. €3.80 per person, €3.20 per child under 10. ❶

María Eugenia, Ctra. Nacional, 342 (☎958 20 06 06; fax 20 94 10), at km 436 on the road to Málaga. Take the Santa Fé or Chauchina bus from the train station (every 30min.). Open year-round. €3 per person, €2.40 per child. ❶

FOOD

Granada offers a variety of ethnic restaurants to relieve those who have had too much fish. North African cuisine and better vegetarian options can be found around the **Albaicín,** while more typical menus await in Pl. Nueva and Pl. Trinidad. The adventurous eat well in Granada—*tortilla sacromonte* (omelette with calf's brains, bull testicles, ham, shrimp, and veggies), *sesos a la romana* (batter-fried calf's brains), and *rabo de toro* (bull's tail) are common. Picnickers can gather fresh fruit and vegetables at the **market** on C. San Agustín (M-Sa 9am-3pm). Get groceries at **Supermercado T. Mariscal,** C. Genil, next to El Corte Inglés. (Open M-F 9:30am-2pm and 5-9pm, Sa 9:30am-2pm.)

NEAR PLAZA NUEVA
Pl. Nueva abounds with large, generic indoor/outdoor cafes located right on the square itself. Those seeking more authentic fare would do better to comb the small side streets that lead out of the plaza. The bars around Pl. Nueva, like most everywhere in Granada, offer tapas for free (with a drink).

Taberna Salinas, C. Elvira, 13 (☎958 22 14 11). For a light but authentic dinner in this rustic tavern, order a *tabla salinas surtida* (plate of cheeses, pâté, and cold cuts; €13.70) to complement a glass of wine. The menu also offers a wide selection of grilled meats and seafood (€7-18). Open daily 12:30pm-2am. V. ❸

Restaurant Sonymar, Pl. Boquero, 6 (☎958 27 10 63). Relish the amazing service and delicious food at this secluded neighborhood eatery. *Menú* €5.90. 4-course *menús* €11.70-13, entrees €7.20-15.20. Open daily 1-4pm and 8-11:30pm. AmEx/V. ❷

La Nueva Bodega, C. Cetti Meriém, 9 (☎958 22 59 34). Cheaper than most restaurants in its vicinity, with affordable yet authentic traditional cuisine. *Menús* €4.20-9. Tapas €4. Beer €1.60. Open daily noon-midnight. ❶

ALBAICÍN
Wander the romantic, winding streets of the Albaicín and you'll discover a number of budget bars and restaurants on the slopes above Pl. Nueva. This is a veritable paradise for connoisseurs of Middle Eastern cuisine; stop anywhere for a cheap Shawarma or falafel sandwich. C. Calderería Nueva, off C. Elvira leading from the plaza, is crammed with teahouses and cafes.

Naturi Albaicín, C. Calderería Nueva, 10 (☎958 22 73 83; www.vivagranada.com/naturi). Excellent vegetarian restaurant with a serene Moroccan ambience. You can venture in many directions with their diverse, exotic menu. No alcohol served. *Menús* €6.90-8.30. Open M-Th and Sa 1-4pm and 7-11pm, F 7-11pm. ❷

Samarcanda, C. Calderería Vieja, 3 (☎958 21 00 04). Delightfully successful kitchen transplanted from Lebanon. For €38, you can order a huge *Mesa Libanesa* platter to share, complete with a bottle of Lebanese wine. The desserts are worth saving room for, especially the *"meghleh,"* usually cooked in honor of a child's birth. Open Su-Tu and Th-Sa 1-4:30pm and 7:30pm-midnight. MC/V. ❷

El Ladrillo II, C. Panaderos, 13 (☎958 29 26 51). Feast on seafood under the stars while listening to the romantic strains of *sevillanas.* The *menú* claims to offer "the biggest portions in Spain." Entrees €6-8. Open daily 12:30pm-1:30am. MC/V. ❷

GRAN VÍA AND ELSEWHERE

Botánico Café, C. Málaga, 3 (☎958 27 15 98). This fresh, hip cafe is a major student hangout where a fusion of cultural food traditions brings new life to Spanish favorites. Converts to a pub on weekend nights. Starters €5-10, main dishes €6-14. Open Su-Th noon-1am, F-Sa noon-2am. ❷

Restaurante Asador Corrala del Carbón, C. Mariana Pineda, 8 (☎958 22 38 10). There's no better place to satisfy your carnivorous cravings. Savor traditional Andalusian meat in an indoor re-creation of an old neighborhood courtyard in Granada. Entrees €11-18. Open daily 1-4pm and 8:30pm-midnight. ❸

Los Italianos, Gran Vía, 4 (☎958 22 40 34). Probably the busiest gelato parlor you'll ever come across, especially when the sun has set. The endless counter offers up a large and original collection of flavors served in many shapes and sizes. *Barquillos* (cups) €1-2; *tarrinas* (cones) from €1. Open daily 9am-3am. ❶

⊙ SIGHTS

A **"bono turístico" pass,** which is good for one week and provides direct access to the Alhambra and several other sights throughout Granada, can be useful. The pass also includes 10 free trips on local bus lines to destinations within the city. (For reservations call CajaGRANADA information and booking office ☎902 10 00 95. For direct sale, ask the tourist office for the numerous outlets around the city. €22.50, with reservation €24.50.)

▧ THE ALHAMBRA

*To reach the Alhambra, take Cuesta de Gomérez off Pl. Nueva and be prepared to pant (20min.; no unauthorized cars 9am-9pm), or take the quick **Alhambra-Neptuno microbus** from Pl. Nueva (every 5min., €0.90). ☎958 22 15 03, reservations for entrance 902 22 44 60; www.alhambratickets.com. Open Apr.-Sept. daily 8:30am-8pm; Oct.-Mar. M-Sa 9am-5:45pm. Also open June-Sept. Tu, Th, Sa 10-11:30pm; Oct.-May Sa 8-10pm. Audioguides available, narrated by "Washington Irving," in Spanish, English, French, German, and Italian (€3). €8, under 8 and the disabled free. Limited to 7700 visitors per day, so get there early or reserve online. You must enter the Palace of the Nasrids (Alcázar) during the time specified on your ticket, but can stay as long as desired. It is possible to reserve tickets a few days in advance at banks for a €0.75 charge; this is recommended especially July-Aug. and Semana Santa. BBVA branches across the country will also book tickets.*

From the streets of Granada, the Alhambra, meaning "the red one" in Arabic, appears blocky and purely practical—a military base planted in the foothills of the Sierra Nevada. This deceptive appearance conceals an unparalleled world of aesthetic and symbolic grandeur born of profound spirituality, heavenly artistic skill, unbreakable determination, and architectural precision. Celebrated by poets, artists, and anyone fortunate enough to visit, the Alhambra never ceases to impress. The age-old saying holds true: *"Si mueres sin ver la Alhambra, no has vivido"* (If you die without seeing the Alhambra, you have not lived).

ALCAZABA. The Christians drove the first Nasrid King Alhamar from the Albaicín to this more strategic hill, where he built the series of rust-colored brick towers that form the Alcazaba, or fortress. A dark, spiraling staircase leads to the **Torre de la Vela** (watchtower), where visitors get a great 360° view of Granada and the surrounding mountains. The tower's bells were rung to warn of impending danger and to coordinate the Moorish irrigation system. At the New Year, during the annual commemoration of the Christian conquest of Granada, an old legend holds that any local girl who scrambles up the tower and rings the bell by hand before

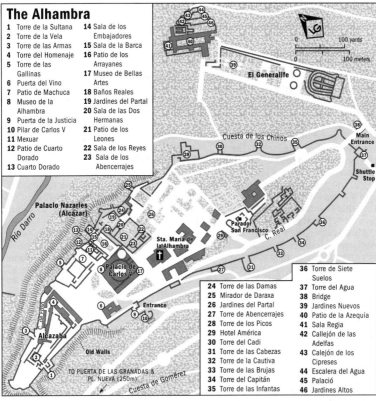

The Alhambra

1 Torre de la Sultana
2 Torre de la Vela
3 Torre de las Armas
4 Torre del Homenaje
5 Torre de las Gallinas
6 Puerta del Vino
7 Patio de Machuca
8 Museo de la Alhambra
9 Puerta de la Justicia
10 Pilar de Carlos V
11 Mexuar
12 Patio de Cuarto Dorado
13 Cuarto Dorado
14 Sala de los Embajadores
15 Sala de la Barca
16 Patio de los Arrayanes
17 Museo de Bellas Artes
18 Baños Reales
19 Jardines del Partal
20 Sala de las Dos Hermanas
21 Patio de los Leones
22 Sala de los Reyes
23 Sala de los Abencerrajes

24 Torre de las Damas
25 Mirador de Daraxa
26 Jardines del Partal
27 Torre de Abencerrajes
28 Torre de los Picos
29 Hotel América
30 Torre del Cadi
31 Torre de las Cabezas
32 Torre de la Cautiva
33 Torre de las Brujas
34 Torre del Capitán
35 Torre de las Infantas
36 Torre de Siete Suelos
37 Torre del Agua
38 Bridge
39 Jardines Nuevos
40 Patio de la Azequía
41 Sala Regia
42 Callejón de las Adelfas
43 Calejón de los Cipreses
44 Escalera del Agua
45 Palació
46 Jardines Altos

El Generalife

Cuesta de los Chinos

Main Entrance

Shuttle Stop

Palacio Nazaries (Alcázar)

Rio Darro

Sta. María de la Alhambra

Parador San Francisco

C. Real

Palacio de Carlos V

Entrance

Alcazaba

Old Walls

TO PUERTA DE LAS GRANADAS & PL. NUEVA (250m)

Cuesta de Gomérez

January 1 begins will receive a wedding proposal within 365 days. Exit through the **Puerta del Vino,** the original entrance to the medina, where inhabitants of the Alhambra once bought tax-free wine (alas, no more).

■**ALCÁZAR.** Follow signs to the *Palacio Nazaries* to see the Alcázar, a royal palace built for Moorish rulers Yusuf I (1333-1354) and Muhammad V (1354-1391). Yusuf I was murdered in an isolated basement of the Alcázar, leaving his son Muhammad V to complete the palace. The entrance leads into the **Mexuar,** a great, pillared council chamber. Note the glazed tile arrangements that reiterate the Nasrid mantra: "There is no victor but God." Attached to the Mexuar is a small prayer hall, with an intricately decorated *mihrab*, marking the direction of prayer to Mecca. The Mexuar adjoins the **Patio del Cuarto Dorado** (Patio of the Gilded Hall). The magnificently carved walls are topped by the shielded windows of the harem, such that the women could see out but no one could see in. The *hammams*, or Arab baths, are behind an iron-grilled door but have been permanently closed for preservation. Off the far side of the patio, leafy horseshoe archways of diminishing width lead to the **Cuarto Dorado** (Gilded Hall), decorated by Muhammad V. Its painstakingly carved wooden ceiling, inlaid with ivory and mother-of-pearl, displays colorful, ceramic, geometric figures.

Next is the **Patio de los Arrayanes** (Courtyard of Myrtles), an expanse of emerald water filled with goldfish and bubbling fountains. Stand at the top of the patio for a glimpse of the 14th-century **Fachada de Serallo,** the palace's elaborately carved facade. The long and slender **Sala de la Barca** (Boat Gallery), with an inverted boat-hull ceiling, flanks the courtyard. The walls are covered with the 99 names of Allah, as well as the familiar Nasrid slogan.

Granada was formally surrendered to the *Reyes Católicos* in the elaborate **Sala de los Embajadores** (Hall of Ambassadors), adjoining the Sala de la Barca to the north, and it was here that Fernando and Columbus discussed finding a new route to India. Every surface of this magnificent square hall is intricately wrought with symbolic inscriptions and ornamental patterns. The Mozárabe dome, carved of more than 8000 pieces of wood and inlaid with cedar, is by far the most impressive part of the room. A section of the original floor remains in the center. From the Patio de los Arrayanes, the Sala de los Mozárabes leads to the **Patio de los Leones** (Courtyard of the Lions), the grandest display of Nasrid art in the palace. A rhythmic arcade of marble columns borders the courtyard, and a fountain supported by 12 marble lions babbles in the middle. Some believe that this fountain originally belonged to one of the sultan's Jewish advisors, but was transferred to this patio and redecorated with Muslim motifs.

Moving counter-clockwise around the courtyard, the next room is the **Sala de los Abencerrajes.** Here, Boabdil had the throats of 16 sons of the Abencerrajes family slit after one of them allegedly had amorous encounters with his concubine Zora-hayda. The rust-colored stains in the basin are said to mark the indelible traces of the butchering; evidently none of this bothered Holy Roman Emperor Charles V, who dined here during the construction of his neighboring *palazzo.* Light bleeds into the room through the intricate domed ceiling, which features an eight-pointed star, a design said to represent terrestrial and celestial harmony.

Through stalactite archways at the far end of the Patio de los Leones is the **Sala de los Reyes** (Hall of Kings). The only human representations in the entire palace—the 21 sultans who ruled from the Alhambra, important assemblies, and hunting parties—are depicted on detailed sheepskin paintings fixed to the walls with bamboo pins. On the remaining side of the courtyard, the resplendent **Sala de las Dos Hermanas** (Chamber of the Two Sisters) has a *muqarnas* (honeycombed) dome comprised of thousands of tiny cells. This stalactite-like structure is typical of Islamic architecture and represents an ascension and the doors of heaven opening. From here, the secluded **Mirador de Daraxa** overlooks the Jardines de Daraxa (Gardens of the Sultana).

Passing the room where American author Washington Irving resided in 1829 and wrote the famous *Tales of the Alhambra* (1832), a courtyard leads to the **Baños Reales,** an unimpressive 14th-century addition, toward the royal gardens and the exit. Do not leave the Nasrid Palace unless you are satisfied with your visit, as—much like Boabdil—you will not be allowed to return.

TOWERS AND GARDENS. Just outside the eastern wall of the Alcázar in the **Jardines del Partal,** lily-studded pools stand beside rose-laden terraces. The **Torre de las Damas** (Ladies' Tower) soars above it all. A series of six additional towers traverses the area between the Alcazaba and El Generalife.

▧ **EL GENERALIFE.** Over a bridge, across the **Callejón de los Cipreses** and the shady **Callejón de las Adelfas,** are the vibrant blossoms, towering cypresses, and streaming waterways of El Generalife, the sultan's vacation retreat. In 1313 Arab engineers changed the Darro's flow by 18km and employed dams and channels to prepare the soil for Aben Walid Ismail's design of El Generalife. Over the centuries, the estate passed through private hands until it was finally repatriated in 1931. The two buildings of El Generalife, the **Palacio** and the **Sala Regia,** connect across the **Patio de la Acequia** (Courtyard of the Irrigation Channel), embellished with a narrow pool fed by fountains that form an aquatic archway. Honeysuckle vines scale the back wall, and shady benches invite long rests. An old oak tree stands at the place where the sultana Zorahayda supposedly had several amorous encounters with a nobleman from the Abencerrajes tribe. Although currently a mere shadow of its past glory, El Generalife still merits a visit.

PALACIO DE CARLOS V. After the *Reconquista* drove the Moors from Spain, Fernando and Isabel restored the Alcázar. Little did they know that two generations later, Emperor Charles V would demolish part of it to make way for his *palazzo*, a Renaissance masterpiece by Michelangelo's disciple Pedro Machuca. A square building with a circular inner courtyard wrapped in two stories of Doric colonnades, it is Machuca's only surviving design. Although the palace is incongruous with the surrounding Moorish splendor, scholars concede that it is one of the most beautiful Renaissance buildings in Spain. Inside, the small but impressive **Museo de la Alhambra** contains the only original furnishings remaining from the Alhambra. (☎958 22 62 79. Open Tu-Sa 9am-2:30pm. Free.) Upstairs, the **Museo de Bellas Artes** displays religious sculptures and paintings of the Granada School dating from the 16th century. (☎958 22 48 43. Open Apr.-Sept. Tu 2:30-6pm, W-Sa 9am-6pm, Su 9am-2:30pm; Oct.-Mar. Tu 2:30-7:45pm, W-Sa 9am-7:45pm, Su 9am-2:30pm. €1.50.)

▨ALBAICÍN

The Albaicín's intricacies are well worth exploring. Although generally safe, the Albaicín is disorienting, so use caution at night. Bus #12 runs from beside the cathedral to C. Pagés at the top of the Albaicín.

A labyrinth of steep streets and narrow alleys, the Albaicín was the only Moorish neighborhood to escape the torches of the *Reconquista*, and it remains a key stop in Granada. After the fall of the Alhambra, a small Muslim population remained here until being expelled in the 17th century. Today, with its abundance of North African cuisine, outdoor bazaars blasting Arabic music, teahouses, and a mosque near Pl. San Nicolás, the Albaicín attests to the persistence of Islamic influence in Andalucía. Spectacular sunsets over the surrounding mountains can be seen from C. Cruz de Quirós, above C. Elvira.

The best way to explore this maze is to proceed along Carrera del Darro off Pl. Santa Ana, climb the Cuesta del Chapiz on the left, then wander through the Moorish ramparts, cisterns, and gates. On Pl. Santa Ana, the 16th-century **Real Cancillería,** with its beautiful arcaded patio and stalactite ceiling, was the Christians' Ayuntamiento. Farther uphill are the 11th-century **Arab baths.** (Carrera del Darro, 31. ☎958 02 78 00. Open Tu-Sa 10am-2pm. Free.) The **Museo Arqueológico** showcases funerary urns, classical sculpture, Carthaginian vases, Muslim lamps, and ceramics. (Carrera del Darro, 41. ☎958 22 56 40. Open Tu 3-8pm, W-Sa 9am-8pm, Su 9am-2:30pm. €1.50, EU citizens free.) The ▨**mirador** adjacent to **Iglesia de San Nicolás** affords the city's best view of the Alhambra—it's especially good in winter when more snow adorns the Sierra Nevada behind it. From C. de Elvira, go up C. Calderería Nueva to C. San Gregorio and continue uphill on this street past Pl. Algibe de Trillo, where it becomes Cta. Algibe de Trillo. At Pl. Camino, make a left onto Cta. Tomasa and another left onto Atarazana Cta. Cabras. The *mirador* will be on your right.

SACROMONTE

If you are not up for the 20min. climb from Pl. Nueva, take bus #31 (€0.90), which runs 8 times per day, night buses Th-Sa 11:25pm-2:30am. Ask at the tourist office for exact schedules and check with the driver that the bus is to Sacromonte before you get on.

Pierce the aura of mystery surrounding the gypsy culture and visit their very unique neighborhood. A whole hillside plastered white with the facades of cave dwellings contains a community worth exploring. Though a stroll in the neighborhood is an experience in itself, the **Centro de Interpretación del Sacromonte** at the top of the hill has a telling display of model caves, from a house and kitchen to a stable and caves for iron-working, basket-weaving, and pottery-making; it also does a good job of answering many frequently asked questions—where else could you learn that the gypsies were originally Punjabis? *(Open M-F 10am-8pm; more information available at the tourist office.)* Since the Sacromonte sits on a neighboring hill, it also offers magnificent views of the Alhambra.

IN THE CATHEDRAL QUARTER

■ **CAPILLA REAL.** Downhill from the Alhambra's Moorish splendor, through the Puerta Real off Gran Vía de Colón, on C. Oficios, the *Capilla Real* (Royal Chapel), Fernando and Isabel's private chapel, exemplifies Christian Granada. During their prosperous reign, the Catholic monarchs funneled almost a quarter of the royal income into the chapel's construction (1504-1521) to build a proper burial place. Their efforts did not go unrewarded; intricate Gothic masonry and meticulously rendered figurines, as well as **La Reja,** the gilded grille of Maestro Bartolomé, grace the couple's resting place. Behind La Reja lie the almost lifelike marble figures of the storied royals themselves. Fernando and Isabel are on the right, when facing the altar; beside them sleep their daughter Juana la Loca (the Mad) and her husband Felipe el Hermoso (the Fair; see **Madly in Love,** p. 180). The lead caskets in which all four monarchs were laid to rest lie directly below the marble sarcophagi in a crypt down a small stairway on the left. The smaller, fifth coffin belongs to the hastily buried child-king of Portugal, Miguel, whose death allowed Carlos V to ascend the throne. In the adjacent **Sacristía,** Isabel's private **art collection** favors Flemish and German artists of the 15th century. The glittering **royal jewels**—including the queen's golden crown and scepter and the king's sword—shine in the middle of the sacristy. Nearby are the Christian banners which first fluttered in triumph over the Alhambra. *(☎958 22 92 39. Capilla Real and Sacristía both open M-Sa 10:30am-1pm and 4-7pm, Su 11am-1pm and 4-5pm. Both sights €2.50.)*

CATEDRAL. Behind the Capilla Real and the Sacristía is Granada's cathedral. Construction of the cathedral began upon the smoldering embers of Granada's largest mosque after the *Reconquista* and was not completed until 1704. The first purely Renaissance cathedral in Spain, its massive Corinthian pillars support a 45m vaulted nave. *(☎958 22 29 59. Open Apr.-Sept. M-Sa 10:45am-1:30pm and 4-7pm, Su 4-7pm; Oct.-Mar. M-Sa 10:30am-1:30pm and 3:30-6:30pm, Su 11am-1:30pm. €2.50.)*

OTHER SIGHTS. The 16th-century **Hospital Real** is divided into four tiled courtyards. Above the main staircase, the *mudéjar* coffered ceiling echoes the ones of the Alhambra. *(Av. Hospicio. Open M-F 9am-2pm. Free.)* The 14th-century **Monasterio de San Jerónimo** is around the corner. Though badly damaged by Napoleon's troops, it has since been restored. *(☎958 27 93 37. Open Apr.-Sept. M-Sa 10am-1:30pm and 4-7pm, Su 11am-1:30pm; Oct.-Mar. M-Sa 10am-1pm and 3-6:30pm, Su 11am-1:30pm. €2.10.)*

🎵 NIGHTLIFE

Granada's "free tapas with a drink" tradition lures students and tourists to the many pubs and bars spread across several neighborhoods, genres, and energy levels. Some great tapas bars are found on the side streets off Pl. Nueva. The most boisterous crowds hang out on C. Pedro Antonio de Alarcón, between Pl. Albert Einstein and Ancha de Gracia, while hip new bars and clubs line C. de Elvira from C. Cárcel to C. Cedrán. Gay bars can be found around Carrera del Darro.

■ **Camborio,** Camino del Sacromonte, 48 (☎958 22 12 15), a 20min. walk uphill from Pl. Nueva. Pop music echoes through dance floors to the rooftop above. Striking view of the Alhambra. Beer €1.80-3. €4.50 cover F-Sa. Open Tu-Sa 11pm-dawn.

■ **Granero,** Pl. Luis Rosales (☎958 22 89 79). A New Age bar pulsing with energy. Low on tourists, high on local style. Salsa and Spanish pop pervade. Beer €2.50, mixed drinks €6. Open Su-Th 8am-3am, F-Sa 8am-4am.

Fondo Reservado, Cuesta de Sta. Inés, off Carrera del Darro. A gay-friendly bar with a trendy crowd. Beer €2.60. Mixed drinks €4-5. Open Tu-Th 11pm-3am, F-Sa 11pm-4am.

Planta Baja, C. Horno de Abad, 11 (☎958 25 35 09). Wildly popular with students and unbeatable on weekends. Shake to electric beats in a futuristic underground garage. Beer €1.80. Open Th 11pm-3:30am, F-Sa 11pm-4:30am.

Kasbah, C. Calderería Nueva, 4 (☎958 22 79 36). Relax amidst the Middle Eastern comforts of this candlelit cafe with silky embroidered pillows and romantic nooks. Busy in the evening; empties out late at night. Arab pastries and an exhaustive selection of Moroccan teas (€1.80). Open daily noon-1:30am.

Granada 10, C. Cárcel Baja, 3 (☎958 22 40 01). Movie theater by evening (shows at 8 and 10pm), raging dance club by night. Perhaps the most flashy and opulent disco you'll ever see (at least in Granada). Club open Su-Th 12:30-4am, F-Sa 12:30-5am.

■ ENTERTAINMENT AND FESTIVALS

The daily paper, *Ideal*, lists entertainment venues in the back under *Cine y Espectáculos;* the Friday supplement highlights bars and special events. The *Guía del Ocio* (€0.90), sold at newsstands, lists clubs, pubs, and cafes.

FLAMENCO AND JAZZ

The most "authentic" flamenco performances, which change monthly, are advertised on posters around town. The tourist office provides a list of nightly *tablaos*. A smoky, intimate setting awaits at **Eshavira,** C. Postigo de la Cuna, in a very secluded alley off C. Azacayas, between C. de Elvira and Gran Vía. This joint is *the* place to go for flamenco, jazz, or a fusion of the two. Photos of Nat King Cole and other jazz greats plaster the walls. Those with musical talent who wish to stage their own impromptu concerts can pick up the guitar or sit down at the piano that the owner has provided specifically for this purpose. (☎958 29 08 29. Call for schedule. Minimum consumption €2.60.)

FESTIVALS

Parties sweep Granada in the summer. The **Corpus Cristi** celebrations, processions, and bullfights in May are world-famous. That same month, avant-garde theater groups from around the world make a pilgrimage to Granada for the **International Theater Festival** (☎958 22 93 44). The **Festival Internacional de Música y Danza** (mid-June to early July) sponsors open-air performances of classical music, ballet, and flamenco in the Palacio de Carlos V and other outdoor venues. (☎958 22 18 44; www.granadafestival.org. Tickets €6-36, senior and youth discounts available.)

■ DAYTRIP FROM GRANADA

GUADIX

From the station on C. Santa Rosa, Maestra buses (☎958 66 06 57) depart for: Almería (1½hr.; 7), Granada (1hr.; €4.10); and Jaén (1½hr.; €7). Call the company for schedules as they are subject to frequent change. Coming in from Granada, ask to be let off at Pl. de las Américas, near Guadix's cathedral, to avoid a 15min. walk from the bus station. The

ANDALUCÍA

Dug (literally) into the rock basin of what was once a prehistoric lake, Guadix (pop. 20,000) has been inhabited for thousands of years. What distinguishes Guadix from other cities in Spain and the rest of the world is that almost half of its residents live in *casas cuevas* (cave houses). If you can't decide where to start touring, there is no better place than the ■Mirador Cerro de la Bala; getting there will acquaint you with the town, and the magnificent 360° view from atop shows you exactly how to prioritize. First come the caves, the town's claim to fame. The Cueva-Museo de Alfarería, C. San Miguel, 47, displays earthenware artifacts and a well dating from 1650, along with a large collection of decorative and domestic pottery from the Moorish and modern ages of Guadix. (☎ 958 66 47 67. Open daily 10:30am-2pm and 4:30-8pm. €2, groups €1.50 per person, children €1.) Another cave open to the public is the Cueva-Museo de Costumbres Populares, on the right off C. Canada de las Perales; it showcases an intact cave house, albeit one over-furnished with anachronistic artifacts. (Open M-Sa 10am-2pm and 4-7pm, Su 10am-2pm. €1.30, groups €0.80 per person, children €0.65.) Though these museums are well worth a visit, residential caves may be more interesting since they're less "dressed up" for tourists and more revealing of the local lifestyle. The home to the right of the Cueva-Museo de Costumbres Populares has a sign explicitly inviting in tourists. The Catedral is another of the town's treasures, where stone is worked like gold. The adjacent Museo del Catedral exhibits a large collection of religious art including paintings, sculptures, and manuscripts. The Alcazaba Árabe, a series of 11th-century turrets, is unfortunately closed to the public.

Despite Guadix's impressive attractions, the city remains relatively untouristed; accommodations are scarce, but prices are reasonable. Experience cave-living at Chez Jean & Julia ❸, Ermita Nueva, 67, run by an amiable French couple in the *barriada de cuevas*. Groups of two to six can rent authentic cave apartments complete with kitchen and bath. (☎ 958 66 91 91. Breakfast included. Reserve months ahead. Cave apartments June-Sept., Christmas, and *Semana Santa* €66; Oct.-May €52; non-cave doubles and triples €35.) Those who prefer more modern comforts should check out Hotel Mulhacen ❸, Av. Buenos Aires, 43, on the highway toward Murcia. Most rooms are wheelchair-accessible. (☎ 958 66 07 50. Singles €33.40; doubles €42.70.) Mesón Granadul ❷, on the corner of C. San Miguel and Av. Mariana Pineda, is popular with locals and serves excellent tapas and *raciones*. (☎ 958 66 61 28. Entrees €4-9.) For a more casual setting, try Pepe ❶, a youthful hot spot with filling *menús* for €7-9.

LAS ALPUJARRAS

Alsina Graells buses (☎ 958 18 54 80) run between Granada and the villages of Las Alpujarras: Pampaneira (2hr., €4.60); Bubion (2¼hr., €5); Capileira (2½hr., €5); Trevélez (3½hr., €5.80) Buses run 3 times per day 10:30am-5:15pm. The 1st does not go to Trevélez. Ask in each town for the return schedule. Discovery Walking Guides, Ltd. publishes a superb guidebook with blow-by-blow accounts of every trail in Las Alpujarras (www.walking.demon.co.uk; €15).

The *pueblos blancos* (white villages) of Las Alpujarras blanket the southern slopes of the Sierra Nevada in an area known as *la Falda* (the skirt). Although busloads of European tourists have recently discovered the rustic beauty of these settlements and their neighboring hiking trails, Las Alpujarras remains one of Spain's poorest areas. The villages' slow-paced lifestyle, well-preserved beauty, and cultural traditions make for a refreshing change from the more bustling cities of Andalucía. Staying a day or two in any village will treat the traveler to the region's hospitality and a taste of Spain's natural beauty. For the more active tourist, the mountains offer plenty of climbing and hiking opportunities, and some backpackers spend months amidst the streams, trails, and wild boars.

Although the roads are now paved and the towns touristed, a medieval Berber influence is still evident in the region's architecture; the low-slung houses rendered from earth and slate quite closely resemble those in Morocco's Atlas Mountains. With the fall of Granada in 1492, the Berbers relocated to Las Alpujarras, and Christian-Muslim conflict continued until 1610, when John of Austria finally ousted the Moors. The legacy of Moorish defiance lives on every June during Trevélez's *Fiestas de Moros y Cristianos*. Galician settlers made the Alpujarras their home after the Moors were expelled, introducing Celtic and Visigothic traditions found nowhere else in Andalucía.

Las Alpujarras is best appreciated by car, but for those without wheels, Alsina Graells buses travel from Granada to many of the high-altitude towns, though service is infrequent and not always punctual. The buses trace switchback after unnerving switchback, hugging the scenic road. Bus drivers often stop to let travelers off at intermediate points. Some hard-core visitors hike from place to place, and locals, well aware of transportation problems, often sympathize with hitchhikers. *Let's Go* does not recommend hitchhiking. Again, having one's own car is highly advisable as it will allow you a flexibility otherwise impossible, enabling you to enjoy the region at your own pace.

Those interested in exploring the wilderness of the Sierra Nevada will find more than their fill of treks leading out from each town, particularly Capileira and Trevélez. Though there are splendid treks at every level of difficulty, serious hikers must be well prepared to face the climatic changes of the high Sierra range. A good map, compass, warm clothes, cooking and camping equipment, and possibly even a GPS system for GPS-waymarked maps and trails are necessary for long stays in the mountains. The short-term hiker need not despair, however; plenty of challenging hikes can be completed with sturdy boots and water by setting out from one village and arriving at another before the late summer sundown.

PAMPANEIRA

As the road winds in serpentine curves up to the high Alpujarran villages, the landscape quickly becomes harsh. Nevertheless, a sign at the entrance to Pampaniera (pop. 360) encourages visitors: *Quédate a vivir con nosotros*—"stay and live with us." Pampaniera (1059m) is the first—and least beautiful—of a trio of hamlets overlooking the **Poqueira Gorge**, a massive ravine cut by the Río Poqueira; the town makes a great springboard for climbing to **Bubión** (about 1hr.) and **Capileira** (2hr.). The trail to both begins from behind the church at the very top of town; a sign points the way. If you lose the trail or start at the wrong point, look toward the church of Bubión and head uphill; through abandoned terrace farms and steep bush, you will rejoin the trail quickly. **Nevadensis** offers hiking tours of the Sierra Nevada, organizes horseback riding, and even arranges accommodations. Located in the small main square, they also serve as the town's **tourist office**. (☎958 76 31 27; www.nevadensis.com. Open Su-M 10am-3pm, Tu-Sa 10am-2pm and 5-7pm.)

Hostal Pampaneira ❷, C. José Antonio Primo de Rivera, 1, has large rooms with private baths and comfortable beds. (☎958 76 30 02. Singles €20; doubles €30; triples €40. MC/V.) **Hostal Ruta del Mulhacén ❸**, Av. de la Alpujarra, 6, opposite Hostal Pampaneira, is slightly more costly but rewardingly so, as it is sure to brighten your stay with its lively colors and communal atmosphere. (☎958 76 30 10. Singles €25-28; doubles €39-45; triples €42-50.) Hostal Pampaneira's **restaurant ❷** is usually buzzing with activity in the evenings, with local men playing card games and families out dining. The food is hearty, no-nonsense fare, and the charming old patrons will pepper your meal with information on the local scene. (Entrees €3.90-7.20. Open for lunch and dinner. MC/V.) Local taverns offer pool tables and music, and the locals joke, "Madrid is peaceful. It's all happening in Pampaneira!"

BUBIÓN

Bubión, a steep 3km (1hr.) hike on a dirt trail from Pampaneira, is resplendent with Berber architecture, village charm, and enough *artesanía* (traditional arts and crafts) to make your head spin. If you begin your hike early, carry some water and snacks with you; everything in this sleepy town opens late. Those not up for the steep hike can catch the "early" bus from Pampaneira at 12:35pm. The town has no tourist office, but locals are glad to assist when they can. **Rustic Blue**, Barrio La Ermita, is a great resource for action-seekers; the intrepid staff has been organizing excursions, rural lodging, guided hikes, and horseback rides into the mountains for a decade. (☎958 76 33 81; fax 76 31 34. English and French spoken. Open M-F 10am-2pm and 5-7pm, Sa 11am-2pm.) If a night stay is on the itinerary, **Las Terrazas** ❷, Pta. del Sol, has several flower-filled terraces and cozy rooms overlooking the valley. (☎958 76 30 34. Singles €22; doubles €30.) **Ciber Monfi Café Morisco** ❷ offers Moorish-flavored food in a setting to match, along with **Internet access.** Follow the signs from anywhere in town. (☎958 76 30 53. Open Su-M and W-Sa, usually in afternoon, but hours vary.) The **Teide** ❷ offers filling portions of traditional food. (Entrees €4-13. Open daily 9-11am, 1:30-4pm, and 8-10:30pm. MC.)

CAPILEIRA

Capileira (1436m), perched atop the Poqueira Gorge (from Granada 2½hr., from Bubión a 1hr. hike on the trail or a 20min. walk on the road), makes a good base for exploring the neighboring villages and the back side of *la Falda*. A tedious ascent to Mulhacén (3479m), mitigated only by views of spectacular gorges, is possible from Capileira via the *refugio* (shelter); however, soft-core climbers might prefer to start from the more commonly used base town Trevélez. Looming peaks tower over cobblestone alleys, with the distant valley below. Enjoy small luxuries at **Hostal Paco López** ❷, Ctra. de la Sierra, 5, where each room has a balcony, TV, and bath. (☎958 76 30 11. Singles €18; doubles €30.) A filling *menú* (€6-9) is served at **Restaurant Poqueira** ❷, C. Dr. Castillo, 6. (Open Tu-Su lunch and dinner.)

TREVÉLEZ

Jamón serrano, and lots of it, distinguishes Trevélez, continental Spain's highest community (1476m). This tiny town is known all over Andalucía for its cured pork. Nearly everything revolves around the ham industry, but the town still has its share of history and charm. Steep roads weave through three *barrios*, and water rushes through Moorish irrigation systems still intact from 1000 years ago.

Trevélez is a logical base for the ascent to **Mulhacén** (3479m), one of the highest peaks of the Sierra Nevada. Every August, throngs of locals visit Mulhacén to pay homage to the **Virgen de las Nieves** (Virgin of the Snows). Summit-bound travelers should prepare with proper cold equipment and head north on the trail leaving the upper village from behind the church; avoid the trail that follows the swampy Río Trevélez. Continue past the Cresta de los Postreros for a good 4-5hr. until you reach the **Cañada de Siete Lagunas** (the largest lake, Laguna Hondera, should be directly in front of you); go right to see the **Cueva del Cura** (the Priest's Cave), a famous refuge. To reach Mulhacén, go up the ridge south of the refuge (3-4hr. further). Since both itineraries take a considerable amount of time, it is not advisable to hike Mulhacén the same day you visit the lake. Regardless of which trail you choose, you should purchase a **map** and hiking guide of the Sierra Nevada, such as the one by **Alpina** (€5.50), available in any souvenir shop.

Budget beds aren't hard to find in Trevélez. **Hostal González ❷**, Pl. Francisco Abellán, behind the restaurant of the same name, has perfectly comfortable, clean rooms waiting beyond the grungy exterior. (☎958 85 85 31. Singles €15; doubles €25. MC.) If you like ham, you're in luck—every **restaurant** in town advertises ham specials and has the meat hanging from the ceiling. To keep your options open, plan on lunch in Trevélez, as most *cocinas* (kitchens) here close for dinner.

JAÉN
☎953

A day or two in Jaén is sure to be pleasant, to say the least. Spain's olive oil capital has much to reward visitors, from its breathtaking museums and cathedral to its mountain-top castle, not to mention a vibrant atmosphere and fun-loving people.

▐ TRANSPORTATION. Trains (☎902 24 02 02) depart from Po. de la Estación at the bottom of the slope and run to **Madrid** (4-5hr., 4 per day 6:15am-5:15pm, €20) via **Córdoba** (1½hr., €8) and **Sevilla** (3hr., €15). **Alsina Graells buses,** Pl. Coca de la Piñera (☎953 25 50 14), serve popular destinations: **Baeza** (1hr., 14 per day 8:30am-9:30pm, €3.20); **Cazorla** (2hr., 3 per day noon-6:30pm, €6.50); **Granada** (1½hr., 13 per day 7:30am-8pm, €6.30); **Málaga** (3hr., 3 per day 7:30am-4:30pm, €14).

▐▐ ORIENTATION AND PRACTICAL INFORMATION. Jaén centers around **Plaza de la Constitución.** From the plaza, **Calle Bernabé Soriano** leads uphill to the cathedral and the old section of town. **Calle Maestra,** home to the tourist office, is up several blocks to the right. To reach the town center from the bus station, exit from the depot and follow Av. de Madrid uphill to Pl. de la Constitución (5min.). From the train station, turn right onto Po. de la Estación, which becomes C. Roldán y Marín. If you're not up for the 25min. walk, take bus #1 along Po. de la Estación (€0.85) or a taxi (€3).

The **tourist office,** C. Maestra, 13, is near the cathedral and has an excellent English-speaking staff. (☎/fax 953 24 26 24; otjaen@andalucia.org. Open July-Aug. M-F 10am-8pm, Sa-Su 10am-1pm; Sept.-June M-F 10am-7pm, Sa-Su 10am-1pm.) Local services include: **Banco Santander Central Hispano,** Pl. de la Constitución (☎902 24 24 24. Open June-Sept. M-F 8:30am-2pm, Sa 8:30am-1pm; Oct.-May M-F 8:30am-2pm); **luggage storage** at the bus station (€1.80 per 24hr.) or the train station (€3 per 24hr.); **police** ☎953 21 91 05. **Internet access** is available at **Cyberam,** Fuente Don Diego, Bajo, C.

ON THE MENU

PIG HEAVEN

If you can't tell the difference between a slaughterhouse and a bar, a slaughterhouse and a souvenir shop, or a slaughterhouse and a supermarket, you must be in Trevélez. If you intend to spend any time in this secluded village of Las Alpujarras, get used to spending most of it under densely suspended pork legs.

Since pork has dominated even the domain of interior decoration here, you shouldn't be surprised to find that it has monopolized menus as well. The standard question is: "how would you like your *jamón?*"

One could say that the triumph of the ham industry in Trevélez is meant to be. One of the highest villages in the region, it enjoys a crisp, cool, and relatively dry microclimate. Not only is this optimal for curing the ham in the Spanish manner, but it also allows the meat to remain unspoiled for nine months to a year and a half, suspended, as it usually is, in open air. Trevélez's reputation for curing the best pig dates back to 1862, when Queen Isabel II held a competition for the best produce in the land and this tiny town won. She honored its victory with the privilege of a denomination to be stamped on the town's pork, as rigidly controlled as the wine of La Rioja or *queso manchego.*

So, pork fans, honeymoon in Trevélez. And don't worry if your meat's been sitting out for over a year.

Adarves Bajos. (☎953 08 87 62. €2 per hr. Open daily 9am-2pm and 5-10pm.) The **post office**, Pl. de Jardinillos, is next to the pedestrian street Miguel de Priego, which becomes Jardinillos at the plaza. From Pl. de la Constitución, turn right onto C. San Clemente and continue to the plaza. (☎953 24 78 00. Open M-F 8:30am-8:30pm, Sa 9:30am-1pm.) **Postal Code:** 23004.

▐▌ ACCOMMODATIONS AND FOOD. Most of Jaén's accommodations are close to the cathedral and along Av. de Madrid. Though not especially roomy, **Hostal Carlos V ❷**, Av. de Madrid, 4, 2nd fl., downhill from Pl. de la Constitución, is very convenient. All six rooms share a single hallway and bath. (☎953 22 20 91. Singles €16.30; doubles €28.30; triples €38.30.) Nearby is the comfortable **Hostal Martín ❷**, C. Cuatro Torres, 5, with clean, medium-sized rooms, some with private bath. Turn right and up onto C. Cuatro Torres from Pl. de la Constitución. (☎953 24 36 78. Singles €20; doubles €30.) Those seeking more modern rooms—some even have massaging showerheads—with TV, phone, bath, and elevator should head to **Hotel Europa ❸**, Pl. de Belén, 1. Walking downhill on Av. de Madrid from Pl. de la Constitución, turn right onto Av. de Granada and then left onto Cuesta de Belén. Walk halfway up the hill; the hotel is on your left. (☎953 22 27 00. Singles €35; doubles €56.50; triples €70.)

Delicious Andalusian fare with a twist, prepared by a talented and experimental chef, can be found at **▨Restaurante La Abadía ❸**, C. Melchor Cobo Medina, 19, where hearty portions (€9-18) are served in a cozy, trendily rustic setting. Heading toward Pl. de la Constitución on Av. de Madrid, turn left onto C. Dr. Sagaz Zubelzu. (☎953 24 50 38. Open daily 1-6pm and 8:30pm-1am.) For more casual fare, try the eccentric **▨Machito ❶**, at the top of C. Dr. Sagaz Zubelzu, on the corner of C. Teodoro Calvache. Order the stunning *"yarda"* for a beer with style (€3.50)—everything else here has it. (Open daily 1-4pm and 8pm-1am.) Alternatively, the extensive menu at **Colón Cafetería ❶**, C. Navas de Tolosa, 7, along the main pedestrian walkway, has everything from *churros* (€0.55-0.75) to *batidos helados* (frappes; €1.50-3), among other dishes. (☎953 22 77 35. Open daily 7am-10pm.)

◪ SIGHTS AND ENTERTAINMENT. Andrés de Vandelvira designed Jaén's trademark **▨Catedral de Santa María**, on C. Bernabé Soriano uphill from Pl. de la Constitución. (☎953 23 42 33. Open M-S 8:30am-1pm and 5-8pm, Su 9am-1pm and 6-8pm. Free.) The attached **Museo de la Catedral** displays sundry objects of interest, among them candlesticks by Maestro Bartolomé. (☎953 22 46 75. Open Tu-Sa 10am-1pm and afternoons when the cathedral is open. €3, groups €2.10.) The Renaissance **▨Palacio de Villardompardo**, in Pl. Santa Luisa Marillac at the far end of C. Maestra, contains baffling and incredibly well-preserved, 11th-century Moorish baths—Spain's largest—and an art museum which houses the second-largest collection of *Naïf* artwork in the world, as well as a fascinating collection of ancient machinery. (Follow C. Maestra from the cathedral to C. Martínez Molina. ☎953 23 62 92. Open Tu-F 9am-8pm, Sa-Su 9:30am-2:30pm. Free.) Jaén's least accessible sight is the 13th-century stone **Castillo de Santa Catalina**, a 5km uphill hike from the center of town. Built by the Moors, expanded by Fernando III, and reinforced by the French during the occupation of Spain (1810-1812), the recently renovated castle provides a glimpse into Jaén's rich and varied past. The spectacular view of the city and surrounding olive groves from the promontory, especially gorgeous at sunset, is as memorable as the castle itself. (☎953 12 07 33. Open Tu-Su 10am-2pm and 5-9pm. €3, with Carnet Joven €2, children €1.) To avoid a sweaty walk, take a taxi (€6) from the bus station.

Uphill from the cathedral and right next to the tourist office, **Peña Flamenca de Jaén,** C. Maestra, 11, serves up drinks and flamenco. Try the *manzanilla*, Andalucía's specialty apple liqueur. (☎953 23 17 10. Beer €1.30, includes your choice of tapas. Mixed drinks from €3. Open daily noon-1am.) For a break from *el tapeo*, hire a taxi to **Moët**, Av. de Andalucía, 10, near the train station. This ultra-hip bar attracts an effervescent crowd of students and young professionals. On weekends, it transforms into a disco, with a DJ spinning the latest in Spanish pop. (☎953 27 30 94. Beer €2, mixed drinks from €4.20. Open daily 4pm-5am.)

BAEZA ☎953

Compared with the rest of Andalucía, Baeza does not have the most impressive cathedrals or the most breathtaking museums, and a half-day stroll can exhaust its intimate *barrio monumental*. Its uniqueness and appeal, though, lie in the preserved authenticity of the old town, beautiful in its simplicity and literally uninterrupted by a single modern building or shop. A more modern, tourist-oriented district is right next to the *casco antiguo*, however. Nearby Jaén may have similar attractions, but Baeza's overall feel still makes it a desirable destination.

TRANSPORTATION. Trains depart from **Estación Linares-Baeza** (☎902 24 02 02), 13km out of town on the road to Madrid (reached from the bus station in Baeza, 15min., 8 per day 7:45am-9pm, €0.90) for **Madrid** and **Málaga**, stopping in other cities and towns along the way. Call to inquire about schedules; they vary greatly. The **bus station** (☎953 74 04 68) offers service to **Granada** (2-3hr., 11 per day 7:55am-6:45pm, €9.60) and **Jaén** (1hr., 13 per day 7:10am-8:10pm, €3.30).

ORIENTATION AND PRACTICAL INFORMATION. In the center of town, **Plaza de España** leads downhill to **Paseo de la Constitución**. To get to Pl. de España from the bus station, follow C. Julio Burell to C. San Pablo and continue straight. The **tourist office** is in Pl. del Pópulo. (☎953 74 04 44. Open July-Sept. M-F 9am-2:30pm and 5-7pm, Sa 10am-1pm and 4-7pm, Su 10am-1pm; Oct.-June M-F 9am-2:30pm and 4-6pm, Sa 10am-1pm and 4-6pm, Su 10am-1pm.) Local services include: **police**, C. Cardenal Benavides, 5 (☎953 74 06 59); **Centro de Salud Comarcal**, Av. Alcalde Puche Pardo, past the bus station (☎953 74 29 00); **Internet access, Microware**, Pl. de la Constitución (☎953 74 70 10. €1.50 per hr. Open daily 11am-2pm and 5-10pm). The **post office** is at C. Julio Burell, 19. (☎953 74 08 39. Open M-F 8:30am-2:30pm, Sa 9am-1pm.) **Postal Code:** 23440.

ACCOMMODATIONS AND FOOD. Baeza's hostels are hidden throughout the city. The pleasant **Hostal El Patio ❶**, C. Conde de Romanones, 13, has the cheapest rooms in town and a location in the middle of the *barrio monumental* that's hard to beat. (☎953 74 02 00. Singles €15; doubles €28.) Several bars and restaurants line Po. de la Constitución, and almost all serve *comida típica*. Of these, **Mesón Restaurante La Góndola ❸**, C. Portales Carbonería, 13, offers an extensive menu, with a fine selection of meat, seafood, and *perdiz* (partridge), the tasty local specialty cooked in a garlic-based vegetable stew. (☎953 74 29 84. Entrees €10-15. Open daily 9am-4pm and 7:30pm-1am.) The more casual bar **Guadalquivir ❶**, C. San Pablo, 42, is popular with a younger local crowd. (☎953 74 15 29. *Bocadillos* €1.70-2.10, *raciones* €4.80-6. Open daily noon-4pm and 8:30pm-midnight.)

SIGHTS. Most major sights in Baeza's intimate and well-preserved **barrio monumental** are free. With your back to the tourist office, walk up the stairs to your right, then take a left onto C. Conde de Romanones; at the street's end is the **Antigua Universidad** (founded in 1595), a structure whose courtyard served as an outdoor classroom where Modernist poet Antonio Machado taught French. (Open M-Tu and Th-Su 10am-1pm and 4-6pm. Free.) Farther down C.

Conde de Romanones stands the astoundingly simple 13th-century **Iglesia de Santa Cruz.** It is Baeza's oldest church, and one of the only Romanesque structures in Andalucía. (Open M-Sa 11am-1:30pm, Su noon-2pm. Free.) Next door to the church is a small ▨**museum,** which houses ornate icons, artifacts, and carriages decorated with gold and silver. Especially exciting (or chilling) are the macabre costumes and old church documents about the procession of the religious brotherhood of Santa Vera Cruz, held during *Semana Santa.* (Open daily 11am-1:30pm and 4:30-7pm. €1.) On the other side of Pl. de la Santa Cruz, adjacent to the imposing 15th-century **Palacio Jabalquinto,** (Open daily 9am-2pm, M-Th and Sa-Su also 5-7pm. Free.) the **seminario's** facade bears the names of some egotistical graduates and a caricature of an unpopular professor, rumored to be painted in bull's blood. Across Pl. Santa María from the seminary, the **Santa Iglesia Catedral** houses *La Custodia de Baeza,* the second most important Corpus Christi icon in Spain, trumped only by that of Toledo. (Open daily June-Aug. 10:30am-1pm and 5-7pm; Sept.-May 10am-1pm and 4-6pm. Free.) The park atop the city wall, reached by walking along Po. de las Murallas, offers a beautiful **view** of the olive tree-carpeted Guadalquivir Valley.

VALENCIA AND MURCIA

The southeast corner of Spain is one of its least well-known to travelers, and for no good reason. From the sunny, sandy beaches of the Costa Blanca and the inland friendliness of Murcia to the cosmopolitan appeal of Valencia and the mountains of Morella, the area is certain to charm anyone who visits.

The region's past is a tangle of power struggles between the whole cast of usual suspects: Phoenicians, Carthaginians, Greeks, Romans, and Moors. It first fell under Castilian control when El Cid expelled the Moors in 1094; he ruled it in the name of Alfonso VI until his death in 1099. Without El Cid's powerful influence, Valencia and Murcia again fell to the Moors, and remained an Arab stronghold until 1238. In the 1930s, it was besieged again, this time by Franco's troops. *Valencianos* resisted with characteristic strength—Valencia was the last region incorporated into Franco's Spain. In 1977, the region finally regained autonomy.

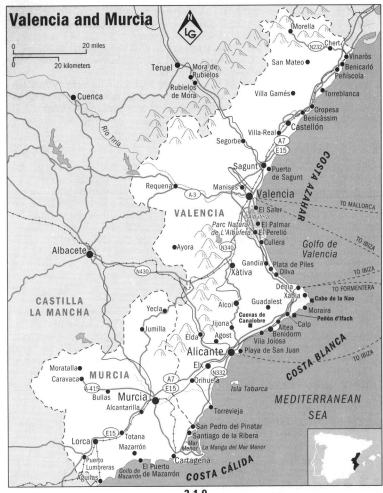

HIGHLIGHTS OF VALENCIA AND MURCIA

RELIVE Spain's Roman past at **Cartagena** (p. 353).

WALK on water in **Valencia,** where a cultural center fills an ancient riverbed (p. 320).

ROCK ON atop Calp's high-flying **Peñón d'Ifach** (p. 344).

INDULGE in luscious truffles in remote, medieval **Morella** (p. 332).

VALENCIA

Valencia is something of a natural wonder. Nearly 500km of Mediterranean shoreline alternate between soft dunes and jagged promontories, while a patchwork of orange orchards and vegetable fields, all fed by Moorish irrigation systems, lies farther inland. Valencia's beauty is found even in its cities, where carefully landscaped gardens display ornate fountains and exotic plants.

Valencià, the regional language spoken more in the north and inland, is a dialect of Catalan. Although Valencia's regionalism is not as intense as Catalunya's, the Generalitat's recent mandate that all students enroll in one course of *valencià* reflects a resurgence of regional pride, and the dialect is used on street signs, maps, menus, and the lips of many a *valenciano*.

Valencia's festivals are some of the wildest in Spain, and its culinary heritage has had a pronounced impact on Spanish cuisine: paella, now considered a quintessentially Spanish dish, was first concocted somewhere in the region's fields, and Valencian oranges are widely accepted as the best in the nation, if not the world.

VALENCIA ☎963

Valencia (pop. 750,000) seems to possess all the best aspects of its sister cities: the bustling energy of Madrid, the vibrancy of Alicante, the off-beat sophistication of Barcelona, and the friendly warmth of Sevilla. An architectural wonder, Spain's third largest city is among the few places in Europe where ultra-modern styles are successfully blended with traditional ones. Just a glance around its central Pl. Ayuntamiento reveals a mix of traditional Spanish architecture, opulent 19th-century palaces, art deco movie theaters, and modern towers. It is a city of great contrasts, from its white beaches to its palm tree-lined avenues to the parks that lie in the dry bed of the Río Turia. Yet despite its cosmopolitan modernity, Valencia manages to retain a certain small-town charm that enchants all those who visit.

▌ TRANSPORTATION

Flights: Airport (☎961 59 85 00), 8km from the city. **Cercanías** trains run between the airport and train station (30min.; M-F every 30min., Sa-Su every hr. 7:03am-10:03pm; €1.20). Subway line #5 is currently being expanded to reach the airport. Many flights to the Islas Baleares. **Iberia,** C. La Paz, 14 (☎963 52 75 52, 24hr. info and reservations 902 40 05 00). Open M-F 9am-2pm and 4-7pm.

Trains: Estació del Nord, C. Xàtiva, 24 (☎963 52 02 02). Ticket windows open daily 7:30am-9:30pm. **RENFE** (24hr. ☎902 24 02 02) to: **Alicante** (2-3hr., 11 per day 7:04am-10:35pm, €10.50-23); **Barcelona** (3hr., every 1-2hr. 5:50am-8:45pm, €28.50-34.50); **Madrid** (3½hr., 12 per day 6:45am-9:15pm, €19.20-37); **Sevilla** (8½hr., 11:30am, €42.50). **Cercanías** trains run at least 2 per hr. to: **Gandía** (1hr., €3.40); **Xàtiva** (45min., €2.60); **Sagunt** (30min., €2.20).

Buses: Estación Terminal d'Autobuses, Av. Menéndez Pidal, 13 (☎963 49 72 22), across the riverbed, a 25min. walk from the city center. Municipal bus #8 runs between Pl. del Ajuntament and the bus station (€1). **ALSA** (☎902 42 22 42) to: **Alicante**

Valencia

🏠 ACCOMMODATIONS
Home Youth Hostel, 13
Hostal Alicante, 25
Hostal Antigua Morellana, 15
Hostal El Rincón, 11
Hostal-Residencia El Cid, 21
Hostal-Residencia San José, 23
Hostal-Residencia Universal, 24
Pensión Paris, 22

🍴 FOOD
El Rall, 16
La Lluna, 3
La Pappardella, 8
The Lounge Café-Bar, 14
Sol i Lluna, 18
Zumería Naturalia, 19

⭐ NIGHTLIFE
Akuarela, 20
Bolsería Café, 9
Café Negrito, 7
Finnegan's, 17
Fox Congo, 6
Jimmy Glass, 4
Johnny Maracas, 5
Radio City, 12
Venial, 10
Warhol, 1
Zenith, 2

(4½hr., 1-3 per hr. 4:45am-12:25am, €14.90-17.10) via the **Costa Blanca; Barcelona** (4½hr., 9 per day 9am-10pm, €21); **Granada** (8hr., 9 per day 4:45am-2:30am, €35.45-42.80); **Málaga** (11hr., 9 per day 4:15am-2:30am, €43.60-52.80); **Sevilla** (11hr., 3-4 per day 10:30am-3am, €42.60-49.80). **Auto Res** (☎963 49 22 30) goes to **Madrid** (4hr., 13 per day 7am-3am, €19.80-24.20).

Ferries: Trasmediterránea, Estació Marítima (☎902 45 46 45; www.trasmediterranea.com). Take bus #4 from Pl. del Ajuntament or #1 or 2 from the bus station. To **Mallorca** and **Ibiza** (1-2 per day, no ferries to Ibiza W; €30-70, depending on speed and class). One 15hr. ferry to **Menorca** per week (Sa 11:30pm, prices vary). Buy tickets at a travel agency or at the port on the day of departure. **Balearia** (☎902 16 01 80) runs to **Eivissa** (2-4 per week). See **By Boat,** p. 356, for more info.

Public Transportation: EMT Office, Pl. Correu Vell, 5 (☎963 15 85 15). Open M-F 8am-2pm. Bus #8 runs to the bus station. Buses #10, 21, 22, and 23 go to Las Arenas and Malvarrosa along Pg. Marítim. Buy tickets (€1) on board; 10-ride ticket (€5.90) or 1-day pass (€3) available at newsstands. Service stops around 11:30pm-midnight. **Late-night buses** go through Pl. del Ajuntament (every 45min. 11pm-1:38am). **Metro** service loops around the *casco antiguo* and into the outskirts. The most central stop is on C. Xàtiva across the street from the train station, or C. Colón by El Corte Inglés. Buy tickets from machines in any station (€1-3 depending on distance, 10-ride pass €5.90).

Taxis: ☎963 70 33 33 or 57 13 13.

■✦ⓘ ORIENTATION AND PRACTICAL INFORMATION

Since **Estació del Nord** lies very close to the center of the city, it is most convenient to enter Valencia by train. **Avenida Marqués de Sotelo** runs from the train station to **Plaça del Ajuntament (Plaza Ayuntamiento),** the center of town. Most lodging and food and many sights are in the **casco antiguo,** nestled in a bend of the now-diverted Río Turia, the dry bed of which loops around the center of the city. Other sights and museums are across the river or on the outskirts of the city. The *casco antiguo* is best explored on foot—most public transportation (except bus #5) barely penetrates the old town. Because of Valencia's size, though, it's best to take advantage of the extensive bus system or subway to see more than just the area within walking distance of the center.

Tourist Office: Regional office, C. de la Paz, 46-48 (☎963 98 64 22; www.valencia.es). Open M-F 9am-7pm, Sa 10am-7pm. **Branch,** Estació del Nord, C. Xàtiva, 24 (☎963 52 85 73). Open M-F 9am-6:30pm. **Municipal office,** Pl. del Ajuntament, 1 (☎963 51 04 17). Open M-F 9am-2pm. **Branch,** C. Poeta Querol (☎963 51 49 07). Open M-F 10am-2:30pm and 4:30-7pm, Sa 10am-2pm, Su 11am-2pm.

Currency Exchange: Most banks have good exchange rates; all have a minimum commission of €6. Banks cluster around Pl. del Ajuntament or just off it on C. las Barcas.

American Express: Duna Viajes, C. Cirilo Amorós, 88 (☎963 74 15 62; fax 34 57 00). From C. Don Juan de Austria, follow C. Sorní to Pl. América. C. Cirilo Amorós is on the right. Open M-F 9:30am-2pm and 4:30-7:30pm, Sa 10am-1pm.

Luggage Storage: 24hr. storage at the **bus station** (€1-3.50) and **train station** (€2.40-4.50). Open daily 7:30am-9:30pm.

El Corte Inglés: 2 locations at C. Colón and C. Pintor Sorolla (☎963 51 24 44). Open M-Sa 10am-10pm. Sells groceries and anything else you could possibly consume.

Laundromat: Lavandería El Mercat, Pl. del Mercat, 12 (☎963 91 20 10). Full-service wash and dry in 2-3hr. for €10. Open M-F 10am-2pm and 5-9pm, Sa 10am-2pm.

Police: Po. de Alameda, 17 (☎963 60 03 52, emergency 092).

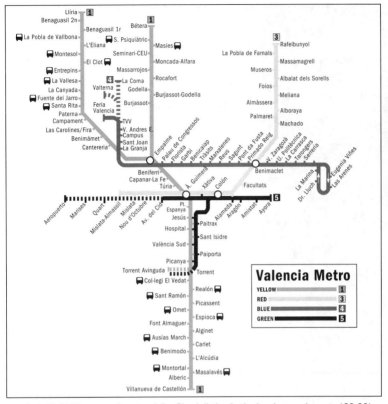

Valencia Metro

YELLOW	**1**
RED	**3**
BLUE	**4**
GREEN	**5**

Late-Night Pharmacy: Rotates daily. Check listing in the local paper *Levante* (€0.80) or the *farmacias de guardia* schedule posted outside any pharmacy.

Hospital: Hospital Clínico Universitario, Av. Blasco Ibáñez, 17 (☎963 86 26 00), at C. Dr. Ferrer. Take bus #41, 71, or 81 from Pl. del Ajuntament. **Ambulance** ☎085.

Internet Access: 🖵 **Ono,** C. San Vicente Mártir, 22 (☎963 28 19 02). Centrally located computer bliss. Huge 2-story complex of super-fast computers. Laptop stations. Info available on what's happening around town. €1.80 per 45min. 9am-2pm, per 30min. 2-10pm, or per hr. 10pm-1am. Open M-Sa 9am-1am, Su 10am-1am. **Fundación Bancaixa,** Pl. Tetuán, 23, 5th fl. (☎963 87 58 64). Free access on somewhat slow computers. Limit 1hr. Passport or student ID required. Open M-F 9am-2pm and 4-9pm, Sa 9am-2pm. **Confederación,** C. de Ribera, 8 (☎963 94 03 11). 46 ultra-modern computers in an industrially decorated space. €3 per hr.

Post Office: Pl. del Ajuntament, 24 (☎963 51 67 50). Open M-F 8:30am-8:30pm, Sa 9:30am-2pm. **Postal Code:** 46080.

🏠 ACCOMMODATIONS

Hostels are abundant in Valencia, but on weekends, especially in summer, finding a room isn't always easy—it's best to call ahead. Reservations are especially necessary during the *papier-mâché* orgy of *Las Fallas* (Mar. 12-19). The best deals are around **Plaça del Ajuntament** and **Plaça del Mercat,** both in the *casco antiguo*.

RICE IS NICE

Paella is known throughout the world as a quintessentially Spanish dish, but any *valenciano* can tell you where it started—here, in the homes of fishermen around L'Albufera. The techniques for preparing it have been perfected for years by rice cultivators, processors, and *paelleros* (traditionally male). Don't call it all paella, however; there are hundreds of different rice dishes, unique in ingredients and preparation.

Paella, for example, is the *valenciano* word for the typical pan in which the rice paella dish (originally called *arroz en paella*) is cooked. The most common is *paella de mariscos*, paella with a variety of fish and shellfish. *Paella valenciana*, though, is served with chicken and rabbit. *Arroz a banda*, similar to paella, is traditionally a more humble dish enjoyed by fishermen, where the fish is cooked separately from the rice, saffron, garlic, and tomato.

If you prefer your rice baked, try *arroz al horno*, popular in la Ribera and la Huerta for its slightly simpler recipe. Also popular is *arroz negro*, cooked with squid and blackened from the ink. If you don't prefer rice at all, try *fideuá*, paella's cousin, made with noodles instead of rice. Whichever you choose, you are certain not to be disappointed, so long as you go for the authentic version. Avoid restaurants bearing pictures of pre-made paellas on signs; what you see is what you get, and it's not the real thing.

Home Youth Hostel, C. Lonja, 4 (☎963 91 62 29; www.likeathome.net). Across Av. Maria Cristina from the Mercat Central, go down C. Ercilla and left on C. Lonjas. Lounge packed with students. Kitchen and friendly staff. Hall baths. Internet €0.50 per 15min. Bike rental €8 per day. Laundry €5.50 per load for wash and dry. Dorms €14; singles €21; doubles €32; triples €48; quads €64. 10% discount with ISIC. **Branches** at C. Cadirers, 11 (☎963 92 40 63), or in Pl. Vicente Iborra (☎963 91 37 97). ❶

Hostal-Residencia El Cid, C. Cerrajeros, 13 (☎/fax 963 92 23 23). A left off C. San Vicente Mártir coming out of Pl. del Ajuntament. Pretty hallways and staircase with Spanish floral tiles, plants, and windows. Room quality varies from TVs and A/C to just a fan. Doubles €25, with shower €32, with bath €35. Prices vary with season. ❶

Pensión Paris, C. Salvá, 12 (☎963 52 67 66). Turn right onto C. Barcas from the Pl. del Ajuntament, then make a left onto C. Poeta Querol; C. Salvá is the 2nd right. 13 spotless rooms with balconies and high ceilings. Marble floors give a luxurious feel in simple surroundings. Singles €19; doubles €29, with shower €32; triples €41/€45. ❷

Hostal-Residencia San José, C. Transits, 5 (☎963 94 01 52). From Pl. del Ajuntament, go down C. Barcelonina and take the 2nd right. Large, sunny rooms behind a beautiful blue and white facade. Doubles €35; triples €45. ❷

Hostal Alicante, C. de Ribera, 8 (☎963 51 22 96). As central as it gets, right off the Pl. del Ajuntament. Clean and well-lit. Hugely popular with backpackers. Singles €22, with bath and A/C €30; doubles €30/€40. MC/V. ❷

Hostal Antigua Morellana, C. En Bou, 2 (☎/fax 963 91 57 73). Across Av. María Cristina from the Mercat Central, go down C. Ercilla, to the corner of C. Tunidores. Bright, quiet, and comfortable rooms with bath, TV, A/C, and phone. Wood furniture and classy, crimson linens. July-Sept. doubles €58; triples €75. Oct.-June €48/€60. ❹

Hostal-Residencia Universal, C. las Barcas, 5 (☎963 51 53 84). Clean rooms with large windows, new furniture, and quilted bedspreads on a main street off Pl. del Ajuntament. Singles €19; doubles €28, with shower €32; triples €40; 1 quint €67. ❷

Hostal El Rincón, C. Carda, 11 (☎963 91 79 98). Left out of the market onto Av. María Cristina (also called Pl. del Mercat). Cross C. Bolsería and it's the 1st street on the left. Bright hallways lead to bare but clean rooms. Improvements underway, but still one of the cheapest places in town. Singles €10, with bath €13; doubles €18/€24. MC/V. ❶

FOOD

Paella may be the most famous, but it is actually just one of 200 Valencian rice dishes. Other specialties include *arroz a banda* (rice and fish with garlic, onion, tomatoes, and saffron), *all i pebre* (eels fried in oil, paprika, and garlic), and *fideuá* (paella with noodles instead of rice). Valencia has a well-deserved reputation as a food lover's city; its restaurants are generally cheap, creative, and perfect for people on the run. Bushels of fresh fish, meat, and fruit are sold at the enormous **Mercat Central,** located in a beautiful Art Nouveau building on Pl. del Mercat. (Open M-Sa 7am-3pm.) For **groceries,** stop by **El Corte Inglés.**

VALENCIA AND MURCIA

▓ **La Lluna,** C. Sant Ramón, 23 (☎963 92 21 46). Feel free to moon over this gem of a veggie restaurant hidden in El Carme just off the Pl. Mossen Sorrel. Fantastic variety of entrees, appetizers, and salads, all delicious, fresh, and €3-5. Funky setting of hanging lampshades, tiled walls, and tablecloths. Serves a 4-course *menú* (€5.80) weekday afternoons. Don't miss the *manzanas asadas con nata y miel* (roasted apples with honey and cream; €4) for dessert. Open M-Sa 1:30-3:30pm and 9-11:30pm. ❶

▓ **Sol i Lluna,** C. del Mar, 29 (☎963 92 22 16). Not your *abuela*'s tapas joint. Delicious, creative, gourmet tapas (€5-9), like avocado and chicken burritos and curry meatballs, abound in this small, eclectically lit restaurant just off Pl. de la Reina. Seafood lovers should try the *calamares al romano.* Open M-F 9am-1:30am, Sa 5pm-1:30am. ❷

▓ **The Lounge Café-Bar,** C. Estamiñera Vieja, 2 (☎963 91 80 94; www.theloungecafe-bar.com), just off Pl. Dr. Collado. Great menu of salads and sandwiches with lots of vegetarian options (€2.80-€4.50). Awesome music and colorful setting. Internet available, first 30min. free with food. Open M-F 10am-1:30am, Sa-Su noon-1:30am. ❶

El Rall, C. Tundidores, 2 (☎963 92 20 90), between the Lonja and Pl. Negrito. Excellent paella (€9-15 per person, 2 person min.) and other seafood served outdoors in a small square. Reservations recommended. Open daily 1-4pm and 8-11pm. ❸

Zumería Naturalia, C. del Mar, 12 bajo (☎963 91 12 11). Cozy basement juice bar with wicker chairs and straw-hat lampshades. 40 blended juices (€3-4, with alcohol €4-6) served in oversized goblets or plastic cups to go. Sweet and savory crepes €2-2.50. Open M-Th 5pm-1:30am, F-Sa 5pm-2:30am, Su 5pm-10:30pm. ❶

La Pappardella, C. Bordadores, 5 (☎963 91 89 15; www.viciositalianos.com), a block from the cathedral. Vast selection of pastas from spaghetti, oil, and garlic to ones with fresh veggies and seafood (€5-8). *Menú* €8. Open daily 2-4pm and 9pm-midnight. ❷

◉ SIGHTS

Most of the museums are by the Turia riverbed. The older sights cluster near Pl. de la Reina, which is linked to Pl. del Ajuntament by C. Sant Vicente Mártir. EMT bus #5, dubbed the **Bus Turístic** (☎963 52 83 99), loops around the old town sights (€1).

▓ **CIUDAD DE LAS ARTES Y LAS CIENCIAS.** Designed by renowned Spanish architect Santiago Calatrava, Valencia's latest urban creation dedicated to the arts and sciences is nothing short of stunning. Ultra-modern, airy, and thoroughly fascinating, this mini-city has already become the fourth biggest tourist destination in Spain, and visitors come as much for the buildings' extraordinary designs as for the attractions themselves. The complex is divided into four large buildings, all surrounding a vast reflecting pool. Even the parking garage is a work of art, with a garden terrace, **L'Umbracle,** on the roof. **L'Hemisfèric,** a sleek glass and steel capsule, wows the eyes with its laser shows, and planetarium, while **L'Oceanogràfic** recreates aquatic environments in an underground water-world. The enormous **Palau de les Arts,** scheduled to be completed by the end of 2005, will house stages for opera, theater, and dance. The **Museu de Les Ciencies Príncipe Felipe,** the gleaming centerpiece, is packed with students and tourists learning through hands-on exhibits. *(Bus #35 runs from Pl. del Ajuntament.* ☎ *902 10 00 31; www.cac.es. Museum open June 15-Sept. 15 daily 10am-9pm; Sept. 16-June 14 M-F and Su 10am-8pm, Sa 10am-9pm. €7, children and students €5.50. L'Oceanogràfic open June 21-Sept. 7 daily 10am-midnight; Mar 15-June 20 and Sept. 8-Oct. 12 M-F 10am-8pm, Sa-Su 10am-10pm; Oct 13-Mar. 14 M-F 10am-6pm, Sa-Su 10am-8pm; €20.50/ €15.50. Combination tickets to the whole complex €28/€21. L'Hemisfèric daily IMAX shows €7, children and students €5.50.)*

CATEDRAL. Begun in the 13th century and completed in 1482, this magnificent cathedral is the region's most impressive building. The three different entrances display a melange of Romanesque, Gothic, and Baroque architectural styles. The **Miguelete** (cathedral tower) has awesome views of Valencia. Novelist Victor Hugo once counted 300 bell towers in the city from this vantage point. The interior is lined with altars, each with its own design and character. The **Museu de la Catedral** squeezes a great many treasures into three tiny rooms—one for the Gothic period, one for the Renaissance, and one Mannerist. Enter the museum through the Gothic, stone **Capilla de Santo Cáliz.** Check out the overwrought tabernacle made from 1200kg of gold, silver, platinum, emeralds, and sapphires, plus a Holy Grail, two Goyas, and the Crucifijo de Marfil statues, which depict "man's passions." *(Pl. de la Reina. Cathedral* ☎ *963 91 01 89. Open daily 7:30am-1pm and 4:30-8:30pm. Closes earlier in winter. Free. Tower open daily 10am-1pm and 4:30-7pm. €2. Museum* ☎ *963 91 81 27. Open Mar.-Nov. M-Sa 10am-1pm and 4:30-6pm, Su 10am-1pm; Dec.-Feb. daily 10am-1pm. €2.)*

MUSEU PROVINCIAL DE BELLES ARTES. One of Valencia's finer attractions, it features a wide array of paintings. One floor is dedicated to 14th- to 16th-century Valencian art and has an impressive collection of triptychs and altarpieces. Other floors feature El Greco's *San Juan Bautista*, Velázquez's self-portrait, Ribera's *Santa Teresa*, and a slew of Goyas. The museum has been named one of Spain's premier art galleries. Be sure to check out the sculpture pavilion. *(C. Sant Pío V, near the Jardines del Real. M: Pont de Fuste. Walk to the river and make a left; the museum is about 2 blocks down on the left. Bus #8 from the Pl. del Ajuntament drops you across the river; cross Puente de la Trinidad.* ☎ *963 60 57 93. Open Tu-Sa 10am-8pm. Free.)*

INSTITUT VALENCIÀ D'ART MODERN (IVAM). See everything from early 20th-century portraits to classic avant-garde sculpture to 1970s clash. IVAM is also home to a collection of abstract works by 20th-century sculptor Julio González, among others. The rotating temporary exhibits are extremely popular. *(C. Guillém de Castro, 118, west across the riverbed. M: Turia. Take a right out of the Po. de Pechina exit and go 5min. down the river, right by the Puente de Artes. Or take bus #5 from the Pl. del Ajuntament.* ☎ *963 86 30 00. Open Tu-Su 10am-10pm. €2, students €1. Su free.)*

MUSEO NACIONAL DE CERÁMICA. An amazing collection of ceramic works, both artistic and artisanal, housed in the spectacular 19th-century Rococo Palacio de Dos Aguas, former home of the Marqueses de Dos Aguas. Half the museum shows ceramics, and the other half is the palace rooms, which contain full-size carriages and paintings. Don't miss the enormous tiled kitchen. *(C. Poeta Querol, 2, Riconada García Sanhiz. From the Pl. Ajuntament, go down C. Barcas and take a left onto C. Poeta Querol.* ☎ *963 51 63 52. Open M-Sa 10am-2pm and 4-8pm, Su 10am-2pm. €2.40.)*

PARKS. Manicured parks surround the city center. Horticulturists will marvel at the **Jardín Botànic,** a university-maintained garden that cultivates 43,000 plants of 300 international species. *(C. Quart, 80, on the western end of Río Turia near*

Gran Vía Fernando el Católico. M: Turia. Go left out of the Po. de Pechina exit down Gran Vía and take a left onto C. Quart. ☎963 91 16 57. Open Tu-Su 10am-9pm, closes earlier in winter. €1.) On the other side of the river, next to the Museu Provincial de Belles Artes, off C. Sant Pío V, are the popular **Jardines del Real,** home to ponds, fountains, a rose garden, and even a small zoo. *(M: Pont de Fuste. Walk to the river, take a left, pass the museum, and enter on C. Sant Pío V. Open Mar. 22-Sept. 20 6:30am-9pm; Sept. 21-Mar. 21 8:30am-8:30pm. €5).*

OTHER SIGHTS. The elliptical **Basílica Virgen dels Desamparats** houses a resplendent golden altar. *(In the Pl. de la Virgen, right behind the Catedral. Open for mass M-F 7am-2pm and 5-9pm, Su 7:30am-2:30pm and 5-9:30pm. Free.)* The old **Lonja de la Seda (Silk Exchange)** is a terrific example of Valencian Gothic architecture and a testament to Valencia's prominence in the medieval silk trade. *(Pl. del Mercat. ☎963 52 54 78. Open Tu-Sa 9:15am-2pm and 5:30-9pm, Su 9am-1:30pm. Free.)* Valencia's beautiful **Palau de Música** is one of the world's premier concert halls, hosting orchestras, soloists, and jazz bands throughout the year. During the **Festiu de Juliol** in July there is are daily jazz concerts; the hall's website has more info. *(Po. de la Alameda, 30. ☎963 37 50 20; www.palauvalencia.com. Ticket window open daily 10:30am-1:30pm and 5:30-9pm.)*

 VALENCIA AND MURCIA

NIGHTLIFE

Use your *siesta* wisely—Valencia's nightlife requires drinking and dancing until sunrise. Bars and pubs in **El Carme,** just beyond the market, start up at 11:30pm. Follow Pl. del Mercat and C. Bolsería to **Plaza Tossal,** where outdoor terraces, upbeat music, and *agua de Valencia* (orange juice, champagne, and vodka) energize the masses. Many bars can also be found along **Calle Caballeros** in El Carme. The gay and lesbian scene centers on **Calle Quart** and around **Plaza Vicente Iborra.**

Discos, which normally don't draw a crowd until at least 3am, dominate the university area, particularly on **Avinguda Blasco Ibáñez.** In summer, some of the best places to be seen are the outdoor discos by the beach at **Platja de Malvarrosa.** There are a few smaller discos in El Carme, most of which are popular with both gay and straight patrons. For more info, consult the *Qué y Dónde* weekly magazine (€1) or the weekly entertainment supplement, *La Cartelera* (€0.75), both available at newsstands. Or check out *24/7 Valencia,* a free English magazine available in most Internet cafes or other hang-out spots. The areas by the beach and the university are far from the *casco antiguo,* and the buses and metro stop running around 11:30pm. Fortunately, though, they start up again around 5am, so if it's a good night, you can take a cab there and the metro home.

EL CARME AND PLAZA DE LA REINA

Café Negrito, Pl. del Negrito, 1, off C. Caballeros (☎963 91 42 33). Escher-esque drawings decorate this loud bar and cafe popular with locals. Prides itself on its *agua de Valencià* (€6; large €21), but watch out for ducks. Open daily 10pm-3am.

Bolsería Café, C. Bolsería, 41 (☎963 91 89 03). Beautiful people of all ages pack the many rooms and corners in this upscale cafe-bar. Forest decor, smaller terraces and bars upstairs, and an industrial back room. Drinks €6. Open daily 7pm-3:30am

Radio City, C. Sta. Teresa, 19 (☎963 91 41 51; www.radiocityvalencia.com). Popular free disco with and live music on weeknights. Young and friendly atmosphere. Beer €3.50, mixed drinks from €5. Flamenco every Tu night. Open daily 7:30pm-3:30am.

Venial, C. Quart, 34 (☎963 91 73 56). A lively and popular gay club with a huge dance floor and lots of crazy clientele. Hosts many of Spain's top DJs. More relaxed atmosphere at the back room bar. Cover €10, includes 1 drink. Open daily 1-7:30am.

Fox Congo, C. Caballeros, 35 (☎963 92 55 27). Dark, spacious, and metallic bar. A mixed crowd of slightly older patrons and beautiful people lounge on leather benches and dance to finely spun house. Beer €3.60, mixed drinks €6. Open daily 7pm-4am.

Jimmy Glass, C. Baja, 28 (☎963 91 05 03). Sip martinis (€4-6) to the soothing sounds of live classic jazz played nightly at this ultra-cool bar. Also offers a full menu of cocktails (€4-6). Open daily 8:30pm-3am.

Johnny Maracas, C. Caballeros, 39 bajo (☎963 91 52 66). Locals and tourists alike get friendly (sometimes too friendly) at this lively salsa bar. Try a *mojito* (€5) at their aquarium bar. Beer €3.50. Mixed drinks €5. Open daily 7:30pm-3:30am.

Finnegan's, Pl. de la Reina, 19 (☎963 91 05 03). American students frequent this huge Irish pub in front of the cathedral. Video screens for soccer matches. Beer €3.10, pints €4. Open M-Th 12:30pm-1am, F-Su 12:30pm-3am.

UNIVERSITY AREA

🎵 **Warhol,** Av. Blasco Ibáñez, 111. Does more than justice to its namesake. Eclectic mix of house, 80s, and rock with Lichtenstein-esque walls and 4 bars. Wild crowd of students and locals. *Festa Brasileira* Tu night, Murray Rock Night featuring classic rock favorites Th. Cover Su-Th €6, F-Sa €9; includes 1 drink. Open daily 1-7am.

Zenith, Av. Blasco Ibáñez, 111. In the same building as Warhol. Crazy disco where students bust a move to Spanish pop and house amidst mirrors and split level bars and dance floors. Cover €6, before 3am women free. Open Th-Sa 1-7:30am.

BY THE BEACH

Akuarela, C. Eugenia Viñes, 152, in Pl. Malvarossa. The only place to be by the beach. Gargantuan disco with different rooms and bars, a patio, and 4 stone staircases leading all around. Every inch packed with a young crowd partying until the sun comes up. Metro right across the street to head home after 5am, but who'd leave that early? Open daily 12:30-8:30am. Cover Th €10; F-Sa until 2:30am €10, after 2:30am €13.

🌊 BEACHES

Sand-seekers can join the topless by bouncing down to the expansive and packed beaches on Valencia's coast. The sand and water quality are less than spectacular, but the blistering heat converts everyone into a sea-lover. The most popular beaches are **Las Arenas** and **Malvarrosa,** connected by a bustling boardwalk. Buses #20, 21, 22, and 23 all pass by the sands. Equally crowded but more attractive is **Salér,** a pine-bordered strand 14km from the city that divides a lagoon from the sea. Cafeterias and snack bars line the shore. **Autobuses Buñol** (☎963 49 14 25) go to Salér (on the way to El Perello) from the intersection of Gran Vía de Germanías and C. Sueca. To get to the bus stop, exit the train station and take the street to the right (between the station and the bullring) to Gran Vía de Germanías. The bus stop is one block down. (25min., every 30min. 7am-10pm, €1.) For a better beach experience, hop the bus or train to **Dénia** (p. 345), **Gandía** (p. 348), or **Xàbia** (p. 347). All make perfect beach daytrips from Valencia.

🎆 FESTIVALS

Valencia's most famous festival is **Las Fallas** (Mar. 12-19). During **Semana Santa** a few weeks later, monks clog the streets enacting Biblical scenes, and children perform the miracle plays of Sant Vicent Ferrer. **Corpus Cristi** follows soon after with its display of *rocas* (carriages symbolizing Biblical mysteries). The **Festiu de Juliol** (Festival of July) brings fireworks, concerts, bullfights, and a *batalla dels flors*— a skirmish in which paradegoers and girls on floats toss flowers at each other.

🔼 DAYTRIPS FROM VALENCIA

SAGUNTO (SAGUNT)

Cercanías trains (☎ 962 66 07 28) from Valencia (C-6 line) stop in Sagunt (30min.; M-F 37 per day 6:10am-10:30pm, Sa-Su 15 per day 7:20am-10:30pm; €2.20), as do ALSA buses (☎ 964 66 18 50; 45min., daily every 30min. 7am-10:30pm, €2.10) and AVSA buses, which run to the beach (7am-10:10pm, €2.60). To get to the old town from the train station, take a right out of the station and then a left before the overpass on C. de los Huertos. Continue for 10min. to the Pl. Cronista Chabret and the tourist office.

The residents of Sagunt are said to be Spain's most courageous. This reputation dates to the 3rd century BC, when the citizens of Phoenician-controlled Saguntum held out during an eight-month siege by Hannibal's Carthaginians. Some sources say that on the brink of annihilation, Sagunt's women, children, and elderly threw themselves into a furnace; others insist that they chose starvation over defeat.

The architectural medley of Sagunt's monuments reflects a long list of conquering forces. The highlight of the old town is its vast medieval **castle,** which lies mostly in ruin above the town and was declared a national monument in 1931. (Open June-Sept. Tu-Sa 10am-8pm, Su 10am-2pm; Oct.-May Tu-Sa 10am-2pm and 4-6pm, Su 10am-2pm. Free.) On the way up to the castle is the equally impressive **Teatro Romano,** which has survived a controversial restoration process to become a state of the art outdoor stage. It is built entirely on the skeleton of the Roman structure, much of which is still visible. Ask at the tourist office for a list of performances. By the port (4km from town), Sagunt's grassy, rolling **beaches** attract summer travelers—**Puerto de Sagunt,** right near the port, is the best. Buses to the beaches leave from Av. Santos Patronos in front of the Ayuntamiento; return buses pick up outside the beach tourist office (every 30min. 7am-9:30pm, €0.85).

The **tourist office** in Pl. Cronista Chabret, across the plaza from the Ayuntamiento, has maps and walking tours. (☎ 962 66 22 13; www.sagunt.com/turismo. Open Sept.-May M-F 8am-3pm and 4-6:30pm, Sa-Su 9am-2pm. Hours vary in summer, but are usually M-Sa 10am-2pm and 4-7pm, Su 9am-2pm.) There's a **branch** at Av. Mediterráneo, 67, by the port. (☎ 962 69 04 02. Open M-Th 10am-2pm and 4:30-7:30pm, F-Sa 10am-2pm, Su 10am-2pm and 4:30-7:30pm.)

L'ALBUFERA

The park is a 40min. bus ride (15km) from Valencia on the tourist bus, which picks up in Pl. de la Reina, or on the Autocares Herca bus, which leaves from Gran Vía Germanías at the intersection of C. Sueca. To catch the return bus, walk with your back to the lagoon and cross the bridge on your right. The bus stop is outside the local high school.

Spain's largest lagoon, L'Albufera, and the surrounding **Parc Natural de L'Albufera** are a nature lover's paradise. Trails for biking and hiking ring the lake (6km in diameter) while small fishing boats hide amid tall wetland reeds. L'Albufera, one of the wettest regions on the Iberian peninsula, is a prime spot for bird watching—over 250 migrant species make temporary camp along its shores. The **Bus Touristic L'Alburfera** runs there four times per day in summer, three in winter, with a guided tour. (€12, includes a boat ride on the lagoon.) **Autocares Herca** runs to El Palmer (the only city on the lagoon) 5 times per day from Valencia (€1.50). Ask at a Valencia tourist office (p. 322) for information on boat tours and cultural excursions.

JÁTIVA (XÀTIVA)

Trains are the best way to get in and out of Xàtiva. RENFE (☎ 963 52 02 02) runs from Valencia to Xàtiva (1hr., every 30min. 6am-10:30pm, €2.60; return 1-4 per hr. 5:30am-3am.) To reach the old village and the tourist office from the train station, walk straight up Baixada de l'Estació and turn left at its end.

Once the second most populous city in Valencia, Xàtiva, a mecca of palaces and churches, was burned to the ground by Felipe V in the 18th century. Today all that remains is an impressive castle, a slew of churches and ruins, and its annual festival. **Alameda de Jaume I** divides the town into the new and the old villages, starting from the foot of a hill topped by an awe-inspiring ▓**castle.** The complex has two sections: the **castell machor,** on the right as you enter, and the pre-Roman **castell chicotet.** The former, used from the 13th through 16th centuries, bears the scars of siege and earthquake. Its vaulted **prison** has held famous wrongdoers, including Fernando el Católico and the Comte d'Urgell, a would-be usurper of the Aragonese throne. The Comte is buried there. The prison's garden also contains the shields and histories of its prisoners. It's a 30min. walk uphill to the castle, but a tourist train chugs up daily at 12:30 and 5:30pm, 4:30pm in winter. (Open summer Tu-F 10am-7pm, Sa-Su 10am-8pm; winter Tu-Su 10am-6pm. €2, under 18 €1.) Held since 1250, Xàtiva's **Fira festival** storms the city August 15-20 with live music, bullfights, and tug-of-war contests. The **tourist office,** Alameda Jaume I, 50, is across from the Ayuntamiento. (☎962 27 33 46; www.ayto-xativa.com. English spoken. Open June 15-Sept. 15 Tu-F 10am-2:30pm and 5-7pm, Sa-Su 10am-2pm; Sept. 16-June 14 Tu-F 10am-2pm and 4-6pm, Sa-Su 10am-1:30pm.)

CASTELLÓN (CASTELLÓ) ☎964

As the halfway point between Valencia and Barcelona, Castelló (pop. 160,000) can easily seem like little more than a transportation hub. In reality, though, it is a thriving, cosmopolitan city with much to offer. Its bustling plazas, wealth of historic monuments and museums, and beaches should be enough to attract anyone, but its distinction as one of the least expensive spots to stay along the Mediterranean, and the fact that it is the home of the large Universidad de Jaime I, makes it popular with both budget travelers and students alike. There is plenty to enjoy in Castelló that is easy on the eyes and the wallet.

▐ TRANSPORTATION. The combined **train** and **bus station** is on Av. Pintor Oliet, between the University and the center of the town (train info ☎964 21 45 32, bus info ☎964 24 07 78). Castelló is most easily reached by train from **Valencia,** as **Cercanías** trains run there frequently (1hr., 1-4 per hr. 6:10am-10:30pm, €3.40). **RENFE** (☎902 24 02 02) trains also run to **Barcelona** (2½hr., 15 per day 7am-9pm, €14.70-46.50). Trains also head to: **Málaga** (10hr., 10:36am and 11:30pm, €25-34); **Granada** (9hr., 10:36am and 11:30pm, €23.50); **Murcia** (6hr., 3 per day 1:30-6:40pm, €15.50-20). **ALSA** (☎902 42 22 42) sends buses to: **Alicante** (4-5½hr., 8 per day 4:45am-2:30am, €16.30); **Almería** (9-10hr., 3 per day 4:45am-10:50pm, €34.60); **Barcelona** (4-5hr., 1-2 per hr. 4am-1am, €18.30-22.18); **Gandía** (2½hr., 9:40 and 10:50pm, €8.30); **Murcia** (5-7hr., 7 per day 4:45am-2:30am, €40); **Sevilla** (12hr., 9:20pm and 2:30am, €47-55.10). **Auto-Res** (☎963 49 22 30) goes to **Madrid** (4-5hr., 4-5 per day 7:30am-11:45pm, €23.40-28.30). **Autos Mediterráneo** (☎964 22 00 54) departs for **Morella** (2½hr.; M-F 7:30am and 3:45pm, Sa 3:45pm; €7.30). **Municipal bus** #9 runs from the train station to Pl. Borrul in the center (€0.60). For a **taxi,** call ☎964 22 74 74.

▐▐ ORIENTATION AND PRACTICAL INFORMATION. The city center is the **Plaza Mayor,** which contains the **Ayuntamiento, Catedral de Santa María,** and **Mercado Central.** C. Mayor runs up to the **Plaza de María Agustina** and the **tourist office.** (☎964 35 86 89; castellon@touristinfo.net. Open Sept.-June M-F 9am-2pm and 4-7pm, Sa 10am-2pm; July-Aug. M-F 9am-7pm, Sa 10am-2pm.) There is another **branch** at the port. (☎964 28 32 02; graocastellon@touristinfo.net. Open M-Th

10:30am-2:30pm and 4-6pm, F-Sa 11am-3pm and 5-7pm, Su 11am-2:30pm.) **Calle Mar** and **Calle Hermanos Bou** both run to the port, 4km east of the town center. Most services, including **banks** and **ATMs,** can be found in and around the Pl. Mayor. Local services include: **Hospital General** (☎964 21 10 00); **police** (☎092); **post office,** Pl. Tetuán, 41. (☎964 21 47 73. Open M-F 8:30am-8:30pm, Sa 9:30am-2pm.) **Postal Code:** 12001.

ACCOMMODATIONS AND FOOD. Castelló is filled with fairly inexpensive hotels, so feel free to splurge a bit on a good night's rest. For budget accommodations, though, one of the nicer hostels in town is **H.V. Ventura ❷,** C. San Vicente, 89, which has large, tasteful rooms with bath and TV a block off Av. Rey Don Jaime. (☎964 25 03 09. Singles €18, with bath €20; doubles €30; triples €45.) Price and location are the best things about **Pensión La Esperanza ❷,** C. Trinidad, 37. Just two blocks off the Pl. Mayor, this hostel offers rooms with sinks and hallway baths. (☎964 22 20 31. Singles €16.50; doubles €27; triples €40.50; quads €50.) For lunch, take a stroll down **Calle Caballeros,** which runs parallel to C. Mayor toward the Pl. Mayor. Here you'll find a variety of places open only for lunch that offer *menús* for under €10. For dinner, your best bet is to head down to the **Grau** (port; see **Beaches,** p. 331) where seafood restaurants line Pl. de la Mar and the streets. Try **Meduse ❷,** Po. Buenavista, 31, for a funky, modern atmosphere and a fine selection of seafood and vegetarian dishes. (☎964 06 34 40. Salads and *bocadillos* €3-5. Entrees €8-12. Live music every Th night; ask for a schedule. Open daily 6pm-2am.) For the more standard fare of rice dishes and seafood, head to **Tasca del Puerto ❸,** Av. del Puerto, 13. (☎964 28 44 81. Entrees €9-27. Open Tu-Sa 1:30-4pm and 8-11pm.)

SIGHTS. Castelló's cultural center and one of its most attractive buildings is the **Museu de Bellas Artes,** C. Hermanos Bou, 28, a seven minute walk from the city center. Bus #4 also runs there from Pl. Bou. The museum deftly manages to combine past and present by housing two floors of 14th-19th century paintings (including an impressive collection of works by Castilian painter Gabriel Puig Roda) and sculptures in a beautiful, modern building of wood, stone, and glass. Don't miss the artisan ceramics or the archaeological exhibits in the basement. (☎964 72 75 00. Open M-Sa 10am-8pm, Su 10am-2pm. Free.) If the museum doesn't quench your thirst for Spanish paintings, stop by the **Convento Capuchinas,** C. Núñez de Arce, 11, a small, easily missed convent which houses nine beautiful portraits of the founders of the order by Francisco Zurbarán. (Open daily for mass 4-8pm. Closed Aug. Free.) In the Pl. Mayor, the octagonal **Torre Campanario de Fadri** stands 58m tall and is the symbol of Castelló. Finished in the 17th century, it was built to be a free standing bell tower for the **Concatedral de Santa María** right next door. Now it is owned by the government, not the church, and can only be toured in groups. Call for information and reservations. (Tower ☎964 22 75 56, cathedral ☎964 22 34 63. Open M-F 9:30am-1pm and 6:30-7:45pm, Sa 9:30am-1pm except during services at 11am, Su 9:30-11:30am. Free.)

BEACHES. Castelló's **Grau** (port), located 4km east of the city, has a scene all its own. Buses run from the Pl. Borrul to the port and the beaches (summer every 15min., winter every 30min.). Surrounding the port is the **Plaça del Mar,** which houses dozens of restaurants and even a small shopping center. To the left of the port when facing the water is **Playa del Pinar,** and farther north lies **Playa del Gurugú.** Both are fairly crowded, but for good reason considering their soft sands and sparkling waters. The **Paseo Buena Vista** runs from the port to the beginning of the beaches, while the **Paseo Marítimo** runs along the shore line.

IN DEEP TRUFFLE

If the Gothic architecture and innate charm aren't enough to draw you to Morella, then go for their delicious cuisine, which centers around flavorful *trufas negras* (black truffles). Dug up from deep in the region's mountains, these delectable delicacies add a touch of class to any dish. The most common (and probably the cheapest) truffle dish you'll find is *paté de trufas* (truffle pâté), which runs about €6-9, depending on the restaurant. Even more mouthwatering is the ◪ *solomillo de cordero relleno de trufas*, truffle-stuffed lamb served either roasted or baked in a pastry with ham (€11-16).

Truffles can also be taken to go and come in several varieties. *Trufas del verano* are the most common and are used as a garnish. A very small jar containing three or four will only cost you €4.50. The most expensive are the *trufas de la reina,* a small jar of which will set you back a whopping €27.50. These, however, are larger, more flavorful, and longer lasting. Locals also make their own *aceite de trufas* (truffle oil) by simply mixing them with olive oil. Stores sell jars of truffle juice especially for this purpose.

For the best variety and prices of truffles, stop by **Guimera,** C. Virgen del Pilar, 27 (☎964 17 31 15), which offers a huge selection of local food specialties including freshly made honey (with free samples), cheeses, and wines.

MORELLA ☎964

Rising majestically above the fertile valley below, the medieval fortress town of Morella (pop. 2000), located in the northernmost extremes of the Comunitat Valenciana, is an isolated gem for the traveler. With picturesque cobblestone streets, impressive medieval walls, and a castle crowning its highest point, it offers soothing vistas and small town charm. Tourists are only the latest in a long line of people who have been drawn to Morella, which has hosted Celts, Romans, and Moors at various times throughout its history.

▐▊ TRANSPORTATION AND PRACTICAL INFORMATION. Morella is hard to reach. Most visitors arrive via Valencia, though the city is also accessible from Barcelona. Travelers must make a connection at **Castelló** on the **Cercanías train** line from Valencia (1hr., 1-4 per hr. 6:10am-10:30pm, €3.40). From Barcelona, the **RENFE** Mediterranean goes to Castelló (2½hr., 15 per day 7am-9pm, €14.70-46.50). **Autos Mediterráneo** (☎964 22 00 54) departs from the bus stop outside of Castelló's train station for **Morella** (2½hr.; M-F 7:30am and 3:45pm, Sa 3:45pm; return M-F 7:45am and 4pm, Sa 4pm; €7.30). The bus from Castelló doesn't start at the bus stop, however, and stops there only briefly, so keep an eye out. It drops you off either at the Pta. de San Miguel, the arched entrance to the city, or at the Torre Beneito, on C. Muralla. The return bus picks up only at Torre Beneito. Morella's **tourist office,** Pl. San Miguel, is right through the archway, across the street, and on the left. (☎964 17 30 32; www.morella.net. Open July-Aug. 10am-2pm and 4-7pm; Sept.-June Tu-Sa 10am-2pm and 4-6pm, Su 10am-2pm.) For **medical assistance,** call ☎964 16 09 62. **Internet access** is available at **Ciberlocutori Nou,** C. Sant Julia, 2. (☎964 16 10 05. €1 per 30min. Open daily 10am-2:30pm and 5:30-10:30pm.)

▐▊ ACCOMMODATIONS AND FOOD. Once you pass through the Gothic archways of Morella, you may never want to leave—and considering the bus schedule, it's likely you'll have to stay at least one night. Fortunately, most lodging here gives you luxury standards at budget prices. ◪**Hostal La Muralla ❷,** C. Muralla, 12, has rooms with TV and private bath. (☎964 16 02 43. Simple breakfast included. Singles €25.60; doubles €38.50. MC/V.) Live royally (on a budget) at **Hotel El Cid ❷,** Portal Sant Mateu, 3, a block to the right of the bus stop when facing the city wall. Gigantic rooms come with colorful plaid bedspreads, TV, phone, and bathtub; some have balconies with great views of the mountainous countryside. (☎964 16 01 25; www.hotelelcidmorella.com. Breakfast or full board available for additional fees. Singles €23.20; doubles €40. V.) Those seeking a touch of elegance will find it in the comfortable rooms of **Hotel Cardenal Ram ❹**, Cuesta Suner, 1, built in a 15th-century palace at the end of the colonnade on C. Don Blasco de Alagón. All rooms have large bath, TV, and phone. (☎964 17 30 85. Breakfast €6, lunch or dinner €14. Singles €40; doubles €60. MC/V.)

The town's gourmet cuisine is filled with *trufas* (truffles) dug up from under the local turf. Specialties include *paté de trufas* and *cordero relleno trufado* (truffle-stuffed lamb; see **In Deep Truffle**, p. 332). Eating out is pricey, and options are limited—most eateries are located on shop-lined C. Don Blasco de Alagón, Morella's main street. **Restaurante Casa Roque ❸**, Cuesta San Juan, 1 serves delicious local favorites in a beautiful dining room decorated with colorful photographs of the town. (☎964 16 03 36. Entrees €9-15. *Menú* €12-25. Open M-Sa 10:30am-5pm and 8:30-11:30pm. MC/V.) Those looking to escape the truffle madness run to **Restaurante Lola ❶**, C. Blasco de Alagón, 21, for the best Italian cuisine in town. (☎964 16 03 87. Entrees €4.80-9.20. *Menú* €10. Open M-Sa noon-4:30pm and 8:30pm-2am.)

◪ SIGHTS. Perched atop a massive rock, the **▨Castell de Morella** dazzles even the most seasoned of castle-goers with its impressive history and lovely pathways filled with wildflowers and butterflies. Celts, Romans, and Moors have all defended Morella's walls as their own. El Cid stormed the summit in 1084, and Don Blasco de Alagón took the town in the name of Jaume I in 1232. Civil wars in the 19th century and an explosion have damaged the castle, but the resulting craters only add to the intrigue. Artillery walls surround it, with openings just wide enough for the sights of archers or a camera lens. Inspect the **Cadro guardhouse** and the **Catxo dungeon,** where the prince of Viana was imprisoned in the 15th century. (Entrance at the end of C. Hospital, uphill from the basilica. ☎964 17 31 28. Open June-Sept. 10:30am-7:30pm; Oct.-May 9:30am-6:30pm. €1.20, students €0.90.) In Pl. Arciprestal, on the way to the castle, the ceiling of the Gothic **Basílica Santa María la Mayor** hovers over a winding stairwell, a large organ, and the ghostly statue of Nuestra Señora de la Asunción. Bracketed by chandeliers, the altar is almost as breathtaking as the basilica's stained glass windows. (Open June-Aug. Tu-Su 11am-2pm and 4-7pm; Sept.-May noon-2pm and 4-6pm. Mass M-F 7pm; Sa 8:15pm; Su 10am, 5, and 6:30pm. Basilica free. Museum €0.90.) For great views of both the countryside and the castle, stop by the **Mirador de la Plaza Colón** at the end of C. Blasco de Alagón. To see the remnants of the Gothic **aqueduct,** exit the city through the enormous **Portal de San Miguel,** turn left, and walk five minutes.

COSTA BLANCA

The "white coast," so named for the color of the fine sand and smooth pebbles that cover its shores, extends from Dénia through Calp to Alicante. A varied terrain of hills blanketed with cherry blossoms, jagged mountains, lush pine-covered slopes, and natural lagoons surrounds densely populated coastal towns, all of which attract their fair share of tourists. It's easy to see why—Altea, Calp, Dénia, and especially Xàbia offer relief from the disco droves that energize Alicante and Benidorm, making their spectacular beaches and charming town centers ideal spots for families or travelers seeking more tranquil locales. In all of these towns, if you're not willing to shell out the money for a beachfront hotel, you may be better off staying in Alicante or Benidorm and daytripping up and down the coast. Fortunately, frequent and cheap modes of transportation make this an easy option.

◄ COASTAL TRANSPORTATION

Trains: Ferrocarrils de la Generalitat Valenciana (☎965 92 02 02, in Alicante 26 27 31), also known as the "Costa Blanca Express," hits almost every town and beach along the coast on its Alicante-Dénia line. Trains run from Alicante to: **Altea** (1½hr., every hr. 5:50am-8:50pm except noon, €3.80); **Benidorm** (1hr., every hr. 5:50am-8:50pm, €3.10); **Calp** (1¾hr., 7 per day 5:50am-8:50pm, €4.80); **Dénia** (2¼hr., 7 per day 5:50am-8:50pm, €6.90). Trains return to **Alicante** from Dénia and Calp (every 2hr. 6:25am-7:25pm) and from Altea and Benidorm (every hr. 6:24am-10:24pm). **Tramsnochador** (☎965 26 27 31), the night train from Alicante, runs to **Altea** and **Benidorm.** (June 18-Sept. 4 per day 10:55pm-12:55am; returning from Altea at 12:24 and 2:24am, from Benidorm 12:36 and 2:36am.)

Buses: Depending on where you're going, buses can be the easiest and most cost-efficient way to get around the Costa Blanca. **ALSA** (☎902 42 22 42) runs between Alicante and Valencia, stopping in towns along the Costa Blanca. From Valencia buses run to: **Alicante** (2-4hr., 12-15 per day 4:45am-10:45pm, €13-15); **Benidorm** (4hr., 15-18 per day 4:45am-9:45pm, €11.55); **Calp/Altea** (3-4½hr., 8-10 per day 6am-5pm, €9.35-10.55); **Dénia** (1hr., 11-12 per day 5:15am-10:45pm, €4.75); **Gandía** (1hr., 9-11 per day 4:45am-9:45pm, €5.05); **Xàbia** (2-3hr., 6 per day 6:30am-9:45pm, €8.30). From Alicante buses run to: **Altea** (1hr., 1-2 per hr. 6:30am-7pm, €3.90); **Calp** (1½hr., 1-2 per hr. 6:30am-7pm, €5.20); **Dénia** (2½hr., 1-2 per hr. 6:30am-8pm, €8.20); **Xàbia** (2hr., 19 per day 7am-8pm, €7.30); **Valencia** (2½hr., 1-3 per hr. 6:30am-9pm).

ALICANTE (ALACANT)   ☎965

A mural in Alicante's bus station proclaims *"Bienvenido seas, viajero: Alicante te ofrece sosiego y luz radiante"* (May you be welcome, traveler: Alicante offers you peace and radiant light). Alicante (pop. 285,000) feels at once expansive and intimate, vibrant and relaxed, urban and natural. While undoubtedly a Spanish city in every way, there is an extra sparkle and a unique energy here. Perhaps it's because the residents are friendlier, the nightlife is livelier (particularly during the explosive festival of Sant Joan in late June), and even the beaches seem sunnier. For whatever reason, Alicante is indescribably unlike any other city in Spain, and is an unforgettable stop along the Mediterranean that no traveler should miss.

◄ TRANSPORTATION

Flights: Aeroport Internacional El Altet (☎966 91 90 00), 11km from town. **Iberia** (24hr. ☎902 40 05 00) and **Air Europa** (☎902 24 00 42) have daily flights to **Madrid, Barcelona,** and the **Islas Baleares,** among other destinations. **British Airways** (☎966 91 94 72) flies to London, England. **Alcoyana** (☎965 16 79 11) bus #C-6 runs to the airport from Pl. Luceros (every 40min., €0.85).

Trains: RENFE, Estación Término (☎902 24 02 02), on Av. de Salamanca. Info open daily 7am-midnight. To: **Barcelona** (4½-6hr., 5-6 per day 6:55am-6:25pm, €43-67); **Elx** (30min., every hr. 6:05am-10:05pm, €1.70); **Madrid** (4hr., 4-9 per day 7am-8pm, €36-56); **Murcia** (1½hr., every hr. 6:05am-10:05pm, €3.80); **Valencia** (1½hr., 10 per day 6:55am-8:20pm, €9-34.50). **Ferrocarrils de la Generalitat Valenciana (TRAM),** Estació Marina, Av. Villajoyosa, 2 (☎965 26 27 31), has service along the Costa Blanca. In summer the **Tramsnochador** (night trains; ☎965 26 27 31) run to beaches including **Altea** and **Benidorm,** with some continuing to **Dénia** (June 18-Sept. 4 F-Sa every hr. 10:55pm-4:55am, with weeknight service June 20-24; €0.90-4.20).

Alicante

▲ ACCOMMODATIONS
Habitaciones Belenguer, 3
Habitaciones México, 8
Hostal Mayor, 19
Hostal Metidia, 16
Hostal Les Monges Palace, 14
Hostal-Residencia Portugal, 2
Residencia La Milagrosa, 22
Residencia Universitaria (HI), 1

● FOOD
Al Peperone, 9
Cafetería Mediterráneo, 20
Kebap, 4
La Bodeguita de Abajo, 6
La Taberna del Gourmet, 21
Restaurante O'Pote Gallego, 18

★ NIGHTLIFE
Astrónomo, 12
Café Directo, 23
Coscorrón, 11
Coyote Ugly, 24
Do-Desafinado, 10
El Forat, 17
La Biblioteca, 13
O'Connell's, 7
Puerto Di Roma, 25
Supporter, 15
Z-Klub, 5

TO PLAYA SAN JUAN
AND PLAYA MUTXAVISTA (4km);
TO BENIDORM (31km);
TO DÉNIA (91km);
TO VALENCIA (166km);

Casco Antiguo

SANTA CRUZ

Mediterranean Sea

Port

TO PUERTO NUEVO (100m)

TO BENIDORM (2km)
TO (11km)

Buses: C. Portugal, 17 (☎965 13 07 00). **ALSA** (☎902 42 22 42) to: **Altea** (1hr., 1-2 per hr. 6:30am-7pm, €3.90); **Barcelona** (7hr., 15 per day 4:45am-2:30am, €34.60-40.10); **Calp** (1½hr., 1-2 per hr. 6:30am-7:00pm, €5.20); **Dénia** (2½hr., 1-2 per hr. 6:30am-8pm, €8.20); **Granada** (6hr., 10 per day 6:45am-3am, €24-29.40); **Xàbia** (2hr., 19 per day 7am-8pm, €7.30); **Madrid** (5hr., 15 per day 8am-12:45am, €23.20-30); **Málaga** (8hr., 8 per day 6:45am-2:45am, €31.70-39.30); **Sevilla** (10hr., 11:30am and 11:45pm, €40.20); **Valencia** (2½hr., 1-3 per hr. 6:30am-9pm, €14.90-15.30). **Mollá** (☎965 13 08 51) runs buses to **Elx** (30min.; M-F 2 per hr. 7am-10pm, Sa every hr. 8am-10pm, Su 8 per day 9am-9:30pm; €1.60).

Public Transportation: TAM (☎965 14 09 36). Buses #21 and 22 run from the train station in Alicante to Playa San Juan (€0.85).

Taxis: Teletaxi ☎965 25 25 11.

✳❷ ORIENTATION AND PRACTICAL INFORMATION

Originating at the train station, **Avenida de la Estación** becomes **Avenida Alfonso X el Sabio** after passing through Pl. Luceros and runs through the center of town. **Explanada d'Espanya** stretches along the waterfront between Av. Federico Soto and Rmbla. Méndez Núñez, which marks the beginning of the *casco antiguo*.

Tourist Office: Municipal office, C. Portugal, 17 (☎965 92 98 02; www.alicanteturismo.com). English spoken. Open M-Sa 9am-2pm and 4-8pm. **Regional office,** Rmbla. Méndez Núñez, 23 (☎965 20 00 00; www.comunitatvalencia.com). English spoken. Open June-Aug. M-F 10am-8pm; Sept.-May M-F 10am-7pm, Sa 10am-2pm and 3-7pm. **Airport branch** open Tu-Sa 10am-2pm and 5-8pm. Other branches by the train station and on the Explanada d'Espanya.

Budget Travel: TIVE, IVAJ, Pl. San Cristóbal, 8 (☎965 93 67 00). ISIC €4.20. HI card €10.80. Open M-F 9am-3pm.

Luggage Storage: Bus station (€2-3.80 per bag. Open M-Sa 8am-9:30pm, Su 10am-1pm and 3:45-7pm) and **train station** (€2.40 per bag. Open daily 7am-midnight).

Police: Comisaría, C. Médico Pascual Pérez, 27 (☎965 10 72 00).

Hospital: Hospital General, C. Maestro Alonso, 109 (☎965 93 83 00).

Internet Access: Fundación BanCaja, Rmbla. Méndez Núñez, 4, 2nd fl. 1hr. free with ISIC. Open M-F 10am-2pm and 5-9pm, Sa 9am-2pm. **CBRie,** Teniente Álvarez Soto, 8, 1 block off the Rambla. €1.50 per hr. Open daily noon-midnight.

Post Office: Corner of C. Arzobispo Loaces and C. Alemania (☎965 21 99 84). Open M-F 8:30am-8:30pm, Sa 9:30am-2pm. **Branch,** Bono Guarner, 2 (☎965 22 78 71), next to the train station. Open M-F 8:30am-8:30pm, Sa 9:30am-1pm. **Postal Code:** 03070.

▌ ACCOMMODATIONS

While hostels are everywhere, good accommodations require an early arrival or a reservation, especially during the Festival de Sant Joan. If you're not particular, though, finding a cheap room in Alicante is fairly easy.

◪ **Habitaciones México,** C. General Primo de Rivera, 10 (☎965 20 93 07; mexrooms@ctv.es). Small but cozy rooms with sea-foam green walls and emerald- tiled hallway baths. The wonderful owners and their huge family make you feel right at home. Free Internet access (noon-10pm) and kitchen use. Laundry €6. Singles €12-15; doubles €27, with bath €33; triples €33/€36. ❶

Residencia La Milagrosa, C. Villa Vieja (☎965 21 69 18). 30 simple, sunny rooms in luxurious marble surroundings blocks from the beach. Huge rooftop garden terrace with a view of the castle makes it even sweeter. Hallway baths. Kitchen on every floor. Dorms June-Aug. €20; Sept.-May €15. ❷

Hostal Les Monges Palace, C. San Agustín, 4 (☎965 21 50 46). Tiles painted with 3 smiling nuns lead you to stately rooms. Some have A/C, jacuzzis, and saunas, but you'll pay more. Internet access available in rooms or at reception (€3 per hr.). Parking €8 per day. Singles €25-29.50; doubles €37-50; triples €44-60. MC/V. ❸

Hostal-Residencia Portugal, C. Portugal, 26 (☎965 92 92 44). Clean, modern rooms across the street from the bus station. Ask for one with a balcony facing the street. In-room TV €3. Singles €21, with bath €26; doubles €32/€35; triples €45/€54. ❷

Habitaciones Belenguer, C. Alemania, 15 (☎965 92 79 47). Simple, clean rooms with tile floors, sinks, and TV. Convenient to bus station, beach, and town center. Free Internet and kitchen use. Laundry €6. Singles €15-18; doubles €25-28; triples €32-36. ❷

Hostal Metidja, Rmbla. Méndez Núñez, 26 (☎965 14 36 17). Great location right next to Havana Café. Clean rooms with hallway baths. All with TV and A/C. Singles €20-22; doubles €35-45; triples €50-58. Prices higher June-Aug. ❷

Hostal Mayor, C. Mayor, 5 (☎965 20 13 83). Centrally located with brightly painted rooms, all with bath. Noisy at night due to its proximity to the bars of the *casco antiguo*. Singles €20; doubles €30; triples €45. ❷

Residencia Universitaria La Florida (HI), Av. Orihuela, 59 (☎965 11 30 44). Take bus #03. Dorms with bath and A/C. Travelers mingle at the snack bar, by the TV, or over foosball. Laundry €1.60 per load. 3-day max. stay. Open July-Sept. Dorms €7.50, with breakfast €8.30, with 3 meals €15.30; over 26 €10.60/ €11.40/€18.40. ❶

🛒 FOOD

Most visitors refuel along the main pedestrian streets; prices are reasonable despite the crowds of tourists. As usual, multilingual menus and posterboards of paella mark the overpriced establishments. The numerous Turkish and Lebanese *kebap* restaurants are the best bargains in the city. Smaller, cheaper *barrestaurantes* in the old city have fewer visitors, but also less variety. The **market** is on Av. Alfonso X el Sabio. (Open M-Sa 8am-2pm.) Buy basics at **Supermarket Mercadona,** C. Álvarez Sereix, 5 (☎965 21 58 94; open M-Sa 9am-9pm) or at **El Corte Inglés.**

🍽 **Kebap,** Av. Dr. Gadea, 5 (☎965 22 92 35), near the corner of C. Italia. Accept no substitutions from its neon competitors; this is the best Middle Eastern cuisine in Alicante. Mouth watering *rollos* (pitas with meat or veggies; €2.40). Heaping entrees €5.70-7. Open daily 1-4pm and 8pm-midnight. 2nd location at C. San Fernando, 12. ❶

NO WORK, ALL PLAY

BONFIRE OF THE EFFIGIES

During the rollicking **Festival de Sant Joan** (June 20-29), Alicante takes parties to the next level. For 75 years the city has ushered in the summer with over a week of parades and parties. The festival springs from a tradition of burning unusable materials on the summer solstice; in 1928 the festivities were expanded to encompass the feast day of Sant Joan, and satiric effigies (*fogueres* or *hogueras*) were added to the flames.

On the 19th, streets are blocked off and huge, colorful *fogueres* are erected throughout the city among tented dancing areas with street bars. Young and old gather from midnight until dawn, dancing and drinking for one week straight. But daylight brings no rest: fireworks explode daily at 2pm, residents gather for spectacular parades, and traditional music fills the air. In the early evening, visitors are treated to the *Bellesa del Foc* (Beauty Queen of Fire) competition.

The festival reaches a fever pitch on the evening of Sant Joan's feast day (June 24). At midnight the effigies are set ablaze in a ceremony known as *la Cremá* (the burning). Firefighters then proceed to soak everyone nearby during *la Banyá* (the bath), and the party continues until dawn—soaking wet.

Make reservations far in advance; the city swells with visitors the week before the festival.

La Bodeguita de Abajo, C. Bailén, 4 (☎965 21 94 80). Great appetizer options (€1-4) and *comida típica* served in a cavernous space adorned with paintings by local artists. Live music Th nights. Entrees €9-13. Open daily 9pm-midnight. ❷

La Taberna del Gourmet, C. San Fernando, 10 (☎965 20 42 33). Traditional restaurant specializes in a *menú* for 2, which includes a selection of paella, fish, and meat dishes (€19-23). Entrees €6-19. Lunch *menú* €13. Open daily 1-4pm and 8pm-12:30am. ❸

Al Peperone, Pl. San Cristóbal, 2-B (☎965 14 65 21; www.viviositalianos.com). In the plaza off Rmbla. Méndez Núñez. Thin crust pizzas (€6-14) and daily pasta specials (€5-6.50) in a modern setting. Take-out available. Open daily 2-4pm and 9pm-midnight. ❷

Cafetería Mediterráneo, C. Altamira, 8 (☎965 14 08 40), 2 blocks from the Explanada. A cafe bursting with locals at all hours of the day. Chrome bar displays an array of nicely priced daily tapas and *raciones.* 4-course *menú* €8.80. Open M-Sa 7am-10pm. ❶

Restaurante O'Pote Gallego, Pl. Santísima Faz, 6 (☎965 20 80 84), in the square behind the Ayuntamiento. Galician and Valencian specialties served in a pleasant setting. Meat and fish entrees €5-15. *Menú* €20.10. Open Tu-Sa 1-4pm and 5-11pm. ❷

👁🎫 SIGHTS AND BEACHES

With drawbridges, dark passageways, and hidden tunnels, the **Castell de Santa Bárbara** keeps silent guard over Alicante's beach. The 200m high fortress built by the Carthaginians boasts a dry moat, dungeon, and ammunitions storeroom. The *Albacar Vell*, constructed during the Middle Ages, holds a vast sculpture garden with exhibits of Spanish greats. A paved road from the old section of Alicante leads to the top, although most people opt for the **elevator** rising from a hidden entrance on Av. Jovellanos, just across the street from Playa Postiguet, near the white pedestrian overpass. (☎965 26 31 31. Castle open Apr.-Sept. 10am-7:30pm; Oct.-Mar. 9am-6:30pm. Free. Elevator €2.40.) The **Museu de Arte del Siglo XX La Asegurada,** Pl. Santa María, 3, showcases modern art, including several works by Picasso, Miró, and Dalí. The museum offers free guided tours if reserved in advance. (☎965 14 07 68. Open May 15-Sept. 14 Tu-F 10am-2pm and 5-9pm, Sa-Su 10:30am-2:30pm; Sept. 15-May 14 Tu-F 10am-2pm and 4-8pm, Sa-Su 10:30am-2:30pm. Free.)

Alicante's **Playa del Postiguet,** just meters to the left of the new port, is bordered by sand sculptures and brims with sunbathers, and families. For more peaceful shores, the 6km of **Playa de San Juan** and **Playa del Mutxavista** are the nearest options. (To San Juan, take TAM bus #21, 22, or 31. For Mutxavista, take #21. Each departs every 15min., €0.80. The Alicante-Dénia train (TRAM) leaves the main station every hr. and stops at Playa del Muxtavista and Playa de San Juan; €0.80.)

🎤 NIGHTLIFE

The discos and port-side pubs of Alicante make for vibrant and varied nightlife. For yet wilder nightlife, **Benidorm,** 45min. away, rocks out with several huge discotecas, all accessible from July to August by FGV's special **Tramsnochador** (see **Trains,** p. 334). There are two main concentrated areas of bars and clubs in town: in the *casco antiguo* behind Rmbla. Méndez Núñez and at the port.

CASCO ANTIGUO

Most night owls kick off the evening with bar-hopping in the *casco antiguo,* though there are enough watering-holes in this insane maze of winding streets to keep anyone busy until morning. The first *"copa"* of the night is usually drunk at one of the cafe-bars in and around **Plaza San Cristóbal.** Keep an eye out for specials posted in the windows. Generally, if one bar has them, its neighbors do too.

Coscorrón, C. Tarifa, 3. For a famous *mojito* (€2.50) served in an antique teapot, head to Coscorrón, so named for the bump on the head you might receive from the 4ft. high door. Open since 1936, it claims to be the oldest bar in Alicante. Head downstairs to admire decades of political stickers or upstairs for more breathing room and writing on the walls. Open Su-Th 10:30pm-2:30am, F-Sa 11pm-4:30am.

Do-Desafinado, C. Santo Tomás, 6 (☎670 40 82 36; www.do-desafinado.com). A sexy, sophisticated crowd packs this eclectically decorated cafe-bar as DJs spin house and pop. Check website for DJ schedule. Open Th-Sa 9pm-4:30am, Su 6:30pm-3am.

O'Connell's, Av. de la Constitución, 14 (☎965 14 05 84). 1 block off the Rambla from the *casco antiguo,* American and British exchange students hang out and hook up at this lively Irish pub. Beer €1.50-3. Open M-F 4pm-4am, Sa-Su 5pm-5am.

El Forat, Pl. Santísima Faz, 4. Glowing bar whose tag line is *"para todos los gustos"*—for every taste. Filled with silk flowers, old headshots, and religious icons. Wild mixed gay/straight crowd, and an occasional drag show. Drinks €3-5. Open daily 11pm-4am.

Astrónomo, C. Virgen de Belén, at C. Padre Maltés. 2 magically decorated floors of dancing and drinking. When it gets too hot on the dance floor, escape across the street to cool off on the large, outdoor terrace. Drinks from €4.50. Open Th-Sa 11pm-6am.

La Biblioteca, C. Montegnon, 5. A slightly older crowd hits the dance floor instead of the books at this 3-story monolithic disco. The name means "the library," so it's natural that books adorn the walls. Beer €3, mixed drinks from €5. Open Th-Sa 11pm-6am.

Supporter, C. San Nicolás, 14. Take a break from Spanish pop with a mix of modern and classic rock in this funky bar with concert tickets from the last 20 years covering its walls. Beer €1.50-3, mixed drinks €3-4. Open Th-Sa 10:30pm-4:30am.

NEAR THE PORT

Alicante's **main port** houses a complex of bars overlooking the water. These tend to fill up a bit later than the bars in town. A dance-happy crowd fills the many vast discos on the **Puerto Nuevo,** to the left when facing the water. None of these charge a cover, though there is sometimes a drink minimum. The liveliest spots are **Puerto Di Roma,** with a well-dressed, mixed-age crowd, and **Café Directo,** which also has a location back in the *casco antiguo.* If English is your language of choice, **Coyote Ugly** is just a few doors down, complete with poles on the bar for...well, you know. The bartenders here are (arguably) hot, but the crowd is uninspiring.

THE BIG SPLURGE

SAIL AWAY, SAIL AWAY, SAIL AWAY

The port of Alicante is its heart and soul. As a center of commerce, nightlife, and travel for this sparkling city on the Mediterranean, the Puerto Nuevo demands a visit on any trip to the city. Yet what stands out among the tourists, clubs, and million-dollar yachts that line the many docks are the dozens of signs declaring *"para alquilar"* (for rent) that hang from masts and dockposts. For around €200, you can truly experience the port of Alicante by renting a boat for the day.

La Reina Azul (☎965 14 68 88; www.lareinaazul.com) rents 5.1m (around 17ft.) Quicksilver 500 motorboats that seat a maximum of five people for €190 during the summer and €170 in the winter. Grab four friends and cruise the Mediterranean for less than €40 per person. The price even includes a waterskiing kit.

If you really know what you're doing and have enough money to burn, consider renting a fully equipped, 11.4m (37ft.), eight-person, Bavaria 36 sailboat. Daily, weekend, and weekly prices are available ranging €250-€2750, depending on the season and amount of time. La Reina Azul also offers larger, eight-person motor boats as well as motor-sail boats. Call for prices or visit their office, located in the *marina deportiva* section of the port.

THE HIDDEN DEAL

SOMEONE ELCHE'S SHOES

The tiny city of Elche (Elx), located just outside Alicante, is primarily known for its lush gardens and surrounding palm forest, but the city also has a little secret: it's Spain's mecca of discount shoe stores. No less than 42% of all the shoes made in Spain come from Elche, making it a prime location for wholesale shoe shopping. It seems that aside from its many botanical offerings (which are also not to be missed), the town exists solely to sell shoes. Even the cafe by the train station offers examples of the famous *"zapatos de Elche"* (shoes of Elche).

For a wider selection than the train station cafe, head to the Pl. Glorieta in the center of town. Known among the locals merely as "La Glorieta," this giant square houses literally dozens of discount shoe stores in its center and surrounding streets. You'll find great deals on Spanish brands like the hip **Camper** and classy **Adolfo Dominguez**, and also lots of cheap imports. Walk down C. Obispe Tormo from the tourist office and you'll run right into it. In January and July, serious sales known as ⚑ **rebajas** create a near frenzy among shoppers—discounts can be up to 70% off already amazing prices. So, when visiting Elche, be sure to bring along your camera for the parks and an extra suitcase for the shoes.

The best choice, though, is ⚑**Z-Klub,** C. Coloma. Coming off Rmbla. Méndez Núñez, go right on Explanada d'Espanya and walk 2 blocks; C. Coloma is a small side street on the right. This is the only club in Alicante that has a cover, but it's well, well worth it. The interior offers chic, beautiful, high-tech surroundings, with multiple rooms and balconies overlooking the huge dance floor. Spain's top DJs spin quality, fun house all night long for a gorgeous mixed gay-straight crowd. (Cover €10-15, includes 1 drink. Open Th-Sa midnight-6am.)

🌺 🎵 FESTIVALS AND ENTERTAINMENT

From June 20-29, hedonism rules during the ⚑**Festival de Sant Joan,** culminating on the 24th. The **Verge del Remei** procession begins in Alicante on August 3; pilgrims then trek to the monastery of Santa Faz the following Thursday. The city honors *La Virgen del Remedio* all summer during the **Fiestas del Verano,** when numerous concerts and theatrical performances are held in the new open-air theater at the port. During July and August, Playa de San Juan becomes a stage for ballet and musical performances, part of the **Plataforma Cultural** series. (Open daily until 9pm. Events on Playa de San Juan free, at the port cover from €9.) Schedules for these festivals appear on a monthly basis. Check the tourist office website (www.alicanteturismo.com) for more info.

🔲 DAYTRIPS FROM ALICANTE

ELCHE (ELX)

RENFE trains run from Alicante (every hr. 6:05am-10:05pm, €1.50-1.80). Mollá buses (☎965 13 08 51) leave Alicante (M-F 2 per hr. 7am-10pm, Sa every hr. 8am-10pm, Su 8 per day 9am-9:30pm; €1.60).

With palm trees planted every ten feet along its streets, Elx feels like a lush green oasis amidst the monochromatic cities lining the rest of the Costa Blanca. Elx's **parks** make for a great daytrip—the city is located 23km from Alicante and surrounded by one of Europe's only palm forests. Heading to nearby beaches is also an option, although better ones are farther north. If horticulture doesn't strike your fancy, Elx is also extremely well-known as the **shoe-shopping** capital of Spain.

Of Elx's many parks and public gardens, by far the most exquisite is the ⚑**Hort del Cura** (Priest's Orchard), C. Porta de la Morera, 49, where magnificent trees shade colorful flower beds; at its heart, you'll find a cactus garden, a beautiful, modern rotating sculpture, and the Palmera Imperial, a 165-year-old beast of a palm tree with eight separate palms growing out of the center of its trunk. To get there from the train or bus station, follow Po. de la Estación for about 10min. through the center of town until you reach C. Porta de la Morena, and take a left. There are many signs to help you along the way. (☎965 45 19 36; www.huertodelcura.com. Open June-Aug. 9am-9pm; Sept.-May 9am-6pm. €4, includes audioguide.) At the corner of Av. Ferrocarril and Po. de la Estación begins the **Parque Municipal,** where palm trees, grassy promenades, and playgrounds make for a cheerful, family-oriented park. (Open daily June-Aug. 7am-midnight; Sept.-May 7am-9pm.) Stop by the tourist office for a complete list of parks and gardens.

Both the train station (Estación Parque; ☎902 24 02 02) and the bus station (☎965 45 58 58) are located along Av. del Ferrocarril. To get to the town center, bear left on Po. de la Estación. The tourist office is on Pl. Parc, at the end of Po. de la Estación and the Parque Municipal. (☎965 45 27 47. English spoken. Open M-F 10am-7pm, Sa 10am-2:30pm, Su 10am-2pm.)

ISLA TABARCA

Cruceros Kon Tiki (☎965 21 63 96) departs daily from the dock on Explanada d'Espanya in Alicante to Tabarca (high-speed 30min., regular 1hr.; July-Aug. 3 per day 11am-2:30pm; Sept.-June 11am; return July-Aug. 4 per day 2-7:30pm, Sept.-June 5pm; round-trip €15). Extra service sometimes added in low season, particularly May and June (Sa-Su 3 per day 11am-3:30pm; return 3 per day 2-7pm).

Still a quiet fishing village, this tiny island 15km south of Alicante offers an old fort, plenty of fresh seafood restaurants, a rocky beach with beautiful turquoise water, and several coves with tide pools perfect for a refreshing dip in the sea. Despite its petite proportions, tourists have begun to make the island a choice day-trip destination for a quieter, more secluded beach experience than Alicante.

The beach is straight ahead when you come off the dock; rent beach chairs and umbrellas from an attendant (chairs €5 per day, 2 chairs and umbrella €10). To the left, the remnants of the tiny fort, once a jail for Spanish exiles, overlook the Mediterranean on three sides. To find the tide pools, head to the right past the beach from the dock and proceed down the main street through town until you reach a large stone gate. Pools of crystal clear water and small, rocky coves lie on the other side. Seafood restaurants line the narrow strip between the fort and the beach—all serve delicious *comida típica* with *menús* ranging €8-11. The tourist office, police station, and even a tiny museum are all located in a small complex on the beach, directly opposite the water (☎965 96 00 58).

BENIDORM   ☎965

Although its name means "good sleep," you'd be hard-pressed to pass a peaceful night in Benidorm—the place is a 24-hour beach party. From the countless rows of beachwear shops and clubs along Playa del Levante to the restaurants, boutiques, and bars in the the heart of the *casco antiguo*, this town will keep you going from dusk till dawn, every day of the week. Thousands of visitors from the British Isles, the Netherlands, and Belgium come to Benidorm every summer, some to sunbathe for days on the city's 5km of white-sand beaches, others just for a night to party until dawn—the Tramsnochador even has a separate stop for the disco gardens (see **Nightlife** below). Those who want to own a piece of the madness settle down in the numerous luxury apartment buildings that dot the skyline. If it's the quintessential tranquility of the Costa

Blanca you seek, bypass this town and head north to calmer Altea and Xàbia; if what you want is a crazy, incomparable carnival, look no further than the streets and sands of Benidorm.

☎☏ TRANSPORTATION AND PRACTICAL INFORMATION. The **train station** (☎965 85 18 95) is located on C. de l'Estació, at the top of a small hill above the city. Local bus #7 departs from the train station for the city center. (☎965 85 43 22. Every 30min. 6:30am-9:50pm, €0.85.) The **bus stop** (there's no real bus station) is on Av. de Europa, at the corner of Av. Gerona about four blocks inland from the beach, close to the city center. For **taxis** call ☎965 86 26 26 (€3-5 to the city center). The *casco antiguo*, which forms the center of the city, divides Benidorm into two sections. To the north, along boardwalk **Avenida d'Alcoi**, is the main beach, **Playa de Levante**, as well as larger streets where most big hotels and apartment buildings are located. To the south is the seaside **Parque de Elche** and a more secluded beach, **Playa de Poniente.**

To get to the **tourist office,** Av. de Martínez Alejos, 16, from the bus stop, continue down Av. de Europa toward the beach, take a right at Av. del Mediterráneo, and continue to **Plaza de la Hispanidad.** Veer left onto C. Dr. Pérez Llorca, and take a left onto Av. de Martínez Alejos. (☎965 85 32 24; www.benidorm.org. Open July-Sept. M-Sa 9am-9pm; Oct.-June M-F 9am-8:30pm, Sa 10am-1:30pm and 4:30-7:30pm.) **Banks** and **ATMs** line C. Dr. Pérez Llorca and the pedestrian street that leads to the boardwalk, Av. de Martínez Alejos. **Internet access** is at **Cybercat Café,** on the bottom floor of the arcade-cafeteria complex **El Otro Mundo de Jaime,** Av. Ruzafa, 2, near the *casco antiguo*. (☎965 86 79 04. €1 per 20min. Open daily 10am-2am.) The **post office** is located at Pl. Dr. Fleming, 1. (☎965 85 34 34. Open M-F 8:30am-2:30pm, Sa 9:30am-1pm.) **Postal Code:** 03500.

☏ ACCOMMODATIONS. Though Benidorm has abundant upscale hotels and resorts—including the tallest hotel in Europe—it has little to offer in terms of affordable lodging for the budget traveler. The most reasonably priced accommodations are found in the *casco antiguo*. A few blocks up the street from the tourist office, spacious rooms with balconies and bath surrounding a skylit staircase can be found at **Pensión La Orozca ❷,** Av. Ruzafa, 37. (☎965 85 05 25. All rooms have private bath. Ask for a fan in the summer. Singles €20; doubles €30.) Back down Av. Ruzafa toward the beach is **Hostal Tabarca ❷,** Av. Ruzafa, 9, with speckled tile floors, beaded curtains, plain rooms, and clean hallway baths. (☎965 85 77 08. June-Sept. singles €18; doubles €30; triples €35. Oct.-May €15/€25/€30.) Those seeking peace and quiet will find it in the cheerful, modern rooms of **Hotel La Santa Faç ❹,** C. La Santa Faç, 18, in the heart of the *casco antiguo*. All rooms have bath, A/C, TV, and phone. (☎965 85 40 63; www.santafazhotel.com. June-Aug. singles €48; doubles €60; triples €80. Sept.-May €42/€60/€90.)

☐ FOOD. The **produce market** (W and F 8am-3pm) is on Vía de Emilio Ortuño, just outside the *casco antiguo*. The main supermarket, **Mercadona,** is on C. Invierno, one block up C. Mirador, off Vía de Emilio Ortuño. (Open M-Sa 9am-9:30pm.) Restaurants are found every few meters along **Calle Esperanto** and **Calle Gerona,** and consist mainly of pizzerias, a couple of Indian and Turkish restaurants, and eateries whose neon signs and huge, illuminated outdoor menus offer "international cuisine"—more varieties of pizza. For pub grub, head to C. Mayor and the many side streets in the *casco antiguo,* but if you want *comida típica*, **Restaurante L'Albufera ❷,** on the corner of C. Gerona and Av. del Dr. Orts Llorca, has a huge menu, including 14 different *menús del día* to choose from, and hearty portions of Spanish fare at reasonable prices. (☎965 86 56 61. Most entrees €8-12. Open daily 1-4pm and 8pm-midnight.) The giant paella on the sign outside showcases the signature dish at **Restaurante Aitona ❷**, Av. Ruzafa. Vegetarians shouldn't miss the heaping grilled vegetable platter (€9.50). Call ahead for reservations. (☎965 85 30 10. Open daily 1pm-midnight.) If you're looking for "a touch of class in the old town," stop by **Queen's ❷**, Pl. de la Constitución, 5, for a great crowd of old-time locals and expats. There's even a cabaret nightly at 11pm. (☎966 81 29 96. *Bocadillos* €2-4. Entrees €6-14. *Menú* €14. Restaurant open daily 7-11:30pm. Bar open daily 9am-2:30am.) A filling meal with the locals can be found at **La Tasca del Pueblo ❷**, Marqués de Comillas, 5, with wooden chairs and tiled walls and offering a huge selection of meat and fish dishes for €7-10. (☎966 80 63 12. Open daily noon-1am.)

SIGHTS AND FESTIVALS. It's difficult to find many remnants of Benidorm's historic past, since most of what was once the old city is now enveloped by modern high-rises and wide roadways. Tucked within the narrow streets of the *casco antiguo*, however, are the ruins of the **Castillo-Mirador de Benidorm,** Pl. del Castell, at the end of **El Carrer dels Gats,** the old main street. Built in the 14th century to protect the city from attacks by Berber pirates, the castle is now almost entirely indistinguishable beneath its famous **mirador,** known as "The Balcony of the Mediterranean." The large blue and white promenade affords excellent views of Playa del Levante to the north and Playa de Poniente to the south, as well as of **Benidorm Island,** the enormous slanted-rock formation in the water directly in front of the main beach. A visit to Benidorm is not complete without a stroll along the 2080m long **Paseo Marítimo de la Playa de Levante.** Dotted with hip cafes and bars, this expansive boardwalk is the place to see and be seen, as the beautiful (and not so beautiful) traverse its length at all hours of the day and night. The city also holds a world-renowned international music festival, **Festival de la Canción de Benidorm,** in early to mid-June. Check out www.festivaldebenidorm.com for schedules.

NIGHTLIFE. Benidorm usually follows an expensive, exhaustive, but hedonistically fulfilling pattern every night in July and August and weekends the rest of the year. Locals and tourists alike begin their party trek through the city around midnight at the various bars and taverns of the *casco antiguo*. Close to the Ayuntamiento is **La Sal,** C. Costera del Barco, 5. Located in an old, half-timbered house, this local favorite is packed on the weekends with an ultra-hip crowd of mainly Spanish and German patrons. (☎966 87 34 94. Beer €4.80. Open daily 10:30pm-4am.) Also wildly popular is **Ándale Ándale,** C. Alameda, 24, which serves mixed drinks (from €4) to well-dressed Spanish yuppies who like to rock out to the latest in Spanish pop.

When most bars close or start winding down (generally 3:30-4am), partygoers head toward the beach, where some of the craziest disco-pubs line the Po. Marítimo de la Playa de Levante, all near the corner of Av. Bilbao. If all you want to do is dance (particularly on top of bars and pool tables), head to **Penelope,** whose multiple bars and packed dance floor make it one of the hippest venues on the beach. If you can make it through the crowd, check out the Egyptian room in the back. A mixed gay-straight crowd grooves to house at **Ku,** while a young crowd of Brits packs the dance floor to a variety of music at **KM.** Most disco-pubs are open nightly in summer and on weekends during the rest of the year 11pm-5am. None charge cover, but drinks can get expensive (beer €5-6). Keep an eye out for club promoters standing outside entrances, as they often give out coupons for free shots at the bars, drink specials, or free admission to discos.

Around 4:30-5am, the party shifts from the beach to the huge disco gardens on **Avenida de la Comunitat Valenciana.** You may not be in a state to walk, and it's a good 15min. on foot, so it is best to take a **taxi** (€3.20). If you do walk, bring a burly friend, since the road becomes a dark highway a few blocks before the clubs. Once there, numerous discos line both sides of the street. All three locations mentioned on the beach also have huge disco counterparts up here. For ambience alone, check out the spaceship-like building that houses ◼**Ku (Disco),** where smooth white walls and crazy red lamps surround a massive dance floor, outdoor terrace, and even a pool. The new club on the scene is **Zona VIP,** which features an underground bar and several rooms. **Pachá,** Spain's largest disco chain, has a venue here that is hugely popular with tourists. Most head to the terrace at **Space** around 6 or 7am to watch the sun rise over the city. The majority of these clubs are open every night in the summer midnight-6am, and on weekends throughout the rest of the year. Cover usually runs around €12, but always includes a drink; mixed drinks start at €6. Again, promoters are everywhere and sometimes offer free admission.

ALTEA   ☎965

Unlike the majority of towns lining the Costa Blanca, Altea's coastline betrays little of its growing tourism industry. Restaurants remain modest (but not necessarily cheap), daily life appears uninterrupted, and skyscraper hotels have yet to spring up. It is also one of the Costa Blanca's leading artist communities, and the town and beachfront are both filled with galleries. A long jetty with a charming walkway protects Altea's calm stretch of shoreline from waves, and serene, pebbly beaches fan out from one end of town to the other. From the beach, narrow cobblestone streets and staircases wind up to **Plaza de la Iglesia.** Shaded by the cobalt dome of the church of the **Virgen del Consuelo,** the square commands breathtaking views of the Mediterranean. The main thoroughfare, **Comte d'Altea** (in which C. La Mar becomes Pl. del Convent), is a block from the sea and filled with shops, while **Calle Sant Pere,** which turns into the **Passeig del Mediterrání,** runs along the beach.

Don't plan on making up for lost euros in Altea, as the vacation vibe here comes with vacation prices. Among the cheapest accommodations options is **Habitaciones La Mar ❷,** C. La Mar, 82, close to the train station and beach, with small, clean rooms. (☎965 84 30 16. June-Aug. singles €24, with bath €30; doubles €30/€36; triples €36/€42. All prices €6 less Sept.-May.) For breakfast Altea has many pastry shops and bakeries along Comte d'Altea, near the Pl. del Ayuntamiento. Among the many waterfront restaurants, try **La Liebre ❷,** Po. Mediterráneo, 39, which specializes in typical Spanish fare and atypically delicious gazpacho. Try their huge salads (€5-7) for a filling lunch. (☎965 84 57 79. *Menú* €9. Open daily 1pm-midnight.) There are a number of bars on the waterfront that cater to an older crowd and close early; local and foreign partygoers head to Benidorm and Alicante for nightlife and entertainment.

Both **trains** and **buses** stop at the foot of the hill on C. La Mar (head left to go toward the town center). If you're arriving by bus from Alicante, get off at the first stop; if arriving from Valencia, get off at the second stop. The **tourist office** is on C. Sant Pere, 9, parallel to C. La Mar, right by the water. From the train station or the bus stop, walk toward the sea. (☎965 84 41 14. Open June-Aug. M-F 10am-2pm and 5-7:30pm; Sept.-May M-Sa 10am-2pm and 5-7:30pm.) Local services include the **police,** C. La Mar, 91 (☎965 84 55 11), and **ambulance** (☎965 84 35 32).

CALPE (CALP)   ☎965

With t-shirt stores lining the streets and beaches packed with foreigners, Calp seems the classic tourist trap—yet the flocks of visitors descend for good reason. The beaches are the town's main draw and lure visitors with kilometers of soft, fine white sand. Calp's main avenue, **Avenida Gabriel Miró,** descends to the **Paseo Marítimo Infanta Elena** and the **Playa Arenal-Bol.** Heading down the *paseo,* be sure to take a look at **Los Baños de la Reina,** the ruins of a Roman beach spa that was later used as a fish farm. A massive, flat-topped rock formation called the ◼**Peñón d'Ifach** (327m) towers above the town, dividing the beaches into two distinct sections, and is an attraction by itself. To hike up (2½hr. round-trip), walk past the tourist office, then turn right onto Av. del Port at the rotunda, and left onto Av. Isla de Formentera, following the signs. On a clear day, you can see Ibiza from the cliffs and caves above Calp. Beyond the Peñón are more inviting shores on the **Playa La Fossa-Levante**. Continue along the **Paseo Marítimo Infanta Cristina** to reach the tiny beach in the secluded cove of ▓**Calalga**.

If you do decide to spend the night, try the tiny, bright **Pensión Céntrica ❶**, Pl. Ifach. All rooms have sinks, but the toilets are relegated to hallway bathrooms. Food and drinks are available in a cozy bar-restaurant where breakfast (€2) is offered. (☎965 83 55 28. €12 per person. Mostly doubles, 2 singles.) Other affordable lodging options are located in the narrow streets of the *casco antiguo*, above **Plaza de la Constitución** off Av. de Gabriel Miró. The most reasonably priced restaurants in Calp can also be found there: **Casa Florencia ❷**, C. del Mar, 21, serves delicious seafood paellas and other rice dishes for two or more people (€9-12). Dine al fresco on the sunny colorfully tiled terrace. (☎965 83 35 84. Call ahead for reservations. Open daily 1-11pm.) A number of small bars can be found behind Pl. de la Constitución and along the beach headed toward the Peñón de Ifach, but for a wilder scene, your best bet is to go to Benidorm or Alicante.

ALSA buses (☎965 83 90 29) stop 2km from the beach at C. Capitán Pérez Jordá (see **Coastal Transportation**, p. 334). The **train station** is about a 15min. uphill walk from the bus stop; some of the roads do not have a sidewalk. Whether you take a bus or a train to Calp, when you arrive, hop on one of the **Autobuses Ifach** to the beach (every hr., €0.90). They run in a circuit between the stations, beach and town, and often time their routes to be at the stations when trains/buses arrive. If all else fails, call a **taxi** (☎965 83 78 78).

The main **tourist office** is by the beginning of the path to the Peñón at Av. Ejércitos Españoles, 44. (Open June-Aug. M-Sa 9am-9pm, Su 10:30am-2pm; Sept.-May M-F 9am-2pm and 4-8pm, Sa 10am-2pm.) The easiest way to get there is on the municipal bus from the bus or train station. Get off at the Pl. Colón, walk up C. la Niña away from the water, and take a right onto Av. Ejércitos Españoles. There are other branches in the old town and at the port, also easily accessible by bus. The **police**, Av. Ejércitos Españoles (☎965 08 90 00), are just down from the main tourist office. **DIP Internet Center**, C. Benidorm, 1, is off Av. de Gabriel Miró, three blocks from the beach. (☎965 83 93 83. €1 per 20min. Open daily 10am-11pm.)

DÉNIA ☎966

Set halfway between Valencia and Alicante along the Golfo de Valencia, Dénia (named by the Greeks for Diana, goddess of the hunt, the moon, and purity) is an ideal upscale family resort destination whose harbor serves as an important ferry connection to the Islas Baleares. The town has little to offer budget travelers in the way of bargains, although its rows of boutiques, charming beachfront hotels, and tasty restaurants are enough to tempt even the most thrifty to splurge. Fortunately, its long stretches of beautifully groomed beaches are available free of charge (sadly, the many watersport opportunities they provide are not). Whatever your price range, however, Dénia makes for a lovely stop along the Mediterranean. The amount of time and money you spend there is up to you.

■▐ **ORIENTATION AND PRACTICAL INFORMATION.** The **train station** (☎965 78 04 45) is on C. Calderón de la Barca, just off C. Patricio Ferrándiz. The **bus station** is on Pl. Arxiduc Carles. For train and bus schedules, see **Coastal Transportation**, p. 334. **Local buses** (☎966 42 14 08) pick up on the Explanada Cervantes. Head to the water from the tourist office and take a left. The stop is about 5min. down from the traffic circle. Take the bus marked "Marina" or "Calma" for the more

WHERE DID YOU GET THAT SALAD?

Spain's different regions are famous for having their own identities, cultures, and traditions, and this individualism surely extends to their cuisine. While each region naturally has its own specialties—like Andalucía's gazpacho or Valencia's paella—its cooks put their own special blend of ingredients into one of the mainstays of tapas all over Spain: the *ensalada*.

Most of the time, an *ensalada* does not consist of the standard combo of lettuce and veggies. Salads in Spain are a mix of meat or fish and produce, prepared to the tastes of a particular region and served cold.

An *ensalada murciana*, for example, consists of black olives, tuna, onions, and peppers tossed in fresh olive oil with a touch of vinegar and garlic. Add sweet corn and hard-boiled eggs and make the olives green for an *ensalada valenciana*. Further south, an *ensalata de Almería* substitutes *bacalao* (cod) for tuna and roasts the vegetables before adding olive oil and chilling.

Of course, these exact ingredients may vary from restaurant to restaurant. If you speak Spanish (or Catalan or Valenciá), feel free to ask what makes your salad special. Most cooks are happy to talk about the relationship between their salad and their regional pride.

secluded beaches; the bus marked "Rotas" heads in the opposite direction. (Marinas depart every hr. on the hr. 8am-8pm; Rotas on the half hr. 8:30am-9:30pm, no bus at 2:30pm; Calmas on the half hr. 8:30am-9:30pm, no bus at 2:30, 3:30, 5:30, or 7:30pm; €0.85.) To reach the Baleares by sea, consult **Baleària Eurolínies Marítimes,** in Pl. Oculista Buigues, between the tourist office and the water. (☎902 16 01 80; www.balearia.net.) **Ferries** run from Dénia to Palma and Ibiza (€49-66). For full ferry info, see **By Boat,** p. 356. For **taxis,** call ☎965 78 65 65.

The **tourist office** sits on Pl. Oculista Buígues, 9, 30m inland from Estació Marítima, at the end of C. Patricio Ferrándiz. To get to the tourist office from the bus station, turn left out of the plaza onto C. Patricio Ferrándiz; from the train station, go straight ahead, then veer right. (☎966 42 23 67; www.denia.net. Open July-Aug. daily 9:30am-2pm and 4:30-8pm; Sept.-June M-Sa 9:30am-1:30pm and 4:30-7:30pm, Su 9:30am-1:30pm.) Three blocks from C. Patricio Ferrándiz, shop- and restaurant-lined **Calle Marqués de Campo** is the main tourist strip. Local services, including local **buses, trains, ferries,** and the **post office,** are located on **Calle Patricio Ferrándiz,** which runs straight to the port from the bus station. In an emergency, contact the **police** at ☎092. **Internet access** is available at **Cyber Mon,** on C. Carlos Sentí in the Mon Blau complex, the large blue building next to the market on the block between C. de la Mar and C. Magallanes. Head upstairs through the arcade. (Coin-operated computers €1.50 per hr. Open daily 10am-11pm.)

■■ ACCOMMODATIONS AND FOOD. Dénia certainly doesn't cater to budget travelers, especially in the lodging department. Be prepared to shell out €30 or more for a single room in the summer, and book accommodations well in advance for festivals in July. **Hostal L'Anfora ❷,** Explanada de Cervantes, 8, has some of the most inexpensive rooms in town and a great location right by the port. (☎966 43 01 01; www.hostallanfora.com. Deposit required. July-Sept. singles €30; doubles €50. Oct.-June €25/€40. MC/V.) Other relatively inexpensive accommodations can be found along **Avenida del Cid** at the foot of the hill leading to the *castillo.* **Hostal Cristina ❷,** Av. del Cid, 5, has small, cozy rooms with wood furniture, floral tiling, and the curtains to match; all have bath, most A/C and TV. (☎966 42 31 58; www.hostal-cristina.com. Breakfast included. July-Aug. singles €24; doubles €42. Oct.-May €20/€35.) For a splurge in the heart of the *casco urbano* try **Hostal Loreto ❹,** C. Loreto, 12, on the other side of the Pl. Constitución from C. de la Mar. Gorgeous rooms in a recently renovated old inn, with a courtyard and restaurant attached. (☎966 43 54 19; www.hostalloreto.com. Breakfast €6. Singles €36-43, with bath €41-66; doubles with bath €50-66. Prices vary with season.) **Camping Las Marinas ❶**, C. Les Bovetes Nord, 4, is a 3km bus ride (€0.80) from Platja Jorge Joan. Take the buses marked "Racón." Hot water, supermarket, restaurant, and beachside setting are all added bonuses. (☎966 47 41 85. Open year-round. €4.80 per person and per tent.) **Restaurants** line C. Marqués de Campo and the Explanada de Cervantes, though most cater to families and tourists. Cheaper eateries sit merely a block or two off the main streets. Despite its portside location, the popular **Clima ❷**, Pl. Drassanes, 5, has a huge, affordable menu consisting of everything from paellas (€7-9) to pizza (€7-10) to sandwiches (€4-6), as well as a wide variety of ice cream sundae concoctions (€3-5), with a pleasant terrace right on the boardwalk. (☎965 78 10 54. Open daily 1pm-midnight.) If you're sick of Spanish cuisine, right next door is **Khyber I ❶**, Pl. Fontanella, 4, which serves up reasonably priced and authentic curries and other Indian cuisine. (☎965 78 56 04. Entrees €4.60-6. *Menú* €14.60. Open daily 1-4pm and 9-11pm.) Vegetarian delights can be found at **Caña de Azúcar ❶**, C. Fora Mur, 3A. Meat-free fare abounds, ranging from soy burgers to salads to couscous. (☎677 09 83 50. Most entrees €4-7. 3-course lunch *menú* €9.50. Smoothies and fresh juices €2-4. Offers vegetarian cooking classes; call for details. Open Tu-Su 1-5pm and 8pm-midnight.) The **market** is on C. Carlos Sentí, 6, in a large orange building (open M-Sa 7am-2pm), and a **Másymás** supermarket is at the bus station in Pl. Arxiduc Carles (open M-Sa 9am-9pm).

◨◪ SIGHTS AND BEACHES. An 18th-century **castle** sprawls across the hill overlooking the marina. Centuries earlier, Jaime II enforced the 1304 separation between the town below and the castle above by displacing all of Dénia's inhabitants to the *villa vella*, or old town, beyond the castle walls. There is a small architectural museum inside. (☎966 42 06 56. Open daily June 10am-1:30pm and 4-7:30pm; July-Aug. 10:30am-1:30pm and 5-8:30pm; Sept. 10:30am-1:30pm and 5-8pm; Oct. 10am-1pm and 3-6:30pm; Nov.-Mar. 10am-1pm and 3-6pm; Apr.-May 10am-1:30pm and 3:30-7pm. Night hours July to mid-Sept. 10pm-12:30am. €1.80.) A **tourist train** chugs to the castle from the tourist office (M and W-Su 4:15 and 5:45pm; €3.60, includes castle entrance), or you can take the stairs next to the town hall.

Dénia's biggest attraction, however, is its 14km of pristine **beaches.** Windsurfers skip over the waves off **Platja Els Molins** (north of the port on the "Marina" bus), while scuba divers explore the depths off **Las Platjas Area de Las Rotes** (south of the port on the "Rotas" bus). Those who want a beach to just sit and relax on have plenty of options—**Platja Les Marines, Platja Les Bovetes,** and **Platja Punta Raset** are all close to the center of town and well within walking distance from the port. The tourist office provides a pamphlet detailing the services available on each beach as well as the trails in nearby **Montgó Natural Park** (☎966 42 32 05).

▧ FESTIVALS. Dénia holds a miniature **Fallas Festival** March 16-20, burning effigies on midnight of the final day. During **Festa Major** (early July), locals prove they are just as gutsy as their fellow countrymen in Pamplona during the **bous a la mar,** a feat in which bulls and fans dive together into a pool of water. In mid-July, the **Fiestas de la Santísima Sangre** feature street dances, concerts, mock battles, and fireworks over the harbor.

JÁVEA (XÀBIA)

Xàbia's harbors shelter tranquil waters free of tourists—while British families come to the well-kept apartment buildings and unspoiled beaches in summer, backpackers head to younger, more popular destinations. Transportation is inconvenient, but you're still better off coming for the day. Watch the time; if you miss the return bus, try **Pensión La Favorita ❷**, C. Magallanes, 4, which is as good as it gets—bright, colorful rooms with a cheerful atmosphere, two blocks from the beach. From the tourist office in the port, with your back facing the water, take a right and go up through a small arch. Then follow signs to the *pensión*. (☎965 79 04 77. Singles €17-26; doubles €26-46; triples €37-47. Prices vary with facilities and season.) **Restaurants** line C. Andrés Lambert and consist of pizzerias and seafood *freidurías* (for the finest in fried fish).

Although the municipal bus runs from the port along a long stretch of pebbled bathing spots, Xàbia's real beauties—its pristine beaches, coves, and cliffs—are not well-connected. A number of secluded coves line the coast south of the port. Xàbia's most popular beaches, **Playa La Granadella, Playa de Ambolo**, and **Playa La Barraca**, about 10km south of the port along Ctra. del Cabo de la Nao, can best be reached by car. Ask the tourist office for a map and driving directions. The **Fiesta de Moros y Cristianos** erupts during the second half of July; fireworks jolt wide-eyed tourists roaming among costumed Moors and Christians as parades, bands, and contests provide a welcome distraction from the summer heat.

ALSA buses stop at the intersection of Av. d'Ondara and Av. Colomer but arrive only six times per day (see **Coastal Transportation,** p. 334). To get to the port and the beaches, take the **municipal bus.** To catch it, take a right out of the rotunda and walk 2min. down C. Dr. Borrul to the bus stop at Placeta del Convent. (☎966 42 14 08. June-Sept. every 30min. 8am-2pm and 4-11pm, every hr. 2-4pm; Oct.-May every hr. 8am-2pm and 4-10pm. €0.80.) If you don't feel like waiting, continue down Av. Príncipe de Asturias from the Pl. del Convent, bear right onto Ronda Norte, then left onto Av. Alicante, which becomes Av. Rey Juan Carlos 1 and then Av. del Port before continuing to the ocean (25min.). Xàbia has three **tourist offices**—most convenient are those near the port, Pl. Almirante Bastarreche, 24 (☎965 79 07 36), and by the Ayuntamiento, Pl. de la Iglesia, 6. (☎965 79 43 56; www.xabia.org. All open M-F 9am-2pm and 5-8pm, Sa 10am-3:30pm and 5-8pm, Su 10am-3:30pm.)

GANDÍA
☎962

Five centuries before the tourism industry hit the Costa Blanca, the powerful Borjas family of Valencia had already discovered Gandía and transformed it into a center of noble beach bumming. Today, Gandía still gets most of its income from visitors seeking the peace of a seaside retreat. Fine sands stretch for kilometers, so it's not surprising that the most popular activity here is sunbathing. Staying in town tends to be rather expensive, but frequent trains from Valencia make Gandía the perfect spot for a relaxing beach daytrip.

RENFE trains (☎902 24 02 02) run from **Valencia** (1hr., every 30min. 6am-10pm, €3.40; return every 15min.). **ALSA,** (☎902 42 22 42) inside the train station, runs **buses** to **Alicante** (3-4hr., 11 per day 7am-10pm, €9.50) and **Valencia** (1hr., 9-11 per day 7:55am-9pm, €5.20). Buses to Alicante stop in **Altea** (€5.60), **Calp** (€4.30), and **Dénia** (€2.60). Departing from the tourist office, **La Marina buses,** Marqués de Campo, 14, run to the **beach** along Pg. Marítim (every 15min.; night buses until 4am in summer; M-Sa €1.05, Su €0.85). The majority of services in Gandía are located near the **train station** on Marqués de Campo; everything else is by the beach. The **tourist office,** Marqués de Campo, is across from the train station. (☎962 87 77 88. English spoken. Open June-Aug. M-F 9:30am-1:30pm and 4:30-7:30pm, Sa 10am-1:30pm; Sept.-May M-F 9:30am-1:30pm and 4-7pm, Sa 10am-1pm.) There is a **branch** by the beach on Pg. Marítim, 45. (☎962 84 24 07. Open M-F 10am-2pm and 5-8pm, Sa 10am-1:30pm and 5-8pm, Su 10am-1:30pm.) The branch building also houses the **Red Cross** and **police** (☎962 87 88 00). The **post office,** Pl. Jaume I, 7, is a few blocks behind the Ayuntamiento. (☎962 87 10 91. Open M-F 8:30am-2:30pm.) **Postal Code:** 46700.

Gandía is full of expensive hotels; those who want to stay cheaply here should make reservations. **Hostal-Residencia El Nido ❸**, C. Alcoy, 22, is the cheapest option near the beach. Ask for an ocean view. (☎962 84 46 40. Sept.-June doubles €40; July €48; Aug. €57.) Most **restaurants** are located along the beach and in the pedestrian streets near the train station. Most offer similar menus and price ranges. The best plan, though, is to have a picnic on the beach with groceries from **Supermarket Mercadona**, C. Perú, behind the train station. (Open M-Sa 9am-9pm.)

MURCIA

The province of Murcia, bordered by Valencia to the north, the Mediterranean to the east, and Andalucía to the west, may be in the shadow of more touristed regions, but its sunny, warm climate, tiny beach resort towns, and thriving capital city give it more than its share of character. Four centuries ago, a bizarre wave of plagues, floods, and earthquakes wreaked havoc throughout Murcia. In the process of utterly destroying some areas, the earthquakes uncovered a rich supply of minerals and natural springs. Today, thermal spas, pottery factories, and paprika mills color the lively coastal towns, and orange and apricot orchards reinforce Murcia's reputation as the *Huerta de Europa* (Europe's Orchard).

MURCIA ☎968

Murcianos will tell you that their city is a pleasant place to visit from September to June; the city thrives off the energy of its university in the fall and explodes into full bloom in the spring with its annual festivals. However, even the most loyal residents flee the oppressive heat of summer in the city for the nearby Mediterranean. Though modern Murcia boasts parks, cafes, and tree-lined avenues, the old quarter's winding lanes reveal the Moorish heart of the historic city of Mursiya, founded by Abderramán II in AD 825.

TRANSPORTATION. **Aeropuerto de San Javier** (☎968 17 20 00), about 30km to the southeast, has flights to Madrid and London. **RENFE trains** (☎902 24 02 02), at Pl. Industria, head to: **Alicante** (2hr., every hr., €3.70); **Barcelona** (7-10hr., 4 per day, €42.50); **Lorca** (1hr., every hr., €3.70); **Madrid** (5-6hr., 5 per day, €35.50); **Valencia** (3½hr., 4 per day, €25). **Buses** (☎968 29 22 11) leave from the station on C. Bolos to: **Alicante** (1½hr., 14 per day 7am-9pm, €4.50); **Almería** (4hr., 4-6 per day 5:15am-7:45pm, €14); **Barcelona** (8½hr., 9 per day 6:15am-12:30am, €38.50); **Dénia** (3½hr., 6 per day 2am-9:10pm, €10.50); **Granada** (4-5hr.; M-Th 5 per day, F-Su 7 per day 8:30am-10pm; €16.50); **La Manga del Mar Menor** (1hr.; Sept.-June M-Sa 3 per day, Su 2 per day, July-Aug. every hr. 9am-9pm; €5); **Lorca** (1½hr., 6-17 per day 7am-9pm, €3.50); **Madrid** (5-6hr., 10-12 per day 7am-1am, €21-34); **Málaga** (7hr., 5 per day 1:25pm-3:35am, €24); **Sevilla** (7-9hr., 3 per day 10:30am-9pm, €31.50); **Valencia** (3¾hr., 4-7 per day 5:30am-8:30pm, €11.50). **Municipal buses** (€0.70) cover the city; bus #9 runs past the bus and train stations.

ORIENTATION AND PRACTICAL INFORMATION. The **Río Segura** divides the city, with sights and services to the north and the train station to the south (take bus #9, 17, or 39 between the two). Murcia has two main streets that cut through the central areas of town: the **Gran Vía Escultor Salzillo** and the **Gran Vía Alfonso X El Sabio.** Both emerge from the Plaza Circular (the former Av. de la Constitución), a giant traffic circle in the center of the city. The **tourist office** is in Pl. Cardenal Belluga across from the cathedral. (☎968 35 87 49; www.murciaciudad.com. Open June-Sept. M-Sa 5:30-9:30pm, Su 10am-2pm; Oct.-May M-Sa 10am-

IN RECENT NEWS

NOT A DROP TO DRINK

A glance around any street in Murcia these days will reveal at least a dozen or so signs that read *"AGUA PARA TODOS"* (Water for Everyone) in large blue letters. These represent the viewpoint of Murcia and Valencia in what has become an incredibly heated debate over how to solve the water shortage plaguing southern Spain.

Over the past decade, droughts have seriously depleted the water supply in the region, leaving the Río Segura, which bisects the city of Murcia, almost dry and causing serious problems for farmers all along the coast. In response, the former president of Spain, José María Aznar, proposed to build an aqueduct that would transfer water to Murcia from the Río Ebro in the north and save both the river and the suffering crops of the *"Huerta de Europa"* (Europe's Orchard).

Unfortunately for the Murcianos, President Zapatero halted construction of the aqueduct on grounds that it hurts the north. He even introduced a law requiring such resource reallocations to benefit all parties, making construction of the aqueduct impossible and sealing the river's fate.

Murcia has looked at other solutions, such as desalinization plants, but they are costly. Until a decision is reached, its beloved river will continue to trickle along, dividing Murcia in half as sharply as Spain is divided on this issue.

2pm and 4-8pm.) The **regional tourist office** is in Palacio González Campuzano—the red building in Pl. Julián Romea. (☎968 27 76 76. Open M-F 9am-2pm and 5-7pm, Sa 10:30am-1pm.) Local services include: **police**, Av. San Juan de la Cruz (☎968 26 66 00); **Hospital Morales Meseguer**, Av. Marqués de Vélez, 22 (☎968 36 09 00). For **Internet** access, visit **Cyber Ocio**, C. Albudeiteros, 3. Take a right off C. Serrano Alcázar, from Pl. Julián Romea. (☎968 93 05 96. 11am-2pm and after 9pm €1 per 30min., €1.50 per hr.; 4:30-9pm €1.20/€2.40. Open 11am-2pm and 4:30pm-late.) The **post office**, Pl. Circular, 8a, is near the intersection with Av. Primo de Rivera. (☎968 24 10 37. Open M-F 8:30am-8:30pm.) **Postal Code:** 30008.

🛏🍴 ACCOMMODATIONS AND FOOD. When Murcia heats up and empties out in summer, finding a room is the only breeze in town; it is a considerably more difficult task in winter. One of the few decent budget options is **Hostal-Residencia Murcia ❷**, C. Vinader, 6, off Pl. Sta. Isabel; take bus #11 from the train station. The ample rooms have TV, phone, and A/C. (☎968 21 99 63. Singles €20, with bath €30; doubles €38/€46.) Another reasonable option is centrally located **Pensión Hispano I ❷**, C. Trapería, 8, in the huge Hispano complex, which also has a much nicer hotel and a restaurant. (☎968 21 61 52. Singles €20, with shower €25, with bath €29; doubles with shower €35, with bath €39; triples with bath €49.)

Although ice cream shops and outdoor cafes seem to be everywhere, finding a decent meal is a bit harder. Start your morning off with a *tostado* and coffee amidst marble, wood, and classic rock at **Cafetería Altea ❶**, C. Sagasta, at the corner of C. Pilar. (☎968 21 53 02. *Tostados* €2.) The area around **Plaza de San Juan**, near the river, is home to a number of popular restaurants and tapas bars. **La Parranda ❷**, Pl. de San Juan, offers local cuisine a cut above average in taste, but not in price. (☎968 22 06 75. Tapas €1-3, *raciones* €6-15. Open daily 11:30am-4:30pm and 8pm-midnight.) For the usual selection of Spanish food served by good-humored *camareros*, head to **Mesón-Restaurante Hermanos Rubio ❶**, Pl. Sta. Isabel, 3. If it's available, be sure to try the *gazpacho murciano*, which adds a savory new twist to the Andalusian favorite—bacon. (☎968 21 20 40. *Menú* €9. Open M-Sa 8am-midnight and Su mornings. AmEx/MC/V.) Sample the venerated Murcian harvest at the two story **market** on C. de Verónicas (open M-Sa 9am-1pm) and C. Sierra del la Pila, near the bus station (open M-Sa 8:30am-3pm).

◙ **SIGHTS.** The **Museo Taurino,** located in the Club Taurino in the Jardín El Salitre, off C. Acisclo Díaz, displays bullfighting memorabilia, matador costumes, and mounted bulls' heads that pay homage to particularly valorous beasts. Among the various shrines to Spain's best *toreros*, take note of the one to José Manuel Calvo Benichon, which features the shredded, bloody shirt he wore the day he was gored to death in Sevilla by his 598kg opponent. (☎968 28 59 76. Open June-Aug. M-F 10am-2pm and 5-8pm; Sept.-May also Su 11am-2pm. Free.) From there, walk through the serene **Jardín El Salitre** and cut across town on C. Acisclo Díaz to the palatial **Casino de Murcia,** C. Trapería, 18, which began as a gentlemen's club for the city's 19th- and 20th-century bourgeoisie. Current members have use of the entire building, from its lounges to its libraries. The rooms were designed thematically, and include the magnificent Byzantine entrance, Versailles ballroom, English billiard room, Arabic patio, and Oxford library; many are open to the public. (☎968 21 22 55. Open daily 10am-9pm. €1.20.) Continue up C. Trapería and take a right onto C. Andres Bacquero, which becomes C. Dr. Fleming. Take a right onto C. Obispo Frutos and you'll come to Murcia's **Museo de Bellas Artes,** C. Obispo Frutos, 12, the region's largest museum, with over 1000 works and an extensive collection of local art. It is currently closed for major renovations and is expected to reopen in January 2005. Call for more information. (☎968 23 93 46.) From the museum, continue on C. Obispo Frutos toward the river, cross it, take a right, and head back toward the center of town. While crossing, note the striking ◙**bridges,** each designed by a different Spanish architect. Lastly, check out the **Museo Hidraúlico,** C. de los Molinos, also known as *"Los Molinos del Río,"* which details the history of the Río Segura and the city's use of hydraulic power. (☎968 22 02 05. Open M-Sa 11am-2pm and 6- 9pm. Free.)

◙◙ **NIGHTLIFE AND ENTERTAINMENT.** Much of Murcia's nightlife centers around the city's numerous plazas. Ornate glass doors, Louis XIV furniture, and a beautiful Mosaic bar adorn ◙**El Diablo Enamorado,** a "chill-out cafe" on C. San José Bajo, 15, just off the Pl. de San Juan. (☎666 71 29 77. Beer €1-3, mixed drinks €3-5. Open daily 3pm-2am.) Most clubs are clustered around **Parque Atalayas,** the large park off Ronda Levante, a major thoroughfare. Others are near the university, along C. Dr. Fleming and Pl. Universidad, where students liven things up from Thursday to Saturday. Unleash your inner animal at **Fauna,** C. Dr. Fleming, 12, among numerous fish tanks and even a well-placed elephant. (☎658 06 27 50. Beer €2, mixed drinks €4. Open Th-Sa 11pm-4am.)

On Holy Saturday, March 26, the **Fiesta de Primavera** starts a week-long celebration that brings jazz and theater performances to the city. Every June and July the **Festival Belluga** draws dance and classical music acts from all over Europe to perform outside the cathedral. Check at the tourist office for schedules.

◙ **DAYTRIPS FROM MURCIA**

LORCA

RENFE Cercanías trains (☎902 24 02 02) run to Lorca's Estación Satullena (the 2nd Lorca stop), Ex. de la Estación (1hr., every hr. 6:45am-10:05pm, €3.70). The bus station (☎968 46 92 70) sends buses to Murcia (1½hr., every hr., €3.40) and Águilas (30min.; M-F 9 per day, Sa-Su 2-3 per day; €2).

The city of Lorca is a veritable patchwork of architectural variety, from its modern train station to the crumbling castle. Medieval ghettos, Renaissance artistry, post-Franco urbanism, and contemporary elitism all flavor the town's neighborhoods. Ancient battles stripped Lorca of the orchards that cover the rest of the region, yet each conquering force left its own peculiar imprint on the **castillo** atop Lorca's central hill, a 20min. walk from Pl. de España. The castle is being converted into a pricey hotel, but the facade is the real attraction. Moors built the **Torre Espolón** shortly before the city fell to Alfonso X, El Sabio of Castilla, who, in a fit of self-adulation, ordered the construction of the **Torre Alfonsín.** Today, a hermitage, the **Ermita de San Clemente,** deteriorates at the castle's eastern edge. When Granada fell in 1492, Lorca's inhabitants moved to the bottom of the slope, leaving in their wake three idyllic churches—**Santa María, San Juan,** and **San Pedro**—which today stand in ruin. Starting anew, they erected six monasteries and the impressive **Colegiata de San Patricio.** One of many well-preserved private residences, the **Casa de los Guevara,** in the same building as the tourist office, features a pre-19th-century pharmacy. (Open M-F 11am-1pm and 5-7pm. Free.)

Enjoy lunch at **Calderón,** in the Pl. de Calderón outside the Teatro Guerra, the region's oldest theater. (☎968 46 37 56. Tapas €1-3, sandwiches €3-5. Open daily 8am-midnight.) Other restaurants serving local fare can be found near Pl. de España. The **tourist office** is on C. Lope Gisbert. (☎968 46 61 57. Open M-F 9am-2pm and 5-7:30pm, Sa-Su 11am-2pm.)

ÁGUILAS

RENFE Cercanías trains (☎902 24 02 02) leave from Murcia (1¾hr., 5 per day, €4.80) via Lorca (50min., 5 per day, €1.20). Buses (☎968 29 22 11) run from Murcia via Lorca (9 per day, €5.10).

Gorgeous beaches line the shores of Águilas, the easternmost town along the *Costa Cálida* (Hot Coast), and frequent buses and trains make it the most accessible beach getaway from Murcia. While the town's sand and turquoise waters are the main draw, the **Torre de Cope** and **Castillo de San Juan de las Águilas,** featuring incredible views of the coast, are popular stops in the city's *casco antiguo* (old quarter). To reach them, take C. Isaac Peral off C. Coronel Pareja out of Pl. de España and follow C. Sánchez Fortuna, which curves to the right toward a staircase from Pl. Asunción Balaguer. (Both the Torre and the Castillo are closed indefinitely for renovations.) **Playa de Levante Puerto,** the best beach close to town, is to the left of the port when facing the water. In the next cove over, **Playa las Delicias** is cleaner and more popular. Paella is the beachfront favorite, and any number of cafes and restaurants along the water serve steaming platters of it. Head back to Murcia for the night, as accommodations here are limited and expensive. The beautiful Plaza de España, brimming with flowers at the center of town, is about a 10min. walk from the train station. Head toward the beach, take a right by the water, and take another right at the pier onto C. Coronel Pareja.

The **tourist office,** C. Coronel Pareja, is a block toward the water from the plaza. (☎968 49 32 85. Open July-Aug. M-F 9am-2pm and 5-10pm, Sa 10am-2pm; Sept.-June M-F 9am-2pm and 5-9pm, Sa 10am-2pm.)

LA MANGA DEL MAR MENOR

Autobuses Hermanos Giménez/Lycar (☎968 29 22 11) run to and from Murcia (1¼-1¾hr., 3-6 per day, €4.70) and make several stops along the strip. Autocares Costa Azul (☎968 50 15 43) go to Alicante (2½hr., 6:30am, €6.20).

A geological fluke created the popular vacation spot known as La Manga del Mar Menor. Centuries of marine deposits settled over a small volcanic ridge and then solidified into a 19km strip of land separating the Mar Menor (Lesser Sea) from the Mediterranean. Windsurfers take advantage of the waveless sea, while beach-lovers relax on the white sands and in the crystal waters of the Mediterranean. The beachfront strip is lined with hotels, shops, restaurants, and even a few new night clubs to accommodate the increasing number of tourists and summer residents.

La Manga has one main road, **Gran Vía,** that runs the length of the peninsula. Addresses are indicated by km point (km 0 is at the mainland pole) and *urbanizaciones* (commercial complexes). Local **buses** zip back and forth along La Manga (Su-Th every 30min. 8am-2:30pm and every hr. 3:30-6:30pm, F-Sa every 30min. 8am-8:30pm and every 15min. 9pm-6am; €0.70-1.80). **Bike Service** rents bikes at rates ranging from €6 for 2hr. to €55 per week. Special rates are available for families and groups. (☎619 99 21 14. Open M-Sa 10am-2pm and 4-9pm.) **Escuela de Vela Pedruchillo,** km 8-9, sells **water sports** equipment. (☎968 14 04 12. Open daily 10am-2pm and 4-8pm.) The **tourist office,** located right at the start of Gran Vía, has a map and accommodations list. (☎968 14 61 36. Open July-Aug. M-F 10am-2pm and 6-8pm, Sa 10:30am-1pm; Sept.-June M-F 10am-2pm and 5-7pm, Sa 10:30am-1pm.) **Centro Comercial Manga del Mar,** Salida 6, km 1, houses a taxi stand, the **El Árbol** supermarket (open M-Sa 9:30am-10pm, Su 9:30am-3pm), and various rental agencies. **Iber Car** rents cars for 1 day (€51-90), 3 days (€115-271), or 1 week (€180-481). (☎968 56 35 54. 25+ with current driver's license only. Open M-F 10am-1:30pm and 5-8pm, Sa 10am-1:30pm. AmEx/V.)

If you spend the night, try **Pensión Mikaela ❶,** C. Amoladeras, 13, in Cabo de Palos, one town away from the strip. From the tourist office, head down the street away from the beach, take a left off C. Subida al Faro and another left off C. Amoladeras. The beautiful building with simple, airy rooms is a little removed from the beach but easily accessible by bus. (Meal plans available in the adjoining restaurant. July-Sept. singles €12; doubles with bath €42. Oct.-June €12/€30.)

CARTAGENA

For those burnt out by the beaches and hungering for a little history, a day in Cartagena might just do the trick. Founded in 227 BC by the Carthaginian general Asdrubal, the city of Qart Hadast ("New City") was modeled after Carthage itself and served as the main Punic metropolis in Iberia, rich in natural resources and privileged by its protected interior port. The Romans, after crushing Carthage in the Punic Wars 20 years later, changed little—not even their name for the city, Carthago Nova. Today, Cartagena remains a bustling port city with much to offer. From fresh seafood restaurants to lush gardens, modern cultural festivals to Roman ruins (and, of course, beaches aplenty), any traveler can see why Cartagena has stood fast through the centuries.

⊞⍰ TRANSPORTATION AND PRACTICAL INFORMATION. The **train station** is in Pl. de México. To get to the city center and tourist office, walk straight on Av. de América to reach Pl. Bastarreche. In the station, the ticket office is open 5am-9:30pm and customer service from 5am-11pm. **RENFE trains** (☎902 24 02 02) head to: **Barcelona** (8-10hr., 8:40am, €45) via **Alicante; Madrid** (5-8hr., 2-4 per day, €33.50); **Murcia** (1hr., 4-7 per day 7:30am-10pm, €3.30); **Valencia** (4hr., 2 per day, €28). The **bus station** is next to Pl. Bastarreche. **Autocares Costa Azul** (☎968 50 15 43) runs to **Alicante** (2hr., 8 per day 8am-5pm, €6.70). **Alsina Graells** buses go to: **Cádiz** (10-12hr., 10:30am and 9pm, €44.60); **Granada** (4-5hr., 4 per day 8:30am-9pm, €19.90); **Málaga** (7-8hr., 8:30am and 3pm, €28.10); **Sevilla** (8-9hr., 3 per day 10:30am-9pm, €35). **ALSA/Enatcar** heads to: **Barcelona** (10hr., 10am, €41.10); **Madrid** (5-6hr., 6-13 per day 6:15am-midnight, €24.70-€39.10); **Valencia** (4hr., 3-5 per day, €15.70). The **tourist office** (☎968 50 64 83; www.ayto-cartagena.com), in Pl. Bastarreche, has walking tours of the city, maps, and an accommodations list. **Luggage storage** is available at the train station for €2.40 per day.

◪◪ ACCOMMODATIONS AND FOOD. There are some luxury hotels in Cartagena, but more affordable accommodations are few and far between; it's probably best to head to Murcia for the night. If you want to stay, **Pensión Liarte ❶**, C. Muralla de la Tierra, 26, has simple rooms at great rates, though in a slightly rundown part of town. The 24hr. watchman ensures a pleasant stay. To get there, follow C. San Diego out of Pl. Bastarreche, take a right after the plaza onto C. Sor Francisca Armendáriz, and then go left up the hill. (☎968 50 58 73. Singles €12; doubles €17, with bath €22; triples €25.) Those hungry for more than history should head to the numerous tapas bars in town, particularly those on C. Puertas de Murcia. For seafood and rice, the port is the place to be. Follow C. Trovero and then C. Cuesta del Batel from Pl. Bastarreche. **Techos Bajos ❷**, at the bottom of the hill on the left, is a good budget option with a picnic atmosphere and seafood specialties; its neighbors can easily accommodate deeper pockets. (☎966 50 50 20. Appetizers €4-8. Entrees €8-15. Open daily for breakfast and lunch 9am-5pm, F-Su for dinner 7:30pm-midnight.)

◪ SIGHTS. Cartagena prides itself on its rich history; the modern, informative, and beautiful museums are the best part of the city. The **Centro de Interpretación de la Muralla Púnica (CIMP)** provides detailed information about the Punic history of the city and displays the only remnants of the original defensive wall of Qart Hadast, the one extant part of the city's Carthaginian heritage. (Pl. Bastarreche. The schedules of this and other sights change on a monthly basis; ask at the tourist office for updated info. €3.50.) Roman artifacts can be found throughout the the city, though most are, sadly, far from complete. The ruins of the **Augusteum,** C. Caballero, 2, a site dedicated to the cult worship of the emperor Augustus (€2.50), and the **Decumanum,** Pl. de los Tres Reyes, a Roman road (€2), shed light on life in Carthago Nova. The **Interpretation Center,** in the lush gardens of the **Castillo de la Concepción** high above the port, is well worth the climb; alternatively, you can ride up in the new panoramic elevator (€1). A semi-preserved Roman theater is on the edge of town. A combination pass to all four sights is available at each location (€11; ask for student discounts). Cartagena's history didn't end with the Roman empire, however; the tourist office also provides architectural **walking tours,** grouped thematically as "Baroque and Neoclassical" or "Modernist and Eclectic."

LAS ISLAS BALEARES

Ages ago, Spain won a centuries-long race to conquer the Islas Baleares; now they are renowned as one the best summer vacation spots in the world. Two million tourists who flood the islands each year can't be wrong, right?

While all four islands—Mallorca, Menorca, Ibiza, and Formentera—share fame for their gorgeous beaches and landscapes, each has its own special character. Mallorca, home to capital city Palma, absorbs the bulk of high-class, package-tour invaders, and, with its museums, nightlife, and international flavor, Palma reigns as the Baleares' cultural hub. Ibiza, a counter-cultural haven since the 1960s, is the stylistic heart of the islands. With monstrous discos and a loyal contingent of wild, beautiful partygoers, Ibiza offers the undisputed best nightlife in Europe, if not the world. Menorca, wrapped in green fields and stone walls, leads a private life of spectacular, empty white beaches, hidden coves, and mysterious Bronze Age megaliths. Formentera, the smallest and most distant island, is more peaceful with unspoiled sands and unpaved roads.

Summers are hot, crowded, fun, and the best time to visit any of the islands; winters are chilly and slow, as nightlife doesn't heat up until early July. Most hours, schedules, and prices listed are for summer only. Low-season prices at hotels can drop by up to half, and sight hours are often limited.

HIGHLIGHTS OF LAS ISLAS BALEARES

PARTY with German tourists at Palma's **El Arenal** beach (p. 362).

PARTY with Brits in **Sant Antoni** (p. 387).

REDEFINE THE PARTY in **Ibiza** (p. 380).

🏹 GETTING THERE

Flying to the islands is cheap and faster than a ferry. Those under 26 can get discounts with **Iberia/Aviaco Airlines** (in Barcelona ☎902 40 05 00). **Servicios de Ocio Marítimo (SOM** ☎971 31 03 99) lines up bus-ferry-and-*discoteca* packages

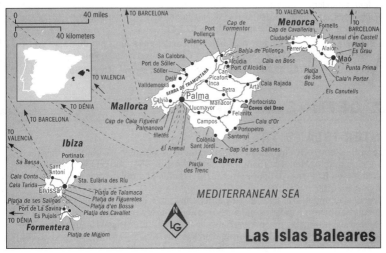

Las Islas Baleares

to Ibiza designed for those who want transportation and an all-night party, but have no use for lodging. Book *those* tickets through a travel agency in Barcelona, Valencia, or on any of the islands.

BY PLANE

Scheduled flights are the easiest to book, and flights from Spain to any of the islands won't break the bank. Frequent flights leave from cities throughout Spain and Europe (including Frankfurt, London, and Paris). Many daily **Iberia** flights (☎902 40 05 00; www.iberia.com) connect Palma and Eivissa to Barcelona, Madrid, and Valencia. The cheapest way to get to Menorca is from Barcelona. Flights from the other cities are infrequent and more expensive. Service from Alicante and Bilbao also exists, but is less frequent.

Iberia offers **student fares** (with an ISIC) on flights from Barcelona (40min., €60-120) and Madrid (1hr., €150-180). ■Vueling (☎902 33 39 33; www.vueling.com), **Air Europa** (☎902 24 00 42; air-europa.com), and **Spanair** (☎902 13 14 15; www.spanair.com) also offer inexpensive flights to the islands. Schedules and prices are subject to change. Another option is a **charter flight,** which can be the cheapest and quickest means of travel. Most deals entail a stay in a hotel, but some companies (called *mayoristas*) sell unoccupied seats on package-tour flights. The leftover spots ("seat only" deals) can be found in newspaper ads or through travel agencies (check **TIVE** and other budget travel havens in any Spanish city). Prices during summer and *Semana Santa* are higher than in low season (Oct.-May). During low season, tickets are easy to get a week or so before departure. Those traveling in July or August should reserve several weeks in advance.

BY BOAT

Ferry service is a little less expensive than flying, but takes longer. On-board discos and small swimming pools on some boats ease the ride, but there are also high-speed ferry options that take only 2-4hr. Ferries run from Barcelona and Valencia to Palma (Mallorca) and Eivissa (Ibiza); ferries also run from Dénia (in Alicante) to Eivissa. Seats may be available up to an hour before departure, but reserve tickets a few days in advance.

Trasmediterránea (☎902 45 46 45; www.trasmediterranea.com) boats depart daily from **Barcelona's** Estació Marítima Moll and **Valencia's** Estació Marítima to **Mallorca, Menorca,** and **Ibiza.** Fares from the mainland are €68-100, depending on speed and distance. Fares between the islands range €28-47.

Balearia (☎902 16 01 80; www.balearia.com) ferries run from **Dénia's** Estació Marítima to **Ibiza** (2-4½hr., 3 per day, from €46), continuing on to **Palma** (from €46).

Buquebus (☎902 41 42 42) has super-fast catamaran service between **Barcelona** and **Palma** (4hr.; 2 per day; €49, cars €112).

▐ GETTING AROUND

INTER-ISLAND TRANSPORT

Iberia flies between Palma and Eivissa (45min., 5 per day, €54-80) and between Palma and Maó, Menorca (35min., 4 per day, from €54). **Air Europa, Spanair,** and **Vueling** (see **By Plane**, p. 356) connect the islands at similar prices. Student discounts are often available.

A cheaper option is to take the **ferry.** Prices and times change with the wind; consult the tourist office or a travel agent. Ferries to and from Maó can be lengthy (6½hr.), but "fast ferries" now make the journey between the other three islands in under 3hr. **Trasmediterránea** (☎902 45 46 45) sails from Palma to Maó (6½hr., Su only, €68) and Eivissa

(2½hr.; 8am and 8:30pm from Palma, Su 8 or 9am and 8pm from Eivissa; €61.70). There is no direct Maó-Eivissa connection. **Trasmapi** (☎971 31 20 71) links Ibiza and Formentera (fast 25min., 12 per day, €35; slow 35min., 6 per day, €22.80). **Umafisa Lines** (☎971 31 45 13) runs car ferries on the same route. **Iscomar Ferries** (☎902 11 91 28) run between Menorca's Port de Ciutadella and Mallorca's Port d'Alcúdia for daytrips.

INTRA-ISLAND TRANSPORT

The three major islands have extensive **bus** systems, although transportation nearly comes to a halt Sundays in most locations, so check schedules. Mallorca has two narrow-gauge **train** systems that are more of a tourist attraction than a major mode of transportation. Intra-island travel is reasonably priced—bus fares between cities range €1.20-6 each way. While it's possible to visit any of the islands without renting a vehicle, cars and mopeds are a great—but pricey—way to explore remote areas not accessible by bus. In Mallorca and Menorca, cars are the best option, while in Ibiza, a moped is more than adequate. On Formentera, bicycles are a great way to get around. A tiny, standard transmission **car** costs around €36 per day including insurance. **Mopeds** are around €18, and **bicycles** a mere €6-10. Prices drop in low season and for long-term rentals.

MALLORCA (MAJORCA)

Mallorca has long attracted the rich and famous. The site of the scandalous honeymoon of pianist Frédéric Chopin and novelist George Sand, Mallorca is also a choice vacation spot for Spain's royal family, as well as Michael Douglas, who has poured time and money into preserving the north coast where he summers.

European package tourists converge on the island in summer, often suffocating the coastline, but there are legitimate reasons for such Mallorca lust. To the northwest, white sand and olive trees adorn the jagged Sierra de Tramontana. To the east, expansive beaches sink into calm bays, while to the southeast, caves mask underground treasure. Inland, towns retain their unique culture, where windmills drawing water for almond groves power a thriving agricultural economy. Although the coastline has been sacrificed to developers, even the most jaded travelers sigh at the expanses of sea, sand, and rock that sprawl across much of the island.

PALMA   ☎971

A stroll along the streets of Palma (pop. 323,000) is like a trip in and out of reality. Wandering through the expansive maze of twisting lanes in the old quarter makes you forget that you are on an island. After a visit to the designer stores near Plaça d'Espanya, it becomes hard to imagine that the city was once a devotional retreat for Fernando and Isabel. Head to the beach, and you feel as though you're no longer in Spain, given the abundance of Germans and Brits sunbathing on the white sand. Still, despite the tourist invasion and growth as a major urban center, Palma retains a genuinely local flavor. In its many cafes and traditional tapas bars, where the native dialect of *mallorquí* is the only language heard, it becomes clear why Palma reigns as the undisputed cultural capital of the Baleares.

▥ TRANSPORTATION

Flights: Aeroport Son San Juan (☎971 78 90 00), 8km from downtown Palma. Bus #1 runs between airport and port, stopping along the way in Pl. d'Espanya (every 15min. 5:50am-2:30am, €1.80). **Air Europa** (☎902 24 00 42), **Iberia** (☎902 40 05 00), and others offer service to Palma. See **By Plane**, p. 356, or **Inter-Island Transport**, p. 356.

LAS ISLAS BALEARES

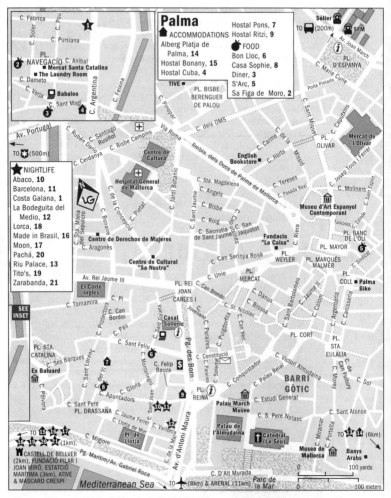

Palma

⌂ ACCOMMODATIONS
Alberg Platja de
  Palma, **14**
Hostal Bonany, **15**
Hostal Cuba, **4**

Hostal Pons, **7**
Hostal Ritzi, **9**

🍴 FOOD
Bon Lloc, **6**
Casa Sophie, **8**
Diner, **3**
S'Arc, **5**
Sa Figa de Moro, **2**

★ NIGHTLIFE
Abaco, **10**
Barcelona, **11**
Costa Galana, **1**
La Bodeguita del
  Medio, **12**
Lorca, **18**
Made in Brasil, **16**
Moon, **17**
Pachá, **20**
Riu Palace, **13**
Tito's, **19**
Zarabanda, **21**

Trains: Ferrocarril de Sóller (☎971 75 20 51; www.trainsoller.com), Pl. d'Espanya.
To: **Sóller** (1hr., 5 per day 8am-7pm, €6.50). **Servicios Ferroviarios de Mallorca
(SFM)**, Pl. d'Espanya (☎971 75 22 45), departs to **Inca** and **Sa Pobla** (35min., 22 per
day 5:45am-9:15pm, €1.80).

Buses: Bus travel to and from Palma is not difficult, but travel between most other areas
is inefficient and restrictive. Nearly all buses stop at the mian stop on C. Eusebi Estada,
several blocks down from Pl. d'Espanya; buy tickets on bus. The tourist office has a
schedule of all buses. More popular destinations include: **Alcúdia** and **Port d'Alcúdia**
(1hr.; M-F 16 per day 8am-9pm, Sa-Su 5 per day 9:30am-9pm; €4.10); **Coves del
Drac** (1hr.; M-F 4 per day 10am-1:30pm, Sa-Su 10am; €6.60); **Covetes/Es Trenc** (M-
F 3 per day 10am-5pm, Sa-Su 10:30am; €4.20); **Port Pollença** (1hr.; M-F 5 per day
9am-7:15pm, Sa 3 per day 11:30am-6pm, Su 10am and 8:30pm; €4.80); **Sóller** and

Port de Sóller via **Deià** (45min.; M-F every hr. 7am-8:30pm, Sa 8 per day 8:30am-7:30pm, Su 3 per day 9am-5:30pm; €2.10); **Valldemossa** (30min.; M-F 13 per day 7:30am-7:30pm, Sa 4 per day 8am-7:30pm, Su 10:30am and 12:30pm; €1.20).

Ferries: Trasmediterránea, Estació Marítima, 2 (☎902 45 46 45). Ferries dock at Moll Pelaires, south of the city. Bus #1 goes along Pg. Marítim/Av. Gabriel Roca (every 15min. 5:50am-2:30am). Tickets sold M-F 9am-1pm and 5-7pm, Sa 9am-noon. Tickets and info also available at travel agencies. Daily ferries to Barcelona, Eivissa, and Valencia. **Balearia** (☎902 16 01 80) sends ferries to Dénia. See **By Boat,** p. 356.

Public Transportation: Empresa Municipal de Transportes (EMT; ☎971 75 22 45). Pl. d'Espanya is the hub. Stops around town and as far as Cala Major and Arenal. €1.10 (buy tickets on board), 10-ride pass (€7.51) available at tobacco stands. Buses run approx. 6am-10pm. The airport bus (#1) runs until 2am (€1.80).

Taxis: (☎971 75 54 40). Airport to center of town approx. €15. Old town to Estació Marítima €8-10.

Car Rental: Ative, Pg. Marítim, 28 (☎971 45 66 02). €18-45 per day with insurance. Open M-Sa 9am-1pm and 3-7:30pm, Su 10am-1pm. **Mascaro Crespi,** Av. Joan Miró, 9 (☎971 73 61 03). €15-30 per day with insurance. Open M-Sa 8am-1pm and 3-7pm, Su 9am-1pm and 5-7pm. €100 deposit required. No credit cards.

Bike Rental: Palma Bike, Pl. Coll, 8 (☎971 71 80 62). €10 per day, 3 days €25, 1wk. €40. Open M-Sa 9am-8pm, Su 10am-1pm.

■ ❖ 🛈 ORIENTATION AND PRACTICAL INFORMATION

To get to town from the airport, take bus #1 to Pl. d'Espanya (15min., every 20min., €1.80). From the dock, take Pg. Marítim/Av. Gabriel Roca or bus #1 to Av. d'Antoni Maura, which leads to Pl. de la Reina and Pg. des Born. From the water, Pg. des Born leads to **Plaça Rei Joan Carles I,** the center of the old town, and **Avinguda Rei Jaume III,** the business artery. To the right, C. de la Unió leads (after some stairs) to **Plaça Major,** the center of Palma's pedestrian shopping district.

Tourist Offices: Palma branch, Pg. des Born, 27 (☎971 72 40 90; www.a-palma.es), in the bookshop of Casa Solleric. Open M-F 9am-8pm, Sa 9am-1:30pm. Sometimes open on Su instead of Sa (same hours). **Info booth** in Pl. d'Espanya. **Island tourist office,** Pl. Reina, 2 (☎971 71 22 16). Open M-F 9am-8pm, Sa 10am-2pm.

Budget Travel: TIVE, C. Jeróni Antich, 5 bajo (☎971 17 77 88). ISIC, HI cards, and tickets. No inter-island travel or charters. Open M-F 9am-2pm and 5-7:30pm.

Currency Exchange: Banco Santander Central Hispano, Pg. des Born, 17 (☎971 72 51 46). Open May-Sept. M-F 8:30am-2:30pm; Oct.-Apr. M-F 8:30am-2:30pm, Sa 8:30am-1pm.

El Corte Inglés: Av. Rei Jaume III, 15 (☎971 77 01 77), and Av. Alexandre Roselló, 12-16. Both open M-Sa 9:30am-9:30pm.

English Bookstore: Book Inn, C. Horts, 20 (☎971 71 38 98). Open June-Sept. M-F 10am-1:30pm and 4:30-8pm; Oct.-May M-F 10am-1:30pm and 4:30-8pm, Sa 10am-1:30pm.

Women's Center: Centro de Derechos de Mujeres, C. Aragón, 26, 1st fl. (☎971 77 49 74, 24hr. hotline 900 19 10 10). Rape crisis assistance. Open M-F 9am-2pm.

Laundromat: 🖼 **The Laundry Room,** Pl. Navegació, 9 bajo (☎645 93 63 60). €10 per load. Ironing (€2 per item), dry cleaning, and a host of other services like storage, currency exchange, even massages (€30 per hr.). Open M-F 7am-3pm.

Police: Av. Sant Ferrà (☎091 or 092).

Late-Night Pharmacy: Rotates daily; see listings in the local paper, *Diario de Mallorca,* or check posting for *farmàcia de guardia* outside pharmacies.

Medical Services: Clínica Rotger, C. Santiago Rusiñol, 9 (☎971 44 85 00), is centrally located. **Clínica Juaneda,** C. Son Espanyolet, 55 (☎971 73 16 47), and **Femenía,** Av. Camilo José Cela, 20 (☎971 45 23 23). All open 24hr.

Internet Access: Babaloo, C. Verja, 2 bajo (☎971 95 77 25). Just off C. Sant Magi. Near Diner and Hostal Cuba. €2 per hr. or €5 for 350min. Open M-Sa 10am-10pm, Su 3-10pm. **Xpace,** C. Sant Gaieta, 4D (☎971 72 92 19). €2.50 per hr., €6 per 4hr. Sign up a friend and get 1hr. free. Open M-Sa 9am-1am, Su 2pm-1am.

Post Office: C. Constitució, 5 (☎902 19 71 97). Parcels upstairs. **Fax** service. Open M-F 8:30am-8:30pm, Sa 9:30am-2pm. **Postal Code:** 07080.

▚ ACCOMMODATIONS

This resort town has few hostels and few bargains; call ahead in summer.

Hostal Cuba, C. Sant Magí, 1 (☎971 73 81 59), at C. Argentina. From Pl. Rei Joan Carles I, turn left and walk down Av. Jaume III, cross the river, and turn left on C. Argentina. Bus #1 from the airport drops you half a block away; get off at Sa Faxima and go downhill. Spotless rooms with high ceilings and wood furniture. All rooms with bath except one: the "penthouse suite," a tiny single on the 3rd fl. with a beautiful view of the city (€18). Singles €20; doubles €37; triples €45. ❷

Hostal Ritzi, C. Apuntadors, 6 (☎971 71 46 10), above "Big Byte" cybercafe, half a block off Pl. de la Reina. Centrally located *hostal* with funky, old-fashioned rooms overlooking interior patio that can get noisy at night. Breakfast (€3.50-5) in Victorian dining room. Laundry €7. Singles €25; doubles €38, with shower €40, with bath €50. ❷

Hostal Bonany, C. Almirante Cervera, 5 (☎971 73 79 24), in a wealthy residential area 3km from town. Bus #3 or 6 from Pl. d'Espanya to the 1st stop on Av. Joan Miró and walk up C. Camilo José Cela. Take the 1st right, then left at the end of the street. More like a hotel than a *hostal:* swimming pool, comfy sitting area, and spacious rooms with bath, TV, and balcony. Breakfast €3. Singles €24; doubles €36. ❷

Hostal Pons, C. del Vi, 8 (☎971 72 26 58). Off the Pl. Drassena by La Llotja. A cheaper option in the Barri Gòtic with small, simple rooms, hallway baths, and a palm-filled patio. Singles €18; doubles €38; triples €54. ❷

Alberg Platja de Palma (HI), C. Costa Brava, 13 (☎971 26 08 92), in El Arenal. Take bus #15 from Pl. d'Espanya or Pl. de la Reina (every 8min., €1.10) and get off at the Hotel Acapulco stop about 45min. from city center. 4-bed dorms with shower. HI card required. Breakfast included. Sheets €2.80, 27 and over €3. Laundry €6/€7. 24hr. reception. Dorms €10-13, 27 and over €10.70-17.40. ❶

▚ FOOD

Palma's many ethnic restaurants are paradise for those sick of tapas. Pricey but popular outdoor restaurants fill **Plaça Mayor** and **Plaça Llotja,** but budget eaters head to the side streets off **Passeig del Born,** to the cheap digs along **Avinguda Joan Miró,** or to the pizzerias along **Passeig Marítim.** Make sure to try the *ensaimadas* (pastries smothered in powdered sugar) and the *sopa mallorquina* (a pizza-like snack of stewed vegetables over brown bread). There are two **markets: Mercat de l'Olivar** in Pl. Olivar off C. Padre Atanasio, and **Mercat Santa Catalina** across town at the corner of C. Pou and C. Dameto. For **groceries,** try **Servicio y Precios** on C. Felip Bauza, near C. Apuntadors and Pl. Reina (☎900 70 30 70; open M-F 8:30am-8:30pm, Sa 9am-2pm), or the supermarket downstairs in either **El Corte Inglés** (p. 359).

Diner, C. Sant Magí, 23 (☎971 73 62 20). Anyone homesick for the good old USA can get their fix (and a great meal) here. American-style favorites served in a kitschy diner setting. Delicious, affordable menu includes burgers (€3-5), hot dogs and grilled cheese (€3.50), tuna melt (€5), ribs (€6.50), and more, all made to order and served with a smile by an awesome international staff. Open 24hr. ●

Bon Lloc, C. Sant Feliu, 7 (☎971 71 86 17). Ultra hip vegetarian restaurant that serves the best (and most popular) lunch in town. Daily 4-course rotating *menú* (€11.10) features options like cool cucumber soup, tasty onion tarts, and delicious chocolate pear cake. Open M-Sa 1-4pm. MC/V. ❷

Sa Figa de Moro, C. Anibal, 21 (☎971 73 10 15). Typical Mallorcan food served in a fun, lively setting with wicker walls and young locals. Delicious selection of salads (€4-6) and *Pá amb olis* (large appetizer platters with bread and olive oil; €5-9). Open M-Sa 1-4pm and 8pm-midnight; summer also Su night. ❷

Casa Sophie, C. Apuntadors, 24 (☎971 21 40 11). Cheap, scrumptious fare in simple, bohemian venue. Home-style menu with vegetarian options like couscous, pasta, and fantastic polenta. Try the *Tabla Mediterránea* (€5.40) as an appetizer—it's an antipasto-like concoction of Spanish and Italian favorites. Entrees €4-7. Open 9pm-1am. ●

S'Arc, Pl. del Banc de l'Oli, 13 (☎971 71 17 20). Just off the Pl. Major, this sleek yet charming restaurant offers great tapas (€5-9) and *pintxos* (bite-size appetizers; €3-5) as well as a creative rotating menu of entrees (€9-15). Open M-Sa 9am-midnight. ❷

👁 🏛 SIGHTS AND MUSEUMS

Palma's architecture melds Arabic, Christian, and Modernista styles into a reflection of the island's multicultural past and present. Many of its landmarks are nestled amidst the narrow streets of the *Barri Gòtic* (Gothic quarter).

CATEDRAL (LA SEU). This Gothic giant towers over Palma and the bay. The cathedral, dedicated to Palma's patron saint San Sebastián, was begun in the 1300s, finished in 1601, and then modified by Gaudí in *modernista* fashion in 1909 to include a stunning stone mobile above the altar, among other ceiling fixtures. The interior and its added ornamentation blend smoothly with the stately exterior. The southern facade, perhaps the most impressive, overlooks a reflecting pool and the ocean. *(C. Palau Reial, 29. ☎971 72 31 30. Main portals are under construction; enter through museum on the left side when facing the front door. Cathedral and museum open June-Sept. M-F 10am-6:15pm; Apr.-May and Oct. M-F 10am-5:15pm; Nov.-Mar. M-F 10am-3:15pm; year-round Sa 10am-2:15pm. €3.50.)*

ES BALUARD. Formerly a 17th-century military fortress, this gargantuan stone building has been gutted and transformed into the new home of Palma's contemporary art museum, which had its grand opening in January of 2004. Its interior was designed by a team of Spain's top architects including Ángel Sánchez Cantalejo, and the clean, modern lines juxtapose beautifully with the severe military exterior. Its collection features three floors of 20th- and 21st-century paintings, sculptures, and installation pieces, and concerts are held weekly in summer in the sculpture garden. *(Pl. Porta Santa Catalina. Open June-Oct. daily 10am-midnight; Nov.-May Tu-Su 10am-8pm. Concerts June-Oct. F 10pm. €6, students €4.50.)*

FUNDACIÓ PILAR I JOAN MIRÓ. Inaugurated in December 1992, this small estate hosts rotating exhibitions about the life and work of the artist, a great collection of his paintings and sculptures, and his preserved studio, which shows works in progress at the time of his death. The studio was designed and built by his good friend, the Catalan architect Josep Lluis Sert. The foundation also provides funding and workspace for young Spanish artists. *(Av. Joan Saridakis, 29. Take* *bus #6 from Pl. de la Reina to Av. Joan Saridakis; the bus drops you about half a block down the hill from the studio. ☎971 70 14 20. Open May 16-Sept. 14 Tu-Sa 10am-7pm, Su 10am-3pm; Sept. 15-May 15 Tu-Sa 10am-6pm, Su 10am-3pm. €4.40.)*

CASTELL DE BELLVER. Overlooking the city and bay, the very rotund Castell de Bellver was a summer residence for 14th-century royalty; it later housed Mallorca's most distinguished prisoners. The castle contains a municipal museum and models of archaeological sites. During the summer, the Castell also hosts concerts and theatrical performances in its central courtyard. Schedules available at the Castell or the tourist office. *(Bus #3 from Pl. d'Espanya or #6 from Pl. de la Reina. Both drop you off in Pl. Gomila. Walk downhill to C. Bellver and take a left, then a right on C. Drecera. Follow the signs up to the massive staircase. Also accessible by car. The Tourist Bus (#50) drives to the top from Pl. de la Reina or Pl. Gomilia; €13. ☎971 73 06 57. Open Apr.-Sept. M-Sa 8am-8:30pm, Su 10am-5pm; Oct.-Mar. M-Sa 8am-7:15pm, Su 10am-5pm. €1.80, students €0.90.)*

PALAU DE L'ALMUDAINA. Built by the Moors, this imposing palace was at one point a stronghold of Fernando and Isabel. The well-preserved interior features rooms from the palace's many different eras and a fantastic collection of tapestries. Guided tours are given in numerous languages. The pleasant garden off Pl. Reina directly in front of the palace also merits a visit. *(C. Palau Reial. ☎971 21 41 34. Open Apr.-Sept. M-F 10am-6:30pm; Oct.-Mar. M-F 10am-2pm and 4-6pm, Sa 10am-2pm. Guided visits €4, unguided €3.20; students and children €2.25. EU citizens free W.)*

MUSEU D'ART ESPANYOL CONTEMPORANI. Now part of the Fundació Joan March, this museum displays an excellent collection of works by the 20th century's most iconic Spanish artists—Picasso, Dalí, Miró, Gris, and Tàpies. *(C. Sant Miquel, 11. ☎971 71 35 15. Open M-F 10am-6:30pm, Sa 10am-1:30pm. Free.)*

OTHER MUSEUMS. The other half of the eclectic Joan March collection (ranging from 14th-century altarpieces to modern sculpture) is housed in the **Palau March Museo** across from the Palau d'Almudaina. *(C. Palau Reial, 18. ☎971 71 11 22. Open M-Sa Apr.-Oct. 10am-6:30pm; Nov.- Mar. 10am-5pm. €4.50.)* **Casal Solleric** houses modern art. *(Pg. des Born, 27. ☎971 72 20 92. Open Tu-Sa 10:30am-1:45pm, Su 10am-1:45pm. Free.)* The **Centre de Cultura "Sa Nostra"** features rotating exhibits and cultural events like lectures, concerts, and movies. Swing by for an upcoming schedule. *(C. de la Concepció, 12. ☎971 72 52 10. Open Tu-F 10:30am-9pm, Sa 10am-1:30pm.)* **La Llotja,** the cavernous former merchant exchange of the island, now houses exhibitions of contemporary painters and sculptors. *(Pl. Llotja. ☎971 71 17 05. Open Tu-Sa 11am-2pm and 5-9pm. Free.)* The **Museo de Mallorca** is ideal for travelers interested in archaeology or medieval painting. The museum guides you through the history of the island from prehistoric times to the Roman conquest and Moorish occupation. *(C. Portella, 5. ☎971 71 75 40. Open Tu-Sa 10am-7pm, Su 10am-2pm. €2.40.)*

▣ BEACHES

Mallorca is a huge island, and many of the best beaches are a haul from Palma. Still, several picturesque (though touristy) stretches of sand are accessible by city bus. The beach at **El Arenal** (S'Arenal; Platja de Palma; bus #15), 11km to the southeast (toward the airport), is the prime stomping ground of Mallorca's most sunburnt German tourists. The waterfront area is full of German signs for restaurants, bars, and hotels—think *Frankfurt am Mediterranean*. Other beaches close to Palma include **Cala Major,** 15km southwest, and **Illetes,** 9km southwest, which are smaller than El Arenal but equally popular (both accessible by bus #3). The tourist office distributes a list of 40 nearby beaches.

📻 🎵 NIGHTLIFE AND ENTERTAINMENT

Entertainment *a la Mallorca* has a Spanish flavor often missing on the other islands. The tourist office keeps a list of sporting activities, concerts, and exhibits. There is also *cine a la fresca*, an outdoor movie showing, a few nights per week during summer in the Parc de la Mar. For info and events, *El Día del Mundo* (€0.75) has an entertainment supplement every Friday that lists bars and discos, and *La Calle* offers a monthly review of hotspots. Also check out the free *Youthing* guide available in many cafes, stores, and restaurants.

Mallorcans use any and every occasion as an excuse to party. One of the more colorful bashes, **Día de Sant Joan** (June 24), brings singing, dancing, and drinking to Parc de la Mar. The celebration begins the night before with a fireworks display.

BARS

In the past, the winding streets between Pl. de la Reina and Pl. Llotja were the place for bar-hoppers, but a recent law requiring downtown bars to close by 1am during the week and 3am on weekends has shifted the late-night action to the waterfront. Still, the *casco viejo* is place to be for your first drink of the night.

> 🏆 **Costa Galana,** Av. Argentina, 45. Run by a squad of Argentine beauties, this funky, upbeat bar away from the touristy part of town has white leather chairs, colorful artwork, and a nice combo of surfing videos and house music. Awesome lounge downstairs. Stop by during the day for a coffee and one of their unbelievable *alfajoras,* an Argentine sandwich cookie made with *dulce de leche,* graham crackers, and chocolate (€1.20). Beer €2. Mixed drinks €3-5. Open daily 8am-3am.

> **La Bodeguita del Medio,** C. Vallseca, 18, plays Cuban rhythms in a tavern with writing on the walls and a shrine to Ernest Hemingway. Tasty *mojitos* €4. Mixed drinks €5. Open Su-Th 8pm-1am, F-Sa 8pm-3am.

> **Lorca,** C. Federico García Lorca, 21. Great spot for gay nightlife, just off the Pg. Marítim. Blue and yellow walls pay homage to the Andalusian poet himself while the mostly gay crowd chats, drinks, and people-watches on the terrace to a mix of pop, rock, and flamenco. Mixed drinks €4. Open daily 11am-3am.

> **Barcelona,** C. Apuntadors, 5. A small, dark bar with lots of atmosphere, Barcelona jams with live music midnight-3am. Cover €4 for live concerts (added to the 1st drink). Beer €3.50, mixed drinks €5. Open Su-Th 8:30pm-1am, F-Sa 8:30pm-3am.

> **Abaco,** C. Sant Joan, 1. For pure decadence head here. Fresh fruit, flowers, candies and classical music fill this 450-year-old mansion, while the upper rooms have tapestries, velvet couches, and oil paintings. Sit at the bar and munch on apricots or get served one of their enormous, fruity cocktails (€15) on the terrace, surrounded by tropical plants and caged birds. Open daily 10am-3am.

DISCOS

The center of the club scene is the **Passeig Marítim/Avinguda Gabriel Roca** strip that runs along the water from Av. d'Antoni Maura to the ferry station. Clubbers start the night in *bares-musicales* that line the street a little closer to town. Each mini-disco boasts different tunes, but Spanish pop dominates. The party then moves down the block to the giant discos (**Tito's** and **Pachá** are the main ones). Look for promoters along the way offering reduced cover prices and extra drinks. It's a 20min. walk from Pl. de la Reina, or you can hop on bus #1 from Pl. d'Espanya. (Bus service stops at 2:30am.) There is also the **Bus de Nit** (Night Bus; #41), which runs 11pm-6am from the Pl. de la Reina, stopping at key points along the strip (€1.10). Be advised, though, that on the way back toward town, the bus often skips stops despite attempts to flag it down. You may be better off taking a cab.

Several clubs and bars (many of them gay, especially on Av. Joan Miró) are centered on **Plaça Gomila** and along **Avinguda Joan Miró**—but exercise caution here at night, as there have been a number of reported instances of petty crime in recent years. The bars and clubs around the beach at **El Arenal** (a.k.a., Berlin) are German-owned, German-filled, and German-centric, but offer some fun options. The last bus back to Palma leaves at 1:35am, though, so you'll most likely have to take a cab home unless you make it to 5:50am, when the first bus of the morning leaves.

Tito's, Pg. Marítim/Av. Gabriel Roca. Don't expect any favors from the bouncers at Palma's hippest disco, but beyond them lies a gorgeous art deco palace with 2 floors, glass elevators, an amazing view of the water, and even the occasional fireworks show. Music moves between house, pop, and hip-hop. Cover €15-18. Open daily 11pm-6am.

Pachá, Pg. Marítim, 42, a couple of blocks farther down Av. Gabriel Roca. A toned-down version of the Eivissa landmark, this little sibling has a massive dance floor, a smaller salsa club attached to it, a tropical terrace, and enthusiastic patrons. Cover €12-18, includes 1 or 2 drinks depending on the night. Open daily 11pm-6:30am.

Riu Palace, C. Llaud, Playa de Palma (www.riupalace.com). 1 block in from the beach in El Arenal. Bus #15 runs until 1:30am and drops you right outside. Cab back to Palma is about €15, but the bus starts again at 6am. If you don't mind partying with Deutschland or cheap alcohol, the Palace is your place. 2 huge rooms fill nightly with young fashion-conscious (and unconscious) German disco fiends. Cover includes open bar all night; bottles of name-brand alcohol and better drinks are available at the "special VIP Bars" (bottles €24-36, drinks €1-2). Come before midnight for a free t-shirt, "rapper cap," and necklace. Cover for women €18, men €20. Open daily 10pm-6:30am.

Made in Brasil, Pg. Marítim, 27. Takes you right to Rio with lively Brazilian music. Be sure to try their specialty drink: the Gai Piriño. (€5.50). Open daily 8pm-4am.

Moon and **Zarabanda,** both along the Pg. Marítim, offer larger venues than the *bares-musicales* and cheaper covers than the big discos. Moon €6, includes 1 drink; Zarabanda €10, includes 2 drinks. Both open daily 11pm-6am.

WESTERN MALLORCA

Ten minutes beyond the urban lifestyle and high-rises of Palma, the road enters a ravine where the island's first cave dwellers lived and rises in tight, narrow curves. North beyond Valldemossa, olive groves pitch toward the sea. This is western Mallorca, one of the most beautiful landscapes in the Mediterranean, alternating between severe, breathtaking cliffs, and serene coves with pebble beaches. It has inspired a range of creative minds, from Chopin and George Sand to Robert Graves and Michael Douglas. However, the villages and beaches will enchant you even if you've never tickled the ivories, spilled any ink, or robbed the cradle.

VALLDEMOSSA

Nord Balear buses (☎ 971 49 06 80) to Valldemossa leave Palma at C. Arxiduc Salvador, 1 (30min.; 13 per day 7:30am-7:30pm, Sa 4 per day 8am-7:30pm, Su 10:30am and 12:30pm; €1.20).

Valldemossa's tiny, shaded streets huddle beneath the slopes of the Sierra de Tramontana. Little in this peaceful village hints at the passion that scandalized townsfolk during the winter of 1838 when Frédéric Chopin and George Sand stayed in the 14th-century monastery **Cartoixa Reial** (see **Prelude to a Breakup,** p. 365). Chopin memorabilia includes the piano which he carried up the mountain and manuscript drafts of some of his most famous works, donated by Chopin societies all over the world. Sand's cell also shows early drafts of *Un Hiver a Majorque*. A ticket (€7.50) includes access to the **Museu Municipal,** which has a brief history of the city, rooms filled with local artwork, and a contemporary art room upstairs with works by Miró and Picasso. The **Palau del Rei Sancho** is a former retreat of Nicaraguan poet Rubén Darío, who also came here to write some of his best work. Folk dances take place (M and Th 11am-1:30pm) in the courtyard, and piano recitals (programs feature all Chopin, all the time) are held in the music room. (☎971 61 21 06. Open M-Sa 9:30am-6:30pm, Su 10am-1pm. Recitals every hr. on the half hr. in summer.) Cafes around the main square serve simple fare—linger over your meal, because once the few stores and sights close, there's nothing else to do.

DEIÀ

Buses heading for Port Sóller from Palma stop in Deià (30min.; M-F every hr. 7am-8:30pm, Sa 8 per day 8:30am-7:30pm, Su 3 per day 9am-5:30pm; €1.50).

Once a secluded artists' colony, the picture-perfect hillside village and peaceful cove of Deià have been transformed into a ritzy, upscale resort town for Europe's most fashionable nouveau-riche. The small pebble **beach** (Cala Deià) is a 30min. hike down the hill or a 10min. drive. To get there by car, continue along the highway until you reach the second bus stop and take a left down the hill. The town retains its original charm and artisan presence: pricey art galleries and handmade jewelry shops seem to be on every corner. On the top of the hill behind the church lies the flowery **Cementari Municipal.** English poet Robert Graves is buried there among a few other early 20th-century artists.

Richard Branson, of the British Virgin empire, owns the most fabulous hotel in town, called **La Residencia.** Converted from a 16th-century manor, the estate is certainly worth checking out, but don't bother checking in unless you've got at least one Oscar or are ready to sell a kidney. The only (relatively) cheap place to stay is the **Pensión Villa Verde ❹**, on C. Ramón Llull, 19, which offers spectacular rooms with views to match surrounding a flora-filled patio where breakfast (included) is served. (☎971 63 90 37. Singles €43; doubles €58, with terrace €80.) Expensive restaurants can be found all over town, but the best bet for food is by the beach at **Can Lluc ❷.** (The lower of the two restaurants. Tapas €3.50-6.50. Entrees €8-14. Open 10:30am-7pm for drinks and snacks; kitchen open noon-5pm). End your day on the terrace at **Café Sa Fora,** right on the main road. Bring your drink outside to chat and watch the sunset over the mountains. (Beer €3, mixed drinks €5-8. Open daily 11am-3am.) There is no tourist office, but large green signs with maps and a list of just about every sight, restaurant, and lodging in town are posted all around.

PRELUDE TO A BREAKUP

Mallorca's most famous vacationers are the Polish composer Frédéric Chopin and his lover, French novelist George Sand (Aurore Dupin), who spent the winter of 1838-39 in the tiny mountain town of Valdemossa. Though it was intended as a honeymoon of sorts for the two lovers, the vacation was doomed from the outset. Chopin suffered from tuberculosis at the time, constantly in pain and prone to black moods. Sand, a passionate free-thinker, felt trapped and alone on the island, as is evident in her writings. The couple's presence, and that of Sand's two children from a previous marriage, caused a stir among the townsfolk, who tormented the couple through the windows of cells #2 and 4 of the Cartoixa Real, which they occupied. Sand documents these incidents in her book *Un Hiver a Majorque (A Winter in Mallorca)* and refers to the locals as "barbarians and monkeys." Despite these less than ideal circumstances, Chopin produced some of his greatest pieces while on the island, drafts of which are now on display in the monastery. Sadly, the love affair ended on a sour note when the two realized that their personalities were too divergent and nothing could bring them together. Thus, in February of 1839, they boarded the same ship which had taken them to Mallorca less than four months before and, after reaching the Spanish mainland, parted forever.

SÓLLER

The old-fashioned Palma-Sóller train, run by Ferrocarril de Sóller, C. Castanyer, 7, is a highlight. The brave ride between cars as they pass through orchards and tunnels. (☎ 971 63 03 01, Palma 971 75 20 51; www.trendesoller.com. 6 per day 8am-7:30pm, €6.40.)

Sóller basks in a fertile valley where oranges and tomatoes are the principal crops, and every plot of land is lined with either citrus groves or sunburnt tourists. The town's backdrop of spectacular mountains and quaint squares makes for a pleasant change from Palma's touristy beaches and urban surroundings. In mid- to late-July, the Ajuntament hosts a **Folk Dancing Festival.** Info is available at the tourist office or posted in front of the church in Pl. de la Constitució. Restaurants fill Pl. de la Constitució, but if you don't need a full meal, try the *coca mallorquina*, a cold pizza-like snack (about €1.80) available in bakeries. Sóller's **tourist office,** in an old trolley car in Pl. d'Espanya downstairs from the train station, has accommodations listings. (☎ 971 63 02 00. Open M-F 9:45am-2pm and 3-5pm, Sa 9am-1pm.)

PORT DE SÓLLER

Nord Balear "tunnel express" buses link Port de Sóller to Palma (1hr.; M-F every hr. 7am-8:30pm, Sa 8 per day 8:30am-6:30pm; €2). Trolleys also connect Sóller and Port de Sóller (1-2 per hr. 7am-8:15pm, €1).

From Sóller it's a 30min. walk (or a short ride on the Nord Balear bus or trolley) to Port de Sóller, where a pebbly beach lines the bay. Two **grocery stores** are on C. Jaume Torrens, and **restaurants** line the beach. The surrounding area's famous **coves** are most easily explored by boat. The **tourist office,** C. Canonge Oliver, 10, has quality maps and a list of accommodations and car rental agencies. (☎/fax 971 63 30 42. Open M-F 9:10am-12:55pm and 2:40-4:55pm, Sa 10:10am-12:45pm.)

SA CALOBRA

Tramontana and Barcos Azules sail to Sa Calobra from the port near the last trolley stop in Port de Sóller. (Info and schedules ☎ 971 63 31 09. May-Oct. 15 3-5 per day 10am-3pm, return 4 per day 10:45am-5pm; round-trip €20.) Buy tickets across the street from the last tram stop. One bus runs from Alcúdia daily 9:30am, return 3pm (€5.90).

Narrow, steep, and serpentine, the road to the dramatic cove of Sa Calobra writhes over 12 nail-biting kilometers while dropping 1000m to the sea. The boat from Port de Sóller is easier on the nerves, but not on the wallet. **Torrent de Pareis,** a spectacular cove that leads into a ravine with freshwater pools, is a 15min. hike from the bottom of the road and a popular photo opportunity (look for a landing packed with tourists). Sa Calobra itself is a smooth pebble beach bordered by cliffs. Like much of the rest of the island, its beauty is somewhat scarred by tourist restaurants, gift shops, and scores of sun-hungry Brits and Germans.

NORTHERN MALLORCA

Known for their long beaches and rocky coves, the northern gulfs of Mallorca are popular among the older, package-tour crowd; much of the coast is swamped beyond belief. The drive can be stunning, and though the region's coves and beaches are far from secluded, they are among the most beautiful on the island.

ALCÚDIA AND PORT D'ALCÚDIA

Buses (☎ 971 54 56 96) run to Alcúdia (€4) and Port d'Alcúdia (€4.10) from Pl. d'Espanya in Palma (1hr.; M-Sa 16 per day 8am-9pm, Su 5 per day 9:30am-9pm). The bus to Port Pollença and Cap de Formentor leaves from the corner of C. del Coral and Pg. Marítim. Municipal buses run back and forth between the port and the town every 15min., or hop on any bus leaving the port—they all stop in town.

Alcúdia and its nearby port are far from undiscovered. The beaches along the shallow bay are packed with hotels, bars, and pizzerias, but the city has an ancient intimacy about it (it dates back to Roman times) and makes for a nice getaway from its southern sister, Palma. The beach is the main attraction here, but for something more than the ocean, the old town has 14th-century ramparts, **Roman ruins** dating from 2 BC, and town walls that have experienced a series of medieval razings and re-buildings. The **Museu Pollentia** documents archaeological discoveries on Mallorca. (☎971 54 70 04. Open Tu-F 10am-1:30pm and 3:30-5:30pm, Sa-Su 10:30am-1pm. €2.) **Parc de s'Albufera des Grau,** within walking distance of the beach, is filled with marshes, flowers, and dunes. (Open daily summer 10am-7pm; winter 10am-5pm. Free.) The tourist office has a brochure of 10 hiking/biking excursions.

Port d'Alcúdia also makes a nice base for exploring the stunning beaches of the northeast coast. If you have a car, take the road toward **Artà** and then **Capdepera** from town. About 20km from Port d'Alcúdia, you will see signs leading to **Cala Torta** along a bumpy dirt road. Cala Torta itself is the most touristed of the three arid coves on this corner of the island. If you hike from this beach over the cliffs to the west, you come to **Cala Mitjana,** a beautiful cove with crashing waves and tide pools filled with seaweed. (Beach chairs and umbrellas €2.) Past Cala Mitjana is **Es Matzoc,** a pleasant white-sanded beach that is not entirely overrun by tourists.

The best places to stay are at the port. **Hostal Calma ❷,** C. de Teodor Canet, 25, is a great deal, offering renovated rooms with A/C, TV, and private bath. (☎971 54 85 85. Breakfast €2. Singles €20; doubles €36; triples €45.) For a light lunch, stop into **Oceano ❶,** C. dels Mariners, 18B, for fresh sandwiches and salads (€3.75-€4.50) in a deep blue setting. (☎971 54 74 14. All food available for take-out.) In town, **Ca'n Simo ❷,** C. d'en Serra, 22, offers a delicious vegetarian menu. (☎971 54 62 73. Salads €5. Omelettes €8. Entrees €10-14. Lunch *menú* €12. Dinner *menú* €18. Open M-Sa 12:30-4pm and 7:30-11:30pm.) Head to **Supermercats Aprop,** C. dels Mariners, 14, for groceries. (Open M-Sa 9:30am-9:30pm, Su 9am-2pm.)

There are two **tourist offices** at the port. One is on Pg. Marítim (☎971 54 72 57; open summer M-Sa 9am-8pm) in a small plaza at the far end of the beach, on the left as you face the water. The other is on the opposite side of the beach, slightly inland at C. d'Artá, 68 (☎971 892 615; www.alcudia.net; schedule varies, call for hours). In town, the office is at C. Major, 17. (☎971 89 71 00.) In an emergency call the **police** at ☎971 54 50 66.

PORT POLLENÇA

Autocares Mallorca buses connect Alcúdia and Pollença (20min., M-Sa every 15min. 8:30am-1:30pm and 2:30-8:15pm, €1). Autocares Villalonga, C. San Isidro, 4 (☎971 53 00 57) go to Palma (1hr., 5 per day 7:15am-5pm, €4.30). Buses stop along the strip and at the rotary at the end of Pg. Saralegui.

Popular among British and northern Europeans, and calmer and classier than the neighboring beach towns, Port Pollença features a beautiful man-made beach along a crescent-shaped bay. Cafes, restaurants, and pubs cater to a more refined crowd of middle-aged tourists and a few families, and the town isn't particularly expensive though the views are spectacular. The area hosts a **music festival** in July and August, with a variety of concerts every Wednesday and Saturday night. A complete schedule of events and list of ticket vendors is available at the tourist office (tickets €16-36). **Hostal Corro ❷,** C. Joan XXIII, 68, offers clean, colorful rooms and hall baths blocks from the beach. (☎971 86 66 83. Singles €25; doubles €30; triples €42, with bath €48.) The **tourist office,** C. Monges, is one block from the last bus stop by the port. (☎971 86 54 67. Open M-F 8am-3pm and 5-7pm, Sa 9am-1pm.) **Rent March,** C. Joan XXIII, 89, rents bikes and mopeds. (☎971 86 47 84. Bikes €6-8 per day; mopeds €24-125 per day. Open Mar.-Nov. M-Sa 9am-1pm and 3-8pm, Su 6-8pm.) In an emergency, call the **police** (☎971 53 04 37).

Highway C-710, which runs along the northwest coast of Mallorca, twists and turns through some of the most breathtaking seaside cliffs and majestic mountains and valleys in all of Europe. It extends for practically the entire coast, from Andratx in in the west to Pollença in the east. This drive will take you north

TIME: 4hr.

DISTANCE: 50-60km/30-35mi.

SEASON: Any time of year except winter, when the weather makes for treacherous driving.

from Palma to pick up C-710 in Valldemossa, and then east through Pollença and out to Cap de Formentor, on the far northeastern coast of the island.

From Palma, drive north toward Valldemossa on PM-111. The Serra de Tramontana, Mallorca's northern mountain range, lies ahead, preceded by citrus orchards and olive groves on all sides.

1 VALLDEMOSSA. 19km on this road takes you into the heart of Valldemossa, the tiny mountain town where Frédéric Chopin and George Sand spent their infamous, doomed "honeymoon" (see **Prelude to a Breakup,** p. 365). In town, stop at the **Cartoixa Reial,** the monastery where the couple stayed, and see the piano Chopin carried up the mountain in order to write some of his most famous pieces. Also on display are some of the original manuscripts of Sand's book *Un Hiver a Majorque,* her chronicle of their disastrous visit. (☎971 61 21 06. Open M-Sa 9:30am-6:30pm, Su 10am-1pm. €7.50.)

2 MONASTIR DE MIRAMAR. Pass through town following the signs toward Deià. Eventually you will have to make a hard right off PM-111; this is highway C-710. On the left, valleys surrounding Valldemossa rise and fall around the town's terra-cotta roofs and Gothic bell towers. Off the short 9km stretch between Valldemossa and Deià there is a small pink sign on the left side of the highway. Turn left there and drive down the steep dirt road to the Monastir de Miramar, a tiny monastery founded in 1276 and rebuilt again in 1872. The picturesque **gardens** and rows of Gothic arches look over the cliffs, peppered with olive trees out to the sea. (Open Tu-Su 10am-7pm. €3.)

SCENIC DRIVE

DEIÀ. The highway leads you through the center of Deià, a former artists' colony that has since become a ritzy mountain retreat for the rich and famous. Park your car in one of the lots on the side of the highway and wander uphill to the **Cementari Municipal,** where English poet **Robert Graves** is buried alongside a host of other artists and writers who used to call Deià home.

FORNALUTX. Continue down the highway toward Sóller and take a left off the main highway into the center of town. If you stay on C-710, you'll end up heading back toward Palma. Follow the signs toward Fornalutx as you navigate the winding, narrow streets of the town. When you reach a fork with only a sign to Palma pointing left, go right and continue on C-710 through the agricultural town of Fornalutx, where **orchards** of lemons, tomatoes, and, of course, **olives** descend into the depths of the Sierra de Tramuntana. Follow signs to Lluc and Pollença at any intersections or traffic circles.

GORG BLAU AND THE ANCIENT COLUMN. Just past Fornalutx, the road drops down, and on your right you'll see two of Mallorca's handful of freshwater lakes. As you pass the second one, Gorg Blau, you may notice a lonely column sitting off to the right side of the road. It was excavated from the lake in 1967 and is thought to be from a 7th-century monastery. As the question mark on its inscription indicates, however, its origins are, in fact, still unknown.

FLOWERS AND GOATS. The long stretch between Fornalutx and Pollença is brimming with jagged peaks and lush valleys. In spring, these landscapes are covered in a rainbow of flowers and the first signs of the coming harvest. In summer, the countryside burns bright green, reflecting the heat the of sun. Watch out for goats on this road—they have a tendency to spring up out of nowhere.

PORT DE POLLENÇA. When you reach the traffic circle just outside of Pollença, you've come to the end of C-710. Head left off the circle toward Port de Pollença (the road here is PM-220), whose beachside cafes and pleasant plazas make for a great lunch or dinner stop. Try **Iberi ❷,** C. Migjorn, 6, for delicious creative cuisine served in a colorful outdoor plaza. (☎971 86 61 95. Appetizers, salads, and entrees €6-9.)

CAP DE FORMENTOR. Follow the brown signs out of Port de Pollença toward Formentor, a popular **beach** destination, and Cap de Formentor, the northeast tip of Mallorca where the journey ends. The 18km stretch from Port de Pollença is the crème de la crème in terms of **dramatic cliffs and views of the sea** on both sides of the road, as is evidenced by the myriad landings off the highway that are more often than not filled with cars full of camera-happy tourists. The more popular ones are indicated by blue signs with camera icons on them, but there are still many others with room for only one or two cars that offer **unbeatable photo-ops.** Keep an eye out for them if you want some great pictures.

THE LIGHTHOUSE. At the end of this long and winding road is the **Far del Cap de Formentor,** the lighthouse at the top of the cliff. The views from the top are nothing short of spectacular and are well worth the climb and possible line for a parking spot. If you time your visit around **sunset** (8-9pm in summer), the sight promises to be stunning as you watch the cliffs turn pink in the light and reflection of the sun sparkling off the deep blue Mediterranean.

BACK TO PALMA. The fastest way back to Palma is to return to Port de Pollença and pick up PM-220, which connects with C-713 heading toward Inca. Just past Inca, take PM-27 toward Palma (also called Vía Cintury and indicated by a blue sign), which is a more direct route (with much higher speed limits) than C-713, and will get you back in about half the time it took to get here.

CAP DE FORMENTOR

Buses stop 6km away from the end of Cap de Formentor. Autocares Villalonga, C. San Isidro, 4 (☎ 971 53 00 57), sends one bus daily from Palma (10:15am, return 3:30pm; €5.30). Autocares Mallorca (☎ 971 54 56 96) leave from Port Pollença (4 per day 10am-4:30pm, €1). A boat (☎ 971 86 40 14) goes to Platja Formentor from Port Pollença's Estació Marítima (every hr. 10am-3pm, no boat 2pm; returns every hr. 11:30am-5:30pm, no boat 2:30 and 4:30pm; round-trip €7.50).

A trek to Cap de Formentor, 15km northeast of Port Pollença, leads to dramatic seaside cliffs, a lighthouse, and a spectacular view—all enjoyed by dozens of tourist families. The road is peppered with landings perfect for photoops, and all are crowded with cars. Before the final 9km drive up to the lighthouse, the road drops to **Platja Formentor,** where a canopy of evergreens seems to sink into the water. If you have your own transportation, head downhill from the lighthouse to the bottom of the road for two of the most beautiful coves in Mallorca. On the right is the small dirt parking lot for **Cala Figuera,** a cove surrounded by jagged cliffs popular with private yachts. Across the road to your right is a small wooden sign pointing in the direction of █**Cala Murta,** perhaps the only secluded cove on the island. From the road, follow the dirt path indicated by the sign to a small electrical station. Bear right and you will see the cove's tiny pebbly beach and turquoise water.

SOUTHEASTERN MALLORCA

Signs along the highway of Mallorca's southeast coast might as well read "Welcome Tourist Hordes;" much of the area has been built up by developers. The scalloped bays on the coast east of Cap de ses Salines, Mallorca's southernmost point, are their most recent discovery. Still, the breathtaking scenery, long, beautiful beaches, and intriguing caves remain relatively unspoiled.

█ **COVES DEL DRAC.** Despite its classification as a bona fide tourist attraction (with the lines to prove it), the Coves del Drac (Dragon's Caves), just south of Porto Cristo, are among the island's most dramatic natural wonders and are a unique experience not to be missed. Scores of striking red and pink stalactites and stalagmites surround crystal clear reflecting pools, all expertly lit to be appropriately mystifying yet visible. At the end of the 30min. walk into the depths of the caves is one of the largest underground lakes in the world, where classical musicians give concerts while floating on illuminated rowboats. Audience members are invited to take boat rides across the lake after the concert. The whole thing lasts about an hour and is breathtakingly beautiful, but can also be described as somewhere between absurd and bizarre; still, it's certainly worth the trip and price. *(A bus to the caves runs from the main station by Pl. d'Espanya in Palma; 1hr.; M-Sa 4 per day 10am-1:30pm, Su 10am; €6.40. If you're driving, head toward Manacor from Palma and then toward Porto Cristo. Follow the signs through town. Open daily 10am-7pm. €8.50; tickets are purchased for entrance at a specific hour and are good until quarter past.)*

PLATJA DES TRENC. West of Cap de ses Salines and east of Cap Blanc sprawls one of Mallorca's best and longest beaches, Platja des Trenc. In most cases, a 1-2km walk is usually enough to put plenty of sand between you and the thickest crowds, but watch out for nudists as you move farther from the more crowded area. *(Buses run to Platja des Trenc in the summer from Pl. d'Espanya in Palma; M-Sa 3 per day 10am-5pm, Su 10:30am; €3.90. Driving from Palma, the road to the beaches is off the highway between Llucmajor and Campos. The sign is small, though, so watch for it. Parking €5.)*

MENORCA

Menorca's fantastic beaches, rustic landscapes, and picturesque towns draw ecologists, sun worshippers, and photographers. In 1993, UNESCO declared the island a biosphere reserve; since then, administrators have emphasized preservation of Menorca's natural harbors, pristine beaches, rocky northern coast, and network of farmlands. The act has also encouraged protection, excavation, and study of Menorca's stone burial chambers and homestead complexes, remnants of the mysterious Talayotic stone age culture dating from 1400 BC. Since its incorporation into the Catalan kingdom in 1287, Menorca (pop. 72,000) has endured a succession of foreign invaders—Arab, Turkish, French, and British. Quieter and more upscale than the other Baleares, Menorca attracts wealthy young families in search of a peaceful beach vacation and has less to offer budget travelers than its larger neighbors. Most families tend to stay in resorts and apartments along the beaches; the towns themselves sometimes offer reasonable prices. Students make their appearance here before the real tourist season starts, in the spring, while everyone else arrives full-force in August. Menorca's main cities, Maó and Ciutadella, located at the east and west ends of the island respectively, serve as gateways to the real attractions: beautiful stretches of sand and a seemingly infinite number of impressive rocky coves.

MAHÓN (MAÓ) ☎971

Maó (pop. 25,000) adds a touch of class to the tourism industry. Even the ever-present sandal and shirt shops that line the port offer more refined items, and the restaurants are certainly not your typical waterfront, paella-postered establishments. The British occupied the city for most of the 18th century, leaving Georgian doors, brass knockers, and wooden shutters in their wake. Two centuries later, the predominance of British tourists testifies to the UK's continuing influence. Most people clear out during the day, using the town as a jumping-off point for the numerous beaches nearby; public buses go to some of the more popular stretches of sand. Others spend their hours window shopping at the numerous boutiques that line Maó's pedestrian streets. The city comes alive in early evening when sea breezes cool the air and sunburnt visitors return from beaches to the city's world-famous restaurants. Despite the presence of bars and clubs, Maó's nightlife is centered more around post-dinner conversation than all-night partying.

▐ TRANSPORTATION

Flights: Airport (☎971 15 70 00), 7km out of town. The **Aerobús** (operated by **Torres** ☎902 07 50 66) runs in a loop between the airport, the Pl. de s'Esplanada, and the Port (every 30min., €1.40). **Iberia/Aviaco** (☎971 36 90 15); **Air Europa** (☎971 24 00 42); **SpanAir** (☎971 15 70 98). Advance booking is essential in summer. See **By Plane,** p. 356, and **Inter-Island Transport,** p. 356.

Ferries: Estació Marítima, Moll de Ponent (☎971 36 60 50). Open M-F 8am-1pm and 5-7pm, Sa 8am-noon, Su 8-10:30am and 3:30-5:15pm. **Trasmediterránea** (☎971 36 29 50) sends ferries daily to **Barcelona** and weekly to **Palma** and **Valencia. Balearia** sends ferries to **Alcúdia, Mallorca,** and **Barcelona.** For more info, see **By Boat,** p. 356, and **Inter-Island Transport,** p. 356.

Buses: The new bus station is at the far end of Pl. de s'Esplanada. Go up C. Vasallo and it's on the left. Though under construction, it's the hub for buses to and from Maó. Check the tourist office or newspapers *Menorca Diario Insular* and *Menorca* for schedules.

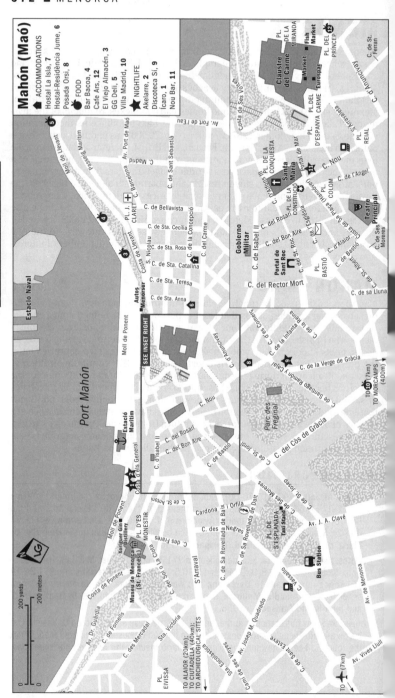

Mahón (Maó)

♠ **ACCOMMODATIONS**
Hostal La Isla, **7**
Hostal-Residéncia Jume, **6**
Posada Orsi, **8**

● **FOOD**
Bar Bacoa, **4**
Cafe Ars, **12**
El Viejo Almacén, **3**
GG Deli, **5**
Villa Madrid, **10**

★ **NIGHTLIFE**
Akelarre, **2**
Discoteca Sì, **9**
Ícaro, **1**
Nou Bar, **11**

Transportes Menorca (TMSA; ☎971 36 04 75) to: **Ciutadella** via **Ferreries** and **Es Mercadal** (1hr.; M-F every hr. 7:15am-10:15pm, Sa 7 per day 8am-10pm, Su 6 per day 8am-7pm; €3.90); **Es Castell** (20min.; every 30min. M-Sa 7:15am-8:45pm, Su 9:15am-1:45pm and 3:45-8:45pm; €1.10); **Platja Punta Prima** (20min.; M-F 9 per day 8:30am-7:30pm, Su 8 per day 9:30am-7:30pm; €1.20); **Son Bou** (30min., 7 per day 8:30am-7:30pm, €1.80). **Autobuses Fornells Roca Triay** (☎971 37 66 21) go to: **Arenal d'en Castell** (30min.; M-Sa 7 per day 9:30am-7pm, Su 3 per day 11am-6:40pm; €1.80); **Es Grau** (20min., 3-5 per day 10am-6pm, €1); **Fornells** (40min., 2-4 per day 10:45am-7pm, €2.30); **Son Parc** (30min., 5 per day 10:45am-7pm, €1.90). Buy tickets on board.

Taxis: Main stand at Pl. de s'Esplanada (☎971 36 12 83), or **Radio Taxi** (☎971 36 71 11). To: **airport** (€9); **Cala Mesquida** (€8); **Cala'n Porter** (€11.80); **Es Castell** (€5).

Car Rental: ▨**Morcamps,** C. Gobernador Ramírez, 31 (☎971 36 95 94). Fully loaded cars (4-doors, A/C, radio, and CD player), for as little as €22 per day. Tourist office provides a comprehensive list of all car rental agencies in the city.

Bike and Scooter Rental: Autos Menorsur, Moll de Llevant, 35-36 (☎971 35 47 86), Puerto de Maó. Bicycles €10 per day, €37-42 per week. Scooters €21-27/€93-150. Also rents cars: Aug. €40 per day, €210 per wk.; July €36/€180; occasionally offers a 3-days-for-€75 deal. Substantial discounts in low season. Open Apr.-Sept. daily 9:30am-1:30pm and 5-7:30pm.

✚⁊ ORIENTATION AND PRACTICAL INFORMATION

The **Plaça de s'Esplanada** is the geographic center of the city. **Calle de Ses Moreres** leads into the nest of pedestrian streets and plazas that end at the **port.** Facing the water at the port, the **Moll de Llevant** is to the right. **Moll de Ponent** is to the left. To reach the heart of the city from the **ferry station,** go left (with your back to the water) about 150m and then right at the steps that cut through the serpentine **Costa de Ses Voltes.** The steps end between Pl. de la Conquesta and Pl. d'Espanya.

Tourist Office: C. de Sa Rovellada de Dalt, 24 (☎971 36 37 90; www.e-menorca.org). English spoken. Open M-F 9am-1:30pm and 5-7pm, Sa 9am-1pm. **Summer offices** open Mar.-Oct. at Moll de Levant, 2 (☎971 35 59 52; open M-F 8am-9pm, Sa 9am-1pm), and the airport (☎971 15 71 15; open daily 8am-11pm) have similar services.

Currency Exchange: Banks with 24hr. **ATMs** line C. Hannóver and C. Nou.

Laundromat: Lavandería Marin, Cami des Castell, 64 (☎971 36 23 79). Wash and dry up to 5kg €11.50. Open M-F 9am-1pm and 4-7:30pm.

Police: Municipal, Pl. de la Constitució (☎971 36 39 61).

Pharmacy: Check the list outside any pharmacy for the *farmàcia de guardia.*

Medical Assistance: Hospital Verge del Toro, C. Barcelona, 3 (☎971 15 77 00). English spoken. **Medical Emergency:** ☎061.

Internet Access: Comunicate, C. Vassallo, 22 (☎971 36 55 11). €3 per hr., students €1.50 per hr. Open M-Sa 10am-11pm, Su 6-11pm. **Ciber Principal,** C. Nou, 25 (☎971 36 26 89). €1.20 per 20min., €2.40 per 40min., €3.50 per hr. Open M-F 9:30am-10pm, Sa 11am-2pm and 6-10pm.

Post Office: C. del Bon Aire, 11-13 (☎971 35 66 34), at C. de l'Església. Open M-F 8:30am-8:30pm, Sa 9:30am-2pm. **Postal Code:** 07703.

⌐ ACCOMMODATIONS

It's easier to find a room in Menorca than on the other islands, but it's still a good idea to call ahead, especially in July and August.

▨**Posada Orsi,** C. de la Infanta, 19 (☎971 36 47 51). Renovated in 2003, rooms are beautiful, exquisitely decorated, modern, and fun. Brightly colored walls and linens. Comfy TV room and sitting room. Call before arriving. Singles €17-23; doubles €28-38, with shower €35-47. Prices vary with season. MC/V. ❷

Hostal-Residència Jume, C. de la Concepció, 6 (☎971 36 32 66; fax 36 48 78). Standard rooms, all with bath. Large windows and efficient fans cool things down nicely in summer. Breakfast included by default for €4 extra; specify if you don't want it. Lots of services available at reception—car rental, books, snacks, even a small pharmacy. June-Aug. singles €21; doubles €42. Sept.-May €18/€36. Closed Dec. 15-Jan. 5. ❷

Hostal La Isla, C. de Santa Catalina, 4 (☎/fax 971 36 64 92). Immaculate rooms all with private bath. Restaurant downstairs serves a typical *menú*. Open June-Sept. Singles €23, with breakfast €26; doubles €43/€47; triples €59/€63. MC/V. ❷

⌔ FOOD

Fine dining is the main activity in Maó, and the city takes its restaurants very seriously. Café-bars spilling into Pl. de la Constitució, Reial, and s'Esplanada serve *platos combinados* (€2.70-5.10) to sidewalk throngs of hungry customers, though the majority of tourists head to eateries along the water, where prices, food, and ambience match the upscale atmosphere. Seafood is a specialty here, but restaurants serve myriad other favorites. Regional specialties include *sobrassada* (soft sausage spread), *crespells* (biscuits), and *rubiols* (turnovers filled with fish or vegetables). *Mahonesa* (mayonnaise), which was invented on the island, is popular in many of the more exotic dishes.

There is a produce **market** in the Claustre del Carme, which extends from Pl. d'Espanya to Pl. de la Miranda. (Open M-Sa 9am-2pm.) Groceries are sold below the produce market at **Eurospar.** (☎971 36 93 80. Open M-Sa 8am-8pm.)

ALONG THE WATER

▨ **Grand General (G.G.) Delicatessen,** Moll de Llevant, 319 (☎971 35 28 05). By far the best-kept secret and best deal along the strip of seaside restaurants. Fresh vegetarian dishes, fish and meat entrees, Italian *bruschetta* sandwiches, and an excellent variety of salads. Try the antipasto for a bit of everything smothered in delicious, fresh olive oil (€8). The 20min. walk from the port is well worth it. Sandwiches €3.50-5, entrees and salads €5-9. Open M-Sa noon-midnight. ❶

El Viejo Almacén, Moll de Llevant, 75 (☎971 36 89 52). Friendly atmosphere and cave-like decor compliment excellent "fusion" tapas (€3-6.50), and a wide variety of creative appetizers and entrees like grouper carpaccio and eggplant with goat cheese (€8-15). Rotating *menú del día* €17.50. Open Tu-Sa 11am-midnight. ❸

Bar Bacoa, Moll de Llevant, 106 (☎630 16 25 04). Affordable tapas and seafood fare among colorful canvas lamps, and a staff of friendly Frenchmen. Tapas €3-9. Pasta €7. Entrees €10-12. Open M-Sa noon-3pm and 8-11pm. ❷

IN TOWN

Cafe Ars, C. del Carme, 13 (☎971 36 80 41). Lighter fare in a bohemian setting. Salads (€5-9), pastas (€5-7), and sandwiches (€2.50-3.50) are tasty and affordable. Dim lights and jazz create a relaxing atmosphere, and large windows frame the outside world. Three-course *menú* €11. Open M-Sa 10am-midnight. ❷

Príncep Café, Pl. del Príncep, 5 (☎971 36 19 84). Perfect place for breakfast, a light lunch, or a *café* surrounded by black and white photos and orange walls. *Bocadillos* €2-3. *Tostadas* €2-4. ❶

OUTSIDE MAÓ

Villa Madrid, S'uestrà, 46 (☎971 15 04 64). Head toward St. Lluís from Maó and take a right onto the road toward Binisafuller. Restaurant is between Binisafuller and Torret de Baix, 10min. from Maó. If you're up for a short drive and a splurge, try this creative Mediterranean paradise in a beautiful 19th-century colonial house. Indulge in the tasting *menú* (€47) and sample just about everything from their huge selection. Open daily 8pm-11:30pm; closed Tu in winter. ❺

🔘 SIGHTS

The most awe-inspiring sights in Menorca are outside of its cities, although Maó does have a few attractions. Get sauced off free liquor samples at the **Xoriguer Gin Distillery** at the port. Through glass windows at the back of the store, visitors can watch their drinks bubble and froth in large copper vats. (☎971 36 21 97. Open M-F 8am-7pm, Sa 9am-1pm.) The **Museu de Menorca,** Av. Dr. Guàrdia, an old Franciscan monastery closed in 1835, displays excavated items and exhibits on Menorca dating back to prehistoric times. (☎971 35 09 55. Open Tu-Su 10am-2pm and 6-8:30pm. €2.40, students €1.20.) Founded in 1287 and rebuilt in 1772, the **Església de Santa María La Major,** Pl. de la Constitució, trembles from the 3210 pipes of its über-organ, built by the Swiss Juan Kilburz in 1810. (Organ concerts M-Sa 11am, €3 "donation." Open for visits 8am-1pm and 6-8:30pm.) The **Portal de Sant Roc,** up C. Sant Roc from Pl. de la Constitució, straddles the streets of Maó. It is the last fragment of the medieval wall built to defend the city against pirates.

Maó is close to numerous **archaeological sites,** including prehistoric caves, settlements, and monuments, but they are accessible only by car; see the tourist office for info on a self-guided driving tour. Perhaps the most famous of these monuments is **Torre d'en Galmes,** off the road to Platges de Son Bou from Alaior. Atop a hill overlooking the island's interior, this Talayotic city dates from 1400 BC and served as both a religious and commercial center for Menorca's original inhabitants. Though much of it has yet to be excavated and seems to be nothing more than piles of disorganized rubble, the eerie **Sala Hipostila,** a prehistoric house, is of special interest; the roof is supported by columns narrower at their bases than at their crowns. (Open daily 10am-8pm. €2.40, students €1.20.)

🔳 🔆 NIGHTLIFE AND FESTIVALS

Maó is not known for its nightlife. Weekdays are quiet except in August, and weekends are still relatively tame. Summers are naturally a little more lively. A string of bars and clubs line the **Costa d'els General,** a small street that slopes upwards from the Moll de Ponent. One of the more fashionable places on the strip is 🔳**Akelarre,** Moll de Ponent, 41-43, a spacious, trendy bar and dance club with stone walls and columns. Chill out downstairs to jazz or rock out upstairs to the latest house and pop. It's also a cafe during the day and hosts many jazz concerts. See posters for details or ask at the bar for a schedule. (☎971 36 85 20. Open daily June-Oct. 8am-5am; Nov.-May 7:30pm-4am.) A few doors down is **Ícaro,** Moll de Llevant, 46, a sleek, stylish bar with two floors, an older crowd, and black and white photos on the walls. (☎971 36 97 35. Mixed drinks €4-6. Open summer daily 8pm-4am; winter F and Sa only.) Away from the port, **Nou Bar,** C. Nou, 1, 2nd fl., serves drinks (€4-6) to a calm crowd of locals overlooking the Pl. de la Constitució. (☎971 36 55 00. Open daily 7:30pm-3am.) **Discoteca Sí,** C. de la Verge de Gràcia, 16, turns on the strobe light after midnight, but doesn't get going until after 4am when the partiers head back from the port. (Open daily midnight-6am.)

Film lovers should check out **cine a la fresca,** held every summer night except Friday in the Claustre del Carme at 10pm. A different film is shown each week in the outdoor courtyard of the cloister. Look for the posters around town advertising the current movie. (Enter from Pl. de la Miranda. €6.)

From May to September, merchants sell shoes, clothes, and souvenirs in **mercadillos** held daily in the town squares of various cities around the island. In Maó, the markets are located in the Pl. s'Esplanada on Tuesday and Saturday. In mid-July, Maó's **Verge del Carme** celebration brings a colorfully trimmed armada into the harbor. The **Festival de Música de Maó** in July and August showcases Església Santa María's Swiss organ and brings renowned classical musicians to the city's **Teatro Principal,** Costa d'en Deià, 40. Check the tourist office or the box office of the theater for schedules and prices. (Box office ☎971 35 56 03. Open Tu-Sa 11am-2pm and 1hr. before performances, F and Sa also 5-7pm.)

CIUTADELLA (CIUDADELA) ☎971

Ciutadella's (pop. 15,000) narrow, cobblestoned paths weave between neighborhoods nearly undisturbed by tourists, while only blocks away, restaurants, shops, and postcard vendors compete for attention in the crowded plazas. There is a seductive charm to the city's ancient streets, broad plazas, and hectic port, and the rugged beauty of the surrounding countryside and nearby beaches provides an easy, exciting escape from city congestion.

▐ TRANSPORTATION

Buses: Transportes Menorca (TMSA) leaves from C. Barcelona, 8 (☎971 38 03 93), to **Maó** (1hr., every hr. 6:45am-9:45pm, €3.90). **Autocares Torres** (☎971 38 64 61) offers daily service from the ticket booth in Pl. de s'Explanada to surrounding beaches, all 15-30min. away. To: **Cala Blanca** and **Santandria** (15min., 1-2 per hr. 7am-10:40pm, €1.10); **Cala Blanes, Los Delfines,** and **Cala Forcat** (10-20min., 1-2 per hr. 7am-11:30pm, €1.10); **Sa Caleta** (25-30min., 1-3 per hr. 7am-12:15am, €1.10).

Ferries: Iscomar de Ferrys (☎902 11 91 28) runs between Ciutadella and **Alcúdia, Mallorca** (2½hr.; M-F 11:30am and 8pm, Sa-Su 8pm; €36). **Cape Balear** (☎902 10 04 44) links Ciutadella to **Cala Ratjada, Menorca** (55min.; May-Oct. 3 per day 7:30am-7:30pm; €45-60).

Taxis: (☎971 38 28 96). Pl. de s'Explanada is a prime hailing spot.

Car Rental: Europcar, Av. de Jaume I, 59 (☎971 38 29 98). 21+. From €39 per day and €210 per wk. Open daily 9am-8pm. The tourist office provides an extensive list of all rental car agencies in the city.

Bike and Scooter Rental: Velos Joan, C. Sant Isidre, 32-34 (☎971 38 15 76). Bike rental €6 per day, €20-26 per wk. 2-day min. scooter rental. Scooters €41-72 for 2 days, €127-236 per wk. Open M-F 8:30am-1:30pm, Sa 9am-1:30pm.

▐ ORIENTATION AND PRACTICAL INFORMATION

To get from the **bus station** to **Plaça de la Catedral** and the tourist office, head left half a block, take a left on C. de Maó, go straight through Pl. d'Alfons III, and continue along C. de Maó as it turns into C. Josep M. Quadrado (ses Voltes) after crossing Pl. Nova. To get from Pl. de la Catedral to **Plaça de s'Explanada** (also called Pl. dels Pins), exit the plaza on C. Major del Born with the cathedral behind you and to the right, cross Pl. d'es Born on its right side, and bear diagonally across to the left. The **port** and its accompanying street, C. Marina, lie below the rest of the city and can be reached via a stone stairway just off the corner of Pl. d'es Born.

Tourist Office: Pl. de la Catedral, 3 (☎971 38 26 93; www.e-menorca.org). Excellent maps available. English spoken. Open June-Sept. daily 9am-9pm; Oct.-May M-F 9am-1pm and 5-7pm, Sa 9am-1pm. **Branch** in Pl. de s'Explanada. Open M-F 9am-2pm.

Banks: BBVA, Pl. d'es Born, 14 (☎971 48 40 04). Open M-F 8:30am-2pm. Other banks with 24hr. **ATMs** can be found around the Pl. de s'Explanada and Pl. d'es Born.

Police: Pl. d'es Born (☎971 38 07 87).

Medical Emergency: Clínica Menorca, C. Canonge Moll (☎971 48 05 05). Open 24hr.

Internet Access: Acceso Directo, Pl. de s'Explanada, 37 (☎971 38 42 15; www.elcafenet.net). €1 per 25min. Open M-Sa 9am-midnight.

Post Office: Pl. d'es Born (☎971 38 00 81). Open May-Oct. M-F 8:30am-8:30pm, Sa 9:30am-1pm; Nov.-Apr. M-F 8:30am-2:30pm, Sa 9:30am-1pm. **Postal Code:** 07760.

ACCOMMODATIONS

Hostels are packed and pricey during peak season (June 15-early Sept.)—double rooms usually run over €30. Always call ahead in the summer. Relax in the centrally located floral paradise of **Hostal Residència Oasis ❹,** C. Sant Isidre, 33. From Pl. de s'Explanada, take Av. del Capità Negrete to Pl. d'Artrutx and C. Sant Isidre. The rooms are clean and bright, but you're better off hanging out on the gorgeous garden patio. (☎971 38 21 97. Breakfast included. Doubles with bath €46.) Another option is **Hotel Geminis ❸,** C. Josepa Rossinyol, 4, whose outdoor terrace has a small pool. Take C. del Sud off Av. del Capita Negrete from Pl. de s'Explanada; turn left onto C. Josepa Rossinyol. The restaurant and plush sitting room complement the fully stocked rooms with wood furniture, phones, baths, A/C, and TV. (☎971 38 58 96; fax 38 36 83. Breakfast included. Mid-June to Sept. singles €50; doubles €80; triples €90. Oct. to mid-May €45/€60/€70.)

FOOD

Most of Ciutadella's options are touristy. Nicer restaurants surround the port, while more generic spots near Pl. de s'Explanada and along C. de Josep M. Quadrado offer cheaper fare. Shop at the **market** on Pl. de la Libertat, or try **Supermarket Super Avui,** C. Sant Onofre, 12. (☎971 38 27 28. Open M-Sa 10am-2pm and 5-8pm.)

HOLD YOUR HORSES!

On the last Thursday in June, Ciutadella celebrates *La Fiesta de San Juan,* a wild festival that rivals the infamous *San Fermín* of Pamplona. It coincides with the shortest night of the year, the summer solstice, and its pagan origins are thought to have marked the triumph of light over dark. One of the most important features of the festivities is fire, and the ashes of the numerous bonfires are thought to cure skin diseases. One is advised (by legend, not by *Let's Go*) to jump through the fire a minimum of three times in order to insure a good year.

The party formally begins with the arrival of the *fabioler* (herald of the ceremony) on a white horse. Playing a drum and flute, he gallops through town for four hours with crowds of drunken Menorcans following close behind. At 6pm, village men ride 250 wild horses through town on their hind legs for as long as the horses can stand it. Successful steeds are rewarded with cheers of *"Olé!"* and the rest charge into the crowd, often knocking over bystanders. In 1999, one horse crashed down on the mayor of Menorca, ending his term for good. Nota bene for future office-holders: some PR opportunities just aren't worth it.

La Guitarra, C. Nuestra Sra. dels Dolors, 1 (☎971 38 13 55). Take C. Major del Born out of Pl. d'es Born and turn right onto C. del Roser, which leads to C. Nuestra Sra. dels Dolors. For traditional island cuisine, descend to this stone cave-turned-restaurant and sample the *sopa mallorquina,* a traditional meat and veggie soup (€5). *Menú* €10. Entrees €6.60-18. Open June-Sept. M-Sa 12:30-3:15pm and 7-11pm. MC/V. ❸

Es Molí, C. de Maó, 1 (☎971 38 00 00). Located inside (yes, inside) the giant windmill across from the Pl. de ses Palmeres, this spacious bar popular with locals serves cheap *bocadillos* and tapas (€1-3). Open daily 5:30am-11pm, later on F and Sa nights. ❶

Pizzeria Restaurant Raco d'es Palau, C. del Palau, 3 (☎971 38 54 02), in an alley off C. Major del Born. Pleasant indoor and outdoor seating complements great pizza (€6.50) and seafood dishes (€9-17.70). Open daily 4pm-midnight. MC/V. ❷

🔘 🎵 SIGHTS AND ENTERTAINMENT

An interesting complement to Menorca's beaches are its various archaeological sites, most of which lie off the highway between Maó and Ciutadella. Keep an eye out for the purple signs. Dating from the Bronze Age, the **⬛Naveta des Tudons,** one of the oldest structures in Europe, is 4km from the city. These ruins of communal tombs are the island's best preserved, and contained the remains of over 100 people. **Torretrencada** and **Torrellafuda** were rounded towers that overlooked the countryside. Both protect Stonehenge-like *taulas,* formations that have stood for over 3000 years. Buses don't come near these sights, so if you don't have a rental car, consider **hiking** (about 5km) along C. Vell de Maó, or **biking** along the highway. The descriptive *Archaeological Guide to Menorca* is available at the tourist office.

The Ciutadella community is one of early-to-bedders. It's more fun heading over to Maó (or better yet, Mallorca or Ibiza) for nightlife. From the first week in July to the beginning of September, Ciutadella hosts the **Festival de Música d'Estiu,** featuring some of the world's top classical musicians. Tickets (€9.60-21) are sold at **Foto Born,** C. Seminari, 14, and at the box office. Concerts take place in the cloisters of the seminary. (☎971 38 17 54. Box office open daily 9:30am-1:30pm and 5-8pm.) On June 22, even veteran partiers from Palma and Eivissa join locals as they burn gallons of midnight oil during **La Fiesta de San Juan** (see **Hold Your Horses!,** p. 377), Menorca's biggest *fiesta.* A week before the festivities, which include jousting and equestrian displays, a man clad in a sheepskin carries a lamb on his shoulders through the city.

BEACHES

Menorca has over 80 beaches. The more popular ones are accessible by bus from Maó and Ciutadella (neither city has its own), but as a result some are overrun by resort hotels, bars, restaurants, and postcard shops, and can get fairly packed during the day. Other beaches are located in small coves, and are naturally more secluded. This fantastic and beautiful variety is best explored with a rental car and the *Let's Go to the Beach* brochure (not affiliated with *Let's Go* guides) and map available at any tourist office. The highway from Maó to Ciutadella is straight and well-maintained; local roads are curvy, pot-holed, and often unpaved. Be careful when driving at night. The list below is divided into stops along the North and South shores, and includes a mix of the more accessible and more remote spots. Given the many options, though, you may discover your own hidden treasure by choosing at random from the map or off the highway.

🔘 NORTH SHORE BEACHES

⬛ **PLATGES D'ALGAIARENS.** This stretch east of Cala Morell is home to the most outstanding beaches on the island, including Cala en Carabó, Penyal de l'Anticrist, Sa Falconera, and Cala Pilar Ets Alocs, all accessible via a path through the woods and over the rocks. Though not as secluded as they used to be, these beaches, surrounded by pine forests in a lush valley, allow you to forget the outside world for a few hours. *(Beaches really only accessible by car, moped, or a long bike ride from Ciutadella. Parking €5, mopeds €2. A taxi from Ciutadella costs €12, but arrange the return trip in advance; there are no pay phones, and cell phones may lose service.)*

ARENAL D'EN CASTELL. Breathtaking views, calm, turquoise water, and soft, white sand make this tiny cove a popular destination for daytrippers from Maó and vacationing families who populate the upscale resorts and condos dotting the slope above the beach. A tourist train, "Arenal Na Macaret Express," makes the short trip from the bus stop in Arenal across a narrow strip of land to **Macaret,** a tiny fishing village with an even tinier beach. *(Autocares Fornells leave from Maó. 30min.; M-Sa 7 per day 9:30am-7pm, Su 3 per day 11am-6:30pm; €1.90.)*

ALBUFERA ES GRAU. A large natural reserve, Albufera Es Grau entices visitors with lagoons, pine woods, and farmland, as well as diverse flora and fauna. Recreational activities include hiking to the coves across the bay. Some of the best swimming areas are across from the main lagoon and uphill from town, along a series of bluffs and secluded coves; only the sound of the water lapping at the rocks can be heard. *(Park info ☎971 43 17 82.)* **Viajes Isla Colom** sends boats from the marina on the lagoon in Es Grau to **Illa d'en Colom,** an island with more beaches. *(☎971 35 98 67. 4 boats per day 10:30am-5pm, last return 7pm; round-trip €14.30. Autocares Fornells leave from Maó. 20min.; M-Sa 3 per day 10:30am-6pm, Su 5 per day; €1.)*

FORNELLS. A long fence made of driftwood leads you into the small fishing village of Fornells. Known primarily for its lobster farms, this charming town has only recently begun to attract tourists. Windsurfers zip around Fornells's shallow port, while beach gurus make excursions to the golden sands of **Cala Tirant,** only a few kilometers to the west. *(Autobuses Fornells leave from Maó. 30min., 5 per day 10:45am-7pm, €2.50.)*

◨ SOUTH SHORE BEACHES

▨**CALA MITJANA.** Thirty minutes from Maó, this small beach overlooks a dramatic cove bordered by limestone cliffs that plunge into the turquoise sea. Though it is not totally secluded, if you climb the staircase on your right upon entering the cove and head down the dirt path for about five minutes, you get to ▨**Cala Mitjaneta,** a smaller cove with a tiny beach and even more dramatic views of white cliffs and the wide expanse of the Mediterranean beyond the inlet. While some visitors wade into the water here, others prove their bravery (or recklessness) by diving from the rocks. *(On the main highway from Maó to Ciutadella, head toward Ferreries, and then take the road to Santa Galdana. Directly on the left before reaching the roundabout above the town is the dirt road that leads to Cala Mitjana. Park in the small dirt lot and continue on foot.)*

ELS CANUTELLS. Situated off the road from Maó to Cala'n Porter (a 15min. drive from Maó), Els Canutells is a pleasant and secluded cove with calm, turquoise waters good for swimming and snorkeling, and dotted with the boats of loyal visitors. A couple of bars and restaurants are on the road above the cove. *(TMSA buses run to and from Maó. 20min., 4 per day 8:45am-7pm, €1.20.)*

CALA'N PORTER. Expansive and touristy, Cala'n Porter greets thousands of visitors each summer with its whitewashed houses, orange stucco roofs, and red sidewalks. Its small, grassy beach lies at the bottom of a steep, bouldered hillside, but pedestrian access is easy via the main road and a marked staircase. *(TMSA buses run to and from Maó. M-Sa 7 per day 9:30am-7:40pm, €1.20.)* A 10min. walk away, at the end of Av. Central, the ▨ **Covas d'en Xoroi** dominate cliffs high above the sea. The caves are inhabited by an amazing network of bars which transforms into a popular disco (attracting mostly a young British crowd) by night, all with a gorgeous view of the vast Mediterranean. (☎971 37 72 36; www.covadenxoroi.com. Cover for bars before 6:30pm €5; 6:30pm–10:30pm €8.50, includes 1 drink. Cover for disco €15-25. Bars open Apr.-Oct. daily 10:30am-10:30pm. Disco open daily 11pm-late. Foam parties Th.)

PLATGES DE SON BOU. The longest beach on the island, Son Bou offers 4km of sand covered with throngs of sunburnt tourists. As the most popular of Menorca's beaches, it's also the most visitor-friendly, with frequent bus service to and from Maó and Ciutadella, ample parking, endless beach chairs, umbrellas for rent, and cafes. There are even *discotecas* only two blocks from the sand. Be aware, though, that part of the beach is also for nudists, and the farther away from the commercial center you walk, the more naked it gets. (TMSA buses to the beaches leave from Maó. 30min., 7 per day 8:45am-7pm, €1.70.) For those who choose to stay late, **Disco Pub Copacabana,** in the Nuevo Centro Comercial, on the left when heading away from the water, is the best place to rock your evening, with a huge dance floor, pool tables, and a full arcade, all with a great view of the water. (Mixed drinks €5.50. Open May-Oct. daily 11pm-3:30am.) If you're just in the mood for a relaxing frozen drink, head across the street to the big rattan chairs and couches of **Bou Hai Hawaiian Bar,** which serves margaritas and daiquiris in its hut for €5.50-8. (Open daily noon-3am.) If you do stay late, make sure you have a rental car or a place to stay—after 7:35pm, there is no public transportation back to Maó until morning.

PUNTA PRIMA. While this beach may not be as secluded or expansive as some, it draws a crowd due to its proximity to Maó. A lighthouse on a strip of land across from the beach overlooks a coastline surrounded by restaurants, supermarkets, and touristy shops. If you're there for lunch, stop by **Bar Agnes ❷,** on the main strip across from the beach, for reasonably priced sandwiches (€2.50) and salads served in ceramic bowls (€5-6.50). They even have a swimming pool on their back terrace that you can use free of charge. (TMSA buses run to and from Maó. 20min.; M-F 9 per day 8:30am-7:30pm, Su 8 per day 9:30am-7:30pm; €1.20.)

IBIZA (EIVISSA)

Nowhere on Earth does style rule over substance (or substances rule over style) more than on Ibiza (pop. 84,000). A hippie enclave in the 1960s, Ibiza has forgotten her roots in favor of a new age of decadence. Disco fiends, fashion gurus, movie stars, and party-hungry backpackers arrive in droves to debauch in the outrageous party culture that permeates the island. However, not every night has to be filled with hedonism and glam; much of Ibiza's wild see-and-be-seen disco culture exists at only a few megaclubs. It's not uncommon to linger over dinner or chill at a waterfront bar. A thriving gay community lends credence to Ibiza's image as a center of tolerance, but the island's high price tags preclude true diversity.

Surprisingly, there is more to Ibiza than spectacular nightlife; its beaches and mountains are some of the most spectacular in all the Baleares. The island's rich history has left its mark in the form of several ancient castles—the most prominent in Eivissa (Ibiza City). Since the Carthaginians retreated to Ibiza from the mainland in 656 BC, the island's list of conquerors reads like a "Who's Who of Ancient Western Civilization." Perhaps the most famous was the 1235 invasion by the Catalans, who brought Christianity and built the walls that still fortify Eivissa.

IBIZA CITY (EIVISSA) ☎971

Eivissa (pop. 35,000) is the world's biggest 24hr. party. The town itself is like Dr. Jekyll and Mr. Hyde. During the day, families meander and sightsee through the walled D'alt Vila, and the city streets remain tranquil while the majority of visitors sleep off hangovers, tanning at nearby beaches. Eivissa could easily be any other seaside village in Spain. At night, however, there's no mistaking this town for any other. Flashy bars appear seemingly out of nowhere, filling street after street with neon lights, blasting music, and fast-talking club promoters; stores take extra-long *siestas* during the afternoon to stay open until 1 or 2am, and throngs of beautiful people walk the streets dressed up for each other. Grab a front-row seat at the outdoor tables to enjoy the prime people-watching action. Come 3am, the scene migrates to the clubs outside of town, where parties last until dawn (and often well into the next day)—then, it all begins again.

▐ TRANSPORTATION

Flights: Airport (☎971 80 90 00), 7km south of the city. Bus #10 runs between the airport and Av. d'Isidor Macabich, 20, in town (30min., every hr. 7am-11.10pm, €1.10). Info open 24hr. **Iberia,** Pg. Vara de Rey, 15 (☎902 40 05 00), flies to Alicante, Barcelona, Madrid, Palma, and Valencia. **Air Europa, Vueling,** and **Spanair** offer similar options. See **By Plane,** p. 356, or **Inter-Island Transport,** p. 356.

Ferries: Estació Marítima. Trasmediterránea (☎971 31 51 00) sells tickets for ferries to **Barcelona, Palma,** and **Valencia.** Office open M-F 9am-1pm, 4:30-7:30pm, and 2hr. before departures. **Trasmapi-Balearia** (☎971 31 40 05) runs daily to **Dénia,** near Alicante, and **Palma.** Office open M-F 9am-2:15pm, 4:30-8pm, and midnight-1:15am; Sa 9am-2:15pm and 6-8pm; Su 9am-2:15pm and midnight-1:15am. **Umafisa Lines** (☎971 21 02 01) sends boats to **Barcelona** 3-4 times per week. For rates and schedules, see **By Boat,** p. 356, or **Inter-Island Transport,** p. 356.

Buses: Eivissa has a fairly extensive bus system, although buses to more remote beaches and villages run only a few times per day, so plan accordingly. The main bus stop is on Av. d'Isidor Macabich, past Pl. d'Enric Fajarnés i Tur walking away from the port. For an exact schedule, check the tourist office or *El Diario.* Intercity buses (€1.80) leave from Av. d'Isidor Macabich, 42 (☎971 31 21 17), to **Sant Antoni** (M-Sa every 15min., Su every 30min. 7am-11:30pm; €1.50) and **Santa Eulària des Riu** (M-F every 30min., Sa-Su every hr. 7:30am-11:30pm; €2). Buses (☎971 34 03 82) to the beaches cost €1.20 and leave from Av. d'Isidor Macabich, 20, and Av. d'Espanya to: **Cala Tarida** (5 per day 10:10am-6:45pm); **Cap Martinet** (M-Sa 11 per day 8:15am-8pm); **Platja d'en Bossa** (every 30min. 8:30am-11pm); **Salinas** (every hr. 9:30am-7:30pm).

Taxis: ☎971 39 84 83.

Car and Moped Rental: Casa Valentín, Av. B.V. Ramón, 19 (☎971 31 08 22). Mopeds €25-30 per day. Cars from €39 per day. Open daily 9am-1pm and 3:30-8:30pm.

▣ ▐ ORIENTATION AND PRACTICAL INFORMATION

Three distinct sections make up the city. **Sa Penya,** in front of Estació Marítima, is crammed with bars and boutiques. Atop the hill behind Sa Penya, high walls circle **D'alt Vila,** the old city. **La Marina** and the commercial district occupy the gridded streets to the far right (with your back to the water) of the Estació. **Avinguda d'Espanya,** continuing from Pg. Vara de Rey, heads toward the airport and local beaches. The local paper *Diario de Ibiza* (€1; www.diariodeibiza.es) has an *Agenda* page that lists essential information, including the bus schedule for the entire island, the ferry schedule, the schedule of all domestic flights to and from Ibiza, water and weather forecasts, info on the island's 24hr. pharmacies, a list of 24hr. gas stations, and important phone numbers.

Tourist Office: Pl. d'Antoni Riquer, 2 (☎971 30 19 00), right across from the Estació Marítima. Open June-Nov. M-F 9am-9pm, Sa 9:30am-7:30pm; Dec.-May M-F 8:30am-3pm, Sa 10:30am-1pm. **Booths** at the end of Pg. Vara de Rey and at the airport (☎971 80 91 18). Open May-Oct. M-Sa 9am-2pm and 3-8pm, Su 9am-2pm.

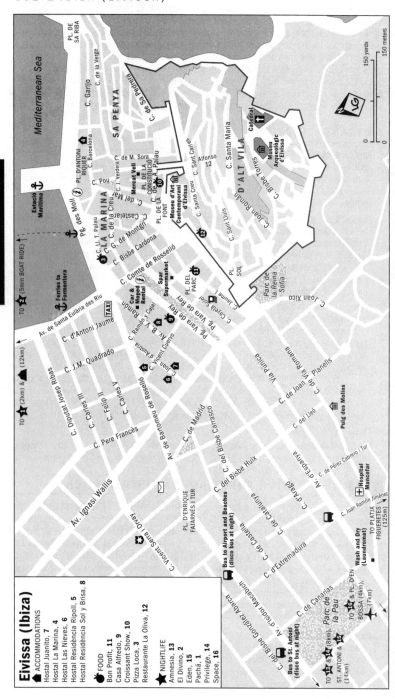

LAS ISLAS BALEARES

Eivissa (Ibiza)

▲ ACCOMMODATIONS
Hostal Juanito, **7**
Hostal La Marina, **4**
Hostal Las Nieves, **6**
Hostal Residència Ripoll, **5**
Hostal Residència Sol y Brisa, **8**

● FOOD
Bon Profit, **11**
Casa Alfredo, **9**
Croissant Show, **10**
Pizza Loca, **3**
Restaurante La Oliva, **12**

★ NIGHTLIFE
Amnesia, **13**
El Divino, **2**
Eden, **15**
Pachá, **1**
Privilege, **14**
Space, **16**

Currency Exchange: Exchanges are all over town; banks and ATMs offer better rates. **La Caixa,** Av. d'Isidor Macabich, has good exchange rates for cash and travelers checks.

Laundromat: Wash and Dry, Av. d'Espanya, 53 (☎971 39 48 22). Self service wash and dry €10 for 8kg, €13 if they do it for you. **Internet access** €1 per 15min., €1.50 per 30min., €3 per hr. Open M-Sa 10am-9pm.

Police: C. Vicent Serra i Orvay, 25 (☎971 31 58 61).

Medical Assistance: Hospital: Barri Can Misses (☎971 39 70 00), west of town, and **Hospital Nuestra Señora** (☎971 39 70 21). **Ambulance:** ☎971 39 32 32.

Internet Access: ◼ **Noon,** C. Cayetà Soler, 9 (☎971 39 48 50). Without a doubt the coolest place to check e-mail. Also a book and clothing store, and a bar in back. €2 per 20min., €5 per hr. Open M-Sa 10:30am-2:30pm and 5pm-midnight. **E-connect,** C. Guillem de Montgrí, 3 (☎971 19 46 07). €0.90 per 15min., €3.50 per hr., €15 for 5hr. Wireless access. Open daily summer 10am-1am, winter 10am-10pm.

Post Office: C. Madrid (☎971 31 43 23). **Lista de Correos.** Open M-F 8:30am-8:30pm, Sa 9:30am-2pm. **Postal Code:** 07800.

🏠 🏕 ACCOMMODATIONS AND CAMPING

Decent, cheap *hostales* in town are rare, especially in the summer—but then again, who actually *sleeps* here anyway? Call several weeks in advance for summer stays, when prices climb and hostels fill fast. The letters "CH" *(casa de huéspedes)* mark many doorways; the owner can often be reached at the phone number on the door. Eivissa has a relatively safe and up-all-night lifestyle, and owners offer keys for 24hr. entry. All prices listed below are for high season and can drop by as much as €12 in the off-season. The tourist office offers an extensive list of all lodging options in the city.

Hostal Residència Sol y Brisa, Av. B. V. Ramón, 15 (☎971 31 08 18; fax 30 30 32). Upstairs from Pizzeria da Franco. Clean and centrally located with a social atmosphere. Singles €25; doubles €44. ❷

Hostal La Marina, C. Barcelona, 7 (☎971 31 01 72; fax 31 48 94), amid the raucous bar scene. Rooms have beautiful, sophisticated mosaic decor. 4 buildings offer lodging ranging from stark to lavish. The best (and priciest) have TV, A/C, private bath, carpet, and balcony. Singles €41-62; doubles €56-150; studio apts. for 5 people €160. ❺

Hostal Residència Ripoll, C. Vicent Cuervo, 10-14 (☎971 31 42 75). Fastidiously clean hallways and baths and unusually large, fan-cooled rooms with pretty bedspreads are among the best in town. Apartments are more spacious and fun. July-Sept. singles €30; doubles €42; triples €57; 3-person apts. with TV, patio, and kitchen €78. Oct.-June €20/€30/€33/€450 per month. ❸

Hostal Juanito/Hostal Las Nieves, C. Joan d'Austria, 17-18 (☎971 19 03 19). Run by the same owner, both hostels offer cheap housing in a central area. Rooms are basic and bare-walled, but more than adequate for sleeping off a hangover. Singles €21; doubles €42, with bath €50. ❷

Camping Es Cana (☎971 33 21 17; fax 33 99 71; www.ibiza-spotlight.com/campes-cana). Reserve by fax. €6.25 per person, €6.50-10 per tent (depending on the number of people). Bungalows €40-62; cabins €18.30.

Camping Cala Nova (☎971 33 17 74). Take bus #13 or 15 from Eivissa to Sta. Eulària des Riu, and then bus #18 from Sta. Eulària d'alt to Es Cana. Sites are a 10min. walk from the bus stop; follow signs. €5.40 per person, €4.60 per tent. ❶

🍴 FOOD

Eivissa has some amazing restaurants, but good, inexpensive cuisine is hard to find; it's not uncommon to see budget travelers stocking up at grocery stores or chowing down at fast food joints to save their euros for the discos. Cafes offering

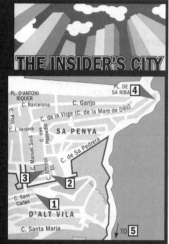

THE INSIDER'S CITY

A GAY OLD TIME

Ibiza is one of the most gay-friendly beach retreats in the world. Although every club here has a mixed crowd, some are gayer than others. The heart of the scene is on C. de la Virge and C. Alfonso XII, where terraces offer cruising opportunities galore. We've picked out the best of the best, but for a more complete list, check out the *Plano Gay de Ibiza* (Gay Map of Ibiza), stop by Socio, C. Madrid, 52b, the center for gay tourism, or browse the listings on www.ibigay.com.

1 **Anfora,** C. Sant Carles, 7, in the D'alt Vila. The city's only completely gay disco. A small maze of tiled bars and terraces; the dance floor is a cave-like pit with a ceiling of disco balls and throngs of shirtless partiers. Don't miss "Night Fever" every Th: all your favorite classics from "I Will Survive" to Whitney Houston. Cover before 2am €8, after 2am €12; includes 1 drink. Open daily midnight-6am.

the usual touristy fare line the port, while cheaper options are around **Plaça del Parc,** just off Pg. Vara del Rey. Eivissan dishes include *sofrit pagès,* a deep-fried lamb and chicken dish; *flao,* a lush lemon- and mint-tinged cheesecake; and *graxonera,* cinnamon-dusted pudding made from eggs and bits of *ensaimada* (candied bread). The **Mercat Vell** sells meat, fruit, and vegetables (open M-Sa 7am-1pm). For **groceries,** try **Spar.** (Open M-Sa 9am-9pm.)

Bon Profit, Pl. del Parc. For the mere 4hr. per day that Bon Profit is open, it overflows with locals waiting for a table to sample the most delicious (and cheapest) Spanish cuisine around. It also has the distinction of being one of the only restaurants in town (and in Spain) that is smoke-free. Entrees €2-9. Open M-Sa 1-3pm and 8-10pm. ●

Croissant Show, Mercat Vell (☎971 31 76 65), at the corner of C. Antoni Palau. Tasty sandwiches, quiches, and salads, a delectable variety of pastries and cakes, and prime people watching by the entrance to the D'Alt Vila make this lively cafe a perfect spot for a late lunch or "breakfast" after a hard night's clubbing. Sandwiches €4.30-5.60, salads €6.50-8, quiche €3.10, pastries €1.10-3.50. Open daily 6am-midnight. ●

Restaurante La Oliva, C. Santa Creu, 2 (☎971 30 57 52). Pricey but scrumptious Italian fare in a cozy, homey atmosphere. For a candlelit outdoor table it's best to make a reservation. Pasta €8-11; meat and fish entrees €9-18. Open daily 8pm-1am. ❸

Casa Alfredo, Pg. Vara de Rey, 16 (☎971 31 12 74). Fish, meat, and heavenly desserts fill the *menú* (€6-9) that locals deem the best in town. Also a good place for a nice dinner. Entrees €10-25. Open M-Sa 1-4pm and 8pm-midnight. ❸

Pizza Loca, C. Lluís Tur i Palau, 15 (☎971 31 45 68). Rectangular pizzas with a variety of toppings including vegetables, tuna, and salami. Eat outside at wooden tables or get it to go and chow down on the beach. Slices €2-3. Open daily noon-5am. ●

⊙ SIGHTS

Wrapped in 16th-century walls, **D'alt Vila** (High Town) rises above the town. Its twisting streets lead to the 14th-century **cathedral,** built in several phases and styles. (Open daily 10:30am-1pm.) Across a small plaza from the cathedral is the **Museu Arqueològic d'Eivissa,** home to a variety of regional artifacts. (Open Tu-Sa 10am-2pm and 6-8pm, Su 10am-2pm. €2.40, students €1.20.) Within stone walls, the small **Museu d'Art Contemporani d'Eivissa** displays a range of art exhibitions. (C. Sa

Carrossa, on the left when entering from Pl. de sa Font. ☎ 971 30 27 23. Open M-F 10am-1pm and 6:30-10pm, Sa 10am-1:30pm. €1.20, students free.) The archaeological museum, **Puig des Molins,** Vía Romana, displays Punic, Roman, and Iberian artifacts. (☎ 971 30 17 71. Open M-Sa 10am-2pm and 6-8pm, Su 10am-2pm. €1.20.)

🏖 BEACHES

In Eivissa, if you're not at a disco, you're at the beach. The power of the rising sun draws thousands of topless solar zombies to nearby tanning grounds. ◪**Platja de ses Salinas** does the beach as only Eivissa can. Bask among the beautiful people and groove to chilled-out house pulsating from **Sa Trincha** bar at the end of the beach, or reserve a beach chair in front of **The Jockey Club** and receive full bar and restaurant service right from the sand while top DJs warm up for their club gigs. Club promoters walk the sands offering bracelets and flyers for discount covers or even free entrance, if you make the cut. (Bus runs every 30min. to Salinas from Av. d'Isidor Macabich.) **Platja Figueretes,** a thin stretch of sand in the shadow of large hotels, is the best foot-accessible beach from Eivissa. To get there, walk about 10min. down Av. d'Espanya and take a left onto Av. del País Vasco. Farther down, and best accessible by bus, **Platja d'en Bossa** is the liveliest of Eivissa's beaches, with numerous beach bars and throngs of sun-seeking tourists who pack its hotels. (Bus runs every 30min. from Av. d'Isidor Macabich.) **Platja des Duros** is tucked across the bay from Sa Penya and Sa Marina, just before the lighthouse. **Platja de Talamanca,** whose water is more an enclosed bay than open sea, is accessible on foot by following the road to the new port and continuing on to the beach (20min.). **Platja des Cavallet** attracts a beautiful, largely gay crowd showing off their bodies—in some cases, their entire bodies. To get there, take the bus from Eivissa to Salinas; get off at the stop before Salinas (called Can Tixedo) and follow the signs to the beach (10min.) or walk from Salinas (20min.). If you choose the latter option, stay on the wide, main path, as it's easy to get lost among the many trails that lead up and down the coast. Getting lost, though, is not the worst thing in the world here, as you're sure to be rewarded: jagged limestone cliffs shelter welcoming tidal pools and even the occasional ruin, white sands, and lush pine forests buzzing with cicadas. The main path is easy to find again.

2 **Angelo,** C. Alfonso XII, 11. Just around the corner from **Dome** lies one of the most popular gay bars in the city. The terrace is a bit of a meat market, but it is everyone's first stop before Anfora or any of the discos. Its beautiful interior is also a restaurant. Beer €3, mixed drinks €5-7. Open daily 10pm-4am.

3 **Dome,** C. Alfonso XII (www.dome.es). Bask among the beautiful people here if you're fabulous enough to get a table on the terrace. Although not exclusively gay, its location alone makes it popular with the gay crowd. Beer €5.50-7.50, mixed drinks €9.50-11.50. Open daily 10pm-4am.

4 **Bar Teatro,** C. de la Virge, 83 (www.barteatro.com). The last bar on C. de la Virge is a must-see for theater fans. Run by a pair of friendly Brits, the walls are plastered with posters from London's theater seasons past and present, and the music is a delightful mix of queeny hits and show-tune dance remixes. Beer €3, mixed drinks €6. Open daily 10pm-3:30am.

5 **Chiringay,** on the sands of Platja des Cavallet, Ibiza's gayest beach. This overflowing bar and restaurant is where you'll find scores of scantily clad guys all day, whether they're having a drink or one of the amazing salads. Beer €5, mixed drinks €7-10. Entrees and salads €6-20. Open daily 10am-9pm.

More private coastal stretches lie in the northern and southwestern parts of the island and are accessible by car or moped. Among these, the German enclave at **Cala de Sant Vicent** (past Santa Eulària des Riu on the road to St. Carles de Peralta) offers white sands and breathtaking views that are far from secluded, but peaceful nonetheless. The small coves in the rocky northernmost point of the island (between Portinatx and St. Agnes de Corona) are worth visiting if you seek serenity or the company of modern-day flower children. **Cala Xarraca** is a beautiful cove popular with families, who fight for spots on its small beach. **Cala Carbó,** south of St. Antoni and west of St. Josep, offers a small but beautiful beach with picturesque cliffs and a fantastic beachfront seafood restaurant. The tourist office has a great map of all the beaches with pictures, descriptions, and driving directions.

▶ NIGHTLIFE

The crowds return from the beaches by nightfall, when even the stores dazzle with throbbing techno and flashing lights. Herds of people representing each club parade through the streets, advertising their disco and trying to outdo others. Meanwhile, seaport bars crawl with aggressive promoters. **Bars** in Eivissa are crowded midnight-3am and are everyone's first stop before hitting the discos. The scene centers on **Carrer de Barcelona** and spins outward into the side streets. **Carrer de la Verge**, **Carrer Alfonso XII,** and the surrounding streets are the center of gay nightlife and outrageous fashion (see **A Gay Old Time,** p. 384). Cocktails can cost as much as €10 and beer rings in at around €6, so if you plan on drinking a lot, either pre-game on your own or head to the cheaper bar scene in Sant Antoni (p. 388).

The island's **discos** are world-famous—veterans claim that you will never experience anything half as wild or fun, and virtually all have a mixed gay-straight crowd. The best sources of information on types of parties and DJs are discogoers and the zillions of posters that plaster the stores and restaurants of La Marina and Sa Penya. There is something different each day of the week, and each club is known for a particular theme party—be sure to hit up clubs on these nights, or you'll end up shelling out a lot of money for a not-so-happening party. For listings, check out *DJ* magazine, free at many hostels, bars, and restaurants. Drinks at Eivissa's clubs cost about €10, and covers start at €30. If you know where you're going ahead of time, buy your disco tickets from a promoter at or in front of the bars in town; you'll pay €6-18 less than what you would pay at the door, and it's completely legit—some tickets even include transportation and admission to **Space,** the beachfront after-hours club, although these deals are more often found in Sant Antoni. Most of the discos have their own bars, restaurants, and clothing stores where tickets are sold. In many of these places it's possible to be "chosen" by promoters and get a wristband that will get you in for free or at least get you a lot of extras with your cover. Look hot and don't be afraid to approach or bargain with them. They almost always give great deals to groups (especially of girls).

Generally, disco-goers bar-hop in Eivissa or Sant Antoni and jet off to clubs via bus or taxi around 3am. Almost all discos are located fairly far from town and require some kind of transport. The exceptions are **Eden** and **Es Paradis** in St. Antoni, which are accessible by foot. The **Discobus** runs to all the hotspots (leaves Eivissa from Av. d'Isidor Macabich every hr. 12:30am-6:30am, schedule for other stops available at tourist office and hotels; €1.75).

Other than the ones listed here, there are a few smaller, cheaper discos that are popular with locals and expats. **Underground** and **La Diosa** are two, but as they're not part of the mega-PR scene, it's harder to get info on them. Ask around where you see posters, but don't leave Eivissa without checking out at least one of the major locales. If you pick a good night, you'll definitely get your money's worth.

Pachá (☎971 31 36 00; www.pacha.com), 15min. walk from the port, 2min. in a taxi. The most famous club chain in Spain, and the most elegant of Eivissa's discos. Locals and tourists get their groove on in the beautiful, airy main room, or chill out on the roof-top terrace with views of the port. Given its prestige and popularity, any night is a good night to go. "Renaissance" on Th brings the best up and coming DJs, and the fabulous "F*** Me I'm Famous" parties on F attract a rowdy crowd, but few celebrities. Only club open year-round in Eivissa. Cover €50. Open daily midnight-7:30am.

Amnesia (☎971 19 80 41; www.amnesiaibiza.com), on the road to Sant Antoni; take the Discobus. Converted warehouse with psychedelic lights and movie screens has 2 gigantic rooms; a largely gay crowd congregates around the upper left corner of the left one, especially on W. Best known for "Cream" on Th, when London DJs play hard house or trance, but the night to go is "La Troya Asesina" on W, when drag performances take over the left room, and foam soaks the crowd on the right. Cover from €40. Open daily midnight-8am.

Privilege (☎971 19 80 86; www.privilege-ibiza.com), on the Discobus to Sant Antoni, or a €9 taxi. The world's largest club, according to the *Guinness Book of World Records*, and an experience like no other. This enormous complex packs in up to 10,000 with bars numbering in the double digits, a glowing open-air dome, and a pool in which the world's best DJs spin a crazy variety of music. While financial problems force the club to open only its main room some nights, it's still the place to be on M for its infamous ▨**"Manumission"** parties, an institution that just celebrated its 10th anniversary. Cover from €40. Open June-Sept. daily midnight-8am.

El Divino, Puerto Ibiza Nueva (☎971 31 83 38; www.eldivino-ibiza.com), 20min. walk from the port (keep right at the round-about), €6 cab ride, or take the shuttle boat from the port (runs until 4am, look for El Divino signs; €1.80). Small, energetic club on the water—worth it just for the view, although exotic dancers, fun, thumping house, and the young British crowd aren't too shabby either. Head to the waterfront terrace for a break from techno insanity. Best nights are "Hed Kandi" on Sa and "Kinky Malinki" on M, if you want an option cheaper than Manumission. El Divino tickets will reimburse you for the shuttle boat. Cover €40. Open mid-June to mid-Sept. daily midnight-7:30am. V.

Space, Platja d'en Bossa (☎971 39 67 93; www.space-ibiza.com). The official after-hours hotspot for just about every club in Eivissa. Starts hopping around 8am, peaks mid-afternoon, and doesn't wind down until after 5pm. The metallic get-up, techno music, video-cubes, and X-Box stations are almost as hardcore as the dancers. An out-door dance terrace has a more low-key atmosphere; music starts there around 10am, and don't forget your sunglasses. "We Love Space" on Su mornings rocks out non-stop for a full 22 hours until 6am on M. "Matinee Group" on Sa mornings and the after par-ties on Tu and Th mornings are also popular. Cover €30-55.

Eden, C. Salvador Espíritu (☎971 34 25 51), across from the beach in Sant Antoni. Gaining in popularity, Eden pulls out all the stops for "Judgement Sunday," when DJ Judge Jules attracts huge crowds, mostly of young Brits staying in Sant Antoni. "Urban Flava," its F hip-hop night, brings in some big names; P. Diddy made an appearance last summer. Retro nights on Tu feature house from the past decade. Garden decor (naturally) and sunken dance floor. Cover €37-45. Open daily midnight-7am.

SAN ANTONIO DE PORTMANY (SANT ANTONI)

Every summer, masses of young Brits migrate to Sant Antoni. The rowdy nightlife and down-to-earth atmosphere combined with its proximity to some of the island's best beaches turn the town into a twenty-something enclave. With two clubs, plenty of bars, and cheaper food and accommodations than Eivissa, Sant Antoni is the perfect budget alternative to its sister city's high prices and lifestyle. While the rowdy, largely British scene dominates some areas (especially C. de Santa Agnés, or "the West End"), Sant Antoni's quieter streets and squares provide a relaxing alternative to the loud, up-all-night atmosphere that prevails on much of the island.

TRANSPORTATION AND PRACTICAL INFORMATION. Buses run from the end of Pg. de la Mar in Sant Antoni to: **Cala Bassa** (20min., 8 per day 9:30am-6:30pm, €1.20); **Cala Conta** (15min., 7 per day 9:10am-6pm, €1.20); **Cala Tarida** (10min., 8 per day 9:30am-7:05pm, €1.20); **Eivissa** (25min.; every 30min. M-Sa 7-9:30am and 10-11:30pm, every 15min. 9:45am-9:30pm, Su every 30min. 7:30am-10:30pm; €1.50); **Santa Eulària** (35min., M-Sa 4 per day 9:30am-6pm, €1.10). **Ferries** leave Sant Antoni for **Dénia** (see **Inter-Island Transport,** p. 356). Smaller companies run daily **boats** to nearby beaches. Signs posted along the port have schedules. For a **taxi,** call ☎971 34 07 79. Sant Antoni is easy to get around, as major streets lie on something of a grid. For **car** and **moped rental,** try **Motos Luis,** Av. Portmany, 5. (☎971 34 05 21. Mopeds from €22. Cars from €39. Open M-Sa 9am-2pm and 4-8pm, Su 9am-2pm.) The **tourist office** is a stone building in the middle of the pedestrian thoroughfare by Pg. de ses Fonts. (☎971 34 33 63. Open M-F 9:30am-2:30pm and 3-8:30pm, Sa 9am-1pm, Su 9:30am-1:30pm.) Local services include: a **laundromat, Wash & Dry La Vaca,** C. Soledad, 36 (☎971 80 38 34; 7kg €13, ironing €2 per item; open daily 7am-9pm); **police,** Av. Portmany, km 14 (☎971 34 08 30); **Centro de Salud,** C. d'Alacant (☎971 34 51 21); **Internet access** at **Surfanet,** C. B.V. Ramón, 5 bajo (☎971 80 39 47; €0.90 per 15min., €1.20 per 30min; open daily 10am-midnight.)

ACCOMMODATIONS AND FOOD. *Hostales* in Sant Antoni are numerous, cheap, and full of Brits. Call well in advance for any summer stay; in the low season, prices drop. **Hostal Residència Roig ❸,** C. del Progrés, 44, has gorgeous, clean rooms with private baths, comfortable couches in the lobby, and access to a nearby hotel's pool. (☎971 34 04 83. Singles €30; doubles €50; triples €75.) The large bedrooms, huge TV lounge, and great location make **Hostal Salada ❷,** C. de la Soledat, 34, one of the best bargains in town. Walk up C. B.V. Ramón from the port and turn left onto C. de la Soledat. (☎971 34 11 30. Singles €15.50-18.50; doubles €30.50-33.50; triples €36.50.) Another option is clean, spacious **Hostal Rita ❷,** C. B.V. Ramón, 17B. All singles share common bath, but some doubles and triples have private ones. (☎971 34 63 32. Singles €24; doubles €35, with bath €42.) **Restaurants** are all over Sant Antoni. A variety of choices are available at the outdoor cafes along Pg. de la Mar or on its side streets leading uphill. Of the more trendy beachfront establishments, ⬛**The Orange Corner ❶,** Av. Dr. Fleming, 24, stands out. The orange building right on the water serves cheap sandwiches, salads, fruit drinks, milkshakes, and alcoholic favorites on a neon terrace. The restaurant also hosts pre-parties and sells tickets to many of the discos, including El Divino. (Entrees €5-8. Alcoholic milkshakes €6, non-alcoholic shakes and smoothies €4. Open daily 10am-4am.) For cheap eats with an ocean view in a slightly less hectic setting, try **Manilla ❷,** C. del General Balanzat, 19, just down the beach from Café de la Mar, next to the apartments of the same name. Pastas (€6-9), Mexican entrees (€8-12), and crepes (€6-8.50) are served by candlelight on an ample terrace with a fountain. (☎971 34 55 24. Open daily noon-midnight.)

BEACHES AND NIGHTLIFE. The town itself is situated on a long, narrow strip of sand, but better beaches are only a stone's throw away. Check out **Cala Bassa,** one of the more popular tanning spots, for a gorgeous (and sometimes nude) beach that's accessible by bus. **Cala Gració,** 1.5km from Sant Antoni, is easily reached on foot. **Santa Eulària des Riu** is more built up and substantially larger than some of the other beaches nearby. Hoof it or bike to the small coves of **Es Povet** and **Caló d'es Moro.** If you have a car or moped, head to **Cala Salada,** just a few kilometers north of town, for calm waters and a picturesque hippie community.

Sant Antoni's **nightlife** revolves largely around three main areas. The area on the far end of town, near the littered beach of Es Ganguil, has several waterfront bars. Most of these have connections to the big discos and can offer great deals on cover and transport. Crowds gather on the small beach to watch the ■**sunset** and chill to mellow house. Chic **Café Mambo** is a popular pre-party bar with a tiny interior and a huge terrace. It's also the official pre-Pachá stop. Spacious **Savannah** attracts a well-dressed, older crowed with its mosaic decor, and, much farther down toward Caló d'es Moro, **Kanya** offers a lively scene in a bright yellow tent overlooking the sea. **Café de la Mar,** "the original sunset bar," serves overpriced drinks in an art deco mansion atmosphere. The crowded streets of town are packed with low-key watering holes and drunk pre-partiers. The beach bar at **Eden** (p. 387), **M Bar,** Manumission's official pre-party bar, and mini-discos facing the main beach round out the options. Compared to the competitive club scene of Eivissa, the nightlife options in Sant Antoni are much more casual and relaxed.

FORMENTERA

The tiny island of Formentera provides a quiet, picturesque getaway from more hectic Ibiza. Despite the recent invasions of bourgeois, beach-hungry Spaniards, Germans, and Italians who have built opulent summer homes here, the island's stunning beaches maintain a sense of hypnotic calm. The most popular one is **Platja des Illetes,** a long stretch north of the port where soft, golden sands meet the rolling, turquoise Mediterranean. Although there are buses, by far the cheapest and most enjoyable way to explore Formentera is by renting a ■**bike;** the island's size and distinction as the flattest of the Baleares makes it a fun and easy place to explore on two wheels. The **tourist office,** located in the port complex, offers a comprehensive list of Green Tours for hikers and cyclists, and bike paths and rental agencies are plentiful. (☎971 32 20 57. Open M-F 10am-2pm and 5-7pm, Sa 10am-2pm.) The island itself is pricey and often visited as an expensive daytrip from Eivissa (a round-trip on the cheapest ferry costs €22.80). With a bike and groceries, though, it can easily be explored for under €40 and is a perfectly beautiful place to recharge for a day before heading back to Ibiza for another night of partying. For transportation to Formentera, see **Inter-Island Transport,** p. 356.

BARCELONA

Barcelona loves to indulge in the fantastic. From the urban carnival that is Las Ramblas to buildings with no straight lines, the city pushes the limits of style in everything it does—and gets away with it. As the center of the whimsical and daring *Modernisme* architectural movement and the home of Picasso and Miro, Barcelona holds fairy-tale creations that are like no others in the world. Yet the draw of Barcelona extends beyond its paintings and architecture. The energy and attention to the visual is just as alive in its people, who spend countless hours at bar-cafes that look as hip and put-together as they do.

The time is now for Barcelona. In the quarter-century since the end of Franco's oppressive regime, Spain has blossomed, with Barcelona at the forefront. It has led the autonomous region of Catalunya in an energetic and unique resurgence of culture. The city's major makeover during the late 1980s and early 1990s, intended as preparation for the 1992 Olympics, was so successful that *barceloneses* have continued to reinvent their home and to forge their own identity. The result is a vanguard city squeezed between the mesmerizing blue waters of the Mediterranean and the green Tibidabo hills, flashing with such vibrant colors and intense energy that you'll see Barcelona long after you have closed your eyes. Take a short siesta, and then stay up as late as you can; you will need every hour available to fully explore this city. Barcelona is a gateway, not only to Catalan art and culture but also to the Mediterranean and the Pyrenees. Pack your swimsuit and your skis, your art history book and your clubbing shoes, and don't worry if you don't speak Spanish—neither does Barcelona.

HIGHLIGHTS OF BARCELONA

SCREAM your lungs out at a *fútbol* match (p. 404).

SHOW OFF your fashion sense in trendy **l'Eixample** (p. 420).

EXPERIENCE the unfinished masterpiece that is **La Sagrada Família** (p. 423).

EXPAND your cultural horizons by taking in the **art** and **architecture** scene.

HOW TO USE THIS CHAPTER. Barcelona is divided into several neighborhoods *(barris)*, four of which are covered here. We have grouped together all of each *barri's* accommodations, food, sights, museums, and night-life listings. General information on these aspects of Barcelona, as well as shopping and specific listings for camping and entertainment (including sports, theater, concerts, and film) appears after the practical information.

✈ INTERCITY TRANSPORTATION

Flights: Aeroport El Prat de Llobregat (**BCN;** ☎932 98 38 38; www.barcelona-air-port.com), 13km southwest of Barcelona. To get to Pl. Catalunya, take the **Aerobus** (☎934 15 60 20) in front of terminals A, B, and C (approx. 40min.; every 12-13min.; to Pl. Catalunya M-F 6:30am-midnight, Sa-Su 6:30am-midnight; to the airport M-F 6am-11:15pm, Sa-Su 6am-11:20pm; €3.50). The better option is a RENFE **train** (17min. to Estació Sants, 23min. to Pl. Catalunya; every 30min., from airport 6:13am-11:40pm, from Estació Sants to airport 5:43am-11:16pm; €2.20). To reach the train, go on the pedestrian overpass in the front of the airport, on the left with your back to the entrance. **Taxis** are in front of terminals A, B, and C (☎932 23 51 51); €12.90 to Pl. Espanya; €15.50 to Pl. Catalunya, €19 to Sagrada Família.

Trains: Barcelona has 2 main train stations. For general info about trains and train stations, call ☎902 24 02 02. **Estació Barcelona-Sants,** in Pl. Països Catalans (M: Sants-Estació) is the main terminal for domestic and international traffic. **Estació França,** on Av. Marquès de l'Argentera (M: Barceloneta), services regional destinations, including Girona, Tarragona, Zaragoza, and some international arrivals. Note that trains often make stops before reaching the main stations; check the schedule. **RENFE** (☎902 24 02 02, international 934 90 11 22) to: **Bilbao** (8-9hr., 5 per day, €34.50-44); **Madrid** (7-9hr., 8 per day, €33.50-59); **San Sebastián** (8-9hr., 5 per day, €33.50-42.50); **Sevilla** (11-12hr., 6 per day, €50-77.50); **Valencia** (3-5hr., 15 per day, €28.50-34.50). International destinations include **Milan,** Italy (via Figueres and Nice) and **Montpellier,** France with connections to Geneva, Paris, and various stops along the French Riviera. 20% discount on round-trip tickets.

Buses: Most buses arrive at the **Barcelona Estació Nord d'Autobusos,** C. Alí Bei, 80 (☎932 65 61 32). M: Arc de Triomf. Info booth open 7am-9pm. Buses also depart from Estació Sants and the airport. **Sarfa** (☎902 30 20 25; www.sarfa.com). Open 7:30am-10:45pm. Stop and ticket office also at Ronda Sant Pere, 21, in Pl. Urquinaona; open M-Su 7:30am-9pm. To: **Cadaqués** (2½hr., 6 per day, €16); **Lloret de Mar** (1hr., 21 per day, fewer off-season; €7.10); **Palafrugell** (2hr.; 18 per day M-F 8:30am-8:30pm, Sa-Su 10:30am-7:30pm; €12.20); **Tossa del Mar** (1½hr., 21 per day, €8.10). **Linebús** (☎932 65 07 00; www.movelia.es) goes to **Paris** via Tours or Lyon (15hr., M-Sa 8pm and 12:15am, €84) and southern France. Under 26 and over 60 10% discount. **ALSA/Enatcar** (☎902 42 22 42; www.alsa.es) goes to: **Alicante** (9hr., 3 per day, €33); **Madrid** (8hr., 20 per day 12:30am-11:59pm, €24); **Naples,** Italy (24hr., 4:45pm, €115); **Paris,** France (15 hr., 1-3 per day, €84); **Valencia** (4hr., 16 per day, €21); **Zaragoza** (3½hr., 20 per day, €12).

Ferries: Trasmediterránea (☎902 45 46 45), in Estació Marítima-Moll Barcelona, Moll Sant Bertran. Summer only to: **Ibiza** (5-8hr., 1 per day M-Sa, €49.60); **Mahón** (8-9hr., 1 per day starting mid-June, €49.60); **Palma** (3½hr., 1 per day, €69).

▣ ORIENTATION

Barcelona's layout is simple. Imagine yourself perched on Columbus's head at the **Monument a Colom** (on Pg. de Colom, along the shore), viewing the city with the sea at your back. From the harbor, the city slopes upward to the mountains. From the Columbus monument, **Las Ramblas,** the main thoroughfare, runs up to **Plaça de Catalunya** (M: Catalunya), the city's center. **Ciutat Vella** is the heavily touristed historic neighborhood, which centers around Las Ramblas and includes the Barri Gòtic, La Ribera, and El Raval. The **Barri Gòtic** is east of Las Ramblas (to the right, with your back to the sea), enclosed on the other side by **Vía Laietana.** East of Vía Laietana lies the maze-like neighborhood of **La Ribera,** which borders Parc de la Ciutadella and Estació de França (train station). To the west of Las Ramblas (left with your back to the sea) is **El Raval,** Barcelona's multicultural neighborhood, with some important museums and equally important artsy bars.

Beyond La Ribera—farther east, outside Ciutat Vella, and curving out into the water—are **Poble Nou** and **Port Olímpic,** with its twin towers (the tallest buildings in Barcelona) and an assortment of discos and restaurants on the beach. Beyond El Raval (to the west) rises **Montjuïc,** crammed with sprawling gardens, museums, the 1992 Olympic grounds, and a fortress. Directly behind your perch on the Monument a Colom is the **Port Vell** (Old Port) development, where a wavy bridge leads across to the ultra-modern (and tourist-packed) shopping and entertainment com-

BARCELONA

Barcelona

ACCOMMODATIONS
Albergue Mare de Déu de Montserrat (HI), 1
Hostal Eden, 28
Hostal Lesseps, 3
Hostal Qué Tal, 22
Hostal Residencia Oliva, 30
Hostal-Residència Windsor, 25
Hotel Antibes, 32
Pensión Aribau, 27
Pensión Fani, 24
Pensión San Medin, 6

FOOD
Agua, 40
Buenas Migas, 15
La Font de Prades, 34
La Gavina, 7
Mandalay Café, 20
OvUm, 9
La Pérgola, 35
El Racó d'en Baltá, 17
Restaurante Casa Regina, 13
Restaurant Illa de Gràcia, 11
Sushi Itto, 12
Tenorio, 29
Thai Gardens, 31
Txapela, 14
Zahara, 39

NIGHTLIFE
Àtame, 19
Bar Marcel, 4
Buenavista Salsoteca, 16
Catwalk, 41
D Mer, 2
Dietrich, 26
La Fira, 18
Gasterea, 8
Les Gens que J'Aime, 23
Luz de Gas, 10
The Michael Collins Irish Pub, 21
Otto Zutz, 5
L'Ovella Negra, 37
Razzmatazz, 38
La Terrazza, 33
Tinta Roja, 36

BARCELONA

BARCELONA

Ciutat Vella
see legend p. 396

Universitat de Barcelona

PL. DE LA UNIVERSITAT — M — UNIVERSITAT

Via de les Corts Catalanes

Ronda Universitat

VIPS

C. Sepúlveda

C. Villarroel

C. Casanova

C. Muntaner

C. Comte d'Urgel

C. Floridablanca

PL. CASTELLA

C. Torres i Amat

C. Gravina

C. Petal

C. Bergara

Triangle Shopping Center

C. Tamarit

Ronda de Sant Antoni

C. Valldonzella

C. Tigre

C. Paloma

Centro de Cultura Contemporania

C. Tallers

Museu d'Art Contemporani

PL. DELS ANGELS

Llibreria de Raval

C. Nou de Dulce

C. Ferlandina

C. San

C. Sant Gil

C. Sant Vicenç

C. la Riera Alta

C. de la Lluna

C. Joaquín Costa

C. Elisabets

Champion Supermarket

PL. VILA DE MADRID

SANT ANTONI — M

C. Princep de Biana

C. la Cendra

C. Bisbe Laguarda

C. d'Erasme de Janer

C. Peu de la Creu

EL RAVAL

C. Angels

C. Dr. Dou

Las Ramblas

C. Sant Antoni Abat

C. Cera

C. de l'Hospital

C. de la Riera Baixa

Esparteries

C. Carme

C. Pintor Fortuny

Palau de la Virreina

C. d'En Roca

C. de la Portafe

C. la Reina Amalia

C. de Vistalegre

C. d'en Roig

C. Floristes de la Rambla

La Boqueria

C. Petritxol

Ronda de Sant Pau

C. de L'Aurora

Biblioteca Sant Pau

C. de l'Hospital

Museu de l'Eròtica

Navegaweb

PL. DEL PI

C. Leialtat

PL. J. MA. FOLCH I TORRES

C. les Carretes

C. la Riereta

C. Sant Jeroni

C. la Cadena

C. Sant Rafael

C. d'Espalter

C. d'en Robador

C. Junta de Comerç

EL CALL

C. la Boqueria

C. Banys Nous

C. Sta. Elena

PL. SALVADOR SEGUÍ

C. de Sant Pau

Gran Teatre del Liceu

LICEU — M

C. Ferran

C. les Flors

C. de l'Hort de Sant Pau

C. S. Ologuer

C. S. Ramón

C. Marqués del Barbera

C. de les Penedides

C. la Unió

C. Avinyo

PARAL.LEL (FUNICULAR) — M

Abat Safont

C. les Taples

C. Nou de la Rambla

Euro NetCenter

Tourist Police

PL. REIAL

C. la Lleona

C. d'Agla

C. Cabanes

C. de l'Est

C. Guardia

C. Lancaster

Palau Güell

PL. GEORG ORWELL (PL. TRIPP)

C. Vila i Vilà

C. de Santa Madrona

C. Arc del Teatre

Easy Internet PL. DEL TEATRE

C. Escudellers

C. Nou Sant Francesc

C. Rull

C. Cid

C. Peracamps

C. Cervello

Centre D'Art de Santa Mónica

Santa Mònica

C. Còdols

Jardins de les Tres Xemeneies

C. Palaudaries

C. Portal Santa Madrona

Museu de Cera

C. Ample

C. Piquer

Pg. de Montjuïc

C. de Puigxuriger

C. Albreda

C. Carrera

TO MONTJUÏC (100m)

Museu Marítim

DRASSANES — M

C. Josep Anselm Clavé

Pg. de Colom

Ronda del L

PL. PORTAL DE LA PAU
■ Monument a Colom

TO MAREMÁGNUM (80m)

BARCELONA

PASSEIG DE GRÀCIA Ⓜ

Jardins de la
Reina Victoria

Pg. de Gràcia

Via de les Corts Catalanes

C. Bruc

C. Girona

C. Bailén

PL.
TETUÁN

TETUÁN Ⓜ

56

57

C. de Pau Claris

C. de Roger de Llúria

C. de Casp

L'EIXAMPLE

0   200 yards
0   200 meters

- DE
ALUNYA

El Corte
Inglés

Ronda de Sant Pere

C. d'Ausiàs

58

UNYA (i)
NFE)

URQUINAONA Ⓜ

59

C. Fontanella

60

Ronda de Sant Pere

C. d'Alí-Bei

TO ESTACIÓ
NORD (300m)

AMÓN
ADEU

61

C. Estruc

C. les Moles

Via Laietana

C. les Jonqueres

C. d'Ortigosa

C. Trafalgar

63

C. Trafalgar

Pg. de
St. Joan

ARC DE
TRIOMF Ⓜ

Corte
glés

62

C. Comtal

PL.
LUIS
MILLET

Palau de la
Música Catalana

C. Sant Pere Més Alt

C. Mare de Déu

C. St. Pere

C. S. Pere

C. Argenters

Pge. Ser Monec

C. Méndez Núñez

PL.
SANT
PERE

Pg. Lluis Companys

Arc de
Triomf

C. Montsió

64

uda

C. Durán i Bas

Biblioteca
Francesca
Bonnemaison

C. Vil Caniis

C. Sant Pere Més Baix

C. Rec Comtal

Pg. Lluis Companys

oters

C. Sagristans

C. Dr. J. Pou

PL.
ANTONI
MAURA

Gral. Álvarez

C. Jaume Giralt

C. Metges

C. en Cortinas

C. Clastics

PL. DEL
COMERÇ

la Palla NOVA

Av. de la Catedral

Av. de
Francesc Cambó

C. dels Mercaders

C. Feixures

C. Fonollar

C. Portal Nou

PL. DE
LA SEU

LA RIBERA

Pg. de Pujades

Església
Catedral de la
Santa Creu

Museu
d'Història
de la Ciutat

C. de Colomines

C. Tantarantana

Museu
de la
Xocolata

65

66

au de la
eralitat

C. Bisbe

(i) C. Llibreteria

68

C. Corders

67

C. Assaonadors

C. Comerç

Museu de
Zoologia

■ Hivernacle

ll PL. DE
SANT JAUME

C. Jaume I

JAUME I Ⓜ

71

C. Princesa

72

Museu
Picasso

C. Flassaders

Pg. de Picasso

Ajuntament

aria
es
vantes

C. Ciutat

BARRI
GÒTIC

Via Laietana

C. l'Argenteria

C. Manresa

C. dels Mirallers

C. Banys Vells

C. Montcada

73

74

76

C. Fusina

Parc de la
Ciutadella

tessa

C. Regomir

78

C. Lledó

C. Sots

C. la Nau

79

PL. DE
COMERCIAL

C. del Rec

C. Comercial

C. d'Avinyó

Santa Maria
del Mar

80

82

80

85

C. Antic St. Joan

C. la Ribera

C. Gignàs

84

El Fossar
de les
Moreres

C. Canvis Nous

C. del Aguliers

C. Espaseria

86

87

Parc
Zoològic

C. la Mercè

C. Marquet

C. Consolat de Mar

PL. DE
LES
OLLES

Av. Marqués de L'Argentera

PL. DEL
PALAU

ller

C. la Fusta

PL.
D'ANTONI
LÓPEZ

Pg. d'Isabel II

89

Canvis Vells

Estació
de
França

Pg. de Circumval·lació

sway tunnel)

a la Fusta

TO MOLL
d'ESPANYA
(50m)

BARCELONETA Ⓜ

Av. d'Icària

TO VILA OLÍMPICA
(800m)

Ciutat Vella

see map p. 394-395

⌂ ACCOMMODATIONS
Albergue de Juventud
  Kabul, **48**
Apart. Rembrant, **12**
Barcelona Mar Youth
  Hostel, **32**
BCN Hostal Central, **2**
Gothic Point Youth
  Hostal, **71**
Hostal Mariluz
  Youngsters, **77**
Hostal Avinyó, **83**
Hostal Benidorm, **50**
Hostal Campi, **13**
Hostal de Ribagorza, **63**
Hostal Fernando, **40**
Hostal Levante, **47**
Hostal Malda, **24**
Hostal Nuevo Colón, **87**
Hostal Òpera, **29**
Hostal Parisien, **23**
Hostal Plaza, **60**

Hostal San Remo, **58**
Hostal Sun & Moon, **37**
Hostal Residencia
  Lausanne, **61**
Hostal-Residencia
  Rembrandt, **21**
Hotel California, **42**
Hotel Lloret, **8**
Hotel Pelayo, **4**
Hotel Peninsular, **30**
Hotel Toledano/Hostal
  Residencia Capitol, **9**
Ideal Youth Hostel, **34**
Mare Nostrum, **28**
Pensión Ciutadella, **86**
Pensión L'Isard, **3**

🍴 FOOD
7 Portes, **89**
L'Antic Bocoi del Gòtic, **78**
Arc Café, **88**
Attic, **17**
The Bagel Shop, **14**
Bar Ra, **20**
Bodega la Tinaja, **82**
Buenas Migas, **11**

Bunga Raya, **67**
Café de l'Òpera, **35**
Los Caracoles, **52**
La Colmena, **68**
Comme-Bio, **1**
DosTrece, **16**
Ès, **10**
Hello Sushi, **27**
Irati, **26**
Laie Llibreria Café, **57**
Maoz Falafel (a), **69**
Maoz Falafel (b), **39**
Maoz Falafel (c), **22**
Mi Burrito y Yo, **70**
Origens 99.9%, **81**
El Pebre Blau, **76**
Pla dels Angels, **7**
Els Quatre Gats, **64**
Les Quinze Nits, **43**
Lupino, **19**
Restaurante Can Lluís, **18**
El Salón, **84**
Taira, **66**
Terrablava, **62**
Tèxtil Café, **72**
Txapela, **56**
Va de Vi, **75**

Vildsvin, **41**
Xaloc, **25**
Xampanyet, **74**

⭐ NIGHTLIFE
El Born, **80**
El Bosq de les Fades, **54**
El Copetín, **79**
Casa Almirall, **6**
Dai Club, **65**
Fonfone, **53**
Glaciar Bar, **49**
Jamboree, **45**
Karma, **46**
London Bar, **44**
Margarita Blue, **55**
Marsella Bar, **33**
Molly Malone, **38**
Moog, **51**
Muebles Navarro
  (El Café que Pone), **15**
Palau Dalmases, **73**
Pas del Born, **85**
La Paloma, **5**
Salvation, **59**
Sant Pau 68, **31**
Schilling, **36**

plexes **Moll d'Espanya** and **Maremàgnum.** North of Ciutat Vella is upscale **l'Eixample,** the gridded neighborhood created during the expansion of the 1860s, which runs from Pl. de Catalunya toward the mountains. **Gran Vía de les Corts Catalanes** defines its lower edge, and the **Passeig de Gràcia,** l'Eixample's wide, tree and boutique-lined avenue, bisects this chic neighborhood. **Avinguda Diagonal** marks the border between l'Eixample and the **Zona Alta** ("Uptown"), which includes Pedralbes, Grà-cia, and other older neighborhoods in the foothills. The peak of **Tibidabo,** the north-west border of the city, offers the most comprehensive view of Barcelona.

🚆 LOCAL TRANSPORTATION

MAPS

El Corte Inglés distributes a good free map. The Barcelona **tourist office** (Pl. de Cat-alunya and Pl. Sant Jaume; see p. 397) has maps with a good enlarged inset of the Barri Gòtic, although the better ones will cost you a couple of euros. The *Guia d'Autobusos Urbans de Barcelona,* free at tourist offices and metro stations, maps out the city's bus and metro lines; the *Guia Fàcil del Bus per Mour't per Barcelona,* also free, describes the routes in more detail.

METRO AND BUS

Barcelona's public transportation (info ☎ 010) is quick and cheap. If you plan to use public transportation extensively, there are several *abonos* (passes) available, all of which work interchangeably for the metro, bus, urban lines of the FGC com-muter trains, and Nitbus. The **T-1 pass** (€6) is valid for 10 rides and saves you nearly 50% off the cost of single tickets. The **T-Día pass** (€4.60) is good for a full day of unlimited travel, the **2 Dies** (€8.40) for two, the **3 Dies** (€11.80) for three, the **4 Dies** (€15.20) for four, and the **5 Dies** (€17.30) for five. These save you money if you use the metro more than three times per day.

Metro: (☎ 934 86 07 52; www.tmb.net). Vending machines and ticket windows sell passes. Red diamonds with the letter "M" mark stations. Hold on to your ticket until you exit—riding without one risks a fine of €40. Trains run M-Th 5am-midnight, F-Sa 5am-2am, Su and holi-days 6am-midnight. Hours are extended on special holidays. €1.10 per *sencillo* (single ride).

Ferrocarrils de la Generalitat de Catalunya (FGC): (☎932 05 15 15; www.fgc.es). Commuter trains to local destinations with main stations at Pl. de Catalunya and Pl. d'Espanya. Note that some destinations within the city (such as parts of Gràcia) require taking the FGC. Blue symbols resembling 2 interlocking Vs mark metro connections. The commuter line costs the same as the metro (€1.10) until Tibidabo. After that, rates go up by zone: zone 2 €1.60, zone 3 €2.30. Metro passes are valid on FGC trains. Info office at the Pl. de Catalunya station open M-F 7am-9pm.

Buses: Go just about anywhere, usually from 5am-10pm (many leave for the last round at 9:30pm). Most stops have maps posted, and you can easily figure out which bus to take; the next one should come within 10-15min. in central locations. €1.10.

Nitbus: (☎901 511 151). 16 different lines run every 20-30min. 10:30pm-4:30am, depending on the line; a few run until 5:30am. All buses depart from Pl. de Catalunya, stop in front of most of club complexes and work their way through Ciutat Vella and the Zona Alta. Maps are available at *estancos* (tobacco shops), posted on some bus stops, online (www.tmb.net), and marked by signs in metro stations. Metro passes are valid.

Bus Turístic: Hop-on, hop-off tours of the city. Passes sold for 1-2 days. See p. 403.

TAXIS

Taxis swarm the city and you can usually hail one in any relatively central location. A *lliure* or *libre* sign or a green light on the roof means vacant; yellow means occupied. On weekend nights you may wait up to 30min. in some locations; long lines form at popular spots like the Port Olímpic. To call a cab, try **RadioTaxi** (☎932 25 00 00) or **Servi Taxi** (☎933 30 03 00). **Disabled travelers** should call ☎934 20 80 88.

CAR RENTAL

Avis, C. Pallars, 457 (☎933 03 10 66; fax 03 22 41.). 3 other locations, including branch at the **airport** (☎932 98 36 00. Open M-Sa 7am-12:30am, Su 7am-midnight), and at **Estació Sants,** Pl. dels Països Catalans (☎933 30 41 93; fax 91 41 07. Open M-F 7:30am-10:30pm, Sa 8am-7pm, Su 9am-7pm).

Budget, C. Caracas, 50 (☎932 74 07 64; www.budget.com). 25+. **Branch** in El Prat de Llobregat airport (p. 390).

Docar/BCN, C. Montnegre, 18 (24hr. ☎933 22 90 08; www.docar.com). M: Les Corts. Open M-F 8am-2pm and 4-8pm, Sa 9am-2pm, Su by appointment.

Hertz, C. Tuset, 10 (☎932 17 80 76; www.hertz.es). M: Diagonal or FCG: Gràcia. Open M-F 9am-2pm and 4-7pm, Sa 9am-2pm. **Branch** office at airport (☎932 37 56 808) and by **Estació Sants,** C. Viriat, 45 (☎934 19 61 56).

Over-Rent S.A., Av. Josep Tarradellas, 42 (24hr. ☎934 05 26 60; fax 19 96 30), rents motorcycles.

Vanguard Rent a Car, C. Viladomat, 297 (☎ 934 39 38 80). 19+. Rents mopeds from €40 per day. More expensive 2-person *motos* also available. Includes insurance and helmet. Open M-F 8am-2pm and 4-8pm, Sa-Su 9am-1pm. **Branch** at C. Caracas, 50 (☎932 74 07 64).

⓰ PRACTICAL INFORMATION

TOURIST AND FINANCIAL SERVICES

Tourist Offices: Plaça de Catalunya, Pl. de Catalunya, 17S (☎907 30 12 82), underground on the bottom left-hand corner if facing south (toward Las Ramblas). M: Catalunya. The main office, along with Pl. de Sant Jaume, has free maps, brochures on sights and public transportation, booking service for last-minute accommodations, a gift shop, money exchange, and box office (Caixa de Catalunya). Open daily 9am-9pm. **Plaça de Sant Jaume,** Pl. de Sant Jaume,

BARCELONA

1. M: Jaume I. Open M-F 9am-8pm, Sa 10am-8pm, Su and holidays 10am-2pm. **Oficina de Turisme de Catalunya,** Pg. de Gràcia, 107 (☎932 38 40 00; www.gencat.es/probert). M: Diagonal. Open M-Sa 10am-7pm, Su 10am-2:30pm. **Institut de Cultura de Barcelona (ICUB),** Palau de la Virreina, Las Ramblas, 99 (☎933 01 77 75). Info office open M-Sa 10am-8pm, Su 11am-3pm. **Estació Barcelona-Sants,** Pl. Països Catalans. M: Sants-Estació. Info and last-minute accommodations booking. Open summer daily 8am-8pm; winter M-F 8am-8pm, Sa-Su 8am-2pm. **Aeroport El Prat de Llobregat** (☎934 78 05 65), terminals A and B. Info and last minute accommodations bookings. Open daily 9am-9pm. **Tourist Office Representatives** booths dot the city in the summer. Open July-Sept. daily 10am-8pm. **Tourist Call Center** (national ☎807 11 72 22, €0.39 per min.; international 933 68 97 30; www.barcelonaturisme.com). **Accommodation Booking,** www.hotelsbcn.com.

Tours: In addition to the Bus Turístic (p. 403), the Pl. de Catalunya tourist office offers 1½hr. walking tours of the Barri Gòtic Sa-Su at 10am (English) and noon (Catalan and Spanish). Apr.-Sept. also Th and F at 10am in English. Group size limited; buy tickets in advance. (☎906 30 12 82 for info. €8, ages 4-12 €3.) They also offer a 1½hr. Picasso tour of Barcelona (includes entrance to the Museu Picasso) Sa-Su 10:30am (English) and 11:30am (Catalan and Spanish). €10, ages 4-12 €5; 1st Su of month €8/€3.

Budget Travel: usit UNLIMITED, C. Rocafort, 116-122 (☎934 83 83 79; fax 83 83 70). Open M-F 10am-2pm and 4-8pm.

Currency Exchange: As always, **ATMs** give the best rates. The next best rates are available at banks. General banking hours M-F 8:30am-2pm. Las Ramblas has many exchange stations open late, but the rates are not as good.

American Express: Pg. de Gràcia, 101 (☎933 01 11 66). M: Diagonal. Open M-F 9:30am-6pm, Sa 10am-noon. Also at Las Ramblas, 74 (☎933 42 73 11). M: Liceu. Open daily 9am-9pm.

LOCAL SERVICES

Luggage Storage: Estació Barcelona-Sants, M: Sants-Estació. Lockers €4.50 per day. Open daily 5:30am-11pm. **Estació de França,** M: Barceloneta. Lockers €3 per day. Open daily 7am-10pm.

Libraries: Biblioteca Sant Pau, C. de l'Hospital, 56 (☎933 02 07 97). M: Liceu. Walk to the far end of the courtyard; the library is on the left. Do not confuse it with the Catalan library that you'll see first, which requires permission to enter. Open W-Th and Sa 10am-2pm, M and F 3:30-8:30pm. Closed Jul.-Aug. **Institut d'Estudis Nordamericans,** Vía Augusta, 123 (☎932 40 51 10). Library open Sept.-July M-F 10am-2pm. **Biblioteca Francesca Bonnemaison,** C. Sant Pere Més Baix, 7 (☎932 68 73 60), across from the Palau de la Músic Catalana. Open M and Th 4-9pm, Tu and F 10am-2pm and 4-9pm, W 10am-9pm, Sa 10am-2pm. **Biblioteca Barceloneta-La Fraternitat,** C. Comte de Santa Clara, 8-10 (☎932 25 35 74), in Port Vell 2 blocks from the beach. Open M-Tu and F 4-9pm, W 10am-2pm and 4-9pm, Th 10am-9pm. Closed Aug. 1-15.

Religious Services: Comunidad Israelita de Barcelona (Jewish services), C. Avenir, 24 (☎932 00 61 48). **Comunidad Musulmana** (Muslim services), Mosque Toarek Ben Ziad, C. de l'Hospital, 91 (☎934 41 91 49). Services daily at prayer times. **Església Catedral de la Santa Creu** (Catholic services), in Pl. de la Seu. M: Jaume I. Cloister open 9am-1:15pm and 4-7pm. Mass at 9, 10, 11am, noon, and 7pm; Su 9am, noon, 1, 6, and 7pm (in Spanish). **Parròquia María Reina,** C. d'Esplugues, 103 (☎932 03 55 39). Mass in English offered. **Iglesia Evangélica Española,** C. Llull, 161 (☎934 85 48 41). **Asociación de los Testigos de Jehová,** Vía Laietana, 13, 4th fl. 1a (☎933 19 69 82). **Casa del Tíbet,** Pg. de Sant Joan, 104 (☎932 07 59 66; www.casadeltibetbcn.org). **Hare Krishna,** Pl. Reial, 12 (☎933 02 51 94; www.iskcon.org). Contact the Tourist Office for info on other services.

Gay and Lesbian Services: Antinous, C. Josep Anselm Clavé, 6 (☎933 01 90 70; www.antinouslibros.com). M: Drassanes. A large bookstore and cafe specializing in gay and lesbian books and films, including several guide books. Decent selection in English.

IT'S AS EASY AS

one, two, three

uno, dos, tres

un, deux, trois

один, два, три

일 , 이 , 삼

Immerse yourself in a language.

Rosetta Stone® software is hands-down the fastest, easiest way to learn a new language — and that goes for any of the 27 we offer. The reason is our award-winning Dynamic Immersion™ method. Thousands of real-life images and the voices of native speakers teach you faster than you ever thought possible. And you'll amaze yourself at how effortlessly you learn.

Don't force-feed yourself endless grammar exercises and agonizing memory drills. Learn your next language the way you learned your first — the natural way. Order the language of your choice and get free overnight shipping in the United States!

Available for learning:
Arabic • Chinese • Danish • Dutch • English French • German • Hebrew • Hindi • Indonesian Italian • Japanese • Korean • Latin • Pashto Polish • Portuguese • Russian • Swahili • Swedish Spanish • Thai • Turkish • Vietnamese • Welsh

The guaranteed way to learn.

Rosetta Stone will teach you a language faster and easier than other language-learning methods. We guarantee it. If you are not satisfied for any reason, simply return the program within six months for a full refund!

Learn what NASA, the Peace Corps, thousands of schools, and millions around the world already know: Rosetta Stone is the most effective way to learn a new language!

Personal Edition. Solutions for Organizations also available.

Open M-F 11am-2pm and 5-9pm, Sa noon-2pm and 5-9pm. **Cómplices,** C. Cervantes, 2 (☎934 12 72 83). M: Liceu. A bookstore with publications in English and Spanish and a decent selection of gay films. Also provides a **map** of Barcelona's gay bars and discos. Open M-F 10:30am-8pm, Sa noon-8pm.

Laundromats: Tintorería Ferrán, C. Ferrán, 11. M: Liceu. Open M-F 9am-8pm. **Tintorería San Pablo,** C. San Pau, 105 (☎933 29 42 49). M: Paral·lel. Wash, dry, and fold €10; do-it-yourself €7.30. Open M-F Sept.-July 8am-2pm and 4-8pm; Aug. 8am-2pm. **Lavomatic,** Pl. Joaquim Xirau, 1 (☎933 42 51 19), 1 block to the right off La Rambla and 1 block below C. Escudellers (open M-Sa 10am-10pm); also at C. Consolat del Mar, 43-45 (☎932 68 47 68), 1 block north of Pg. Colon and 2 blocks to the right off Vía Laietana (open M-Sa 9am-9pm). Wash €3.75, dry €0.75 per 5min. **Wash @ Net,** C. les Carretes, 56, in El Raval near Las Ramblas. Wash €4-6, dry €1 per 10min. Internet €0.50 per 30min. Open 10am-11pm. **Lavandería Cervantes,** C. Cervantes, 5. Open M-F 9am-2pm and 4-8pm, Sa 9am-1:30pm.

EMERGENCY AND COMMUNICATIONS

Local police: ☎092. **National police:** ☎091. **Medical Emergency:** ☎061.

Police: Las Ramblas, 43 (☎933 44 13 00). M: Liceu. Multilingual officers. Open 24hr. **Turisme Atenció,** C. Nou de la Rambla, 80 (☎933 44 13 00), off La Rambla in El Raval 3 blocks from the port. A police station specifically for tourists. This is where to go if you've been pickpocketed.

Late-Night Pharmacy: Rotates; check any pharmacy window for the nearest on duty, or contact the police.

Hospital: Hospital Clínic, C. Villarroel, 170 (☎932 27 54 00). M: Hospital Clínic. Main entrance at the intersection of C. Roselló and C. Casanova. **Hospital de la Santa Creu i Sant Pau** (☎932 91 90 00, emergency 91 91 91). M: Hospital de Sant Pau. **Hospital Vall d'Hebron** (☎932 74 60 00). M: Vall d'Hebron. **Hospital del Mar,** Pg. Marítim, 25-29 (☎932 48 30 00), right on the beach before Port Olímpic. M: Ciutadella or Vila Olímpica.

Internet Access:

■ **Easy Internet Café,** Las Ramblas, 31 (www.easyinternetcafe.com). M: Liceu. With reasonable prices and over 300 terminals in a bright, modern center, this is Internet heaven. CD burning, faxing, copying, and scanning. €1.80 per hr., 1-day unlimited pass €4, 7-day €10, 30-day €20. Open 8am-2:30am. **Branch** at Ronda Universitat, 35. M: Catalunya. €1.60 per hr., 1-day pass €3, 7-day €7, 30-day €15. Open 8am-2am.

Navegaweb, Las Ramblas, 88-94 (☎933 17 91 93; navegabarcelona@terra.es). M: Liceu. Good rates on international calls. Internet €0.90 per 30min.; €1.80 per hr. Open daily 10am-10pm.

Bcnet (Internet Gallery Café), C. Barra de Ferro, 3, down the street from the Museu Picasso. M: Jaume I. €2.40 per hr.; 10hr. ticket €18. Open M-F 10am-10pm, Sa-Su noon-10:30pm.

Cybermundo Internet Centre, C. Bergara, 3, and C. de Balmes, 8. M: Catalunya. Just off Pl. de Catalunya, 2 branches behind the Triangle shopping mall. Disks allowed. €1.20 per hr. Open M-F 9am-1am, Sa 10am-1am, Su 11am-1am.

Euro NetCenter, C. Marquès de Barbera, 19, a block off Las Ramblas. M: Liceu. €0.50 per 30min., €1 per hr. Open daily 11am-10pm.

MS Internet, C. Pintor Fortuny, 30 (☎933 17 55 62), 3 blocks off Las Ramblas in El Raval. M: Liceu or Catalunya. €1 per hr. Open M-Sa 9:30am-9:30pm.

CiberOpción, Gran Vía, 602. M: Universitat. €0.60 per 30min. Open M-F 9am-1am, Sa 10am-1pm, Su 11am-1am.

People @ Web, C. Provença, 365. M: Verdaguer. €0.60 per 20min. Open M-F 11am-11pm, Sa-Su 5-11pm.

Workcenter, Av. Diagonal, 441. M: Hospital Clínic or Diagonal. **Branch** at C. Roger de Llúria, 2. M: Urquinaona. A last resort, expensive at €4.80 per hr. Open 24hr.

Telephones: Buy phone cards at tobacco stores and newsstands. **Directory Assistance:** ☎1003 for numbers within Spain, 1008 within Europe, 1005 outside Europe.

BARCELONA

Post Office: Pl. d'Antoni López (☎902 19 71 97). M: Jaume I or Barceloneta. **Fax** and **Lista de Correos.** Open M-F 8:30am-9:30pm, Su (access on side street) 8:30am-2:30pm. **Postal Code:** 08003.

ACCOMMODATIONS

While accommodations in Barcelona are easy to spot, finding an affordable one can be more difficult. If it is one of the busier travel months (June-Sept. or Dec.), wandering up and down Las Ramblas looking for a place to stay can quickly turn into a frustrating experience. If you want to stay in the touristy areas—Barri Gòtic or Las Ramblas—reserve weeks or even months ahead. Consider staying outside heavily trafficked Ciutat Vella; there are plenty of hostels in the Zona Alta, particularly in Gràcia, that will have more vacancies. For the best rooms, l'Eixample has many good deals and is also a quiet area at night. Be careful in La Ribera and El Raval on small streets far from the main avenues. Accommodations are listed by neighborhood and ranked by decreasing quality.

CAMPING

A handful of sites lie in the outskirts of the city, accessible by intercity buses (20-45min.; €1.50). The **Associació de Càmpings de Barcelona,** Gran Vía de les Corts Catalanes, 608 (☎934 12 59 55; www.campingsbcn.com) has more info. A good choice is **Filipinas ❶,** Autovía de Castelldefells, km12. Take bus L95 (€1.60) from Pl. de Catalunya to the campsite, 12km south. (☎936 58 28 95; reservas@infonegocio.com. €5.30 per person, per 2-person tent, and per vehicle; €0.40 extra for larger tent. Electricity €4. AmEx/MC/V.)

ACCOMMODATIONS BY PRICE

B Barri Gòtic **E** Elsewhere **G** Gràcia **L** La Ribera **R** El Raval **X** L'Eixample

UNDER €15 (❶)	
Albergue Mare de Déu de Mont. (HI) (430)	G
Camping Filipinas (400)	E
☒ Hostal Malda (409)	B

€15-25 (❷)	
Alberg Residència La Ciutat (430)	G
Albergue de Juventud Kabul (409)	B
Barcelona Mar Youth Hostel (418)	R
Gothic Point Youth Hostel (415)	L
Hostal Avinyó (408)	B
Hostal Campi (409)	B
☒ Hostal Fernando (408)	B
Hostal Mariluz Youngsters (409)	B
Hostal Residència Lausanne (410)	B
Hostal Sun & Moon (408)	R
☒ Hostal-Residència Rembrandt (409)	B
Ideal Youth Hostel (418)	R
☒ Pensión L'Isard (417)	R

€26-35 (❸)	
BCN Hostal Central (421)	X
Hostal Benidorm (408)	B
Hostal Eden (421)	X
☒ Hostal Levante (408)	B
Hostal Nuevo Colón (415)	L

Hostal Ópera (418)	R
Hostal Parisien (409)	B
☒ Hostal Residència Oliva (421)	X
Hostal San Remo (421)	X
☒ Hotel Peninsular (418)	R
Hotel Toledano/Hostal Res. Cap. (409)	B
Pensión Ciutadella (415)	L
Pensión Fani (421)	X
Pensión San Medín (430)	G

€36-45 (❹)	
Hostal Lesseps (430)	G
☒ Hostal de Ribagorza (414)	L
☒ Hostal Qué Tal (421)	X
Hostal Residència Windsor (421)	X
Hotel Lloret (410)	B
Pensión Aribau (421)	X

ABOVE €45 (❺)	
Apart. Rembrandt (409)	B
☒ Hostal Plaza (409)	B
Hotel Antibes (421)	X
Hotel California (409)	B
Hotel Pelayo (418)	R
Mare Nostrum (410)	R

⬚ FOOD

Barcelona offers every kind of food and ambience you could possibly desire. Whether it's Basque, Chinese, Indian, or American, chances are you'll find an establishment that will exceed your culinary expectations. While it's tempting to stick to the ubiquitous familiar foods, be sure to sample the local flavors and Barcelona's more experimental cuisine. As a world-class food city, Barcelona has sleek restaurants that rival New York's, yet it also offers countless neighborhood bars frequented by the same handful of people. Inexpensive options can be found with a little legwork, but if you want to live cheap and do as *barceloneses* do, buy your food fresh at one of the extensive *mercats* (markets) and hit up a grocery store for other essentials. Pick up the extensive *Guía del Ocio* (€1) at a newsstand for a list of most restaurants in Barcelona, including listings by type of food, descriptions, hours, some reviews, and contact information.

FOOD BY TYPE

B Barri Gòtic **G** Gràcia **L** La Ribera **M** Montjuïc **R** El Raval **W** Waterfront **X** l'Eixample

ASIAN

Bunga Raya (415)	L ❸
Hello Sushi (419)	R ❷
Mandalay Café (423)	X ❸
Sushi Itto (430)	G ❸
Taira (415)	L ❹
Thai Gardens (423)	X ❸

CAFES AND PASTRY SHOPS

Arc Café (410)	B ❷
Buenas Migas (418)	R ❶
Café de l'Òpera (410)	B ❶
La Colmena (411)	B ❶
Laie Llibreria Café (423)	X ❷
Tèxtil Café (416)	L ❸
Zahara (428)	W ❷

CATALAN AND SPANISH

7 Portes (416)	L ❹
🏠 Agua (428)	W ❸
DosTrece (418)	R ❸
🏠 Els Quatre Gats (411)	B ❹
La Font de Prades (426)	M ❸
La Pérgola (426)	M ❸
🏠 L'Antic Bocoi del Gòtic (410)	B ❷
🏠 Les Quinze Nits (410)	B ❶
Los Caracoles (410)	B ❸
Mi Burrito y Yo (410)	B ❹
Restaurante Can Lluís (419)	R ❸
Xaloc (411)	B ❶

INTERNATIONAL

Attic (411)	B ❸
🏠 El Pebre Blau (415)	L ❹
🏠 El Racó d'en Baltá (421)	X ❸
El Salón (410)	B ❸
És (418)	R ❹
🏠 HBN BCN (428)	W ❸
La Gavina (430)	G ❸
Lupino (418)	R ❹
🏠 Orígen 99.9% (415)	L ❷
Tenorio (423)	X ❸
The Bagel Shop (411)	B ❶
Vildsvin (410)	B ❸

TAPAS

Bodega La Tinaja (415)	L ❷
Irati (410)	B ❹
Txapela (Euskal Taberna) (423)	X ❷
Va de Vi (415)	L ❷
Xampanyet (415)	L ❶

VEGETARIAN

🏠 Bar Ra (418)	R ❷
🏠 Comme-Bio (423)	X ❷
Maoz (411)	B ❶
🏠 OvUm (430)	G ❷
🏠 Pla dels Angels (418)	R ❷
Restaurante Casa Regina (431)	G ❸
Restaurante Illa de Gràcia (431)	G ❶
Terrablava (411)	B ❷

Markets: La Boquería (Mercat de Sant Josep), off Las Ramblas. M: Liceu. Wholesale prices for a picture-worthy selection of vegetables, fruit, cheese, meat, and wine. Worth visiting even if just to buy fresh juice on the go. **Mercat de la Concepi**, C. València, between C. Bruc and C. Girona. M: Girona. Smaller version of La Boquería.

BARCELONA

Supermarkets: Champion, Las Ramblas, 113. M: Liceu. Open M-Sa 9am-10pm. **El Corte Inglés,** Pl. de Catalunya, 14. M: Catalunya. Supermarket in basement. Open M-Sa and 1st Su of the month 10am-10pm (see **Malls,** p. 406, for more info).

TAPAS

Hopping from one tapas bar to another is a fun and often cheap way to pass the evening. When you arrive, don't wait to be seated and don't look for a waiter to serve you; most tapas bars are self-serve and standing (or crowding) room only. Ask for a *plato* (plate) and help yourself to the toothpick-skewered goodies that line the bars. Keep your toothpicks—they'll be tallied up on your way out to determine your bill. If you're tired of standing at the bar, most places offer more expensive sit-down menus as well. Barcelona's many tapas (sometimes called *pintxos*) bars, concentrated in La Ribera and Gràcia, often serve *montaditos*, thick slices of bread topped with all sorts of delectables from sausage to *tortilla* (omelette) to anchovies. Vegetarian tapas are rare— be aware, for example, that slender white strands on some *montaditos* are really eels masquerading as noodles. Generally served around lunchtime and dinnertime, *montaditos* are presented on platters at the bar. They go well with a glass of *cava*—Catalan champagne—or a cup of *sidra*, a Basque alcoholic cider generally poured from several feet above the glass.

◎ 🏛 SIGHTS AND MUSEUMS

Barcelona has always been on the cutting edge of the art world. Many visitors cross continents not only to see the paintings in one of the fantastic museums but also to admire imaginative modern architecture and parks designed by world-renowned artists. Even the streets come alive with Barcelona's artistic spirit, marked by intricate lampposts or murals. The city's museums range from Surrealist and classical masterpieces to historical exhibits and one-of-a-kind mind-bending curiosities. The main architectural attractions are the *Modernista* treasures spread throughout the city, but concentrated in l'Eixample, while parks like Parc Güell and Parc Diagonal Mar offer an unsurpassed setting for relaxation surrounded by innovative designs and sculptures.

RUTA DEL MODERNISME

For those with a few days in the city and an interest in seeing some of the most popular sights, the Ruta del Modernisme is the cheapest and most flexible option. The route is not a tour precisely, in the sense that it doesn't offer a guide or organized transportation; it's a ticket that provides discount admission to dozens of Modernista buildings throughout the city. Passes (€3.60; students, over 65, and groups over 10 people €2.60) are good for 30 days and give holders a 25-30% discount on entrance to the Palau de la Música Catalana, Fundació Antoni Tàpies, the Museu d'Art Modern, Museu de Zoologia, tours of l'Hospital de la Santa Creu i Sant Pau and the facades of La Manzana de la Discòrdia (Casas Amatller, Lleó i Morera, and Batlló), and map tours of Gaudí, Domènech i Montaner, and Puig i Cadafalch buildings, among other attractions. The pass comes with a map and a pamphlet that gives the history of different sites, which is helpful for prioritizing visits. Purchase passes at **Casa Amatller,** Pg. de Gràcia, 41 (☎ 934 88 01 39; www.rutamodernisme.com. M: Pg. de Gràcia.), near the intersection with C. Aragó. Many of these sights have tour times and length restrictions; visiting all of them on the same day is virtually impossible.

BARCELONA CARD

Another discount option is the **Barcelona Card.** The card is sold for 1-5 days and includes free public transportation and over 100 discounts (and free admission to a few attractions and walking tours) at museums, cultural venues, theaters, a small selection of bars and clubs, shops, and restaurants. Sold at tourist offices or at Casa Batlló, Corte Inglés, Estació d'Autobus Barcelona Nord, the Aquarium, and Poble Espanyol. Prices for 1-5 days range from €17 for adults and €14 for ages 4-12 to €27/€24. Keep in mind that for students (usually with ISIC card), it may be cheaper to just use student discounts to get into attractions.

BUS TURÍSTIC

Sit back and let the sights come to you. The Bus Turístic stops at 40 points of interest along three different elliptical routes (red for the north area, blue for the south, and green for the eastern waterfront). Tickets come with a comprehensive eight-language brochure with information about each sight. A full ride on both routes takes 3-3½hr. depending on traffic, but the idea is to get off at any place of interest and use the bus (as many times as you want in your allotted days) as a comfortable and convenient means of transportation. Getting around between some of these sights without it would require a taxi or familiarity with the local bus system. You can buy tickets once on board, or ahead of time at **Turisme de Catalunya**, 17 Pl. de Catalunya (☎906 30 12 82), in front of El Corte Inglés. Many of the museums and sights covered by the bus offer discounts with the bus ticket; keep in mind that some are closed on Mondays. Overall, the bus is a good idea if you want to see the whole city quickly, and don't worry about not blending in—Barcelona is a city invaded by tourists, and *barceloneses* don't seem to mind. (Buses run daily except Dec. 25 and Jan. 1, every 10-30min. 9am-9:30pm; 1-day pass €16, ages 4-12 €10; 2-day pass €20/€13.)

🎟 ENTERTAINMENT

MUSIC, THEATER, AND DANCE

Barcelona offers many options for theater aficionados, though most performances are in Catalan (*Guía del Ocio* lists the language of the performance). Reserve tickets through **Tel Entrada** (24hr. ☎902 10 12 12; www. telentrada.com) or **ServiCaixa** at any branch of the Caixa Catalunya bank (24hr. ☎902 33 22 11; www.servicaixa.com; open M-F 8am-2:30pm). The **Grec** summer festival turns Barcelona into an international theater, music, and dance extravaganza from late June to the end of July (www.grec.bcn.com). For info about the festival, which takes place in venues across the city, ask at the tourist office or, during the festival, stop by the booth at the bottom of Pl. de Catalunya. For information on non-tourist-specific cultural activities in the city, swing by the **Institut de Cultura de Barcelona (ICUB)**, Palau de la Virreina, Las Ramblas, 99. (☎933 01 77 75. Info office open M-Sa 10am-8pm, Su 11am-3pm. Ticket sales M-Sa 10am-7pm. Most performances around €25.) Another resource is www.travelhaven.com/activities/barcelona/barcelona.html, which offers 10% discounts on performances at the Palau de la Música Catalana, Gran Teatre del Liceu, and l'Auditori.

Palau de la Música Catalana, C. Sant Francesc de Paula, 2 (☎932 95 72 00; www.palaumusica.org). M: Jaume I. To the right off Vía Laietana at the level of Pl. Urquinaona. Concert tickets €6-330. Box office open M-Sa 10am-9pm, Su from 1hr. prior to the concert. No concerts in Aug.; check the *Guía del Ocio* for listings. MC/V.

Centre Artesà Tradicionàrius, Tr. de Sant Antoni, 6-8 (☎932 18 44 85; www.tradicionarius.com), in Gràcia. M: Fontana. Catalan folk music concerts Sept.-June F 10pm. Tickets €10. Open M-F 11am-2pm and 5-9pm. Closed Aug.

Gran Teatre del Liceu, Las Ramblas, 51-59 (☎934 85 99 13, 24hr. ticket sales at ServiCaixa; www.liceubarcelona.com). M: Liceu. Founded in 1847, destroyed by fire in 1994, and recently reopened, Liceu has regained its status as the city's finest venue. Tickets start at €7 and rise fast. Reserve tickets in advance. Box Office open M-F 2-8:30pm, Sa and holidays 1hr. before showtime.

L'Auditori, C. Lepanto, 150 (☎932 47 93 00; www.auditori.com), in l'Eixample between M: Marina and Glòries. The Auditori is home to the city orchestra. Concerts from late Sept. to mid-July, with performances generally F at 7pm, Sa at 9pm, and Su at 11am; confirm times in advance. Tickets F-Sa €15-44, Su €11-31; special performances go up to €120. Available by phone, through ServiCaixa, or at ticket windows (open M-Sa noon-9pm, Su 1hr. before show starts to 1hr. after it has begun). MC/V.

El Tablao de Carmen (☎933 25 68 95; www.tablaodecarmen.com), on Av. Marquès de Comillas, inside Poble Espanyol. M: Espanya. Restaurant with very popular flamenco shows. Dinner and show €55, drink and show €29. Open Tu-Su from 8pm; shows Tu-Th and Su 9:30pm and 11:30pm, F-Sa 9:30pm and midnight. Call for reservations. AmEx/MC/V.

FILM

Most screens show the latest Hollywood features, some in the original English. The *Cine* section in the *Guía del Ocio* denotes subtitled films with *V.O. subtitulada (versión original);* other foreign films are dubbed *(doblado),* usually in Catalan. Many theaters have a discount day (usually Monday). **Filmoteca,** Av. Sarrià, 33, screens classic, cult, and otherwise exceptional films, in the original language with subtitles in Spanish or Catalan. (M: Hospital Clínic. ☎934 10 75 90. €2.70, students and seniors €2.) **Méliès Cinemas,** C. de Villarroel, 102, shows classics. (M: Urgell. ☎934 51 00 51. M €2.70, Tu-Su €4.) **Icària-Yelmo,** C. Salvador Espriu, 61, in the Olympic Village, boasts 15 screens and *V.O.* (☎932 21 75 85; www.yelmocineplex.es. M matinees €4.50, Tu-Su €6.) The brand-new **Cinesa Maremàgnum,** Port Vell, in Moll d'Espanya next to the Aquarium, has 11 screens. (M: Drassanes. Tickets by phone ☎902 33 32 31 or ServiCaixa. €5.80, W €4.20.) Next door, the new **IMAX Port Vell** has an IMAX screen, an Omnimax 30m in diameter, and 3-D projection. Get tickets at the door, through ServiCaixa, or by phone. (☎902 40 02 22. €10, matinees €7. Showtimes 10:30am-12:30am.) **Arenas Cine-Gay,** C. Tarragona, at the corner with Príncipe Jorge, offers contemporary gay-themed films. (M: Espanya. ☎934 23 11 69. €5.80.)

FÚTBOL

For the record, the lunatics covered head-to-toe in red and blue didn't just escape from an asylum—they are **F.C. Barcelona (Barça)** fans. Grab some face paint and head to the 120,000-seat **Camp Nou,** Europe's largest *fútbol* ground. On game days, the stadium is packed with thousands of screaming, rabid fans cheering on the home team, one of the world's most popular. The box office is on C. Arístedes Maillol, 12-18. Get tickets (€30-60) early; after finishing in second place in 2004, ahead of rival Real Madrid, Barca's even more optimistic about next season. **R.C. Deportivo Espanyol,** a.k.a. *los periquitos* (parakeets), Barcelona's second professional soccer team, spreads its wings at **Estadi Olímpic,** Pg. Olímpic, 17-19. This team isn't as renowned as Barça, but the games are fun and cheaper (€20-45). Get tickets from Banca Catalana or call TelEntrada (24hr. ☎902 10 12 12).

RECREATIONAL SPORTS

The tourist offices can provide info about swimming, cycling, tennis, squash, sailing, hiking, scuba diving, whitewater rafting, kayaking, and most other sports.

DiR Fitness Club, 12 branches throughout Barcelona, including one at C. Gran de Gràcia, 37 (☎934 15 55 50; www.dir.es). A popular Barcelona gym chain to see and be seen with the city's physical crème de la crème. Has every commodity you can imagine, from steam-bath, solarium, and personalized fitness programs to a finger-print-scan entrance. Prices depend on time of day, age, and number of days per week, but generally €3.90 per day (€2 extra for the card, purchased once); monthly passes range €20-100 depending on location and services. Open M-F 7am-10:15pm, Sa 9am-7:15pm.

Piscines Bernat Picornell, Av. Estadi, 30-40 (☎934 23 40 41), to the right when facing the stadium. Test your swimming in the Olympic pools—2 gorgeous facilities nestled in stadium seating overlooking the city. €4.40 for outdoor pool (long-term passes available); €8.20 for workout facilities including sauna, massage parlor, and gym. Outdoor pool open M-F 7am-midnight, Sa 7am-9pm, Su 7am-8pm. Workout facilities open M-F 7am-midnight, Sa 7am-9pm, Su 7:30am-8pm.

Club Sant Jordi, C. París, 114 (☎934 10 92 61). M: Sants. Passes available for facilities including sauna, weights, and stairmaster. Bring your passport. Pool use €3.70. Open M-F 7am-5pm, Sa 8am-6pm, Su and holidays 9am-2pm.

Beaches: The entire strip between Vila Olímpica and Barceloneta is a long public beach accessible from M: Ciutadella or Barceloneta. The closest and most popular is **Platja Barceloneta,** off Pg. Marítim. Beware (or be aware) of nudity on **Platja San Sebastià.** Barcelona's beaches, although good for a city, are crowded at almost any time of day. To avoid the crowds, it is easy to take the commuter rail along the coast and get off when you see one you like.

BULLFIGHTS

Although the best *matadors* rarely venture out of Madrid, Sevilla, and Málaga, Barcelona's **Plaça de Toros Monumental,** Gran Vía de les Corts Catalans, 743 (☎932 45 58 02; fax 32 71 58), is an excellent facility. Catalunya is currently considering a ban on bullfighting (which could take effect as soon as 2005), so this Plaça de Toros may soon see a fate similar to the one by Pl. Espanya—conversion into a shopping mall. (☎932 45 58 04. M: Monumental.) Bullfights take place during the summer tourist season, since tourists are about the only people who go (May-Sept. Su at 6:30pm). Tickets are available at travel agencies, ServiCaixa, or at the office on C. Muntaner, 24. (L'Eixample. ☎934 53 38 21; fax 51 69 98. Open W-Sa 11am-2pm and 4-8pm.) The box office at the Plaza de Toros sells tickets before the fight.

IN RECENT NEWS

LIFE IN THE AFTERNOON

In spite of the flamenco and bull-fight-themed souvenirs lining the shelves of Las Ramblas tourist shops, those coming to Spain to see this stereotypical image will have to venture beyond Catalunya. With its own culture and dance—the *sardana,* that is—Catalans have good reason to differentiate themselves from the rest of the country. The clearest example of this is the potential ban on bullfighting looming over the region. While the rest of the country continues to revere the *matadores* splashed across tabloid covers, Catalunya is very close to banning the bullfight for its cruelty. Already unpopular in the region, more than 250,000 people have signed a petition calling for its abolition, following a campaign by animal rights groups. Although the few *aficionados* have threatened to protest, the ban now hinges on a vote by the regional government, and secret ballots predict an overwhelming victory. It seems Catalunya would rather focus on the finer things in life—like art, architecture, and fashion. Only 100 bulls are killed in Barcelona each year, compared to 20,000 in Spain. Catalan distaste for the sport may include a desire to continue to forge an identity separate from that of Spain. While the living statues of matadors on Las Ramblas may persist for the amusement of tourists, soon enough, Catalunya will take a further step in defining its own personality.

☐ SHOPPING

Barcelona is cosmopolitan, trendy, trashy; shopping options reflect all these personalities. Above all, however, the city is shopaholic. Almost any main street is lined with stores, but the **Barri Gòtic** in particular bursts with hip and alternative clothing and accessories. If you're on the prowl for typical European women's clothing, check out C. Portaferrissa, C. Pelai in front of Pl. Catalunya, and Av. Portal de l'Angel. If you're more into the alternative scene, take a stroll down C. Avinyó and its smaller side streets. You can find all sorts of less expensive jewelry, accessories, and other cool knick-knacks perfect for gift-giving on C. Boquería. If you're looking for more legitimate jewelry, meander into one of the gems on C. Call. If you have extra cash or just want to go drool on the windows of European designers, check out Pg. de Gràcia in **l'Eixample.** One place to try for bargains is **Calle Girona,** between C. Casp and Gran Vía, in l'Eixample, where you'll find a small line of discount shops offering girls' and women's clothing, and men's dress clothes, shoes, bags, and accessories. (M: Tetuán. Walk 2 blocks down Gran Vía and take a left on C. Girona.) **Calle Bruc,** one street over, offers more retail delights for bargain-hunters. Be aware that stores marked "Venta al Mejor" are wholesalers who don't take kindly to browsing. Another area to try for discounts is the **Mercat Alternatiu (Alternative Market)** on C. Riera Baixa in **El Raval.** (M: Liceu. Take C. de l'Hospital—a right off Las Ramblas facing the ocean—and follow it to C. Riera Baixa, the 7th right, shortly after the stone hospital.) This street is crammed with second-hand and thrift stores stocked with everything from music to clothes.

MALLS

Spain has a series of laws against franchises in order to protect the economic prosperity of small businesses. The theory is that if franchises are allowed to be open all the time, small business, whose limited staff must take off Sundays and for *siesta,* will have no way to compete. Thus, these monstrous department stores are open only Monday to Friday and the first Sunday of each month. Perhaps due to this unwelcoming environment, or to Barcelona's preference for street-shopping, there are very few actual malls in the city.

El Corte Inglés, Pl. de Catalunya, 14 (☎933 06 38 00; www.elcorteingles.es). M: Catalunya. **Free map** of Barcelona. Sells everything from musical instruments to sneakers. Also has English books, hair salon, roof-top cafeteria, supermarket, the *oportunidades* discount department, currency exchange, and telephones. You could easily survive in this building for a couple of years. Open M-Sa and first Su of the month 10am-10pm. **Branches:** across the street from the tourist office, Portal de l'Àngel, 19-20 (M: Catalunya); Av. Diagonal, 471-473 (M: Hospital Clínic); Av. Diagonal, 617 (M: María Cristina).

Triangle, Pl. de Catalunya, 4 (☎933 18 01 08; www.triangle.es). M: Catalunya. Since its opening in 1999, architecture buffs have bemoaned this shopping center's utter lack of imagination and style. Shopaholics, however, are more enthusiastic. It consists mainly of the huge **FNAC** media and electronics store and the **Sephora** branch, the largest cosmetics store in the world in square footage. The first floor has a few clothing and sunglasses shops. Open M-Sa 10am-10pm.

Maremàgnum, Moll d'Espanya (☎932 25 81 00; www.maremagnum.es), in Port Vell. M: Drassanes. Small stores fill the first 2 floors of this mall and all-around leisure superstop that dominates the waterfront skyline. A must-see for *fútbol* (soccer) fans is the **Botiga del Barça,** a smaller version of the official F.C. Barcelona souvenir shop at Camp Nou stadium (p. 404). Aside from some shops, this is not the best place for fashion. Stores open daily, most 11am-11pm. At night, bars and clubs open as Maremàgnum transforms into a nightlife playground.

BOOKS

Come-In English Bookstore, C. Provença, 203 (☎934 53 12 04). Entirely English books. Bulletin boards in front advertise people looking for travel partners or language instructors. Open M-Sa 9:45am-2pm and 4:30-8:15pm.

VIPS, Rmbla. de Catalunya, 7 (☎933 17 49 23). M: Catalunya. Convenience store and American-style restaurant with many English magazines and some books. Open daily 9am-3am. AmEx/MC/V.

FNAC (www.fnac.es), 3 locations: in the Triangle mall in Pl. Catalunya, M: Catalunya (☎933 44 18 00; triangle@fnac.es; open M-Sa 10am-10pm); on Av. Diagonal, 3-35, where it reaches the shore, M: Besòs Mar (☎935 02 99 00; open M-Sa 10am-10pm); and in L'Illa Centre Comercial, Av. Diagonal, 549, M: María Cristina (☎934 44 59 00; illa@fnac.es; open M-Sa 10am-9:30pm). AmEx/MC/V.

Happy Books, Pg. de Gràcia, 77 (☎933 17 07 68). English and discounted books. Open M-Sa 9:30am-9pm. AmEx/MC/V.

Llibreria del Raval, C. Elisabets, 6 (☎933 17 02 93), off Las Ramblas in El Raval. M: Catalunya. Literature and nonfiction in 4 languages (Catalan, Spanish, English, and French) fill the shelves of this spacious bookstore, born in 1693 as the Gothic-style Church of la Misericòrdia. Pocket Catalan/English and Catalan/Spanish dictionaries (€11) are useful for travelers. Open M-Sa 10am-9pm. AmEx/MC/V.

Crisol Libros y Más, Rmbla. de Catalunya, 81 (☎932 15 27 20; www.crisol.es), in l'Eixample. M: Pg. de Gràcia. This Madrid transplant stocks a wide range of music (lots of international titles), books (fiction, plays, self-help, cooking, travel guides, road maps), magazines, videos, DVDs, small gifts, and stationery. There is also a large children's section, some English novels, and original English-version videos. Open M-Sa 9am-10pm. Wheelchair-accessible. AmEx/MC/V.

NIGHTLIFE

The nightlife in Barcelona needs no introduction: whether you're looking for psychedelic absinthe shots, a sunrise foam party, a cosmopolitan bar with shiny countertops, or just someplace quiet to sit back and enjoy a drink surrounded by fake gnomes, this city has it all. Things don't get going until late (don't bother showing up at a club before 1am) and keep going for as long as you can handle it. Check the *Guía del Ocio*, available at newsstands, for even more up-to-date listings of nighttime fun, as the hot spots change often.

FESTIVALS

While Barcelona is quite different from other parts of Spain, the city shares at least one thing in common with the rest of the country—it knows how to have fun. Festivals abound in this happening city; the trick is to know what will be going on during your visit. For information on all festivals, call the tourist office ☎933 01 77 75 (open M-F 10am-2pm and 4-8pm). Remember to double check sight and museum hours during festival times as well as during the Christmas season and *Semana Santa*. The **Festa de Sant Jordi** (St. George; Apr. 24) celebrates Catalunya's patron saint with a feast. Men give women roses, and women give men books. In the last two weeks of August, city folk jam at Gràcia's **Festa Mayor;** lights blaze in *plaças* and music plays all night. The **Sónar** music festival comes to town in mid-June, attracting renowned DJs and electronic enthusiasts from all over the world for three days of concerts and partying. During July and August, the **Grec Festival** hosts dance and concert performances, as well as film screenings, in different concert venues. On September 11, the **Festa Nacional de Catalunya** brings traditional costumes, dancing, and Catalan flags hanging from balconies. The **Festa de Sant Joan** (see **C'mon Baby, Light My Fire,** p. 420) takes place the night before June 24; you might as well surrender to the all-night partying, because ceaseless fireworks will prevent sleep anyway. The largest Barcelona celebration, however, is the **Festa de Mercè,** the week before and after Sept. 24. To honor the patron saint of the city, *barceloneses* revel with fireworks, *sardana* dancing, and concerts. **Santa Eulàlia,** the city's other patron saint, is celebrated Feb. 12-13.

BARRI GÒTIC AND LAS RAMBLAS

As the oldest sections of Barcelona, the Barri Gòtic and Las Ramblas are the tourist centers of the city. Originally settled by the Romans in the 3rd century BC, the Barri Gòtic is built on top of the original Roman city, Barcino. Subsequent layers of medieval Catholic rule cover Barcino in a maze of narrow, cobbled streets (from dark and grimy to charming) dense with historic and artistic landmarks. The modern tourist industry has added shops, hostels, and bars to the churches and other monuments left over from the Middle Ages. Take a stroll down **Carrer Avinyó** and you'll see some of Barcelona's most treasured architectural landmarks, just meters away from the area's most popular bars and restaurants. Whether you are drawn in by the new or the old, there is something for everyone in this labyrinth.

 ACCOMMODATIONS

LOWER BARRI GÒTIC

The following hostels are between C. Ferran and the water. Backpackers flock here to be close to hip Las Ramblas and in the middle of the late-night reveling. Beware of the cheapest options if you want breathing room.

🏨 **Hostal Levante,** Baixada de San Miquel, 2 (☎933 17 95 65; www.hostallevante.com). M: Liceu. The best deal in Barri Gòtic. 50 large, bright, tastefully decorated rooms with light wood interiors and balconies or fans, and a relaxing TV lounge. Ask for one of the newly renovated rooms. 6 very chic apartments also available; each has room for 4 to 8 people, and most include kitchen, living room, wood floor, and laundry machine. Singles €33; doubles €56, with bath €65; apartments €30 per person per night. MC/V. ❸

🏨 **Hostal Fernando,** C. Ferran, 31 (☎/fax 933 01 79 93; reservas@hfernando.com). M: Liceu. This clean hostel is so well-located it fills up almost entirely from walk-in requests. Beds in air-conditioned dorms come with lockers. Common TV-dining room. Dorms €18-21; doubles €46-47, with bath €60-64; triples with bath €70. MC/V. ❷

Hostal Sun & Moon, C. Ferran, 17 (☎932 70 20 60; www.smhostel.net). Although the 6-and 8-bed rooms are a bit cramped and the decor is sparse, it has one of the lowest prices and an unbeatable location. By 2005 will have Internet, bike rental, kitchen, and laundry. Breakfast must be pre-arranged (through hostelworld.com, which gets lower prices). Sheets €1.50, towel €1, blanket €2. Dorms €20. AmEx/MC/V. ❷

Hostal Benidorm, Las Ramblas, 37 (☎/fax 933 02 20 54). M: Drassanes or Liceu. In lobby, go left and up 3 flights. The best value on Las Ramblas, with phone and bath in each clean room, balconies overlooking Las Ramblas, and excellent prices. Singles €35; doubles €55; triples €75; quads €90; quints €105. €5 more in Aug. MC/V. ❸

Hostal Avinyó, C. Avinyó, 42 (☎933 18 79 45; www.hostalavinyo.com). M: Drassanes or Jaume I. Rooms with couches, high ceilings, fans, safes, and stained-glass windows. Great, calm location. Prices change frequently; check website for updates. Singles €16-25; doubles €24-42, with bath €40-57; triples €36-57/€54-75. ❷

Hotel Toledano/Hostal Residència Capitol, Las Ramblas, 138 (☎933 01 08 72; www.hoteltoledano.com). M: Catalunya. Rooms with cable TV and phones; some have balcony, interior ones have A/C. Free Internet in lobby, free wireless throughout. 4th fl. hotel (all rooms with bath): singles €34; doubles €49-59; triples €75; quads €84. 5th fl. hostel: singles €28; doubles €40; triples €53; quads €61. AmEx/MC/V. ❸

Hostal Mariluz Youngsters, C. Palau, 4 (☎/fax 933 17 34 63), up 3 flights. M: Liceu. Tidy 4- to 6-person dorm rooms and a few comfortable doubles border a rough-around-the-edges courtyard in this dark but historic old building. Reservations require credit card. July to mid-Sept. dorms €25; 1-bed double €50, 2-bed double €60; mid-Sept. to Nov. €20/€42/€45; Feb.-Mar. €18/€45/€51; Apr.-June €20/€50/€55. MC/V. ❷

Hostal Parisien, Las Ramblas, 114 (☎933 01 62 83). M: Liceu. Well-kept rooms keep young guests happy. Quiet hours after midnight. Prices vary, but generally singles M-F €38, Sa-Su €42; doubles with bath €48/54; triples with bath €57. ❸

Albergue de Juventud Kabul, Pl. Reial, 17 (☎933 18 51 90; www.kabul.es). M: Liceu. Legendary among backpackers; squeezes in up to 200 frat boys in rooms of 4 to 8. Keeps the party going by blasting American music in common areas. Located in backpacker central. Key deposit €15. Laundry €2.50. No reservations. Dorms €15-23. ❷

Hotel California, C. Rauric, 14 (☎933 17 77 66; www.seker.es/hotel_california), at the corner with C. Ferran. M: Liceu. Enjoy one of the 31 clean, sparkling rooms, all with TV, phone, bath, and A/C. Convenient location. Bar with social area in lobby. Safe box. Reception 24hr. Singles €55; doubles €85; triples €105. AmEx/MC/V. ❺

UPPER BARRI GÒTIC

This section of the Barri Gòtic is between C. Fontanella and C. Ferran. **Portal de l'Àngel,** a popular and chic pedestrian avenue, runs through the middle. Rooms are pricier than in the lower Barri Gòtic but more serene. Early reservations are essential in summer.

🖼 **Hostal-Residència Rembrandt,** C. de la Portaferrissa, 23 (☎/fax 933 18 10 11; hostrembrandt@yahoo.es). M: Liceu. This fantastic hostel has 28 rooms that are much nicer than others in the area; all are unique, some with large bath, patio, TV, and/or sitting area. Be sure to take advantage of the restaurant-quality dining area for breakfast (€5). Fans €2 per night. Reception 9am-11pm. Reservations require credit card. Singles €28, with bath €38; doubles €45/€55; triples €65/€70. MC/V. ❷

🖼 **Hostal Malda,** C. Pi, 5 (☎933 17 30 02), entrance inside small shopping center. M: Liceu. The friendly and concerned owner keeps the hostel occupied year-round by offering 30 quality rooms with shared baths at unbeatable prices. No reservations; show up between 9-11am to claim a space. Singles €13; doubles €28; triples with shower (shared WC) €40. ❶

🖼 **Hostal Plaza,** C. Fontanella, 18 (☎/fax 933 01 01 39; www.plazahostal.com). Savvy, super-friendly Texan owners; fun, brightly painted rooms with eclectic art; great location. Laundry €9. Internet access €1 per 15min. Singles €50, with bath €60; doubles €65/€75; triples €86/€96. 10% discount Nov. and Feb. AmEx/MC/V. ❺

Apart. Rembrandt, C. Canuda, 13 (☎933 01 31 57). This hotel, owned by the same people as Hostal-Resedencia Rembrandt, offers enormous, brand-new rooms with A/C, TV, full and luxurious baths, balconies facing the plaza, and even small kitchens. Breakfast €5. Reception 9am-10pm. Singles €50; doubles €90; large suite €120. MC/V. ❺

Hostal Campi, C. Canuda, 4 (☎/fax 933 01 35 45; hcampi@terra.es). Centrally located and cozy, it's a great bargain. Most rooms have large balconies. Call to reserve. Prices vary, but generally singles €22; doubles €44, with bath €52; triples €60/€72. ❷

Hotel Lloret, Las Ramblas, 125 (☎933 17 33 66). M: Catalunya. New modern rooms in an amazing location (hence the price) include large bathrooms, tasteful furniture, A/C, TV, and phone. Worth the splurge. Singles €45-48; doubles €75-81; triples €89-95; quads €105. AmEx/MC/V. ❹

Hostal Residència Lausanne, Av. Portal de l'Angel, 24 (☎933 02 11 39). M: Catalunya. Small hostel with stark white walls includes a posh lounge with TV. Amazing location between high-end boutiques. Doubles €40-48, with bath €65. ❷

Mare Nostrum, Las Ramblas, 67 (☎933 18 53 40; fax 934 12 30 69). M: Liceu. Hotel-level facilities and prices. Rooms have A/C and satellite TV, and some overlook Las Ramblas. You pay for the location. Breakfast €4. Laundry €12 per load. Singles €56, with bath €70.20; doubles €64.40/€74.60; triples €86/€98; quads €104/€120. ❺

◨ FOOD

LOWER BARRI GÒTIC

 L'Antic Bocoi del Gòtic, Baixada de Viladecols, 3 (☎933 10 50 67). M: Jaume I. Formed in part by an ancient 1st-century Roman wall, this dimly lit, rustic restaurant is tiny and romantic. Excellent salads (€4.25-7.50), exquisite pâtés (€9-12), and fine cheese platters (€11.50-12.10) are a nice change from over-prepared food. Reservations recommended. Open M-Sa 8:30pm-midnight. AmEx/MC/V. ❷

▨ **Les Quinze Nits,** Pl. Reial, 6 (☎933 17 30 75). M: Liceu. One of the most popular restaurants in Barcelona, with nightly lines halfway through the plaza (though they move quickly). Delicious Catalan entrees at unbeatable prices (pasta and rice €3.30-5.60, fish €6-8, meat €5-9). Try the Catalan dessert dish with almond ice cream and *crema catalana.* No reservations. Open daily 1-3:45pm and 8:30-11:30pm. AmEx/MC/V. ❶

El Salón, C. l'Hostal d'en Sol, 6-8 (☎93 315 21 59). M: Jaume I. A mellow bar-bistro serving gnocchi, chicken, pork, and fish (€8-18). Wine €2-8. Cocktails €4-5. *Menú* €20. Open M-Sa 8:30pm-midnight; bar open 7pm-2am. AmEx/MC/V. ❸

Café de l'Òpera, Las Ramblas, 74 (☎933 17 75 85). M: Liceu. A drink in this antique-mirror-covered cafe used to be a post-opera bourgeois tradition; now it is a hidden favorite amidst tourist traps. The hot chocolate (€2.70) is as thick as a melted bar. *Churros* €2.20. Tapas €2-4. Salads €2-8. Open daily 8am-2:30am. ❶

Mi Burrito y Yo, C. del Pas de l'Ensenyança, 2 (☎933 18 27 42). M: Jaume I. Not a Mexican joint (*burrito* here means "little donkey"), but inviting and lively with salads, meat dishes, and Catalan specialties. Live music 9:30pm. Entrees €12-23. *Menú* €15-20. Open daily 1pm-midnight. MC/V. ❹

Los Caracoles, C. Escudellers, 14 (☎933 02 31 85). M: Drassanes. What started as a snail shop has evolved into a delicious Catalan restaurant with a dark, rustic interior. Specialties include (surprise) *caracoles* (snails; €8.10) and rabbit (€12). Open daily 1pm-midnight. AmEx/MC/V. ❸

Arc Café, C. Carabassa, 19 (☎933 02 52 04). M: Drassanes. Away from the crowds, this cafe serves creative soups and salads. Entrees €5-15. Lunch *menú* €8.50. Open M-Th 9am-1am, F 9am-3am, Sa 11am-3am, Su 11am-1am. AmEx/MC/V. ❷

Irati, C. Cardenal Casañas, 17 (☎902 52 05 22; reservas@sagardi.com). M: Liceu. An excellent Basque tapas bar. Keep toothpicks to figure out the bill. Bartenders pour *sidra* (cider) behind their backs. Entrees €15-20. Open daily noon-1am. AmEx/MC/V. ❹

Vildsvin, C. Ferran, 38. M: Liceu. (☎933 17 94 07, reservations 43 53 10). Oysters and international beers (€4-8) are the specialties at this Norwegian bar that offers salads, salmon, and home-made cheeses and sausages. Tapas €3-5. Desserts €3.50-5. Entrees €8-14. Open M-Th 9am-2am, F-Sa 9am-3am. AmEx/MC/V. ❸

Maoz, 3 locations: at C. Ferran, 13; Las Ramblas, 95; and C. Jaume I, 7 (☎934 12 12 61; www.maozfalafel.com). A satisfying quick fix. Vegetarian chain staffed by friendly, young hippies has only one menu option (falafel, with or without hummus) and an array of fresh vegetable toppings. Falafel €2.70-3.50. Open daily 11am-1:30am. ❶

UPPER BARRI GÒTIC

 Els Quatre Gats, C. Montsió, 3 (☎933 02 41 40). M: Catalunya. Picasso's old Modernista hangout with lots of Bohemian character; he loved it so much he designed a personalized menu. High-quality cuisine such as Catalan salad with goat cheese and nuts (€9), millefoilles of Iberian pork in wild mushroom sauce (€15.20), and rack of lamb with roasted potatoes (€13.20). Entrees €12-26. Lunch *menú* €11. Live piano 9pm-1am. Open daily 1pm-1am. Closed Aug. AmEx/MC/V. ❹

Attic, Las Ramblas, 120 (☎933 02 48 66). M: Liceu. It's hard to believe this chic, modern restaurant with top-rate service is right on touristy Las Ramblas. Fusion Mediterranean cuisine, including fish (€10-13), meat (€6-14), and rice (€6-9) dishes. Open 1-4:30pm and 7:30pm-12:30am. AmEx/MC/V. ❸

Terrablava, Vía Laietana, 55 (☎933 22 15 85). Popular with professional *barceloneses* in a hurry, an all-you-can-eat buffet of veggies, pasta, pizza, a meat dish of the day, fruit, dessert, coffee, and one of the most extensive salad bars in the area. Buffet €7, at night €8.40. Open daily 12:30pm-1am. ❷

The Bagel Shop, C. Canuda, 25 (☎933 02 41 61). M: Catalunya. Barcelona meets New York City in this small, bright cafe. Diverse bagel selection (€0.70), bagel sandwiches (€3-5), and varied spreads, from cream cheese to caramel (€3-6). Open M-Sa 9:30am-9:30pm, Sept.-June also Su 11am-4pm. ❶

La Colmena, Pl. de l'Àngel, 12 (☎933 15 13 56). M: Jaume I. This divine pastry and candy shop tempts all; don't walk in unless you're prepared to buy, because you will—no one can resist the "beehive." Pastries €1-4. Open daily 9am-9pm. AmEx/MC/V. ❶

Xaloc, C. de la Palla, 13-17 (☎933 01 19 90). M: Liceu. This big, classy delicatessen popular with locals is centered around a butcher counter with pig legs hanging from the high ceiling. Meat and poultry sandwiches on tasty baguettes €4-14. Lunch *menú* €9.80. Open daily 9am-midnight. AmEx/MC/V. ❶

🎟 🏛 SIGHTS AND MUSEUMS

LAS RAMBLAS

Las Ramblas, a pedestrian-only strip roughly 1km long, is a world-famous cornucopia of street performers, fortune-tellers, human statues, pet and flower stands, artists, and even a sex shop, all for the benefit of the visiting droves of tourists. A stroll along this bustling avenue can be an adventure at almost any hour, day or night. Watch out for the man in an ostrich suit that jumps out screaming at innocent tourists. The wide, tree-lined thoroughfare dubbed Las Ramblas is actually composed of five (six if you count the small Rambla de Mar) distinct Ramblas (promenades) that together form one boulevard starting at the Pl. de Catalunya and the **Font de Canaletes** (more of a pump than a fountain)—visitors who want to come back to Barcelona are supposed to sample the water. Halfway down Las Ramblas, **Joan Miró's** pavement mosaic brightens up the street. Pass the **Monument a Colom** on your way out to the Rambla de Mar and a beautiful view of the Mediterranean.

GRAN TEATRE DEL LICEU. Once one of Europe's top stages, during its 150-year history the Liceu has been ravaged by anarchists, bombs, and fires. This theater, featuring Catalan opera, is adorned with palatial ornamentation, gold facades, and sculptures—there's even a fantastic hall of mirrors. *(Las Ramblas, 51-59, by C. Sant Pau. M: Liceu, L3. ☎ 934 85 99 13; for tours 85 99 14; www.liceubarcelona.com. Tickets sold at box office M-F 2pm-8:30pm and Sa 1hr. before show or by ServiCaixa. Open to public M-Su 10am-1pm. Guided 30min. tours 10am, by reservation only; call between 9am-2pm. €5.)*

CENTRE D'ART DE SANTA MÓNICA. One can only imagine what the nuns of this former convent would have thought of the edgy art installations (such as "How Difficult it is to Sleep Alone" and "Transsexual Express") that rotate through this large gallery, worth a visit for modern art fans. *(Las Ramblas, 7. M: Drassanes. ☎ 933 16 27 27. Open Tu-Sa 11am-2pm and 5-8pm; Su 11am-3pm. Call for info on exhibitions. Free.)*

MONUMENT A COLOM. Ruis i Taulet's Monument a Colom towers at the port end of Las Ramblas. Nineteenth-century *Renaixença* enthusiasts convinced themselves that Columbus was Catalan, from a town near Girona. In addition to that mistake (he was Italian), Columbus points proudly out over the horizon—toward Libya, not the Americas. Take the elevator to the top to enjoy a stunning view. *(Portal de la Pau. M: Drassanes. Elevator open Oct.-May 10am-6:30pm; June-Sept. 9am-8:30pm. €2, children and over 65 €1.30.)*

LA BOQUERIA (MERCAT DE SANT JOSEP). Besides being one of the cheapest and best places to get food in the city, La Boqueria is a sight in itself: a traditional Catalan market located in a giant, all-steel Modernista structure. Specialized vendors sell delicious produce, fish, and meat from one of a seemingly infinite number of independent stands inside. *(Las Ramblas, 89. M: Liceu. Open M-Sa 8am-8:30pm.)*

MUSEU DE L'ERÒTICA. As Spain's only erotica museum, the exhibits attract many of Barcelona's most intrepid tourists. The random assortment of pictures and figurines spans human history (somewhat unevenly) and depicts a variety of seemingly impossible sexual acrobatics that pushes the limits of human flexibility. The seven-foot wooden phallus is an irresistible photo-op. *(Las Ramblas, 96. M: Catalunya, L1/3. ☎ 933 18 98 65; www.erotica-museum.com. Open June-Sept. 10am-midnight; Oct.-May 11am-9pm. €7.50, students €6.50.)*

PALAU DE LA VIRREINA. Once the residence of a Peruvian viceroy, today this 18th-century palace houses rotating contemporary photography, music, and graphics exhibits. Also on display (for free in the lobby) are 3-5m tall dolls, the most symbolic figures of the celebrations of Carnival and Corpus Christi. Be sure to check out the famous rainbow stained-glass facade of the **Casa Beethoven** next door at Las Ramblas, 97, now a well-stocked music store. *(Las Ramblas, 99. M: Liceu. ☎ 933 16 10 00. Open Tu-Sa 11am-8pm; Su 11am-3pm. Free; exhibitions vary, but around €3.)*

MUSEU DE CERA (WAX MUSEUM). Some 300 wax figures form an endless parade of celebrities, fictional characters, and European historical figures you've probably never heard of; the most recognizable are generally ones with distinctive facial hair, like Fidel Castro and Chewbacca from Star Wars. *(Las Ramblas, 4. M: Drassanes. ☎ 933 17 26 49. Open July-Sept. daily 10am-8pm; Oct.-June M-F 10am-2:30pm and 4-8pm, Sa-Su and holidays 11am-2:30pm and 4:30-9pm. €6.70, ages 5-11 and seniors €3.80.)*

BARRI GÒTIC

While the ancient cathedrals and palaces give the impression that this neighborhood's time has passed, the area is still very lively, as evident in the ever-crowded narrow streets. As the oldest part of Barcelona, the Barri Gòtic came into existence well before the use of the grid layout (found in l'Eixample), taking shape during Roman times and continuing to develop during the medieval period. Today it is the site of Catalan commercialism in all its glory, with store-lined streets, coupled with historical landmarks.

⧆ MUSEU D'HISTÒRIA DE LA CIUTAT. There are two components to the Museu d'Història de la Ciutat: the Palau Reial Major and the subterranean excavations of the Roman city Barcino. Built on top of the fourth-century city walls, the **Palau Reial Major** served as the residence of the Catalan-Aragonese monarchs. When restoration on the building began, the **Saló de Tinell** (Throne Room) was discovered, wholly intact, under a baroque chapel. The huge Gothic room is believed to be the place where Fernando and Isabel received Columbus after his journey to America. Today, it houses year-long temporary exhibitions. The second part of the museum lies underground; this 4000m² not-to-be-missed **archaeological exhibit** was excavated from 1930 to 1960 and displays incredibly well-preserved 1st- to 6th-century remains of the Roman city of Barcino. *(Pl. del Rei. M: Jaume I. ☎ 933 15 11 11; www.museuhistoria.bcn.es. Pamphlets available in English. Open May 11-Oct. M-Sa 10am-8pm, Su 10am-3pm; Oct.-May 10 Tu-Sa 10am-2pm and 4-8pm, Su 10am-3pm. Museum €4, students €2.50. Exhibition €3.50/€2. Combined museum and exhibition €6/€4.)*

ESGLÉSIA CATEDRAL DE LA SANTA CREU. This cathedral is one of Barcelona's most popular and recognizable monuments. Beyond the choir are an altar with a bronze cross designed by Frederic Marès in 1976 and the sunken Crypt of Santa Eulàlia. The cathedral museum holds Bartolomé Bermejo's *Pietà*. Catch a performance of the *sardana* in front of the cathedral on Sunday after mass; services begin at noon and 6:30pm. *(M: Jaume I. In Pl. Seu, up C. Bisbe from Pl. St. Jaume. Cathedral open daily 8am-12:45pm and 5:15-7:30pm. Cloister open 9am-12:30pm and 5:15-7pm. Elevator to the roof open M-Sa 10:30am-12:30pm and 5:15-6pm; €2. Choir area open M-F 9am-12:30pm and 5:15-7pm, Sa-Su 9am-12:30pm; €2. English audioguide €4. Special guided tours daily 1-5pm include everything for €4.)*

PLAÇA DE SANT JAUME. Pl. de Sant Jaume has been Barcelona's political center since Roman times. Two of Catalunya's most important buildings have dominated the square since 1823: the grandiose **Palau de la Generalitat,** headquarters of Catalunya's government, and the **Ajuntament,** or city hall. *(Generalitat open 2nd and 4th Su of the month 10:30am-1:30pm. Closed Aug. Mandatory tours in English, Spanish, or Catalan every 30min. starting at 10:30am. Free. Ajuntament open 2nd and 4th Su 10am-1:30pm. Free.)*

EL CALL (JEWISH QUARTER). Although today there is little indicating the Jewish heritage of the area, for centuries El Call was the most vibrant center of intellectual and financial activity in all of Barcelona. One synagogue was transformed into a church, the **Església de Sant Jaume** (C. Ferran, 28). The only remaining tangible evidence of Jewish inhabitants is the ancient **Hebrew plaque** on tiny C. Marlet; the rest of the area has been commercialized. *(M: Liceu.)*

PLAÇA REIAL. This is the most crowded, happening *plaça* in the entire Barri Gòtic, where tourists and locals congregate to eat and drink at night, and to buy and sell at the Sunday morning flea market. Near the fountain in the center of the square there are two street lamps designed by Antoni Gaudí. If only he could have witnessed the antics of the drunk backpackers that flood this plaza until sunrise. *(M: Liceu or Drassanes.)*

⧉ NIGHTLIFE

Here, traditional *cervecerías* and bar-restaurants, with the occasional unique locale, can be found every five steps on main streets such as C. Ferran. The Barri Gòtic is perfect for chit-chatting your night away, sipping sangria, or scoping out your next dance partner. C. Escudellers is a more lively location for post-bar dancing, and Pl. Reial remains packed until early morning. Las Ramblas becomes a bit sketchy late at night, as prostitutes emerge where families roamed in the daylight.

🏵**Jamboree,** Pl. Reial, 17 (☎ 933 01 75 64). M: Liceu. In the corner to your right coming from Las Ramblas. What was once a convent is now one of the city's most popular live music venues and a crowded hip-hop club later at night (with a mostly American crowd). Daily jazz or blues performances. Cover M €3, Tu-Su €8. Drinks €8-10, so try to hit up a bar before. Open daily 11pm-1am; nightclub 2-5am. Upstairs, the attached club **Tarantos** (☎933 18 30 67) hosts flamenco shows (€3). Open M-Sa 10pm-2am.

Fonfone, C. Escudellers, 24 (☎933 17 14 24; www.fonfone.com). M: Liceu or Drassanes. Atmospheric blue and green lighting and sounds of "funky" music draw crowds from 1-3am. Different DJs every night from all over the world (Tu hip-hop, W Latin; check the website). Beer €3.50. Mixed drinks €6-8. Open daily 10pm-2:30 or 3am.

Molly Malone, C. Ferran, 7 (☎933 42 40 26). M: Liceu. The place to go if you're looking to meet English-speaking tourists guzzling pricey but strong mixed drinks (€7-8). Guinness on tap €5. Bottled beer €4. Open Su-Th 8pm-2:30am, F-Sa 7pm-3am.

Karma, Pl. Reial, 10 (☎933 02 56 80; www.karmadisco.com). M: Liceu. This multicolored tunnel-shaped club keeps a varied Pl. Reial crowd dancing to music ranging from pop to oldies to techno. Drinks (€4-6) and beer (€3) are less of a rip-off than at other clubs. Open Tu-Su noon-2:30am; club midnight-5am.

Schilling, C. Ferran, 23 (☎933 17 67 87). M: Liceu, L3. One of the more chill and spacious wine bars in the area, with dim lighting and velvet seat cushions. Excellent sangria (pitcher €14). Wine €2, bottles €13. Serves breakfast and sandwiches during the day (€3-8). Open daily 10am-2:30am, Su noon-2:30am; bar opens 8pm.

El Bosq de les Fades, Pg. de la Banca, 5 (☎933 17 26 49), near the Wax Museum. M: Drassanes. Complete with trees and gnomes. A good place to chill before hitting up a club. Open M-Th 2pm-1am, F 2pm-2am, Sa 11am-2am, Su 11am-1am.

Margarita Blue, C. Josep Anselm Clavé, 6. (☎933 17 71 76; www.margaritablue.com). M: Drassanes. This Mexican-themed, modern bar-restaurant draws a 20- and 30-something crowd with its tequila cocktails, *mojitos,* and good Mexican food (lunch *menú* €7, entrees €4-9). Blue margaritas €3. W night drag shows around 11:30pm. Open Su-W 7pm-2am, Th 7pm-2:30am, F-Sa 7pm-3am. AmEx/MC/V.

Glaciar Bar, Pl. Reial, 3 (☎933 02 11 63). M: Liceu. A popular hangout for those looking for a casual, dressed-down night. Plenty of outside tables in the plaza. Beer €1.50-2. Mixed drinks €4. Liter of sangria €10. Open daily 4pm-3am.

LA RIBERA

As the stomping ground of Barcelona's many fishermen and merchants, La Ribera has always had a working-class feel. However, its confines were witness to two of the most major events to shape Barcelona's history. In the 18th century, Felipe V demolished much of La Ribera, then the city's commercial hub, to make space for the impressive Ciutadella fortress, then the center of Madrid's oppressive control and now the site of a beautiful park. In 1888, the former site of the Ciutadella hosted the Universal Exposition, and La Ribera was injected with a dose of cosmopolitanism through the new flare of Modernisme. In recent years, the neighborhood has evolved into Barcelona's bohemian nucleus, attracting a young, artsy crowd of locals and a few expats and tourists in the know.

⛏ ACCOMMODATIONS

🏵**Hostal de Ribagorza,** C. Trafalgar, 39 (☎/fax 933 19 19 68; www.hostalribagorza.com). M: Urquinaona. Rooms in a Modernista building complete with marble staircase and tile floors. TVs, fans, and homey decorations. Doubles €40, with bath €50-55. Prices lower in winter. MC/V. ❹

Pensión Ciutadella, C. Comerç, 33 (☎933 19 62 03). M: Barceloneta. Small hostel with 6 spacious rooms, each with A/C, TV, and balcony. Family feel. Bike rental €15 for 5hr. 1 single, with shared bath and no balcony €35; doubles €36-40, with bath €45-50; 1 triple €60. ❸

Gothic Point Youth Hostel, C. Vigatans, 5 (☎932 68 78 08; www.gothicpoint.com). M: Jaume I. Creatively decorated lobby area with free Internet access and large TV is usually filled with young backpackers, and even a weekly crafts fair. 150 beds in dorm-style rooms with A/C. Biweekly Gaudí and city walking tours €5. Breakfast included. Lockers €1.20 per day. Sheets €1.80, towels €1.80. Refrigerator access. High season dorms €21.50; low season €17. AmEx/MC/V. ❷

Hostal Nuevo Colón, Av. Marquès de l'Argentera, 19 (☎933 19 50 77; www.hostalnuevocolon.com). M: Barceloneta. 26 modern rooms in hotel-quality building with a common area and TV. Singles €35; doubles €48, with bath €62; 6-person apartments with kitchens €150 per day. ❸

🍴 FOOD

🖹 **Orígen 99.9%,** C. Enric Granados, 9 (☎/fax 934 53 11 20; 99.9origens@terra.es), and at C. Vidrierias, 6-8 (☎933 10 75 31). This rustic but hip restaurant and gourmet store sticks to natural, fresh ingredients at unbeatable prices. Diners are greeted by a black-and-white photo display with a quote: "The virtue of the countryside is the fruit of the relation between man and earth." Small portions. Soups €3-9; vegetarian, meat, and seafood dishes €3-5. Try the beef-stuffed apple (€4) or rabbit in chocolate sauce (€3.60). Open 12:30pm-1:30am. ❷

🖹 **El Pebre Blau,** C. Banys Vells, 21 (☎933 19 13 08). M: Jaume I. Ring the doorbell to get into this hidden gourmet restaurant, which serves delicate dishes that creatively fuse Mediterranean and Middle Eastern flavors. The specialties—foie gras with apricots and honey and seared duck with berries—are to die for. Reservations recommended on weekends. Wheelchair-accessible. Kitchen open daily 8:30pm-midnight. MC/V. ❹

Taira, C. Comerç, 7 (☎933 10 24 97). From M: Jaume I, follow C. Princesa, then turn left on C. Comerç. Chill on floor-level futons and funky chairs at this swank sushi hot spot. Splurge on the *moriawase* (€17.20), and finish up with a *sorbete de sake* (€4). *Sashimi* €14-17. *Maki* €11-12. *Menú* €8.10. Shiatsu massages W 9pm. Cafeteria open M-F 8am-4pm. Restaurant open Tu-Sa 1-4pm and Tu-Su 9pm-midnight. At night, **Dai Club** (☎679 24 12 51), entrance through Pg. de Picasso, 6, attached to the back of the restaurant, becomes a chill nightspot marked by avant-garde Asian-inspired decor. No cover. Open Th-Sa 11pm-3am. Wheelchair-accessible. AmEx/MC/V. ❹

Bodega La Tinaja, C. Espartería, 9 (☎933 10 22 50). M: Jaume I. Excellent wine selection (€1.50-5 per glass). The cheese, pâté, fish, and meat accompaniments to the bread are mouthwatering. Open Su and Tu-Sa 6pm-2am. MC/V. ❷

Xampanyet, C. Montcada, 22 (☎933 19 70 03). M: Jaume. Next to the Museu Picasso and packed with people. The house special—*cava* (choose from 17 varieties)—is served with anchovies and, of course, *pa amb tomàquet* (bread with tomato; €1.50). Bottles €7 and up. Open Tu-Sa noon-4pm and 7-11:30pm, Su noon-4pm. Closed Aug. ❶

Va de Vi, C. Banys Vells, 16 (☎933 19 29 00). M: Jaume I. Possibly the most romantic restaurant in La Ribera, candle-lit in a 16th-century stone building. Choose from over 170 varieties of wine and *cava* (glasses €1.60-4), a wide selection of cheeses (€4-15.50) and tapas (€1.80-13). Wheelchair-accessible. Open Su-W 6pm-1am, Th 6pm-2am, F-Sa 6pm-3am. ❷

Bunga Raya, C. Assaonadors, 7 (☎ 933 19 31 69). M: Jaume I. One of the first *locales* in La Ribera to specialize in exotic food, this intimate restaurant offers Malaysian delicacies like *rendang,* or beef cooked with milk and coconut butter. *Menú* €13. Entrees €10-15. Open Tu-Su 8pm-12am. ❸

Tèxtil Café, C. Montcada, 12 (☎932 68 25 98). M: Jaume I. Across from Museu Picasso in the gothic courtyard of the Museu Tèxtil i d'Indumentària, this fresh and charming terrace cafe serves mostly tapas and sandwiches with *cava* and wine. Approx. €12-21 per person. Open Tu-Su 10am-11:45pm. Wheelchair-accessible. ❸

7 Portes, Pg. de Isabel II, 14 (☎ 933 19 30 33; www.7puertas.com). M: Barceloneta. This dark wood-beamed upscale restaurant proudly claims to have hosted several famous customers such as Orson Welles. Traditional dishes and personal service. Great paella €15, fish and shellfish €8-50, meat dishes €10-20, cannelloni €8.80. Reserve on weekend nights. Open daily 1pm-1am. AmEx/MC/V. ❹

🜚 ⬚ SIGHTS AND MUSEUMS

▨ MUSEU PICASSO. The most-visited museum in Barcelona traces the development of Picasso as an artist, with the world's best collection of work from his formative Barcelona period; he donated over 1,700 works to the museum himself, and it now boasts 3,600. It is amazing to see the transition from the classical techniques he used to the unique stylistic developments that made him an icon. Crucial works include *Portrait of Aunt Pepa*, the most important from his formative period, *First Communion*, his first large exhibited work, and the 57 canvases of the *Las Meninas* series. *(C. Montcada, 15-19. M: Jaume I. Open Tu-Sa 10am-8pm, Su 10am-3pm. Last entrance 30min. before close. €5, students and seniors €2.50; with temporary exhibition €8/€4.70. Under 16 free. 1st Su of the month free.)*

▨ PALAU DE LA MÚSICA CATALANA. In 1891, the Orfeo Catalán choir society commissioned Modernista Luis Domènech i Montaner to design this must-see concert venue. The music hall glows with tall stained-glass windows, an ornate chandelier, marble reliefs, intricate woodwork, and ceramic mosaics. Scupltures of wild horses seem to come alive out of the walls flanking the stage. Concerts held at the Palau include symphonic and choral music in addition to more modern pop, rock, and jazz. *(C. Sant Francesc de Paula, 2. ☎932 95 72 00; www.palaumusica.org. M: Jaume I. Mandatory 50min. tours in English every hr. Reserve 1 day in advance. Open daily Aug. 10am-7pm; Sept.-July 10am-3:30pm. €7, students and seniors €6. Check the Guía del Ocio for concert listings. Concert tickets €6-330. MC/V.)*

PARC DE LA CIUTADELLA. Host of the 1888 Universal Exposition, the beautiful park contains several museums, well-labeled horticulture, the wacky and imposing Cascada fountains, a pond, and a zoo. The sprawling lawns are filled with strolling families, students playing instruments and smoking, and couples doing the standard Spanish PDA-overload. Buildings of note include Domènech i Montaner's Modernista **Castell dels Tres Dracs** (Castle of Three Dragons, now the Museu de Zoología), the geological museum, and Josep Amergós's **Hivernacle.** The **Parc Zoològic** is also worth a look. *(M: Ciutadella. Zoo open daily May-Aug. 9:30am-7:30pm; Apr. and Sept. 10am-7pm; Mar. and Oct. 10am-6pm; Nov.-Feb. 10am-5pm. €12.90, over 65 €7.20.)*

MUSEU DE LA XOCOLATA. Arguably the most delectable museum in Spain. If you can halt the inevitable salivation for a few moments, the museum presents gobs of information about the history, production, and ingestion of this sensuous treat. Perhaps more interesting are the exquisite chocolate sculptures, particularly the edible Sagrada Família, soccer star Ronaldo, and Dalí-inspired pieces. The small cafe offers workshops on cake baking and chocolate tasting. *(Pl. Pons i Clerch, by C. Comerç. ☎932 68 78 78; www.museudelaxocolata.com. M: Jaume I. Open M and W-Sa 10am-7pm, Su 10am-3pm. Workshops from €6.30; reservations required. €3.80, students and seniors €3.30, Barcelona Card €2.70. Under 7 free.)*

SANTA MARÍA DEL MAR. This architectural wonder was built in the 14th century in only 55 years. At a distance of 13m apart, the supporting columns span a width greater than any other medieval building in the world. It's a beautiful and fascinating example of the limits of Gothic architecture—were it 2 ft. taller, the roof would have collapsed from structural instability. *(Pl. Santa María, 1. M: Jaume I. Open M-Sa 9am-1:30pm and 4:30-8pm, Su 10am-1:30pm and 4:30-8pm. Free.)*

EL FOSSAR DE LES MORERES. The Catalans who resisted Felipe V's conquering troops in 1714 to defend the rights and constitution of Catalunya lie here in a mass grave, commemorated by a modern sculpture with a flame at the peak, mulberry trees *(moreres)*, and a plaque with a verse by poet Serafí Pitarra: "In the Mulberry Cemetery no traitors are buried. Even though we lose our flags, this will be the urn of honor." Demonstrators converge here on *La Diada* (Catalan National Day, September 11), to commemorate the siege of Barcelona and subsequent ban on displays of Catalan nationalism. *(Off C. de Santa María behind the church.)*

NIGHTLIFE

El Copetín, Pg. del Born, 19. M: Jaume I. Cuban rhythm invades everything in this dim, casual nightspot. Awesome *mojitos* €5. Open Su-Th 7pm-2:30am, F-Sa 7pm-3am.

El Born, Pg. del Born, 26 (☎933 19 53 33). M: Jaume I. Sit at the marble counter over the basins where fish were once sold or follow the spiral staircase upstairs for a meal. Fondues €12-15. Cocktails €4-6. Open M and W-F 6pm-2:30am, Sa-Su 6pm-3am.

Palau Dalmases, C. Montcada, 20 (☎933 10 06 73). M: Jaume I. A self-labeled "Baroque space" in a 17th-century palace filled with lavish paintings, statues, and furniture. Cocktails €7-10. Fresh juices €8. Live opera performances Th 11pm (€20, includes 1 drink). Open Tu-Sa 10pm-2am, Su 6-10pm.

Pas del Born, C. Calders, 8 (☎933 19 50 73). M: Barceloneta or Jaume I. The bright pink exterior is an indication of the stylish yet laid-back clientele and decoration of this bar. Open M-Th 7pm-2am, F-Sa 7pm-3am.

EL RAVAL

Located next to Las Ramblas and the Barri Gòtic, the northern part of El Raval tends to be a favorite of Barcelona's natives rather than its tourists. This diverse and culturally rich working-class neighborhood has a special charm, with small, quirky shops and eateries, welcoming bars, and hidden historical attractions. At one time a small rural area outside of the city walls, El Raval was enveloped by the new city boundaries in the 14th century and has been squeezing people in ever since. The situation became critical in the late 19th and early 20th centuries, when over-crowding led to an urban nightmare of rampant crime, prostitution, and drug use. Revitalization efforts, especially since the '92 Olympic games, have worked wonders, however; new museums and cultural centers have paved the way for trendy restaurants and bars, and today El Raval is emerging as one of Barcelona's most dynamic areas. At night, bars and restaurants in the northern part light up and this becomes one of the city's hippest hangouts, definitely worth checking out.

ACCOMMODATIONS

Be careful in the areas nearer to the port and farther from Las Ramblas; they can be dark and eerily deserted late at night.

Pensión L'Isard, C. Tallers, 82 (☎/fax 933 02 51 83). M: Universitat. The friendly owners offer the absolute lowest price in the *barri* on 14 impeccable rooms; 4 have balconies. Singles €21; doubles €39, with bath €53; triples €55. AmEx/MC/V. ❷

🏨 **Hotel Peninsular,** C. de Sant Pau, 34 (☎933 02 31 38). M: Liceu. This building is now one of the sights on the Ruta del Modernisme. 80 beautiful rooms with phone and A/C. Breakfast included. Singles €30, with bath €50; doubles €50/€70. MC/V. ❸

Hostal Ópera, C. de Sant Pau, 20 (☎933 18 82 01; www.hostalopera.com). M: Liceu. Recently renovated rooms feel new. Bath, phone, and A/C in every room. Internet in the common room. Singles €35-38; doubles €55-58; triples €80-82. MC/V. ❸

Hotel Pelayo, C. Pelai, 9, 1st fl. (☎933 02 37 27; www.hotelpelayo.com). M: Universitat. A great deal in an amazing location, this hotel is worth the extra bucks to avoid the ubiquitous overpriced hostels. Full bath, TV, A/C, and phone in each spotless room. Singles €55; doubles €75. MC/V. ❻

Barcelona Mar Youth Hostel, C. de Sant Pau, 80 (☎933 24 85 30; www.youthostel.com). M: Paral·lel. This new hostel crams in 120 dorm-style beds (6-16 per rm., curtains around each bed). A/C and music in the lounge area. All beds come with safe. Internet €1 per 30min. Breakfast included. Sheets €2.50, towels €2.50, both €3.50. Self-serve laundry €4.50. Laundry service available. Summer €21-23; winter €14-18. AmEx/MC/V. ❷

Ideal Youth Hostel, C. la Unió, 12 (☎933 42 61 77; www.idealhostel.com). M: Liceu. One of the best deals in the city. Free Internet access in the swanky lobby area. Breakfast included. Sheets €6.50. Laundry €4. Dorms €22. ❷

🍴 FOOD

🍴 **Bar Ra,** Pl. de la Garduña (☎933 01 41 63; www.ratown.com). M: Liceu. Everything about Ra exudes cool, from the clientele to the incense-infused outside seating under multi-colored lights. Lots of vegetarian options, including a daily specialty that is bound to amaze. Creative fusion cuisine, like chicken curry salad with tropical fruit (€10). Entrees €9-15. Dinner by reservation only. Open daily 9:30am-1:30am; kitchen open 1:30-4pm and 9:30pm-midnight. AmEx/MC/V. ❷

🍴 **Pla dels Angels,** C. Ferlandina, 23 (☎933 49 40 47). M: Universitat. The funky decor of this colorful, inexpensive eatery, with equally funky dishes and a large vegetarian selection, is fitting for its proximity to the contemporary art museum. Entrees €5-6. Open M-Th 1:30-4pm and 9-11:30pm, F-Sa 1:30-4pm and 9pm-midnight. MC/V. ❷

Lupino, C. Carme, 33 (☎934 12 36 97). M: Liceu. Next door to Ra, a slightly more upscale and sophisticated locale, also with terrace seating and simple, creative decor. Lunchtime menu €8.50, entrees (try the goat cheese salad with grapes) €6-18. The sleek, modern bar inside, blue-lit catwalk and all, attracts the hippest of El Raval's trendy locals. Open Su-Th 10am-1am, F-Sa 10am-3am. ❹

És, C. Dr. Dou, 14 (☎933 01 00 68). M: Liceu. One of the coolest restaurants in El Raval, entirely white and red restaurant, proudly declares that "all of their cooks are in love." Try fusion dishes like calamari with lemon sorbet and orange salad (€10.20), roast duck with potatoes and cherries (€14.20), or tuna with grapefruit puree. Meat entrees €9.60-14.20, fish €10.20-14.60. Open daily 1pm-12:30am. AmEx/MC/V. ❹

Buenas Migas, Pl. Bonsuccés, 6 (☎933 18 37 08; buenasmigas@buenasmigas.com). M: Catalunya. Enjoy coffee or tea (€0.90-1.70) at one of the shaded outside tables in the plaza, or stay in the rustic interior with your focaccia (€2-4) topped with everything from vegetables to bacon and brie. Open Su-W 10am-11pm, Th-Sa 10am-midnight. ❶

DosTrece, C. Carme, 40, (☎933 01 73 06; www.dostrece.net). M: Catalunya. Crowds of young locals dine in the fine decor of stained glass Frida Kahlo portraits and candles, while listening to live music (jazz Tu, flamenco W, hip-hop Th, soul F, house Sa). Lunch *menú* €9. Entrees €7-15. Open M-Sa 1:30-4pm and 9pm-midnight. M closed at night. Terrace open until 3am. AmEx/MC/V. ❸

Hello Sushi, C. Junta de Comerç, 14 (☎934 12 08 30; www.hello_sushi.com). M: Universitat. In keeping with the diverse and young vibe of the upper El Raval, this modern sushi bar has eclectic red-and-blue-lighted decor and occasional live music (call for more details). Lunch *menú* €8.50, student *menú* €4, night *menú* €15. Salads and soups €2-4. Tempura €8-16, sushi €0.90-2 per piece. AmEx/MC/V. ❷

Restaurante Can Lluís, C. Cera, 49 (☎934 41 11 87). M: Sant Antoni. From the metro, head down Ronda S. Pau and take the 2nd left on C. Cera. Eschewing trendiness, the menu is filled with traditional Catalan favorites including rack of lamb (€10.90) and *fideuà* (€12.90), a traditional noodle and seafood dish. Lunch *menú* €7. Dinner *menús* (€20-35) include wine. Open M-Sa 1:30-4pm and 8:30-11:30pm. V. ❸

🜚 🏛 SIGHTS AND MUSEUMS

🜚**PALAU GÜELL.** Gaudí's recently renovated 1886 Palau Güell—the Modernista residence built for patron Eusebi Güell (of Parc Güell fame)—has one of Barcelona's most spectacular interiors. Güell spared no expense on this house, considered to be the first true representation of Gaudí's unique style. *(C. Nou de La Rambla, 3-5. M: Liceu. ☎ 933 17 39 74. Mandatory tour every 15min. Open Mar.-Oct. Su 10am-2pm, M-Sa 10am-8pm, last tour 6:15pm; Nov.-Dec. M-Sa 10am-6pm. €3, students €1.50.)*

MUSEU D'ART CONTEMPORANI (MACBA). This cleanly designed building was constructed with the idea that sparse decor would allow the art to speak for itself. The MACBA has received worldwide acclaim for its focus on interwar avant-garde art, as well as Surrealist and contemporary works. The main attraction is not the limited permanent exhibition (which is modified to fit with the temporary), but the innovative rotating three-month exhibitions. *(Pl. dels Àngels, 1. M: Catalunya. ☎ 934 12 08 10; www.macba.es. Open July-Sept. M-F 11am-8pm, Sa 10am-8pm, Su 10am-3pm; Oct.-June M and W-F 11am-8pm, Sa 10am-8pm, Su 10am-3pm. Tours in Spanish and Catalan W and Sa 6pm, Su noon. €7, students €3, under 17 free; temporary exhibitions €2.50.)*

CENTRE DE CULTURA CONTEMPORÀNIA DE BARCELONA (CCCB). The center stands out for its mixture of architectural styles, consisting of an early 20th-century theater and its 1994 addition, a sleek wing of black glass. The institute shows a variety of temporary exhibits, including film screenings and music performances; check the *Guía del Ocio* for scheduled events. *(Casa de Caritat. C. Montalegre, 5. M: Catalunya or Universitat. ☎ 933 06 41 00; www.cccb.org. Open June 21-Sept. 21 Tu-Sa 11am-8pm, Su 11am-3pm. Sept. 22-June 20 Tu and Th-F 11am-2pm and 4-8pm; W and Sa 11am-8pm; Su and holidays 11am-7pm. Tours Tu and F 6pm, Sa-Su and holidays 11:30am. €4, students €3, W all €3, children free.)*

🜚 NIGHTLIFE

If glamorous clubs and all-night dancing are your scene, El Raval is not for you. It is too cool for that. The streets are densely packed with a bar for every variety of bar-hopper—Irish pubbers, American backpackers, absinthe sippers, social drinkers, lounge lizards, and foosball maniacs. However, true to the artsy nature of the area, El Raval's specialty is a hip, creatively decorated, colorful bar with a young, laid-back crowd. Make sure to check out the area between C. Joaquim Costa and C. Carme, around the MACBA.

🜚 **Casa Almirall,** C. Joaquín Costa, 33. M: Universitat. Cavernous space with weathered couches, cool, dim lights, and equally laid-back clientele. Staff walks you through your first glass of *absenta* (absinthe; €6.50)—and cuts you off after your second. (Bring your own lighter.) Beer €3-4, mixed drinks €6-8. Open Su-Th 7pm-2:30am, F-Sa 7pm-3am.

C'MON BABY, LIGHT MY FIRE

It seems appropriate that the shortest night of the year is also the most sleepless. In fact, sleep is a luxury for weeks before the **Festa de Sant Joan,** as children rehearse with fireworks at all hours. June 23 is the day when the sun is highest in the sky, sinking lower each day thereafter. The festival venerates the sun as a symbol of wealth and fertility, and fireworks and bonfires are lighted to give it back some of the power it is losing. At the same time, fire—believed to be a purifying element—is used to cleanse the past and eradicate bad luck by burning old furniture in bonfires. One fire, the *Flama del Canigó,* is carried from town to town before the celebration.

While all this fire might seem a bit dangerous (especially in the hands of toddlers, not rare during the festival), the idea is that "he who lights the fire for Sant Joan doesn't get burned all year." Water and herbs are believed to have curative powers on this night, but they take a back seat to the flames. Across the city *barceloneses* gather in the few hours of darkness: children light fireworks while adults eat *coca de Sant Joan,* a special pastry. Younger crowds revel all night at large parties on the beach. The next morning news programs show the dazed and confused celebrators being woken up and cleared off the sand. It's a good thing the entire city shuts down on June 24.

London Bar, C. Nou de la Rambla, 34 (☎933 18 52 61). M: Liceu. Rub shoulders with unruly, fun-loving expats at this Modernista tavern, one of the oldest (the brass and mirrors have been around 94 years) in the city and a favorite of young tourists. Live music (usually rock or blues) nightly at 12:30am with no cover. Beer, wine, and absinthe €2-3; mixed drinks €6-7, whiskey €6. Open Tu-Sa 7:30pm-4am. AmEx/MC/V.

La Paloma, C. Tigre, 27 (☎933 01 68 97). M: Universitat. An older crowd clears the way for the youth around midnight; live salsa and popular Spanish music in this 100-year-old dance hall with a theater-like interior, chandelier and all. Th night is the popular "Bongo Lounge" session. Mixed drinks €7 and up. Cover €7. Open Th-Sa 6-9:30pm and 11:30pm-5am, Su and holidays 6-10pm.

Marsella Bar, C. de Sant Pau, 65. M: Liceu. Religious figurines grace the walls of Barcelona's oldest bar, open since 1820; perhaps they're praying for the absinthe (€3.40) drinkers who frequent the place. Mixed drinks €2-6. Live music. Open M-Sa 10pm-3am.

Muebles Navarro (El Café que Pone), C. la Riera Alta, 4-6 (☎607 18 80 96). Enjoy the mellow ambience and watch friends get friendlier as they sink into the comfy couches together. Beer and wine €2-3. Mixed drinks €5-7. Open Tu-W 2pm-2am, Th 6pm-2am, F-Sa 6pm-3am.

Sant Pau 68, C. de Sant Pau, 68. M: Liceu. The red lighting and flowered wallpaper set the mood for a relaxed ambience in one of El Raval's hippest bars. Drinks €2-5. Open Tu-Th 8pm-2:30am, F-Sa 8pm-3am.

Moog, C. Arc del Teatre, 3 (☎933 18 59 66; www.masimas.com/moog). M: Liceu or Drassanes. Fitting with the industrial metal walls and floor, this is the techno headquarters of Barcelona, though the upstairs dance floor sticks to the 80s and 90s. Look for the flyers on the street to get in free. Cover €12. Open daily 11pm-5am.

L'EIXAMPLE

Barcelona's l'Eixample (Enlargement; luh-SHOMP-luh) is remarkable for the unusual circumstances that led to its development. Right around the time when the oppressive Bourbon walls around the old city were finally demolished in 1854, the Catalan cultural *Renaixença* was picking up. As the number of wealthy benefactors of industrialization grew, utopian socialist theories spread like wildfire through philosophical circles, including those of l'Eixample designer **Ildefons Cerdà i Sunyer.** The gridded streets wound up filled with relatively wealthy residents (not the blending of classes as he'd imagined), designer shops, corporate buildings, and great eateries from around the world. Most tourists only see the

Pg. de Gràcia and Sagrada Família areas, but if you have the energy to explore the whole neighborhood, you'll get a great lesson in Modernisme, and a better feel for the Barcelona that lies beyond tourist attractions.

ACCOMMODATIONS

Hostal Residència Oliva, Pg. de Gràcia, 32, 4th fl. (☎934 88 01 62; www.las-guias.com/hostaloliva). M: Pg. de Gràcia. Elegant wood-worked bureaus, mirrors, ceilings, and a light marble floor give this hostel a classy ambiance. 5 of the 16 rooms look onto Pg. de Gràcia or neighboring streets, and all have high ceilings, TVs, and fans. The location of this old building (as the perilous ride up the ancient elevator indicates) is enviable. Singles €32; doubles €55, with bath €62; triples with bath €90. ❸

Hostal Qué Tal, C. Mallorca, 290 (☎/fax 934 59 23 66; www.quetalbarcelona.com), near C. Bruc. M: Pg. de Gràcia or Verdaguer. This high-quality gay- and lesbian-friendly hostel has one of the best interiors in the city, with murals, a plant-filled terrace, and snazzy decor in all 13 rooms. Singles €39; doubles €58, with bath €74. ❹

Hostal San Remo, C. Bruc, 20 (☎933 02 19 89; www.hostalsanremo.com). M: Urquinaona. All 8 spacious rooms in this small, personal hostel have TV, A/C, and soundproof windows; 4 have terraces. Reserve early. Singles with bath €32-35; doubles €52-59, with bath €57-58, one without WC €50. Nov. and Jan.-Feb. reduced prices. MC/V. ❸

BCN Hostal Central, Ronda Universitat, 11, 1st fl. (☎933 02 24 20; www.bcnhostal-central.com). M: Universitat. In an old building with marble staircases and ornate ceilings, this hostel is freshly painted with breezy colors and has an unbeatable location. There are 4 amazing triples with large balconies. Singles with shared bath €25-33; doubles €50-55, with bath €60-65; triples €54/€78; larger triple for 4 without bath €60; quads €60, with bath €85-90. Extra bed €12-18. Reservation by phone or email with credit card (MC/V) required, but must pay cash for room. ❸

Hostal Eden, C. Balmes, 55 (☎934 52 66 20; http://hostaleden.net). M: Pg. de Gràcia. Modern rooms with high ceilings are equipped with TV and fan; most have big, new bathrooms. Apr.-Oct. singles €30, with bath €45; doubles €45/65; triples €75; quads €85. Nov.-Mar. €25/€35/€35/€50/€60/€70. AmEx/MC/V. ❸

Pensión Fani, C. València, 278 (☎932 15 36 45). M: Catalunya. Oozes quirky charm. Rooms rented by month; single nights also available, but only in triples. Singles €350 per month; doubles €540 per month; triples €22 per person per day. ❸

Pensión Aribau, C. Aribau, 37 (☎/fax 934 53 11 06). M: Pg. de Gràcia. All 16 rooms (half with balconies) have TV and A/C. Reservations recommended. Singles €36, with bath €50; doubles €55/€65; triples with bath €85. €10 less in low season. MC/V. ❹

Hostal Residència Windsor, Rmbla. de Catalunya, 84 (☎932 15 11 98). M: Pg. de Gràcia. All 15 rooms with high ceilings in this more peaceful Las Ramblas location come equipped with comfy sleep sofas and heat in winter. Renovations will bring new floors and TVs, fans, and baths to every room by the end of 2004. Singles €38, with bath €45; doubles €55/€64. Extra bed €10. ❹

Hotel Antibes, C. Diputació, 394 (☎932 32 62 11; www.hotelantibes.net). An amazing deal for a 2-star hotel, the spacious, modern rooms with A/C, bath, phone, and TV are worth a short commute to the center of the city. Breakfast €4.40. Laundry service available. Parking €12. Singles €57; doubles €70; triples €95; quads €109. MC/V. ❺

FOOD

El Racó d'en Baltá, C. Aribau, 125 (☎934 53 10 44). M: Hospital Clínic. Founded in 1900, offers eccentric decor and innovative Mediterranean dishes like duck sirloin with rosemary caramel (€13). Fish and meat entrees €12-18. Open M 9-11pm, Tu-Th 1-3:30pm and 9-10:45pm, F 1-3:30pm and 9-11pm, Sa 9-11pm. AmEx/D/MC/V. ❸

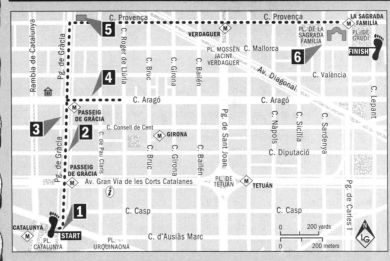

As Barcelona became unbearably crowded within the walls of the old city, a call for designs for an "expansion" (*eixample* in Catalan) was held. Ildefons Cerdà's chosen plan for gridded streets with ample park space and low buildings was not exactly closely followed. However, l'Eixample's spacious, right-angled streets provided the perfect setting for 19th-century experimentation with Modernist architecture, with its bright colors and no-straight-lines designs that need to be admired from a distance.

1 PL. CATALUNYA. Start off in Pl. Catalunya, on the lower border of l'Eixample. Make sure to get your **free map** at El Corte Inglés.

2 PG. DE GRÀCIA. Walk up along the wide, tree-lined Pg. de Gràcia and **resist the temptation** to enter (or at least spend money in) the endless array of expensive designer boutiques. You can already begin to see a significant difference from the cramped, old buildings of the Barri Gòtic.

3 LA MANZANA DE LA DISCÒRDIA. One of the most notable Modernist landmarks is this entire block, known as *La Manzana de la Discòrdia,* between C. Aragó and C. Consell de Cent. It is known as the "block of discord" because of the clash between three designs: **Casa Amatller, Casa Lleó,** and **Casa Batlló** (p. 423). In Casa Amatller you can buy a **Ruta del Modernisme** pass (p. 402). The first floor, the attic, and the chimneys of Gaudí's Casa Batlló are open to the public.

4 C. ARAGÓ. C. Aragó, to the east of Pg. de Gràcia, has affordable quality restaurants and is a great spot to **people-watch** the parade of perfectly dressed *barceloneses*.

5 CASA MILÀ (LA PEDRERA). Three long blocks up Pg. de Gràcia is perhaps Gaudí's best-known work aside from La Sagrada Família, Casa Milà or "La Pedrera." This building, designed to mimic the ocean's waves and seaweed, is definitely worth a visit, especially for the whimsical **rooftop** with its views of Barcelona.

6 LA SAGRADA FAMÍLIA. The last stop is definitely worth the long walk. Take a right onto C. Provença and follow it for 11 blocks (make sure to stay straight and not turn onto the slanted Av. Diagonal). You cannot miss La Sagrada Família, Gaudí's masterpiece, still nowhere near finished (119 years and counting), as well as the site of his tomb.

There is a metro stop (L5 and L2) here to go back to the center of the city. Other Gaudí works not in this immediate area include **Parc Güell** (p. 431), **Palau Güell** (p. 419), the **Calvet House,** the **Teresianes Order School,** the **Bellesguard Tower,** the **Güell Pavillions,** and the **Vicenç House.**

Comme-Bio, Av. Gran Vía, 603 (☎933 01 03 760); also at Vía Laietana, 28 (☎933 19 89 68). The antithesis of traditional Catalan food, this place has hummus, tofu, and yogurt. Restaurant and small grocery store. Pasta, rice, and veggie pizzas €9. Salads €6-8. Specialties €8-12, pasta and rice €7-10. *Menú* €15-23. Buffet €12-16. Open daily 9am-11:30pm. ❷

Tenorio, Pg. de Gràcia, 37 (☎932 72 05 92/94). A hip, modern setting right on Pg. de Gràcia, with patio seating. International fusion cuisine (€7-18); ravioli is a specialty. Open daily 1pm-1:30am. AmEx/MC/V. ❸

Laie Llibreria Café, C. Pau Claris, 85 (☎933 18 17 39; www.laie.es). M: Urquinaona. This urban oasis offers a fresh, plentiful all-you-can-eat buffet (€8.30) on the floor above a great bookstore. Internet €1 per 15min. Open M-F 9am-1am, Sa 10am-1am. Kitchen open 1pm-midnight, M until 9pm. AmEx/MC/V. ❷

Mandalay Café, C. Provença, 330 (☎934 58 60 17; www.mandalaycafe.net). Exotic pan-Asian cuisine, including gourmet dim sum and elegant salads in extravagant decor (eat in bed if you wish). Entrees €9-13. F night trapeze artist around 11pm. Open Tu-F for lunch and dinner until midnight, Sa only for dinner. AmEx/MC/V. ❸

Thai Gardens, C. Diputació, 273 (☎934 87 98 98). M: Catalunya. Extravagant decor livens up classic Thai dishes. *Menú* €28. Pad thai €7.50. Entrees €9-18. Open Su-Th 1-4pm and 8pm-midnight, F-Sa 1:30-4pm and 8pm-1am. ❸

Txapela (Euskal Taberna), Pg. de Gràcia, 8-10 (☎934 12 02 89). M: Catalunya. This Basque restaurant is a godsend for the tapas-clueless traveler who wants to learn, with an exhaustive offering of over 100 types, which you order by number. Tapas €1-1.60. Wheelchair-accessible. Open M-Th 8am-1:30am, F-Su 10am-2am. AmEx/MC/V. ❷

🜂 🏛 SIGHTS AND MUSEUMS

The Catalan *Renaixença* and the growth of Barcelona during the 19th century pushed the city past its medieval walls and into modernity. Ildefons Cerdà drew up a plan for a new neighborhood where people of all social classes could live side by side; however, l'Eixample did not thrive as a utopian community but rather as a playground for the bourgeois. Despite gentrification, the original Modernista architecture that draws visitors remains intact.

▨ LA SAGRADA FAMÍLIA. Although Antoni Gaudí's unfinished masterpiece is barely a shell of the intended finished product, La Sagrada Família is without a doubt the world's most visited construction site. Despite the fact that only eight of the 18 planned towers have been completed (and those the shortest, at that) and the church still doesn't have an "interior," millions of people make the touristic pilgrimage to witness its work-in-progress majesty. Of the three proposed facades, only the Nativity Facade was finished under Gaudí. A furor has arisen over recent additions, especially sculptor Josep Subirachs's Cubist Passion Facade, which is criticized for being inconsistent with Gaudí's plans. Those with claustrophobia will prefer the elevator over the stairs. *(C. Mallorca, 401. M: Sagrada Família. Open daily Apr.-Sept. 9am-8pm, elevator open 9:30am-7:45pm; Oct.-Mar. 9:30am-5:45pm, elevator open 9:30am-5:45pm. €2. Excellent guided tours in English 11am and 1pm, in Spanish noon. In summer, also at 3 and 5:30pm in English, 4pm in Spanish. €3. Entrance €8, students with ISIC card €5. Combined ticket with Casa-Museu Gaudí €8/€6.)*

▨ LA MANZANA DE LA DISCÒRDIA. A short walk from Pl. de Catalunya, the odd-numbered side of Pg. de Gràcia between C. Aragó and Consell de Cent is popularly known as *la manzana de la discòrdia* (block of discord). Its name comes from the stylistic clashing of three buildings. Regrettably, the bottom two floors of **Casa Lleó i Morera,** by Domènech i Montaner, were destroyed to make room for a fancy store, but you can buy the **Ruta del Modernisme pass** there and take a short tour of the upstairs, where sprouting flowers, stained glass, and legendary doorway sculptures adorn the interior. Puig i Cadafalch opted for a geometric, Moorish-influenced pattern on the facade of **Casa Amatller** at #41. Gaudí's balconies ripple like water, and tiles sparkle in blue-purple glory on **Casa Batlló**, #43. The most popular interpretation of Casa Batlló is that the building represents Catalunya's patron Sant Jordi (St. George) slaying a dragon; the chimney plays the lance, the scaly roof is the dragon's back, and the bony balconies are the remains of his victims. The ChupaChups lollipop company now owns the Casa Batlló, and it is closed to the public except for tours. (*Open M-Sa 9am-2pm, Su 9am-8pm. €8, students €6.*)

█ CASA MILÀ (LA PEDRERA). Modernism buffs argue that the spectacular Casa Milà apartment building, an undulating mass of granite popularly known as *La Pedrera* (The Quarry), is Gaudí's most refined work. Note the intricate ironwork around the balconies and the irregularity of the front gate's egg-shaped window panes. A popular interpretation of the design is that it represents the sea—the undulating walls are the waves and the iron balconies are seaweed. The roof sprouts chimneys that resemble armored soldiers, one of which is decorated with broken champagne bottles. Rooftop tours provide a closer look at the Prussian helmets. The winding brick attic has been transformed into the **Espai Gaudí,** a multimedia presentation of Gaudí's life and works. (*Pg. de Gràcia, 92. ☎902 40 09 73. Open daily 10am-8pm, last admission 7:30pm. Free guided tours in English M-F 4pm; in Spanish summer 6pm, winter 4pm. €7, students and over 65 €3.50.*)

FUNDACIÓ ANTONI TÀPIES. Antoni Tàpies is one of Catalunya's best-known artists; his works often defy definition, though they clearly spring from Surrealism. Tàpies's massive and bizarre wire sculpture *(Cloud with Chair)* atop Domènech i Montaner's red brick building announces this collection of contemporary abstract art. The top floor of the foundation is dedicated to famous Catalans, particularly Tàpies, while the first two floors feature temporary exhibits of other modern artists' work. (*C. Aragó, 255. M: Pg. de Gràcia. ☎934 87 03 15. Museum open Su and Tu-Sa 10am-8pm. Free guided tours Sa noon. €4.20, students and seniors €2.10.*)

HOSPITAL DE LA SANTA CREU I SANT PAU. This is not your ordinary green-walled hospital. Designated a UNESCO monument in 1997, the brilliant Modernista Hospital de la Santa Creu i Sant Pau was Domènech i Montaner's lifetime master-piece. The entire complex covers nine full l'Eixample blocks (320 acres) and the pavilions are whimsically decorated, resembling gingerbread houses. The outdoor spaces are an oasis in the desert of urban gridding; they once included a small forest and still boast more than 300 different types of plants, as well as plenty of shaded paths. (*Sant Antoni M. Claret, 167. M: Hospital de St. Pau. ☎934 88 20 78. Hospital grounds open 24hr. 50min. guided tours every 30min. Sa-Su 10am-2pm. Last tour leaves 1:30pm. Call ahead for tours M-F. English tours available. €4.20, students and over 65 €3, groups €3.60.*)

■ NIGHTLIFE

L'Eixample has upscale bars and some of the best—though not exclusively—gay nightlife in Europe, as evident in the area's nickname, "Gaixample."

- **█ Buenavista Salsoteca,** C. Rosselló, 217 (☎932 37 65 28; www.salsabuenavista.com). M: Diagonal. This over-the-top club manages to attract a chill mixed crowd. Free salsa lessons W 10:30pm. Rueda Cubana Th. F-Sa cover €9, includes 1 drink. Open W-Th 11pm-4am, F-Sa 11pm-5am, Su 8:30pm-2am.

- **█ Dietrich,** C. Consell de Cent, 255. M: Pg. de Gràcia. An unflattering cartoonish painting of Marlene Dietrich in the semi-nude greets a mostly gay crowd. Beer €3.50. Mixed drinks €5-8. Nightly trapeze show at 1:30am. Open Su-F 6pm-2:30am, Sa 6pm-3am.

La Fira, C. Provença, 171. M: Hospital Clínic or FGC: Provença. Bartenders serve a hip crowd dangling from carousel swings and surrounded by creepy fun-house mirrors and even a fortune teller. DJs spin funk, disco, and oldies. Open Tu-Th 10pm-3am, F-Sa 7pm-4:30am, Su 6pm-1am.

Les Gens que J'Aime, C. València, 286 (☎932 15 68 79). M: Pg. de Gràcia. Relax in one of the red velvet sofas and travel back to Gaudí's time in this intimate and very peaceful bar. Background soul, funk, and jazz, as well as drinks ranging from *caipirinhas* to dry martinis, sooth patrons. Beer €3. Half-bottles of wine €9. Open daily 7pm-2:30am, weekends until 3am.

Àtame, C. Consell de Cent, 257. M: Pg de Gràcia. Next door to Dietrich, with an industrial green interior, this bar is frequented mainly by gay men but is not as scandalous as its name ("tie me up") might imply. A great, relaxed spot for drinks and conversation. Cocktails €3-8, beer €3. Open daily 5pm-3am.

Luz de Gas, C. Muntaner, 246. M: Diagonal. Chandeliers and deep red walls set the mood in this hip *sala-teatre* that clears out for the dancing clientele later at night. Beer €6, mixed drinks €9. Live music every night, from rock to 60s. Concerts €15; check *Guia del Ocio* for listings and times. Open daily 11pm-5am; July-Aug. closed Su.

Salvation, Ronda de St. Pere, 19-21. M: Urquinaona. The place to come if you've sinned and want to keep on sinning. A popular gay club with a crowd in their late 20s and 30s. Beer €5. Mixed drinks €8. Cover €11, includes 1 drink. Open F-Su midnight-6am.

The Michael Collins Irish Pub, Pl. Sagrada Família, 4 (☎934 59 19 64; www.michael-collinspubs.com). M: Sagrada Família. 100% Irish, from the waitstaff and live music (check the site for schedule) to the smoky, wooden decor. American and European sports on the TV. Draft beer €4, mixed drinks €5. Open daily noon-3am.

MONTJUÏC

Montjuïc (mon-joo-EEK), the hill at the southwest end of the city, is one of the oldest sections of Barcelona; throughout Barcelona's history, whoever controlled Montjuïc's peak controlled the city. The Laietani collected oysters near Montjuïc before they were subdued by the Romans, who erected a temple to Jupiter on its slopes. Since then, dozens of despotic rulers have constructed and modified the **Castell de Montjuïc,** built atop the ancient Jewish cemetery (hence the name Montjuïc, Hill of the Jews). In the 20th century, Franco made the Castell de Montjuïc one of his "interrogation" headquarters; somewhere deep in the recesses of the structure, his *ben-eméritos* ("honorable ones," a.k.a. the militia) are believed to have shot Catalunya's former president, Lluís Companys, in 1941. The fort was not re-dedicated to the city until 1960. Since re-acquiring the mountain, Barcelona has given Montjuïc a new identity, transforming it from a military stronghold into a vast park by day and a playground by night. Today the park is one of the city's most visited attractions, with a little bit of something for everyone—world-famous art museums and theater, Olympic history and facilities, walking and bike trails, a healthy/unhealthy dose of nightlife, and an awe-inspiring historical cemetery. Since it is out of the way, Montjuïc is a nice change from the packed streets of downtown, and most attractions guarantee a view of the city that confirms just how big Barcelona is.

▐ FOOD

Food options are not as plentiful in Montjuïc as in the rest of the city. The Fundació Miró, MNAC, Castell de Montjuïc, and Teatre Grec all have pleasant cafes, but to find more than drinks and sandwiches, enter the depths of Poble Espanyol. *Menús* of all sorts run €10-15; otherwise, try one of the listings below. Some restaurants, bars, and grocery stores also line **Avinguda Paral.lel** in Poble Sec.

La Font de Prades, (☎934 26 75 19) at the Plaça de la Font in Poble Espanyol. M: Espanya. Set back in a quiet, less-trafficked area of Poble Espanyol, is this surprisingly elegant restaurant. *Menú* €13. Open Tu-Th 1-4pm and 8:30-11pm, F-Sa 1-4pm and 8:30pm-midnight, Su 1-4pm. Bar open until the restaurant clears out. ❸

La Pérgola, (☎933 25 20 08) at the corner of Av. Reina María Cristina and Av. del Marquès de Comillas. M: Espanya. During the day (1-4pm), this is a classic full-service dining room in which the tuxedoed staff will serve you such carefully prepared favorites as Perigord duck marinated in ginger (€13). *Menú* €42. From late afternoon on it is a bar-cafe popular with both international businessmen and tourists. Offers a tasty buffet-style *menú* (€10). Open daily 9:30am-9pm. After 4pm, drinks only. Closed in Aug. ❸

👁 🏛 SIGHTS AND MUSEUMS

🖼 FUNDACIÓ MIRÓ. Designed by Miró's friend Josep Lluís Sert and tucked into the side of Montjuïc, the Fundació links modern white interior and exterior spaces with massive windows and outdoor patios. Skylights illuminate an extensive collection of statues and paintings from Miró's career, ranging from sketches to massive, wall-sized canvases. His best-known pieces in the museum include *El Carnival de Arlequín*, *La Masia*, and *L'or de l'azuz*. Room 13 displays experimental work by young artists. The Fundació also sponsors music and film festivals. A must for art-lovers. Also check out the sculpture garden on the side; you can follow the garden paths down the hill to the Palau Nacional. *(Av. Miramar, 71-75. Take the funicular from M: Paral.lel. Open Tu-Sa 10am-7pm, Th 10am-9:30pm, Su and holidays 10am-2:30pm. Doors close 15min. early. Library open Tu-F 10am-2pm and 3-6pm, Sa 10am-2pm. €7.20, students and seniors €3.90. Temporary exhibitions €3.60/€1.80. Under 14 free.)*

🖼 MUSEU NACIONAL D'ART DE CATALUNYA (PALAU NACIONAL). Designed by Enric Catá and Pedro Cendoya for the 1929 International Exposition, the beautiful Palau Nacional has housed the Museu Nacional d'Art de Catalunya (MNAC) since 1934. Its main hall is a public event space, while the wings are home to the world's finest collection of Catalan Romanesque art and a wide variety of Gothic pieces. The Romanesque frescoes, now integrated as murals into dummy chapels, were salvaged in the 1920s from their original, less protected locations in northern Catalunya's churches. The museum's Gothic art corridor displays paintings on wood, the medium of choice during that period. The chronological tour of the galleries emphasizes the growing influence of Italy over Catalunya's artistic development, and ends with a breathtaking series of paintings by Gothic master Bernat Martorell. As soon as 2005, the historical art of the museum will be complemented by the modern art from the Museu d'Art Modern, which is being moved in its entirety into the Palau Nacional from its previous home in the Parc de la Ciutadella. In front of the building the **Fonts Luminoses** (the Illuminated Fountains) are dominated by the central **Font Mágica,** which come alive during weekend laser shows in the summer. *(From M: Espanya, walk up Av. Reina María Cristina, away from the twin brick towers, and take the escalators to the top. Open Tu-Sa 10am-7pm, Su and holidays 10am-2:30pm. €4.80 for permanent Romanesque exhibit. Temporary exhibits €3-4.20; both temporary exhibits €5; 1 temporary plus permanent €6; all exhibits €7.50. 30% discount for students and seniors.)*

🖼 CASTELL DE MONTJUÏC. A visit to this historic fortress and its **Museum Militar** is a great way to get an overview of the city's layout and history. Gaze over the city from the castle's exterior *mirador*. Enjoy coffee at the cafe while cannons stare you down. Make sure to take the *teleféric* to and from the castle, since that is half the fun. A good place to go just for the views, if military history isn't your thing. *(From M: Paral.lel, take the funicular to Av. Miramar and then the cable* *car to the castle. Teleféric de Montjuïc open M-Sa 11:15am-9pm, and 11am-7:15pm low season. One-way €3.60, round-trip €5. Or, walk up the steep slope on C. Foc, next to the funicular station. Open daily 9am-10pm. Castle and mirador €2.)*

⚑ NIGHTLIFE

Lower Montjuïc is home to **Poble Espanyol,** a recreation of famous buildings and sights from all regions of Spain. The courtyards host performances, and the entire complex is filled with interesting crafts shops. (Av. Marquès de Comillas. ☎935 08 63 00; www.poble-espanyol.com. M: Espanya or bus #13, 50, or 100. Open Su 9am-midnight, M 9am-8pm, Tu-Th 9am-2am, F-Sa 9am-4am. Ticket booth closes 1hr. before park. English guided tours €2. €7, students and seniors €5. Prices may vary when there are concerts.) A visit is perhaps best at night, when it turns into Barcelona's epic "disco theme park." Fall in love with the craziest clubbing experience in all of Barcelona at some of the most popular (and surreal) venues: **La Terrazza,** an outdoor madhouse. (☎934 23 12 85; www.laterrazza.com. Open May 28-Aug. Su midnight-6am; Sept.-June Su and Th-Sa midnight-6am.) Its winter counterpart, **Discothèque,** has a strict door policy (dress up as trendily as you can muster, and then skank it up a bit) and an €18 cover, which includes 1 drink. (Open Oct.-May F-Sa 12-7am.) ◪**Tinta Roja,** near Poble Espanyol, is for tango lovers, with a live show. Dancing starts at 1am and ends after 8am. (C. Creus dels Molers, 17. ☎934 43 32 43. Open W-Su 8pm-2:30am.)

THE WATERFRONT

In addition to the piers of **Barceloneta** and **Port Vell, Poble Nou** and **Port Olímpic** are also part of Barcelona's coastline. Barceloneta, or "Little Barcelona," was born out of necessity. In 1718, La Ribera was butchered to make room for the enormous **Ciutadella** fortress; the destruction of this historic neighborhood left thousands homeless, and it was not until 30 years later that the city created Barceloneta to house the displaced refugees. This area follows a carefully planned grid pattern, which would later influence the design of l'Eixample. Because of its seaside location, Barceloneta became home to the city's sailors, fishermen, and their families. Barcelona's drive to refurbish its waterfront resulted in the expansion of Port Vell. After moving a congested coastal road underground, the city opened Moll de la Fusta, a wide pedestrian zone that leads to the beaches of Barceloneta and connects the bright **Maremàgnum** and the **Moll d'Espanya.** Today, the entire stretch from here (in front of the Columbus monument), through the rejuvenated **Port Vell**—the "Old Port"—until Port Olímpic, is as hedonistic and touristy as Barcelona gets.

Until the last few decades, Poble Nou consisted mainly of factories, warehouses, and low-income housing. Auto shops and commercial supply stores still abound, but the major factories were all removed for the **1992 Olympics.** When Barcelona was granted its Olympic bid in 1986, this privilege presented a two-sided challenge: comfortably housing 15,000 athletes while beautifying the city's long-ignored coastline. Oriol Bohigas, Josep Martorell, David Mackay, and Albert Puig Domènech designed the solution: the **Vila Olímpica,** a residential area with wide streets, symmetrical apartment buildings, pristine parks, and open-air art. Most social activity in the area takes place in the L-shaped **Port Olímpic,** home to docked sailboats, over 20 restaurants, a large casino, and a long strip of brash nightclubs. The promenade right on the beach between Barceloneta and Port Olímpic is a great place to run, walk, sit, or people-watch.

⚡ FOOD

■ **HBN BCN,** C. Escar, 1 (☎932 25 02 63), right on Platja San Sebastián in Barceloneta, at the end of Pg. Joan de Borbó on the right. The perfect place for those craving Latin American cuisine, with both typical Mediterranean and Cuban fare served by a beautiful staff. Try the *picadillo* and *arroz congrí,* or the combined plate of Cuban tapas (plantains, yuca, avocado, shredded beef, rice, and beans). Bar serves great *mojitos* with live band Th and Su at 6pm. Dinner reservations recommended. Kitchen open 1-4pm and 9pm-midnight. AmEx/MC/V. ❸

■ **Agua,** Pg. Marítim de la Barceloneta, 30 (☎932 25 12 72; www.grupotragaluz.com), the farthest establishment before Barceloneta, to the right of the copper fish. This upscale restaurant attracts large numbers of tourists, trendy *barceloneses,* and GQ-business-types. Stare at the eclectic photos and paintings that dot the dark blue walls as you enjoy Agua's specialties: delicate seafood and rice dishes. Vegetarian options. Entrees €5.50-14; prawns €30. Wheelchair-accessible. Open daily 1:30-4pm and 8:30pm-midnight. Reservations recommended. AmEx/MC/V. ❸

Zahara, Pg. Joan de Borbó, 69 (☎932 21 37 65; www.zahara.com). This hip cocktail bar is a diamond in the rough of mainstream Barceloneta bar-cafes. The extensive menu uses color-codes and icons to show the contents and potency of each cocktail (€6-9). Tasty salads €8-9, sandwiches €4-5, beer €2.50. Open daily 1pm-3am. MC/V. ❷

👁 🏛 SIGHTS AND MUSEUMS

■ **TORRE SAN SEBASTIÀ.** One of the easiest and best ways to view the city is from these cable cars, which span the entire Port Vell, connecting beachy Barceloneta with mountainous Montjuïc. The full ride, which takes about 10min. each way and makes an intermediate stop at the Jaume I tower near Colom, gives an aerial perspective of the entire city. (*Pg. Joan de Borbó. M: Barceloneta. In Port Vell, as you walk down Joan de Borbó and see the beaches to the left, stay right and look for the high tower. Open daily 11am-8pm. To Jaume I round-trip €7.50; to Montjuïc one-way €7.50, round-trip €9; short round-trip to the closer tower €7.50; just the elevator to the top €3.50.*)

L'AQUÀRIUM DE BARCELONA. Barcelona's aquarium is an aquatic wonder, featuring a large number of octopi and penguins. The highlight is a 75m glass tunnel through an ocean tank of sharks, sting rays, and a two-dimensional fish. (*Moll d'Espanya, next to Maremàgnum. M: Drassanes or Barceloneta. Advanced tickets ☎932 21 74 74; www.aquariumbcn.com. Open July-Aug. daily 9:30am-11pm; Sept.-June 9:30am-9:30pm. €13.50, students €12.50, under 12 and seniors €9.25.*)

VILA OLÍMPICA. The Vila Olímpica, beyond the east side of the zoo, was built to house 15,000 athletes and entertain millions of tourists for the 1992 Summer Olympics. It's home to several public parks, a shopping center, and offices. It's worth checking out to see the newest, most modern part of Barcelona. In **Barceloneta,** beaches stretch out from the old port around a small working-class neighborhood. (*M: Ciutadella or Vila Olímpica. Walk along the water on Ronda Litoral toward the 2 towers.*)

MUSEU MARÍTIM. The *Drassanes Reiales de Barcelona* (Royal Shipyards of Barcelona) are considered the world's greatest standing example of civil (i.e. non-religious) Gothic architecture and are currently awaiting nomination as a UNESCO World Heritage Site. The complex consists of a series of huge indoor bays with slender pillars, in which entire ships could be constructed and stored over the winter. Since 1941, the building has housed the Maritime Museum, which traces (a bit dryly) the evolution of shipbuilding and life on the high seas. It also has a nice cafe. *(Av. Drassanes, off the rotary around the Monument a Colom. M: Drassanes. ☎933 42 99 20. Open daily 10am-7pm. Free audio guide. €5.40; under 16, students, and seniors €2.70. Museum and ride on Las Golondrinas boat €6.60/€5.10. Museum and ride on TriMar €10.10/€7.70.)*

PARC DIAGONAL MAR. The center of a new neighborhood to the east of Port Olímpic, this 14-hectare park was designed by Enric Miralles. Its innovative design incorporating plants, water, and a tubular structure, is noteworthy, and the park is perfect for relaxing and escaping the masses of Barcelona. *(At the end of Av. Diagonal, where it meets the sea. Walk 1 block toward the water. M: Selva de Mar.)*

 NIGHTLIFE

POBLE NOU AND PORT OLÍMPIC

L'Ovella Negra (Megataverna del Poble Nou), C. Zamora, 78 (☎933 09 59 38). What was once a warehouse is now the place to come for the first few beers of the night. Foosball games on the 2nd floor are nearly as intense as the real-life Barça-Real Madrid matches. Large beers €2. Cocktails from €2. Open F-Sa 5pm-3am, Su 5-10:30pm. Kitchen open until 12:30am.

Razzmatazz, C. Pamplona, 88 and Almogàvers, 122, across the street (☎932 72 09 10; pedro@sinnamon.es). M: Marina. A huge warehouse-turned-entertainment complex now houses 5 clubs, each with its own ambience: Pop, The Loft, Razz Club, Lo*Li*Ta, and Temple Beat Room. The overall feel is decidedly rock and techno, with strobe-lit dance floors and concert space for indie rock. Concert prices vary; call ahead. Beer €3. Cocktails €6. Cover €12, includes access to all 5. Open F-Sa and holidays 1-5am. MC/V.

Catwalk, C. Ramón Trias Fargas, 2-4 (☎932 21 61 61). The sleek interior makes this one of the hottest (and most exclusive) places in town, if not to get a date then at least to watch other people. Previously Club Danzatoria. All house music all the time. Inquire about cover. Open Th-Su midnight-6am.

MAREMÀGNUM

Like Dr. Jekyll, Barcelona's biggest mall (p. 406) has another personality. At night, the complex turns into a tri-level maze of clubs, each playing its own music for a throng of tourists and the occasional Spaniard. Some highlights are **Nayandei,** which houses two clubs in one: **Disco** has an open-door policy, but the **Boîte** has a more strict dress code. (Spanish and American dance-pop. Open 9pm-4:30am, until 6am on weekends.) Other clubs include: **Irish Winds** (an Irish bar with live Celtic music), **Star Winds** (non-stop house; open 9pm-sunrise), and **Mojito Bar** (slightly more affordable cocktails at €6; straight-up Latin music—Salsa and merengue with current tunes mixed in; open 5pm-5am). Though not the most authentic experience in Barcelona, it is extremely fun, and crowds are guaranteed all week. None charge cover; clubs make their money from exorbitant drink prices (beer €5, mixed drinks €8-10). Good luck catching a cab after closing time; the night isn't over until a drunken tourist falls into the harbor on the way home.

ZONA ALTA: GRÀCIA AND OUTER BARRIS

Zona Alta ("Uptown") is the section of Barcelona that lies at the top of most maps: past l'Eixample, in and around the Collserola mountains, and away from the low-lying waterfront districts. The Zona Alta is made of several formerly independent towns. Although all of these have now been incorporated into Barcelona's city limits as residential areas, each neighborhood retains its own character.

The most visited part of Zona Alta is Gràcia, which was incorporated into Barcelona in 1897, much to the protest of its residents. Calls for Gràcian independence continue even today, albeit with less frequency. The area has always had a political streak—a theme that appears in the names of Mercat de Llibertat, Pl. de la Revolució, and others. After incorporation, the area continued to be a center of leftwing activism and resistance, even throughout the oppressive Franco regime. Gràcia packs a surprising number of Modernista buildings and parks, international cuisine, and chic shops into a relatively small area, making it a good choice for exploring. Relatively untouched by tourism, Gràcia retains a local charm that has been sapped from some of Barcelona's more popular sections; staying here is worth the short commute to the center of the city.

ACCOMMODATIONS

Gràcia is Barcelona's "undiscovered" quarter, so last-minute arrivals may find vacancies here, although options are few.

Pensión San Medín, C. Gran de Gràcia, 125 (☎932 17 30 68; sanmedin@telefonica.net). M: Fontana. Embroidered curtains and ornate tiling adorn this family-run pension's 12 rooms, 4 with balcony. Small common room with TV. Reception open 8am-midnight. Singles €30, with bath €39; doubles €48/60. MC/V. ❸

Hostal Lesseps, C. Gran de Gràcia, 239 (☎932 18 44 34; fax 17 11 80). M: Lesseps. Spacious, classy rooms sport red velvet wallpaper. All 16 rooms have TV and bath; 4 have A/C (€5 extra). Rooms facing the street are a bit noisy. Singles €40; doubles €65; triples €80; quads €95-100. MC/V. ❹

Albergue Mare de Déu de Montserrat (HI), Pg. Mare de Déu del Coll, 41-51 (☎932 10 51 51; www.tujuca.com). This gorgeous 220-bed hostel is a great way to meet other backpackers, in spite of its distance from the city center. Breakfast included. Flexible 3-day max. stay. Dorms €21.60, under 25 €18.10. HI members only. AmEx/MC/V. ❶

Alberg Residència La Ciutat, C. L'Alegre de Dalí, 66 (☎932 13 03 00). M: Joanic. Follow C. Escorial up for 5 blocks, then cross one street over to the right onto C. L'Alegre de Dalí; the Alberg will be on the right. This Alberg is roomier and cleaner than many downtown options and a great way to meet other travelers. Several lounge areas with satellite TV and kitchen access. Private rooms have TV, phone, and bath. Breakfast and Internet included. Laundry €5.40. Reception 8am-11pm. Renew/check-out before 10am. 4- to 12-bed dorms €19.30; singles €32.10; doubles €51.40. MC/V. ❷

FOOD

OvUm, C. Encarnació, 56 (☎932 19 82 13). M: Joanic. Follow C. Escorial for 2 blocks and turn left on C. Encarnació. True to its name, this charming low-lit restaurant features egg specialties (such as roast egg with pineapple and parmesan; €5) and vegetarian options with a Catalan twist. Salads (yes, with eggs) €6, entrees (with egg as well) €5-6, omelettes €6-7. Open Su and Tu-Sa 8:30-11:30pm. Closed 1st week of Aug. Reservations recommended for dinner. AmEx/MC/V. ❷

La Gavina, C. Ros de Olano, 17 (☎934 15 74 50), at the corner of C. St. Joaquím. Funky Italian pizzeria complete with a life-size patron saint. Pizzas €5.50-16. Wheelchair-accessible. Open Tu-Su 2pm-1am, F-Sa 2pm-2am. ❸

Sushi Itto, C. Londres, 103 (☎932 41 21 99; www.sushi-itto.com). This classy sushi place combines Japanese cuisine with Western flavors, such as in the eclectic roll options. Lunch *menú* M-F €9.90. Open M-Su 1:30-4:30pm and 8:30pm-midnight. ❸

Restaurant Illa de Gràcia, C. Sant Domenec, 19 (☎932 38 02 29). M: Diagonal. Follow Gran de Gràcia for 5 blocks and make a right onto C. Sant Domenec. This small locale boasts a huge vegetarian menu with tons of well-balanced options. Entrees €4-6. Open Tu-Su 2-4pm and 9pm-midnight. Closed last 2 weeks of Aug. D/MC/V. ❶

Restaurante Casa Regina (El 19 De La Riera), C. Riera de Sant Miquel, 19 (☎932 37 86 01). M: Diagonal. This semi-casual restaurant with simple decor serves only organic food, including grilled meats and vegetarian options. *Menú* €9.40, entrees €5-42, most around €10. Open M-Sa 1-4pm and 9-11:30pm. MC/V. ❸

◉ 🏛 SIGHTS AND MUSEUMS

▨ PARC GÜELL. This fantastic park was designed entirely by Gaudí but—in typical Gaudí fashion—was not completed until after his death. Gaudí intended Parc Güell to be a garden city, and its dwarfish buildings and sparkling ceramic-mosaic stairways were designed to house the city's elite. However, only one house was built, which is now the **Casa-Museu Gaudí.** Two mosaic staircases flank the park, leading to a towering Modernista pavilion that Gaudí originally designed as an open-air market but now houses only the occasional street musician. The longest park bench in the world, a multicolored serpentine wonder made of tile shards, decorates the top of the pavilion. (*Bus #24 from Pl. Catalunya stops at the upper entrance. Park free. For tours, contact the Museu d'Historia de la Ciutat which will make a group for one. Open May-Sept. daily 10am-9pm; Mar.-Apr. and Oct. 10am-7pm; Nov.-Feb. 10am-6pm. Museum open daily Apr.-Sept. 10am-8pm; Oct.-Mar. 10am-6pm. €4, students with ISIC card €3.*)

▨ MUSEU DEL FÚTBOL CLUB BARCELONA. A close second to the Picasso Museum as Barcelona's most-visited museum, the FCB museum merits all the attention it gets from soccer fanatics. Sports fans will appreciate the storied history of the team. The high point is the chance to enter the stadium and take in the enormity of Camp Nou. It costs extra to see the facilities, such as dressing room and the field. (*C. Arístides Maillol, next to the stadium. ☎934 96 36 08. M: Collblanc. Enter through access gates 7 or 9. Open M-Sa 10am-6:30pm, Su and holidays 10am-2pm. €5.30, under 13 €3.70, students and seniors €4.50. Facilities and museum €9.50/€6.60/€8.10.*)

▨ NIGHTLIFE

The area around C. Marià Cubí has great nightlife unspoiled by tourists, but you'll have to take a taxi. For more accessible fun in Gràcia, head to Pl. del Sol, where you will find relaxed bars like **Eldorado** (Pl. del Sol, 4; ☎932 37 36 96; open 7pm-2:30am) and **Café del Sol** (Pl. del Sol, 16; ☎934 15 56 63; open daily 1pm-2:30am).

▨ Otto Zutz, C. Lincoln, 15 (☎932 38 07 22; www.ottozutz.com). FGC: Pl. Molina. Groove to house, hip-hop, and funk while Japanimation lights up the top floor in one of Barcelona's most famous clubs. Beer €5. Cover €15, includes 1 drink; email ahead or look for flyers at bars and upscale hotels in the city for a discount. Open Tu-W midnight-5am; Th-Sa midnight-6am.

Gasterea, C. Verdi, 39. M: Fontana. Yellow walls cast a warm glow in this table-less bar. Tapas €1.05. Mixed drinks €5. Su-Tu and Th 7pm-1am, F-Sa 7pm-2am.

D Mer, C. Plató, 13 (☎932 01 62 07). FCG: Muntaner. A blue-hued heaven for lesbians of all ages. A touch of class, a dash of whimsy, and a ton of fun in this small club. Cover €7, includes 1 drink. Beer €3.50. Mixed drinks €6. Open Th-Sa 11pm-3:30am.

Bar Marcel, C. Santaló, 42. When midnight strikes, locals pack this cafe-bar in search of cheap booze. Certainly not the fanciest bar in the neighborhood, but possibly the most loved by locals. Beer €1.60. Mixed drinks €5. Prices vary. Open daily 8pm-3am.

⚡ DAYTRIP FROM BARCELONA

MONTSERRAT ☎938

A 1235m peak protruding sharply from the Río Llobregat Valley with a colorful interplay of limestone, quartz, and slate, Montserrat (Sawed Mountain) inspires poets, artists, and travelers. A millennium ago, a wandering mountaineer saw the Virgin Mary here; as the story spread, pilgrims flocked to the mountain. The Monastery of the Virgin, founded in 1025 by the opportunistic Bishop Oliba, is tended today by 80 Benedictine monks. During the Catalan *Renaixença* of the 19th century, politicians and artists, like poets Joan Maragall and Jacint Verdaguer, turned to Montserrat as a source of Catalan legend and tradition. Under Franco, it became a center of regional resistance. Today, the site attracts devout worshippers and tourists who come to see the Virgin of Montserrat, her ornate basilica, the art museum, and panoramic views of the mountain's stunning rocks.

▯ TRANSPORTATION. FGC (☎932 05 15 15) line R5 runs to Montserrat from M: Espanya in Barcelona (1hr.; every hr. 8:36am-5:36pm; return from Montserrat 10:37am-7:37pm; round-trip including cable car €12); get off at Montserrat-Aeri, not Olesa de Montserrat. From there, catch the **Aeri cable car** right by the station, the coolest way of ascending to the monastery. (Daily July-Aug. every 15min. 9:23am-1:45pm and 2:40-6:45pm; price included in FCG fare or €6 by itself. Schedules change frequently; call ☎938 77 77 01 to check.) Another option (more suitable for those who don't like dangling from a cable over 100m in the air) is to take the FGC's new **Cremallera de Montserrat.** (☎902 31 20 20; www.cremallerademontserrat.com.) Purchase a combined R5 train plus the Cremallera (Rack Railway) instead of the Cable Car (Cremallera alone €6, children €3.30, retired €5.40; combined, including train from Pl. Espanya, €11.80/€9.10/€11.20). Get off the FGC one station later, at Olesa de Montserrat, and take the railway up (every 20-30min.). **Autocars Julià** buses run to the monastery, from near Estació Sants. (Leaves Barcelona daily 9am and returns June 25-Sept.14 6pm, rest of the year 5pm. Call ☎933 17 64 54 for reservations. €10. MC/V.) If you plan to use the funiculars (railways from the monastery that take you to hiking paths) to hike, consider the **Tot Montserrat,** available at tourist offices or in M: Espanya; it includes tickets for the FGC, cable car, funiculars, Museu de Montserrat, and a meal, all for €34 (€20 if you buy it at Montserrat without FGC fare). Call ☎938 35 03 84 for a **taxi.**

⚡ PRACTICAL INFORMATION. Montserrat is not a town, but a monastery with very limited adjacent lodging and food for religious and camera-toting pilgrims. Visitor services are in Pl. Creu, the area straight ahead from the top of the Aeri cable car steps and the Cremallera station. The **info booth** in Pl. Creu provides free maps, schedules of religious services, and advice on mountain navigation. An audio guide with booklet to Montserrat that you return before leaving is €5. Audio-guide with headphones for two is €6.50. (☎938 77 77 77. Open July to mid-Sept. daily 9am-7pm; Oct.-June M-F 9am-5:30pm, Sa-Su 9am-7pm.) For much more detailed information, buy the *Official Guide to Montserrat* (€7.30) or the guide to the museum (€4). Services include: **ambulance** or **mountain rescue team** (☎936 92 80 80); the **Patronat del Parc Natural** (☎938 35 05 91); **ATMs** and bank at La Caixa, next door to the info office (open M-F 9:15am-2pm, Sa 9:15am-1:30pm; June-Sept. closed Sa); **post office** (open M-F 10am-1:30pm and Sa 10am-noon).

☐ FOOD. Food options in Montserrat are extremely limited and aimed entirely at tourists trapped on a mountainside with no other alternatives. A great idea is to pack food for your hike before coming. You can also pick up some at the small **Queviures supermarket** in Pl. Creu. For a quick meal, **Bar de la Plaça ❶** is next to the supermarket. (*Bocadillos* and hamburgers €2.60-3.60. Open M-F 9:30am-5pm, Sa 9:30am-4:40pm.) A new **cafeteria ❶** in Pl. Creu has limited self-service food options. (Sandwiches €3-4, steak and fries €5, salads €4. Open M-F 8:45am-7:45pm, Sa-Su 8:30am-8:15pm. MC/V.) The barren (but with a great view) **self-service cafeteria ❷** for Tot Montserrat card-holders is up the hill to the right from the cable car steps (2 dishes, chosen from paella, pasta, and meat, plus dessert and bread, drinks not included, for €9.70, Sa-Su €10.35; children under 12 €6; open Feb.-Dec. daily noon-4pm), as is **Restaurant de Montserrat ❷**. (*Menú* €13, holidays €14.10, children €6; special *menú* €20.50. Open Mar. 15-Nov. 15 daily noon-4:30pm. MC/V.) The **Restaurant Hotel Abat Cisneros ❺** offers an expensive *menú* (€23.30) of Catalan food in a nice setting. (Open daily 1-4pm and 8-10pm. AmEx/MC/V.)

◙ SIGHTS. Above Pl. Creu (from the info office, take the stairs up and to the right), the beautiful **basílica** looks onto Pl. Santa Noría. Inside the courtyard, next to the main chapel entrance, a hallway through side chapels leads to an elevated shrine with the 12th-century Romanesque **La Moreneta** (the black Virgin), an icon of Mary. (Walkway open July-Sept. daily 8-10:30am and noon-6:30pm; Nov.-June M-F 8-10:30am and noon-6:30pm, Sa-Su 8-10:30am and noon-6:30pm; holidays 7:30am-8:15pm.) Legend has it that San Pedro hid the figure, carved by San Lucas, in Montserrat's caves. For many years it was revered as a black virgin, until it was discovered that the statue was merely very dirty; the custom stuck, however, and it was painted black. It is now showcased in an ornate silver case surrounded by intricate color and gold mosaics of Biblical figures. For luck, rub the orb in Mary's hand. Behind the shrine is a beautiful chapel. If you can, catch a performance of the renowned **Escalonia boys' choir** in the basilica. (Daily 1 and 7:30pm, except late June and July.) Also in Pl. Santa María, through a walkway to the right of the basilica, the small **Museo de Montserrat** has a variety of art, from an Egyptian mummy to Picasso's *Old Fisherman* and Dalí's *El Mariner*. The Impressionist works, particularly Joaquim Torres Garcia's wide, colorful landscapes, are the highlight. (Open July-Sept. M-F 10am-7pm, Sa-Su 9:30am-7:40pm; Nov.-June M-F 10am-6pm, Sa-Su 9:30am-6:30pm. €5.50, students and over 65 €4.50, ages 6-12 €3.50, under 6 free.)

◪ WALKS. Some of the most beautiful areas of the mountain are accessible only on foot. The **Santa Cova funicular** descends from Pl. Creu to paths which wind to ancient hermitages. (Apr.-Oct. daily every 20min. 10am-6pm; Nov.-Mar. Sa-Su only 10am-5pm. Round-trip €2.50, students €2.30, ages 3-14 €1.30.) Take the **St. Joan funicular** up the hill for inspirational views of Montserrat. (Apr.-Oct. daily every 20min. 10am-6:40pm; Nov.-Mar. M-F 11am-5pm, Sa-Su 10am-5pm. Round-trip €6.10; joint round-trip ticket with the Sta. Cova funicular €6.90, over 65 €6.20, ages 10-14 €3.50.) The dilapidated **St. Joan monastery** and **shrine** are only a 20min. tromp from the highest station. The real prize is **Sant Jerónim** (the area's highest peak at 1235m), with its views of Montserrat's mystical rocks. The serrated outcroppings are named for human forms, including "The Bewitched Friars" and "The Mummy." The hike is about 2½hr. from Pl. Creu or a 1hr. trek from the terminus of the St. Joan funicular. The paths are long and winding but not difficult—after all, they were made for guys wearing long robes. En route, take a sharp left after about 45min. to reach a small old chapel—otherwise you'll hit a helicopter pad. On a clear day, the hike offers views of Barcelona and surrounding areas.

CATALUÑA (CATALUNYA)

From rocky Costa Brava to smooth Costa Dorada, the lush Pyrenees to chic Barcelona, Catalunya is a vacation in itself. It has been graced with many of the nation's richest resources, making it the most prosperous region in Iberia. *Catalanes* are famous for their work ethic; as the saying goes, *"El Català de les pedres fa pa"* (the Catalan makes bread out of stones).

Colonized first by the Greeks and the Carthaginians, Catalunya was later one of Rome's favored provinces. Only briefly subdued by the Moors, Catalunya's counts achieved independence in 987. Catalunya grew powerful as she joined the throne of Aragón in 1137; still, while this union empowered Catalunya to pursue her own empire for a time, it ultimately doomed her to be subjugated to Spanish rule. King Felipe V was finally able to suppress Catalunya fully in the early 18th century, after the Catalans sided against him in the War of the Spanish Succession (1702-1714). In the late 18th century, the region's fortunes revived when it developed into one of Europe's premier textile manufacturers and pursued trade with the Americas. Nineteenth-century industrial expansion nourished arts and sciences, ushering in an age known as the Catalan *Renaixença* (Renaissance). The 20th century gave birth to the Modernista movement and an all-star list of artists and architects, including Pic-

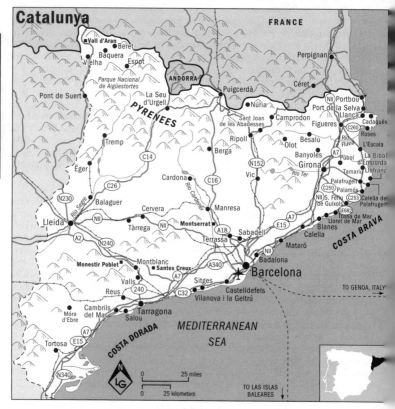

asso, Miró, Dalí, Antoni Gaudí i Comet, Lluís Domènech i Montaner, and Josep Puig i Cadafalch. Home to staunch opponents of the Fascists during Spain's Civil War, Catalunya lost its autonomy in 1939. During his regime, Franco suppressed Catalan language instruction (except in universities) and limited Catalan publications.

Since Catalunya regained regional autonomy in 1977, Catalan media and arts have flourished; Catalan is once again the official language. While some worry that the use of the regional dialect will discourage talented Spaniards from working or studying in Catalunya, effectively isolating the region, others argue that extensive regional autonomy has generally led to progressive ends. Many *catalanes* will answer inquiring visitors in Catalan even if asked in *castellano*. Catalunya offers visitors the chance to experience a different side of Spain's multifaceted persona.

HIGHLIGHTS OF CATALUNYA

SURRENDER to Dalí's egotism at the Teatre-Museu Dalí in **Figueres** (p. 464).

BATTLE the ghosts of gladiators in **Tarragona's** Roman amphiteater (p. 442).

UNWIND in the charming village of **Calella** on the Costa Brava (p. 455).

LEARN the secrets of the Kabbala where it was created, in **Girona's** El Call (p. 460).

COME OUT of your culinary shell in **Lleida** at the snail festival in May (p. 469).

COSTA DORADA

SITGES ☎ 938

Forty kilometers south of Barcelona, the beach town of Sitges deserves its self-ordained title of the "jewel of the Mediterranean," offering visitors crystalline water, sweeping bays, and beautiful tanning grounds baked by 300 sunny days per year. First prominent in the late 19th century as one of the principal centers of the *Modernisme* art movement, today Sitges is swarmed by tourists from around the world who have heard tales of its thriving gay community and vibrant nightlife. Although the flood of daytripping Spaniards, tourist families, and twenty-something partiers may drown other towns, in Sitges it only seems to supply an exhilarating flavor. So close it shares a phone code with Barcelona, Sitges makes an ideal daytrip but is also worth a couple of nights' stay.

▐ TRANSPORTATION

Cercanías trains (☎934 90 02 02) run from Estació Barcelona-Sants to Sitges (40min., every 15-30min. 5:40am-11:06pm, €2.20). Trains also run from Sitges to **Cambrils** (1hr., €3.30) via **Salou** and **Tarragona. Mon Bus** (☎938 93 70 60) connects the Barcelona Airport to Pg. Villafranca in Sitges (M-F every hr., Sa-Su every 2hr.). More importantly, **late night buses** operate from Pg. Villafranca to Rmbla. Catalunya in Barcelona and back (12:11-4am, €2.85). **Bus Urba** runs local buses 8am-9pm (9:30am-9pm on weekends) every 30min. (☎938 14 49 89. €0.80-0.85.)

A **taxi** (☎938 94 13 29) between Barcelona and Sitges costs €45-50. To reach the beaches and *calas* between them, rent a car in Barcelona or in Sitges at **Europcar** (☎938 11 19 96), on the first floor of the Mercat to the right from the train station.

▬ ▐ ORIENTATION AND PRACTICAL INFORMATION

Most people coming to Sitges arrive at the train station, on **Carrer Carbonell,** in the northern section of town. From here, the town center is 5min. by foot, the beach about 10min. To reach either, take a right as you leave the station and then the third left onto **Carrer Sant Francesc.** This leads straight to the old town, and intersects with **Carrer Parellades,** the main path of stores and restaurants, which runs parallel to the ocean. Any street off Parellades will lead to the waterfront. **Passeig Ribera** runs along the central and most crowded beaches.

For a good free map and info on accommodations, nightlife, and beaches, stop by the **tourist office,** Sínia Morera, 1. From the station, turn right onto C. Carbonell and take a right a block later at the plaza. The office is across the street, a block to the left—look for the sign with the big "i." Make sure to ask for the monthly bulletin of events, expositions, and tours called ◪**Sitges Daily.** (☎938 94 50 04; www.sitges.org. Open July-Sept. daily 9am-9pm; Oct.-June M-F 9am-2pm and 4-6:30pm.) A smaller branch is by the museums on C. Fonollar. (☎938 11 06 11. Open W-F 10:30am-1:45pm, Sa 11am-2pm and 4-7pm, Su 11am-2pm.) **Agis** offers guided tours of the city (☎619 79 31 99; www.sitges.com/agis), while **Jafra Natura** takes visitors through the bordering Garraf Natural Park. (☎686 59 50 99; jafranatura@hotmail.com.) The supermarket **Super Avui,** C. Carbonell, 24, can be found across from the train station. (Open M-Sa 9am-9pm.) Local services include: **medical assistance** (☎938 94 64 26); the **police** (☎904 10 10 92) in the Pl. Ajuntament (to get there from C. Parellades, take C. Major toward the coast; the station is on the right); **Internet access** and **fax** service at **Café Art,** C. Sant Francesc, 44 (☎938 94 52 09; €1.25 per 30min., €1.75 per hr.; open daily 11am-1am), and at **Locutori Intycom,** C. Parellades, 39 (☎938 94 59 94; €1.40 per 30min., €2.40 per hr.). The **post office** is in Pl. d'Espanya. (☎938 94 12 47. Open M-F 8:30am-2:30pm, Sa 9:30am-1pm. No package pick-up Sa.) **Postal Code:** 08870.

■ ACCOMMODATIONS

Accommodations are expensive and, although abundant, difficult to reserve on summer weekends; call far ahead if you plan on staying. One possibility is to day-trip into Sitges from Barcelona; in the end, Sitges' nightlife is so crazy you may not end up needing a bed of your own.

Hotel El Cid, C. Sant Josep, 39 (☎938 94 18 42; fax 94 63 35). From the train station, pass the rotunda, and take the 4th left off C. Carbonell (look for the yellow sign). One of the best deals in town and popular with young travelers. All 77 of the colorful and comfortable rooms come with bathrooms, safety deposit box, and fan. Small pool, bar, and garden in back. Breakfast included. Doubles €38.20-66. MC/V. ❸

Hostal Parellades, C. Parellades, 11 (☎938 94 08 01), 1 block from the beach. Clean rooms and an airy terrace. Dirt cheap for Sitges, with easy entry after late nights (early mornings, rather). Singles €27; doubles €40, with bath €50; triples with bath €65. ❷

Hostal Bonaire, C. Bonaire, 31 (☎938 94 53 26). 12 bright, if small, rooms half a block from the beach. Ask for one of the new rooms with private bath and a terrace overlooking party-happy C. Bonaire. 24hr. reception. Summer singles €35, with bath €39; doubles €55. Spring and fall €33/€35/€49. Winter €30/€33/€45. MC/V. ❷

Hotel Montserrat, C. Espalter, 27 (☎938 94 03 00; www.hotelmontserratsitges.com). From the train station, turn left onto C. Sant Francesc and right onto C. Espalter. Rooms have lounging area, bath, phone, TV, and fridge. Internet access in lobby. Breakfast included. Aug.-Sept. 10 and *Semana Santa* singles €50, superior (larger) €56; doubles €75, superior €80; triples €104. July and late Sept. €50/€56/€68/€74/€97. Apr.-June €39/€45/€54/€60/€84. Closed Oct.-Mar. €6 extra for terrace. Reservation with deposit only. MC/V. ❹

FOOD

Sitges is filled with tourist-trap restaurants, especially on the beachfront, where it is easy to get ripped off. C. Parellades has cheaper fare; venture far to the left (when facing the coast) to escape the generic at small, friendly bars.

Izarra, C. Mayor 24 (☎938 94 73 70), behind the museum area. This friendly Basque tapas bar can be either a quick fix before a long night of club-hopping or a more substantial and leisurely meal. Ask for a *plato* and grab whatever tapas look tasty, from Basque fish to more traditional Spanish *croquetas*. Big entrees (€6-13.80) and *sidra* (cider; €2) are also available. Open daily 1:30-4pm and 8:30-11pm. MC/V. ❷

Restaurante La Oca, C. Parellades, 41 (☎938 94 79 36). Chicken roasting on an open fire, salads, pasta, and pizza attract lines of hungry tourists. Try the succulent *pollastre* (roast chicken) for €5.75-6.20. Open Su-F 1pm-midnight, Sa 1pm-1am. MC/V. ❷

Restaurante Lizarran, C. Sant Pau, 3 (☎938 11 03 20) at the intersection with C. Parellades. This hip tapas bar attracts a 20-something crowd and features a mix of sea- and land-dwellers, such as *pulpo* (octopus), *merluza* (hake), and *entrecot de buey* (beef). Try the *rabo de toro al vino tinto* (bull's tail in wine), which is much better than it sounds (€9.50). Tapas bar and entrees €6-14. Open daily noon-midnight. MC/V. ❷

Xalet Restaurant, Illa de Cuba, 35 (☎938 11 00 70), inside a castle-like hotel. A break from the crowds of the beachfront, the seating in the beautiful courtyard is reason enough to come. Delicate entrees range from gazpacho to veal (€13.30-24). *Menú* €19.75. Open Su-M and W-Sa 8:30-11:30pm. ❹

SIGHTS

The pedestrian walkway **Carrer Parellades,** which features shopping, eating, and drinking galore, is the central attraction for most tourists. However, the side streets and the peaceful beaches farther up the coast are where the wise locals go. Visitors may come just for the beach, but Sitges has some can't-miss sights, including Morell's whimsical **Modernista clock tower,** Pl. Cap de la Vila, 2, above Optica at the intersection of C. Parellades and Sant Francesc.

Seven blocks from the clock on C. Fonollar, the **Museu Cau Ferrat** (☎938 94 03 64) hangs high over the water's edge. Once home to Modernista Santiago Rusiñol (1861-1931) and a meeting point for the young Pablo Picasso and Ramón Casas, the building is a shrine to Modernista iron work, sculpture, ceramics, glass work, and painting, featuring pieces by El Greco and Picasso. The extensive collection of wrought iron was amassed by Rusiñol in an effort to preserve various 18th-century traditions. Next door, the **Museu Maricel del Mar** (☎938 94 03 64) has a select collection of Romanesque and Gothic painting and 19th-century Catalan sculpture, as well as an interesting marine collection showcasing models of the Catalan navy and fishing fleet. These two museums have some of the best views of Sitges and of the **Parish Church,** Sitges's signature building, looming high over the rocky coast. Farther into town, the **Museu Romàntic,** C. Sant Gaudencio, 1, off C. Parellades, is a 19th-century house filled with period pieces like music boxes and over 400 17th- to 19th-century dolls from all over the world. (☎938 94 29 69; www.diba.es/museus/sitges.asp. All museums open June 15-Sept. Tu-Su 10am-2pm and 5-9pm; Oct.-June 14 Su 10am-3pm, Tu-F 10am-1:30pm and 3-6:30pm, Sa 10am-7pm. Guided tours summer 4 per day 11am-6pm, winter 3 per day; every hr. in Museu Romàntic. Combo ticket good for one visit to each museum €5.40, students €3; otherwise €3 per museum, students and seniors €1.50.)

SEX ON THE BEACH

During the first week of February, finding housing in Sitges can be quite a feat. It may seem strange that anyone would flock to this summer town in the dead of winter, when all the beaches have surrendered to the winds, but it's not for the sun that gay tourists spare no expenses to get here—it's for the annual celebration of Carnaval, when excessive glitter becomes a must and a massive party overtakes the streets.

The town first established itself as a tourist destination in the early 20th century, when artists from Barcelona and, later, all of Europe, would come for the creative ambience. However, at the end of Franco's regime, lots of gays took up residence in Sitges, and the town garnered its reputation as a gay haven on the Mediterranean.

While Sitges has mostly embraced this calling, it was not without a recent struggle. Two years ago, the mayor of Sitges declared open war on the cruising culture by shining lights on the beaches at night to stop people from using the area as a public bedroom. The gay population of Sitges found this discriminatory, and reacted quickly and effectively. Protests were held, and gay and lesbian groups threatened to boycott the city, which relies on their tourism. Noting the situation's gravity, the government intervened. Today, Sitges's gay community is stronger than ever.

Across the street from the museums, the stately **Palau Maricel,** on C. Fonollar, built in 1910 for American millionaire Charles Deering, wows visitors with its sumptuous halls and rich gardens. Guided tours are available on summer nights and include a glass of *cava* (champagne); on Friday, Saturday, and Sunday nights, a piano concert completes the evening. Call ahead for reservations and times. (☎938 11 33 11. Tours €6; F-Su concert and tour €8.)

▲ BEACHES

Sitges's sky-blue waters and proximity to Barcelona make it a viable alternative to the crowded sands of Barceloneta or Port Olímpic. Plenty of sand accommodates hordes of sun worshippers on hot summer days. At **Platja de la Fragata,** the beach farthest to the left as you face the sea, sand sculptors create new masterpieces every summer day. By midday, the beaches close to downtown can become almost unbearably crowded. The best beaches, with calmer waters and more open space, **Platja de la Barra** and **Platja de Terramar,** are a one or two kilometer walk away. Along the way you will pass several small beaches, including **Platja de La Bassa Rodona,** popular with gay sunbathers. Rocks shield these beaches from waves, creating a shallow ocean swimming pool that extends far into the water and is ideal for children. The farther you are willing to walk, the bluer the water and the more sand you will get to claim. If you want total seclusion, Sitges is known for its peaceful **nude beaches.** Gay-friendly **Platja de L'Home Mort** can be reached by walking past Terramar until you hit a golf course at the end of the sidewalk. Walk on the beach past the golf course, and L'Home Mort is in a small cove behind the hills, where the train tracks are right on the coast. Don't venture into the forest here unless you want to see people having a much better time than you. A tamer nude beach is **Platja dels Balmins,** on the opposite side of the city. To reach it, walk past the church and **Platja de Sant Sebastià,** and take the dirt walkway on the coast, following it up and down a slope; the beach is a small, quiet cove before the port with a restaurant and water ideal for snorkeling.

🎭 🎵 NIGHTLIFE AND ENTERTAINMENT

While Sitges is an easy daytrip, it's almost better to go for a night-trip. The wild clubs are the perfect escape from the confines of the decidedly more cosmopolitan night scene of Barcelona. The places to be at sundown are ⊠**Carrer Primer de Maig** (which runs directly from the beach and Pg. Ribera) and **Carrer Marqués Montroig**, off C. Parellades. Bars and clubs line both sides of the small streets, overflowing onto the roads and blasting pop and house from 10pm until 3am. The clubs here are wide-open and accepting, with a vibrant mixed crowd of gay and straight people, along with the occasional drag queen. There's no cover anywhere, making for great bar- and club-hopping. Beers at most places go for about €3, mixed drinks €6. Even crazier is the "disco-beach" **Atlàntida**, in Sector Terramar (☎938 94 26 77; foam parties on Th and Su nights), and the legendary **Pachá**, on Pg. Sant Didac in nearby Vallpineda (☎938 94 22 98), which plays 80s, 90s, and house music, and has a Latin room. Buses run all night on weekends to the two discos from C. Primer de Maig. Other popular spots can be found on C. Bonaire and C. Sant Pau, but most open only on weekends. **Gay clubs** and cafes include **Ricky's**, C. St Pau, 25 (☎938 94 96 81; open daily midnight-6am), **Trailer**, C. Angel Vidal, 14 (☎938 94 04 01), with infamous foam parties, and **Perfil**, C. Espalter, 7 (☎938 94 44 52). The tourist office has information on nightlife—ask for a *Guía del Ocio.*

In celebrating holidays, Sitges spares no extravagance and pushes the boundaries of style. During the **Festa de Corpus Cristi** (May 29), townspeople collaborate to create intricate fresh-flower carpets in the Concurs de Catifes de Flors. For papier-mâché dragons, devils, and giants dancing in the streets, visit during the **Festa Major**, held August 22-27 in honor of the town's patron saint Bartolomé. Nothing compares to **Carnaval**, a preparation for fasting during the first week of Lent (Feb. 3-9). Spaniards crash the town for a frenzy of parades, dancing, outrageous costumes, and vats of alcohol. The last night is the wildest, as hundreds of drag queens parade through the streets. A pistol shot starts the **Rally de Coches de Época** in October, an antique car race from Barcelona to Sitges. June brings the **International Theater Festival** (€10-22 per show), and July and August the **International Jazz Festival** (€10.50 per concert). In September, competitors tread on fresh grapes on the beach for the annual **Grape Harvest**, and September 22-23 brings the **Festivitat de Santa Tecla**. In October is the famous **Festival Internacional de Cinema de Catalunya**, which is perhaps Sitges's biggest event.

▶ DAYTRIP FROM SITGES

VILANOVA I LA GELTRÙ

Cercanías trains (RENFE) run from Vilanova to Sitges (7min., every 15-30min., €1.10) and continue to Barcelona (40-50min., €2.70). Mon Bus (☎938 93 70 60) and La Plana (☎938 14 58 48) connect Vilanova to Sitges (€1.30), Vilafranca (€1.60), and Barcelona (€3) every hr. 7:20am-10:20pm. The bus station is in the plaza in front of the train station. A taxi (☎938 93 32 41) from Vilanova to Sitges costs about €9-12.

One of Catalunya's most important ports, Vilanova i la Geltrù actually turns out to be two cities in one: an industrial hub and a well-groomed beach town. There is little in the dusty uptown area save old churches and stone facades; most visitors spend the day on the **beach** (10min. from the train station). To get there, exit the station, turn left onto C. Forn de Vidre, and take the third left onto Rmbla. de la Pau, a wide avenue with a tree-lined walkway in the middle. You'll know you're going the right way on Rmbla. de la Pau when you head into a tunnel under a train overpass; after that, follow it all the way to the port and onto **Passeig del Carme.** The wide **Platja de Ribes Roges** is past the tourist office; to the left is the smaller **Platja del Far.** Expect fine sand, sun, and a bit of company at both; the beaches are refreshingly calm. There are a handful of museums in town, including the **Biblioteca Museu Víctor Balaguer,** Av. Victor Balaguer, which has a collection of 19th- and 20th-century Catalan paintings and sculptures. (☎938 15 42 02; www.victorbalaguer-bmb.org. Open Tu-W and F-Sa 10am-1:30pm and 4:30-7pm, Th 6-8:30pm, Su and holidays 10am-1:30pm.) The **Museu Romàntic Can Papiol** recreates the lifestyle of a wealthy 18th- to 19th-century household. (☎938 93 03 82; www.diba.es/museuslocals. Open Tu-Sa 10am-2pm and 4-6pm, Su 10am-2pm.)

If you decide to stay in town, the popular **Can Gatell ❸,** C. Puigcerdà, 6-16, has 63 clean rooms with TV and bath. With your back to the station, head down C. Victor Balaguer and at the end turn right onto La Rambla and take the first left. (☎938 93 01 17. Wheelchair-accessible. June-Aug. singles €33-75; doubles €48-92. Sept.-May €25-59/€35-76. Extra bed €10.) The hostel's *menú* (€8, served M-F, includes wine) is popular with locals. (Restaurant open daily 7-10:30am, 1-5pm, and 8:30-10pm.) Numerous pricey restaurants serve fresh seafood along Pg. del Carme. An inexpensive alternative is **Supermarket Orangután,** Rmbla. de la Pau, 36. (Open M-Th 9:30am-2pm and 5-8:30pm, F-Sa 9:30am-8:30pm.) The **tourist office,** about 100m to the right on Pg. del Carme in a small park called **Parc de Ribes Roges,** offers excellent maps. (☎938 15 45 17. Open July-Aug. M-Sa 10am-8pm, Su 10am-2pm; Sept.-June M-Sa 10am-1pm and 4-7pm.)

TARRAGONA
☎977

The strategic position of Tarragona (pop. 120,000) on the Mediterranean coast made the city a provincial Roman capital under Augustus; today an amphitheater and other ruins pay homage to the city's imperial days. These vestiges of Tarragona's august past are some of the city's most compelling attractions, but the labyrinthine roads of the old city are a prime place to sit out on a cafe terrace or to wander around and get lost on purpose.

▐ TRANSPORTATION

Trains: ☎902 24 02 02, on Pl. de la Pedrera by the water, downhill from the old city. Wheelchair-accessible. Ticket booth open daily 4:30am-midnight. Customer service open daily 6am-8pm. The best transportation option. To: **Alicante** (4hr., 10 per day, €34.50-62); **Barcelona** (1¼hr., 55 per day 5:15am-11:04pm, €4.35-16); **Bilbao** (8½hr., 3 per day 1:24am-11:25pm, €32-42.50); **Cambrils** (20min., 12 per day 7:41am-10:24pm, €1.20-12.50); **Madrid** (6½-8hr., 5 per day 8:20am-11:57pm, €31-87.50); **Pamplona** (7hr., 3 per day 1:24am-11:25pm, €26.50-35); **Salou** (15min., 19 per day 4:34am-10:03pm, €1.20-12); **Sitges** (5:52am and 9:32pm, €1.20-12); **Valencia** (2-3hr., 16 per day 4:34am-9:49pm, €24-45); **Zaragoza** (4hr., 12 per day 1:24am-11:57pm, €18.50-47).

Buses: Pl. Imperial Tarraco (☎977 22 91 26). Follow Rmbla. Nova away from the water; the station is to the left of the rotunda. **ALSA/Enatcar** (☎902 42 22 42) runs buses to **Barcelona** (1½hr., 8 per day, €8) and **Valencia** (4hr., 6 per day, €15.20). **HIFE** (☎977 22 40 00) and **Plana** (☎977 21 44 75) also leave from the station.

Public Transportation: EMT Buses (☎977 54 94 80) run daily 6am-11pm. Convenient for trips to beaches and ruins in the outskirts. €1, 10-ride *abono* ticket €4.70.

Taxi: Radio Taxi (☎977 22 14 14).

Car Rental: AVIS (☎977 21 17 01), by the train station in Pl. de la Pedrera.

▐ ▐ ORIENTATION AND PRACTICAL INFORMATION

Most sights are clustered up the coast from the train station, on a hill surrounded by remnants of Roman walls. On the slope of the hill, **La Rambla Vella** and **La Rambla Nova** (parallel to one another and perpendicular to the sea) are the main thoroughfares of the new city. Rmbla. Nova runs from **Passeig de les Palmeres** (a walkway overlooking the sea) to **Plaça Imperial Tarraco,** the large rotunda and home of the bus station. To reach the old quarter from the train station, turn right and walk 150m to the stairs parallel to the shore.

Tourist Office: C. Major, 39 (☎977 25 07 95; www.tarragonaturisme.com), half a block downhill from the bottom of the cathedral steps, in the center of the old quarter. Open June 21-Sept. 26 M-F 9am-9pm, Sa 9am-2pm and 4-9pm, Su 10am-2pm; Sept. 27-June 20 M-Sa 10am-2pm and 4-7pm, Su and holidays 10am-2pm. **Catalunya Regional Tourist Office:** C. Fortuny, 5 (☎977 23 34 15; www.catalunyaturisme.com). 1 block off of Rmbla. Nova. Information on nearby towns and the whole Catalunya region. Open M-F 9:15am-2pm and 4-6:30pm, Sa 9:15am-2pm.

Tourist Information Booths: Clear domes at 3 locations: Pl. Imperial Tarraco, at the inland end of La Rambla Nova by the bus station, and the end of Rmbla. Vella where Av. de Catalunya meets Vía de l'Impera Romi. Open daily June 21-Sept. 26 10am-1:30pm and 4:30-8pm; Sept. 27-June 20 Sa 10am-2pm and 4-7pm, Su 10am-2pm.

Luggage Storage: At the train station. Open 4:30am-midnight. €3 for 24hr.

Comisaria de Policía, Pl. Orleans (☎977 24 98 44). From Pl. Imperial Tarraco, walk down Av. President Lluís Companys and take the 3rd left to the station.

Medical Assistance: Hospital de Sant Pau i Santa Tecla, Rmbla. Vella, 14 (☎977 25 99 00). Large, old building in the middle of the Rambla. **Hospital Joan XXIII,** C. Dr. Mallafré Guasch (☎977 29 58 00).

Internet Access: Netgaming Tarragona, C. Méndez Núñez, 7 baixos, 3 blocks up the coast and half a block to the left from Rmbla. Nova. €1.50-2 per hr. Open daily 9:30am-9:30pm. Closes for lunch in the summer. **Tarraconecta,** C. del Cós del Bou. Half a block toward the coast from Pl. de la Font. €2 per hr. **Biblioteca Pública,** C. Fortuny, 30 (☎977 24 05 44). Free use of computers with passport.

Post Office: Pl. Corsini, 12 (☎977 24 01 49), 6 blocks from the coast and 2 blocks below Rmbla. Nova off C. Cañellas. Open M-F 8:30am-8:30pm, Sa 9:30am-1pm. **Postal Code:** 43001.

ACCOMMODATIONS AND CAMPING

Most of the city's accommodations are two- to four-star hotels near the center and on the water. Pl. de la Font in the old quarter (parallel to Rmbla. Vella) and the area around Pl. Imperial Tarraco are filled with quality lodging; the former is a more charismatic location.

Hostal Noria, Pl. de la Font, 53 (☎977 23 87 17), in the heart of the historic town. Enter through the low-key restaurant on the corner of the plaza. 24 clean and bright rooms, all with pretty-in-pink bathrooms. Summer singles €21-28; doubles €34-45. Winter €19-24/€30-40. ❷

Pensión Forum, Pl. de la Font, 37 (☎977 23 17 18), upstairs from the restaurant. 30 clean rooms with bath don't leave much space for lounging, but provide a decent place to sleep. Ask for a room with a good view. Singles €16-19; doubles €32-38. MC/V. ❷

Camping: Several campsites line the road toward Barcelona (Vía Augusta or CN-340) along the northern beaches, especially around km 1. Take bus #9 (every 20min., €1) from Pl. Imperial Tarraco. **Tarraco** (☎/fax 977 29 02 89 or 29 02 89) is the closest campsite, at Platja de l'Arrabassada. Well-kept facilities near the beach. €2.75-3.75 per person, per tent, and per car; €2-2.50 per child. Open Apr.-Sept. MC/V. ❶

⚡ FOOD

Ramblas Nova and Vella and the streets in between are full of restaurants serving cheap *menús del día* and greasy *platos combinados* (€6-8). The winding streets of the old quarter, especially Pl. de la Font, have more personal restaurants, but they're more expensive. Tarragona's **Mercado Central** takes place in Pl. Corsini next to the post office. (☎977 23 15 51. Open M-W and Sa 8am-2pm, Th-F 7am-2pm and 5:30-8:30pm. Flea market Tu and Th.) For **groceries**, head to **Champion,** C. Augusta, at Comte de Rius, between the Ramblas. (Open daily 9am-9:15pm.) **El Serrallo,** the fishermen's quarter, next to the harbor, has excellent seafood. Try your fish with Tarragona's typical ⚡**romesco sauce,** consisting of red peppers, garlic, toasted almonds, and hazelnuts simmered in olive oil.

Restaurant Les Coques, Nou Patriarca, 2 (☎977 22 83 00), on a small street to the right of Pl. La Seu when facing the cathedral from the steps. Roman walls, chandeliers, modern paintings, and antiques create an eclectic interior. Relaxing and familial, with first class service. Try the *almejas en salsa verde* (clams in green sauce; €16.25), grilled baby goat (€14.50), or fresh *pulpitos de Tarragona* (baby octopus; €23.50). Entrees €10-32. Open M-Sa 1:30-3:45pm and 9-10:45pm. AmEx/MC/V. ❹

La Teula, C. Mercería, 16 (☎977 23 99 89). Head half a block in the direction of the cathedral from Pl. del Fòrum in the old city. Small, wood-paneled locale great for salads (€4-6) and toasted *entrepans* with interesting Catalan veggie and meat combos (€7-12). Lunch *menú* €7.90. Open daily around noon-4pm and 8pm-midnight. MC/V. ❷

Restaurant El Caserón, C. Ces del Bou, 9 (☎977 23 93 28), parallel to La Rambla Vella. From Pl. de la Font, facing the two streets toward the coast, take the one on the left. Popular local diner serving typical entrees for €3-14, such as the excellent *combinado de bistec* (egg, steak, salad, and fries for €6.60) and grilled fish (€13.50). *Menú* €7.50. Open Su-M 8:30-11pm, Tu-F 1-4pm and 8:30-10:30pm. MC/V. ❷

Forum, Pl. de la Font, 37 (☎977 23 17 18). An elegant restaurant run by an attentive staff. Beautiful seafood entrees €10-24. Open daily 1-4pm and 8:30pm onward. ❹

👁 ⚡ SIGHTS AND BEACHES

Tarragona's status as a Roman provincial capital transformed the small military enclosure into a glorious imperial port. Countless Roman ruins stand silently amid 20th-century hustle and bustle, all just minutes uphill from the beach.

⚡**ROMAN RUINS.** Below Pg. de les Palmeres between Ramblas Vella and Nova, set amid gardens above Platja del Miracle is the **Roman Amphitheater.** Gladiators once killed wild animals and each other for captive audiences in this massive structure. It was also a site for public executions; in 259, the Christian bishop Fructuosus and his two deacons were burned alive here. In the sixth century, these martyrs were honored with a basilica built in the arena.

Up the hill from here, between the theater and the city, is the entrance to the **Pretori I Circ Romans,** which houses the **Praetorium Tower,** the former administrative center of the region, and the **Roman Circus,** built in the first century AD for chariot races and other spectacles. Visitors descend into the long, dark tunnels that led fans to their seats, and see a miniature model of what Roman Tarragona (or Tarraco) looked like. The Praetorium was also the governor's palace in the first century BC; rumor has it that the infamous hand-washer Pontius Pilate was born here.

The scattered **Fòrum Romà,** with reconstructed Corinthian columns, is near the post office on C. Lleida, three blocks below Rmbla. Nova and six from the coast, an area with few remaining ruins. Once the center of town, its distance from the other ruins demonstrates how far the walls of the ancient city extended. To see what remains of the second-century BC walls that stretched all the way to the sea, stroll through the **Passeig Arqueològic** in the inland part of the city, near the cathedral. *(Amphitheater ☎ 977 24 22 20; Praetorium ☎ 977 22 17 36. All ruins open May-Sept. Su 9am-3pm, Tu-Sa 9am-9pm; Oct.-Apr. Tu-Su 9am-7pm. Admission to each €2, students and seniors €1, under 16 free.)*

MUSEUMS. The **Museu Nacional Arqueològic,** across the small Pl. del Rei and next to the Praetorium, displays ancient architecture, sculptures, personal effects, bronze tools, and mosaics (including the famous "Head of Medusa"), and offers insight into daily life in the Roman Empire. It is considered the most important collection of Roman artifacts in Catalunya. *(☎ 977 23 62 09. Wheelchair-accessible. Open June-Sept. Tu-Sa 10am-8pm, Su 10am-2pm; Oct.-May Tu-Su 10am-1:30pm and 4-7pm. €2.40, students and seniors €1.20, under 16 free. Tu free. Includes entrance to the necropolis.)* The early Christian burial site at the Museu i Necròpolis Paleocristians, Av. Ramón y Cajal, 78, on the opposite end of the city, has yielded a rich variety of urns and tombs, the best of which are on display in the small museum. *(☎ 977 21 11 75. Open June-Sept. Tu-Sa 10am-1pm and 4:30-8pm, Su 10am-2pm; Oct.-May Tu-Sa 10am-1:30pm and 3-5:30pm, Su 10am-2pm. €2.40, students €1.20. Tu free.)* Tarragona's historical offerings are not limited to Roman ruins. To see the beautiful 18th-century house where the Viscounts of Castellarnau lived, go up C. Nau (which turns into C. Cavellares) seven blocks from the Museu Nacional Arqueologic and the Roman Circus; the **Casa-Museu Castellarnau** will be on your left before the dead end. *(☎ 977 24 22 20. Open May-Sept. Tu-Sa 9am-9pm, Su 9am-3pm; Oct.-Apr. Tu-Su 9am-7pm. €2, students €1, under 16 free.)* If you'd like to get a better feel for Tarragona, there is the small but interesting **Museu d'Art Modern de Tarragona,** C. Santa Anna, 8, featuring 20th-century photography, painting, and sculpture from famous and local artists (including art competition winners), with a focus on art from the past few decades. Between Pl. del Fórum and Pl. del Rei. *(☎ 977 23 50 32; www.altanet.org/MAMT. Open Tu-F 10am-8pm, Sa 10-3pm and 5-8pm, Su and holidays 11am-2pm. Free.)*

BEACHES. The hidden access to **Platja del Miracle,** the main beach visible from the hill, is along Baixada del Miracle, starting from Pl. Arce Ochotorena. Walk to the left from the Roman theater until you reach the underpass, under the train tracks, to the beach. Though not on par with the region's other beaches, this secluded spot is not bad for a few hours of relaxation. A bit farther away are the larger beaches, **Platja Llarga,** and the favorites for those in the know, **Platja l'Arrabassada** and **Platja de la Mora.** *(Take bus #1 or 9 from Pl. Imperial Tarraco or any of the other stops.)*

OTHER SIGHTS. In the center of the old quarter, lit by octagonal rose windows flanking the transept, is the gigantic Romanesque-Gothic ▨**cathedral,** which dates from 1331 and is one of the most magnificent cathedrals in Catalunya. It was at one point an Arab mosque, evident in the blending of exterior styles. The dark interior holds the tomb of Joan d'Aragó, and the outside courtyard (or "cloister") is a perfect place to relax. The adjoining **Diocesan Museum** has a handful of rooms showcasing religious relics from the last 700 years. *(Entrance to both on C. Claustre, near Pl. La Seu. Open M-Sa Mar. 16-May 30 10am-1pm and 4-7pm; Jun. 1-Oct. 15 10am-7pm; Oct. 16-Nov. 15 10am-5pm; Nov.16-Mar.15 10am-2pm. Closed holidays. €2.40, students and seniors €1.50, under 16 free.)* The **Pont del Diable** (Devil's Bridge), a Roman aqueduct 10min. outside of the city, is visible on the way in and out of town. Take municipal bus #5 (every 20min., €1) from the corner of C. Cristòfer Colom and Av. Prat de la Riba or from Pl. Imperial Tarraco.

🅿 🎆 NIGHTLIFE AND FESTIVALS

Weekend nightlife in Tarragona takes place on a much smaller scale than in Sitges or Barcelona, but the more intimate atmosphere is a nice change. Between 5 and 10pm, Ramblas Nova and Vella (and the surrounding area) are packed with strolling families, and the outside seating at restaurants dotting the old quarter begins to fill up. After 10pm, the pedestrian streets that run up and down the hill and the bars that line them liven up; fireworks often brighten the sky in summertime. Later at night, the place to be is **Port Esportiu,** a plaza full of restaurant-bars and mini-discos; the flow of people from the city center to the port along the streets is a party in itself. Heading up Rmbla. Nova away from the beach, take a left onto C. Unió; bear left at Pl. General Prim and follow C. Apodaca six blocks to its end. Cross the tracks; the fun awaits on the port to the left.

The end of July ushers in the **Fiesta de Tarragona,** which goes through the first week of August (info ☎ 977 24 47 95, tickets 24hr. 33 22 11). The small but unique festival of **Sant Magí** takes place August 14-19 with exhibitions, music, processions, and theater. Pyromaniacs shouldn't miss the end of the first week of July when fireworks light up the beach in **El Concurso Internacional de Fuegos Artificiales** (International Fireworks Display Contest; www.piroart.com). On even-numbered years, the first Sunday in October brings the **Concurs de Castells,** a competition of tall human towers, as high as seven to nine "stories," called *castells.* More *castells* appear during the annual **Fiesta de Santa Tecla** (Sept. 14-24). If you're unable to catch the *castellers* in person, don't miss their life-size monument on Rmbla. Nova, two blocks from Pl. Imperial Tarraco.

🅿 DAYTRIPS FROM TARRAGONA

SALOU

Getting to Salou is very easy by Cercanías trains (☎ 977 38 19 37) which stop at the corner of C. Carles Roig and Pg. de L'Estació, a 10min. walk from the beach. RENFE (☎ 902 24 02 02) runs trains from Barcelona (1½hr., every 1-1½hr. 6:06am-9:00pm, €5.10-15.50), stopping at Tarragona along the way. Plana (☎ 977 21 44 75; www.auto-carsplana.com) buses run from Tarragona to Salou (every 30min. 6:20am-10:30pm. €1.70-1.90) and drop you off at the station on the beach in the middle of Pg. de Jaume I. (☎ 977 38 10 44. Open 10am-1pm and 4-8pm.) If all else fails, a Radio Taxi (☎ 977 38 50 90) will get you to Tarragona or Cambrils for €6-10.

A tourist town in all its glory, Salou (pop. 20,000) is stretched out along the coast and calls for crowd-control at the height of August. On a visit in winter, however, you would be lucky to spot cars on the road. The main street is **Passeig de Jaume I,** a wide promenade lined with palm trees and fountains on the crowded **Platja Llevant.** To get here, take two rights when you get off the train, cross the tracks on C. Barcelona, and continue to the coast. Home to both Universal Studio's **Port Aventura** theme park and the **Costa Caribe** water park, beaches aren't Salou's only attraction. The water park is one of Europe's largest and has its own stop on the train before Salou; the Plana bus also runs there from the Salou beach front. (☎ 902 20 22 20. Open daily June 19-Sept. 12 10am-midnight; Sept. 13-June 18 10am-8pm. Theme park tickets €33-35; water park tickets $18-19. Discounts for under 11 and over 60. 2-day and 2-park passes available.) At night, activity is centered on the north end of town past the end of Pg. de Jaume I. Head to the **Tropical Heat Cafe** at the corner of C. Murillo and Av. Carles Buigas, and **1a Línea Pub** two blocks up.

The **tourist office,** Pg. Jaume I, 4, with free maps and guides, is a cream-colored mansion on the left, half a block up the coast; other locations at Pl. de Venus and Pl. d'Europa. (☎ 977 35 01 02; www.salou.org. Open daily 9:30am-1:30pm and 4:30-

8pm.) Room prices run high, but if you must spend the night, try **Hostal La Cabaña ❸**, C. València, 46, off of C. Barcelona. The hostel has a peaceful location relatively close to Platja de Ponent as well as a social courtyard and a talkative, thoughtful owner. (☎977 38 03 46; fax 35 15 73. Breakfast €2.20. Reception 9am-10pm. Doubles with bath €32-45.) Don't miss ◙**La Gelateria di Ornella** (☎977 35 22 96), Pg. Miramar, 10, to the right from the port.

CAMBRILS DEL MAR

Trains run to and from Tarragona (20min., every 20min., €1.40-9.50) and Barcelona (1¾hr., every 20min., €5.10-15.50). The station is on Av. Virgen de Montserrat, 1km inland from the port. (☎902 24 02 02. Open daily 6am-9:30pm. Ticket booth open daily 8:15am-7:45pm) The bus station is situated where the train tracks meet Pg. Sant Joan Baptista de la Salle. HIFE and Plana run buses to Barcelona, Tarragona, and Salou. (☎902 11 98 14. Ticket booth open daily 10am-noon and 4:30-7:30pm.)

A fishing village that has evolved into a small resort town, Cambrils provides a quieter alternative to Salou. Although it is a year-round destination, Cambrils's 9km of beach fill up mainly during high season. The attractions of Cambrils are centered along its coast and beaches. **Platja Prat d'En Forés,** past the port, is the most crowded, but the payoffs are the many beautiful people and beach activities. **Estació Nauticà,** Pg. de les Palmeres, 1, (☎661 73 33 10) offers plenty of watersports. Check the tourist office for other companies that rent equipment and give lessons.

Cambrils's second claim to fame is its cuisine. The coastal road is packed with expensive beachside restaurants (€10-22). Go inland two or three blocks (around the port) for cheaper fare, such as pizzerias and tapas bars. The portside restaurants are ideal for sampling the town's fine seafood. Ask for the *rossejat,* a dish unique to Cambrils made with fine pasta cooked in fish broth. **Acuamar "Casa Matas" ❹,** Consolat de Mar, 66, between the port and the Nautical Club across from the beach, has personality. Painted bright green and, most importantly, air-conditioned, Acuamar offers rice, fish, and shellfish dishes ranging from *dorada a la sal* (salted dorado; €12.70) to *caracoles de mar* (sea snails; €9). (☎977 36 00 59. Open M-Tu and F-Su 1-3:45pm and 8-10:45pm, W 1-3:45pm.) Many ice cream shops border the hot seaside walkways, but **Sirvent Geladeria,** Consolat de Mar, 44, offers unusual flavors like rose petal, as well as the more traditional *crema catalana* (€1.60-3). **Nightlife** is limited and focused on Av. de la Diputació along the beach. The cheapest accommodation option near the beach is the **Pensió Platja ❶,** C. Roger de Llúria, 16. (☎977 36 00 29. Dorms €10-15.) The **tourist office** is located on Pg. de les Palmeres. (☎902 15 47 41; www.turcambrils.info. Open daily summer 9am-9pm; winter 10am-1:30pm and 4:30-8pm)

REUS ☎977

Reus (pop. 90,000) lacks the coastline of other nearby towns but attracts visitors looking to learn more about Antoni Gaudí, the famous architect born here. Gaudí moved to Barcelona as a teenager, but don't mention that to the locals—they are proud of its importance during his formative years, which arguably influenced the architectural genius that ensued. In the 19th century, a period of industrial growth put Reus on the map as a major trader of *aguardent* (firewater). Today, the city offers great shopping, elegant museums, and peaceful plazas. If you are after more than this, however, you might want to skip Reus and head straight for Barcelona.

▐ TRANSPORTATION

Flights: Aeroport de Reus (☎977 77 98 32), Autovía Reus, km 3. Reus Transport Públic runs 12 buses per day from the airport to the train and bus stations.

Trains: (☎902 24 02 02), on Pl. de la Estación. Ticket booth open daily 8:15am-10pm. Station open daily 4:20am-12:25am. By far the best transportation to Reus. Trains to: **Barcelona** (2hr., 23 per day 4:41am-9:18pm, €5.10-23.50); **Madrid** (4-7½hr., 4 per day, €30.50-86.50); **Pamplona** (5hr., 3 per day, €26-34.50); **Tarragona** (15min., 26 per day 3:56am-9:18pm, €1.20-14.50).

Buses: (☎977 75 14 80), at Av. Jaume I and Av. President Macià Fortuny. Call the company directly to get exact times and prices. **Hispano Igualadina** (☎977 77 06 98) goes to Tarragona every 15min. during the day on weekdays and every hr. at night, early in the morning, and on weekends. Buses leave from the station but stop at Pl. de les Oques in the city before leaving town.

Public Transportation: Reus Transport Públic (☎977 30 00 06) runs buses daily 6am-10pm. Buses #10, 22-23, and 26 stop at the train station.

Taxis: Radio Taxi (☎977 34 50 50).

⚑ ⓘ ORIENTATION AND PRACTICAL INFORMATION

Reus's sights are concentrated in *"el tomb,"* the center of town, where **Plaça Prim** is also located. From the train station, walk straight out past the small **Plaça Joan Rébull** onto **Passeig Sunyer,** a wide tree-lined promenade, and follow it for four blocks until **Plaça de les Coques.** Then turn left onto **Carrer de Sant Joan,** one of the city's main streets, which leads to the tourist office and the center of town.

Tourist Office: C. Sant Joan, 34 (☎977 77 81 49; www.reus.net/turisme). Coming from the train station, the office is on the right after the large Mercat Central building. Free map and *Guia del Modernisme* for a self-guided walking tour of the city's buildings. Guided walking tours available if you call ahead. Open daily June-Aug. 9:30am-2pm and 4-8pm; Sept.-May 9:30am-1:30pm and 4-7pm.

Luggage Storage: At the train station. €3 for 24hr. 4:30am-midnight.

Police: Comissaria de Policía, C. General Moragues, 54 (☎977 32 80 00), 3 blocks from the train station.

Pharmacy: Mariné-Miranda, Pl. Prim, 1 (☎977 12 77 12). 24hr. pharmacies alternate; check the window of any pharmacy for the current one.

Medical Assistance: Hospital de Sant Joan, C. Jacint Barrau (☎977 32 04 24).

Internet Access: CyberKafè.com, C. Batán, 2 (☎977 75 04 92), 2 blocks southeast of Pl. Baluard. €2-2.40 per hr. Open daily 11am-10pm.

Post Office: Pl. Llibertat, 12 (☎977 31 46 62) and Pl. de l'Estació, by the train station (☎977 31 97 90). Look for the yellow "Correus" signs. **Postal Code:** 43201

⌂ ACCOMMODATIONS

Reus has a surprisingly wide range of accommodations in comparison with other coastal towns, all within the city center.

Hotel Ollé, Pg. de Prim, 45 (☎977 31 10 90; www.costadoradaonline.net), by Pl. La Pastoreta. Hotel-quality rooms at hostel prices, all with TV, A/C, and bath, in a central location. Wheelchair-accessible. Singles €25; doubles €42. ❷

Hostes Potau, C. del Vidre, 13 (☎977 34 50 01; http://hostes.potau.com). From the tourist office, in a narrow street to the right, 2 blocks after crossing Pl. Prim (with the equestrian statue). Modest but clean rooms with sink, towel, and sheets. Singles with shared bath €14; doubles €27.50, with bath €37.50. ❶

Hotel Hostal Simonet, Raval de Santa Ana, 18 (☎977 34 59 74; www.hostalsimonet.com). Entrance in the hidden narrow street 1 block from C. del Vidre. 39 plush rooms with bath, satellite TV, A/C, and more. Bar-restaurant with a terrace downstairs. Singles €32-37.50; doubles €51.50-72. ❸

FOOD

The narrow streets around Pl. Prim and Pl. Mercadal are filled with bakeries and small tapas bars in between the stores. Prices vary widely (€6-20), but there are many *menús* for under €10. Reus prides itself on its Siurana olive oil, a special oil derived from the *arbequina*, a small olive of concentrated flavor. For a local, delicious dessert, try the *menjablanc*. A spectacle in itself, the ■Mercat Central, in the center of the city, offers a colorful array of fresh produce as well as other delicacies. (Open M-Th 8am-2pm, F 7:30am-2:30pm and 5:30-8:30pm, Sa 7:30am-3pm.)

La Bajoqueta, C. de la Mar, 5 (☎977 34 54 53), right off Pl. Mercadal. One of the best-priced restaurants you will find in the chic shopping streets. Typical Catalan food and delicacies from La Mancha, such as tapas and sausages. The *Bajoqueta* salad consists of artfully displayed tomato slices, green beans, olives, and eggs. Entrees around €9; *menú* €7.50, €10 on Sa. Open M-Sa 9am-5pm and 8pm-midnight. ❷

El Celler del Padrí, C. Roger de Belfort, 35 (☎977 33 15 99). A large, cozy restaurant serving Mediterranean food, such as escargots *a la llauna*. An assortment of fish with many local sauces. Entrees €8-16; *menú* €10. Open daily 1-5pm and 8-11pm. ❸

⑥ SIGHTS

Reus attracts visitors for two reasons: Gaudí and the insane amount of shopping. Streets such as **Raval de Jesús** and **Calle Monterols,** leading down from Pl. Prim, as well as **Calle Galera** and **Calle Jesús,** are filled with modern boutiques selling clothes and shoes. They serve all tastes and ages, with an emphasis on young and innovative fashion. Walking through these streets—except during the siesta shutdown—can fill a day in itself while emptying your wallet.

A visit to Reus is not complete without walking ■The Reus Modernist Trail. Either with a guide or following the pamphlet (available at the tourist office) and the various signs, this walk will take you through the beautiful and uniquely detailed Modernista buildings scattered throughout the old town. Its crown jewel is the **Casa Natal d'Antoni Gaudí,** the architect's childhood home, which features the "Gaudí adolescent" sculpture, an homage to his birth. Another highlight is the **Casa Navàs** (1901) by Lluis Doménech i Montaner, one of the most significant Modernista architects. The trail starts and ends at the tourist office, and covers a small section of the city center and areas ranging from private homes to industrial buildings. If you are particularly interested in Gaudí, ask at the tourist office for guided tours focused on his heritage. The main shopping options are conveniently located along the same streets as the trail. Reus has two minor museums. The **Museu Salvador Vilaseca,** Raval de Santa Anna, 59, by Pl. Catalunya, features archaeological finds from the area. The exhibit **"Gaudí & Reus,"** also located here, includes drawings, personal items, and texts from both his youth and his time as an architect. (☎977 34 52 49; www.reus.net/museus. Open Tu-Sa 10am-2pm and 5-8pm, Su and holidays 11am-2pm. €2, seniors and students €1.) The **Museu d'Art i Història,** Pl. de la Llibertat, 13, has an exhibit on the culture of olive oil in Reus and Siurana as well as Gothic art and sculpture. (☎977 34 48 33; www.reus.net/museus. Open Tu-Sa 10am-2pm and 5-8pm, Su and holidays 11am-2pm. €2, seniors and students €1.)

⑤ ▓ NIGHTLIFE AND FESTIVALS

Reus has more quiet plazas than crazy parties; however, a handful of entertaining pubs dot the city. Several cluster in front of the train station, such as **Orisha,** on C. Espronceda a block from Pl. Joan Rebull, and **La Fábrica** and **Suau** on Pg. Mata (across Pl. Joan Rebull). Local partiers prefer to hop on the bus and head to Salou.

The biggest festival in Reus is **La Festa de Sant Pere** during the third week of June. The town builds giant puppets and costumes for the festivities, featuring concerts and dances, as well as the famous *castells* (human towers). More *castells* appear for the **Festes de Misericòrdia** (3rd week of September), with exhibitions on Pl. del Mercadal. For additional festival information, contact the **Oficina de Festivals,** C. Sant Joan, 27 (☎ 977 77 81 11; www.reus.net/cultura).

◆ DAYTRIP FROM REUS

VALLS

Getting to Valls requires depending on the unreliable Reus bus system. Make sure to leave several return options so as to not be stranded. Hispano Igualadina (☎ 977 77 06 98) goes to and from Valls 9 times per day 7:05am-8:15pm. It leaves Reus from the bus station, but also stops at Riera Miró, in front of the bar Dallas. There is no information office at the station, so find the marked bus (with a "Reus-Valls" sign) and buy your ticket on board (€2.10 each way). The Valls station (☎ 977 60 65 96) is located at C. Anselm Clavé and has both Plana (☎ 977 21 44 75) and Hispano Igualadina buses, which service Barcelona 6 times per day.

Valls is the proud birthplace of the *castell* tradition. If you can make it for the **Festa de Sant Joan** (June 23-25), you can see the "Xiqets de Valls" castellers in action (www.ajvalls.org for more information). The town also features a picturesque downtown area and the beautiful 12th-century **Monestir de Santes Creus**. The **tourist office** is located at C. de la Cort, 61, and offers a good map. (☎ 977 61 25 30; turisme.valls@altanet.org. Open May-Sept. M-Sa 10am-2pm; Oct.-Apr. Tu-Sa 10:30am-1:30pm and 5-8pm, Su 10am-2pm.) The **police** are located at Baixada de l'Església (☎ 977 60 13 13). For a **taxi,** call ☎ 977 60 10 10.

COSTA BRAVA ☎ 972

Skirting the Mediterranean Sea from Barcelona to the French border, the Costa Brava's jagged cliffs and pristine beaches draw throngs of European visitors, especially in July and August. Early June and late September can be remarkably peaceful; the water is warm and the beaches much less crowded. In winter the Wild Coast lives up to its name, as fierce winds batter quiet, near-empty beach towns. A more interesting landscape than the smooth beaches of the Costa Dorada, the rocky shores have attracted romantics and artists like Marc Chagall and Salvador Dalí, a Costa Brava native. Dalí's house in Cadaqués and his museum in Figueres display the largest collections of his work in Europe. Though it may be hard to escape the summer masses, the Costa Brava rewards visitors with beautiful weather, clear water hidden below peaks, and towns with distinct personalities.

TOSSA DE MAR ☎ 972

Falling in love with (or in) Tossa de Mar is easy. In 1934, French artist Marc Chagall began his 40-year love affair with this seaside village, deeming it "Blue Paradise." During the filming of *The Flying Dutchman* here in 1951, Ava Gardner fell hard for Spanish bullfighter Mario Cabrera, much to the chagrin of Frank Sinatra, her husband at the time. Like many coastal towns, Tossa (pop. 4000) suffers from tourist industry blemishes: souvenir shops, inflated prices, and crowded beaches. That said, it resists a generic resort ambience, drawing from its historical legacy, artistic foundation, and mountainous landscape to preserve a small-town feel.

TRANSPORTATION

Buses: (☎972 34 09 03) on Av. Pelegrí at Pl. de les Nacions Sense Estat. Ticket booth open daily 7:15am-12:40pm and 3:30-7:40pm. **Pujol i Pujol** (☎610 50 58 84) takes the scenic route to **Lloret del Mar** (20min.; June-Aug. every 30min., Sept.-May every hr. 7:40am-8:40pm; €1.15). **Sarfa** (☎97 234 09 03; www.sarfa.com) goes to **Barcelona** (2hr., 18 per day 7:40am-noon and 3-7:40pm, €8.10) and **Girona** (1hr., 7:30am, €4).

Boats go (very slowly) to towns and *calas* along the coast, including Lloret and St. Feliu. **Viajes Marítimos** (☎616 90 91 00; www.viajesmaritimos.com) depart every 30-60min. 9:35am-5:25pm (€5.50-18). Buy tickets and board on Pg. de Mar, on the beach in front of the First Aid stand. Take these to reach uncrowded beaches.

Car Rental: Viajes Tramontana, Av. Costa Brava, 23 (☎972 34 28 29). **Avis** (☎902 13 55 31) and affiliates **Olimpia** (☎972 34 02 41) and **SACAR** (☎972 34 10 73) operate from the same store. 21+; under 25 surcharge €6 per day. Credit card, driver's license (International Driving Permit for longer rentals), and passport. 1-day rentals €43-65. Open daily July-Aug. 9am-9pm, Apr.-June and Sept.-Nov. 9am-3pm and 4-8pm.

Bike and Moped Rentals: Jimbo Bikes, Rmbla. Pau Casals, 12 (☎972 34 30 44; jimbotossa@logicontrol.es). Staff gives bike route information; license required for moped rental. Mountain bikes €3.50-4.50 per hr., €17-21 per day. Mopeds €10-15 per hr., €25-31 per 6 hr., €40-50 per day. Open M-Sa 10am-8pm, Su 9:30am-2pm and 4-8pm. AmEx/MC/V.

Taxis: Stand outside the bus station (☎972 34 05 49).

ORIENTATION AND PRACTICAL INFORMATION

Buses arrive at **Plaça de les Nacions Sense Estat** where **Avinguda del Pelegrí** and **Avinguda Ferrán Agulló** meet; the town slopes down to the waterfront. From the station, make a right onto Av. del Pelegrí, and go straight until making a left onto C. La Guardia. The street narrows, curving around to become C. Socors and then C. Portal; any street to the left will get you to the beach, while staying on C. Portal will get you to the old quarter (10min.). **Passeig del Mar** is the main road, along **Platja Gran** (Tossa's main beach), ending on the west side at the old quarter, **Vila Vella.**

Tourist Office: Av. del Pelegrí, 25 (☎972 34 01 08; www.infotossa.com), in the bus terminal at Av. Ferrán Agulló and Av. Pelegrí. English and French spoken. Advice on hiking trails and sights and a posted schedule of upcoming events. Leads weekend guided hikes and walks in the mountains (usually Sa-Su 8am from the office, but schedule varies). Open June-Sept. M-Sa 9am-9pm, Su and holidays 10am-2pm and 5-8pm; Apr.-May and Oct. M-Sa 10am-2pm and 4-8pm; Nov.-Mar. M-Sa 10am-2pm and 4-7pm.

Currency Exchange: Banco Santander Central Hispano, Av. Ferrán Agulló, 2 (☎972 34 10 65). Open M-F 8:30am-2pm.

Police: Municipal Police, Av. del Pelegrí, 14 (☎972 34 01 35). English spoken. They'll escort you to a **24hr. pharmacy** at night if necessary.

Pharmacy: Farmàcia Castelló, Av. Ferrán Agulló, 12. Open daily 9:30am-1:30pm and 4:30-9pm; closes at 8pm in winter. Check posting for *Farmàcia de Guardia.*

Medical Services: Casa del Mar, Av. de Catalunya (☎972 34 18 28). Primary care and immediate attention. The nearest hospital is in Blanes, 30min. south.

Internet Access: Tossa Bar Playa, C. Socors, 6, on the main beach. €1 per 15min. Open May-Oct. daily 10am-10pm. **Tossa Communication Center,** C. Nou, 1 (☎660 12 60 29; locutoss@hotmail.com), by the corner with La Guardia. Internet (€0.75 per 15min.) and long-distance phone calls. Open daily Apr.-Sept. 10am-midnight; Oct.-Nov. and Mar. 10:30am-11pm; Dec.-Feb. Sa-Su 4-9:30pm.

TOSSA'S INLAND TREASURES

The moment you arrive at Tossa de Mar it's hard to escape the publicity for boat tours, snorkeling gear, and other aquatic pastimes. However, if you dare to venture inland from the crowded beaches you will find one of Catalunya's majestic national parks, Parc de Garraf, and the Massif of Cadiretes wildlife reserve. Luckily, the Tossa de Mar tourist office has created a program of guided excursions into the wilderness for beach-weary and more adventurous travelers. These aren't only mountain hikes—many of them go up the beach coasts, providing great views of the rough junction of land and sea. Aside from providing an escape from the masses for a few hours, the tours are led by professionals (for the brain) and have different difficulty levels (for the body). For those who think a 4-6hr. hike is not all that short, make sure to take the green, not red, route (still 3-4hr.).

The tourist office compiles a tri-monthly schedule of routes, and they usually leave on Saturday (for the Green) and Sunday (Red) at 8am from the office on Av. del Pelegrí. There are different itineraries each week, including a "Visit to a hidden valley," a "Megalithic" route to admire the evidence of ancient humans in Tossa, and a visit to the "last virgin *cala.*" The cost? Just €6. Ask for the current schedule at the Tourist Office, and don't forget your sneakers and a water bottle.

Post Office: C. María Auxiliadora, 4 (☎972 34 04 57), down Av. del Pelegrí from the tourist office. Open M-F 8:30am-2:30pm, Sa 9:30am-1pm. **Postal Code:** 17320.

ACCOMMODATIONS

Tossa is a seasonal town; many hostels, restaurants, and bars are open only from May to October. The **old quarter** hotels are the only ones really worth considering. The tourist office website (www.infotossa.com) also lists rooms.

Fonda/Can Lluna, C. Roqueta, 20 (☎972 34 03 65). From Pg. del Mar, turn right onto C. Peixeteries, veer left onto C. Estalt, walk uphill until the dead end and go left. Family-run hostel has immaculate singles, doubles, and triples with baths. Breakfast included—eat on the roof for a breathtaking view. A popular choice with Spanish tourists; booked months ahead in summer. Lunch €10. July-Aug. €17 per person; Sept.-June €15. ●

L'Hostalet de Tossa, Pl. de l'Església, 3 (☎972 34 18 53; www.hostelettossa.com), in front of the Església de Sant Vicenç. Clean and annually renovated with hotel-quality rooms. Many of the 32 colorful doubles overlook the terrace and face the church. Common areas boast foosball, pool table, and TV. Doubles with bath *Semana Santa* and July 15-Aug. €60-68; June-July 14 and Sept. €46; Apr.-May and Oct. €38. MC/V. ❷

Pensión Carmen Pepi, C. Sant Miguel, 10 (☎972 34 05 26). Turn left off Av. del Pelegrí onto C. María Auxiliadora and veer right through Pl. de l'Antic Hospital and onto C. Sant Miguel. This traditional house with small courtyard has an authentic feel and good location. Baths past their prime, but rooms are spacious and comfy. Breakfast €4.20. July-Aug. singles €22; doubles €43. June and Sept. €19/€38; Sept.-May €17/€34. ❷

Hotel Sant March, Av. del Pelegrí, 2 (☎972 34 00 78). Has a family-friendly ambience and outside terrace. Not on the beach, but a big pool makes up for it. Doubles June 27-Sept. 15 and *Semana Santa* €67; Apr. 13-June 26 €61; Sept. 16-Oct. 6 €52. MC/V. ❸

Pensión Moré, C. Sant Telmo, 9 (☎972 34 03 39), 1 block up from Pl. d'Espanya. Cozy lounge with TV; large doubles and triples with views of the old quarter. Common bath, but sinks in rooms. July-Aug. doubles €28; triples €40. Sept.-June €24/€34. ●

Camping: Can Martí (☎972 34 08 51), at the end of Rmbla. Pau Casals, off Av. Ferrán Agulló, 15min. from the bus station and a 20min. walk from the beach. Popular campsite on fringes of a wildlife reserve. Hot showers, telephones, swimming pool, and restaurant. Near the municipal sports area. June 20–Aug. €7 per person, €7 per tent, €3 per car; May 14-June 19 and Sept. 1-19 €6/€6/€2. Accepts traveler's checks. ●

FOOD

Tossa's old quarter has the best cuisine and ambience. Restaurants catering to tourists have *menús* at reasonable prices; most specialize in seafood. For groceries, head to **Can Palou**, C. La Guardia, 25. (Open daily 9am-2pm and 4-9pm. MC/V.)

■ **Restaurant Santa Marta,** C. Francesc Aromi, 2 (☎972 34 04 72), just inside entrance to the old fortress off C. Portal; veer right. In a medieval dwelling with log-cut tables and a patio covered with flowering vines. Contemporary cuisine with innovative dishes like salmon with raspberry and kiwi sauce (€12.95). Entrees €9.85-28, *menú* €13.50. Open *Semana Santa* to Oct. 15 daily 12:30-4pm and 7:30-11pm. AmEx/MC/V. ❸

La Taverna de Tossa, C. Sant Telmo, 26 (☎972 34 19 39). In the heart of the old quarter, right off La Guardia. Serves up inexpensive house wine (€5.20 per L), traditional tapas (€1.90-9.90), and provincial specialities in a large old-world style dining room. Popular among Spanish tourists. Entrees €3.70-12.10. Open Apr.-Sept. daily 1-4pm and 7pm-midnight; Oct.-Mar. F-Su 1-4pm and 7pm-1am. V. ❷

Restaurant Marina, C. Tarull, 6 (☎972 34 07 57). Faces the Església de Sant Vincenç and has outdoor seating for tranquil people-watching. A nice family restaurant with benches bedecked with green-checked tablecloths. Menu features pizza, meat, fish, and lots of paella. Try the vegetarian *fideuá* (vermicelli with garlic; €6.75). Entrees €3.50-12.30. *Menús* €8.50 and €10.50. Open daily 10am-midnight. MC/V. ❷

Pizzeria Anna, Pont Vell, 13 (☎972 34 28 51). Turn right on Pont Vell from Pg. Mar; it's the small restaurant on the left corner of C. Portal, at the entrance to the old city. Though homesick Italians may be let down, the seafood-sick traveler will be in heaven. Pasta €6; pizza €7. Open daily Mar.-Nov. noon-4pm and 7pm-midnight. MC/V. ❶

SIGHTS AND BEACHES

Inside the walled fortress of the **Vila Vella,** an escalating spiral of medieval alleys and steep stairways take you all the way to a picture-perfect view of the city and the surrounding *calas* (small coves). At the tiny Pl. Pintor J. Roig y Soler is the ■**Museu Municipal,** which has a collection of 1920s and 30s modern art, including a whole room dedicated to Marc Chagall with one of his few paintings still in Spain, *"El violinista Celest."* Tossa's Roman mosaics (dating from the 4th to the 1st century BC), and other artifacts from the nearby Vila Romana are displayed in a 12th-century palace-turned-museum; there are also temporary monographical expositions. (☎972 34 07 09; museu.tossa@ddgi.es. Open June 16-Sept. 15 daily 10am-8pm; June 1-15 and Sept. 16-Oct 31 M-F 11am-1pm and 3-5pm, Sa-Su 11am-6pm. €3, students and seniors €1.80.)

Tossa's main beach, **La Platja Gran,** drawing the majority of beachgoers, is surrounded by cliffs and the Vila Vella. To escape the crowds, visit some of the neighboring *calas,* accessible by foot. The tiny ■**Es Codolar** sits just under the tower of the Vila Vella palace, hugged by precipices cloaked in foliage. To get there, follow C. Portal to the end. Snorkeling and diving are popular sports in these crystal-clear waters; pick up gear at **Andrea's Diving Center,** C. San Raimon de Penyafort, 11 (☎972 34 20 26). For less strenuous activity, several companies, like **Fondo Cristal,** send glass-bottomed boats to nearby beaches and into caves, where you can jump in for a swim or stay and take a later boat back. Tickets are available at booths on the Platja Gran. (☎972 34 22 29; www.fondocristal.com. 1hr.; 17 per day; €8, children €6.) **Club Aire Libre,** on the highway to Lloret, organizes various excursions and rents equipment for water sports. To get there, hop on the bus to Lloret. (☎972 34 12 77. Canoeing and kayaking €13; water skiing €26 for 2 lessons; scuba diving €264 for 5-day certification course; sailing €11 per hr.; windsurfing €10.30 per hr.)

◙ NIGHTLIFE

Bars line the narrow streets of the old quarter and occasionally offer live music; since there are so many close by, walk around C. Portal and Pg. del Mar, and take your pick. At ◙**Bar Trinquet,** C. Sant Josep, 9, flirt over dripping candles under romantic chandeliers or stare at the stars in the ivy-covered courtyard. The small **Bar El Pirat,** C. Portal, 32, and its companion bar **Piratín,** C. Portal, 30, have outdoor tables overlooking the sea down below at Es Codolar. (☎972 34 14 43. Open Apr.-Oct. daily 11pm-3am.) For live music try **Don Pepe,** C. Estalt, 6, one block up from C. Peixeteries, a small bar that hosts a flamenco guitarist or rumba musician every night. (☎972 34 22 66. 18+. Open Apr.-Oct. daily 9:45pm-4:30am.)

◙ DAYTRIPS FROM TOSSA DE MAR

BLANES

RENFE trains run from the Blanes station (accessible by the #4 bus from the town center) to Barcelona (every ½hr. 6:10am-9:39pm). Buses (☎972 35 04 87) run to Lloret de Mar (#1; every 20min. 7am-9:40pm, later in July and Aug.). Sarfa buses go to the nearby Girona airport (5 per day, 8am-7:35pm).

The beach town of Blanes is split into two parts. To the east is the old town—the actual city of Blanes. Far to the west lies a strip of hotels with a few tourist-hungry locales. Blanes attracts tourists for two reasons: its beaches and its botanical garden. The beaches can range from decent, such as the main **Platja de S'Abanell** to the right of Pl. Catalunya, to the far superior, if smaller, **Platja de Blanes,** right in front of the old town. If you are willing to walk, however, ◙**Cala de Sant Francesc** is the best choice. With breathtakingly blue water surrounded by jagged cliffs, and, more importantly, few people, this beach is worth the hike; it even has its own restaurant. Take the bus to the botanical gardens (see below), then keep walking down that road past the hill. The Cala will be on your right. Those with more time can walk all the way up Pg. de L'Esperança from town.

The **Marimurtra Botanical Garden** is famous for a reason. Containing three different climate regions and over 40 acres of gardens with 20,000 plants and 6000 species—many nearly extinct—from all over the world, it is also the headquarters for the International Station of Mediterranean Biology. The amazing views from the garden are plastered on postcards all over town. (Open Apr.-Oct. daily 9am-6pm; Nov.-Mar. M-F 10am-5pm, Sa-Su and holidays 10am-2pm. €3.) **Urbans** buses (☎972 33 10 84) run to the garden from Pl. Catalunya (every 15min. 9am-6:30pm).

Although accommodations are abundant, cheap pensions are hard to find. The affordable **Hostal Regina ❶,** C. Esperança, 47-49 is in the old part of town and has 27 rooms with bath. (☎972 33 04 26; hostalregina@eresmas.net. July-Aug. and *Semana Santa* €18.25; Apr.-June and Sept. €16. Singles €3 extra.) For innovative cuisine, check out **El Ceretà,** C. del Mirador de S'Auguer, 17, a block from Pl. Catalunya. The *menú* (€11) includes salad, calamari or pasta, steak or eggplant, and homemade dessert. (Paella for 2 €15. Entrees €6.10-13.80.) The **tourist office,** Pg. de Catalunya, 2, has information on sights and transportation. (☎972 33 03 48; www.blanes.net. Open M-Sa 9am-8pm; July-Aug. also Su 9am-2pm.)

LLORET DE MAR

Pujol (☎972 36 44 76) and Sarfa (☎972 36 42 95) go to: Girona (45min., €3.80); Tossa (15min., every 30min. 8:15am-8:45pm, €1.20); Barcelona (€7.10).

Lloret de Mar may seem like any other beach town, but it is perhaps the biggest and most commercialized of them all; countless hotel highrises and neon signs line the main avenue. Lloret revels in its reputation as a resort destination and keeps vacationers coming. Those weary of packed beaches and souvenir shops should skip Lloret and head to Tossa de Mar. Nightlife in Lloret is big, loud, and flashy. Very large clubs line Av. Vilarrodona. The neon-orange **Revolutions** and **Londoner** are two blocks from the beach. More big and brash clubs can be found along the pedestrian streets, such as the **Broadway** discotheque two blocks up from Pl. de L'Església. On the beach there are also several clubs; **Univers** and **Zodiac,** up Pg. Camprodon on the east end of the coast, promise a good time.

Numerous reasonable hotels are located on the beach and Av. Just Marlés i Vilarrodona. A great deal just a block from the beach is **Hostal Sol Playa ❶,** C. Sant Elm, 9. Singles, doubles, and triples have flowered bedspreads, and some share a bath. (☎972 36 44 36; fax 37 17 83. View to the sea €18-35; to the street €15-30; to the interior courtyard €12-25. MC/V.) Cheap food options are available along the numerous streets two to three blocks from the beach, especially on C. de la Vila. There are a good number of Argentine restaurants, such as **El Gaucho Steakhouse ❸,** C. José de Tagones, 10. The *menú del día* provides enough food for two, with pasta, salad, a large steak, and fries, all for €7. (☎972 36 74 91. Entrees €5.50-20; salads €4-6. Open daily noon-3:30pm and 7-10:30pm.) To get to the **tourist office,** Av. de les Alegries, 3, take a left from the bus terminal onto Av. Just Marlés i Vilar-rodona, and follow it to the beach, taking a left. The office is to the left after five blocks, in Pl. de la Vila. Pick up the **Viva** monthly guide to the city here.

PALAFRUGELL   ☎972

In AD 988, inhabitants of the beach town of Llafranc founded inland Palafrugell, seeking refuge from the constant plundering of Mediterranean pirates. Today, budget travelers come here to flee the wallet-plundering of seaside hotels and res-taurants. Forty kilometers east of Girona, Palafrugell (pop. 18,000) serves as a base for trips to the beach towns Calella, Llafranc, and Tamariu, which, only 3km away, cater mostly to wealthy Europeans. However, Palafrugell has charming, peaceful plazas in addition to its great accommodations, and proves a soothing escape not just from the pirates, but from the hordes of sunburnt tourists as well.

▮ TRANSPORTATION

Buses: Sarfa, C. Lluís Companys, 2 (☎972 30 06 23), half a block up from Pl. de Modest Cuixart. To: **Barcelona** (2hr., 10-13 per day 6:30am-7:30pm, €12.15); **Calella** and **Llafranc** (15-20min.; July-Aug. 24 per day, June and Sept. 12-16 per day, Oct.-May 4-5 per day; €1.10); **Figueres** (1½hr., 3-4 per day 7:30am-6:30pm, €5.05); **Girona** (1hr., 22 per day 6:30am-9:45pm, €3.75) via **La Bisbal d'Emporda** (15min.).

Taxis: Radio Taxi (☎972 61 00 00). 24hr. service throughout the area. **Taxi Costa Brava,** C. Lluís Companys, 4 (daytime ☎972 61 22 22, 24hr. 659 93 67 72).

Car Rental: Rent Services, Begur, 44-46 (☎972 30 62 11; rentservices@viajesrei-tur.e.telefonica.net). Can be arranged at **Viatges Reitur,** C. Cavallers, 17 (☎972 30 09 26), 1 block from tourist office. 1-2 days €23-54 per day, 3-6 days €20-51, 7-13 days €18-49. Insurance €10-15 per day. (Open M-F 9am-1:30pm and 4:30-8:30pm, Sa 9am-1pm and 5-8pm. Credit cards only. AmEx/MC/V.)

▰▱ ORIENTATION AND PRACTICAL INFORMATION

To get from the bus station to the center of town, walk away from the Pl. de Mod-est Cuixart to the first street, C. del Vilar, taking a right and then a left onto C. de la Font, the middle of three roads. Follow it as it curves to the left and narrows into a little street, Raval Interior. After four blocks it will run into **Plaça de l'Església,** where you'll find the church and tourist office. The central **Plaça Nova** is one block before to the right. To get to the nearby beach towns of Calella, Llafranc, and Tamariu, take a bus, spin away on a moped or mountain bike, or take a picturesque 3km walk southeast through the countryside. Signs from Pl. de Josep Pallach will point you toward these neighboring towns.

Tourist Office: Can Rosés, Pl. de l'Església (☎972 61 18 20; www.palafrugell.net). 1st right off C. Cavallers walking away from Pl. Nova. Ask for the indispensable *Guía Municipal* and the *Agenda de Palafrugell*, updated monthly, with relevant nightlife information. **Branch** at C. Carrilet, 2 (☎972 30 02 28). From the bus station, walk left and take the 1st left off the plaza; it will be 1 block down. Both open May-Sept. M-Sa 10am-1pm and 5-8pm, Su and holidays 10am-1pm; Oct.-Apr. M-Sa 10am-1pm and 4-7pm, Su and holidays 10am-1pm; branch also open July-Aug. during siesta.

Currency Exchange: Banesto, C. Torres Jonama, 43 (☎972 30 18 22), at the corner of C. l'Estrella. Open M-F 8:30am-2pm, Sept.-Apr. also Sa 8:30am-1pm. **Caja de Madrid,** C. Torres Jonama, 45 (☎972 30 60 22), across from Banesto, and also at Pl. Nova, 10 (☎972 30 63 16). Cashes **traveler's checks.** Open daily 8:15am-2pm.

Luggage Storage: At the Sarfa **bus station.**

Laundromat: Hiper-Net, Pl. de les Palmeres, 46, on the corner with C. Barris i Buixó. Open M-F 9am-1pm and 4-8pm, Sa 9am-1pm.

Police: ☎092. **Municipal police:** ☎972 61 31 01, on Av. de García Lorca. Call them for the location of the current **24hr. pharmacy.**

Medical Services: Centro de Atención Primaria (CAP), C. d'Àngel Guimerà, 6 (☎972 61 06 07, urgent 30 00 23). Open 24hr.

Internet Access: CiberEmpord@, C. Martí Jordi Frigola, 6 (☎972 30 43 45), in Pl. de les Palmeres, 1 block down and 2 to the left from Pl. Nova. €0.60 per hr. Open daily 10am-1pm and 4:30-8:30pm. The *Guía Municipal* lists Internet cafes.

Post Office: C. Barris i Buixó, 23 (☎972 30 06 07). **Lista de Correos.** Open M-F 8:30am-2:30pm, Sa 9:30am-1pm. **Postal Code:** 17200.

ACCOMMODATIONS AND CAMPING

Though the options are few in Palafrugell, room prices are reasonable and quality and service high. Be sure to call ahead on summer weekends.

Fonda l'Estrella, C. Quatre Cases, 13-17 (☎/fax 972 30 00 05), at the corner of C. la Caritat, a right off C. Torres Jonama. Though the low-key side entrance seems unremarkable, this bright 17th-century building has 10 high-ceilinged rooms off a Moorish courtyard bursting with plants, flowers, and caged parrots. Breakfast (€4.50) served in high season. July-Aug. doubles with sink €41, with bath €52. Sept.-June €37/€48. ❷

Hostal Plaja, C. Sant Sebastià, 34 (☎972 30 05 26; www.hostalplaja.com), 2 blocks off Pl. Nova. This 127-year-old house, home to the Plaja family for 50 years, has 8 rooms, with 16 more next door. Frescoed foyer gives way to a courtyard surrounded by spotless rooms, all with balconies, baths, TVs, new beds, free postcards, and mints. Meals €7-10. Singles €26-28; doubles €46-50. Triples and quads also available. ❸

Camping: Moby Dick, Av. Costa Verda, 16-28 (☎972 61 43 07; www.campingmobydick.com). Take the Sarfa bus to Calella and ask the driver to let you off, or enjoy the nice walk. No white whale in sight, but it is close to the water. Open Apr.-Sept. €2.70-4.40 per adult, €1.50-2.60 per child, €2.70-4.60 per tent, €2.70-4.40 per car. ❶

FOOD

Restaurants near the beach are predictably expensive, making meals in Palafrugell proper a wiser option. Plazas Nova and de l'Església, and the streets in between, have several cafes, burger places, and pizzerias. **L'Arcobaleno ❷**, C. Major, 3, between the two plazas before the tourist office, brings a touch of Tuscany to Catalan classics. The delicious all-inclusive lunchtime *menú* (€8) has everything from *gnocchi* to roast chicken, though most other entrees are €15-20. (☎972 61 06 95. Open Apr. to mid-Sept. daily 1-4pm and 6:30pm-midnight; mid-Sept. to Mar. closed M. AmEx/MC/V.) **Restaurant La Taverna ❷**, C. Giralt i Subiros, 3, across from the Església de Sant Martí, serves traditional fare, such as lamb, *entrecot*, and tomato salad. (☎972 30 04 30. Salads €3-5. Entrees €5-14. Open daily 1-4pm and 7:30-11:30pm.) For more creative takes on the local fare, try **Ca La Rita ❷**, C. de les Botines, 21, a polished, modern, and casual restaurant with *bistec*, chicken, and interesting side dishes. (☎972 30 57 03. *Menú* €8. Open daily noon-midnight.)

🔅 📰 SIGHTS AND ENTERTAINMENT

In addition to its nearby beaches, Palafrugell boasts a couple of attractions, including one of the world's few cork museums. The **Museu del Suro,** C. Tarongeta, 31, has everything you ever (never?) wanted to know about cork and its production, including the crucial role it played in the region's history. Where else can you hear a cork choir and see a cork sculpture exhibit? (☎972 30 78 25; www.museudelsuro.org. Free tours in English July-Aug. Tu 5pm. Open mid-June to mid-Sept. daily 10am-2pm and 4-9pm; mid-Sept. to mid-June Tu-Sa 5-8pm, Su 10:30am-1:30pm. €1.20, students and seniors €0.60.) If cork's not your thing, Palafrugell just inaugurated the **Can Mario Contemporary Art Museum,** Pl. de Can Mario, 7, a large brick-colored renovated factory two blocks from Pl. de l'Església. The site features permanent exhibitions of contemporary Catalan painting and scuplture, as well as international photography. (☎972 30 62 46; www.fundacionvilacasas.org. Wheelchair-accessible. Open mid-June to mid-Sept. M and W-Su 5-9:30pm; mid-Sept. to mid-Dec. and Feb. to mid-June M and W-Sa 11am-2pm and 4:30-8.30pm, Su and holidays 11am-2pm.) In addition, the **Teatre Municipal (TMP),** C. Santa Margarida, 1, has weekly screenings of recent films, as well as theater and musical productions. (☎972 61 11 72. Box office open M-Sa 10am-1pm and 5-8pm, Su 10am-1pm. Theater tickets €21, students and seniors €18. Movie tickets less; prices vary.)

Palafrugell is one of the few places where you can see the famous Catalan *sardana* dance in action (in Pl. Nova July-Aug. F 10:30pm). The town's biggest festival takes place around July 20, when the **Festa Major** dances into the streets. Calella honors **Sant Pere** June 26-29 with lots of *sardana* dancing. The **Festivals of the Habaneras** (melancholic Spanish-Cuban sea songs) come to town the first Saturday of July and August. Around June 19 is the **Festa de la Pela del Suro,** featuring unique demonstrations of cork-peeling, as well as food and live music. The **Mercado de Artesanía** (crafts) takes place in Pl. Nova the first Sunday of each month.

📍 DAYTRIP FROM PALAFRUGELL

CALELLA AND LLAFRANC

*Buses run from the station in Palafrugell to Calella and Llafranc (15-20min.; July-Aug. 24 per day, June and Sept. 12-16 per day, Oct.-May 4-5 per day; €1.10). For walking directions (3km), see the **Orientation** section of Palafrugell (p. 453).*

Calella's breathtaking bay sneaks up on you as you turn the corners of its whitewashed, narrow streets. This magnificent landscape is hidden in a small town that, along with Llafranc and Tamariu, is technically part of Palafrugell. The school, hospital, police, and post office for Calella are all in Palafrugell, meaning the residents of the coast live in constant commute. Llafranc is a 20min. walk along the coast, which slowly gives way to another beautiful pine-bordered bay.

The **beaches** are what draw people here, and they don't disappoint. Although the ones on the boardwalk are small and can get very crowded, a walk farther to the right will get you more space in the sand. The beaches are all small, clear-water bays bordered by high, rocky coasts; strolls on the walkways along the coast, especially between Calella and Llafranc, are a must. Walk left along the beach, through **Passeig del Canadell, Passeig de la Torre, Passeig de Xavier Miserachs,** and ◪**Passeig de la Marinada,** the last forested stretch.

Nightlife in Calella consists mostly of pubs that close relatively early. There are some festivals, such as **Festival Jardins de Cap Roig** (formerly the Costa Brava Jazz Festival) held in July and August and featuring a series of concerts by big-name international artists like Cesária Évora. (For more information contact Fundación Caixa de Girona ☎972 20 98 36. Tickets €15-65.) The **Sant Pere Festival** takes place mainly in Calella; the **Cantada de Habaneras** is celebrated the first Saturday in July in Calella and the first Saturday in August in Llafranc. Also in August Llafranc holds the **Fiesta Mayor de Santa Rosa** with dances and activities. If you are here the first Saturday of September, check out the **Mercado Loco** in Pl. del Promontori, where anything and everything is sold (mostly crafts and antiques).

There are no hostels in Calella, and only two in Llafranc, both with hotel prices. Hotels in Calella range from expensive to outrageous—the **Hotel Mediterrani ❹,** C. Francesc Estrabau, 40, is, believe it or not, the most reasonable. The hotel has views of the bay. (May-Oct. ☎972 61 45 00, Nov.-Apr. 932 09 91 13; www.hotelmed-iterrani.com. Breakfast included. Singles €41.10-57.75; doubles €72.50-136.30. MC/V.) The **Hostal Celimar ❸,** C. Carudo, 12-14, is one block up from the beach and Pl. del Promontori in Llafranc. (☎972 30 13 74; celimar@grn.es. Singles €27-35; doubles €48-52; triples €63-70; quads €82-88. MC/V.) Food options are similarly pricey. One exception is **Pizzeria Sol Ixent ❷,** Barri Sant Roc, a small pizzeria on the rightmost end of the bay facing the water. Salads, pizzas, and other items run €5-15, with good vegetarian options. (☎972 61 50 51. Open daily 11am-11pm.)

GERONA (GIRONA) ☎972

Girona (pop. 81,000) is a world-class city that most people have yet to notice. A Roman *municipium* and then an important medieval center, the "city of four rivers" was an exemplar of the Spanish settlements where Christians, Arabs, and Jews were able to peacefully coexist—for a time. Girona was the home of the renowned *cabalistas de Girona*, a group of 12th-century rabbis who created a school of mystic thought called the Kabbala. Today you can walk the streets of the old Jewish quarter. Girona went on to garner a reputation as a stronghold against French invasion, proven by their legendary resistance against Napoleon.

▛ TRANSPORTATION

Flights: Aeropuerto de Girona-Costa Brava, Termino Municipal de Vilobi d'Onyar (☎972 18 66 00), is small and services a few regular flights on **Basiq Air** (www.basiqair.com), **British Airways** (☎972 11 13 33; www.ba.com), **Iberia** (☎972 47 41 92; www.iberia.com), and **Ryanair** (☎972 47 36 50; www.ryanair.com). **Barcelona Bus** (☎902 36 15 50) runs shuttles from Girona, Barcelona, and the Costa Brava to the airport (from the Girona bus station every hr. 5am-9pm, €1.75; from Barcelona €11). A **taxi** to the Old City is roughly €17 (12km).

Trains: RENFE (☎972 24 02 02), in Pl. d'Espanya to the west of the city center. Info open daily 5:45am-10pm, customer service 6:30am-10pm. To: **Barcelona** (1½hr.; M-F 25 per day 6am-9:30pm, Sa-Su 9:48am-9:30pm; €5.60-5.85), change at **Maçanet** for coastal train; **Figueres** (30-40min., 23 per day 7:18am-10:04pm, €2.20-2.50) via **Flaçà** (15min., €1.40); **Madrid** (10½hr., 1 per day, €36); **Milan,** Italy (11½hr.; 9:47pm; €109, under 26 €87); **Paris,** Italy (11hr.; 10:17pm; €109, under 26 €86).

Buses: Next to the train station, 5min. from the city center. **Sarfa** (☎972 20 17 96) info open M-F 7:30am-8:30pm, Sa-Su 8:45am-noon and 4:30-8:30pm. To: **Cadaqués** (2½hr., 2 per day, €7.10); **Palafrugell** (1hr., 17 per day, €4), for connections to **Calella** and **Llafranc; Tossa de Mar** (40min.; July-Aug. 2 per day, Sept.-June 1 per day; €4). **Teisa** (☎972 20 02 75) info open M-F 9am-7:15pm with 20min. breaks throughout, Sa-Su 9am-1pm, Su also 4:30-5:30pm . To: **Lérida** (3½hr.; 2 per day; €16.30, students €14.70); **Ripoll** (2hr.; M-F 3 per day, Sa-Su 2 per day; €8.40-9.35). **Barcelona Bus** (☎972 20 24 32; www.barcelonabus.com) buy tickets on bus. MC/V. Express buses to **Barcelona** (1¼hr.; M-F 6 per day, Sa-Su 3 per day; €9.50-11.50) and **Figueres** (50min.; M-F 6 per day, Sa-Su 3 per day; €3.90-4.60).

Car Rental: Europcar (☎972 20 99 46; www.europcar.es), in the train station. Also in the airport (☎972 18 66 18). Open M-F 9am-1:30pm and 4:30-7pm, Sa 9am-2pm. 21+, must have had a license for 1yr. From €58 per day, €6 extra for under 25. AmEx/MC/V. **Avis** (☎972 22 46 64; www.avis.es) is across from Europcar inside the train station. Also at airport (☎972 18 66 77). Must be 23+ and have had a license for at least 1yr. From €17 per day, €10 extra for under 25. Open M-Sa 8am-9pm. AmEx/MC/V.

Bike Rental: Alberg Cerverí, C. Ciutadans, 9, ☎972 21 80 03. €16 per day. **Bicicletes TRAFACH** (☎972 23 49 43) in Salt, 2km away. Open Th-F 1:30-8:30pm. €14 per day. **Centre BTT** (☎972 46 82 42), in Quart, 3km away. Open Sa-Su 8am-3pm.

Taxis: Radio Taxi (☎972 20 33 77) and **Taxi Girona** (☎972 20 33 77) have 24hr. service. Taxis are scarce on the street.

◰ ▯ ORIENTATION AND PRACTICAL INFORMATION

The Riu Onyar divides the city into old and new sections. Nine bridges, mostly pedestrian, connect the two banks. The **Pont de Pedra** leads into the old quarter by way of C. Ciutadans, one block off the bridge, which turns into C. Peralta and then C. Força, leading to the cathedral and **El Call,** the historic Jewish neighborhood. The **train** and **bus terminals** are situated off C. Barcelona, in the modern neighborhood. To get to the old city, exit the parking lot, turn left onto C. Barcelona, and head to the right until you reach the river. The old town is on the other side.

Tourist Offices: Rmbla. de la Llibertat, 1 (☎972 22 65 75; www.ajuntament.gi/turisme), by Pont de Pedra on the old bank. English spoken. Pick up the biweekly *La Guía,* in Catalan but with clear listings of events. Open M-F 8am-8pm, Sa 8am-2pm and 4-8pm, Su 9am-2pm. The **Punt de Benvinguda** office, C. Berenguer Carnicer, 3 (☎ 972 21 16 78) is 7 blocks up and across the river. Open M-Sa 9am-2pm and 3-5pm, Su 9am-2pm.

Luggage Storage: Lockers in the train station €3 per 24hr. Open M-F 6:30am-10pm.

Police: Policía Municipal, C. Bacià, 4 (☎092).

Hospital: Hospital Universitari de Girona, Av. França (☎972 94 02 00).

Internet Access: Centre/Punt de Joves, C. Santa Eugènia (☎972 22 00 70), 3 blocks up from train station. **Free** access for students with a passport or ID. Open 9:15am-2pm and 3:30-7pm. **El Magatzem d'Internet,** C. Ballesteries, 20 (www.megaciber.com), by the river and El Call, 4 blocks up from tourist office. €2 per hr. Open M-F 10:30am-2:30pm and 4:30-10pm, Sa 11am-2:30pm and 4-10pm, Su 3-10pm.

Post Office: Av. Ramón Folch, 2 (☎972 22 21 11), a brick building with a golden dome. **Lista de Correos.** Open M-F 8:30am-8:30pm, Sa 9:30am-2pm. **Postal Code:** 17070.

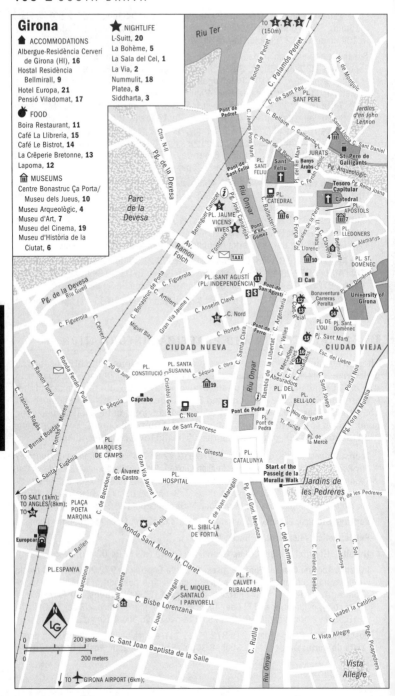

Girona

♠ **ACCOMMODATIONS**
Albergue-Residència Cerverí
de Girona (HI), **16**
Hostal Residència
Bellmirall, **9**
Hotel Europa, **21**
Pensió Viladomat, **17**

🍴 **FOOD**
Boira Restaurant, **11**
Café La Llibreria, **15**
Café Le Bistrot, **14**
La Crêperie Bretonne, **13**
Lapoma, **12**

🏛 **MUSEUMS**
Centre Bonastruc Ça Porta/
Museu dels Jueus, **10**
Museu Arqueològic, **4**
Museu d'Art, **7**
Museu del Cinema, **19**
Museu d'Història de la
Ciutat, **6**

★ NIGHTLIFE
L-Suitt, **20**
La Bohème, **5**
La Sala del Cel, **1**
La Via, **2**
Nummulit, **18**
Platea, **8**
Siddharta, **3**

⌐ ACCOMMODATIONS

There are enough hostels in Girona to find a room without much trouble, but some are no less expensive than the hotels in the new city. The best locations are within a couple of blocks of the river on either bank. Call ahead in the summer.

Hostal Residència Bellmirall, C. Bellmirall, 3 (☎972 20 40 09). Expensive but worth the splurge. Delightful rooms, all with private bath, in a 14th-century stone house on a narrow cobblestone street by the cathedral. Breakfast included and served by the friendly hostess in the cozy dining area or plant-filled garden patio. Perfect romantic environment. Closed Jan.-Feb. Singles €33, doubles €58, triples €75. ❸

Hotel Europa, C. Juli Garreta, 21-23 (☎972 20 27 50; fax 20 03 86), 2 blocks from the train station. Two-star hotel with the same prices as a high-end hostel. Not in the historic district, but within walking distance. Amazing service. 25 modern rooms with TV and bath. Bar and restaurant in sleek lobby. Wheelchair-accessible. Breakfast €5. Singles €32; doubles €60; triples €80; quads €90. Ask for lower prices in the winter. ❸

Pensió Viladomat, C. Ciutadans, 5 (☎972 20 31 76; pensioviladomatgirona@yahoo.es). Sparkling, well-furnished rooms in an old apartment building in an historic neighborhood. Rooms with bath have TV. Long-term options and apartments available. Singles €17; doubles €33-35, with bath €56; triples with bath €75. ❷

Albergue-Residència Cerverí de Girona (HI), C. Ciutadans, 9 (☎972 21 80 03; www.tujuca.com). The whitewashed walls and blue metal bunks in this college dorm may cause flashbacks to sleepaway camp, but the price and location make it worthwhile. 42 beds Oct.-June; 110 beds July-Sept. Sleek sitting rooms with TV/VCR, board games, videos, and ping-pong. Rooms of 2, 3, 8, and 10 beds with lockers. Internet €1 per 30min. Breakfast €3; other meals €4.50-5.50. Sheets and towel €3. Wash €2, dry €1. 24hr. check-in. Reception 8:30am-2:30pm, 3:30-9:30pm, and 10-11pm. Dorms €14.80, over 25 €18; weekends and high season €2 more. MC/V. ❶

⌐ FOOD

Girona boasts great and varied cuisine. Local specialties are *botifarra dolça* (sweet sausage made with pork, lemon, cinnamon, and sugar) and *xuixo* (sugar-sprinkled pastries filled with cream). The best place to find good, moderately priced food is on C. Cort Reial, at the top of C. Argentería. La Rambla is home to tourist cafes with ubiquitous terrace seating, and Pl. de L'Independència offers both high-end and cheap options, with seating facing the beautiful plaza. In summer, an open **market** can be found near the Polideportivo in Parc de la Devesa (open Tu and Sa 8am-3pm). Get your **groceries** at **Caprabo,** C. Sequia, 10, a block off the Gran Vía. (☎972 21 45 16. Open M-Sa 9am-9pm.)

▨ La Crêperie Bretonne, C. Cort Reial, 14 (☎972 21 81 20). Proof of Girona's proximity to France, this popular crepe joint combines a funky atmosphere with great food, right in the historic district. Old French posters decorate the stone walls, and your food is cooked inside a small bus bound for "Cerbère." *Menú* €9.50. Crepes €2.50-7. Unusual salads €7-8. Open Tu-Sa 1-4pm and 8pm-midnight, Su 8pm-midnight. MC/V. ❷

Café Le Bistrot, Pj. Sant Domènech, 4 (☎972 21 88 03). An elegant, turn-of-the-century atmosphere, with a great view overlooking one of the old city's slanting streets. Excellent food like fresh specialty pizzas (€5-6). Lunch *menú* €10-12. Homemade desserts €3.50-4. Terrace dining 10% extra. Open M-Th 1-4pm and 8pm-1am, F-Sa 1-4pm and 7pm-2am, Su 1-4pm and 8pm-midnight. AmEx/MC/V. ❷

Boira Restaurant, Pl. de l'Independència (☎972 21 96 05). Fine cuisine served on the terrace by the regal plaza or in the colorful restaurant with a view of the river. Local favorite offering creative dishes such as lentil salad with salmon, veal with arugula and onions, and black noodles. Vegetarian options available. *Menú del día* €12. Entrees €5.90-13.50. Open daily noon-4pm and 9pm-midnight, Su closes at 11pm. ❸

C
A
T
A
L
U
N
Y
A

Café la Llibrería, C. Ciutadans, 15 (☎972 20 48 18; lallibreria@teleline.es), serves cocktails (€4), beer (€1.50), tapas (€2.50-3), and various entrees (€6-10) to chic intellectuals and posers in its hip lounge area or outside. Also a bookstore (specializes in fiction and Jewish literature), Internet station (€2 per 20min.), and cocktail bar at night, with occasional poetry readings. Open daily 9am-midnight. MC/V. ❷

Lapoma, C. Cort Reial, 16 (☎972 21 29 09). The helpful service and delicious dishes entice many to this recently revamped, dim and romantic restaurant. Entrees are a contemporary French twist on Catalan fare (€4-12), including many vegetarian options. Price can skyrocket depending on drink and food selection. Wine tasting also available. Open M and W-Su 8pm-midnight. Closed first 2wk. of Aug. AmEx/MC/V. ❷

◙ SIGHTS

The narrow, winding streets of the medieval old city, interspersed with steep stairways and low arches, are ideal for wanderers. Start your self-guided historical tour at the **Pont de Pedra** and turn left at the tourist office down tree-lined **Rambla de la Llibertat.** Continue on C. Argentería, bearing right across C. Cort Reial. C. Força begins on the left up a flight of stairs.

▨ **EL CALL.** The part of the old town around C. Força and C. Sant Llorenç was once the center of Girona's thriving medieval Jewish community ("call" comes from kahal, Hebrew for "community"). The site of the last synagogue in Girona now serves as the **Centre Bonastruc Ça Porta,** named for Rabbi Moshe Ben-Nachman (Nachmanides or Ramban), a scholar of Jewish mysticism (Kabbala) and the oral tradition. The center includes the **Museu d'Història dels Jueus Girona,** notable for its detailed wooden model of the original Call. Other highlights include its collection of inscribed Hebrew tombstones and objects found in excavation that relate Jewish community life at the time. A new room has opened dedicated to Jewish religion, traditions, and community. *(The entrance is off C. Força, halfway up the hill.* ☎972 21 67 61. *Both open June-Oct. M-Sa 10am-8pm, Su 10am-3pm; Nov.-May M-Sa 10am-6pm, Su 10am-3pm. Museum €2, students and over 65 €1, under 16 free. The tourist office offers guided tours of El Call in July and Aug. €6 during the day, €12 at night.)*

CATHEDRAL COMPLEX. Girona's imposing Gothic **cathedral** rises 90 steps from the plaça, making its stairway the highest in Europe and defining the Girona skyline. The **Torre de Charlemany** and cloister are the only structures left from the 11th-12th centuries; the rest of the building dates from the 14th-17th centuries. The world's widest Gothic **nave** (22m) is surpassed in size only by St. Peter's in Rome. A door on the left leads to the trapezoidal cloister and the **Tesoro Capitular** museum, home to some of Girona's most precious paintings, sculptures, decorated bibles, and other treasures. The tesoro's (and possibly Girona's) most famous piece is the **Tapis de la Creació,** an 11th-century tapestry depicting the story of creation. *(Tesoro* ☎972 21 44 26; www.lacatedraldegirona.com. *Wheelchair-accessible. Open Tu-Sa July-Sept. 10am-8pm; Mar.-June 10am-2pm and 4-7pm; Oct.-Feb. 10am-2pm and 4-6pm; Su and holidays 10am-2pm. Cathedral free; Tesoro €3, students €2.)*

WALKS. Girona's renowned ▨**Passeig de la Muralla,** a trail along the fortified walls of the old city not for the faint of heart, can be accessed at several points: at the Jardins de la Francesa (behind the Cathedral), from the Jardins d'Alemanys (behind the Museu d'Art, nearby), and at the main entrance at the bottom of La Rambla in Pl. de la Marvà. *(Open daily 8am-10pm.)* At the St. Pere de Galligants church (by the Museu Arqueològic) you can go up on a *mirador* for great views of the city. Behind the Cathedral, the walk coincides with the equally beautiful **Passeig Arqueològic.** Partly lined with cypresses and flower beds, this path skirts

the northeastern medieval wall and also overlooks the city. For the less athleti-
cally inclined, a small green train gives a 30min. guided tour of the main sights of
the old town, including the town hall, cathedral, Església de St. Feliu, El Call, and
the walls. Leave any pretense of blending in at the curb. *(In summer leaves daily from
the Pont de Pedra every 20-25min. 10am-8pm. Less frequently in the winter; check at the tourist
office. Available in English. €3.50, children €3.)*

MUSEU DEL CINEMA. This unusual collection of artifacts, clips, and interactive
displays documents the rise of cinema from the mid-17th to 20th centuries, with a
few Asian shadow theater pieces from as early as the 11th century. It walks you
through film's history from the invention of the camera obscura (9th-12th centuries) to the birth of the modern film industry (featuring movie memorabilia like a
Marilyn Monroe dress), and more, with several hands-on displays and short films.
A must for movie buffs, especially given Catalunya's central role in the early Spanish cinema. *(C. Sèquia, 1. ☎972 41 27 77; www.museudelcinema.org. Wheelchair-accessible.
Open May-Sept. daily 10am-8pm; Oct.-Apr. M-F 10am-6pm, Sa 10am-8pm, Su 11am-3pm. €3,
students and over 65 €1.50, under 16 free. AmEx/MC/V.)*

OTHER MUSEUMS. The **Museu d'Art,** next to the cathedral, holds an important
collection of art ranging from Gothic to modern. *(☎972 20 38 34;
www.museuart.com. Wheelchair-accessible. Open Tu-Sa Oct.-May 10:30am-1:30pm and 4-6pm;
June-Sept. 10:30am-1:30pm and 4-7pm; Su and holidays 10am-2pm. €2, students and over 65
€1.50.)* The remarkably well-done **Museu d'Història de la Ciutat,** C. Força, 27,
showcases 2000 years of Girona's history and prominent figures, from the first
settlers in Catalunya to the present day. *(☎972 20 69 89; www.ajuntament.gi/museu-
ciutat. Wheelchair-accessible. Open Tu-Sa 10am-2pm and 5-7pm, Su and holidays 10am-2pm.
Some descriptions in English. €2, students €1, under 16 free.)* The **Banys Àrabs,** inspired
by Muslim bath houses, once contained saunas and baths of varying temperatures; now the graceful 12th-century structure, with its fascinating insight into
the ritual of bathing, amazing heating system, and notable architecture, occasionally hosts outdoor art exhibits. *(☎972 21 32 62. Open daily July-Aug. 10am-8pm;
Apr.-June and Sept. 10am-7pm; Oct.-Mar. and holidays 10am-2pm. €1.50, students €0.80.)*
The **Museu Arqueològic** complements its archaeological displays with detailed
booklets on the area's history. *(Pl. dels Jurats. ☎972 20 26 32; www.mac.es. Open Tu-Sa
10:30am-1:30pm and 4-7pm, Su 10am-2pm. €1.80, students €1.40, under 16 free.)*

🎦 🎴 NIGHTLIFE AND FESTIVALS

Nightlife in Girona is extensive and ranges from finger-snapping coffeehouses
to sleek artsy bars and crowded *discotecas.* Bars cluster around the **Plaça de
l'Oli** (in the old quarter), **Plaça de l'Independència, Calle Figuerola,** and the
expansive, impeccably designed **Parc de la Devesa,** where in the summer the
forest explodes with temporary outdoor bars and occasional live music.
(Drinks €4.50-5.80. Open June-Sept. 15 Su-Th 10pm-3:30am, F-Sa 10pm-
4:30am.) The artsy bars and cafes in the old quarter are particularly mellow,
and a good way to start the evening. **Platea,** C. Fontclara, 4, right off the river
at the train tracks, is a popular early morning dance spot with a unique spin.
Housed in an antique theater, it has concerts on Wednesday nights and other
performances Friday to Saturday. *(☎972 41 19 02; www.localplatea.com. Open
W-Sa 11pm-5am. University night Th.)* Across the street in Pl. Viçens Vives, 6,
La Bohème is a trendy bar to drink at beforehand.

More popular bars and clubs are just a 10min. walk across the river. **La Sala del
Cel,** C. Pedret, 118, is a great dance club with a techno vibe, and **Siddharta,** C.
Pedret, 116, next door, is the place to pre-game. **La Via,** C. Pedret, 66, down the

street, is another choice bar. If you are willing to walk 30min. (or take a €6 taxi ride), **L-Suitt,** west of the city next to the Cinemes Lauren, is a popular, large club with house and funk music (☎972 23 72 25; www.lsuitt.com). Finally, within the city center, **Nummulit,** C. Nord, 7-9, between the river and Pl. Constitució, is a local favorite, blasting rock and pop from midnight to 3am (closed M).

Starting on the second Saturday in May and lasting into the following weekend, government-sponsored **Temps de Flores** exhibitions spring up all over the city; local monuments and pedestrian streets swim in blossoms, and the courtyards of Girona's fine old buildings are open to the public. Summer evenings often inspire spontaneous *sardana* dancing in the *plaças*. Girona lights up for the **Focs de Sant Joan** on the night of June 23, the summer solstice, with an outdoor party of fireworks and large bonfires where, in the distant past, old books were burned. On this night, try the traditional Coca de Sant Joan dessert—with *cava*, of course. For **Viernes Santo,** the Friday of *Semana Santa,* Girona organizes the parade of the *Manaies*, over 100 men decked out in full Roman soldier gear, including horses and weapons. From the end of June into July, the **Religious Music Festival** (☎872 08 01 62; www.ajuntament.gi/musiquesreligioses) takes place, drawing choirs and artists from all over the world.

FIGUERAS (FIGUERES) ☎972

In 1974, the mayor of Figueres (pop. 35,000) asked native Salvador Dalí to donate a painting to an art museum the town was planning. Dalí refused to donate just a painting—he was so flattered by his hometown's recognition that he donated an entire museum. With the construction of the Teatre-Museu Dalí, Figueres was catapulted to international fame; ever since, a multilingual parade of Surrealism fans has been entranced by Dalí's bizarre spectacles and erotic visions. Though it is a beachless sprawl, Figueres is the capital of Alt Empordà county and a major gateway city to France and the rest of Europe. The city has other quality museums and some pleasant cafes and plazas; if you choose to extend your visit beyond Dalí's spectacle, the town's lovely Rambla is a good place to start.

▐ TRANSPORTATION

Trains: Pl. de l'Estació. ☎902 24 02 02. To: **Barcelona** (2hr.; M-F 23 per day, Sa-Su 13 per day; €7.30-8.40); **Girona** (30min.; M-F 23 per day, Sa-Su 13 per day; €2.20-2.50); **Portbou** (30min., 11 per day, €1.70-2).

Buses: All buses leave from the **Estació d'Autobusos** (☎972 67 33 54), in Pl. de l'Estació. **Sarfa** (☎972 67 42 98; www.sarfa.com) is open 7:45am-8:30pm, weekends and holidays 9am-1pm and 3:45-8:30pm. If closed, buy tickets on bus. To **Cadaqués** (1hr.; July-Aug. 5 per day, Sept.-June 3-4 per day; €3.70) and **Palafrugell** (1½hr.; M-F 4 per day, Sa-Su 3 per day; €5.80). **Barcelona Bus** (☎972 50 50 29; www.barcelona-bus.com) runs to **Barcelona** (2¼hr.; 2-4 per day M-F 7:45am-6:15pm, Sa 11am-4:15pm; €12.50) and **Girona** (1hr.; M-F 5 per day, Sa-Su 2-3 per day; €3.60).

Taxis: Taxis line the Rambla (☎972 50 00 08) and the train station (☎972 50 50 43).

Car Rental: Hertz, Pl. de l'Estació, 9 (☎972 67 02 39). 23+, must have had driver's license for 2yr. All-inclusive rental from €59 per day. Open M-F 8am-1pm and 4-8pm, Sa 9am-1pm. AmEx/D/MC/V. **Avis,** Pl. de l'Estació (☎972 51 31 82), in the train station. 23+, credit card only. Rental, including taxes, insurance, and unlimited kilometers, from €63 per day. Open M-Sa 9am-1pm and 4-7pm. AmEx/MC/V.

⊕ 🛈 ORIENTATION AND PRACTICAL INFORMATION

From **Plaça de l'Estació,** bear left on C. Sant Llàtzer, walk six blocks to C. Nou (the third main road), and take a right to get to Figueres's tree-filled Rambla. To reach the **tourist office,** walk up La Rambla and continue on C. Lasauca straight out from the left corner. The blue, all-knowing "i" beckons across the rather treacherous intersection with Ronda Frial.

Tourist Offices: Main Office, Pl. Sol (☎972 50 31 55). Very helpful, with good map, information on all sights, and a free list of accommodations. Offers 2 guided tours through the city: one Dalí themed, the other a night tour. Call ahead for more info. Open July-Aug. M-Sa 9am-8pm, Su 9am-3pm; Sept. M-Sa 9am-8pm; Apr.-June and Oct. M-F 9am-3pm and 4:30-7pm, Sa 10am-2pm and 3:30-6:30pm; Nov.-Mar. M-F 9am-3pm. Two **branch offices** in summer, one in the train station (open July-Sept. 15 M-Sa 10am-2pm and 4-6pm), and the other in a yellow trailer in front of the Dalí museum (open July to mid-Sept. M-Sa 9am-8pm, Su 9am-3pm).

Currency Exchange: Banco Santander Central Hispano, La Rambla, 21. Open Apr.-Sept. M-F 8:30am-2pm; Oct.-Mar. M-F 8:30am-2pm, Sa 8:30am-1pm.

Luggage Storage: Large lockers (€3) at the train station. Open daily 6am-11pm. At the bus station €2. Open daily 6am-10pm.

Foreign Language Bookstore: Llibreria J. Mallart, C. Besalu, 12 (☎972 50 01 33) sells regional, Spanish, and European travel guides in English, Spanish, Catalan, and French. Open M-F 9am-1pm and 4-8pm, Sa 9:30am-1pm and 4:30-8pm.

Police: Ronda Firal, 4 (☎972 51 01 11). To report a crime, contact the **Mossos d'Esquadra,** C. Ter (☎972 67 50 89).

Medical Assistance: Hospital Comarcal de Figueres, Ronda Rector Arolas (☎972 50 14 00), behind the Parc Bosc to the left of the Dalí Museum. **Red Cross,** C. Albert Cotó, 1 (☎972 50 00 90).

Internet Access: Youth Center (Departamento de la Juventud), on C. Poeta Marquina, has **free** access. Veer right past the tourist office and make a left; it's a red brick building behind the library. Open daily 8am-2pm. **Tele Haddi,** C. Joan Reglá, 1 (☎972 51 30 99). €1 per 15min., €1.50 per 30min., €2.50 per hr. Open daily 9:30am-10pm.

Post Office: C. Santa Llogaia, 60-62 (☎972 50 54 31). Open M-F 8am-1pm. **Postal Code:** 17600.

▛ ACCOMMODATIONS

Most visitors to Figueres make the journey a daytrip from Barcelona, but quality, affordable accommodations in Figueres are easy to find. Most hostels tend to be on upper floors above bars or restaurants. Some cluster on **Carrer Jonquera,** around the Dalí museum; others are located closer to **La Rambla** and **Carrer Pep Ventura.** The tourist office has a list of all pensions and hostels.

🏶 **Hostal La Barretina,** C. Lasauca, 13 (☎972 67 64 12). From the train station, walk up La Rambla to its end; look for C. Lasauca directly ahead on the left; the hostel is a block up on the left. An almost hotel-like luxury experience—each of the 11 relatively new rooms has TV, A/C, heat, and bath. Reception in the restaurant downstairs. Breakfast €3, other meals €7.20. Reservations recommended. Wheelchair-accessible. Singles €22.50; doubles €38.60. AmEx/MC/V. ❷

CATALUNYA

Hostal San Mar, C. Rec Arnau, 31 (☎972 50 98 13). Follow C. Girona off La Rambla (from the station, at the beginning on the right) and continue as it becomes C. Jonquera; take the 5th right onto C. Isabel II, then the 2nd left. Enter through the bar. The long walk is rewarded with clean, modern rooms with bath and TV at very low prices. Breakfast €3.50, other meals €8.50. Singles €14-15; doubles €26-28. Cash only. ❶

Pension Bartis, C. Méndez Núñez, 2 (☎ 972 50 14 73), is a tourist favorite by the train station. Breakfast €2.50. Singles €15-24; doubles €21-36. ❷

◘ FOOD

Restaurants near the Museu Dalí serve overcooked paella to the masses; better choices surround La Rambla on smaller side streets. The **market,** which draws Spaniards from nearby towns with its amazing fruit and vegetable selection, is at Pl. Gra. (Open Tu, Th, Sa 5am-2pm. Best selection on Th.) Buy groceries at **Bonpreu,** Pl. Sol, 5. (Open M-Th 9am-2pm and 5-9:30pm, F-Sa 9am-9:30pm. MC/V.)

Taquería Mexicana, Restaurant Jalisco, C. Tapis, 21 (☎972 50 53 52). For those looking for a change in their diet, this Jalisco-styled restaurant serves Mexican classics (entrees €4.70-15). Try the *fajitas de pollo* (chicken; €6.50). Vegetarian options. Open M-Tu and Th-Su 12:30-3:30pm and 8-11:30pm. MC/V. ❷

La Llesca, C. Mestre Falla, 15 (☎972 67 58 26), near Pl. Sol and the tourist office. Specializes in *llesques,* toasted sandwiches topped with almost anything (€4-11). *Menú* €8; salads €3-5. Open M-Sa 8am-midnight, Su 6pm-midnight. AmEx/MC/V. ❷

Hotel Duran Restaurant, C. Lasauca, 5 (☎972 50 12 50). From the train station, walk up La Rambla to the end and look for C. Lasauca directly ahead. Serves traditional Catalan cuisine with a distinctive French influence in the luxurious lobby. Lunch *menú* €15. Meat and seafood entrees €16.30-31.20. Open daily 1-3:30pm and 8:30-10:30pm. ❹

◙ SIGHTS

▨ **TEATRE-MUSEU DALÍ.** Welcome to the world of the Surrealist master. This building, the self-proclaimed "largest surrealistic object in the world," was the municipal theater for the town of Figueres before it was destroyed at the end of the Spanish Civil War—hence the name. When Dalí decided to donate a museum to Figueres, he insisted on using the ruins of the old theater for three reasons: he believed he was a "theatrical painter," it is in front of the church where he was baptized, and its lobby was where he had his first exhibit as a teenager. The resulting homage to this first gallery is the reconstructed theater, covered in sculptures of eggs and full of Dalí's painting, sculptures, other creations, and his own tomb, all in an atmosphere created meticulously by Dalí.

In keeping with his reputation as a Fascist self-promoter, Dalí's personally designed mausoleum/museum/monument is ego-worship at its finest. Nevertheless, it should be approached as a multimedia experience—an electrifying tangle of sculpture, painting, music, and architecture. It's all here: Dalí's naughty cartoons, mind-bending sculptures (if you will), dramatically low-key tomb, and many paintings of Gala, his wife and muse. The treasure trove of paintings includes, among others, the remarkable *Self Portrait with a Slice of Bacon, Poetry of America, Galarina, Meditating Rose,* and *Galatea of the Spheres.* There is also a small offering of works by other artists selected by Dalí himself, including pieces by El Greco, Marcel Duchamp, and architect Peres Piñero. Although the rooms are numbered, the museum warns that, in keeping with Dalí's idiosyncrasy, perhaps you should follow no dictated order. The museum is large, however, and will take several hours to see regardless of the route you take. (☎972 67 75 00; www.salvador-

dali.org. From the Rambla, take C. Girona past Pl. Ajuntament as it becomes C. Jonquera. Steps by a Dalí statue to your left lead to the pink and white egg-covered museum. Open July-Sept. daily 9am-7:45pm; Oct.-June Tu-Su 10:30am-5:45pm. Ticket office closes 30min. earlier. €9, students and seniors €6.50, under 9 free. Night entrance in summer €10. Call ahead for night hours.)

OTHER SIGHTS. Although it is, like the city itself, often overshadowed by the Dalí Museum, the **Museu Empordà,** La Rambla, 2, is one of the best in the region and features works varying from archaeological objects of the region to Medieval, Baroque, and contemporary Catalan art. It also provides a breather from the hyper-analytical Dalí-obsessed masses. *(☎972 50 23 05; www.museuemporda.org. Open Tu-Sa 11am-7pm, Su and holidays 11am-2pm. Free with entrance to Dalí Museum, temporary exhibitions always free. €2, students and seniors €1.)* Next door, delight once again in the wonders of your favorite childhood toys at the **Museu del Joguet,** winner of Spain's 1999 National Prize of Popular Culture and the second most popular museum in Figueres. The colorful collection of over 4,500 objects features antique dolls, board games, comics, rocking horses, toys for the blind, and more, including toys that belonged to Federico García Lorca and, predictably, Dalí. *(Sant Pere, 1, off La Rambla. ☎972 50 45 85; www.mjc-figueres.net. Open June-Sept. M-Sa 10am-1pm and 4-7pm, Su 11am-1:30pm and 5-7:30pm; Oct.-May Tu-Sa 10am-1pm and 4-7pm, Su 11am-1:30pm. €5, students and under 12 €4.)* Ten minutes from the Museu Dalí, the 18th-century **Castell de Sant Ferràn** commands a view of the countryside and, at 12,000 square meters, is the largest stone fortress in Europe. Still a military building until two years ago, the fortress offers 2hr. guided visits by Jeep and bus, over and underground, with headlight-helmets and all. *(Av. Castell de Sant Ferràn; follow Pujada del Castell from the Teatre-Museu Dalí. ☎972 50 60 94. Open daily July-Sept. 15 10:30am-8pm; Mar.-June and Sept. 16-Oct. 10:30am-2pm and 4-6pm; Nov.-Feb. 10:30am-2pm. €2.10, guided visits €12, audio guide €3.)*

🅿 🌿 NIGHTLIFE AND FESTIVALS

Nightlife is focused on the street by Pl. Sol, behind the tourist office. There are six bars here, including the biker hangout **Selva de Mar.** The obligatory Irish pub, **Jem Casey's,** C. Manuel de Falla, has live music occasionally. To its left is the popular dance club **La Serradora,** which, like many bars in summer, has pleasant outdoor seating. Further into town, the **Bar-Cafe Hotel Paris,** on La Rambla in the same building as the Museu del Joguet, has cushy couches and a decidedly more laid-back atmosphere. For those yearning for Latin music, two blocks to the right and three up from La Rambla is **Noche Latina,** C. Muralla Ample, which features merengue, bachata, and salsa, with occasional live music.

In September, classical and jazz music flood Figueres during the **Festival Internacional de Música de l'Empordà.** (Tickets available at Caixa de Catalunya. Call ☎972 10 12 12 for info.) From September 9-12, the **Mostra del Vi de L'Alt Empordà,** a tribute to regional wines, brings a taste of the local vineyards to Figueres. The week of May 3, the **Fires i Festes de la Santa Creu** sponsors cultural events and art exhibitions. Parties and general merrymaking can be expected at the **Festa de Sant Pere,** held June 28-29, which honors the town's patron saint. The **Festival de Jazz** takes place during the second half of June.

CADAQUÉS AND PORT LLIGAT ☎972

The whitewashed houses and small but deep bay of Cadaqués (pop. 2000) have attracted artists, writers, and musicians ever since Dalí built his summer home in neighboring Port Lligat in the 1930s. While Cadaqués is the larger of the two towns (Port Lligat is basically just Dalí's house), the nerve-wracking bus ride up the mountain on a winding street explains why it has evaded the typical fate of other beach towns. The rocky, nearly sandless beaches and dreamy landscape attract their share of tourists, but Cadaqués preserves a pleasantly laid-back and intimate atmosphere. If you're traveling here from September to May, it's best to make it a daytrip, as most food and entertainment establishments close in the low season; however, keep in mind the limited transportation options for a same-day return.

█▐ TRANSPORTATION AND PRACTICAL INFORMATION. Cadaqués has no train station. Sarfa **buses** (☎972 25 87 13; ticket office open 7-8:30am, noon-2:30pm, and 4:30-7:30pm) run to: **Barcelona** (2½hr.; 7:15am and 4:15 or 7pm, depending on day; €16.20); **Figueres** (1hr.; 3-4 per day 7:15am-5pm, weekends 8:25am-7:10pm; €3.65); **Girona** (2hr., 1-2 per day, €7.10). The bus stop is to the right of the ticket office. From there, walk downhill to the right on Av. Caritat Serinyana to the waterfront **Plaça Frederic Rahola,** where a signboard map with indexed services and accommodations will orient you. **Rent@Bit,** Av. Caritat Serinyana, 9, rents scooters and bikes, which are convenient for exploring the remote areas surrounding Cadaqués. (☎972 25 10 23; www.rentabit.net. Bikes from €18 per day, scooters from €40; hourly rates available.) **Bikes & Boats Cadaqués,** Platja es Poal, rents—you guessed it—bikes and boats. (☎972 25 80 27. Scooters from €16 per hr. or €86 for 3 days, boats from €65 per 4hr. or €100 for 8hr.)

The **tourist office,** C. Cotxe, 2, off Pl. Frederic Rahola, is to the right of the plaza, on a small street on the right opposite the beach. (☎972 25 83 15. Open July-Aug. M-Sa 9am-2pm and 3-8pm, Su 10:30am-1pm; Sept.-June M-Sa 9am-2pm and 4-7pm.) **Banco Santander Central Hispano** is at Av. Caritat Serinyana, 4. (☎972 25 83 62. Open Apr.-Sept. M-F 8:30am-2pm; Oct.-Mar. M-F 8:30am-2pm, Sa 8:30am-1pm.) Local services include: **police,** C. Carles Rahola, 9 (☎972 15 93 43); **medical assistance,** C. Nou, 6 (☎972 25 88 07); **Internet access** at **Telecomunicaciones Cadaqués,** C. Riera, 4, a block off Pl. Frederic Rahola (☎972 15 92 09. €1.50 per 30min. Open daily 10am-11pm); the **post office,** on Av. Rierassa off Av. Caritat Serinyana, two blocks down from the bus station. (☎972 25 87 98. Open M-F 8:30am-12:30pm, Sa 9-11am.) **Postal Code:** 17488.

▐▐ ACCOMMODATIONS AND FOOD. As Cadaqués is a beach town, many accommodations are open only during the summer. **Hostal Vehí ❷,** C. de L'Església, 6, is across from the tall white church. A short walk from the water, this is, by far, the best deal in town. (☎972 25 84 70. Doubles with sink €32, with bath €42; triples €42. MC/V.) **Hostal Cristina ❸,** C. Riera, is right by the water, to the right of Av. Caritat Serinyana on the plaza. Cristina offers bright, newly renovated rooms with great views of the plaza and a rooftop terrace overlooking the water. (☎972 25 81 38. Reception 9am-1pm and 3-8pm. Summer prices include breakfast. May-Sept. singles €30; doubles €40, with bath €50. Oct.-Apr. €25/€35/€45. MC/V.) **Camping Cadaqués ❶,** Ctra. Port Lligat, 17, is 100m from the beach on the way to Dalí's house; follow the signs for Hotel Port Lligat. The campground is popular and crowded, but still relatively clean. (☎972 25 81 26. Open Apr.-Sept. €5.20 per person, €6.40 per tent, €5.20 per car.)

Cadaqués harbors the usual slew of overpriced waterfront tourist restaurants that seem to have photocopied each other's menus—wander into the back streets for more interesting options. C. Miguel Rosset, off Pl. Frederic Rahola, has some good ones. Picnicking on the beach is always a good idea; **groceries** can be purchased at **Suma,** C. Riera, a block from Pl. Frederic Rahola. (Open M-Sa 8:30am-1:30pm and 4:30-8:30pm, Su and holidays closed in the evening.) ⬛**Can Tito ❷,** C. Vigilant, 8, up from the tourist office, is an exceptional historical and culinary experience. The stone archway at the entrance to this elegant restaurant is one of five portals dating back to AD 1100, when

Cadaqués was still a fortified village at the mercy of roving pirates. The menu features local specialties like cod carpaccio, calamari croquettes, and black (squid ink) rice. (☎972 25 90 70. Fish and meat entrees €5-16.50. Open daily Mar.-Jan. 1:30-3pm and 8-10:30pm. MC/V.) Although the area around the waterfront and on Pl. Fredreric Rahola is filled with generic pizzerias, one block inland on Av. Caritat Serinyana is the cozy **Bar La Cala ❷**, with salads (€2.90-5.10), paella (€7.20), and fish and meat plates (€4-13.20) at reasonable prices. (☎972 25 85 04. Open daily 1-3:30pm and 8-10:30pm.) **Restaurant Vehí ❸**, C. de l'Església, 6, on the third floor with a view of the church, serves traditional Catalan seafood, like peppers stuffed with fish in Cap de Reus sauce for €10.50. (☎972 25 84 70. *Menú* €12-13.50. Entrees €5.80-25. Open Mar.-Oct. daily noon-3:15pm and 7:15-10:30pm.)

🎦 📱 **SIGHTS AND ENTERTAINMENT. Església de Santa María** is a 16th-century Gothic church with a Baroque altar. Two blocks up and to the right, the **Museu de Cadaqués,** C. Narcis Monturiol, 15, displays rotating exhibits with varied themes that often revolve around Dalí. (☎972 25 88 77. Open daily mid-June to Sept. 11am-1:30pm and 4-8:30pm. €4.50, students €3.)

From the museum, it's a pleasant walk (30min.) to 🎦**Casa-Museu Salvador Dalí,** in Port Lligat, the house where Dalí and his wife Gala lived until her death in 1982. With your back to the Sarfa station, take the right fork and follow the signs to Port Lligat until *Casa de Dalí* signs appear. At C. President Lluís Companys, where signs to the house point in two different directions, follow the one to the right. A **trolley** leaves from Pl. Frederic Rahola for the scenic 10km route to Port Lligat (1hr.; 4 per day 11am-5pm; €6, children €4). This modest fisherman's abode was transformed to meet the artist's eccentric needs. Though only two unfinished Dalí originals remain in the house, decorations that include a lip-shaped sofa and pop-art miniature Alhambra are works of art themselves. (☎972 25 10 15; pllgrups@dali-estate.org. Open mid-June to mid-Sept. daily 10am-9pm, last tour at 8:10pm; mid-Sept. to Nov. and mid-Mar. to mid-June Tu-Su 10am-6pm, last tour at 5:10pm. Tours are the only way to see the house; make reservations 4-5 days in advance. Ticket office closes 45min. before the house. €8; students, seniors, and children €6.) **Boat rides** in his *Gala* depart from the front of the house on the hour for a 55min. trip to Cap de Reus. (☎617 46 57 57. Open daily 10am-7pm, depending on weather. €10.) On the beach, **Escola de Vela Ones,** C. Sa Riera, 4, in Platja Gran, rents kayaks, sailboats, and windsurfing gear, and also runs adventure tours. (☎972 25 90 29. Open daily July-Sept. 15 10am-8pm.)

Nightlife in Cadaqués is limited to summer weekends and focused on C. Miguel Rosset, off Pl. Frederic Rahola. Five bars occupy a couple of blocks; the most popular is **Shadows,** C. Miguel Rosset, 19, which, with its sleek metal decor, seems almost out of place in Cadaqués. Also popular is the **L'Hostal** club, right on the Pg. Llorens by the plaza.

INLAND CATALUNYA

LÉRIDA (LLEIDA) ☎973

From the well-kept parks and plazas to the fashion retail frenzy of C. Major, Lleida (pop. 120,000) has modernized poignantly in the face of history's constant presence; trendy boutiques are framed by old churches and palaces. Founded in the 6th century BC, Lleida has a past marked by struggle as a result of its strategic location. After recession, disease, and war in the 16th and 17th centuries, it was invaded by Napoleon's brutal army. Left in ruin many times, Lleida is a city defined by reconstruction and today is the economic center of interior Catalunya.

F TRANSPORTATION. RENFE trains, Pl. Berenguer IV (☎902 24 02 02). Trains to: **Barcelona** (2-4hr., 14 per day 5am-8:53pm, €8.10-19); **Madrid** (5hr., 3 per day 8:41am-1:25am, €35.50-54); **Tarragona** (1½-2hr., 9 per day 2:48am-5:55pm, €4.40-13.50); **Zaragoza** (2½hr., 9-12 per day 6:20am-1:25am, €9.20-24). **AVE** or **Altaria** high-speed trains run to: **Catalayud** (1½hr., 4 per day 9:48am-9pm, €31); **Guadalajara** (2½hr., 4 per day 9:48am-9pm, €49); **Madrid** (3hr., 10 per day 7am-9pm, €54); **Zaragoza** (1hr., 11 per day 7am-10:30pm, €24). **Central Bus Station** (☎973 26 85 00), on Av. Catalunya half a block up from the river (open daily 6am-10pm). Buses to: **Andorra** (2-3hr., M-Sa 3 per day 9:30am-7:30pm, €15); **Barcelona** (2¼-2¾hr., 9 per day 6am-7:30pm, €15); **Girona** (3½hr.; Sept. 12-June 3-4 per day 5:45am-6:45pm; July-Sept. 11 M-F 7:30am and 5:30pm, Sa-Su 8:30am and 5:30pm; €16); **Tarragona** (2hr.; M-F 6 per day 7:30am-9:15pm, Sa-Su 9:30am and 9:15pm; €4); **Zaragoza** (2¼hr., 5 per day 8am-6pm, €8-9). Yellow **city buses** (☎973 27 29 99) run throughout the city; the tourist office has a map and schedule. The most useful lines are the "Exterior" bus (#10, 7am-10pm) from the train station to the center, which stops along Av. de Madrid, and the "Seu Vella" bus (#15, 10am-7:30pm, 5:30pm in the winter) between the train station and Seu Vella (€0.75; 10-ride passes €5 at tobacco shops). For a **taxi,** call **Radio Taxi** (☎973 20 30 50).

■ 🔢 ORIENTATION AND PRACTICAL INFORMATION. There is a **map** posted on the street to the right of the rotunda in front of the train station to help you navigate to the tourist office. Bordered by the Río Segre, Lleida sprawls up the hill toward Seu Vella, the imposing cathedral. **Calle Major,** one block inland from the river, is the city's principal commercial street, lined with hip boutiques. **Rambla de Ferran,** the street straight out from the train station, runs parallel to C. Major. Av. de Madrid, Av. de Catalunya, Rmbla. d'Aragó, and Seu Vella frame the center of the city. **Plaça Sant Joan,** at the end of C. Major (from the bus station, Av. de Blondel becomes C. Major), or four blocks straight from the train station (starting on C. Cardenal Remolins, which becomes C. Sant Joan), is the tourist center, with several hostels and cafes right at the foot of the stairs to the cathedral. Lleida has two **tourist offices.** The main one is at C. Major, 31, the street parallel to the river and one block inland, 3 blocks past Pl. Sant Joan when coming from the train station. Make sure to get your free **map** and the very useful **Guía del Ocio,** with information on food and nightlife. (☎902 25 00 50; www.turismedelleida.com. Open M-Sa 10am-8pm, Su and holidays 10am-1:30pm.) The office at Av. de Madrid, 36, around the corner from the bus station, has regional info. (☎973 27 09 97; fax 27 09 49. Open June-Sept. M-Sa 10am-1pm and 5-7pm.) **Banks** with 24hr. **ATMs** line Rmbla. de Ferran and C. Major. Other services include: **luggage storage,** at the train station (€4.50 per 24hr., €3 for small locker; open 4:30am-2am), but none at the bus station; **police,** Gran Passeig de Ronda, 52 (☎088; 973 24 40 50); **Arnan de Vilanova Hospital,** Av. de l'Alcalde Rovira, 80 (☎973 24 81 00); **Internet access** at **C@fe Cyber M@ik,** C. Francesc Macià (☎973 24 76 54; €0.75 per 30min.; open M-Sa 8am-midnight, Su 9am-midnight) and at **Cafetó Internet,** C. del Bonaire, 8 (☎973 72 51 48; €2 per hr.; open M-F 9am-2pm and 4pm-midnight, Sa 9am-2pm and 4pm-2am, Su 5pm-midnight); and the **post office,** Rmbla. de Ferran, 16, 4 blocks toward town from the train station (☎973 24 70 00; open M-F 8:30am-8:30pm, Sa 9:30am-2pm). **Postal Code:** 25007.

🏠 ACCOMMODATIONS. Most budget accommodations (including those listed) double as student housing, so term-time (Oct.-June) space is limited. Sunny, freshly painted rooms at the central 🏷**Hostal Mundial ❶,** Pl. Sant Joan, 4, provide abundant floor space, even with large beds, shower or bath, sink, and desks in every room. Ask for one with a balcony overlooking the plaza. (☎973 24 27 00; fax 24 26 02. Breakfast €3. M-F *menú* €7. Singles with bath or shower €15; doubles with shower €22, with bath and TV €26, with free Internet €30. AmEx/MC/V.) **Hotel Goya ❷**, C. Alcalde Costa, 9, up Av. de Catalunya from the river, at the end of the store-lined main street by the bus station, provides comfortably sized rooms with squeaky-clean bathrooms and framed posters. Each of the 18 rooms comes with a desk, dresser, phone, and small TV. (☎973 26 67 88; fax 26 69 22. Singles €22; doubles €36; triples €50.) **Alberg Sant Anastasi (HI) ❶**, Rmbla. d'Aragó, 11, offers a noisy, social atmosphere with clean 4-person rooms, Internet (€1 per hr.), washer (€2) and dryer (€1), two TV lounges, and a game room. Very few rooms are available Sept.-June. (☎973 23 60 99; www.tujuca.com. Breakfast included. Sheets €2, towels €2, both €3. Reception 7am-1am. Wheelchair-accessible. HI card required. Dorms €13.70-14.90; over 25 €16-18. €3 extra for rooms with bath.)

⚑ FOOD. Lleida's local specialty is *caragoles* (snails), and the city manages to consume over 12 slimy tons of them each year, most notably during their popular gastronomic festival, the *Aplec del Caragol*, which features feasting and snail races, held the third weekend (F-Su night) in May. The tourist office has a list of restaurants that serve a special *menú Xec Caragol* (€24) composed entirely of various snail dishes—some of the more popular ones are snails cooked on a *llauna* (metal sheets), served with *ali-oli* (mayonnaise and garlic), *a la vinagreta* (cooked with veggies on a stone tile), and *a la gormanta* (fried with seasonings). To experience this unique cuisine, **El Celler del Roser ❸**, C. Cavallers, 24, offers an idyllic yet elegant country setting with very personal service. Delicate snail, meat, and fish entrees run €7-15. (Open M-Sa 1-4:30pm and 8:30-11pm, Su 1-4:30pm. AmEx/MC/V.) For those who would rather chop off one of their less-important fingers than eat snails, the area surrounding C. del Bonaire and Av. de l'Alcalde Rovira has the majority of Lleida's restaurants, and the area around Seu Vella has a variety of tiny hole-in-the-wall establishments serving African cuisine. The options on C. Major and its surrounding streets are limited, but one good option is **La Tassa ❷**, Rmbla. de Ferran, 11, across from the post office, with a rustic setting and varied *entrepans* (€3-4.30) and breakfast combos (€1.05-12.80). (☎973 23 88 01. Open daily 7:30am-10pm. MC/V.)

Though a bit far from the tourist hub, **Iruña ❸**, Pl. de Sant Llorenç, is a local favorite set inside a 17th-century farmhouse exterior, with a comfortable family setting and huge courses of delicious Navarran and Basque specialties. (☎973 27 47 55. *Menú* €12. Open Tu-Su 1-4pm and 8-11pm.) Across from the bus station on Av. de Catalunya, the supermarket **Esclat** meets all your grocery needs. (Open M-Sa 9am-9:15pm.) With its attractive interior and friendly vibe, **Natural Blend,** C. Villa de Foix, 2 (in Pl. de la Catedral), is the perfect place to recharge with a coffee before heading back to C. Major for more shopping. (Open daily 8am-10pm.)

◎ SIGHTS. Perched atop the hill above the city, **▨Seu Vella** (nicknamed *"el castillo"* by *leridanos* since it resembles a fortress), Lleida's amazing 14th-century cathedral and cloister, was built on the grounds of a mosque. For an excellent historical and architectural account of Seu Vella, get the audio-tour for an additional €0.60. The long climb up to the **bell tower** is worth every step; two of the seven bells (with names like Bárbara) are Gothic originals from the 15th century. To reach the cathedral, ride the elevator (€0.40) up from Pl. Sant Joan or take the path and stairs to the left of it. (☎973 23 06 53. Open daily June-Sept. 10am-1:30pm and 4-7:30pm; Oct.-May 10am-1:30pm and 3-5:30pm. Bell tower closes 30min. before rest of complex. €2.40, under 21 €1.80, under 5 and over 65 free. Tu free.)

At ground level there are also several beautiful churches, most notably the 19th-century **Església de Sant Joan** in Pl. Sant Joan and the 18th-century **Catedral Nova,** in the Pl. de la Catedral at the end of C. Major.

The new **Centre d'Art de la Panera,** Pl. de la Panera, 2, the large warehouse by the church, houses rotating temporary exhibitions of contemporary art in its spacious galleries. (☎973 70 03 99; lapanera@paeria.es. Open Tu-Sa 10am-2pm and 4-8pm, Su 10am-2pm. Free tours by appointment M-Sa noon and 6pm, Su noon. Free.) Lleida's Romanesque Ayuntamiento, the **Palau de la Paeria,** houses a small basement museum dedicated to the art and archaeology of the city. (C. Major. Open M-Sa 11am-2pm and 5-8pm, Sa 11am-2pm. Free.) The tiny and free **Museu d'Art Jaume Morera** houses a rotating display of 19th- and 20th-century works; the permanent collection begins with realist landscapes by Morera himself and depicts the chronological evolution to more contemporary *leridano* art. (C. Cavallers, 15, 2nd fl. ☎973 27 36 65. Open June 15-Sept. 15 Tu-Sa 10am-1pm and 6-9pm, Su 10am-1pm; Sept. 15-June 15 Tu-Sa 11am-2pm and 5-8pm, Su 11am-2pm.)

■ ■ **NIGHTLIFE AND FESTIVALS.** The area around C. del Bonaire is the best place to go bar-hopping in Lleida, with great spots like **Can-Can, O'Sullivan's,** and **Maracas.** The tourist office's **Guía del Ocio** lists various nightlife alternatives.

The month of May is chock full of festivals, besides the **Aplec del Caragol.** From May 7-11, the **Festa Major** is held in honor of hometown hero St. Anastasius, a *leridano* who served in the Roman army until he was martyred in 303 by order of Diocletian. The *festa* offers colorful parades which culminate in a floral offering to the saint and the *batalla dels flors* (flower battle), as well as the ubiquitous presence of *Lo Marraco,* Lleida's resident dragon, and giant puppets of Marc Anthony and Cleopatra built in 1840 (the oldest in Catalunya). The 15th sees a merry reenactment of the victory over the Moors (arguably merrier for the Christians), while the week of May 29 is spent celebrating **Sant Miquel,** Lleida's patron saint.

From the end of June through September, the hillsides of Gardeny become **Gurugú,** a vast tent-city of drunken merriment, presented by many of Lleida's bars. From Av. de Catalunya, turn left on C. Lluís Companys and follow it until Pl. dels Pagesos. Go through the plaza and turn left on C. de Saturn. Follow C. de Saturn until it ends at C. del Cardenal Cisneros, and turn left. Gurugú will be on your left. The walk isn't through the safest of neighborhoods, so try not to stray from the main streets, and travel in a group if possible, or just take a taxi (€4).

THE PYRENEES

Nowhere in Spain is the wear of time more marked than along the sprawling stretch of the Pyrenees. Throughout the region, antique cobbled towns persist among severe cliffs and gently eroded valleys, and vast nature preserves welcome travelers fleeing the revelry in nearby Pamplona, San Sebastián, and Barcelona. The French portion of the Camino de Santiago crosses into Spain at Roncesvalles, and pilgrims on their way to Santiago de Compostela in Galicia rest in mountainside *refugios* alongside more adventurous tourists. In winter, ski resorts await demanding downhillers in Aragón and Catalunya.

Those who tire of the Pyrenees' expansive natural landscapes can get their fill of the synthetic in the tiny shopping-state of Andorra, a duty-free mecca for bargain hunters throughout Spain and France. Beyond a spending high, however, the Pyrenees offer little in the form of artificial stimulation—travelers looking for wild nightlife should get on the first bus to Barcelona.

Early June to late September is the best time for trekking; any earlier and avalanches are a potential danger, and it can get prohibitively cold later. Tourist offices distribute pamphlets on scenic areas and outdoor activities. The Pyrenees are best explored by car, as public transportation links are few and far between.

HIGHLIGHTS OF THE PYRENEES

ROUGH IT in the glorious **Parque Nacional de Ordesa** on the French border (p. 497).

RETREAT to **Roncesvalles** and blow your horn with Roland (p. 502).

SKI in three countries at slope-filled **Puigcerdà** (p. 476).

FEAST at the **Pirineos Sur** international cultural festival in July (p. 491).

CATALAN PYRENEES

While beachgoers and city-dwellers flock to Barcelona and the Costa Brava, Catalunya's portion of the Pyrenees draws a different breed of tourist. Bikinis are tossed aside for slightly better insulation as hikers and high-brow skiers, mostly from Spain and France, come for the refined ski resorts and some of Spain's wildest mountain scenery. Meanwhile, history and architecture buffs, notebooks in hand, eagerly explore the tranquil mountain towns filled with well-preserved Romanesque buildings. Skiers will find the *Snow in Catalonia* or *Ski España* guides most useful, and the website www.pirineo.com is a fantastic general planning resource (for both skiing and hiking) for those who can read Spanish.

RIPOLL   ☎972

Although the sleepy town of Ripoll (pop. 10,800), with its host of carefully preserved, centuries-old monuments, may seem trapped in a permanent time-warp, it continues to attract visitors in search of Spain's Romanesque architectural legacy; the elaborately carved portal of the Monasterio de Santa María is one of the most famous in all of Spain. Ripoll also serves as a convenient base for excursions to the nearby town of Sant Joan de les Abadesses.

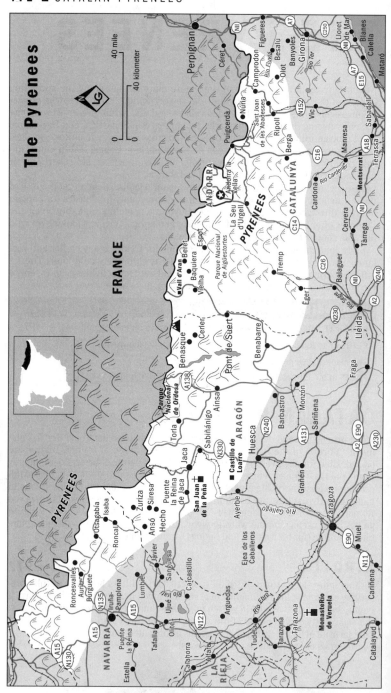

F TRANSPORTATION. RENFE, Pl. Mova, 1 (☎972 70 06 44), runs **trains** to **Barcelona** (2hr., 9-12 per day 6:32am-8:31pm, €5.10) and **Puigcerdà** (1hr., 6 per day 8:56am-8:54pm, €2.70). The **bus station** (across a small park from the train station) sends **Teisa buses** (☎972 70 20 95) to **Barcelona** (4hr., 12 per day, €11.50) and **Sant Joan de les Abadesses** (15min.; 6-7 per day 11:35am-8:30pm, July 15-Sept. 11 also 9:35am; €1.20). **Taxis** stop in front of the train station, or call ☎659 43 74 30.

ℱ PRACTICAL INFORMATION. The **tourist office,** next to the monastery on Pl. Abat Oliba, gives out free maps with listings of accommodations and food. (☎972 70 23 51. Open M-Sa 9:30am-1:30pm and 4-7pm, Su 10am-2pm and 4-7pm.) **Local services** include: **laundromat, La Rapida,** Pl. St. Eudald (open M-F 9:30am-1pm and 5-8pm, Sa 9:30am-1:30pm); **municipal police,** Pl. Ajuntament, 3 (☎972 71 44 14); **Guardia Civil** (☎972 70 08 82); **pharmacy,** located in Pl. St. Eudald (☎972 70 01 41; open M-F 9am-1:30pm and 3:30-8pm, Sa 9am-2pm). The **locutorio,** Pg. el Regull, on the other side of the Pont l'Arquer which bridges the Riu Fresser, has **Internet access.** (☎972 70 42 70. €2 per hr. Open daily 10am-2pm and 4-9:30pm). The **post office,** C. d'Estació, faces the tree-lined park. (☎972 70 07 60. Open M-F 8:30am-2:30pm, Sa 9:30am-1pm.) **Postal Code:** 17500.

ℱℂ ACCOMMODATIONS AND FOOD. Ripoll is an ambitious daytrip; the town's few but budget-friendly accommodations make an overnight stay possible. For more information on accommodations in the entire valley, visit www.elripolles.com. The luxurious and friendly ▓**Fonda La Paula ❷,** C. Pirineus, 6, on Pl. Abat Oliba, is just past the tourist office. Listen as the good-natured owner, Agustín, tells you all about the quirky local history of Ripoll. Cream-colored rooms sport comfortable beds, TVs, and tiled bathrooms. (☎972 70 00 11. Singles €22.50; doubles €36; triples €53.50; quads €68.50. MC/V.) **Hotel La Trobada ❸,** Pg. Compositor Honorat Vilamanyá, 4-5, about 500m up the same street as the train station, rambles up the hill, with fully furnished, immaculate rooms overlooking the town and valley below. (☎972 70 23 53; www.elripolles.com/latrobada. Private baths. Reception 1-9pm, at other times inquire in the bar next door. Wheelchair-accessible. Singles €32; doubles €56; triples €64; quads €78. MC/V.)

Restaurants surround Pl. Gran. Follow C. Bisbe Morgades and take a right before the river on C. Mossen; the *plaça* is to the left. If you are looking for fancy, exquisitely prepared Catalan fare chased by unique mouthwatering desserts, try ▓**Reccapolis ❹,** Ctra. Sant Joan, 68, about a 15min. walk down Ctra. Sant Joan from Pl. Ajuntament. (☎972 70 21 06; www.reccapolis.com. Entrees €10-18. Open Su-Tu and Th-Sa 1-4pm and 8:30-10:30pm, W 1-4pm. AmEx/MC/V.) At **La Piazzetta ❷,** Pl. Nova, 11, the ambience may be Catalan, but the food is Italian. (☎972 70 02 15. Pizzas €5.50-9, pasta €5.50-8. Open M-Sa 1-3:15pm and 8:15-11:30pm, Su 8:15-11:30pm. MC/V.) Stock up on **groceries** at the supermarket across from the bus station, **Champion,** C. Progrés, 33-37. (☎972 70 26 32. Open M-Th 9am-9pm, F-Sa 9am-9:30pm, Su 10am-2pm. AmEx/MC/V.)

◪ SIGHTS. Most visitors to Ripoll come to see the incredibly intricate 11th-century portal of the ▓**Monasterio de Santa María.** Founded in AD 879 by Count Guifré el Pelú (Wilfred the Hairy), the Santa María monastery was once the most powerful in all of Catalunya. The curved doorway, nicknamed the "Stone Bible," depicts survival scenes from the Old and New Testaments as well as a hierarchy of the cosmos and a 12-month calendar. Panels (in Catalan) attempt to decode the doorway. Adjoining it is a beautiful two-story Romanesque and Gothic **cloister.** To reach the monastery, look for the monumental bell tower rising above the town's skyline. Take a left on C. Progrés from the train and bus stations, following it until it merges with C. d'Estació. Take the first left after the colorful modern "metal dancers" onto Pont d'Olot, cross the river, then continue straight on C. Bisbe Morgades to Pl. Ajuntament and Pl. Abat Oliba. *(Church open daily 10am-1pm and 3-7pm. €2, with student ID €1; includes entrance to the cloister.)*

⚑ DAYTRIPS FROM RIPOLL

SANT JOAN DE LES ABADESSES

Sant Joan is accessible by Teisa bus (☎ 972 74 71 81) from Ripoll (15min.; 6-7 per day 11:35am-8:30pm, weekends and July 15-Aug. also 9:35am; return 8:35am-5:25pm, July 15-Aug. also 6:10pm; €1.20), which continues to Camprodon (20min., €3.40).

Sant Joan de les Abadesses (pop. 3600) is a small place best known for its famous 12th-century **monestir**, the work of Guifré el Pelú, who founded the nunnery in AD 887, installing his daughter Emma as the first abbess. Unfortunately, the *monestir* fell short of its holy cause and was closed in the 13th century due to the nuns' licentious activities, which evolved into a local variant of the legend of the evil Comte Arnau, who seduces the abbess. Next door is the impressive collection of religious artifacts from the valley in the **Museu del Monestir.** The oldest piece is a set of pages from an 11th-century book of service, which have survived miraculously intact. You can still make out the lettering, though you have to read Latin to understand it. (Museum and monestir open Nov.-Feb. M-F 10am-2pm, Sa 10am-2pm and 4-6pm; Mar.-Apr. and Oct. M-Sa 10am-2pm and 4-6pm; May-June and Sept. M-Sa 10am-2pm and 4-7pm; July-Aug. daily 10am-7pm. Combined entry to both €2.)

While Sant Joan makes for the perfect daytrip, **Casa Fonda Janpere ❷,** C. Mestre Andreu, 3, a block from the monestir, has 12 big rooms with private baths and TVs for those who want a longer stay. (☎ 972 72 00 77. Breakfast €5, dinner €8. Up to 4 people per room, €20 per person. MC/V.) The **tourist office** in Sant Joan is located next to the *monestir*, which is to the left from the bus stop. Check out the small **contemporary art museum** in the same building. (☎ 972 72 05 99; www.sant-joandelesabadesses. Open M-F 10am-8pm, Sa-Su 10am-2pm and 4-8pm.)

CAMPRODON

Camprodon is accessible by Teisa bus (☎ 972 74 71 81) from Ripoll (35min.; 6-7 per day 11:35am-8:30pm, weekends and July 15-Aug. also at 9:35am; return 8:15am and 3:30pm, July 15-Aug. also at 5:50pm; €3.40).

The best hiking in the Ripollés area is found along the 900km of trail in the Valle de Camprodon (pop. 2350), 20min. up the highway from Sant Joan de les Abadesses. Biking routes are also very popular, and in the winter Spaniards dig their skis out of the closet and head for the Vallter 2000 resort. The tourist office sells a pack of 28 hiking routes in the valley (€3.60, individual routes €0.30), ranging from easy strolls between towns to difficult expeditions in the higher reaches of the surrounding mountains. Each route listing includes a detailed description and map. One of the more popular routes is the loop from **Camprodon** to the **Chapel of Sant Antoni** (Ruta 3 at the tourist office). The well-marked path starts on the road to Coll d'Ares from Camprodon and climbs 400m to the chapel for excellent views before descending back to Camprodon (1¾hr.; low difficulty). There are also many **mountain biking** trails in the valley; inquire at the tourist office for specific routes. **Bike rental** is available at **Esports VIVAC,** Ctra. C-38, across from the tourist office at the entrance to the town. (☎ 972 13 04 26. Half day €12, full day €15.) The ski resort **Vallter 2000,** several kilometers uphill from Camprodon, has a number of good slopes, as well as on-site hotels and restaurants. (☎ 972 13 60 57; www.vallter2000.com. Various classes offered; inquire in person. €23 per day, afternoon pass €21; reduced rates for children under 12.)

For overnight stays, try **Hotel Sant Roc ❸,** Pl. Carme, 4, on the left walking up the main road into town from the bus station. The spacious, clean rooms have private baths. (☎972 74 01 19. Dinner €10. Singles €28-56; doubles €56-64. MC/V.) The **tourist office** is located about three blocks to the right of the bus station in the middle of a traffic rotary. The helpful staff provides extensive information on hiking, biking, skiing, and other outdoor activities. (☎972 54 09 36. Open Tu-F 10am-2pm and 3-6pm, Sa 10am-2pm and 4-8pm, Su 10am-2pm).

VALLE DE NÚRIA   ☎972

Legend has it that in about AD 700, Sant Gil lived for a time in the Valle de Núria, preaching the gospel to mountain shepherds. Before he left to spread his teachings to other lands, he carefully hid several items that would eventually become hallmark symbols of the valley: the bell he used to call the shepherds in for the congregation, the pot from which he spooned his dinner, his cross, and a wooden statue he had carved himself known as the Virgen de Núria. A pious pilgrim purportedly uncovered Gil's hidden treasures in the year 1079 after seeing them in a vision, and so the valley's famous *santuari* was born. Today, the once remote and isolated sanctuary has grown into a full-blown ski resort, the church and hermitage almost lost amidst the restaurants, hotel, and hordes of tourists.

📱 TRANSPORTATION. Núria is accessible only from the town of **Ribes de Freser,** and then only by foot (see **Hiking,** below) or by the antiquated ratchet-rail known as the **Cremallera.** Inaugurated in 1931, the Cremallera provided the easy access necessary to make the valley into the tourist hub it is today. The 40min. ride up the mountainside costs a hefty €14.50 (round-trip), but the beautiful valley above is worth the price. (Cremallera operates year-round. July-Sept. 15 and weekends every hr. 8:30am-5:40pm, return 8:30am-6:30pm; rest of year 6 per day 9:25am-5:40pm, return 8:20am-6:30pm.)

   RENFE trains run to Ribes from **Puigcerdà** (50min.; 6 per day 6:33am-6:50pm, return 9:14am-9:16pm; €3) and **Ripoll** (30min.; 7 per day 8:56am-8:54pm, return 7:21am-7:45pm; €2.20). The much less practical **buses** run to Ribes from **Ripoll** (45min.; M-F 6:45 and 9:20pm, Sa 1 and 6:45pm; return M-F 3:45 and 8:05pm, Sa 9:45am and 3:35pm). **Taxis** can be reached at ☎616 64 48 84.

📷📱 ORIENTATION AND PRACTICAL INFORMATION. The lower Cremallera station in Ribes is next to the train station. To get to the center of town, pass behind the Cremallera station and follow C. Pedrero, which becomes C. St. Quinti. As the road crosses the river, veer right into the Pl. Ajuntament (about 600m). The Ribes **tourist office,** with information on accommodations and transportation, is to the left. (☎972 72 77 28. Open Tu-Sa 10am-2pm and 5-8pm, Su 11am-1pm). Get hiking information at the **information office** in Núria, in the lobby of the hotel in the main sanctuary complex, visible from the upper Cremallera stop. (☎972 73 20 20. Open daily 8:30am-6:45pm.) Local services include: **police** (☎627 41 75 35); **medical assistance** at **Centro Assisténcia Primaria** (☎970 72 77 09); **Internet access** in Ribes at **Televall,** on C. Major, about one block from the tourist office away from the river. (€3 per hr. Open M 4-9pm, Tu-F 9am-2pm and 4-9pm, Sa 10am-2pm and 4-8pm.) The **post office** is on C. St. Quinti between the train station and tourist office. (☎972 72 74 62. Open M-F 8:30am-2:30pm, Sa 9:30am-1pm). **Postal Code:** 17534.

📷📱 ACCOMMODATIONS AND FOOD. Núria itself has only one hotel, one *albergue,* and one campsite. For more options, stay in Ribes. In Núria, the **Hotel Val de Núria ❺,** located next to the sanctuary, has fully furnished rooms. (☎972 73 20 30. Rooms €102-150 per person for 2-night min. stay, additional nights €44-

67; apartments range from €150 for a double for 2 nights to €190 for a quint for 2 nights. MC/V.) Families are welcome at the **Albergue Pic de l'Àliga ❶**, an 800m walk up the hill from the upper Cremallera station, or take the free chair-lift, which leaves from just above the Cremallera station. (☎972 73 20 48. Reception 9am-1pm and 2:30-7pm. Dorms €16-18, over 25 €19.50-21.60.) Limited **camping ❶** is available behind the sanctuary complex (☎972 73 20 20. €1.80 per person and per tent.) In Núria there are a few dining options, all operated by the same people. The most upscale is the **hotel restaurant ❸**, which serves a €20.40 *menú* and meat dishes for €10-20. (Open daily 1-3pm and 8-10pm. MC/V.) The tavern-like **La Cabana dels Pastors ❷**, a little past the hotel restaurant, serves heartier fare. (Open daily 11am-6pm.) Dish up your own food at the **Autoservei ❶**, under the hotel restaurant, the cheapest place in the valley with cafeteria fare ranging from €6 to €10. (Open daily 1-3:30pm.)

� **HIKING.** The beautifully conserved mountainsides surrounding the *sanctuari* complex on the floor of the valley are laced with hiking trails. The Núria information office sells a map (€1) with descriptions of over 40 hiking routes in the valley ranging from easy walks to difficult treks. If you plan on any serious hikes, get Editorial Alpina's Puigmal sector map, available for €8 in the hotel lobby shop. The most popular hike is the **Cami-Vell,** an ascent from **Queralbs,** the last town accessible by car along the Cremallera line, to the **Valle de Núria.** The trail dates back to the period before the construction of the Cremallera and was only recently reopened. The most difficult part of the 2½hr. hike is the 700m elevation gain, though other than that the trail is wide and well-marked. Remember that the bottom of the valley is already above 2000m, so any hiking among the peaks, the tallest of which is **Puigmal** at 2913m, can get cold very quickly, and nasty weather conditions can spring up unexpectedly.

PUIGCERDÀ

Despite a name that challenges foreigners, Puigcerdà (pop. 7000; pooh-chair-DAH) has become a popular town by virtue of its stunning location in the mountainous Cerdanya region. Puigcerdà's view of the valley is beautiful, and the town serves as a cheap base for hiking, biking, or skiing in the surrounding hillsides. Puigcerdà is perhaps best known for appearing in the *Guinness Book of World Records* for the world's longest *butifarra* (sausage), a Freudian nightmare measuring 5200m.

▐▐ TRANSPORTATION

RENFE trains (☎972 88 01 65) run to **Barcelona** (3hr., 6 per day 6:33am-6:50pm, €7) and **Ripoll** (1¼hr., 6 per day 6:33am-6:50pm, €2.60). **Alsina Graells buses** (☎973 35 00 20) run to: **Barcelona** (3¼hr.; M-Sa 2-4 per day 5:15am-1:15pm, Su 4pm; €12); **La Seu d'Urgell** (1hr., 3 per day 7:30am-5:45pm, €4); **Lleida** (3¼hr., 3:10pm, €17.10). Buses depart in front of the train station and from Pl. Barcelona; buy tickets on board. The schedule is at Bar Estació, in the train station. **Taxis** (☎972 88 00 11) wait on Pl. Cabrinetty. For **bike rental,** try **Sports Iris,** Av. de França, 16. (☎972 88 23 98. Bikes €10 per half day, €15 per day. Open M-Sa 10am-2pm and 4-8pm. MC/V.)

▐▖⊁ ▐ ORIENTATION AND PRACTICAL INFORMATION

Puigcerdà's center is at the top of the hill. Off the main plaza, **Plaça Ajuntament** is nicknamed *el balcón de Cerdanya* for its commanding view of the valley. The less picturesque **train station** is at the foot of the western slope. Buses stop at the train station and then Pl. Barcelona; get off at the second stop. To reach Pl. Ajuntament from the inconvenient train station, walk past the stairs in the station's *plaça* until you reach the first real flight of stairs (between 2 buildings). Turn right at the top, then look for the next set of stairs on your left, just before a sign for C. Hostal del Sol. Turn left at the top onto Raval de les Monges where the final set of stairs winds up to the right (make sure not to take the prior set). To save your legs, take the spiffy, free cable car, which leaves from a station about 50m straight in front of the train station, halfway up the hill. From the top of the cable car, look for the elevator, in front of the upper station and a little to the left, which will take you the rest of the way to Pl. Ajuntament. From the *plaça* walk one block on C. Alfons I to **Carrer Major,** the principal commercial street. Turn left on C. Major to Pl. Santa María. From Pl. Santa María, with your back to the bell tower, head out diagonally to the left to Pl. Barcelona.

Tourist Office: C. Querol, 1 (☎/fax 972 88 05 42), off Pl. Ajuntament. Look for their multilingual booklet with info on historical sights, hiking and skiing, and lists of food and accommodations. Open M and F 9am-1pm and 4-8pm, Tu-Th and Sa 9am-2pm and 3-8pm, Su 10am-1pm.

Bank: Banco Santander Central Hispano, on Pl. Cabrinetty. 24hr. **ATM.** Open Oct.-Mar. M-F 8:30am-2pm, Sa 8:30am-1pm; closed Sa Apr.-Sept.

Municipal police: Pl. Ajuntament, 1 (☎972 88 19 72). **Guardia Civil,** Camí Pedragosa (☎972 88 44 11). **Hospital: Hospital de Puigcerdà** in Pl. Santa María (☎972 88 01 50), behind the *campanari.*

Internet: Punt Com, C. d'Espanya, 10 (☎972 88 31 55). €2 per 30min. Open Tu-Sa 10am-1:30pm and 4-8:30pm, Su 10am-2pm.

Post Office: Av. Coronel Molera, 11 (☎972 88 08 14). 1½ blocks down from Pl. Barcelona. Open M-F 8:30am-2:30pm, Sa 9:30am-1pm. **Postal Code:** 17520.

🛏🍴 ACCOMMODATIONS AND FOOD

Rooms in Puigcerdà come easily, if not relatively cheaply. Most less-expensive pensiones are off Pl. Santa María in the old town. Try the inexpensive **Hostal Muntanya ❷,** Av. Coronel Molera, 1, which offers basic, well-kept rooms, though the hallways are a bit dim. From Pl. Barcelona head down Av. Coronel Molera; it's on the left. (☎972 88 02 02. Breakfast €3. Singles €19; doubles €38.) **Alfonso Habitaciones ❷,** C. d'Espanya, 5, has decent, dimly lit, carpeted rooms with TVs, private baths, and colorful bedspreads, plus a good-natured owner. Heading away from the church, take a left off C. Alfons I. (☎972 88 02 46. Singles €21; doubles €42, triples €60.) If you're looking for a real treat, try the three-star **Avet Blau Hotel ❺,** Pl. Santa María, 14 (overlooking the plaza and bell tower), which has six spacious and comfortable doubles. You can even bring your dog, provided you don't leave it alone in the room. (☎972 88 25 52. Breakfast included. Reservations recommended. Doubles €75-95. Up to 2 extra people €25 each. MC/V.) If you're planning to ski at the nearby resort La Molina, try **Mare de Déu de les Neus (HI) ❶,** on Ctra. de Font Canaleta, which has modern facilities and an excellent location just 500m from the La Molina RENFE station and 4km from the slopes. In winter a bus goes up to the slopes every 30min. (☎972 89 20 12; reservations 934 83 83 63. Breakfast included. Sheets €2. Reserve in high season. Dec. dorms €18.50, over 25 €22. Jan.-Nov. €14/€15. Doubles and triples available, same price per person. MC/V.) **Camping Stel ❷,** 1km from Puigcerdà on the road to Llivia, offers full-service camping with the benefits of a chalet-style restaurant, bar, and lounge. (☎972 88 23 61. Site with tent and car €17, plus €4.80 per person, €4.20 per child. Electricity €3.20. May 28-Sept. 26 and Oct. 22-May 1).

The neighborhood off C. Alfons I has many food options. For fresh produce, try the weekly **market** at Pl. 10 d'Abril. (Su 6am-2pm.) Get **groceries** at **Bonpreu,** Av. Coronel Molera, 12, the small supermarket diagonally across from the post office. (Open M-Sa 9am-9pm, Su 10am-2:30pm. MC/V.) At ▨**Cantina Restaurant Mexicà ❷**, Pl. Cabrinetty, 9, you can kick back with a margarita and take in some excellent and surprisingly authentic tacos, fajitas, and quesadillas. (☎972 88 16 58. Entrees €7-9. Open Su-W and F-Sa 1:30-3:30pm and 8:30-11pm.) **El Pati de la Tieta ❷**, C. Ferrers, 20, serves large portions of pasta and pizzas (€7-11) and heavenly desserts (€6-7) on an ivy-covered patio. (☎972 88 01 56. Fish and meat entrees €11.50-17. Open daily 1-3:30pm and 8-11:30pm.)

◉ ⚐ SIGHTS AND SLOPES

Between ski runs and cycling, dash over to the **campanario,** the octagonal bell tower in Pl. Santa María. This 42m high, 12th-century tower is all that remains of the **Església de Santa María,** an eerie reminder of the destruction wreaked by the Civil War. The 13th-century **Església de Sant Domènech,** on Pl. 10 d'Abril, contains several Gothic paintings considered to be among the best of their genre. (Open 9:30am-8pm. Free.) Puigcerdà's picturesque **estany** (lake), a 2min. walk up C. Pons i Gasch from Pl. Barcelona, was created in AD 1380 for irrigation purposes. It now serves as a lovely place for an evening's row among the waterfowl. (Rowboat rental €2.50 per person per 30min.; inquire at the cafe on the far side.)

Puigcerdà calls itself the "capital of snow." **Ski** in your country of choice (Spain, France, or Andorra) at one of 19 ski areas within a 50km radius. The closest and cheapest one on the Spanish side is **La Molina** (☎972 89 20 31; www.lamolina.com). Nearby **Masella** (☎972 14 40 00; www.masella.com) offers the longest run in the Pyrenees at 7km. For cross-country (nordic) skiing, the closest site is **Guils-Fontanera** (☎972 19 70 87), with 45km of forest paths. A little farther out, try **Lles** (☎973 29 30 49) or **Aránser** (☎973 29 30 51). The Puigcerdà area is also popular for **biking;** the tourist office has a map with 17 routes. **Club Poliesportiu Puigcerdà,** on Av. del Poliesportiu, has a pool, tennis courts, basketball courts, and a skating rink. (☎972 88 02 43. €4.60 per sports facility, skating rink €6.80, or €8.50 per day for all facilities. Open M-F 10:30am-10pm, Sa 10:30am-9:30pm, Su 10:30am-8pm, though each facility also has its own hours.)

PARC NACIONAL D'AIGÜESTORTES I ESTANY DE SANT MAURICI

Catalunya has only one official national park, but it's a big one. The **Estany de Sant Maurici,** the park's largest lake, in the east, and the wild tumbling of the Riu de Sant Nicolau in the west have earned it the nickname "Aigües Tortes" (Twisted Waters). Flocks of sheep roam the wildflower dusted alpine meadows as golden eagles soar above its snow-capped peaks. With more than 100 glacial lakes and over 14,000 hectares to explore, the park merits at least two days—using public transportation, it's hard to do it in fewer than three.

◼✳ ⓘ ORIENTATION AND PRACTICAL INFORMATION

The two main gateway towns to the park are **Boí** to the west and **Espot** to the east. To enter the park from either side, you can drive or take a taxi to the main trailheads. To drive from Boí, take the main highway (L-500) north for about 2km past the Boí turnoff to the park entrance on the right, stopping at the last parking lot just within the park's peripheral borders. The public **taxi** service (☎973 69 63 15 or

629 20 54 89) operates jeeps that take visitors from the main plaza in Boí to the last information booth about 6km past the official park entrance. (20min.; July-Sept. 15 8am-7pm, rest of summer 9am-6pm. In winter call the mobile number for service. Taxis leave when groups of six or more clients form, and arrange for return service. One-way €4, round-trip €8.) From the Espot side, drive up the main road to the last parking lot just before the park entrance or take a jeep **taxi** into the park, leaving from the plaza next to the park office and Ayuntamiento. (☎973 62 41 05. July-Sept. 15 8am-7pm, rest of summer 9am-6pm. In winter call for service.) Taxis go to: **Estany de Sant Maurici** (15min.; €4); **Estany de Ratera** (25min., €12); **Estany d'Amitges** (30min., €15.50); **Estany Negre** (30min., €19).

REFUGIOS

Since camping is not permitted within park borders, *refugios* are the only option for wilderness adventures of more than one day; just make sure to bring your own sheets or sleeping bag. Call several days in advance to reserve a spot, or it will be a rough (and illegal) night out in the woods. A night's stay runs €7-11, and most guarded *refugios* serve dinner and breakfast for an additional €8-12.

INSIDE THE PARK

Refugio de Ernest Mallafré (☎973 25 01 18, winter 25 01 05), uphill from the information office on the southern side of Estany de Sant Maurici.

Refugio d'Amitges (☎973 25 01 09, winter 933 18 15 05), near Estanys de Amitges.

Refugio de Josep María Blanc (☎973 25 01 08, winter 934 23 23 45), near Estany Negre.

Refugio de Estany Llong (☎629 37 46 52), next to Estany Llong.

Refugio de Ventosa i Calvell (☎973 29 70 90, winter 934 50 09 66), in the northern portion of the park on the Boí side, next to Estany Negre de Boí.

OUTSIDE THE PARK

Refugio de Calomers (☎973 25 03 08, winter 64 05 92), on the north side of the park by Lac Major de Calomers.

Refugio de Restanca (☎608 03 65 59), north of Refugio de Ventosa i Calvell next to Lac dera Restanca.

Refugio de Saboredo (☎973 25 30 15, winter 933 29 97 36), north of Refugio d'Amitges across the Serra de Crabes.

Refugio de Colomina (☎973 25 20 00, winter 68 10 42), the park's southernmost refuge, across the Serra de Sobremonestero from Estany de Sant Maurici, or across the Dellui Saddleback from the Boí side.

Refugi Gerber-Mataró (☎973 25 01 70), north of Estany de Sant Maurici across the Serra de les Agudes.

Refugi Pla de la Font (☎619 93 07 71), just north and a little west of Espot near the Coll de Foguerix.

HIKES

Free maps from the park information offices in Espot and Boí list well-defined itineraries, but explorers may want to drop the extra cash to buy a more detailed 1:25,000 scale map (€8 in the offices; available in area stores for a bit more). The red *Editorial Alpina* guides (€3) for Montardo, Vall de Boí, and Sant Maurici are particularly useful. For more detailed hiking info, contact the park **tourist offices**

(Espot ☎973 62 40 36, Boí 69 61 89). Trail accessibility and difficulty varies by season. As with all hikes, check trail conditions and weather with a park office before heading out, and be prepared for all types of weather in the mountains.

 STORMY WEATHER. The mountains may appear calm from afar, but the region's notoriously unpredictable weather can be quite dangerous, especially in winter. Casual wandering is not recommended. Though the main trails are clearly marked, it is easy to become lost should one stray into the mountains.

BOÍ SIDE

The **Ruta de la Nutria** leaves from the main public parking lot, heading along the Riu de Sant Nicolau to the last information booth at the Aigüestortes, passing Estany de Llebreta on the way (1¾hr.; low difficulty). The **Camino de Estany Llong** heads from the Aigüestortes to Estany Llong and its *refugio* (1¼hr.; low difficulty). For the more intrepid and experienced hiker, Estany Llong can also be reached from the Aigüestortes via ◪**El Valle de Dellui,** a beautiful hike among alpine meadows and glacial lakes (4½hr.; moderate difficulty due to duration, steepness, and rock scramble over large boulder field). Those seeking the best views of the park should continue past Estany Llong to **Portarró de Espot** (2424m), an amazing lookout spot in the center of the park with vistas of both the Boí and Espot sides. A side trail leads to the top of the **Pic del Portarró** (2736m), where the view is a 360° panorama (3hr.; moderate difficulty due to elevation gain).

ESPOT SIDE

From the park entrance, the wide, well-traveled **Ruta del Isard** leads to the Estany de Sant Maurici (1¼hr.; low difficulty with wide gravel path). For great views of the big lake and the surrounding valley, take the hiking tour **El mirador del Estany de Sant Maurici,** which runs around the lake to the Cascada de Ratera and the Estany de Ratera before looping back to the starting point (2¼hr.; low difficulty). To get to the **Estanys de Amitges** and the popular **Refugio d'Amitges,** start at the Estany de Sant Maurici and continue up the trail past Estany de Ratera (1¾hr.; low difficulty to Estany de Ratera, moderate difficulty continuing on to Amitges). The **Portarró de Espot** is also accessible from Estany de Sant Maurici, a slightly shorter hike than from the Boí side, but a better bet to catch a glimpse of an *isard* (*chamois* or mountain antelope) bounding on the rocky slopes and patches of snow (2½hr.; moderate difficulty due to steepness and elevation gain). From Espot itself, a less-traveled hike leads to the **Estany Negre** and the **Refugio J.M. Blanc** (3½hr.; moderate difficulty due to steepness of trail). To traverse the entire park, from Aigüestortes to Estany de Sant Maurici, is a good day's hike, leading over the Portarró, but make sure to reserve a bed for the night at the Refugio de Malafré or you'll be sleeping in the cold (5½hr.; moderate difficulty due to length and elevation gain).

ESPOT AND ESTANY DE SANT MAURICI ☎973

The official gateway to the eastern half of the park and the best point of entrance coming from Barcelona, the tiny town of **Espot** is comprised mostly of rustic restaurants and quiet accommodations for the weary hiker. Espot is a good 4.5km from the actual entrance to the park, but the walk there is quite scenic. Those with cars can park at the last parking lot, just outside the park entrance.

▉ TRANSPORTATION. Unfortunately for those relying on public transportation, buses only come within 7km of Espot, on highway C-147 at the La Torrassa crossing. The nearest actual stop is at **La Guingueta d'Aneu,** about 9km from Espot, with service to **Barcelona** (5½hr., 7:30am, €25.50) and **Lleida** (3hr., 4:30pm). From La Guingueta you can either walk to Espot (2½hr.) or call the jeep service for pickup. (☎973 62 41 05. €12 to Espot.)

🛈 **PRACTICAL INFORMATION.** The bustling **park information office** (on the right as you enter Espot) provides brochures on accommodations in and around Espot, itineraries, maps, and trekking advice. (☎973 62 40 36. Open daily Apr.-Oct. 9am-1pm and 3:30-6:45pm; Nov.-Mar. M-Sa 9am-2pm and 3:30-6pm.) The local **bank,** with 24hr. **ATM,** is **La Caixa,** next to the park office. (Open M-F 11am-2pm.) The **police** can be reached at ☎085. In a medical **emergency,** call ☎973 62 10 05. For groceries, a **supermarket** is located across the main bridge toward the park. (☎973 62 40 51. Open M-Sa 9:30am-2pm and 4:30-9pm.)

🏠🏕 **ACCOMMODATIONS AND CAMPING.** The park office has a list of the many local residences that take in travelers; you can often find good deals. Cross the main bridge to **Residència Casa de Pagés Felip** ❷ for comfortable rooms with a down-home touch and private baths. Follow the bridge road for two blocks and then take a left; the *residència* is just behind Hotel Roya. (☎973 62 40 93. Laundry €15. Doubles €30-40; triples €45-60.) Those devoted to an ascetic life may be disappointed by the camping in Espot: all locations provide food, games, water, showers, and a selection of other amenities. **Casa Peret de Peretó** ❶ and **Camping Solau** ❶ run a joint establishment, offering spacious, sunny rooms inside with private bath and 22 campsites outside on the sprawling front yard. (☎973 62 40 68; www.casa-peretdepereto.com or www.campingsolau.com. Doubles €34-36; campsites €3.80-4 per person, per tent, and per car.) Located 1.3km down the park entrance road on the right, **Camping Vora Parc** ❶ offers the closest camping to the park, with sites along the riverbank. The stone entryway and manicured lawn are indicative of the carefully maintained sites. (☎973 25 23 24. €4.40 per person, children 6-14 €4, under 6 free. €4.40 per tent, and per car. Electricity €3.80. MC/V.)

BOÍ ☎973

Despite the nearby ski resort in **Taüll,** Boí hasn't lost its country charm. The village's cobblestone streets wind their way through low arches and mini-plazas. Boí is the most convenient base from which to explore the western half of the park. Green RCPs *(Residèncias Casa de Pagés)* indicate the many local residences offering lodging for

THE BIG SPLURGE

BOÍ OH BOÍ!

You may have thought that the invigorating fresh air of the mountains and serenity of the outdoors would be enough to enliven your spirit while traveling through the Pyrenees. Soon you will realize that hiking is just exhausting. Never fear--just up the mountain from the tiny village of Boí lie the Caldes de Boí, natural hot springs long famous for the mineral water that is still bottled here. Today the **Hotel Caldas,** newly renovated from a 17th-century hotel-and-church complex, and the **Hotel Manantial** provide the perfect places to stay while enjoying the therapeutic properties of the celebrated waters. The hotel complex has several salons as well as outdoor terraces, swimming pools, and miniature golf, all at a breathtaking 1500m. The spa complex offers a variety of health treatments ranging from specialized massages to anti-stress programs. Be sure not to miss the *estufas naturales:* unique in all of Europe, these natural saunas are built directly into the mountainside and draw their heat from deep within the mountain itself.

☎932 72 26 47; www.caldesdeboi.com. Hotel Caldas ❺ €60-112 per person per night, Hotel Manantial ❺ €86-147 per person per night, with a variety of 2-8 day therapeutic packages available for €250-1250 per person. For more information contact: Caldes de Boí, Pau Claris, 162, Barcelona, 08037.

travelers. Although very safe, most of these private residences do not accept credit cards, have very limited space (usually only 1-2 rooms), and change hours depending on the whim of the host.

Public transportation from the east to the medieval village is inconvenient but possible. From **Vielha,** take the bus (M-Sa 1pm) to Boí via **Pont de Suert** (1¼hr.; leaves Pont de Suert at 1:45pm, returns to Vielha at 9am; €3.50). Boí's **park info office** is near the bus stop on the *plaça,* inside the old stone building. Look for the signs for Casa del Parc. (☎973 69 61 89; www.parcsdecatalunya.net/aiguestortes.htm. Open daily June-Sept. 9am-1pm and 3:30-7pm; Oct-May 9am-2pm and 3:30-6pm.) Reach the **Mossos d'Esquadra** (Catalan police) at ☎973 69 08 15, or the **police** at ☎088.

Hostal Beneria ❸, C. Treijo, just past Hotel Pey off the main road, offers affordable, big, clean rooms with bath, and a comfortable TV lounge with huge leather chairs. (☎973 69 60 30. Breakfast included. Singles €26; doubles €45.) **Hostal Fondevila ❷,** to the right of the main road through Boí, has palatial rooms with baths and plenty of socializing space in the big TV room, game room, and bar. (☎/fax 973 69 60 11. Reception 9am-11pm. Wheelchair-accessible. July 18-Aug. 25 and Christmas-*Semana Santa* singles €34; doubles €48; triples €60; quads €75. Otherwise €27/€43/€55/€70. MC/V.) **Camping Taüll ❶,** uphill about 3km on the main road just before Taüll. (☎973 69 61 74. €4 per person, per car, and per tent; €3.50 per child. Bungalows for 2 people €50, for 4 people €80-90, for 6 people €90-100, for 8 people €120, for 10 people €150). **Restaurante Pey ❸,** Pl. Treijo, 3, has a homey, sunny dining room and generous servings of tasty entrees; the roasted chicken is delicious. (☎973 69 60 36. *Menú* €12. Open daily 1-4pm and 8-11pm.)

VAL D'ARAN

Some of the Catalan Pyrenees's most dazzling peaks cluster around green Val d'Aran, Catalunya's northernmost valley. Val d'Aran's main river flows into France and is hemmed in tightly by the highest peaks in the eastern range; consequently, the area's original native language is not Catalan but Aranés, a dialect close to *langue d'oc,* the medieval Romance language spoken in southern France. Today, modern transportation and the tourist industry have made substantial inroads into the valley's isolation.

BAQUIERA-BERET AND SALARDÚ ☎973

Baquiera-Beret, with its budget-busting cluster of hotel complexes, is Spain's most chic ski resort; after all, the Spanish royal family's favorite slopes are here. Currently, about 80 alpine trails and a few cross-country ones wind down the surrounding peaks. For skiing info and reservations, contact the **Oficeria de Baquiera-Beret** (☎973 63 90 00; fax 64 44 88). However, if you're not here to ski, skip this small town, which shuts down after ski-season.

Budget accommodations have disappeared from the ski resort itself, but never fear; reasonably priced options abound along the cobbled streets of **Salardú,** just 4km down the highway from Baquiera on the way to Vielha. The main parking lot is uphill from the town center along the broad C. Des Estudis. Coming from Vielha along highway C-142, veer left at the fork after the first hard left at the town's eastern end. Above the umbrella tables of Bar Montanha, the rooms of **Pensión Montanha ❷,** C. Major, 8, provide a cheap, comfortable sleep, and several of the bright, clean rooms have private bath. From the parking lot, head downhill on C. des Estudis, turning right just before the highway. Montanha is several doors down. (☎973 64 41 08. Singles €24; doubles €30, with bath €35; triples €37/€42.) The **Auberja Era Garona (HI) ❶,** Ctra. de Vielha, is in neighboring Salardú. Dorms have four or six beds, and the reception desk offers bike and ski rentals. (☎973 64 52 71; www.aranweb.com/garona. Internet available. Breakfast included. Sa-Su Dec.-Apr. and *Semana Santa* €17, over 25 €19.40; M-F Dec.-Apr. and July-Sept. 15 €14.80/€17.20; May-June and Sept. 16-Nov. €12.60/€13.)

Upscale restaurants abound in Baquiera-Beret and Salardú, but you haven't really eaten in style until you've hit **Eth Cabilac ❸**, C. Mayor, 12, next door to Pensión Montanha. Elegant food and service at reasonable prices makes Eth Cabilac a must. (☎973 64 42 82. *Menú* €16, special "*Aromas del Valle*" *menú* €24. Entrees €7-15. Open daily 1-3:30pm and 8:30-10:30pm. AmEx/MC/V.) Just down the street from the church is **El Horno ❶**, C. Sant Andreu, 3, whose cheap, delicious pastries you can smell a block away. (☎636 32 58 20. Pastries €0.80-€1.20. Orange juice €1. Open M-Sa 9am-1pm and 5-8pm, Su 10:30am-1pm.)

While in town, don't miss the beautifully restored 16th-century murals on the ceiling of Salardú's 13th-century **Església de Sant Andreu** and its incredible garden view. Shuttles connect Vielha and Salardú in July and August (15min.; leaving Vielha 11:44am, Salardú 2:19pm). Check at the tourist office in Vielha for the most recent schedule.

VIELHA   ☎973

The biggest town in Val d'Aran, Vielha (pop. 7000) combines the warmth of its small old quarter with the bustling activity of the main commercial thoroughfare. From its prime location, Vielha welcomes hikers and skiers to its lively streets with every sort of service the eager wilderness adventurer might desire.

TRANSPORTATION AND PRACTICAL INFORMATION. Alsina Graells (Lleida office ☎973 27 14 70) runs buses from Vielha to: **Barcelona** (5hr.; 5:30am and 1:30pm, July-Sept. 15 also 11:45am; €23.70); **Boí** (1hr., 1pm, €3.50); **Lleida** (2hr., 5:30am and 1:30pm). Schedules in the Val d'Aran and Val d'Áneu change frequently; for updated info consult the tourist office. For a **taxi**, call ☎973 64 01 95. Rent **bikes** at **Bodysport,** Aptos. Sapporo II, down the main road toward Salardú. (☎973 64 04 84. €15 per 4hr., €20 per day. Open M-Sa 11am-8pm.) The **tourist office,** C. Sarriulèra, 10, is one block up river from Pl. de Gléisa in the center of town (look for the big wooden "i" past the post office). Staff assists hikers, skiers, and sightseers by providing transportation info and accommodations listings. (☎973 64 01 10; www.aran.org. Open daily 9am-9pm.) **ATMs** pepper the main thoroughfare, Av. Castièro, which intersects the river before turning into Av. Pas d'Arró. Local services include: **Mossos d'Esquadra** (local police; ☎973 64 09 72) and **Guardia Civil** (☎973 64 00 05); **Farmàcia Palá,** across the river from Pl. de Gléisa about 1 block down on the left before the traffic rotary (☎973 64 23 46); **Hospital Val d'Aran** (☎973 64 00 04); **Internet access** at Ciber Battle Zone, Av. Maladeta, 8, across the Riu Garona on the footbridge in the newly built section of town, Av. Maladeta is the second street parallel to the river (☎973 64 05 70; €3 per hr.; open daily 5-10pm). The **post office,** C. Sarriuléra, 6, is by the tourist office. (☎973 64 09 12. Open M-F 8:30am-2:30pm, Sa 9:30am-1pm.) **Postal Code:** 25530.

ACCOMMODATIONS AND FOOD. Budget travelers in need of a treat can put their feet up at the elegant yet homey ▨**Hotel El Ciervo ❸**, Pl. Sant Orenç, 3. Standing on the bridge with your back to the tourist office, head downhill to the left side of the river. Upon entering the plaza, turn left to face the hotel's light green, mural-bedecked exterior. Wonderful full baths, some with massage-tub, and huge breakfast feasts included with the room. (☎973 64 01 65; fax 64 20 77. Closed May-June and Oct.-Nov. Singles €30-45; doubles €45-72. Rooms with jacuzzi bath €9 extra. MC/V.) Another reliable option is **Ostau d'Óc ❷**, C. Castéth,

THE SMALL REPUBLIC

Isolated up in their remote mountain valley, the Aranese people have traditionally been an aloof and self-ruling bunch. Maintaining relative autonomy through its early history, Aran was finally brought under the provincial system of government in 1834, but remained relatively cut off from the rest of Spain due to the southern ring of mountains impassable in winter months. This all changed in 1948, however, with the completion of the Túnel de Vielha, a 5km passage cut through the rock at the base of the mountains.

Despite the vast influx of tourism sparked by the tunnel, the Aranese people have managed to hold on to their cultural identity. Today, the natives still speak Aranese, a dialect of Gascon, a language from southern France. If you want to sound like the locals, instead of *sí* for "yes," say *óc*, which is the source of the name Occitan, the family to which Gascon belongs. All street signs are, by special privilege, labeled in Aranese instead of Catalan, and children are still taught to read first in this language.

The Oficina de Foment Eth Ensenhanent der Aranés del Conselh Generau d'Aran, *literally "office for promotion of teaching Aranese," offers courses (2hr. per week) in Aranese from October to May (for info contact* ☎973 64 18 01; *ofea@aran.org).*

13, across the traffic rotary on the main road and up the hill to the left. All the clean, spacious rooms have full baths and are a little removed from the bustle of the downtown area. (☎973 64 15 97. Singles €16-32, doubles €30-42, quads €51-70.) Several other inexpensive pensiones fill the end of C. Reiau, off Pg. Libertat (which intersects Av. Castièro at Pl. Sant Antoni). **Pensión Casa Vicenta ❷**, C. Reiau, 3, is a good place to spend the night, with its great mattresses and clean private baths, some with skylights. (☎973 64 08 19. Closed Oct.-Nov. Dec.-*Semana Santa* and July 15-Sept. 15 singles €22; doubles €33, with bath €37. Otherwise €19/€27/€32.)

Restaurant Basteret ❷, C. Mayor 6b, is tucked into a corner facing the tourist office just across the river. Friendly staff and well-priced dishes (€8-20) make this a great spot. (☎973 64 07 14. Open daily June-Sept. 15 1-4pm and 8:30-11pm. Closed last 2 weeks of Oct. and M from Sept. 16-May. MC/V.) **Eth Breç ❶**, Av. Castièro, 5, beneath Hotel d'Aran along the main road, serves incredible pastries and a selection of teas. (☎973 64 00 50. Open daily 8am-2pm and 4-9pm. MC/V.) **Era Plaça ❶**, Pl. dera Glèisa, serves up big pizzas (€5.50-7.50) and even bigger sandwiches (€3.50-4), as well as a wide selection of *raciones* for €4-8. (Off Pl. dera Glèisa on the main road. ☎973 64 02 49. Open daily 9am-1:30am.)

🎦🎵 **SIGHTS AND ENTERTAINMENT. Iglesia de San Miguel,** a simple 12th-century Romanesque church, houses the intricate *Crist de Mijaran,* one of Val d'Aran's signature artifacts. The church is to your left on the main plaza, facing the tourist office. (Open daily 11am-8pm.) The ethnographic collection at the **Muséu de Val d'Aran,** C. Mayor, 26, explains the intricacies of the unique Aranese culture and language. Ask for a language translation pamphlet from the front desk, as all the exhibits are written in Aranese. (☎973 64 18 15. Open Tu-Sa 10am-1pm and 5-8pm, Su 11am-2pm. €2.) Vielha is a good base for many **outdoor activities. Camins del Pirineu,** Av. Pas d'Arró, 5, in the shopping gallery, is a great place to start. Staff organizes **treks** into the Aigüestortes (from €22), leads **rafting** and **horseback riding trips,** and rents **mountain bikes.** Ask about the popular half-day bike trip (26km one-way) to Camino Real/Vielha-Les, which promises a great workout and spectacular views. (☎973 64 24 44. Bikes half-day €15, full-day €21.) In conjunction with the **Escola Snowboard Val d'Aran,** Camins can also teach you how to **snowboard** (☎973 64 58 81; www.esva.es. Open only in winter; call ahead.)

When the sun goes down, the ready-to-rage of all ages run to **Eth Clót,** just beyond Hotel El Ciervo near Pl. Sant Orenç, a self-proclaimed *bar-musical.* Warm up at tables below before heading to the upstairs dance floor. The bar is the perfect place to quench your grind-induced thirst and refuel for a fierce game of foosball. (Beer €3, mixed drinks €5. Open daily 10:30pm-3am; closed Su in Oct.)

LA SEU D'URGELL ☎973

La Seu (pop. 10,000) serves as Spain's gateway to the tiny Pyrenean country of Andorra, just a few kilometers to the north. While the neon glow and snowy slopes of the tiny *principat* may beckon travelers onward, don't hasten to leave the quiet haven of La Seu too soon. The winding streets of the historic center and the beautiful Parc Olímpic del Segre are worth exploring before heading across the border.

TRANSPORTATION. The **bus station** (☎973 35 00 20) is located on Av. de J. Garriga i Massó at the end of town nearest to Andorra, about 400m from the town center. To get there, walk down Av. de J. Garriga i Massó, passing C. del Bisbe Benlloch on your left, until you come to the traffic rotary at the intersection with Av. de Pau Claris. Follow Av. de Pau Claris down two blocks to the main plaza. (Info open M-F 9am-1pm and 3-7pm, Sa 9am-12:15pm and 3-7pm, Su 3-7pm.) **Alsina Graells** runs **buses** to: **Andorra la Vella** (40min.; M-Sa every hr. 7am-8pm, Su 5 per day 7:45am-6:30pm; €2.40); **Barcelona** (3½hr., 7:24am and 5:24pm, €18.70); **Lleida** (2½hr.; M-Sa 6am and 4:10pm, Su 9am and 4:10pm; €12.80); **Puigcerdá** (1hr., 3 per day 9:15am-7pm, €4.60). A shuttle runs to **Sort** (1½hr., 10:15am and 7:30pm, €3).

ORIENTATION AND PRACTICAL INFORMATION. The main road in La Seu is **Avinguda de Pau Claris,** which runs south from the highway to Andorra, becoming C. de Sant Ot along the way, to the Parc Olímpic del Segre. The main plaza, **Passeig de Joan Brudieu,** is at the Parc Olímpic end of the street. The historic center is located to the left when heading down Av. de Pau Claris toward the passeig from the bus station. The **tourist office,** Av. de les Valls d'Andorra, 33, is inconveniently located at the very edge of town, just before the start of the highway to Andorra. Head up Av. de Pau Claris, veering left at the fork onto Av. de les Valls d'Andorra. (☎973 35 15 11. Info on accommodations, outdoor activities, and cultural events. Open June-Sept. M-F 9am-8pm, Sa 10am-2pm and 4-8pm, Su 10am-2pm; Oct-May daily 10am-2pm and 4-6pm.) Local services include: **banks** and 24hr. **ATMs** lining C. de Sant Ot; **municipal police** (☎973 35 04 26); **Mossos d'Esquadra** (emergencies ☎088, non-emergencies 973 36 00 73); the **hospital** (☎973 35 00 50); **Internet access** at **World Locutorio,** Av. del Salória, 37 (€1.50 per hr.; open M-F 10am-2pm and 3-10pm, Sa 3-10pm). The **post office** is on C. de Josep Zulueta at Av. del Salória (open M-F 8:30am-2:30pm, Sa 9:30am-1pm). **Postal Code:** 25700.

ACCOMMODATIONS AND FOOD. Rooms in La Seu are not hard to locate, but budget accommodations are scarce. A reliable night's stay can be found at the conveniently located **Hotel Avenida ❸,** Av. Pau Claris, 24, just 100m from the bus station at the intersection of Av. de J. Garriga Massó and Av. de Pau Claris, down the street from the main plaza. Rooms are fully equipped with all the modern amenities including TV and full bath. (☎973 35 01 04; www.avenhotel.com. Singles €28-31.50; doubles €46.50-53. AmEx/MC/V.) One of La Seu's most luxurious accommodations is **Hotel Andria ❹,** Pg. Joan Brudieu, 24. The halls and lobby are lined with antiques, including a genuine turn-of-the-century telephone operator's console, while outside is a shady garden in the courtyard perfect for afternoon relaxation. The palatial rooms come with A/C and marble floors; hydro-massage baths are €20 extra. (☎973 35 03 00; www.hotelandria.com. Dinner and breakfast

€24. Singles €42-75; doubles €50-90; triples €80-120. MC/V.) To get to the **Alberg de la Seu d'Urgell (HI) ❶,** also known as La Valira, at C. Joaquim Viola, 57, head toward town from the bus station on Av. de J. Garriga Massó, taking a right at the traffic rotary onto Joaquim Viola. (☎973 35 38 97. 96 places. Dinner €5. Wheelchair-accessible. €17, over 25 €19.40.)

Restaurants line C. de Sant Ot and Pg. de Joan Brudieu. Try the tavern-style eating experience at **Mesón Teo ❸,** Av. de Pau Claris, 38, where medieval weapons and animal heads line the walls above your hearty dinner. (☎973 35 10 29. *Menú* €12, entrees €6-16. Open M-Th 1-4pm and 8:30-10:30pm, F-Sa 1-4pm and 8:30-11:30pm.) **Restaurant Andria ❹,** under the hotel of the same name, has an excellent wine selection and beautifully prepared meals (€11-19) in an elegant dining room or out on the romantic terrace. (Open daily 12:30-4pm and 8:30-11pm. MC/V.) Stock up on groceries at **Suma** (☎973 35 39 93), located off of Av. de Pau Claris past Hotel Avenida. (Open M-Sa 9am-2pm and 5:30-9pm. MC/V.)

◙ **SIGHTS.** The 12th-century **Catedral d'Urgell** is the only preserved Romanesque cathedral in Catalunya. The oldest piece in the connected **Museu Diocesá d'Urgell** is a set of 10th-century illustrations of the Apocalypse known as *Beatus*. (☎973 35 32 42; www.museudiocesaurgell. Cathedral and museum open June-Sept. M-Sa 10am-2pm and 4-7pm, Su 10am-1pm; Oct.-May M-F noon-1pm, Sa-Su 11am-1pm. €2.50.) The **Parc Olímpic del Segre** was constructed to host the canoe and kayak events for the 1992 Barcelona Olympic Games. Today, visitors can pay to rent canoes or kayaks and try their own hands at the raging waters of the course (€9.50 per person per hr., includes canoe or kayak, equipment, and water; classes €27 per hr.). The less experienced can paddle on calm water (€5 per hr., classes €27 per hr.) and still have fun. (☎973 36 00 92; www.parcolimpic.com. Park open summer 8am-8:30pm).

ANDORRA

The tiny Principat d'Andorra (pop. 70,000) bills itself as "El País dels Pirineus," the country of the Pyrenees. Perhaps, however, Andorra is best described not as Pyrenean, but as pyre-neon: the natural beauty of its mountainous surroundings is easily matched by the artificial glitz of its flashy capital. For every nature-loving visitor in search of the perfect hike or bike trail, there are a dozen bargain-hunters lured here by the sheer abundance of duty-free shopping. But Andorra is not at all embarrassed about its role as Europe's shopping mall. Far from it: the country embraces its unique culture and is as proud of its flashy present as it is of its noble past. Andorra has a rich history; according to legend, Charlemagne founded Andorra in 784 as a reward to the valley's inhabitants for having led his army against the Moors. For the next 12 centuries, the country was the rope in a game of tug-o'-war between the Spanish Counts of Urgell, the Church of Urgell, and the King of France. Not until 1990 did the country create a commission to draft a democratic constitution, adopted on March 14, 1993. For all its modern amenities, Andorra today is far less progressive than other EU nations. In the 1993 election, only the 13,000 native Andorrans (out of 65,000 total inhabitants) were granted the vote, and women have only had suffrage since 1970.

Sandwiched between France and Spain, Andorra's citizens are comfortably trilingual, though proud of their place as the only nation where Catalan is the sole official language. Euros flow like water, as the absence of a sales tax draws consumers from all over Europe. Excellent skiing and biking opportunities, as well as frequent soccer matches, lure sports buffs across the border. With Andorran towns mere minutes apart thanks to the extensive local bus system, a single day can include wandering through aisles of duty-free perfume, hiking through a pine-scented valley, and relaxing in a luxury spa.

TRANSPORTATION

The only way to get to Andorra is by car or bus. All traffic from Spain enters through the town of **La Seu d'Urgell;** the gateway from France is **Pas de la Casa.** Upon exiting Andorra, you may be required to stop at customs for a brief and rubber-glove-less search.

BY BUS

Catch international buses to destinations other than La Seu d'Urgell at **Estació Central d'Autobusos,** C. Bonaventura Riberaygua, in **Andorra la Vella. ALSA/Samar** buses (in Madrid ☎914 68 41 90, in Andorra 80 37 89) run from Andorra la Vella to **Madrid** (9hr.; Tu-Th and Su 11:30am, F and Su also 10pm; €38). **Eurolines** (in Andorra ☎80 51 51, in Madrid 915 06 33 60) runs to **Barcelona** (4hr., 4-7 per day 6:30am-8:15pm, €20) and Madrid (Tu-Th and Su 11:30am, F and Su also 10pm; €40). To go anywhere else in Spain, you first must go to the town of La Seu d'Urgell on a **La Hispano-Andorra** bus (☎82 13 72; 30min.; M-Sa every hr. 8am-9pm, Su 5 per day 8:15am-7:15pm; €2.50) departing from Pl. de la Rotunda, across from the tourist office.

BY CAR

Driving in Andorra la Vella is an adventure for some, a nightmare for others. Road signs in Andorra are confusing, and navigating the crowded, twisting streets can prove a maddening chore for the most patient driver. It's far better to ditch the car in a parking lot and use the extensive public transportation system.

PUBLIC TRANSPORTATION WITHIN ANDORRA

Efficient intercity buses connect the villages along the three major highways that converge in Andorra la Vella, though figuring out when and where buses stop and which ones go to your destination can be somewhat of a puzzle. The tourist office offers a schedule that will tell you where to wait for specific destinations. Since most towns are only 10min. apart, cities can be seen in a day via public transportation. Additionally, rides are cheap, ranging from €0.70 to €1.70.

ANDORRA LA VELLA ☎376

Andorra la Vella (pop. 20,760), the capital, is anything but *vella* (old): virtually a single cluttered road flanked by shop after duty-free shop, most of the old buildings have been upstaged by shiny new electronics and sporting goods stores. After doing a little shopping, you're best off escaping to the countryside for a walk in the much less crowded mountains.

■ ▶ ORIENTATION AND PRACTICAL INFORMATION. Coming from Spain, visitors first pass through Sant Julià de Lòria and then tiny Santa Coloma, which runs directly into Andorra la Vella. The main thoroughfare **Avinguda Santa Coloma** becomes **Avinguda Príncep Benlloch** several blocks into the city, which in turn becomes **Avinguda Meritxell** at Pl. Príncep Benlloch before continuing on as the highway to areas northeast of the capital. There are several **tourist offices** scattered throughout Andorra la Vella; the largest is on Pl. de la Rotonda. The multilingual staff offers free *Sports Activities* and *Hotels i Restaurants* guides. (☎376 82 71 17. Open July-Aug. M-Sa 9am-9pm, Su 9am-7pm; Sept.-June daily 9:30am-1:30pm and 3:30-7:30pm.) Local services include: **Banc Internacional,** Av. Meritxell, 32 (☎376 88 47 05; open M-F 9am-1pm and 3-5pm, Sa 9am-noon); **medical emergency**

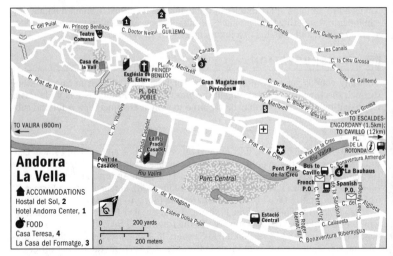

Andorra La Vella

▲ ACCOMMODATIONS
Hostal del Sol, **2**
Hotel Andorra Center, **1**

● FOOD
Casa Teresa, **4**
La Casa del Formatge, **3**

(☎116); **police,** Prat de la Creu, 16 (emergencies ☎110, non-emergencies ☎376 87 20 00); **Hospital Nostra Senyora de Meritxell** (☎376 87 10 00); **weather and ski conditions** from **Ski Andorra** (☎376 86 43 89). For **taxi** service, call ☎376 86 30 00.

Placing an international **telephone call** in Andorra is a chore. Many mobile plans do not service the area, and outside calling cards are just as futile; collect calls to most countries—including the US—are not possible. Buy an STA *teletarjeta* (telecard) at the tourist office or the post office for calls within the country (€3-6). Ask for an international calling card for calls out of the country, since the STA card will only get you a few minutes. To call Andorra from Spain or France, you must dial the international code (☎376) first. For directory assistance dial ☎111 or 119 (international). **Internet access** is available at **Future@Point,** C. de la Sardana, 6. (☎376 82 82 02. €1 per 15min, €2.80 per hr. Open M-Sa 10am-11pm, Su 10am-10pm. MC/V.) The **Spanish post office** is at C. Joan Maragall, 10. (☎376 82 02 57. **Lista de Correos** upstairs. Open M-F 8:30am-2:30pm, Sa 9:30am-1pm.)

⚅⚅ ACCOMMODATIONS AND FOOD. The mid-range hotels in Andorra la Vella are almost universally run-down and overpriced; you're better off saving some dough at the cheaper ones or sucking it up and living in the lap of luxury at one of Andorra la Vella's numerous finer hotels. At the lower end, **Hostal del Sol ❶,** Pl. Guillemó, 3, provides small, no-frills rooms with hall baths. Ask to see your room before committing; the corner ones are bigger and nicer. (☎376 82 37 01. Dorms €12.50. MC/V.) At the high end, check out **Hotel Andorra Center ❹,** C. Doctor Nequi, 12. Conveniently located, it offers beautiful, fully furnished rooms as well as a piano bar, in-house restaurants, a fitness center with swimming pool and sauna, and parking for €11 per day. Inquire about custom massages. (☎376 82 48 00. Breakfast included. Dinner €3. Call ahead. Prices change frequently; expect to pay about €25-35 per person. AmEx/MC/V.) You don't exactly rough it at shaded **Camping Valira ❶,** Av. de Salou, behind the Estadi Comunal d'Andorra la Vella, which has satellite TV, hot showers, a restaurant, laundry, and an indoor pool. (☎376 72 23 84; www.campvalira.com. Wheelchair-accessible. Call ahead. €4.20 per person, per tent, and per car.) Or, get away from the hustle and bustle of Andorra la Vella completely and head 12km up the highway toward France to the little town of **Canillo.** Catch the bus to Canillo in front of the French post office on C. Bonaventura Armengol (15min., every hr. 8am-8pm, €1.80). The three-star **Hotel Roc de Castell ❹**, Ctra. General, has well-equipped rooms, leather-couched lounges and a restaurant (entrees around €13). From Andorra la Vella, drive straight through Canillo; the hotel will be on your left as you leave town. (☎376 85 18 25. Breakfast €4-6.50. Singles with shower €31-46, with full bath €38-59; doubles €49-73; triples €67-100; quads €87-112. MC/V.) **Camping Janramon ❶**, Ctra. General, offers friendly service and the satisfaction of knowing you are as far away from Andorra la Vella as possible while remaining in Andorra. The services, less cushy than other sites in the valley, include laundry, electricity, and a bar. (☎376 85 14 54. Reception 9-11am and 6-9pm. If you arrive late, park and pay later. Open June 15-Sept. €3.10 per person, per tent, and per car.)

If you need proof of Andorra's cheesiness, look no further than ◪**La Casa del Formatge ❶**, C. les Canals, 4. Cheese, cheese, and more cheese await in this two-story extravaganza. A big cow above the door lets out a long, low "Moooo" every so often. Enjoy the ample free samples while you browse the shelves of bovine statuary, or head to the shop upstairs for some wine with that cheese. At the house restaurant you can dine on cheese entrees (€5-10) under the knowing gaze of a decidedly less-modest Mona Lisa draped in nothing but—what else?—cheesecloth. (☎376 80 75 75; www.lacasadelformatge.ad. Open M-F 10am-8pm, Sa 9:30am-9pm, Su 9:30am-7pm.) **Casa Teresa ❸**, C. Bonaventura Armengol, 11, has phenomenal spaghetti (€6.80). If that's not enough, they also serve a variety of other delicious dishes, including large, creative pizzas, all in an elegant setting with servers who are both formal and friendly. (☎376 82 64 76. Entrees €9-16, pizzas €6.50-7.50. Open daily 8am-4pm and 8-10:30pm; closed June 24-July 15.)

For shopping, check out one of the three-story department store monstrosities in nearby Santa Coloma, or the **Grans Magatzems Pyrénées**, Av. Meritxell, 11, the country's biggest department store, where an entire aisle is dedicated to chocolate bars. A **supermarket** is on the 2nd floor. (Open Aug. and holidays M-Sa 9:30am-9pm, Su 9:30am-7pm; Sept.-July M-F 9:30am-8pm, Sa 9:30am-9pm, Su 9:30am-7pm.) Or head to **La Bauhaus**, C. Bonaventura Armengol, 11, next to Casa Teresa, and realize how much cooler you could actually be. A wide selection of stylish books, furniture, and other necessities of the hipster lifestyle. (☎376 86 32 36; www.labauhaus.com. Open M-F 10am-8pm, Sa 10am-9pm, Su 10am-2pm.)

◪ **EXCURSIONS.** The best thing to do in Andorra la Vella is drop your bags in a hostel and get out. Have fun in Canillo's colossal **Palau de Gel d'Andorra**, a recreational complex with swimming pool, ice-skating rink ("ice disco" by night), gym, tennis, and squash courts. Brace yourself on Fridays for the awesome power of ice-rink go-carts! (☎376 80 08 40. €5.50-8 each or €12.50 for all in 1 day. Go-carts F 10:30pm-midnight; €13.50. Equipment rental €2.30-4.50. Open daily 10am-11:30pm; each facility has its own hours.) You won't believe the fantastically gaudy **Caldea-Spa**, Parc de la Mola, 10, in bordering **Escaldes-Engordany**, until you see it. It's what the Emerald City would be if the Wizard of Oz drank a lot of chablis and was really into Yanni. Enjoy an exfoliating Japanese Garden Grapefruit Bath, or some ◪**Lymphatic Facial Draining**. (☎376 80 09 99. €24.50 for 3hr., plus fees for each service. Open daily 9am-11pm.)

Nowhere is the contrast of old and new, or the uniquely Andorran acceptance of it, better on display than at the **Santuari de Meritxell**, 2km from **Canillo** toward Andorra la Vella. The original Romanesque chapel was completely remodeled in the 18th century, which in turn burned down in 1972. The new chapel, built by Catalan architect Ricardo Bofill in 1976, is an ultra-modern building which strives, with questionable success, to incorporate elements of Andorra's disparate past: from the copper-sheeted bell tower reminiscent of medieval monasteries to large

BIRD'S-EYE VIEW

While every other tourist in Andorra is busy trudging up the surrounding mountains on foot to see the spectacular views of the valley, for the right price you can skip this wearying pursuit and go straight to the top without ever having to set one foot in front of the other. That's right, you can see the whole valley from the comfort of a helicopter cockpit with the experienced pilots of **Heliand**. The valley is not very large, and a short flight will get you a bird's-eye view of the entire country—but it's not cheap. A 10min. flight costs €50 per person, and 20min. costs €100.

For those who want to experience the mountain refuge lifestyle but don't have the time, or perhaps the energy, to hike up, the service also offers daytrips to remote mountain lakes. Get a little fishing done, sit down for some grilled trout, and be comfortably back in your hotel room by nightfall. The most popular destinations are the *Estanys Forcats*, *Angonella*, *Truites*, and *Tristaina*, all at well over 2000m in elevation. Flights to any of these lakes cost €240 each way. Heliand will make trips to other lakes as well, but the price jumps to €360 each way.

Heliand is located just outside the town of La Massana, to the left while driving on the highway toward the town of Ordino. (For more information and booking call ☎376 83 79 29; fax 83 86 14.)

apertures cut in an Islamic style. The Santuari houses a permanent collection dedicated to the patron saint of Andorra: the Virgin of Meritxell. To get there, either ask the bus driver to be let off at the entrance on the way to Canillo, about 200m from the actual *santuari*, or hike over from Canillo (25min.). Head down the stairs next to the tourist office and look for the highway heading up into the hills. Follow that road until it forks. Veer right toward the village of Prats, where you will find a sign pointing to the trail to the monastery. From there it is only 10min. (☎376 85 12 53. Open M and W-Su 9:15am-1pm and 3-6pm. Guided tours July-Oct. Free.)

🏔️🏔️ **HIKING AND THE OUTDOORS.** An extensive network of hiking trails traverses Andorra. The free, multilingual, and extremely helpful and detailed tourist office brochure *Mountain Activities* includes 41 hiking itineraries, 9 mountain biking itineraries, and even several rock-climbing routes, as well as bike rental services and cabin and refuge locations within the principality. La Massana is home to Andorra's tallest peak, **Pic Alt de la Coma Pedrosa** (2946m). For organized hiking trips, try the **La Rabassa Sports and Nature Center** (☎376 32 38 68; www.campdeneudelarabassa.ad), in the parish of Sant Julía de Lòria. In addition to *refugio*-style accommodations, the center has mountain biking, guided hikes, horseback riding, archery, and field sports.

⛷️ **SKIING.** With five outstanding resorts, Andorra offers skiing opportunities galore from November to April; lift ticket prices range from €25-40. **Pal** (☎376 73 70 00; fax 83 59 04), 10km from La Massana, is accessible by bus from La Massana (5 per day 8:45am-7:45pm, returning 9:10am-5:05pm; €0.90). Pal's sister resort, nearby **Arinsal** (☎376 73 70 00), is accessible directly from Andorra la Vella (1 per hr. 8:15am-8:45pm, returning 8:25am-8:45pm; €0.90). On the French border, **Pas de la Casa-Grau Roig** (☎376 80 10 60) is the valley's highest resort at 2050m, with 53 slopes, the most of any other resort, totalling 100km. It is accessible by bus from Andorra la Vella (4 per day 9am-6:45pm, returning 9:30am-7:45pm; €4.70). The more horizontal **La Rabassa** (☎376 84 38 98) is Andorra's only cross-country ski resort. If you want someone else to propel you, try taking the old doggies—sled dogs that is—out for a spin (lessons €24). Andorra's tourist office publishes a winter edition of *Ski Andorra*, a guide of all things related to skiing in the valley. Call **SKI Andorra** (☎376 86 43 89; www.skiandorra.ad) or the tourist offices for extensive information on services, reservations, prices, and transportation.

ARAGONESE PYRENEES

Aragón claims 90km of Pyrenean grandeur, bracketed by the Río Gallego in the west and the Río Nobuera in the east. Between these two frontiers, alpine meadows and 20 crystalline glaciers are tucked amid gorges and jagged cliffs. Such terrain has had its use—founded in the mid-9th century upon these fortifying slopes, the Kingdom of Aragón was unconquered by northern enemies. The most popular entry point for the Aragonese Pyrenees is Jaca, from which most head to the spectacular Parque Nacional de Ordesa. In the east, Benasque draws hardcore mountaineers with its access to the highest peaks in the Pyrenees, while the western valleys of Ansó and Hecho are ideal for less strenuous mountain rambling. For details on winter in Aragón, get the free tourist office pamphlets *Ski Aragón* or *El Turismo de Nieve en España*. If you're there in summer, make sure to get to the █**Pirineos Sur** international cultural festival during the last three weeks of July, featuring a host of concerts, markets, and foods from all over the world, focusing mainly on the Americas. For more information, head to www.pirineos-sur.com, or call ☎974 29 41 51.

JACA ☎974

The whole Western side of Jaca (pop. 12,500) is dominated by the enormous, pentagonal **Ciudadela,** a military fortification from the 16th century complete with full moat, curtain wall, arrow slits, and replica cannon. The complex is still the site of the Command and Headquarters of the 64th Galicia High Mountain Regiment, the oldest regiment in the Spanish military, though it is mostly a tourist attraction these days. Make sure to check out the captive herd of deer kept in the moat. The town used to serve as a refuge for weary pilgrims crossing the Pyrenees to Santiago. Though the city also had a brief stint as capital of Aragón (1035-1095), for centuries it had little to offer in the way of diversion. At present, Jaca provides not only the perfect base for excursions into the Pyrenees and nearby ski resorts but also holds many festivals of its own, most notably the **Fiestas de Santa Orosia y San Pedro** (June 23-29) and the biennial **Festival Internacional del Camino de Santiago** (Aug. 8-26), which showcases medieval religious themes and music. During these *fiestas*, the city is awash in various concerts and plays. Formal processions like **La Comparsa de Gigantes**—a company of characters in oversized costumes—and numerous ad hoc parades usually occur under the influence of many a malted beverage. For more information on specific events, pick up a *Programación Cultural y Deportiva* from the tourist office.

▐ TRANSPORTATION. RENFE trains leave from the train station, about 1km from the *ciudadela* at the end of Av. Juan XXIII. (☎974 36 13 32. Ticket booth open daily 9am-1pm and 4-8pm.) To **Zaragoza** (3hr., 3 per day 7:50am-6:40pm, €11.40) via **Huesca** (1¼hr., €5.10-6.40). **La Oscense buses** (☎974 35 50 60) run to: **Pamplona** (2hr.; M-F 8:15am and 1:15pm, Sa 8:15am, Su 1:15 and 7pm; €6); **Sabiñánigo** (20min., 5 per day 8:15am-7:15pm, €1.30); **Zaragoza** (2hr.; 6 per day July-Aug. 8:15am-8:15pm, Sept.-June 8:15am-7:15pm; €10.70). From Sabiñánigo, **Empresa Hudebus** (☎974 21 32 77) connects to **Torla** (1hr.; July-Aug. 11am and 6:30pm, Sept.-June 11am only; €2.60), near Ordesa and Aínsa. **Josefa Escartín buses** (☎974 36 05 08) go to **Ansó** (1½hr., M-Sa 6:30pm, €3.50) via **Hecho** (55min., €2.50) and **Siresa** (1hr., €2.80). Catch a **taxi** (☎974 36 28 48) at the intersection of C. Mayor and Av. Regimento Galicia.

▐▐ ORIENTATION AND PRACTICAL INFORMATION. Buses drop passengers on Av. Jacetania, at the northern edge of the city center. From the station, walk through Pl. de Biscos to C. Zocotín and continue for two blocks to **Calle Mayor.**

Take a right onto C. Mayor to Pl. Cortes de Aragón, with **Avenida Regimiento Galicia** on the left and **Calle Primer Viernes de Mayo** on the right. The green city bus runs from the **train station** to the center of town (every hr.). To walk from the station to the town center, take Av. Juan XXIII to its end, turn left onto Av. de Francia, continue as it becomes C. Primer Viernes de Mayo, and then make a left onto C. Mayor. The staff at the **tourist office,** Av. Regimiento de Galicia, 2, one block down from Pl. Cortes de Aragón, speaks English and will give you more tourist literature than you can carry. (☎974 36 00 98; www.aytojaca.es. Open July-Aug. M-F 9am-2pm and 4:30-8pm, Sa 9am-1:30pm and 5-8pm, Su 10am-1:30pm; Sept.-June M-F 9am-1:30pm and 4:30-7pm, Sa 10am-1pm and 5-7pm.) **Alcorce Aventura,** Av. Regimiento de Galicia, 1, organizes **hiking, rock climbing, spelunking,** and **rafting** trips. (☎974 35 64 37; www.alcorceaventura.com. Guided hiking trips from €21 per person per day; rafting from €36; ski and snowboard rentals €15 per day. Open June-Sept. M-Sa 9:30am-1:30pm and 5:30-9pm; Oct.-May M-Sa 9:30am-1:30pm. MC/V.) Ski season is December to April. For ski conditions, call **Teléfono Blanco** (☎976 20 11 12). Local services include: **Banco Santander Central Hispano,** C. Primer Viernes de Mayo (open Apr.-Sept. M-F 8:30am-2pm; Oct.-Mar. M-F 8am-2:30pm, Sa 8:30am-1pm); **police,** C. Mayor, 24 (☎092, emergencies 974 35 57 58); **Centro de Salud,** Po. de la Constitución, 6 (☎974 36 07 95). For **Internet access,** try **Ciber Civa,** two stores down from the tourist office on Av. Regimiento de Galicia. (☎974 35 67 75. €1.90 per hr. Open M 11:30am-1:30pm and 5-9:15pm, Tu-Sa 11:30am-1:30pm and 5-11:15pm, Su 5:30-11pm.) The **post office** is at C. Correos, 13, just down the street from the tourist office. (☎974 35 58 86. Open M-F 8:30am-2:30pm, Sa 9:30am-1pm.) **Postal Code:** 22700.

⌐⌐ ACCOMMODATIONS AND FOOD. Jaca's hostels and *pensiones* cluster around C. Mayor and the cathedral. The generous owners of ◧**La Casa del Arco ❷,** C. San Nicolás, 7, will welcome you into their home with incense, cool music, and delicious food in the downstairs restaurant. The common room has a TV and library. Look for the yellow building off Pl. de Ripa, adjacent to Pl. de Biscos, just across the street from the bus station. (☎974 36 44 48. Breakfast €4. Rooms €18-20 per person.) A more luxurious stay is available at **Hotel Bucardo ❸,** Av. de Francia, 13, whose bright, large rooms with private baths and comfortable common room downstairs will relax the weary traveler. From the bus station, walk along Av. Jacetania toward the Ciudadela and turn right onto Av. de Francia; look for the big sign about two blocks farther down. (☎974 36 24 85; www.lospirineos.com/bucardo. Breakfast included. Singles €23.60-30.20; doubles €45.30-54.50; triples €53.90-70. MC/V.) To reach the large, old-fashioned rooms of **Hostal Paris ❷,** C. San Pedro, 5, from the bus station, head toward the *ciudadela* on Av. Jacetania, taking a left onto C. San Pedro toward the cathedral. Look for the sign to your right. Rooms share hall baths. (☎974 36 10 20; www.jaca.com/hostalparis. Breakfast €2.50. Reception 7am-3am. July 15-Sept. 15 and *Semana Santa* singles €19.50; doubles €31. Rest of year €18/€28. MC/V.) **Albergue Juvenil de Escuelas Pías (HI) ❶,** Av. Perimetral, 6, offers rows of two-bunk bungalows. From C. Mayor, turn left onto Av. Regimiento de Galicia, then left again onto Av. Perimetral. (☎974 36 05 36. Breakfast €2. Quads €11 per person, over 25 €12.)

Bocadillos fill the menus on Av. Primer Viernes de Mayo, and locals fill the many cafes on Pl. de la Catedral. ◧**Restaurante Vegetariano El Arco ❷,** C. San Nicolás, 74, serves an outstandingly creative, all-veggie *menú* for €10. Try the *cebolla asada con pisto y roquefort* (roasted onions with mixed vegetables in roquefort sauce) and top it off with a delicious *batido de plátano* (fresh banana smoothie). (Open M-Sa 1-3pm and 8:30-11:30pm.) **Ulzama ❶,** Pl. Cortes de Aragón, 8, has a wide selection of sandwiches (€2-3), tapas (€1-2), and *platos combina-*

dos (€4-8), as well as big ice cream cones in many flavors (€2.10). Feel free to test your endurance on the Super Ulzama, a giant cone (€3.30). **Supermercado ALVI**, C. Correos, 9, sells groceries. (Open M-Sa 9:30am-2pm and 5:30-8:30pm. V.)

DAYTRIPS FROM JACA

MONASTERIO DE SAN JUAN DE LA PEÑA

Taxis (☎974 36 28 48) will make the journey for €33, with a 1hr. wait before bringing you back. If you are driving, park at the lot above the monastery; a shuttle transports visitors every 30min. from the Monasterio Alto to the Monasterio Viejo (1.5km). The adventurous can catch a bus from Jaca to Pamplona and ask to be dropped at Santa Cruz de la Seró (CN 240, km 295). From there, it's a 7km hike to the monastery.

The spectacular **Monasterio de San Juan de la Peña** is purposefully difficult to reach: the Holy Grail was supposedly concealed here for three centuries. Determined hermits hid the original monastery, *monasterio viejo*, in a canyon 22km from Jaca and maintained such extreme privacy that both church and cup were kept safe from invading Moors. It's worth a visit, both for the 10th-century underground church carved directly into the rock and the 12th-century cloister wedged under a massive boulder. The carved capitals of the cloister's arcade are not to be missed. The 17th-century *monasterio alto* sits 1.5km uphill; it is currently undergoing massive renovations and will reopen as the **Centro de Interpretación de los Reyes de Aragón**. (☎974 35 51 19; www.monasteriosanjuan.com. Open June-Aug. daily 10am-2:30pm and 3:30-8pm; Mar. 16-May and Sept.-Oct. 15 daily 10am-2pm and 4-7pm; Oct. 16-Mar. 15 Tu-Su 11am-2pm and 4-5:30pm. €3.50, includes entrance to church in Santa Cruz de la Seró; €5, includes parking lot shuttle.) A **snack bar ❶** next to the parking lot sells *bocadillos* (€2-3) and other items.

CASTILLO DE LOARRE

Only serious hikers and those with cars can reach the castle. La Oscense (☎974 35 50 60) sends 1 bus from Jaca to Loarre, 5km from the castle (1hr., M-F 7:15am, €6); the return bus (5pm, €4.13) stops only in Ayerbe, 7km away from Loarre. Trains run only from Jaca to Ayerbe (1¼hr.; 3 per day 7:50am-6:40pm, €3.40; return 3 per day 9:06am-5:06pm, €3.30-4.20). From there, take a taxi or trek 2hr. to Loarre and then uphill to the castle.

The power and magnificence of the **Castillo de Loarre** are visible for kilometers in all directions. Every inch of this imposing fortress, with steep cliffs at its rear and thick walls protecting it on the hillside, is open to exploration; visitors are free to investigate on their own or go on the guided tour. Though you may want to spend your time admiring the vast countryside below, the castle's history is equally fascinating. Around 1020, Navarra's King Sancho the Elder annexed Loarre into his kingdom as a defensive bastion against the nearby Muslim stronghold of Bolea. In 1071, King Sancho Ramírez founded an Augustinian monastery here, and the castle's dual nature as both fortress and monastery is still readily apparent. A crypt, which opens to the right of the steep entrance staircase, holds the remains of Demetrius, the patron saint of gladiators, who died in Loarre. Be sure to climb the Queen's Tower for a great view of the countryside below. The dark staircase leading to the crypt, as well as other dark areas of the castle, can be difficult to navigate as electric lighting has not yet been installed here. (☎974 38 26 74. Open daily July-Aug. 10am-1:30pm and 4-7pm; Sept.-June 11am-2pm and 4-5:30pm. Free. Tours in Spanish, English, and French July-Aug. daily every 30min.; Sept.-June Sa-Su only, call in advance. €2)

Apart from the castle, the tiny town of **Loarre** offers a chance to really get away from it all. Spend the day relaxing in the countryside, or take advantage of one of the many nearby hiking trails. From the castle itself, you can continue up Monte

Pusilibro to its 1569m peak on the **Rasal Pusilibro** trail (1½hr., easy to medium difficulty), or ask at the helpful tourist office at the base of the castle for more area hikes. **Camping Castillo de Loarre ❶,** down the road from the castle toward Loarre, offers friendly service, a swimming pool, a supermarket, and a brightly decorated bar and restaurant. (☎974 38 27 22. €2.90 per person, €2.30 per child; €2.90 per tent; €2.60 per car. Electricity €2.60. 3-person bungalows €50, 5-person €63. Restaurant open 8:30am-11pm. *Menú* €11.) **Casa O'Caminero ❷,** Ctra. Huesca, 8, has delicious paellas (€11), and an €12 *menú*. (☎974 38 26 96. Open daily 1:30pm-until last customer leaves.)

VALLE DE HECHO

The craggy Valle de Hecho and its picturesque hamlets 40km west of Jaca are an almost-forgotten wilderness offering some of the most undiscovered hiking opportunities in Aragón. Under the humid influence of the Atlantic, these western slopes and glacial valleys encourage dense forest growth, including the lush *Selva de Oza* filled with beech and fir trees. The valley is best visited during the summer, as it is extremely quiet during the rest of the year. An Alosa/La Oscensa **bus** (☎974 36 05 08) leaves Jaca (M-Sa 6:50pm), stopping at **Hecho** (7:30pm) and **Siresa** (7:40pm) before continuing to **Ansó** (8pm). Every morning except Sunday, the bus returns from **Ansó** (6:30am) via **Siresa** (6:50am) and **Hecho** (7am) on its way back to **Jaca** (7:45am). Outside of the towns, check out the new **El Megalitismo Pirináico,** Ctra. de Oza, km 8, a museum devoted to the ancient stone constructions of the megalithic period. (From Hecho, take the highway to Oza and look for the sign at 8km. ☎619 71 06 24. Open summer daily 11am-7:30pm; call for visiting times during winter. €2.)

HECHO (ECHO)   ☎974

Hecho (pop. 1000) is the valley's geographical and administrative center, a serious title that doesn't suit the small and inviting town. The **tourist office** is in the Pallar d'Agustín, an old renovated farmhouse that also houses Hecho's **Museo de Arte Contemporáneo.** Look for the modern sculptures dotting the lawn on the main road toward Ansó and the funky green and blue splotched paint job, a work of art in and of itself. (Museum and tourist office open M-Sa 10am-1:30pm and 5:30-8pm, Su 10am-2pm. Free.) The tourist office is closed October to June, but the staff at the **Ayuntamiento** in Pl. Conde Xiquena (next to Pl. Alta, off C. Mayor) either upstairs in the office (M-F 8am-3pm) or downstairs in the library (M-F 5-7pm) are happy to answer questions during this time. The hiking experts of **Compañía de Guías Valle de Echo,** C. Lobo, lead trips and rent cross-country skis. (☎974 37 52 18; www.guias-dehecho.com. Call ahead for information.) A **bank** with 24hr. **ATM** is on Pl. Alta, off C. Mayor. (Open Apr.-Oct. M-F 9am-2pm; Nov.-May M-W and F 8:15am-2:30pm, Th 8:15am-1:45pm and 5:15-7:30pm. MC/V.) The **Guardia Civil** can be reached at ☎974 37 50 04. A **pharmacy** is on the main road from Ansó. (☎974 37 51 02. Open M-F 10am-1:30pm and 5-9pm.) The **post office,** Pl. Alta, is also off C. Mayor. (Open M-F 8:30am-2:30pm, Sa 9:30am-1pm.) **Postal Code:** 22720.

Look for any of a number of *casas rurales*, which provide enjoyable company in an intimate atmosphere. Follow signs toward the *centro de salud* to the white building with the jungle of potted plants out front, **Casa Blasquico ❹,** Pl. Fuente, 1. After one night, you're part of the family. Enjoy the familiarity or escape into your beautifully decorated, flower-patterned room. All rooms have TV, and some have a balcony. (☎974 37 50 07. Closed Sept. 7-15 and Dec. 22-26. Doubles €48. IVA not included. MC/V.) Downstairs, the acclaimed **Restaurante Gaby ❹,** with one wall covered in cooking awards, serves up out-of-this-world dishes, specializing in wild game. (Breakfast €3.50. Entrees €10-18. Reservations required. Open 1:30-3:30pm and 8:30pm-until last customer leaves.) On the other side of town on the main road, the less personal **Hotel de la Val ❷**, Ctra. Selva de Osa, has nice but plain rooms with full private baths and great views upstairs. (☎974 37 50 28. Closed Nov. Breakfast €5, lunch and dinner €12 each. Singles €19-24.50; doubles €32-45. MC/V.) At the entrance to Hecho from Jaca, the well-kept sites and *albergue*-style bunks of **Camping Valle de Hecho ❶** are just a short walk from town down the main road to Huesca. The campsite also includes a swimming pool, laundry, bar, and supermarket. (☎/fax 974 37 53 61. Reception 8:30am-11pm. €3.74 per person, per tent, per car. Bunks €7. IVA not included. AmEx/MC/V.) Get your groceries at **Supermercado Alvi**, C. Mayor. (Open July-Sept. M-Sa 9:30am-2pm and 5-8pm, Su 10am-2pm; Oct.-June M-Sa 10am-2pm and 5-8pm. MC/V.)

VALLE DE ANSÓ

Farther down the road from Jaca, the little town of Ansó rests in one of the most appealing valleys in the Pyrenees, a lush growth of oak and pine trees. You might see the very last Pyrenean bears; they live only in this particular valley. Like Hecho, the Valle de Ansó lives for July and August, when the bulk of its visitors pour in over the mountain ridges. Visitors stop in cobblestoned Ansó before heading farther up the valley to Zuriza, the departure point for the valley's best hikes.

ANSÓ ☎974

Just east of Navarra, the cobblestone streets and matching houses of tiny Ansó (pop. 530) immediately expose its gentle warmth. The drier terrain and relatively fewer trees remind you that you have arrived in Aragón. In an old movie theater, the **nature center**, C. Santa Bárbara, 4, houses several permanent displays on the Valle de Ansó and surrounding valleys. Most interesting are the scale models of the Aragonese Pyrenees on the first floor and the entire second floor, which is devoted to the habitats, habits, history, and doubtful future of endangered Pyrenean bears (see **El Oso Perdido**, right) and other wildlife. (☎974 37 02 10. Open June 15-Sept. 15 daily 10am-2pm and 3-8pm; Sept. 16-June 14 Sa-Su 10am-2pm and 4-8pm. Free.) At the **Museo de Etnología** inside the **Iglesia de San Pedro**, antique chorus books are displayed beside mannequins modeling traditional dress. (☎974 37 00 22. Open July-Sept. 15 daily 11am-1:30pm and 4:30-8pm; during the rest of the year, call first to set up a visiting time. €2.) A fairly easy 4.8km round-trip hike that begins in Ansó will take you along the paved road to a weather-sculpted rock for-

THE LOCAL STORY

EL OSO PERDIDO

The range of the *Oso pardo*, the native gray bear of Spain, once stretched from the Pyrenees to Portugal and south to where Madrid stands today. Over the centuries, though, humans have slowly shrunk the bounds of this range, until today the bears persist only in remote areas of the Picos de Europa and the Pyrenean valley of Ansó, treading ever closer to the realm of extinction.

Traditionally, humans have done their best to make life difficult for *osos*. In medieval times there were great bear hunts; later, the bears were captured to serve short lives as street entertainers, a practice that continued up through the end of the 19th century. And there were always farmers, who, afraid for their livestock, annually set aside a sum of their money for the *cazata del oso*, a bear hide bounty. Hunters, equipped with steel traps, snares, and poison pellets, wiped whole ranges clear of the bears.

In 1967, the government placed a ban on hunting the bears. Still, poaching continued, as did habitat destruction. As humans encroach, the bears have less and less space to live and breed. Many conservation plans have been proposed, but no consensus can be reached. It has all been too little too late—there are just 5 bears left in the Pyrenees. When they die, the beloved *Oso pardo* will become *el oso perdido*, the lost bear.

mation called *El Fraile y la Monja* (The Monk and the Nun). Start at the town's southern edge and walk 2km downhill to the Hecho-Huesca fork. Going toward Hecho, the formation is atop the first tunnel, about 400m up the hill.

Though the owner may also be the town mayor, ◪**Posada Magoria ❸**, C. Milagro, 32, is the perfect place to avoid getting down to business. With a meticulously attended backyard garden, covered porch, and balcony all overlooking the quiet Río Verál, Magoria is an ideal place to spend a lazy afternoon before enjoying a lengthy massage (€20) and heading down to dinner in the family-style dining room, which claims to have been the first organic restaurant in Spain, started 25 years ago (*menú* €12, breakfast €6; home-grown vegetarian meals also offered). Once stuffed, hit the sack in one of the *posada*'s airy bedrooms, bedecked in antique furniture. They might even let you play yourself a lullaby on the house guitar. (☎974 37 00 49. Singles €30; doubles with 1 bed €43, with 2 beds €50.) For convenience, you can't beat **Hostal Kimboa ❹**, on your right heading toward Zuriza. Enjoy its restaurant's typically Aragonese *menús* (€10-11), featuring such staples as *migas* (fried bread chunks, mushrooms, onions, and sausage; similar to stuffing) and *carnes a brasa* (flame grilled meat). Comfortable rooms have new, clean bathrooms; some have balconies. (☎974 37 01 84. Singles €40, with dinner and breakfast €45; doubles €50/€70. MC/V.) The more impersonal **Hostal AISA ❷**, just beside the post office, offers big rooms with great views and private baths. (☎974 37 00 09. Breakfast €6. Singles €22; doubles €40-42; triples €54.) The new **Camping Valle de Ansó ❶**, Ctra. Extramuros, located below town, features gorgeous views, two swimming pools (non-guests €2, children €1), restaurant, bar, and cafeteria. (Bar and cafeteria open daily 8am-midnight. Restaurant open daily 1:30-4pm and 8:30-11pm. *Menú* €8 or €15. €3.60 per person, per tent, and per car.) The **tourist office** is on Pl. Domingo Miral. (☎974 37 02 25. Open June 15-Sept. 15 daily 9:30am-2pm and 4:30-8pm.) The **Guardia Civil** can be reached at ☎974 37 00 04. Next to the tourist office is the **post office**. (☎974 37 02 25. Open M-F 10-10:45am, Sa 10-10:20am.) **Postal Code:** 22728.

ZURIZA

In the northern part of the Valle de Ansó (15km north of Ansó itself) lies Zuriza, which consists of little more than a single camping location, **Camping Zuriza.** Surrounding terrain alternates between the shallow hills and valleys of the campsite and the steep summit of southwestern **Ezcaurri.** Many hikers use the area as a base for the arduous trek to **Sima de San Martín,** a gorgeous trail along the French border. To get there, drive from Zuriza 12km towards Isaba until you come to the Isaba-Belagua crossroads. Take the road to Belagua, heading north along the Río Belagua. After about 12km of smooth terrain and a gentle 2km ascent, you'll near the French border and will see signs for the trail. **Camping Zuriza ❶** lies along the banks of a stream running between Ezcaurri and Hondonada. It's a great spot for fishing, hiking, and kayaking (April-May). The campground also provides a **supermarket, hostel,** and **pub/restaurant** where you can get info and maps (€4-7.50) of nearby trails. (☎974 37 01 96. Breakfast €2.80. Hot showers included. Campsite €3.50 per person, €2.90 per child; €3.50 per tent and per car. IVA not included. Hostel doubles €29, with bath €39. Bunks €8.50. MC/V.) Alternatively, exhausted campers and hikers can find accommodations in the nearby **Refugio de Linza ❶,** only 5km from Zuriza. (☎974 37 01 12. 100 beds in 25 rooms. Breakfast €3, dinner €10. Dorms €9.) From the *refugio*, it's a reasonable and well-marked day hike (7hr. round-trip) to **Mesa de los Tres Reyes** (2444m), a series of three impressive peaks that spans the borders of France, Navarra, and Aragón.

PARQUE NACIONAL DE ORDESA

The majestic beauty of ⬛**Parque Nacional de Ordesa** invites you to spend a week as a vagabond. After staying the night in a crowded *refugio*, extremely well-maintained trails draw you through the park, cutting across forest, rock face, snow-covered peak, and river. No luxury living here: you sleep where you are and eat what you carry. If you're lucky, you might just catch a glimpse of an endangered *quebrantahuesos* (literally, bone-breaker), the largest bird of prey in the Pyrenees, famous for its habit of dropping large bones from high in the air in order to break them into small enough pieces for a tasty meal. Ordesa is located just south of the French border, and includes the canyons and valleys of Ordesa, Añisclo, Escuaín, and Pineta. Huge crowds descend into Ordesa through the village of **Torla** in July and August to traipse along the park's diverse trails.

🚉 TRANSPORTATION. All **trains** along the Zaragoza-Huesca-Jaca line stop in Sabiñánigo. **La Oscense** (☎974 48 00 45) runs a **bus** between Sabiñánigo and **Jaca** (20min.; M-Sa 6 per day 8:15am-7:15pm, Su 4 per day 8:15am-7:15pm, July-Aug. also daily 8:15pm; €1.50). From there, **Compañía Hudebus** (☎974 21 32 77) runs to **Torla** (55min.; July-Aug. 11am and 6:30pm; Sept.-June M-Sa 11am, Su 5pm; €2.50.) During *Semana Santa* and July to October 12, a shuttle runs between Torla and **Ordesa** (15min.; June 28-Aug. every 15min. 6am-7pm, *Semana Santa* and Sept. 6am-6pm, Oct. 7am-6:30pm; €2.10, round-trip €3.10). When the shuttle is running, cars are prohibited from entering the park. (Parking lot in Torla €0.60 per hr. 9am-8pm; overnight parking free; after first 24hr. €0.48 per hr.). It's also possible to find free roadside parking, even in high season. In low season, those without a car will have to either hike the 8km to the park entrance or catch a **Jorge Soler taxi** (☎974 48 62 43; €12), which also offer a variety of van tours for up to 8 people. Buses leave Torla for **Sabiñánigo** (1hr.; daily 3:30pm, July-Aug. also 8pm; €2-3) and **Aínsa** (1¼hr., daily at noon, €2.70).

📋 PRACTICAL INFORMATION. Don't try to drive off the main road in any of the towns near the park, especially Torla. The narrow, steep streets were not designed with cars in mind. Just park and walk; your sanity (and suspension) will thank you. The **visitors center** is on the left 1.8km beyond the park entrance. The shuttle stops here on the way to the **pradera,** the parking lot within the park (2km farther on). You can get off, tour the center's exhibits on park geology, biology, and history, and catch another bus (free) to the *pradera* every 15min. (Open daily 9am-2pm and 4-7pm.) The **park info center** in Torla, across the street from the bus stop, takes over in low season, which runs mid-September to May. (☎974 48 64 72. Open Oct.-June M-F 8am-3pm; July-Sept. M-F 8am-3pm, Sa-Su 9am-2pm and 4:30-7pm.) You can pick up free maps and the **Senderos Sector Ordesa** trail guide from the park info center, or the indispensable *Editorial Alpina* guide (€7.50) in town. For more information on Torla and surrounding towns, head to the **tourist office** on Pl. Nueva at the end of C. Francia. (☎974 48 63 78. Open M 9am-1:30pm, Tu-Sa 9am-1:30pm and 5-9pm, Su 9am-noon.) Across from the pharmacy on C. Francia, **Compañía Guías de Torla** organizes rafting (€40), canyoning (€35-50), and year-round mountaineering (€30-70) expeditions. (☎974 48 64 22; www.guiasdetorla.com. Open daily May-June 15 and Oct.-Nov. 5-9pm; late June-Sept. 8:30am-1:30pm and 5-10pm; Dec.-Apr. available by phone. MC/V.) In neighboring **Broto** (4km from Torla), **Casteret Grupo Explora** offers year-round seasonal expeditions, as well as spelunking, rafting, and hydrospeeding (basically white-water rafting without the raft), and **Internet** access. To get there, head back down the highway and bear left at the fork, or take the beautiful 45min. hike; look for the sign on the left side of the road about 50m past the parking lot. (C. Santa Cruz, 18. ☎974 48 64 32;

www.grupoexplora.com. Activities €20-50; Internet €0.50 per 15min., €3 per hr. Open daily 10am-2pm and 5-9pm. MC/V.) Local services include: **Guardia Civil** (☎974 48 61 60); a **pharmacy**, between Restaurant la Brecha and Refugio l'Atalaya (☎619 48 72 64; open M-F 10am-1:30pm and 5-8pm); and the **post office**, on C. Francia at Pl. de la Constitución (open M-Sa 9-11am). **Postal Code:** 22376.

▐▌▐▌ ACCOMMODATIONS AND CAMPING. Hotels and higher-end accommodations are located beside the highway before entering Torla; a few lie along the road closer to Ordesa. Torla itself offers the greatest number of budget accommodations, but they tend to fill up fast in July and August—reserve ahead. Don't worry about oversleeping here; the reliable town rooster sounds daily at 7:30am. Located smack in the center of town right across from the tourist office, **La Casa de Laly ❷**, C. Fatas, is a comfortable place to spend the night after a day of hard hiking. Get the inside scoop on the park from the owner's daughter, who works at the park visitors center. The very clean rooms with firm beds share a bath in the hall. (☎974 48 61 68. Doubles €26, with bath €32.) Named for Ordesa's best-known poet, **Refugio Lucien Briet ❶**, C. Francia, has the most comfortable bunks local *refugios* have to offer. Go up C. Francia, following the sign across the street to the left of the bus stop pointing to "Centro Población," then continue 1 block uphill. (☎974 48 62 21; www.refugiolucienbriet.com. Sheets €3. Bunks €8.50; doubles with bath €34. MC/V. **Restaurante la Brecha ❸** downstairs has a €12 *menú*.) Across the street, the funky **Refugio L'Atalaya ❶**, C. Francia, 45, is hippie-hiker heaven. The adjoining bar and restaurant, bedecked with modern art and finger paintings by Gerard Aguirre, the owner, deserve a visit even if you stay elsewhere. An extensive and affordable wine menu has a map indicating the origin of each wine. Inquire at the bar about purchasing your very own Gerard Aguirre one-of-a-kind placemat. A small kitchen is available for use. (☎974 48 60 22. Open *Semana Santa*-Oct. 11. *Menú* €11-17. Loft mats €8 per person. Refugio and bar open daily 7am-2am, restaurant 1-3pm and 8-11pm. MC/V.) **Camping Ordesa ❶** and the enormous **Hotel Ordesa ❹**, just outside Torla en route to Ordesa, share a pool, restaurant, tennis courts, outdoor ping-pong, and free parking for guests. The hotel rooms offer great views, as well as full bathrooms and TV. (☎974 48 61 25. Camping *Semana Santa* and July-Aug. €3.50 per person, per tent, and per car; rest of year €2.80. Hotel singles €27-39; doubles €37.50-54; triples €51-72.30; quads €60-86. Wheelchair-accessible. AmEx/MC/V.) The prettiest setting is at **Camping San Antón ❶**, closest to the park, which also rents 4-person bungalows and 4-6 person apartments. (☎974 48 60 63. Camping open *Semana Santa*-Sept. €3.70 per person, €3.50 per child; €3.70 per tent, €4.30 per large tent; €3.70 per car. Electricity €3.20. Bungalows and apartments open year-round. Wood bungalows *Semana Santa* and July-Aug. €82; rest of the year €74. Stone bungalows €61/€50.)

▐▌ FOOD. Most accommodations serve a very filling dinner (€13-15) and simple breakfast (included). In Broto, the low-ceilinged stone grottoes and stone-and-thatch cottage of **Restaurante La Bóveda ❷**, Av. de Ordesa, 4, make the perfect place to take a break from all your assorted outdoor activities. Seamlessly blending its rustic decor with simply elegant cuisine, La Bóveda offers delicious soups and appetizers (€4-9), as well as a hearty *menú* (€12). Try the house sangria (€5.80 per liter), and be sure to save room for one of the beautiful desserts (€3-4). Finish your meal off with a shot of sweet homemade *pacharán* (€1.20), a specialty of the Aragonese Pyrenees. (☎974 48 60 79; www.vallebroto.com/laboveda. Open May-Dec. 1:30-3:30pm and 8:30-10:30pm.) In Torla, up C. Francia, **Restaurante Bar El Rebeco ❸** serves a satisfying *menú* (€14) in three dining rooms, all decorated in a delightful mish-mash of antique photos, oil paintings, country-kitchen crafts, and miniature Renaissance statuary. (☎974 48 60 68. Open May-Oct. daily 1-

3:30pm and 8-10:30pm. MC/V.) **Bar Restaurante Taillon ❷,** C. Francia, has sand-wiches (€3) and a hearty *menú* (€12). Grab a beer (€1.50) and head out to the garden for an amazing view of Mt. Mondaruego. (☎974 48 63 04. Open Mar.-Nov. daily 7:30am-1am; dining room open daily 8:15am-10:30pm.) In Pl. Nueva up the ramp to the right of the tourist office, **Pizzeria-Bocatería Santa Elena ❶,** C. Furquieto, offers a friendly, casual setting and cheap, hearty eats. The pizzeria proffers a wide selection of salads (€3-3.50), *bocadillos* (€3-4), and pizzas (€6-12), as well as huge *jarras* of beer for €3. (☎974 48 63 59. Open daily 1:30pm-midnight.) To pick up your own food, **Supermercado Torla,** on C. Francia, is a few buildings down from Refugio L'Atalaya on the opposite side of the street. (☎974 48 63 88. Open May-Oct. daily 8:30am-2pm and 5-8:30pm. Nov.-Apr. closed Su. MC/V.)

🄽 **HIKING.** If you can spend only one day in Ordesa, the main trail that runs up the Río Arazas to the foot of Monte Perdido and **Refugio Góriz,** with three spectacular waterfalls within 1hr. of the trailhead, is the most practical and rewarding hike, especially for inexperienced mountaineers. The full hike to the Refugio takes about 8hr. (round-trip), but it is possible to turn back at any point along the trail. Turning around at the **Cola de Caballo** (Horse's Tail), one of the most photographed waterfalls in the park, with an excellent view, is about 6hr. round-trip on the same trail; turning at the **Gradas de Soasa** waterfall is about 4hr. round-trip; ◪**Cascadas de Estrecho,** a breathtaking waterfall that drops a solid 30m through a narrow shoot, has viewing platforms both at the base and above, and makes for a 2hr. hike roundtrip. Check weather forecasts with the park office (☎974 48 64 72) before starting out; heavy snow makes the trail impassable in winter and spring, and paths becomes dangerous in the rain. For more experienced hikers, **Sendero 3** (in the Senderos Sector Ordesa trail guide) makes for a good day hike. From the parking lot at the Pradera de Ordesa, take the trail right, which leads across the Río Arazas, and follow the signs for trail 3 and the **Senda de los Cazadores.** The trail includes the Soaso Circle, as well as the steeper, more dangerous **Senda de los Cazadores** and the beautiful lookout point at **Calcilarruego.** Be especially careful on the descents (6-7hr. round-trip.) To see the impressive **Cascada de Cotatuero,** which drops an unbelievable 200m from the Cotatuero glacier, it's a more difficult 4hr. round-trip hike. Take the left-hand trail that breaks away from the main trail at the Virgen de Pilar monument. Try to arrive early, especially July-August, as the park is flooded with visitors by noon and you won't have the wilderness all to yourself.

AÍNSA (L'AINSA)   ☎974

Romantic, if slightly touristy, the village of Aínsa (pop. 1800)—a 1hr. drive from Ordesa—is the ideal stop for less rugged travelers, especially families. From the friendly souvenir shops along its main intersection, Aínsa leads visitors up a winding cobblestone staircase to its perfectly preserved medieval quarter.

🄵🄽 **TRANSPORTATION AND PRACTICAL INFORMATION. Compañía Hudebus** (☎974 21 32 77) runs daily buses from **Sabiñánigo** to Aínsa, stopping in **Torla** along the way (2¼hr.; 11am; returning at 2:30pm, July-Aug. also 6:40pm; €5). **Compañía Cortés** (☎974 31 15 52) runs from Aínsa to **Barbastro** (1hr., M-Sa 7am and 3:15pm, €4.20), where buses make the connection to **Benasque** (2hr., M-F 11am and 5:20pm, €6.50). The **tourist office,** Av. Pirenáica, 1, is at the highway crossroads, visible from the bus stop. (☎974 50 07 67. Open July-Aug. daily 9am-9pm; Mar.-June and Sept. daily 10am-2pm and 4-8pm; Oct.-Feb. Tu-Sa 10am-2pm and 4-8pm.) Although Aínsa is not as well situated for hiking as Torla and Benasque are, companies surrounding the tourist office can arrange countless outdoor activities. **Intersport,** Av. de Sobrarbe, 4 (☎974 50 09 83) and **EKM,** Av. Pirenáica, 5 (☎974 51

00 90; www.ekm.es) rent out bikes and lead backpacking trips; **Aguas Blancas,** Av. Sobrarbe, 11 (☎974 51 00 08) coordinates rafting and kayaking excursions. A **pharmacy** is on Av. Sobrarbe just before bridge (☎974 50 00 23). **Internet** access is available at the **library,** C. los Murros, 2, on the top floor of the big brick building at the base of the medieval quarter. (☎974 50 03 98. Open M-Tu and Th-Su 11am-1pm and 5-9pm, W 3-7pm. €1.50 per hr.) The **post office** is located on Av. Sobrarbe, down the street across from the tourist office. (☎974 50 00 71. Open M-F 9am-2:30pm, Sa 9am-12:30pm.) **Postal Code:** 22330.

⌐⌐ ACCOMMODATIONS AND FOOD. Hotel Dos Ríos ❸, Av. Central, 4, just around the corner from the bus stop, is visible from the tourist office. Rooms are plain but comfortable with full bath, TV, and A/C. Some have balconies and minibars. (☎974 50 09 61; www.pirineo.com/hotel.dos.rios. Singles €26-29; doubles €39-43. V.) **Casa Rural El Hospital ❷,** C. Santa Cruz, 3, has beautiful rooms, but the views are lacking. Only a small sign on the door marks the residence; you'll find the reception in the t-shirt shop on the corner about a block uphill. (☎974 50 07 50. June 16-Sept. doubles with bath, TV, and A/C €39-42. Oct.-June 15 €33. MC/V.) While more luxurious establishments line the main road and aren't difficult to locate, less expensive options surround the bus stop in the new part of town. Outside of the center, **Camping Aínsa ❶,** Ctra. Aínsa-Campo, km 1.8, offers a swimming pool, supermarket, bar, and restaurant. (☎974 50 02 60; www.pirineo.com/camping_ainsa. Open *Semana Santa*-Oct. 15. €4.40 per person, per car, and per tent. Restaurant open until Sept.7 9am-11pm. MC/V.)

Essential groceries, and a few delicacies can be picked up at **Alimentación M. Cheliz,** Av. Ordesa. (☎974 50 00 62. Open July-Sept. daily 8am-9pm; Oct.-June M-Sa 8:30am-2:30pm and 4-8:30pm, Su 8:30am-2:30pm. MC/V.) **Restaurante (Medieval) Bodegas de Sobrarbe ❹,** Pl. Mayor, offers an elegant dining experience out on the beautiful garden terrace or deep within the dark, 11th-century interior. Order the *menú* (€18), or relax with a drink on the terrace (beer €1.70, wine €1.10, mixed drinks €4). Facing the castle upon entering Pl. Mayor, Bodegas de Sobrarbe is in the bottom left corner. (☎974 50 02 37. Open daily 12:30-4pm and 8:30-11pm; bar open noon-1am.) Across from the tourist office, the aptly named **Cafetería Dos Ríos ❶,** Av. Central, 4 (☎974 50 09 61), offers a wide variety of stone-oven pizzas (€7.80) and *bocadillos* (€3.50-4) for sidewalk dining. (Open daily 8am-2am.)

◙ ☀ SIGHTS AND FESTIVALS. A thousand years ago, Aínsa was the capital of the Kingdom of Sobrarbe (incorporated into Aragón in the 11th century), and the ruins of its 11th-century **castle** on Pl. Mayor remind visitors of its past prominence. In 1181, priests consecrated the **Iglesia de Santa María,** across the plaza from the castle, whose spiraling tower steps can be climbed for €1. At the top, an incredible view of the Parque Nacional de Ordesa's peaks awaits. For those exhausted from the uphill hike to the plaza, a stairless view can be found just behind the church. The **Eco Museo,** located inside the *castillo,* is dedicated to teaching visitors the value of protecting wildlife in the Pyrenees. (☎974 50 05 97. Open *Semana Santa*-June W-Th 10:30am-2pm and 5-8:30pm; July-Sept. 12 daily 10:30am-2pm and 5-8:30pm; Sept. 13-Nov. 1 Sa-Su 10:30am-2pm and 5-8:30pm; rest of year call for visiting times.) The **Museo de Oficios y Artes Tradicionales,** Pl. San Salvador, 5, offers a glimpse into the Pyrenean home, with exhibits ranging from traditional ceramics to metallurgy to basket-weaving. (☎974 51 00 75; www.huexpo.net. Open daily Apr.-June 11am-2pm and 4:30-7:30pm; July-Sept. 15 10:30am-2pm and 4:30-9pm; rest of year call for visiting times. €2.50, students €1.80.) The third week of August marks the annual **Festival Músicas de Europa,** a week long festival with performances by artists from countries all across Europe. (For more information on events and ticket sales, call the Aínsa tourist office ☎974 50 07 67 or visit www.festivales.aragon.es. Tickets €10, entrance to all shows €60.)

VALLE DE BENASQUE: BENASQUE

The Valle de Benasque is a haven for no-nonsense hikers, climbers, and skiers. Countless trails wind through the mountains, and the area teems with *refugios*, allowing for longer expeditions. With its many excursion companies and nearby trailheads, mellow **Benasque** (pop. 1900) is an excellent base for outdoor activities. Casual hikers are often scared off by the valley's reputation for serious mountaineering—the Pyrenees's highest peaks, including awe-inspiring Mt. Aneto (3404m), are here—but relaxing nature walks are within every visitor's reach.

☐☑ TRANSPORTATION AND PRACTICAL INFORMATION. La Alta Aragonesa (☎974 21 07 00) runs buses to **Zaragoza** (4hr.; M-Sa 6:45am and 3pm; Su 3pm; €14.80) via **Huesca** (3hr., €10) and to **Lleida** (4hr., 6:45am and 3pm, €12) via **Barbastro** (2hr., €6.40). In July and August, the shuttle bus **Pirineos 3000** makes frequent runs from the town to the trailhead parking lots Senarta (€2, round-trip €3) and La Besurta (€5, round-trip €8). To get to the **tourist office,** C. San Pedro, face Hotel Aragüells at the main bus stop and walk one block down the alley between BBVA bank and the building with the KHURP sign. (☎/fax 974 55 12 89; www.turismobenasque.com. Open daily July-Aug. 9am-2pm and 4-9pm; Sept.-June 9:30am-1:30pm and 4:30-8:30pm.) In case of a **medical emergency,** call ☎974 55 21 38. For the **Guardia Civil,** call ☎974 55 10 08. A **pharmacy** is at Av. de Francia, 38, about 2 blocks past the BBVA. (☎974 55 28 10. Open M-F 10am-2:30pm and 5-9pm, Sa-Su 10am-2pm and 5-9pm.) The hip **Cybercafé Surcos,** C. San Pedro, offers **Internet** access upstairs; the bar downstairs is a local favorite. Just up C. San Pedro from the tourist office, back toward the main road; look for the red door. (€3 per hr. Coffee €1. Beer €1.50. Mixed drinks €4. Open daily 9pm-2:30am.) Earlier in the day, **Locutorio Telefónico,** on C. Los Huertos off of C. San Marsial, also provides Internet access. (€2 per hr. Open daily 10am-midnight.) The **post office,** Pl. del Ayuntamiento, is in the Ayuntamiento across from the church. (☎974 55 20 71. Open M-F 9am-noon, Sa 10:30am-noon.) **Postal Code:** 22440.

☐☐ ACCOMMODATIONS AND FOOD. Although lodgings are available within Benasque proper, you're better off staying in one of the many reasonably priced, more-or-less modern hotels on the main road. Of these, the best are **Hotel Aneto ❷**, with its spacious wooden interiors and private baths, and the adjoining **Hostal Valero ❶**, with its smaller, less expensive rooms and hall baths, both of which provide a comfortable night's rest for the travel-weary. The two share a modest pool, gym, and tennis court. (Both ☎974 55 10 61. Hotel singles €27-33; doubles €43-58; triples €55-72. Hostal 5- to 10-bed dorms €11-17; singles €13-18; doubles €25-44. Wheelchair-accessible. MC/V.) **Hotel Argüells ❹**, Av. los Tilos, 1, is across from the main bus stop. Rooms have TV, private bath, safe, and phone. (☎974 55 16 19; www.hotelarguells.com. Singles €30-46; doubles €48-68; triples €66-93; quads €78-96. MC/V.) Better yet, head 3km up the highway toward France to **Camping Aneto ❶**, which serves as a convenient starting point for a day's hike, and offers rooms, apartments, and bungalows as well as campsites. There's also a supermarket, playground, TV lounge, bar-restaurant, and heated pool. (☎974 55 11 41; www.campinganeto.com. Rooms with shared kitchen, living room, and bathrooms €12 per person year-round. *Semana Santa,* Christmas, and July-Aug. camping €4.10 per person, per car, and per tent; otherwise €3.50. 2 person bungalows €58-70; 4 person bungalows €70-82. IVA not included. MC/V.)

For an elegant treat, head to **La Parrilla ❹**, Ctra. de Francia (☎974 55 11 34). Heading north on the highway, look for La Parrilla's yellow sign after Av. de Luchón. Award-winning chef Benito Ostarin Canals serves up creative, one-of-a-kind cuisine, perfectly balanced by the traditional Aragonese fare whipped up by La Parrilla's other chef—Benito's grandma. (*Menú* €14. Open daily 1-4pm and 9-10:30pm.) Signs from C. Ministro Cornel off Pl. del Ayuntamiento will lead you to **Pub-Terraza Les Arkades ❷**, a piece of town history occupying an old stone building built in 1647. (☎974 55 12 02. *Menú* €12. Restaurant open June 22-Oct. 12 daily 1-4pm and 8-11pm; bar open 5:30pm-3:30am.) Stock up at **Supermercado Aro Rojo**, C. Molino. From the highway, take Av. de los Tilos (the first left after passing the Río Esera upon entering town from the south) one block, and then the first left onto C. Molino, which dead ends at the supermarket. (☎974 55 28 79. Open daily 9:30am-2:30pm and 5-9pm.)

🈵 **HIKING.** Experienced hikers can head for the **Lago de Cregüeña**, the highest lake in the area at 2657m. Start out early from Benasque and hike uphill 8km on the valley road toward France or take a shuttle to Senarta. From Senarta, turn right onto the trail off the main road and climb up, up, and away, following the falls of the Río Cregüeña. The sometimes steep but not yet technical ascent winds through glens, but never strays far from the river's edge. Four arduous hours later, you'll reach the lake. Another longer, though less tiring, route (5hr. one-way) leads to the **Lagos de Vallibierna** (2432m and 2484m) from Senarta. Take the GR-11 along the river up the Valle de Vallibierna to the **Refugio de Vallibierna.** From there, look for the signs to the lakes, another 2hr. up the mountainside. Those wishing to scale **Mount Aneto** (3404m), the highest of the Pyrenees, can pick up some gear and head out at 5am with the experts from the **Refugio de la Renclusa ❶.** To reach the *refugio*, take the main road (follow the signs to France) north 14km until the paved road ends at Besurta, or take the shuttle; from there it's a 45min. hike to the *refugio*. (☎974 55 21 06. Open June 22-Sept. 24.) For less strenuous nature-wandering, head in the opposite direction down the main road and follow the signs to **Forau de Aigualluts,** a lovely pond at the base of a waterfall (40min.). These trails are sometimes impassable in the winter months, so ask at the tourist office in advance.

NAVARRAN PYRENEES

The Navarran Pyrenees are not for the sedentary; only pilgrims, athletes, and wanderlust-stricken journeyers can appreciate their well-preserved forests and topographical diversity. Forbidding peaks dominate the eastern Valle de Roncal, while the mountain slopes to the west allow easy access to the area's streams, waterfalls, and green meadows. Mist and fog obscure visibility at high altitudes to create a dreamy atmosphere, or nerve-racking driving conditions, depending on your point of view. Navarra's *casa rurales* (rural lodging houses) are particularly beautiful and great budget options (€21-29; reservations ☎948 20 65 40). Pick up a free copy of the *Guía de alojamientos de turismo rurales* in any of Navarra's tourist offices. Pamplona is a sensible base for those dependent upon public transportation; you can head east toward Valle de Roncal, or north toward Roncesvalles.

RONCESVALLES   ☎948

As the first stop in Spain on the Camino de Santiago, Roncesvalles's dozen mist-enshrouded buildings rest amid miles of thickly wooded mountains. The devout aren't the only ones who pass through this mountain town (pop. 30); folklore buffs come in search of the remains of French hero Roland, Charlemagne's favorite soldier, who died just up the hill in AD 778 while leading the rear-guard as the Frank-ish forces crossed back over the Pyrenees. The heavily restored Capilla de Sancti Spiritus, less than 2km up the road from the monastery, stands over the remains of the bone heap (courtesy of dead soldiers and pilgrims) where his tomb is thought to be. (The chapels can be visited only on guided tours.)

✆⚐ TRANSPORTATION AND PRACTICAL INFORMATION. La Montañesa buses (☎948 22 15 84) run between **Pamplona** and Roncesvalles via **Burguete.** (1½hr.; M-F 6pm, Sa 4pm; €4.20. Return buses M-Sa 6:50am.) For **taxis,** call Pedro at ☎948 76 02 82 or 609 43 62 26. A **tourist office** in the mill behind Casa Sabina Hostería provides maps and guides to the sights of Roncesvalles and the Camino de Santiago. (☎948 76 03 01. Open *Semana Santa* and July-Aug. M-Sa 10am-2pm and 2:30-7pm, Su 10am-2pm; Sept.-*Semana Santa* and Apr.-June daily 10:30am-2pm.) There is an **ATM** inside the lobby of La Posada. For **Banco Santander Central Hispano** (open Apr.-Sept. M-F 8:30am-2:30pm; Oct.-Mar. M-F 8:30am-2:30pm, Sa 8:30am-1pm), head to nearby Burguete (2km south).

⚐❐ ACCOMMODATIONS AND FOOD. For a pleasant stay in Roncesvalles, try **La Posada ❸,** the first building on your right upon entering town. Featuring airy, spacious rooms and a wood-beamed common room with couches, TV, and an exercise bike, La Posada offers the best lodgings in town, although it's pretty much the only option. (☎948 76 00 02. *Semana Santa* and July-Aug. doubles €45; triples €50.50; quads €56. Sept.-Oct. and Dec.-June €42/€48/€53. *Menú* €15. Restaurant open 1-3:30pm and 8:30-10pm. Bar open 8:30am-10pm.) The **monastery ❶** in Roncesvalles has lodging for pilgrims—enter the door to the right as you face it. To attain "official pilgrim" status, you'll have to make a €1 symbolic payment and obtain proper credentials: a stamped piece of paper that verifies your sacred mission. The attached **Oficina de Peregrinos** provides this service. But don't become official just to get cheap lodging; true pilgrims look down on such vagrancy, and you won't be able to use the credentials until the next stop on the path anyway. (☎948 76 00 00. Reception M-Sa 10am-1:30pm and 4-7:30pm, Su 4-6pm. Rooms €5. MC/V.) Behind the monastery is **Albergue Juvenil Roncesvalles (HI) ❶,** a somber building that served as a pilgrims' hospital in the 18th century. There are rec rooms in the basement. (☎948 76 03 64. Internet access available. Meals only for large groups. Reception 3-10pm. HI members only; cards for sale €5, over 29 €10. Call ahead for reservations June-Aug. 4- to 11-bed dorms €7.50.) Accommodations, including several *casas rurales*, are more plentiful in nearby **Burguete.** Those following the **Camino de Hemingway** can check out **Hostal Burguete ❸,** C. San Nikolás, 71 (est. 1880). With its springy beds and big, old-fashioned rooms, not much has changed since Papa Hemingway did some resting and writing here on his way back to Paris from Pamplona. (☎948 76 00 05. Breakfast €3.25. *Menú* €11.50. Restaurant open daily 1:30-3pm and 8:30-10pm; curfew 11:30pm. Wheelchair-accessible. Doubles €41-53. AmEx/MC/V.)

Besides La Posada's dining room, Roncesvalles's lone restaurant is the cramped **Casa Sabina Hostería ❶,** which serves up decent *bocadillos* for €4. (Open 8am-10pm.) You're better off heading to **Asador Aritza ❸,** C. Kanaleburua, 6, in Burguete. The colorful dining room and country setting are perfect complements to the filling entrees (€12-18) and *menú* (€10-14). From Roncesvalles, Artiza is one of the first buildings on the left as you enter Burguete; look for the sign. (☎948 76 03 11. Open Su-M and W-Sa 12:30-3:15pm and 8:30-10pm. Closed M evening. MC/V.)

◔ SIGHTS. Inside the **Colegiata,** up the driveway from the *capilla,* the tombs of King Sancho El Fuerte (the Strong) and his bride rest in solitary splendor, lit by the huge stained-glass windows of the **Capilla de San Agustín.** (☎948 79 04 80. Chapel and cloister open *Semana Santa*-Sept. daily 10am-1:30pm and 3:30-6:30pm; Oct.-*Semana Santa* M-F 10am-5pm. €1.50.) In the decisive battle of Las Navas de Tolosa, Sancho reputedly broke the chains protecting the Arab king Miramomolin with his own hands and summarily decapitated him. The heavy iron chains hanging from the walls of the chamber are represented in Navarra's flag. The monastery's lovely French Gothic **church,** endowed by Sancho and consecrated in 1219, is its main attraction. (☎948 76 00 00. Open M-Sa 10am-8pm, Su 7am-8am. Free.) Ask at the tourist office about **guided visits,** including all monuments and the Roncesvalles museum (€3.20; students, seniors, and pilgrims with credentials €2.40).

OCHAGAVÍA (OTSAGABIA)   ☎948

At the confluence of the Ríos Anduña, Zatoia, and Salazar is Otsagabia (pop. 600), a picturesque mountain village typical of Navarran Pyrenees *pueblos* in appearance, if not in population. The Valle de Salazar's largest town spans both sides of the cheerful Río Anduña, 85km from Pamplona. Otsagabia's whitewashed houses and cobbled streets lead to forested mountains great for hiking, trout fishing, and cross-country skiing. The 12th-century **Ermita de Muskilda,** housing a 15th-century Virgin, is the spiritual and cultural nexus of the town. From Otsagabia, it's a 6.2km (1½hr.) circular hike or 3km round-trip (40min.) out and back; follow the path from behind the church, or take the road toward **Izalzu** and look for the stone cross. (☎948 89 00 38. Open June 15-Sept. 15 daily 11am-2pm and 4-8pm; Sept. 16-June 14 M-F 4-7pm, Sa-Su 4-8pm. Guided tours June-Sept. daily 6pm, €1.50.) Local dances featuring elaborate costumes are performed at the sanctuary on September 8, the first day of Otsagabia's annual **Festival de la Virgen de Muskilda.**

The tourist office sells good trail maps and descriptions of hikes in the area for €1-2. A lengthy but smooth hike (20km; 6hr. one-way) follows the Río Irati past the **Embalse de Irabia** lake and through the **Selva de Irati** to the town of **Orbaitzeta;** hikers can leave their cars at the **Ermita de las Nieves** 24km north of Otsagabia and head west along the river. Another slightly closer hike, **Altos de Abodi** (6km, 2½hr.), crests the peak of Abodi (1496m), and leads past several ancient mountain ruins along the crest of the Sierra de Abodi. The trailhead is on the road to Irati, about 15km from Otsagabia; look for the sign. **Cross-country skiers** can also enjoy two circuit trails originating farther down the same highway. None of these hikes are accessible by bus, so those without cars must either hoof it or take a **taxi** (☎948 89 02 94) to the beginning of the trails. **Ekia** (☎696 89 99 95; www.ekiapirineo.com) has an office at the campground and runs everything from hiking (€18-28) to spelunking (€27) to canyon descent (€33-48).

The **tourist office,** on the main road, Ctra. Aísaba, is in the same building as a nature center and offers a free lodging guide, *Guía de Alojamientos Turísticos.* (☎948 89 06 41; fax 89 06 79. Open June 15-Sept. 15 M-Sa 10am-2pm and 4:30-8:30pm, Su 10am-2pm; Sept. 16-June 14 daily 10am-2pm, F-Sa also 4:30-7:30pm.) The **nature center** has info on local flora and fauna and operates under the same hours as the tourist office. (☎948 89 06 41. €1.20.) If looking for accommodations ask at the tourist office or look for the "CR" signs advertising one of the town's 25 *casas rurales.* A left down the street just beyond the post office will take you to the warm and welcoming ■**Casa Navarro** ❷, C. Lavadia, 6, which rents large, immaculate rooms with balconies. Look for the corner building with a wide entryway. (☎948 89 03 35. Breakfast €3. Reservations recommended. Doubles €25, with bath €30; triples €33.) Follow the blue "free parking" signs across the river from the main road to get to **Kixkia** ❷, C. Urrutia. With huge cider casks embedded in the far wall and long wooden tables, Kixkia is a perfect example of the typical *sidrerías* of the area. (☎948 89 05 17. Entrees €4-15. *Menú* €24, including all-you-can-drink cider. Open daily 1:30-4pm and 8-11pm.)

Río Irati (☎948 22 14 70) runs buses to **Pamplona** (1½hr., M-Sa 9am, €5.90) with return service to Otsagabia (M-Th 3:30pm, F 7pm, Sa 1:30pm).

VALLE DE RONCAL

Carved by the Río Esca, Valle de Roncal is a handsome valley stretching south from the French border. Its intimate towns, inviting *casas rurales*, and prime hiking trails should not be missed.

RONCAL   ☎948

Smack in the center of the Valle de Roncal, diminutive **Roncal** (pop. 250) prides itself on two things: its famed *queso Roncal*, a sharp, sheep's milk cheese, and its world-renowned tenor, Julián Gayarre (1844-1889). **Casa Museo Julián Gayarre,** on C. Arana, occupies the singer's birthplace, showcasing assorted memorabilia and ▨**the tenor's preserved larynx.** (☎948 47 51 80. Open Apr.-Sept. Tu-Su 11:30am-1:30pm and 5-7pm; Oct.-Mar. Sa-Su 11:30am-1:30pm and 4-6pm. €1.80; seniors and students €1.60; under 12 free.) **La Tafallesa buses** (☎948 22 28 86) run to **Pamplona** (2hr., M-F 7am, €6). The **tourist office** on Roncal's main road, Po. de Julián Gayarre, has an English-speaking staff and info on hiking and *casas rurales*. (☎948 47 52 56; fax 47 53 16. Open June 15-Sept. 15 M-Sa 10am-2pm and 4:30-8:30pm, Su 10am-2pm; Sept. 16-June 14 Su-Th 10am-2pm, F-Sa 10am-2pm and 4:30-7:30pm.) Services include the **Guardia Civil** (☎948 47 50 05) and a **pharmacy,** next door to the tourist office (☎948 47 51 52; open July-Sept. M-F 10am-2pm and 5-8pm, Sa 10am-2pm; Oct.-June M-F 10am-2pm and 5-7:30pm, Sa 10am-2pm). For a full meal, head up the road to Isaba. Go to **Panadería Lus ❶**, C. Iriondoa, 3, down the path next to Caja Navarra, for some wine and a taste of the lauded Roncal cheese. (☎948 47 50 10. Open July-Aug. 9:30am-2pm and 5:30-8:30pm; Sept.-June 9:30am-1:30pm and 5-7pm.) If you spend the night, head to the wonderfully homey **Casa Villa Pepita ❶**, Po. Julián Gayarre, 4, across from the dirt playground just before the bridge. Each room has its own beautiful and ornate decoration scheme. (☎948 47 51 33. Breakfast €3.50. Meals €11. Doubles €25, with bath €33.)

ISABA   ☎948

Isaba (pop. 500) draws hikers and skiers north of Roncal to explore the surrounding mountains. A stunning hike that leaves from Isaba climbs to Zuriza in the Valle de Hecho (15.6km, 5-6hr.). The ascents from Collado Argibiela to Punta Abizondo (1676m) and Peña Ezkaurre (2050m) are shorter but steeper. Another recommended hike leads from Isaba to neighboring Otsagabia, in the Valle de Salazar (21.4km, 5-6hr.). For more routes in the area, ask at the tourist office. Ski trails run north of Isaba, at the Estación de Ski Larra-Belagna, km 18 on NA-1370, the highway towards France (call the tourist office ☎948 89 32 51). A village festival, featuring stone-throwing contests and games of *pelotas*, a local variation of polo, runs July 25-28 in honor of Santiago. Isaba breaks out in dancing and general merriment on September 15 in honor of San Cipriano, the town's patron saint.

La Tafallesa buses (☎948 22 28 86) run to **Pamplona** via Roncal (2hr., M-F 6:50am, €6); wait at the park benches in the plaza on the main road. For **taxis,** call ☎948 47 70 80 or 626 26 54 76. Isaba's **tourist office,** C. Bormapea, 5, is on the right as you enter town, heading north, just before the boardwalk. (☎948 89 32 51. Open *Semana Santa*-Oct. 12 Tu-Sa 10am-2pm and 4:30-7:30pm, Su 10am-2pm; rest of year M-F 10am-2pm, Sa 4:30-7:30pm.) A **pharmacy** (☎948 89 31 48) is available in town. **Telephones** and **ATMs** can be found just uphill from the tourist office.

THE PYRENEES

On the north side of town, next to the parking lot, is **Hotel Ezkaurre ❹**. Weary travelers can take an afternoon to bask in the garden out back or sit down for a relaxing board game lit by sky-lights in the comfortable common room upstairs. The cozy, sunny rooms and beautiful woodwork are complemented by the **restaurant ❷** downstairs. Bedraggled backpackers appreciate the generous portions and down-home feel. (☎948 89 33 03. *Menú* €9.90. Breakfast €3.25. Restaurant open 8:30-10:30am and 8:30-10:30pm. July-Sept. singles €36; doubles €48; triples €64. Oct.-June €30/€40/€54. MC/V.) For a comfortable but pricey night's sleep, **Hotel Isaba ❹**, C. Bormapea, 51, below the tourist office, is the polar opposite of rugged *refugios*. A large, circular fireplace and two big common rooms—both filled with comfortable couches and chairs—make Isaba a great place to relax after a long day of hiking, with a pool just outside the door. All rooms have full bath and TV; some look out on stellar views of the mountains. The hotel's **restaurant ❷** serves a *menú* (€15) and entrees (€7-12). (☎948 89 30 00; www.hotelisaba.com. Restaurant open daily 7:30-10:30am, 1-3:30pm, and 8:30-10:30pm. Wheelchair-accessible. *Semana Santa* and July 12-Aug. singles €39-50; doubles €60-78. IVA not included. AmEx/MC/V.) For a more economical choice without a loss in quality, head to **Hotel Txiki ❷**, up the main road from the tourist office on the right. The plain but clean rooms all have private bath. (☎948 89 31 18. Doubles €39. MC/V.) **Albergue Oxanea ❶**, C. Bormapea, 47, offers wooden bunks and a TV lounge with VCR and board games. (☎948 89 31 53. Breakfast €2.40. Meals €9. Open daily Jan.-Apr. and July-Sept.; Oct.-Nov. 22 and May-June open Sa-Su only. Dorms €8, with sheets €10.) **Camping Asolaze ❶**, 6km up the road toward France, offers a restaurant, store, bunkbeds, and wheelchair-accessible private bungalows in addition to campsites. (☎948 89 30 34. Sheets €2.80. Dorm €9.50. Camping €3.75 per person, per tent, and per car; €3.30 per child. Bungalow quads high season €70, low season €60; 6 people €85/€75. Closed mid-Nov. to Nov. 30. MC/V.) Those venturing into the wilderness can stock up for the trail at **Vendi Supermercado** on C. Mendigatxa (☎948 89 31 91).

2pm.) **Luggage storage** is available at the train station (€3 per day) and the bus station (€0.75 per piece per day, overnight counts for two days; both open daily 6:30am-10:30pm). **Banco Santander Central Hispano** is at Pl. del Torico, 15. (☎978 60 11 35. Open M-F 8:30am-2:30pm; Oct.-May also Sa 8:30am-1pm.) **Internet, international calls, fax,** and Western Union **money transfers** are available at **Mister Phone** on C. San Andrés. Take a right a block past the tourist office; it will be on the left two blocks down. (☎978 61 77 39. Internet €0.50 per 15min. Open M-Sa 11am-2pm and 5:30pm-10pm, Su 5:30-10pm.) The bar across from the cathedral on C. Santa Emerenciana also has one computer. Viajes Teruel Tours, on C. Nueva, 7, off Pl. del Torico, also accepts Western Union **money transfers.** (Open M-F 10am-2pm and 5-8pm, Sa 10am-1:30pm.) The **post office,** C. Yagüe de Salas, 19, can also send **faxes.** (☎978 60 11 90. Open M-F 8:30am-8:30pm, Sa 9:30am-2pm.) **Postal Code:** 44001.

⌂⌂ ACCOMMODATIONS AND FOOD. Lodgings are scarce during August and *Semana Santa* and impossible during the *fiesta* in early July—call months ahead. Thought to be the oldest hostel in all of Spain, **Fonda el Tozal ❷,** C. Rincón, 5, promises the rustic charm and comfort of a *casa rural* with several features of typical *mudéjar* design, including stunning and spacious tiled bathrooms. Along with great beds, guests will enjoy the impressive stable-turned-bar. To reach it, continue past Pl. del Torico on C. Joaquín Costa for three blocks and take a left. (☎978 61 02 07. Doubles €27-33, with bath €38-45; triples €37-42/€48-55. Extra beds €9.) To get to **Hostal Aragón ❷,** C. Santa María, 4, head in the direction that the Torico statue faces and take the first left as you leave Pl. del Torico. Friendly owners keep airy, spacious rooms with colorful tiled floors and sparkling baths, some with TV. (☎978 61 18 77. English spoken. Singles €17, with bath €22; doubles €24-25/€35-39; triples with bath €47-49.) If you are willing to pay a little more, **Hotel Plaza ❺,** Pl. Tremedal, 3, offers stocked rooms (TV, phone, mini-bar, A/C) with modern decor and a restaurant. (☎978 60 88 17; www.bacohoteles.com. *Menú* €9. Singles €51.60; doubles €76; suites €94. MC/V.)

Teruel is famous for its salty, flavorful cured ham, *jamón de Teruel,* featured in tapas bars and the popular **Rokelín** ham stores and bar-restaurants; there are several in the town (on C. Comandante Foreta, 9, and at C. Rincón, 2), but the one on C. Ramón y Cajal off Pl. del Torico offers outside seating to savor the plentiful and fresh trays of ham, cheese, salads and sandwiches (€4-12). Lovers of all things Italian will appreciate the pastas (€5.40-7.20) and crisp specialty

THE LOCAL STORY

KISS OF DEATH

The tombs of Juan Diego de Marcilla and Isabel de Segura in the **Mausoleo de los Amantes** are the source of Teruel's nickname: *Ciudad de los Amantes* (City of Lovers). Teruel celebrates love in a rather morbid retelling of a true tragic story—dubbed the most beautiful love story of all time by poet Federico Muelas. It began in the early 13th century when Diego left Teruel to make his fortune and prove his worth to Isabel's affluent family. Five years later, he returned on the very day of Isabel's wedding to his childhood rival. Diego begged Isabel for one last kiss but was refused; he died immediately of grief. At the funeral, in the same church where they lie today, Isabel kissed the corpse and, overcome with sorrow, died herself.

At the beautiful alabaster mausoleum by sculptor Juan de Ávalos—constructed after adamant fundraising and protests at the sight of the exposed mummified bodies—the lovers are commemorated with life-size statues, their hands reaching out, a few centimeters from touching, a gesture of their impossible love. For a peek at the lovers' mummified remains—discovered during church renovations in 1555 and moved enough times to rival Evita's body—duck down near their heads.

pizzas (€5-10), along with local wines, served at the cozy **Los Caprichos ❷**, C. Caracol, 1, from Pl. del Torico, two blocks up C. Hartzenbusch (to the left when looking out in the direction of the Torico) on the right. (☎978 60 03 30. Take-out available. Open Tu-Su 1:30-4pm and 8:30-11:30pm.) **Restaurante La Parrilla ❸**, C. Esteban, 2, two blocks uphill from the tourist office, specializes in regional dishes and has a magnificent €10 *menú* with succulent meat grilled on a stone fireplace. (☎978 60 59 17. Meat entrées €10.50-25, fish €7-12, salads €6-12. Open M-Sa 1-4:30pm and 8:30-11:30pm. AmEx/MC/V.) Better yet, skip a meal and stuff yourself with mouth-watering goodies from pastry shops throughout the city, particularly the vast array at **Pastelería Sanz ❸**, C. Ramón y Cajal, 2, half a block from the plaza. (Open M-F 9am-2pm and 6-8pm, Sa 9am-2pm and 6-8:30pm, Su 10am-2pm.) If you insist on eating "real" food, there is a **market** on Pl. Domingo Gascón; from Pl. del Torico, take C. Joaquín Costa for two blocks. (Open M-F 9:30am-2pm and 6-8:30pm, Sa 9am-2pm.)

◪ SIGHTS. The mother of all Teruel's *mudéjar* monuments is the 13th-century **Catedral de Santa María de Mediavilla.** The vast difference between the chapels is noteworthy—the gilding of the baroque *Capilla de la Inmaculada*, dating from the 19th century, is brilliant in comparison to the more subdued wooden carvings of the 16th-century *retablo mayor.* Also interesting is the shrine to a destroyed Virgin Mary statue, with a prayer asking for forgiveness for the defacing. What brings the cathedral fame is the intricate *Techumbre mudéjar*, a decorative ceiling that covers the entire central nave with everything from vegetable motifs to religious scenes, but overall a clearly Islamic feel. Behind the cathedral in the Episcopal Palace is the **Museo de Arte Sacro,** exhibiting religious paintings, carvings, and sculptures from Medieval to Baroque origin. (Cathedral open daily 11am-2pm and 4-8pm. Free guided visits in Spanish, 3-6 per day depending on demand. Museum open July-Sept. 10am-2pm and 4-8pm; Oct.-June M-Sa 10am-2pm. Cathedral or museum €1.20, both €2.) Muslim artisans built the brick-and-glazed-tile **Torres Mudéjares,** found throughout the city, between the 12th and 15th centuries, after a Christian church adapted the Almohad minarets to their own purposes. The most intricately designed of the towers, in detailed white and green patterns, is the 14th-century **Torre de El Salvador,** C. del Salvador; it is the only one open to visitors. Climb 123 steps through several chambers to the bell tower and its panoramic views. (☎978 60 20 61; www.teruelmudejar.com. Open Tu-Su 11am-2pm and 4:30-7:30pm; closed July 10-13. €2.50, ages 6-12 and seniors €1.) Teruel's famous love story is kept alive at the **Mausoleo de los Amantes,** currently undergoing lengthy renovations (check with the tourist office). Behind the cathedral, the **Museo Provincial,** devoted to archaeological and ethnographic pursuits, is in the 16th-century **Casa de la Comunidad,** Pl. Fray Anselmo Polanco, a leading example of the Aragonese Renaissance style. Rotating small temporary exhibits, typically of modern art, complement the permanent collection. (☎978 60 01 50. Open Tu-F 10am-2pm and 4-9pm, Sa-Su 10am-2pm. Free.)

▓ FESTIVALS. The most renowned celebration of Teruel is the 10-day joint celebration of the **Fiestas del Ángel,** also known as "La Vaquilla," that takes place the Sunday closest to the **Fiesta del San Cristóbal** (July 10), usually the second Sunday of July. The festivities are in loving honor of the little Torico (he wears an honorary red handkerchief for the week); traditional attire is worn for the *corridas*, puppet parades, public picnics, fireworks, and, most importantly, the continuous liquored-up nighttime celebrations (Sa-M). The second guest of honor is Santa Emerenciana. Teruel's population quadruples for this celebration, so plan accordingly. If you arrive on the weekend closest to Valentine's Day and find the entire town dressed in medieval attire, don't be surprised—they are merely recreating the **Wedding of Isabel de Segura,** one of the two tragic lovers. Lastly, September 19-20 brings the somewhat commercial **Feria del Jamón,** where ham producers set up stands to sample (and advertise) their particular mouth-watering delicacies.

LA RIOJA

La Rioja and great wine are literally synonymous. "Rioja" is an internationally acclaimed wine classification with an 800-year-old tradition; both the 1994 and 1995 grapes received the highest ratings possible, and since 1991 its wine has been the only in Spain to earn the coveted *Calificada* rating. The region's name derives from the Ebro tributary Río Oja, whose waters trickle through the vineyards. The best *bodegas* (wine cellars) draw from the lands in western Rioja Alta, around Haro. Try to stay sober enough to walk at least part of the Camino de Santiago, which passes through much of the region. The mountainous Sierra, with tranquil fields at the feet of towering peaks, lines La Rioja's southern border.

LOGROÑO ☎941

The best entry point into the vineyard towns of La Rioja, capital city Logroño (pop. 140,000) has always looked out for its *bodegas*: in 1635, the mayor banned carts from streets next to wineries "for fear that the vibration caused by these vehicles might affect the must." But Logroño is more than just wine. From haute couture shops to bustling avenues lined with bars serving the region's renowned *vinos* and tapas—not to mention the best burger in Spain—Logroño provides a more down to earth alternative to Spain's chic cities. Its origins dating as far back as 956, Logroño's name came from *"illo Gronio"* (the passageway), since rock elevations along the Río Ebro permitted its crossing at various spots by the city. Logroño was a prized target for conquest and had to defend its borders constantly—most notably on June 11, 1521, against the French, who still celebrate their success today. Locals have claimed that Logroño feeds both the body and the soul. Although the Camino de Santiago passes through here, the soul will find little but bustling commerce for nourishment. The body, however, can feast.

▐▀ TRANSPORTATION

Trains: RENFE, Pl. de Europa (☎902 24 02 02), off Av. de España on the south side of town, southeast of the bus station. Info open daily 7am-11pm. To: **Barcelona** (7hr., 3 per day 2:03am-12:46pm, €29-38); **Bilbao** (4hr., 3 per day 4:20am-6:33pm, €15-19); **Burgos** (2hr., 4 per day 12:46am-6:33pm, €9.50-19); **Madrid** (3¾hr., 8am, €45.50); **Vitoria-Gasteiz** (1½hr., 7pm, €6.40); **Zaragoza** (2-2½hr.; 6 per day 2:03am-8:10pm, F additional train 10:14pm; €9.45-15).

Buses: Av. de España (☎941 23 59 83), on the corner of C. del General Vara de Rey and Av. de Pío XII. More convenient for nearby destinations. Info open M-Sa 6am-11pm, Su 7am-11pm. To: **Barcelona** (6hr., 6 per day 1:30am-4:25pm, €24); **Burgos** (2hr.; M-Sa 5 per day 8:30am-7:30pm, Su 3 per day 11am-9:45pm; €6.35); **Madrid** (4hr.; 5-6 per day M-Th and Sa 6:45am-7pm, F 6:45am-10pm, Su 9:30am-10pm; €19-25); **Pamplona** (2hr.; M-Sa 5 per day 7am-7pm, Su 3 per day 10am-7pm; €6.50); **Santo Domingo de la Calzada** (1hr.; M-F 11 per day 7:15am-8pm, Sa 7 per day 8:30am-7:30pm, Su 3 per day 11am-9:45pm; €2.80); **Soria** (1½hr.; 5-6 per day M-Th and Sa 6:45am-7pm, F 6:45am-10pm, Su 9:30am-10pm; €5.70); **Vitoria-Gasteiz** (2hr.; M-F 6 per day 7am-8pm, Sa 4 per day 10am-8pm, Su 5 per day 10am-9:30pm 4-6 per day 7am-8pm; €7.20); **Zaragoza** (2hr.; 6 per day M-Th and Sa 7am-6:30pm, F additional train at 3pm, Su 10:30am-9pm; €10).

Public Transportation: All local buses (☎941 20 27 77) run to Gran Vía del Rey Juan Carlos I at the intersection with C. del General Vara de Rey, 1 block from Parque del Espolón. There is an info booth here. Buses #1 and 3 pass the bus station. €0.56.

Taxis: Stands at the bus station (☎941 23 75 29) and Parque del Espolón (☎941 22 42 99). **Radio Taxi** (☎941 50 50 50).

Car Rental: Hertz, Pl. de Europa (☎941 25 59 89), outside the train station. 21+ and have had license for 2 years. From €53 per day. Open M-F 9am-1pm and 4-7pm, Sa 9am-1pm. AmEx/MC/V. **AVIS,** Gran Vía, 67 (☎941 20 23 54), 6 blocks to the left from bus station. 23+. Open M-F 9am-1pm and 4-7pm, Sa 9am-1pm. AmEx/MC/V.

■✵ 🛈 ORIENTATION AND PRACTICAL INFORMATION

Gran Vía del Rey Juan Carlos I is Logroño's main thoroughfare. Both the old and new towns radiate from **Parque del Espolón.** The **casco antiguo** stretches between the park and the Río Ebro on the far north side of the city. To reach the park (and tourist office, located in the park by C. del General Vara de Rey) from the **train station,** angle left on Av. de España. At the **bus station** (the next major intersection), turn right onto C. del General Vara de Rey, which leads north to the park on your left (8min.) and the *casco antiguo* bordering it on the top.

Tourist Office: Po. del Espolón (☎941 29 12 60; www.larioja.org/turismo). English, French, and German spoken. Tours of the *casco antiguo* July 9-Aug. 28 F-Sa 11am and 7pm, €3. Open June-Oct. M-F 9am-9pm, Sa 10am-2pm and 5-8pm, Su 10am-2pm; Nov.-May M-Sa 10am-2pm and 4-8pm, Su 10am-2pm.

Currency Exchange: Banco Santander Central Hispano, on C. del General Vara de Rey at the corner of Parque del Espolón. **ATM.** Open Apr.-Sept. M-F 8:30am-2pm; Oct.-Mar. M-F 8:30am-2pm, Sa 8:30am-1pm.

Luggage Storage: At **bus station.** €2 per locker. Open M-Sa 6am-11pm, Su 7am-11pm. At **train station** (€3). Open 24hr.

English-Language Bookstore: Santos Ochoa, C. de Sagasta, 3 (☎941 25 86 22) has a decent English book selection. Open M-F 10:30am-1:45pm and 5-8:30pm, Sa 10:30am-2pm. MC/V. **Second location** at Gran Vía del Rey Juan Carlos I, 47. Open 9:30am-2pm and 5-9pm, Sa 10am-2pm and 5:30-9pm. MC/V.

Police: C. Ruavieja (☎091 or 092), near Iglesia de Palacio.

Medical Services: Hospital San Millán, Av. de la Autonomía de la Rioja, 3 (☎941 29 45 00). Follow Av. de La Paz away from the *casco antiguo,* and go right after 7 blocks.

Internet Access: Free Internet at **Cibertecas,** across the street from the bus station at Av. de Pío XII, 5. Tourist office has list of other, less central branches. Hours vary, but generally open M-F 9:30am-1:30pm and 4-8pm, F 8pm-midnight, Sa 10am-2pm and 8pm-midnight. **Mercadoteca** on C. del Peso, between C. Capitán Eduardo Gallarza and C. de Sagasta, next to the Mercado de Abastos in the *casco antiguo,* also has free Internet. Open M-F 10am-2pm and 5:30-8:30pm, Sa 10am-2pm.

Post Office: C. Pérez Galdós, 40. From the bus station, turn left and walk 5 blocks. Open M-F 8:30am-8:30pm, Sa 9:30am-2pm. **Branch** beside the train station on Av. de Lobete. Open M-F 8:30am-2:30pm, Sa 9:30am-1pm. **Postal Code:** 26002.

🏠 ACCOMMODATIONS

For budget accommodations, the *casco antiguo* is probably your best bet. Try C. San Juan, the second left past Parque del Espolón from the stations, or C. San Agustín and C. Laurel. Reservations are crucial for *fiesta* week near September 21.

Fonda Bilbaína, C. Capitán Eduardo Gallarza, 10, 2nd fl. (☎941 25 42 26). Take C. de Sagasta, the street perpendicular to the park on the opposite end from C. del General Vara de Rey, into the *casco antiguo,* turn left onto C. Hermanos Moroy and then right onto C. Capitán Eduardo Gallarza. Bright rooms with high ceilings, wood floors, big beds, and sinks. Insist on a room facing the street with a balcony. Singles €21, with shower €24, with bath €27; doubles €25/€30/€33. ❷

Hostal Niza, C. Capitán Eduardo Gallarza, 13 (☎941 20 60 44; www.hostalniza.com), 1 block before Bilbaína. A great deal for doubles. 16 light blue rooms with TV, A/C, beautiful new baths, coffee and cookies trays, and even hair dryers and (in some) DVD players. June-Sept. doubles €60, for individual use €40, for 3 with extra bed €75; Sept.-June €55/€36/€70. AmEx/MC/V. ❸

Residencia Universitaria (HI), C. Caballero de la Rosa, 38 (☎941 26 14 30). From C. del General Vara de Rey turn right after the Parque El Espolón onto Mura de Cervantes, which becomes Av. de la Paz. After 7 long blocks, turn left on C. Caballero de la Rosa and walk 3 blocks; beige building on the right. University dorms during the school year; used by athletic teams in summer. Public phone and 2 common rooms with TV. Doubles with bunks and private bath; rooms usually not shared. Lively and young atmosphere. Sheets €2.80. Open July-Aug. 15. €7.70, with breakfast €9.20. ❶

FOOD

Logroñeses take their grapes seriously—wine is the beverage of choice with everything. C. Laurel and C. San Juan brim with bars and cafes. **Mercado de San Blas** offers fresh fruit and vegetables in a concrete building on C. Capitán Eduardo Gallarza. (Open M-F 7:30am-1:30pm and 4-7:30pm, Sa 7:30am-1:30pm.) For **groceries,** head to **Champion,** Av. La Rioja, left off C. Miguel Villanueva past the tourist office. (☎941 22 99 00. Open M-Sa 9am-9:30pm.)

El Merendero II, Gran Vía, 67. If you came to Logroño looking for the best wine in Spain, you're in luck; they also have the best burger. It may not look like much, but one bite into an *especial* (€3.10) and you'll be convinced. Open Tu-Su 6pm-2am. ❶

Joshua, C. Laurel, 10, off C. Capitán Eduardo Gallarza. The specialty at this cozy restaurant is the *musaka,* a mouthwatering lasagna made with eggplant, veal, bechamel, and cheese. Also offers traditional fare: *lomo, ternera,* and *croquetas. Platos combinados* €6.80. *Menú* €9.80. Open daily 1-5pm and 9:15pm-12:30am, F-Sa until 1am. ❶

En Ascuas, C. Hermanos Moroy, 22 (☎941 24 68 67; www.enascuas.com). Elegant rustic decor marked by large black-and-white pictures depicting wine culture. Delicious appetizers (€2.80-9.30) and salads (€4.90-7) include *jamón iberico* with mushrooms and cheese and salmon salad. Lots of *parrilla* (grill) options, from *cordero* (lamb) to duck (€3.50-17.90), including the massive 4-person serving. For white meat fans, fish entrees €7.50-14. Open Tu-Su 1:30-3:30pm and 8:30-11:30pm. D/MC/V. ❸

Bar Soriano, Tr. de Laurel, 2 (☎941 22 88 07), where C. Laurel turns. No indoor seating. The specialty is *champiñones con gambas* (mushrooms with shrimp; €0.75) washed down with a shot of *vino* (€0.45). Open daily 11am-3am. ❶

SIGHTS

Aside from the beautiful **Parque del Espolón** and, in the ring around it, numerous shopping streets that include the pedestrian walkways of Av. de Juan and the streets that intersect it (creatively dubbed the "street with 100 shops"), Logroño offers a few more historically significant attractions. In an 18th-century Baroque palace, the **Museo de la Rioja** has a collection of art, mostly religious works, spanning the last eight centuries, most of which came from the 1835 state seizure of monastic properties, and a rotating contemporary art exhibit. (Pl. San Agustín, 23, along C. Portales. ☎941 29 12 59. Open Tu-Sa 10am-2pm and 4-9pm, Su 11:30am-2pm. Free.) The twin towers of the 19th-century **Catedral de Santa María de la Redonda,** which hides a Michelangelo inside, dominate Pl. del Mercado in the *casco antiguo*. From C. del General Vara de Rey turn left on C. Portales; the cathedral is two blocks away. (Open M-Sa 8am-1:30pm and 6:30-8:45pm, Su 9am-2pm and 6:30-8:45pm. Free.) Since the cathedral may still be undergoing renovations, get your pretty church dose at the Renaissance **Iglesia de Santiago El Real,** a mandatory stop on the Camino de Santiago and home of the Virgen de la Esperanza, in the Pl. de Santiago bordering the river. Follow C. Sagasta until C. Marqués de San Nicolás and it will be two blocks to the right. (Open 8:15am-1:15pm and 6:30-7pm.) To do a miniature, less draining (but perhaps less spiritually enlightening) version of the Camino de Santiago, follow C. Ruavieja (the oldest street in the city, where the pilgrims sleep) or C. de Barriocepo from the church four blocks east to the **Murallas de Revellín** at the end. The pilgrims exit the city through this arch, all that remains of the medieval walls that once surrounded it. The grassy knolls along the **Río Ebro** make for a peaceful walk; a path runs by **Puente de Hierro** and **Puente de Piedra.**

NIGHTLIFE AND FESTIVALS

Logroño **nightlife** begins along C. Laurel in the *casco antiguo*, making use of some of that wine they talk so much about. After midnight it moves to C. Mayor along Pl. del Mercado, C. de Sagasta, and C. Carnicerías. Two of the best spots are the equally elegant and artsy **Traz Luz,** C. Portales, 71 (☎947 21 41 94; open M-Th 10am-10pm, F-Sa 10am-3am), and sophisticated **Noche y Día,** C. Portales, 63 (☎949 20 64 06; open M-Th 8am-2am, F-Sa 8am-2:30am). A block away, on C. Sagasta, 9, **La Granja** provides a more creative setting, with a huge illuminated blue sky backdrop. (☎941 23 02 62. Open M-Th 8am-11pm, F-Sa 8am-2am.) Or, head down to **Café Casablanca,** Av. de Portugal, 30 (☎941 22 09 45. Drinks €5. *Pinchos* €1.50. Coffee €1. Open M-Th 9am-1am, F-Sa 9am-2:30am.) Warning: this classy but casual dive may be adorned with posters and photos from the film, but that doesn't mean you should ask the bartender to play anything again. His name isn't Sam, he's heard it before, and you'll only piss him off. The **Fiestas de San Bernabé** (June 11) bring revelry and fireworks along with historically significant processions around the Murallas de Revellín, but the biggest party in town begins the week of September 21 for the **Fiesta de San Mateo.** That same week, locals celebrate the grape harvest with the **Fiestas de la Vendimia,** during which they make a ceremonial offering of crushed grapes to the Virgin of Valvanera. Participants crush the grapes with their bare feet in the Parque del Espolón.

DAYTRIP FROM LOGROÑO

HARO

RENFE trains (☎941 31 15 97) connect Logroño to Haro. (40min.; daily 7:36am and 7pm; also M, W, F 2:30pm; €3.10, 2:30pm train €9.50. Return trains run daily 1:22, 8:55 and 9:47pm; €3.10, additional train at 12:09pm €9.50.) Buses (☎941 31 15 43) from Logroño to Haro. (1hr.; 7 per day M-F 7:30am-8pm, Sa 4 per day 10:15am-8pm, Su 3 per day 10:15am-8:30pm; €2.50. Return buses M-F 6 per day 7:45am-8:30pm, Sa 3 per day 8:45am-6pm, Su 3 per day 8:45am-7pm.)

Though Logroño proudly boasts of its wines, few places are as dominated by *vino* as Haro. Rubí, Paternina, Rioja Santiago, Carlos Serres: these are the names of just a few of its 17 *bodegas*. Awash with the warming drink, Haro (pop. 10,000) is the heart of La Rioja's wine industry due to its grape varieties, climate, and soil, and should be a priority stop for any connoisseur or aficionado. Most wineries, the majority located strategically across the river by the train station, offer free tours of their facilities in Spanish (some in English) between 9am and 2pm, typically including a tasting; reservations are almost always required.

The large **Bodegas Muga** (the most popular Spanish wine in the USA), a 10min. walk across the Río Tirón, to the left beyond the train tracks, can be visited without calling ahead. They also sell bottles from €4 to €70. (☎941 31 04 98. Tours M-F 11am in English, 11am and noon in Spanish. €5. MC/V.) **Bodegas Bilbaínas,** located across the river but before the train tracks, can be visited by appointment, except on Friday, when you can walk in. (☎941 31 01 47. Tours July Tu-F 11am, Sa 10am and noon, Su 11am; Aug. M-Sa 11am. Free.) **Bodegas Cune** also offers tours in English. (☎941 30 48 09. Tours, by appointment, M-Sa 10am, 1, and 4pm in Spanish, 11am in English.) If the samples just aren't enough, hit up the numerous **wine shops** on C. Santo Tomás and take a bottle to the flower-filled **Jardines de la Vega,** on C. Virgen de la Vega three blocks up from the tourist office. Most charge €1.40-3 (and up) per bottle, but *jarreros* (Haro locals) insist that any bottle less than €2.80 should not be consumed. The **Estación Enológica y Museo del Vino,** Av. Bretón de los Herreros, 4, has sleek exhibits in Spanish detailing everything you could possibly want to know about wine, its production, and the many cultural activities in La Rioja that revolve around it. (☎941 31 05 47. Open M-Sa 10am-2pm and 4-8pm, Su 10am-2pm. €2, children free. W free.) Join the locals as they *ir de vinos* (go for wine) in the evening in the many *vinotecas* in **La Herradura,** the area around C. Santo Tomás, off Pl. de la Paz. Order *vino* and you'll get the vintage of the year (€0.40); for higher quality, order *crianza,* wine over three years old (€0.80). There are numerous food options in this same area, most identical; for large portions of salads (€3-5), pizzas (€7-10), pasta (€6), and *platos combinados* (€6-10), try **Popy's ❷,** C. Arrabal, 3, right off Pl. de la Paz. (☎941 30 35 74. Open 1-4pm and 7:30-11:30pm.) Haro breaks out in festivities on June 29, the day of San Pedro, when participants spray wine at innocent bystanders during the **Batalla del Vino.**

To reach **Plaza de la Paz** from the **train station,** take the road downhill, turn right and then left across the river, and follow C. Navarra uphill to the plaza (15min.). From the **bus station,** follow signs to *centro ciudad* along C. la Ventilla, continuing 2 blocks past Consum. Head diagonally left across Pl. de la Cruz (6 blocks from the station) onto C. Arrabal, which leads straight into Pl. de la Paz. The **tourist office,** in Pl. Florentino Rodríguez, provides a listing in English of all the *bodegas* and their tours. Take C. Virgen de la Vega from the corner of Pl. de la Paz; the office is in the plaza to the left around the bend, located in the corner of the large stone building. (☎941 30 33 66. Open July-Sept. 20 M-Sa 10am-2pm and 4:30-7:30pm, Su 10am-2pm; Sept. 21-June Tu-Sa 10am-2pm and 4-7pm, Su 10am-2pm.)

NAVARRA (NAVARRE)

Navarran cities are somewhat of an oddity. Though subdued, quiet, picturesque, and religiously and politically conservative, they throw the country's wildest parties—Pamplona's outrageous *San Fermín* (July 6-14) is undoubtedly the most (in)famous. But there hasn't always been reason to celebrate. In the 13th century, the Kingdom of Navarra was divided into six districts and since then has long experienced the difficulties of Spain's on-again/off-again regionalism. It gained autonomy in 1512, then lost it in 1833 by supporting the losing candidate in Spain's first Carlist War. To avoid another such loss, Navarra sided with the "winners" in the 20th century, allying themselves with Nationalist forces in the Spanish Civil

War. They soon found that Franco's conservatism outstripped their own and had no tolerance for regional differences. Nevertheless, Navarra's spirit has remained relatively undaunted. It continues to support regionalist causes, most recently the re-establishment of autonomy in 1983. Visitors, however, will have a harder time separating themselves from one of Spain's most serene and storied regions.

PAMPLONA (IRUÑA) ☎948

El encierro, la Fiesta del San Fermín, the Running of the Bulls, utter debauchery: call it what you will, the outrageous festival of the city's patron saint is the reason people come to Pamplona (pop. 200,000). *San Fermín* is rightly touted as the biggest and craziest festival in all Europe. Though the city's somewhat limited parks, museums, and monuments await exploration, it is the famous *encierro*, the focal point of the July 6-14 celebration, that draws visitors from around the world. Ever since Ernest Hemingway immortalized the *San Fermín* chaos in *The Sun Also Rises*, hordes of visitors have come to witness and experience the legendary running. At the bullring, Hemingway's bust welcomes fans to the eight-day extravaganza of dancing, dashing, and of course, drinking—no sleeping allowed.

Although *San Fermín* may be the city's most irresistible attraction, Pamplona's lush parks, Gothic cathedral, massive citadel, and winding *casco antiguo* entertain those who show up at other times—though beware of the 1-2 week post-*San Fermín* recovery period, when many stores and restaurants close. Despite being the capital of Navarra, Pamplona's roots are actually Basque; the area was settled by the Basques long before the Roman "founders" arrived and named the city after Pompey the Great. Today you can still sense the traces of Basque patriotism.

■ TRANSPORTATION

Flights: Aeropuerto de Noaín (☎948 16 87 00), 6km from town. Accessible only by taxi (€9). **Iberia** (☎948 31 79 55) to **Barcelona** (Sept.-July 4 per day, Aug. M-F 1 per day) and **Madrid** (Sept.-July M-F 7 per day, Sa 5 per day, Su 4 per day; Aug. 2-4 per day). **Lagunair** (☎902 34 03 00) flies to **Mallorca, Málaga,** and **Valencia.**

Trains: Estación RENFE, Av. de San Jorge (☎902 24 02 02). Bus #9 from Po. Sarasate (20min., €0.80). Info open daily 6am-10pm. **Ticket office,** C. Estella, 8 (☎948 22 72 82). Open M-F 9am-1:30pm and 4:30-7:30pm, Sa 9:30am-1pm. Trains are not the best option, as Pamplona is not well-connected by rail and the station is far from the city center. To: **Barcelona** (6-8hr., 3-9 per day 12:33pm-12:57am, €29.50-38); **Madrid** (3¾hr., 3 per day 7am-7pm, €45.50); **Olite** (40min.; M-Sa 4 per day 9:25am-8pm, Su 7:05pm; €2.50); **San Sebastián** (2-3 per day 5:36am-6:31pm, €12.50-16); **Vitoria-Gasteiz** (1¼hr.; M-Sa 4 per day 8:45am-7:40pm, Su 3 per day 12:17-7:40pm; €4-11); **Zaragoza** (2hr., 4-5-per day 12:33pm-12:57am, €15-19.50).

Buses: Estación de Autobuses (☎948 22 38 54), at the corner of C. Conde Oliveto and C. Yanguas y Miranda. **Bilman** (☎948 22 09 97) to **Barcelona** (5½hr.; 4 per day M-Th and Sa 8:05am-1:05am, F and Su 8:35am-1:05am; €20) and **Valencia** (9:45am and 11pm, €19.15) via **Teruel. La Burundesa (ALSA;** ☎948 22 17 66) to **Bilbao** (2hr.; M-Th and Sa 4-6 per day 7am-7pm, F 6 per day 7am-8pm, Su 4 per day 11am-8pm; €11.20) and **Vitoria-Gasteiz** (1½hr.; M-F 11 per day 7am-8:30pm, Sa 8 per day 7am-8:30pm, Su 6 per day 9am-9pm; €6.20). **Conda** (☎948 22 10 26) to **Madrid** (5hr.; M-Th 4 per day 7am-6:30pm, F and Su 7 per day 7am-9:30pm, Sa 4 per day 7am-6:30pm; €22.20) and **Zaragoza** (2-3hr., 5-9 per day 7:15am-8:30pm, €10-11). **La Estellesa** (☎948 22 22 23) to **Estella** (1hr.; M-Sa 10 per day 7:30am-8:30pm, Su 4 per day 10am-7pm; €3.20) and **Logroño** (1hr.; M-Sa 5 per day 7:30am-7pm, Su 4 per day 10am-7pm; €6.40). **La Tafallesa** (☎948 22 28 86) to **Olite** (50min.; M-F 8 per

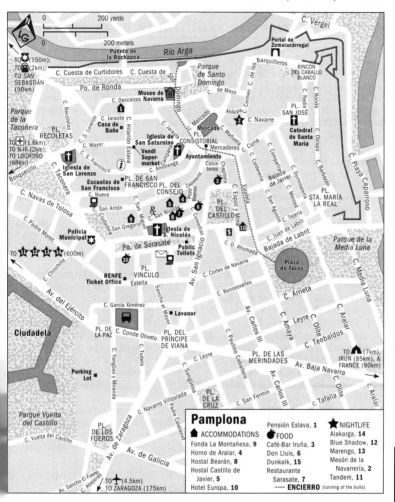

Pamplona

⌂ ACCOMMODATIONS
Fonda La Montañesa, **9**
Horno de Aralar, **4**
Hostal Bearán, **8**
Hostal Castillo de
Javier, **5**
Hotel Europa, **10**

● FOOD
Café-Bar Iruña, **3**
Don Lluis, **6**
Dunkalk, **15**
Restaurante
Sarasate, **7**

Pensión Eslava, **1**

---- **ENCIERRO** (running of the bulls)

★ NIGHTLIFE
Alakarga, **14**
Blue Shadow, **12**
Marengo, **13**
Mesón de la
Navarrería, **2**
Tandem, **11**

day 8:15am-8:30pm, Sa 7 per day 9:30am-8:30pm, Su 1 and 8:30pm; €2.70). **La Veloz Sangüesina** (☎948 87 02 09) to **Sangüesa** (M-Sa 3 per day 1-8pm, Su 8:15pm; €3). **Vibasa** (☎948 10 13 63) to **Barcelona** (6-8hr., M-Th and Sa 4 per day 8:05am-1:05am, F and Su 5 per day 8:35am-12:55am; €24).

Taxis: Teletaxi (☎948 23 23 23) or **Radiotaxi** (☎948 22 12 12); stand at Parque de la Taconera at the intersection of C. Navas de Tolosa and C. Taconera.

Car Rental: Europcar, Hotel Blanca Navarra, Av. de Pío XII, 43 (☎948 17 60 02). Take bus #15, 4-1 or 4-2 from Po. Sarasate and get off after the traffic circle on the way out of town. 21+. Open M-F 8:30am-1pm and 4-7:30pm, Sa 9am-1pm. AmEx/MC/V. **AVIS,** C. Monasterio de la Oliva, 29 (☎948 17 00 36; fax 17 00 69) and at airport (☎948 16 87 63). Open 8am-1pm and 4-7pm, Sa 9am-1pm. At airport open to coincide with flight arrivals (M-F morning and evening, Sa morning, Su evening). AmEx/MC/V.

✦❓ ORIENTATION AND PRACTICAL INFORMATION

The **casco antiguo**, in the northeast quarter of the city, contains almost everything of interest. **Plaza del Castillo** is Pamplona's center. To reach it from the **bus station**, turn left onto Av. Conde Oliveto, then left after two blocks at Pl. Príncipe de Viana onto Av. de San Ignacio (the second from the left), which runs into the plaza. From the **train station**, take bus #9 to the last stop; cut across Po. de Sarasate and walk diagonally left to Pl. del Castillo. North of Pl. del Castillo, the Baroque **Casa Consistorial (Ayuntamiento)** is a helpful marker in the swirl of medieval streets.

Tourist Office: C. Hilarión Eslava, 1 (☎948 20 65 40; www.navarra.es). Aside from maps, regional info, accommodations, food, and cultural information, offers a crucial minute-by-minute *San Fermín* **Fiesta Programme** guide that lists every event, also available at www.pamplona.net. Special *San Fermín* info, including monument and bank schedules, transportation, Internet, laundry and showers, luggage storage, etc. Ask about guided tours. English spoken. Open during *San Fermín* daily 8am-8pm; July-Aug. M-Sa 9am-8pm, Su 10am-2pm; Sept.-June M-F 10am-2pm and 4-7pm, Sa 10am-2pm.

Currency Exchange: Banco Santander Central Hispano, Pl. del Castillo, 21 (☎948 20 86 00), has an **ATM**. Open *San Fermín* 9am-1pm; May-Sept. M-F 8:30am-2pm; Oct.-Apr. M-F 8:30am-2pm, Sa 8:30am-1pm. Note that schedules right after *San Fermín* are cut short—make sure to get money before the weekend.

Luggage Storage: At the **bus station**. Bags €2 per day, large packs €3 per day. Open M-Sa 6:15am-9:30pm, Su 6:30am-1:30pm and 2-9:30pm. Closes for *San Fermín*, when the **Escuelas de San Francisco,** the big stone building at the end of Pl. San Francisco, opens instead (Open from July 3 at 8pm to July 15 at 2pm). Lines are long, and you must have passport or ID. €2 per day and each time you check on luggage. Open 24hr.

Laundromat and Public Baths: Casa de Baño, C. Hilarión Eslava (☎948 22 17 38). 4.5kg wash €4, dry €3.75. Allow 2hr. for wash and dry cycles. Showers (€0.85), bath (€1.80). Towel €0.25, soap €0.25. Open during *San Fermín* daily 8am-9pm; otherwise Tu-Sa 8:30am-8pm, Su showers only 8:30am-1pm. **Lavanor,** C. Sancho el Mayor, 7 (☎948 22 88 15). Open M-F 9:20am-1:30pm and 5-8pm, Sa 9:20am-1:30pm; during *San Fermín* daily 9am-1:30pm.

Public Toilets: Squat toilet booths are set up for *San Fermín*, but the bathrooms in **Parque de la Taconera** (beyond Hotel Tres Reyes at the corner of the park, by C. Taconera) and **Paseo de Sarasate** (at the end by Av. S. Ignacio) are more comfortable.

Municipal Police: C. Monasterio de Irache, 2 (☎092 or 948 42 06 40). **National Police,** C. General Chinchilla, 3 (☎091).

Pharmacy: FarPlus, C. San Nicolás, 76 (☎948 21 07 04). Open M-F 9am-1:30pm and 5-8pm, Sa 9:30am-1:30pm. **Late-night pharmacy** changes daily. All pharmacies post info for that evening's location, or call ☎948 22 21 11.

Medical Services: Hospital de Navarra, C. Irunlarrea (☎948 42 21 00), at the corner with Av. de Pio XII. The **Red Cross** sets up stands at the bus station and along the *corrida* during *San Fermín*. The **Ambulatorio Solchaga** is in the Pl. de Toros year-round.

Internet Access: Kuria.Net, C. Curia, 15 (☎948 22 30 77). €3 per hr. Open M-Sa 10am-10pm, Su 1-10pm; during *San Fermín* daily 9am-11pm. **Ciberarroba.com,** C. San Antón, 70. €3 per hr. Open M-F 11am-2pm and 4:30-10pm.

Post Office: Po. de Sarasate, 9 (☎948 20 68 40). Open M-F 8:30am-8:30pm, Sa 9:30am-2pm; during *San Fermín* M-Sa 8:30am-2pm. **Postal Code:** 31001.

🏠📷 ACCOMMODATIONS AND CAMPING

If you think you're going to get a good night's sleep on a shoestring budget during *San Fermín*, think again. Unless you've booked a hotel room at least five months in advance—or a quality hostel six months in advance—start fluffing up your sweatshirt: it's going be your pillow on the crowded, noisy, litter-laden park grass, or a crowded and not-always-pristine *pensión* floor. Some early birds may be lucky enough to secure space at campgrounds, which don't take reservations. They may be the only affordable option, and buses run back and forth to them all night (the tourist office has a schedule); however, these can be cramped and uncomfortable. Expect to pay rates up to four times those normally listed (anywhere from €45-90 and up per person) in most budget hotels. Early in the week, people accost visitors at the train and bus stations, offering couches and floor space in their homes. Be wary—you might find yourself blowing your money for a few hours of sleep on an unclean floor in a bad part of town. Check the newspaper *Diario de Navarra* for *casas particulares*, though many advertisers are hesitant to let anyone other than native Spaniards or fluent Spanish speakers into their home; inquire at the tourist office for other listings. Many who can't find rooms (or never planned on finding them at all) sleep outside on the lawns of the Ciudadela, Pl. de los Fueros, and Pl. del Castillo, or along the banks of the river. Those who choose this risky option should store their luggage or, at the very least, sleep on top of it. Try to stay in a large group or near other tourists. A lucky few with cars go to nearby Estella to catch some shut-eye or snooze in their back seat—parking is free on most streets during *San Fermín*.

During the rest of the year, finding a room in Pamplona is no problem. Hostels line C. San Nicolás and C. San Gregorio off Pl. del Castillo, as well as the parallel C. Zapatería and C. Nueva, off Pl. de San Francisco. On weekends, rabble-rousing in Pl. del Castillo may make it difficult to sleep. Most hostels have different prices for *temporada alta (San Fermín)*, *temporada media* (usually only July and August, but sometimes including June or September), and *temporada baja* (the rest of the year). Price icons reflect *temporada media* prices.

Hotel Europa, C. Espoz y Mina, 11 (☎948 22 18 00; www.heuropa.com). Although it offers no rooms during *San Fermín* due to a permanent festival clientele, its bright rooms are away from loud C. San Nicolás and serve as a luxurious treat the rest of the year. Breakfast €8. Singles F-Su €61.50, M-Th €68.50; doubles €74/€78. MC/V. ❺

Pensión Eslava, C. Eslava, 13, 2nd fl. (☎948 22 15 58). Not as crowded as other *pensiones* and relatively quieter, but still central. Bigger rooms with balconies and shared baths, perfect for the traveler without reservations. *San Fermín* doubles only €50 per person. Otherwise singles €10-15; doubles €20-30. Discounts for longer stays. ❶

Horno de Aralar, C. San Nicolás, 12 (☎948 22 11 16). This homey restaurant has 5 fresh, spotless rooms with TV and full bath. During *San Fermín* all rooms €180; otherwise singles €30; doubles €50. AmEx/MC/V. ❸

Fonda La Montañesa, C. San Gregorio, 2 (☎948 22 43 80), down C. San Nicolás a block from Po. de Sarasate. Older, non-luxurious rooms, but adequate when space and/or budget is tight. Pleasant, safe environment with gracious owner. Ask for a room on a higher floor during the festival or be prepared to get no sleep. No reservations. *San Fermín* singles €47; doubles €94. Otherwise singles €14; doubles €28. ❶

Hostal Castillo de Javier, C. San Nicolás, 50-52 (☎948 20 30 40; www.hostalcastillodejavier.com). This new modern hostel has a swanky lobby area and 19 rooms with A/C, TV, phone, and full bath. Breakfast €3.50. *San Fermín* (breakfast included) singles €130; doubles €200. Otherwise singles €42.80, with bath €46.30; doubles €59/€66. Extra bed €21.40. AmEx/MC/V. ❹

Hostal Bearán, C. San Nicolás, 25 (☎948 22 34 28). Squeaky-clean rooms with phone, TV, bath, safe box, but you're paying more for its location. *San Fermín* singles €104, doubles €110; July-Sept. €37/€43; Oct.-June €31/€37. MC/V. ❹

Camping Ezcaba (☎948 33 03 15), in Eusa, 7km down the road to Irún. Take city bus line 4-V (dir: Oricaín) from Pl. de las Merindades (4 per day, during *San Fermín* 26 per day). Hop off at the final gas station stop. Fills fast during *San Fermín*, but frequent 24hr. transportation makes it worth it. No reservations. Call for *San Fermín* prices. Otherwise €3.60 per person, per tent, and per car. MC/V. ❶

🍴 FOOD

Tiny neighborhood cafe-bars advertise hearty *menús:* try the side streets near C. Jarauta, C. Descalzos, near Po. de Ronda, and the area above Pl. San Francisco. C. Navarrería and Po. de Sarasate are lined with numerous *bocadillo* bars. C. San Nicolás and Pl. del Castillo have many bars and restaurants, but they tend to be overpriced; however, these are the places to go for outside seating in the heart of the action. The *barracas políticas* (bars organized by political interest groups that don't expect any interest in their platforms), next to the amusement park in the Ciudadela offer cheap drinks. Many cafes and restaurants close for one to two weeks after *San Fermín* to recover. The **market,** C. Mercado, is to the right of the Casa Consistorial, down the stairs. (Open M-Sa 8am-2:30pm.) **Vendi Supermarket** is at the corner of C. Hilarión Eslava and C. Mayor. (Open M-F 9am-2pm and 5:30-7:30pm, Sa 9am-2pm; *San Fermín* M-Sa 9am-2pm. MC/V.)

🍴 **Café-Bar Iruña,** Pl. del Castillo (☎948 22 20 64). With its ornate pillars and ceilings, this former casino that Hemingway made famous in *The Sun Also Rises* is even more notable for its large, beautiful interior than for its delicious *menú* (€10), the only option for table dining. Drinks and *bocadillos* at the bar and terrace seating on the famed plaza. Open M-Th 8am-11pm, F 8am-2am, Sa 9am-2am, Su 9am-11pm. MC/V. ❸

🍴 **Restaurante Sarasate,** C. San Nicolás, 19 (☎948 22 57 27), above a seafood store. Mellow, friendly atmosphere. Organic vegetarian dishes including both typical options (stuffed eggplant, vegetable lasagna, mushroom risotto) as well as more innovative ones (mango and papaya salad, blue cheese soufflé). Lunchtime *menú* €10, F-Sa night and Su *menú* €16. Open daily 1-4pm, F-Sa also 8:30-11pm. AmEx/MC/V. ❸

Dunkalk, C. Alhóndiga, 13 (☎948 21 19 62; www.dunkalk.com), off Po. de Sarasate. This pub/eatery overflows with boomerangs, crocodile barstools, and murals of a kangaroo-filled outback. Mellow in the day and lively at night. Inexpensive menu with a wide selection of beers. Large *bocadillos* €3-5. *Menú* €12.50. Chicken and other entrees €5-8. Open Su-Th 9am-2:30am, F-Sa 9am-3am. MC/V. ❸

Don Lluis, C. San Nicolás, 1 (☎948 22 17 31). Located where C. San Nicolás runs into Pl. del Castillo, the location could not be better. Filling €9 *menú del día* with choices among paella, salad, *lomo, cordero,* and other traditional dishes. At night, Don Lluis packs in a crowd of all ages. Open M-Th 8:30am-midnight, F-Sa 8:30am-4am. ❷

👁 SIGHTS

CATHEDRAL AND CHURCHES. Pamplona has a rich architectural legacy. Carlos III and his wife Queen Leonor are entombed in an alabaster mausoleum in the recently restored 14th-century Gothic **Catedral de Santa María.** Off the cloister is a kitchen with five chimneys, one of only four of its kind in Europe. *(☎948 21 08 27. Open M-F 10am-7pm, Sa 10am-2:30pm; during San Fermín 10am-1:30pm; closed July 7 and 11. Guided tours, including church, cloister, and Museo Diocesano, M-F 7 per day, Sa 3 per day. €4, group rates available.)* The 13th-century **Iglesia de San Saturnino,** C. Ansoleaga, 4, is near the Ayuntamiento. *(☎948 22 45 22. Open 10am-1pm and 5-8pm; July 6, 7, and 13 9:30am-1:30pm and 6:30-8pm. Free.)* The Romanesque **Iglesia de San Nicolás,** in Pl. San Nicolás, is also close by. *(C. San Miguel, 15. ☎948 22 12 81. Open daily 10am-2pm and 4-8pm. Modified hours during San Fermín. Inquire about free guided tours in the summer. Free.)* For a peek at the legendary San Fermín, head to **Iglesia de San Lorenzo,** also known as Capilla San Fermín, next to the tourist office. *(C. Mayor, 74. ☎948 22 53 71. Open daily 8:30am-12:30pm and 6:30-8pm. Modified hours during San Fermín. Free.)*

CIUDADELA. Felipe II built the pentagonal Ciudadela in an effort to secure the city from attack. Today, it's part of a grassy park that hosts an amazing *San Fermín* fireworks display and free exhibits and concerts during the summer. Its impressive **walls** scared off even clever Napoleon, who refused to launch a frontal attack and staged a trick snowball fight instead; when Spanish sentries joined in, the French entered the city through its gates. For a scenic walk to the **Ciudadela** from the old quarter, pick up C. Redín at the far end of the cathedral plaza. A left turn follows the walls past the **Portal de Zumalacárregui** and along the Río Arga. Bear left through the lush and manicured gardens of the **Parque de la Taconera**— where deer, swans, and peacocks roam—until reaching the Ciudadela. *(To get to the intimidating walls directly from Pl. del Castillo, follow Po. de Sarasate to its end, then take a right onto C. Navas de Tolosa. Take the next left on C. Chinchilla; you'll see the massive entrance at the end of the street, 2 blocks down Av. del Ejército. ☎948 22 82 37. Open M-Sa 7:30am-9:30pm, Su 9am-9:30pm. Closed July 6-14. Free.)*

MUSEO DE NAVARRA. The museum shelters Roman mosaics, regional murals, and a collection of 14th- to 20th-century paintings, including Goya's portrait of the Marqués de San Adrián. *(Up C. Santo Domingo from Pl. Consistorial. ☎948 42 64 92. Open Tu-Sa 9:30am-2pm and 5-7pm, Su 11am-2pm; San Fermín Tu-Sa 11am-2pm, closed July 7 and 12. €2, students €1; under 18 and retired free, Sa afternoons and Su mornings free.)*

MUSEO OTEIZA. Although it is only accessible by car or bus, this unique, modern museum is worth the short drive. 1,650 sculptures and 2,000 "experimental" pieces by Jorge Oteiza, an important 20th-century sculptor, are housed in a unique building of smooth wooden and stone surfaces that has a fascinating use of natural light. The museum also allows you to visit the artist's former workshop. *(C. de la Cuesta, 7, in Alzuza, 9km northeast of Pamplona. Río Irati buses go to Alzuza M-Sa 8:45am and 1:30pm, Su 4 and 7:30pm; return buses M-Sa 9:30am and 2:15pm, Su 4:40 and 8:15pm; €1. ☎948 33 20 74; www.museooteiza.org. Open Tu-Su 10am-8pm. €3, students and retired €1.50, under 12 and F free.)*

🎵 ENTERTAINMENT

There is (night)life after *San Fermín*, and it's not difficult to find. **Plaza del Castillo** is the social heart of Pamplona, with outside seating in all directions around the beautifully lit plaza. High school students gather at bars in the *casco antiguo* to demonstrate their vocal abilities: singing, shouting, and any other type of loud carousing are *de rigueur*. Bar-hopping down C. San Nicolás and C. San Gregorio is a favorite nighttime activity, or head to the bars on C. Calderería, C. San Agustín, and C. Jarauta. **Mesón de la Navarrería**, C. Navarrería, draws crowds day and night. (☎948 21 31 63. Open Su-Th noon-4pm and 6:30pm-midnight, F-Sa noon-4pm and 6:30pm-2:30am.) If you don't mind the trek, follow the example of claustrophobes and college students who escape the cramped streets of the *casco antiguo* to the bars in Barrio San Juan on Av. de Bayona. **Alakarga**, Pl. Monasterio Azuelo, draws an open-minded late-night crowd. (☎948 26 60 05. Ring the bell to enter. Beers €3. Mixed drinks €4.80. Open Su-W 10:30pm-6am, Th-Sa midnight-7am.)

You'll find the university crowd at **Travesía de Bayona**, a small plaza of bars and *discotecas* off Av. de Bayona, just before it forks into Monasterio de Velate. The best bars are **Blue Shadow** and **Tandem**, Tr. de Bayona, 3 and 4, both of which offer good dancing, big crowds, and friendly bartenders. (Beer €3. Mixed drinks €5. Blue Shadow open Th-Sa 9pm-3:30am, Tandem open Th-Sa 6pm-6am.) Av. de Bayona also boasts the most popular and pricey of nightspots. Half a block from Pl. Juan XXIII, the enormous **Marengo**, Av. de Bayona, 2, needs five doormen to guard its threshold from sneaky fun-seekers. A ticket and clubbing gear are required. (☎948 26 55 42. Beer and mixed drinks €6. Tickets €10. Open Th-Sa 11pm-6am.)

❄ FIESTA DEL SAN FERMÍN (JULY 6-14)

No limits, no lethargy, and no liability make Pamplona's ◪**Fiestas de San Fermín**—known to most as "The Running of the Bulls"—Europe's premier party. At no other festival will you witness mayhem quite like this eight-day frenzy of parades, bullfights, dancing, fireworks, concerts, wine, and more wine. *Pamploneses*, clad in white with *fajas* (red sashes) and *pañuelos* (bandanas), throw themselves into the 204 hours of merry-making, displaying obscene levels of physical stamina and alcohol tolerance that even the most enthusiastic visitors can't keep up with.

 While Pamplona is usually a very safe city, assaults and muggings skyrocket during *San Fermín*. Apparently, some characters come with shadier intentions, more interested in tourist cash than *fiesta* excitement. Never keep your wallet in your back pocket, and carry little cash and no important documents on you. Do not roam alone at night, and be extremely cautious in the parks and dark streets of the *casco antiguo* and along riverbanks.

Around 10am on July 6, the whole city crowds around the Ayuntamiento, overflowing into adjacent streets, in anticipation of the mayor's noon appearance. As the midday hour approaches, the mass sings and chants *"San Fermín!"* raising *pañuelos* high above their heads. Don't commit the faux pas of wearing your *pañuelo* before the first *chupinazo* (rocket blast); tie it around your wrist to keep it safe. Also, the plaza can get unbearably packed; wear closed-toed shoes and prepare to get up close and personal with hundreds of fellow revelers. As the mayor emerges, fires the awaited *chupinazo* from the balcony, and screams "People of Pamplona! Long live *San Fermín!*" in Spanish and Basque, a howl explodes from the sea of red triangles in the plaza below. Champagne (and corks) rains along with eggs, ketchup, wine, flour, and yellow *pimiento*. Within minutes the streets of the *casco antiguo* flood with improvised singing and dancing troupes. The *peñas*, societies more concerned with beer than bullfighting, lead the hysteria. At 5pm on the 7th and at 9 or 9:30am every other day, they are joined by the *Comparsa de Gigantes y Cabezudos*, a troupe of beloved *gigantes* (giant wooden monarchs) and *zaldikos* (courtiers on horseback). *Kilikis* (swollen-headed buffoons) run around chasing little kids and hitting them with play clubs. These misfits, together with the city band and church and town officials, escort *San Fermín* on his triumphant procession through the *casco antiguo*, serenading him with a *jota*, the local folk song. The saint's 15th-century statue is brought from the Iglesia de San Lorenzo at 10am on July 7, the actual *Día de San Fermín;* in exchange for this promenade, he is asked to protect the runners of the *encierro*, who sing to him three times before their fateful sprint. (Virtually everything closes on July 7 and July 11; hours listed refer only to July 6, 8-10, and 12-14.)

THE RUNNING OF THE BULLS

The *encierro* (running of the bulls), is the highlight of *San Fermín*. The ritual dates back to the 14th century, when it served the practical function of getting the bulls from their corrals to the bullring, until someone decided it would be fun to run in front of—not behind—the bulls. These days, the first and grandest *encierro* of the festival is at 8am on July 7 and is repeated every day for the next seven. Hundreds of bleary-eyed, hyper-adrenalized runners flee from large bulls with even larger horns, as smart bystanders cheer from barricades, windows, and balconies.

A rocket marks the release of the bulls and another announces that all the bulls have left the enclosure into the 825m course. Six to nine animals are released from their pens as runners scurry away ahead of them. If you want to participate in the bullring excitement without the risk of running with the beasts, you can line up by the Pl. de Toros well before 7:30am and run in before the bulls are even in sight (though such a "cowardly" act will bring booing from the locals). Three to six steers accompany the bulls—watch out, they have horns, too. Both the bulls and the mob are dangerous, and lately overcrowding has resulted in the bulls actually getting blockaded by the masses. Runners, all convinced the bull is right behind them, flee for dear life and act without concern for those around them. Experienced runners, many of whom view the event as an athletic art form, try to get as close to the bull as possible. The course has three sharp turns, which the bulls often have difficulty cornering; when their legs slide out from under them, they falter, creating a pile of bull. Avoid outside corners to prevent getting crushed under said pile, and be especially careful at the Mercaderes-Estafeta corner.

After the final dangerously downward-sloping stretch (alcoves where runners can seek refuge are placed here for a reason) the run cascades through a perilously narrow opening (where a large proportion of injuries occur), and pours into the bullring amid shouts and cries from appreciative spectators. After the bulls have been safely rounded into their pens inside the Pl. de Toros, less dangerous black cows are released into the ring to "play" with the mass of 350 people. The safer alternative is to follow Hemingway's example: don't run—watch the *encierro* from the bullring instead. Music, waves, chanting, and dancing pump up spectators until the headline entertainment arrives. Bullring spectators should arrive around 6:45am. Tickets for the *Grada* section are available at 7am (M-F €3.80, Sa-Su €4.40). You can watch for free, but the free section is overcrowded, and it can be hard to see and breathe.

To watch one of the actual bullfights, you must wait in the line that forms at the bullring around 6:30pm every evening; earlier is always better. As one day of bullfighting ends, tickets go on sale for the next one. (Tickets vary depending on the day, starting at €5 for the Andanada section and rising up to €888; check www.feriadeltoro.com for detailed prices.) Cheaper, more subdued spectacles occur in the days preceding and following *San Fermín*—bargain with the scalpers outside the bullring for the best price (€5-13). Though the *sol* section can get hot, it is cheaper, closer, and generally more fun, as it is where the *peñas* are located, loudly making their opinion on the *toreador*'s performance known.

THE PARTYING OF THE PARTICIPANTS

Once the running is over, the insanity spills into the streets, gathering steam until nightfall, when it explodes with singing in bars, dancing in alleys, spontaneous parades, and a no-holds-barred party in Pl. del Castillo, which quickly becomes a huge open-air dance floor. The attire for this dance-a-thon includes sturdy, closed-toed shoes (there's glass everywhere), white t-shirt and pants or skirt (soon to be wine-soaked), a red *pañuelo* (bandana), and a cheap bottle of champagne (to spray, of course; don't pay more than €3). English speakers often congregate where C. Estafeta hits Pl. de Toros, at an outdoor consortium of local *discotecas*. A word to the wise: avoid the fountain-jumping (you'll know it when you see it); it is stupid. It is *not* a traditional part of the festivities—it was inaugurated by Americans, Aussies, and Kiwis, and several people have died in recent years. The truly inspired partying takes place the first few days of *San Fermín*. After that, crowds thin out, and the atmosphere goes from dangerously crazed to mildly insane. After the peak of deafening noise takes place at the midnight march of the Estruendo "band," (if a cacophonous amalgamation of eardrum-shattering sounds counts as a band), the party begins (or ends) each day at 6am, when bands with shrill trumpets march down the streets, waking everyone for the running. The city eases the transition with tamer concerts, outdoor dances, including a popular folk festival at 1pm on July 6 in Pl. de los Fueros, a mule and horse procession, a rural sports fes-

ARAGÓN, LA RIOJA, AND NAVARRA

RUN FOR YOUR LIFE. So, you're going to run with the bulls (keep in mind it's 18 and up only, and it's suggested you be physically fit with good reflexes). Partaking in the encierro gives you a lifetime of bragging rights, but those who decide to run should seriously consider the risks involved. Some have been gored to death (the last fatality was an inexperienced American in 1995), and each day, gruesome newspaper photos of injuries are posted for all to behold. If you choose to run, try to prevent ending up on evening news programs around the world and heed a few words of San Fermín wisdom:

Research the *encierro* before you run. The tourist office dispenses a pamphlet that outlines the exact route of the 850m, 4min. run and offers tips for inexperienced runners. You should also watch it once on TV to get a glimpse of what you're in for, and then once in person, if possible.

It's a long course, and running the whole thing safely while evading six bulls running 24km per hr. and avoiding the mobs is nearly impossible. You must choose beforehand which part of the route (usually 50m) is most suitable for you (avoid the first stretch, the Cuesta de Santo Domingo, which, with its sharp slope, favors the bulls' longer hind legs over yours; most runners start at the Ayuntamiento, midway through the course), and wait at the appropriate entrance point behind the barriers. Make sure you know where you're pulling out (always on the same side you entered), and don't stop there—others behind you want to get out just as badly, and they won't hesitate to trample you. If you are doing the final stretch, run all the way into the bullring, get behind the fence, and make room for others. At this point, let the bulls be.

Do not stay up all night carousing. Not surprisingly, hung-over or still drunk foreigners have the highest injury rate. Experienced runners get a good night's sleep and arrive no later than 7am. Many locals arrive at 6am. The course closes at 7:30am.

Wear proper clothing (the snazzy red-and-white garb with nothing loose or baggy) and shoes. Do not carry anything with you (especially a backpack or video camera).

Give up on getting near the bulls and concentrate on getting to the bullring in one piece. Although some whack the bull with rolled newspapers, the point is to defy the animals from a distance, never distracting or touching them; anyone who does is likely to anger the bull and locals alike.

Try not to cower in a doorway or stand in corners or blind bends; people have been trapped and killed this way.

Be particularly wary of isolated bulls—they seek company in the crowds.

Run straight ahead (never, ever stop) the entire time; think of how appreciative you'd be if someone cut you off and caused you to trip.

If you fall, **stay down.** Curl up into a fetal position, lock your hands behind your head, and **do not get up** until the clatter of hooves has passed.

tival, funfairs, bull-leaping and swerving demonstrations in the bullring, and other performances. To catch an important event that doesn't involve binge-drinking, check out the Pamplona Cathedral Choir performance of the Vespers, a religious song just for the occasion, at 8pm on July 6 in the chapel of *San Fermín*. The festivities culminate at midnight on July 14 with the singing of *Pobre de mí:* "*Pobre de mí, pobre de mí, que se han acabado las Fiestas de San Fermín*" (Poor me, poor me, the festivals of *San Fermín* have ended).

Attending all eight days of the festival is a challenge. Noisy crowds and increasingly disturbing street odors drive many away after a few days. But if you want more, several nearby towns sponsor *encierros:* **Tudela** has its festival the week of

July 24, **Tafalla** celebrates the week of Aug. 15, and **Sangüesa** during the second week of September. Many *pamploneses* take part in a festival less touristed than their own, but the majority begins a countdown to the celebration on New Year's.

◪ DAYTRIPS FROM PAMPLONA

▨ LUMBIER GORGES

Río Irati buses (☎ 948 30 35 70) run to Lumbier from Pamplona (1hr., M-Th 3 per day 1-7pm, F 1 and 7pm, Sa 1:30pm; return M-F 7:30am and 2:30pm, Sa 9:45am; €3). The Centro de la Interpretación de las Foces in Pl. Mayor in Lumbier provides more info on the gorges; ask about guided tours. Open June 16-Sept.15 Tu-Su 10am-2pm and 4:30-8:30pm; Sept. 16-June 15 Tu-Th 10am-2pm, F-Su 10am-2pm and 4:30-7:30pm. €1.20, over 65 and under 18 free. From Lumbier to Iso, it's a 12km walk, drive, or taxi ride down NA-178 in the direction of Domeño. Pedro Iso taxi ☎ 636 48 58 50. Parking at Foz de Lumbier is €1.50.

Over millions of years, two fantastic gorges were carved by the flow of rivers through the mountains near Pamplona. Outside the little town of Lumbier, the **Foz de Lumbier** (Lumbier Gorge) drops 50-150m down to the Río Irati over a length of 1.3km, and a path alongside leads through old railway tunnels. There are two marked walking routes. Starting at the parking lot is a 2.6km walk through the interior of the gorge on the old Irati Railroad route and its tunnels (a flashlight for the curved tunnels would not hurt, but isn't necessary). At the end of the route you will see the one-arched 17th-century **Puente del Diablo** (Devil's Bridge, 4km). Destroyed by the French in the 1812 War of Independence, its name comes from a legend that its creator invoked the devil to help him finish such a difficult feat. Adjacent are the ruins of a Roman village. From here you can retrace your steps to the parking lot. The second, also easy, 5.5km option (with a 175m altitude change) departs from the parking lot as well, to the left of the gorge (following the N-113 signs) and circumnavigates the gorge, returning through the inside to see the tunnels and Puente del Diablo found along the shorter walks. Stop along the mostly flat, well-marked path at **Corral de Atzuela** (1.2km) during the first half to take in an astounding view. The entire path is well-marked with white and green signs. Just before the town of Iso, 12km down the road, the even more impressive **Foz de Arbayún** cuts a chasm through to the river below. The Mirador de Iso, by the NA-178, affords glimpses of the 250 pairs of swooping griffin vultures that live here, while a small footpath below follows the Río Salazar toward its source.

CASTILLO DE JAVIER

La Tafallesa (☎ 948 22 28 86) runs a bus from Pamplona to Javier (1hr.; M-F 5pm, Sa 1pm; €3.70). Buses return M-Sa 8am. A taxi (☎ 948 87 03 09) from Sangüesa costs approx. €10 plus the wait. Buses to Sangüesa on La Veloz Sangüesina (☎ 948 87 02 09; M-Sa 3 per day 1-8pm; Su 8:15pm; €3.50) return to Pamplona (3 per day 8am-6:30pm, €3.50). Castillo de Javier ☎ 948 88 40 00.

Near the entrance to the small village of Javier, 8km from Sangüesa, is the majestic 11th-century **Castillo de Javier,** the birthplace of San Francisco Javier (St. Francis Xavier), one of the first Jesuits and the patron saint of Navarra. This picture-perfect castle on the strategic border between the kingdoms of Navarra and Aragón changed hands numerous times over the last millennium, landing finally in the Jesuits' possession. Its **Chapel of the Holy Christ** houses a 14th-century effigy that is said to have suffered a spontaneous blood-sweating fit at the moment of San Francisco Javier's death. The Castillo de Javier is undergoing extensive renovation but is expected to reopen in late summer. The adjoining 19th-century Basílica de Javier is still open before mass. (M-Sa 8:30am and 1pm, Su 1 and 6pm. Free.)

SANGÜESA   ☎948

It is said of Sangüesa (pop. 4600) that there is a monument on every street. Granted, that's not difficult in a town with so few streets, but Sangüesa is indeed a city full of history and culture. Situated in the middle of Navarra, 45km southeast of Pamplona, Sangüesa was founded by Alfonso el Batallador in the 11th century, so that the kingdom would have an important town on the Camino de Santiago. Sangüesa was ultimately catapulted into a mandatory stop on the pilgrimage, as its twelve historical hospitals attest. Today, some of Sangüesa's streets seem untouched by time, and the pilgrims (and tourists in the know) continue to pour in. With its serene riverside location and richly historical buildings, it is a rewarding stop for both sacred and secular tourists.

▐▀▐▌ TRANSPORTATION AND PRACTICAL INFORMATION. Buses stop across from the tourist office where C. Mayor meets the river. **Veloz Sangüesina Buses** (☎948 87 02 09) run from **Pamplona** (45min.; M-Sa 3 per day 1-8pm, Su 8:15pm; return buses M-Sa 3 per day 8am-6:30pm, Su 7:15pm; €3.10). **Gómez** (☎976 67 55 29) runs to **Zaragoza** (M-F 6:50am). For **taxis** call ☎948 87 00 85.

On the banks of the Río Aragón, Sangüesa consists basically of the main C. Mayor, perpendicular to the river and leading to the bridge, and the six streets that intersect it. From the bus stop, walk away from the river to reach most accommodations, sights, and restaurants. The **tourist office**, C. Mayor, 2, has a **map** and other regional information. (☎/fax 948 87 14 11; oit.sanguesa@cfnavarra.es. English and French spoken. Open May-Sept. M-Sa 10am-2pm and 4-7pm, Su 10am-2pm; Oct.-Apr. M-F 10am-5pm, Sa-Su 10am-2pm.) Local services include: **Banco Santander Central Hispano,** C. Mayor, 41 (☎902 24 24 24; open Apr.-Sept. M-F 8:30am-2pm; Oct.-Mar. M-F 8:30am-2pm, Sa 8:30am-1pm); **municipal police** (☎948 43 00 04), in the Ayuntamiento on C. Mayor, a block up from the tourist office; **Centro de Salud** (☎948 87 14 41), on Po. de Cantolagua by the campgrounds; **Internet access** at **Elicad,** C. Fermín de Lubián, 15, next to the **post office.** (☎948 87 09 80; www.elicad.com. €3 per hr. Open M-F 4-11pm, Sa-Su 11am-1pm and 4-11pm.)

▐▛▐▘ ACCOMMODATIONS AND FOOD. Lodging is limited in Sangüesa, but the few options available make up for their shortcomings with friendly service and a small-town feel. **Pensión Las Navas ❶,** C. Alfonso el Batallador, 7, one block up from the tourist office, is the most affordable option. Ask for a room with an outside window. (☎948 87 00 77. Singles €14, with bath €18; doubles €28/€36. MC/V.) Across the bridge from the tourist office, **Hostal J.P. ❷,** C. Padre Raimundo Lumbier, 3, offers spacious rooms with TV and full bath. (☎948 87 16 93; www.ciberwebs.com/jp. Breakfast €3.90. Singles €30; doubles €44. Extra bed €15, under 14 €12. IVA not included. MC/V.) To take advantage of Sangüesa's serene riverfront, **Camping Cantolagua ❶,** Camino de Cantolagua, just a 10min. walk along the river to the left when facing the bridge, is a great option. (☎948 43 03 52/87 13 13; www.mardelpirineo.com. €3.50 per person, €3 per child; €3.50 per tent, €4.50 per large tent; €3.50 per car; €10.80 per site. Doubles with shared bath €36; quads with kitchen €54; bungalows for 5 €72.20. MC/V.)

Restaurant options are limited to a few tapas bars along C. Mayor and the perpendicular streets C. Santiago and C. Alfonso el Batallador. Groceries are available at **Autoservicios Gallo,** C. Fermín de Ripalda, three blocks to the left on C. Alfonso el Batallador from C. Mayor. (Open M-F 9am-1:30pm and 5-8pm, Sa 9am-2pm.) **Las Navas ❷,** C. Alfonso el Batallador, 7, offers a delicious and filling *menú del día* (weekdays €10, weekends €14.50) and friendly service alongside cheerful poker-playing retirees. (☎948 87 00 77. Open daily 1-2:30pm and 8-11pm. MC/V.)

Acuario ❷, C. Santiago, 9, is a friendly bar with a *menú del día* (€8.50, €7 for pilgrims). The €12 jar of sangria would make any pilgrim forget where he was heading. (☎948 87 01 02. Salads €5, gazpacho €4.25. Open daily 8am-11pm.)

🔲 **SIGHTS. Sangüesa Tours,** C. Mayor, 1, in the back of the Iglesia Santa María la Real across from the tourist office, offers guided tours of monuments (5-6 per day, €1.80) and of the entire town (5 per day, €3.50); this is also the only way to visit the Convento de San Francisco and its museum. (☎620 11 05 81. Open M-Sa 10am-2pm and 4-6:30pm.) **Iglesia de Santa María la Real** was constructed in the 13th and 14th centuries and has a sculpted stone facade worth checking out. (Across from the tourist office. Open daily 10am-1:30pm and 4:30-6:30pm. €1.80; ages 12-18, pilgrims, and retired €1.40; under 12 free.) One block up, through the Pl. de las Arcadas to the left, is the 13th-century **Palacio-Castillo del Príncipe de Viana,** once home to Navarra's last royal couple, Juan de Labrit and Catalina de Foix. Now it just houses the public library. (Open June 15-Sept.15 M-F 8:30am-2:30pm; Sept. 16-June 14 M-F 3-9pm. Free.) The **Iglesia de Santiago,** at the end of C. Santiago, could easily be mistaken for a fortress. (Open 30min. before mass M-F 8:30pm, Su noon and 8pm. Free.) Lastly, the **Palacio de Ongay-Vallesantoro** displays a unique blend of Baroque elements with Mexican and Peruvian colonial art; look up to see the interesting roof details. The interior houses rotating cultural exhibits. (Open M-F 8am-2pm. Exhibit room open Tu-Sa 7-9pm; holidays noon-2pm. Free.)

🔲 **FESTIVALS.** One of the largest in the vicinity, Sangüesa's **Fiestas Patronales** (Sept. 11-17) in honor of San Sebastián, its patron saint, draw crowds from nearby towns. *Encierros,* processions, music, and, of course, lots of wine and merrymaking, ensue. During the town-wide **medieval dinners,** on select Fridays from July to August, every detail from the food to the entertainment transports you back in time. (Info ☎948 87 02 51. €40 per person.) January 6 brings the **Three Kings** reenactment, while January 20 is the actual **Día de San Sebastián,** though he is more enthusiastically revered during the Fiestas Patronales.

OLITE ☎948

Small Olite (pop. 3000) was once the home of Navarran kings—most notably Carlos III—and it still retains a regal air about it. Locals are proud of Olite for its charming, manicured beauty—after all, they point out, it was the city of kings. It has markedly resisted commercialization and expansion, except in 1347, when the old town moved past its Roman walls into the outskirts, resulting in the rounded shape it has today. Olite's appeal extends beyond its courtly past—it is the wine capital of Navarra. With spotless plazas and peaceful, winding streets, Olite possesses an allure that those in the know appreciate, yet it remains a hidden treasure for most visitors to the area. It has a surprising amount of sights for its size, but, above all, it serves as the perfect idyllic location to kick back, choose which vice to enjoy—wine or pastries?—and watch time screech to a halt.

🔳🔳 **TRANSPORTATION AND PRACTICAL INFORMATION. Trains** (☎948 70 06 28) run to: **Pamplona** (40min.; M-Th and Sa 3 per day 7:58am-4:05pm, F 4 per day 7:58am-5:40pm, Su 3 per day 1:05pm-7:27pm; €2.50) via **Tafella** (5min., €1.30); **Zaragoza** (1½hr.; 5:17pm, Su also 7:39pm; €7) via **Tudela** (45min., €3.10) and other points on the **Vitoria-Gasteiz-Zaragoza** line. To get from the station to **Plaza de Carlos III** in the center of town, take C. de la Estación to Bar Orly, walk through the archway, and follow R. de San Francisco past **Plaza de los Teobaldos** through another arch to Plaza de Carlos III. **Buses** are cheaper and more convenient. **Conda** (☎948 22 10 26) and **La Tafallesa** (☎948 22 28 86) both run buses to **Pamplona** (45min.; M-F

10 per day 6:45am-6:30pm, Sa 8 per day 7:55am-6:30pm, Su 7 per day 8:15am-8pm; €2.60-2.70). Buses out of Pamplona to Tudela and Zaragoza stop at Olite approximately 30min. after their departure. Conda stops at Bar Orly; to reach Pl. de Carlos III, see the directions from the train station. La Tafallesa arrives a block away. To reach Bar Orly, follow **Rúa Romana** left (past Bodega Cooperativo Olitense and Bodega Carricas). **Taxis** (☎948 74 01 43) are available at the end of R. de San Francisco, before Pl. de Carlos III. The **tourist office** is located in Pl. Teobaldos in the Museo del Vino, on the corner to the left when coming from the buses on R. de San Francisco. (☎/fax 948 74 17 03; oit.olite@cfnavarra.es. Open Apr.-Sept. M-F 10am-7pm, Sa 10am-2pm and 4-7pm, Su 10am-2pm; Oct.-Mar. M-F 10am-5pm, Sa-Su 10am-2pm.) **Guiarte,** located on the corner of R. Mayor on Pl. de Carlos III, offers guided tours of Olite in English (1½hr. "Secrets of Olite" includes all monuments, Roman and medieval, the two churches, and R. Mayor) and the surrounding natural areas. (R. Mayor. ☎948 74 12 73; www.guiartenavarra.com. €3.30, longer tour €4.25.) Local services include: **Banco Santander Central Hispano,** R. de Medios, 4 (☎902 24 24 24; open M-F 8:30am-2pm, Sa 8:30am-1pm); **Centro de Salud** (☎948 74 17 01) at the opposite end of R. de Medios from Pl. de Carlos III, to the left; **Internet access** at **Cyber Camelot,** R. de Medios, 4, off Pl. de Carlos III (€2.50 per hr.; open daily 11am-1pm and 7-11pm, closed W evening); the **post office,** R. Portillo, 3, across the plaza from the palace. (☎948 74 05 82. Open M-Sa 8:30-11am.) **Postal Code:** 31390.

⌐▢ ACCOMMODATIONS AND FOOD. Olite's courtly airs are preserved in menu and accommodations prices everywhere. The sole exception is the 4 spacious and bright rooms above **Restaurante Gambarte ❷,** R. del Seco, 15, off Pl. de Carlos III, which share a clean common bath. The restaurant serves a filling 2-course *menú* for €9. (☎948 74 01 39. Restaurant open M-Th 1-3:30pm, F-Su 1-4:30pm and 8:30-10:30pm. Meat and fish entrees €10-15. Singles €16; doubles €25. MC/V.) The pricier, medieval-flavored rooms of **Hotel García Ramírez ❺,** R. de Medios, 1, on the plaza, all have satellite TV, fan, private bath, phone, and mini-bar; splurging on the rooms with large balconies onto the Pl. de Carlos III is well worth it. (☎948 74 13 00; www.hotelgarciaramirez.com. Breakfast €3. July-Aug. doubles €64, with balcony €75; Sept.-June €47/€64. AmEx/MC/V.) The extraordinary medieval **dining room** offers a *menú* (M-F) for €10.50 and a larger *menú* (Sa-Su) for €15. (Open daily 1-4pm and 9-11pm. Adjoining Café-Bar Ducay open daily 8am-11pm. MC/V.) The extravagant Parador Nacional, **Príncipe de Viana ❾,** Pl. de los Teobaldos, 2, housed in the 16th-century medieval castle, contains details like tapestries and stained-glass windows that transport you back in time. Alternatively, you can splurge on a meal (€24) in its luxurious **restaurant.** (☎948 74 00 00; www.parador.es. Breakfast €9.70. Mar.-Oct. doubles €107; suites €122. Nov.-Feb. €94/€110. AmEx/MC/V.) **Camping Olite ❶** is 1km outside of town heading south on C. Santa Brígida from Bar Orly, which becomes GR1; another option is to head on Ctra. N-115 toward Peralta, and it will be at km 2300. (☎948 74 06 04; colite@can.es. €3.30 per person and per car, €2.75 per child, €3.70 per tent; 5-person bungalows €55. AmEx/MC/V.)

At ▧ **Casa Vidaurre, Obredor Artesano ❶,** C de la Estación, 3, the Vidaurre family has been making delicious pastries, cakes, and candies since 1900. You can sample all of these, as well as a wide selection of local wines and homemade meats, cheeses, and preserves at the in-house cafe, a bright, simple mix of old and new architectural styles. (☎948 74 05 79. Coffee, roll, and juice €3.75. Desserts €1.20. Coffee €1. Open Tu-Sa 7:30am-3pm and 4:30-10pm. MC/V.) Several restaurant-cafes line Pl. de Carlos III, charging exorbitant amounts for palace-side seating. Venture down R. de Mirapies (a block down R. Mayor) to **Asador Pizzería Casa del Preboste ❷,** R. de Mirapies, 8, for affordable pizzas (€6.40-9.50) or nighttime drinks in a friendly atmosphere. (Meat entrees €9.80-13, fish €9-18. M-F *menú* €10, Sa-Su larger *menú* €15. Open M-F noon-4:30pm and 8pm-12:30am, Sa-Su noon-2am. AmEx/MC/V.) **Supermarkets** line C. Mayor off Pl. de Carlos III, including **Coviran Supermarket,** C. Mayor, 9; an **Ali-7-Ahorro** food store is at R. de San Francisco, 31.

◪ **SIGHTS.** Medieval Olite's ◪**Palacio Real** was the 15th-century home of Carlos III (1387-1425) and his court, not to mention one of the most luxurious European palaces of its time. Though the town's 1937 restoration was far from subtle, the palace's three towers and spiral staircases are great fun to explore, reminiscent of many a childhood fairy tale. (☎948 74 00 35. Guided tours in English and Spanish Sa-Su every hr. Open July-Aug. daily 10am-2pm and 4-8pm; Apr.-June and Sept. daily 10am-2pm and 4-7pm; Oct.-Mar. M-Sa 10am-2pm and 4-6pm, Su 10am-2pm and 4-6:30pm; *Semana Santa* and holidays daily 10am-7pm. Guiarte offers guided tours. €2.70; over 65 and ages 6-13 €1.80; under 5 free.) The **Museo del Vino,** Pl. de los Teobaldos, 10, houses artful exhibits dedicated as much to the aesthetics of vines, wines, and winemaking as to wine-making's history and traditions. From Bar Orly, head up R. de San Francisco. (☎948 74 07 54; www.centrodelvino.com. Open W-Su 10:30am-2pm and 4:30-8pm, Tu 4:30-8pm. €3.50, over 65 and ages 6-13 €1.50, under 5 free.) Between the Palacio Real and the Castillo Viejo at the base of Pl. de los Teobaldos is the Gothic **Iglesia de Santa María,** noted for its intricately sculpted facade and Renaissance belfry. (Open before mass M-Sa 9:30-10am, Su 10:30-11am and 6-6:30pm. Guided tours available. Free.) The equally beautiful medieval **Iglesia de San Pedro,** Pl. del Dosal, stands out for its cloister, Roman facade, and its elegant pointy tower. (Follow R. Mayor for 2 blocks to R. de San Pedro, and it will be to the left on the end. Open M-Sa 6:30-7pm, Su 9:30-10am and noon-12:30pm. Free. Guiarte offers 20min. guided tours every 30min.; €1.80.). The **Galerías Medievales,** dating to the 16th-century, down the stairs in the center of Pl. de Carlos III, house exhibitions on Olite's medieval court and life back in the day. (☎948 74 18 85. Open M 10am-3pm and 5-8pm, Tu-F 10am-3pm and 5-7pm, Sa 11am-2pm and 5-7pm, Su 10am-3pm and 5-8pm. €1.50, includes guided tour.)

▓ **FESTIVALS.** Equally proud of its past and present, Olite puts both on display: **Las Fiestas Patronales,** around Sept. 13-19, are a miniature, tamer version of *San Fermín,* with *encierros,* live music, and the like. September 5th brings the **Fiesta Vendimia,** the perfect occasion to celebrate

IN RECENT NEWS

THE 130-MILLION-YEAR SIESTA

Clearing stones from their almond orchards in the province of Aragón, the farmers of Riodeva, were unaware that they were tossing aside parts from a trail of dinosaur bones. It took a pair of paleontologists to identify their precious findings, and digging began in early 2003 to see how good it would get. They were not disappointed—they found the largest dinosaur ever unearthed in Europe, including an upper limb bone as big as 6 ft. The entire skeleton was 114 ft. long and weighed 40 to 50 tons (that's seven elephants). Dating back to 130 million years ago when what is now Spain enjoyed wet, tropical weather, much of its remains are perfectly preserved, including toe bones and a nail bigger than a human hand. The evidence points to it being a Sauropod, a bird-brained vegetarian.

The province of Teruel was known as a region rich in fossils, but the largest dinosaurs are typically found in the Americas and Asia, not here. Spain's first dinosaur was discovered in the Teruel region, and Riodeva's new potential for the field brings a tear to many a paleontologist's eye. If you don't have the patience to comb through the dirt yourself, maybe the nearby dinosaur theme park **Dinopolis** will satisfy your curiosity; if anything, you'll help fund the discoverers digging away under the sun, as profits from the park go to them.

the many wines of Olite, including *verjus*, the sour local specialty. Ideal for families, **Las Festivales Medievales,** for three days during the last week of August, seek to recreate the splendor of Carlos III's royal court and are reason enough for the entire town to decorate itself medieval-style, garb and all: it features a fair complete with crafts, concerts, knights, witches, magicians, and knight face-offs (including archery), along with a royal parade. Lastly, perfect for Shakespeare aficionados, the **Classic Theatre Festival** (☎ 948 74 17 03) takes place during the third and fourth weeks of August.

ESTELLA
☎ 948

Hiding between the cities of Logroño and Pamplona, charming Estella (pop. 13,000) rests in a bend of the Río Ega. What it lacks in size and glamor it makes up for in hospitality toward the faithful. With telltale walking sticks in hand, pilgrims traversing the Camino de Santiago have been descending on Estella since the town's founding in 1090. Sancho Ramírez reworked the route to include this historic town because the medieval pilgrim found there "good bread, excellent wine, and an abundance in meat and fish." You can still find all of these, and, with an appealing plaza, mellow cafes, and a pastry shop on every corner, the town also makes a perfect place to stay for other, somewhat more dazed pilgrims—it's a great alternative if you can't find Pamplona accommodations for *San Fermín*.

■ ▐ **ORIENTATION AND PRACTICAL INFORMATION.** Two streets intersect at the heart of town. **Calle San Andrés/Baja Navarra** runs north-south from the bus station on Pl. de la Coronación to the **Plaza de los Fueros,** while **Paseo de la Inmaculada** runs east-west from C. Dr. Huarte de San Juan and **Avenida de Yerri** to the **Puente del Azucarero.** Another main road, **Calle Mayor/Zapatería/Ruiz de Alda/Espoz y Mina,** runs parallel to Po. de la Inmaculada one block away and is the main commercial hub. The river divides the city disproportionately, and the older sites, along with the tourist office, are on the other, smaller side. To reach the bridge from the bus station, go right and follow C. Sancho el Sabio to the river and across the bridge; turn left on the other side and the **Plaza de San Martín** with its Renaissance Fuente de los Chorros will be on the right. The tourist office is by the other side of the plaza, to the right in front of the large church.

La Estellesa buses (☎ 948 55 01 27) leave from the **station** (☎ 948 32 65 09) on Pl. de la Coronación to: **Logroño** (1hr., 8-12 per day 8:30am-8:45pm, €3.70); **Pamplona** (1hr.; 7-8 per day M-Sa 7am-8pm, Su 4 per day 11am-8pm; €3.20); **San Sebastián** (1½-2hr., 6 per day 8:45am-7:45pm, €8.90); **Zaragoza** (2½hr., M-Sa 8:30am, €11.70). Check the second page of the local newspaper, *Noticias,* for daily schedules and destinations. The **tourist office,** C. San Nicolás, 1, is straight across the Puente del Azucarero (or to the left if crossing from the bus station) through Pl. de San Martín; look for the red sign across from the elevated church. Offers accommodation listings and map of restaurants, along with map of city. (☎/fax 948 55 63 01; oit.estella@cfnavarra.es. Open daily 10am-2pm and 4-7pm.) Tours of the San Pedro de la Rúa and San Miguel churches (30min. each; 5 per day; €2.20, both €3.50; pilgrims €2.05/€3.25; children €1.85/€2.85) as well as a general monuments visit (daily 12:15 and 5:15pm; €3.85, pilgrims €3.50, children €3.15) can be arranged through **Cultura 5,** C. San Nicolás, 3, across the hall from the tourist office (☎ 948 55 00 70). The **police,** Po. de la Inmaculada, 1, are inside the modern Ayuntamiento. **Medical attention** (☎ 948 55 10 11) is available at the opposite end of Po. de la Inmaculada from the river, and at the **Hospital Comarcal** (☎ 948 54 80 00). Nighttime **pharmacy** shifts (until 10pm) rotate but general hours are 9am-1:30pm and 4:30-8pm, Sa 9am-1:30pm. The **library,** C. Ruiz de Alda, 34-36, provides free **Internet** on four computers to patient patrons; drop by to reserve a 30min. slot. (☎948 55 64 19. Open July-Sept. 8:30am-2:30pm; Oct.-June M-F 9am-9pm.) The cafe **La Aljama,** to the left when exiting the tourist office, has a few terminals. (€3 per hr. Open 1:30-4pm and 7-9pm. MC/V.) The **post office** is at Po. de la Inmaculada, 5. (☎948 55 17 92. Open M-F 8:30am-2:30pm, Sa 9:30am-1pm.) **Postal Code:** 31200.

⊓ ⊓ ACCOMMODATIONS AND CAMPING. With its proximity to Pamplona, Estella is a good place to catch some shut-eye during *San Fermín.* Reservations are advisable then and during its own *encierro* (running of the bulls) the first week of August. Straight out from the bus station, follow C. San Andrés to C. Mayor and turn left to find **Pensión San Andrés ❶,** C. Mayor, 1. Rustic but airy, bright, and impeccably clean rooms have TVs, and some have refrigerators. Balconies overlooking the peaceful plaza below become exhilarating lookout points during the *encierro.* (☎948 55 41 58. Singles €12-21, with bath €21-23; doubles €24-27/€32-35; triples with bath €40; quads with bath €50. IVA not included. MC/V.) The spacious wood-floored rooms of **Hostal Cristina ❹,** C. Baja Navarra on the corner of Pl. de los Fueros, come with large windows, baths, and TVs. (☎948 55 04 50; fax 55 07 72. July-Aug. and *Semana Santa* singles €35; doubles €45. Sept.-June singles €35; doubles €39; triples €52-56.) From the left of the tourist office, it's 1km (20min.) downriver and past the factory to **Camping Lizarra ❶,** C. Ordoiz; let the Pamplona bus driver know and he'll stop. The grounds include a supermarket, pool, laundry, playground, money exchange, horseback-riding, fishing, an 18-bed hostel, and a bar. (☎948 55 17 33; www.campinglizarra.com. Open year-round. €3.80 per person, €3.40 per child; €3.80 per tent; €10.30 per *parcela* (plot with room for tent and car), €7 per smaller plot; hostel bunks €6.20. MC/V.)

⊓ FOOD. Estella is known throughout the region for its *gorrín asado* (roast piglet, also called *gorrín de Estella*). For groceries, head to **Alimentación Choma,** C. Mayor, 93. (Open M-F 7am-1:30pm and 5:30-8, Sa-Su 7am-2pm.) Save fresh fruit and vegetable shopping for the numerous fruit vendors along C. Mayor. More importantly, save a little cash for the sublime **La Mallorquina,** C. Mayor, 63, a pastry and sweets shop. (Open M-Sa 9am-2pm and 5-9pm, Su 9am-3pm.) The overwhelming portions of regional food served upstairs at **Restaurante Casanova ❷,** C. Obispo Oñate, 7, are sure to slow any pilgrim's progress. Entering Pl. de los Fueros from C. Baja Navarra, take the first left and look for the wooden sign. (☎948 55 28 09. *Menú* M-F €8.40, Sa-Su €14.50. Fish and meat entrees €5.50-18. Open M 1-3:30pm, Tu-Su 1-3:30pm and 8-11pm. MC/V.) **Asador Astarriaga ❹,** Pl. de los Fueros, 12, offers Navarran fare on the wide plaza. Offers *gorrín* (€12.70) and various other meat entrees (€10-15) including rack of lamb. (☎948 55 00 32. Fish entrees €11-19. *Menú* M-F €10.70, F-Sa €18. Open daily 1-4pm and 9-11pm; closed Su night. MC/V.) For a more economical alternative, try the *chorizo* or other *bocadillos* (€1.50) at the homey but polished **Café-Bar Lerma ❶,** Po. de la Inmaculada, between C. San Andrés/Baja Navarra and C. Escultor Imberto. (*Bocadillos* from €1.50; beer €1.50; fresh orange juice, coffee, and pastry €2.50. Open daily 8am-11pm.)

⊓ ⊓ SIGHTS AND ENTERTAINMENT. Next to the tourist office, the world's oldest representation of medieval French hero Roland jousts with Farragut the Moor on the columns of the 12th-century Romanesque **Palacio de los Reyes de Navarra,** the city's "architectural jewel" and now the **Museo Gustavo de Maetzu.** Inside are the impressive and uniquely styled works of painter Gustavo de Maetzu, who spent his last years in Estella. (☎948 54 60 37; fax 55 32 57. Open Tu-Sa 11am-1pm and 5-7pm, Su 11am-1pm. Free.) The 12th-century **Iglesia de**

San Miguel commands a view of Estella from the hilltop Pl. de San Miguel, to the right after crossing the Puente del Azucarero from the tourist office. Its ornately carved stone portal depicts San Miguel fighting dragons, weighing souls, and taking care of celestial business. Opposite the tourist office, the late Romanesque-early Gothic **Iglesia de San Pedro de la Rúa,** with its half-destroyed cloister, towers above **Calle de la Rúa.** A sight in itself, Estella's **mercado,** one of the oldest in the world, takes place Thursday morning in the Pl. de los Fueros. The week-long **Fiestas de la Virgen del Puy y San Andrés** kick off the Friday before the first Sunday in August, featuring an *encierro* of baby bulls (less ferocious than Pamplona's), kiddie entertainment, a fair, Navarrese dancing, and *gaitas* (traditional instruments of northern Spain similar to bagpipes, but without the bags). July 19-25 the city's more enthusiastic residents dress up in medieval garb for **Semana Medieval,** featuring parades, concerts, an "Arab Market" with food and crafts in Pl. de Santiago, theater performances, a roaming storytelling character, and even a jousting match. To attend the city-wide Medieval Dinner on the night of the 23rd, appropriate attire is required.

PAÍS VASCO (EUSKADI)

As the Basque saying goes, "Before God was God and the rocks were rocks, the Basques were Basque." The País Vasco is officially composed of the provinces Gipuzkoa, Álava, and Vizcaya, but the Basque homeland extends into Navarra and southwestern France. The varied landscape of the País Vasco resembles a nation unto itself, with cosmopolitan cities, verdant hills, industrial wastelands, and quaint fishing villages. The people are marked by their deep attachment to the land and immense cultural and national pride. However, it is *euskera*, a language unrelated to any other in Europe, that binds and quite literally defines them. Even the Basque name for themselves, *Euskaldinuak*, means "speakers of Euskera."

Though their origins are shrouded in mystery, the Basques are thought to have descended from the first Europeans (some theories place Cro-Magnon man directly in their family line, while others argue that they migrated from Africa via the Caucasus Mountains), whose arrival predated that of the Indo-European tribes that would go on to populate the rest of Eurasia. They might once have inhabited all of Iberia; by the time of the Romans, however, they were already confined to the Pyrenees region. Under the Romans, the Basques lived semi-autonomously until the 18th-century abolishment of the Basque *fueros* (ancient rights of self-gov-

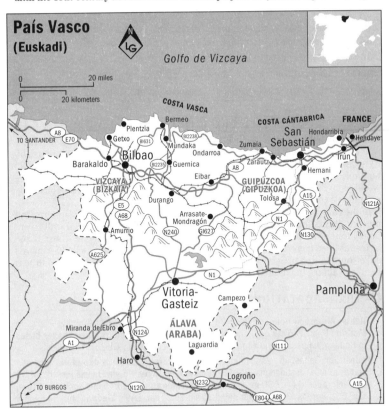

PAÍS VASCO

ernment). The Basques enjoyed a brief return to independence under the Second Spanish Republic, but the Republican defeat in the Spanish Civil War ushered in the Fascist rule of General Francisco Franco, who oppressed the Basques, banning *euskera* and other forms of cultural self-expression. In 1968, in response to such injustices, the organization *Euskadi ta Askatasuna* (ETA; "Basque Country and Freedom") began a terrorist movement that continues to exist today and has caused over 800 deaths. A short-lived 1998 cease-fire did little to quell the violence; their most recent victim was a policeman from Sangüesa in 2003. Anti-ETA sentiment is now quite strong among Basques—posters and banners denouncing the organization line streets throughout the region—but many also argue that the methods employed by the government to suppress (or exterminate) ETA undermine free speech and disregard human rights.

Most Basques share a strong desire to preserve their cultural identity. Although *castellano* is the predominant language, *euskera* has enjoyed a resurgence since Franco's death. Other regional traditions like *cesta punta* or *pelota vasca* (known outside Spain as the deathly fast sport of *jai-alai*) continue to thrive. Basque cuisine is some of Iberia's finest, including *bacalao a la vizcaína* (salt cod in tomato sauce) and dishes *a la vasca* (in parsley-steeped white wine sauce). Tapas, considered a regional specialty, are called *pintxos* (PEEN-chos); locals wash them down with *sidra* (cider) and the local white sparkling wine, *txakoli*.

HIGHLIGHTS OF PAÍS VASCO

BASK in the seaside splendor of **San Sebastián** (p. 544).

GROOVE to summer tunes at **Vitoria-Gasteiz's** International Jazz Festival (p. 565).

REFLECT on disaster and renewal at the Guernica Peace Museum (p. 560).

SEE your reflection (and some art) in the **Museo Guggenheim** in Bilbao (p. 557).

SAN SEBASTIÁN (DONOSTIA)   ☎943

San Sebastián (pop. 180,000) glitters on the shores of the Bay of Biscay. An elaborate ivory boardwalk and wide white-sand beaches give the city an air of gentility—Queen Isabel II summered here—but mask the 21st-century edge found in its boutiques, surf-shops, and nightclubs. Still, its cosmopolitan air doesn't interfere with the city's strong sense of regional culture. Residents and posters constantly remind you that you are not in Spain, you are in the Basque country.

In the early 19th century, San Sebastián stood as one of Spain's great ports, but much of it was destroyed during the 1813 Peninsular War. The ruined walls were finally torn down in 1863, and construction of a new city began, one whose popularity has been increasing ever since. Today, foreigners and land-locked Spaniards alike journey to San Sebastián in search of its world-famous beaches, countless bars, and almost unparalleled scenery.

⌐ TRANSPORTATION

Flights: Airport in Hondarribia (☎943 66 85 00), 20km east of the city. Flights to **Madrid** (1¼hr., 3-6 per day) and **Barcelona** (1¼hr., 1-4 per day). **Interurbanos buses** to Hondarribia pass by the airport (45min., every 15-20min., €1.25). A **taxi** costs €25.

Trains: San Sebastián has 2 train stations; **Euskotren, Estación de Amara,** runs *cercanías* to local destinations. **RENFE, Estación del Norte,** Po. de Francia (☎902 24 02 02). Info open daily 7:30am-11pm. To: **Barcelona** (9hr.; 10:45am, Su-F also 11pm; €33.50); **Burgos** (3½hr., 8 per day 8:32am-10:37pm, €19); **Madrid** (8hr.; Su-F 3 per day 8:32am-10:37pm, Sa 9:33am and 10:37pm; €33-41); **Paris,** France via **Hendaye** (9-11hr.; 4 per day 7:45am-10:25pm; €85); **Salamanca** (6½hr.; Su-F 3 per day 8:32am-10:20pm, Sa 1:37 and 10:20pm; €27.50-36.50); **Vitoria-Gasteiz** (1¾hr.; M-Sa 9 per day 6:57am-10:37pm, Su 8 per day 8:32am-10:37pm; €7.70-17).

Buses: San Sebastián has no actual bus station, only a platform and a series of ticket windows on Av. de Sancho el Sabio, 31-33, and Po. de Vizcaya, 16.

ALSA, Po. de Vizcaya, 16 (☎942 10 12 10), runs internationally to **Paris** (12hr., 8pm, €61).

Continental Auto, Av. de Sancho el Sabio, 31 (☎943 46 90 74). To: **Burgos** (3-3½hr., 7 per day 9am-12:30am, €13); **Madrid** (6hr., 7-9 per day 7:15am-12:30am, €26.70); **Vitoria-Gasteiz** (2hr., 8 per day 7:15am-12:30am, €6.60).

La Estellesa, Po. de Vizcaya, 16 (☎943 47 01 15), to **Logroño** (2½hr., 4 per day 8am-7pm, €13).

Transportes PESA, Av. de Sancho el Sabio, 33 (☎902 10 12 10), to **Bilbao** (1¼hr.; M-F every 30min. 6:30am-10pm, Sa every hr. 7:30am-10pm, Su every hr. 8:30am-10pm; €8).

Interbus, Pl. Gipuzkoa (☎943 64 13 02), to **Hondarribia** (45min., every 15-30min. 7:45am-10:15pm, €1.70) and **Irún** (35min., every 15-30min., €1.40).

La Roncalesa, Po. de Vizcaya, 16 (☎943 46 10 64), to **Pamplona** (1hr., 6-10 per day 7am-9:15pm, €6).

Vibasa, Po. de Vizcaya, 16 (☎943 45 75 00), to **Barcelona** (7hr., 3 per day 7am-11:40pm, €25).

Public Transportation: Local Buses (☎943 28 71 00). Map/schedule available at tourist office. €1. **Bus #16** runs from Alameda del Boulevard to campground and beaches.

Taxis: Vallina (☎943 40 40 40) and **Donostia** (☎943 46 46 46).

Bike Rental: Bici Rent Donosti, Po. de la Zurriola, 22 (☎943 29 08 54). Provides bike trail maps. Bikes €12 per 4hr., €18 per day. Tandem bikes €6 per hr., €20 per 4hr., €36 per day. For mopeds, call ahead.

◪ ⚉ ORIENTATION AND PRACTICAL INFORMATION

The **Río Urumea** splits San Sebastián down the middle, with the **parte vieja** (old town) and **El Centro** (the new downtown) to the west, separated by the wide walkway **Alameda del Boulevard.** The **RENFE train station** and the neighborhood **Gros** lie on the east side. **Buses** stop in the south of the city on the west side.

Tourist Office: Municipal Centro de Atracción y Turismo, C. Reina Regente, 3 (☎943 48 11 66; www.sansebastianturismo.com). English, French, and German spoken. Open June-Sept. M-Sa 8am-8pm, Su 10am-2pm and 3-8pm; Oct.-May M-Sa 9am-1:30pm and 3:30-7pm, Su 10am-2pm. **Branch office** at bus station open June-Sept. daily 11am-1pm and 4-8pm.

Hiking Information: Club Vasco de Camping, C. Iparraguirre, 8 (☎943 27 18 66; www.vascodecamping.org). Local mountaineering and hiking club organizes and coordinates excursions. Info on hiking opportunities in País Vasco. Open M-F 6-8:30pm.

Luggage Storage: Train station (€3 per day; buy tokens at the ticket counter). Open daily 7am-11pm.

Laundromat: 5 á Sec, inside Mercado de la Bretxa. Open M-Sa 9am-9pm.

Police: Guardia Civil, C. Easo, 41 (☎092, lost items 943 48 13 20).

Medical Services: Casa de Socorro, C. Bengoetxea, 4 (☎943 44 06 33). Services only available to EU citizens, but others should come here to be redirected to a private clinic.

Internet Access: Zarr@net, C. San Lorenzo, 6 (☎943 43 33 81). Come meet the owner, Juan, the nicest man in Spain. €0.05 per min., €3 per hr. Also sells **phone cards.** Open M-Sa 10am-10pm, Su 4-10pm.

Post Office: C. Urdaneta (☎902 19 71 97), behind the cathedral. Open M-F 8:30am-8:30pm, Sa 9:30am-2pm. **Postal Code:** 20012.

PAÍS VASCO

PAÍS VASCO

San Sebastián (Donostia)

▲ **ACCOMMODATIONS**
Albergue Juvenil
la Sirena (HI), **1**
Pensión Amaiur, **3**
Pensión Anne, **12**
Pensión Añorga, **20**
Pensión Boulevard, **15**
Pensión Easo, **19**
Pensión La Perla, **22**

Pensión Larrea, **8**
Pensión Loinaz, **13**
Pensión Puerto, **7**
Pensión San Lorenzo, **10**
Pensión Urkia, **21**
Pensión Fermín, **5**

♨ **FOOD**
Arrai Txiki, **6**
Café Santana, **17**
Caravanserai Café, **23**
La Cueva, **4**
Juantxo, **11**
Kursaal, **26**
Restaurante-Café
Oquendo, **25**
Va Bene, **16**

★ **NIGHTLIFE**
Akerbeltz, **2**
Bideluze, **24**
Molly Malone, **18**
Ostadar, **9**
Zibibbo, **14**

Parte Vieja
Santa María
del Coro
Museo de San Telmo
C. Sta. Corda
C. 31 de Agosto
C. Juan de Bilbao
San Jerónimo
San Juan
PL. DE LA CONSTITUCIÓN
C. Esterlines
C. Embeltrán
C. Mayor
C. Iñigo
PL. DE SARRIEGI
C. San Lorenzo
Mercado de la Bretxa
Alameda del Boulevard
Super Todo Todo
C. Calbetón
Puerto Kaleoz
C. Igentea
Ayuntamiento
C. Koruko Andra Mari
Billabona

Mar Cantábrico
Isla de Santa Clara
Monte Igueldo
Funicular
Aquarium
Cementerio de los Ingleses
Castillo de Santa Cruz de la Mota
Monte Urgull
PUERTO
Bahía de la Concha
Real Club Náutico
Parque del Palacio Real de Miramar
Playa de Ondarreta
Playa de la Concha

TO MONTE ULÍA (1km)
Playa de la Zurriola
GROS
Pukas Surf Club
Bici Rent Donosti
Po. de la Zurriola
C. Usandizaga
Club Vasco de Camping
C. Miracruz
San Francisco
Secundino Esnaola
C. Zabaleta
PL. DE CATALUÑA
C. Colón
Puente de Zurriola
C. Ramón M. Lili
Puente de Santa Catalina
RÍO Urumea
Estación del Norte (RENFE)
Parque Cristina Enea
Virgen del Carmen
Po. de Duque de Mandas
Po. de Francia
Po. del Muelle
Puente de María Cristina
Po. del Árbol de Guernica
C. Prim
Po. de los Fueros

Bus to Museo Chillida-Leku
Po. Rep. Argentina
PL. DE SARRIEGI
C. Aldamar
C. San Juan
Po. de Salamanca
C. Oquendo
C. Legazpi
Elkano
Kurruka
Alameda del Boulevard
C. Bengoetxea
C. Etxaide
C. Bergara
C. Getaria
C. Peñaflorida
Garibai
C. Andia
C. Loiola
C. Fuenterrabia
C. San Jerónimo
Parque de Aldelri Eder
Po. Nuevo
Po. Anderero Ebira
Camino de la Santa Cruz
C. Hernani
C. San Marcial
C. Arrasate
Arasate
Urdaneta
PL. DE LA LIBERTAD
Av. de la Libertad
PL. DE BILBAO
C. Reyes Católicos
C. Urbieta
C. Easo
C. Triunfo
PL. DE CERVANTES
Catedral del Buen Pastor
Estación de Amara (Euskotren)
C. San Martín
C. San Bartolomé
PL. DE ZARAGOZA
Po. Zuñiga Zarauz
Po. de la Concha
PL. DE LA CONCHA

TO (20km)
TO (200m)
TO PALACIO DE AIETE (600m);
TO MUSEO CHILLIDA-LEKU (4km)
TO (5 km)

Av. de Satrústegui
Po. del Peine de los Vientos
Av. de Zumalacárregui
Av. de Brunet
C. Pamplona Irunea
C. Matia
Parque de Pamplona Inunea
Po. de Sartústegui

SEE PARTE VIEJA INSET

200 yards / 200 meters
150 meters / 150 yards

ACCOMMODATIONS AND CAMPING

Small *pensiones* are scattered throughout the noisy *parte vieja*. For a more restful night's sleep farther from the action, look for *hostales* and *pensiones* on the outskirts of El Centro. In July and August, *"completo"* signs—the Spanish equivalent of "no vacancy"—begin to appear in many doorways. Particularly tight times are during *San Fermines* (July 6-14) and *Semana Grande* (Aug. 21-28); September's film festival (starting just before the last week of Sept.) is not much better. To make matters worse, many *pensiones* don't take reservations in summer. Come early in the day and be prepared to shop around, as finding a room may take some time. Solo travelers should be prepared to pay for a double if unable to find a willing roommate; single rooms are virtually impossible to come by. The tourist office has a list of all registered accommodations in the city.

PARTE VIEJA

Where the younger backpackers go for a night's rest (or more accurately a night's partying), the *parte vieja* is brimming with reasonably priced *pensiones* and restaurants. Its proximity to Playa de la Concha and the port makes this area a prime nightspot; scores of places offer a night's sleep above loud *pintxos* (tapas) bars. Call in advance for reservations.

◙ **Pensión Amaiur,** C. 31 de Agosto, 44, 2nd fl. (☎943 42 96 54; www.pensionamaiur.com). Virginia, the wonderful English-speaking owner, offers 14 beautiful rooms, 4 with balconies, each with a personal touch. 7 common baths and 2 fully equipped, tidy kitchens for when you're all *pintxo*-ed out. Internet €1 per 18min. Single €18-35; doubles €28-45, with balcony €32-50; triples €39-72; quads €48-85. MC/V. ❷

◙ **Pensión San Lorenzo,** C. San Lorenzo, 2 (☎943 42 55 16; www.infonegocio.com/pensionsanlorenzo), off C. San Juan. This sunny hostel features bright rooms, immaculate private baths, and an incredibly helpful owner. Doubles with TV, hi-fi stereo, fridge, and safe. All rooms with sink and shower, some with bath. Internet €2 per hr.; free Internet connection in all rooms. July-Aug. doubles €48. June and Sept. €36. Oct.-May €24. ❸

Pensión Boulevard, Alameda del Boulevard, 24, 1st fl. (☎943 42 94 05; www.pensionboulevard.com). All rooms in this luxurious *pensión* come with balcony, minibar, TV, and bath. Doubles €36-60. ❹

Pensión Larrea, C. Narrica, 21, 2nd fl. (☎943 42 26 94). Rooms are plain but spacious and welcoming. All have balconies. Kitchen with microwave. Internet €1 per 18min. July-Aug. singles €24; doubles €45; triples €60. Sept.-June €18/€30/€45. ❸

Pensión Fermín, C. Fermín Calbetón, 6, 1st fl. (☎943 43 15 73). Perfect for young travelers hoping to take advantage of the *parte vieja* nightlife. Balcony rooms noisy late into the night, but all are spacious with fridge and TV. Clean common baths; some rooms have private bath. July-Aug. doubles €44. June and Sept. €30. Oct.-May €20. ❷

Pensión Loinaz, C. San Lorenzo, 17 (☎943 42 67 14; www.pensionloinaz.com). English-speaking owner. Common baths; all rooms have balconies. Internet €1 per 18min. Laundry €7 per load. July-Aug. doubles €45; triples €60. June and Sept. €36/€45. Oct.-May €27/€39. AmEx/MC/V. ❹

Pensión Puerto, Puerto Kalea, 19, 1st fl. (☎943 43 21 40). Spotless, sunny rooms with big comfy beds. Doubles €45-50. ❸

Pensión Anne, C. Esterlines, 15, 2nd fl. (☎943 42 14 38; www.pensionanne.com). Plain, comfortable rooms in a convenient location. €12 extra for small private bath. Singles €24-38; doubles €50-60; triples €67-81. ❷

OUTSIDE THE PARTE VIEJA

Most of these places tend to be quieter than those in the *parte vieja*, but are still close to the port, beach, bus, and train stations, no more than 5min. from the old city. This area also has some of the city's most elegant boulevards and buildings.

Pensión La Perla, C. Loiola, 10, 2nd fl. (☎943 42 81 23; www.pensionlaperla.com), on the street directly in front of the cathedral. English spoken. Soak in your private bath, then waltz across your beautiful wood floor and step out onto your balcony. Heat and TV. July-Sept. singles €30-32; doubles €45. Oct.-June €24/€32. MC/V. ❸

Pensión Urkia, C. Urbieta, 12, 3rd fl. (☎943 42 44 36; www.pensionurkia.com), across from what will eventually be a brand new department store. Big, clean rooms with full bath and TV, all but 1 with balcony. June-Sept. doubles €45; 1 triple €60. Oct-May singles €28; doubles €35; 1 triple €42. ❷

Pensión Easo, C. San Bartolomé, 24 (☎943 45 39 12; www.pensioneaso.com). Huge windows and common coffee machine; all rooms have sink and TV. Singles with sink €25-34, with bath €35-50; doubles €35-43/€45-62; triples €45-58/€60-83. MC/V. ❸

Pensión Añorga, C. Easo, 12 (☎943 46 79 45). Quiet pension for travelers in search of a peaceful night's sleep. Shares entryway with 2 other *pensiones*. Spacious rooms have shiny wood floors and comfy beds. 2 quads available. July-Aug. singles €25; doubles €34, with bath €43. Sept.-June €19/€25/€32. Quads €16 per person. ❷

Albergue Juvenil la Sirena (HI), Po. Igueldo, 25 (☎943 31 02 68), a light pink building 3min. from the beach. Bus #16 runs to Po. Igueldo, right in front of the *albergue* (every hr. 7:30am-10pm, €1). Clean rooms, multilingual staff. HI members and ISIC-carriers only. Laundry and kitchen available. Breakfast included. Sheets €2.60. 3-night max. stay if full. Curfew Sept.-May Su-Th midnight, F-Sa 2am. May-Sept. €14.40-16, 26 and over €16-17.60. Oct.-Apr. prices reduced 20%. MC/V. ❶

Camping: Camping Igueldo (☎943 21 45 02; www.campingigueldo.com), 5km west of town. The 268 spots fill quickly. Beautiful views of the ocean make the drive worth it. Bus #16 ("Barrio de Igueldo-Camping") runs between the site and Alameda del Boulevard (every hr. 7:30am-10pm, €1). *Parcelas* (spot for 2 people with room for car and tent) June 16-Sept. 15 and *Semana Santa* €12, extra person €3.50. Water and electricity add €8.80. Rest of year call ahead for prices. MC/V. ❶

🍴 FOOD

Pintxos, chased down with *txakoli*, the fizzy regional wine, are a religion here; bars line the streets in the *parte vieja*, spreading an array of enticing tidbits on toothpicks or bread across the countertops. In the harbor, many places serve tangy sardines with slightly bitter *sidra*. The clean and modern **Mercado de la Bretxa**, in an underground shopping center, sells everything from fresh produce and meat to *pintxos*. (Open M-Sa 8am-9pm, though most vendors take lunch 3-5pm.) For **groceries**, stop by **Super Todo Todo**, Alameda del Boulevard, 3. (☎943 42 82 59. Open M-Sa 8:30am-9pm, Su 10am-2pm. MC/V.)

PARTE VIEJA

🏷 **Arrai Txiki,** C. del Campanario, 3 (☎943 43 13 02; www.arraitxiki.com), accessible from C. Fermín Calbetón or C. 31 de Agosto. The Argentina-born, San Francisco-trained chef-owner cooks up delicious, organic, vegetarian cuisine in a simple, elegant setting. The waiters are also chefs, and they'll gladly share the secrets of the kitchen with interested diners. Entrees €3-6. Open Su-M and W-Sa 1-4pm and 8-11pm. ❷

Juantxo, C. Esterlines, 6 (☎943 42 74 05), main entrance off C. Embeltran. Try the *filete* with onions, cheese, and peppers (€2.90). The bread definitely makes the sandwich. Wide selection of excellent *bocadillos* (€2-3), *pintxos* (€1-2), and *raciones* (€2-5). Open M-Th 9am-11:30pm, F-Su 9am-1:45am. ❶

Café Santana, C. Reina Regente, half a block toward the river from tourist office. Huge, if slightly pricey, selection of *pintxos* (€2-3.50), all nicely labeled for the layman *pintxo*-hopper. Open daily 7am-10pm, breakfast until 11am. MC/V. ❶

La Cueva, Pl. de la Trinidad (☎943 42 54 37). A cavernous restaurant with a covered outside terrace serving traditional seafood. Quite a fancy place to eat fish. M-F *menú* €15. Grilled sea creature entrees €8-15. Open Tu-Su 1-3:30pm and 7-11pm. MC/V. ❸

Va Bene, Alameda del Boulevard, 14 (☎943 42 24 16). Frequented by tourists and locals alike. The place to go for high-quality, low-price hamburgers and hot dogs served in the tradition of the best American diners. Norman Rockwell prints make for a retro setting inside with great patio seating. Burgers €2.50-4.50. Open daily 11am-2am. ❶

OUTSIDE THE PARTE VIEJA

Kursaal, Po. de la Zurriola, 1 (☎943 00 31 62), in a Guggenheim-esque glass cube building across the river from the *parte vieja*. Treat yourself to an elegant gourmet lunch on their breezy patio. The chef is a legend among locals. *Menú* 1-3:30pm M-F €14, Sa-Su €16.60. Entrees €12-30. Open daily 10am-3:30pm and 8-11pm. MC/V. ❹

Caravanseraí Café, Pl. del Buen Pastor, 1 (☎943 47 54 18), along the right side of the cathedral when facing its front doors. Chic and artsy, without the pretentious prices. Fabulous vegetarian options (€3.60). Entrees €5-7, pasta €6-6.60. €0.60 surcharge for patio dining. Open M-Sa 8am-11:30pm, Su 10:30am-11:30pm. MC/V. ❷

Restaurante-Café Oquendo, C. Oquendo, 8 (☎943 42 09 32). Pictures of Spanish celebrities line the walls, many signed with high praise. Quality meals of fish and other seafood (€13-30) and meats (€11-15). *Menú* €21. Lunch 1-3:30pm, dinner (except Su) 8-11pm. Bar open daily 8am-midnight. MC/V. ❹

🔆 SIGHTS

San Sebastián's sights, while impressive on their own, are nothing compared to the splendor of the city as a whole. The best way to absorb it all is on an evening stroll along Playa de la Concha, which has breathtaking views of Santa Clara, the Estatua del Sagrado Corazón, and the city's bustling skyline.

MUSEO CHILLIDA-LEKU. The Museo Chillida-Leku houses a beautiful permanent exhibit of Eduardo Chillida's work, spread throughout the extensive garden of a 16th-century farmhouse restored by the sculp-

TOUGH SHELL

September 2005 will mark the 52nd annual **Donostia-San Sebastián Festival Internacional de Cine,** one of the biggest film festivals in Europe, second only to Cannes. Since it began in 1953, the festival's official goal has stayed the same: to recognize the year's most innovative films, those that push the boundaries of social and cultural norms. Famous actors like Gregory Peck, Susan Sarandon, Michael Caine, and John Malkovich, to name but a few, have accepted the prestigious Donostia Award, which honors outstanding lifelong contributions to the art of film. Other big names such as Hitchcock, Spielberg, Audrey Hepburn, and Johnny Depp have graced the screen, and the audience.

The festival annually shells out a variety of awards—some voted on by the audience—the most coveted of which are shaped like sea shells. A golden one is awarded to the best film and a silver to the best director, actor, and actress. To keep things fair, each film (out of the huge number screened each fall) is allowed no more than one prize.

For more information, visit the official website at www.sansebastianestival.com. For ticket information and advance booking, call the office (☎943 48 12 12) or send a letter to: San Sebastian International Film Festival, P.O. Box 397, 20080 Donostia-San Sebastián.

tor himself. The farmhouse, a spectacular construction of huge wood beams and arching stone, now houses some of Chillida's earliest pieces. Make sure to peruse the whole sculpture garden, though, as pieces are hidden around every turn of the path. *(Bo. Jauregui, 66. 15min. from the town center. Autobuses Garayar, line G2, leave from C. Oquendo every 30min, €1.20. By car, take N-1 out of San Sebastián south toward Vitoria-Gasteiz, turning toward Hernani on GI-2132. Museum is on the left. ☎943 33 60 06; www.museochillidaleku.com. Open July-Aug. and Semana Santa M and W-Sa 10:30am-7pm, Su 10:30am-3pm; Sept.-June Su-M and W-Sa 10:30am-3pm. Closed Christmas and New Year's. Daily tours provided, as well as 45min. audio-tours in 5 languages. €6, under 12 and seniors €3.)*

▩ MONTE IGUELDO. Both of San Sebastián's mountains afford spectacular views, but those from Monte Igueldo win hands down. By day, the countryside meets the ocean in a line of white and blue; by night, Isla de Santa Clara seems to float in a halo of light. The sidewalk toward the mountain ends just before the base of Monte Igueldo, by Eduardo Chillida's sculpture *El Peine de los Vientos* (Comb of the Winds). The road leading to the top is bordered by a low cliffside stone wall, a local favorite for romantic picnic dinners while watching the sun slip into the sea. If you're interested in taking the quick route to the summit, though, try the funicular instead. *(☎943 21 02 11. Open June-Sept. daily 10am-10pm; Oct.-Feb. Sa-Su 11am-8pm; Mar.-June Sa 11am-8pm, Su 11am-9pm. Funicular runs every 15min.; €0.90, round-trip €1.60.)*

MONTE URGULL. Across the bay from Monte Igueldo, the paths on Monte Urgull wind through shady woods, monuments, and stunning vistas. The overgrown **Castillo de Santa Cruz de la Mota** tops the summit with 12 cannons, a chapel, and the statue of the *Sagrado Corazón de Jesús* blessing the city. *(Paths lead to the summit from Po. Nuevo; the official Subido al Castillo starts at the end of Pl. de Kaimingaintxo, past the Iglesia de Santa María toward Santa Clara. Castillo open daily 8am-sunset. Free.)*

MUSEO DE SAN TELMO. The Museo de San Telmo resides in a Dominican monastery and houses the world's largest collection of keystone funerary monuments. The overgrown cloister is strewn with funerary relics, while the main museum beyond displays an eclectic collection including a fascinating array of prehistoric Basque artifacts, a few dinosaur skeletons, and some contemporary art. *(Pl. Zuloaga, 1. ☎943 48 15 80. Open Tu-Sa 10:30am-1:30pm and 4-7:30pm, Su 10:30am-2pm. Free.)*

PALACES. When Queen Isabel II started vacationing here in the mid-19th century, fancy buildings sprang up like wildflowers. The **Palacio de Miramar** has passed through the hands of the Spanish court, Napoleon III, and Bismarck; it now serves as the Universidad del País Vasco, but anyone can stroll through the adjacent **Parque de Miramar** and contemplate the views of the bay. *(Between Playa de la Concha and Playa de Ondarreta. Open daily June-Aug. 8am-9pm; Sept.-May 8am-7pm. Free.)* The other royal residence, **Palacio de Aiete,** is also closed to the public, but surrounding trails are not. *(Head up Cuesta de Aldapeta or take bus #19 or 31. Grounds open daily June-Aug. 8am-9pm; Sept.-May 8am-7pm. Free.)*

AQUARIUM. If you can't stand to eat any more of your finned friends, watch 'em. On rainy days, the aquarium, one of Europe's most modern, is worth a visit. The second floor holds a permanent exhibit on naval history in the region. *(Po. del Muelle, 34, on Pl. de Carlos Blasco de Imaz. Arrows point the way from the port. ☎943 44 00 99; www.aquariumss.com. Open July-Aug. daily 10am-9pm; Apr. 8-June and Sept. daily 10am-8pm; Oct.-Apr. 7 M-F 10am-7pm, Sa-Su 11am-8pm. €10, children €5.)*

◪ BEACHES AND WATER SPORTS

The gorgeous **Playa de la Concha** curves from the port to **Pico del Loro,** the promontory home of the Palacio de Miramar. The flat beach virtually disappears during high tide. Sunbathers jam onto smaller and steeper **Playa de Ondarreta,** beyond

Miramar, and surfers flock to the bigger waves of **Playa de la Zurrida,** across the river from Mt. Urgull. Picnickers head for alluring **Isla de Santa Clara** in the bay. (☎943 00 04 50. Motorboat ferry 5min., June-Sept. every 30min., round-trip €1.95.) The portside kiosk has more info.

Several sports-related groups offer a variety of activities and lessons. For **canoeing** and **kayaking,** call the **Real Club Náutico,** C. Ijentea, 9, located on the water at the Monte Urgull end of Playa de la Concha and shaped like a small cruise ship. (☎943 42 35 75. Open 10am-1pm and 4-6:30pm. 2 wk. courses €48-120.) Surfers can check out the **Pukas Surf Club,** Av. de la Zurriola, 23, or the hut on the beach, for info on lessons and rentals. (☎943 42 12 05. Open M-Sa 9:30am-9pm. AmEx/MC/V.) For general information on all sports, pick up a copy of the *UDA-Actividades Deportivas* brochure at the tourist office.

■ NIGHTLIFE

The *parte vieja* pulls out all the stops in July and August, particularly on C. Fermín Calbetón, three blocks in from Alameda del Boulevard. During the year, when students outnumber backpackers, nightlife tends to move beyond *parte vieja*. Keep an eye out for coupons on the street, but be aware that the deals usually aren't as sweet as they sound.

Ostadar, C. Fermín Calbetón, 13 (☎943 42 62 78). This little bar is among the most popular places for tourists and locals to mix and break it down to one of the best dance mixes in *parte vieja*. Beer €1.80, mixed drinks €4.50. Open daily 5pm-4am.

Akerbeltz, C. Koruko Andra Mari, 9. Face Iglesia de Santa María on C. 31 de Agosto, take a left, and go up the stairs; it's on the corner at the road's end, just before the port. A tiny, sleek, local bar more appropriate for lively conversation than crazy partying. Beer €1.60. Open M-Th 3pm-2:30am, F-Sa 3pm-3:30am.

Molly Malone, C. San Martín, 55 (☎943 46 98 22). An Irish pub with impressive brew selections and a mellow upstairs loft. Murphy's Irish Red and Guinness on tap €2. Other beers €2-3. Open M-F 11am-4am, Sa-Su 3pm-4am.

Zibbibo, Pl. de Sarriegi, 8 (☎943 42 53 34). Perhaps the most popular bar for young tourists in the *parte vieja*, Zibbibo is practically a disco, just on a smaller scale. Nice, if somewhat repetitive, blend of top 40 and techno. *"Grande"* sangria €4.50. Happy hour Su-Th 10:30-11:30pm. Open daily 2pm-4am. MC/V.

Bideluze, Pl. Gipuzkoa, 14 (☎943 42 28 80). For a relaxed evening out, this cafe has chill music, good coffee (€1.50), and plush red chairs. *Bocadillos* €3-6. Open M-Th 8am-1am, F 8am-2am, Sa-Su 11am-1am.

HONDARRIBIA   ☎943

Less than 1hr. east of San Sebastián by bus, Hondarribia (pop. 15,000) is a charming getaway from its popular neighbor. Its quiet streets, lined with cafes and art galleries and dotted with parks and modern sculptures, are the perfect place to spend a day recovering from the hustle and bustle of San Sebastián. The suburbanized coastal town stretching along Txingudi Bay boasts old wharfs and new shops along a golden sand beach. Compared to chic San Sebastián, Hondarribia is small and simple, but not old-fashioned. In the peak days of summer, the beach can become ridiculously crowded with vacationers from Madrid and Barcelona, but it's usually pleasantly calm through June.

■ **PRACTICAL INFORMATION.** Green and white **Interurbanos buses** (☎943 64 13 02) to **San Sebastián's** Pl. Guipuzkoa stop in front of the post office at Pl. San Cristóbal; pay onboard (45min.; every 15-30min. M-Sa 6:45am-9pm, Su 7:45am-9pm; €1.50). **AUIF buses** (☎943 63 31 45) go to **Irún** (10min., every 15min. 7am-10pm,

€0.95). The **airport, Gabarrari Kalea** (☎902 40 05 00), serviced exclusively by **Iberia** (☎943 66 35 00), is within walking distance of the town center toward Irún. The **tourist office, Bidasoa Turismo,** Jabier Ugarte Kalea, 6, is right off Pl. San Cristóbal; from the bus stop walk across the plaza. (☎943 64 54 58; www.bidasoaturismo.com. Open July-Sept. M-Sa 9:30am-2pm and 4:30-8pm; Oct.-June M-F 9am-1:30pm and 4-6:30pm, Sa 10am-2pm. English spoken.) Local services include: **bank, Caja Laboral/Kutxa,** San Pedro Kalea, 9, across from the post office (open M-F 8:15am-2:15pm; **ATM** open 6:30am-10:30pm); **police,** Mayor Kalea, 10 (☎943 64 43 00). The **English Corner,** Itsasargi Kalea, 2, which also runs small-scale, English-language tours of the area, offers **Internet** access. From the bus station, walk back up Beñat Matxin de Arzu Kalea with the bay on your right to Zuloaga Kalea, which becomes Itsasargi Kalea. (☎943 64 54 35; www.hondarribiatours.com. €1 per 15min. Open M-F 11am-2pm and 5-7pm. Reservations for tours online. MC/V.) The **post office** is at Pl. San Cristóbal, 1. (☎943 64 12 04. Open M-F 8:30am-2:30pm, Sa 9:30am-1pm.) **Postal Code:** 20280.

⌂ ⚑ ACCOMMODATIONS AND CAMPING. A brand new hotel in a seemingly old building, **◙Hotel Palacete ❺,** Pl. Gipuzkoa, 5, combines the best of both worlds: simple, elegant interiors with thatched chairs, whitewashed walls, and a castle-esque spiral stone staircase mixed with fully modern baths and electronic keys. From the tourist office, walk up Jabier Ugarte Kalea and take the first right onto Santiago Kompostela Kalea, which runs into Pl. Gipuzkoa. (☎943 64 08 13; www.hotelpalacete.net. Breakfast €6. Singles €48-72; doubles €55-80. AmEx/MC/V.) **Hostal Txoko Goxoa ❷,** Margolari Etxenagusia, lies in the other direction from Pl. San Cristóbal. From the tourist office, head up Jabier Ugarte Kalea, take the second right onto Juan Laborda Kalea. Follow it uphill until it ends at the city's old walls and take a right. The friendly English-speaking owner will greet you and show you to your airy, completely relaxing room with spotless private bath. (☎/fax 943 64 46 58; www.txokogoxoa.com. Breakfast €4.20. July-Sept. singles €37.50; doubles €52. Oct.-June €28.50/€44.50. MC/V.) **Hostal Álvarez Quintero ❸,** Bernat Etxepare Kalea, 2, with an entrance through the tunnel, offers conveniently located rooms with large private baths. Other amenities include a comfortable downstairs common room and access to municipal tennis courts and swimming pool. (☎943 64 22 99. Breakfast €4.50. Reception 8am-midnight. Wheelchair access on 1st fl.. Singles €28-34; doubles 1st fl. €36-44, 2nd fl. €44-53. MC/V.) **Albergue Juan Sebastián Elcano (HI) ❶,** Higer Bidea, 7, sits on a hillside overlooking the beach and mountains. From the bus stop near the port on Foru Kalea, turn inland to C. Baserritar Etorbidea and look for the signs pointing uphill to the Albergue. The hostel has a TV room and tennis and basketball courts. (☎943 64 15 50; fax 64 00 28. Breakfast included. Sheets €2. 3-night max. stay when full. Reception daily 9am-noon and 4-8pm. Curfew midnight, but doors open at 1 and 2am. Reserve ahead in Dec. and Jan. HI members only; HI cards €6-10. Dorms €9.30, over 30 €14. MC/V.) **Camping Jaizkibel ❶** is 1km from town on Ctra. Guadalupe toward Monte Jaizkibel and can be reached only by car or foot. The campground has hot showers, cafeteria, restaurant, and laundry. Bungalows have bath and kitchen. (☎943 64 16 79. Reception 9am-10pm. €3.70 per person, per tent, and per car. Bungalows €67.40-75.20.)

⌂ FOOD. Several **markets** spill onto San Pedro Kalea, 3 blocks inland from the port. Stock up at **Aliprox,** Santiago Kalea, 19. (☎943 64 15 40. Open M-Sa 8:30am-1:30pm, M-F also 5-7:30pm. MC/V.) Eat like rural royalty at **◙Antontxo ❸,** Santiago Kalea, 47, where you'll find unbelievably generous portions served up under the rafters of an old farmhouse. Bright yellow-and-blue wall decorations and reliefs celebrating traditional Basque culture bring the dining room to life. The *rabo de buey* (oxtail; €9) is amazing. From Pl. San Cristóbal with your back to the bay,

Vitoria-Gasteiz

🏠 ACCOMMODATIONS
Hostal-Residencia Nuvilla, **9**
Hotel Iradier, **10**
Pensión Araba, **8** & **11**

🍴 FOOD
Bocatería Boca a Boca, **5**
Museo del Órgano, **12**
Restaurante Argentino La
Yerra, **1**
El Siete, **4**
La Taberna de Los
Mundos, **6**

⭐ NIGHTLIFE
Cervecería Txistu, **3**
The Man in the Moon, **7**
Scheherazade, **2**

Currency Exchange: Banco Santander Central Hispano, Pl. del Arca, 1-3 (☎945 14 45 30). 24hr. **ATM.** Open May-Sept. M-F 8:30am-2pm; Oct.-Apr. M-F 8:30am-2pm, Sa 8:30am-1pm.

Luggage storage: Lockers at the **train station** (€3; buy tokens at the ticket counter 6am-1am) and the **bus station** (€2 per item per day). Open M-Sa 8am-8pm, Su 9am-7pm.

El Corte Inglés: (☎945 26 63 33), on C. de la Paz. Supermarket downstairs. Open M-Sa 10am-10pm. AmEx/MC/V.

Police: C. Olaguíbel (☎091 or 092), across from the hospital.

Medical Services: Hospital General de Santiago, C. Olaguíbel, 29 (☎945 00 76 00). **Osakidetza Servicio Vasco de Salud,** Av. de Santiago, 7 (☎945 24 44 44), off C. de la Paz. Free medical attention; passport required. Open M-F 5pm-midnight, Sa 2pm-midnight, Su 9am-midnight.

Internet Access: Ponte Cómodo.com, C. los Herrán, 37. €2.40 per hr. Copies €0.10. Open M-F 10am-8pm, Sa 11am-8pm, Su 4-8pm. **Cuatro Azules,** C. Postas, 28 (☎945 13 45 13), across from the post office. A slow, coin-operated machine. €0.50 per 7min., €1 per 30min. Open Su-Th 12:30pm-2:30am, F-Sa 12:30pm-4am.

Post Office: C. Postas, 9 (☎945 15 46 92). Open M-F 8:30am-8:30pm, Sa 9:30am-2pm. **Lista de Correos** on C. Nuestra Señora del Cabello. **Postal Code:** 01008.

PAÍS VASCO

ACCOMMODATIONS AND CAMPING

Vitoria-Gasteiz has only a few *pensiones*, though more deluxe hostels abound. If you plan to come during the jazz festival (first 2 weeks of July) or the *Fiestas de la Virgen Blanca* (Aug. 4-9), make reservations at least one week in advance.

Hotel Iradier, C. Florida, 49 (☎945 27 90 66; www.hoteliradier.com). Ring buzzer to enter. Big but cozy blue and yellow rooms, very modern, some with balconies, all with private bath, TV, and phone. Singles €30; doubles €48; triples €66. MC/V. ❸

Hostal-Residencia Nuvilla, C. de los Fueros, 29, 3rd fl. (☎945 25 91 51). Common baths. Rooms have balconies and sinks. Singles €23; doubles €33; triples €42-45. ❷

Pensión Araba, C. Florida, 25, 1st fl. (☎945 23 25 88). Attractive rooms, some with sinks and all with TV (some with VCR). Singles €20-24, with bath €28; doubles €30/€36; triples €40/€48. ❷

Camping: Camping Ibaya, Ctra. Nacional, 102 (☎945 14 76 20), 4km from town toward Madrid. Follow Portal de Castilla west from the new cathedral. Restaurant, hot showers, and laundry. Open year-round. €3.50 per person, per tent, and per car. MC/V.

FOOD

You can't go wrong in the *casco viejo*. The area around Pl. de España has *pintxos* galore. Buy groceries at **Champion,** C. General Álava, 10. (Open M-Sa 9am-9:30pm.)

El Siete, C. Cuchillería, 3 (☎945 27 22 98). Popular with locals in search of traditional food—and lots of it. 38 varieties of sandwiches (€2.50-3.60). *Menú* served M-F 1-4pm (€8-12). Open Su-Th 9am-12:30am, F-Sa 10am-3am or later. ❶

Museo del Órgano, C. Manuel Iradier, 80 (☎945 26 40 48), on the corner just before the Pl. de Toros. With fresh, filling vegetarian cuisine, this is a favorite among locals, who create big lines at lunch. M-F 4-course *menú* €9. Open M-F 1-4pm. MC/V. ❷

Restaurante Argentino La Yerra, C. Correría, 46 (☎945 26 37 59), in the *casco viejo*. Good beef entrees (€11-18, unless you're brave enough to take on all 800g of the monster €30 steak) and enticing pasta dishes (€7.30). M-F luncheon *menú* (€8). Open Su and Tu-W 1:30-4pm, Th-Sa 1:30-4pm and 9:30pm-midnight. MC/V. ❸

La Taberna de Los Mundos, C. de la Independencia, 14 (☎945 13 93 42). Serves mouth-watering, affordable sandwiches (€4). Fish and pork entrees €8-11. Restaurant open M-Th 1:30-4pm, F-Sa also 9:30pm-midnight, Su 2-4pm. Bar and *bocadillos* open M-W 9am-midnight, Th 9am-1am, F-Sa 10:30am-2am, Su noon-midnight. ❷

Bocatería Boca a Boca, C. Nueva Fuera, 13 (☎945 27 84 18), right across from the Metropolis Sex Shop. The swinging tiki lounge interior is the perfect place to enjoy one of their specialty *kebaps* (€3-5.50) or many *bocadillos* (€2-4). Open M-Th 11am-4pm and 8pm-midnight, F-Sa 11am-4pm and 8pm-4am, Su 8pm-midnight. ❶

SIGHTS

The tree-lined pedestrian walkways of the new city and steep narrow streets of the *casco viejo* make for pleasant wanderings. **Plaza de la Virgen Blanca** is the focal point of the *casco viejo* and site of Vitoria-Gasteiz's *fiestas*. Beside Pl. de la Virgen Blanca is the broad, arcaded **Plaza de España,** which marks the division between the old and new towns. **Los Arquillos,** a series of arches that rise above Pl. de España, were designed by architect Justo Antonio de Olaguíbel from 1787 to 1802 to connect the *casco viejo* with the rapidly growing new town below. ◪**El Anillo Verde,** a ring of parks and grassy promenades entirely encircling the city, make for a beautiful afternoon walk, bike ride, or birdwatching sojourn.

MUSEUMS AND PALACES. The permanent collection at ▨**Artium,** the contemporary art museum that opened in 2001, boasts multimedia works and paintings by 20th-century greats such as Dalí, Picasso, Miró, and Arroyo. Equally as worthwhile, two galleries feature a regular rotation of macabre and unconventional works by local favorites like surrealists Vicente Ameztoy and Javier Pérez. *(C. de Francia, 24. ☎945 20 90 00. Open Tu-F 11am-8pm, Sa-Su 10:30am-8pm. Adults €3.50; students, seniors, and ages 14-17 €1.80; under 14 free; W by donation.)* Many of the *casco viejo*'s Renaissance *palacios* are open to the public as museums. The gorgeous **Palacio de Augusti** houses the **Museo de Bellas Artes,** with works by regional artists. *(Po. Fray Francisco de Vitoria. ☎945 18 19 18. Open Tu-F 10am-2pm and 4-6:30pm, Sa 10am-2pm, Su 11am-2pm. Free.)* The world's largest deck of playing cards, recognized by the Guinness Book of World Records, weighs 10kg and measures 94 by 61.5cm, and you'll find it (along with 20,000 others) at the **Fournier Playing Card Museum.** *(C. de la Cuchillería, 54. ☎945 18 19 18. Tours can be booked for W and F mornings. Open Tu-F 10am-2pm and 4-6:30pm, Sa 10am-2pm, Su 11am-2pm. Free.)*

CATHEDRALS. The apse of the 20th-century neo-Gothic **Catedral Nueva,** in the new town, hosts the ▨**Museo Diocesano de Arte Sagrado,** a surprisingly extensive collection of paintings and religious artifacts from Basque churches, including canvases by El Greco and Ribera. *(C. Monseñor Cadena y Eleta. ☎945 18 19 18. Cathedral open M-Sa 11am-2pm. Free. Museum open Tu-F 10am-2pm and 4-6:30pm, Sa 10am-2pm, Su 11am-2pm.)* Construction of the Gothic **Catedral de Santa María** in the *casco viejo* began in the 12th century. Though the cathedral is closed during a €24 million restoration project until 2010, it offers English tours of the restoration process and archaeological studies. *(☎945 25 51 35; www.catedralvitoria.com. Tours Mar.-Sept. Open 11am-2pm and 5-8pm. €3, under 12 free.)*

▨ ▨ NIGHTLIFE AND FESTIVALS

After nightfall, the *casco viejo* lights up. Bars line C. Cuchillería ("La Cuchi"), C. Herrería ("La Herre"), C. Zapatería ("La Zapa"), and C. San Francisco. For intimate socializing, crash ▨**Scheherazade,** C. Correría, 42, a sumptuous Moroccan tea room with small tables, embroidered cushions, and an intoxicating ambience. Sip a kiwi shake (€1.80) or hot tea with fresh herbs blended to order (€1.50) and let your creative juices flow—crayons and paper are provided. *(☎945 25 58 68. Open Su-Th 4:30-11pm, F-Sa 4:30pm-midnight.)* For a chance to catch a conversation in English, try **The Man in the Moon,** C. Manuel Iradier, 7. Locals come here to practice their English with foreign travelers. *(☎945 13 43 27. Open daily 8am-3am.)* Finally, head over to **Cervecería Txistu,** C. San Vicente, 1, for a great selection of international beers in a relaxed environment. *(Beer €2-3. Open M-Th 8:30am-1am, F-Sa 8:30am-3am.)*

For info on **theater** and special events, pick up the weekly *Kalea* (€1.40) from tobacco stands or newsstands. During the first two weeks of July, world-class jazz grooves in the city at the **Festival de Jazz de Vitoria-Gasteiz.** Tickets for big-name performers cost €10-35, but there are plenty of free performances on the street. Call or visit the Asociación Festival de Jazz de Vitoria, C. Florida, 3, for specific info (☎945 14 19 19; www.jazzvitoria.com). On July 24-25, *Las Blusas* ("The Blouses") hold their own festival with wine, music, and games. The blue shirts represent the old shepherds that used to live in Vitoria. Rockets mark the start of Vitoria's biggest, craziest party of the year, the **Fiesta de la Virgen Blanca** (Aug. 4-9), at 6pm on the 4th in Pl. de la Virgen Blanca. Various processions, parades, music, partying in the streets, and general debauchery follow soon after.

Basque Identity as Simultaneously Traditional and Post-Modern

What exactly is meant by "Basque ethnic identity," and what is "Basque ethnicity"? The phenomenon of ethnic identity emerges where the subjects of anthropology, sociology, political science, and psychology converge. It includes the language one speaks and the civic territory in which one lives, and in the case of the Basques, shared ancestry and culture play crucial roles in this determination. Today, the majority of people living in the Basque Country would define "being Basque" as those people who are born in, or permanently live in the Basque Country; those who speak Basque; those who have Basque ancestry; as well as those around the world who love the Basque culture and work for its protection and promotion.

Despite five centuries of speculation by linguists and philologists concerning the possible relationships between Basque and other languages, no studies have indicated a conclusive relationship between Basque and any other language (Michelena 1985; Tovar 1957; Collins 1986:8-12). This makes Euskera, the Basque language, unique among Western and Central European languages. Euskera is the only surviving pre-Indo-European language on the continent. Visitors will see that most signs in Araba, Bizkaia, and Gipuzkoa are posted in both Basque and Spanish. Outside of these three provinces, Euskera is not heard as often, nor is it as visible. Although the Basque term for "Basque people" is *Euskaldunak*, (those who have the Basque language) defining Basque people as those who speak Basque becomes problematic in that so many of those who live in Euskal Herria no longer utilize Euskera regularly. The Basque language was prohibited as a means of communication in Spain during the dictatorship (1939-1975) and it had been lost in many areas of the hispanicized urban centers in the 1800s. The current system of *ikastola*, or schools where the language of instruction is Euskera, and especially the education system of Araba, Bizkaia, and Gipuzkoa, has significantly reversed the decline in Basque knowledge and usage. Today, the majority of youth in those provinces understand or have studied Euskera, though they do not necessarily use it. The political parties in power in Navarre have not prioritized the maintenance of Euskera in their territory, and the historic language has suffered immeasurable decline.

According to anthropologist Julio Caro Baroja, the most important element in stimulating emigration out of Euskal Herria was the rules of inheritance followed in Basque society (Caro Baroja 1971; Bilbao 1992). Population density, high fertility, coupled with the scarcity of agricultural lands and low output, resulted in limited expansion potential. The lack of industrial and urban growth until the 1800s also limited options for employment and migration within Euskal Herria. Each farmstead could support a single family. Those who owned their property and animals kept their holdings in the same family, and Basque common law discouraged fragmentation or division through sales or inheritance. Consequently, most Basque farmsteads remained unchanged for many centuries, with each generation having a single heir.

The *fueros* guaranteed the practice of selecting only one of the former owner's offspring as the new owner. This meant that in most families there were three or four candidates for emigration. Even today in certain villages the traditional rules of male primogeniture are followed, in other areas a female is selected, while in parts of Nafarroa the heir or heiress is chosen according to individual merit without reference to gender or birth order (Lafourcade 1999:167-174). Until recently, the remaining siblings would have to depend upon the new owner for employment, accommodation, and care. For thousands, a more viable alternative was emigration.

The Industrial Revolution of the 19th century disrupted traditional agricultural economic activities and displaced workers from both rural and urban areas. The cheaper manufacture of products left artisans searching for markets, which were abundant in the Americas. Displacement from rural society, changing urban society, unemployment, unrest, labor strikes, arrests and imprisonments related to a lack of civil rights all preceded the Spanish Civil War (1936-1939). After the Republican and Basque nationalist forces were defeated, Franco's victory guaranteed a central policy of Spanish identity-building and Basque nation-destroying. The horrendous indignities suffered, the dismantling of Basque institutions, the outlawing of manifestations of Basque culture, the dictatorial repression and lack of human and civil rights, and multitudes of death warrants pushed Basques out of their homeland in pursuit of safe havens. Hundreds of thousands of Basques were exiled through political and economic repression, and the majority were never able to return to their homeland. The political factors of Basque identity remain critical and are a part of daily life, from choosing which bar or restaurant to frequent to the purchase of daily newspapers with a certain political bias.

Today's Basques are affected by these historical factors, but also add another layer of identity with a post-modern 'Basqueness' that includes trilingualism (Basque, Spanish, and English or French). Despite political wrangling with Madrid, the Basque provinces rank among the highest in economic output and quality of life indicators.

Dr. Gloria Totoricagüena Egurrola received her Ph.D. from the London School of Economics and Political Science and is currently an Assistant Professor at the University of Nevada, Reno Center for Basque Studies.

ASTURIAS AND CANTABRIA

Jagged cliffs and precipitous ravines lend an epic feel to the tiny lands of Asturias and Cantabria, tucked between the País Vasco and Galicia. Though connected by location and landscape, Asturias and Cantabria have distinct provincial personalities. With the world-class resort towns of Santander and Comillas, Cantabria appeals to Spain's vacationing elite. Asturias instead draws hearty mountaineers looking to conquer the peaks of its national parks, including the Parque Nacional Picos de Europa and the Parque Natural de Oyambre.

The impassable peaks of the Cordillera Cantábrica halted the Moorish advance, enabling Visigoth Christians to make the land their northern stronghold. Asturian hero Don Pelayo officially began the *Reconquista* in 722 in the Picos hamlet of Covadonga; the campaign would last until the fall of Granada in 1492. Today, Spain's heir to the throne is titled the Príncipe de Asturias, in honor of the region's preservation of true "Spain" during the Moorish invasions. This legendary spirit of defiance found an outlet during and before the Spanish Civil War in blue-collar resistance to the Fascists, most prominently during a bloody miners' revolt. The terrain has continued to limit the number of rail lines through the region, leaving lone roads to wind along its steep mountainsides and scalloped shores.

Asturias is famous for its apples, cheeses, wholesome fresh milk, and *arroz con leche* (rice pudding). *Sidra* (cider) and *fabada asturiana* (a hearty bean-and-sausage stew) grace menus everywhere. True Asturians can be recognized by the way they take their cider, poured from several feet above the glass and downed immediately. Cantabrian cuisine comes from the mountains and the sea, adding anchovies, tuna, and sardines to the mix. Local favorites include *cocido montanés* (bean stew) and *marmita* (tuna, potato, and green pepper stew).

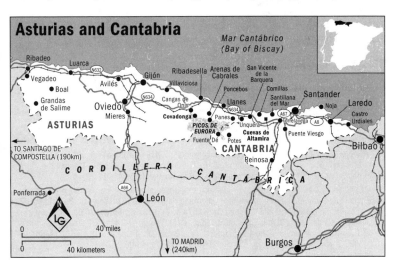

Asturias and Cantabria

> ## HIGHLIGHTS OF ASTURIAS AND CANTABRIA
>
> **LOSE** your breath at the beauty of the **Parque Nacional Picos de Europa** (p. 583).
>
> **RELAX** on the renowned Península de Magdalena in **Santander** (p. 592).
>
> **PONDER** human existence (and evolution) at the **Cuevas de Altamira** (p. 599).
>
> **SWIM** in the teal sea at **Llanes,** below winding streets, ruins, and cows (p. 577).
>
> **FOLLOW** your nose to **Arenas de Cabrales,** home to Spain's stinkiest cheese (p. 581).

ASTURIAS

Impenetrable peaks and dense alpine forests define the Asturian landscape, as well as its history. Thanks to the foreboding Picos de Europa, Asturias never fell to bands of marauding Moors; the legacy of the Visigoths who kept the cross on the peninsula can still be seen in the many pre-Romanesque churches and monasteries dotting Asturian hillsides. A different sort of invasion is at work today: tourists rushing to take advantage of the booming adventure tourism industry in the Parque Nacional Picos de Europa. Although better known for its peaks, Asturias also has a popular coast. The wide swaths of sand and lively waves in Gijón draw swarms of beachgoers, but plenty of quiet, cliff-lined coves lie just off the beaten path, where tropical and alpine vegetation commingle and await the lucky visitor.

OVIEDO ☎958

Oviedo's name comes from the Latin *urbis* (city), and for a few centuries, it really was the city in Spain. As a haven from Moorish attacks, Oviedo (pop. 200,000) became the epicenter of the Reconquista and was made the capital of the Kingdom of Asturias as early as 810. Although the city has since faded into the background of Spanish political geography, its immense park, lively street musicians, beloved *churrerías*, underrated art museum, and endless shopping are more than enough to keep visitors busy for several days. If the urban scene isn't for you, the mountains on the horizon, with the quiet Monte Naranco minutes away and the Picos de Europa beyond, allow you to explore the beauty of the Asturian countryside.

■ TRANSPORTATION

Flights: Aeropuerto de Ranón/Aeropuerto Nacional de Asturias (☎985 12 75 00), in Avilés, 28km from Oviedo. **Prabus,** C. Marqués de Pidal, 20 (☎985 25 47 51), runs frequent buses from the ALSA station to the airport. **Aviaco** (☎985 12 76 03) and **Iberia** (☎985 12 76 07) fly to **Barcelona, London,** and **Madrid.**

Trains: Both RENFE and FEVE serve Oviedo from **Estación del Norte,** Av. de Santander.

FEVE (☎985 29 76 56), 3rd fl. Info open daily 9am-11:30pm. To: **Bilbao** (7hr., 9:05am, €17.80); **El Ferrol** (6½hr., 7:47am and 2:47pm, €16.70) via **Ribadeo** (4hr., €8.70); **Llanes** (2hr., 5 per day 9:05am-6:55pm, €6); **Santander** (4½hr., 9:05am and 3:35pm, €11.20).

RENFE (☎902 24 02 02), 1st fl. Pay attention to the type of train; a slow local train through the mountains can double your travel time. Info open daily 7:45am-11:15pm. To: **Barcelona** (12-13½hr.; Su-F 10:50am and 7:48pm, Sa 10:57am; €40-53) via **Burgos** (5-6hr., €21.50-28); **Gijón** (30min., every 30min. 5:18am-11:28pm, €1.90); **León** (2-2½hr.; M-F 5 per day 7:30am-11pm, Sa 3 per day 9:50am-4:25pm, Su 4 per day 9:50am-11pm; €6.10-19.50); **Madrid** (6-9hr., 3 per day 9:50am-11pm, €34.50-38.50) via **Valladolid** (4hr., €24-27).

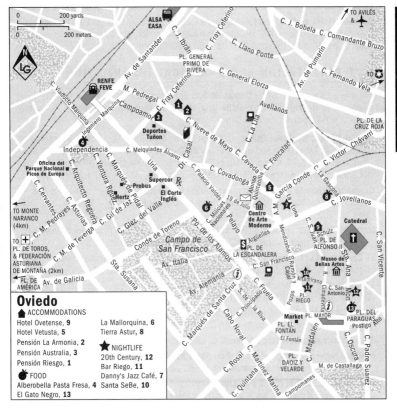

Oviedo

▲ ACCOMMODATIONS

Hotel Ovetense, **9**

Hotel Vetusta, **5**

Pensión La Armonia, **2**

Pensión Australia, **3**

Pensión Riesgo, **1**

La Mallorquina, **6**

Tierra Astur, **8**

★ NIGHTLIFE

20th Century, **12**

Bar Riego, **11**

🍎 FOOD

Alberobella Pasta Fresa, **4**

El Gato Negro, **13**

Danny's Jazz Café, **7**

Santa SeBe, **10**

Buses: ALSA (national) and **Económicos/EASA** (regional) buses operate out of the station on C. Pepe Cosmen (☎902 49 99 49). Open daily 6:30am-12:30am.

ALSA (☎985 96 96 96). To: **Barcelona** (12hr.; 8am and 8pm, Su also 7:30pm; €43.70); **Burgos** (4¼hr., 8am and 8pm, €14.30); **La Coruña** (4½-6¾hr.; 4 per day M-Sa 6:30am-4pm, Su 6:30am-7pm; €22-29); **León** (1½hr., 9-13 per day 7:30am-10:30pm, €7.10); **Madrid** (5hr.; M-Sa 10-11 per day 6:30am-1:30am, Su 9 per day 7:30am-12:30am; €26.40-41.50); **Santander** (3-4hr., 8-10 per day 7am-12:45am, €11-14.30); **Santiago de Compostela** (5½-7hr.; 4 per day M-Sa 6:30am-4pm, Su 6:30am-7pm; €26-33); **Vigo** (7-9hr., 6:30am and 3pm, €30.90); **Valladolid** (4hr., 4 per day 7am-6pm, €15.10).

Económicos/EASA (☎985 29 00 39). To: **Arenas de Cabrales** (2hr.; M-F 5 per day 7:45am-6pm, Sa-Su 9:30am and 6pm; €7.20); **Cangas de Onís** (1-1½hr.; M-F 22 per day 6:30am-9:30pm, Sa-Su 13 per day 8:30am-9:30pm; €5.10); **Covadonga** (1¾hr.; M-F 5 per day 6:45am-5:30pm, Sa-Su 4 per day 8:30am-6:30pm; €5.80); **Llanes** (1½-2hr.; M-F 20 per day 6:45am-12:45am, Sa-Su 17 per day 7am-12:45am; €7.30).

Public Transportation: TUA (☎985 22 24 22) runs **buses** 8am-10pm (€0.80). All stops have bus maps. #4 runs from the train station up C. Uría, turning off just before Campo de San Francisco. #2 goes from both stations to the hospital. #2, 3, 5, and 7 run from the train station along C. Uría to the old city. #3 also runs from Campo de Santa Cruz and C. Uría up to Monte Naranco.

Taxis: Radio Taxi (☎985 25 00 00). 24hr. service. €3-4 from the stations to the old city.

Car Rental: Hertz, C. Ventura Rodríguez, 4 (☎985 27 08 24; fax 27 26 31). From €55 per day with 350km limit. 23+, must have had license for 1yr.; ages 23-25 €6 extra per day. Open M-F 9am-1pm and 4-7:30pm, Sa 9:30am-noon.

■★⚡ ORIENTATION AND PRACTICAL INFORMATION

At Oviedo's city center is the **Campo de San Francisco,** a massive park on the slope of a hill. At its downhill base is **Calle Uría,** the city's main thoroughfare. The **cathedral** lies down C. San Francisco from C. Uría.

Tourist Office: Regional Office, C. Cimadevilla, 4 (☎985 21 33 85). Brochures on Oviedo and Asturias, including the Picos de Europa. English spoken. Open M-F 9am-2pm and 4:30-6:30pm, Sa-Su 10am-2pm and 4-7pm. **Municipal Office,** C. Marqués de Santa Cruz, 1 (☎985 22 75 86). Open daily 10:30am-2pm and 4:30-7:30pm.

Currency Exchange: Banco Santander Central Hispano, Pl. de la Escandalera (☎985 20 83 30), across from Campo de San Francisco. Open Apr.-Sept. M-F 8:30am-2pm; Oct.-Mar. M-F 8:30am-2pm, Sa 8:30am-1pm.

Luggage Storage: Lockers at the **RENFE station** (€1.80 per day). Open daily 7am-11pm. Also at the **bus station** (€2 per day). Open daily 6:30am-12:30am.

El Corte Inglés: C. Uría, 33. Gigantic department store with supermarket downstairs. Open M-Sa and the 1st Su of the month 9:30am-9:30pm. AmEx/MC/V.

English-Language Bookstore: Librería Cervantes, C. Dr. Casal, 9 (☎985 20 77 61). Open M-Sa 10am-1:30pm and 4:15-8:15pm. MC/V.

Police: Municipal (☎092 or 985 24 03 00). **Guardia Civil** (☎062 or 985 28 02 04). Both are in the municipal building on C. Quintana.

24hr. Pharmacy: Farmacia Nestares, C. Uría, 36. Across from El Corte Inglés.

Medical Services: Hospital Central de Asturias, Av. de Julián Clavería (☎985 10 61 00), near the Pl. de Toros. **Ambulance:** ☎985 10 89 00.

Internet Access: CiberCentro La Lila, C. la Lila, 17 (☎984 083 400). 24 fast computers. 1hr. limit if there's a wait; spots can be reserved. Free. Open M-F 9am-9pm. **Laser Internet Center,** C. San Francisco, 9 (☎985 20 00 66). €3 per hr. Open 24hr.

Post Office: C. Alonso Quintanilla, 1 (☎985 21 41 86). Open M-F 8:30am-8:30pm, Sa 9:30am-2pm. **Postal Code:** 33060.

⌂ ACCOMMODATIONS

Although *pensiones, hostales,* and *hoteles* pack the new city on C. Uría, C. Campoamor, and C. 9 de Mayo, cheap accommodations aren't easy to find, especially in July and August. However, all are clean and many are in restored buildings, offering comfort and convenience at a higher price than nearby cities.

Pensión Australia, C. Campoamor, 14, 2nd fl. (☎985 22 22 67). All of the expansive rooms in this centrally located *pensión* have 2 beds, TV, sink, and lots of sunlight. Clean common bath. Singles €15; doubles €25. ❶

Pensión Riesgo, C. 9 de Mayo, 16, 1st fl. (☎985 21 89 45). Pleasant *pensión* in the city center. Singles €15; doubles €30, with shower €33. ❷

Hotel Ovetense, C. San Juan, 6 (☎985 22 08 40; fax 21 62 34). Comfortable rooms in a noisy neighborhood only a few steps away from the cathedral. July-Sept. singles €35; doubles €50; triples €60; quads €80. Oct.-June €30/€45/€55/€70. AmEx/MC/V. ❸

Hotel Vetusta, C. Covadonga, 2 (☎985 22 22 29; fax 22 22 09). A modern 3-star hotel, Vetusta offers jacuzzis and saunas in half of its elegant rooms. Singles €53-62; doubles €75-82. IVA not included. AmEx/MC/V. ❺

Pensión La Armonia, C. Nueve de Mayo, 14 (☎985 22 03 01). Comfy rooms with TV and spotless hall bath run by a hospitable owner and her dog. Singles €18; doubles €30. ❷

🍴 FOOD

If you have enough euros for only one drink in Oviedo, be sure to try *sidra* (cider) by the bottle (€1.50-3.60). It goes fast, and much of it ends up on the floor due to the unconventional pouring method. For the best experience, head to the wood-beamed **sidrerías,** where waiters pour from above their heads and expect you to swallow in one gulp. Cheap restaurants line C. Fray Ceferino between the bus and train stations. The indoor **market** at Pl. el Fontán (open M-Sa 8am-3pm) and **Supercor,** C. Uría, 15 (open M-Sa 9:30am-9:30pm), sell produce and groceries.

Tierra Astur, C. La Gascona, 1 (☎985 20 34 11). At the top of *La Calle de la Sidra,* Tierra Astur's wooden *terraza* and cavernous interior are the perfect spots to down bottle after bottle of *sidra* (€2) with traditional Asturian ham and cheese platters (€3.60-12). Generous fish and meat entrees €6.80-15, specialty *fabada asturiana* (black pudding stew) €9. Open daily 11am-2am. AmEx/MC/V. ❸

El Gato Negro, C. Mon, 22 (☎985 21 70 86). This dark, refined restaurant on a narrow street offers delicious Asturian fare with a generous *menú* (€8.50). *Raciones* €4.20-15.30, entrees €10.20-15.60. Open Tu-Su 11:30am-5pm and 7pm-midnight. MC/V. ❷

Alberobella Pasta Fresca, C. de la Independencia, 22 (☎985 27 57 15). Concocts delicious and authentic Italian fare, perfect for the tapas-weary traveler. Lunch buffet €5.20. Huge pasta dishes €7.50-9. Pizza €6-9. Salads €2.20-2.50. MC/V. ❷

La Mallorquina, C. Milicias Nacionales, 5 (☎985 22 40 75). Sunny cafe offers light, vegetarian-friendly fare. Salads €7-12. *Menú* €7.50. Open daily 10am-midnight. ❷

📷 SIGHTS

CATEDRAL DE SAN SALVADOR. A recent renovation restored Oviedo's cathedral to its original splendor. Two chapels have brilliant blue ceilings above the altar. The **Capilla de Santa María del Rey Casto,** which contains the royal pantheon, was chosen by Alfonso II el Casto in 802 to house the remains of Asturian monarchs and Christian relics rescued from the Moors. In this chapel, also look for the statue of San Pedro holding a metal key in his hand; according to legend, if you make three wishes and turn the key around three times, one of the wishes will come true. The cathedral complex also includes the famous **crypt** of Santa Leocadia, which holds the remains of the martyrs Eulogio and Leocadia, a *cámara santa* (holy chamber), a **cloister,** and a church **museum.** *(Pl. de Alfonso II. ☎985 22 10 33. Open July-Sept. M-F 10am-8pm, Sa 10am-6pm; Oct.-June M-F 10am-1pm and 4-7pm, Sa 4-6pm. Cámara santa €1.25. Museum €3, children €0.95. Th evening free.)*

MUSEO DE BELLAS ARTES. The two buildings of the Museo de Bellas Artes in the **Palacio de Velarde** display the fifth-largest collection of Spanish art in the country. While the upper floors have devotional art on loan from Madrid's Prado, the ground floor has a collection of astonishing modern works by local artists. In addition to the Klimt-esque work of Herme Anglada Camaresa, highlights include the gigantic *Retablo de Santa Marina* and works by El Greco, Goya, Velázquez, and Picasso. *(C. Santa Ana, 1, just up from Pl. de Alfonso II. ☎985 21 30 61. Open July-Aug. Tu-Sa 11am-2:30pm and 5-9pm, Su 11am-2:30pm; Sept.-June Tu-F 11am-2pm and 4:30-8:30pm, Sa 11:30am-2pm and 5-8pm, Su 11:30am-2:30pm. Free.)*

MONTE NARANCO. Asturian Pre-Romanesque style was the first European attempt to blend architecture, sculpture (including human representations), and murals after the fall of the Roman Empire. The style was developed under Alfonso II (789-842) and refined under his son Ramiro I, for whom the *Ramirense* style is named. Two examples, the recreational palace **Santa María del Naranco** and the royal church of **San Miguel de Lillo,** both elegant in their slender simplicity, stand 4km outside Oviedo on Monte Naranco. *(From C. Uría, take bus #3 toward the train station; daily 8:30am and every hr. 9:40am-9:40pm, €0.75. ☎985 29 56 85. Both open Apr.-Sept. Su-M 9:30am-1:30pm, Tu-Sa 9:30am-1:30pm and 3:30-7:30pm; Oct.-Mar. Su-M 10am-1pm, Tu-Sa 10am-1pm and 3-5pm. €2.20, children €1.20. M free.)*

OTHER SIGHTS. The tourist offices can provide you with a list of Gothic **churches.** The **Centro de Arte Moderno** hosts temporary exhibits of regional and national cutting-edge artists. *(C. Alonso Quintanilla, 2. Open M-F 5-9pm, Sa 11:30am-2:30pm and 5-9pm, Su 11:30am-2:30pm. Free.)*

⚄ OUTDOOR ACTIVITIES

Though not the best base for hiking in the Parque Nacional Picos de Europa (p. 583), Oviedo is definitely the place to stock up on gear and supplies, as shops within the park and in gateway towns can be prohibitively expensive.

☒ **Federación Asturiana de Montaña,** Av. de Julián Clavería, 11 (☎985 25 23 62; www.fempa.net), near the bullring, a 30min. walk from the city center, or take bus #2 or 12 (dir.: Hospital) from C. Uría. This office is in charge of all outdoor activities in the national park and can direct visitors to branches throughout the area. Organizes excursions and provides guides and advice on weather and the best hiking routes. Instructors for everything from paragliding to kayaking. Open M-W and F 10am-2pm, Th 5-8pm.

Deportes Tuñon, C. Campoamor, 7 (☎985 21 48 40). Extensive selection of camping and rock-climbing gear, long underwear, and a few maps. Open M-F 10am-1:30pm and 4:30-8:30pm, Sa 11am-2pm. AmEx/MC/V.

⚄ NIGHTLIFE

The streets south of the cathedral, especially C. Mon and the areas around Pl. Riego, Pl. el Fontán, and Pl. el Paraguas, teem with noisy *sidrerías* and clubs. Stylish **Bar Riego,** on Pl. Riego, serves tasty *batidos* (milkshakes; €2-3.60) on a breezy *terraza.* (Open M-Sa noon-4pm and 8pm-2am.) After a few *chupitos* and *copas*, most students head to one of the clubs nearby. **20th Century,** C. Mon, 12, and **Santa SeBe,** C. Altamirano, 6, pick up after 2am and are popular with locals. (Beer €2.20-2.50, mixed drinks €3.50-5. Open 10:30pm-6am.) Between C. Alcalde M. García Conde and C. Jovellanos, **Danny's Jazz Café,** C. Luna, 11, is a lively spot even in mid-week, with Nat King Cole and Miles Davis LP's on the walls. (☎985 21 14 83. Beer €1.80, mixed drinks €3.60. Open daily 8pm-4am.) Wine connoisseurs follow **la ruta de los vinos** (the wine route) from *bodega* to *bodega* along C. El Rosal (*copas* €1.80-3.60). For about 10 days around September 21, Oviedo throws a **fiesta** with concerts and processions in honor of its patron saint, San Mateo.

GIJÓN ☎985

Gijón (pop. 275,000) may harbor nine beaches along its shoreline, but sand, sun, and sea are not the only reasons to visit this lively coastal town. Gijón (Xixón in the local dialect) has made the transition to a modern city while remaining solidly connected to its history, as evidenced by its Roman wall—parts of which have been reconstructed—and the name of Gaspar Melchor de Jovellanos, an illustrious 18th-century thinker (and close friend of Diego Velázquez), which still adorns many of Gijón's main buildings. The fiesta-like energy of the Plaza Mayor with its open-air market and *sidrerías* will make any stay in the city an exciting one.

▐ TRANSPORTATION

Trains: Gijón has two train stations, **Estación FEVE-RENFE,** C. Alvarez Juarez and **Estación Jovellanos RENFE,** C. Sanz Crespo (☎985 17 02 02).

RENFE: (☎985 98 13 63). To: **Barcelona** (13hr., 10:30am and 7:20pm, €40.50-53.50); **Madrid** (6-7hr., 9:30am and 3:55pm, €35.50; overnight 9hr., 10:30pm, €40); **Oviedo** (35min., every 30min. 6am-11:25pm, €2.15).

FEVE: (☎985 34 24 15). To **Avilés** (40min., every 30min. 7am-10pm, €0.90) and **Cudillero** (1½hr., 7 per day 7am-7:30pm, €0.90).

Buses: (☎985 35 75 82), Av. Magnus Blikstad at Av. Llanes. Runs **ALSA** buses to: **Barcelona** (12-13hr., 7:30am and 7:30pm, €45); **Bilbao** (5hr., 5 per day 6:30am-4:45pm, €18); **Madrid** (5½hr., 2 per day, €35-41.50); **Oviedo** (1hr., every hr. 8am-10:30pm, €1.75); **Ribadesella** (1¾hr., 6 per day 6:30am-8pm, €5.72); **San Sebastián** (6½hr., 4 per day 6:30am-4pm, €24); **Santander** (2½-3½hr., 6 per day 6:30am-8pm, €12); **Villaviciosa** (30min., 6 per day 6:30am-8pm, €4.10).

Taxis: Radio Taxi, Antolín de la Fuente Cla, 4 (☎985 14 11 11).

▐▌ ORIENTATION AND PRACTICAL INFORMATION

The high headland of the peninsula known as **Cimadevella** marks the old town, centered about the Plaza Mayor. The main beach, **Playa de San Lorenzo,** to the east and the **Puerto Deportivo** dock to the west sandwich the modern downtown; public gardens, the **Jardines de Begoña,** lie to the south.

Tourist Offices: Municipal office (☎985 34 17 71), on the big dock in the Puerto Deportivo. Excellent listings of accommodations, beaches, restaurants, museums, and upcoming festivals. Open summer daily 8am-10pm, winter 8am-8pm. 2 smaller offices at Playa de San Lorenzo and Pl. de los Campinos next to the Jardines de Begoña. **Regional Office** (☎902 30 02 02) at the east end of the Puerto Deportivo in the Jardines de la Reina. Open summer daily 10am-8pm, winter 10am-2pm and 4-6pm.

Police: Municipal Police Station Av. Hermanos Felgueroso (☎092).

Medical Services: Health center, C. Donato Argüellas, 300m east of the Teatro Jovellanos. The nearest hospitals are **Hospital de Jove** (☎985 32 00 50) and **Hospital de Cabueñes** (☎985 81 50 00). **Ambulance:** ☎985 16 85 13.

24hr. Pharmacy: Farmacía Begoña (☎985 34 25 18), next to the Teatro de Jovellanos.

Laundromat: Lavarama, C. Dindurra, 3. Open M-F 9am-1:30pm and 3:30-8:30pm.

Post Office: (☎902 19 71 97), Pl. 6 de Agosto. **Postal Code:** 33200.

▐▐ ACCOMMODATIONS AND CAMPING

▨ **Hotel Albor,** Pl. Estación de Langrea, 2 (☎/fax 985 34 75 89), next to the train station. Comfortable, well-lit rooms with clean bathrooms and satellite TV. Friendly, eco-conscious owner speaks some English. Singles €30; doubles €45. MC/V. ❸

Hotel Gijón, Pedro Duro, 6 (☎985 35 60 36; fax 35 99 57). Spacious rooms with big windows looking out onto the Puerto Deportivo. All rooms with bath, TV, safe, and telephone. Singles €51-72; doubles €66-93. ❺

Camping: Camping Deva-Gijón (☎985 13 38 48), exit A-66 Salida Deva from the Cta. N-632, 4km east of the city. 2 pools, tennis courts, a restaurant, and a lounge make this campground seem like a hotel. €4 per person, €4 per tent, €4 per car. ❶

FOOD

The tourist office hands out brochures for the best restaurants, including many *sidrerías*, which serve up delicious seafood dishes such as clam and mussel paella in addition to *sidra* (cider). The most popular are **La Galana**, in the plaza next to the Ayuntamiento, and **La Zamorana**, C. Hermanos Felgueroso, 38. In restaurants, *sidra* is generally sold by the bottle (€2-8).

> **TIP**
> **SALUD!** The quality of an establishment's *sidra* can be measured by the server's style of pouring. Generally, the higher they hold the bottle over their heads and the farther down and more horizontally they hold the glass, the better the *sidra* is. Remember to down your glass quickly, in true Asturian style, to get all the good fizz at the top. Watch your shoes, as servers care more about the height of their pour than the amount they spill.

Café Dindurra, Paseo Begoña, 11 (☎985 35 26 20), next to the Teatro Jovellanos. One of the nicer cafes in the Jardines de Begoña, with over 18 different specialty coffees (€3.25-4.25). Attentive servers wait on diners in the plaza or underneath fluted pink columns. Sandwiches €4.50-5, *raciones* €4.25-5. Open daily 1-4pm and 8pm-2am. ❷

Al Pairo, C. San Bernardo, 10 (☎984 29 23 71). Serves standard cafe selections including salads (€4-6), sandwiches (€1.80-3.60), tortillas (€5) and seafood such as *calamares a la Romana* (fried calamari; €7). Open daily 8am-11:30pm. ❷

Banus, (☎985 35 64 10), next to the main tourist office in the Puerto Deportivo. A good spot to slow down for an afternoon or evening drink on the dock with a slightly older crowd. Gourmet ice cream €4-5. Open daily 11am-midnight. ❸

SIGHTS AND BEACHES

TEATRO JOVELLANOS. A city landmark located at the end of the Jardines de Begoña, closer to the old town, this theater was built in 1899 as the Teatro Dindurra, but was rehabilitated and reopened as the Teatro Jovellanos after surviving the 1930s civil war. With productions year-round (10-15 per month, €3-10), the theater also organizes Gijón's summer entertainment agenda. *(☎985 18 29 29; www.teatrojovellanos.com. Open for shows, generally starting at 8:30pm.)*

TERMAS ROMANAS. The Roman baths, first discovered in 1903 and fully excavated and opened as a museum in 1990, are the main remnants of the fortified Roman city that originally sat on the Cimadevilla. Other parts of this ancient city include sections of the old wall, some of which have been reconstructed near the baths. *(Campo Valdés, underground at the old town end of the Playa de San Lorenzo. ☎985 34 51 47. Open July-Aug. Tu-Sa 11am-1:30pm and 5-9pm, Su and holidays 11am-2pm and 5-8pm; Mar.-June and Sept. Tu-Sa 10am-1pm and 5-8pm, Su and holidays 11am-2pm and 5-7pm; Oct.-Feb. Tu-Sa 10am-1pm and 5-7pm, Su and holidays 11am-2pm. Free.)*

CENTRO CULTURAL CAJASTUR AND PALACIO REVILLAGIGEDO. Gijón's modern art museum has contemporary exhibitions that rotate once a month; with free admission, it's worth a visit. *(Plaza del Marqués, 2. ☎985 34 69 21; revillagigedo@cajastur.es. Open July-Aug. Tu-Sa 11am-1:30pm and 4-9pm, Su and holidays noon-2:30pm; Sept.-June Tu-Sa 10:30am-1:30pm and 4-8pm, Su noon-2:30pm. Free.)*

MUSEO DEL FERROCARRIL DE ASTURIAS. This museum is dedicated to preserving the history of trains and railways in Asturias and examining their effects on the cultural development of the region. Situated in the historic North Station, dating from the late 1800s, it reveals a chapter of Gijón's history that visitors would otherwise miss. *(In the old Estación del Norte, in front of the Playa de Poniente. ☎985 30 85 75. Open July-Aug. Tu-Sa 10am-2pm and 5-9pm, Su and holidays 11am-2pm and 5-9pm; Sept.-June Tu-Sa 10am-2pm and 4-8pm, Su 11am-2pm and 4-8pm. Free.)*

BEACHES. When the sun is shining, the beaches are the place to be in Gijón. The city's main beach, **Playa San Lorenzo**, attracts throngs of eager sunbathers, though it virtually disappears at high tide. On the other side of the Puerto Deportivo, the **Playa de Poniente** is sheltered by breakwaters, resulting in gentler waves and a more relaxed—if still crowded—atmosphere. Farther away, past San Lorenzo, is a series of beaches strung out at the foot of the cliffs and isolated from the bustle above. While rockier and rough, these beaches still offer a serene break.

RIBADESELLA ☎985

This quiet coastal town sits nestled between the Mar Cantábrico to the north and the Picos de Europa to the south. Ribadesella (pop. 4500) is split by the mouth of the Río Sella, with the older part on the eastern side of the town's main bridge, and the newer additions on the western side. While adventurous travelers come here to explore the prehistoric cave paintings at Cueva de Tito Bustillo or to canoe on the Sella, others choose Ribadesilla for its beautiful beaches.

⊏ TRANSPORTATION. The **train station** is located in the far southeast corner of town, up Ctra. de la Estación about 400m from the intersection with Av. Palacio Valdés. **FEVE** runs trains to **Llanes** (35min.; 3 per day 10:59am-8:54pm, M-F also at 7:10am and 12:41pm; €1.60) and **Oviedo** (2hr., 3 per day 7:55am-6:13pm, €4.70).

The **bus station** is about 300m south of the bridge off of Av. Palacio. **ALSA** (☎902 42 22 42) runs to: **Gijón** (1½hr.; M-F 8 per day 6:30am-8pm, Sa-Su 5 per day 11am-8pm; €5); **Llanes** (35min.; M-F 9 per day 8:25am-8:10pm, Sa-Su 6 per day 11:40am-8:10pm; €2); **Oviedo** (2hr.; M-F 10 per day 7:05am-7:35pm, Sa-Su 7 per day 9:10am-8:25pm; €6); **Villaviciosa** (30min.; M-F 7:15am and 4pm, Sa-Su 4pm; €5).

For 24hr. **taxi** service, call **Riosellana del Taxi,** S. Coop (☎985 86 15 40).

◼▢ ORIENTATION AND PRACTICAL INFORMATION. The center of Ribadesella is the **Puente del Sella,** the city's main bridge. The downtown area is on the eastern side; C. Marqueses de Argüelles, the main thoroughfare, runs along the river. The municipal **tourist office** is at the east end of the bridge off of C. Marqueses de Argüelles. It offers brochures for canoe rentals, hotels, and information on the caves. (☎985 86 00 38. Open July-Aug. daily 10am-10pm; Sept.-June M-Sa 10am-2pm and 4-8pm, Su and holidays 11am-2pm.) Local services include: **municipal police** (☎619 76 95 76); **Guardia Civil** (☎985 86 01 53), next to the bus station on Av. Palacio Valdés; **pharmacy** (☎985 86 01 53) on the corner of C. Comercio and Santa Marina; **health clinic** on C. Manuel Caso de la Villa (open daily 8am-3pm and 4-9pm for emergencies only); **laundromat, Lavandería Anna,** at C. Comercio, 30 (☎985 86 13 64; open M-F 9:30am-1pm and 4:30-7:30pm, Sa 9:30am-1:30pm); **Inter-**

ASTURIAN MYTHOLOGY

The streets of Ribadesella may not be filled with hordes of tourists, but they are haunted by beings just as scary, at least in our imaginations. On the way up to the Ermita de la Guía is the **Ruta de Mitología Asturiana,** a mystical road where strange creatures wait around each bend. Seven different signposts line the path, each describing a different creature from Asturian mythology, which dates to the days when most of Asturias was Celtic.

Today, the Asturian people are working to hold onto the stories their ancestors told of greedy *cuélebres* (dragons), the demons *Diañu Burlón* and *Pesadiellu,* who can only be vanquished by invoking *Dios,* and the tempest-summoning old wizard *El Nuberu.*

Many Asturians still blame the tiny thieving gnomes, known as *Sumiciu,* for misplaced items, though it is understood that their mischief is good-natured. The *trasgu,* short gnome-like beings with raggedy clothes and bright red hats, are perhaps the most famous, or infamous, of all—as they can either tidy up your house or turn it upside down depending on their mood, and once one becomes attached to you, it won't ever leave, even if you move.

So take a moment as you hike to look back to the days when mythological creatures roamed Asturias. But, men, keep an eye out as you read, lest the seductive *Xanes,* with their nymph-like bodies, lure you away at night.

net access at **Telefónica Movistar,** on the Pl. Nueva. (☎985 85 82 67. €1 per 30min. Open M-F 10am-2pm and 4:30-8:30pm, Sa 10am-2pm.) The **post office** (☎902 197 197), on C. Manuel Fernández Juncos, is on the eastern edge of town. (Open M-F 8:30am-2:30pm, Sa 9:30am-1pm.) **Postal Code**: 33560.

ACCOMMODATIONS AND FOOD. The best bargain in town is **Hotel Boston ❷,** C. El Pico, 7, just past the west end of the bridge. Rooms are clean, well-lit, and come with TV and private bath. (☎985 86 09 66. Singles €20; doubles €28.) Inexpensive rooms are available at the youth hostel **Albergue Roberto Frassinelli ❶,** C. Roberto Cangas, 1. Dorms have big lockers for storage. (☎985 86 11 05. Dinner €5. €11.50, over 30 €13.50.) The **Hotel Covadonga ❸,** C. Manuel Caso de la Villa, 9, has a more classic hotel appeal, though it's dark and the aging rooms are a bit overpriced. (☎985 86 01 10. July-Sept. singles €30; doubles €55, with bath €68. Oct.-June €30/€35/€45.) Upscale hotels can be found on the west side of the river, like the majestic shoreside **Villa Rosario ❺,** C. Dionisio Ruisánchez, 6. (☎985 86 00 90. Singles €52-120; doubles €68-150.)

The many *sidrerías* in Ribadesella are always a good bet for food; most have *menús* for €6-12. C. Marqueses de Argüelles and C. Manuel Caso de la Villa house at least half a dozen of these establishments. The **Restaurante Puerto Dos ❷,** at the east end of the bridge, serves great *cocidos de mariscos* (seafood stew; €15) for two people. (☎985 86 01 29. Daily specials €7-12. Open for breakfast and lunch, closes around 5pm.) The **Pizzería Bahia ❶,** C. Comercio across from the Pl. Nueva, offers quasi-American fare, including pizzas (€5-6), hamburgers (€2.30), and pasta dishes (€3.75), but it stops serving around 10pm. (☎985 86 03 83.) At night, sit and sip your gourmet coffee or Foster's at **El Malecón ❷,** on C. Manuel Caso de la Villa, while listening to a hip mix of jazz and Irish punk rock.

SIGHTS AND EXCURSIONS. Ribadesella's main spelunking attraction is the cave of **Tito Bustillo,** located on Av. de la Cueva de Tito Bustillo, about 300m south of the bridge on the west side of the river. The cave has protected prehistoric pictographs for thousands of years, but to see them you must make reservations at least one day in advance either by phone or online. (☎902 190 508; http://temat-ico.princast.es/cultura/yacimientos/index.html. Max. 5 people per reservation. Open Apr.-Sept. 8 W-Su 10am-4:15pm. 25min. tours €3, students €1.50, under 13 €1.) Other caves without pictographs are located around Ribadesella and are open for touring Wednesday through Sunday.

On the east side of the river, the **Ruta de Mitología Asturiana** (path of Asturian mythology) gives a lesson in the ancient folklore of Asturias as it leads up to the **Ermita de la Guía,** with perhaps the best view of the entire valley.

▐ ADVENTURE TOURISM. Nearly a dozen adventure tourism outfitters are based in Ribadesella, ready to take willing adventurers up the river for day float-trips, into the canyons for hikes, or out to the bridges for bungee jumping. **Trasgu Aventura,** C. Marqueses de Argüelles, opposite the tourist office, offers descents of the Sella complete with food and a brief training course (☎669 70 30 93. 4-5hr.; leaving at 10:30, 11:30am and 12:30pm; €23 per person), potholing (1½-2½hr.; leaving at 9:30 and 11:30am, €23), and canyoning (2-3hr., leaving at 9:30 and 11:30am, €36 per person). Prices include guides, transportation, and a bag lunch for longer trips. Trasgu also rents bicycles and four-wheelers and teaches courses in canoeing and climbing. Reserve a spot on any trip at least two days in advance, as they tend to fill up quickly.

▓ FESTIVALS. On the first Saturday of August, Ribadesella fills to the brim with expert canoers and kayakers from around the world as they gather for the annual **International Descent of the Sella,** an immensely popular river race from Arriondas to the mouth of the Sella at Ribadesella. When visiting during this week, make reservations at least a month in advance, or plan to sleep on the beach in your canoe.

LLANES ☎985

Perched on a narrow ledge between the heights of the Picos de Europa and the cliffs over the Bay of Biscay, Llanes seems like an apparition out of myth. While the small beaches here are crowded, this is no resort town; rather, it's a small village rising above the frothing sea that has not yet given way to the tides of tourism.

▐ TRANSPORTATION. Trains leave from the FEVE station, C. Alonso Vega (☎985 40 01 24) to **Oviedo** (2½hr., 3 per day 7:55am-6:13pm, €6) and **Santander** (2hr., 11:32am and 6:14pm, €6). To get to the tourist office and the center of the city from the train station, walk down C. Alonso Vega, take a right at the end onto C. Egidio Gavito, walk for two blocks, and turn left onto C. Alfonso IX.

ALSA-Turytrans runs **buses** from the new station on C. la Bolera (☎985 40 24 85), across town from the train station, next to the intersection of C. Pidal and Av. de la Concepción. (Ticket office open M-F 10am-1:30pm and 3:30-8pm, Su 3:15-8pm.) To: **Bilbao** (3-4hr., 6 per day 2am-6:45pm, €10.70); **Santiago de Compostela** (8½hr., 4:45am and 1:15pm, €32) via **A Coruña** (7¼-7½hr., €28); **Gijón** (2hr., 7 per day 4:45am-9:15pm, €7.36); **Oviedo** (1½-2½hr.; M-F every hr. 4:45am-9:15pm, Sa-Su every hr. 8am-9:15pm; €7.30); **San Sebastián** (4-5hr., 5 per day 2am-4:45pm, €16.80); **Santander** (1½hr., 7 per day 2am-9:45pm, €5.10). To reach the town center from the bus station, head up C. Pidal to the post office and turn onto C. las Barqueras, which leads across the bridge to the Ayuntamiento and tourist office. For a **taxi,** call ☎985 40 11 77 (24hr.). For **car rental,** head to **EuropCar,** on Av. de la Paz just before Cyber Spacio. (☎985 40 10 07. 21+, must have had license for 1yr. From €55 per day for 350km. Open M-F 9:30am-1:30pm and 4-8pm, Sa 9am-1:30pm.)

▐ PRACTICAL INFORMATION. The **tourist office** is housed inside a 13th-century tower on C. Alfonso IX, directly behind the yellow Casa de Cultura/Ayuntamiento on C. Castillo Mercaderes. Ask here for information on adventure tourism, beaches, and accommodations. (☎985 40 01 64. English spoken. Open mid-June to mid-Sept. M-Sa 10am-2pm and 5-9pm, Su 10am-2pm; mid-Sept. to mid-June M-F 10am-2pm and 4-6:30pm, Sa 10:30am-1:30pm.) Local services include: **Guardia Civil**, C. La Galea (☎985 40 00 70); **Farmacia Mariano Ruiz**, Pl. Parres Sobrino, 1 (open summer M-F 9:30am-1:30pm and 4:30-8pm, Sa 10:30am-1pm; winter M-F 9:30am-2pm and 4-7:30pm; late-night pharmacy location posted in window, though it may be a few towns over); **health center**, Av. de San Pedro (☎985 40 36 15); **Lavandería San Antonio**, C. Pidal, 11 (☎985 40 18 35; open M-F 10am-1:30pm and 4:30-8pm, Sa 10am-1:30pm); **Internet access** at **Cyber Spacio**, Av. de la Paz, 6 (☎985 40 03 44; €3 per hr.; open M-F 9am-midnight); **post office**, C. Pidal. (☎985 40 11 14. Open M-F 8:30am-2:30pm, Sa 9:30am-1pm.) **Postal Code:** 33500.

🛏🍴 ACCOMMODATIONS AND FOOD. Rooms fill early in July and August, making one-month advance reservations a necessity. **Casa del Río ❷**, Av. de San Pedro, 3, is a restored mansion two blocks from the beach with airy, spacious rooms, some with balconies. Doubles have tall windows. (☎985 40 11 91. Singles €15-23; doubles €33-40, with bath and TV €40-53.) With clean, bright rooms and a beautiful 17th-century stone arcade, **Pensión La Guía ❷**, Pl. Parres Sobrino, 1, is a central and comfortable choice. (☎/fax 985 40 25 77. Check-out 2pm. Doubles with bath €35-55; triples with bath €50-75. MC/V.) **Albergue de la Estación ❶**, C. Alonso Vega, in the same building as the FEVE station, is Llanes's only hostel, frequented by Spanish teens enjoying a beach weekend. (☎679 57 42 35. Breakfast €3. Wheelchair-accessible. Lockout 2-6pm. 4- to 8-bed dorms €11-14; doubles €30-36. MC/V.) For those looking to splurge on something unique, next door to Casa del Río is the worn limestone facade of **Hotel Don Paco ❺**, Av. de San Pedro, 1, a three-star hotel in a 17th-century manor with handsome rooms and welcoming soft beds. Its **restaurant ❹**, in the old church at the side of the mansion, updates its *menú* (€19) daily, serving up dishes of local game beneath vaulted ceilings and ornate chandeliers. (☎985 40 01 00; www.llaneshoteldonpaco.com. Singles €48-73; doubles €68-102. Restaurant open daily 8-11am, 1-4pm, and 8:30-11pm.) On a small bluff overlooking the ocean, **Camping Entreplayas ❶**, off Av. de Toró between Playas de Puerto Chico and Toró, is wildly popular, if not for its scenic views, then for the neighboring bar, where bathing-suit clad campers laze away their days. (☎985 62 99 94. €4.40 per person, per tent, and per car. Electricity €3.30.)

Cafes and *sidrerías* line C. las Barqueras, C. Castillo Mercaderes, and C. Nemesio Sobrino near the town center; close to the beaches, Av. de Toró and C. Marqués de Argüelles have many local eateries. **Café Bitácora ❶**, C. las Barqueras, 1, serves salads (€2-5), *platos combinados* (€5-6), and a whole menu of desserts (€2-4) in a lively, social outdoor terrace close to the river. (☎985 40 03 88. Open daily 8am-2am.) The less crowded, though no less social, setting at **Cafetería Xana ❶**, C. Marqués de Comillas, 6, around the corner from Bitácora, is a haven for a bit of quiet contemplation amidst portraits from Asturian mythology. (☎985 40 12 58. *Platos combinados* €6-7. Open daily 10am-1:30am.) However, the most exotic fare in town is undoubtedly served at **El Latino ❷**, C. Venezuela, 1. From the Ayuntamiento, walk up C. Nemesio Sobrino, turn right on Av. de San Pedro, and then left onto C. Genaro, which becomes Av. de Méjico and leads to C. Venezuela. This tropical cantina serves all the Mexican favorites, including guacamole, enchiladas, and fajitas. (☎985 40 32 40. Entrees €3-10. Restaurant open daily 8pm-midnight. Bar open 10am-2am.) **El Pescador ❷**, C. Manuel Cué, in the center of the old city, serves delicious Asturian entrees (€6-10) to loyal patrons who fill the restaurant's outdoor seating sections. (☎985 40 32 93. Open daily 11am-5pm and 7pm-1am.) To satisfy that sweet tooth, try the specialty chocolates or deliciously fresh pastries

(€0.80-1.50) at **Confitería Vega ❶**, next to the old section on C. Castillo Mercaderes. (Open daily 8am-10pm.) For groceries, go to **El Árbol**, Av. de Méjico, across from El Latino. (☎985 40 10 50. Open M-Sa 9am-9pm.)

◪ BEACHES. Though some of the most popular beaches in Asturias, these are not the wide swaths of sand common to many other resort towns in the region. Rather, Llanes's beaches are tucked into coves and inlets along the coast, made all the more idyllic by whimsical rocky outcroppings. As these are protected waters, the sea is often calm (and rather seaweedy), though waves can still build to a reasonable force on windy days. Compact **Playa de Sablón**, in the center of town, is the most popular—and the most crowded. From the Ayuntamiento, turn right onto C. Alfonso IX, which runs straight to the beach. **Playa de Toró** is by far Llanes's prettiest and most swimmer-friendly beach, though it's also fairly crowded. From the Ayuntamiento, walk up C. Castillo Mercaderes across the river, and at the post office, turn left onto Av. de la Guía, which turns into Av. de Toró. **Playa de Puerto Chico** will please those looking for total seclusion, but only if they can stand the mountains of seaweed and their accompanying stink. Don't come at high tide, as the beach virtually disappears. To get away from the sand for a change, follow the directions to Playa del Sablón, above, and take the steps up the hill to the ◪**Paseo de San Pedro**, a grassy promenade running along the edge of the cliffs above the sea, serenaded by the crashing waves below. Plenty of benches, shady palm trees, and lizards share the wide-open, breezy sea views.

CANGAS DE ONÍS ☎985

During the summer months, when the streets are packed with mountaineers and vacationing families, it can seem like the sole purpose of Cangas (pop. 6285) is to help travelers spelunk and hang glide. The town's accessibility by bus makes it a useful and ideal base for those interested in a taste of the famous Parque Nacional Picos de Europa. Those seeking a central base for extensive exploring should move on to towns within the park such as Posada de Valdeón, Sotres, or Poncebos. With all the hubbub about the Picos, however, it is easy to forget that Cangas has its own claim to fame. For 70 years, it was the very first capital of what would come to be the country of Spain, founded in 718 by Don Pelayo when his victory over the Moors marked the beginning of the *Reconquista*. Between arranging adventures, take a break to explore the legacies left behind by Pelayo and the previous Paleolithic, Celtic, and Roman inhabitants.

◪ TRANSPORTATION. ALSA, Av. de Covadonga, 18 (☎985 84 81 33), in the Pícaro Inmobiliario building across from the tourist office, runs **buses** to: **Arenas de Cabrales** (40min.; M-F 5 per day 9:10am-7:25pm, Sa-Su 10:55am and 7:25pm; €2.10); **Covadonga** (20min.; M-F 11 per day 8:30am-7:30pm, Sa-Su 7 per day 9:10am-8pm; €0.95); **Madrid** (7hr., 2:35pm, €26.26); **Oviedo** (1½-2hr.; M-F 12 per day 6:15am-8:30pm, Sa-Su 6 per day 9:15am-8:30pm; €5.05); **Valladolid** (5hr., 2:35pm, €14.95). For a taxi, call **Radio Taxi** (☎985 84 87 97 or 84 83 73, 24hr.). Rent cars at **EuropCar**, C. San Pelayo, 17. (☎985 94 75 02. €66 per day for 350km. Open Tu-Sa 9:30am-1:30pm and 4:30-8:00pm, Su 10:00am-2pm. V.)

◪ PRACTICAL INFORMATION. The main street in Cangas de Onís is **Avenida de Covadonga**. The **tourist office**, Jardines del Ayuntamiento, 2, is in the Plaza del Ayuntamiento across from the bus stop and has information about the town, accommodations, and adventure tourism offices, located in other park border towns. (☎/fax 985 84 80 05. Some English spoken. Open daily May-Sept. 10am-10pm; Oct.-Apr. 9am-2pm and 4-7pm.) Park information is available at the **Picos**

de Europa National Park Visitors' Center, Av. de Covadonga, 43, in the **Casa Dago.** From the bus stop, walk up Av. de Covadonga for two blocks past the Iglesia Santa María. The office has a list of mountain *refugios*, maps, hike suggestions, and a fantastic three-dimensional model of the park. (☎/fax 985 84 86 14. Open M-Sa 9am-2pm and 4-6:30pm, Su 9am-3:30pm.) Local services include: **Banco Santander Central Hispano,** C. Emilio Loria across from the Ayuntamiento (☎902 24 24 24; open M-F 8:30am-2pm, Sa 8:30am-1pm); **municipal police,** Av. de Covadonga, 21, in the Ayuntamiento (☎985 84 85 58); **pharmacy,** Av. de Castilla, 24, just off Av. de Covadonga near the *puente romano* (☎985 84 80 38; open daily 9am-7:30pm); **health center,** C. de la Cárcel, down C. Emilio Laria from Av. de Covadonga (☎985 84 85 71); **Internet access** next to the tourist office (€2 per hr.; open M-F 4-9pm); **post office,** Av. Constantino González, to the right off Av. de Covadonga heading toward the *puente.* (☎985 84 81 96. Open M-F 8:30am-2:30pm, Sa 9:30am-1pm.) **Postal Code:** 33550.

◪◩ ACCOMMODATIONS AND FOOD. A few clean *pensiones* along Av. de Covadonga will gladly accept your euros. **Hospedaje Principado ❷,** Av. de Covadonga, 16, 3rd fl., has limited occupancy, but immaculate rooms with TVs. (☎985 84 83 50; fax 84 83 15. Singles €12-19; doubles €20-30, with bath €33-39.) **El Chofer ❷,** C. Emilio Laria, 10, has clean rooms and firm beds with nice sheets that sore bodies will enjoy. TVs, sinks, and hall baths are standard, with Oriental rugs to spice things up. (☎985 84 83 05. Singles €20-35; doubles €25-45.) Serenely set at the western end of the Puente Romano, the newly remodeled **Hotel Imperion ❺,** C. Puente Romano, has all the amenities of a modern hotel—satellite TV, Internet, A/C, massage baths—in a stately 19th-century manor. (☎985 84 94 59. Singles €40-85; doubles €50-100; suites €68-124. AmEx/MC/V.) **Camping Covadonga ❶,** in Soto de Cangas, 4km up the road toward Arenas de Cabrales, has a cafeteria, bar, supermarket, and hot showers. (☎985 94 00 97. Open June-Sept. 20 and *Semana Santa.* €4.50 per person, €4.20 per child, €5 per tent, €4 per car.)

Choose from sandwiches (€2.50-3.50), pasta and pizza (€6.20), tapas, and hamburgers (€2-5) at **Cafetería Reconquista ❶,** Av. de Covadonga, 6. (☎985 84 82 75. Open daily 8am-11pm.) **Restaurant Pizzería Eladia ❷,** Av. de Covadonga, 14, next to the bus stop, serves pizzas (€6-7), entrees (€7-9), and three-course *menús* (€9) across from the town's main social plaza. (☎985 84 80 00. Open daily 10am-midnight.) For a do-it-yourself-meal, try **Alimerka Supermercado,** Av. de Covadonga, 13. (☎985 84 94 13. Open Su-M 9am-2pm, Tu-Sa 9am-9:30pm.)

◪◪ SIGHTS AND EXCURSIONS. At the far end of Av. de Covadonga is the **Puente Romano,** an ancient bridge with an ornate golden cross hanging from the main arch, particularly beautiful at night. From the bridge, follow Av. de Covadonga into town, turn left onto C. Constantino González, and cross the river to reach the **Capilla de Santa Cruz.** This Romanesque chapel, built in 737, sits atop the town's oldest monument, a Celtic *dolmen* (monolith) dating from 3000 BC, which can be seen from the chapel's cave. (Open Tu-Su 10am-2pm and 4-6:30pm.) Not to be missed is **Cueva del "Buxu"** (BOO-shoo), whose walls are adorned with 15,000-year-old paintings by Cangas's paleolithic residents. To reach the cave, follow the main road to Covadonga for 3km until the signs for the *Cueva del Buxu* and Cardes, the closest town, direct you left. Cardes is up the hill about 600m, and the path to the cave starts in front of Bar Buxu. From the bar, it's about 1km to the actual cave. Buses to Arenas de Cabrales, Covadonga, and Llanes (see **Transportation,** p. 579) run near the cave; ask to be dropped off at the **Cruce de Susierra.** Come by 9:30am, as only 25 people are allowed in each day. (☎985 94 00 54. Open W-Su Apr.-Sept. 9:30am-3pm; Oct.-Mar. 9:30am-1pm and 3-5pm. €1.40.)

The Picos de Europa are filled with many rare and exotic animals, but even locals are lucky to see most of them once in a lifetime. However, at **La Grandera Zoo**, up Highway AS-114 about 4km toward Soto, gray bears *(osos sardos)*, Iberian wolves *(lobos)*, wild boars *(jabali)*, Iberian lynx, and 200 other native species can be viewed from the comfort of a short, flat path. (☎985 94 00 17. Open daily 11am-8pm. €6, children €4.) Those with wheels will want to head south from Cangas on highway N-625, which winds along the Río Sella. This route heads through Santillan and Sames, finally coming to the awe-inducing **Desfiladero de los Beyos,** an 11km gorge with wet rocks and blossoming beech trees.

▲ ADVENTURE TOURISM. Cangas de Onís is the perfect place to arrange outdoor activities, but it is imperative to reserve at least two days ahead of time, three to five days from June to August. There are several outfitters in town, but all are closed from December to February. **Cangas Aventura,** Av. de Covadonga, 23, sets up various expeditions, including hiking (low season only), *espeleología* (spelunking, €15-22), **barranquismo** (canyoning, swimming, and spelunking, €36), canoeing (2½hr., 11am-1:30pm, €30-36), and horseback riding (1hr. route €30, 2hr. €36). (☎985 84 92 61; fax 84 88 87. Open daily 9:30am-10pm. Prices include equipment, a guide, transportation to and from Cangas, and sometimes a bag lunch. Discounts for large groups and multiple activities, except in Aug. Call for departure times and destinations.) **Deportes Tuñon,** C. San Pelayo, 31, sells hiking shoes (€40-129), backpacks (€20-180), and all the other gear you'll need to conquer the Picos. (☎985 94 70 61. Open Tu-Sa 10am-1:30pm and 4-8pm, Su 10am-2pm. MC/V.)

ARENAS DE CABRALES ☎985

Some say the small town of Arenas de Cabrales (pop. 800) sits "as close to the sky as to the ground," and that's not so far from the truth. The town rests on several craggy peaks, and the fog, wandering mountain goats, and breathtaking vistas make Arenas seem almost like a mountain mirage. Outdoor enthusiasts flock here, eager to take advantage of the excellent hiking and climbing just 6km away in the Parque Nacional Picos de Europa (p. 583).

▐ TRANSPORTATION. The only reliable buses that come through Arenas are the **ALSA buses** (☎902 42 22 42) that head to **Cangas de Onís** (40min., M-F 5 per day 9:10am-7:25pm, €2.10) and continue to **Oviedo** (2hr., €7.15). Even these buses are often 15 min. behind or ahead of schedule and do not wait. Schedules for buses on other routes change frequently; at times they don't run at all. Check with the **tourist office** (see below) for current schedules. For a **taxi,** call Joaquín (☎985 84 64 87), who claims *"un cliente, un amigo"* ("a client, a friend") and will go almost anywhere in the Asturian Picos. Other taxi services are listed on the tourist hut.

▐ PRACTICAL INFORMATION. The **municipal tourist office** is in a hut on the main road just before the bridge. (☎985 84 64 84; http://turismo.cabrales.org. Open July-Sept. 20 Tu-Su 10am-2pm and 4-8pm.) However, **Ascatur** (Association of Cabrales Tourism) runs a **private tourist office,** Pl. Cuatro Caños, just across the street in the small park, that is much more reliable and has more information available on the park and on accommodations, adventure tourism, and just about every other service in the area. (☎985 84 67 47. Open summer daily 9am-10pm, spring and fall Tu-Su 10am-1pm and 5-9pm.) Local services include: **Guardia Civil** (☎985 84 50 04), on the main road toward Cangas near the post office; **Consultorio Médico** (☎985 84 67 86), uphill on the main road across from the **ATM** and the **pharmacy** (☎985 84 50 16), which is next to Cajastur; **Internet access** in **Bar El Chibiski del Chilito** next to the **Disco Xana** up the main street from the tourist office, or at **El Mirador**

THE CHEESE STANDS ALONE

It's an odd selling point, but somehow Arenas de Cabrales has become famous for its unbridled moldy blue cheese, *queso de Cabrales*. Every year, local farmers empty the udders of their cows, goats, and ewes to make a starting mix for the cheese. The exact consistency varies, producing subtle differences in different Cabrales cheeses detectable only by the *queso* connoisseur.

The current production standards are as follows: after heating for several hours, rennet is added to curdle the milk, and the whey is slowly siphoned off. When only curds remain, they are placed in circular molds to sit for a day or two to drain, before being brought to the caves. Humidity, cool temperatures, and good ventilation provide a perfect home for the Penicillium bacteria, which give the cheese its characteristic blue color. Over the next six months, the bacteria hold a fiesta in the cheese, until, when it's removed and rolled onto the streets of every tourist spot in Asturias, it's become the speckled globs that make Cabrales famous. Brave tasters rave about the pungent flavor, creamy texture, and a knock-out kick.

*The **Cueva el Cares,** on the road to Poncebos, gives daily 1hr. tours in summer 10:15am-1:15pm and 4:15-7:15pm; fall and winter Sa-Su only. €2.50, children €1.50.*

Cibercafe in Po. de Cabrales, 15min. down the road to Cangas de Onís (☎985 84 54 30; €3 per hr.; open daily 7am-midnight, Su noon-midnight); **post office,** near the bus stop toward Cangas de Onís (open M-Sa 9-11am). **Postal Code:** 33554.

ꟾ◰ ACCOMMODATIONS AND FOOD. For a laid-back attitude, the ◧**Hotel Torrecerredo ❷**, known as the "one-star hotel with a five-star view," about 600m up the road to Cangas, is the perfect choice. Vegetarian-friendly meals are served regularly. The good-humored owners also operate an adventure tourism business by the same name. (☎985 84 67 05; fax 84 66 40. Reservations encouraged. Breakfast €5. Singles €20-40; doubles €30-55. AmEx/MC/V.) The homey **Pensión Covadonga ❷**, down C. Pedro Niembro near the tourist office, offers spotless rooms with incredible mountain views, with an impressive jungle of potted plants wrapping around the main staircase. (☎985 84 65 66. Reserve 1-2 months ahead for July and Aug. Doubles July €24, Aug. €35, Sept.-June €12-14.) **El Castañeu ❷**, right next to Pensión Covadonga, offers comfortable doubles, some with breathtaking views of the Picos. (☎985 84 65 73. Reserve a month ahead for Aug. One single €10-12; doubles with bath €24-32.) **Hotel Picos de Europa ❹**, Ctra. General, is located on the main road in an orange building visible from the bus stop. It offers spacious, fully equipped rooms and an outdoor pool. (☎985 84 64 91. Reserve a month in advance for Aug.; recommended for July. Singles €41-75; doubles €53-90. AmEx/MC/V.) **Naranjo de Bulnes Camping ❶**, 1km east on AS-114, has campsites and cabins, as well as a cozy TV room, a cafeteria, a bar, and shower facilities. (☎/fax 985 84 65 78. Camping €4.25 per person, €4 per tent, €3.80 per car. Cabins for 1-2 people €29-34; each additional person €6.)

Of the few eateries in Arenas, ◧**La Panera ❸**, left of Banco Bilbao Vizcaya (BBVA) and up a small hill, is by far the best. Over 100 years old and isolated on the top of a hill surrounded by the Picos on all sides, the building has the look and feel of an intimate alpine lodge. The restaurant serves delicious local specialties such as Asturian steak in smooth Cabrales cheese sauce (€16) on its romantic outdoor balcony, followed up by equally heavenly deserts. (☎985 84 68 10. *Menú* €11, entrees €11-20. Open daily noon-4pm and 7:30-11:30pm. MC/V.) For a typical *cafetería*, head down the main road to **Cafetería Santelmo ❷**, beside Hotel Picos de Europa. The restaurant offers a wide variety of *carnes* (meats, €8-12), salads (€7-9), and tapas (€3-8).

(Open daily 7am-4pm and 8pm-midnight. AmEx/MC/V.) The **Casa Tres Palacios** market, opposite the tourist office, carries a limited selection of grocery items. (☎985 84 65 05. Open M-F 6:30am-9:30pm, Sa-Su 7:30am-9pm.)

🔆 **ADVENTURE TOURISM. Novedades Cendón,** across the street from the tourist office, sells basic gear, guidebooks, and maps. (☎985 84 64 74. Open daily June-Aug. 9am-10:30pm; Sept.-May 10am-8pm. MC/V.) **SNP Viajes,** Pl. del Casteñedo, located 50m past Pensión Covadonga, organizes canoeing (€25 per person), caving (3-4hr., €22), and hiking (€25-40) daytrips, but you must gather at least four people together to reserve a trip. Package includes guide, technical equipment, and lunch. (☎985 84 64 55; www.snptravel.com. Reservations required at least 2 days in advance. English spoken. Open 11am-1:30pm and 3-6pm.) **Torrecerredo** offers longer packages ranging from four to eight days, such as the self-guided hiking week, which includes room, board, maps, advice, and transportation (7 days, €400). Daytrips may be possible, especially for those staying at the hotel. Opportunities vary; call or visit the website for current info. (☎985 84 67 05; www.picosadventure.com. Reserve at least 3 days in advance. English spoken. MC/V.)

PARQUE NACIONAL PICOS DE EUROPA

Three hundred million years ago, Mother Nature flapped her limestone bedsheet and erected the Picos de Europa, a mountain range of curious variation and chaotic beauty. This accident of nature created a formidable border between the Asturias and Cantabria regions and the rest of Spain, and residents found protection from the Moors and divine inspiration in their impenetrable range. Although the mountains and towns here often feel as isolated as they were centuries ago, they are now part of the very civilized Parque Nacional Picos de Europa. Founded in 1918 as the Parque Nacional de Covadonga, Spain's first national park, it grew into the largest national park in Europe, spanning three massifs and three provinces (Asturias, Cantabria, and Castilla y León).

The ancient crags and summits of the Picos de Europa shelter some of Europe's most elusive and endangered species, including wild horses, boars, wolves, bears, and *chamois* (a goat-type animal), as well as long-eared owls, Egyptian vultures, songbirds, and eagles. The scrub-spotted peaks lure thousands of outdoor enthusiasts who come to explore the myriad caves and caverns carved out by centuries of glacial activity and the backcountry trails that trace the contours of the mountains. Highlights include the distantly regal Naranjo de Bulnes, the sparkling Lagos de Enol y Ercina (p. 588), and the vertigo-inducing Teleférico de Fuente Dé (p. 591).

⛏ ORIENTATION

Part of the larger Cordillera Cantábrica, the Picos de Europa consist of three massifs: the **Occidental (Cornión),** the **Central (Urrieles),** and the **Oriental (Ándara).** The highest peak, Torrecerredo (2646m), rises out of the Central massif. Several rivers wind through the park; the three largest are the Sella, Dobra, and Cares. The **Garganta del Cares** (Cares Gorge) cuts a dramatic line between the Macizo Oriental and Macizo Central, the latter of which holds the park's most popular trails and famous peaks: the treacherous **Peña Vieja** (2613m) and **Pico Tesorero** (2570m), the stark **Llambrión** (2642m), and the mythic **Naranjo de Bulnes** (Picu Urriellu; 2519m).

Those interested in day hikes and guided adventure tourism start in **Cangas de Onís** (p. 579) and **Potes** (p. 590); experienced and well-equipped hikers head to **Arenas de Cabrales** (p. 581), which serves as a good base for exploring the Urrieles. Although independent adventures are definitely possible, most visitors opt for guided hikes and expeditions unless they have extensive experience.

TRANSPORTATION

Getting to the Picos is relatively easy—it's getting around once there that's difficult. **ALSA buses** link **Cangas de Onís** (p. 579) and **Arenas de Cabrales** (p. 581), the gateways in the west and the north, to towns just inside the park's borders. In summer, these buses run from Arenas to **Panes** as well. The most important towns within the park are **Covadonga** and **Poncebos; La Palomera buses** link **Potes,** the gateway in the east, with **Panes** to the north and **Fuente Dé** to the south. With a bit of creativity and the help of knowledgeable locals, it is possible to reach more towns than bus schedules allow. It is, however, much more efficient to travel by car, as buses run infrequently, irregularly, and make many stops. Route **AS-114** runs along the northern edge of the Picos from Cangas de Onís through Arenas de Cabrales and on to Panes, where it intersects Route N-621. N-621 runs 50km south and west to Potes, where a branch leads to Fuente Dé.

PRACTICAL INFORMATION

The key to hiking in the Picos is planning ahead. Water sources and campsites are hard to come by, there are no real supermarkets in the park, and few ATMs are available at towns in the region. The only phones are in town and at *refugios*.

THERE IS A SEASON. Although hiking is possible from May to September, the best times to visit are July and August, despite the crowds. In early summer, it is cold and stormy, with snow still a real possibility; September weather can be equally unpredictable. If visiting during July and August, you must make reservations in the gateway cities to the park (Cangas de Onís, Arenas de Cabrales, and Potes) a month in advance, possibly even earlier in August.

Park Information: In **Asturias:** Cangas de Onís, Av. de Covadonga, 43 (☎985 84 86 14; p. 579); in **Cantabria:** Camaleño (☎942 73 05 55); in **Castilla y León:** Posada de Valdeón, Ctra. Cordinanes (☎987 74 05 49; fax 74 05 79).

Guidebooks: In English, Robin Walker's *Picos de Europa* is the best. In Spanish, the guides of Miguel Ángel Andrados provide extensive information. The park office in Cangas sells a guide book (in Spanish) listing hiking trails, with maps and photos (€9).

Gear: Basic amenities and hiking gear are available in all of the gateway towns, but **gear** is cheapest in Oviedo (p. 568). Inside the park, **food and water** are scarce, even in the towns of Poncebos, Covadonga, and Fuente Dé, none of which have supermarkets. **Water purification** packets are only available in Oviedo. Inside the park, only water from identified springs is safe to drink without treatment. The free **maps** of the park provided by tourist offices are insufficient for hiking if you plan on following any trails other than the most touristed. Sufficiently detailed and current trail maps can be purchased in just about every store in Cangas de Onís, Arenas de Cabrales, and Potes for €3-4.

Refugios and Rangers: Before embarking on any hikes in the park, consult the list of *refugios* below, which, in addition to providing shelter in the mountains in the form of dorm-style bunks (sometimes mattresses, no sheets), also double as ranger stations.

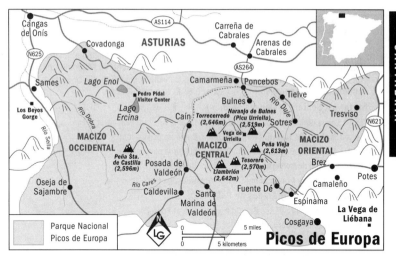

The stations are typically open from 8 or 9am to 5 or 6pm, except during winter, when most are unmanned. However, there is always at least one building open free of charge for brave winter hikers. Some *refugios* are known by several names. You can also pick up the most complete and current list at any park office. Most *refugios* cost €6-7 per night; the larger ones, such as Vegarredonda and Vega de Urriellu, generally have nicer amenities.

Macizo Occidental

▓ Casa Municipal de Pastores/Vega de Enol (☎985 84 92 61), next to Lake Enol. 26 spots.

Vegarredonda (☎985 92 29 52, alt. 1410m), south of Lake Enol. 68 spots.

Marqués de Villaviciosa/Vega de Ario (☎639 81 20 69, alt. 1630m), by Vega de Ario southeast of Lake Enol. 45 spots, little water available during winter months.

Vegabaño (☎987 29 21 47), in the southwest corner of the park. 25 spots.

Ordiales (☎987 29 21 47, alt. 1750m), at the Ordiales lookout. 4 spots. No rangers in residence, free access.

Macizo Central

▓ Delgado Úbeda/Vega de Urriellu. (☎985 92 52 00), by Vega de Urriellu. 96 spots, open with rangers in residence during winter months.

Cabaña Verónica, near Pico Tesorero. 3 spots, call the Guardia Civil to reserve (☎942 73 00 07, alt. 2325m).

El Redondo/Fuente Dé (☎942 73 66 99), by Fuente Dé in the park's southeast corner. 68 spots.

Diego Mella/Collado Jermoso (☎636 99 87 27, alt. 2060m), next to Collado Jermoso. 28 spots.

Toño Odriozola/Hotel de Áliva (☎942 73 09 99), in the Ptos. de Áliva. Several hotel-style doubles. The most expensive *refugio* in the park. Doubles €45.

José Ramón Lueja/Jou de Los Cabrones (☎985 92 52 00, alt. 2034m), by Jou de los Cabrones. 24 spots.

La Terenosa, near the Collado Pandébano en route to Vega de Urriellu (alt. 1315m). 30 spots. Reserved for emergency use only; don't plan ahead to stay here. When necessary, keys in neighboring *cabaña* (cabin).

Macizo Oriental

Casetón de Andara (☎689 89 70 14, alt. 1725m), by Vegas de Andara and Pica del Mancondiú. 18 spots.

Tours and Guided Hikes: For information on adventure tourism outings, see **Cangas de Onís** (p. 579), **Arenas de Cabrales** (p. 581), and **Potes** (p. 590). The park service offers free guided day-hikes from towns throughout the park. Simply show up at the departure point at the listed time to participate. Below is a list of guided hikes, with difficulty (L=Low, M=Medium, H=High), map route number, location, schedule, and departure point. Shortly before your hike begins, call the region park office to confirm the information. You can also pick up schedules at any park office.

Northwest Sector (by Cangas de Onís)

L: A-1 **Lagos de Covadonga.** (3hr.; Tu-W, F 10:30am; Buferrera parking lot at Los Lagos.)

M: A-3 **Majada del Tolleyu.** (4hr., W 9:30am, Buferrera parking lot.)

M: A-4 **Majada de Belbín.** (4hr., Th. 9:30am, Buferrera parking lot.)

M/H: A-2 **Vega de Comeya.** (5hr., M 9:30am, Buferrera parking lot.)

M/H: A-5 **Vega de Orandi.** (5hr., F 9:30am, Covadonga (Escolanía).)

Northeast Sector (by Arenas de Cabrales):

M: B-2 **Bulnes.** (4hr.; Tu and Sa 10am; info booth at Poncebos.)

M: B-3 **Minas de Ándara.** (4½hr.; W and Su 10am; Hoyo del Tejo, between Sotres and Tresviso.)

M/H: B-1 **Monte Camba.** (4hr.; M and F 10am; Plaza de Tielve.)

H: B-4 **Peña Maín.** (6hr., Th 9:15am, Plaza de Sotres.)

Southeast Sector (Liébana—by Potes and Fuente Dé)

L: C-2 **Hayedo de las Íces.** (4½hr., Tu 10am, Plaza at Espinama.)

L: C-3 **Vega Linares.** (4hr., W 10am, Cosgaya town border.)

L: C-4 **Canal Arredondas.** (4hr., Th 10am, Brez town border.)

L: C-6 **Sierra de Bejes.** (4hr., Sa 10am, Plaza at Bejes.)

L: C-7 **Puertos de Áliva.** (4hr., Su 10am, Fuente Dé at the top of the *teleférico* station.)

M: C-1 **Horcados Rojos.** (4hr., M 10am, Fuente Dé at the top of the *teleférico* station.)

M: C-5 **Espinama-Áliva.** (5½hr., F 10am, Plaza at Espinama.)

Southwest Sector (by Sajambre and Valdeón)

L: D-6 **El Cuebre.** (4hr., Sa 10am, Posada de Valdeón park info booth.)

L: D-7 **El Odrón.** (4hr., Su 10am, Posada de Valdeón park info booth.)

M: D-1 **Majada de Vegabaño.** (4½hr., M 9:30am, Soto de Sajambre at Escuelas.)

M: D-2 **Vega de Llos.** (6hr., Tu 9:30am, Posada de Valdeón park info booth.)

M: D-3 **Monte Piergua.** (4½hr., W 9:30am, Posada de Valdeón park info booth.)

M: D-4 **Valle de Sajambre.** (4½hr., Th 9:30am, Oseja de Sajambre Ayuntamiento.)

M: D-5 **Barbujó.** (6hr., F 9:30am, Plaza at Santa Marina)

▶ ACCOMMODATIONS

The most convenient accommodations are in Cangas de Onís, Arenas de Cabrales, and Potes; however, these only permit day hiking. For multi-day hikes, the **refugios** (cabins with bunks but not blankets; see **Refugios and Rangers,** p. 584) scattered throughout the park are the best option for staying overnight in the backcountry as strict bivouacking regulations have recently been imposed. All of the park offices have a complete list of the *refugios*. There are only four **campgrounds** inside the park (at Caín, Santa Marina, Caldevilla, and Fuente Dé), and they are all in the southern half. However, many towns close to its borders, including Cangas and Arenas de Cabrales, have campsites. Other lodging options include **albergues** (hostels, usually in ancient buildings with bunks and cold water) and **casas** (buildings with bunks, hot water, and stoves); these, however, are also only in or near towns, and not useful farther out in the mountains. In all cases you should bring a sleeping bag. Prices for *refugios* and camping range from €3-7 per person and/or tent, and reservations are usually not accepted. It's wise to call ahead to see if space is available. Towns within the park also have **pensiones** and **rooms** in private homes; look for *camas* and *habitaciones* signs (typically €20-30 per double).

 OUTDOOR ACTIVITIES AND HIKING

For multi-day routes, consult one of the Picos de Europa park offices. In addition to the following suggested day hikes, there are numerous free guided hikes arranged through the park offices (see **Tours and Guided Hikes,** p. 586). The following hikes are listed according to the nearest trailhead or town. Before embarking on any hike, secure a good map that has all trails clearly marked. The following are merely suggestions; be sure to gather more information before departing.

> **SUGGESTIONS FOR HIKERS.** Always consider the difficulty level and length of route when planning your hike. If you don't get a guide or hike with someone who knows the area, stay on marked trails. Never start a hike without a compass and a detailed map of the area (min. scale 1/25000). Also, make sure to bring at least 2L of water per person. Some clean water sources are available in the park, and you can also bring water purification tablets, but check ahead of time to find safe water sources. Before you start hiking, tell someone, such as a hostel owner or park office, where you are heading and when you expect to be back. If you want to spend the night in the *refugios* scattered throughout the park, call ahead, either to the *refugio* itself or to a park office, and make sure they're open (p. 584). In case of fog, it is better to sit down and wait rather than walk around without knowing where you are.

COVADONGA

Covadonga is accessible only through Cangas, on the Bustio-Arriondas route. ALSA buses (☎902 42 22 42) run from Cangas (20min.; M-F 5 per day 8:30am-7:30pm, Sa-Su 4 per day 8:30am-6:45pm; €1) and back (20-30min.; M-F 5 per day 8:50am-7:15pm, Sa-Su 4 per day 10:30am-8pm; €1). Buses stop at the Hospedería and uphill at the basilica.

"This little mountain you see will be the salvation of Spain," Don Pelayo, the first King of Asturias, prophesied to his Christian army in 718, gesturing to the rocky promontory above what is now Covadonga. The mountain soon became the site of the first successful battle in the *Reconquista*, although legend claims that it was not geography but the intervention of the Virgin Mary that made victory over the Moors possible. Today, pilgrims crowd the quiet, candlelit **Santa Cueva,** where legend claims the Virgin appeared to Pelayo. (Open daily summer 9am-9pm; winter 9am-7pm. Free.) Afterward, head to the **Santuario de Covadonga,** a neo-Gothic basilica built in 1901 that towers next to the cave. (Open daily summer 9am-9pm; winter 9am-7pm. Free.) The **Museo del Tesoro,** next to the bus stop, displays the treasures, including paintings, swords, books, and jewelry, donated to the Virgin over the years. (Open daily 10:30am-2pm and 4-7:30pm. €2, children €1.)

Covadonga's **info office,** at the top of the hill by the Cueva, has details on local accommodations and sights. (☎985 84 60 35. Open daily May-Oct. 10am-2pm and 3-7pm; Nov.-Apr. 11am-2pm and 3-5pm.) Cangas offers cheaper accommodations, but it's hard to resist the friendly atmosphere and stunning views of the mountains at the **Hospedería del Peregrino ❷,** on the main road next

SKY HIGH

While the mountaineers and shepherds in the Picos tend to shy away from Spain's usual crazy party life, they do indulge themselves at least one day a year.

The *Fiesta del Pastor* (July 25) in Vega del Enol, is *the* party in the Picos. Called the *Romería cerca del cielo* (feast near the sky) for its location, the crafts, dancing, and games are held in honor of the pastoral tradition. People from every corner of the Picos come to revel in the festivities, and this gathering has helped to foster a sense of community in the area.

The region's youth begin the party the night before, sleeping in tents by the Lago de Enol until the games start early on the morning of the 25th. Around 8am, the rest of the town treks up to the lakes for competitions, like the *Escalada a la Porre de Enol* (a type of local alpinism race), a bareback horse race, and a town tug-of-war that pits lifelong friends against each other for the glory of being champion of the Picos for the year. Since it's one of the few times that the whole Picos community comes together, the *Fiesta del Pastor* also serves as a forum for discussing community concerns, like continuing friction between environmental preservation and the livelihood of local farmers—it's not uncommon to see one of the morning's champions metamorphose into a spokesperson for an issue like predator control later in the evening.

to the bus stop below the basilica. (☎985 84 60 47; fax 84 60 51. Singles €18-29; doubles with hall bath €22-36. AmEx/MC/V.) **Gran Hotel Pelayo ❹** is the Ritz of the town. Built a century ago, the hotel will open from its complete renovations in May 2005, showing off a new classy interior. Big rooms complete with all modern amenities, such as Internet, A/C, and full baths, overlook the basilica and the surrounding peaks. (☎985 84 60 61; fax 985 84 60 54. English spoken. Doubles €60-110. AmEx/MC/V.) At ▨**El Huerto del Ermitaño ❹**, savor local dishes ranging from baked *jabalí* (wild boar, €11) to steak with *queso de Beyos* (€15), a cheese native to the Picos, to the tune of the Cueva's waterfall just across the road. (Halfway up the hill to the basilica. ☎985 84 60 97. Entrees €7-12, *menú* €10-20. Open daily noon-11:30pm.) **Merendero Covadonga ❶,** where the main highway meets the road to the Lagos, caters to visitors in a hurry to get to the basilica or the lagos. In a timely fashion, enjoy a wide variety of sandwiches (€2-3), *raciones* (€4), *platos combinados* (€6), and paellas (€8) on the outdoor terrace. (☎985 84 60 67. Open daily 9am-9pm, or later if there are enough customers.) The only **groceries** in town arrive for Hospedería guests twice a week (W and Sa) by truck—buy them from the driver at the hostel.

▨ LAGOS DE ENOL Y ERCINA

These tarns, or mountain lakes, are accessible from Cangas de Onís and Covadonga (see above). ALSA buses (☎902 42 22 42) run from Covadonga to the lakes (20min., July-Sept. 15 5 per day 10am-4pm, €1.50). In Covadonga, buses leave from the basilica to follow a frightening but spectacular road lined with pastures and precipitous cliffs; the right side of the bus has the best views en route. Alternatively, Turataxis runs shuttles several times daily between the lakes and the basilica (20min., schedule varies, €8).

Seemingly defying gravity, the **Lagos de Enol y Ercina** sparkle silently among limestone slopes and open valleys between the peaks of the mountains past Covadonga. The **Centro de Visitantes Pedro Pidal,** past Lake Enol on the way to Lake Ercina (follow the signs) has extensive info on the Lagos region and on the entire park, including hikes and refugios (☎985 84 86 14. Open Apr.-Nov daily 10am-6pm). Free **guided hikes** around the lakes depart from the Buferrera parking lot. See **Tours and Guided Hikes** (p. 586) for more info.

Two especially good hikes, at a slightly higher level of difficulty, take travelers east from the lakes to the **Vega de Ario,** which offers a panoramic view of the Urrieles mountains (8-9hr. round-trip, medium to high level of difficulty), or south to the **Mirador de Ordiales,** a vantage point overlooking the Pico de las Vidriosas, Río Dobra, and a frightening gorge (7-8hr. round-trip, high level of difficulty). Alternatively, head west 2km to the **Mirador del Rey** lookout point, then wander among the beech trees of the **Bosque de Pome** (4hr. round-trip), also accessible by car off the main road from Covadonga; take a right just before Lake Enol to the Vega de Enol, then continue a little past, taking another right at the fork. For more hiking options, check with the visitor center. The ◙**Refugio del Pastor ❶,** just past Lake Enol on the road to the Mirador del Rey in the Vega de Enol, has 45 spots year-round and provides meals and guides. The refuge finished a year-long renovation in July 2003 and is now practically a hotel with a bar, dining area, hall bath, and dorm-style bunks with clean mattresses and pillows. Bring your own sheets or sleeping bag. (Meals at 1pm and 8pm. No reservations accepted. €7.)

PONCEBOS

*Poncebos is accessible only from Arenas de Cabrales. **ALSA** buses run from Arenas (15min., July-Sept. 15 7 per day, €0.95) and arrive at the Bar-Restaurante Garganta del Cares. By car, take AS-114 to Las Arenas; cross the river where the signs point to Poncebos onto AS-264. Taxis also go to Poncebos at almost any time of day (€5).*

Poncebos, just within the park's borders and about 6km from Arenas, is the actual starting point for many of Arenas's hiking trails. The walk to the main trailhead from Arenas threads through the feet of surrounding mountains; tight, winding roads make some corners dangerous. To stay overnight in Poncebos, try either **Hostal Poncebos ❷** (☎985 84 64 47. Singles €24-36; doubles €39-60; triples €51-72. MC/V) or the comfortable beds in **Hostal-Restaurante-Bar Garganta del Cares ❷.** (☎985 84 64 63. Dorm-style rooms for 2 with TV €24-30, for 3 €34-42, for 4 €44-54; doubles with bath and TV €45-75. MC/V.) All rooms in both hostels have winter heating and windows either facing the mountains or overlooking the river.

Poncebos marks the start of one of the Picos's most famous trails, the 12km **Ruta del Cares.** The gorge's walls drop 200m down to the Río Cares below. The Ruta del Cares is an easy 6hr. hike along a trail that starts in Poncebos and ends in **La Posada del Valdeón.** A shorter alternative is to walk from Poncebos to **Caín** (3hr.) and take a taxi or bus from there to Posada del Valdeón. (Taxi Pidal ☎985 84 51 77.) On the ◙**Caín-Poncebos** portion of the trail, many lush and secluded spots lie along the river waiting to be found by hikers looking for a lunch break with a view. Stay overnight in Caín at either **La Ruta ❷** (☎987 74 27 02. Singles €21; doubles €40; closed Oct. 1 to *Semana Santa*) or **La Posada del Montaña ❹.** (☎942 31 86 50. Doubles €36; triples €50; reserve a month in advance for Aug.)

The **Poncebos-Bulnes** route, an easy 3hr. hike, follows the Río Tejo to **Bulnes,** a small village seemingly frozen in time. Consider tucking in at **El Chiflón ❶,** which has 17 beds, a bar, showers, guides, weather reports, and meals. (☎985 84 59 43. One- to three-week advance reservations suggested. Breakfast €3.60. Doubles €38; triples €45; quads €51.) The park service offers free **guided hikes** to Bulnes on Tuesday and Saturday at 10am (4hr.; departs from the small information hut on Poncebos's main highway). The ◙**Poncebos-Collado Pandébano-Naranjo de Bulnes** route, a killer 17km hike (8-10hr. one-way), crawls first to saddleback Collado Pandébano and then inches 9km farther to the foot of the Picos's most famous mountain, **Naranjo de Bulnes,** named for its unmistakable sunburnt orange face. From here you can see the major *picos* in the area and the dancing blue waves of the Bay of Biscay in the distance. Most climbers choose to start the hike in **Sotres,** the highest town in the Picos, and continue from there (9-10hr. round-trip). There are two *refugios* in the Naranjo de Bulnes area: ◙**Refugio**

Vega de Urriellu ❶ (☎985 92 52 00), at the foot of the Naranjo, and **Refugio Jou de Los Cabrones ❶** (☎985 78 03 81); see **Refugios and Rangers,** p. 584. If the trail is open, it's worth going beyond the **Poncebos-Camareña** path, up a rocky slope, to **Puertos de Ondón,** where the view is incomparable.

POTES

La Palomera buses (☎942 88 06 11) travel to Fuente Dé July-Aug. (45min.; M-F 3 per day 8am-8pm, Sa-Su 1pm; €1.80) and back (M-F 3 per day 8:45am-8:45pm, Sa-Su 5pm). During the rest of the year, buses run to Espinama, 4km below Fuente Dé (40min., M-F 1pm, €1.10) and back (M-F 9am and 2:10pm). Buses also go to Santander (2½hr.; July-Aug. M-F 3 per day 7am-5:45pm, Sa 9:30am and 5:45pm, Su 5:45pm; Sept.-June M-F 3 per day 7am-5:45pm, Sa 8am and 5:45pm, Su 5:45pm; €6) via Panes (40min.) and Unquera (1hr.). There are two taxi stops in town, one about 100m toward the town center from the tourist office on Pl. de la Serna and the other across town on C. Dr. Encinas.

A Potes (pop. 2000) tourist brochure prophesies "*Y volverás*" (you'll return), and you probably will—this down-to-earth town in the shadow of the mountains makes a great base for outdoor activities in the eastern section of the Picos de Europa or for daytrips to the many churches and hermitages that dot the surrounding hillsides. But Potes's ancient cobblestone streets, arches, and main street arcade, brimming with shops selling cheese, wine, and all manner of other local specialties, make spending the day in town just as rewarding.

Urdón, 15km north of Potes on the road to Panes, is the start of a challenging 6km (2½hr.) hike to **Tresviso,** a tiny town where chickens outnumber humans. Trail details can be found on posters all over Potes. Another option is the peak **El Cuernón** in **Sierra de Peña Sagra,** about 13km (2hr.) east of the towns of **Luriezo** and **Aniezo.** From the summit (2042m), you can survey the Picos and the sea, 51km away. On your way down, visit the **Ermita de Nuestra Señora de la Luz,** where the patron saint of the Picos lives 364 days a year. The Virgin, known affectionately as *Santuca* (tiny saint), is honored on May 2. A 3km uphill hike from the tourist office toward Fuente Dé is the **Monasterio de Santo Toribio de Liébana,** which protects the *Lignum Crucis,* reportedly the largest surviving piece of the true cross of Christ in the world. The building itself is enchantingly illuminated. (Open daily summer 9am-1pm and 3:30-8pm; winter 9am-1pm and 3:30-7pm. Free.)

The streets of Potes are lined with outfitters specializing in the latest outdoor fads. The tourist office has a list of all the outfitters in town. In summer, book several days in advance for expeditions. **Picos Aventura,** C. Cervantes, 3, organizes horseback riding, mountain biking, paragliding, and canyoning. The office is at the base of the bridge on C. Dr. Encinas. (☎942 73 21 61. €21-48. Open daily 10:30am-9pm. MC/V.) **La Liébana,** between Potes and Fuente Dé, organizes similar outings. The office is behind the gazebo on the river on C. Dr. Encinas. (☎942 73 10 00; fax 73 10 21. Open Mar.-Dec. 10am-2pm and 4-8pm. €22-70.)

Several hostels are scattered on C. Dr. Encinas and on C. Cántabra, a side street. The cheapest rooms fill early in the day, so make reservations a day or two in advance for June and July and a couple weeks in advance for August. The beautiful ▓**Casa Cayo ❸,** C. Cántabra, 6, a right off C. Dr. Encinas when walking into town from the bus stop, with exposed rafters and bright white walls, has the feel of a country cottage in the middle of town. All the rooms are spacious and immaculate with TV, phone, and bath. There's also a cozy lounge with a big TV. (☎942 73 01 50. Singles €20-30; doubles €30-45. MC/V.) Closer to Panes up a stairway off C. Dr. Encinas, **El Fogón de Cus ❷,** C. Capital Palacios, 2, has friendly owners and sunny, spacious rooms that are a little worn around the edges. The adjoining **restaurant ❷** serves hearty mountain fare (*menú del día* €8.50); for a livelier atmosphere, ask for a table in the back room with the TV. (☎ 942 73 00 60. Some English spoken. All rooms have sinks and heat. Singles €15-20; doubles €24-33, with bath €25-36. Restaurant open daily 1:30-4pm and 8:30-11pm. AmEx/ MC/V.) The closest camping site is the first-class **Camping La Viorna ❶**, about 1km up the road to Monasterio Santo Toribio, which helps organize excursions and has a restaurant-bar, supermarket, and pool. (☎ 942 73 20 21. Open *Semana Santa*-Oct. 30. €3.40 per person, car, or tent.)

Potes can feed plenty of hungry hikers; C. Dr. Encinas, C. Cántabra, and C. San Cayetano are packed with restaurants, tapas bars, and cafeterias. A delicious dining option in a dim but joyful atmosphere is riverside **Restaurante La Caseta II ❷**, C. Cántabra, 8, next-door to Casa Cayo, where veal, lamb, and game are the specialties. (☎/fax 942 73 07 13. *Menú* €11, entrees €7-10. Open daily 10am-11pm.) Supermarket **El Árbol** is across from the bus station. (☎ 942 73 05 26. Open M 9:30am-8:30pm, Tu-Sa 9:30am-2pm and 5-8:30pm, Su 10am-2pm.)

The **tourist office** has information on adventure tourism, *refugios*, and accommodations as well as good hikes in the surrounding area. (☎/fax 942 73 07 87. Open daily 10am-2pm and 4-8pm.) Local services include: **Banco Santander Central Hispano,** C. Dr. Encinas, 11, with a **24hr. ATM** (☎ 902 24 24 24. Open M-F 8:30am-2pm, Sa 8:30am-1pm); **Guardia Civil** (☎ 942 73 00 07), on C. Obispo off C. Dr. Encinas; **Farmacia F. Soberón,** C. Cántabra (☎ 942 73 00 08. Open daily 9:30am-9:30pm); **Centro de Salud** (☎ 942 73 03 60) on C. Eduardo García de Enterría, inside the **Cruz Roja** (Red Cross; ☎ 942 73 01 02) building; **Internet access** at **CyberLiebana,** in the arcade off of C. Dr. Ercinas (€1.80 per hr. Open 10am-midnight).

FUENTE DÉ

Fuente Dé is accessible only during July and Aug. from Potes on La Palomera buses (☎ 902 42 22 42. 45min.; M-F 3 per day 8:45am-8:45pm, Sa-Su 5:45pm; return M-F 3 per day 8am-8pm, Sa-Su 1pm; €1.80). The bus stops in front of the Parador de Fuente Dé, just below the teleférico (cable car) base. During other months, take the bus to Espinama and walk the rest of the way to Fuente Dé (4km).

Only 23km from Potes, the ◨**Teleférico de Fuente Dé** is well worth an excursion. The goosebump-inducing *teleférico*, the third largest cable car system in the world, jets 800m to the mountain top (1834m) in less than four minutes. (☎ 942 31 89 50. Open daily July-Aug. 9am-8pm; Sept.-June 10am-6pm. €6; round-trip €10, under 8 €3.) A zig-zagging trail ascends just left of the cable (3hr.) for those up for a hike. At the top, there are many possible hikes along the four-wheel drive tracks. Those up for an extended stay can take the northern trail to **Sotres,** a fairly difficult hike usually taking at least 2 days. A less demanding option is the 4km walk from the top of the *teleférico* to **Refugio de Áliva ❹** (1666m), the most expensive and luxurious "refuge" in the park. All rooms come with full bath and heat in winter; there is also a cafe on site. (☎/fax 942 73 09 99. Doubles €45. MC/V.) Alternately, continue on the next 8km as the track winds its way down the mountainside to the village of Pido and finally back to **Espinama** (11.5km, 5hr. from upper cable car station), where **Habitaciones Sebrango ❷** offers respite for those who've had their fill of the wilds. (☎ 942 73 66 15. Singles €24; doubles €30). From the cable car's lower station, the easier **Somo Waterfall Route** (11½km, 4½hr.) swings through the Berrugas cattle sheds, the soft Bustantivo meadows, and on to the Somo waterfall. Hikers wearied by a day's descent can find rustic lodging with spectacular views at **El Redondo Camping ❶,** just above the base of the *teleférico*. (☎ 942 73 66 99. Bar, market, and hot showers. Reception daily 9am-9pm. €5 per person, €3 per child, €6 per site. Electricity €3.)

CANTABRIA

From the spectacle of Santander's El Sardinero beaches to the pristine provincial park of Oyambre, it's the shore that makes Cantabria famous. Though they have yet to see the resort build-up of Spain's more famous southern coasts, the region's beach towns are by no means untouched or secluded. The beach scene, declared to have some of the world's cleanest surfing water, particularly in Santander, is what lures visitors, but Cantabria also has hiking in the Picos de Europa, Paleolithic cave drawings, and renowned architecture including Gaudí's El Capricho and the 13th-century Colegiata de Santa Juliana in Santillana del Mar.

SANTANDER   ☎942

In Santander (pop. 185,000), palm trees rub shoulders with pines, pasty Brits bake on the beach next to bronzed Spaniards, and the grime of the city center is easily forgotten on a walk down El Sardinero's bougainvillea-filled boardwalks. Santander has been destroyed three times by natural and not-so-natural disasters—a fire at the start of the 15th century incinerated everything in sight, an explosion on a dynamite ship in 1893 leveled the peninsular city, and in 1941 another fire gutted it. Its most recent incarnation has resulted in a nearly ideal city, complete with surf, sand, and sometimes sun. Those looking to get away from it all should avoid Santander, as it is "all" and then some. Those willing to share beach space with a thousand other sun-starved bodies, however, will reap great rewards. A mountainous horizon with cliff-top lighthouses is the Bay of Biscay at its best.

◪ TRANSPORTATION

Flights: Aeropuerto de Santander, Av. de Parayas (☎942 20 21 00), in nearby Camargo (4km away). Serviced exclusively by Iberia. Accessible only by taxi (€12). **Iberia ticket office,** Po. de Pereda, 18 (☎902 40 05 00). Open M-F 9am-1:30pm and 4-7pm.

Trains: FEVE (☎942 20 95 22) and **RENFE** (☎902 24 02 02), Pl. de las Estaciones. RENFE serves only a few destinations, as Santander is the terminus of a rail line; take a slower FEVE train to larger cities east or west of Santander. RENFE info open daily

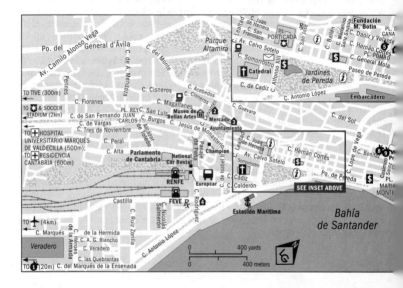

7:30am-10pm. RENFE goes to **Madrid** (6hr.; M-F 3 per day 8:10am-11pm, Sa 6 per day 8:10am-11pm, Su 4 per day 8:10am-11pm; €33, Su at 5:15pm €23.80) and **Valladolid** (4½hr., 5-7 per day 8:10am-11pm, €12.80-22.50). FEVE goes to: **Bilbao** (3hr., 3 per day 9:22am-6:50pm, €6.30); **Oviedo** (4¼hr., 9:10am and 4:10pm, €11.40).

Buses: C. Navas de Tolosa (☎942 21 19 95). Info open daily 8am-10pm. To: **Barcelona** (10hr., 9am and 9pm, €41.80); **Bilbao** (1½hr., every hr. 6am-9:30pm, €5.60-10); **Burgos** (4hr.; M-Sa 5 per day 12:30am-7pm, Su 6 per day 12:30am-11:59pm; €9.50); **León** (3½hr.; M-Sa 1-2 per day 9am-4pm, Su 7:30pm; €10.40); **Madrid** (6hr.; M-Sa 6 per day 12:30am-7pm, Su 8 per day 12:30am-11:59pm; €23.10-30.80); **Oviedo** (3½hr.; M-F and Su 9 per day 6:30am-8pm, Sa 6 per day 6:30am-8pm; €11-18.70); **Palencia** (3hr.; M-Th and Sa 9am and 5pm, F and Su 9am and 4pm; €7.90); **Salamanca** (6hr., 9am and 5pm, €14.20).

Ferries: Brittany Ferries, Estación Marítima (☎942 36 06 11; www.brittany-ferries.es), by the Jardines de Pereda. Reservations recommended in summer 2wk. in advance. Info open M-F 9am-7pm. To **Plymouth,** UK (8-10hr.; 2 per wk.; €85-132 plus €7 for a seat, €97 for a basic cabin). **Los Reginas,** C. Embarcadero (☎942 21 67 53), by the Jardines de Pereda. To **Pedreña, Somo,** and the **Playas del Puntal** (45min., every 30min. 11am-7pm, round-trip €3.10). Runs **tours** of the bay (1hr., June-Sept. 3-6 per day, €6.20).

Public Transportation: Municipal buses (☎942 20 07 71) run throughout the city (every 15min.; July-Aug. 6am-midnight, Sept.-June 6am-10:30pm; night buses every hr. midnight-6am; €1). Buses #1-4, 7, 9, 13, and 14 run from the Ayuntamiento stop (buses coming from El Sardinero stop in front of the plaza; buses going there stop in front of Foot Locker) to El Sardinero along Po. de Pereda and Av. de la Reina Victoria, stopping at Pl. de Italia and Jardines de Piquío. Detailed route info posted at stops, often with a screen showing when the next bus will arrive.

Taxis: Radio Taxi (☎942 33 33 33). 24hr. service to greater Santander. Taxis wait outside the train and bus stations, on C. Vargas, and near the Ayuntamiento. The tourist office has a map showing all taxi stops throughout the city.

Car Rental: EuropCar, (☎942 26 25 46), next to National Car Rental. 21+, must have had license for 1 year. From €55 per day for 350km. Open M-F 9am-1pm and 4-7:30pm, Sa 9am-1pm.

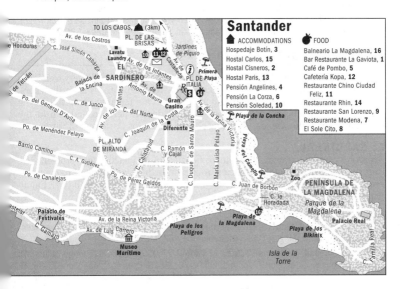

✠ 🛈 ORIENTATION AND PRACTICAL INFORMATION

Santander sits on a peninsula in the Bay of Biscay; its southern shores form the Bahía de Santander. There are two main sections to the city: **El Centro** (the center), around the train and bus stations and the Jardines de Pereda in the west, and **El Sardinero**, to the east. The main thoroughfare starts at the Ayuntamiento in the center as **Avenida Calvo Sotelo** and runs along the shore to the Jardines de Piquío in El Sardinero, changing its name to **Paseo de Pereda** and **Avenida de la Reina Victoria** along the way. At the western tip of Santander is **La Península de la Magdalena**, the famed park. Santander is surprisingly large; the best way to get around is by bus.

Tourist Office: Jardines de Pereda (☎942 20 30 00; www.ayto-santander.es). Maps and accommodations listings. Open July-Aug. daily 9am-9pm; Sept.-June M-F 9:30am-1:30pm and 4-7pm, Sa-Su 10am-2pm. **Branch** in El Sardinero open July-Aug. daily 10am-9pm; June Sa 10:30am-2:30pm and 3:30-7:30pm, Su 10:30am-2:30pm.

Currency Exchange: Banco Santander Central Hispano, on Av. Calvo Sotelo. **Branch** at Pl. de Italia. Open May-Sept. M-F 8:30am-2pm, Oct.-Apr. M also Sa 8:30am-1pm.

Luggage Storage: Lockers at the **train station** (€3 per day). Open daily 7am-11pm. Lockers at the **bus station** bottom level (€2.40 per day). Open daily 6am-12am.

Laundromat: Lavatu, Av. de los Castros, 29 (☎942 27 70 00). Open M-F 9am-1pm and 5-8pm, Sa 9am-1pm. 7kg €12 wash and dry. AmEx/V.

Police, Pl. Porticada and Av. del Deporte (☎942 20 07 44, emergencies 062).

Hospital: Hospital Universitario Marqués de Valdecilla, Av. de Valdecilla, 25 (☎942 20 25 20). **Residencia Cantabria,** Av. Cardenal Herrera Oria (☎942 20 25 20).

Pharmacy: Farmacia Lavin y Camus, C. Hernán Cortés, 2 (☎942 21 12 69). Open 24hr. In El Sardinero, **Somacarrera,** Pl. de Italia, 1 (☎942 27 05 96), underneath the Gran Casino. Open 10am-1:30pm and 4:30-8pm. For locations of late-night pharmacies, call ☎942 22 02 60 or check the schedule at any pharmacy.

Internet Access: Divernet Informática, C. Cisneros, 29 (☎942 24 14 25). English spoken. €2 per hr. Open M-Sa 9:30am-2pm and 3:30-9:30pm, Su 3:30-9:30pm. **La Copia,** C. Lealtad, 13. Next to cathedral. Open daily 9am-1:30pm and 5-8pm.

Post Office: Av. Alfonso XIII (☎942 21 26 73). Open M-F 8am-9pm, Sa 8:30am-1pm. **Branch** in El Sardinero on Av. Las Cruces. Open M-F 8:30am-8:30pm, Sa 8:30am-1pm. **Lista de Correos** and **fax** only at Av. Alfonso XIII location. **Postal Code:** 39080.

🏠 ACCOMMODATIONS AND CAMPING

In July and August, showing up in town without a reservation could very well leave you out in the cold. The train and bus stations are filled with *pensión* hawkers, but beware: this practice is illegal, and many rooms are far from the beaches. The highest hotel densities are near the market on Pl. de la Esperanza, across from the train station on C. Rodríguez, and along elegant Av. de los Castros in El Sardinero.

EL SARDINERO
Everyone wants to stay in El Sardinero because of its beaches and promenades. Unfortunately, such popularity means rooms are expensive and hard to come by. From the Ayuntamiento stop in the city center, take bus #1-4, 7, or 9 to El Piquío (Hotel Colón); Av. de los Castros is directly opposite the beach.

▨ **Hostal Carlos,** Av. de la Reina Victoria, 135 (☎942 27 16 16). This building, an officially designated historical site, has big, sunny rooms. English and German spoken. Breakfast €3.20. Singles €33-57; doubles €47-67. MC/V. ❸

Pensión Soledad, Av. de los Castros, 17 (☎942 27 09 36). 16 large rooms with sinks and good views. Common TV room. Breakfast €1.50. Singles €22; doubles €25-38. ❷

Hostal Paris, Av. los Hoteles, 6 (☎942 27 09 36). A 19th-century mansion-turned-luxury hostel overlooking the beach. High ceilings and white walls lined with black and white photos of historic Santander. Rooms have clean baths, some with balconies. Open June-mid-Oct. Singles €60-82; doubles €83-105; triples €110-140; quads €130-165; quints €150-190. AmEx/MC/V. ❺

Camping: Cabo Mayor, Av. del Faro (☎ 942 39 15 42). On the scenic bluff of Cabo Mayor, 3km from Playas Primera and Segunda. From the Ayuntamiento, take bus #2, 7, 9, or 13 to "Av. del Faro," 7 stops after El Piquío. Turn left onto Av. del Faro and follow it 10min. into the Cabos. Alternatively, head north along coastal Av. de Castañeda, bear right at the rotary, and then turn left onto C. Gregorio Marañón; Av. del Faro is on the right. Pool, currency exchange, supermarket, bar, and tennis courts. Reception 8am-11pm. Open Apr.-Oct. €4 per adult, €4 per tent, €3.60 per car. Electricity €2.40. ❶

CITY CENTER

One should stay near the stations only out of necessity, though accommodations there are plentiful and cheap. By day, the area is grimy, noisy, and far from the beach; by night, it's unsettling. The area north of the Ayuntamiento and Av. de Calvo Sotelo is a far more pleasant collection of restaurants, shops, and bars crowded with locals trying to escape the glassy-eyed stares of vacationers. At night, catch a cab to El Sardinero (€4), or take a pleasant, if lengthy, stroll.

Hospedaje Botín, C. Isabel II, 1, 1st fl. (☎942 21 00 94; www.hospedajebotin.com). The owners have a healthy obsession with cleanliness, and their crazy 80s comforters keep guests warm. Balconies overlook the market behind the Ayuntamiento. All rooms have TV and sink. Singles €18-30; doubles €26-44; triples €41-76; quads €50-83. ❷

Pensión Angelines, C. Rodríguez, 9, 2nd fl. (☎942 31 25 84). Large, recently renovated rooms are immaculate and have huge windows, TV, and heat. TV lounge. July-Aug. singles €18; doubles €28. Sept.-June €12/€22. ❷

Hostal Cisneros, C. Cisneros, 8, 1st fl. (☎942 21 16 13). A clean, comfortable option. All rooms have TV, beautiful wooden headboards, a sunny terrace, and bath. Reservations, sometimes with first night's payment, required. Discounted parking on same street. July-Sept. doubles €43; *Semana Santa*-June €39; Oct.-*Semana Santa* €30. ❹

Pensión La Corza, C. Hernán Cortés, 25, 3rd fl. (☎942 21 29 50), has a posh reception area and luxurious rooms with bath and TV, some with balconies over Pl. José Antonio in the center of town. Doubles €42-50. MC/V. ❹

 FOOD

EL SARDINERO

The best grocery option is **Diferente,** C. Joaquín de la Costa, 18, in the **Hotel Santemar** shopping complex. (Open M-F 9am-2:30pm and 5-9pm, Sa 9am-2:45pm and 5:15-9pm, Su 9:30am-3pm. AmEx/MC/V.) El Sardinero is packed with ice cream stands and expensive restaurants. For more value for your dining euro, head to the city center, where good, cheap food is plentiful.

Restaurante Chino Ciudad Feliz, Pl. de las Brisas (☎942 27 32 30). Serves all the westernized Chinese staples, with an ocean view. Alas, no fortune cookies, but other post-meal gifts in the souvenir shop. Lunch *menú* €7.50. Entrees €5.80-9. Open daily 1-4pm and 7:30pm-midnight. MC/V. ❷

Cafetería Kopa, Pl. de las Brisas, in the same building as Ciudad Feliz. Though not the most exciting fare, Kopa has what most restaurants in El Sardinero lack: good standard Spanish and British fare at reasonable prices. Sandwiches €2-4, burgers €3-4.50, *platos combinados* €6-8. *Menú* €10. Open daily 9am-midnight. AmEx/MC/V. ❷

Balneario La Magdalena, C. la Horadada (☎942 03 21 07), on Playa de la Magdalena. Quiet restaurant perched above the beach with a menu of meat (€10-16) and fish (€11-16). Great for a beer after a long day on the beach. Open daily 10am-midnight. ❸

Restaurante Rhin, Pl. de Italia (☎942 27 30 34). Right next to the sand and surf above Playa la Primera. Be sure to rinse off the sand and put on a shirt and some shoes before you sit down for dinner. *Menú del día* €21, entrees €10-18, fish €17-22. MC/V. ❹

CITY CENTER

Seafood restaurants crowd the Puerto Pesquero (fishing port), grilling up the day's catch at the end of C. Marqués de la Ensenada. From the main entrance of the train station, turn right onto C. Rodríguez and right again onto C. Castilla; walk eight blocks down and turn left on C. Héroes de la Armada; cross the tracks and turn right after about 100m (20min.). Alternatively, buses #4 and 14 run from the Ayuntamiento to C. Marqués de Ensenada. Across the street from the Ayuntamiento, **Champion,** C. Jesús de Monasterio, sells groceries. (Open M-Sa 9am-9:30pm.)

▨ **El Sole Cito,** C. Bonifaz, 19 (☎942 36 06 33, takeout 32 51 18). The plates are the only square things in this undeniably hip bistro. Autumn leaves, African masks, and a vegetarian menu (€4-7.50). Try the incredibly tender *croquetas de solomillo* (sirloin croquettes, €5) or their large selection of pastas (€5.50-8). Pizzas €6-9, meats €9-15. Open Su-Th 1-4pm and 8-11:30pm, F-Sa 1-4pm and 8pm-12:30am. MC/V. ❷

Restaurante San Lorenzo, C. Bonifaz, 21 (☎942 05 51 74), next door to El Sole Cito. Suave, upstairs dining area under blue lights. Perfect for a late-night dinner and intimate conversation. Exquisite food, especially the *solomillo de cerdo* (pork loin) stuffed with Tresviso cheese and covered in a pine nut and raisin sauce (€11.40). While not easy on the wallet, its well worth the splurge. Meats €10-15, full dinners €9-15. Open Tu-Su 9pm-1am. MC/V. ❸

Café de Pombo, C. Hernán Cortés, 21 (☎942 22 32 24). On Pl. de Pombó, just behind Banco de Santander. Coffees, pastries, ice creams, crêpes, sandwiches—all delicious, all huge, all €1-3, served in an elegant dining area that conjures up images of *fin de siecle* French cafes. What more could you want? Open daily 8am-9pm. ❶

Restaurante Modena, C. Eduardo Benot, 6 (☎942 31 33 71). Delectable Italian standards, from lasagna to 4-cheese tortellini, served in a comfortable, if small, dining room. Not particularly budget (pasta €6-10), but the filling, vegetarian-friendly fare and *tiramisú* are worth the extra euros. Open daily 8pm-midnight. MC/V. ❷

Bar Restaurante La Gaviota, C. Marqués de la Ensenada (☎942 22 11 32), at the corner of C. Mocejón in the *barrio pesquero* (fishermen's neighborhood). An elegant dining room hidden behind a rough exterior. Try the fresh grilled sardines (12 for €3.60) or the *paella de mariscos* (€5). Menu fresh from the sea €6-12, *menú del día* €8. Open daily 12:30pm-4:15pm and 7:30pm-midnight. AmEx/MC/V. ❷

🎥 SIGHTS

While Santander is proud of its few official architectural sights and museums, skip them in favor of its beaches and parks unless it rains, in which case Santander's amusing—and free—museums are worth perusing. The tourist office has a list of one- to two-hour walking tours, the best way to get to know the city and feel like you actually did something during the day.

▨ **PENÍNSULA DE LA MAGDALENA.** Although it can feel a bit like an amusement park at times, La Magdalena is Santander's prime attraction and one of the most beautiful parts of the city. The entire peninsula is filled with palms and pines and ringed by bluffs plunging into the sea along slender, calm beaches. Crowds of people line the main walkways, but you can find a bit of peace and quiet among the paths in the middle or in a secluded, guaranteed romantic nook along the cliffs. The park's crowning landmark is the **palacio**, a modern, neo-Gothic mansion Alfonso XIII used as a summer home. Today, the palace hosts the elite Universidad Internacional Menéndez Pelayo's summer sessions on oceanography. The calls of the big male sea lion can be heard across the park from the small mini-zoo that also houses penguins and seals. A **tourist train** runs past the zoo and a display of historic ships next to it and through the rest of the peninsula. (☎639 51 36 72. €1.80.) Walking, however, is the best way to explore, and the 2km path ends with nourishment: *churrerías* flank the park's entrance. (☎942 27 25 04. Park open daily June-Sept. 8am-10pm; Oct.-May 8am-8:30pm. The palace has no scheduled visiting hours.)

▨**LOS CABOS.** More peninsular parks lie just north of the El Sardinero beaches. While Cabos Menor and Mayor lack the attractions and action of La Magdalena, their bluffs and vistas are more scenic and good places for quiet reflection. Cabo Menor, the more southern of the two, houses Santander's golf course and another mini-zoo; it also has postcard-worthy views of Cabo Mayor's 19th-century lighthouse. From Pl. de Italia, walk up Av. de Castañeda past Glorieta del Dr. Fleming, and turn right onto Av. de Pontejos, which turns into Av. del Faro and takes you out onto the capes. Check out the unparalleled views from the path that runs around the cliffs encircling the Cabos. To reach it, follow Av. García Lago to the end of Playa la Segunda and look for stairs that lead up to the top of the peninsula. (Parque Municipal de Matalenas on Cabo Menor open summer 9am-9pm; winter 9:30am-6pm.)

CATEDRAL DE SANTANDER. Built in the 13th century, Santander's Gothic cathedral is often called the city's first monument. The remains of the heads of martyred Roman soldiers Emeterio and Celedonio are kept in the crypt below the cathedral in two 16th-century silver reliquaries formed in the image of their faces. After dropping into the guillotine basket in AD 300 in La Rioja, they were brought to Santander in the 8th century for safekeeping during the Moorish invasion, where they were kept in the ruins of an oven once used to heat Roman baths. These ruins have now been excavated, and you can see them through a section of glass flooring below the church. The relics are occasionally taken out for religious processions. (Pl. del Obispo José E. Eguino, behind the post office and Banco España. ☎942 22 60 24. Open M-F 10am-1pm and 4-7:30pm, Sa 10am-1pm and 4:30-8pm, Su 8am-2pm and 5-8pm. July-Aug. free tours in Spanish daily at 10:30, 11:30am, 12:45, 4:30, 5:45, 6:30, and 7:30pm.)

MUSEO DE BELLAS ARTES. Devoted to the works of local artists, Santander's Museo de Bellas Artes is surprisingly impressive, if eclectic. Modern photographs share wall space with canvasses from such classic artists as El Greco. The majority of the works are by local artists, featured in rotating exhibitions on the ground floor. Art history buffs will enjoy the collection of 20th-century pieces. (C. Rubio, 6. ☎942 23 94 85. From the Ayuntamiento, walk up C. Jesús de Monasterio and turn right onto C. Florida. Open June 16-Sept. 14 M-F 10:30am-1pm and 5:30-8pm, Sa 10:30am-1pm; Sept. 15-June 15 M-F 10am-1pm and 5-8pm, Sa 10am-1pm. Special exhibitions open until 9pm. Free.)

MUSEO DE PREHISTORIA Y ARQUEOLOGÍA DE CANTABRIA. Exhibits on the life and times of the region's inhabitants in the era before history was invented. Also features displays of artifacts from the Iron Age through medieval times, including stellas and sarcophagi. (C. Casimiro Sainz, 4. ☎942 20 71 09. Open summer Tu-Sa 10am-1pm and 4-7pm, Su 11am-2pm; winter Tu-Sa 9am-1pm and 4-7pm, Su 11am-2pm.)

◪ BEACHES

In Santander, every day is a beach day: rain or shine (but most often rain), locals flock to the beach as soon as work gets out and spend the late afternoon and evening soaking up the last rays of sun. It's easy to understand why, as Santander's beaches, particularly those in El Sardinero, are wide swaths of powdery sand. The waves, however, can get very rough; it's not uncommon for five-foot breakers to crash onto the beach. Calmer water and rockier beaches can be found on the bay side. The best and most popular beaches are undoubtedly ⊠**Playas Primera y Segunda** in El Sardinero. Not only does the soft sand go on forever, but the EU has declared these one of its eight cleanest beaches. Primera and Segunda are also hangouts for Santander's surfing crowd, which emerges during and after rain. Crowds rush to the calmer waters on the southern shore of La Magdalena. Rock-framed **Playa de Bikinis** is the most secluded and the haunt of Santander's guitar-strumming teens; **Playa de la Magdalena** and **Playa de los Peligros,** stretching from the peninsula to below Av. de la Reina Victoria, are virtually waveless and therefore very popular with families. To escape the beachgoing hordes, either head across the bay by ferry to **Playas Puntal, Somo,** and **Loredo** lining a narrow peninsula of dunes, or hoof it up to the remote beaches of Los Cabos where ⊠**Playa de Matalenas** and **Playa de los Molinucos** await you without the throngs.

⊠ ⊠ NIGHTLIFE AND FESTIVALS

Exhausted from sunbathing, everyone in Santander seems to hit the sack early. In **El Sardinero,** cafes and bars line the promenade along Playas Primera and Segunda, with street performers offering live entertainment to families and teenagers. Others spend their evenings blowing euros at the **Gran Casino,** Pl. de Italia. Passport, proper dress (pants and shoes), and a minimum age (18 to gamble) are required. (Open daily 8pm-4am. €3 to enter main casino.) In the city center, university students and older couples tapas-hop around Pl. Cañadío, C. Daoíz y Velarde, and C. Pedrueca. Around 2 or 3am on Friday and Saturday nights or during festivals, crowds flood **Calle Río de la Pila** and **Calle Casimiro Sainz.**

The July **Concurso Internacional de Plano de Santander** and the huge, month-long **Festival Internacional de Santander** in August bring crowds of people and myriad music and dance performances to town. For more info, contact the **Oficina del Festival,** Palacio de Festivales de Cantabria (☎942 21 05 08; www.festival-santander.com), on C. Gamazo. The **Baños de Ola** is a turn-of-the-century-style celebration of Alfonso XIII's discovery that, lo and behold, playing in the waves is fun. The festival takes place the third week of July on the El Sardinero promenades, with bathers clad in antique-looking swimsuits. That same week, the *barrio pesquero* celebrates **Santiago,** the patron saint of fishermen.

⊠ DAYTRIPS FROM SANTANDER

⊠ COMILLAS

Comillas and Santillana del Mar are on the Santander-San Vicente de la Barquera line. La Cantábrica (☎942 72 08 22) buses depart from Navas de Tolosa in Santander (1hr.; M-F 4 per day 10:30am-7:15pm, Sa-Su 3 per day 11:30am-10:30pm; return trips M-F 4 per day 7:15am-5:45pm, Sa-Su 3 per day 10am-7:15pm; €3).

The coast of Comillas (pop. 2500) is intoxicating. From desolately calm inlets to the wind-swept swaths of sand directly on the Bay of Biscay, Comillas's beaches are its main attraction, drawing everyone from Spanish nobles to foreign visitors, all equally amazed by their splendor. This small resort town's central beach, **Playa Comillas,** is a vast expanse of silky sand and raging waves; on windy days, ten-foot breakers can pound the shores.

From the main bus stop, follow C. Marqués de Comillas uphill into town. At the top of the hill, turn left onto C. los Infantes, which will turn into C. Antonio Garelly. Follow this road down through the tunnel to arrive at the parking lot and the beach's main entrance. Heading in the opposite direction on C. Marqués de Comillas from the bus stop will bring you, 4km later, to **Playa Oyambre,** an equally beautiful but uncrowded and less developed beach. An easier alternative is to take the La Cantábrica bus toward San Vicente and ask the driver to let you off at Oyambre. For very gentle waters and excellent wading, make sure to walk over to the tidal estuary of the Ría de Rabia, on the Comillas side of the beach.

Comillas is equally proud of its architectural attractions. Most notable—and amusing—is ▨ **El Capricho,** Gaudí's summer palace. While it's not open to tourists, most visitors are content to see the swirling turrets and gingerbread-esque windows from outside. From the bus stop, you can see the colorful palace on the hill; follow the footpath across the street for a closer view. One way to get a look inside El Capricho is to eat in its **restaurant ❸.** (Reservations ☎924 72 03 65. Entrees €12-13. Open M-Sa 1-3:30pm and 9-11pm, Su 1-3:30pm.) Next to it on the same hill are the neo-Gothic **Palacio de Sobrellano,** designed by Catalan architect Doménech i Montaner, and the **Capilla-Pantheon,** containing furniture designed by Gaudí. (Open July-Aug. daily 10:30am-1:30pm and 4-7pm; Sept.-June W-Su 10:30am-1:30pm and 4-7pm. Guided tours €3.) From the tourist office, turn uphill and sneak a peek at the impressive facade of the **Universidad Pontificia** (closed to the public). Comillas goes up in a blaze of fireworks, pole-walking, goose-chasing, and dancing July 15-18 during the town's major **fiesta.**

The **tourist office** is at C. María del Piélago, 2. From the bus stop, follow C. Marqués de Comillas to the turn-off for the beach, turn right, and head down C. Gaudí two blocks until you see signs to the office. (☎942 72 07 68. Open July-Aug. daily 9am-9pm; Sept.-June M-Sa 10:30am-1:30pm and 4:30-7:30pm, Su 10:30am-1:30pm.)

CUEVAS DE ALTAMIRA

The Altamira caves are on the way to Santillana del Mar on the San Vicente de la Barquera line. La Cantábrica (☎942 72 08 22) sends buses from Pl. de las Estaciones, in Santander, to Altamira (45min., 10:30am, €2). However, the best way to visit to the caves is to take the beautiful 3km (30min.) walk up from Santillana del Mar. By foot or by car, take CA-133 out of town, turning onto CA-134 when the signs point to Altamira.

Bison roam, horses graze, and goats butt heads on the ceilings of the limestone ▨**Cuevas de Altamira,** dubbed the "Sistine Chapel of Paleolithic Art." The large-scale polychromatic paintings, created by Cro-Magnon people over 15,000 years ago, are renowned

THE LOCAL STORY

ANCIENT GRAFFITI?

Some 18,000 years ago, the first Cro-Magnon graffiti artist stepped foot inside the cave known as Altamira, looked at the ceiling, and thought, "Gee, that bump on the ceiling looks like a buffalo." Over the next few millennia, generations of his successors filled the entire ceiling with creatures like *bisontes* (bison) and *ciervas* (deer). They even "signed" their work with handprints created by blowing fine red pigment over their hands, making a negative on the cave walls. Modern archaeologists think these were components of elaborate ritual ceremonies, perhaps intended to bring success in the hunt.

About 11,000 years ago the endeavor came to a sudden halt when a collapse at the cave mouth sealed it until its discovered in 1879. In 1917, Altamira was opened to the public, and dubbed the "Sistine Chapel of prehistory." Unfortunately, this almost proved its undoing. The 100,000+ people who visited each year weakened the surface, causing the paintings to crumble, until they were in danger of disappearing. Eventually, the Spanish government realized the danger, and closed them to the public in the 90s. However, in 2001 the scientists were able to replicate the most impressive parts in full, and made a perfect life-sized replica, known as the *Neocueva*. They still won't let you draw on the walls, though. You'll have to go find your own cave for that.

for their scrupulous attention to naturalistic detail and resourceful use of the caves' natural texture. Unfortunately, tourism has caused substantial damage, and the actual caves are now closed indefinitely while scientists try to stop the decay. The **Museo de Altamira** has, with the aid of modern science, constructed the Neocueva, a near-perfect replica of the entrance to the original cave as well as the Sala de Policromos, the most spectacular gallery. The Neocueva is accessible to all visitors, including those in wheelchairs. Guides lead groups every 30min. back through time to the days of cave bears and stone tools. While you wait to go on the tour, peruse the excellent permanent exhibit on human evolution. (☎942 81 80 05. Open June-Sept. Tu-Sa 9:30am-7:30pm, Su 9:30am-5pm; Oct.-May Tu-Su 9:30am-5pm. €2.40, Sa afternoon and all day Su free.) The Museo Arqueológico Nacional in Madrid also has replicas of the cave.

SANTILLANA DEL MAR

Buses take the same route as those to Comillas. La Cantábrica (☎942 72 08 22) sends buses from the station in Santander (45min.; M-F 4 per day 10:30am-7:15pm, Sa-Su 3 per day 11:30am-10:30pm; €1.80). In Santillana del Mar, buses stop on C. Santo Domingo in front of the Museo Diocesano; the return bus stops at the stairway across the street in front of the centro de salud. For a taxi, call ☎608 47 34 41.

French philosopher Jean-Paul Sartre proclaimed Santillana del Mar (pop. 4000) the most beautiful town in Spain. He also said that hell is other people, so his enthusiasm for Santillana might well be tempered by the hordes of tourists that now flock here. Santillana is a tourist town and knows it: the tangled, medieval cobblestone streets are crowded with ice cream stands and souvenir shops. The crowds are here for a reason, though: Santillana *is* beautiful, and it's worth suffering a few other tourists to see it. If you detest crowds and tourist commercialism, though, avoid Santillana altogether and go straight to Altamira.

The town is named for Santa Juliana Cino del Mar, a martyr who refused to renounce her virginity and her faith in God. The **Colegiata de Santa Juliana**, a 12th-century Romanesque church founded by Turkish monks, houses her remains. The sepulchre guards her relics, and the gorgeous high altarpiece is a 15th-century Spanish-Flemish painting depicting the saint's martyrdom. From the bus stop, walk uphill into town and veer to the right at the first fork onto C. de la Carrera, which becomes C. Cantón and eventually C. del Río and leads directly to the church. (Open summer daily 10am-1:30pm and 4-7:30pm; winter Tu-Su 10am-1:30pm and 4-6:30pm. €2.50, includes entrance to the Museo Diocesano.) From the front of the Colegiata, a trek back up C. del Río leads to the ▨**Museo de la Tortura y de la Inquisición,** Av. de Jesús Otero, 1. Four words: abdomen-gouging vaginal pear. If this freaks you out, skip this small museum, which displays more than 70 instruments of pain and suffering and whose exhibits of terrifying torture methods used during the Spanish Inquisition reveal the darker side of Christianity. However gruesome, though, the museum is very informative and posts full descriptions of the instruments in four languages, including where, when, and for what transgression each instrument was used. (☎942 84 02 73. Open daily 10am-10pm. €3.60.) The **Museo Diocesano,** C. el Cruce, across the street from the stop on C. Santo Domingo in the Monasterio Regina Coeli, has an extensive, if mediocre, collection of religious relics and artwork. Most interesting, other than the ancient building itself, once a monastery, is the collection of over 300 miniature crucifixes. (Open summer daily 10am-1:30pm and 4-7:30pm; winter Tu-Su 10am-1:30pm and 4-6:30pm. Adults €2.50, includes entrance to the Colegiata.)

The **tourist office** is at Av. Escultor Jesús Otero, 20. From the bus stop, walk up C. Santo Domingo and bear right onto C. de la Carrera. Then take the first right onto C. Gándara and go right again onto Av. Escultor Jesús Otero. (☎942 81 82 51; http://turismo.cantabria.org. Open daily 9:30am-1:30pm and 4-7pm.)

GALICIA (GALIZA)

If, as the old Galician saying goes, "rain is art," then there is no gallery more beautiful than the skies of northwestern Spain. Galicia looks and feels like no other region of the country. Often veiled in a silvery mist, it is a province of fern-laden woods, slate-roofed fishing villages, and endless beaches. Rivers wind through hills and widen into estuaries that empty into the Bay of Biscay and the Atlantic.

A rest stop on the Celts' journey to Ireland around 900 BC, Galicia harbors enduring Celtic influences. Ancient *castros* (fortress-villages), inscriptions, and *gaitas* (bagpipes) testify to this Celtiberian past, and lingering lore of witches, fairies, and buried treasures has earned Galicia a reputation as a land of magic. The rough terrain has historically hampered trade, but ship building, auto manufacturing, and even renowned fashion labels are contributing to the region's gradual modernization and development. Tourists have begun to visit even the smallest of towns, and Santiago de Compostela, the terminus of the Camino de Santiago, continues to be one of the world's most popular backpacking destinations.

Galicians speak *gallego*, a linguistic missing link of sorts between Castilian and Portuguese. While newspapers and street signs alternate between languages, most conversations are conducted in Spanish. Regional cuisine features *caldo gallego*

(a vegetable broth), *vieiras* (scallops, the pilgrim's trophy), *empanadas* (turnovers stuffed with assorted fillings), and *pulpo a gallego* (boiled octopus). Regionalism in Galicia doesn't cause quite the stir it does in the País Vasco or Catalunya, but you still may see graffiti calling for *"liberdade."*

HIGHLIGHTS OF GALICIA

SANCTIFY yourself by making the pilgrimage to **Santiago de Compostela** (p. 602).

COMMUNE with the Celts at the ruins of their castle in **O Castro de Baroña** (p. 610).

GULP down the fiery local concoction during the Fiesta de San Xuan in **Vigo** (p. 615).

EXPLORE the untouched coves and beaches of the **Islas Cíes** (p. 615).

CLIMB the lighthouse Hercules built in **A Coruña** (p. 622).

WITNESS the end of the world at **Cabo Finisterre** (p. 609).

SANTIAGO DE COMPOSTELA ☎981

Santiago (pop. 94,000) is a city of song. From the impromptu orchestra concerts on R. do Vilar to the thumping of all-night discos, from the roving bands of *gaita* players to the cathedral's morning chimes, every street and plaza is filled with celebration. Perhaps these are the chords of weary pilgrims, elated to have, at long last, reached the apostle's tomb. Or perhaps these are the tunes of the *Apóstolo*, the city's extravagant two-week fiesta in honor of its namesake in late July. But more likely, these are just the sounds of joy at waking up to another day in Santiago, where narrow, Baroque streets empty into vast plazas, where idlers and revelers spill out of the myriad cafes and bars, and where every day in this sun- (and perhaps Apostle-) blessed city is worthy of celebration.

▰ TRANSPORTATION

Flights: Aeropuerto Lavacolla (☎981 54 75 00), 10km toward Lugo. A bus goes to Santiago, stopping at the bus and train stations and C. General Pardiñas, 26 (8 per day 6:40am-10:30pm, €1.55). Schedule in the daily *El Correo Gallego* (€0.75). **Iberia,** R. do Xeneral Pardiñas, 36 (☎981 57 20 24). Open M-F 9:30am-2pm and 4-7pm.

Trains: R. do Hórreo (☎981 52 02 02). Info open daily 7am-11pm. To: **Bilbao** (10¾hr., 9:04am, €35.50) via **León** (6½hr., €24.50) and **Burgos** (8hr., €31); **La Coruña** (1hr.; M-Th 14 per day 6:30am-8:32pm, F 17 per day 6:30am-10:35pm, Sa 14 per day 6:30am-10:35pm, Su 12 per day 7:35am-10:35pm; €3.30-4.30); **Madrid** (8hr.; Su-F 2 and 10:30pm, Sa 10am and 10:30pm; €38.50); **Vigo** (2hr.; M-Sa 14-17 per day 6:25am-9:45pm, Su 12 per day 7am-9:45pm; €5.10-6.60) via **Pontevedra** (1½hr., €3.20-4.30).

Buses: Estación Central de Autobuses, R. de Rodríguez (☎981 54 24 16), a 20min. walk from downtown. Bus #10 goes from the station to the R. de Montero Ríos side of Pr. de Galicia (10min., 7:30am-10:30pm M-Sa every 20min., Su every 30min.; €0.80). Info open daily 6am-10pm.

ALSA (☎981 58 61 33, reservations 902 42 22 42). Open daily 7:30am-9:30pm. To **Madrid** (8-9hr.; M-Sa 5-6 per day 6am-9:30pm, Su 4 per day 10am-9:30pm; €35.40, round-trip €58) and **San Sebastián** (13½hr.; 3 per day 8:30am-6pm; €49.30, round-trip €93.70) via **Bilbao** (11¼hr., €43.80/€59).

Arriva/Finisterre (☎981 58 85 11) to **Finisterre** (2½hr.; M-F 7 per day 8am-7:30pm, Sa 3 per day 8am-4:30pm, Su 3 per day 9am-6:30pm; €10).

Castromil (☎981 58 97 00). To: **La Coruña** (1½hr.; M-Th every hr. 7am-9pm, F every hr. 7am-10pm, Sa every hr. 9am-8pm, Su 9 per day 10am-9pm; €6); **El Ferrol** (2hr.; M-F 8 per day 9:15am-9pm, Sa 6 per day 9:15am-9pm, Su 6 per day 9:15am-10pm; €6.80); **Noia** (1hr.; M-F

GALICIA

Santiago de Compostela

▲ ACCOMMODATIONS
Hospedaje Fonseca, 2
Hospedaje Ramos, 4
Hospedaje Rodríguez, 16
Hostal Alfonso, 1
Hostal Barbantes/
Libredón, 3
Hostal Pazo Agra, 15
Hotel Virxe da Cerca, 17

Meson La Cigala d'Oro, 6
O Cabaliño do Demo, 18

★ NIGHTLIFE
A Reixa, 14
Casa das Crechas, 8
Conga 8, 10
Modus Vivendi, 12
Retablo Café Concerto, 13
Xaveste, 11

◆ FOOD
A Tulla, 7
Cre-Cotté, 9
Hamburguesería Raíña, 5

Map labels:

Centro Gallego de Arte Contemporáneo
Convento de Santo Domingo de Bonaval
Museo do Pobo Gallego
R. de Teo
R. de San Pedro
R. de Bonaval
R. do Rosario
R. do Medio
R. Dos Lagartos
Campo da Angustia
Corredoira das Fraguas
Av. de Quiroga Palacios
Av. de Lugo
R. da Batalla de Clavijo
R. do Obispo Teodomiro
Av. de Gonzalo Torrente Ballester
TO + (10km)
Ramón del Valle Inclán
Porta do Camiño
R. das Rodas
Santa María del Camiño
Costiña de S. Anotonio
Calzada de S. Antonio
R. de Belvís
Parque de Belvís
Convento de San Agustiño
MATADOIRO
San Benito
R. das Casas Reais
Calzada de San Pedro
MERCADO
R. das Trompas
Convento de Belvís
Seminario Menor
R. de Andar
R. de Xoana de Abaxo
R. da Virxe da Cerca
R. de Santo Agostiño
R. de CERVANTES
Cinco Rúas
Museo das Peregrinacións
PR. SAN MARTIÑO PIÑARIO
PR. DA INMACULADA
R. da Acibechería
San Martiño Pinario
R. de Anteallares
Paio de Antealtares
PR. DA QUINTANA
PR. DE FEIJÓO
R. de Xelmírez
R. da Conga
Tr. de Salomé
Santa María Salomé
Universidade
R. da Ensinanza
Parque de Belvís
R. de Andar
Praceiras
R. do peligo de abaixo
R. de Sar
R. do Olvido
Catedral
PR. DE OBRA DOIRO
PR. DAS PRATERIAS
Travesía de Cádelería
Tr. da Universidade
PR. MAZARELOS
Convento de las Madres Mercedarias
R. do Castro de Ouro
R. do Patio de Madres
Hotel Reyes Católicos
Pazo de Raxoi
PR. DE FONSECA
R. de Fonseca
Tr. de Fonseca
Av. de Rodrigo de Padrín
Av. de Figueroa
R. do Vilar
R. do Franco
Office for Peregrinos
TAXI
R. de Entrerrías
PR. DO TOURAL
Cantón do Toural
Supermercado Lorenzo Froiz
R. da Senra
Fonte de Santo Antonio
R. de Pitelos
R. da Concepción Arenal
R. do Castro de Ouro
R. de Pérez Constanti
R. de Curros Enríquez
R. de López Ferreiros Fontán
R. de debomingo Fontán
Campo de S. Clemente
R. do Pombal
R. de Gómez Ulla
PR. DE GALICIA
R. de Santiago de Guayaquil
R. de Lavexe Ruiz
R. de Ramón Piñeiro
R. do Horreo
Parlamento de Galicia
Av. de Lugo
Caballería de Santa Susana
Av. de Xoán Carlos I
Carreira do Conde
Av. de Rosalía de Castro
TO + (1.5km)
R. Nova de Abaixo
R. de Montero Ríos
R. de Alfredo Brañas
R. de República
R. do Xeneral Pardiñas
R. do Salvador
Dr. Teixeiro
R. de Montero Ríos
Iberia Airlines
R. de Antonio Casares
PR. ROXA
R. da República de Antenina
R. da Rosa
Santiago León de Caracas
R. de Ramón Caballinos
Servilimp
R. de Frei Rodeiro Salvado
R. de San Pedro o Santo
R. de Fernando III o Santo
Av. de Lugo
Avis

200 yards
200 meters
0

TO (1.5km) & ▲ (2km)

14 per day 8:15am-10pm, Sa 10 per day 10am-10pm, Su 6 per day 10am-8pm; €2.90); **Vigo** (2hr.; M-F every hr. 9am-10pm, Sa every hr. 9am-1pm and 5-9pm, Su 9 per day 10am-9pm; €7) via **Pontevedra** (1½hr., €4.70).

Public Transportation: Local buses (☎981 58 18 15). Bus #6 to the train station (10am-10:30pm), #4 to the campgrounds (7am-10:30pm), and #10 to the bus station. In the city center, almost all buses stop at Pr. de Galicia, where there are 2 stops, one on the R. do Dr. Teixeiro side and one along R. de Montero Ríos. Except for #6, buses run daily 7:30am-10:30pm every 20-30min. €0.75.

Taxis: Radio Taxi, at the bus station (☎981 58 24 50) and Pr. de Galicia (☎981 56 10 28). 24hr. For late-night service, try near the clubs in Pl. Roxa.

Car Rental: Avis (☎981 59 04 09), at the train station. 23+, must have had license for 1 yr. Open M-F 9am-1:15pm and 4-7pm, Sa 9am-12:45pm, Su 9:30am-12:30pm. From €86 per day for 350km, €450 per wk. 25 and under add €10.50 per day. Discounts for longer rentals.

■★🛈 ORIENTATION AND PRACTICAL INFORMATION

The **cathedral** marks the center of the old city, on a hill above the new city. The **train station** is at the far southern end of town. To reach the old city from the station, either take bus #6 to **Praza de Galicia** or walk up the stairs across the parking lot from the main entrance, cross the street, bear right onto R. do Hórreo and continue uphill about 10min. The **bus station** is at the town's far northern end. The walk is over 20min.; instead, take bus #10 to Pr. de Galicia (10min.). In the old city, three main streets lead to the cathedral: **Rúa do Franco, Rúa do Vilar,** and **Rúa Nova.**

Tourist Office: Municipal Office, R. do Vilar, 63 (☎981 55 51 29; www.santiagoturismo.com). English, German, Italian, and French spoken. Open June-Sept. 9am-9pm; Oct.-May 10am-3pm and 5-8pm. **Branch** in Pr. de Galicia. Open M-F 10am-2pm and 4-7pm, Sa 11am-2pm and 5-7pm, Su 11am-2pm. **Regional Office,** R. do Vilar, 43 (☎981 58 40 81), provides information about Galicia and daytrips from Santiago. Open M-F 10am-2pm and 4-7pm, Sa 11am-2pm and 5-7pm, Su 11am-2pm.

Currency Exchange: Banco Santander Central Hispano, Pr. de Galicia, 1 (☎981 58 61 11). Open May-Sept. M-F 8:30am-2pm; Oct.-Apr. M-F 8:30am-2pm, Sa 8:30am-1pm. Western Union services and 24hr. **ATM** outside.

Religious Services: Mass in the cathedral M-Sa 9:30am, noon *(Misa del Peregrino)*, 6, and 7:30pm (vespers); Su 10:30am, 1, 5, and 7pm (vespers). Most nights also offer a special **pilgrim's mass,** featuring the *botafumeiro* (a gigantic incense burner).

Laundromat: ServiLimp, R. Ramón Cabanillas, 16 (☎981 59 29 52). 4.5kg of laundry €6. Open M-F 9:30am-1:30pm and 4-8pm, Sa 10am-2pm.

Police: Av. de Rodrigo de Padrón (☎981 54 23 23).

24hr. Pharmacy: Farmacia M. Jesús Valdés Cabo, Cantón do Toural, 1 (☎981 58 58 95). **Farmacia R. Bescanses,** Pr. do Toural, 1 (☎981 58 59 90), built in the mid-19th century, is worth seeing.

Medical Assistance: Hospital Clínico Universitario, Tr. da Choupana (☎061 or 981 95 00 00), 2km west of town.

Internet Access: CyberNova 50, R. Nova, 50 (☎981 57 51 88). 26 fast computers. 9am-10pm €1.20 per hr., 10pm-1am €1 per hr. Open M-Sa 9am-1am, Su 10am-1am.

Post Office: Tr. de Fonseca (☎981 58 12 52). **Lista de Correos** and **fax** at R. do Franco, 6. Open M-F 8:30am-8:30pm, Sa 9:30am-2pm. **Postal Code:** 15701.

ACCOMMODATIONS AND CAMPING

Nearly every street in the old city has at least one or two *pensiones*. The liveliest and most popular, however, are on R. do Vilar and R. da Raíña. Call ahead in winter, when university students occupy most rooms.

Hospedaje Ramos, R. da Raíña, 18, 2nd fl. (☎981 58 18 59), above O Papa Una restaurant. In the center of the *ciudad vieja*, these well-lit rooms are newly renovated with shining floors, tight windows that keep out the noise, and private bath. Reserve 2 wk. in advance during summer. Singles €16; doubles €27.50. ❶

Hostal Barbantes/Hostal Libredón, Pr. de Fonseca, 5 (☎981 57 65 20; fax 58 41 33). 2 hostels under the same owner share a reception area. Both have spacious, sparklingly clean rooms with sunlight and private bath. Barbantes's rooms are newly renovated with TVs and overlook Pr. de Fonseca. Barbantes Apr.-Oct. singles €40; doubles €60. Nov.-Mar. €36/€54. Libredón €30-36/€45/€27-32/€40. MC/V. ❹

Hostal Pazo Agra, R. da Calderer   ía, 37 (☎981 58 35 17). Clean rooms with tall ceilings and private hallway baths have glass doors opening to balconies. Some have TV. Reception 9am-11pm in Restaurante Zingara, Cardenal Payá, 2, just around the block. May-Oct. singles €25; doubles €36. Nov.-Apr. €17/€26, or approx. €300 per mo.

Hostal Alfonso, R. do Pombal, 40 (☎981 58 56 85; www.hostalalfonso.com). Rooms in this warmly decorated hostel each have a view of either the park or the cathedral as well as TV, private bath, and fresh fruit. Breakfast included. Reserve a month ahead in Aug. May-Oct. singles €45; doubles €64. Oct.-Apr. reduced prices. AmEx/MC/V. ❹

Hospedaje Rodríguez, Ruela do Pisón, 4 (☎981 58 84 08), on a quiet street 3 blocks from Pr. de Galicia. The owner will make you feel right at home in the clean, sunny, marble-tiled rooms. Laundry, kitchen, hall bath. Singles €14, €60 per wk.; doubles €24.

Hotel Virxe da Cerca, R. da Virxe da Cerca, 27 (☎981 56 93 50). Peaceful and relaxing, in a former 18th-century Jesuit house with a garden and a view of the nearby hills and the Convento de Santo Domingo. Standard rooms in the new building are less expensive. All the amenities and more. Apr.-Oct. standard singles €75, *especial* €85; doubles €95/€105. Nov.-Mar. €65/€84/€85/€95. IVA not included. V. ❺

Hospedaje Fonseca, R. de Fonseca, 1, 2nd fl. (☎981 57 24 79). Colorful, sunny rooms. Common kitchen with TV. Shared baths. Singles, doubles, triples, and quads all €15 per person. Approx. €70 per person per wk., €180 per mo. ❶

Camping: As Cancelas, R. 25 de Xullo, 35 (☎981 58 02 66). 3km north of the cathedral. Take bus #6 heading uphill on R. de Hórreo, or #4 from R. da Senra, 1 block off of Pr. de Galicia heading toward it. Laundry, supermarket, and pool. Reception 8am-11:30pm. July-Aug. €4.60 per person, €4.80 per car and tent. Sept.-June €3.70 per person, car, and tent. Electricity €3. ❶

FOOD

Tapas-weary budget travelers will appreciate Santiago's selection of restaurants. Bars and cafeterias line the streets with remarkably inexpensive *menús*. Most restaurants are on **Rúa do Vilar, Rúa do Franco, Rúa Nova,** and **Rúa da Raíña;** in the new city, look near Pr. Roxa. End your meal with a *tarta de Santiago*, a rich almond cake emblazoned with a sugary St. James cross. The best bakery in town is **Confitería El Coral,** R. Dr. Teixeiro, 32, which has a tantalizing selection of homemade chocolate, ice cream, and pastries. (☎981 56 20 10. Open daily 9:30am-2:30pm and 4:30-9pm.) Santiago's **mercado,** near the Convento de San Agustín, is a sight in its own right, going strongest on Thursdays and Saturdays.

GALICIA

WALK LIKE A HERMIT

One night in 813, a hermit trudged through the hills on the way to his hermitage. Suddenly, miraculously bright visions flooded his senses, revealing the long-forgotten tomb of the apostle James. Word eventually reached King Alfonso II, who ordered the construction of a cathedral around this *campus stellae* (field of stars), marking the birth of the world-famous pilgrimage hotspot.

Since the 11th century, thousands of pilgrims have traveled the *Camino de Santiago*. Many have made the pilgrimage in search of spiritual fulfillment: most as true believers, some to adhere to a stipulation of inheritance, a few to absolve themselves of sin, and at least one to find romance (the wife of Bath in Chaucer's *Canterbury Tales* sauntered to Santiago in bright red stockings to find herself a husband).

Clever Benedictine monks built monasteries to host pilgrims along the *camino,* giving rise to the world's first large-scale international tourist route and helping make Santiago's cathedral the world's most frequented Christian shrine. In the 12th century, an enterprising French monk, Aymery Picaud, added a book to the *Codex Calixtinus,* a collection of stories about the apostles, that was filled with information on the quality of water at various rest stops and descriptions of vil-

(Open M-Sa 7:30am-2pm.) **Supermercado Lorenzo Froiz,** Pr. do Toural, is one block from Pr. de Galicia. (Open daily 9am-10pm. MC/V.)

O Cabaliño do Demo, R. Ayer Ulloa, 7 (☎981 58 81 46). Enjoy a variety of global vegetarian entrees, from Middle Eastern to Mexican, in this creative and resourcefully decorated restaurant. *Menú* €8, appetizers and entrees €4.80-6.50. Open M-W 2-4pm and 9-11:30pm, Th-Sa 2-4pm and 9pm-midnight. ❷

A Tulla, R. de Entrerúas, 1 (☎981 58 08 89). Literally a hole in the wall, this tiny family restaurant is accessible only through an obscure alley between R. do Vilar and R. Nova. Delicious homemade dishes draw large, energetic crowds of locals for lunch and dinner. Entrees €6.50-8.50, *menú* €11.80, vegetarian *menú* €9. Open M-Sa noon-midnight. ❷

Cre-Cotté, Pr. de Quintana, 1 (☎981 57 76 43). Savor crepes (€5.50-8) and an extensive selection of enormous salads (€6.50-7.50) at this popular spot, on the beautiful terrace or in the softly lit dining room. Open daily noon-midnight. AmEx/MC/V. ❷

Mesón La Cigala d'Oro, R. do Franco, 10 (☎981 58 29 52). Has a terrace in the back and specializes in seafood. The *mariscada* (€55) serves 2 and contains every kind of seafood imaginable. Entrees €10-30, three-course *menú* €18.80. Open daily 1-3:30pm and 8-11:30pm. AmEx/MC/V. ❹

Hamburguesería Raíña, R. da Raíña, 18. An oasis for the starving, broke traveler. Huge hamburgers €1.80-2.30. Open daily 1-4pm and 8pm-1am. ❶

⊙ SIGHTS

◼ CATEDRAL DE SANTIAGO DE COMPOSTELA
☎981 58 35 48. Open daily 7am-7pm. Free.

Santiago's cathedral has four facades, each a masterpiece from a different era, with entrances opening to four different plazas: Praterías, Quintana, Inmaculada, and Obradoiro. From the southern **Praza das Praterías** (with the sea horse), enter the cathedral through the Romanesque arched double doors. The Pórtico Real and Porta Santa face **Praza da Quintana,** to the west of the cathedral. To the north, a blend of Doric and Ionic columns, rebuilt after a fire in the 18th century, grace **Praza da Inmaculada,** combining Romanesque and Neoclassical styles. Consecrated in 1211, the cathedral gradually acquired Gothic chapels (in the apse and transept), a dome, a cloister, and the Baroque **Obradoiro facade** with two towers that soar above the city. This facade faces **Praza do Obradoiro,** an immense plaza scattered with souvenir hawkers and *tunas* (lute-strumming students in medieval garb).

Many consider Maestro Mateo's **Pórtico de la Gloria,** encased in the Obradoiro facade, the crowning achievement of Spanish Romanesque sculpture. This apocalyptic 12th-century amalgam of angels, prophets, saints, sinners, demons, and monsters forms a compendium of Christian theology. Unlike most rigid Romanesque statues, those in the Pórtico seem to smile, whisper, and lean. The revered **remains of St. James** (Santiago) lie beneath the high altar in a silver coffer, while his bejeweled bust, polished by the embraces of thousands of pilgrims, rests above the altar. The **botafumeiro,** an enormous silver censer used in religious rituals and intended to overpower the stench of dirty pilgrims, swings from the transept during High Mass and liturgical ceremonies. Much older than the towers that house them, the **bells** of Santiago were stolen in 997 by Moorish invaders and transported to Córdoba; when Spaniards later conquered Córdoba, they had their revenge by forcing Moors to carry the bells back.

MUSEUM AND CLOISTERS. Inside the museum are several gorgeous 16th-century tapestries, manuscripts from the *Codex Calixtinus,* and Romanesque remains from one of many archaeological excavations conducted in the cathedral. The 12th-century *Codex,* five volumes of manuscripts of the stories of the Apostle James, includes travel information for early pilgrims. There is also a room dedicated to the stone choir that once stood inside the cathedral. It was built by the Maestro Mateo to represent the "New Jerusalem that descends from heaven," described in Revelation 3:12. (☎981 58 11 55. Museum open June-Sept. M-Sa 10am-2pm and 4-8pm, Su and holidays 10am-2pm; Oct.-May M-Sa 10am-1:30pm and 4-6:30pm, Su and holidays 10am-1:30pm. €5, students €3; includes entrance to crypt.)

OTHER SIGHTS

PAZO DE RAXOI. The majestic facade of the Pazo de Raxoi shines with gold-accented balconies and monumental columns. Once a royal palace, it now houses the Ayuntamiento and the office of the president of the *Xunta de Galicia* (Galician government). At night, floodlights illuminate the remarkable bas-relief of the 844 Battle of Clavijo, during which, according to legend, Santiago helped the fight off the Moors. (Across Pr. do Obradoiro, facing the cathedral.)

MUSEO DAS PEREGRINACIÓNS. This three-story Gothic building is full of creatively displayed historical info about the *Camino* and pilgrimages in general. It includes statues of the Virgin as a baby-Jesus-

lages, inhabitants, and monuments along *La Ruta Francesa,* beginning near the French border in Roncesvalles, Navarra (p. 502)—in essence, the world's first travel guide.

Although they no longer don the typical brown cape, pilgrims nowadays are easily spotted by their crook-necked walking sticks, sunburnt faces, and scallop shells tied to weathered backpacks. The shells, the emblem of fisherman St. James and a pagan symbol of travelers on foot, were first acquired by pilgrims after visiting the cathedral. Although only pilgrims on their way home used to carry the shell, it soon became a mark of immunity, respected by bandits and robbers, and pilgrims began to carry it on the voyage to Santiago as well.

True *peregrinos* (pilgrims) must cover 100km on foot or horse or 200km on bike to receive La Compostela, an official certificate of the pilgrimage issued by the cathedral. A network of *refugios* and *albergues* offers free lodging to pilgrims on the move and stamps the "pilgrims' passports" to provide evidence of completion of the full distance. At a rate of 30km per day, walking the entire French route (from Roncesvalles in the Pyrenees to Santiago de Compostela, 750-870km) takes about a month and places you in the ranks of such illustrious pilgrims as royal couple Fernando and Isabel, St. Francis de Assisi, Pope John Paul II, and Shirley MacLaine.

GALICIA

toting pilgrim, illustrations of the different routes to Santiago, and exhibits on the rituals of pilgrimage and the iconography of Santiago. *(Pr. de San Miguel. ☎981 58 15 58. Open Tu-F 10am-8pm, Sa 10:30am-1:30pm and 5-8pm, Su 10:30am-1:30pm. €2.40, children and seniors €1.20, free during special expositions and most of the summer.)*

CENTRO GALLEGO DE ARTE CONTEMPORÁNEO. The expansive galleries and rooftop *terraza* of the sparkling Centro Gallego de Arte Contemporáneo (CGAC) house temporary cutting-edge exhibitions of boundary-bending artists from around the world. In 2005, programs will feature works by Arturo Herrera, Manolo Paz, and Din Matamoros, among other artists. *(R. de Ramón del Valle Inclán. Next to the Museo de Pobo Gallego. ☎981 54 66 19; www.cgac.org. Open Tu-Su 11am-8pm. Free.)*

MUSEO DE POBO GALLEGO. Find out everything you have ever wanted to know about traditional Galician living. Exhibits on ship building, pottery, house construction, and *gaitas* (the Galician bagpipe) fill the rooms branching off of three intertwining spiral staircases. *(Inside the Convento de Santo Domingo de Boneval. ☎981 58 36 20. Open Tu-Sa 10am-2pm and 4-8pm, Su 11am-2pm. Free.)*

MONASTERIO DE SAN MARTIÑO PINARIO. Once a religious center almost as prestigious as the cathedral, the monastery is a mixture of Romanesque cloisters, Plateresque facades, and Baroque sculpture. Its composite style makes it an outstanding architectural study. *(In Pr. de San Martiño Pinario.)*

🎭 🎆 NIGHTLIFE AND FESTIVALS

The local newspaper *El Correo Gallego* (€0.75) and the free monthly *Compostela Capital* list art exhibits and concert information. Consult any of three local monthlies, *Santiago Días Guía Imprescindible, Compostelán,* or *Modus Vivendi,* for updates on the live music scene. At night, crowds flood cellars throughout the city. To boogie with local students, hit the bars and clubs off Pr. Roxa. One of the city's biggest festivals, **Fiestas de la Ascensión,** on May 20, features concerts, a famous cattle market, and the consumption of many octopi in the Santa Susana oak grove. The city celebrates the **Día de Santiago** (July 25) for a full two weeks (July 15-31), in a celebration called *Apóstolo;* on the night of the 24th, a Pontifical Mass is held in the cathedral during **Las Vísperas de Santiago.**

🏆 **Casa das Crechas,** Vía Sacra, 3 (☎981 56 07 51). A 2-story pub with a witchcraft theme and a black-and-white photo collection downstairs. Renowned for Tu night jazz and Galician folk concerts. Beer €2. Open daily summer noon-4am; winter 4pm-3am.

Retablo Café Concerto, R. Nova, 13 (☎981 56 48 51). Heavenly decor in rich reds, purples, and golds as well as low prices keep tourists and students coming back. Eclectic music selections include techno, pop, rock, and house. Beer €2, mixed drinks €4.50. Open daily noon-5am.

Conga 8, R. da Conga, 8 (☎981 58 34 07). The mix of salsa, merengue, and Spanish dance music in this dark stone basement draws an older crowd to the dance floor. Popular hangout for local *tunas* (student music groups) around 3am. Beer €1.80, mixed drinks €4. Open daily 10pm-5am.

Xavestre, R. de San Paolo de Antaltares, 31. Get up close and personal with *santiaguinos* in this crowded bar. 20-somethings spill out into the street, to the tune of the latest hits in Spanish pop music. Beer €2.50, mixed drinks €5-6. Open daily 11am-late.

Modus Vivendi, Pr. de Feijo, 1 (☎981 57 61 09). Galicia's oldest pub was a clubhouse for revolutionary Galician youth in the 1970s. Today, the relaxed interior entertains Santiago's youth into the wee hours of the night with live music W and Th. Beer €2, mixed drinks €4. Open daily 7pm-late.

A Reixa, Tr. Salomé, 3 (☎ 981 56 07 80). A smoky, low-ceilinged pub dedicated to 60s rock. Sporadic concerts advertised on posters throughout the city. Homemade *aguardiente*, a coffee liqueur, €1.80-2.20. Beer €1.80. Open daily 4:30pm-late.

◪ DAYTRIPS FROM SANTIAGO DE COMPOSTELA

The northern part of the Rías Baixas hides undiscovered hamlets frequented only by pilgrims. These small towns make good daytrips from Santiago, although buses in this area tend to stop frequently, making travel times quite lengthy. Go anyway; otherwise, you'll regret missing the views of the turbulent coastline and the peace of small Spanish fishing towns.

▨ CABO FINISTERRE (CABO FISTERRA)

Arriva/Finisterre buses run from Santiago to Finisterre (2½hr.; M-F 7 per day 8am-7:30pm, Sa 3 per day 8am-4:30pm, Su 3 per day 9am-6:30pm; €9.90, round-trip €18) and back (M-F 4 per day 7:50-4:30pm, Sa 3 per day 10:30am-4pm, Su 3 per day 9:45am-6pm). The bus stop is next to the Albergue de Peregrinos, 50m uphill from the water.

Jutting out precariously from the infamously rocky Costa de la Muerte ("Coast of Death"; Costa da Morte in *gallego*), Cabo Finisterre was once considered Europe's westernmost point, and for centuries it was a crucial port for all naval trade along the Atlantic. Finisterre was also famous due to the ancient belief that it was off these shores that the world ended—hence its name: *finis* (end), *terre* (earth). Even today, it feels like the end of the earth after a seemingly endless bus ride out to a desolate town on a lonely, wind-swept peninsula. On July 1, 2003, Cabo Finisterre became the first port on the Costa de la Muerte to send out fishermen since the sinking of the oil tanker *Prestige* in November 2002.

The 1½hr. hike from the port to **Monte San Guillermo** is long, but those who complete it are rewarded with incredible views of the tumultuous sea and Finisterre's famous bed-shaped **fertility rocks.** Couples having problems conceiving are advised to make a go of it on the rocks under a full moon (harvest moons are even better). On another hill on San Guillermo are **As Pedras Santas,** two fairly large rocks which cannot be lifted by themselves, but which slide effortlessly side-to-side if you press the right spot. Try it yourself—the contact point is well marked. The **lighthouse** that has beckoned ships for years is 45min. from the center of town and can be reached by descending the trail that continues down the other side of the mountain. The best **beach** in Finisterre is

FROM THE ROAD

MUSINGS FROM THE END OF THE WORLD

As I sat on the bus back to Santiago from Finisterre, a question wracked my mind: Why is it called the end of the earth? Couldn't it just as easily be the beginning? The more I considered it, the more arbitrary the name "Finisterre" seemed.

My only possible answer has to do with the pilgrimage. *Peregrinos* have made the trip to the apostle's tomb for over a millennium, and they have to finish somewhere. While Santiago's majestic cathedral may seem like the appropriate point for weary hikers to pat themselves on the back and go home, somehow it's not; many have continued an extra 120km toward Finisterre, a jagged peninsula that reaches out into nothingness.

In Santiago, there's no such thing as starting or stopping. As a violinist in one corner finishes a string of Vivaldi pieces, a harpist in another begins his own serenade. Ethereal mists brighten into cheerful sunlight, which fades out into a calm grayness again. The pilgrimage simply can't end in Santiago because Santiago defies endings. So while it may be called the end of the earth, Finisterre might just create that crucial sense of resolution for the *peregrinos* who know that they can go no farther. The end of the journey just marks the beginning of the trip home.

—Defne Ozgediz

KING OF THE WHITES

Like many kings, it is short-lived, inbred, and gets drunk young. It has thousands of devotees who espouse its charm, grace, and taste. Indeed, since its ascension in the 1980s, after wine producers in Galicia shifted their attention to this difficult-to-grow grape, *El Albariño* has become king of Spanish white wines, transforming Galicia's hillsides forever.

The mild temperatures and high rainfall in Galicia have always hampered attempts at growing red wine grapes. However, the sturdy, rot-resistant *albariño* grape thrives in Galicia. Not only is it well-suited to the climate, but its wine, light, with a distinctive perfume and crisp taste, perfectly compliments the region's celebrated seafood. Thanks to the popularity of *albariño*, which is considered the best white wine in Spain and one of the best in the world, wine production is now Galicia's fastest growing industry.

The controversy over *albariño*'s bloodlines only adds to its mystique. Some claim French monks brought it to Santiago during the 12th- and 13th-century crusades, further asserting that *albariño* is genetically linked to Germany's Riesling grape. However, locals hold steadfastly to the explanation that *albariño* is indigenous to Galicia. No matter what region gave birth to the grape, the Rías Baixas are now the uncontested parents of the regal wine.

on the flat isthmus that connects the peninsula with the mainland. The beaches are powdery and wide, the waters calm but frigid. Either walk 4km along the road to Santiago or take the bus and ask to stop.

The **Albergue de Peregrinos,** C. Real, 2, has maps, brochures, and tourist info. From the bus stop, facing the water, turn left. At the pink statue, turn left again. (☎981 74 07 81. Open May-Oct. M-F 8:30am-11pm, Sa-Su 1-11pm; Nov.-Apr. daily 10am-1pm and 5-11pm.) Nearby, **Bazar de Artesanía da Costa da Morte** also has maps and info on bike rentals. (☎981 74 00 74. Bikes €4 per hr., €12 per day. Open June-Sept. daily 9:30am-2pm and 5-9pm; Oct.-May M-Sa 10am-1:30pm and 5-8:30pm.) If you miss the last bus back to Santiago, you can stay at **Hospedaje López ❶,** R. de Carrasqueira, 4. The clean, inexpensive rooms with shared baths all have views of the coast. From the bus stop, cross the street and walk uphill, then turn left onto the narrow street; the hostel has dwarf figurines in the front yard. (☎981 74 04 49. Apr.-Aug. singles €15; doubles €18-21. Sept.-Mar. €12/€15-18.)

O CASTRO DE BAROÑA

To reach O Castro de Baroña, you'll need to make a connection in Noia. Castromil (☎981 58 90 90) runs buses from Santiago to Noia (1hr.; M-F 14 per day 8:15am-10pm, Sa 10 per day 10am-10pm, Su every 2hr. 10am-8pm; €2.90). From Noia, Hefsel buses stop at O Castro de Baroña (in front of Café-Bar O Castro) en route to Riveira (30min.; M-F 14 per day 6:50am-9:30pm, Sa 7 per day 8am-9pm, Su 10 per day 9am-1pm; €1.60). Be sure to tell the bus driver where you're going, as the stop is easy to miss. From the bus stop, follow signs to the fortress, downhill toward the water. Catch the bus home across the road from Café-Bar O Castro.

One of Galicia's best-preserved coastal Celtic villages, **O Castro de Baroña** lies 19km south of Noia. The seaside remains of a 5th-century Celtic **fortress** cover the neck of the isthmus, ascending to a rocky promontory above the sea and then descending to the soft sands of an excellent crescent **beach,** where clothing is *"prohibido."* Don't be intimidated by the hostile graffiti denouncing those who don swimsuits; beachgoers are friendly and some cover their bodies as well. For those who need a shower, **Café-Bar O Castro ❸,** Lugar Castro de Baroña, 18, in **Porto do Son** (the O Castro bus stop), offers spotless rooms under the care of a very nice owner. (☎981 76 74 30. June-Aug. doubles €25-30; Sept.-May reduced prices.) Should you get stuck in **Noia** on the way back to Santiago, several hotels are a short walk from the bus station on R. da Galicia. From the bus station, walk uphill on R. Pedra Sartaña, turn right onto R. Rosalía de Castro, and then left onto R. da Galicia. The bus station offers free **luggage storage.**

(Open 6:30am-11pm.) The closest hostel to the station, **Hostal Valadares ❷**, C. Alameda, offers comfortable rooms with firm mattresses, most with views of the surrounding mountains. TV, winter heat, bath, and breakfast are included. From the bus station, walk uphill on R. Pedra Sartaña and turn left at the street's end. (☎981 82 04 36. July-Aug. singles €25-40; doubles €30-42. Off-season reduced prices.)

MUROS AND LOURO

Castromil runs buses between Santiago and Muros (2hr.; M-F 11 per day 8:15am-9pm, Sa 10 per day 10am-9pm, Su every 2hr. 10am-8pm; €4.50-5.60) via Noia.

Muros is a small but lively fishing village recognized in 1970 as a historical site for its unique examples of traditional Gothic urban design, including narrow one-person lanes, arcades, sailor houses, and bite-size plazas. Its neighbor Louro, 4km away, is home to some of the most untouched, soft-sanded beaches in all of Galicia. The combination of the two makes an ideal daytrip—Muros, with its transportation facilities, accommodations, and restaurants, provides the amenities necessary for a day in the surf at Louro. From Muros, after walking around the old city's steep and winding streets, visitors can walk along the **Paseo Marítimo** (to the right, facing the water) to Louro, with views of sparkling cobalt waters on the way. The first beach in Louro, **Playa San Francisco,** is less than 3km from Muros. Stay overnight right on the beach at **A Vouga Camping ❶**, which has a restaurant, bar, hot showers, and a small market. (☎981 82 76 07. Reception 9am-11:30pm. Call a couple days ahead to reserve a space. €3.20 per person, €2.80-3.40 per tent, €17-20 per site, depending on size. Electricity €2.40.)

The Ayuntamiento in Muros houses a small **tourist office** open only in summer. From the bus stop, facing the water, walk right. The Ayuntamiento is in the plaza where the street bends. (☎981 82 60 50. Open June-Sept. 15 M-F 10:30am-2:30pm and 5:30-8:30pm, Sa 11:30-2:30pm.) For **bike rentals,** try **TriKi** farther along the same street. (☎981 76 20 02. Open M-Sa 10am-1:30pm and 5-8:30pm. €8 per day, €24 per week. MC/V.) If you'd like to stay in Muros, closer to the restaurants (all with boat-themed furniture), try **Hospedaje A Vianda ❸**, Av. de Castelao, 47. Some rooms have a view, and all are very clean with winter heat and shared baths. (☎981 82 63 22. Reserve a month ahead for Aug. stays. Doubles €30, with view €36; triples with view €42.) Three blocks uphill from the bus stop, in a stone building off of Pr. de Mercado, Muros also holds a popular clothing and food **mercado** (Tu and F 9am-2:30pm).

RÍAS BAJAS (RÍAS BAIXAS)

According to Galician lore, the Rías Baixas (Low Estuaries) were formed by God's tremendous handprint, with each river stretching like a finger through the land. The deep, navy blue bays, countless sandy coves, and calm, cool waters have lured vacationing Spaniards for decades. Only recently have foreign tourists discovered the area's charm. While not nearly as cool or rainy as their Galician neighbors— the Baixas are, after all, the sunniest part of the northern Spanish coast—the Baixas are blessed with an ocean wind that makes for a refreshing break from the scorching heat (and hordes of tourists) of central and southern Spain.

VIGO ☎986

Spanish poet José María Álvarez once wrote that "Vigo does not end, it goes on into the sea." Often called Spain's door to the Atlantic, Vigo (pop. 300,000) began as an unobtrusive fishing port; with the arrival of the Citröen manufacturing plant, it exploded into the biggest city in Galicia. Its compactness and increasing popu-

GALICIA

larity among European travelers have prompted extensive construction projects to expand pedestrian space near the city center and the marina. While Vigo isn't the place to escape the bustle, the nightlife and shopping are among the best in the region. It's also a good base for daytrips to nearby villages and beaches.

▐ TRANSPORTATION

Flights: Aeropuerto de Vigo, Av. del Aeropuerto (☎986 26 82 00), 15km from the city center. The local #R9 bus runs regularly from R. Urzáiz near R. Colón to the airport (€1). **Iberia** (☎986 26 82 28) and **Air Europa** (☎986 26 83 10) have offices at the airport. Daily flights to **Barcelona, Bilbao, Madrid,** and **Valencia.**

Trains: RENFE, Pr. de la Estación (☎902 24 02 02), downstairs from R. Urzáiz. Open daily 7am-11pm. To: **La Coruña** (2½hr., 10-14 per day 5:45am-8:55pm, €8.30-10.60); **Madrid** (8-9hr.; Su-F 1:50 and 10:20pm, Sa 9:55am and 10:20pm; €38.50); **Pontevedra** (30min., 11-14 per day 5:45am-9:38pm, €1.10-2.20); **Santiago de Compostela** (2hr., 11-14 per day 5:45am-9:38pm, €5.10-8.30).

Buses: Estación de Autobuses, Av. de Madrid (☎986 37 34 11), on the corner of R. Alcalde Gregorio Espino.

ATSA (☎986 61 02 55) to: **Bayona** (50min.; every 30min. M-F 7am-10:15pm, Sa 7:30am-10:30pm, Su 8am-11pm; €1.90); **La Guardia** (1½hr.; M-F every 30min. 7:30am-9:30pm, Sa 12 per day 8:30am-9:30pm, Su 6 per day 10am-9:30pm; €4.30); **Túy** (45min.; M-F every 30min. 7:30am-9:30pm, Sa 9 per day 8:30am-9:30pm, Su 4 per day 10am-9:30pm; €2.40). Buy tickets on board.

Auto Res (☎986 37 78 78) to **Madrid** (9hr., 6-8 per day 8:30am-11:30pm, €29.50-34.10).

Castromil (☎986 27 81 12) to: **La Coruña** (2½hr.; M-F 9 per day 6:15am-8:15pm, Sa 8 per day 7:30am-8:15pm, Su 7 per day 8:30am-8:30pm; €4.50); **Pontevedra** (45min.; M-F every 30min. 6:15am-9:30pm and 10:40pm, Sa every 30min. 7:30am-8:30pm and 10:40pm, Su every hr. 7:30am-9:30pm and 10:40pm; €2.20); **Santiago de Compostela** (1¼hr.; M-F 6:15am and every hr. 7:30am-7:30pm, Sa 11 per day 7:30am-7:30pm, Su 11 per day 8:30am-9:30pm; €6.90).

Ferries: Estación Ría, R. As Avenidas (☎986 22 52 72), past the nautical club on the harborside walkway. To: **Cangas** (20min.; M-F every 30min. 6:30am-10:30pm, Sa-Su every hr. 6:30am-10:30pm; €1.70); **Islas Cíes** (50min.; June-Sept. 4 per day 11am-7pm, Oct.-May 3 per day 11am–4pm; round-trip €15); **Moaña** (30min.; every hr. M-Sa 6:30am-10:30pm, Su 8:30am-10:30pm; €1.60).

Taxis: Radio Taxi, at Porta do Sol (☎986 47 00 00). About €0.40 per km.

Car Rental: National, R. Urzáiz, 84 (☎986 41 80 76). 23+, must have had license at least 2 yr. Open M-F 9am-1:30pm and 4:30-7pm, Sa 9am-1pm. 3-day rental from €96, 1 wk. from €180.

▦▐ ORIENTATION AND PRACTICAL INFORMATION

Gran Vía is Vigo's main thoroughfare, stretching south to north from Pr. de América through Pr. de España and ending at **Rúa Urzáiz.** A left turn onto R. Urzáiz leads to Pta. do Sol and into the **casco antiguo;** most of the city's action is here in the old city and along the waterfront. As you exit the train station onto R. Urzáiz (upstairs from the main entrance), go right two blocks to reach Gran Vía. Keep walking on R. Urzáiz for 10min. to reach the waterfront. The city center is a 25min. trek from the bus station. Exit right uphill along busy Av. de Madrid. Eventually, a right on Gran Vía at Pr. de España leads to the intersection with R. Urzáiz. It's easier to take the #R4, 7, 12a, or 12b bus from Av. de Madrid in front of the bus station to Gran Vía, R. Urzáiz, or R. Colón (€0.90).

Tourist Office: R. Cánovas de Castillo, 22 (☎986 43 05 77). From the train station, turn right onto R. Urzáiz and follow it to R. Colón; veer right. When R. Colón reaches the water, turn left onto R. de Montero Ríos. The office is on the left as the street curves left. English-speaking staff provides information about the city and the region of Galicia. Open June-Sept. M-F 9:30am-2pm and 4-7:30pm, Sa-Su 10am-2pm and 5-6:30pm; Oct.-May M-F 9:30am-2pm and 4:30-6:30pm, Sa 10am-noon. The **Vigo branch** is just uphill and to the right. (☎986 22 47 57; www.turismodevigo.org. Open June-Sept. daily 10am-2pm and 4:30-8:30pm; Oct-May reduced hours).

Currency Exchange: Banco Santander Central Hispano, R. Urzáiz, 20 (☎902 24 24 24). Open Apr.-Sept. M-F 8:30am-2:30pm; Oct.-Mar. M-F 8:30am-2:30pm, Sa 8:30am-1pm. 24hr. **ATM** outside.

Luggage Storage: At the **train station** (€3). Open daily 7am-11pm. At the **bus station** (€2.50). Open M-F 9:30am-1:30pm and 3-7pm, Sa 9am-2pm.

English-Language Bookstore: Casa del Libro, C. Velázquez Moreno, 27 (☎986 44 16 79), off of C. Príncipe. Travel guides and novels. Open M-Sa 9:30am-9:30pm.

Police: Pr. do Rei (☎986 43 22 11).

Pharmacy: C. Ronda don Bosco, 3 (☎986 43 84 08), on the corner of R. Venezuela. Open daily 10am-1:30pm and 4:30-8pm.

Medical Assistance: Hospital Xeral, R. Pizarro, 22 (☎986 81 60 00). **Ambulance:** ☎061 or 986 41 62 26.

Internet Access: CiberStation, Pta. do Sol (☎986 22 36 35), across the street from the end of C. del Príncipe. €1.80 per hr. Open daily June-Aug. 10am-12:30am; Sept.-May 10am-1am. Also available at **Imaxin@,** R. Ecuador, 16 (☎986 42 11 87). €1.60 per hr. Open M-Th 10am-2pm and 4-10pm, F-Sa 10am-2pm and 4pm-2am, Su 4-10pm.

Post Office: Av. de García Borbón, 50-52 (☎986 43 81 44), downhill from the train station. **Lista de Correos** and **fax.** Open M-F 8:30am-8:30pm, Sa 9:30am-2pm. **Postal Code:** 36201.

▌ ACCOMMODATIONS

Vigo's inexpensive rooms make the city a logical base for exploring surrounding areas. Most accommodations are clustered around the train station on R. Alfonso XIII (to the right upon exiting the train station) and its side streets.

Hostal Ría de Vigo, R. Cervantes, 14 (☎986 43 72 40), a left off R. Alfonso XIII 4 blocks from the station. Cheerful rooms with private bath, TV, and balconies overlooking busy R. Cervantes. Check-out 11am. Singles €15-18; doubles €20-25. ❷

Hostal Atlántico, Av. García Borbón, 35 (☎986 22 05 30). From the train station, follow R. Alfonso XIII downhill to Av. García Borbón. In a central location near the *casco antiguo,* Hostal Atlántico offers bright and spacious rooms with TV, bath, A/C, and phone. Aug. singles €36; doubles €48; triples €60. June-July and Sept. €30/€48/€60. Oct.-May €27/€42/€54. AmEx/MC/V. ❹

Hospedaje La Estrella, C. Martín Codax, 5 (☎986 22 50 35), a left off R. Alfonso XIII, 3 blocks down from the station. Unadorned but large rooms complete with TVs and clean baths. Singles €15, with bath €22; doubles €20/€25. ❷

Hostal La Colegiata, Pl. de la Iglesia, 3 (☎986 22 09 52). Simple, comfortable rooms with private baths only 2 blocks uphill from the waterfront. June-Sept. singles €15; doubles €30; triples €33. Closed in winter. ❷

Hotel Celta, C. México, 22 (☎986 41 46 99; fax 48 06 56). From the train station, walk up the stairs to R. Urzáiz and make a right; the 1st street on your left is C. México. Private baths, phones, TVs, and friendly service. June-Sept. singles €41; doubles €53. Oct.-May €25/€42. AmEx/MC/V. ❹

◘ FOOD

Gran Vía and C. Venezuela, four streets uphill from R. Urzáiz off Gran Vía, are brimming with bright cafeterias and *terrazas*. Many seafood restaurants lie around the As Avenidas boardwalk by the water, near the touristy *casco viejo*. For 24hr. cheap hot food or dessert visit **Ecos Cafetería ❶**, R. Urzáiz, 35. For groceries, hit **Supermercado Froiz**, R. do Uruguai, 14. (Open M-Sa 9am-2pm and 5-9pm.)

Tapas Areal, C. México, 36 (☎986 41 86 43). A typical Spanish *taparía* specializing in seafood. Delicious food and a broad selection of wines in a traditional, dark-paneled setting. Entrees €3.10-13; tapas from €2.80. Open M-Sa 1pm-12:30am. MC/V. ❷

Restaurante Curcuma Vegetariano, C. Brasil, 4 (☎986 41 11 27). Serves a killer gazpacho (€2.50) and immense portions of fresh dishes, from Mediterranean classics to soy burgers. Appetizers €1.50-3.50, entrees €5-6.50. Open M-Th 1-4pm and 8pm-midnight, F-Sa until 12:30am. MC/V. ❶

Cafetería El Coral, on the corner of C. Ecuador and C. Cuba (☎986 41 07 19). From R. Urzáiz, take a left onto Gran Vía and a left again onto C. Ecuador. Whether you want an early breakfast or an inexpensive dinner, El Coral is the place for *cocina gallega*. Entrees €4.50-7, 3-course *menú* €6. Open daily 6:30am-midnight. ❶

Restaurante El Gallinero, R. Concepción Arenal, 1 (☎986 22 82 83). This busy, cheerful spot near the marina draws downtown lunch crowds to its chicken-decorated interior, naturally specializing in poultry and egg dishes. Entrees €5-9. Open M 1-4pm, Tu-Sa 1-4pm and 9pm-midnight. ❷

El Capitán, C. Triunfo, 5 (☎986 22 09 40), off Pr. de la Princesa. In a simple dining area, choose from popular fish specialties (€9-30), including *lubina a la sal* (sea bass in salt) and *besugo* (sea bream). Many tapas, beef dishes (€8.50-12), and a fine wine selection. Open daily 11:30am-5:30pm and 7:30pm-late. MC/V. ❸

◙ NIGHTLIFE

There isn't much to see or do in Vigo besides party. Starting in the late afternoon, students pack the *casco antiguo*, where cafes, bars, and discos abound. The area around **Rúa Areal** and **Rúa Concepción Arenal** is jam-packed with discos, nightclubs, and bars playing the latest Spanish hits for trendy crowds. Near the train station—R. Cervantes, R. Lepanto, and R. Churruca, in particular—are dark, smoky bars and clubs drawing a young scene. For the latest hotspots, check the posters hanging around town advertising discos and techno music.

Black Ball, R. Churruca, 8. The perfect bar for anyone who longs for the feathered hair and leisure suits of the 70s. With an incredible collection of vintage kitsch and groovin' music from the likes of Jimi, James, and Janis, Black Ball offers a relaxed atmosphere and cheap mixed drinks (€2.50-4.50) to start the night. Open daily 11pm-4:30am.

20th Century Rock American Classic Bar, R. Areal, 22 (☎637 50 71 54). With a full-size Cadillac, Harley Davidson motorcycle, and the Statue of Liberty adorning its halls, your beer (€3) or mixed drink (€5) is only an excuse to stare at the Americana collection with the rest of the jam-packed crowd. Open Su-Th 7pm-2am, F-Sa 7pm-3:30am.

Budha Bar, R. Areal, 42 (☎670 84 16 74). Sip a drink on a leopard-skin sofa or get down on the mirror-lined dance floor with the energetic crowd. Beer €3, mixed drinks €5. Open M-Sa 12:30am-5:30am.

La Bola de Cristal, R. Churruca, 12. Like its neighbor Black Ball, La Bola de Cristal specializes in the 70s. Come for the retro decor; stay for the funk and disco. A mixed-age crowd dances to the beats of The Jackson 5 and Gloria Gaynor. Beer €3, mixed drinks €4.50. Cover F-Sa €3. Open Su-Th 11:45pm-4:30am, F-Sa until 5:30am.

Versus, R. Areal, 18. Break out your most stylish ensemble for this upscale club. The numerous video screens and dim lighting create a decadent techno-minimalist ambience, and the mix of Top 40 to classic rock gets the crowds moving. Open July-Aug. M-Sa midnight-6am; Sept.-June Th-Sa midnight-6am.

Posada de las Almas, Pr. de Compostela, 19. A luscious mix of medieval castle and theater, this club has red velvet curtains, crystal chandeliers, and predictable pop tunes, attracting an older chic crowd. Drinks €6. Open Su-W 6pm-3am, Th-Sa 6pm-4:30am.

El 7-4, R. Areal, 74 (☎986 12 89 59). An energetic club where a mixed gay-straight crowd dances to funk and groove. Beer €3, mixed drinks €5. Open M-Sa midnight-5am.

FESTIVALS

Watch for the magical **Fiesta de San Xuan** on June 23, when neighborhoods light huge cauldrons of *aguardiente* (firewater) to make an infusion called *la queimada*, which consists of *aguardiente*, coffee, lemon, and sugar; revelers pass around the sweet mixture while dancing among bonfires on the beach. You can catch a similar display, as well as concerts and processions, during the **Fiestas del Cristo de la Victoria** at the end of July.

DAYTRIPS FROM VIGO

▨ ISLAS CÍES (ILLAS CÍES)

4 ferries per day (sometimes more in nice weather) make the 14km trip between Estación Marítima in Vigo and the islands. Though fairly expensive, it's worth it. (40min.; June-Sept. daily, Oct.-May Sa-Su only; departs 11am, 1, 5, 7pm; returns noon, 2, 6, 8pm; round-trip €15, under 12 free.) Ferries fill quickly, so buy tickets in advance.

The Romans called them the "Islands of the Gods," and one can hardly doubt that the deities happily left Olympus to spend their weekends in the Illas Cíes. Guarding the mouth of the Ría de Vigo, two connected islands—**Illa de Monte Agudo** or **del Norte** and **Illa do Medio** or **del Faro**—offer irresistible beaches and cliffside hiking trails for travelers. The islands were declared a natural park in 1980; only 2200 people are allowed in per day, ensuring wide stretches of uncrowded beach. **Playa de Figueiras** and **Playa de Rodas** gleam with fine white sand and sheltered waters. For smaller, wavier, and more secluded spots, head right on the trail from the juncture near the dock, beyond Playa de Figueiras, which leads to a plethora of coves and rocky lookouts. A 4km hike to the left of the dock on the main "road" leads to a bird observatory and two lighthouses with breathtaking views. On the same trail is a campsite, a restaurant, and a supermarket that sells bottles of water, which will come in handy once you get to the **Faro de Cíes,** the big lighthouse on the southern tip of the island. Watch out for territorial seagulls that dive-bomb hikers walking too close to the birds' spotted chicks.

If you plan to spend the night, you can **camp ❶** on the island. Facilities include a small market, bar, baths, and hot showers. (Reservations ☎986 43 83 58; fax 44 72 04. Reception 8:30am-1pm and 2:30-7pm. Open June-Sept. and *Semana Santa.* Camping €5.90 per person, €4.50 per child 3-12, €5.90 per small tent, €7.50 per large tent. IVA not included.) Before leaving Vigo, be sure to make reservations and get a "Tarjeta de Acampado" in the **Camping Office** at the Estación Marítima.

CANGAS

Ferries run from Estación Ría (☎986 22 52 72) in Vigo to Cangas (20min.; M-F every 30min. 6:30am-10:30pm, Sa-Su every hr. 6:30am-10:30pm; round-trip €3.40). From Cangas, an equal number return (M-F every 30min. 6am-10pm, Sa-Su every hr. 6am-10pm).

THE BIG SPLURGE

GET PAMPERED IN THE PARADOR

If the idea of crossing back and forth between Spain and Portugal at your whim sounds appealing, you might want to spend a few days in Túy. If that idea isn't quite as enticing as lying in a four-poster bed and looking out your window at Valença do Minho's imposing fortress and the smooth hillsides on the Portuguese horizon, you have yet another reason to stay. And to enjoy it all in luxury, there's no better option than the *Parador Nacional de San Telmo*.

Built in 1968 in the style of a *casa típica gallega*, this newly renovated parador will indulge your desire for opulence. The hotel has two kinds of rooms: the elegantly rustic ones, with dark wood paneling and plush maroon furniture, and the contemporary ones with private terraces leading to the garden. But that's are just the beginning; once you drop your bags, grab your swimsuit, a tennis racket, and head outside. If your appetite is a priority, the parador's acclaimed restaurant boasts Galician specialties like *arroz con bogavante* (€38 for two people) and an array of fresh seafood. It may dent your budget, but a night or two in Túy will recharge you for the rest of your trip.

The *Parador* (☎ 986 60 03 00; fax 60 21 63) is located on Av. de Portugal. Singles €77.70-90.70; doubles €113.30-97.10. IVA not included. AmEx/MC/V.

Just across the bay from Vigo, tiny Cangas's main draw is its placid, nearly deserted beach, **Praia de Rodeira.** With your back to the ferry terminal, turn right onto Po. Marítimo, the pedestrian waterside walkway, which brings you to the beach (10min.). The cobalt waters here are virtually waveless, perfect for actual swimming. While there are no snack bars near the beach, restaurants lie near the ferry station. The most popular is undoubtedly **Restaurante-Bar Celta ❷,** R. Alfredo Saralegui, 28, which serves endless seafood tapas to the hungry hordes gathered at long tables along the street. With your back to the ferry terminal, cross the street and head up the stairs to your left; the restaurant is at the top. (Tapas €1-6. Fish entrees €5-12. Open daily 10am-1am, serves meals 1-4pm and 8:30pm-1am.) On Fridays, Cangas attracts crowds from surrounding towns for its extravagant **market,** selling clothes and fresh food in the harborside gardens immediately to the left of the ferry terminal (9am-2pm).

LA GUARDIA (A GUARDA)

Buses return to Vigo (1½hr.; M-F every 30min. 5:45am-8pm, Sa 12 per day 7am-8pm, Su 6 per day 8:30am-8pm; €4.30) from the bus stop at the corner of C. Domínguez Fontela and C. Concepción Arenal. Ticket office open daily 9am-9pm.

Between the mouth of the Río Miño and the Atlantic Ocean, A Guarda (pop. 10,000) thrives on an active fishing industry and the 500,000 tourists who annually make their way up its mountain. The town itself is a sleepy, dust-filled maze overlooking a bay; most visitors skip it and head to the majestic **Monte Santa Tecla.** From the bus stop, turn right onto C. Domínguez Fontela and again onto C. José Antonio. From C. José Antonio, bear right uphill onto C. Rosalía de Castro, which continues to the top (6km). Alternatively, 5min. up the road, take the steps off to the left that mark the start of a shorter, steeper pedestrian pathway through the woods (3km). Three-quarters of the way up the mountain is the highlight of the climb: the ruins of a **Celtic castle.** The interlocking circles of the foundations of this ancient fortress village overlook a blurry blue horizon and the twisting coastline below. Near the peak is a **chapel** dedicated to Santa Tecla, the patron saint of headaches and heart disease. Cured worshippers gave the wax body parts inside (hearts, heads, and feet) as gifts.

TÚY (TUI)

An ATSA bus (☎ 986 61 02 55) from Vigo stops on C. Calvo Sotelo at Hostal Generosa and returns from the other side of the street (45min.; M-F every 30min. 6:30am-8:45pm, Sa 9 per day 7:45am-8:45pm, Su 4 per day 9:15am-8:45pm; €2.40).

While the medieval border town of Túy (pop. 16,000) offers the novel opportunity to walk into Portugal, it's more notable for its beautiful *casco antiguo* and its views of the Río Miño valley. The centerpiece of the old city is the **cathedral;** constructed in 1120, it was the first Gothic structure in Iberia. It now houses the relics of San Telmo, patron saint of sailors, and boasts an impressive organ hanging over the nave. One ticket gets you into both the cathedral and the **Museo Diocesano,** home to sarcophagi and regional religious art. (Museo Diocesano ☎986 60 31 07. Cathedral and museum open May-Sept. daily 10am-1:30pm and 4-8pm; Oct-Apr. closed Sa. €2.40.) A 1km metal walkway over the Río Miño, **El Puente Internacional** extends to Portugal's Valença do Minho (p. 787). To get to the **tourist office,** R. Colón, from the bus stop, continue in the direction of the bus on Po. de Calvo Stelo and turn right onto R. Augusto González Besada. The office is on the right, just after the intersection with Av. de Portugal. (☎986 60 17 89. Open July-Aug. M-F 10am-2pm and 5-7:30pm, Sa-Su 10am-2pm and 5-6:30pm; Sept.-June shortened hours.)

BAYONA (BAIONA)

ATSA buses run to Vigo (50min.; every 30min. M-F 6am-9:15pm, Sa 6:30am-9:30pm, Su 7am-10pm; €1.90).

Bayona (pop. 10,000) was the first Iberian town to receive word of the New World when Columbus returned to its port in March 1493. The town even boasts a reconstructed version of the famous globe-trotting ship, **La Caravela Pinta,** in the harbor and reenacts the landing every March. (Open M and W-Su 10am-8pm. €0.80.) While the ship is Bayona's main historic attraction, you can't visit without bringing your swimsuit. The entire town is surrounded by blustery Atlantic beaches, where brightly colored fishing boats bob offshore and only the bravest dare to swim in the icy blue waves. The golden sand, however, is perfect for lounging among the myriad other sun worshippers. The 2km pedestrian Po. Alfonso IX loops around the grounds along the shore. As you get off the bus, walk along Po. Alfonso IX to your right for 15-20min. to get to the enormous crescent-shaped stretch of sand at **Praia Ladeira.** To your left, the path will take you to the shell-filled **Praia Cruncheira** and loop around the fortress walls to the rocky and quieter **Praia de los Frailes.** The path continues along the water around the grounds of the 16th-century **Fortress of Monte Real,** now a cushy *parador nacional*, which stands just above the beaches. Although you have to pay a ridiculous €1 just to enter the gate, the fortress is a perfect place to explore if you get bored of the beach.

PONTEVEDRA   ☎986

According to legend, Pontevedra (pop. 80,000) was founded by the Greek archer Teucro as a place to convalesce after his Trojan War exploits. Today, it continues to provide a place to crash by offering reasonably priced beds for visitors flitting to and from various high-priced coastal towns. Although it makes a good base, Pontevedra on the whole is not the most interesting town, and the new city is a bit of an eyesore. The old city, however—filled with palm trees, flowering balconies, stately cathedrals, and squares lined with traditional arcaded *gallego* buildings—is pleasant and inviting, making for a surprisingly enjoyable stay.

▐ TRANSPORTATION

Trains: Av. Alféreces Provisionales (☎902 24 02 02), a 20min. walk southeast of the old city. Info open daily 7am-9:45pm. To: **La Coruña** (3hr.; M-Th 12 per day 6:16am-7:12pm, F 15 per day 6:16am-9:21pm, Sa-Su 13 per day 6:16am-9:21pm; €7.60-

9.50); **Madrid** (11hr.; Su-F 1 and 9:30pm, Sa 9:08am and 9:30pm; €39.50); **Santiago** (1½hr.; M-F 14-17 per day 6:16am-10:15pm, Sa 12 per day 6:16am-9:21pm, Su 13 per day 6:16am-10:15pm; €3.30-4.30); **Vigo** (20min.; M-Sa 14-17 per day 7:40am-10:56pm, Su 13 per day 8:55am-10:56pm; €2.20).

Buses: Av. Alféreces Provisionales (☎986 85 24 08). Info open daily 8am-10pm. To: **Cambados** (1hr.; M-F 10 per day 8:30am-8:35pm, Sa 4 per day 11:30am-8:35pm, Su 3 per day 12:15-8:35pm; €2.20); **La Coruña** (2½hr.; M-F 9 per day 6:45am-9pm, Sa 8 per day 8am-9pm, Su 7 per day 9am-9pm; €10.50); **El Grove/La Toja** (1hr., every 30min. 7:45am-10pm, €3.20); **Madrid** (8hr., 6 per day 9am-11pm, €27.90); **Santiago** (1hr.; M-Th 13 per day 6:45am-8pm, F 14 per day 6:45am-9pm, Sa 11 per day 8am-8pm, Su 11 per day 9am-10pm; €4.70); **Vigo** (1hr.; M-F every 20min.-1hr. 7am-10:50pm, Sa 15 per day 9:30am-9:50pm, Su 13 per day 10:50am-9:50pm; €3.50).

Taxis: Radio Taxi (☎986 85 12 85). 24hr. €3-4 from the stations to town.

Car Rental: Avis, R. da Peregrina, 49 (☎986 85 20 25). 23+, must have had license for at least 1 yr. From €90 per day for 350km. 23-25 add €10 per day for insurance. Discounts for longer rentals. Open M-F 9am-1:15pm and 4-7pm, Sa 9am-12:45pm.

✈🛈 ORIENTATION AND PRACTICAL INFORMATION

Six streets radiate out from **Praza da Peregrina,** the main plaza connecting the new and old cities. The main streets are R. Oliva, R. Michelena, R. Benito Corbal, and R. da Peregrina. **Praza de Galicia** is a 5min. walk from Pr. da Peregrina; from Pr. da Peregrina, head down R. da Peregrina and veer right at the first fork onto R. Andrés Muruais. The **train** and **bus stations,** located across from each other, are about 1km from Pr. da Peregrina. From the bus station entrance, turn left onto Av. Calvo Sotelo; from the train station, walk straight out onto Av. Calvo Sotelo after crossing the rotary. Continue on Av. Calvo Sotelo for 10-15min. as it changes to the one-way Av. de Vigo and then R. da Peregrina before leading to Pr. da Peregrina.

Tourist Office: R. General Mola, 3 (☎986 85 08 14). From Pr. da Peregrina, get on R. Michelena and take the 1st left onto R. General Mola. English spoken. Open July-Sept. M-F 9am-2pm and 4:30-7:30pm, Sa 9am-2pm and 4-7pm, Su 9am-2pm; Oct.-June M-F 10am-2pm and 4:30-6:30pm, Sa 10am-2:30pm. **Branch** in a hut on Pr. de España. Open June-Nov. M-Sa 10am-2pm and 5-9pm, Su 11am-2pm and 5-8pm.

Currency Exchange: Banco Santander Central Hispano, Pr. da Peregrina, 5 (☎986 85 42 16). Open M-F 8:30am-2pm, Sa 8:30am-1pm. 24hr. **ATM** outside.

Bookstore: Librería Michelena, R. Michelena, 22 (☎986 85 87 46). Selection of books in English. Open M-F 9:30am-1:30pm and 4:30-8pm, Sa 9:30am-1:30pm. MC/V.

Police: R. Joaquín Costa, 19 (☎091 or 986 85 38 00).

Pharmacy: R. Oliva, 30 (☎986 85 13 69). Open daily 9:30am-10pm.

Hospital: Hospital Provincial, R. de Joaquín Costa (☎061 or 986 85 21 15).

Internet Access: Ciber Las Ruinas, R. del Marqués de Riestra, 21, 2nd fl. (☎986 86 63 25), just off Pr. de España. €1.60 per hr. Open M-Sa 10:30am-1:30am, Su 5pm-1:30am; open until 2am if crowded.

Post Office: R. Oliva, 21 (☎986 87 16 77). **Lista de Correos, fax,** and Western Union services available. Open M-F 8:30am-8:30pm, Sa 9:30am-2pm. **Postal Code:** 36001.

🛏 ACCOMMODATIONS

Hotels and hostels are not particularly abundant in Pontevedra, and hostels with private baths are especially hard to come by. Reservations are necessary in August, when Spaniards head to coastal towns and cities.

Casa Maruja, Av. de Santa María, 12 (☎986 85 49 01). From Pr. da Peregrina, walk up R. Michelena through Pr. de España and turn right onto R. Mestre Mateo. Most of the small, homey rooms in this family-run *pensión* have pleasant views with big windows. All have private bath and TV. July-Aug. singles €18-25; doubles €37; triples €40. Sept.-June €12-16/€25-27/€35. MC/V. ❷

Hotel México, R. de Andrés Muruais, 10 (☎986 85 90 06; fax 84 59 39). Follow the directions from the stations (p. 618), but take a sharp left onto R. de Andrés Muruais before you reach Pr. da Peregrina. Very simple, carpeted rooms with plenty of light, laundry, TV, elevator, and a cafeteria. Singles €27; doubles €40. AmEx/MC/V. ❸

Casa del Barón-Parador, R. Barón, 19 (☎986 85 58 00; fax 85 21 95), in the *casco antiguo*. Occupying a 16th-century palace, the hotel has a beautiful terrace, reading room, bar, and restaurant. Refreshingly huge rooms have cable TV, A/C, minibar, safe, and phone. Access to windsurfing, horseback riding, and rafting. Reserve in advance. Rooms €97.10-113.30. Inquire about discounts for ages 20-30. AmEx/MC/V. ❺

Hospedaje Penelas, R. Alta, 17 (☎986 85 57 05). Wonderful location close to bars and clubs in the *casco antiguo*. Spacious, well-furnished rooms with common baths. Singles €10-18; doubles €15-30, depending on length of stay. ❶

Casa Alicia, Av. de Santa María, 5, 1st fl. (☎986 85 70 79). From Pr. da Peregrina, walk up R. Michelena through Pr. de España and turn right onto R. Mestre Mateo. Av. de Santa María will be on the right. Small rooms amidst a collection of family photos. Immaculate hall bathrooms. Singles €20-25; doubles €25-30; quads €45. ❷

FOOD

Pontevedra prides itself on seafood. In the evenings, locals crowd tiny bars in the streets around Pr. da Peregrina. C. Figueroa, Pr. da Leña, and C. San Sebastián harbor some of the most popular *marisquerías* and tapas bars. For groceries, try **Supermercado Froiz,** Av. de Vigo, 31. (Open daily 9:30am-10pm.)

Bodegón Micota, R. da Peregrina, 4 (☎986 85 59 17). This basement *bodega* serves Spanish takes on global classics like fajitas (€8-9), *kebaps* (€9.50-15), and fondue (€13-15.50). *Menú del día* €6.70. Open daily noon-4:30pm and 8pm-1am. MC/V. ❷

La Algueria Mudéjar, C. Churruchaos, 2 (☎986 85 12 58). On the other side of the Ayuntamiento from Pr. de España. Enjoy fresh *revueltos* (scrambled eggs; €4.50-13), house specialties, and an extensive wine selection in a warm, tavern-like atmosphere. Entrees €6.50-21. Open M-Sa noon-4pm and 7:30pm-late, Su evenings only. MC/V. ❸

Mesón La Peregrina, R. da Peregrina, 16 (☎986 86 27 50). This *restaurante típico* specializes in seafood and regional meat dishes. 3-course *menú*, entrees €8-14. Open daily 1-4pm and 8pm-midnight. MC/V. ❷

SIGHTS

Pontevedra's primary sight is the extensive and impressive ▨**Museo Provincial,** R. Pasantería, 10. From Pr. da Peregrina, walk up Po. de Antonio Odriozola, which runs between the gardens and Pr. da Ferrería; this eventually curves into R. Pasantería and leads to the museum off Pr. da Leña. Occupying four buildings in the *casco antiguo*, its exhibits include religious sculpture in a crypt-like basement, models of a traditional Galician kitchen and ship interior, and contemporary art. (☎986 85 14 55. Open June-Sept. Tu-Sa 10am-2:15pm and 5-8:45pm, Su 11am-2pm; Oct.-May Tu-Sa 10am-1:30pm and 4:30-8pm, Su 11am-2pm. €1.20, EU members and students free.) In Pr. de España are the 13th-century Gothic **ruinas de Santo Domingo.** With moss-encrusted sepulchres and the sun filtering through cracks in what remains of the structure, the ruins are an eerie glimpse into the past in the midst of the new city. (Open June-Sept. Tu-F 10am-2pm. Free.) The **Basílica de Santa María a Maior** features a golden Plateresque door constructed in the 16th century, which depicts several versions of Mary; at night, it's illuminated by flood-lights. From Pr. de España take Av. de Santa María downhill to the left of the Ayuntamiento. (☎986 86 61 85. Open daily 10am-1pm and 5-9pm.)

🎵 🌿 ENTERTAINMENT AND FESTIVALS

Sunny days bring a crowd to the white-sand **beaches** in the coves of nearby Marín. Monbus buses make the journey from the outer corner of Pr. de Galicia on Av. Augusto García Sánchez (30min., every 15min., €0.90). From the bus stop in Marín, facing the water, head left on C. Angusto Miranda around the military school and up the hill. To reach **Playa Porticelo**, turn right on C. Tiro Naval Janer, continue for 15min., and bear right when the road splits. Another 10min. on the same path brings you to the larger **Playa Mogor.** The festival of **Santiaguiño del Burgo** (July 25) is marked by religious processions throughout Pontevedra, and **La Pereg-rina** (the 2nd week of August, peaking on Sunday) brings films, concerts, loads of honey, and bullfights to the city.

At night, you'll find bar after pub after *tapar ía* on the triangle of streets made by R. Princesa, R. Paio Gómez Charino, and R. Tetuán. A popular place among residents of all ages is **Café Teatro,** R. Michelena, 11, a karaoke bar complete with stage and comfy-couch audience seating. (Open daily 10pm-6am.)

▶ DAYTRIPS FROM PONTEVEDRA

The following towns are perfect daytrips from Pontevedra, as buses run frequently and drop off passengers in the heart of town. The towns can also be reached easily from Santiago de Compostela.

🗺 CAMBADOS

26km from Pontevedra. Plus Ultra buses run from Pontevedra to the bus station in Cambados near Pr. Concello (1hr.; M-F 10 per day 8:30am-8:35pm, Sa 4 per day 9:30am-8:35pm, Su 3 per day 12:15-8:35pm; €2.20). Check return schedule at the bus station bar.

Offering a precious glimpse of small-town life and a glass of renowned *albariño* wine accompanying a platter of fresh shellfish, harborside Cambados (pop. 15,000) makes for a refreshing daytrip from Pontevedra. The lack of a beach has left Cambados out of the tourist loop, but the resulting isolation adds to the town's charm, as do its enchanting sights.

Conveniently, all of these can be visited in a simple loop-route. Follow your nose to the **Palacio de Fefiñanes,** an attractive 16th-century palace-turned-*bodega* that brims with giant, sweet-smelling barrels of *albariño*. You can also request to visit the quiet *viñedo* and small forest hidden behind the walls across the street; a stroll among the grapevines and plum trees will make you forget that you're still in the town center. From the tourist office, walk away from the bus station along the tree-covered Po. da Calzada. At the walkway's end, walk up the street on the right, R. Príncipe, lined with stores selling *albariño* at bargain prices. At the end, turn left onto R. Real, which leads into Pr. de Fefiñanes, crowned by the palace. (Open for visits Apr.-Oct. 10am-2pm and 4-8:30pm.) The 15th-century *bodega* and hotel **Pazo A Capitana** (see **A Haven for Wine Tasters,** p. 621) is a short walk from the pal-ace. Its hanging vines, patio fountains, and wine cellars merit at least a few min-utes, if not a couple of nights. From Pr. de Fefiñanes, return down R. Real and continue until its end. Turn left onto Av. de Vilariño, right onto R. Barcelona, and left onto R. Sabugueiro at the street's end. (☎986 54 32 10. Open for visits daily 11am-1pm and 4-8pm.) On a quiet hill 10min. away, solemnly watching over the town cemetery, lie the beautiful ruins of the **Iglesia Santa Mariña.** From Pazo A Capitana, return down R. Sabugueiro. At the four-way intersection turn left on Av. da Pastora and continue to the end. The church is up on the left. Walk up the wide, flat stairs just behind it to a *mirador* with a view of the *ría*, including El Grove and La Toja. Just below the church is the new **Museo Etnográfico a do Viño,** Galicia's first wine museum, which takes its visitors through the history and process of wine-making. (☎986 52 61 19. Open Tu-Su 10am-2pm and 4:30-7:30pm. €3, ages 10-17 and seniors €1.50.) For a second privileged view of the *ría*, walk straight down Po. os Olmos (on the right facing the museum gate), cross the main street, and continue walking through the oldest, most tangled and worn-in section of town until you hit the water and see the **Torre de San Sadorniño.** The remains of this 12th-century fortification stand on a seemingly dissolving island connected to the mainland by a tiny bridge. The first weekend in August brings in famous poets and politicians for the town's well-known **wine festival.** The culinary specialities, including shellfish and cheese, are just an excuse to keep sampling the *albariño*, whose vines peek out from backyard fences and porch rooftops throughout Cambados.

Visitors may find it helpful to start at the **tourist office.** With your back to the bus station and the water, walk left. The office, a small cabin-like building, will be on the left. If you have a car inquire here about *La Ruta del Vino*, through nearby vineyards. (☎986 52 07 86. Open July-Sept. M-F 10am-2pm and 4:30-8pm, Sa-Su from 10:30am; Oct.-June M-F 10am-2pm and 4:30-7:30pm, Sa-Su from 10:30am.)

EL GROVE (O GROVE) AND LA TOJA (A TOXA)

Monbus (☎902 15 87 78) runs buses from Pontevedra to O Grove (1½hr.; June-Sept. 20-22 per day 7:45am-10pm, fewer in winter; €3.30); an equal number return (20-22 per day 6:30am–8pm). Buses also run from Santiago. Buses run from O Grove to Cambados (30min.; M-F 7 per day 7:30am-6pm, Sa-Su 5 per day 8:45am-6pm; €0.90). Schedules are posted in the O Grove bus station.

Every July and August, affluent Europeans come in Land Rovers and BMWs to the fishing town of O Grove (pop. 14,000) and its swanky island partner, A Toxa. Proudly calling itself "Paraiso de Marisco," O Grove runs along a tranquil strait west of Pontevedra and is lined with mussel farms, colorful boats, and clam-diggers. Even though there's no beach in town and few on-the-water activities, the waterfront is the main attraction; from here, tourists gawk at fishermen hauling in their catches and inevitably end up

THE BIG SPLURGE

A HAVEN FOR WINE TASTERS

If you've fallen in love with Cambados, or if you're just feeling weary and wobbly after a day of *bodega*-hopping, you can do no better than to indulge in a night or two at **Pazo A Capitana,** R. Sabugueiro, 46. Besides boasting its own vineyard laden with *albariño* grape vines and orange trees, as well as an endless selection of homemade wines and overwhelmingly pungent liqueurs, this 16th-century *bodega* also houses elegant rooms that just beg for a splurge. Individually designed with natural colors and dark wood paneling, they successfully create an aura of modest, rustic elegance perfect for a small Spanish wine town. All have huge windows that flood the furniture with sunlight, and several overlook the vineyard and private garden. The dining hall, built in the palace's original *cocina gallega,* includes a stone hearth as well as antique cutlery on its ledges. While it may be pricey, it's worthwhile—as long as you can take a break from the wine-tasting and sober up to enjoy its unassuming beauty in the middle of Cambados.

From the rotary next to the tourist office, walk up Av. de Vilariño and turn right on the narrow street 1 block past R. Barcelona. ☎986 52 05 13; www.pazoacapitana.com. Breakfast included. July to mid-Sept. singles €70; doubles €90. Mid-Sept. to June singles €60/€70. MC/V.

munching on enormous platters of fresh seafood in any of the local restaurants. Fridays also provide a chance to peruse clothing, local food, and crafts at the waterside market from 8am to 2pm. The **tourist office** has plenty of information on boat rides, free bike rentals, sea museums, beaches, the country club and casino at A Toxa, and the town's popular **seafood festival** during the first two weeks of October. With your back to the main entrance of the bus station, walk right and follow the water. The tourist office is in a small cabin near ice cream stands. (☎986 73 14 15. Open June-Sept. M-F 10am-2:30pm and 4:30-8:30pm, Sa 10am-2pm and 4-8pm, Su 10am-2pm; Oct.-May closed Su.)

LA LANZADA

Monbuses (☎902 15 87 78) en route to O Grove stop at La Lanzada, returning to Pontevedra from across the street (1hr., June-Aug. every hr. 7:45am-10pm, €3).

Ten kilometers toward Pontevedra from O Grove, La Lanzada—arguably the best beach in Galicia—seduces bathers with its fine white sands and irresistible waves. This mile-long beach is protected by dunes and rocky promontories jutting into sea. Unlike many other beaches in the region, it also provides plenty of beach chairs and umbrellas so visitors won't end up fried after an afternoon of playing in the sand. While most bathers come to relax and lounge beside the Atlantic, quite a few come seeking the elusive "Ninth Wave"—according to pagan legend, women who swim in exactly nine waves at moonlight will be forever cured of infertility.

RÍAS ALTAS

Thick fogs and misty mornings have kept the Rías Altas secret from most visitors. With the exception of La Coruña, the area's busy capital, the Rías Altas seem to have been nearly forgotten, and that's the very reason to visit: residents of the tiniest of coastal towns welcome travelers with open arms, and visitors who actually make it here have miles of green estuaries and secluded beaches all to themselves.

LA CORUÑA (A CORUÑA)   ☎981

Unlike most of its Galician neighbors, A Coruña (pop. 260,000) is a big city, complete with high-rises, expressways, and urban sprawl. Somehow, though, A Coruña manages to preserve the feel of an old-time fishing port. The center is a maze of tangled, narrow alleys, teeming with raucous bars and popular *marisquerías* (seafood restaurants). The miles of harborside walks echo with Galician legend and lore: Greek hero Hercules supposedly built the lighthouse, and the city's nickname, the Crystal City, was earned for the blinding sunset reflected on its rows of tightly packed windows. As any proud *coruñese* will tell you, Santiago might be the northwest's most popular city, but A Coruña is the *real* Galicia.

▐▛ TRANSPORTATION

Flights: Aeropuerto de Alvedro (☎981 18 72 00), 9km south. Served by **Air Europa** (☎981 18 73 08), **ERA** (☎981 18 72 86), and **Iberia** (☎981 18 72 59). Daily flights to **Paris** via **Barcelona** and **London**.

Trains: Estación San Cristóbal, Pr. San Cristóbal (☎902 24 02 02). Info open daily 7am-10:30pm. To: **Barcelona** (15-16hr.; daily 6pm, Th-F and Su-M also 7:10am; €44-51.50); **Madrid** (8½-11hr.; M-F and Su 12:55 and 9:22pm, Sa 9am and 12:55pm; €40.50); **Santiago** (1hr.; M-F 14-17 per day 6:10am-10:30pm, Sa 12 per day 6:20am-8:20pm, Su 13 per day 6:20am-10:30pm; €3.30-4.30); **Vigo** (2hr.; M-F 13-16 per day 6:10am-8:20pm, Sa-Su 12 per day 6:20am-8:20pm; €8.30-10.60) via **Pontevedra.**

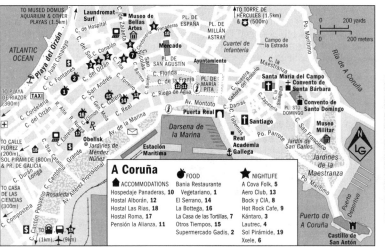

A Coruña

♦ **FOOD** ★ **NIGHTLIFE**
▲ **ACCOMMODATIONS**

▲ ACCOMMODATIONS	♦ FOOD	★ NIGHTLIFE
Hospedaje Panaderas, **10**	Bania Restaurante	A Cova Folk, **5**
Hostal Alborán, **12**	Vegetariano, **1**	Aero Club, **13**
Hostal Las Rias, **18**	El Serrano, **14**	Bock y CIA, **8**
Hostal Roma, **17**	La Bottega, **16**	Hot Rock Cafe, **9**
Pensión la Alianza, **11**	La Casa de las Tortillas, **7**	Kántaro, **3**
	Otros Tiempos, **15**	Lautrec, **4**
	Supermercado Gadis, **2**	Sol Pirámide, **19**
		Xxele, **6**

Buses: C. Caballeros (☎ 981 23 96 44).

ALSA/Enatcar (☎ 981 15 11 00) to: **Madrid** (8½hr.; M-Sa 6-7 per day 5am-10:30pm, Su 5 per day 11am-11:30pm; €35-49); **Oviedo** (4½-6¾hr., 3-4 per day 9:30am-7pm, €22-29); **San Sebastián** (14hr., 9:30am and 7pm, €46.80) via **Santander** (10hr., €29.70).

Castromil (☎ 981 24 91 92) to **Santiago** (50min.-1½hr.; M-F 6:35 and 6:50am and every hr. 8am-10pm, Sa every hr. 8am-3pm and 5-10pm, Su every 2hr. 9am-3pm and every hr. 5-10pm; €6) and **Vigo** (2-2½hr.; M-F 9 per day 8am-8pm, Sa 8 per day 8am-8pm, Su 6 per day 11am-8pm; €12.50) via **Pontevedra** (1½-2hr., €10.50).

IASA-Arriva (☎ 981 23 90 01) to: **Betanzos** (40min.; M-F every 30min. 6:30am-10:30pm, Sa 24 per day 6:30am-10:30pm, Su 22 per day 6:30am-11pm; €1.80); **Ferrol** (2hr.; M-F every hr. 7:30am-9:30pm, Sa 7 per day 10:30am-8:30pm, Su 8 per day 11:30am-9:30pm; €5.70); **Ribadeo** (4hr.; M-F 5 per day 8am-4pm, Sa 6 per day 8am-4pm, Su 3 per day 8am-2:30pm; €14.10); **Viveiro** (3½hr.; M-Sa 6 per day 6:30am-7:30pm, Su 4 per day 6:30am-7:30pm; €11.30) via **Betanzos.**

Public Transportation: Red **Compañía de Tranvías de La Coruña** buses (☎ 981 25 01 00) run frequently (7am-11:30pm; €0.85). Buy tickets on board.

Taxis: Radio Taxi (☎ 981 24 33 33) and **TeleTaxi** (☎ 981 28 77 77). Both 24hr. From the tourist office with the ocean to the right, walk along the sidewalk to the taxi stand. €5 from the train and bus stations to the *ciudad vieja.*

Car Rental: Autos Brea, Av. Fernández Latorre, 110 (☎ 981 23 86 45). 21+, must have had license for 1yr. From €60 per day with unlimited mileage. Open M-F 9am-1pm and 4-7pm, Sa 9am-2pm.

■✶ ORIENTATION AND PRACTICAL INFORMATION

A Coruña sits on a narrow peninsula between the Atlantic Ocean and the Ría de A Coruña. The new city stretches across the mainland; the peninsula encompasses the *ciudad vieja* (old city). Beaches are on the Atlantic side and the harbor is on the river. **Avenida de la Marina** runs along the harbor and leads past the obelisk and the tourist office to **Puerta Real,** the entry into **Plaza de María Pita** and the *ciudad vieja.* From the bus station, take bus #1 or 1a straight to the **tourist office** at the Puerta Real stop. To get from the train station to the *ciudad vieja*, take the city bus from the bus station; from the main entrance of the train station on Pr. San

Cristóbal, cross the plaza and walk right on R. de Outeiro. At the rotary, turn left onto R. Estaciones and follow the pedestrian paths over the highway. The bus station and stop for buses #1 and 1a are across the street from the base of the pedestrian stairs. Bus #14 connects the center with the museums and monuments along **Paseo Marítimo**.

Tourist Office: Regional Office, Av. de la Marina (☎/fax 981 22 18 22; www.turgalicia.es). English spoken. Info on regional travel and daytrips from A Coruña. Open M-F 10am-2pm and 4-7pm, Sa 11am-2pm and 5-7pm, Su 11am-2pm. **Turismo A Coruña** (☎981 18 43 44; www.turismocoruna.com), in a glass building in a corner of Pl. María Pita. Open M-Sa 10am-2pm and 4-8pm, Su 10am-2pm.

Currency Exchange: Banco Central Santander, C. Cantón Grande, 4 (☎981 18 88 00). Open M-F 8:30am-2pm, Sa 8:30am-1pm.

Laundromat: Surf, C. Hospital San Roque, 35 (☎987 20 44 20). Wash and dry up to 6kg €10. Open M-F 9:30am-1:30pm and 4:30-8pm.

Police: Municipal, C. Miguel Servet (☎981 18 42 25).

24hr. Pharmacy: C. Real, 92 (☎981 22 21 34).

Medical Services: Ambulatorio San José, C. Comandante Fontanes, 8 (☎981 22 60 74). **Ambulance** ☎061.

Internet Access: Cyber, C. Zalaeta, 13 (☎981 20 38 41). Speedy connections. €0.75 per 30min., €1.20 per hr. Open daily 10am-2am. **Estrella Park,** C. Estrella, 12. €0.50 per 20min. Open daily 11am-midnight.

Post Office: C. Alcalde Manuel Casas (☎981 22 51 75). **Lista de Correos** and **fax** service. Open M-F 8:30am-8:30pm, Sa 9:30am-2pm. **Postal Code:** 15001.

♪ ACCOMMODATIONS

Most accommodations are near the old city. Bed-hunters should head to C. Riego de Agua and R. Nueva. Reservations are necessary only during August's festival.

Hostal Roma, R. Nueva, 3 (☎981 22 80 75). Spotless, sunny rooms with TV and bath. Mingle with guests in the lounge, complete with TV, couches, and Internet on 5 computers. Breakfast available. Reception 7:30am-midnight. Aug. singles €36; doubles €50; triples €72. Sept.-July €24-30/€36-42/€54-64. MC/V. ❸

Pensión la Alianza, C. Riego de Agua, 8, 1st fl. (☎981 22 81 14). Small but comfortable rooms with character in the *ciudad vieja* and a hospitable owner. Be sure to request a room with a window. Singles €18; doubles €30. ❷

Hostal Las Rias, C. San Andrés, 141, 2nd fl. (☎/fax 981 22 68 79). With bath, TV, and phone, these comfortable rooms come at a bargain. July-Aug. singles €20; doubles €37. Sept.-June €15/€28. ❷

Hostal Alborán, C. Riego de Agua, 14 (☎981 22 65 79). Small rooms with bath and TV. 1st fl. common room with sofas and big screen TV. Aug. singles €26; doubles €46. Sept.-July €23-24/€33-37. AmEx/MC/V. ❷

Hospedaje Panaderas, C. Panaderas, 1st fl. (☎981 20 50 80). Austere but adequate rooms in an old building, only minutes from the beach and nightlife. Hall bath. Singles €12; doubles €17. ❶

♫ FOOD

The streets around C. Estrella, C. de la Franja, and C. la Galera teem with cheap *marisquerías* and other restaurants. The area around Av. Rubine off Playa de Riazor is fancier. Culinary delights include the usual Galician fare, from *cocido* (stew) and *empanadas* (pies) to hams beckoning from the ceilings of *jamonerías*. This is also one of the best places to sample *pulpo* (octopus). The **market** is in the oval building on Pr. San Agustín, near the old town. (Open M-Sa 8am-3pm.) For groceries, stop by **Supermercado Gadis,** C. del Orzán, 86. (☎981 21 62 63. Open daily 9am-9pm.)

La Casa de las Tortillas, C. del Orzán, 5 (☎981 22 67 18). In a warm, homey setting, La Casa offers salads (€3-8), sangria (€9), and dozens of creative varieties of *tortilla española* (€4.50-8). Go after 10pm if you want company. Open Su-M and W-Th 8pm-12:30am, F-Sa 8pm-2am. ❶

Otros Tiempos—Cervecería-Jamonería, C. la Galera, 54 (☎981 22 93 98). Founded in 1914, this restaurant has vintage furniture complemented by black-and-white movie stills and a lively clientele. Big, hearty *raciones* €3-11, sandwiches €2.60-4.50, *empanadas* €4-5. *Menú* €8.50. Wide selection of beer (€2.20-4). Open daily 11am-4pm and 7pm-12:30am. MC/V. ❷

La Bottega, C. Olmos, 25 (☎981 91 46 76). Decorated in a subaquatic theme, this relaxing restaurant serves delicious crepes (€4.80-6.80), exotic salads (€4.60-7), and typical Spanish *raciones* (€5.10-6.50). Open Su-Th 1:30-4:15pm and 8pm-12:15am, F-Sa until 12:45am. AmEx/MC/V. ❷

Bania Restaurante Vegetariano, C. Cordelería, 7 (☎981 22 13 01). Fresh, creative vegetarian cuisine, including a hearty *estofado de mar y tierra* (seaweed and vegetable stew; €6.10) served in a sunny environment. Salads €6-7, entrees €5-7.10. Open M-Sa 1:30-4pm and 9-11:30pm. ❶

El Serrano, C. la Galera, 21. The giant *tablas,* including various Galician hams, cheeses, and fish (€12.40-30), are perfect for groups. Generous *raciones* (€4.20-10.40), specializing in *calamares* (€8). Open daily noon-4pm and 8pm-midnight. MC/V. ❷

👁 SIGHTS

While A Coruña lacks many of the historic monuments of other towns, it has several phenomenal attractions along Po. Marítimo. To visit them all in one afternoon, start from Playa del Orzán and follow waterside Po. Marítimo to the major museums and Torre de Hércules. Trolleys also follow the *paseo* with stops at all the museums and the Torre. The route begins at the start of Po. Marítimo, near Puerta Real, and ends at Playa del Orzán. (Trolleys daily every 30min. noon-9pm; €1.)

TAKE THE *PIMIENTO* PLUNGE

They're a test of wits, a risky game of Russian Roulette not to be played by the faint of heart or the soft of tongue. If you like the spiciest Indian food or salsa that's so hot it has labels warning against making contact with the skin, this game's for you. Otherwise, there are plenty of tamer Galician specialities on the menu in Vigo's traditional restaurants.

Pimientos de Padrón, small green peppers grown in a town near Santiago, have become a distinctive regional favorite for their rich, full flavor, their satisfying crunch combined with a soft flesh—and, of course, for the gamble that each one poses to the innocent pepper connoisseur who hardly realizes that his next bite might be his last. The preparation is simple; the peppers are fried in olive oil for about 3 minutes, then sprinkled generously with salt and served either on their own as tapas or alongside meat dishes in some restaurants. You'd better have some fresh bread and a full glass of water nearby as you get started. The catch with these babies is that every so often a piping hot pepper comes along, and there's nothing to do once you've realized it but chew quickly and swallow. Nothing sets apart the fiery few in color, smell, or texture; it's only after the point of no return that you'll know. Most of the time, they're simply mouth-watering, but occasionally they'll be eye-watering as well.

LAS TRES CASAS CORUÑESAS

A €10 bono ticket allows same-day admission to all 3 museums.

■**AQUARIUM FINISTERRAE.** Also known as the **Casa de los Peces,** this aquarium is A Coruña's magnificent homage to the sea. Over 200 species of local marine life are displayed in vast tanks, while the downstairs room features exhibits on marine ecosystems the world over. Try to catch speedy fish with your bare hands, and learn about the largest marine creature ever to exist. Don't miss Nautilus, an enormous, eerie aquarium in the basement that recreates Captain Nemo's adventure. *(On Po. Marítimo at the bottom of the hill from the Torre de Hércules. Bus #14 from the Puerta Real. ☎981 18 98 42. Open July-Aug. daily 10am-9pm; Sept.-June M-F 10am-7pm, Sa-Su 10am-8pm. €8, children and seniors or with Carnet Joven €3.)*

■**MUSEO DOMUS.** The Domus, also called the **Casa del Hombre** (House of Man), is an anthropology, natural history, and science museum rolled into one, featuring interactive, high-tech exhibits on human cultures and anatomy. Watch "blood" spurt at 50km/hr. from a model heart; hear "Hello, I love you" in over 30 languages; and spend hours playing with microscopes, computers, and other gizmos. *(C. Santa Teresa, 1, on Po. Marítimo between the aquarium and Playa Orzán. ☎981 18 98 40. Open daily July-Aug. 11am-9pm; Sept.-June 10am-7pm. €2, children and seniors or with Carnet Joven €1. IMAX supplement €1.20; check at ticket booth for schedule.)*

CASA DE LAS CIENCIAS. Casa de las Ciencias is an interactive science museum for kids designed for hands-on learning about physics, geology, and the environment. The four-story building features a giant Foucault's pendulum and a planetarium. *(Parque Santa Margarita. ☎981 18 98 46; www.casaciencias.org. Open daily July-Aug. 11am-9pm; Sept.-June 10am-7pm. Casa €2, children and seniors €1. Planetarium €1; check show schedules.)*

OTHER SIGHTS

TORRE DE HÉRCULES. A Coruña's tourist magnet, the Torre de Hércules looms over rusted ships at the peninsula's end. The tower originally dates from the 2nd century BC, but was renovated in a Neoclassical style in 1790. Legend has it that ■**Hercules** erected the tower, the world's oldest working lighthouse, over the remains of his defeated enemy, Geryon. The long climb to the top is rewarded with stunning views of the city and bay. *(On Po. Marítimo, a 20min. walk from Puerta Real. From C. Millán Astray, turn left onto C. Orillamar, which turns into Av. de Navarra and brings you to the tower. Open July-Aug. Su-Th 10am-8:45pm, F-Sa 10am-11:45pm; Apr.-June and Sept. daily 10am-6:45pm; Oct.-Mar. daily 10am-5:45pm. €2, children and seniors €1.)*

MUSEO DE BELLAS ARTES. This museum displays classic Spanish, French, Italian, and Flemish art from the Renaissance to the 20th century in a renovated convent; don't miss the display of Goya's engravings. It also houses the work of *gallego* artists. *(☎981 22 37 23. Open Tu-F 10am-8pm, Sa 10am-2pm and 4:30-8pm, Su 10am-2pm. €2.40, with Carnet Joven €1.20, children and seniors free.)*

MUSEO HISTÓRICO ARQUEOLÓGICO CASTILLO DE SAN ANTÓN. A Coruña flaunts its archaeological treasures in this former fortress and prison, with displays from other Galician fortresses and artifacts from the Megalithic, Bronze, and Roman Ages. *(☎981 20 59 94. Open July-Aug. Tu-Sa 10am-7:30pm, Su 10am-2:30pm; Sept.-June Tu-Sa 10am-7pm, Su 10am-3pm. €2, children and seniors or with Carnet Joven €1.)*

🅒 BEACHES

A Coruña's best beaches are the long, narrow **Playa de Riazor** and **Playa del Orzán,** which flank Po. Marítimo on the Atlantic side of the peninsula and are separated from one another only by a small walkway. On weekends, the sand along these calm waters is packed with bodies, but crowds thin out on week-days. Small, secluded beaches, including **Playas del Matadero, de San Amaro,** and **das Lapas,** hide farther down Po. Marítimo near Torre de Hercules, although these tend to be rockier, wavier, and seaweedier.

NIGHTLIFE

In the early evening, *coruñeses* linger in Celtic pubs throughout the old city, bar-hopping around C. del Orzán, C. del Sol, and the mess of streets near C. de la Franja and C. de la Florida. **Xxele,** C. del Orzán, 11, is filled with Led Zeppelin post-ers, Boy George look-alikes, and exotic flavored *chupitos* including chocolate and *"perfecto amor."* (Beer €0.60, *chupitos* €1.20. Open Su-W 9pm-2:30am, Th-Sa 9pm-3am.) For a brighter, more mainstream scene, head to the packed tables in **Hot Rock Cafe,** C. Panaderas, 24. (Beer €1.70. Open M-Sa 9pm-2am.) Popular Celtic pubs playing folk and rock along C. del Orzán include **Bock y CIA,** C. del Orzán, 2 (beer €2.50, mixed drinks €3; open Th-Sa 11pm-4am) and **A Cova Folk,** C. del Orzán, 38 (open daily 11pm-3am).

When bars die down around 2am, **discos** pick up along the two beaches and on C. Juan Flórez. **Sol Pirámide,** C. Juan Flórez, 50, plays dance music loud enough to rouse the dead (☎981 27 61 57; open 3-6am), while **Aero Club,** in the basement of C. Torreiro, 11, promises a raging time with a young, energetic crowd and house music (beer €2.50, mixed drinks €4.50; open Th-Sa 11pm-4am). Bubbly locals pack the small, top-40-infused dance floor of **Kántaro,** C. del Sol, 21, and across the street **Lautrec** draws crowds with electronica. (Kántaro open Th-Sa midnight-5am. Lautrec open daily 1-5:30am.)

FESTIVALS

The city's main festival is **Las Fiestas de María Pita,** which lasts the entire month of August. Party-hardy *coruñeses* spend the month celebrating with various concerts, parades, and medieval fairs. To kick off the events, the city holds a mock naval battle in the harbor on July 31 to honor María Pita, the woman who single-handedly rallied a defense against the invading army of Sir Francis Drake in 1589 after the town's men had fled the port in fear. Although it is celebrated in many parts of Europe, A Coruña greets **La Noche de San Juan** (June 23) with particular fervor since it coincides with the opening of sardine season. Locals light *aguardiente* (firewater) bonfires before spending the night leaping over flames and gorging on sardines. Contrary to what you might assume, the rite is supposed to ensure fertility. If you drop an egg white in a glass of water on this night, it will supposedly assume a form symbolic of your future spouse's occupation.

THE NORTHERN COAST

The northern estuaries of Galicia are among the cleanest, loveliest, and emptiest in all of Spain. To explore the Rías Altas often means spending hours on quiet coastal roads in the misty rain; if you want to leave the beaten path, this is where to do it. Though public transportation is reliable, renting a car is more convenient.

VIVEIRO

Arriva buses from Viveiro connect to: A Coruña (4hr., 3-4 per day 6:15am-7:45pm, €11.70); El Ferrol (2¼hr., 3-4 per day, €6.60); Ribadeo (1½hr.; M-F 9:35am and 3:45pm, Sa 3:45pm; €4.80).

A beautiful old city poised between forest and sea, **Viveiro** (pop. 16,000) is known throughout Spain for its beaches, peaceful atmosphere, and July *fiestas*, especially **Las Rapas das Bestas,** which takes place the first Sunday of July in the nearby town of Candaoso. The second weekend of July, Galicia's free-spirited youth camp out on the beaches of Ortiguera, 36km from Viveiro, for the town's **Celtic Music Festival.** For 25 years, folk bands from every region of Spain as well as Ireland, Scotland, and even Sweden have played free concerts. During the festival, a special bus runs from A Coruña to Ortiguera Wednesday through Sunday. Although Viveiro is surprisingly pleasant, with a well-preserved web of streets in its *casco histórico*, at the edge of a large inlet, the main draw is **Playa Area** 5km away. Arriva buses, headed for Burela, drop off beachgoers 100m uphill from the sand (M-Sa 9 per day 9:50am-8pm, Su 11:45am and 8pm). Right in town, across the bridge from the tourist office, is the soft-sanded expanse of **Playa de Covas,** offering a more convenient opportunity to toast under the sun. Viveiro's **tourist office,** C. Benito Galcerán, has town maps and can offer info on adventure tourism. Exit through the bus station's front entrance; the office is a small wooden cabin on the left. (☎982 56 08 79. Open July-Aug. daily 11am-2pm and 5-8pm; Sept.-June closed Su.) If you decide to spend the night, **Fondo Nuevo Mundo ❷,** C. Teodoro de Quirós, one block uphill from Pr. Maior, has big wood-paneled rooms and clean common baths. (☎982 56 00 25. Singles €20; doubles €30.)

RIBADEO

Arriva buses run from Ribadeo to: A Coruña (2½-3½hr.; M-Sa 4 per day 7:15am -6:20pm, Su 2:40 and 6:20pm; €14.10); Santiago de Compostela (3¼hr., 6pm, €12.50); Viveiro (1½hr.; M-F 3 per day 9am-6pm, Sa 11:30am and 6pm; €4.80).

The official boundary between Galicia and Asturias, **Ribadeo** lays claim to one of the most beautiful beaches in Spain, ■**Praia As Catedrais,** 8km outside of town. Jagged cliffs rise sharply from the alcoves of soft sand, natural rock archways droop into the sea, and low tide reveals caverns, coves, and warm lagoons perfect for exploring and swimming. The first Sunday in August marks the rowdy **Xira de Santa Cruz,** during which locals trek to the top of Monte Santa Cruz, 3km from town, and spend the day dancing and feasting on traditional dishes. **Hostal Orol ❷,** C. Rinconada de San Francisco, 9, just off of Pl. de España, has sunny rooms with TVs. (☎982 12 87 42. Mid-July to mid-Sept. singles €20, with bath €24; doubles €33. Mid-Sept. to mid-July €15/€20/€24. AmEx/MC/V.) You can also camp at **Camping Playa de Reinate ❶,** 1km down the wooden walkway from Praia As Catedrais. (☎982 13 40 05. €3 per person and per car, €3-3.50 per tent. Electricity €2.50. 2-person bungalows with shower and electricity €45; 4-person bungalows €65.) **FEVE trains** run from Ribadeo to **Esteiro,** the stop closest to the beach (10min.; 4 per day 6:45am-6:17pm, return 4 per day 11am-9:40pm; €0.90). From the train stop, walk through the grass and onto the gravel path past the yellow house. Turn right onto the paved road, follow it over the train tracks, and follow the signs about 1km to the beach. The town itself has a quiet, almost ghostly air. The **tourist office,** Pl. de España, is in Parque de San Francisco. (☎982 12 86 89. Open M-Sa 10am-2pm and 4-7pm, Su 10am-2pm.)

VALDOVIÑO AND CEDEIRA

Rialsa buses (☎981 31 59 55) run from El Ferrol to Cedeira (40min.; M-F 9 per day 7:30am-10pm, Sa 6 per day 8:30am-10:30pm, Su 5 per day 11am-10:30pm; €2.60) via Valdoviño. In El Ferrol, connections can be made to and from A Coruña (1hr., every hr. 6:30am-9:30pm, €5.70).

Valdoviño, 61km northeast of A Coruña, is home to many gorgeous, isolated beaches and hosts the Pantín Classic **surfing competition** at its famous **Playa de Pantín** (Sept. 6-8). Valdoviño itself has a large stretch of sand with slightly calmer waters. The neighboring town of **Cedeira** prides itself on its festivals. On the last Sunday of July, the townspeople hop in their cars and drive up to Sierra de la Capelada to watch the annual horse-shearing festival. The mountain is not accessible by train or bus, so you'll have to hitch or walk along the side of the highway if you don't have a car. The **Festa do Percebe** honors the barnacle on the first weekend in August. In summer, you can pitch a tent at the well-equipped **Camping A Lagoa ❶,** just off of the beach. (☎981 48 71 22. Open June 15-Sept. 15. €2.60 per person and per car, €2.60-3.55 per tent. Electricity €2.60.)

GALICIA

LAS ISLAS CANARIAS

From the snowy peak of Mount Teide to the fiery volcanos of Timanfaya, the Islas Canarias have enchanted humanity since the beginning of time. Homer and Herodotus referred to them as gardens of astounding beauty, and the lost civilization of Atlantis was said to have left behind these seven islands when it sank into the ocean. The Spanish spoken in the Canaries bears stronger resemblance to the Spanish of Cuba or Puerto Rico than that of mainland Spain, while Canarian fare is marked by a heavy Mediterranean influence. Remnants of pre-Spanish Guanche culture—names like Tenerife, for example—stand as reminders of island culture before the 1402 Spanish conquest and the subsequent development of plantation economies. Since then, the Canaries have been known as the "Fortunate Isles" for their incomparable and diverse natural beauty, from volcanic deserts in the south to wind-swept dunes in the south to misty forests in the north. Many beautiful coastlines (mostly in the south of each island) are now marred by ugly tourist developments, which are spoiled, expensive, and bland: do whatever you can to avoid these areas. The Canaries reward anyone who steps off the beaten path, so rent a beat up old car, grab a map, and discover the isolated beaches, lush forests, rolling surf breaks, dormant volcanoes, and tiny mountain villages that grace these strange, seemingly inhospitable islands, and your trip will be unforgettable.

HIGHLIGHTS OF LAS ISLAS CANARIAS

REVEL in the volcanic beauty of **El Teide National Park** (p. 647).

ESCAPE from the hordes of other travelers on distant **La Gomera** (p. 657).

INDULGE in the beach paradise of **Morro Jable** (p. 651).

FANTASIZE about Martians in the barren bliss of **Timanfaya National Park** (p. 654).

SURF the sweet waves off the coast of tiny **El Cotillo** (p. 649).

✈ GETTING THERE

When properly informed and guided, a trip to the Canaries can be amazing. For do-it-yourself island adventure, purchase tickets to and from the mainland, arriving to and departing from opposite sides of the Canaries, then hop from island to island by boat, make your way through island interiors with cheap rental cars, and stay in rural houses, beach-side apartments, or *hostales*. Otherwise, browse travel agencies in Spain, England, and Germany for 8-day packages to the Canaries, including hotel and airfare, for €350-550. You won't be staying at the Ritz, but expect much more than the average budget hostel. These packages usually restrict you to a specific part of one island and are not ideal for backpackers looking to explore.

Located off the western coast of Morocco, the Canaries make for a long haul by boat (15hr.-2 days from Cádiz), but a relatively quick flight (2½-3½hr.) from mainland Spain. Competitive fares make flying the best option. Many airlines fly direct from Spain, Portugal, and northern Europe. Flights from Madrid are the cheapest and most frequent. European tourists, primarily German and British, flock to the islands in January and February; airfares during this time are the most expensive. Still, if you plan ahead, getting there will not break the bank. Buying from consolidators can cut costs in half (www.travelocity.com has good deals). A one-way ticket in summer should cost no more than €115.

Air Europa (24hr. ☎ 902 24 00 42; www.aireuropa.com) and **Spanair** (☎ 902 13 14 15; www.spanair.com) fly to the islands cheaply (round-trip €150-360).

Las Islas Canarias

ATLANTIC OCEAN

Lanzarote

Isla Montaña
Clara
La Isla Graciosa
Haría
Famara
Teguise
Arrecife
Tinajo
P.N. de
Timanfaya
Puerto del Carmen
Playa Blanca

Fuerteventura

Isla de Lobos
Puerto del Rosario
Corralejo
El Cotillo
La Oliva
Gran Tarajal
Betancuria
Pájara
Tuineje
Península
de Jandía
Morro
Jable

Gran Canaria

Las Palmas
Playa de las
Gáldar Canteras
Arucas
Teror
Telde
Agaete
Maspalomas
S. Nicolás
de Tolentino
Puerto
de Mogán
Playa del
Inglés

Tenerife

La Laguna
Santa Cruz de Tenerife
Bajamar
Tacoronte
Tegueste
La Orotava
Güímar
Puerto de la Cruz
Granadilla de Abona
Icod de
El Teide
los Vinos (3718m)
P.N. El Teide
Las Galletas
Guía de Isora
Los
Playa de
Cristianos
las Américas

La Gomera

Vallehermoso
Hermigua
P.N. de Garajonay
San Sebastián
de la Gomera
Valle Gran Rey
Playa de
Santiago

El Hierro

Valverde

La Palma

Santa Cruz de la Palma

0   20 miles

0   20 kilometers

Iberia (24hr. ☎902 40 05 00; www.iberia.com) flies from Madrid and Barcelona to Gran Canaria, Fuerteventura, Tenerife, and Lanzarote (round-trip €170-350).

⌐ GETTING AROUND

INTER-ISLAND TRANSPORT

If time is not an issue, traveling between the islands by ferry is the cheapest choice (see **chart**, p. 633). However, jetfoils and inter-island flights are competitively priced to facilitate quicker transit. All ferries carry cars. **Fred Olsen** and **Naviera Armas** have both launched new fleets of luxury ships, making longer trips more pleasant. Jetfoils are faster but cost almost twice as much—consider taking them on longer voyages. Prices for ferries and jetfoils vary with accommodations; travelers can choose between a reclinable *butaca* (similar to bus sets) and, on especially long trips, a *camarote a compartir* (a dorm bed). Tickets can be purchased one-way *(ida)* or round-trip *(ida y vuelta)*. Three major lines serve the islands and provide substantial student discounts. The offices at each city's ports list timetables and fares, although it is much easier and faster to check them via the Internet. Arrive at least 1hr. before departure to buy your ticket.

BY PLANE

Binter Canarias (www.bintercanarias.com or www.bintercanarias.es; verify flight information with parent company **Iberia** ☎902 40 05 00). Daily flights connect almost all islands. Prices listed are one-way, normal fare first, followed by student rate; round-trip is always cheaper. The number of flights per day varies by season; check website for more info. **Gran Canaria** to: **Fuerteventura** (40min., €62/€49); **La Gomera** (40min., €83/€64); **Lanzarote** (45min., €69/€54); **La Palma** (50min., €83/€64); **Tenerife Norte** (40min., €54/€43); **Tenerife Sur** (35min., €54/€43).

BY BOAT

Fred Olsen (☎922 62 82 00; www.fredolsen.es). Jetfoils throughout the islands. MC/V.

Naviera Armas (☎902 45 65 00; www.naviera-armas.com). Ferry routes. MC/V.

Trasmediterránea (24hr. ☎902 45 46 45; www.trasmediterranea.com). Ferries from Cádiz and jetfoils and ferries between islands. 15hr.-2 days; departs from Cádiz Tu, returns W and Sa; round-trip with dorm bed €847. Ticket windows open 1hr. prior to departure; reservations can be made online. MC/V.

INTRA-ISLAND TRANSPORT

Outside of Gran Canaria and Tenerife, the limits of **public transportation** prevent budget travelers from accessing the natural and cultural treasures of the Canaries. On islands such as Lanzarote, Fuerteventura, and La Gomera, buses to national parks and secluded beaches are either very limited or nonexistent. Dependency on public transportation will leave you in one of the abysmal capital cities of the smaller islands, where buses run only to and from the main bus station. Renting a **car** (€30 per day) is an invaluable, cost-effective investment for groups, opening up a new world of pristine landscapes, secluded beaches, and remote villages.

CAR RENTAL

Choose a car rental agency with several offices throughout an island so you can pick up and drop off the car in different locations for no extra charge. Reserve ahead to ensure good prices, since walk-ins are often charged double. Almost all cars are manual. Most agencies follow the same schedule (9am-1pm and 5-8pm); cars must be picked up and dropped off during these times. Prices quoted are per day (based on 1-2 day rental), including tax, insurance, and unlimited mileage. Prices drop significantly when renting for more time. The minimum age is 21, and you must have a driver's license, though it need not be international. Some agencies let you take the car from island to island (via ferry), but only with a hefty fee.

CiCAR (Canary Islands Car; reservations ☎ 928 82 29 00; www.cicar.com), with 27 offices throughout the islands, is the best option for car rental. Certain offices arrange for a representative to pick you up upon arrival and take you to the car rental office free of charge. Economy cars are available for €30 per day. Other reliable companies include: **Auto-Reisen** (☎ 922 63 59 78; €27 per day); **Avis** (☎ 902 13 55 31; €65 per day); **Betacar/Europcar** (☎ 922 37 28 82; €29 for 1 day, €50 for 2 days); **Felycar** (☎ 900 21 10 40; €38 per day); **Hertz** (☎ 902 14 37 89; €34 per day).

ORIGIN	DESTINATION	LENGTH	FREQUENCY	TIME	PRICE
Arrecife	Las Palmas	8hr.	W, F	noon	€29
Arrecife+	Las Palmas	8hr.	Tu, Th, Sa	1pm	€29
Arrecife+	Santa Cruz, Tenerife	10hr.	Th	10:15am	€34
Corralejo+	Playa Blanca	30min.	5-7 per day	8am-8pm	€13
Corralejo*	Playa Blanca	30min.	5-7 per day	M-Sa 7:45am-7pm, Su 9am-7pm	€14
Las Palmas	Arrecife	8hr.	Tu, Th, Sa	Tu-Th midnight, Sa 2:30pm	€29
Las Palmas+	Arrecife	10hr.	M, W, F	11:50pm	€29
Las Palmas	Morro Jable	1½hr.	1 per day	M-Sa 10 or 11am, Su noon or 2pm	€50
Las Palmas+	Morro Jable	4hr.	1 per day	M-Sa 7:10am, Su 1:30pm	€27
Las Palmas	Puerto Rosario	8hr.	M, W, F	midnight	€29
Las Palmas+	Puerto Rosario	8hr.	Tu, Th	11:50pm	€29
Las Palmas	Santa Cruz, Tenerife	1½hr.	2-3 per day	varies 7:30am-7pm	€23
Las Palmas+	Santa Cruz, Tenerife	3½hr.	M-F 2 per day, Sa-Su 1 per day	M-F 6:45am and 3:30pm, Sa-Su 7am	€14
Las Palmas* (bus to Agate)	Santa Cruz, Tenerife	1½hr.	M-F 8 per day, Sa-Su 6 per day	M-F 6:30am-9pm, Sa-Su 8am-9pm	€31
Los Cristianos	San Sebastián	1½hr.	1-3 per day	daily 8:30am; M-F 2pm; Su 7:17pm	€18
Los Cristianos*	San Sebastián	40min.	6 per day	8am-8:30pm	€18-21
Morro Jable	Las Palmas	1½hr.	1 per day	1,3,or 5pm	€50
Morro Jable+	Las Palmas	3hr.	1 per day	7pm	€27
Playa Blanca+	Corralejo	30min.	5-7 per day	7am-7pm	€13
Playa Blanca*	Corralejo	30min.	5-7 per day	M-F 7:10am-6pm, Su 8:30am-6pm	€14
Puerto del Rosario	Las Palmas	8hr.	Tu, Th, Sa	1pm	€29
Puerto del Rosario+	Las Palmas	8hr.	W, F	noon	€29
Puerto del Rosario+	Santa Cruz, Tenerife	12hr.	F	2:30pm	€34
San Sebastián	Los Cristianos	1½hr.	1-2 per day	daily 5pm; M-F 11:45am	€18
San Sebastián*	Los Cristianos	40min.	5-6 per day	7am-6:30pm	€18-21
Santa Cruz, Ten.+	Arrecife	10hr.	Th	10pm	€34
Santa Cruz, Ten.+	Las Palmas	3½hr.	1-2 per day	M-F 11:10am and 8:10pm, Sa-Su 7:30pm	€14
Santa Cruz, Ten.+	Puerto del Rosario	10hr.	Th	10pm	€34
Santa Cruz, Ten.+	Santa Cruz, La Palma	8hr.	M-W, Sa	M-W 11:50pm, Sa 1am	€16

Unless otherwise noted, ferries are run by Trasmediterránea. * denotes Fred Olsen. + denotes Naviera Armas.

LAS ISLAS CANARIAS

GRAN CANARIA

Often called the "miniature continent," Gran Canaria sports a wide range of landscapes, from green, tropical vegetation in the north to the rolling dunes of Maspalomas in the south. Las Palmas is a vibrant and eclectic city with attractive museums and the famous Playa de las Canteras, but European tourists flock primarily to the south, reveling in Gran Canaria's perpetual sunshine and beautiful beaches. Mountain towns in the interior, where daily life does not revolve around tourists, provide visitors with a rare glimpse into the vibrance of local culture. An ideal visit to Gran Canaria is a well-rounded one. Be sure to take it all in—the beach will still be there when you're ready for it. Also, unlike the other islands, Gran Canaria is explorable without a car thanks to its extensive bus system.

LAS PALMAS

The urban mecca of the Canaries, Las Palmas (pop. 365,000) features all the qualities of any normal big city—shopping, decent eating, theater, cafes, and bars. The city boasts a quaint historic district in the south, which holds some of the Canaries' best museums. Playa de las Canteras, one of Europe's most famous beaches, is packed with locals—tourists prefer the guaranteed sun on the southern coast.

▐ TRANSPORTATION

Flights: (info ☎928 57 90 00). **Buses** *(guaguas)* run from Parque de San Telmo's Estación de Guaguas to the airport (#60; 45min., every 30min. 6:30am-1:30am, €1.80).

Buses: Estación de Guaguas (☎928 36 83 35), on the sea side of Parque de San Telmo. Office open M-F 7am-6:45pm, Sa-Su 8am-12:45pm. **Líneas Global** (☎902 38 11 10; www.globalsu.net) connects Las Palmas to the rest of the island's many bus lines, some of which run long into the night. For those exploring extensively by bus, the blue **tarjeta insular** pass (€15) gives a 20% discount on municipal and island-wide buses. Bus schedules change on weekends, especially on Su; pick up a timetable in the ticket office. To: **Arucas** (#205, 209, 210, and 234; every 30min.-1hr. 6am-2am, €1.40-1.80); **Maspalomas-Playa del Inglés** (#5 and 30; 1hr.; every 20min. 5:20am-3am; Playa Inglés €4.20, Maspalomas €4.60); **Puerto de Mogán** (#1; 1½hr.; every 20min. 5am-7pm, also 8:30, 9:30, 10:30, and 11:30am; €6.50); **Puerto Rico** (#91; every hr. 6:15am-8:15pm, €5.60); **Teror** (#216; every 30min. 6am-11pm, €1.80).

Inter-City Buses: Guaguas Municipales, C. León y Castillo, 330 (☎928 44 65 00), are yellow buses (€0.90) that travel within the city. Stops are frequent. When in doubt, hop on bus #1 (24hr.), which runs north to south from Muelle de la Luz to Teatro Pérez Galdós, passing Parque de Santa Catalina and Parque de San Telmo. 10-ride *"bono"* (€5.20) available at tobacco shops or at the main bus station.

Ferries: Trasmediterránea (☎928 45 56 45) runs jetfoils from Muelle de Santa Catalina. **Naviera Armas** (☎902 45 65 00) ferries depart from Muelle León y Castillo. Ferry tickets can be purchased at the docks 1hr. before departure. **Fred Olsen** (☎922 62 82 00) ferries to **Tenerife** depart from **Agaete.** A free bus leaves Parque de Santa Catalina 1hr. before the ferry leaves. Buy your ferry tickets and board the bus at the Fred Olsen office in the northwest corner of the park. Tickets also sold at travel agencies for a small fee. For more info, see **Inter-Island Transport,** p. 632.

Car Rental: CiCAR (airport ☎928 57 93 78, Muelle de Santa Catalina 928 26 40 89). **Hertz** (☎928 57 95 77) has offices scattered around the island, including at the airport and in the Jetfoil office at Muelle de Santa Catalina.

Taxi: Radio Taxi (☎928 46 22 12).

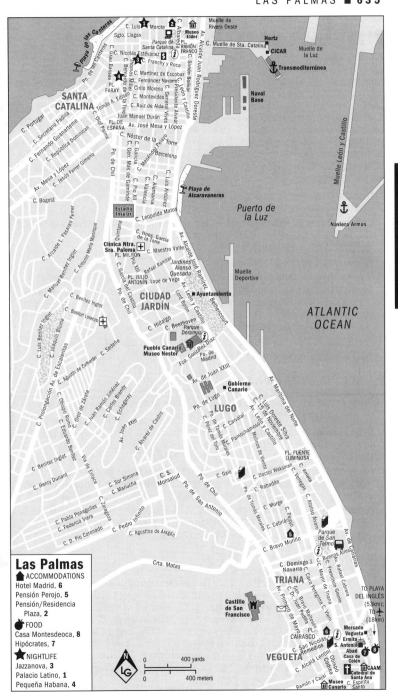

LAS ISLAS CANARIAS

Las Palmas

🏠 ACCOMMODATIONS
Hotel Madrid, **6**
Pensión Perojo, **5**
Pensión/Residencia
   Plaza, **2**

🍴 FOOD
Casa Montesdeoca, **8**
Hipócrates, **7**

⭐ NIGHTLIFE
Jazzanova, **3**
Palacio Latino, **1**
Pequeña Habana, **4**

✳ 🛈 ORIENTATION AND PRACTICAL INFORMATION

The bus system is the easiest way to get around Las Palmas. The city is loosely divided into a series of districts, connected by both a major highway and avenues running north to south along the east coast. **Calle León y Castillo** cuts through the city center. **Playa de Las Canteras** and **Muelle de la Luz** frame the north of the city, packed with accommodations, bars, discos, and sex shops. Farther south through a series of residential neighborhoods lies **Triana**, a shopping district close to the city's main bus station. Quaint, beautiful **Vegueta**, home to the city's historical district, branches south from there. Buses #1, 12, 13, 15, and 41 run between **Parque de Santa Catalina** and Vegueta. The northern area of the city, though home to much of the nightlife, is not perfectly safe at night. La Isleta, north of Santa Catalina, can get particularly hairy; use common sense and caution.

Tourist Offices: The **Patronato de Turismo**, C. León y Castillo, 17 (☎928 21 96 00; www.grancanaria.com), is a good resource. Open M-F 8am-2pm.

Currency Exchange: Banco Santander Central Hispano, C. Nicolás Estévanez, 5 (☎902 24 24 24), at the south end of Parque de Santa Catalina. No commission. Open M-F 8:30am-2pm, Sa 8:30am-1pm.

Police: Parque de Santa Catalina (☎092 or 928 26 05 51).

Hospital: Hospital Insular, Pl. Dr. Pasteur (☎928 44 40 00). 24hr. English spoken.

Internet: Free Internet at the **Biblioteca Pública,** Pl. Hurtado de Meduza (☎928 384 672), in the Triana neighborhood. Internet daily 9am-8:30pm. Library open 24hr. Or, try **Cyber's@Zero** (☎928 27 47 75), in Parque de Santa Catalina, with cheap access and speedy computers. €1 per 40min. Open daily 9am-midnight

Post Office: Av. Primero de Mayo, 62 (☎928 36 13 20). Open M-F 8:30am-8:30pm, Sa 9:30am-2:30pm. **Postal Code:** 35007.

🛏 ACCOMMODATIONS

Without advance notice, it's nearly impossible to find lodging during high season (Dec.-Feb., especially during *Carnaval*).

Hotel Madrid, Pl. Cairasco, 4 (☎928 36 06 64; fax 38 21 76). Elegantly furnished rooms retain their historical feel. Franco stayed in #3 the night before the Civil War began. Singles €24, with bath €30; doubles €35/€40. ❷

Pensión Perojo, C. Perojo, 1 (☎928 37 13 87). Located in an airy older building, Perojo's rooms are spacious and spotless. Short walk from the old city and bus station makes up for lots of noise. Hall baths. Singles €15; doubles €24; triples €30. ❶

Pensión/Residencia Plaza, C. Luis Morote, 16 (☎928 26 52 12). Location near Parque de Santa Catalina is great, as are the large corner rooms. Laundry €7. Singles €17, with bath €20; doubles €23/€26. Extra bed €6. ❷

🍴 FOOD

Las Palmas's cuisine is as international as its fluctuating population. Restaurants along Playa de las Canteras and in Vegueta often cater specifically to tourists. For groceries, head to **Mercado de Vegueta,** on C. Mendizábal. (☎928 33 41 29. Open daily M-F 8am-2pm and 5-8pm, Sa 8am-2pm.) **Hipócrates ❷**, C. Colón, 4, across from Casa de Colón in Vegueta, offers vegetarian dining and a €9.20 lunch *menú*. (☎928 31 11 71. Open daily 1-4pm and 8:30pm-midnight, closed Su evenings and M afternoons.) **Casa Montesdeoca ❸** serves Spanish entrees (€7-14) in a 16th-century courtyard. (☎928 33 34 66. Open M-Sa 12:30-4pm and 8pm-midnight.)

🅞 SIGHTS

Las Palmas's sights can be toured in a single day. Begin in the south in Vegueta, the city's **historic neighborhood;** its colonial and Neoclassical architecture and open markets make for a sweet respite from the new city's commercial buildings. A plethora of small side streets makes maps difficult to follow; from the Parque San Telmo Bus Station, head down C. Triana and cross C. Lentini to enter the historic neighborhood.

CASA DE COLÓN. To follow the footsteps of Columbus, visit this mansion as your last stop before the New World. The museum contains various artifacts from early transatlantic voyages, including an extensive collection of old maps. Appropriately enough, artifacts from pre-Columbian cultures can be found downstairs in the crypt. Each room has multilingual descriptions of exhibits. *(C. Colón, 1. ☎928 31 23 86; www.grancanariacultura.com. Open M-F 9am-7pm, Sa-Su 9am-3pm. Free.)*

MUSEO CANARIO. The collection provides a comprehensive background to the Canaries' pre-conquest history. Ponder your own mortality while perusing the extensive collection of Cro-Magnon skulls and mummies, which documents the evolution of man and Guanche society. Of special interest are exhibitions on Guanche architecture, fertility rites, and trepanation, an ancient, crude form of brain surgery. *(C. Verneau, 2. ☎928 33 68 00; www.elmuseocanario.com. Open M-F 10am-8pm, Sa-Su 10am-2pm. All exhibits in Spanish. Guided tours in Spanish every 45min. 10am-2pm and at 6 and 7pm. €3, students €1.20.)*

CENTRO ATLÁNTICO DE ARTE MODERNO. This open steel and glass structure hosts free, well-curated modern art exhibits that rotate every two months; expect to see some big names (last year's exhibition "Landscape and Memory" had work from the 1960s-2004 by Thomas Struth, Sam Taylor-Wood, Hiroshi Sugimoto, and Bruce Nauman) alongside work by more local artists. The center has great multimedia spaces and presents film and video art. Elegantly translated English blurbs help explain the unexplainable. *(C. Los Balcones. ☎902 311 824; www.caam.net. Open Tu-Sa 10am-9pm, Su 10am-2pm. Call ahead to arrange a free guided tour.)*

MUSEO ELDER DE LA CIENCIA Y LA TECNOLOGÍA. The city's new pride and joy, the museum, on the port side of Parque de Santa Catalina, is a state-of-the-art exploration of topics from ancient Egyptian mathematics to the racecar engine. It also houses a

ON THE MENU

EATING LIKE A BIRD

Canarian cuisine is delightful, though sometimes hard to find in more touristed areas where food caters to European visitors. Restaurants in rural areas and seaside towns are the best places to look, though some larger restaurants (like **El Restaurante del Campesino** on Lanzarote) serve delicious authentic food. Main dishes include a variety of fresh fish (*vieja*, parrot fish, is very popular) served *a la plancha* (grilled). *Potaje*, a stew made from pork, corn, potatoes, beans, and whatever else is in the kitchen, is a heavier dish. *Ropa Vieja* is a hearty mix of potatoes, peppers, mutton, goat, and onion. Most meals are accompanied by delicious *papas arrugadas* (small "wrinkly" potatoes) and served with a variety of *mojos* (sauces). The most popular of these are *mojo picón* (spicy red sauce) and *mojo verde* (parsley sauce). *Gofio*, which consists of ground toasted cereals, is put in soup or eaten with milk for breakfast.

Goat has always been a staple, whether as roasted *cabrito* (kid) or goat cheese. Fuerteventura is famous for its *majorero* cheese, a creamy artisanal delicacy. Gran Canaria is known for its flower-infused *queso de flor*. The islands grow a variety of tropical fruit like bananas, avocados, mangos, and cactus fruits—often the dessert of choice. Creamy *bienmesabe*, made from honey, almonds, eggs, and rum, is also popular.

space station, screens IMAX documentaries, and has computers with free Internet. (☎828 01 18 28; www.museoelder.org. Open Oct.-June Tu-Su 10am-8pm; July-Sept. Tu-Su 11am-9pm. €3, children €2.10; with IMAX ticket €4.50/€3.)

CATEDRAL DE SANTA ANA. This 16th-century Gothic cathedral houses the **Diocesan Museum of Religious Art.** José Luján Pérez designed the Neoclassical facade. The museum is not spectacular, but the church is home to the mummified body of Bishop Codina, whose uncorrupted corpse was disinterred and is now on display. (C. Espíritu Santo, 20. ☎928 31 49 89. Open M-F 10am-4:30pm, Sa 10am-1:30pm. €3.)

PUEBLO CANARIO. The white-washed **Pueblo Canario** (Canarian Village), dedicated to *canario* culture, is home to the **Museo Néstor,** a collection of painter Néstor Martín-Fernández de la Torre's pastel celebrations of body and spirit. As per his request, on Sunday mornings Pueblo Canario is filled with traditional Canarian folk dance and music from 11:30am to 1pm. (Take bus #1, 15, or 41. ☎928 24 51 35. Open Tu-F 10am-8pm, Su 10:30am-2:30pm. Call ahead for free guided tours. €2, students free.)

◪ ♫ BEACHES AND ENTERTAINMENT

The waters along **Playa de Las Canteras** are protected during low tide by a natural reef, turning the ocean into a tranquil swimming pool. Locals flock to the far left, where the waves are great for bodyboarding. Surfers and windsurfers head to the far extremes where waves and wind are plentiful. **Medusa Sub,** C. Bernardo de La Torre, 58, specializes in diving courses and equipment rental and sales. (☎928 26 27 86. €22 per dive, €40 with equipment. 2wk. certification course €300. Open M-F 10am-2pm and 5-9pm, Sa 10am-1pm and 6-8pm.)

Nightlife in Las Palmas is unremarkable. Most popular spots (including karaoke bars) are located near Parque de Santa Catalina; be careful there at night. Take advantage of year-round outdoor terraces on Pl. de España and along Po. de las Canteras. A brand new stand-out is **Jazzanova,** C. Nicolás Estévanez, 24. The bar hosts live jazz, Latin, or R&B every night. (☎647 401 638. Beer €2, mixed drinks €5. Open daily 8pm-4am). **Palacio Latino,** C. Luis Morote, 51, is a typical *discoteca.* (Cover €6, includes 1 drink. Open F-Su midnight-5:30am.) **Pequeña Habana,** C. Fernando Guanarteme, 45, sizzles with salsa until 4am on weekends.

◪ DAYTRIPS FROM LAS PALMAS

MASPALOMAS

Buses run to and from the airport (#66; 40min., every hr. 6:15am-9:15pm, €3.10); Las Palmas (#5 and 30; 1hr., every 20min. 5am-2:30am, €4.15-4.60); Puerto de Mogán (#32 and 61; 30min., schedule varies 8:30am-8:30pm, €3.05); Puerto Rico (#32, 39, and 61; 30min., schedule varies 7am-8:30pm, €1.60.)

Located on the southern tip of Gran Canaria, Maspalomas's 17km of shoreline offer some of the finest beaches in the Islas Canarias. The famed **Playa del Inglés** is ideal for parasailing, surfing, jet-skiing, scuba diving (though the sandy bottom is not home to many fish), and deep-sea fishing in Puerto Rico. The secret has long been out, and planeloads of European tourists swarm the coast every year. The crowds are worth putting up with, though, to see the awesome, wind-swept ◪**Dunas de Maspalomas** beyond the beach, a subtle reminder that the Canaries share their latitude with the Sahara. From Playa del Inglés, head right (facing the sea) on the beach and walk about 20min.—you can't miss them.

Other good beaches include the flawless, quieter **Playa de Maspalomas** and the rocky **Playa de la Mujer** and **Playa Meloneras. Water Sports Center,** in the Kasbah shopping center, rents jet skis. (☎928 76 66 83. €30-36 for 20min.) **Diving Center**

"Sun-Sub" offers daily diving trips with optional equipment. (☎928 77 81 65; www.sunsub.com. €28 without equipment, €60 for a 7hr. "taster's course.") **Happy Biking,** in Hotel Continental, rents bikes, equipment, guides, and picnic supplies. (☎928 76 68 32. €7.50-22.50 per day. Guided tours half-day €24, full-day €42. Open M-Sa 8:30am-1:30pm and 6-8pm.) Beyond the fantastic beaches, most people come to Playa del Inglés and Maspalomas to eat, drink, and party. Cement buildings and market bazaars house the town's **nightlife.** Once you get over the ostentatious party atmosphere, marvel at the sparkler in your drink, accompanied by a plastic frog and token orange slice. The frequent night bus between Las Palmas and Maspalomas makes nighttime entertainment that much easier. **Yumbo Centrum,** located between Av. Tirajana and Av. de España and facing Av. de EEUU, houses an entire block of restaurants, gay and straight bars, clubs, Internet cafes, laundromats, and grocery stores. Before you hit the comical kitsch there, head to **Detox/ Retox,** Av. de Tiranjara, 9, halfway between Yumbo and the beach, a smart, stylish little cafe bar that refreshes with fruit cocktails (€4) and debauches with hard ones (€4-6). Caters to a primarily gay clientele, but all are welcome. (☎928 76 74 59; www.detoxretox.com. Open Tu-Su 4:30pm-1am.) Also nearby, on the corner of Av. de España and Av. de EEUU, is the **tourist office.** (☎928 77 15 50. Open summer M-F 9am-2pm and 3-8pm, Sa 9am-1pm; winter M-F 9am-9pm, Sa 9am-1pm.)

Residencia San Fernando ❶, C. La Palma, 16, is the only budget accommodation in town, though nicer hotels are affordable through tour packages. Follow Av. Tirajana uphill away from the beach; La Palma is the second right after the highway. The *residencia* is across from Centro San Fernando. The dunes and beach are easily accessible, but rooms are bare. (☎928 76 39 06. Singles €12.50; doubles €18.50.) Dining in Maspalomas is quite awful. Hustlers lure you to tourist-themed restaurants serving over 120 generic entrees. The town's culinary savior is the dirt-cheap **Pepe Chiringo ❶,** at Av. Tirajana and Av. Francia, with heaping portions of chicken breast covered in homemade *alioli* (€3).

ARUCAS

Buses #205, 206, 210, 222, and 234 travel from the Las Palmas station to Arucas (every 30min.-1hr. 6am-2am, €1.50-1.90).

Arucas, a delightful mountain town set on a dormant volcano, has a stunning neo-Gothic church and a genuine, relaxed atmosphere. An enjoyable daytrip from Las Palmas or any spot on the island, it is worth tearing yourself away from the beach to take in the town's splendor. While tourist kiosks in Las Palmas and tourist offices in Maspalomas can provide maps and guides for the city, a local **tourist office** is in the Jardín Municipal, near Pl. de la Constitución. (☎928 62 31 36; www.arucasturismo.com. Open M-F 8am-3pm.) Overlooking a set of gardens, the **Iglesia de San Juan Bautista,** constructed mostly by local artisans between 1909 and 1977, is an enormous structure for such a small town. (Open daily 9am-12:30pm and 4-7pm. Free.) A short walk out of town leads to **Montaña de Arucas,** which has breathtaking views. Since 1884, Arucas has been home to the **Arehucas factory,** which produces the island's delicious rum; the free 30min. tour ends with a tasting. (☎928 62 49 00. Open summer 9am-1pm; winter 9am-2pm.) Though all of Arucas can be seen in a morning, there is one (and only one) budget lodging in town: a little *albergue* called **La Granja Escuela Anatot ❷,** C. Ruz de Pineda, 5, which provides a home for scholars—and you, too, if you reserve in advance. (☎/fax 928 60 55 44. Taxi from the bus station €4. Breakfast included. €21 per person.)

TEROR

Buses #216, 220, and 229 serve Teror from Las Palmas (40min., every 30min. 6am-11pm, €1.80). Buses #215 and 220 run from Arucas to Teror (20min., every 30min. 6:30am-11pm, €0.90).

Don't let the name scare you: if you're looking for rural charm, a bit of culture, and great walking trails, Teror is the perfect break from the beach crowds and the city. Teror has worked hard to preserve its small-town identity and history while actively promoting a quiet, contemplative type of tourism. An ideal day in Teror would begin by exploring the historic sights and wandering the cobbled streets, then taking a hike on one of the many surrounding trails. The tourist office provides comprehensive maps of trails and sights in the even smaller communities that surround the town. Teror becomes the religious focal point of the entire island during the **Fiesta del Pino** (Sept. 8-19), a celebration of the patron saint of the island, whose image resides in the Basílica. In addition to the thousands of *canarios* who flock to eat, drink, and be merry, representative groups from each of the 21 Gran Canarian municipalities make a pilgrimage to dedicate the best foods and crafts to the saint. If you would like to stay for more than a day, contact one of the many *casas rurales* through the tourist office. There is one residence in the center of town, the **Casa Rural de Doña Margarita ❺**, which has three wonderfully furnished apartments, each with two bedrooms, full kitchens, and access to a sun room with hammocks. (☎928 35 00 00; info@margaritacasarural.com. Reservations highly recommended. To stay during the festival, reserve at least 6 months in advance; prices go up about €30 per night. Doubles €75; triples €85; quads €96.)

The center of town is the **Plaza de Pino,** with a small, Baroque **Basílica** and its fine wood sculptures (☎928 63 01 18; open M 1-8:30pm, Tu-F 9am-1pm and 3-8:30pm, Sa 9am-8:30pm, Su 7:30am-7:30pm; free), the **tourist office** (☎928 63 20 54; open summer M-F 9:30am-3:30pm; winter 9:30am-4:30m), and the **Casa Museo de la Patrona,** a creaky old aristocrat's house doubling as a museum (open M-Sa 11am-6pm, Su 10am-2pm). Behind the square is the **Casa de la Cultura,** which hosts rotating art exhibits. The modern **biblioteca** (library) is in the same building and has free **Internet.** (C. de la Escuela, 3. ☎928 63 02 16. Open M-F 10am-1pm and 5-8pm.)

TENERIFE

The volcanic peak of El Teide (3718m) juts into the blinding blue sky, peering down on Tenerife's diverse landscapes and tranquility. Though it is the Canaries' second most populous island, Tenerife has countless solitary walking trails that start just outside the capital. The microclimates of the island have generated a land of ever-changing flora and terrain, best characterized by the verdant gardens of the north, the rocky beaches of the south, and the mesmerizing mountainous and volcanic spectacles of the interior. Though the island's beauty lies more in its people and spectacular vistas than its beaches, sun-worshippers can still get their fix down south. Nature-lovers, backpackers, and families will find Tenerife a rewarding travel destination, a peaceful outlet from the urban sprawl of mainland Spain. For those in search of greater seclusion, the island provides transportation to the more untouched western islands of La Gomera and La Palma.

SANTA CRUZ DE TENERIFE ☎922

The first shots of the Spanish Civil War rang out in this capital city in 1936. The Canaries' General-in-Chief, Francisco Franco, would go on to orchestrate the war for the next three years. Today, with more than 250,000 residents, the small port city is a pedestrian utopia, with endless *ramblas* (promenades), quaint historical houses, *zumerías* (juice bars), and lush parks. Santa Cruz de Tenerife also maintains a strong sense of culture that was lost in the capitals of the eastern islands.

▐ TRANSPORTATION

Flights: National flights land at the northern **airport, Los Rodeos** (☎922 63 56 35; www.aena.es/ae.tfn), 6km west of Santa Cruz. From Los Rodeos, buses #102, 107, and 108 run to town (25min., every 20min. 6am-10:15pm, €1.20). International flights dominate the south's **Reina Sofía airport** (☎922 75 90 00; www.aena.es/ae.tfs). From Reina Sofía, buses #111 and 341 head to town (1½hr., every hr. 5am-2:30am, €5.20). **Iberia** (Los Rodeos ☎922 635 855, Reina Sofía 759 391, Central 902 400 500), **Spanair** (Los Rodeos ☎922 63 58 19, Reina Sofía 759 244, Central 902 131 413), **Air Europa** (Los Rodeos ☎922 635 819, Los Cristianos 63 59 55, Central 902 401 501), and **Binter Canarias** (☎922 63 50 81) all fly to the island.

Buses: TITSA (info ☎922 53 13 00, Santa Cruz station 21 56 99; www.titsa.com) serves all towns from the **Estación de Guaguas**, Av. Tres de Mayo, 57, down Av. José Antonio Primo de Rivera from Pl. de España. Open daily 6am-9pm. Some lines do not run in summer; call ahead or check online for info. To: **Los Cristianos/Playa de las Américas** (#110 and 111; 1hr.; every 30min.-1hr. 5:30am-11:30pm, last bus at 2:30am; €6.30-6.70) and **Puerto de la Cruz** (#102 has stops, #103 runs direct; 45min.-1hr.; every 30min.-1hr. 6am-9:30pm; also 10:15, 11:15pm, 1:15, 1:45, and 4:15am; €3.60). If you plan on using buses often, buy a **bonobus ticket** (Card Titsa; €12), which gives 31% discount on cost of individual tickets on short rides and 50% for distances greater than 21km. For passengers who return within 2hr., the return trip is free.

Ferries: Trasmediterránea (Central ☎902 45 46 45, Santa Cruz 84 22 43, Los Cristianos 79 61 78). **Fred Olsen** (☎922 62 82 00) runs a **free bus** from the main station to Los Cristianos for trips to La Gomera, 1½hr. prior to departure. Arrive at the station early. See **Inter-Island Transport**, p. 632, for more info.

Car Rental: Local offices include **Auto-Reisen** (☎922 26 22 02), **Avis** (☎922 25 87 13), and **CiCar** (☎922 63 59 25). See **Intra-Island Transport**, p. 632.

Taxis: Radio Taxi ☎922 311 012.

◪ 🛈 ORIENTATION AND PRACTICAL INFORMATION

Despite its extensive bus system, Santa Cruz is easily navigable on foot. The port city branches out from **Plaza de España**. Directly across from Pl. de España is **Plaza de la Candelaria**; C. del Castillo runs perpendicular to the water from here into the commercial district. Av. José Antonio Primo de Rivera and Av. Francisco La Roche originate at Pl. de España and run along the waterfront, separating the port and the city. To get to Pl. de España from the **ferry terminals,** turn left onto Av. Francisco la Roche/Av. Anaga, and follow it to the plaza (10min.). From the **bus station,** head right down Av. Tres de Mayo towards the water, then take a left on Av. José Antonio Primo de Rivera, continuing on to the plaza (15min.).

Tourist Office: Pl. de España (☎922 23 95 92), on the corner of Av. José Antonio Primo de Rivera. Facing the monument in the plaza, it is in the near left corner. Open July-Sept. M-F 8am-5pm, Sa 9am-noon; Oct.-June M-F 8am-6pm, Sa 9am-1pm.

Police: Av. Tres de Mayo, 72 (☎922 60 60 92). Follow Av. Tres de Mayo past the intersection with Av. La Salle; the station is on the right.

Pharmacy: Farmacia La Marina, C. de la Marina, 7 (☎922 24 24 93), 1 block from Pl. de España. Open M-F 8am-8pm, Sa 9am-1:30pm. Many more are on C. del Castillo.

Hospital: Hospital Universitario de Canarias, Urbanización Ofra (☎922 67 80 00), in La Laguna, north of Santa Cruz. Take bus #014 or 015.

Internet Access: Tóp Anaga, Av. Francisco la Roche/Av. Anaga, 11 (☎922 28 24 96), next to the 24hr. convenience store. €1 per 30min. Open daily 9am-midnight.

CANARY CARNAVAL

If you've been in Spain a week, you've probably stumbled upon at least one fiesta, but nothing can prepare you for the debauched madness that awaits revelers in the Islas Canarias' all-out, no-holds-barred celebration of Carnaval. All of the islands go wild, but Santa Cruz in Tenerife takes the cake. Every year from early February to March, the city erupts in celebration with parades, fireworks, drinking, dancing, music, drinking, costumed balls, and more drinking. Santa Cruz holds a world record for getting over 200,000 people to attend an outdoor costume ball in 1987. Celia Cruz played, accompanied by a laser light show. The party gets bigger every year, so be sure to reserve accommodations at least a few months in advance. The epicenter of the celebrations is the Pl. de España, which hosts the opening parade, the election of the Carnaval queen, the Burial of the Sardine, and the cute children's parade. Each year has a theme that provides the inspiration for decadent costumes (many are drag, but you may see some Star Wars Storm Troopers, too). Mixed with the hedonism is a bit of politics; Carnaval was banned under Franco's regime, and much of the entertainment is provided by *murgas*, musical groups that sing satirical songs lampooning politicians, celebrities, and other likely targets.

For more information, visit www.carnavaltenerife.com.

Post Office: Pl. de España (☎922 53 36 29). Open M-F 8:30am-8:30pm, Sa 9:30am-2pm. **Postal Code:** 38007.

ACCOMMODATIONS

Budget accommodations in Santa Cruz tend to be less desirable than one- and two- star hotels. Affordable places to spend the night are scattered on C. del Castillo and C. Bethencourt Alfonso. The tourist office has lists of accommodations and a map of the hotels; make use of their free 2min. phone calls to reserve a room.

Hotel Horizonte, C. Sta. Rosa de Lima, 11 (☎/fax 922 27 19 36). From C. de la Marina, turn left at C. Emilio Calzadilla, then right on C. Sta. Rosa de Lima. Rooms are spotless and all have baths. Superb service. Singles €20-26; doubles €40-45; triples €45. ❷

Pensión Casablanca, C. Viera y Clavijo, 15 (☎922 27 85 99). C. Bethencourt Alfonso becomes C. Pérez Galdós and then C. Viera y Clavijo. Funky rooms are cramped but lively with pink, blue, or green color schemes. Common baths. Reservations highly recommended. Singles €15; doubles €21. ❶

Hotel Anago, C. Imeldo Seris, 19 (☎922 24 50 90; fax 24 56 44). Off C. General Gutiérrez. Basic rooms with TV and phone, many with balcony. Singles with shower €25.50, with bath €32; doubles €42/€53; triples €53/€75. AmEx/MC/V. ❸

FOOD

Eating is a cheap and delicious activity in Santa Cruz. The numerous *zumerías* and sandwich shops lining the city streets serve over 50 combinations of fresh fruit juices and shakes for around €1.80. **La Hierbita ❷**, C. del Clavel, 19, offers delicious Canarian specialties including fresh fish (entrees €2.75-9), local wines, and homemade desserts. Try the *almagote*, a sort of cheese pâté. The owners, from La Palma and La Gomera, restored and converted this former *pensión* into a cozy local favorite with multiple dining rooms. From Pl. de España, take C. General Gutiérrez, a right onto C. Imeldo Seris, and another right onto C. Cruz Verde; Clavel is your first left. (☎922 24 46 17. Open M-Sa noon-4pm and 8pm-midnight.) Among the best in town, **Zumería Tropicana ❶**, C. Portlier, 71, is a bit of a hike from Pl. de España, but if you're near Pl. de Weyler, go uphill on Rmbla. de Pulido and turn left after one street onto C. Portlier. This *zumería* specializes in vegetarian food (like pumpkin burgers) and drinks made from fruits and vegetables. (☎929 84 44 90. Open Su-F

5pm-midnight.) Another great option is **Crepería la Bohème ❶**, C. Emilio Calzadilla, 8, which serves huge, delicious specialty crepes (savory €3-5.90, sweet €1.20-2.30, with fruit €3.60). The Guanche crepe has an eclectic *canario* mix of fruits, cheese, corn, and chicken. (From Pl. de España, turn right along C. Marina and left up C. Emilio Calzadilla. ☎922 29 62 96. Open M-F 10am-5pm and 8-11:30pm, Sa-Su 8-11:30pm). For cheap Canarian classics try **Bodeguita Canaria ❶**, C. Imeldo Seris, 18; from Pl. de España go through Pl. Candelaria, take a left onto C. Cruz Verde, and a right onto C. Imeldo Seris. The hearty *ropa vieja*, a mix of goat, mutton, potatoes, and peppers, is good and filling. (☎922 29 32 16. Main dishes €3.90-5.70. Open M-F 1-4pm and 8-11:30pm, Sa 8-11:30pm.) Cafes, restaurants, and bars crowd Pl. de España, but **Avenida Francisco la Roche/Avenida Anaga** has better deals (*menús* from €6) and chic *terrazas*. **Mercado de Nuestra Señora de Africa,** an indoor market across the river and one block inland from the Museo de la Naturaleza, sells meat, fish, cheese, and produce. (Open daily 8am-3pm.)

🎢 🎵 SIGHTS AND ENTERTAINMENT

The greatest sights in Santa Cruz are outside the city limits along lookout points off the main highway and smaller side roads. Renting a car allows you to explore the hidden treasures that encircle the city. Especially enchanting are the forested trails of the Anaga headlands and the black sand beaches of **Almáciga.** Within the city itself, the beautiful plazas and parks are perfect for coffee sipping, people-watching, and deep thinking. Besides **Plaza de España,** the **Plaza de Weyler** is a popular spot and a gateway to the great **shopping** southward. Be sure to walk along the promenade by the port to get a close look at the ☑**Auditorio de Tenerife.** Finished in 2003, Santiago Calatrava's immense white structure looks like a tidal wave crashing over a small version of the Sydney opera house. (Facing the water, head right from Pl. de España. Ticket office open M-F 8am-3pm. No performances July-Sept.) If it's shade you're after, walk up C. Bethencourt Alfonso from Pl. de España and turn right onto C. Valentín Sanz to **Plaza del Príncipe de Asturias,** which has huge trees and some interesting sculptures. **Parque Municipal García Sanabria** doubles as a garden and open-air sculpture museum with some impressive ficus trees and avant-garde works by Pablo Serrano and Rafael Soto. (From Pl. del Príncipe de Asturias, follow C. El Pilar uphill to the Parque.) The **Museo de la Naturaleza y el Hombre,** C. Fuente de Morales, 1, off C. San Sebastián, transports you to the archaeological past, detailing everything from pre-historic marine biology to Guanche burial practices. On the lighter side, try sculpting your own ceramic pots in its classroom. (☎922 53 58 16; fax 29 43 45. Open Tu-Su 9am-7pm. €3, students €1.50. 50% discount with *bonobus* pass. Su free.) The intricate woodwork of the 16th-century **Iglesia de la Concepción** is worth the walk. (To reach Pl. de la Iglesia, turn left onto C. Bravo Murillo from the tourist office. ☎922 24 23 84. Mass M-F 9am and 7:30pm; Sa 6 and 7:30pm; Su 9, 11am, noon, 1, 6, and 8pm. Open M-F 8am-7:30pm.)

🏖 🍹 BEACHES AND NIGHTLIFE

Many flock to Tenerife for a beach vacation, and some of the best beaches are accessible by frequent buses leaving from the main station. If you are in the area be certain to check out the small black sand beaches of **Almáciga** (bus #246) and **Benijo** (bus #246). For surfers, there is a good swell at Almáciga, even in the summer. The drive (or bus ride) is a sight in itself, winding along hairpin turns up and down the mountainous Anaga headlands. Those who want to tan where the sun don't shine should head to **Las Gaviotas** (bus #245), a nude beach. The artificial golden sand of **Las Tereistas** (bus #910) is an option closer to the city center. **Trekkers** should be sure to pick up a guide of hiking trails from the tourist office. With proper planning, one can get off a bus high up in the Anaga mountains and hike down to the black sand beaches, making for a great daytime activity.

In Santa Cruz, warm summer nights beckon Latin lovers. The young'uns stop to down cheap rum and cokes in the plaza, since drinks in the clubs run €4.80-6, while the older crowd heads to Av. Francisco la Roche/Av. Anaga's bar-discos. Around 4am, the drunken parade of stilettos marches to the sizzling **terrazas del verano,** running down Av. José Antonio Primo de Rivera's waterfront. If you're in the mood for flamenco, head to **Lerele,** Av. Francisco la Roche/Av. Anaga, 41, where there's live music (Th-Sa) starting at midnight. (☎637 17 57 25. Drinks €5. Wear shoes or leather sandals. No cover. Open W-Sa 8pm-3am.) A night at **El Primero,** one of three adjoining outdoor clubs, goes by in a blur of booze promotions, seductive platform dancers, and bursting sequined halters. (Mixed drinks €5. Open 11pm-dawn.) Posh **MoMA,** Pl. del Auditorio, takes its cues from the New York museum and plays commercial dance music. (☎922 23 20 11. Drinks €6. Come well dressed. Open W-Sa 10:30pm-3:30am.)

LOS CRISTIANOS AND PLAYA DE LAS AMÉRICAS

The white sand of Playa de las Américas is the first hint of what awaits visitors to Tenerife's main southern attractions: from the frat-boy nightlife to the fast food chains, just about everything here quivers with a flavor of modern kitsch. Brought in from the Sahara desert, the beach sand is a tasteful contrast to the gray of nearby Los Cristianos. Exploding into full-fledged resorts in the 1960s and 70s, these two popular island towns probably have more sub-par five-star hotels than natives. Paling in comparison to the beaches of Fuerteventura, Playa de las Américas and Los Cristianos still serve as useful bases for exploring other shores in the south, including Playa del Médano, one of Tenerife's best and a windsurfing mecca. Most importantly, ferries to La Gomera depart from Los Cristianos.

▮ TRANSPORTATION. Although Los Cristianos and Playa de las Américas are actually two separate towns and municipalities (accounting for the high taxi fare between the two, about €3-5), they are considered one by tourists and tourist offices alike. The pedestrian **Paseo Marítimo** connects Los Cristianos to its northern neighbor, Playa de las Américas. **Buses** run from stops on Av. Juan Carlos in Los Cristianos to: **Puerto de la Cruz** (#343; 4 per day 9am-5:45pm, €10.40); **Reina Sofía airport** (#487; every hr. 7:20am-9:20pm, €2.20); **Santa Cruz** (#110 and 111; every 30min. 6am-10pm, also 11:15pm, 12:30, 4:30am; €6.30-6.70); **El Teide** (#342; 9:15am, round-trip €7.10). In Playa de las Américas, buses stop along Av. Rafael Puig Lluvina. Buses #342, 416, 441, 442, 450, 467, 470-73, and 487 link Playa de las Américas and Los Cristianos, stopping frequently along the shore. Buses from Santa Cruz run directly from Los Cristianos along the outer highway to Costa Adeje's bus station. To get to Playa de las Américas, get off at Los Cristianos and take one of the above buses. **Ferries** leave from Los Cristianos, connecting Tenerife to the western islands. **Fred Olsen** (☎922 79 02 15) and **Trasmediterránea** (☎902 45 46 45, Los Cristianos 922 79 61 78) run ferries to **Santa Cruz, San Sebastián,** and **Valverde** (see **Inter-Island Transport,** p. 632). **Garajonay Express** (☎922 788 014) runs a passenger ferry to **San Sebastián de la Gomera,** with subsequent stops in the towns of **Playa de Santiago** and **Valle del Gran Rey.**

⚡ PRACTICAL INFORMATION. To reach the **tourist office** from Los Cristianos bus stop, walk downhill on Av. Juan Carlos and take a right onto Av. de Amsterdam; it's on your left in the Centro Cultural. (☎922 75 71 37. Open summer M-F 9am-3pm, Sa 9am-1pm; winter M-F 9am-3:30pm, Sa 9am-1pm.) Local services include: **banks,** near Pl. Carmen and Av. General Franco in Los Cristianos (most open M-F 9am-1pm and 4-7pm); **police,** in the Centro Cultural in Los Cristianos (☎922 75 71 33); **Internet access** at **Salon Oper Teide,** C. General Franco, a block from the plaza (€1 per 30min.; open daily 10am-midnight). The **post office** is on a pedestrian street off C. Sabadeños. From Pl. Carmen, go up Av. General Franco, turn left at the gas station onto C. Montaña Chica, and right onto C. Sabadeños. (☎922 79 10 56. Open M-F 8:30am-8:30pm, Sa 9:30am-1pm.) **Postal Code:** 38650.

⚡⚡ ACCOMMODATIONS AND FOOD. Playa de las Américas is full of resorts, but unless you want to splurge, stick to Av. General Franco or C. Paloma in Los Cristianos. The many *pensiones* are almost always full; be sure to call ahead. One option is **Pensión La Playa ❷,** C. Paloma, 9. From Av. General Franco, turn uphill onto C. Estocolmo; C. Paloma is the first left. The basic rooms have warm, orange walls and lush plant life. (☎922 79 22 64. Singles €15-20; doubles €24; triples €30.) Another option is **Pensión Corisa ❷,** C. Amalia Alayón, 18. From Pl. Carmen, bear right onto C. Amalia Alayón, parallel to Av. General Franco; across from the gas station. The neat furniture forges comfort out of small rooms, and the common baths are spotless. (☎922 79 07 92. Doubles €18-20. Monthly rental €300.) **Food** in both towns caters to international tastes and big budgets but is marginally better in Los Cristianos, away from the beachfront. For groceries, go to **Supermercado Carolina,** Av. General Franco, 8. (☎922 79 30 69. Open M-Sa 8am-8:30pm. V.)

⚡⚡ BEACHES AND NIGHTLIFE. Playa de las Américas makes a picture-perfect postcard, but **Playa Vistas** in Los Cristianos is more appealing if heavy crowds aren't your style. Either way, break out the bronzer. Kiosks and parked info-vans fortify the beaches, full of fliers for **water sports** and **scuba diving.** Booths on the far end of Los Cristianos beach offer daily **fishing** excursions for €12-18 per hour. **Water Sports & Charters** monopolizes the water sports centers on several beaches around Playa de las Américas (☎922 71 40 34; parasailing €25-30 for 10min.; booking office open daily 9am-7pm). If cetaceans float your boat, head to the stands by the port for whale-watching. The **Travelin' Lady** is a small, eco-conscious boat that heads out for 2hr. cruises (11am, 1, 3pm) with a stop for a quick swim. (☎609 429 887. €15.) Nightlife centers on Playa de las Américas, where a pastiche of vibrant lights, bikini contests, and beer (€2-5) awaits. A battery of two-story discos hawking 2-for-1 drink promotions to thirsty foreigners ensure that the city's nightlife stays charged and energetic. The **Verónicas** complex offers an imitation Ministry of Sound and your standard Shamrock Pub. Facing the sea at Playa de las Américas, walk to your right around the point along Av. Andrade Fumero. A late-night taxi to Los Cristianos will set you back €5-7. For a more local salsa flavor closer to Los Cristianos, try **Centro Comercial San Telmo** on Playa de Las Vistas.

PUERTO DE LA CRUZ

Its colorful streets filled with a wholesome energy, this port town (pop. 25,000) is one of the most enjoyable urban spots on the islands. Once a capital of the wine trade and an important 17th-century connection to the New World, Puerto de la Cruz draws an assorted mix of sailors and visitors; the steep streets are filled with African vendors, Spanish fishermen, tanned Europeans, and some unusually large lizards. Puerto de la Cruz serves as a base for exploring the Orotava region, as frequent buses depart from this western destination. There is also one bus for the Teide National Park every morning (9:15am); be sure to get there early.

⬛⁊ TRANSPORTATION AND PRACTICAL INFORMATION. From the main **bus station** on C. del Pozo, 1 (☎922 38 18 07), buses leave for: **La Orotava** (#101, 345, 350, 352, 353; 25min., every 30min.-1hr. 6:30am-1:10am, €1.10); **Playa de las Américas** (#340 and 343; 1hr., 4 per day 9am-5:45pm, €10.40); **Santa Cruz** (#101 makes stops, 102 and 103 are direct; 1-2hr.; every 30min. 6:15am-9:40pm, also 11pm, 12:45, 3:15, and 4:45am; €3.70); **El Teide** (#348; 1½hr., 9:15am, round-trip €7.90). Puerto de la Cruz expands from Playa San Telmo past **Plaza del Charco,** ultimately reaching the sands of Playa Jardín. To get to Pl. del Charco from the bus station, turn right onto C. del Pozo as you exit, continue onto C. Dr. Ingram, and turn left onto C. Blanco (10min.). The **tourist office** sits on Pl. Europa. From Pl. del Charco, head toward the port on C. Blanco, and turn right onto C. Santo Domingo; the office is on the left at the far end of the plaza. (☎922 38 60 00. Open July-Sept. M-F 9am-7pm, Sa 9am-noon; Oct.-June M-F 9am-8pm, Sa 9am-1pm.) The **police** are on Pl. Europa (☎922 37 84 48), and the **post office** is at C. del Pozo, 14, across from the bus station (☎922 38 58 05; open summer M-F 8:30am-2:30pm, Sa 9:30am-1pm; winter M-F 8:30am-8:30pm, Sa 9:30am-1pm.) **Postal Code:** 38400.

⬛◰ ACCOMMODATIONS AND FOOD. *Pensiones* are comfortable and plush in Puerto de la Cruz—reserve in advance. For bright, newly renovated rooms with balconies, comfy chairs, full baths, and great value, head to **Pensión Rosa Mary ❷,** C. San Felipe, 14. (☎922 38 32 53. Singles €20; doubles €30.) Another excellent option is **Pensión los Geranios ❷,** C. del Lomo, 14. From Pl. del Charco, turn left on C. San Felipe, right on C. Pérez Zamora, and left on C. del Lomo. A great location, comfortable rooms, and a friendly owner all add to this hostel's charm. (☎922 38 28 10. Doubles €22-24.) **Cafes** line Pl. del Charco. For something more refined, try ◰**La Rosa de Bari ❷,** C. del Lomo, 23, featuring fresh pasta and other Italian fare. (☎922 36 85 23. Entrees €6.50-12. Open Tu-Su 12:30-2:45pm and 6:30-11pm. AmEx/MC/V.) For cheap *canario* food in a flowered courtyard head to **Bodegon Cha 'Paula ❶,** C. Blanco, 19. From Pl. del Charco, head uphill on C. Blanco. Try the *conejo al ajillo* (rabbit in garlic sauce; €5) for a savory treat. (☎922 38 07 30. Open daily noon-midnight.)

◳◳ SIGHTS AND ENTERTAINMENT. The parade of flowers, tourists, bathing suits, and palm trees makes Puerto de la Cruz a sight in itself. **Loro Parque** houses the world's largest penguinarium, marine mammal shows, and great ape exhibits. (Free shuttle from Playa Martiánez. ☎922 37 38 41; www.loroparque.com. Open daily 9am-5pm. €22.) The small **Museo Arqueológico,** C. del Lomo, 9, features exhibits on the processes and ceremonies used by the prehistoric natives to produce pots, urns, jewelry, and decorations. (☎922 37 14 65. Open Tu-Sa 10am-1pm and 5-9pm, Su 10am-1pm. €1, students €0.50.) Far more interesting are the city's **botanical gardens,** C. Retama, 2, hosting a jungle of tropical plants from around the world. Be sure to check out the *Dama de Noche* (Lady of the Night), with its peach-colored lampshade flowers, and the thorny-barked Bottle Tree. The centerpiece is a huge, unbelievable ◰**ficus tree;** the upper branches drop down tendrils that become trunks with roots of their own. (To reach the gardens, climb from Playa de San Telmo onto C. la Hoya and continue onto C. Calzada de Martiánez until you reach Av. Marqués Villanueva del Prado. Follow the road past the Canary Centre; the gardens are on your left. Buses to La Orotava and Santa Cruz pass by as well. ☎/fax 922 38 35 72. Open daily Apr.-Sept. 9am-7pm; Oct.-Mar. 9am-6pm.

€3.) For beaches, **Playa Jardín** is preferable to the smaller **Playa Martiánez.** The amusing **Lago Martiánez** is a nature-based water park with saltwater pools and waterfalls designed by César Manrique. (Open daily 10am-7pm. €3.30.)

Party-primed locals and tourists mix in Puerto's nightlife. **Azúcar,** at the intersection of C. Dr. Ingram and C. Blanco, is a Cuban-themed bar and local favorite. (☎922 38 70 14. Drinks €3.40-4. Open Tu-Su 8:30-3:30am.) The cool younger crowd relaxes at **Limbo,** C. Blanco, 19, an artsy living-room/rooftop terrace with great music and cheap drinks. (☎922 92 41 25. Beer €1, mixed drinks €3. Open summer Su-W 9pm-3am, Th-Sa 9pm-4:30am; winter Su-W 5pm-3am, Th-Sa 5pm-4:30am.) Tourists are also drawn to the **Fiestas de Julio,** two weeks of live performances, festive meals, and much drinking, centered around July 16th's **Fiesta de la Virgen del Carmen,** in which an image of the saint is paraded through town and into the ocean.

▶ DAYTRIPS FROM PUERTO DE LA CRUZ

◼ PARQUE NACIONAL EL TEIDE

Bus #348 departs from the main station in Puerto de la Cruz at 9:15am and returns from the Parador de Turismo of El Teide at 4pm. From Playa de las Américas, bus #342 departs from Torviscas at 9:15am, passing by Los Cristianos at 9:30am, on its way to the park (1½hr., round-trip €7.10). The bus returns to Playa de las Américas and Los Cristianos at 3:15pm from El Portillo Visitor's Center, 3:40pm from the teleférico, and 4pm from the Parador de Turismo. Renting a car provides flexibility and allows exploration of the wildly different but equally beautiful views from the eastern (from the Puerto de la Cruz) and western (from Los Cristianos) access roads.

Towering 3718m over Tenerife, Spain's highest peak presides over a vast, unspoiled wilderness. El Teide itself forms the northern ridge of a much larger volcano that erupted millions of years ago; the remaining 17km wide crater, the **caldera,** only hints at the size of the explosion. El Teide shadows peaceful fields of the most vibrant wildflowers on earth. In 1798, during the last major eruption, lava seeped down the slopes of **Pico Viejo** (3102m), creating a stunning, 800m crater. **Las Cañadas,** comprised of collapsed craters, is another product of the lava. Though dormant, the area's volcanic activity has not yet ceased. Over 400 species inhabit the diverse terrain, but watch out for the **Lagarto Tizón,** a stone-camouflaged lizard, lurking in the park. If you notice an abundance of bees, it is because they have been introduced to the park to help pollinate the gorgeous **wildflowers;** be sure to look out for the purple **violetas del Teide,** a native species.

El Portillo Visitor's Center offers comprehensive park maps and a short but excellent video on the history and geology of El Teide. (☎922 35 60 00. Open daily 9am-4:15pm.) The bus will make a stop for those who want to climb Montaña Blanca before arriving at the **teleférico** (cable car), which climbs the final 1000m almost all the way to El Teide's peak. (Open daily 9am-5pm; €20.) For ecological and safety reasons, access to the crater is restricted. To get to the top, hikers must first get a permit (in person) from the **Oficinas del Parque,** C. Emilio Calzadilla, 5, in Santa Cruz. (☎922 29 01 29. Open M-F 9am-2pm.) The park gives out only 50 permits per day, so go at least two days before you plan to hike. The bus stops last at the **Parador de Turismo.** Next to the Parador is a brand new **visitor's center,** and although less helpful than the visitor's center at El Portillo, it offers plenty of maps, advice, and exhibits. (☎922 37 33 91. Open 9am-4:15pm.)

Call the national park information service in Santa Cruz (☎922 29 01 29 or 29 01 83; open M-F 9am-2pm) to reserve a spot on one of the **free guided hikes** that depart daily or to inquire about the most scenic routes for the day. Nine **unguided hiking trails** allow for independent pacing and meandering. The Parador occupies an idyllic setting next to the emblematic **Roques de García**

(2140m), rock chimneys and remnants of eruptions that face their creators, Mt. Teide and Pico Viejo. Though tourists crowd the lookout, you'll be alone on the trail (easy 2hr. hike), which has fantastic views of the bizarre formations. An enjoyable 3hr. hike circles the huge formations of **Guajara's** peak and leaves plenty of time to spare for bus-riders. Hikes to El Teide's peak require strong legs and an early start to complete in a day, though it is possible. Be sure to get your permit first. Alternatively, hikers spend the night at **Refugio Altavista ❶**, past Montaña Blanca, and hike the last hour in the morning to catch the sunrise. The *refugio* has cooking facilities, but bring your own food and water. To reserve a spot, contact the office in Santa Cruz. (☎901 50 19 01. Open Mar.-Oct. M-F 9am-2pm, weather permitting. €12, students €3.)

LA OROTAVA

Buses #101, 350, and 353 run from Puerto de la Cruz's main bus station (30min., every 30min.-1hr. 6:30am-1:25am, €1.20).

Named for the lush valley that spreads out below, the small town of La Orotava warrants a daytrip from Puerto de la Cruz. It was once the richest and largest of Tenerife's nine Guanche fiefdoms and finally fell to the conquistadors in 1496, 94 years after they first landed in the archipelago. In the 17th and 18th centuries, Spanish, Italian, and Flemish nobility resided here, leaving elegant squares, streets, and churches renowned for their facades. If you intend to visit the sights, plan for a weekday jaunt—most establishments here are closed on weekends.

The tourist office map lists over 15 sights; though it would take a full day to see them all, the following walking tour should take only two hours. From the **bus station,** head uphill on C. Alfonso Trujillo, turn right onto Av. Emilio Luque Moreno, which becomes Av. José Antonio and then Carrera del Escultor Estévez. Continue past Pl. de la Constitución to the **tourist office,** C. Carrera del Escultor Estévez, 2. (☎922 32 30 41. Open M-F 8:30am-6pm.) From the tourist office, turn left down C. Tomás Zerolo to find **Iglesia de Santo Domingo,** whose chapel houses several notable paintings. Next door is the **Museo Iberoamericano de Artesanía,** which houses handicrafts of Spain and Latin America. Especially interesting are contrasting ceramics from Iberia and festival masks from the Americas. (C. Tomás Zerolo, 34. ☎922 32 33 76. Open M-F 9am-6pm, Sa 9am-2pm. €2.10.) Next, **Iglesia de la Concepción,** off C. Cologan, is a National Artistic Monument and perhaps the Canaries' most graceful Baroque building. Rebuilt in the late 18th century after earthquakes ravaged it, the church has a marble dome over the altar. On a sunny day, the red and blue stained glass gives the place a strange violet glow. Especially impressive is Angelo Olivari's delicate rendition of the Immaculate Conception. Check out the church's collection of jewels from the Americas. (Open daily 11am-1pm and 5-7pm. Free.) From the church, go uphill on C. Tomás Pérez and right on Carrera del Escultor Estévez to the neoclassical **Palacio Municipal** and the **Plaza del Ayuntamiento.** The cobblestones in the plaza are the result of regal egotism—Alfonso XIII ordered the streets paved before he visited. (Open 8:30am-3pm. Free.) Just up C. Tomás Pérez, the sensory explosion of **Hijuela del Botánico,** behind iron gates, offers celestial walkways through displays of tropical flora and a fine specimen of the **drago tree,** a long-living species considered sacred by the Guanche people. (Open M-F 9am-2pm. Free.) Exiting the Hijuela, cross the street into the **Jardines de la Quinta Roja,** more formal terraced gardens with fountains and views of the sea. (Open M-F 9am-6pm. Free.) Going downhill, exit the gardens on C. San Agustín, turn right, and head to the **Iglesia de San Agustín,** a 17th-century church with a fine coffered wood *mudéjar* ceiling. (Open daily 4-7pm, Su also for mass 10:30am-1pm. Free.) From there, you can complete the circuit to the **tourist office** by walking left down Carrera de Escultor Estévez.

FUERTEVENTURA

Named Fuerteventura after the strong winds that whip along its western coast, the second-largest island in the archipelago is a varied physical and cultural landscape. The island is home in the south to the Canaries' best stretch of beach and in the east to the Canaries' most abysmal city. Beyond coastal towns, Fuerteventura provides undeveloped, mountainous serenity. Car rental is a must for those venturing to Fuerteventura on their own. For more information, see **Intra-Island Transport,** p. 632.

PUERTO DEL ROSARIO

Until 1957, Fuerteventura's whitewashed capital was known as Puerto de Cabras (Goats' Harbor). The goats knew what was good for them when they migrated out of the city, which has since become the armpit of the Canaries. Unless you long for a depressing vista of dilapidated, crumbling cement buildings, use Puerto del Rosario (pop. 21,000) only as a transportation hub and skip town for the south.

TRANSPORTATION. **Trasmediterránea** (☎928 85 24 08) and **Naviera Armas** (☎902 456 500) run ferries to and from Las Palmas; see **Inter-Island Transport,** p. 632. **Tiadhe buses** (☎928 85 21 66) run to: the **airport** (#3 Caleta de Fuste bus; 20min.; every 30min. 6:30am-6pm, every hr. 7-11pm; €2); **Corralejo** (#6; 45min.; every 30min. 7am-6:30pm, every hr. 7-11pm; €2.50); **El Cotillo** (#7; 40min., 3 per day 10am-7pm, €2.50); **Morro Jaī.e** (#1; 2hr.; M-Sa 10 per day 7am-8:30pm, Su 4 per day 6:30am-6pm; €7).

ORIENTATION AND PRACTICAL INFORMATION. **Calle León y Castillo,** the main thoroughfare of Puerto del Rosario, runs downhill to the port and ferry station. **Avenida Primero de Mayo,** perpendicular to C. León y Castillo and parallel to the water, is the town's commercial drag. The **tourist office,** Av. de la Constitución, 5, is down the street from the bus station and two blocks from Av. Primero de Mayo. (☎928 53 08 44. Open July-Sept. M-F 8am-2pm; Oct.-June 8am-3pm.) In an emergency, call the **Guardia Civil,** C. 23 de Mayo, 16 (☎928 85 11 00). A **hospital** (☎928 86 20 00) is on Ctra. Aeropuerto, and a **pharmacy** at Av. Primero de Mayo, 51. (☎928 53 17 21. Open M-F 8:30am-1pm and 5-8pm.) **Free Internet** is available at the **Consejera de Educación y Juventud,** C. Virgen del Rosario, 13. (Open M-F 9am-2pm.) The **post office** is at Av. 23 de Mayo, 76. (☎928 85 04 12. Open M-F 8:30am-8:30pm, Sa 9:30am-1pm.) **Postal Code:** 35600.

ACCOMMODATIONS AND FOOD. You may find yourself stuck in Puerto del Rosario for a night until accommodations in more scenic towns open up. Most budget accommodations are at the end of C. León y Castillo and its continuation past the port, C. Almirante Lallermand. **Hostal Tamasite ❷,** C. León y Castillo, 9, has clean rooms on the waterfront. All have TV, phone, and bath with shower. (☎928 85 02 80. Singles €27; doubles €36.) Food in Puerto del Rosario is equally basic; *cafeterías* are scattered along Av. Primero de Mayo and C. León y Castillo. A good one is **Tanguaro V ❶,** Pl. España, 7. From C. León y Castilla, turn right onto C. Fernández Casteñeyra; there's a nice view and great *churros*. (Sandwiches €1.50-2.50. Burgers €2. Combo plates €5.50-9. Open daily 7am-11pm.)

DAYTRIP FROM PUERTO DEL ROSARIO

EL COTILLO

From Puerto del Rosario, follow the FV10 all the way to the coast, bearing left before La Olivia. El Cotillo is at km 37. Bus #7 runs to Puerto del Rosario (40min., 3 per day 6:45am-5pm, €2.50). Bus #8 runs to Corralejo (30min., every 2hr. 8am-7pm, €2.50).

On the northwest coast of Fuerteventura, El Cotillo is a breath of fresh air for those looking to escape the touristy kitsch that plagues some of the towns on the island. Still uncorrupted, this tiny fishing village has recently become a surfers haven for the waves just south of town from September to April. The town's center is the old harbor, a short walk downhill from the bus stop. If you've come to play, head to **Onit,** the local surf shop run by a kindly English couple who are as happy to rent you a board and wetsuit (€16) as an apartment. The shop also offers **Internet** for €2 per hr. (☎928 538 676; www.onit-surf.com, apartment info www.fuerteproperty.co.uk. Open M-Sa 10:30am-1:30pm and 5-8pm.) El Cotillo makes a great daytrip or surfing and windsurfing excursion, but if you plan on staying longer head for ▨**La Graviota ❷,** C. La Graviota, perched on a cliff above the old harbor. All the rooms are carefully decorated and creatively laid out, with kitchens and common space. There are only seven suites, so book in advance. (☎/fax 938 53 85 67. Doubles €33-45. Extra bed €10.) Those looking for a more conventional hotel experience should try **Hotel María Hierro ❸,** C. María Hierro, 1, by the main bus stop, for good, standard rooms, some with views and all with bath, TV, phone, A/C, breakfast, and use of a rooftop pool. (☎928 538 598; http://usarios.lycos.es/fuertehotels. Singles €28; doubles €42. Extra bed €9.50.) El Cotillo has numerous restaurants serving fresh local seafood. Sit on the patio overlooking the old harbor and order a *vieja a la plancha* with *papas arrugadas* at **Restaurante Playa ❸,** Muelle Viejo de Cotillo. Filling seafood plates are €12-15. (☎928 53 86 39. Open daily 1-5:30pm.) Just above is **El Veril ❸,** a classy (but not stuffy) spot whose owner cooks his own creative variations on Spanish and Canarian cuisine. The place also serves as a gallery for local artists. The rooftop **grill ❷** is less expensive and more casual. (☎928 53 87 80. Main courses €11-15, local kid €10.50. Open Tu-Su noon-11pm.)

CORRALEJO

Corralejo's center is a zoo of northern European families, car rental shops, and restaurants. To the south, however, sunbathers and water sport enthusiasts will appreciate the protected sand dunes and crystal ocean. Hourly ferries to Playa Blanca in Lanzarote make Corralejo an easy stop for island hoppers.

⎘ TRANSPORTATION. Fred Olsen and Naviera Armas run daily **ferries** to **Playa Blanca, Lanzarote** (see **Inter-Island Transport,** p. 632). To reach the center from the **port,** take C. General García Escámez and turn left onto C. la Milagrosa, then turn left to reach **Avenida General Franco** (10min.). Tiadhe runs **buses** from the **station** on Av. Juan Carlos I (☎928 85 21 66), off C. Lepanto, to **El Cotillo** (#8; 35 min., 7 per day 9am-10pm, €2.30) and **Puerto del Rosario** (#6; 45min., every 30min. 7am-10pm, €2.40). For a **taxi,** call ☎928 86 61 08 or hail one by Supermercado Los Corales.

⑦ ORIENTATION AND PRACTICAL INFORMATION. All activity extends along **Avenida General Franco,** where tourists walk from the southern sand dunes to their hotels in the north, by the port. The **tourist office** is in Pl. Pública, off the end of Av. General Franco nearest the port. (☎928 86 62 35. Open summer M-F 8am-2pm.) There is also a smaller one in the main building at the port. Local services include: **police,** Po. Atlántico (☎928 86 61 07), near the intersection with Av. General Franco; **pharmacy,** Av. General Franco, 46 (☎928 86 60 20; open M-F 9am-1:30pm and 5-9pm); **Internet access** at **Coolers Internet and Wine Bar,** C. la Milagrosa, 31, behind the tourist office (☎928 86 63 35; €2 per hr.; open M-Tu and Th-Sa 10am-10pm, Su 10am-2pm and 7-10pm); and the **post office,** C. Isaac Peral (☎928 53 50 55; open M-F 8:30am-2:30pm, Sa 9:30am-1pm). **Postal Code:** 35660.

⌐⌐ ACCOMMODATIONS AND FOOD. Apartments and hotels line the beach, but budget accommodations are rare. The English-speaking crew at **Hostal Manhattan ❷,** C. Gravina, 24, a left off Av. General Franco when heading toward the port, offers plain, cool rooms, all with bath. (☎928 86 66 43. Singles €22; doubles €30; triples €42; quads €50. MC/V.) For modern rooms with stone floors, private bath, and access to a tiny rooftop pool, try **La Posada Hotel ❹,** Pl. María Figueroa, 1. (☎928 86 73 44; www.hotellaposada.com. Breakfast included. July-Aug. singles €41; doubles €47; triples €53. Sept.-June €36/€41/€44.) Food is nothing special, catering almost exclusively to tourists. Restaurants line Av. General Franco; breakfast deals abound. For standard supplies, try **Supermercado Los Corales,** Av. General Franco, 40. (☎928 86 70 43. Open M-Sa 9am-9:30pm, Su 2-9pm.)

⌐⌐ ENTERTAINMENT AND BEACHES. The *Fiestas del Carmen*, beginning July 16 and lasting two weeks, make for a lively visit. During the festival, such decidedly unholy events as volleyball competitions and outdoor dances help celebrate the town's patron saint before she is led on a watery parade through the port. Nightlife in Corralejo is a parade of tipsy tourists and leering locals. Bars are generally small and loud; most of them are found along Av. General Franco and in the connecting shopping centers. The **Caleta Dorada Complex** and **Centro Commercial Atlántico** are filled with various second-rate bars and pubs. There is one stand-out exception; going on its 12th year, **Oink!,** C. Commercial Atlántico, bottom floor, ocean side, is a lively surf bar with great music and the perfect place to get friendly with expat Brits and pick up tips for finding good waves. Beer runs €2.80 and mixed drinks €3.10-5.70, but to make friends with Jay (the owner), order a shot of Jägermeister for €2. (oink_bar@hotmail.com. Open daily 8pm-2:30am.)

The main attraction in Corralejo is the **Parque Natural de Corralejo y Lobos,** which contains protected, Sahara-like sand dunes. For those without cars, the dunes are accessible via the #6 bus bound for Puerta Rosario (every 30min. 7am-11pm, €.90). Adventure companies compete for business along Av. General Franco, catering to all athletic tastes and abilities. **Dive Centro Corralejo,** C. Nuestra Señora del Pino, 36 (☎928 53 59 06), offers dive trips, lessons, and equipment rental. **Catamaran Celia Cruz** rigs daily trips on glass-bottomed catamarans. (☎639 14 00 14. €10-12 per person; more expensive cruise includes fish-feeding and a drink.) **Ventura Surf,** in the Apartamentos Hoplaco complex on Av. General Franco, rents windsurfing equipment (€40 per day) and offers a 3hr. (€75) beginner's course and an 8hr. (€126) course for extra assistance. (☎928 86 62 95. Open daily 10am-6pm.) **Matador Surf School** offers lessons in units of three (€120), five (€195) and ten days (€390) at different levels of experience. Certified instructors take students to remote beaches in search of the right waves. Lesson includes board, wetsuit, and insurance. (☎/fax 928 86 73 07; www.matadorsurfschool.com. Groups meet at C. Palangre, 1; from the roundabout near the clock tower on Av. Gen. Franco, turn uphill, then right, then left. Students should book a day in advance via Internet or at the office. (Open M-Sa 10am-noon and 6-8pm.)

MORRO JABLE

Expanding 30km across the south of Fuerteventura, the Península de Jandía and its beaches Playa de Sotavento and Playa de Barlovento are the island's biggest draws. The heavenly white sands and turquoise waters that frame the southern coast have transformed the former fishing village of Morro Jable into a mecca of accommodations, food, and transport. The strip of generic restaurants and shops along the beach are a tourist zoo, but the town itself remains relatively pleasant.

⊑ TRANSPORTATION. There is no designated bus station in town. **Tiadhe** buses (☎928 85 21 66) stop at the Centro Comercial de Jandía before terminating on C. Gambuesas in Morro Jable. **Buses** run to **Costa Calma** (#5; 1hr., 11 per day 9:30am-11pm, €2) and **Puerto del Rosario** (#1; 2hr., 8 per day 6am-10pm, €7.20; #10 direct; 1¼hr., 3 per day 6am-3:45pm, €7.20). **Taxis** (☎928 54 12 57) gather at the port. A ride to one of the two main *playas* of Jandía costs €3. **Orlando,** in Apartamentos El Matorral, rents 4WD vehicles for navigating the peninsula's rough dunes. (☎928 54 04 09. 21+. From €35 per day. AmEx/V.)

⊠ ORIENTATION AND PRACTICAL INFORMATION. Morro Jable hugs the beach, most notably the **Playa de la Cebada** and the **Playa del Matorral. Avenida Jandía,** which becomes **Avenida del Saladar,** connects the east and west sides of the city center. Most hotels and restaurants line these two streets; the town's roads inevitably lead to the beach. The **tourist office,** Av. del Saladar, is in the Centro de Comercial de Jandía, local 88. (☎928 54 07 76; www.playasdejandia.com. Open summer M-F 8am-2pm; winter 8am-3pm.) Local services include: **police,** C. Hibisco, 1 (☎928 54 10 22); **pharmacy,** C. Senador Velázquez Cabrera, 28 (☎928 54 10 12; open M-F 9am-1pm and 5-7pm, Sa 9am-1pm); the **Centro Médico Jandía,** at the Jandía Beach Center, Urb. Solana (☎928 54 04 20; open 24hr.); **Internet access** at **Videoclub Canal 15,** C. del Carmen, 41, one street away from C. Maxorata. (☎928 16 60 30. €1 per 30min. Open M-Sa 10am-10pm.) The **post office** is on the corner of C. Buenavista and C. Gambuesas. (☎928 54 03 73. Open M-F 8:30am-2:30pm, Sa 9:30am-1pm.) **Postal Code:** 35625.

⊓⊡ ACCOMMODATIONS AND FOOD. Budget accommodations cluster around the town center, most notably along C. Maxorata and C. Senador Velázquez Cabrera, two parallel streets that lead to the sea. Visitors should not be alarmed by the occasional bugs that take up residence; they also like to vacation in Morro Jable. **Hostal Omahy ❷,** C. Maxorata, 47, has small, clean rooms a short walk from the beach. (☎928 54 12 54. Call ahead for reservations. Doubles with bath €25.) **Apartamentos Altavista ❸,** C. Abubilla, 8, rents out fully furnished, newly decorated suites, with access to a very nice terrace. The prices are not bad, considering each apartment has a kitchen and common space. The same owners are renovating Hostal Maxorata, a local, inexpensive lodging; inquire to see if the work is complete. (☎/fax 928 54 91 64, mobile 686 98 60 51. 1 person €36; 2 people €42; 3 €47; 4 €50.) Restaurants in the area are tailored to the tourist crowds; Italian bistros, dime-a-dozen seafood joints, and German *konfiterias* line the beach. **Piccola Italia ❶,** toward the beach from Videoclub Canal 15 on C. del Carmen, serves scrumptious and authentic pizzas to a mostly local crowd. (☎928 54 12 58. Pizza €4.25-7. Open M-W and F-Su 1-4pm and 7pm-midnight. MC/V.) For good seafood by the shore, try Morro Jable's best, near the port. **Avenida del Mar ❷,** Av. del Mar, 1, at the end of the string of restaurants, offers fresh fish (€10.90) served on a fabulous patio. (☎928 54 13 12. Open daily 10am-11pm.)

◪⊔ BEACHES AND ENTERTAINMENT. The main attractions on the peninsula and in Morro Jable are fierce tanning and water sports in the welcoming turquoise ocean. Morro Jable's ▨**beaches** are lined with bodies in various states of undress from early morning to late night. The most pristine ones on the peninsula are those in the south along Playa de Sotavento, followed by those in Playa de Barlovento and Playa del Matorral (close to the city center). The beaches are ideal for reflective walks and adventurous drives (in places where cars are allowed on the beach). Blessed with the islands' calmest waters and lushest sea life, Morro Jable offers excellent opportunities to practice **water sports.** Stiff breezes off the peninsula's southern tip justify the innumerable **windsurfing** and **kitesurfing** schools that set up camp on the beach (the coast has hosted the World Championships for Professional Windsurfing the last two weeks of July every year since 1985). **Barakuda Club,** Av. del Saladar, offers **scuba diving** and equipment rental. (☎928 54 14 18. Dives Su-F 9am and 2pm. €32 per dive; €26 with your own equipment. €160 for 12hr. of basic instruction. Good package deals available. Open daily 8:30am-6pm.) Sparse **nightlife** revolves around the resorts along Av. del Saladar. Start the night with drinks in one of the many bars of the **Centro Comercial de Jandía** and continue in the city's two *discotecas*, **La Cara Disco** and **Stella Discoteque,** two blocks away.

LANZAROTE

Declared a World Biosphere Reserve by UNESCO in 1993, Lanzarote is both a natural and cultural treasure. Volcanic activity from nearly 300 years ago has left the earth barren and dry, with an unusual landscape resembling the surface of the moon. Driving through the island can best be described as inspirational, most notably en route to the unique Parque National de Timanfaya. Even better, though, is hiking up the sides of long-dead volcanoes, and swimming on empty, perfect beaches. The local government and island native César Manrique made remarkable efforts to develop a tourism industry that complements, rather than detracts from, the island's natural beauty. That said, the south of the island is built-up with tourist traps; head north and west for local culture and less-crowded shores. When visiting, do not rely on public transportation—as on Fuerteventura, the vast majority of the islands' sights can be accessed only by car. Many people hitchhike, but *Let's Go* does not recommend it. Taxis are everywhere and expensive; a ride from Arrecife to Playa Blanca runs about €30. The best choice is to rent a car, pick up an island map at any tourist office, and start exploring.

PUERTO DEL CARMEN

Primarily British tourists flock to Puerto del Carmen, packaged and lobster-tied by one of many tour companies. As Lanzarote's biggest tourist destination, the area provides typical beach fare and decent sunbathing spots. **Avenida de las Playas** squeezes in endless restaurants, bars, and bazaars, many of which are Disney-themed. Offshore reefs offer some of the islands' best **scuba diving.** For more information try **Lanzarote Dive Service,** Av. de las Playas, 35 (☎928 51 08 02; www.lanzarote-

SURF'S UP

There may be no greater physical sensation than surfing down the face of your very own wave. Surfing isn't just for the pros; if you like the ocean, are in decent shape, and have enough balance to ride a bike, you can probably stand up after a couple of days in the water. The Islas Canarias have fantastic surf breaks, and, if toasting yourself in the sun feels slow, you should rent a board and hit the waves.

In the summer months, waves are generally small and perfect for beginners. Those who have mastered the sport and the lingo should come in the fall and winter, when the *olas* really begin to curl. Surf shops here are great resources and can provide clients with housing, cars, boards, and advice on where to go.

Lanzarote has numerous breaks. La Caleta de Famara in the northwest part of the island is a small surf town with a great beach. Once there, head to **Surf San Juan** (C. Arrufo, 5; ☎ 928 52 85 48) and make friends with the jolly owner, Juan. **Famara Surf** (☎928 52 86 76), down the street, offers similar services, but without Juan. A little farther west is the town of La Santa, home to the world-famous *Derecha de la Santa,* a great ride for experts. More breaks can be found on Isla Graciosa, off the northern coast of the island. Be sure to be extra courteous if you are going to a local spot; wait your turn and don't ever cut anyone off.

dive.com). The town's saving grace is ⬛**Pension Magec,** C. Hierro, 11, in the center of the old town. Take a short walk down C. Juan Carlos from the bus stop, past the Biosfera shopping plaza; turn left onto C. Bajamar and right onto C. Hierro. The friendly owner, bright rooms (with shared bath), ocean views, and convenience to the bus stop make it a good base for those unfortunate souls without cars. (☎928 51 51 20; fax 52 38 74. Singles €21; doubles €24, with shower €30.)

Bus #2 runs between Arrecife and Puerto del Carmen, stopping along Av. de las Playas (40min.; M-F every 20min. 6:20am-11:20pm, Sa-Su every 30min. 6:20am-11:20pm; €1.40). **Fred Olsen** (☎902 10 01 07) and **Naviera Armas** (☎902 45 65 00, in Corralejo 928 867 080) also run buses to Playa Blanca to meet their ferry departures. The **tourist office** is at Av. de las Playas near the beach. (☎928 51 33 51; fax 51 56 15. Open M-F July-Aug. 10am-4pm; Sept.-June 10am-5pm.) To explore the island to its fullest, rent a car—there are good deals along Av. de las Playas. **Lanzauto,** Av. de las Playas, 19, rents from €30 per day (€20 per day for a week) with insurance and unlimited mileage. (☎928 51 06 18. 21+. Open daily 8:30am-1pm and 5-8pm.)

⬛PARQUE NACIONAL DE TIMANFAYA

Known as the **Montañas del Fuego** (Fire Mountains), the barren landscape of Lanzarote's national park is filled with evidence of the six-year explosion that began in 1730. Resembling the surface of the moon, copper *hornitos* (mud-volcanos) and blackened folds of solidified lava carve their way into the loose soil; only lichen seem to survive in the scorching ground. The winding roads leading to the national park entrance provide countless photographic opportunities. Note that no public transportation runs to the park; you need your own car. The park itself is explored through a trilingual 40min. **bus tour** (sit on the right for better views). The roller coaster tour is made even more entertaining by a melodramatic soundtrack culminating in the theme from *2001: A Space Odyssey.* Buses leave from the main parking lot in front of El Diablo Restaurant. The magic tricks of **Islote de Hilario's** geothermal heat are the tour's highlight. Legend has it that the hermit Hilario, who lived here with his lone camel, planted a fig tree whose fruit was consumed by the underground fires; today, park employees demonstrate the effects of the 600°C temperatures below the earth, unleashing jets of steam from the ground and setting brush on fire. (☎928 84 00 57. Park open daily 9am-5:45pm; last bus leaves at 5pm, last car enters park at 4:20pm. €8.) The **El Diablo** ❹ restaurant that now occupies the *islote* was designed by Manrique and constructed, using only stone, metal, and glass, to withstand the high temperatures. Volcanic heat seeping from the earth powers the kitchen's grill (meat entrees €9-20). The panoramic view from the dining room is the best on the island, extending from the arid mountains to the azure sea. (☎928 84 00 56. Open daily noon-3:30pm, bar 9am-4:45pm.)

Self-exploration of the national park is prohibited, but free **walking tours** can be arranged through the Spanish National Park State Network. The 3.5km Termesana trail in English or Spanish gives tourists a rare opportunity to explore the natural volcanic beauty on foot. Walking tours (M, W, F 10am) must be arranged at least two weeks ahead of time with the **visitor's center** in Mancha Blanca, where they begin. (5min. from park main entrance. Take the road from Yaiza to Tinajo, km 11.5. ☎/fax 928 84 08 39; www.mma.es. Reservations via phone or email. Open daily 9am-5pm.) Half-hour tours by **camel** are run separately but do nothing more than go up a hill near the southern park entrance for a view (2 adults and 1 child per camel; €10 per camel). The visitor's center provides detailed directions in English for exploring two spectacular and accessible craters outside the national park. The ⬛**Caldera de Montaña** is awesome and gorgeous.

Climb it in the morning so you don't melt. They also host a challenging guided walk, the *Ruta del Litoral*, along the coast of the park, which lasts roughly 6hr. Dates change monthly; contact the visitor's center well in advance. The more adventurous can do the walk on their own, as the coastline is public. To get to the trail, go to the town of Tinajo. Opposite the supermarket is a paved road. Follow the road, and do not bear off to the right. The pavement becomes a track, which goes to a parking area near the sea. The trail follows the coast south and is 5hr. one way. Wear boots, but don't wear yourself out. About 7km away, in the town of Tiagua, is Lanzarote's quaintest and coolest lodging, ▨**La Casa Rural Molina ❷**. Turn into the driveway directly next to the km 13 sign off the highway in Tiagua. Lounge around the country house, sip fresh juice, and peruse the *casa*'s library of guidebooks and novels in a quiet and secluded setting. The gay-friendly Molina is an ideal base for exploring the entire island, and is also home to an artsy *tetería* (tea house) that serves crepes, teas, and salads. Have a cool drink and conversation at the bar. The delicious buffet-style breakfast is free. (☎928 52 92 66; www.casalamolina.com. Reservations recommended. Singles €38; doubles €48, with bath €63. *Tetería* open Su and Th-Sa 6-11pm.) Head even farther south toward Mozaga to dine at Lanzarote's most delicious restaurant, ▨**Monumento al Campesino Restaurante ❷**, adjacent to the monument itself. Feast on *papas arrugadas* drowned in homemade Canarian sauces. Diners can choose to eat outdoors or in a subterranean chamber designed by Manrique. (☎928 52 01 36. Tapas and entrees €5-18. Open daily 10am-6pm.)

LA ISLA GRACIOSA

If you're looking to escape the touristy south, head all the way up to La Isla Graciosa (pop. 650), a small island spread below the dramatic northern cliffs. The isolated beaches and barren volcanic landscapes are worth a day of exploring. Free **camping** is allowed on Playa Francesa; facing the town from the harbor, walk left along the coast, around the point. The more adventurous can **rent bikes** from **La Graciosa Bike** (☎928 84 21 38; €8) or **Natural Bike** (☎928 84 21 42; €7) within the town itself and head for ▨**Playa de las Conchas,** a perfect white-sand paradise, with crystal clear water and hardly any visitors. Try to get a bike with shocks, as the roads are washboarded. Battered old Land Rovers also ferry visitors from town to the beach (round-trip €20 per person). Be sure to inquire about the vagaries and dangers of each new spot, as the rocky bottom is unforgiving. Double-check ferry schedules if you don't plan on staying, or call well in advance for space at **Pension Girasol Playa,** Av. Virgen del Mar, which has clean, bright rooms in the center of town. (☎928 84 21 18. Doubles €17, with balcony €20.) La Isla Graciosa goes wild during **La Fiesta del Carmen** (July 14-19), when hundreds of young people storm the island to drink and dance until the morning. Accommodations are booked months in advance. (**Líneas Romero** runs daily ferries between Orzola and La Isla Graciosa. ☎928 84 20 70. From Orzola: July-Sept. 4 per day 10am-6:30pm; Oct.-June 3 per day 10am-5pm. From La Isla Graciosa: July-Sept. 4 per day 8am-6pm; Oct.-June 3 per day 8am-4pm. Round-trip €13.)

PLAYA BLANCA

Island-hoppers will invariably end up at Playa Blanca, a beach town and transportation hub at the southern tip of Lanzarote. Budget accommodations are limited in the area. If you need a place to stay, try **Apartamentos Gutiérrez ❹**, Pl. Nuestra Señora del Carmen, 8. (☎928 51 70 89. Doubles €36; triples €48; quads €50.) A **tourist office** is located in the port. (☎928 51 90 18. Open M-F 9am-1:30pm.) Playa Blanca is great for **scuba diving;** contact **Centro de Buceo "Toninas"** for classes and activities. (☎928 51 73 00; www.arrakis.es/~divingtoninas. Open daily 10am-6pm.)

OTHER PLACES OF INTEREST

Most of Lanzarote is best explored by taking daytrips from whatever town you're staying in, as sights are often located far from accommodations. Two themes run through the possibilities: the island's natural beauty, and the ways in which artist César Manrique worked with the government to embellish that beauty and preserve it from the destructive potential of too much tourism. Born in Arrecife, Manrique (1919-1992), who took part in the new-wave abstract art movement in Spain, is a legendary figure throughout the Islas Canarias. Dreaming of a sustainable tourism for his native island, however, Manrique spent much of his energy during the 1950s and the rest of his life working to preserve Lanzarote's natural culture, architecture, and landscape while developing a tourism industry to aid the local economy. His art exists in harmony with its surroundings; buildings rise organically from lava bubbles, and his kinetic *"juguetes de viento"* (wind toys) spin playfully in the breeze. Today, visitors can see and experience the fruits of Manrique's labor. The **Centros de Arte, Cultura y Turismo** are all influenced by Manrique, most created by the artist himself. Within the Parque Nacional de Timanfaya, take note of Manrique's uniquely designed **El Diablo** restaurant (p. 654).

■ **FUNDACIÓN CÉSAR MANRIQUE.** This fabulous two-story house, once home to the famous artist, was constructed over five large volcanic bubbles and lava caves in the late 1960s, resulting in a series of unprecedented subterranean chambers and rooms connected by volcanic passageways. Frozen lava flows seep through the windows of the upstairs gallery, which hosts rotating contemporary art exhibitions. *(6km north of Arrecife. Take the highway to Tahiche and turn onto Taro de Tahiche, off C. San Bartolomé. Alternatively, from Arrecife take bus #7 to Teguise and ask to be let off at the Fundación. A taxi from Arrecife costs approximately €5.50. ☎928 84 31 38. Open July-Oct. daily 10am-7pm; Nov.-June M-Sa 10am-6pm, Su 10am-3pm. €7.)*

■ **MUSEO INTERNACIONAL DE ARTE CONTEMPORÁNEO.** The original building, an 18th-century fortress, was built by Carlos III to defend the island from pirate attacks. Its simple stonework epitomizes César Manrique's revitalization of the island's history and architecture. Exhibits (mostly photography) rotate frequently, but geometric and abstract works (including some by Manrique himself) form part of the permanent collection, affixed to the fort and hanging into the restaurant below. *(Located to the west of Arrecife, off Av. Naos. A 40min. walk; taxis from Arrecife cost €2.60 and are safer than walking after dark. ☎928 81 23 21. Open daily 11am-9pm. Free.)*

JAMEOS DEL AGUA. Built into the subterranean tubes formed by volcanic activity 3000-4500 years ago, the Jameos del Agua constitute a natural and architectural marvel. In the luminous underground lake, keep an eye out for tiny blind crabs—you'll see them before they see you. Jameos del Agua is home to the internationally renowned **Casa de los Volcanes**, dedicated to the study of volcanoes. An auditorium built into the grotto holds the **Festival de Música Visual de Lanzarote** every October. At night, the restaurant fills with well-dressed patrons. *(On the northeastern coast 4km north of Arrieta. ☎928 84 80 20. Open M and W-Th 10am-6:30pm; folk music performances Tu and F-Sa 6:30pm-2am. €8 during the day, €9 at night.)*

LA CUEVA DE LOS VERDES. This 6km lava tube was formed when the nearby Corona volcano erupted 3000-4500 years ago. As the lava flowed to the sea, the outer shell cooled in the air, and the inner lava spilled into the ocean, leaving a fantastic cave for amateur spelunkers to tour. The human additions to La Cueva were designed in 1964 by Jesús Soto, though the subterranean chambers were used much earlier by Canarians as refuge from pirate attacks in the 17th century. The caves' colorings and textures are stunning, ranging from smooth basalt to porous red oxide-rich stone. A natural auditorium similar to that of Jameos del Agua is another site of the October music festival. The end of the mandatory 50min. tour includes a clever surprise. *(3km inland from Jameos del Agua in the northeast. ☎928 84 84 84. Open daily 10am-6pm, last entrance 5pm. €8.)*

MIRADOR DEL RÍO. Manrique successfully designed the Mirador del Río to blend into its surroundings; the building remains hidden from view almost until you've reached it. The breathtaking view from over 1400 ft. makes you feel as though you are hovering over La Isla Graciosa. The rest of the Chingo archipelago rise up from the sea like great beasts. Take note of Manrique's hanging metal sculptures, designed to absorb sound within the Mirador. *(At the northern tip of the island, 7km north of Máguez. ☎928 52 65 51. Bar-cafe and Mirador open daily 10am-6pm; last entrance 5pm. €4.70.)* For an equally good (free) view, go past the turnoff for the Mirador, continue west past the tiny town of Ye, turn off the road at the **Vistilla de Ye** sign, and drive down the windy track to the cliff's edge. A 300m walk east along the cliff will reward the intrepid.

MONUMENTO AL CAMPESINO. Manrique's monument to Lanzarote's peasants is a white abstract sculpture of a farmer and a camel, surrounded by basalt windbreaks. The sculpture (and adjacent crafts museum) are not worth a trip for their own sake, but make a great stop for photos and a meal if you're returning from surfing at Caleta de Famara or the Parque Nacional de Timanfaya. *(Located just off the highway heading north from San Bartolomé, before Mozaga. ☎928 52 01 36. Open daily 10am-6pm, restaurant open daily noon-4:30pm, bar open daily 10am-5:45pm. Free.)*

JARDÍN DE CACTUS. Constructed in the style of a Roman amphitheater, Manrique's prickly paradise boasts 1420 species of spiky, flowering, many-armed, and globular cacti from around the world, as well as a 24 ft. cactus sculpture. Visitors can also tour a traditional windmill that locals occasionally use to grind barley for *gofio*. *(Off the highway in Guatiza. If not driving, catch the bus from Arrecife or the roundabout near Fundación César Manrique. From Arrecife take bus bound for Punta Mujeres; M-F 5 per day 6:40am-8pm, Sa also 2pm. Last bus back to Arrecife leaves M-F 4:45pm, Sa-Su 9:10pm. ☎928 52 93 97. Open daily 10am-6pm, bar open 10am-5:45pm. €5.)*

LA GOMERA

Many believe the verdant island of La Gomera, with its terraced gorges and steep mountain passes, is the most blessed of all the Canaries. La Gomera's relative isolation and small, stony beaches keep the droves of tourists at bay. Surrounded by banana and avocado plantations and cooled by a constant breeze, the island's capital, San Sebastián, is refreshingly provincial, unspoiled by day-trippers from Tenerife. La Gomera's crown jewel, however, is the spectacular Parque Nacional de Garajonay and last remaining refuge in the world of laurisilva forests, which died out elsewhere millions of years ago. Navigation by bus is possible, but the limited schedules and gut-wrenching rides will squelch less adventurous spirits.

SAN SEBASTIÁN DE LA GOMERA

On his way to find the mythical Middle Passage to India, Christopher Columbus dropped anchor here for a few days. He gathered water from the well, prayed at the church, and fell in love with a girl before "discovering" the Americas. These days most explorers breeze through this charming town on their way to the beaches in the south. Still, as a transportation hub filled with affordable accommodations, good restaurants, and welcoming locals, San Sebastián makes an excellent base for discovering the rest of La Gomera.

▐ TRANSPORTATION

Flights: Though most people arrive via ferry from Tenerife, the island's new **airport** (☎922 87 30 00) has a few daily flights from Tenerife and Gran Canaria.

Buses: The main bus stop is by the ferry station on the port. 3 lines start in the port and branch out across the island (up to €5, depending on destination). Not all buses stop at the **bus station,** Vía de Ronda (☎922 14 11 01), on the corner of Av. de Colón, so the port is your best bet. Line 1 to **Valle Gran Rey** with stops in **Parque Nacional de Garajonay** (M-Sa 4 per day 10:10am-9pm; Su 10:10am and 6:30pm). Line 2 to **Playa Santiago** and **Alajeró** (M-Sa 4 per day 10:10am-9pm; Su 10:10am and 6:30pm). Line 3 to **Vallehermoso** via **Agulo** and **Hermigua** (M-Sa 4 per day 10:10am-9pm; Su 10:10am and 6:30pm). Line 5 to the island's new **airport** (M-Sa 6:30am and 1pm).

Ferries: Trasmediterránea (☎922 87 13 24) and **Fred Olsen** (☎922 87 10 07) run daily ferries to **Los Cristianos** and **El Hierro** (see **Inter-Island Transport,** p. 632). **Garajonay Exprés** (☎922 87 24 07, Central 902 34 34 50; www.garajonayexpres.com) runs a passenger ferry to **Los Cristianos, Tenerife,** and to **Playa de Santiago** and **Valle del Gran Rey.** The ferry is cheaper and faster than a bus. (45min.; 3 per day 9:45am-8:10pm; €3.28, students €2.62.)

Car Rental: CiCar (☎922 14 17 56; open M-F 9am-7pm, Sa-Su 8:30am-1:30pm and 3:30-7pm) and **Hertz** (☎922 87 15 44; open M, W, F 8am-7pm; Tu, Th, Sa-Su 8:30-11:30am and 1:30-6:30pm), both in the port terminal. 21+. AmEx/MC/V.

Taxis: ☎922 87 05 24 or 922 89 53 00.

▐ ▐ ORIENTATION AND PRACTICAL INFORMATION

Navigating San Sebastián is a breeze. From the port, **Paseo de Fred Olsen** becomes **Avenida de los Descubridores** and runs along the entire coast, intersected midway by **Calle Real,** the town's main drag, at **Plaza de las Américas.** To get to the plaza from the **port,** turn left on Po. de Fred Olsen; the plaza is on the right (5min.). If you arrive after sunset, consider taking a quick taxi into town (€2), as the streets aren't clearly marked and are difficult to maneuver in the dark. **Buses** stop at the port, meeting most ferries (though they're quick to leave once the ferry has arrived). If you've rented a car, turn right onto Vía de Ronda and left onto Ctra. General de Sur (TF-713) to head out of town toward **Valle del Gran Rey.** Use extreme caution driving on the island; blind corners on narrow mountain passes and wide-turning buses can be treacherous—honk that horn.

Tourist Office: C. Real, 4 (☎922 14 15 12; www.gomera-island.com), behind Pl. de las Américas in the Pozo del Aguada. Open M-Sa 9am-1:30pm and 3:30-5pm, Su 10am-1pm. **Park Service,** Ctra. General de Sur (TF-713), 20 (☎922 87 01 05). Go left on Av. de Colón from C. Real and continue across the bridge following signs to Valle Gran Rey; the office is on the right at the 2nd bend. Open M-F 8:30am-2:30pm.

Currency Exchange: Banco Santander Central Hispano, C. Real, 7. Open M-F 8:30am-2pm, Sa 8:30am-1pm. 24hr. **ATM. Banks** line Pl. de las Américas.

Laundromat: Lavandería HECU, C. Real, 76 (☎922 14 11 80). Open M-F 8:30am-1:30pm and 5-8pm, Sa 8:30am-1:30pm. €4.20 per wash and per dry.

Police: Pl. de las Américas, 4 (☎922 141 572), in the Ayuntamiento.

Pharmacy: Pl. de la Constitución, 14 (☎922 14 16 05). Open M-F 9am-1:30pm and 5-8pm, Sa 9am-1:30pm.

Hospital: Nuestra Sra. de Guadalupe (☎920 14 02 00). From Pl. de las Américas, walk away from the port, turn right onto Av. del Quinto Centenario, then left across the bridge, and take the 1st right.

Internet Access: Aguajedum, C. Prof. Armas Fernández, 15 (☎922 14 19 20). From Pl. de las Américas, go uphill on C. Real, turn left onto C. Chil, and then right onto C. Prof. Armas Fernández. €2 per hr. Open daily 10am-1:30pm and 5-10pm.

Post Office: C. Real, 60 (☎922 87 10 81). Open M-F 8:30am-2:30pm, Sa 9:30am-1pm. **Postal Code:** 38800.

▐ ACCOMMODATIONS

San Sebastián's budget accommodations are more affordable than anywhere in the Canaries. *Pensiones* offer double rooms in old Canary-style homes; most have hall baths. For longer stays, *apartamentos* are a better option. *Pensión* signs hang in windows on C. Real. Pricier hotels can be found on C. Ruiz de Padrón.

Pensión Victor, C. del Medio, 23 (☎607 51 75 65; fax 922 87 13 35). A renovated 350-year-old house with flower beds and vines along the patio. High wood-beamed ceilings and common baths. Ask Victor, the terrific, cigar-smoking owner, for the room with terrace. Bar downstairs has beer (€1) and *copas* (€2.50). Singles €20; doubles €25. ❷

Apartamentos San Sebastián, C. Real, 20 (☎922 14 14 75). Breezy, newly furnished apartments with 2 twin beds, kitchen, TV, and living room. Min. stay 2 nights. Reception 9am-1pm and 4:30-8pm. €40 per night; after a week, €35 per night. ❸

Pensión Colón, C. Real, 59 (☎922 87 02 35). Tiled floors and austere rooms surround a quiet courtyard; avoid stuffy rooms without windows. Singles €20; doubles €25. ❶

▐ FOOD

San Sebastián is filled with authentic Canarian restaurants and cheap tapas bars. Nicer options surround Pl. de la Constitución, and typical bars and *mesones* line C. Ruiz de Padrón and C. del Medio. **Bar-Restaurante Casa del Mar ❷,** Po. de Fred Olsen, 1, serves great food; the *bacalao a la vizcaína* (cod in tomato and zucchini sauce with local potatoes; €8.50) is delicious. (☎922 87 03 20. Entrees €5-8.50. Open Su-M and W-Sa noon-4pm and 7-11pm.) **Tasca Restaurante El Pejin ❸,** C. Real, 15, serves Canarian specialties (mostly seafood; €8-15) in a lively atmosphere. The owner may entertain with folk songs if there's a crowd, especially on weekend nights. (☎922 87 15 30. Open M-Sa noon-4pm and 7pm-midnight.) **Bar-Restaurant Cubino ❷,** C. Virgen de Guadalupe, 2,

THE LOCAL STORY

SIBILANT SILBO

If a *gomero* whistles in your direction, don't take offense; most likely he's just practicing his *Silbo* skills. *Silbo Gomero* is a whistled language dating to well before the Spanish conquest. Natives, and later Spaniards, would whistle across the rugged terrain to communicate across distances of up to 5km. It probably started as simple warnings and greetings but evolved into a full-blown system of communication. Similar whistled languages have been found in Turkey, West Africa, Nepal, Burma, Bolivia, and New Guinea—in areas with low population density and rough terrain.

Silbo Gomero is not a language-as-such; it does not have its own vocabulary or grammar. Rather, it is a method of amplifying spoken words and replacing them with whistled equivalents. The *silbador* manipulates his tongue with one hand and amplifies with the other, modulating pitch, volume, and duration to form words. A good *silbador* can whistle in any language, and, if you listen closely, you may understand. *Silbo* was on the brink of extinction until recently, but it has undergone a revival, and *gomeros* receive 30min. of instruction per week in school. But *Silbo* isn't limited to humans—Gomeran birds are rumored to mimic some of the common words. To hear it, ask at local bars around San Sebastián, El Valle del Gran Rey, Las Rosas, and El Cercado.

off Pl. de la Constitución, serves healthy portions of delicious seafood and meat dishes to locals. (☎922 87 03 83. Entrees €4-9. Open Su-M and W-Sa 9am-4pm and 7pm-midnight.) Buy groceries at **Hiper Trebol** in the market complex at the intersection of C. Colón and Av. del Quinto Centenario. (☎922 87 13 66. Open M-Sa 9am-9pm, Sa-Su 9am-3pm.) A **produce market** fills the plaza on Wednesdays and Saturdays from 8am-2pm.

◉ SIGHTS

The few sights in San Sebastián are centered around a famous foreigner: Cristóbal Colón. Before he left, Colón prayed at the **Iglesia de la Asunción,** C. Real. The carved woodwork adorning the simple church is typical of *canario* architecture. The **Torre del Conde,** a small 15th-century fort, peers out over the coast from a small park. In 1488, the wife of the murdered governor, Hernán Peraza, bolted herself inside as she watched the citizens take control of the port. Now it displays Gomeran cartography. Be sure to read the amusing letter to the governor of San Sebastián from English Capt. Charles Windham, who tried to seize the town in 1743 but was repulsed by the *gomeros*. (Open M-F 10am-1pm. Free.) The tourist office is inside **La Casa de la Aguada,** C. Real, 4, featuring the well from which Colón drew water to "baptize the Americas." No Canarian city would be complete without a **beach.** Although there is a small patch of black sand in front of Pl. de las Américas, **Playa de la Cueva** is better, offering more sand, calmer waters, caved cliffs, and a view of Tenerife. From Pl. de las Américas, follow Po. de Fred Olsen toward the port and curve left away from the wharf.

▶ DAYTRIP FROM SAN SEBASTIÁN

▧ PARQUE NACIONAL DE GARAJONAY

Take the bus (line #1) to Valle Gran Rey and get off at Pajarito; if you bear right, the trailhead is 1km up the road. A car greatly facilitates exploration of the park, but several of the best trails are reachable by bus.

Blanketed in thick mist and fog that produces a "horizontal rain" year-round, Garajonay National Park sustains some of the last **laurisilva forests** on earth. Once ubiquitous in the Mediterranean basin, the rest of these mossy forests fell victim to an ice age millions of years ago. Hikers in Garajonay wade through lush ferns, myriad streams, and dripping plants to reach a stunning mountaintop view of the other islands. The park maintains numerous trails and **three self-guided paths,** most originating from **Contadero.** Remnants of volcanic activity, **Los Roques,** line the roadside. The **visitor's center** is in **Agulo,** 9km outside the park. (☎922 80 09 93. Open daily 9:30am-4:30pm.) It provides info on the park's three self-guided hikes. To get there, take bus #3 from San Sebastián (45min., 4 per day 10:30am-9pm) and get off at the Las Rosas stop. The **Park Service,** Ctra. General de Sur (TF-713), 6, in San Sebastián, has the same info. (☎922 87 01 05. Open M-F 8am-2:30pm.) The Agulo office makes reservations required for the **free guided tours** (W and Sa 10am, meet in La Laguna Grande; tour in Spanish only). Both offices carry the booklet whose descriptions correspond to the numbered wooden signs on the park trails.

VALLE GRAN REY ☎922

Green terraced farms step back from sandy beaches into the deep gorge of the "Valley of the Great King." The mellow shores keep the German tourists content with sunbathing, cliff-exploring, and water sports, while farmers work the peaceful valley. Because of its beaches, Valle Gran Rey is probably the nicest place to base a stay in La Gomera, but can be slightly expensive. **Garajonay Exprés** runs passenger ferries (p. 634) to **San Sebastián** and **Los Cristianos.**

Bus #1 runs from San Sebastián to Valle Gran Rey's four small villages: **La Calera, La Playa, La Puntilla,** and **Vueltas,** in that order. (2hr.; M-F 4 per day 10:10am-9pm, Su 10:10am and 6:30pm; €5.) La Calera sits up higher in the valley, while La Playa, La Puntilla, and Vueltas cover the shores below. The four are geographically aligned in a triangular form less than a kilometer long. Street signs are nonexistent, but the area is easy to navigate—for help, stop at the **tourist office** in La Playa. From the La Playa bus stop, face the beach, head right on the main road, and turn left on C. Noria. (☎/fax 922 80 54 58. Open winter M-Sa 9am-1:30pm and 4-6:30pm, Su 10am-1pm; summer M-Sa 9am-2pm.)

The most popular beaches are **Playa de Argaga** and **Playa las Arenas,** a short walk left of Vueltas when facing the beach. The sandy **Playa de Calera** and **Playa de Puntilla,** which stretch left from La Playa, have calm waters. **Playa del Inglés,** featuring more waves, nearby cliffs, and naked bodies, is a 10min. walk from La Playa. With your back to the tourist office turn right, take the first right, and follow the road, as it becomes dirt, to the beach. For scuba diving, try **Fish and Co.,** La Playa, Apt. 99, which heads out every day at 9am. (Dive with equipment €35, 5-day certification course €295, taster's lesson €29.) The **tourist office** is across the street. (☎922 80 56 88; www.gomera.net/tauchen.) For cheap rentals of top-end bikes, head to **Bike Station Gomera,** La Puntilla, 7, which offers €34-43 excursions (book a day in advance; includes lunch) and €9 shuttle service to **La Laguna,** 1260m up. (☎/fax 922 80 50 82; www.bike-station-gomera.com. Beach cruisers €6 per day, hard tails €13, full suspension €18, discounts for more days. Open M-Sa 9am-1pm and 5-8pm.)

Valle Gran Rey's charm and scenery are best experienced with an overnight stay, though call ahead, as the area is no secret to tourists. The few *pensiones* in the area only offer doubles. *Apartamentos* provide more amenities; one place to inquire is the **San José ❷** restaurant, just to the right of the tourist office in La Playa. Apartments are small, but clean, with kitchens. (☎922 80 53 31. "Single" apartment for 2 people €27; "double" apartment for 3-4 people €34.) **Casa Bella Cabellos ❶,** on C. la Alameda in La Calera, offers great views from modern, balconied apartments, and simple wooden doubles in an antique home. From the bus stop, head back up the valley and take the first left (almost a U-turn), follow the road past the San Sebastián bar, then bear right at the "do not enter" sign, and follow the road up. It's on the left. (☎922 80 51 82. 3-night min. House rooms (winter only) €20. Double with fridge €30; quad with kitchen €36.) Also in La Calera, **Pensión Parada ❶,** right next to the bus stop and a 10min. walk from the beach, offers simple doubles with shared baths. (☎922 80 50 52; fax 28 13 10. Doubles €24.)

PORTUGAL

Today's Portugal is a product of a turbulent history that ranged from rule over one of the most glorious trading empires in the world to vassal status under the Moors, Spanish, and French. The relics of that history are now the country's major attraction, but its modern landscape holds treasures of its own, from Lisboa's museums to the hiking trails in the pristine mountains of Trás-Os-Montes. Sheltered from many of the modernizing forces of the 20th century by an oppressive fascist dictatorship, Portugal is emerging from those shadows with a unique mix of the traditional and the cosmopolitan, where rows of olive trees and ancient castles give way to trendy nightclubs. The result is a surprising and worthwhile destination for those tired of the more conventional travel spots in Europe.

HISTORY

In the 14th and 15th centuries, Portugal was one of the most powerful nations in the world, ruling a wealthy empire that stretched from America to Asia. Although the country's international prestige declined by 1580, Portuguese pride did not. Over the following centuries, Portugal struggled to assert its national identity and its uniqueness from Spain. Modern Portugal, with a stable democracy and fast-growing economy, has proven the strength of its national character.

EARLY HISTORY (5500 BC-AD 469). Settlement of Portugal began around 5500 BC when neolithic tribes arrived from Andalucía. These hunters and fishermen remained in ancient Portugal unchanged until 2000 BC, when the Megalithic culture emerged. Remnants of this era still exist in the many neocropolises scattered throughout the country. Several tribes began to populate the Iberian Peninsula during the first millennium BC, including the **Celts,** who settled in northern Portugal and Galicia in the 9th century BC, and the **Phoenicians,** who founded fishing villages in the Algarve and ventured as far north as Lisbon. The **Greeks** and **Carthaginians** soon followed, settling the southern and western coasts. After their victory over Carthage in the Second Punic War (218-201 BC) and their defeat of the Celts in 140 BC, the **Romans** gained control of Portugal, integrating the region into the Iberian province of Lusitania. Six centuries of Roman rule, which introduced the *Pax Romana* and "Latinized" Portugal's language and customs, also paved the way for Christianity.

VISIGOTHS AND MOORS (469-1139). Rome's decline in the 3rd and 4th centuries AD heavily impacted the Iberian Peninsula. By 469, the **Visigoths,** a tribe of migrating Germanic people, had crossed the Pyrenees, and for the next two centuries they dominated the peninsula. In 711, the Muslims (also known as the **Moors**) invaded Iberia, toppling the Visigoth monarchy. Muslim communities were established along the southern coast, which they called the *al-Gharb* (Algarve), and after nearly 400 years of rule, the Muslims left a significant legacy of agricultural advances, architectural landmarks, and linguistic and cultural trends.

THE CHRISTIAN RECONQUISTA AND THE BIRTH OF PORTUGAL (1139-1415). Though the *Reconquista* officially began in 718, it didn't pick up steam until the 11th century, when Fernando I united Castilla and León, providing a strong base from which to reclaim territory. In 1139, **Dom Afonso Henriques** (Afonso I), a noble from the frontier territory around Porto, declared independence from Castilla y León. Soon thereafter, he named himself the first king of Portugal.

Portugal

ATLANTIC OCEAN

SPAIN

Valença do Minho
Vila Nova de Cerveira
Parque Natural da Peneda-Gerês
Caminha
Minho
MINHO
Viana do Castelo
Lima
Serra do Gerês
Parque Natural de Montesinho
Caldas de Gerês
Bragança
Cávado
TRÁS-OS-MONTES
COSTA VERDE
Barcelos
Braga
Guimarães
Tâmega
Parque Natural do Alvão
Mirandela
Miranda do Douro
Amarante
Vila Real
Porto
DOURO LITORAL
Serra do Marão
Parque Natural do Douro Internacional
Espinho
DOURO ALTO
Douro
Ovar
Aveiro
BEIRA LITORAL
Viseu
BEIRA ALTA
COSTA DA PRATA
Luso
Buçaco
Mondego
Guarda
Serra da Estrêla
Manteigas
Coimbra
Parque Natural da Serra da Estrêla
Figueira da Foz
Conímbriga
Zêzere
Serra da Gardunha
Leiria
BEIRA BAIXA
Nazaré
Batalha
Castelo Branco
São Martinho do Porto
Alcobaça
Fátima
Ilhas Berlengas
Caldas da Rainha
Tomar
Serra de Aire
Cabo Carvoeiro
Óbidos
Tejo
Peniche
RIBATEJO
Serra de São Mamede
Castelo de Vide
ESTREMADURA
Santarém
Crato
Marvão
Ericeira
Vila Franca de Xira
Portalegre
Mafra
Sintra
Queluz
ALTO ALENTEJO
Cascais
Lisboa
Estremoz
Elvas
Estoril
Parque Natural de Arrábida
Setúbal
Serra de Ossa
Évora Monte
Cabo Espichel
Tróia Peninsula
Sado
Évora
Sesimbra
Alcácer do Sal
Baía de Setúbal
COSTA AZUL
Sines
Santiago do Cacém
Beja
Guadiana
BAIXO ALENTEJO
COSTA DOURADA
Mira
Mértola
Serra de Monchique
ALGARVE
Lagos
Silves
Portimão
Albufeira
Tavira
Cabo de São Vicente
Sagres
Faro
Olhão
Vila Real de Santo António
Golfo de Cádiz

0   50 miles
0   50 kilometers

With the help of Christian military groups like the Knights Templar, the new monarchy battled Muslim forces, capturing Lisboa in 1147. By 1249, the *Reconquista* under **Afonso III** defeated the last remnants of Muslim power with campaigns in the Alentejo and Algarve. The Christian kings, led by **Dinis I** (1279-1325), promoted the Portuguese language above Spanish and with the **Treaty of Alcañices** (1297) settled border disputes with neighboring Castilla, asserting Portugal's identity as the first unified, independent nation in Europe.

PORTUGAL SAILS THE OCEAN BLUE (1415-1580). **João I** (1385-1433), the first king of the House of Aviz, ushered in a period of unity and prosperity. Dom João increased the power of the crown, establishing a strong base for future Portuguese expansion and economic success. The Anglo-Portuguese alliance, which he secured with the **Treaty of Windsor** (1386) and his marriage to Phillipa of Lancaster, would come to influence Portugal's foreign policy well into the 19th century.

The 15th century was one of the greatest periods in the history of maritime travel and naval advances. Under the leadership of João's son, **Prince Henry the Navigator,** Portugal became a world leader in maritime science and exploration. Portuguese adventurers captured the Moroccan city of Ceuta in 1415, discovered Madeira in 1419, happened upon the uninhabited Açores in 1427, and began to exploit the African coast for slaves and riches a few years later.

Bartolomeu Dias changed the world forever when he rounded Africa's Cape of Storms, later renamed the Cape of Good Hope, in 1488. Dias opened the route to the East and paved the way for Portuguese entrance into the spice trade. The Portuguese monarchs may have rejected **Christopher Columbus,** but they funded a number of other momentous voyages. In 1497, they supported **Vasco da Gama,** who led the first European naval expedition to India; successive expeditions added numerous East African and Indian colonies to Portugal's collection. Three years after da Gama's voyage, **Pedro Álvares Cabral** claimed Brazil for Portugal, establishing a far-flung empire. Portugal's monarchy peaked with **Dom Manuel I the Fortunate** (1495-1521). Known as "the King of Gold," Manuel controlled a spectacular empire. Competition from other commercial powers with alternative routes to the east took its toll, however, and the House of Aviz lost its predominance in 1580.

THE HOUSES OF HABSBURG AND BRAGANÇA (1580-1807). In 1580, Habsburg King of Spain **Felipe II** claimed the Portuguese throne, and the Iberian Peninsula was briefly ruled by one monarch. For 60 years, the Habsburgs dragged Portugal into several ill-fated wars, including the Spanish-Portuguese Armada's crushing loss to England in 1588. Inattentive King Felipe didn't even visit Portugal until 1619, and by the end of Habsburg rule, Portugal had lost its once-vast empire. In 1640, the **House of Bragança** engineered a nationalist rebellion against King Felipe IV. After a brief struggle they assumed control, asserting Portuguese independence from Spain. To secure sovereignty, the Bragança dynasty went to great lengths to reestablish ties with England. In 1661, Portugal ceded Bombay to England, and the marriage of Catherine of Bragança to England's Charles II cemented the Portuguese-British alliance. Nearly half a century later, **João V** (1706-1750) restored a measure of prosperity, using newly mined Brazilian gold and diamonds to finance massive building projects, including the construction of extravagant palaces. The momentous **Earthquake of 1755** devastated Lisboa and southern Portugal, killing over 50,000 people. Despite the damage, dictatorial minister **Marquês de Pombal** was able to rebuild Lisboa while instituting economic reforms.

NAPOLEON'S CONQUEST AND FAMILY MATTERS (1807-1910). Napoleon took control of France in 1801 and set his sights on the rest of Europe. When he reached Portugal, his army encountered little resistance as the Portuguese royal family fled to Brazil. **Dom João VI** returned to Lisboa in 1821 only to face an extremely unstable political climate. Amidst turmoil within the royal family, João's son **Pedro** declared independence for Brazil, becoming the country's first ruler. The **Constitution of 1822,** drawn up in Portugal during the royal family's absence, severely limited the power of the monarchy, and after 1826, the **War of the Two Brothers** (1826-1834) between constitutionalists (supporting Pedro, the new king of Brazil) and monarchists (supporting Miguel, Pedro's brother) divided the country over the question of the Portuguese throne. Eight gory years later, with Miguel in exile, Pedro's daughter **Maria II** (1834-1854) ascended the throne at the tender age of 15. The next 75 years were marked by continued tension between liberals and monarchists.

FROM THE FIRST REPUBLIC TO SALAZAR (1910-1974). Portugal spent the first few years of the 20th century trying to recover from the political discord of the 19th. On October 5, 1910, the king, 20 year-old **Dom Manuel II,** fled to England. The new government, known as the **First Republic,** earned worldwide disapproval for its expulsion of the Jesuits and other religious orders, while conflict between the government and labor movements heightened domestic tensions. Portugal's decision to enter **World War I** (even on the side of the victorious Allies) proved economically fatal and internally divisive. The weak republic wobbled and eventually fell in a 1926 military coup. General **António Carmona** took over as leader of the provisional military government and, in the face of financial crisis, appointed **António de Oliveira Salazar,** a prominent economics professor, minister of finance. In 1932, Salazar became prime minister but soon devolved into a dictator. His *Estado Novo* (New State) granted suffrage to women, but did little else to end the country's authoritarian traditions. While Portugal's international economic standing improved, the regime laid the cost of progress squarely on the shoulders of the working class, the peasantry, and colonial subjects in Africa. A terrifying secret police (PIDE) crushed all opposition to Salazar's rule, and African rebellions were quelled in bloody battles that drained the nation's economy.

REVOLUTION AND REFORM (1974-2000). The slightly more liberal **Marcelo Caetano** dragged on the unpopular African wars after Salazar's death in 1970. In just a few years, international disapproval of Portuguese imperialism and the army's dissatisfaction with colonial entanglements led General António de Spinola to call for decolonization. On April 25, 1974, a left-wing military coalition calling itself the Armed Forces Movement overthrew Caetano in a quick coup. This **Revolution of the Carnations** sent citizens dancing into the streets; today every town in Portugal has its own "Rua 25 de Abril." The Marxist-dominated armed forces granted a variety of civil and political liberties and withdrew Portuguese claims on African colonies by 1975, resulting in a flood of over 500,000 refugees into the country.

The socialist government nationalized several industries and appropriated large estates in the face of substantial opposition. The country's first elections in 1976 put the charismatic socialist prime minister **Mario Soares** into power. When a severe economic crisis hit, Soares instituted "100 measures in 100 days" to shock Portugal into shape. Through austere reforms, he helped stimulate industrial growth. 1986 brought Portugal into the European Community (now the European Union), ending its age-old isolation from northern Europe. Despite challenges by the newly formed Social Democratic Party (PSD), Soares won the election in 1986, becoming the nation's first civilian president in 60 years. Soares was eventually replaced by the Socialist former mayor of Lisboa, **Jorge Sampaio,** in 1995.

CURRENT EVENTS

The European Union declared Portugal a full member of the EU Economic and Monetary Union (EMU) in 1999, and the nation continues its quest to catch up economically with the rest of Western Europe. In 1999, Portugal ceded Macau, its last overseas territory, to the Chinese. Portugal and Indonesia have agreed to cooperate over the reconstruction of East Timor, an ex-Portuguese colony that Indonesia invaded in 1975. Jorge Sampaio returned to the presidency after the January 2001 parliamentary elections, but Socialist prime minister **Antonio Guterres** resigned in December of 2001 after their party suffered heavy losses in Parliamentary elections. President Sampaio then appointed Socialist Democrat **Jose Manuel Durão Barroso** as prime minister to represent the newly merged parties.

PEOPLE AND CULTURE

LANGUAGE

Although this softer sister of Spanish is closely related to the other Romance languages, modern Portuguese is an amalgam of diverse influences. A close listener will catch echoes of Italian, French, Spanish, Arabic, and even English and Slavic. Global escapades spread the language to other regions: today, Portuguese (the world's 6th most-spoken language) binds over 200 million people worldwide, most of them in Portugal, Brazil, Mozambique, and Angola. Prospective students of the language should note the differences between Brazilian and continental Portuguese, mainly in pronunciation and usage.

Some may be heartened to know that English, Spanish, and French are widely spoken throughout Portugal, especially in tourist-oriented locales. The *Let's Go* **Phrasebook** (p. 812) contains useful phrases in Portuguese, and the **Glossary** (p. 814) lists terms used in this guide.

RELIGION

Though the constitution mandates that there is no state religion in Portugal, it might as well—roughly 97% of the Portuguese population practices Roman Catholicism. Composing the remaining 3% are Protestants, Jehovah's Witnesses, and Mormons, along with 35,000 Muslims and a mere 700 Jews. A major force in shaping Portugal's history, the Catholic Church is a respected and powerful influence in modern-day Portugal as well; attendance is high at Sunday masses, and festivals honoring patron saints (*romarias*) are celebrated everywhere.

FLORA AND FAUNA

The push to conserve nature, landscape, and heritage in harmony with the needs of a growing population has inspired the establishment of protected areas. The **Costa Azul** alone boasts a natural park and two reserves. The chalky hills of the **Serra da Arrábida** date back 180 million years, while the Natural Reserve of the **Sado Estuary** protects river birds, the European otter, and bucks, among other species. Bird-watching is especially rewarding in the **Tejo Estuary,** where the bird population in winter months reaches 80,000, largely due to the gathering of half the **avocets** in Europe. Wild goats, pigs, and deer are common sights throughout the country, and wolves and lynxes populate remote regions. The protected **Arriba Fossil Area** of the Costa da Caparica showcases 15 million-year-old sedimentary rock, in which fossilized fauna from the Miocene epoch are visible.

FOOD AND DRINK

LOCAL FARE

The Portuguese season their dishes with the basics: olive oil, garlic, herbs, and sea salt. Despite their historic role in bringing Eastern flavorings to Europe, they use relatively few spices. Portugal's miles of coastline mean that **seafood** forms the core of Portuguese cuisine; it is usually prepared as simply as possible to emphasize freshness. Seafood lovers will enjoy *choco grelhado* (grilled cuttlefish), *linguado grelhado* (grilled sole), and *peixe espada* (swordfish), to name a few. The more adventurous should try the *polvo* (boiled or grilled octopus), *mexilhões* (mussels), and *lulas grelhadas* (grilled squid). **Meat** is treated in the opposite manner from seafood; the taste is extensively embellished and even masked by heavy sauces. Pork, chicken, and beef appear on most menus, often combined in *cozida à portuguesa* (boiled beef, pork, sausage, and vegetables). True connoisseurs add a drop of *piri-piri* (mega hot) sauce to their *cozida*. An expensive delicacy is freshly roasted *cabrito* (kid). No matter what you order, leave room for *batatas* (potatoes), prepared countless ways, which accompany each meal.

The availability of excellent produce means that **sopas** (soups) are usually made from local vegetables. Substantial soups can serve as a cheap alternative to a full meal. Common varieties include *caldo de ovos* (bean soup with hard-boiled eggs), *caldo de verdura* (vegetable soup), and the tasty *caldo verde* (a potato and kale mixture with a slice of sausage and olive oil). **Sandes** (sandwiches) such as the *bifana* or *prego no pão* (meat sandwich) may be no more than a hunk of meat on a roll. Cows, goats, and ewes do their share, providing raw material for Portugal's renowned **queijos** (cheeses). Vegetarians should accustom themselves to cheese sandwichs and Portugal's delectable *broa* bread.

Portugal's favorite dessert is **pudim**, or flan, a rich, caramel custard similar to *crème bruleé*. Satisfy your sweet tooth with **marzipan** made with almonds from the groves of the Algarve. For something different, try *pêras* (pears) drenched in sweet port wine and served with raisins and hazelnuts on top. The most common sweets are the countless varieties of inexpensive, high-quality **sorvete** (ice cream)—look for vendors posting the colorful, ubiquitous "Olá" sign. *Pastelarias* (bakeries) are in most towns, and tasty **pastries** make for a cheap breakfast.

MEALS AND DINING HOURS

Portuguese eat their hearty midday meal—*almoço* (lunch)—between noon and 2pm and *jantar* (dinner) between 9pm and midnight. Both meals entail at least three courses. There are no greasy lumberjack breakfasts to be found in Portugal—a pastry from a *pastelaria* (bakery) and coffee from a cafe suffices for *pequeno almoço* (breakfast). If you get the munchies between 4 and 7pm, snack bars sell **sandes** (sandwiches) and sweet cakes. It is advisable to make reservations when dining in some of the more upscale city restaurants.

EATING OUT

A full meal costs €6-15, depending on the restaurant's location and quality. **Meia dose** (half portions) cost more than half-price but are often more than adequate—a full portion may satisfy two. The ubiquitous **prato do dia** (special of the day) and **ementa** of appetizer, bread, entree, dessert, and beverage will satisfy even the largest appetite. The **ementa turística** (tourist meal) is usually not a good deal—restaurants with menus translated into multiple languages are more likely to charge exorbitant prices. Standard pre-meal bread, butter, cheese, and pâté may be served without your asking, but these pre-meal munchies are not free (€1-3 per person). You may appreciate them, however, since chefs start cooking only after you order; be prepared to wait. In restaurants (but not cafes), a service charge of 10% is usually included in the bill. When service is not included, it is customary to leave 5-10% as a tip. Vegetarians may find themselves left out in the cold in Portugal, but given the availability and high quality of fresh produce, it may prove fruitful to make special requests. Smoking is still generally accepted in most establishments, although there has been a recent move to institute no smoking zones. Signs stating *"proibida fumar"* (no smoking) mark these areas.

DRINK

The exact date marking the birth of Portuguese wine is unknown, though 5000 BC is often used as an estimate. Though it is not quite an international star, the quality and low cost of Portuguese *vinho* (wine) is truly astounding. The pinnacle, **vinho do porto** (port), pressed (by foot) from the red grapes of the Douro Valley and fermented with a touch of brandy, is a dessert in itself. Chilled, white port can be a snappy aperitif, while ruby or tawny port makes a classic after-dinner drink. Sparkling *vinho verde* is picked and drunk young and comes in either red or white. Excellent local table wines include Colares, Dão, Borba, Bairrada, Bucelas, and Periquita. If you can't decide, experiment with the **vinho de casa** (house wine); either the *tinto* (red) or the *branco* (white) is a reliable standby. Tangy **sangria** comes filled with fresh orange slices and makes even a budget meal festive at a minimal expense (usually around €2.50 for a half-pitcher). Your Portuguese drinking vocabulary should contain the following terms: *claro* (new wine), *espumante* (sparkling wine), *rosado* (rosé wine), *vinho de mesa* (table wine), and *vinho verde* (young wine). Bottled Sagres and Super Bock are excellent beers. If you don't ask for it *fresco* (cool), it may come *natural* (room temperature). A tall, slim glass of draft beer is a **fino** or an **imperial,** while a larger stein is a **caneca.** To sober up, order a **bica** (cup of black espresso), a **galão** (coffee with milk, served in a glass), or a **café com leite** (coffee with milk, served in a cup).

CUSTOMS AND ETIQUETTE

Portuguese are generally friendly, easygoing, and receptive to foreign travelers. Even if your Portuguese is a little rusty, a wholehearted attempt at speaking the native tongue will be appreciated.

TABOOS. Be cautious of shorts and flip-flops; they may be seen as disrespectful in some public establishments or in more rural areas, even during a heat wave. Though dress in Portugal is obviously more casual in the hot summer months than in the cold of winter, strapless tops on women and collarless t-shirts on men are generally unacceptable. Skimpy clothes are always a taboo in churches, as are tourist visits during masses or services.

PUBLIC BEHAVIOR. On any list of Portuguese values, politeness would be at the top. Be sure to address Portuguese as *senhor* (Mr.), *senhora* (Ms.), or *senhora dona* (Mrs.) followed by the first name. To blend in, it is a good idea to be as formal as possible upon first meeting. Introduce yourself in detail, giving more than just your name. You'll be welcomed openly and made to feel at home if you mention who you are, where you're from, and what you are doing in Portugal. Don't be surprised if you get pecked on both cheeks by younger Portuguese, but handshakes are generally the standard introductory gesture.

THE ARTS

ARCHITECTURE

Portugal's signature **Manueline** style celebrates the prosperity and imperial expansion of Dom Manuel I's reign (see **Portugal Sails the Ocean Blue,** p. 664). Manueline works routinely merge Christian images and maritime motifs. Their rich and lavish ornaments reflect a hybrid of Gothic, Plateresque, and Moorish influences. The

Manueline style found its most elaborate expression in the **Torre de Belém** (p. 704), built to honor Vasco da Gama. Close seconds are the **Mosteiro dos Jerónimos** (p. 704) in Belém and the **Mosteiro Santa Maria de Vitória** (p. 761) in Batalha.

Though few Moorish structures survived the Christian *Reconquista*, their style influenced later Portuguese architecture. One of Portugal's most beautiful traditions is the colorfully painted ceramic tiles **(azulejos)** that grace many walls and ceilings. Carved in relief by the Moors, these ornate tiles later took on Italian and Flemish designs. Though many are blue, their name doesn't come from *azul* (blue), but rather from the Arabic word *azulayj*, meaning "little stone." Museums like Lisboa's Museu Nacional do Azulejo (p. 702) showcase *azulejo* collections.

PAINTING AND SCULPTURE

The Age of Discovery (1415-1580) was an era of vast cultural exchange with Renaissance Europe and beyond. Flemish masters such as **Jan van Eyck** brought their talent to Portugal, and many Portuguese artists polished their skills in Antwerp, Belgium. Dom Manuel's favorite, High Renaissance artist **Jorge Afonso,** created realistic portrayals of human anatomy. Afonso's best works hang at the **Convento de Cristo** in Tomar and **Convento da Madre de Deus** in Lisboa. In the late 15th century, the talented **Nuno Gonçalves** led a revival of the primitivist school.

Portuguese Baroque art featured even more diverse styles and themes. Woodcarving became extremely popular in Portugal during the Baroque period. **Joachim Machado** carved elaborate crèches in the early 1700s. On canvas, portraiture was head and shoulders above other genres. The prolific 19th-century artist **Domingos António de Sequeira** depicted historical, religious, and allegorical subjects using a technique that would later inspire French Impressionists. Porto's **António Soares dos Reis** brought his Romantic sensibility to 19th-century Portuguese sculpture.

In the 20th century, Cubism, Expressionism, and Futurism trickled into Portugal despite Salazar-instituted censorship. More recently, **Maria Helena Vieira da Silva** has won international recognition for her abstract works, and the master **Carlos Botelho** has become world-renowned for his wonderful vignettes of Lisboa life.

LITERATURE

Portugal's literary achievements—mostly lyric poetry and realist fiction—can be traced back to the 12th century, when the lyrical aspects of Portuguese were standardized by poet-king **Dinis I.** Dom Dinis made Portuguese the region's official language, one of the first "official" non-Latin Romance vernaculars. **Gil Vicente** (1465-1537), court poet to Manuel I, is considered the Portuguese Shakespeare for his dramas about peasants, nature, and religion. The witty realism of his *Barcas* trilogy (1517-1519) influenced contemporaries like Shakespeare and Cervantes.

Portuguese literature blossomed during the Renaissance, most notably in the letters of **Francisco de Sá de Miranda** (1481-1558) and the poetry of **António Ferreira** (1528-1569). An explorer during the Age of Discovery, the humanist **João de Barros** (1496-1570) penned *Décadas da Ásia*, a history of Portuguese conquest in Goa. Influenced by the *Décadas*, **Luís de Camões** (1524-1580) celebrated Vasco da Gama's sea voyages to India in Portugal's greatest epic, *Os Lusíadas* (*The Lusiads*, 1572), modeled on the *Aeneid* (see **Ladies' Man,** p. 704).

Spanish hegemony, intermittent warfare, and imperial decline made the literature of the 17th and 18th centuries less triumphant than that of earlier eras. The 19th century, however, saw a dramatic rebirth with poet **João Baptista de Almeida Garrett** (1799-1854). Both he and historian **Alexandre Herculano** (1810-1877), were exiled for their liberal political views. When political thinkers dominated the rise of the literary intelligentsia in the **Generation of 1870,** literature shifted from romantic to realist. The most visible figure to influence this shift was novelist and life-long diplomat **José Maria Eça de Queiroz.** He conceived a distinctly Portuguese social realism and documented 19th-century Portuguese society, sometimes critical of its bourgeois elements. His best works were *O Crime do Padre Amaro (The Sin of Father Amaro)* and *Os Maias (The Mayas)*.

Fernando Pessoa (1888-1935), Portugal's most famed writer of the late 19th and early 20th centuries, wrote in English and Portuguese under four different names: Pessoa, Alberto Caeiro, Ricardo Reis, and Alvaro de Campos. His semi-autobiography, *Livro do Desassossego (The Book of Disgust)* is his only prose work, posthumously compiled and viewed as a modernist classic. Contemporary writers like **Miguel Torga** have gained international fame for their satirical novels. **José Saramago,** winner of the 1998 Nobel Prize for Literature, is without a doubt Portugal's most important living writer. His work, written in a realist style and laced with irony, has achieved new acclaim in the post-Salazar era; it dominates in all genres, from the dystopian parable of *Blindness* to the historical fiction of *Baltasar and Blimunda*. The end of the dictatorship also saw the emergence of female writers. In **Novas Cartas Portuguesas** *(New Portuguese Letters)*, the "Three Marias" expose the mistreatment of women in a male-controlled society. Other acclaimed post-Salazar authors include **António Lobo Antunes** and **José Cardoso Pires**. Antunes has achieved the status of Saramago but with a different style, one known for its scattered form and psychoanalytic themes. Pires's works often comment on the repression of the Salazar regime, and his novel *Balada da Praia dos Cães (Ballad of Dogs' Beach)* exposes the terror of Salazar's secret police.

MUSIC

With a name meaning "fate," **fado** (FAH-doe) is a musical tradition unique to Portugal, identified with a sense of *saudade* (yearning or longing) and characterized by tragic, romantic lyrics and mournful melodies. Solo ballads, accompanied by the acoustic *guitarra* (a flat-backed guitar like a mandolin), appeal to the romantic side of Portuguese culture. **Amália Rodrigues** (1920-1999) gained international renown as a singer of *fado* and Portuguese folk music.

Apart from its folk tradition, the music of Portugal has yet to achieve international fame. Portuguese opera peaked with **António José da Silva** (1705-1739), a victim of the 1739 Inquisition. The Renaissance in Portugal led to the development of pieces geared for solo instrumentalists and vocals. Coimbra's **Carlos Seixas** thrilled 18th-century Lisboa with his genius and contributed to the development of the sonata form. **Domingos Bomtempo** (1775-1842) introduced symphonic innovations from abroad and helped establish the first Portuguese *Sociedade Filarmónica*, modeled after the London Philharmonic, in Lisboa in 1822.

Although the Portuguese Civil War decreased funding and stifled experimentation, folk music and dancing are still popular in rural areas. In the late 19th century, Joly Braga Santo led a modern revival of Portuguese classical music. The Calouste Gulbenkian Foundation in Lisboa has also kept Portuguese music alive, sponsoring a symphony orchestra since 1962, and hosting local folk singers (including Fausto and Sérgio Godinho), ballets, operas, and jazz festivals. The *Teatro Nacional de São Carlos*, with its own orchestra and ballet company, has further bolstered Portuguese music. The Teatro has spawned a group of talented young composers, including Filipe Pires, A. Vitorino de Almeida, and Jorge Peixinho, all of whom have begun to make their mark in international competitions.

THE MEDIA

Portugal's most widely read daily newspapers are *Público* (www.publico.pt), *Diário de Notícias* (www.dn.sapo.pt), and *Jornal de Notícias* (www.jn.sapo.pt). If you haven't mastered Portuguese, check out *The News*, Portugal's only online English language newspaper, at www.the-news.net. Those interested in international news stories can also pick up day-old foreign papers at larger newsstands.

Portuguese TV offers four main channels: the state-run Canal 1 and TV2, and the private SIC (Sociedade Independente de Communicação) and TVI (TV Independente). Couch potatoes can also enjoy numerous cable channels, most of which air Brazilian and Portuguese soap operas and subtitled foreign sitcoms.

SPORTS

Futebol (soccer to Americans) is the game of choice for just about all Portuguese sports fans. Team Portugal has had its moments in the sun—the national team lost to Greece on home turf in the Finals of the 2004 European Championships and garnered a third-place finish in 2000 at the European Championship with the help of 2001 FIFA World Player of the Year, Luis Figo—but has also fallen short at crucial moments, such as the World Cup '98 qualification matches. Games create a crazed fervor throughout Portugal. Lisboa's **Benfica,** with some of the world's best players, is now led by former Spanish national team coach, José Antonio Camacho.

Native Portuguese have also made names for themselves in long-distance running, where marathon-queen **Rosa Mota** dominated her event for years. For recreation other than jogging and pick-up soccer, native Portuguese often turn to the sea. Wind, body, and conventional **surfers** make waves along the northern coast; **snorkelers** and **scuba divers** set out on mini-explorations to the south and west.

NATIONAL HOLIDAYS

The following table lists the national holidays for 2005.

DATE	FESTIVAL
January 1	New Year's Day
January 6	Epiphany
February 8	Carnival
March 20-27	Semanha Santa (Holy Week)
March 24	Senhor Ecce Homo (Maundy Thursday)
March 25	Good Friday
March 27	Easter
April 25	Liberation Day
May 1	Labor Day
May 29	Corpus Christi
June 10	Portugal Day
August 15	Feast of the Assumption
October 5	Republic Day
November 1	All Saints' Day
December 8	Feast of the Immaculate Conception
December 25	Christmas
December 31	New Year's Eve

RECOMMENDED READING

FICTION: PORTUGUESE AND FOREIGN. For Portuguese classics, check out **Literature** (p. 669). The more famous works have been translated into English. *Selected Letters and Journals*, by Lord Byron, narrates the days Byron spent in Portugal. The classic *The Lusiads*, by Luís de Camões, chronicles Portuguese exploration during the Age of Discovery. *The Last Kabbalist of Lisboa*, by Richard Zimler, is a fantastic murder mystery exploring the world of Portugal's 16th-century Jewish mystics. *The History of the Siege of Lisbon* and *All the Names* are some of the finest works by Nobel Prize-winning José Saramago.

HISTORY AND CULTURE. David Birmingham's *A Concise History of Portugal* (1991) packs an amazing quantity of historical and cultural information in one handy volume. Elanea Brown's *Roads to Today's Portugal: Essays on Contemporary Portuguese Literature, Art, and Culture* (1983) provides a good introduction to 20th-century Portuguese culture. *Modern Portugal* (1998), edited by António Costa Pinto, covers 20th-century Portuguese history from the rise of Salazar to the evolution of the nation's resilient democracy. *Europe's Best-Kept Secret: An Insider's View of Portugal* (1997), by Costa Matos, is a witty account of Portuguese culture and history, including amusing anecdotes about peculiar Portuguese personalities. Finally, for a more literary than historical examination of Portuguese life, read José Saramago's *Journey Through Portugal*.

PORTUGAL ESSENTIALS

The information in this section is designed to help travelers get their bearings once in Portugal. For information about general **travel preparations** (including passports, money, health, packing, and more), consult the **Essentials** chapter (p. 8), which also has important info for those with **Specific Concerns** (p. 46). See **Alternatives to Tourism** for opportunities to work and study in Portugal (p. 53).

EMBASSIES AND CONSULATES

Embassies and consulates are usually open Monday through Friday, mornings and late afternoons, with *siestas* in between—call for specific hours.

Australia: Embassy: Av. da Liberdade, 200, 2nd fl., 1250-147 Lisboa (☎213 10 15 00; www.portugal.embassy.gov.au).

Canada: Embassy: Av. da Liberdade, 196-200, 3rd fl., 1269-121 Lisboa (☎213 16 46 00; fax 16 46 92). **Consulate:** R. Frei Lourenço de Santa Maria, 1, 1st fl. Apartado 79, 8001 Faro (☎289 80 37 57; fax 88 08 88).

Ireland: Embassy: R. da Imprensa à Estrela, 4th fl., Ste. 1, 1200 Lisboa (☎213 92 94 40; fax 97 73 63).

New Zealand: Embassy: Refer to New Zealand Embassy in Spain: Pl. de la Lealtad, 2, 3rd fl., 28014 Madrid (☎915 23 02 26; fax 23 01 71). **Consulate:** Av. António Augusta de Aguiar, 122, 9th fl., 1097 Lisboa (☎213 50 96 90; fax 57 20 04).

United Kingdom: Embassy: R. de São Bernardo, 33, 1249-082 **Lisboa** (☎213 92 40 00; fax 92 41 83). **Consulate:** Av. da Boavista, 3072, 4100-120 **Porto** (☎226 18 47 89; fax 10 04 38).

United States: Embassy and Consulate: Av. das Forças Armadas, 1600-081 **Lisboa** (☎217 27 33 00; www.american-embassy.pt).

TRANSPORTATION

Portugal is easily accessible by plane. Long-distance trains run from **Madrid** (p. 85) to Lisboa, and buses run from **Sevilla** (p. 221) to Lagos. Closer to the border, trains run from **Huelva** (easily accessible from Sevilla, p. 221) and **Cáceres** (p. 207) to Portugal. Trains and buses run from **Badajoz** (p. 207), only 6km from the border, to

Elvas and elsewhere. **Ciudad Rodrigo** (p. 168) is only 21km from the border. In the north, trains run from **Vigo** (p. 611) to Porto; from **Túy** (p. 616), you can walk across the Portuguese border to Valença do Minho (p. 787).

BY PLANE

Most major international airlines serve Lisboa; some serve Porto, Faro, and the Madeiras. **TAP Air Portugal** (in US and Canada ☎800-221-7370, in UK 845 601 09 32, in Lisboa 707 20 57 00; www.tap.pt) is Portugal's national airline, serving all domestic locations and many major international cities. **Portugália** (www.pga.pt) is a smaller Portuguese airline that flies between Porto, Faro, Lisboa, all major Spanish cities, and other Western European destinations. Offices are located in Portugal (☎218 42 55 59), Spain (☎913 93 64 39), and the UK (☎087 0755 0025), with other locations in Belgium, France, Germany, and Italy.

BY TRAIN

Caminhos de Ferro Portugueses (☎808 20 82 08; www.cp.pt) is Portugal's national railway, but for long-distance travel outside of the Braga-Porto-Coimbra-Lisboa line, the bus is better. The exception is around Lisboa, where local trains are fast and efficient. Most trains have first- and second-class cabins, except for local and suburban routes. When you arrive in town, go to the station ticket booth to check the departure schedule; trains often run at irregular hours, and posted schedules *(horarios)* aren't always accurate. Unless you own a Eurailpass, the return on **round-trip tickets** must be used before 3am the following day. Don't ride without a ticket; if you're caught *sem bilhete*, you'll be fined exorbitantly. Children under 12 and adults over 65 receive a 50% discount. **Youth discounts** are only available to Portuguese citizens. Though there is a Portugal Flexipass, it is not worth buying.

BY BUS

Buses are cheap, frequent, and connect just about every town in Portugal. **Rodoviária** (national info ☎213 54 57 75), the national bus company, has recently been privatized. Each company name corresponds to a particular region of the country, such as Rodoviária Alentejo or Minho e Douro, with a few exceptions such as EVA in the Algarve. Private regional companies also operate, among them **AVIC, Cabanelas,** and **Mafrense.** Be wary of non-express buses in small regions like Estremadura and Alentejo, which stop every few minutes. Express coach service *(expressos)* between major cities is especially good; inexpensive city buses often run to nearby villages. Schedules *(horarios)* are usually printed and posted, but double-check with the ticket vendor to make sure they are accurate.

Portugal's main **Euroline** affiliates are Internorte, Intercentro, and Intersul. **Busabout** coach stops in Portugal are at Porto, Lisboa, and Lagos. Every coach has a guide on-board to answer questions and make travel arrangements en route.

BY CAR

Portugal has the highest rate of car accidents per capita in Western Europe. The new highway system (IP) is quite good, but off the main arteries, the narrow, twisting roads are difficult to negotiate. Speed limits are ignored, recklessness is common, and lighting and road surfaces are often inadequate. Buses and trucks are safer options. Moreover, parking space in cities borders on nonexistent. **Gas** comes in super (97 octane), normal (92 octane), and unleaded; prices are high by American standards—€0.70 per liter. Portugal's national automobile association, the **Automóvel Clube de Portugal (ACP),** Shopping Center Amoreiras, Lojas 1122 **Lisboa** (☎21 3714720), provides **breakdown** and **towing service** and **first aid.**

PORTUGAL

Rental prices start at around €50 a day from national companies, €35 from local agencies. Expect to pay more for larger cars and for 4WD. Cars with **automatic transmission** can cost up to €30 a day more than standard manuals (stick shift), and in some places, automatic transmission is hard to find in the first place. It is virtually impossible, no matter where you are, to find an automatic 4WD.

BY THUMB

In Portugal, **hitchhikers** are rare. Beach-bound locals occasionally hitch in summer, but otherwise stick to the inexpensive bus system. Rides are easiest to come by between smaller towns. Best results are reputedly at gas stations near highways and rest stops. *Let's Go* does not recommend hitchhiking (p. 33).

MONEY

Official **banking hours** are Monday through Friday 8:30am to 3pm, but play it safe by giving yourself extra time. For more information on **money,** see p. 12. **Taxes** are included in all prices in Portugal and are not redeemable like those in Spain, even for EU citizens. **Tips** are customary only in fancy restaurants or hotels. Some cheaper restaurants include a 10% service charge; if they don't and you'd like to leave a tip, round up and leave the change. Taxi drivers do not expect a tip unless the trip was especially long. **Bargaining** is not customary in shops, but give it a shot at the local *mercado* (market) or when looking for a *quarto* (private room).

SAFETY AND HEALTH

EMERGENCY Dial ☎ **112** for **POLICE, MEDICAL,** or **FIRE.**

In Portugal, the highest rates of crime have been in the Lisboa area, especially on buses, in train stations, and in airports. Exercise the most caution in the Alfama district, the Santa Apolonia and Rossio train stations, Castelo de São Jorge, and in Belém. The towns around Lisboa with the most reported crimes in recent years are Cascais, Sintra, and Fátima. Thieves try to distract people by staging loud arguments, passing a soccer ball back and forth on a crowded street, asking for directions, pretending to dance with their victim, or spilling something on their victim's clothing. Motorists should be wary of Good Samaritans who have been known to help ailing motorists by the side of the road and then steal their cars.

Portugal poses no particular health risks to travelers. The public health system is quite good, and many doctors speak English. A private clinic may be worth the money for convenience and quick service; most travel insurance providers will cover the tab. For small concerns, Portuguese *farmacias* offer basic drugs and advice and are easy to find in most towns. For general **health** info, see p. 15.

ACCOMMODATIONS

PENSÕES AND HOTELS

Pensões, also called **residencias,** are a budget traveler's mainstay. They're far cheaper than hotels and only slightly more expensive (and much more common) than crowded youth hostels. Like hostels, *pensões* generally provide sheets and towels. All are rated on a five-star scale and are required to post their category and legal price limits. (If you don't see this, ask for it.) In the high season, many do not take reservations; for those that do, booking a week ahead is advisable.

Hotels in Portugal tend to be pricey. Room prices typically include breakfast and showers, and most rooms without bath or shower have a sink. When business is weak, try bargaining in advance—the "official price" is just the maximum allowed. **Pousadas,** like Spanish *paradores*, outperform standard hotel expectations (and, unfortunately, rates). Most are castles, palaces, or monasteries converted into luxurious, government-run hotels. "Historical" *pousadas* play up local crafts, customs, and cuisine and may cost as much as expensive hotels. Most require reservations. Priced less extravagantly are *regional pousadas*, situated in national parks and reserves. For info, contact **ENATUR,** Av. Santa Joana Princesa, 10, 1749-090 Lisboa (☎ 218 44 20 01; fax 44 20 85; www.pousadas.com).

YOUTH HOSTELS

Movijovem, Av. Duque de Ávila, 137, 1069-017 Lisboa (☎707 20 30 30, fax 217 23 21 02; www.pousadasjuventude.pt), the Portuguese Hostelling International affiliate, oversees the country's HI hostels. All bookings can be made through them. A bed in a *pousada da juventude* (not to be confused with plush *pousadas*) costs €9-15 per night (breakfast and sheets included) and slightly less in the low season (Oct.-Apr.). Lunch or dinner usually costs €5, snacks around €2. Rates may be higher for guests 26 and older. Though often the cheapest option, hostels may lie far from the town center. Check-in hours are 9am to noon and 6pm to midnight. Some have lockouts 10:30am to 6pm, and curfews might cramp club-hoppers' style. The maximum stay is eight nights unless you get special permission. An **HI card** is usually mandatory to stay in an affiliated hostel. Although they are sold at Movijovem's Lisboa office, it is more convenient to get an HI membership before leaving home. To reserve a bed in the high season, obtain an **International Booking Voucher** from Movijovem (or your country's HI affiliate) and send it from home to the desired hostel four to eight weeks in advance. In the low season, double-check to see if the hostel is open. Large groups should reserve through Movijovem 30 days in advance. For more info, see **Hostels,** p. 39.

ALTERNATIVE ACCOMMODATIONS

Quartos are rooms in private residences, similar to *casas particulares* in Spain. These rooms may be your only option in smaller, less touristed towns, or the cheapest one in bigger cities. The tourist office can usually help you find a *quarto*. When all else fails, ask at bars and restaurants for names and addresses, but try to verify the quality of the rooms. Prices are flexible and can drop with bargaining.

CAMPING

In Portugal, over 150 **official campgrounds** *(parques de campismo)* feature amenities and comforts. Most have a supermarket and cafes, and many are beach-accessible. Given the facilities' quality and popularity, happy campers are those who arrive early; urban and coastal parks may require reservations. Police are cracking down on illegal camping, so don't try it. Tourist offices stock *Portugal: Camping and Caravan Sites*, a free guide to official campgrounds. Otherwise, write the **Federação de Campismo e Montanhismo de Portugal,** Av. Coronel Eduardo Galhardo, 24D, 1199-007 Lisboa (☎218 12 68 90; fax 218 12 69 18; www.fpcampismo.pt).

KEEPING IN TOUCH

Most useful communication information (including **international access codes, calling card numbers, country codes, operator** and **directory assistance,** and **emergency numbers**) is listed on the **inside back cover.**

PORTUGAL

TELEPHONES

Portugal's national telephone company is **Portugal Telecom.** Though phone offices exist in most cities, all services are available in phone booths on the street and in post offices. Pay phones are either coin-operated or require a phone card. The country uses the **Credifone** and **Portugal Telecom** systems. For both systems, the basic unit for all calls (and the price for local ones) is €0.10. Telecom phone cards, using "patch" chips, are most common in Lisboa and Porto and increasingly elsewhere. Credifone cards, with magnetic strips, are sold at drugstores, post offices, and locations posted on phone booths, and are most useful outside these two big cities. Private calls from bars and cafes cost whatever the proprietor decides; a posted sign usually indicates the rates. City codes all have a two before them, and local calls do not require dialing the city code.

Calling cards probably remain the best method of making international calls (p. 35 for more details). The numbers to access major calling card services (including AT&T, MCI, Canada Direct, BT Direct, Ireland Direct, Telstra Australia, Optus Australia, Telecom New Zealand, and Telkom South Africa) are listed on the **inside back cover.** To **call home with a calling card,** contact the operator for your service provider in Portugal by dialing the appropriate toll-free access number (p. 35).

MAIL AND EMAIL

Mail in Portugal is somewhat inefficient—**Air mail** *(via aerea)* can take from one to two weeks (or longer) to reach the US or Canada. It is slightly quicker for Europe and longer for Australia and New Zealand. **Surface mail** *(superficie),* for packages only, takes up to two months. **Registered** or **blue mail** takes five to eight business days (for roughly 3 times the price of air mail). **EMS** or **Express Mail** will probably get there in three to four days for more than double the blue mail price. **Stamps** are available at post offices *(correios)* and at automatic stamp machines outside post offices and in central locations around cities. **Fax** machines are also available for public use at post offices.

Cybercafes are common in cities and most smaller towns, and are listed in the Practical Information section. When in doubt, try the library, where there is often at least one computer equipped for Internet access.

LISBOA

It's sunset, and the glow cast over the Rio Tejo is matched only by that of the *vinho do Porto*. Welcome to Lisboa, where locals and visitors translate a history of eminence and glory into a passion for the best in food, wine, and music. The city's compactness and simple themes allow even the most inexperienced visitor to explore it in the better part of a week. But don't be deceived; many have tried and failed to define Lisboa in such a short time.

Part of the difficulty in describing Lisboa has to do with its multi-layered history. Half a dozen civilizations claim parenthood of the city, starting with the Phoenicians, Greeks, and Carthaginians. The Romans arrived in 205 BC; under Julius Caesar, Lisboa became the most important city in Lusitania. In 1255, it was made the capital of the kingdom of Portugal, and the city, along with the empire, reached its zenith at the end of the 15th century, when Portuguese navigators pioneered explorations of Asia, Africa, and South America. A huge earthquake on November 1, 1755, touched off the nation's fall from glory—close to one-fifth of the population died in the catastrophe and two-thirds of Lisboa crumbled. Under the authoritarian leadership of Prime Minister Marquês de Pombal, the city recovered through a massive reconstruction effort. In the 20th century, Lisboa saw more than its share of changes. During WWII, Portugal's neutrality and Atlantic connections made the city a frequent meeting spot for spies on both sides. In 1974, when Mozambique and Angola won independence, hundreds of thousands of refugees converged on the city. Today, Portuguese of African, Asian, and European origin coexist peacefully. The temples, castles, and cathedrals contributed by each of Lisboa's past civilizations constitute a consequential part of its personality; nevertheless, Lisboa's diverse history doesn't quite capture the city's uniqueness.

Above all, travelers feel the difference in Lisboa because of the rare combination of glorious history and bittersweet memory. The Portuguese have an infamous word for it: *saudade*. Anyone interested in patriotic discourse is invited to ask locals for their perception of the term. Unique to the Portuguese, *saudade* involves an almost aching, wistful longing; as a noun it is a possession of the people of Lisboa and Portugal. Travelers hear it in the traditional *fado* music, drink it in the celebrated wines, and above all, see it in the Portuguese faces. That is the glory of Lisboa—it can fill you with wonder and break your heart all at once. So while the ornate cathedrals, hip clubs, and captivating history might initially bring travelers to Lisboa, *saudade* keeps them there, and draws them back.

The neighborhoods of Alfama, Bairro Alto, and Baixa are not to be missed. They are home to Lisboa's most definitive sights and are representative of the history that continues to flavor the city today. Whether you seek the open spaces of lush parks or the intensity of labyrinthine streets, Lisboa's neighborhoods await.

HIGHLIGHTS OF LISBOA

SEE grown men cry over traditional **fado** (p. 687).

EXPERIENCE the new Lisboa in the happening **Bairro Alto** (p. 693).

ESCAPE into Portugal's sweet, pastry-filled past in **Belém** (p. 704).

DEFY gravity walking atop the walls of an 8th-century castle in **Sintra** (p. 713).

LOSE yourself in labyrinthine **Alfama,** the former Arabic quarter (p. 699).

FIND your own spot in the sun on the beaches of the **Tróia peninsula** (p. 717).

LISBOA

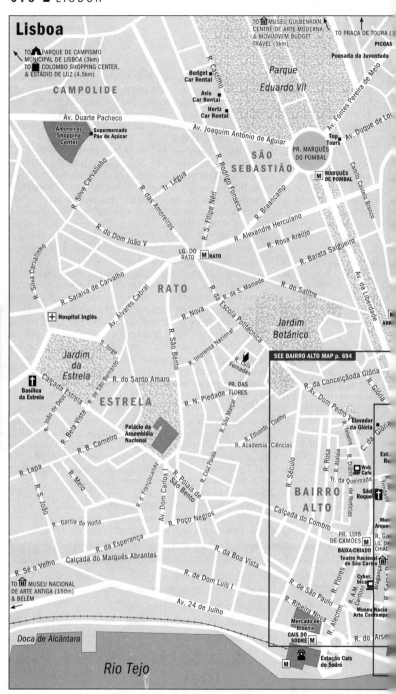

Lisboa

TO ⚑ PARQUE DE CAMPISMO
MUNICIPAL DE LISBOA (3km)
TO ■ COLOMBO SHOPPING CENTER,
& ESTÁDIO DE LUZ (4.5km)

TO 🏛 MUSEU GULBENKIAN,
CENTRE DE ARTE MODERNA,
& MOVIJOVEM BUDGET
TRAVEL (1km)

TO PRAÇA DE TOURA (1

PICOAS

Pousada da Juventude

CAMPOLIDE

Budget
Car Rental

Avis
Car Rental

Hertz
Car Rental

*Parque
Eduardo VII*

Av. Duarte Pacheco

Amoreiras
Shopping
Center

Supermercado
Pão de Açúcar

Av. Joaquim António de Aguiar

SÃO
SEBASTIÃO

PR. MARQUÊS
DO POMBAL

Top
Tours

Ⓜ MARQUÊS
DE POMBAL

R. Silva Carvalinho

Tr. Légua

R. das Amoreiras

R. do Dom João V

R. Rodrigo Fonseca

R. S. Filipe Néri

R. Braancamp

R. Alexandre Herculano

R. Rosa Araújo

R. Barata Salgueiro

LG. DO
RATO Ⓜ RATO

R. Saraiva de Carvalho

RATO

R. da R. de S. Mamede

R. do Salitre

R. Silva Carvalinho

Av. Álvares Cabral

R. Nova

R. da Escola Politécnica

✚ Hospital Inglês

*Jardim
da
Estrela*

S. Jorge

R. São Bento

R. Imprensa Nacional

*Jardim
Botânico*

SEE BAIRRO ALTO MAP p. 694

R. do Santo Amaro

R. Luís
Fernades

R. da Conceiçãoda Glória

Calçada Estrela

✝
Basílica
da Estrela

R. de São Bernardo

ESTRELA

Palácio da
Assembléia
Nacional

PR. DAS
FLORES

R. N. Piedade

R. Marçal

Av. Dom Pedro

Elevador
da Glória

R. João de Deus Estrela

R. Bela Vista

R. Eduardo
Coelho

R. Academia Ciências

R. Século

R. Rosa

R. Atalaia

R. Diário

Web
Cafe

São
Roque

C. da Glória

R. B. Carneiro

R. Lapa

R. Meio

R. d Franciscanas

R. Carlos I

R. Poiais de
São Bento

Cruz Polis

BAIRRO
ALTO

Tr. da Queimada

de Notícias

Mus
Arque

R. S. João

R. Garcia da Horta

R. da Esperança

Av. Dom Carlos I

R. Poço Negros

R. da Boa Vista

Calçada do Combro

PR. LUIS
DE CAMÕES Ⓜ

BAIXA-CHIADO

Teatro Nacional
de São Carlos 🏛

R. Ga
LG. D
CHIAD

R. Sé o Velho

Calçada do Marquês Abrantes

R. de Dom Luís I

R. de São Paulo

R. Flores

Cyber.
bica

R. A.M.
Cardoso

TO 🏛 MUSEU NACIONAL
DE ARTE ANTIGA (150m)
& BELÉM

Av. 24 de Julho

R. Ribeira Nova

R. Alecrim

Museu Nacio
Arte Contempo

Doca de Alcântara

Mercado de
Ribeira

CAIS DO
SODRÉ Ⓜ

Ⓜ

Estação Cais
do Sodré

R. do Arse

Rio Tejo

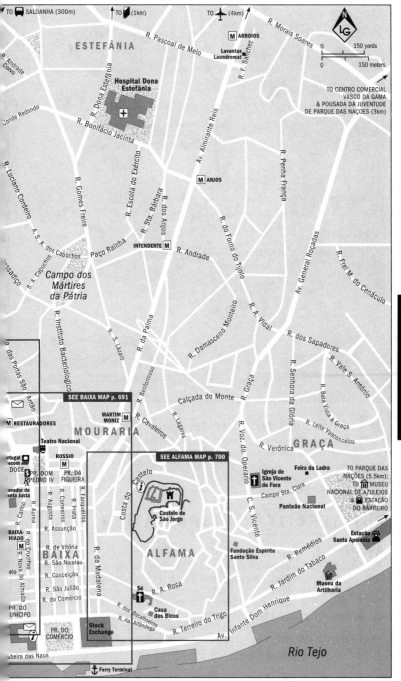

TO ▪ SALDANHA (300m)

TO ▪ (1km)

TO ✈ (4km)

R. Pascoal de Melo

M ARROIOS

R. Morais Soares

ESTEFÂNIA

R. Andrade
Corvo

Lavantax
Laundromat

R. F. Sanchez

N

0 — 150 yards
0 — 150 meters

TO CENTRO COMERCIAL
VASCO DA GAMA
& POUSADA DA JUVENTUDE
DE PARQUE DAS NAÇÕES (3km)

Conde Redondo

R. Dona Estefânia

**Hospital Dona
Estefânia**

R. Bonifácio Jacinta

Av. Almirante Reis

R. Penha França

R. Luciano Cordeiro

R. Gomes Freire

R. Escola do Exército

R. Sta. Bárbara

R. dos Anjos

M ANJOS

R. do Forno do Tijolo

Av. General Roçadas

R. Frei M. do Cenáculo

A. S. A. dos Capuchos

S. A. Capuchos

Paço Rainha

INTENDENTE **M**

R. Andrade

R. A. Vidal

R. da Palma

R. Damasceno Monteiro

R. dos Sapadores

*Campo dos
Mártires
da Pátria*

R. Instituto Bacteriológico

R. S. Lázaro

R. Bemposta

Calçada do Monte

Graça

R. Senhora da Glória

R. Vale S. António

R. Bela Vista à Graça

R. Leite Vasconcelos

das Portas São

Antão

✉

M RESTAURADORES

SEE BAIXA MAP p. 691

**MARTIM
MONIZ** **M**

R. Cavaleiros

R. Lagres

R. Voz do Operário

R. Verónica

GRAÇA

MOURARIA

Teatro Nacional

Portugal
ecom
DOCE

ROSSIO
M

PR. DOM
PEDRO IV

PR. DA
FIGUEIRA

R. Fanqueiros

Costa do Castelo

SEE ALFAMA MAP p. 700

Feira da Ladra

**Igreja de
São Vicente
de Fora**

TO PARQUE DAS
NAÇÕES (5.5km);
TO ▥ MUSEU
NACIONAL DE AZULEJOS
& ▪ ESTAÇÃO
DO BÁRREIRO

evador de
nta Justa

R. Áurea

R. Correeiros

R. Prata

R. Augusta

Campo Sta. Clara

Panteão Nacional

BAIXA-
HIADO **M**

R. do Crucifixo

R. Nova do Almada

R. de Vitória

R. Assunção

BAIXA

R. São Nicolau

R. Conceição

R. São Julião

R. do Comércio

R. da Madalena

**Castelo de
São Jorge**

ℹ

ALFAMA

C. S. Vicente

**Fundação Espírito
Santo Silva**

**Estação
Santa Apolónia** ▪

R. Remédios

PR. DO
UNICIPO

Sé
✝

R. A. Rosa

**Casa
dos Bicos**

R. Jardim do Tabaco

**Museu da
Artilharia**

ibeira das Naus

PR. DO
COMÉRCIO

**Stock
Exchange**

R. dos
Bacalhoeiros

R. da Alfândega

R. Terreiro do Trigo

Av. Infante Dom Henrique

Rio Tejo

⚓ **Ferry Terminal**

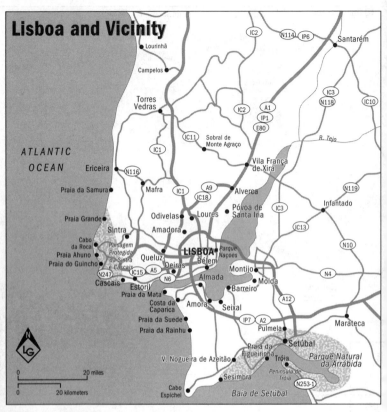

Lisboa and Vicinity

HOW TO USE THIS CHAPTER. Lisboa is divided into several neighborhoods. We have grouped together all of each area's accommodations, food, sights, museums, and nightlife listings. General information on these aspects of Lisboa, as well as shopping and specific listings for camping and entertainment (including sports, theater, concerts, and film) appears after the practical information.

■ INTERCITY TRANSPORTATION

BY PLANE

All flights land at **Aeroporto de Lisboa** (☎218 41 35 00), on the city's northern edge. Walk out of the terminal, turn right, and follow the path around the curve to the bus stop. Take **bus** #44 or 45 (15-20min., every 12-15min. 7am-9pm, €1) to Pr. dos Restauradores; the bus stops in front of the tourist office, located inside the Palácio da Foz. The express **AeroBus** #91 runs to the same locations (15min., every 20min. 7am-9pm, €1); it's a better option during rush hour. A **taxi** downtown costs about €6 (plus a €1.50 baggage fee) at low traffic hours, but trips are billed by time, not distance. Once drivers realize that you are foreign, some may try to keep your change or take a much longer route. To avoid this, ask at the **tourist office** (☎218 45 06 60) inside the airport about the **voucher** program, which allows visitors to pre-pay for cab rides from the airport. Major airlines have offices at Pr. Marquês de Pombal and along Av. da Liberdade.

BY TRAIN

Train service in and out of Lisboa routinely proves to be the bane of every traveller's existence, as there are three stations in Lisboa and one across the river in Barreiro, each serving different destinations. Long-distance trains in Portugal tend to be quite slow; buses, although more expensive, are both faster and more comfortable. However, the two train lines with service to locations near Lisboa (to Cascais and Sintra, with stops along the way) are both reliable. Contact **Caminhos de Ferro Portugueses** for further information about Portugal's rail system. (☎800 20 09 04 for Lisboa connections, 808 20 82 08 elsewhere; www.cp.pt. Open daily 7am-11pm.) The friendly, English-speaking staff at the information desk on the ground floor of Estação Rossio is another reliable source of train information.

Estação do Barreiro (☎213 47 29 30), across the Rio Tejo. Serves points south. Station accessible by ferry from the Terreiro do Paço dock off Pr. do Comércio. (30min., every 30min., €1.30.) To: **Évora** (2½hr., 5 per day 6am-8pm, €12); **Lagos** (5½hr., 5 per day 8:30am-7:30pm, €12); **Setúbal** (1½hr., every 30min. 6am-1am, €1.70).

Estação Cais do Sodré (☎213 47 01 81), just beyond the end of R. do Alecrim, a 5min. walk from Baixa. M: Cais do Sodré. Take the metro or bus #1, 44, or 45 from Pr. dos Restauradores or bus #28 from Estação Santa Apolónia. To: the monastery in **Belém** (10min., every 15min. 5:30am-2:50am, €1); **Cascais** and **Estoril** (30min., every 15min., €1.30); the youth hostel in **Oeiras** (20min., every 15min., €1.30).

Estação Rossio (☎213 46 50 22). M: Rossio or Restauradores. Services points west. **Information** on ground level open daily 10am-1pm and 2-8pm; domestic ticket window open 7am-4pm; international window open 9:15am-noon and 1-5:30pm. English spoken. To **Sintra** (45min., every 15-30min. 6am-2am, €1.30) via **Queluz** (€0.90).

Estação Santa Apolónia, Av. Infante Dom Henrique (☎218 88 40 25). Runs the international, northern, and eastern lines. All trains to Santa Apolónia also stop at **Estação Oriente** (M: Oriente) by the **Parque das Nações**. The international terminal has **currency exchange** and an **info desk** (English spoken). To reach downtown, take bus #9, 39, 46, or 90 to Pr. dos Restauradores and Estação Rossio. To: **Aveiro** (3-3½hr., 20 per day 5:20am-7:55pm, €12); **Braga** (5hr., 19 per day 5:20am-6:55pm, €25); **Coimbra** (2½hr., 23 per day 5:20am-7:55pm, €15); **Madrid** (10hr., 10:05pm, €54); **Porto** (4½hr., 20 per day 5:20am-7:55pm, €13.50).

BY BUS

The bus station is the **Arco do Cego**, Av. João Crisóstomo, around the block from M: Saldanha. Exit the metro onto Av. da República, walk one block up from Pr. Duque de Saldanha, and take a right onto Av. João Crisóstomo. The bus station is a beige building on the corner of Av. João Crisóstomo and Av. Defensores de Chaves. All Saldanha buses (#36, 44, 45) stop in Pr. Duque de Saldanha (€0.60).

Rede Expressos (☎707 22 33 44; www.rede-expressos.pt). To: **Braga** (5hr., 13 per day 7am-12:15am, €14.50); **Coimbra** (2½hr., every 15min. 6:15am-2am, €9.50); **Évora** (2hr., 26 per day 7am-10:30pm, €9.80); **Faro** (5hr., 16 per day 7am-12:15am, €14.50); **Lagos** (5hr., 16 per day 7am-1am, €15); **Peniche** (2hr., 13 per day 7am-10pm, €6.40); **Portalegre** (4½hr., 13 per day 7:30am-7pm, €10.50); **Porto** (4hr., 19 per day 7am-12:15am, €13.50) via **Leiria** (2hr., €8); **Tavira** (5hr., 10 per day 5am-1am, €15).

LISBOA

▟ ORIENTATION

The city center is made up of three neighborhoods: **Baixa** (low district, located in a valley), **Bairro Alto** (high district), and hilly **Alfama**. The suburbs extending in both directions along the river represent some of the fastest-growing sections of the city and are interesting for their contrast with the historic districts. Areas of interest, several kilometers from downtown, include **Belém** (p. 703), **Alcântara,** whose docks are home to much of Lisboa's party scene, and the **Parque das Nações** (p. 703), the site of the 1998 World Exposition and host of a number of attractions.

Alfama, Lisboa's famous medieval Moorish neighborhood, was the lone survivor of the 1755 earthquake. The city's oldest district, it is a labyrinth of narrow alleys, unmarked streets, and *escandinhas*—narrow stairways that only seem to lead to more unmarked streets: expect to get lost, and without a detailed map, expect to get doubly lost. The street-indexed **GeoBloco Planta Turística de Lisboa** and the **Poseidon Planta de Lisboa** (including Sintra, Cascais, and Estoril) are good maps, but expensive (both sold in Estação Rossio and at newsstands, €10). The maps at the tourist offices are also reliable and, most importantly, free.

▟ LOCAL TRANSPORTATION

Lisboa and its surrounding areas have an efficient public transportation system with subways, buses, trams, and funiculars run by **CARRIS** (☎213 61 30 00; www.carris.pt). Use it to full advantage—no suburb takes longer than 90min. to reach. If you plan to stay in Lisboa for any length of time, consider a *passe turístico*, good for unlimited travel on all CARRIS transports. Passes are available for one, three, four, and seven days (€2.35/€5.65/€9.95/€14.10). CARRIS booths, located in most network train stations and the busier metro stations (e.g., M: Restauradores), sell multi-day passes. (Open daily 8am-9pm.) As you pass through various metro stations, enjoy the murals, poetry, and sculptures that celebrate talent in Portugal. If you don't speak Portuguese, taxi drivers may try to charge an exorbitant fare or keep your change; try to find out the approximate fare in advance.

Buses: €1 within the city; pay on the bus.

Metro: (☎213 55 84 57; www.metrolisboa.pt). €0.65 per ride, unlimited daily use ticket €1.40, book of 10 tickets €5.10, 1wk. pass €4.80. Covers downtown and the modern business district with 4 lines. A red "M" marks metro stops. Trains run daily 6:30am-1am, though some stations close earlier.

Trams: €1. Many date from before WWI. Line #28 is great for sightseeing in Alfama and Mouraria (stop in Pr. do Comércio). Line #15 heads from Pr. do Comércio and Pr. da Figueira to Belém and the nightlife districts Av. 24 de Julho and Docas de Santo Amaro.

Funiculars: €1. Funiculars link the lower city with the residential areas in the hills. Elevador da Glória goes from Pr. dos Restauradores to Bairro Alto (3min., every 5min.).

Taxis: Rádio Táxis de Lisboa (☎218 11 90 00), **Autocoope** (☎217 93 27 56), and **Teletáxis** (☎218 11 11 00). Along Av. da Liberdade and Rossio. Luggage €1.50.

Car Rental: A car is an unnecessary burden if your travels take you only to Lisboa, though one can be useful for daytrips. Agencies have offices at the airport, train stations, and downtown; contact them for specific locations. **Avis,** Campo Grande, 390, 2nd fl. (☎800 201 002; fax 217 54 78 52); **Budget,** R. Castilho, 167B (☎213 86 05 16; fax 55 69 20); **Hertz,** R. Castilho, 72A (☎800 238 238; fax 218 87 41 64).

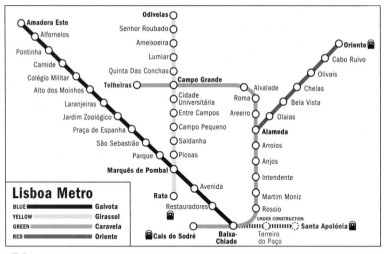

Lisboa Metro

BLUE ■■■■■■■	Gaivota	
YELLOW	Girassol	
GREEN	Caravela	
RED ■■■■■■	Oriente	

⌷ PRACTICAL INFORMATION

TOURIST AND FINANCIAL SERVICES

Tourist Office: Palácio da Foz, Pr. dos Restauradores (☎213 46 33 14). M: Restauradores. The largest tourist office has information about the entire country. Open daily 9am-8pm. The **Welcome Center,** Pr. do Comércio (☎210 31 28 10), is the main office for the city. Sells tickets for sightseeing buses and the "Lisboa Card," which includes transportation and entrance to most sights for a flat fee (1-day €13.25, 2-day €22.50, 3-day €27.50; children €5.90/€9.10/€11.90). A real bargain, but it requires an exhausting schedule to take full advantage of its offers. English spoken. Open daily 9am-8pm. **Branch** at the airport (☎218 45 06 60), just outside the baggage claim area. English spoken. Open daily 8am-midnight. For more info, look for kiosks that read "Ask me about Lisboa" at Santa Apolónia, Belém, and other locations.

Budget Travel: Movijovem, Av. Duque d'Ávila, 137 (☎213 52 86 21; www.pousadasjuventude.pt). M: São Sebastião. Open daily 9am-7pm. V.

Embassies: See **Embassies and Consulates,** p. 672.

Currency Exchange: Banks are open M-F 8:30am-3pm. **Cota Câmbio,** Pr. Dom Pedro IV, 41 (☎213 22 04 80). Open M-Sa 9am-8pm. The main post office, most banks, and travel agencies also change money. Exchanges line the streets of Baixa. Ask about fees first—they can be exorbitant.

American Express: Top Tours, Av. Duque de Loulé, 108 (☎213 19 42 90). M: Marquês de Pombal. Exit the metro and walk up Av. da Liberdade toward the Marquês de Pombal statue, then turn right. English spoken. Open M-F 9:30am-1pm and 2:30-6:30pm.

LOCAL SERVICES

English-Language Bookstore: Livraria Británica, R. Luís Fernandes, 14-16 (☎213 42 84 72; britanica.lis@dinternal.pt), in Rato (see **Lisboa Overview,** p. 678). Walk up R. São Pedro de Alcântara from Bairro Alto; keep straight as it becomes R. Dom Pedro V and then R. Escola Politécnica. Turn left onto R. São Marcal, then right after 2 blocks onto R. Luís Fernandes (20min.). Open M-F 9:30am-7pm. AmEx/MC/V.

Library: Biblioteca Municipal Central, Palácio Galveias (☎217 97 38 62). M: Campo Pequeño. Open M-F 10am-7pm, Sa 11am-6pm.

Shopping Centers: Colombo, Av. Lusíada (☎217 11 36 36), in front of Benfica stadium. M: Colégio Militar-Luz. The largest and most popular shopping mall in Portugal, with over 400 shops, a 10-screen cinema, and a small amusement park. Open daily 10am-midnight. **Centro Comercial Amoreiras de Lisboa,** Av. Eng. Duarte Pacheco (☎213 81 02 00), near R. Carlos Alberto da Mota Pinto. M: Marquês de Pombal. Take bus #11 from Pr. dos Restauradores. 383 shops, including a huge **Pão de Açúcar** supermarket, English bookstores, and cinema. Open daily 10am-11pm. **Centro Comercial Vasco da Gama,** Av. Dom João II (☎218 93 06 00). M: Oriente. Open daily 9am-midnight.

El Corte Inglés, Av. António Augusto de Aguiar at Av. Duque d'Ávila (☎213 71 17 00; fax 83 21 42). M: São Sebastião. Portugal's first branch of the Spanish department store giant has everything, including electronics, designer clothes, groceries, and the largest movie theater in Lisboa (14 screens). Open M-Th 10am-10pm, F-Su 10am-11:30pm.

Laundromats: Lavatax, R. Francisco Sanches, 65A (☎218 12 33 92). Wash, dry, and fold €2 per kg. Open M-F 8:30am-1pm and 3-7pm, Sa 8:30am-1pm. **Lavandaria Clin,** R. de São João da Praça, 5-7, in Alfama. Wash, dry, and fold €4 per kg. Open M-F 8:30am-7:30pm, Sa 8am-3pm.

EMERGENCY AND COMMUNICATIONS

Police: R. Capelo, 13 (☎213 46 61 41 or 42 16 34). English spoken.

Late-Night Pharmacy: ☎118 (directory assistance). Look for the green cross at every intersection, or specifically at **Farmácia Azevedos,** Pr. Dom Pedro IV, 31 (☎213 43 04 02), at the base of Rossio in front of the metro.

Medical Services: Hospital Inglês, R. Saraiva de Carvalho, 49 (☎213 95 50 67). **Cruz Vermelha** (Red Cross), R. Duarte Galvão, 54 (**ambulance** ☎219 42 11 11).

Telephones: Portugal Telecom, Pr. Dom Pedro IV, 68 (☎808 21 11 56). M: Rossio. Has pay phones and booths for international calls. Pay the cashier after your call or use a phone card. Also has **Internet access.** (€1.25 for the first 30min., €0.75 per 15min. after that.) Office open daily 8am- 8pm. V. Buy Portugal Telecom **phone cards** (50 units €3, 100 units €6, or 150 units €9) at the office or at neighborhood bookstores and stationers. Local calls cost at least 2 units. Minutes per unit vary with type of call and type of phone. PT cards should only be purchased for local use; better deals on non-local calls can be found elsewhere, such as at **Casa Viola,** R. Augusta, 222, on the main pedestrian walkway in Baixa. 120min. calling card to the U.S. €5.

Internet Access: Web C@fé, R. Diário de Notícias, 126 (☎213 42 11 81). €2 per 15min., €2.50 per 30min., €3.50 per 45min., €4 per hr. Open daily 4pm-2am. **Cyber.bica,** R. Duques de Bragança, 7 (☎213 22 50 04), in Bairro Alto. €0.75 per 15min., €3 per hr. Open M-Th 11am-midnight, F 11am-2am.

Post Office: Main office, Pr. dos Restauradores (☎213 28 87 00). Open daily 8am-7pm. Often extremely crowded. To avoid the lines, go to the **branch,** Pr. do Comércio (☎213 22 09 20). Open M-F 8:30am-6:30pm. Cash only. **Postal Code: 1100.**

⌕ ACCOMMODATIONS

The local government enforces a price ceiling on *pensões* and hostels, but some try to ignore it. If prices seem inflated, ask for the printed price list. Also, room quality may vary significantly, so ask to see the room beforehand. During the summer, expect to pay €20-30 for a single and €35-45 for a double, depending on amenities. In low season, prices generally drop €5 or more, so try bargaining. Many establishments have rooms with only double beds and charge per person.

Several hotels are in the center of town on Av. da Liberdade, while many more convenient budget hostels are in Baixa along the Rossio and on R. da Prata, R. dos Correiros, and R. do Ouro (R. de Aurea). Lodgings near Castelo de São Jorge are quieter and closer to the sights. If central accommodations are full, head east to the hostels along Av. Almirante dos Reis. Generally, the farther you get from Baixa, the cheaper the accommodations. Be careful at night, especially in Alfama and Bairro Alto; many streets are isolated and poorly lit. Bairro Alto's barely concealed drug trade is another reason for caution in this neighborhood. While these areas are certainly not lairs of rampant crime and debauchery, it pays to be alert.

YOUTH HOSTELS

Pousada da Juventude de Lisboa (HI), R. Andrade Corvo, 46 (☎213 53 26 96). M: Picoas. Exit the metro station onto R. Andrade Corvo and it will be right in front of you. Spacious, recently renovated rooms with fantastic meal options (enormous breakfast included; lunch and dinner available, €5 each). A bar and reading room allow for some quiet time. HI card required. Always reserve ahead; this place is usually packed. June-Sept. dorms €15; doubles with bath €42. Oct.-May €12.50/€35. MC/V. ❶

Pousada da Juventude de Parque das Nações (HI), R. de Moscavide, 47-101 (☎218 92 08 90; fax 92 08 91). M: Oriente. Exit the station and go left on Av. Dom João II for about 20-30min., walking past the Parque das Nações until the street intersects with R. de Moscavide. The hostel is the striped building on the corner, inside the Instituto Português da Juventude. Rooms are cheap but far from the central city. Internet €0.50 for 15min. HI card required. June-Sept. dorms €13; doubles €37. Oct.-May €11/€30. ❶

CAMPING

Camping is popular in Portugal, but campers can be prime targets for thieves. Be aware of your surroundings and use common sense; stay at an enclosed campsite and ask ahead about security. Info is available from the tourist office in the free booklet *Portugal: Camping and Caravan Sites.* There are 30 campgrounds within a 45min. radius of the capital; listed below is the only one in Lisboa proper.

Parque de Campismo Municipal de Lisboa (☎217 60 96 20; fax 217 62 31 06), on the road to Benfica. Take bus #14 to Parque Florestal Monsanto; campsite is at entrance to park. Pool and supermarket. Reception daily 9am-9pm. July-Aug. €4.80 per person, €5 per tent, €3.20 per car. Sept.-June prices vary, but generally run €3.20-3.70. ❶

ACCOMMODATIONS BY PRICE

A Alfama **B** Baixa **BA** Bairro Alto **E** Elsewhere **PN** Parque das Naçoes			
UNDER €15 (❶)		Pensão Estrela (701)	A
Campismo Municipal de Lisboa (685)	E	Pensão Ninho das Águias (700)	A
Pensão Beira Mar (701)	A	Pensão Prata (690)	B
Pousada da Juventude de Lisboa (685)	E	Pensão Verandas (701)	A
Pousada da Juventude de P.N. (685)	PN		
		€26-35 (❸)	
€15-25 (❷)		Residencial Duas Nações (690)	B
Casa de Hóspedes Globo (695)	BA		
Hospedagem Estrela da Serra (690)	B	**€36-45 (❹)**	
Luar Guest House (695)	BA	Pensão Londres (695)	BA
Pensão Estação Central (690)	B	Residencial Florescente (690)	B

🖪 FOOD

Lisboa has some of the least expensive restaurants and best wine of any western European capital. A full dinner costs about €9-11 per person (even in touristy Baixa) and the *prato do dia* (daily special) is often only €4-6. Until then, snack on surprisingly filling, incredibly cheap, and addictively delicious Portuguese pastries; *pastelarias* are everywhere. Incidentally, calorie-counters should proceed with caution in any Portuguese eatery besides supermarkets. In Lisboa, the closer to the industrial waterfront, the cheaper the restaurant. The south end of Baixa, near the port, and the area bordering Alfama are particularly inexpensive. In Baixa, moving just a block off R. de Augusta, the main pedestrian street, can save you a few euros. Lisboa abounds with seafood specialties such as *amêijoas à bulhão pato* (steamed clams), *creme de mariscos* (seafood chowder with tomatoes), and *bacalhau cozido com grão e batatas* (cod with chick peas and boiled potatoes, doused in olive oil). For a more diverse food selection, head up to the winding streets of Bairro Alto, where restaurants specialize in everything from shark to dishes from Góa, a former Portuguese colony on the Indian coast.

SUPERMARKETS

Pingo Doce (☎213 42 74 95), on R. 1 de Dezembro. A small branch of Portugal's major supermarket chain and the only one in central Lisboa. Open M-Sa 8:30am-9pm.

Mercado da Ribeira (☎213 46 29 66), on Av. 24 de Julho. M: Cais de Sodré. Accessible by bus #40 or tram #15. A vast market complex inside a warehouse, just outside Estação Cais do Sodré. Go early for the freshest selection of fruit, fish, and a variety of other foods. Open M-Sa 6am-2pm for produce, 3-7pm for flowers.

Supermercado Pão de Açúcar, Amoreiras Shopping Center de Lisboa, Av. Duarte Pacheco (☎213 82 66 80). Take bus #11 from Pr. dos Restauradores or Pr. da Figueira. Open daily 9am-11pm.

FOOD BY TYPE

A Alfama **B** Baixa **BA** Bairro Alto **G** Graça

INTERNATIONAL				
🍴 Churrasqueira Gaúcha (692)	B ❷		🍴 Martinho da Arcada (692)	B ❸/❶
Restaurante Ali-a-Papa (696)	BA ❸		O Eurico (701)	A ❷
Restaurante Calcuta (695)	BA ❷		Pastelaria Anunciada (692)	B ❷
Restô (703)	G ❷		Restaurante Bomjardim (692)	B ❷
Ristorante Valentino (692)	B ❸		Restaurante Tavares Rico (695)	BA ❺
🍴 Sul (695)	BA ❸		Restaurante Tripeiro (692)	B ❷
			SANDWICHES	
PORTUGUESE			🍴 A Brasileira (695)	BA ❷
A Lanterna (692)	B ❶		Casa das Sandes (692)	B ❶
Churrasqueira O Cofre (701)	A ❷		Ninho Dourado (692)	B ❷

🖸 SIGHTS

To refer to the wonders that attract visitors to Lisboa as "sights" is a bit misleading. From the most modern of art to the most natural of beauty, Lisboa is a city to be experienced. Relaxed *parques* sprinkled throughout the city are complemented by the energy of electrified crowds and crawling commercial districts.

Each intricate neighborhood unravels at the feet of the curious traveler to reveal its history and modern spirit. Those who plan on seeing the whole city might consider purchasing the Welcome Center's "Lisboa Card" (see **Tourist Office,** p. 683).

NIGHTLIFE

Bairro Alto is the first place to go for nightlife, especially before 2am. In particular, **Rua do Norte, Rua do Diário de Notícias,** and **Rua Atalaia** have many small bars and clubs packed into three short blocks, making club-hopping as easy as crossing the street. Several gay and lesbian establishments are between Pr. Luis de Camões and Tr. da Queimada, as well as in the **Rato** area near the edge of Bairro Alto, past Pr. Príncipe Real. For later hours, the options outside Bairro Alto are flashier and more diverse; **Docas de Santo Amaro** hosts a strip of waterfront bars, clubs, and restaurants while the **Avenida 24 de Julho** and the **Rua das Janelas Verdes,** in the **Santos** area above, have some of the most popular clubs and discos. Newer expansions include the area along the river across from the **Santa Apolónia** train station, where the glitzy club Lux is located. At clubs, jeans and sneakers are generally not allowed—some places have uptight fashion police at the door. Inside, beer runs €3-5. Some clubs also charge a cover (generally €10). There's no reason to show up before midnight; crowds flow in around 2am and stay past dawn.

ENTERTAINMENT

Agenda Cultural and *Follow Me Lisboa,* free at the tourist office and at kiosks in the Rossio on R. Portas de Santo Antão, have information on concerts, movies, plays, and bullfights. They also have lists of museums, gardens, and libraries.

FADO

A mandatory experience for anyone visiting the city, Lisboa's trademark entertainment is the heart-wringing *fado,* an expressive art combining elements of singing and narrative poetry (see **Music,** p. 670). *Cantadeiras de fado,* cloaked in black dresses and shawls, relate emotional tales of lost loves and faded glory. Their melancholy wailing is expressive of *saudade,* an emotion of nostalgia and yearning; listeners are supposed to feel the "knife turning in their hearts." On weekends, book in advance. Bairro Alto has many options off R. da Misericórdia and on side streets radiating from Igreja de São Roque; it's the best place in the city for top-quality *fado.* All of the popular houses have high "minimum consumption" requirements (normally €15-20). To avoid shelling out, explore nearby streets; various bars and small venues often offer free shows with less notable performers, but are harder to find. Otherwise, eat dinner beforehand and enjoy dessert and a glass of port instead of an overpriced meal. These places may be touristy, but they do feature Portugal's top names in *fado.* All have acts every 20 minutes.

O Faia, R. Barroca, 56 (☎213 42 67 42; www.ofaia.com), between R. Atalaia and R. Diário de Notícias. Performances by famous *fadistas* like Anita Guerreiro and Lenita Gentil as well as some of the finest Portuguese cuisine available make O Faia worth your time and money. Minimum consumption €17.50, includes 2 drinks. Entrees €20-25. Open M-Sa 8pm-2am; *fado* starts at 9:30pm. AmEx/MC/V. ❹

Machado, R. Norte, 91 (☎213 22 46 40; fax 46 75 07). Founded in 1937, Machado is one of the larger *fado* restaurants and features some of the best known *cantadeiras* and guitarists. Don't be surprised if you run into someone famous here, as Machado has been known to entertain celebrities intent on experiencing *fado* at one of Lisboa's

SINGING YOUR SORROWS

If your heart is broken, *fado* will not only captivate it but nurse it back to health. The melodies and lyrics of *fado* drip with the wrenching pain of unrequited passion. *Let's Go* researcher Peter Brown had an opportunity to interview one of Lisbon's famed *fado* singers, Sara Reis.

LG: So, what makes *fado* different from other traditional songs about heartbreak?

SR: *Fado* comes from the Latin, *fatum,* which means destiny. it's a feeling that is born with us. Either you understand it or you don't. I do because I was born in the middle of *fadistas.* At home I never heard Rock 'n' Roll, and by the time I reached age 7, I was already singing *fado.* To feel *fado* in its totality is to understand life—it's love, death, birth, passion, hatred. It's very complex. In order to really feel *fado,* you have to have reached a certain level of maturity and suffering. There you have it. *Fado* is nostalgia. In my opinion, it is one of the most revolutionary kinds of music. It was created by and for the people. The original *fadistas* would sing about murder and prostitution.

LG: That makes sense. Now, with so much suffering in the world, so much pain, why did *fado* come about here? What makes it specifically Portuguese?

SR: I've heard a lot of different answers to that question during these 42 years. I read a lot, and

best-known locales. Minimum consumption €16. Entrees €25-35. Open Su and Tu-Sa 8pm-3am; *fado* starts at 9:15pm. AmEx/MC/V. ❹

O Forcado, R. da Rosa, 219-221 (☎213 46 85 79; fax 47 48 87). Features *fado* from Coimbra and Lisboa as well as folk music and dance. Decorated with bullfighting pictures and *azulejos* (tiles). Prides itself on its menu as well, with part of the restaurant removed from the performance area. Minimum consumption €15. Entrees €16-25. Open Su-Tu and Th-Sa 8pm-1:30am; *fado* starts at 9pm. AmEx/MC/V. ❹

Cristal Fados, Tr. da Queimada, 9 (☎213 42 67 87). Less famous singers and less luxurious meals; have dinner without blowing your budget. Minimum consumption €8. Entrees €12. Open 8:30pm-1am; *fado* Th-Su. AmEx/MC/V. ❸

BULLFIGHTING

Portuguese bullfighting differs from the Spanish variety in that the bull is not killed, a tradition that dates back to the 18th century. These spectacles take place most Thursdays from late June to late September at ◪**Praça de Touros de Lisboa,** Campo Pequeno. (☎217 93 21 43. Open daily 10pm-2am.) Take the metro to Campo Pequeno or bus #1, 44, 45, or 83. The newly renovated Praça is the perfect venue in which to observe the distinctly Portuguese *toureio equestre,* or horseback bullfighting (see **There's More Than One Way to Fight a Bull,** p. 732). True aficionados should include **Setúbal** (p. 715) in their travel plans, as it is the capital of Portuguese bullfighting and hosts some of the most celebrated *matadores.*

FUTEBOL

The lifeblood of many a Portuguese citizen, the sport that *"gringos"* know as soccer, *futebol* is clearly king in Portugal. The recent success of FC Porto, which won the UEFA Champions League, the most prestigious European club tournament, in 2004, has sparked a renewed sense of pride in Portuguese club *futebol.* With Portugal in the finals of Euro 2004 (the European championship, which Portugal hosted), the fever over this national pastime has reached new heights. Lisboa has two professional teams, **Benfica** and **Sporting,** both of which feature some of the world's finest players. (**Benfica** at Estadio da Luz; ☎217 26 61 29; M: Colégio Militar-Luz. **Sporting** at Alvalade Stadium; ☎217 56 79 14; M: Campo Grande.) Be careful of whom you support in public—Benfica and Sporting are bitter rivals and both have diehard fans who won't buy the excuse that you're "just a tourist." Check the ABEP kiosk in Pr. dos Restauradores or the sports newspaper *A Bola* for games.

THEATER, MUSIC, AND FILM

Teatro Nacional de Dona Maria II, Pr. Dom Pedro IV, stages performances of classical Portuguese and foreign plays and houses the **Orquesta Nacional** (☎213 47 22 26; €3.50-10, 50% student discount). At Lisboa's largest theater, **Teatro Nacional de São Carlos,** R. Serpa Pinto, 9, near the Museu do Chiado in Bairro Alto, **opera** reigns from late September through mid-June. (☎ 213 46 59 14. Open daily 1-7pm.)

The **São Jorge** movie theater (☎212 42 25 23) is at the corner of Av. da Liberdade and Av. dos Condes, across from the Pr. dos Restauradores tourist office. Ten-screen cinemas are also located in the **Amoreiras** (☎217 81 02 00; M: Marquês de Pombal) and **Colombo** (☎217 11 36 36; M: Colegio Militar Luz) shopping centers and on the top floor of the **Centro Vasco da Gama** (☎218 93 06 01; M: Oriente). The largest theater, with 14 screens, is part of the new **El Corte Inglés** shopping complex (☎213 71 17 00; M: São Sebastião). American films are shown with Portuguese subtitles.

🌸 FESTIVALS

Those who love to mingle with the public will want to visit Lisboa in June. Open-air *feiras*—smorgasbords of eating, drinking, live music, and dancing—fill the streets. After savoring *farturas* (huge Portuguese pastries) and Sagres beer, join in traditional Portuguese dancing. On the night of June 12, the streets explode into song and dance in honor of St. Anthony during the **Festa de Santo António.** Banners are strung between streetlights, and confetti falls in buckets during a parade along Av. da Liberdade; young crowds absolutely pack the streets of Alfama, and grilled *sardinhas* (sardines) and *ginja* (wild cherry liqueur) are sold everywhere. Lisboa also has a number of commercial *feiras* (fairs). Bookworms burrow for three weeks in the **Feira do Livro** (in Parque Eduardo VII behind Pr. Marquês de Pombal from late May to early June). The **Feira Internacional de Lisboa** occurs every few months in the Parque das Nações, while in July and August the **Feira de Mar de Cascais** and **Feira de Artesania de Estoril** (celebrating famous Portuguese pottery) take place near the casino. Year-round *feiras* include the **Feira de Oeiras** (Antiques) on the fourth Sunday of each month and the **Feira de Carcanelos,** for clothes (Th 8am-2pm). Packrats should catch the **Feira da Ladra** (flea market), held behind Igreja de São Vicente de Fora in the Graça neighborhood (Tu and Sa 7am-3pm). Take bus #104 or 105 or tram #28.

nobody has ever come to a conclusion. But my own opinion is simple.

Just by virtue of the fact that in 1500 we were already exploring the world, and shipwrecks, and these 42 years. I read a lot, and nobody has ever come to a conclusion. But my own opinion is simple.

LG: Do you think *fado* has anything to do with Portugal's influence on the African continent?

SR: I think that obviously there was a lot of mixing going on. We've got some Arab blood in us, some Spanish blood. So I wouldn't be surprised. There's always a mix.

LG: Can somebody who has never had a broken heart sing *fado*?

SR: Sweetheart, I have already heard young girls no older than 16 sing about life in a way that would move you with emotion. And, on the other hand, I've heard old *fado* singers 50 years old sing from here (points to her head). It all depends on the sensibility and ability of the person.

Modern fadistas, *including* **Amália Rodrigues** and **Argentina Santos,** *have made* fado *a cultural fixture since the legendary* **Maria Severa** *first made it popular in the early 19th century.*

BAIXA

Baixa, Lisboa's old business hub, is the center of town, its neatly laid streets lined with cafes and shoe stores. The grid begins at **Praça Dom Pedro IV** (better known as **Rossio**) and ends at **Praça do Comércio** on the **Rio Tejo.** The *praças* work well as decorative bookends to new Lisboa, completely rebuilt after the earthquake of 1755 totaled it (if Mr. Richter had invented his scale back then, records show that this quake would have tipped 8.9). Pr. do Comércio was actually built on the site of the former Royal Palace, and hence bears the nickname *Terreiro do Paço* (the Palace Lot). Expect to meet many travelers in Baixa; a central train station and the main Portuguese tourist office make Rossio the city's tourist hub (visitors seem to reproduce there at an exponential rate). Linked to Rossio is **Praça dos Restauradores,** where buses from the airport stop and those to other destinations start. Pr. dos Restauradores lies just above Baixa, and from it, sprawling **Avenida da Liberdade** runs uphill to the new business district around **Praça do Marquês de Pombal.**

ACCOMMODATIONS

Dozens of *pensões* surround the three connected *praças* that form the heart of downtown Lisboa. Staying in this area is quite convenient, as it serves as a good base for visiting sights in and around the city. On the other hand, Baixa's prices are noticeably higher than other neighborhoods, particularly during the summer. Most *pensões* are on the top floors of buildings (a hassle for luggage-laden travelers), often overlooking noisy streets; keep your head up (literally) when looking for a place to stay in Baixa because *pensões* are often poorly advertised and easy to miss. Few are especially memorable, though they do differ slightly in amenities. If you didn't reserve at least a week ahead in summer, don't despair; it's usually possible to track something down without too much effort.

▨ **Pensão Estação Central,** Calçada da Carmo, 17, 2nd-3rd fl. (☎213 42 33 08; fax 46 94 97). M: Rossio. Small, plain rooms, but inexpensive and centrally located right off Rossio. TV lounge with a tapestry depicting the Last Supper draped on the wall. Watch out for the swiftly swinging door that leads to the street. Singles have shared bath. June-Sept. singles €20; doubles €35; triples €45. Oct.-May €15/€25/€35. ❷

Hospedagem Estrela da Serra, R. dos Fanqueiros, 122, 4th fl. (☎218 87 42 51). M: Baixa-Chiado. The 5-floor hike doesn't pass by unnoticed, but neither does the resulting view; half the rooms have terraces from which you can see all of Baixa. Away from the area's busiest streets, you're guaranteed a quiet night's rest. June-Aug. singles €15-20; doubles €25-30. Sept.-May €10-15/€20-25. ❷

Pensão Prata, R. da Prata, 71, 3rd fl. (☎213 46 89 08). M: Baixa-Chiado. Basic rooms, some with small bath. July-Sept. singles €25, with bath €30; doubles €30/€35; triples with bath €35. Oct.-June €18-20/€20-25/€20/€25/€30. Must pay ahead. ❷

Residencial Florescente, R. das Portas de Santo Antão, 99 (☎213 42 66 09; www.residencialflorescente.com). M: Restauradores. A more elegant place to hang your hat, as evidenced by the marble foyer. All rooms with marble baths, French doors, small terraces, phone, A/C, and satellite TV. Continental buffet breakfast included. June-Sept. singles €45; doubles €60; triples €75. Oct.-May €40/€50/€70. AmEx/MC/V. ❹

Residencial Duas Nações, R. da Vitória, 41 (☎213 46 07 10), on the corner of R. Augusta, 3 blocks from M: Baixa-Chiado. Large rooms that look out onto the noisy main pedestrian street of Baixa. Staff speaks English. Singles €30, with bath €50; doubles €35/€60. AmEx/MC/V. ❸

FOOD

Despite the fact that Baixa is home to Lisboa's most tourist-oriented restaurants, a little hunting and insider tips uncover prices that compete with anything in Portugal. Venture away from R. da Augusta, the main pedestrian walkway, to Calçada de

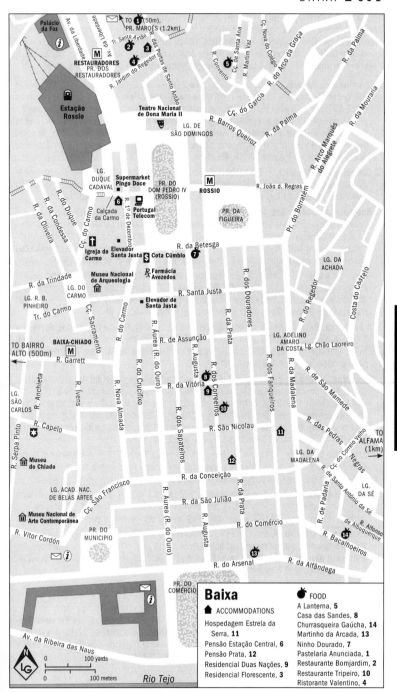

LISBOA

Baixa

🏠 ACCOMMODATIONS

Hospedagem Estrela da
  Serra, 11
Pensão Estação Central, 6
Pensão Prata, 12
Residencial Duas Nações, 9
Residencial Florescente, 3

🍅 FOOD

A Lanterna, 5
Casa das Sandes, 8
Churrasqueira Gaúcha, 14
Martinho da Arcada, 13
Ninho Dourado, 7
Pastelaria Anunciada, 1
Restaurante Bomjardim, 2
Restaurante Tripeiro, 10
Ristorante Valentino, 4

Santa Ana, above Pr. da Figueira, to find cheaper restaurants (under €6) that aren't brimming with tourists. Those with Portuguese-only menus serve more affordable meals. Look for *pastelarias:* more than pastry shops, they often have good lunch deals. R. das Portas de Santo Antão has great seafood, but be warned; they love tourists there and have the bright signs and steep prices to match.

Martinho da Arcada, Pr. do Comércio, 3 (☎218 87 92 59). Founded in 1782, this is the oldest restaurant in Lisboa. The restaurant side offers mildly expensive entrees (€11-17) in an elegant dining room; guests can read poems by renowned Portuguese poet Fernando Pessoa, a regular during his lifetime. A less expensive option (and one of the best in town) is the **cafe ❶,** with *pratos do dia* (€4) served noon-3pm. Outside seating has a view of the hustle and bustle of Pr. do Comércio. Open daily noon-3pm and 7pm-10:30pm. AmEx/MC/V. ❸

Churrasqueira Gaúcha, R. Bacalhoeiros, 26C-D (☎218 87 06 09). Argentine-style meat dishes, friendly waiters, and affordable *pratos do dia* (€6.50-14, ½ portions €5-7.50) make this place worth your while. Open M-Sa 9am-midnight. AmEx/MC/V. ❷

Restaurante Bomjardim, Tr. Santo Antão, 12 (☎213 42 43 89). 2 restaurants with the same name and same management (facing each other on the *travessa*) claim the titles of *Rei dos Frangos* (king of chicken) and *Rei da Brasa* (king of the grill). Their Highnesses deliver with style and distinctive flavor. *Frango assado* (rotisserie chicken) €8.50. Other grilled meats €8-11. Open daily noon-11:30pm. AmEx/MC/V. ❷

Ninho Dourado, R. Augusta, 278. Pleasant outdoor seating, a huge menu, and decent prices (sandwiches €3-4, pizzas €7.50, entrees €8) make Ninho Dourado perfect for a dinner at sunset. Amazingly large individual pitchers of beer (€6), however, are the real reason to stop here. Open daily 10am-midnight. AmEx/MC/V. ❷

A Lanterna, Calçada de Santa Ana, 99 (☎218 86 42 04), up the hill from R. Portas de Santo Antão, toward Alfama. A pleasant escape from the tourist traps and inflated prices on the streets below. Entrees €3.50-4.50. Open M-Sa 9am-9:30pm, meals served noon-3pm and 7-9:30pm. ❶

Casa das Sandes, R. da Vitória, 54. A chain of sandwich shops found throughout Lisboa (though particularly prevalent in Baixa), Casa das Sandes sells sandwiches locals know and love (such as salmon with lemon and cream cheese) and others that travelers will immediately recognize (like club, tuna, and turkey). Outside terraces offer great seating and prices are the lowest in town. Large baguette €3-5, combo with french fries and drink €4-5. Open daily 10am-10pm. AmEx/MC/V. ❶

Ristorante Valentino, R. Jardim do Regedor, 45 (☎213 46 17 27). A break from Portuguese cuisine, Ristorante Valentino offers quality Italian food with a touch of elegance and charm. Entrees €6-15, pizzas €3-9. AmEx/MC/V. ❸

Pastelaria Anunciada, Lg. da Anunciada, 1-2 (☎213 42 44 17). Specialties include *bacalhau à minhota* (codfish; €7) and *cozida à portuguesa* (boiled carrots, meats, potatoes, and more; €4.90). Open daily 6:30am-10pm, serves meals noon-10pm. ❷

Restaurante Tripeiro, R. dos Correeiros, 70A (☎213 42 25 12). A staple in Baixa for 25 years, this small, quaint restaurant specializes in fish, but offers plenty of other options with large portions and piles of vegetables on the side. Entrees €6.50-12.50. Open M-Sa noon-4pm and 6:30pm-midnight. ❷

◎ SIGHTS

Although Baixa claims few historic sights, the lively pedestrian traffic and dramatic history surrounding the neighborhood's three main *praças* make it a monument in its own right. Beware the thousands of cooing pigeons, spoiled by so many statues of distinguished leaders on which to make their mark.

AROUND ROSSIO. Begin your tour of Lisboa's 18th-century history at its heart: ⊠**Rossio,** or **Praça Dom Pedro IV** as it is more formally known. The city's main square was once a cattle market, public execution stage, bullring, and carnival ground. Today, it is the domain of tourists and ruthless local drivers circling Pedro's statue. Take extra caution when crossing the streets here, as motorists will speed up to discourage you from crossing rather than slow down and permit you to pass. Another statue, of Gil Vicente, Portugal's first great dramatist (see **Literature,** p. 669), peers from atop the **Teatro Nacional de Dona Maria II** (easily recognized by its large, Parthenon-esque columns) at one end of the *praça.* Adjoining Rossio is the elegant **Praça da Figueira,** which lies on the border of the hilly streets of Alfama.

AROUND PRAÇA DOS RESTAURADORES. Anyone who mistakes Portuguese for a dialect of Spanish or Portugal for a province of Spain has obviously never been to **Praça dos Restauradores,** where a giant obelisk celebrates the hard-earned (read: a king died) independence from Spain in 1640 after 60 years of captivity. The obelisk is accompanied by a bronze sculpture of the "Spirit of Independence." The less monumental tourist office and numerous shops line the *praça* and C. da Glória— the hill that leads to Bairro Alto. Pr. dos Restauradores is also the start of **Avenida da Liberdade,** one of Lisboa's most elegant promenades. Modeled after the boulevards of 19th-century Paris, this mile-long thoroughfare ends at **Praça do Marquês de Pombal;** from there an 18th-century statue of the Marquês overlooks the city.

AROUND PRAÇA DO COMÉRCIO. The grid of pedestrian streets on the other side of Rossio from Pr. dos Restauradores caters to people-watchers and window shoppers, as well as politicians flitting in and out of the many government buildings. After the earthquake of 1755 leveled this section of Lisboa, the Marquês de Pombal designed the streets to serve as a conduit for goods from the ports on the Rio Tejo to the city center. Pombal envisioned an enlightened city of efficiency and utility, and the final product is just that. The grid forms perfect blocks, with streets designated for specific trades: *sapateiros* (shoemakers), *correeiros* (couriers), and *bacalhoeiros* (cod merchants) each had their own avenue. Although much has changed over the last 250 years (good luck finding a cod merchant), Baixa remains first and foremost a commercial center. The roads lead to **Praça do Comércio,** on the banks of the Tejo. Now, Pr. do Comércio, with its 9400 lb. statue of **Dom João I,** serves as a wide and inviting space between the Tejo's crowds of boats and the city's crowds of people.

BAIRRO ALTO

When people talk about "going to Lisboa," they often mean going to Bairro Alto, and they often mean going at night. The reason why scores of young partygoers come to Lisboa in the first place, Bairro Alto is clearly the center of Lisboa's nightlife. At night, its narrow cobblestone streets come alive with music emanating from the scores of hip bars and clubs located in this district. Here, barhopping is made easy by the number of watering holes and their proximity to each other; if you don't like the looks of a place, or if the party doesn't suit your tastes, just cross the street or go next door, especially on R. da Atalaia, R. do Norte, and R. do Diário Notícias. Even though the area is known for its *casas de fado* and scores of hip bars and clubs, there is still enough to behold during the daytime to warrant a visit.

A mix of narrow streets, idyllic parks, and churches, Bairro Alto is harder to reach than Baixa. At the center of the neighborhood is **Praça Luís de Camões,** which adjoins **Largo do Chiado** at the top of R. Garrett, a good place to rest and orient yourself. Those who want to stay close to the heart of Lisboa's parties should

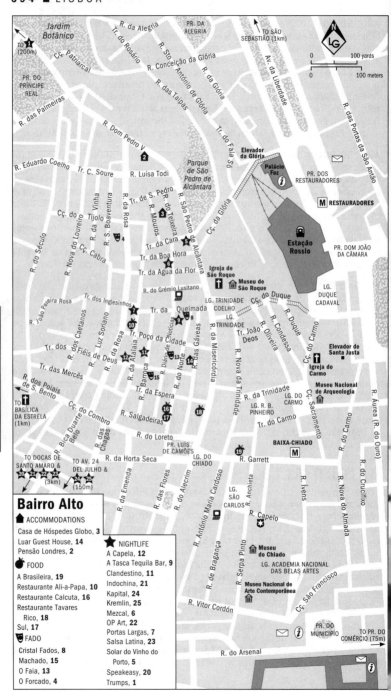

Bairro Alto

▲ ACCOMMODATIONS

Casa de Hóspedes Globo, **3**
Luar Guest House, **14**
Pensão Londres, **2**

🍴 FOOD

A Brasileira, **19**
Restaurante Ali-a-Papa, **10**
Restaurante Calcuta, **16**
Restaurante Tavares
   Rico, **18**
Sul, **17**

🍷 FADO

Cristal Fados, **8**
Machado, **15**
O Faia, **13**
O Forcado, **4**

★ NIGHTLIFE

A Capela, **12**
A Tasca Tequila Bar, **9**
Clandestino, **11**
Indochina, **21**
Kapital, **24**
Kremlin, **25**
Mezcal, **6**
OP Art, **22**
Portas Largas, **7**
Salsa Latina, **23**
Solar do Vinho do
   Porto, **5**
Speakeasy, **20**
Trumps, **1**

surely stay here; also, the district's hills afford a beautiful view of the city, particularly from Parque de São Pedro de Alcântara. Don't plan on getting much sleep though, since Bairro Alto's parties are renowned for lasting well past dawn.

Other nightlife areas close to Bairro Alto include **Avenida 24 de Julho** and **Docas de Santo Amaro,** as well as the developments across from **Estação Santa Apolónia.**

ACCOMMODATIONS

☒**Luar Guest House,** R. das Gáveas, 101 (☎/fax 213 46 09 09). Owned by a friendly young couple that speaks perfect English. Simple, clean rooms, all with phone, bath, and double windows to keep out the noise; far enough away from the center of the nightlife to guarantee you a good night's sleep. Laundry €10. Check-in after noon. Check-out 11:30am. Singles €15; doubles €20-30; triples €35; quads €40. ❷

☒**Casa de Hóspedes Globo,** R. Teixeira, 37 (☎/fax 213 46 22 79). From the park , cross the street and go 1 block on Tr. da Cara, then turn right. Popular with young travelers. All rooms with phone and TV; all but 2 have bath. Away from most bars and nightclubs. English spoken. Laundry €10. Negotiate in winter. Singles €15, with bath €22.50; doubles €25/€30; triples with bath €40; quads with bath €50; quints with bath €55. ❷

Pensão Londres, R. Dom Pedro V, 53, 2nd-5th fl. (☎213 46 22 03; www.pensaolondres.com.pt). Take the elevator to these well-appointed rooms; all with phone, some with TV and panoramic view. Marble baths add to the charm. English spoken. Breakfast included. Singles (only in winter) €35, with bath €50; doubles €59/€70; triples €73/€84; quads with bath €94. Prices €5-10 less in winter. MC/V. ❹

FOOD

The narrow streets of Bairro Alto are lined with bars, restaurants, and the famous *casas de fado.* Prices range from modest to supremely immodest, as in the *casas.* Budget eaters and those searching for veritably Portuguese locales are best off in Baixa, since Bairro Alto's eateries are for the most part international; those that do serve typical Portuguese dishes are the *casas de fado,* where high minimum consumption requirements scare away those looking for a cheap meal.

☒**A Brasileira,** R. Garrett, 120-122 (☎213 46 95 41; www.abrasileira.pt). A former stomping ground of early 20th-century poets and intellectuals, the cafe almost doubles as a tourist sight. Today, it continues to serve as the official hotspot for starving artists in Lisboa; stop in during the afternoon and you'll find yourself in a sea of poets scribbling furiously in worn-out notebooks and painters sketching images of daily life in Bairro Alto. The esplanade out front is a hopping day and night (though eating outside is more expensive) and the restaurant serves a famous *bife à brasileira* (steak and eggs served in cream sauce; €11). Sandwiches and croissants €2-5, entrees €10-14, mixed drinks €5. Open daily 8am-2am. ❷

☒**Sul,** R. do Norte, 13 (☎/fax 213 46 24 49). Dark wood paneling and candlelight give this restaurant and wine bar a romantic feel; relaxing house music and tree-trunk bar stools give it a swanky one. The mix is unique and comfortable. Creative presentation on each plate, and food tastes as good as it looks. Comes alive after 10pm, when it turns into a bar. International entrees with a slew of house sauces €12-16. Open Tu-Su noon-midnight; meals served noon-7pm. ❸

Restaurante Calcuta, R. do Norte, 17 (☎213 42 82 95), near Lg. Camões. Indian restaurant with several curry-based dishes as well as a wide selection of vegetarian options (€5.50-6). Meat entrees €6.50-9. Open M-F noon-3pm and 7-11pm, Sa-Su 7-11pm. AmEx/MC/V. ❷

Restaurante Tavares Rico, R. da Misericórdia, 35 (☎213 41 21 12; www.tavaresrico.pt). Founded in 1784, this restaurant is one of Lisboa's oldest and finest. Don't be surprised if you run into someone famous in its elegant dining room; Tavares Rico has

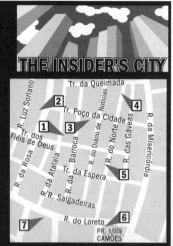

THE INSIDER'S CITY

ALTO FASHION

Though Bairro Alto is best known for what goes on after sunset, it also features some excellent (if slightly eccentric) shopping.

1 **Fátima Lopes,** R. da Atalaia, 36 (☎213 24 05 40). The very definition of chic, Fatima Lopes sells a lot of clothes that would be just as at home on the runway as in any of Portugal's trendy clubs. Looking good doesn't come cheap however; this is one of Bairro Alto's most expensive shops (shirts €100, pants €40). (Open M-F 10am-9pm, Sa noon-2pm and 3:30-9pm. AmEx/MC/V.)

2 **Maomao Shop,** R. da Rosa, 85 (☎213 89 34 21). Although it's highly unlikely that the Chairman would have approved of this store, this wacky locale is worth a visit. To describe its clothes as colorful would be an understatement; check out the Bruce Lee purses. (Open M-Sa 11am-midnight.)

long been a haunt for vacationing celebrities (recent sightings include Victoria Beckham, former Spice Girl and wife to soccer superstar David Beckham). Meat entrees €25-29, fish entrees €25-30. Tu-F 12:30pm-11pm. Tea room open daily 8am-7pm. ❺

Restaurante Ali-a-Papa, R. da Atalaia, 95 (☎213 47 41 43). Serves generous helpings of traditional Moroccan food in a quiet atmosphere; dishes include couscous and tagine. Vegetarian-friendly. Entrees €9-11.50. Open M-Sa 7-11pm. AmEx/MC/V. ❸

⊚ SIGHTS

◼ BASÍLICA DA ESTRELA. Directly across from the Jardim da Estrela, the Basílica da Estrela dates back to 1796 and casts an imposing presence over the Praça da Estrela. Its dome, poised behind a pair of tall belfries, towers over surrounding buildings and trees to take its place in the Lisboa skyline. Half-mad Dona Maria I promised God anything and everything if she were granted a son. When a baby boy was finally born, she built this church, and admirers of beautiful architecture and ornate decor have been grateful ever since. Ask to see the 10th-century nativity. *(Pr. da Estrela. Accessible by metro or tram #28 from Pr. do Comércio. ☎213 96 09 15. Open daily 7:30am-1pm and 3-8pm. Free.)*

MUSEU DO CHIADO. The Museu do Chiado's collection features works by Portugal's most famous post-1850 artists, adding an interesting twist by juxtaposing works from the Fascist era with pre- and post-Salazar pieces. However, the museum also showcases 19th- and 20th-century French art (including a Rodin), not to mention exhibits on famous contemporary artists like Gerhard Richter. *(R. Serpa Pinto, 4. ☎213 43 21 48. Open Tu 2-6pm, W-Su 10am-6pm. €3; students, seniors, and teachers €1.50. Su before 2pm free.)*

IGREJA DE SÃO ROQUE. When the Church decided to bring Sr. Roque's bones and other relics to Lisboa from Spain in the 1500s, they had not intended to build a church in his name. But when the pesky rodents and their epidemic-inducing germs miraculously dissipated upon his arrival, Sr. Roque became a *São*, and a Jesuit church with all the bells and whistles of the era was quickly built. Inside, the **Capela de São João Baptista** (fourth from the left) blazes with agate, lapis lazuli, and precious metals; considered a masterpiece of European art, the chapel caused a stir upon its installation in 1747 because it took three ships to transport it from Rome, where it was built. The ceiling is covered entirely by a magnificent painting portraying scenes from the life of Jesus. *(Lg. Trinidade Coelho. ☎213 23 53 83. Open daily 8:30am-5pm, holidays*

8:30am-1pm.) Next door, the **Museu de São Roque,** with its own share of gold and silver, features religious art from the 16th to 18th centuries. *(☎213 23 53 82. Open Tu-Su 10am-5pm. €1.50, students and seniors free. Su free.)*

MUSEU NACIONAL DE ARTE ANTIGA. This museum hosts a large collection of Portuguese art as well as a survey of European painting, ranging from Gothic primitives to 18th-century French masterpieces. *(R. das Janelas Verdes, Jardim 9 Abril. Buses #40 and 60 stop to the right of the museum exit. Tram #15, from Pr. da Figueira or Pr. do Comércio, also stops nearby. ☎213 91 28 00. Open Tu 1-5 pm, W-Su 10am-7:30pm. €3, students €1.50. Su before 2pm free.)*

ELEVADOR DE SANTA JUSTA. The Elevador de Santa Justa, a historic elevator built in 1902 inside a Gothic wrought-iron tower, once served as transportation up to Bairro Alto, but now just takes tourists up to see the fantastic view and back down again. Avoid the elevator on weekends unless you want to wait in line. *(Runs M-F 7am-11pm, Sa-Su 9am-11pm. €2.20.)*

PARKS. Across from the basílica on Lg. da Estrela, the wide paths of the ⊠**Jardim da Estrela** wind through flocks of pigeons, ducks quacking happily in the pond, and lush flora. A perfect spot for a family outing, with lots of playgrounds and activities for children, the park leaves ample room to do as you please amid the plentiful benches, shady cypress trees, and intoxicating aroma of tropical flowers. *(M: Rato. With your back to the metro stop, take R. Pedro Álvares Cabral, the 2nd road from the left in the traffic circle, for 10min. Open daily 6am-midnight.)* More greenery awaits uphill along R. Dom Pedro V at the Parque Príncipe Real, which connects to the extensive **Jardim Botánico.** For a pretty view of Lisboa, head to the **Parque de São Pedro de Alcântara.** The Castelo de São Jorge in Alfama stares back from the cliff opposite the park, and Bairro Alto twinkles below. *(A 5min. walk from Pr. Luis de Camões.)*

⊠ NIGHTLIFE IN AND NEAR BAIRRO ALTO

BAIRRO ALTO AND NORTH TO THE JARDIM BOTÁNICO

⊠ **A Tasca Tequila Bar,** Tr. da Queimada, 13-15 (☎213 43 34 31). This classy Mexican bar is ideal for some after-dinner cocktails, and the hip house music and powerful shots are perfect for revving you up before you head off to the louder bars and discos. Cocktails €5. "Quickies" (specialized shots including Blow Job, Orgasmo, and Multi-Orgasmo) €3. Open daily 6pm-2am.

3 Lena Aires, Tr. Poco da Cidade, 24 (☎213 48 92 43). The perfect stop for summer shopping, Lena Aires has very affordable clothing, without skimping on style. (Open M-Sa 10am-8pm. MC/V.)

4 Agência 117, R. do Norte, 117 (☎213 46 12 70). Cut-off tees and chic retro-inspired shirts and dresses beckon from this style hub in the heart of Bairro Alto's fashion world. There's even a hair salon and a tiny bar inside, for further prep-work and a spot to flaunt your good taste. (Open M-Sa 2pm-midnight. AmEx/MC/V.)

5 Bad Bones, R. do Norte, 73 (☎213 46 08 88). Just walk in off the street to up your cool factor with a body piercing; if you want a tattoo, though, call in advance—they're by appointment only. (Open M-Sa 11am-7pm.)

6 Diesel Lisboa, Pr. Luís Camões, 30 (☎213 42 19 80). Though Diesel is a more commercial brand, the Lisboa shop is definitely worth a stop, with its cool house music and two floors of the chic Italian label. (Open M-Sa 10am-11pm. AmEx/MC/V.)

7 De Lá Longe, R. do Loreto, 48 (☎213 42 24 24). Quaint little t-shirt shop that also sells bead necklaces and flip flops in almost every imaginable color. (Open daily 11:30am-12:30pm and 1:30-8pm.)

Trumps, R. Imprensa Nacional, 104B (☎213 97 10 59), down R. Dom Pedro V from Bairro Alto, on the 5th street to the left after Pr. Príncipe Real. Lisboa's biggest gay club, Trumps doesn't get going until after 1:30am, but when it does it's a sight to behold, with masses of people crowding its plaza-like dance floor. Features lounge areas for when you've danced yourself silly, billiards tables, and live shows. Come Su for the weekly foam party. Minimum consumption €10. Shots €6. Beer €4. Open Su and Tu-Th 11:30pm-4:30am, F-Sa midnight-6:30am.

Portas Largas, R. da Atalaia, 105 (☎213 46 63 79), at the end of Tr. da Queimada. Located in the heart of Bairro Alto, Portas Largas is one of the district's most popular bars. A mixed crowd dances to Portuguese music before midnight and techno afterwards. To truly experience this place, come after 11:30pm, when things really get wild. Open daily July-Sept. 7pm-4:30am; Oct.-June 8pm-3:30am.

A Capela, R. da Atalaia, 45. Although there are seemingly hundreds of options on R. da Atalaia and the surrounding streets, A Capela is particularly popular later in the evening, providing a much more comfortable environment than nearby holes in the wall thanks to plush velvet cushions and large seating capacity. Large beer €3. Mixed drinks €5. Open daily 9pm-2am.

Clandestino, R. Barroca, 99. Cavernous bar with messages from former patrons sprawled all over the rock walls. Groups of people in their early twenties chat at low tables while rock plays in the background. Listen for at least 1 Pearl Jam song; it's the bar's trademark. Beer €2. Small mixed drinks €4-5. Open Tu-Su 10pm-3am.

Mezcal, on the corner of Tr. Agua da Flor and R. Diário de Notícias. This tiny Mexican bar with the cheapest drinks in Bairro Alto is the perfect stop before hitting more upscale establishments. Find the answer to late-night munchies here with tacos, burritos, and nachos (€2-4). Sangria €1.75. *Caipirinhas* €2.75. Shots €2. Their specialty: €2 margaritas. Open daily 7pm-3:30am.

Solar do Vinho do Porto, R. São Pedro de Alcântara, 45 (☎213 47 57 07), at the top of the steps through the large doorway. Product of a government institute created in 1933 to certify and promote port wine, Solar is a mature setting ideal for sipping and playing grown-up. Complete with fancy cheeses, plush red chairs, and tuxedoed waitstaff. Port runs €1-25 per glass, depending on age and quality. Open M-Sa 2pm-1am.

SOUTH OF BAIRRO ALTO: AVENIDA 24 DE JULHO AND SANTOS

Kapital, Av. 24 de Julho, 68 (☎213 24 25 90). The classiest club in Lisboa has a ruthless door policy that makes admission a competitive sport. Don't expect to get in, especially if you're an unaccompanied male or if it's clear that you're a tourist. For the best chance, go with regulars, smile politely, and keep your mouth shut. 3 floors, with a terrace. At closing, take the back tunnel directly into neighboring Kremlin to continue partying. Cover usually €15. Open M-Sa 11pm-6am.

Kremlin, Escandinhas da Praia, 5 (☎213 95 71 01), off Av. 24 de Julho. Run by the same management as Kapital, but a more mixed crowd including Kapital rejects and migrants. Door policy is harsh but not impossible; come nicely dressed and you should get in eventually. Set in a former bishop's residence, Kremlin has giant plastic statues and 3 rooms throbbing with house music. Cover usually €7 for women, €12 for men. Open Tu-W midnight-6am, Th midnight-8am, F-Sa midnight-9:30am.

WEST OF BAIRRO ALTO: DOCAS DE SANTO AMARO

▨ **Speakeasy,** Docas de Santo Amaro (☎213 95 77 308; www.speakeasy-bar.com), between the Santos and Alcântara stops near the river. More of a concert with waiters and beer than a bar, Speakeasy is Lisboa's premiere jazz and blues center. Live shows nightly, with famous performers once a month. Beer €3. Open M-Sa 9pm-4am.

Indochina, R. Cintura do Porto de Lisboa, Armazém H (☎213 95 58 75), a 10min. walk from the Santos station. Part of a 3-club strip (along with **Blues** and **Dock's**). The Far East decorations give this club, otherwise patronized by a young crowd, a classy feel. Cover €5 for women, €10 for men. Open Th-Sa 11:30pm-6am.

Salsa Latina, Gare Marítima de Alcântara (☎213 95 05 55), across the parking lot from the cluster at Doca de Santo Amaro. A hot spot for older, more sophisticated nightlife-seekers, who come for the live salsa dancing on weekends (lessons by appointment, €15). Terrace with a view. Minimum consumption €10. Open M-Th 8pm-1am, F-Sa 8pm-4am.

OP Art, R. da Cozinha Economia, 11 (☎213 95 67 87), almost directly under the 25 de Abril bridge on the Lisboa side. By day it's a cafe, by night it's a bar, and by early morning, it slaps on a strobe light and starts blasting electronica. The only cafe-bar-disco right on the river. Beer €3. Open Tu-Su noon-5am.

SÃO SEBASTIÃO

Located north of Baixa, São Sebastião offers a more modern setting, complete with busy avenues, modern department stores (including the Spanish superstore El Corte Inglés) and scores of strip malls. That's not to say that those in search of a little culture should avoid São Sebastião, as it also houses two of the finest art museums to be found in Portugal, both legacies of oil tycoon Calouste Gulbenkian.

◙ SIGHTS

▩**MUSEU CALOUSTE GULBENKIAN.** Perhaps Portugal's biggest fan ever, Calouste Gulbenkian became enamored of the Iberian nation when he visited in 1942. In fact, he liked the country so much that he stayed in the same luxury hotel in Lisboa for 13 years, until his death in 1955. In his will, the billionaire of Armenian descent left his extensive art collection (some of it purchased from the Hermitage in St. Petersburg, Russia) to his beloved Portugal. The collection is divided into sections of ancient art—Egyptian, Greek, Roman, Mesopotamian, Islamic, and Oriental—and European pieces from the 15th to 20th centuries. Highlights include the Egyptian room, Rembrandts, Monets, Renoirs, Rodins, and Manets. *(Av. Berna, 45. M: São Sebastião; exit the metro onto R. Testa, take a right when you reach El Corte Inglés, follow the road until it ends, and take another right. Bus #18, 46, 56. ☎217 82 30 00; www.museu.gulbenkian.pt. Open Tu-Su 10am-6pm. €3. Free Su.)*

CENTRO DE ARTE MODERNA. Though not as famous as its neighbor, this museum houses an extensive modern collection dedicated to promoting Portuguese talent. Don't miss the sculpture gardens that separate the two museums. *(R. Dr. Nicolau Bettencourt. M: São Sebastião. From the station, head downhill past a palace, or take bus #16, 31, or 46. ☎217 95 02 41. Open Tu-Su 10am-5pm. €3, Sa free.)*

ALFAMA

Alfama, Lisboa's medieval quarter, was the lone neighborhood to survive the infamous 1755 earthquake. The area descends in tiers from the dominating Castelo de São Jorge facing the Rio Tejo. Between Alfama and Baixa is the Mouraria (Moorish quarter), ironically established after Dom Afonso Henriques expelled the Moors in 1147. A visit to Alfama provides the opportunity to observe a slice of Lisboa far from the bright lights and touristy enclaves of Baixa; here, restaurants are crowded with the friends and family of local owners. This labyrinth of escandinhas, alleys, and unmarked streets is a challenge to navigate; be especially wary

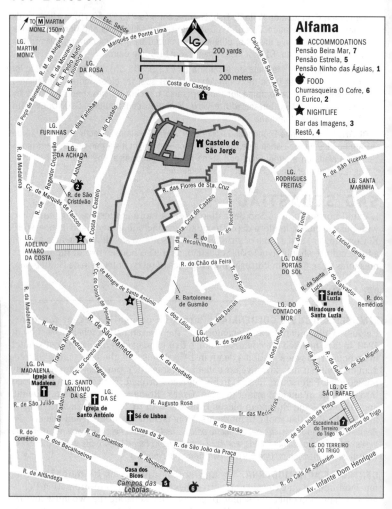

after nightfall, and leave handbags in hostel lockers. Though the constant hike through Alfama's streets is half the fun, visitors can also hop on tram #28 from Pr. do Comércio (€1), which winds past most of the neighborhood's sights.

ACCOMMODATIONS

Alfama has fewer accommodations options and less price competition, but staying here can be a nice change of pace (especially after Baixa). Nonetheless, the steep, unmarked streets can make each trip back to the hostel a grueling workout.

■ **Pensão Ninho das Águias,** Costa do Castelo, 74 (☎218 85 40 70). Climb the spiral staircase, greet the funny squawking bird at the entrance, and ring the bell to get into the garden. Among the best views Lisboa has to offer, especially from rooms #5, 6, 12,

13, and 14. Friendly owner whose hospitality makes for a pleasant stay. English and French spoken. Call ahead in the summer. May-Aug. singles €25; doubles €42, with bath €45; triples (some with bath) €60. Sept.-Apr. €25/€35/€40/€50. ❷

■ **Pensão Beira Mar,** R. Terreiro do Trigo, 16 (☎218 87 15 28; beira@iol.pt). Probably the cheapest option in Alfama for solo travelers. Some rooms with a view of the river cost a bit more. June-Aug. singles €15-20; doubles €30-40; quads €60. Oct.-May €10-15/ €20-30/€40. Be tough and bargain for lower prices in low season. ❶

Pensão Estrela, R. dos Bacalhoeiros, 8 (☎218 86 95 06). An under-utilized option in the lower part of Alfama. Rooms with the basic amenities, including TV, look out on the square below. Spanish spoken. Check-out 11am. June-Sept. singles €20-25; doubles €40; one triple €60. Oct.-May €15/€30-35/€45. Bargain in low season. 1 floor up, the similar **Pensão Verandas** (☎218 87 05 19) has comparable rooms and prices. ❷

🍴 FOOD

The winding streets of Alfama conceal a number of tiny, unpretentious restaurants, often packed with locals. Lively chatter bounces through the narrow alleys.

Churrasqueira O Cofre, R. dos Bacalhoeiros, 2C-D (☎218 86 89 35). A display case shows what's available; though almost everything on the menu is meat, they also have a selection of seafood (all grilled, of course). Outside seating in summer. Entrees €7-13. Open daily noon-11pm, meals served noon-4pm and 7-11pm. AmEx/MC/V. ❷

O Eurico, Lg. de São Cristóvão, 3-4 (☎218 86 18 15), at C. do Marques de Tancos. Run by owner Eurico Ferreira since 1969, this simple restaurant serves generous portions of grilled meat and is packed with workers at lunchtime. Entrees €5-7. Open M-F 9am-10pm, meals served noon-4pm and 7-10pm; Sa noon-4pm. ❷

🎯 SIGHTS

■ **CASTELO DE SÃO JORGE.** At the end of a winding uphill walk is the Castelo de São Jorge, which offers spectacular views of Lisboa and the ocean. Built in the 5th century by the Visigoths and enlarged 400 years later by the Moors, this castle was again improved and converted into a playground for the royal family between the 14th and 16th centuries; today, a lively village bustles within its walls. Wander around the ruins, soak in the views, explore the ponds, or gawk at exotic birds in the gardens. For shoppers, the castle also offers a string of souvenir shops and restaurants. (☎218 82 36 70. Castle open daily Apr.-Sept. 9am-9pm; Oct.-Mar. 9am-6pm. Free.)

LOWER ALFAMA. R. da Alfândeo, which begins two blocks away from Pr. do Comércio, connects Baixa and lower Alfama. Veer right when you see **Igreja da Madalena** in Lg. da Madalena on the right. Take R. de Santo António da Sé and follow the tram tracks to the small **Igreja de Santo António,** built in 1812 over the beloved saint's alleged birthplace. The construction was funded with money collected by the city's children, who fashioned miniature altars bearing saintly images to place on doorsteps—a custom reenacted annually on June 13, the saint's feast day and Lisboa's biggest holiday. Although it may be in celebration of a saint, this event turns into a wild, debaucherous melee that involves *sardinhas*, alcohol, and all-night partying. (☎218 86 91 45. Church open daily 8am-7pm. Mass daily 11am, 5, and 7pm.) In the square beyond the church is the 12th-century **Sé de Lisboa.** Although the cathedral's interior lacks the excessive ornamentation of the city's other churches, its sheer age and relic-filled treasury make it an intriguing visit. (☎218 86 67 52. Open M 10am-5pm, Tu-Su 10am-6pm. Treasury open 10am-1pm and 2-5pm. €2.50.)

GRAÇA

In addition to its sights that approach the heart of what it means to be Portuguese, the reason to visit Graça is its nightlife, some of the hottest and most cosmopolitan in Lisboa.

👁 SIGHTS

🏛 **PANTEÃO NACIONAL.** A massive structure, the building that is now the National Pantheon was originally meant to be the Igreja da Santa Engrácia; the citizenry of Graça started building the church in 1680 to honor their patron saint. However, their ambitions outstripped their finances, and the building project was abandoned without the projected dome, leaving a massive hole in the top. The military regime led by General Salazar eventually took over construction, completing the project and dedicating it as the National Pantheon, the burial ground for important statesmen, in 1966 (a marble plaque commemorating this event can be found on the first floor, near the entrance). In a final twist of irony, when democracy was restored in 1975, the new government relocated the remains of prominent anti-Fascist opponents to this magnificent building and prohibited those who had worked with Salazar from entering. The dome juts out from amongst the other old buildings of Graça, providing an amazing view of Lisboa from the outdoor terrace. Other highlights include the tombs of presidents such as Teófilo Braga, Sidónio Pais, and Oscar Carmona, as well as cenotaphs (honorary tombs for people buried elsewhere) for explorers like Vasco da Gama and Pedro Cabral, the man who discovered Brazil in 1500. The Pantheon also houses the remains of important Portuguese artists, including its most recent arrival, Amália Rodrigues, the queen of *fado*. *(To reach Graça and the Panteão, take the #12 bus or the #28 tram from the bottom of R. dos Correeiros. ☎ 218 85 48 20; fax 85 48 39. Open Tu-Su 10am-5pm. €2, children and seniors €1.)*

IGREJA DE SÃO VICENTE DE FORA. Built between 1582 and 1629, the Igreja is dedicated to Lisboa's patron saint. Ask the church attendant to see the *sacristia* with its inlaid walls of Sintra marble, and be sure to check out the geometrically confused walls at the base of the center dome. *(From the bottom of R. dos Correeiros in Baixa, take bus #12 or tram #28. Open Tu-Sa 9am-6pm, Su 9am-12:30pm and 3-5pm. Free. Chapel next door with scenic view €3.)* At the **Feira da Ladra** (flea market), in the expanse between the Panteão and Igreja de São Vicente, the din of curious and talkative passersby drowns out the cries of merchants hawking new and used goods, from Beatles paraphernalia to African sculptures.

MUSEO NACIONAL DO AZULEJO. Housed within the 16th-century Convento da Madre Deus, this museum is devoted to the art of the *azulejo* (tile), which was first introduced by the Moors (see **Architecture**, p. 668). Through a Manueline doorway, the Baroque interior of the former convent features a large variety of oil paintings, and azulejos of greater variety than can be found anywhere else in Portugal. *(R. Madre de Deus, 4. East of Alfama in Xabregas. From Pr. do Comércio, take bus #104 or 105. ☎ 218 10 03 40. Open Tu 2-6pm, W-Su 10am-6pm. €3, students €1.50.)*

🎵 NIGHTLIFE

Lux/Frágil, Av. Infante D. Henrique, A (☎ 218 82 08 90). Take a taxi to the area across from the Sta. Apolónia train station to get to this enormous 3 fl. complex. In a class and location all its own, Lux continues to be one of the hottest spots in Lisboa since opening in 1998. Top 2 levels are dominated by large bars and seating areas, while the subterranean level is dedicated to the mass of dancers. Minimum consumption €10. Open Tu-Sa 6pm-6am; arrive after 2am if you want company. AmEx/MC/V.

Restô, R. Costa do Castelo, 7 (☎ 218 86 73 34). In early evening, the moderately priced **restaurant ❷** serves Argentine steaks (€13), New Zealand lamb chops (€15), and Spanish tapas (€4). Between 10pm and midnight, Restô fills with a young crowd there to drink and soak in the twilight view of the city from the huge patio. Live Portuguese guitar F-Su. *Caipirinhas* €4. Beer €1.30. Open daily 7:30pm-2am. AmEx/MC/V.

Bar das Imagens, Calçada de Marquês de Tancos, 11-13 (☎ 218 88 46 36). An outdoor patio between the castle wall and the final descent to Baixa. The DJ brings hip-hop to a whole new level, while tasty finger foods and "mocktails" (non-alcoholic fruit cocktails; €3.50) get people pumped for the more popular *caipirinhas* (€4.50). Su brings live Portuguese folk music. Open Su 3-9pm, W-Sa 4pm-3am.

◪ LISBOA'S OUTER DISTRICTS

▨ PARQUE DAS NAÇÕES

From Lisboa, ride to M: Oriente at the end of the red line. The station has escalators to the park's main entrance at the Centro Vasco da Gama. (☎ 218 93 06 01; www.parquedasnacoes.pt. Open daily 10am-midnight.) Alternatively, city buses #5, 10, 19, 21, 25, 28, 44, 50, 68, and 114 all stop at the Oriente station (€1). Cable cars (☎ 218 96 58 23) connect one end of the park to the other. (8min.; summer M-F 11am-8pm, Sa-Su 10am-9pm; winter M-F 11am-7pm, Sa-Su 10am-8pm; €5, under 14 €2.50, over 65 €3.) Oceanário (☎ 218 91 70 02; www.oceanario.pt) open daily Apr.-Sept. 10am-7pm; Oct.-Mar. 10am-6pm. €9, under 12 €4.50, over 65 €5. Pavilhão do Conhecimento (☎ 218 91 71 00; www.pavconhecimento.pt) open Tu-F 10am-6pm, Sa-Su 11am-7pm. €5, under 18 and over 65 €2.50. Torre Vasco da Gama open daily 10am-8pm. €2.50, under 15 and over 65 €1.25.

Until the mid-1990s, this area was a muddy wasteland with a few run-down factories and warehouses along the banks of the Tejo. However, the city rapidly transformed it to prepare for the 1998 World Exposition. Afterward, the government took a risk and pumped millions of euros into the land to convert it into the Parque das Nações (Park of Nations). Fortunately, the gamble paid off. Today, the park is packed day and night with people enjoying its futuristic yet graceful setting and, above all, its bewildering diversity. Perhaps best described as a bastion of capitalism (with stores such as the Vodafone Action Store and the Praça Sony), this park is a testament to the reaches of globalization. The area has everything from an enormous movie theater to an indoor neighborhood of restaurants, a shopping mall, and a science museum. If the proposed construction goes according to plan, the park will soon become a small city, with residential areas added both north and south. The park entrance leads through the Centro Vasco da Gama shopping mall to the center of the grounds, where several information kiosks provide maps. Even the ▨**Estação Oriente** itself is a draw, its arches and spans designed by Santiago Calatrava, Spain's most famous contemporary architect.

The park is a playground for children, its biggest attraction being the ▨**Oceanário,** one of the largest oceanariums in Europe. The new aquarium has interactive sections showcasing the four major oceans (down to the sounds, smells, and climates). All of these connect to the main tank, which houses over 470 different species of fish, sharks, and other creatures. Visitors can get within an arm's length of playful sea otters and penguins. The multilevel design allows for unique views of sea life from underneath the tank. Kids will also enjoy the **Pavilhão do Conhecimento** (Pavilion of Knowledge), an interactive science museum. Other pavilions are scattered throughout the park, including the **International Fairgrounds,** have rotating exhibits during the year. The **Atlantic Pavilion** (site of many big concerts), the **Virtual Reality Pavilion,** with a ride that challenges the senses, and the 145m **Torre Vasco da Gama** (the city's tallest building) grab visitors' attention with their striking 21st-century architecture. The entire city can be seen from the observation tower.

THE LOCAL STORY

LADIES' MAN

Have you ever been forced into exile by the jealous husbands of the countless ladies that you wooed into your arms? No? In that case, you could learn a lot from Luis de Camões, considered to have been Portugal's greatest poet—and greatest lover. Although sources claim that he was actually banished for his politics, there's no doubt that he was quite the charmer among the ladies of Lisboa's royalty. Born in 1524, he led an adventurous life for a poet, enlisting as a soldier in the army in 1547; his service took him around the world, including the Arab and Indian coasts, as well as throughout Portugal's expanding empire.

As he traveled, Camões worked on his poetry while getting himself into as much trouble as possible, losing one eye in battle, being injured in a sword duel, and surviving a shipwreck off the coast of Cambodia in 1570. He published *Os Lusíadas*, his opus magnum, in 1572; this epic poem chronicles Portugal's discoveries in lyric verse. *Os Lusíadas* was an extremely successful work, yet Camões died in poverty somewhere in Asia in 1580. Although Portugal was never able to recover his body, Belém's magnificent Mosteiro dos Jerónimos has an honorary tomb for him; given his importance to Portuguese culture, as well as his penchant for travel, it's fitting that Camões lies in spirit across from another great traveler, Vasco da Gama.

BELÉM

To get to Belém, take tram #15 from Pr. do Comércio (15min.), bus #28 or 43 from Pr. da Figueira (15min.), or the train from Estação Cais do Sodré (10min., every 15min., €0.90). If taking the tram or the bus, get off at the "Mosteiro dos Jeronimos" stop, one stop beyond the regular Belém stop. From the train station, cross the tracks, then cross the street and go left. The Padrão dos Descobrimentos is by the water, across the highway on your left (use the underpass), while the Mosteiro dos Jerónimos is to the right, through the public gardens.

Belém can best be described as a living monument to Portugal's rich tradition of seafaring discoverers; everywhere you go, you will find shrines and museums honoring notable Portuguese seamen and patrons of overseas exploration such as Vasco da Gama, Prince Henry the Navigator, and Diogo Cão. Its combination of architectural beauty, small-town charm, and centuries-old tradition make it a necessary stop for anyone visiting Lisboa.

If you've worked up an appetite after taking in so many Belém jewels of hallowed antiquity, stop by **Pão Pão Queijo Queijo ❶**, R. Belém, 124 (☎213 62 33 69), right next to the Mosteiro dos Jerónimos. This small, quaint locale is perfect for a quick bite, serving delicious pitas (€3-4), sandwiches (€2-3), and entrees (€4-6) at great prices. (Open M-F 8am-midnight, Sa-Su 8am-8pm.)

▨ MOSTEIRO DOS JERÓNIMOS. Established in 1502 to give thanks for the success of Vasco da Gama's expedition to India, the Mosteiro dos Jerónimos was granted UN World Heritage status in the 1980s. The combination of excruciatingly minute Renaissance detail and Gothic arches and architecture is a sight to behold. The main door of the church, to the right of the monastery entrance, is a sculpted anachronism: Prince Henry the Navigator mingles with the Twelve Apostles on both sides of the central column. The symbolic tombs of Luís de Camões and navigator Vasco da Gama lie in opposing transepts. Inside the monastery, the octagonal cloisters of the courtyard continue with the almost haunting attention to detail that is a pleasant contrast to the simple rose gardens in the center. For a beautiful example of Manueline architecture, observe the intricate carvings and vaulted ceilings of the Mosteiro's cloister, considered by many art historians to be a Manueline masterpiece. (☎213 62 00 34. *Open daily summer 10am-6:30pm; winter 10am-5pm. €4.50, students €1.80. Free Su 10am-2pm. Cloisters open daily 10am-5pm. Free.*)

▨ TORRE DE BELÉM. The best-known tower in all of Portugal, the Torre de Belém rises from the north bank of the Tejo and is surrounded by the ocean on three sides. Don't let the name fool you; instead of a looming tower, the Torre de Belém looks more like a small seaside fort. Built under Manuel I from 1515-1520 as a harbor fortress, it originally sat directly on the shoreline; today, due to the receding beach, it is accessible only by a small bridge. Nevertheless, this symbol of Portuguese grandeur has a cameo in dozens of paintings, postcards, and photographs of Lisboa. A UN World Heritage site, it offers panoramic views of Belém, the Tejo, and the Atlantic beyond. Climb up the extremely narrow spiral staircase to the top for the best vista. *(A 10min. walk along the water from the monastery away from Lisboa. Take the underpass by the gardens to cross the highway. ☎213 62 00 34. Open daily summer 10am-6:30pm; winter 10am-5pm. €3, students and seniors €1.50.)*

PADRÃO DOS DESCOBRIMENTOS. Along the river and directly across from the Mosteiro is the Padrão dos Descobrimentos, built in 1960 to celebrate the 500th anniversary of Prince Henry the Navigator's death. The great, white monument is shaped like a narrow cross and features Henry leading celebrated compatriots (among them Vasco da Gama and Diogo Cão) as they wistfully ponder their famous journeys. The view is better than that from the *Torre*, with the added bonus of an elevator (rather than stairs) that transports visitors 50m up to a small terrace. The Padrão also hosts temporary exhibits. *(Across the highway from the Mosteiro. ☎213 03 19 50. Open Tu-Su 9am-5pm. €2, students €1.)*

PALÁCIO NACIONAL DA AJUDA. A short bus ride up the emerald hills above the town brings you to this palace, home of the Portuguese royal family for 110 years. Built in 1802, the 54 chambers are a display of opulence. *(Lg. da Ajuda. Take tram #18 (Ajuda) to the palace's back door, or walk up the Calçada de Ajuda (20min.). ☎213 63 70 95. Open Su-Tu and Th-Sa 10am-4:30pm. Guided tours €3, students €1.50.)*

CENTRO CULTURAL DE BELÉM. Contemporary art buffs will bask in the glow of this luminous complex, which could best be described as a contemporary-looking Mayan fortress. With three pavilions holding rotating world-class exhibitions and a huge auditorium for concerts and performances, the center provides the only modern entertainment in a sea of imperial landmarks. Aficionados of the arts will be glad to find that the Centro Cultural de Belém holds a wide variety of performances, ranging from puppet shows to plays, orchestral music, and even Indonesian music and dance. *(Across the street from the monastery museums. ☎213 61 24 00; www.ccb.pt. Open daily 9am-10pm. Exhibitions 11am-7:15pm; prices vary.)*

◪ DAYTRIPS FROM LISBOA

Lisboa, with all its history and passion, can be daunting after several days. If nature calls, answer it with daytrips to some of the following coastal towns. The beaches and related outdoor activities are a great escape from the city's museum/cathedral/bar crawl pattern. Pay close attention to transportation links as you plan; many of these places lie en route to other, larger destinations such as Sintra (p. 710) and Setúbal (p. 715).

ESTORIL

Trains from Lisboa's Estação Cais do Sodré (☎213 42 48 93. M: Cais do Sodré) run to Estoril (30min., every 20min. 5:30am-2:30am, €1.30), continuing to Cascais (which is also a pleasant 20min. walk along the beach from Estoril). Stagecoach bus #418 to Sintra, which stops in Estoril, departs from Av. Marginal, in front of the train station (35min., every hr. 6:10am-11:40pm, €2.50).

Essentially a casino with a town built around it (imagine a Portuguese Monte Carlo), Estoril nonetheless has a nice coast, lined with bars and restaurants. One of the city's five beaches, **Praia Estoril Tamariz,** greets visitors upon arrival.

When exiting the train station, use the underpass; take a left to get to the beach or a right for the casino and the rest of town. One of Europe's largest casinos, ▨ **Casino Estoril** in Pr. José Teodoro dos Santos is well worth a visit even for non-gamblers; directly across from the train station, the casino is easily identifiable by its expansive, well-maintained front lawn (not to mention the huge sign). As you navigate through the Mercedes- and Porsche-filled parking lot, you may get the impression that it caters only to high rollers. However, besides the fashionable game room and over 1200 slot machines, the casino offers free shows and concerts. Every Wednesday at 11:30pm in the Wonder-Bar, a *fado* concert features some of Portugal's most acclaimed singers; be sure to reserve at least a day in advance. (☎214 66 77 00; www.casino-estoril.pt. Dress code: no sneakers, jeans, shorts, swimwear, or hats anywhere in the casino. Jackets required for the game room (with tie during the winter); can be borrowed at the entrance if you leave an ID. 18+ to gamble, passport required for game room. Open daily 3pm-3am.)

The **tourist office,** on Arcadas do Parque, across the street from the train station and to the left of the park, offers **luggage storage;** its friendly and knowledgeable staff speaks English, Spanish, and French, and will gladly provide you with a mountain of information on the beaches and other attractions of Estoril and neighboring Cascais. (☎214 66 38 13; www.estorilcoast.com. Wheelchair-accessible. Open summer M-Sa 9am-8pm, Su 10am-6pm; winter M-Sa 9am-7pm, Su 10am-6pm.) If you need a place to stay after the casino closes, the cheapest alternative in town is **Pensão Marylus ❷,** R. Maestro Lacerda, 13. From the train station, turn right and follow Av. Marginal three blocks until it intersects Av. dos Bombeiros Voluntários. Turn left, walk 5min., and turn right onto R. Maestro Lacerda. In an old house, the spacious rooms offer an inexpensive respite from gambling losses and overpriced seafood. All rooms have bath and cable TV. (☎214 68 27 40. Breakfast included 7:30am-noon. Singles €25; doubles €45; triples €50.) For those coming off a high euro-winning streak, the lovely **Pensão Pica Pau ❹,** R. Dom Afonso Henriques, 48, is the best place to crash. From the train station, take a left and walk past the tourist office, take the next right after the church onto R. Fausto Figueiredo. Walk to the junction and continue going straight; it will be on your right. *Azulejos* line each hallway, and the private bar with satellite TV, posh swimming pool, as well as personal safes and cable TV in each room give the *pensão* a beach resort feel. (☎214 66 71 40; fax 67 06 64. Breakfast included. Summer singles €50; doubles €75; triples €97.50. Winter €35/€65/€75.) The *pensão* also features its own restaurant, **Restaurante Pica Pau ❷,** which serves charcoal-grilled meats. (Entrees €9-12. Open daily noon-11pm.)

CASCAIS

To get to Cascais from neighboring Estoril, take a right onto the walkway at Praia Estoril Tamariz and walk along the coast about 20min. Trains from Lisboa's Estação Cais do Sodré (☎213 42 48 93; M: Cais do Sodré) head to Cascais via Estoril (30min., every 20min. 5:30am-2:30am, €1.30). Stagecoach bus #417 leaves from outside the train station for Sintra via Estoril (40min., every hr. 6:35am-7:08pm, €2.80). To visit Praia de Guincho, a popular windsurfing beach considered by many to be best on the coast, take the circular route bus #405/415 to the Guincho stop (22min., every 1-2hr. 7:39am-5:34pm, €1.80).

Although the town is pleasantly serene during the off-season, the summer crowds seem to define the flavor of Cascais rather than spoil it; drop by during the warmer parts of the year and you will find the town alive, its beachside restaurants packed with newly tanned bodies and its normally tranquil avenues transformed into a sea of designer shopping bags. In balmy weather, the beaches, especially **Praia da**

Ribeira, **Praia da Rainha,** and **Praia da Duquesa,** are filled with tanners. To reach Praia da Ribeira, take a right upon leaving the tourist office and walk down Av. dos Combatantes de Grande Guerra until you see the water. As is often the case, the better beaches require a little more effort; Praia da Rainha and the large Praia da Duquesa are a short walk out of town towards Estoril. Those in search of shade should head to the expansive **Parque Municipal da Gandarinha** (open daily 10am-6pm). About 1km outside Cascais, another 20min. walk up Av. Rei Humberto de Itália, lies the natural wonder **Boca de Inferno** (Mouth of Hell), so named because of the cleft carved in the rock by the Atlantic surf and the haunting sound of the waves pummeling the cliffs. As the sun sets, the nightlife picks up on **Largo Luís de Camões,** the main pedestrian square.

To get to the **tourist office,** Av. dos Combatantes de Grande Guerra, 25, exit the train station through the ticket office, cross Lg. da Estaçaõ, and take a right at McDonald's onto Av. Valbom; the office is at the end of this shop-lined street. The staff speaks English, Spanish, and French, and **luggage storage** is available. (☎214 86 82 04. Open summer M-Sa 9am-8pm, Su 10am-6pm; winter M-Sa 9am-7pm, Su 10am-6pm.) If you feel like discovering Cascais on wheels, there are free bicycle rentals located a block away from the tourist office; exit the office, turn right, and when you hit the beach you'll see a big stand of bicycles. (Rentals with ID for 1 day only. Open daily 8am-10pm.) Sleeping in Cascais isn't the cheapest thing in the world; try staying at a base in Lisboa (a 30min. train ride away) or at the youth hostel outside nearby Oeiras. If you feel like staying anyway, consider **Residencial Valborn ❹,** Av. Valbom, 14. Enormous rooms with aquamarine bathtubs and breakfast included. (☎214 86 58 01; fax 86 58 05. July-Sept. singles €48-53; doubles €63-68. Nov.-Mar. €30/€35. Apr.-June and Oct. €43-58/€58-63.)

QUELUZ

The best way to get to Queluz is by train. Take the Sintra line from Lisboa's Estação Rossio (M: Rossio) or Estação Sete Rios (M: Jardim Zoológico) and hop off at the Queluz-Belas (not Queluz-Massomá) stop (25min., every 15min., €0.95). To get to the palace, exit the train station through the ticket office and head left on Av. António Ennes, continuing straight as the street becomes Av. da República. Follow the signs until you see the expansive pink palace; the entrance is to the left of the statue of Dona Maria I.

En route to Sintra, stop by Queluz and marvel at the **Palácio Nacional de Queluz;** in addition to being the only reason that you should stop in this unremarkable town, the palace presents an opportunity to observe the marriage of Portuguese architect Mateus Vicente de Oliveira's work (read: lots and lots of *azulejos*) with French sculptor Jean-Baptiste Robillon's Rococo carvings. The result is an interesting mix of French and Portuguese art and architecture that make this palace unique. Originally a hunting lodge, Dom Pedro III turned it into a summer residence in the mid-18th century. Inside, the first stop on the tour is the striking **Sala do Trono;** although Oliveira intended it to be five rooms, the King instead decided to make it one large one, "the biggest and richest in Queluz," and Robillon's influence is clearly visible, with rich carvings adorning the walls. Also be sure to visit the **Sala dos Embaixadores,** with its gilded thrones, marble floors and Chinese vases, as well as the **Quarto Don Quijote,** where the first and only emperor of Brazil, Dom Pedro I, drew his first and last breaths. While you pass through the palace, actors play out scenes from the daily life of its residents; of particular interest is the arithmetic and etiquette lesson that young prince José (1781-1788) receives from his tutor. Outside, enjoy a leisurely stroll through the gardens or the equestrian show. (Palace open M and W-Su 10am-5pm. €4, students and seniors €2; includes gardens. Gardens open M and W-Su May-Oct. 10am-6pm; Nov.-Apr. 10am-5pm. Equestrian show May-Oct. W 11am. €8.)

LISBOA

MAFRA

Mafrense buses, labeled with a green and white "M," run from Lisboa's Campo Grande and stop in the square across from the palace; the buses serve Lisboa (1-1½hr., every hr. 5:30am-9:30pm, €3) and Ericeira (20min., every hr. 7:30am-midnight, €1.50). Don't take the train from Lisboa's Estação Santa Apolónia unless you're up for the 7km walk to Mafra; the station is out where cabs are rare.

An attractive stop on the way to Ericeira from Lisboa, Mafra is home to one of Portugal's most impressive sights and one of Europe's largest historical buildings, the ◪**Palácio Nacional de Mafra.** Built by Dom João V as a "hunting palace," the building took 50,000 workers and 30 years to build. The massive structure built of *pedra lioz,* a type of faux marble, covers nearly 40,000 square meters and includes over 1200 rooms, a monastery, a library, and a cathedral patterned after St. Peter's in Rome. The monastery has its own hospital and infirmary, as well as a **Sala de Penitencia,** where the Franciscan monks punished themselves—note the whip on the wall and the skull above the bed. The **Sala do Trono** (Throne Room), where the king gave his speeches, is covered with murals representing his eight ideal virtues. Look for the **Sala da Caça** (Hunting Room), garishly decorated with antlers and heads of all kinds; even the chairs and tables are made of elk antlers. The most impressive space in the palace is the **biblioteca** (library) containing 40,000 volumes from the 16th to 18th centuries, many of which were bound by the monks. For the tour of the palace and monastery, enter through the door to the left of the main palace steps. (☎261 81 75 50. Open M and W-Su 10am-5pm, last entrance at 4pm. Daily 1hr. tours in English and Portuguese 11am and 2:30pm. €3, students and seniors €1.50, under 14 free. Su before 1:30pm free.)

To reach the **tourist office,** simply walk to the entrance on the other side of the palace; the recently renovated office is now inside the palace compound. In addition to maps and brochures, the office has free **Internet access** (10min. limit). (☎261 81 71 70. Open M-F 9:30am-6pm, Sa-Su 9:30am-1pm and 2-6pm.) If you get hungry for meat (and lots of it), try **Churrasqueira Brasão ❷,** Tr. Manuel Esteves, 7, across the street from the Palácio Nacional; turn onto Tr. Manuel Esteves and it will be on your left. Try their *picanha brasileira* (€11), an assortment of Brazilian-style meats. (☎261 81 56 87. Open daily 10am-2am.)

ERICEIRA

Mafrense buses run from Lisboa's Campo Grande (1¼-1½hr., every hr. 6:30am-11:20pm, €4). Ask to be dropped at the stop nearest the center, or just get off at the bus station. Buses run from Ericeira to: Lisboa (1½hr., every hr. 5:15am-9:05pm, €4); Mafra (25min., every hr. 5:15am-9:05pm, €1.45); Sintra (50min., every hr. 6:30am-8:30pm, €2.80).

Ericeira is a pleasant fishing village whose beaches have been discovered by surfers. Despite its rising popularity, the town seems to handle the attention responsibly, more or less maintaining its traditional way of life while visitors frolic in the waves of the internationally renowned beaches. Beachgoers find their way quickly to nearby **Praia do Norte,** a long beach to the right of the port, and **Praia do Sul** on the left. Although the waves close to town are great for novices, experienced surfers head beyond Praia do Norte to the more pristine **Praia de São Sebastião, Praia da Ribeira d'Ilhas** 3km away (site of a former World Surfing Championship), or the motherlode: **Praia dos Coxos** (Crippled Beach) just beyond Ribeira d'Ilhas. **Utilmar,** near the town center at R. 5 de Outubro, 25A, rents surfboards and bodyboards. (☎261 86 23 71. €15 per day, €25 with wetsuit. AmEx/MC/V.)

To get to the **tourist office,** R. Dr. Eduardo Burnay, 46, from the bus station, cross the road (EN 247-2), turn left, and walk uphill. Take a right onto R. Prudêncio Franco da Trinidade and head straight until you hit Pr. da República; the tourist office is on the left side, at the end of the square. The multilingual staff rents out bikes during the summer. (☎261 86 31 22. Open daily July-Sept. 9:30am-10pm; Oct.-June 9:30am-1pm and 2-7pm. Bike rental Apr.-Sept. half-day 9:30am-2:30pm or 2:30-8pm, €4; full day 9:30am-8pm, €7.)

If you choose to stay or if you miss the last bus back to Lisboa (9:05pm), you might have some trouble finding a cheap room in summer. Check with the tourist office for a list of rooms in private homes. The cheapest option, and a favorite of those staying to hit the waves for more than a day, is **Hospederia Bernardo ❷**, R. Prudêncio Franco da Trinidade, 11 (☎261 86 23 78). This place is a combination apartment (€400-500 per week for 3 people), hotel-style *residencial* with all the amenities (singles €25; doubles €40), and hostel with a common kitchen (€15 per person). Prices drop €5-10 Sept.-May and are negotiable. One of the most comfortable places to stay is **Residencial Fortunato ❹**, R. Dr. Eduardo Burnay, 7, a few blocks past the tourist office. All rooms have bath, TV, gleaming tile, and shiny wood. (☎261 86 28 29. Doubles July €45; Aug. €50; Sept. €42; Oct. €37; Nov.-June €30.) **Restaurante O Jogo da Bola ❷**, Tr. do Jogo da Bola, 3, just behind the tourist office, is a popular local hangout due to its cheap beer, seafood, and other local dishes. (☎261 86 46 46. Entrees €4.50-11, seafood €11-20. Beer €0.60-0.85. Open Su-Tu and Th-Sa noon-2am.) More seafood restaurants and several bars can be found along **Rua Dr. Eduardo Burnay,** which runs from Pr. da República. In the evening, head over to **Neptuno Pub,** R. Mendes Leal, 12. Face Pr. da República from the tourist office and take a left onto Tr. do Jogo da Bola, then take the first left. This friendly Irish pub offers live, traditional *fado* music every Thursday night starting at 10pm, keeping tourists and locals entertained. (☎261 86 20 17. Beer €2. Open M-F 7pm-2am, Sa-Su 7pm-3pm. Summer opens at 4pm.)

ALMADA

To get to Almada, take the Transtejo ferry from Lisboa's Estação Cais do Sodré (every 30min. 5:40am-10:30pm, €0.60) to Estação Cacilhas across the Rio Tejo.

Perhaps the best view of Lisboa is from the top of the ▩**Cristo Rei,** a towering statue of Jesus across the river in neighboring Almada. To reach the Cristo Rei, take bus #101 (€0.80) from Estação Cacilhas and get off at the last stop, the monument itself. Standing 110m high, the massive structure took 7 years to build, not to mention a 10 year fundraising campaign. At a meeting of Portuguese bishops during World War II, a solemn pledge was made to build a large monument to God if Portugal managed to stay out of the war. When the war ended, the Catholic Church and the Portuguese government submitted a public call for contributions. The whole of Portugal responded fervently, with children carrying collection boxes door to door and housewives gladly donating their necklaces and rings, which were melted and made into the beautiful gold ornaments that adorn the monument's chapel. Modeled after Rio de Janeiro's famous Cristo de Corcovado statue, the Cristo Rei overlooks the city with arms outstretched, a symbol of peace for Portugal and the world. (Open daily 8am-7pm. Elevator to the top €2.50.)

SESIMBRA

To get to Sesimbra, take a Transtejo ferry from Lisboa to Cacilhas (10min., every 15min. 5:50am-9:30pm, €0.60) from the dock at Pr. do Comércio and then catch a TST bus to Sesimbra (45min.-1hr., 15 per day 6:40am-12:40am, €2.60). Alternatively, TST buses go directly to Sesimbra (1hr., 7 per day 8am-7:30pm, €2.90) from Lisboa's Pr. de Espanha (M: Pr. de Espanha), but heavy traffic can delay them. TST buses leave from Sesimbra's main bus station on Av. da Liberdade (☎212 23 31 03) to: Cacilhas (45min.-1hr., every 30min. 5:40am-12:30am, €2.60); Lisboa (1hr., 7 per day 6:30am-6:10pm, €3.10); Setúbal (45min., 9 per day 6:20am-6:50pm, €2.50).

LISBOA

The agenda in Sesimbra (pop. 6000) is refreshingly simple: go to the beach, gape at the Moorish castle, eat seafood, and unwind. Unlike other port towns and beaches that have been transformed by tourism (like Tróia), Sesimbra offers an untouched beachside experience. Although the beaches tend to get more crowded during the summer, you won't find yourself fighting for a place to lay down your beach blanket or waiting 30 minutes for a table at one of the charming seafood locales that line the water. A steep hour-long hike to the ⬛**Moorish castle** rewards one with a luminous view of the ocean and surrounding mountains. To reach the castle from the beach, follow the signs that lead to R. Conselheiro Ramada Curto. Continue until you see an incredibly steep dirt road, which leads to the castle. (☎212 268 07 46. Castle open daily June-Sept. 7am-8pm; Oct.-May 7am-7pm. Free.)

To get to the **tourist office,** Lg. da Marinha, 26-27, from the bus station take a left onto Av. da Liberdade and walk downhill to the end, then take a right. (☎212 28 85 40. Open daily June-Sept. 9am-8pm; Oct.-May 9am-12:30pm and 2-5:30pm.) Inexpensive rooms are difficult to find, especially in summer, but **Residencial Mateus ❷,** Av. da Liberdade, across the street from Mini-Preço, is the exception. The owners go out of their way to accommodate guests. Clean rooms, long bathrooms and old wooden furniture add an "at home" feeling. (☎212 23 30 39. June-Aug. €20 per person; Sept.-May €15 per person.) Restaurants cluster in the plaza above the tourist office along Lg. da Marinha. Don't miss **Casa Isaías ❷,** R. Coronel Barreto, 2, up the street from Lg. do Município, at the end of the block on the right. Isaías grills fish (€5-8; pick your fish from the daily catch) in an outdoor brick oven. (☎914 57 43 73. Open M-F noon-10pm; serves food noon-3pm and 7-10pm.)

SINTRA ☎ 219

No visit to Portugal is complete without at least a day among the palaces and sheer bucolic beauty of Sintra. Charmingly nestled into the surrounding hillside, the town is adept at welcoming those exasperated with Lisboa's crazy city life; over the years sultans, kings, and wealthy citizens have found the same pleasures that backpackers and travelers find today. Of course, the former left behind castles, palaces, and mansions that attract the latter even more than Sintra's natural endowments. Many daytrippers from Lisboa take pleasure in walking the town's geranium- and bougainvillea-lined streets and dreaming of long-gone royalty.

▆ TRANSPORTATION

Trains: Estação de Caminhos de Ferro, Av. Dr. Miguel Bombarda (☎219 23 26 05). To Estação Rossio and Estação Sete Rios in **Lisboa** (45min., every 15min. 5:11am-1:11am, €1.30).

Buses: Stagecoach buses (☎214 83 20 55; fax 86 81 68) on Av. Dr. Miguel Bombarda run to **Cascais** (#417; 40min., every hr. 7:13am-8:23pm, €2.80) and **Estoril** (#418; 40min., every hr. 6:50am-midnight, €2.80). **Mafrense** buses, just down the street, go to **Ericeira** (50min., every hr. 7:25am-8:25pm, €2.30).

▆ ▆ ORIENTATION AND PRACTICAL INFORMATION

Situated 25km northwest of Lisboa and 10km north of Estoril, Sintra is split into three parts: the modern **Estefânia** around the train station, where most budget accommodations and banks are located; **Sintra-Vila,** where the historic sights nestle on the mountainside; and **Portela de Sintra,** where shops and municipal offices cluster. Though all three make up the delightful tourist town that is Sintra, Sintra-Vila is particularly beautiful and worth getting to know in detail. The historic sec-

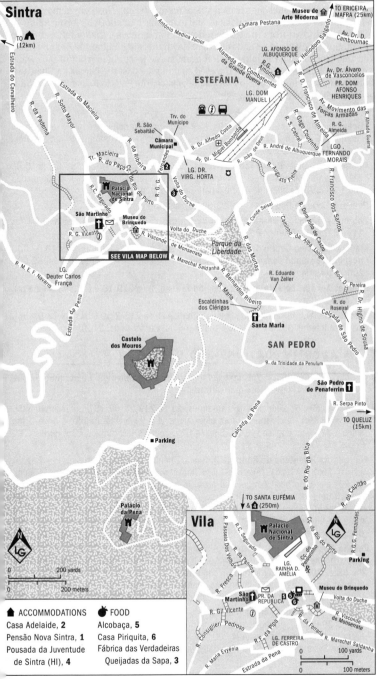

Sintra

TO ▲ (12km)

Estrada do Carvalheiro

TO ERICEIRA, MAFRA (25km)

Museu de Arte Moderna 🏛

R. Câmara Pestana

R. António Medina Júnior

Av. Dr. D. Cambournac

R. Heliodoro Salgado

ESTEFÂNIA

Alameda dos Combatentes da Grande Guerra

LG. AFONSO DE ALBUQUERQUE

R. G. Amorim 1

Av. Dr. Álvaro de Vasconcelos

PR. DOM AFONSO HENRIQUES

Av. Movimento das Forças Armadas

R. D. Francisco de Almeida

R. G. Almeida

R. Gago Coutinho

R. S. Cabral

R. Almada Guerra

LGO. FERNANDO MORAIS

R. André de Albuquerque

R. João de Deus

R. Augusto Freire

R. Francisco dos Santos

LG. DOM MANUEL I

Trv. do Município

R. São Sebatão

Câmara Municipal

R. Dr. Alfredo Costa

R. Dr. Miguel Bombarda

Av. Dr.

Estrada do Macieira

R. Soito Mayor

R. da Paderna

R. da Ribeira

Tr. Macieira

R. do Paço

R.C. Seganedo

R.G.G. Fernandes

Volta do Duche

LG. DR. VIRG. HORTA

2

3

Palácio Nacional de Sintra 🏰

São Martinho ✝

✉

Museu do Brinquedo 🏛

R. G. Vicente

ⓘ

Visconde de Monserrate

Volta do Duche

R. do Rio do Porto

R. Conde Seisal

R. Dom João de Castro

Caminho da Alta Longa

Parque da Liberdade

R. das Murtas

SEE VILA MAP BELOW

R. Marechal Saldanha

R. Bernardim Ribeiro

R. S. Maria

R. Eduardo Van Zeller

R. Rod. D. Pereira

R. do Roseiral

R. Dr. Higino de Sousa

R.M.E.F. Navarro

LG. Deuter Carlos França

Estrada da Pena

Escaldinhas dos Clérigos

Santa Maria 🏴

Calçada de São Pedro

SAN PEDRO

Castelo dos Mouros 🏯

R. da Trinidade da Penulum

São Pedro de Penaferrim 🏴

R. Serpa Pinto

→ TO QUELUZ (15km)

Calçada da Pena

■ Parking

R. do Rio da Bica

R. do Capitão

Palácio da Pena 🏰

TO SANTA EUFÉMIA ▼ & 🏠 (250m)

N

LG

| 0 | | 200 yards |
| 0 | | 200 meters |

Vila

R. Passeio dos velhos

R.C. Segurado

R. da Pendoa

R. Fresca

R. Gil Vicente

R. Consiglieri Pedroso

R. Maria Exyénia

São Martinho ✝

R. da Pipa

R. da Ferraria

PR. DA REPÚBLICA

ⓘ

LG. RAINHA D. AMÉLIA

Palácio Nacional de Sintra 🏰

Cc. do Rio do Porto

R. G. G. Fernandes

LG

■ Parking

Cc. do Pelourinho

R 3

5

6

✉

Museu do Brinquedo 🏛

Volta do Duche

R. Visconde de Monserrate

R. Marechal Saldanha

LG. FERREIRA DE CASTRO

Estrada da Pena

N

LG

| 0 | | 100 yards |
| 0 | | 100 meters |

🏠 **ACCOMMODATIONS**
Casa Adelaide, **2**
Pensão Nova Sintra, **1**
Pousada da Juventude
  de Sintra (HI), **4**

🍎 **FOOD**
Alcobaça, **5**
Casa Piriquita, **6**
Fábrica das Verdadeiras
  Queijadas da Sapa, **3**

LISBOA

tion of town, its appeal stems from a mix of natural beauty (lush green mountains) and opulent excess (the many palaces and mansions that adorn its fertile hills). To get to the old town from the train station (a 15min. walk), take a left out of the train station's ticket office, and turn right down the small hill at the next intersection. One block down the hill, turn left again at the fountain in front of the castle-like **Câmara Municipal,** following the road as it curves past the **Parque da Liberdade.** From there, head up the hill to **Praça da República;** the **Palácio Nacional de Sintra** is the large white building on the right.

Tourist Office: Pr. da República, 23 (☎219 23 11 57; fax 23 87 87), in Sintra-Vila. Open daily June-Sept. 9am-8pm; Oct.-May 9am-7pm. **Branch** office in the train station (☎/fax 219 24 16 23) with the same hours. Both only offer information on the area; English, French, and Spanish spoken.

Currency Exchange: Banco Totta e Açores, R. Padarias, 4 (☎219 10 68 70; fax 10 68 71). On an uphill side street off the main *praça* in Sintra-Vila. Open M-F 8:30am-noon and 1-3pm. **ATMs** also line Av. Heliodoro Salgado in modern Sintra.

Police: R. João de Deus, 6 (☎219 23 09 35), next to the bus station.

Pharmacy: Farmácia da Misericórdia de Sintra, Lg. Dr. Gregório d'Almeida, 2 (☎/fax 219 23 03 91). Open M-F 9am-7pm, Sa 9am-1pm.

Medical Services: Centro de Saúde, R. Dr. Alfredo Costa, 34, 1st fl. (☎219 10 69 00); **Hospital Fernando Fonseca (Amadora-Sintra)** in nearby Amadora (☎214 34 82 00), 20min. by train (€1.10).

Internet Access: Loja do Arco, R. Arco do Teixeira, 2 (☎219 10 61 51; www.rigra.pt). €2.50 per 30min., €1.25 per additional 15min.

Post Office: Av. Movimento das Forças Armadas, 1 (☎219 23 91 51; fax 23 91 56). Also has Internet access. Open M-F 8:30am-6pm. **Postal Code:** 2710.

◪◪ ACCOMMODATIONS AND CAMPING

Sintra makes a good base for daytrips to surrounding historical sights and coastal towns, as accommodations are quite affordable.

▨ **Casa Adelaide,** R. Guilherme G. Fernandes, 11 (☎219 23 08 73). Enter through the back. Well-kept, rustic rooms in an older home. Ask for private bath; the price is the same either way. English spoken. Singles €25; doubles €25; triples €35; quads €35. Prices €5-10 less in winter. ❷

Pousada da Juventude de Sintra (HI), Santa Eufémia at S. Pedro de Sintra (☎219 24 12 10; fax 23 31 76). Take bus #435 from the train station to São Pedro (15min., €1.20) and then hike 2km, or hail a taxi in front of the train station (€9-10). Dining room, sitting room, TV with VCR, stereo, and winter heating. The rooms are on the high end of the youth hostel price range—cleaner than most, yet plain. Breakfast included. HI membership required. Summer dorms €11; doubles €26, with bath €30. Winter €8.50/€21/€24. MC/V. ❶

Pensão Nova Sintra, Lg. Afonso de Albuquerque, 25 (☎219 23 02 20; www.novasintra.com). The *pensão* is the yellow building above a row of shops, recognizable by all the flags. Offering space and luxury, all 9 rooms include marble floors, cable TV, A/C, Internet access, bath, and phone. The open patio at the restaurant-bar is a good place to relax. Breakfast included. Summer singles €60; doubles €80. Winter €45/€51. ❺

Camping: Parque de Campismo da Praia Grande, Av. Maestro Frederico de Freitas, 28 (☎219 29 05 81), on the coast 12km from Sintra. Take bus #441 from Portela de Sintra to Praia Grande. Campsite is 200m from the beach, surrounded by the forest, and near the Serra de Sintra. Reception daily until 7pm. €3 per person. ❶

⬛ FOOD

Pastelarias (pastry shops) and restaurants crowd **Rua João de Deus** and **Avenida Heliodoro Salgado.** In the old town, R. das Padarias (near the Palácio Nacional) is lined with great lunch spots. On the 2nd and 4th Sundays of every month, take bus #435 from the train station to nearby São Pedro (15min., €1.10) for the spectacular **Feira de São Pedro,** featuring every kind of local food you can imagine without the unfortunate price embellishments seen in town.

🔲 **Fábrica das Verdadeiras Queijadas da Sapa,** Volta do Duche, 12 (☎219 23 04 93). Founded in 1756 and at its current location since 1890, Sapa is still run by the same family. A Sintra institution, its owners proudly display media references to their legendary *queijada* recipe on the front wall. Try a pastry (€0.70) or buy a *pacote* (package) for the road (€3.60). Open July-Aug. daily 9am-7pm; Sept.-June Tu-F 9am-6pm, Sa-Su 9am-7pm. ❶

Casa Piriquita, R. Padarias, 1 (☎219 23 06 26), up a small side street off Pr. da República. One of the 4 classic pastry shops of Sintra, Piriquita has the advantage of being right in the central tourist area. Bright yellow tiles cover the facade, and *fado* music floats into the narrow street. The counter is flanked by a marble-floored coffee and tea room. Try one of their *queijadas* (€0.75, *pacote* €3.60) or their premium *travasseiros* (almond cream-filled pastry; €1). A favorite with tourists and locals, so expect a line. Open Su-Tu and Th-Sa 9am-10pm. ❶

Alcobaça, R. Padarias, 9 (☎219 23 16 51). Conveniently located on a heavily transited pedestrian street right off the main square. Stacks of fresh seafood in the window. Shellfish lovers will enjoy the *arroz de marisco* (seafood and rice; €8). Other entrees €5-10. Open daily noon-11pm. Closed mid-Dec. AmEx/MC/V. ❷

🧭 SIGHTS

🔳 **CASTELO DOS MOUROS.** Built during the 8th century by the Moors, the castle was abandoned during the Moorish retreat to the south but repaired in the 19th century under the orders of Dom Fernando II. A walk along its walls rewards you with some of the most awe-inspiring views you will ever see; gaze out at the horizon and watch the fertile green plains of the Ribatejo unroll before your eyes. *(Bus #434 runs to the top from outside the tourist office. All-day bus pass €3.50. Those looking to get some exercise can walk (1-1½hr.); start at the Museu do Brinquedo off Pr. da República and follow R. Visconde de Monserrate up the hill. Continue straight as it becomes R. Bernardim Ribeiro, then take a right up the*

ON THE MENU

PASTRIES WITH A PAST

There's a lot of history packed into the little cheese pastries sold proudly in the *pastelarias* of Sintra. *Queijadas* date back to the 13th century and were once used as a form of currency. The *queijada*'s ascent to fame began in 1756, when a woman named Maria made the pastries to sell at the entrance of town. After the railroad tracks linking Sintra to Lisboa were completed in 1887, famous writers began to pass through. Some were so impressed by the little sweet that it soon made its way into many classic works of Portuguese literature.

Maria's descendants still run **Sapa,** the oldest pastry shop in Sintra, and they have joined with the three other prestigious names of the *queijada* tradition—Preto, Gregorio, and Piriquita—to form an association for the protection of the authenticity and integrity of *queijadas de Sintra*. All shops use the same ingredients: cheese, flour, sugar, egg yolk, water, and cinnamon. But according to Francisco Barreto das Neves, the guardian of the Sapa tradition, there are countless variables in the process that make all the *queijadas* different.

To try these delicious pastries, stop by the Sapa shop (Volta do Duche, 12. ☎219 23 94 83) or ***Casa Piriquita*** *(R. Padarias, 1. ☎219 23 06 26), two of the most famous in the industry. Individual quiejadas cost €0.60-0.75, while a pacote (pack) runs about €3.50-3.60.*

Escadinhas dos Clerigos and walk to the fork at the end. Turn left onto the Calçada da Santa Maria (toward the church), then right when you see a sign for Casa do Adro. Take another right at the 1st side street and follow it up the mountain. Open daily June-Sept. 9am-7pm; Oct.-May 9:30am-5pm. €3.50, seniors and children €1.50. Guided tours €3.50.)

■ **PALÁCIO DA PENA.** Built in the 1840s by Prince Ferdinand of Bavaria, husband of Portugal's Dona Maria II, this royal retreat embraces romantic and fantastic style with its excessive detail. The prince, nostalgic for his country, rebuilt and embellished the ruined monastery with the assistance of a Prussian engineer, combining the artistic heritages of both Germany and Portugal. The result is a Bavarian castle decorated with Arabic minarets, Gothic turrets, Manueline windows, and a Renaissance dome. Interior highlights include the chapel, a fully furnished kitchen, incredible views from the Queen's enormous terrace (rivaling those from the Castelo dos Mouros), and her majesty's toilet—crafted entirely from *azulejos*. *(About 1km uphill from the Castelo dos Mouros. Also accessible with the all-day bus pass, €3.50. ☎ 219 10 53 40; www.parquesdesintra.pt. Open Tu-Su June-Sept. 9am-7pm; Oct.-June 9:30am-6pm. €6, seniors and students €4. Guided tours in English, Spanish, and Portuguese; €3.50.)*

PALÁCIO NACIONAL DE SINTRA. Also known as the Paço Real or Palácio da Vila, the palace presides over Pr. da República. Once the site of a summer residence for Moorish sultans and their harems, the Palácio da Vila was taken over by the Portuguese following the Muslim defeat, as clearly evidenced by the paintings portraying Portuguese noblemen on horseback gunning down Moorish soldiers. The palace and gardens were built in two stages: Dom João I built the main structure in the 15th century and, a century later, Dom Manuel I amassed the best collection of *azulejos* in the world. He added various wings to create a mix of Moorish, Gothic, and Manueline styles. The palace has more than 20 rooms, including the *azulejo*-covered **Sala dos Árabes** and the majestically gilded **Sala dos Brasões;** look up to see the royal coat of arms on the ceiling, surrounded by the armorial bearings of 72 noble families. Equally noteworthy is the bedchamber of Afonso VI, where the imprisoned king spent the last nine years of his life, until his death in 1683. You may notice a bird theme: doves symbolizing the Holy Spirit line the walls of the **Capela,** magpies holding a piece of paper proclaiming the motto of D. João I (*"por bem"* or "for good") cover the ceiling of the **Sala das Pegas,** and swans grace the ceiling of the **Sala dos Cisnes.** *(Lg. da Rainha Dona Amélia. ☎ 219 10 68 40. Open M-Tu and Th-Su 10am-5:30pm. Buy tickets by 5pm. €3, seniors and students €1.50. Su before 2pm free.)*

MUSEU DO BRINQUEDO. The toy museum, in Sintra's old fire station, grew out of the private collection of João Arbués Moreira (a local engineer and toy enthusiast) and displays a fascinating three-floor assortment of over 20,000 toys. According to Moreira, the unifying idea of his museum is to show the history of humanity by way of toys; this philosophy unifies his eclectic collection of cars, trains, Legos, dolls, lead soldiers, and more from around the world. Moreira also highlights the manner in which toys have been used as propaganda; notice how the Hitler toys are taller than any of the others, so as to add grandeur to his image. For an extra treat, look for Moreira himself, who usually hangs around the museum, eager to answer questions and discuss his beloved collection. Especially intriguing is the second floor, which presents the history of war from the dawn of man to WWII. *(R. Visconde de Monserrate, 28. ☎ 219 24 21 71; www.museu-do-brinquedo.pt. Open Tu-Su 10am-6pm, last visit 5:30pm. €3, under 3 and seniors €1.50.)*

SETÚBAL ☎ 265

No question about it, Setúbal is a port city—you can smell it in the air and see it on the menus. But unlike the port cities in the Algarve, Setúbal leaves travelers with more options than just beaches and *bacalhau* (cod). Are you here to commune with Mother Nature? The wild dolphin population in the Reserva Natural do Estuário do Sado can take care of that. Or perhaps you're fleeing from campy tourist traps in a quest to discover "Portugal?" Setúbal meets that need too, with central city squares full of traditional *lojas* (shops), cobblestones, and, of course, statues of obscure Portuguese statesmen. Setúbal is well-equipped to tickle your fancy and should take no more than a day to visit.

⌐ TRANSPORTATION

Trains: leave from either **Estação Praça de Quebedo,** which is the most convenient to the city center, or **Estação de Setúbal** (☎265 23 88 02), in Pr. do Brasil (a 10min. walk down the same street) for **Faro** (4hr., 3 per day 9:20am-8:25pm, €11) and **Estação do Barreiro** (50min., every 30min. 5am-1am, €1.20), where you transfer to a boat to get to **Lisboa.**

Buses: Setubalense, Av. 5 de Outubro, 44 (☎265 52 50 51). From the local tourist office, walk up R. Santa Maria to Av. 5 de Outubro and turn left; the station is about 2 blocks down on the right, in the building with "Rodoviária" written vertically down the front. To: **Évora** (2-2½hr., 4 per day 6:30am-6:45pm, €5.15); **Faro** (4hr., 3pm, €3.40); **Lisboa's** Praça de Espanha (1hr., 21-29 per day 5am-11:30pm, €3.15); **Sesimbra** (45min., 9 per day 7:20am-8:00pm, €2.45).

Ferries: Transado, Doca do Comércio (☎265 23 51 01), off Av. Luísa Todi at the eastern end of the waterfront. To **Tróia** (15min.; every 20 min. around the clock; €1, children 5-10 €0.50, under 5 free).

Taxis: Rádio Táxi (☎265 23 33 34), Av. Luísa Todi and by the bus and train stations.

❖ ❷ ORIENTATION AND PRACTICAL INFORMATION

Setúbal's spine is **Avenida Luísa Todi,** a long boulevard parallel to the Rio Sado. Inland from the river and the *avenida* lies a dense district of shops and restaurants centered around **Praça de Bocage.** Another major thoroughfare, **Avenida 5 de Outubro,** runs along the opposite side of the main district from Av. Luísa Todi to Pr. de Bocage. Perpendicular to Av. 5 de Outubro, **Avenida da Portela** runs past the train and bus stations.

Regional Tourist Office: Posto de Turismo da Costa Azul (☎265 53 91 20), on Tr. Frei Gaspar, just off Av. Luísa Todi near Lg. da Misericórdia. In addition to Portuguese, the staff speaks English, Spanish, and French. Wheelchair-accessible. Open May-Sept. Su 9:30am-12:30pm, M-Sa 9:30am-12:30pm and 3-7pm; Oct.-Apr. M-Sa 9:30am-12:30pm and 2-6pm. **Municipal branch,** R. Santa Maria, 2-4 (☎265 52 44 02). From the bus station, turn left (with your back to the big Rodoviária sign) and walk down Av. 5 de Outubro for 2 blocks; then take a right on R. Santa Maria and the office is on your right. More convenient to train and bus stations than the regional office with the same information. Staff speaks Spanish, French, and German. Open daily June-Sept. 9am-7pm; Oct.-May 9am-noon and 2-5:30pm.

Currency exchange: Banks line Av. Luísa Todi. All open M-F 8:30am-3pm. **Caixa Geral de Depositos** (☎265 53 05 00), on Av. Luísa Todi.

Bike Rentals: Planeta Terra (☎919 47 18 71). Rents street, hybrid, and mountain bikes starting at €7.50 per day. Service includes delivery; reserve ahead.

Police: Av. Luísa Todi (☎265 52 20 22), at Av. 22 de Dezembro.
Medical Services: Hospital São Bernardo, R. Camilo Castelo Branco (☎265 54 90 00).
Laundromat: Lavandaria Donini, R. Tenente Valedino, 9. Open M-F 9am-1pm and 3-7pm, Sa 9am-1pm.
Pharmacy: Farmácia Normal do Sul, Pr. de Bocage, 135 (☎265 52 22 16). Open M-Sa 9:30am-12:30pm.
Internet Access: Sobicome, Av. Luísa Todi, 331 (☎934 72 59 52). €2 per hr. with student ID. Open daily noon-4am. **Ciber Centro,** Av. Bento Gonçalves, 21A (☎265 23 48 00). €2.50 per 30min., students €2.25. Open M-F 9am-11pm.
Post Office: (☎265 52 86 20), on Av. Mariano de Carvalho at Av. 22 de Dezembro.
Posta Restante. Open M-F 8:30am-12:30pm and 2:30-6:30pm. **Postal Code:** 2900.

⚑ ACCOMMODATIONS

There are a few good *pensões* along Av. Luísa Todi and near Pr. de Bocage. Alternatively, ask at either tourist office for a list of *quartos* in private houses.

▨ **Pousada de Juventude de Setúbal (HI),** Lg. José Afonso (☎265 53 44 31; fax 53 29 63), has clean rooms, a common room with TV, and a friendly multi-lingual staff more than willing to help you find the best party spots in Setúbal. Reception 9am-noon and 6pm-midnight. Checkout 10:30am. Dorms €8.50; doubles €18, with bath €20. €2 extra without HI card. AmEx/MC/V. ❶

Residencial Bocage, R. São Cristóvão, 14 (☎54 30 80), off Av. Luísa Todi. Fully loaded suites without fully loaded prices. Rooms include bath, phone, TV, A/C, and breakfast. June-Sept. singles €40; doubles €45. Sept.-June singles €27.50; doubles €32.50. AmEx/MC/V. ❹

Pensão O Cantinho, Beco do Carmo, 1-9 (☎52 38 99), in an alley off Av. Luísa Todi behind Lg. do Carmo. The simple, clean, and spacious rooms above the restaurant have private baths and are by far the cheapest in Setúbal. Reserve a month ahead in summer. Singles €10; doubles €15. ❶

🍴 FOOD

Setúbal is full of restaurants offering town specialties (including grilled fish and fried calamari) at very affordable prices; there's no reason to pay more than €8 for a memorable meal. A row of seafood places lines Av. Luísa Todi just up the street from Doca do Comércio; you can watch as they cut and fry your fish right along the sidewalk. Pick up **groceries** and fresh baked goods at **Pingo Doce,** Av. Luísa Todi, 249. (☎52 61 05. Open daily 8am-10pm.)

Snack-Bar Dona Pança, R. José António Januário Silva, 32 (☎52 54 98), a block off Av. Luísa Todi, through the big arch. Serves five main dishes and about every kind of salad imaginable. Eat for €5-6 in the well-lit dining area with the crowd of locals on their lunch break, or come later in the day for a quieter dinner. Open M-Sa 8am-8pm. ❶

Novo 10, Av. Luísa Todi, 422-426 (☎52 54 98). One of many seafood restaurants with sidewalk grills so that you can watch your lunch being prepared, Novo 10 differentiates itself from the others with fantastic service and a huge selection of traditional entrees. Meat lovers won't leave disappointed; the variety of pork and beef (€9-15) is among the best in town. Open daily noon-2am. ❸

O Cantinho, Beco do Carmo, 1-9 (☎52 38 99), off Av. Luísa Todi in an alley behind Lg. do Carmo. Quality grilled seafood and other traditional dishes. Fish meals run €5-7.50. Be sure to try the *baba do camelo* ("camel's drool," a dessert made of condensed milk and eggs)—it's much better than the name suggests (small bowl €0.60). Open Su-W and F-Sa 9am-11pm; meals served noon-3pm and 7-10pm. ❷

👁 🌿 SIGHTS AND FESTIVALS

The most impressive sight in town is not really in town. The 16th-century ◪**Forte de São Filipe** sits just outside the city. Designed by Italian engineer Filipe Terzi, the fortress was built during the Spanish occupation of Portugal in 1582 and took almost 20 years to finish. A phenomenal view of the Rio Sado rewards visitors, but not before making them earn it; the walk is 20min. uphill from the base of the mountain, on top of the 30min. hike from the town center. Be forewarned: this is not an easy climb. To get there, take Av. Luísa Todi to its end (toward the beaches), following the signs that indicate the directions to the castle. Turn right where the sign indicates, then take the first left onto R. S. Filipe; follow this, which will become Estada do Castelo de S. Filipe, up to the fortress.

During the last week of July and first week of August, the **Feira de Santiago** in Lg. José Afonso brings a carnival, folk music, and enormous outdoor market with local snacks and souvenirs. Coinciding with the fair, Portuguese bullfighting (which spares the bull) takes over the Pr. dos Touros. (Pr. dos Touros is on the opposite side of town, by the train station).

🏖 BEACHES

Perhaps the main reason to come to Setúbal (other than to sample its fine seafood), the beaches along the peninsula of ◪**Tróia** are accessible via a short ferry ride. Boasting 70km of pristine sand and turquoise water, Tróia and its expensive hotels are overrun by tourists during the summer. To find the best spots, ditch the crowds and follow the main road behind the hotels. *(Tróia is a brief ferry ride (15min.; every 15-45min.; €1, children 5-10 €0.50, under 5 free) from Doca do Comércio.)*

🔀 DAYTRIPS FROM SETÚBAL

PARQUE NATURAL DA ARRÁBIDA

Though there are no buses that go through the whole park, your best bet would be to take a bus to Vila Nogueira de Azeitão from Setúbal. During the summer, buses are available daily and leave every 30min. from the Setúbal station. €2.50 per person.

A 10,800 hectare nature reserve, the Parque Natural da Arrábida is known for the majestic vistas from its cliffs, as well as its beautiful beaches and diverse mountain wildlife, which includes wildcats, badgers,

---

🍸 **THE BIG SPLURGE**

BOM DIA, FLIPPER!

Although Portugal doesn't exactly come to mind when you think of dolphin watching, the Parque Natural da Arrábida and the Reservado Natural do Estuário do Sado offer the perfect environment for this exciting activity.

Take one of **Vertigem Azul's** dolphin watching tours and marvel at the sight of the Sado Estuary's pod of approximately 50 dolphins, known locally as "roazes," playing delightfully in the waters against the gorgeous backdrop of the Parque da Arrábida's rocky beaches and cliffs. These animals have been known to venture as far inland as the local marshes in search of the 20 kilograms of food (cuttlefish, grey mullet, eels, rock bass, shad, etc.) necessary for each adult's daily consumption.

Combine your aquatic mammal viewing with a choice of either snorkeling, canoeing or jeep tours through the Sado Estuary and the Parque Natural da Arrábida for a perfect day spent in this gorgeous expanse of untouched wilderness.

For more information, or to book a tour, contact Vertigem Azul, Av. Luísa Todi, 375 (☎265 23 80 00 or 917 84 33 04; www.vertigemazul.com). Most tours are between €58-64 per person, €30-32 per child.

buzzards, and Bonelli eagles. The park is renowned for the fabulous view from its highest peak, the Serra da Arrábida, which towers over the ocean and surrounding cliffs at 500m.

Unfortunately, aside from the four walking trails set up by the park's rangers, individual exploration is not permitted. Nonetheless, several guides are available, offering a variety of tours with different modes of transportation. Most tours cost approximately €50 per person and last all day; some of the best known guides include: **Mil Andanças,** Av. Luísa Todi, 121 (☎265 53 29 96); **Nautur,** R. António Feliciano Castilho, 9 (☎53 29 14); **Tróia Cruze,** R. das Barrocas, 34 (☎265 22 84 82); **SAL** (☎22 76 85; www.sal.jgc.pt). The park's headquarters, located at Doca de Recreio in Setúbal, offers information, pamphlets and sample guide prices. (☎265 54 11 40; fax 54 11 55. Open M-F 9am-12:30pm and 2-5:30pm.)

PRAIA DE FIGUEIRINHA

Figueirinha is accessible via bus from Setúbal. During the summer, buses leave every 30min. and cost €1.20 per person.

The best-known beach in the Parque Natural da Arrábida, Figueirinha's ivory sand and transparent waters have long beckoned those in need of a little R&R. Conveniently located 15 minutes from Setúbal, Figueirinha provides a quick escape from the traffic and endless hustle and bustle of Setúbal. The best time to go is during the week, so as to avoid the swarms of tourists and work-weary locals that invade Figueirinha during the weekend, transforming its white beach into a mass of colorful beach towels and bathing suits.

Sprawl out on the beach and work on your tan; it's what you came for, after all. **Restaurante Bar Mar ❸,** the only restaurant on the beach, is a popular dinner choice after a day of sunbathing. Though the seafood entrees are slightly pricey at €10-15, the air-conditioned interior and freshly caught seafood are worth it. (☎218 01 96 26. Open daily 9am-10pm. MC/V.)

ALGARVE AND ALENTEJO

The Algarve and Alentejo form a perfect balance in Portugal's central and southern regions. The Alentejo's small towns, seemingly stuck in the past, provide an escape from the Algarve's wild tourist-filled beaches—and vice-versa. Nearly 3000 hours of annual sunshine have transformed the Algarve from a fishermen's backwater into one of Europe's favorite vacation spots. In July and August, visitors mob its resorts, packing bars and discos from sunset until long after sunrise. Still, not all is excess in the Algarve. The region between Faro and the Spanish border remains relatively untouched, and to the west of Lagos towering cliffs shelter immaculate beaches. However, life slows down even more as you enter the Alentejo, where arid plains, punctuated only by olive trees, stretch to the horizon. This vast region appeals to travelers in search of relaxation, history, and plenty of wine. With quiet rolling landscapes in the interior and thumping beach parties along the coast the Algarve and Alentejo provide visitors with the best of both worlds and the guarantee that if they tire of one the other is just a bus ride away.

HIGHLIGHTS OF ALGARVE AND ALENTEJO

JOURNEY to **Lagos,** one of the world's great backpacker meccas (p. 719).

STORM the walls of the 13th-century castle in **Marvão** (p. 740).

CHANNEL the spirit of Prince Henry the Navigator at his outpost in **Sagres** (p. 725).

FEEL it in your bones at Évora's **Capela dos Ossos** (p. 737).

MARVEL at the colossal aqueduct in **Elvas,** the largest in Europe (p. 738).

ALGARVE

Behold the Algarve: a vacationland where happy campers from the world over bask in the sun. With nearly a hundred miles of coastline, travelers can find just what they're looking for, from see-and-be-seen beaches to the most remote and desolate stretches of sand. The Algarve has also perfected the art of delicious seafood; local favorites include *sardinhas assadas* (grilled sardines) and *caldeirada* (seafood chowder). Almonds and figs also make their way into most regional cooking, especially in divine desserts like *figos cheios* (figs filled with a thick paste made of ground almonds, cacao, cinnamon, and lemon peel) and delicious varieties of almond-pumpkin cake. During low season, the resorts empty and wildlife of a different sort arrives, as roughly one-third of Europe's flamingos migrate to the wetlands surrounding Olhão.

LAGOS ✆282

In the 17th century, travelers ventured here for the indigo and sugar markets; today they come for the meat market after the sun goes down. Visit for two days and you'll be tempted to stay a month or even longer. Just ask any one of the innumerable expatriate bartenders, surf guides, or restaurant owners. They came, they saw, and they decided to stay and take advantage of the tourist culture that dominates every aspect of a commercial life that goes back centuries; the Algarve's capital for almost 200 years, Lagos launched many of the caravels that brought Portugal power and fortune in the 15th and 16th centuries. Then came the late 20th century and the golden age of tourism. Today no one cares much for its history, but the legendary beaches and swinging northern European bars keep people coming back year after year.

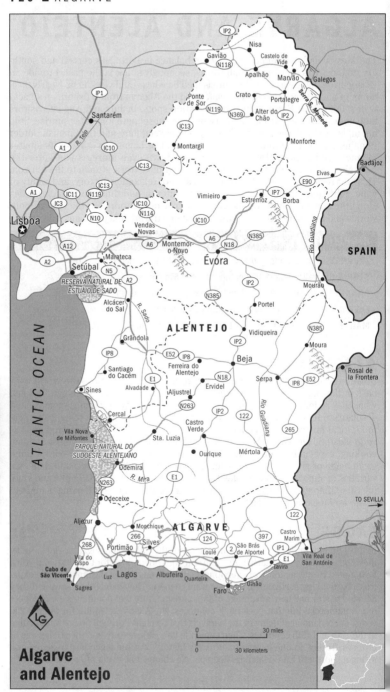

Algarve
and Alentejo

TRANSPORTATION

To reach Lagos from northern Portugal, you must go through Lisboa; trips originating in the east transfer in Faro.

Trains: (☎282 79 23 61), across the river (over the pedestrian suspension bridge) from the main part of town. To: **Beja** (3¼hr.; 3 per day 8:24am-3:04pm; €13.50) via **Faro** (1¾hr., 8 per day 6:07am-7:04pm, €5); **Évora** (5-5½hr.; 3 per day 6:07am-3:04pm; €15.50) via Faro; **Lisboa** (3½-4½hr., 5-6 per day 6:07am-5:31pm, €15.90); **Silves** (40min., 1:39pm, €1.70); **Vila Real de Santo António** (3hr., 7 per day 7:03am-7:04pm, €6.50) via Faro.

Buses: The **EVA** bus station (☎282 76 29 44), off Av. dos Descobrimentos, is just before R. Porta de Portugal (when walking into town) and across the channel from the train station and marina. To: **Albufeira** (1¼hr., 6 per day 7am-5:15pm, €3.80); **Faro** (2½hr., 6 per day 7am-5:15pm, €4); **Huelva,** Spain (4¾hr., 7:30am and 2pm, €10.30); **Lisboa** (5hr., 6 per day 5:30am-6:15pm, €15); **Sagres** (1hr., 16 per day 7:15am-8:30pm, €3).

Taxis: Lagos Central Taxi (☎282 76 24 69) 24hr. service to Lagos and environs.

Car Rental: 21+ for cars, 16+ for mopeds.

Marina Rent A Car, Av. dos Descobrimentos, 43 (☎282 76 47 89). July-Aug. cars including tax and insurance from €45 per day; May-June and Sept. €35; Oct.-Apr. €30. Rent for 2 days and get a 3rd free. AmEx/MC/V.

Motoride, R. José Afonso lote, 23-C (☎282 76 17 20), rents bikes (€10 per day) and scooters (€30 per day). 16+, license required. Open daily 9:30am-7pm.

Hertz-Portuguesa, Rossio de S. João Ed. Panorama, 3 (☎282 76 98 09), behind the bus station off Av. dos Descobrimentos. Cars from €45 per day, tax and insurance included. MC/V.

ORIENTATION AND PRACTICAL INFORMATION

Running the length of the channel, **Avenida dos Descobrimentos** carries traffic to and from Lagos. From the **train station,** walk through the pink marina and cross the pedestrian suspension bridge; turn left onto Av. dos Descobrimentos. From the **bus station,** walk straight until Av. dos Descobrimentos and turn right. **Praça Gil Eanes** is the center of the old town. The **tourist office** is on Lg. Marquês de Pombal up R. Lima Leitão, which extends from Pr. Gil Eanes. Follow R. Silva Lopes to R. General Alberto da Silveira to reach the grotto-lined beach of **Praia Dona Ana.**

Tourist Office: Municipal office (☎282 76 41 11), on Lg. Marquês de Pombal. Open June-Sept. M-Sa 10am-8pm; Oct.-May M-F 10am-6pm.

Luggage Storage: Futebol Mania, R. Prof. Luís de Azevedo, 4 (☎962 74 63 42), off R. Cândido dos Reis. €5 per day.

Currency Exchange: Cota Cambios, Pr. Gil Eanes, 11 (☎282 76 44 52). Open June-Sept. daily 8:30am-10pm; Oct.-May M-F 9:30am-7:30pm, Sa-Su 10am-7:30pm.

English-Language Bookstore: Loja do Livro, R. Dr. Joaquim Telo, 3 (☎282 76 73 47). Small selection of English and other foreign language books including best-sellers and travel guides. Open June-Aug. M-F 10am-1pm and 3-11pm, Sa 10am-1pm; Sept.-May M-F 10am-1pm and 3-7pm.

Laundromat: Lavandaria Miele, Av. dos Descobrimentos, 27 (☎282 76 39 69). Wash and dry €6.50 per 5kg. Open M-F 9am-1pm and 3-7pm, Sa 9am-1pm.

Police: R. General Alberto da Silveira (☎282 76 29 30).

Pharmacy: Farmácia Silva, R. 25 de Abril, 9 (☎282 76 28 59).

Medical Services: Hospital, R. Castelo dos Governadores (☎282 77 01 00).

Internet Access: The Em@il Box (Caixa de Correio), R. Cândido dos Reis, 112 (☎282 76 89 50). €1.25 per 15min., €3.50 per hr. Open M-F 9:30am-8pm, Sa-Su 10am-3pm. Several bars in Lagos have a computer or two; check along R. Lançarote de Freitas and at the youth hostel.

Post Office: R. das Portas de Portugal (☎282 77 02 50), between Pr. Gil Eanes and the river. **Fax** €4.10 per 2 pages. Open M-F 9am-1pm and 3-6pm. **Postal Code:** 8600.

ACCOMMODATIONS AND CAMPING

In the summertime, *pensões* (and the youth hostel) fill up quickly; reserve more than a week in advance. If full, the youth hostel will happily refer you to a *quarto* nearby (close to the nightlife) for about the same price. Locals trying to rent rooms in their homes will probably greet you at the station. Though these rooms are often inconveniently located, they can be the best deals in town at €10-15 per person in summer. Haggle with owners; room quality varies greatly.

■ **Pousada da Juventude de Lagos (HI),** R. Lançarote de Freitas, 50 (☎282 76 19 70; fax 76 96 84). Friendly staff and lodgers congregate in the courtyard and form a core of bar-hoppers later in the evenings. Internet access (€1 per 20min.), a well-equipped kitchen, and a TV room with billiards. Reception has an extensive collection of bilingual dictionaries and travel guides. For July-Aug. book through the central **Movijovem** office (☎213 59 60 00) as far ahead as possible. June 16-Sept. 15 dorms €15; doubles with bath €45. Sept. 16-June 15 €10/€28. MC/V. ●

■ **Olinda Teresa Maria Quartos,** R. Lançarote de Freitas, 37, 1st and 2nd fl. (☎282 08 23 29). Clever Sra. Olinda converted her large home into the answer to the crowded hostel, mirroring the prices and dorm-style atmosphere. Doubles or dorm rooms with shared kitchen, terrace, and bath. If the owner is out, check at the youth hostel. June 16-Sept. 15 dorms €15; doubles €24. Sept. 16-June 15 €10/€30. ●

Residencial Caravela, R. 25 de Abril, 8 (☎282 76 33 61), just up the street from Pr. Gil Eanes. 16 small and basic but well-located rooms off a courtyard, some with balconies. Singles €30; doubles €35; triples €55. ❸

Residencial Lagosmar, R. Dr. Faria da Silva, 13 (☎282 76 37 22). Friendly staff and comfortable rooms, all with bath, TV, and phone. July-Aug. singles €64.50; doubles €74.50; extra bed €22.50. June and Sept. €38/€45/€14.50. Mar.-May and Oct. €32.50/€38/€12.50. Nov.-Feb. €23.50/€27.50/€10. MC/V. ❺

Camping Trindade (☎282 76 38 93), just outside town. Follow Av. dos Descobrimentos toward Sagres. €3.40 per person, €3.70 per tent, €4.20 per car. ●

Camping Valverde (☎282 78 92 11), 6km outside Lagos, 1.5km west of Praia da Luz. Restaurant and pool. €5 per person, €4.10 per tent, €6.50 per car. Showers free. ●

FOOD

Tourists can peruse multilingual menus around Pr. Gil Eanes and R. 25 de Abril, but the cheapest dining options in Lagos are the local produce **market** (Sa only) on Av. dos Descobrimentos and **Supermercado São Roque,** R. das Portas de Portugal, 61 (☎282 76 28 55; open July-Sept. M-F 9am-8pm, Sa 9am-7pm; Oct.-June M-F 9am-7:30pm, Sa 9am-7pm). You'll pay more on R. de Silva Lopes and R. 25 de Abril.

■ **Casa Rosa,** R. do Ferrador, 22 (☎968 37 71 15). A backpacker's culinary mecca, this Lagos mainstay serves whopping portions for next to nothing and side-splitting humor for free. Ask for one of their flyers. The sociable staff serves a wide range of entrees including many vegetarian options (€4.50-7.50). M all-you-can-eat spaghetti €5. Free Internet for diners. Open daily 5-11pm. ●

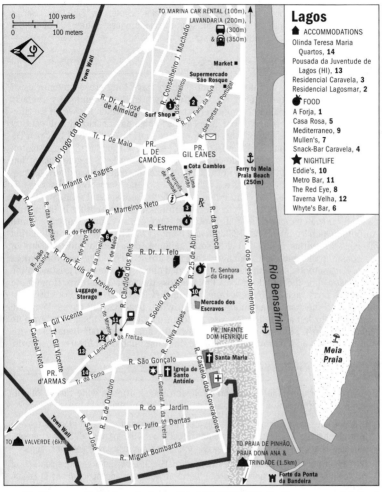

Lagos

♠ ACCOMMODATIONS
Olinda Teresa Maria
  Quartos, **14**
Pousada da Juventude de
  Lagos (HI), **13**
Residencial Caravela, **3**
Residencial Lagosmar, **2**

🍎 FOOD
A Forja, **1**
Casa Rosa, **5**
Mediterraneo, **9**
Mullen's, **7**
Snack-Bar Caravela, **4**

★ NIGHTLIFE
Eddie's, **10**
Metro Bar, **11**
The Red Eye, **8**
Taverna Velha, **12**
Whyte's Bar, **6**

ALGARVE AND ALENTEJO

Mediterraneo, Tr. Senhora da Graça, 2 (☎282 76 84 76). Mediterranean and Thai cuisine, including great seafood and meat dishes, salads, and desserts. The town's best veggie option. Eat indoors or outside. Entrees €7.50-9. Open Tu-Sa 6:30-10:30pm. ❷

Mullen's, R. Cândido dos Reis, 86 (☎282 76 12 81). A funny combination of great Portuguese and international cuisine, stereotypical Irish pub (complete with stacked barrels of beer), and jazz. People come from afar to try the legendary duck in orange sauce and the spicy *frango grelhado* (grilled chicken). Entrees €7-9.50. Bar open daily noon-2am; restaurant open 6pm-midnight. ❷

Snack-Bar Caravela, R. 25 de Abril, 14 (☎282 76 26 83), just off Pr. Gil Eanes. Well-touristed, but for good reason—it's casually classy, a great place to people-watch, and has the best pizza in town. Outdoor seating. Caravela is famous for its supreme 🍧**strawberry ice cream.** Seafood and meat dishes €6-12, pizzas and pastas €4.90-7.30. Open daily June-Sept. 9am-midnight; Oct.-Mar. 9am-11pm. AmEx/MC/V. ❷

A Forja, R. dos Ferreiros, 17 (☎282 76 85 88). Few traditional Portuguese restaurants exist in Lagos, but locals swear by A Forja, known affectionately as "Blue Door." Serves Algarvian seafood with all its tricks but sans the steep prices. Entrees €5.50-12.50. Open daily noon-3pm and 6:30-10pm. ❷

👁 🏖 SIGHTS AND BEACHES

Although sunbathing and non-stop debauchery have long erased memories of Lagos's rugged, sea-faring past, most of the city is still surrounded by a nearly intact 16th-century wall enclosing interesting sights for which it's worth sacrificing a little time at the beach or bar. The **Forte da Ponta da Bandeira,** a 17th-century fortress with maritime exhibitions, overlooks the marina. (☎282 76 14 10. Open Tu-Sa 10am-1pm and 2-6pm, Su 10am-1pm. €1.85, students €1, under 13 free.) Also on the waterfront is the old **Mercado dos Escravos** (slave market). Legend has it that the first sale of African slaves in Portugal took place here in 1441, and now a Scandinavian artist uses the space as a gallery. Opposite the Mercado dos Escravos is **Igreja de Santo António.** The church houses artifacts from several ruling powers in Lagos, from the Neolithic age to the Republic. Most interesting is the mural painted on the chapel ceiling that depicts the life of the church's patron, Santo António. (Open Tu-Su 9:30am-12:30pm and 2-5pm. €2.) The waterfront and marina offer jet-ski rentals, scuba diving lessons, sailboat trips, and motorboat tours of the coastal rocks and grottoes. Lagos's **beaches** are seductive any way you look at them. Flat, smooth, sunbathing sands (crowded during the summer, pristine in the low season) line the 4km long **Meia Praia,** across the river from town. Hop on the 30-second ferry near Pr. Infante Dom Henrique (€0.50 each way). For cliffs that plunge into the sea hiding smaller, less-crowded beaches and caves, keep the ocean to your left and follow Av. dos Descobrimentos toward Sagres to **Praia de Pinhão** (20min.). Five minutes farther down the coast lies **Praia Dona Ana,** with sculpted cliffs and the grottoes that appear on at least half of all Algarve postcards.

🛶 WATER ACTIVITIES

If you're up for more than lazing on the beach, Lagos offers a wide variety of outdoor sports—from scuba diving to surfing to (booze) cruising.

Grotto Boat Tours: Companies offering tours of the coastal cliffs and grottoes (caves) set up shop on Av. dos Descobrimentos. Most tours 45min., from €25 for 2 people. Smaller boats are preferable, as they can maneuver into rock caves and formations.

Surf Experience: R. dos Ferreiros, 21 (☎282 76 19 43; www.surf-experience.com). 1- or 2-week surfing trips including lessons, transportation, and accommodations in Lagos. All levels welcome. Daytrips when space available. Apr.-Nov. 1wk. €424, 2wk. €727; Dec.-Mar. €378/€682. Board and wet suit rental €75/€114.

Booze Cruise: (☎963 01 26 92). This extremely popular cruise offers swimming, snorkeling, tours of the nearby grottoes, a live DJ, and, of course, cheap drinks. Cruises M, W, and Sa. €15. For tickets, call or purchase at the youth hostel.

🔊 NIGHTLIFE

Lagos knows how to keep things sunny, especially after the sun has set. The streets get busy around 10pm, climaxing at midnight. On alternate Sundays from 4-10pm, **Bahia Beach Bar** on Meia Praia hosts live music, volleyball, and a crowd of local workers from Lagos's bars and restaurants. In town, the area between **Praça Gil Eanes** and **Praça Luis de Camões** is filled with cafes. **Rua Cândido dos Reis, Rua do**

Ferrador, and the intersection of **Rua 25 de Abril, Rua de Silva Lopes,** and **Rua Soeiro da Costa** are packed with bars and clubs that start closing at around 2am, with some carrying on until sunrise.

■ **Taverna Velha (The Old Tavern),** R. Lançarote de Freitas, 34 (☎282 76 92 31). Backpackers, expats, and rugby enthusiasts mingle with the amicable, shirtless staff—and each other—over a drink or on the busy dance floor. The only bar in Lagos with A/C, it has free nightly showings of American movies at 5:30pm, a Simpsons double-header immediately following, and regular rugby parties. Beer €1.25-2.50. Mixed drinks €3.50-4. Excellent strawberry-banana daiquiris €7.50 per pitcher. Happy hour with 2-for-1 drinks 9pm-midnight. Open Apr.-Jan. 14 M-Sa 4pm-2am, Su 8pm-2am.

The Red Eye, R. Cândido dos Reis, 63. 20-something Brits and Aussies flood in around midnight for classic rock, cheap liquor, or a casual pool game. Some dancing, but mostly a pick-up scene. Free shot with first drink. Beer €2.80. Mixed drinks €3-4. Shots €2.50-3. Happy hour with 2-pint cocktails for €5 8-10pm. Open daily 8pm-2am.

Metro Bar, R. Lançarote de Freitas, 30. Stylish cosmopolitan atmosphere enhanced by acid jazz mixes. One of the only bars in town tailored to gay audiences, although the clientele is diverse. Beer €1.80. Mixed drinks €2.30-2.90. Open daily 7pm-2am.

Whyte's Bar, R. do Ferrador, 7A (☎968 13 90 62). Live DJ keeps this Lagos institution packed all night long. Dancing on basement level during the summer. If you're brave enough, try the 9 Deadly Sins shot drinking contest. Beer €2-3. Huge variety of mixed drinks €2.50-5. Happy hour nightly. Open daily 8pm-2am.

Eddie's, R. 25 de Abril, 99. Hospitable, easygoing bar popular with backpackers sees more guys than girls. Busy at night, but still comfortable. Beer €1.50. Mixed drinks €3-4. Happy hour 4-9pm. Open M-Sa 4pm-2am, Su 8pm-2am.

▶ DAYTRIP FROM LAGOS

■ PRAIA DA ROCHA

To reach Praia da Rocha from Lagos, take the bus to Portimão (40min., 14 per day 7:15am-8:15pm, round-trip €5) and get off at the Praia da Rocha stop.

A short jaunt from Lagos, locals and tourists agree that this beach is perhaps the very best the Algarve has to offer. With vast expanses of sand, surfable waves, rocky red cliffs, and secluded coves, Praia da Rocha has a well-deserved reputation (and the crowds to match). The **tourist office,** at the end of R. Tomás Cabreina, offers maps and lists of accommodations and restaurants. (☎282 41 91 32. Open May-Sept. daily 9:30am-7pm; Oct.-Apr. M-F 9:30am-12:30pm and 2-5:30pm, Sa-Su 9:30am-12:30pm.)

SAGRES ☎282

Marooned atop a plateau at the most southwestern point in Europe, Sagres (pop. 2500) was for centuries considered the end of the world. Battered by ceaseless winds, the surrounding cliffs plunge hundreds of feet into the Atlantic. It was at Sagres that Prince Henry founded his school of navigation and organized exploratory voyages to the far reaches of the globe. Large tour groups and upscale vacationers are discouraged by the desolate location and relative lack of recreation, making Sagres a perfect destination for travelers in search of uncharted beauty. It also attracts more and more surfers each year.

▐▊ TRANSPORTATION AND PRACTICAL INFORMATION. EVA buses (☎282 76 29 44) run from **Lagos** (1hr., 17 per day 7:15am-8:30pm, €3). Buses also run to **Lisboa** (5¼hr., July-Sept. daily 4pm, €15). The **tourist office** on R. Comandante

Matoso, up the street from the bus stop, dispenses maps and info on Sagres's illustrious history. (☎282 62 48 73. Open Tu-Sa 9:30am-1pm and 2-5:30pm.) The **police** are in Vila do Bispo (☎282 63 91 12). At **Turinfo**, helpful staff members recommend accommodations, offer **Internet access** (€3 per 30min.), rent **bikes** (€6 per half-day, €9.50 per day), give info on **jeep tours** of the nearby nature preserve, A Costa Vicentina (€38, includes lunch), and offer **scuba** advice and **currency exchange**. (☎282 62 00 03. Open daily 10am-12:30pm and 1:30-6:30pm.)

⚬⚬ ACCOMMODATIONS AND FOOD. Windows everywhere display multilingual signs for rooms, many in boarding houses with guest kitchens. Prices range €15-30 for singles and doubles, €25-40 for triples, with lower rates in winter. Follow R. Comandante Matoso toward the tourist office and take a left onto R. Patrão António Faustino to reach ▨**Atalaia Apartamentos ❷**. The beautiful, fully furnished rooms with bath, TV, and refrigerator, and apartments with kitchen, bath, living room, and terrace, are great deals. (☎282 62 46 81. Apartments: July-Sept. 2 people €50, 3-4 people €70-80; Apr.-June €30/€50-60; Oct.-Mar. €25/€40-50. Rooms: July-Sept. doubles €40; Apr.-June €25; Oct.-May €25.) Open-air **camping** is strictly forbidden, so head to the **Orbitur Campground ❶**, 2.5km toward Cabo de São Vicente, just off EN 268. (☎282 62 43 71; fax 62 44 45. Reception daily 9am-7pm. June-Sept. €4.30 per person, €3.60 per tent, €2-2.50 per car. Oct.-May €2.70/€2.25-3.40/€2.20-2.50.) For groceries, try the **market** on R. Mercado, at the intersection with R. Comandante Matoso (open M-Sa 7am-1pm), or **Alisuper**, a larger supermarket on R. Comandante Matoso (☎282 62 44 87; open daily 9am-8pm). ▨**O Dromedário Bistro ❷**, on R. Comandante Matoso, whips up innovative crepes (€2.20-4) and a multitude of vegetarian dishes. Try the fresh fruit juices and shakes (€1.80-2.80). The bar is a night hotspot. (☎282 62 42 19. Restaurant open daily 10am-midnight; bar open M-Th and Su until 2am, F-Sa until 4am. Closed Jan.-Feb.)

◼⚬ SIGHTS AND ENTERTAINMENT. Near town is the ▨ **Fortaleza de Sagres,** the outpost where Prince Henry received the big shots of Portuguese navigation and talked about his fancy instrumentation, including the **Rosa dos Ventos,** a large circle used to measure air pressure and wind speed. The pentagonal 15th-century fortress and surrounding paths yield vertigo-inducing views of the cliffs and sea. (Open May-Sept. 10am-8:30pm; Oct.-Apr. 10am-6:30pm. Closed May 1 and Dec. 25. €3, under 25 €1.50.) Six kilometers farther west lies desolate **Cabo de São Vicente,** which features the second most powerful lighthouse in Europe, a towering structure that overlooks the southwestern tip of the continent and shines more than 90km out to sea; tours are not available, though occasionally a caretaker can be persuaded to give one. On weekdays, take the bus from the station on R. Comandante Matoso near the tourist office (10min., 3 per day 11:15am-4:15pm, €1). On weekends, you're on your own—rent a bike or take an hour-long walk.

Several **beaches** fringe the peninsula, most notably **Mareta**, at the bottom of the road from the town center. Rock formations jut into the ocean on both sides of this sandy crescent. Though not as picturesque as the coves of Salema and Luz, Mareta is popular for its length and isolation; just remember, Sagres is known for its wind, and the beach is no exception. Just west of town is one of the best beaches for windsurfing, **Praia de Martinhal.** Less windy **Praia da Beliche** is located 3km outside of town on the way to Cabo de São Vicente.

Although Sagres may seem dead on arrival, its pulse picks up around 10pm in the summer. At night, a young crowd fills the lively **Rosa dos Ventos** in Pr. da República. (☎282 62 44 80. Beer €1-2. Mixed drinks €3-5. Famous sangria €5.50. Open 10am-2am. Closed W.) Another hotspot is the pulsing **Água Salgada,** on R. Comandante Matoso, 75m beyond the tourist office, going away from the fortress, which has an extensive drink menu and plays a fantastic music mix. (☎282 62 42 97. Beer €1-2. Mixed drinks €4.50. Open daily 10am-4am. Sept.-May closed Tu.) Next door is **O Dromedário** (see **Accommodations & Food**), where trendy young locals let loose and a responsive DJ keeps the party raging. (☎282 62 42 97. Beer €1-2. Mixed drinks, daiquiris, and coladas €3.50-5. Open M-Th and Su 10am-2am, F-Sa 10am-4am.)

ALBUFEIRA   ☎289

Welcome to a land where summer populations more than double and locals dedicate themselves to a single enterprise: hosting the tourists. Sandwiched between two hills, Albufeira's intriguing landscape is covered in sprawling hotel and condominium developments, and the lively international night scene brings such stellar (impersonation) performances as the Rolling Stones and Neil Diamond. But don't let the hype and glamour of Swedish hotels and English pubs scare you off; you are in the Algarve, and that means fabulous beach space. Soak it up, especially since your hotel is most likely only a 5min. walk from the shore.

⊏ TRANSPORTATION. EVA buses connect the **train station** (☎289 57 26 91) to the town center 6km away (10min., every hr. 7:05am-8:20pm, €1.50). To: **Faro** (30min., 13 per day 6:39am-11:13pm, €5); **Lagos** (1hr., 10 per day 6:06am-9:17pm, €4); **Lisboa** (3-5½hr., 5-7 per day 6:06am-6:28pm, €13.50); **Olhão** (1hr.; M-F 9 per day 7:17am-10:31pm, Sa-Su 6-7 per day 8:13am-10:31pm; €2.20); **Tavira** (1-1¾hr., M-F 9 per day 7:17am-10:31pm, Sa-Su 6-7 per day 8:13am-10:31pm, €4); **Vila Real de Santo António** (1½-2¼hr., 7-9 per day 8:13am-10:31pm, €5). The EVA **bus station** (☎289 58 97 55) is in nearby Caliços. Buses head to: **Faro** (1hr., 6 per day 8:40am-7:15pm, €3.60); **Lagos** (1½hr., 7 per day 10:55am-11:10pm, €4.60); **Lisboa** (3½-4hr., 6 per day 7:05am-7pm, €15); **Tavira** (1½hr., 7:20am and 2:40pm, €2.70) via **Faro**. Or grab a ride from **Táxi Rádio** (☎298 58 32 30).

▆▐ ORIENTATION AND PRACTICAL INFORMATION. Albufeira spreads along the Atlantic, with R. Latino Coelho, R. Bernardino Sousa, and R. da Bateria bordering the coast. **Rua 5 de Outubro** and **Avenida da Liberdade** run perpendicular to the ocean and separate the town's busy cafe- and bar-filled section to the east from the slightly more sedate area to the west. From the new "bus station," a parking lot in a field outside of the city, it is at least a 30min. trek to the town center. Take the city bus marked "local" from the station to Av. da Liberdade (every 20min. 9am-8pm, €1.40). To reach the **tourist office**, R. 5 de Outubro, 8, follow Av. da Liberdade downhill to Tr. 5 de Outubro and take a right. Turn left when this small street intersects R. 5 de Outubro. The English-speaking staff at the office offers maps and info on water sports, including fishing and scuba diving. (☎289 58 52 79. Open daily June-Sept. M-Th 9:30am-7pm, F-Su 9:30am-1pm and 2:30-6pm; Oct.-May M-Th 9:30am-5:30pm, F-Su 9:30am-12:30pm and 1:30-5:30pm.) Local services include: **banks,** surrounding the touristy Lg. Eng. Duarte Pacheco; **police** on Av. 25 de Abril (☎289 51 22 05); **Farmácia Piedade** on R. João de Deus, which also posts listings of on-call pharmacies (☎289 51 22 54); **Centro de Saúde** in nearby Caliços (☎289 58 75 50). **Internet access** and **used books** can be found at **Windcafe.com** in the Shopping Center California, R. Cândido dos Reis, 1. (☎289 58 64 51. Open June-Sept. M-F 10am-10pm, Sa-Su noon-10pm; Oct.-May closes daily 8pm.) The **post office** is next to the tourist office on R. 5 de Outubro. (☎289 58 08 70; fax 58 32 30. Open M-F 9am-12:30pm and 2:30-6pm.) **Postal Code:** 8200.

▐▐ ACCOMMODATIONS AND FOOD. Most lodgings in Albufeira are booked solid by package tours from late June through mid-September. The trick is learning to find and **haggle** with the old women who live above the main

ALGARVE AND ALENTEJO

square. Head to R. Cemitério Velho, R. do Saco, R. Igreja Nova, and R. Igreja Velha. Simply looking expectantly at anyone around and saying "Rooms?" will automatically start the process. Don't pay more than €20 for a single in the summer and €25-30 for a double, and be sure to see the room before you agree. It's easy to bargain if you're staying more than a day. There are a few pensions closer to the center of town. ◨**Pensão Dianamar ❸**, R. Latino Coelho, 36, is close to the beach but removed from the commotion. It features a charming courtyard, guest kitchen, TV lounge, roof terrace with a gorgeous view of the sea (for a few extra euros), and clean and comfortable rooms with bath and balconies. (☎ 289 58 78 01; www.dianamar.com. July singles €28-35; doubles €38-45. Aug. €30-40/€50-65. June and Sept. €25-30/€35-43. Mar.-May and Oct. €20-25/€30-33. Closed Nov.-Feb.) **Residencial Capri ❸**, Av. da Liberdade, 83, offers basic white-walled rooms, many with verandas and all with TV and bath. Ask Mark, the young owner, for info on the hottest local clubs. (☎ 289 51 26 91. June-July singles €35; doubles €40; triples €45. Aug.-Sept. and Mar.-May €30/€35/€40. Oct.-Apr. €25/€30/€35. Prices vary, so call ahead to be sure.) Open-air camping is illegal, but weary travelers can pay for the ritz and glitz of **Parque de Campismo de Albufeira ❶**, 2km outside town on the road to nearby Ferreiras, home of the train station. It's more like a shopping mall or a commune than a campground, with three swimming pools, a restaurant, tennis courts, a supermarket, and a disco. (☎ 289 58 76 29; fax 58 76 33. June-Sept. €5 per person, €4.50 per car, €5.10 per tent. Oct.-May 15-50% discount. AmEx/MC/V.)

For fresh produce and seafood, check out the **mercado municipal.** Follow R. da Figueira from the main bus station and take a right onto Es. Vale Pedras. (Open Tu-Su 8am-1pm; Th offers the most variety.) Restaurants and cafes abound in Albufeira, mostly around, and often in, the local bars on R. Cândido dos Reis. Light meals run €5-6, and more interesting local dishes creep up to €9-10. If you're in the mood for a quick fix to interrupt your busy day at the beach, R. 5 de Outubro offers ample options with many inexpensive, fast-service eateries.

◪ **BEACHES.** Albufeira's spectacular slate of **beaches** ranges from the popular **Galé** and **São Rafael** (4-8km toward Lagos) to the chic local favorite **Falésia** (10km toward Faro), both accessible by car, taxi, or bus. Check the tourist office for seasonal schedules. To get to the centrally located **Inatel beach** from the main square, Lg. Eng. Duarte Pacheco, follow Av. 25 de Abril to its end and continue down R. Gago Coutinho until you hit sand. Beautiful but packed **Praia de Albufeira** awaits through the gate to the tourist office. Explore beyond these popular options; the farther you venture, the greater the reward in lack of crowds and quantity of sand.

◪ **ENTERTAINMENT.** As always, days on the sand are best complemented by nights on the dance floor. Bars and restaurants line all the town's streets, but really all you need to do for a great night out is head for R. Cândido dos Reis. Clubs blast everything from salsa to techno as soon as the sun sets—and continue until it rises. The locals recommend **Atrium Bar**, R. Cândido dos Reis, especially for karaoke. The interesting contrast between the professional musicians outside the bar and the amateurs playing inside remind guests that you don't necessarily need talent to hit a groove. (Karaoke nightly 9pm-4am. Beer €3. Mixed drinks €6-7.50. Light food served until 11pm. Open daily 10am-4am.) **Classic Bar**, R. Cândido dos Reis, 10, is a rocking spot with elaborately concocted drinks and a gaggle of tourists getting down to everything the nightly DJ gives them, mostly Latin and English pop. (☎ 289 51 20 75; www.rua-dosbares.com. Beer €2-3. Mixed drinks €5-7.50. Open daily June-Sept. noon-4am; Oct.-May noon-midnight.)

FARO ☎289

Many northern Europeans begin their holidays in Faro (pop. 55,000), the Algarve's capital and largest city, though few stay long enough to absorb its charm. While here, visitors can take advantage of the town's diversity, including a modern shopping district, museums of all sorts, a quiet historical neighborhood within the walls of the well preserved *cidade velha*, and calm beaches on the estuary's islands.

▐▀ TRANSPORTATION

Flights: Aeroporto de Faro (☎289 80 08 00; flight info 80 08 01), 5km west of the city, has a **police station, bank, post office, car rental,** and **tourist info booth.** Open daily 10am-midnight. Buses #14 and 16 run there from opposite the bus station. (20min.; M-F 18 per day 7:10am-8:40pm, Sa-Su and holidays 12 per day 8am-7:30pm; €1.20).

Trains: Lg. da Estação (☎289 82 64 72), near the center of town next to the bus station, not to be confused with a secondary station 2km away but still in Faro. To: **Albufeira** (30min., 14 per day 5:45am-8:46pm, €1.90); **Beja** (2½hr.; M-F 3 per day 9:10am-3:32pm, Sa-Su 9:10am and 2:10pm; €9.50); **Évora** (4½-6hr.; M-F and Su 3-4 per day 6:45am-4:04pm, Sa 6:45 and 9:10am; €11); **Lagos** (1½hr., 9 per day 7:07am-8:46pm, €14); **Vila Real de Santo António** (1hr., 9-12 per day 7:24am-11:05pm, €4).

Buses: EVA, Av. da República (☎289 89 97 00). To: **Albufeira** (1hr.; M-F 7 per day 7am-6:30pm, Sa-Su 3-4 per day 7:20am-5:45pm; €3.50); **Beja** (3-3½hr., 5 per day 8:30am-5pm, €10); **Lagos** (2hr., 8 per day 7:30am-5:30pm, €4.30); **Olhão** (20min., every 20-40min. 7:15am-8:35pm, €1.30); **Tavira** (1hr., 11 per day 7:15am-8:30pm, €2.50); **Vila Real de Santo António** (1½hr., 9 per day 7:15am-6:20pm, €3.70). **Renex,** Av. da República (☎289 81 29 80), provides long-distance service to **Braga** (8½hr., 9 per day 5:30am-1:30am, €22.50) and **Porto** (7½hr., 6-13 per day 5:30am-1:30am, €22) via **Lisboa** (4hr., 12-15 per day, €17). €2-2.50 discount with ISIC.

Taxis: Táxis Rotáxi (☎289 89 57 95). Beige, poorly marked taxis gather near Jardim Manuel Bívar (by the tourist office) and at the bus and train stations.

▄╋▐ ORIENTATION AND PRACTICAL INFORMATION

Faro's center hugs the **Doca de Recreio,** a marina lined with luxuriously apportioned ships and bordered by the Jardim Manuel Bívar and **Praça Dr. Francisco Gomes.** From the train or bus stations, follow Av. da República toward the harbor. Enter the **cidade velha,** or old city, through the **Arco da Vila,** a stone arch next to the tourist office, on the far side of the garden bordering Pr. Dr. Francisco Gomes.

Tourist Office: R. da Misericórdia, 8 (☎289 80 36 04). From the bus or train station, turn right down Av. da República along the harbor, then left past the garden. English and French spoken. Open daily May-Sept. 9:30am-7pm; Oct.-Apr. 9:30am-5:30pm. **Regional office,** Av. 5 de Outubro, 18-20 (☎289 80 04 00). Open M-F 9am-7pm.

Currency Exchange: Cota Cambios, R. Dr. Francisco Gomes, 26 (☎289 82 57 35). Open June M-F 8:30am-8pm, Sa-Su 10am-6pm; July-Sept. M-F 8:30am-9pm, Sa 10am-8pm, Su 10am-7pm; Oct.-May M-F 8:30am-6:30pm, Sa 10am-2:30pm.

Laundromat: Sólimpa, R. Batista Lopes, 30 (☎289 82 29 81). Wash and dry €7 for 4kg, €2 per additional kg. Open M-F 9am-1pm and 3-7pm, Sa 9am-1pm.

Police: R. Polícia da Segurança Pública (☎289 82 20 22).

Hospital: R. Leão Penedo (☎289 89 11 00), just north of town.

Internet Access: Free at the **Instituto Português de Juventude,** next to the youth hostel. 30min. limit. Open M-F 9am-7pm. Also at the **Ciência Viva** museum, R. Comandante Francisco Manuel (☎289 89 09 20; www.ualg.pt/ccviva), near the old city. From Pr. Dr.

Francisco Gomes, walk through the gardens and turn right, heading toward the docks. €2 per hr., students €1. W 50% off. Open July-Sept. 15 Tu-Su 4-11pm; Sept. 16-June Tu-F 10am-5pm, Sa-Su 3-7pm.

Post Office: Lg. do Carmo (☎289 89 25 90), across from Igreja do Carmo. Open M-F 8:30am-6:30pm, Sa 9am-12:30pm. **Postal Code:** 8000.

▗ ACCOMMODATIONS

Lodgings surround the bus and train stations. Most of the low-end budget *pensões* are plain but adequate.

Pousada da Juventude (HI), R. Polícia de Segurança Pública (☎289 82 65 21), near the police station. Sleep easy at the cheapest place in town. Bunk beds, sunny TV atrium, kitchen, and large balcony with tables. Breakfast and lockers included. June 16-Sept. 15 dorms €10; doubles €24, with bath €29.50. Sept. 16-June 15 €8/€18/€21. AmEx/MC/V. ❶

Pensão-Residencial Oceano, Tr. Ivens, 21, 2nd fl. (☎289 82 33 49). From Pr. Dr. Francisco Gomes, head up R. 1 de Maio; it's 1 block up on the right. Pleasant rooms with bath, phone, and TV. July-Sept. singles €35; doubles €45; triples €58. Oct.-June €25/€35/€45. AmEx/MC/V. ❸

Residencial Madalena, R. Conselheiro Bívar, 109 (☎289 80 58 06; fax 80 58 07), close to the train and bus stations. Follow R. Gil Eanes to R. Infante Dom Henrique and take a right. 21 warmly decorated rooms with dark wood molding and big windows, all with TV and large, free-standing closets. Breakfast included. July-Sept. 15 singles €35, with bath €50; doubles €50/€60. Sept. 16-June €20/€25/€35/€40. ❸

Pensão São Filipe, R. Infante Dom Henrique, 55, 2nd fl. (☎/fax 289 82 41 82). From the train station, go up R. Ventura Coelho 3 blocks and turn right onto R. Infante Dom Henrique. Therapeutically warm, comfortable rooms, all with TV, fan, and bath. Doubles summer €50-55; winter €35-40. Discounts for solo travelers. ❸

Pensão-Residencial Central, Lg. Terreiro do Bispo, 12 (☎289 80 72 91), near the pedestrian area up R. 1 de Maio. Clean, bright rooms, all with bath and TV, some with terraces. Doubles €40-50, depending on size and whether it has a terrace. ❹

▗ FOOD

Almonds and figs are native to the Algarve; local bakeries take advantage of this and transform them into delicious ▨**marzipan** and **fig desserts.** Faro has many cafes along **Rua Conselheiro Bívar** and **Praça Dr. Francisco Gomes.** At the **mercado** in Lg. Dr. Francisco Sá Carneiro, locals barter fresh seafood. (Open daily 8am-1:30pm.) Stroll to R. Santo António, a pedestrian district with more (expensive) fresh seafood than you can shake a credit card at. Budget travelers might also opt for the local favorite: the **Minipreço** grocery store, Lg. Terreiro do Bispo, 8-10. (☎289 80 77 34. Open M-Sa 9am-8pm.)

O Ribatejano, R. São Luis, 32A (☎289 81 21 10). Whether you're in the mood for tempeh or stewed pork tongue, the sociable cook whips up delicious protein-conscious vegetarian platters and exotic carnivorous fare, not to mention his homemade sugar- and milk-free raspberry sorbet. Entrees €4.60-5. Open daily 7-11pm. ❶

Mister Frango, R. Cruz das Mestras, 51 (☎289 82 84 44). From R. Santo António, turn left on R. Portugal and follow it 2 blocks. The name says it all. *Frango assado* (roast chicken) as only the Portuguese can make it and at the best price around. €5 buys you a half chicken, rice, and fries. Ask for the not-so-hot hot sauce, *piri piri,* for a pleasant kick. Open daily noon-2:30pm and 7-10pm. ❶

Creperia, Pr. Ferreira d'Almeida, 27, at the end of R. 1 de Maio. Delight in a variety of gourmet crepe options, from asparagus and cream to chocolate, kiwi, banana, and apple (€2-5.50). Open July-Sept. M-Sa 8am-midnight; Oct.-June M-Sa 8:30am-8pm. ❶

Sol e Jardim, Pr. Ferreira de Almeida, 22-23 (☎289 82 00 30). Great restaurant featuring salads and soups (€1-7.40) and—what else?—fresh seafood, along with meat dishes (€6-15). Casual, airy atmosphere pleases an international crowd with draping flags and diverse music. Traditional Portuguese music performed July and Aug. F 8:30pm. Open daily 10:30am-3:30pm and 6:30-10:30pm. AmEx/MC/V. ❷

🖝 SIGHTS

Faro's *cidade velha* is an uncorrupted haven for those looking for the Old World. This medley of ornate churches and museums is punctuated by shops selling local handicrafts in addition to housing multi-generational families.

▨**CAPELA DOS OSSOS.** Step into **Igreja de Nossa Senhora do Carmo** to inspect the small Capela dos Ossos (Chapel of Bones), built from the remains of monks originally buried in the church's former cemetery. More than 1245 skulls and multitudes of bones are arrayed in geometric designs on the walls and ceiling. A sign above the door reads "Stop here and think of the fate that will befall you." *(Lg. do Carmo. ☎289 82 44 90. Open May-Sept. daily 10am-1pm and 3-6pm; Oct.-Apr. M-F 10am-1pm and 3-5pm, Sa 10am-1pm. Church free, chapel €0.75.)*

CATEDRAL (SÉ). A narrow road leads through an Arab portico to the Renaissance cathedral, in a square lined with orange trees and blindingly white buildings. The cathedral is particularly inviting and has three separate sub-altars—each impressive and unique—as well as unconventionally decorated side chapels and a gorgeous, unusual square shape. The cloister is an ideal spot to relax with a book. *(☎289 806 632. Open M-F 10am-5:30pm, Sa 10am-1pm. €2.)*

MUSEU REGIONAL DE FARO. Showcasing the history of the Algarve from various perspectives and time periods, this museum includes a Roman mosaic of Neptune, Moorish candles, Christian art, and a trip through the 20th century. A former convent, it has beautiful architecture and a comfortable, cool cloister. *(Pr. Afonso III, behind the cathedral in the old city. Open June-Sept. M and Sa 2-6pm; Tu-F 10am-6:30pm; Oct.-May M and Sa 2-5:30pm, Tu-F 9:30-5:30pm. €2, families €5.)*

CEMITÉRIO DOS JUDEUS. So you've seen a million cathedrals and churches (however beautiful) since coming to Portugal. Now is your chance to add some diversity to your repertoire in this, one of only a few Jewish cemeteries left in Europe. The cemetery has the graves of inhabitants of "Little Jerusalem," a community of descendants of Jewish exiles fleeing the Spanish Inquisition. After returning from North Africa, they settled in Faro and established, among other things, this obscure but interesting cemetery. *(R. Leão Penedo, between the hospital and the soccer stadium. A 20min. walk from the tourist office. Open M-F 9:30am-12:30pm. Free.)*

🖝🖼 BEACHES AND NIGHTLIFE

Faro's sandy beach, **Praia de Faro,** hides on an islet off the coast with the **Parque Natural da Ria Formosa** on one side. Take bus #16 from the bus station or the stop in front of the tourist office. (5 per day 9:30am-6pm, return 9 per day 10:15am-7pm; €1.) Ferries go to nearby **Ilha do Farol,** a beautiful and less-crowded beach. (45min., June-Sept. every 2hr. 7am-7:30pm, €2.)

ALGARVE AND ALENTEJO

THERE'S MORE THAN ONE WAY TO FIGHT A BULL

Bullfighting has been a part of Iberian culture for centuries, dating back to the Moorish occupation. Eager to expel the Muslim invaders, Iberian noblemen trained themselves on horseback for combat. This spawned the original form of bullfighting; soon, bullfighting on horseback (*toureio equestre*) became a national tradition in both countries.

It was a Portuguese nobleman, Dom Pedro Alcântara y Meneses, who truly founded the activity as we now know it, laying down the formal rules of the fight. However, when Spanish King Carlos II died childless in 1700, the crown passed to Felipe V, of the French house of Bourbon. Disgusted by bullfighting's brutality, the Bourbons banned it in the mid-1700s, much to the people's dismay; to avoid the ban, they took to fighting bulls on foot, thus giving birth to the Spanish variety.

In Portugal, however, the traditional art of *toureio equestre* has persisted uninterrupted. The only difference is that, from the 18th century on, it became illegal to actually kill the bull. The objective of the *toureio equestre* has thus turned from slaughter to showing off the grace of the bullfighter's horse. Fights last only 10 minutes and consist of the bullfighter navigating his horse so as to plant six darts in the bull's neck, a more humane version of the timeless battle between man and beast.

Sidewalk **cafes** crowd the pedestrian walkways off the garden in the center of town, and several **bars** with young crowds liven R. Conselheiro Bívar and its side streets. **O Conselheiro,** in the middle of R. Conselheiro Bívar, is a great evening chill-out spot with a youthful ambience, pool table, and excellent music, which often turns the bar into an exciting dance floor. (Beer €1.50, mixed drinks €4-5.50. Open July-Sept. daily 10pm-2am; Oct.-June Th-Sa 10pm-2am.)

OLHÃO ☎ 289

Olhão (ol-yown), 8km east of Faro, is the largest fishing port in the Algarve. For hundreds of years, the few inhabitants of the area have been fishermen, and modern locals continue the tradition, helping to create one of Portugal's most productive fishing industries. Still, there is more to Olhão than tuna and cuttlefish. Locals pride themselves on their "genuineness;" don't be surprised if restaurants and other places aren't in the kind of hurry you might see elsewhere. Beyond this no-frills town are gorgeous beaches and the Parque Natural da Ria Formosa (see **Daytrips,** p. 733), with numerous species of exotic birds.

== TRANSPORTATION. The **train station** is on Av. dos Combatentes da Grande Guerra, one block from Av. da República. (☎289 72 17 00. Open daily 6am-9pm.) Trains run to: **Faro** (10min.; M-Sa 11-15 per day 6:21am-9:27pm, Su 10 per day 6:21am-8:30pm; €0.80); **Tavira** (30min., 10-14 per day 7:36am-11:14pm, €1.30); **Vila Real de Santo António** (1hr., 9-12 per day 7:36am-11:14pm, €2.40). The **bus station** is on R. General Humberto Delgado, one block from Av. da República. (☎289 70 21 57. Open daily 7am-8pm.) **EVA** buses run to: **Faro** (20min., 13 per day 7:35am-7:50pm, €1.30); **Tavira** (40min., 11 per day 7:35am-7:50pm, €1.90); **Vila Real de Santo António** (1½hr., 9 per day 7:35am-6:40pm, €3.20).

== ORIENTATION AND PRACTICAL INFORMATION. To reach the **port** from the train station, turn left onto Av. dos Combatentes da Grande Guerra and take a right onto **Avenida da República** past the Palácio da Justiça (10-15min.). From the bus station, turn right onto R. General Humberto Delgado and then take another right onto Av. da República (5-10min.). Once on Av. da República, go straight until reaching Olhão's main church. Veer left on R. do Comércio and continue as far as possible. From the end of R. do Comércio, turn left onto R. Olhanense and follow the street until it reaches Av. 5 de Outubro and the sea. The **tourist office** is on Lg. Sebastião Martins

Mestre, a small road that intersects the end of Av. da República, opposite the Câmara Municipal. Its English-speaking staff has maps, ferry schedules, and sometimes free **luggage storage** during the day—ask nicely. (☎289 71 39 36. Open M-Sa 9:30am-1pm and 2:30-6pm.) The **post office** is at Av. da República, 17. (☎289 70 06 03. Open M-F 8:30am-6pm.) **Postal Code:** 8700.

⌂☐ ACCOMMODATIONS AND FOOD. An inexpensive choice is **Pensão Bela Vista ❷**, R. Teófilo Braga, 65-67. Exit the tourist office and follow Tr. da Lagoa to R. Teófilo Braga. Comfortable, modern rooms have TVs; some have bath. (☎289 70 25 38. June-Sept. singles €25-30; doubles €35-40.) From the train or bus station, take Av. da República and turn right onto R. 18 de Junho. After four blocks, turn left again. Here you'll find **Pensão Boémia ❸**, R. da Cerca, 20. Boémia is away from the shore at the center of town, but its cheerful, sunny, and immaculate rooms all have bath, TV, and small refrigerators, and some have large terraces. Boémia is also the only pension in town with A/C. The friendly owner will give you all the info you need—in English, Portuguese, French, or German—to explore the town and beaches. (☎/fax 289 71 45 13. Summer singles €40; doubles €50; winter €35/€40.) Olhão's year-round campground is the **Parque de Campismo dos Bancários do Sul e Ilhas ❶**, off the highway outside of town and accessible by "Câmara Municipal de Olhão" buses (9 per day 7:45am-7:15pm) which leave from in front of the gardens on Av. 5 de Outubro. Amenities include a swimming pool, tennis court, market, bar, and restaurant. (☎289 70 03 00; fax 70 03 90. Showers included. July-Aug. €3.60 per person, €2.60-4 per tent, €3 per car. Sept.-June €3.10/€2.30-3.50/€2.50.)

Supermercado São Nicolau, R. General Humberto Delgado, 62, lies up the block from the bus station. (Open M-Sa 8am-8pm.) The **market** is housed in two red brick buildings adjacent to the city gardens along the river, near Pr. Patrão J. Lopes. (Open daily 7am-1:30pm.) Many eateries on Av. 5 de Outubro serve the day's catch, including **Casa de Pasto O Bote ❷**, Av. 5 de Outubro, 122. While waiting for your fresh fish to grill, enjoy the must-have tomato-herb salad along with other mouthwatering appetizers. Though meat is also offered, the seafood is the star here—experiment with "exotic specials" (€7.50-10) like "razorfish rice." Leave room for dessert; a stunning variety of fresh fruit and almond-based Algarvian specialties are only an order away. (☎289 72 11 83. Entrees €5.50-8. Open M-Sa 11am-4pm and 7pm-midnight.)

▶ DAYTRIPS FROM OLHÃO

ILHAS ARMONA, CULATRA, AND FAROL

Ferries go to Armona from Olhão's dock (15min.; July-Aug. 13 per day 7:30am-8pm; June and Sept. M-F 9 per day 7:40am-7:30pm, Sa-Su 11 per day 8am-7:30pm; Oct.-May 3 per day 8:30am-5pm; last return July-Aug. 8:30pm; June 8pm; €2.20). Another fleet serves Culatra (30min.; June-Aug. every 2hr. 7am-7:30pm; Sept.-May 4 per day 7am-6:30pm; last return June-Aug. 8pm; €2.20) and Farol (45min.; June-Aug. every 2hr. 7am-7:30pm; Sept.-May 4 per day 7am-6:30pm; last return June-Aug. 8:20pm; €2.80).

Long expanses of uncrowded, sandy beach and sparkling sapphire sea surround **Ilhas Armona** and **Culatra**, the two major islands off the coast of Olhão. Armona is the closest, followed by Culatra and then **Farol**, off the far end of Culatra; all three are easy daytrips from Olhão. The farther away you go, the quieter the beaches become, and, of course, the better they are. Farol is easily the most handsome. Even so, none of the three has the volume of tourists seen in other sections of the Algarve, and the inconvenience of getting there will soon be forgotten when you arrive. The islands and sandbars just offshore fence off the Atlantic, creating the **Parque Natural da Ria Formosa**, an important wetland habitat for an amazing variety of sea creatures. During the winter, roughly one-third of Europe's flamingo population can be found here. If you miss the last ride back from Armona, bungalows are available at **Camping Orbitur** ❺ on the central path 5min. from the dock, but at these prices, it's probably better not to get stranded. (☎289 71 41 73. July-Aug. 4-night min. stay; otherwise 2-day min. Cheapest bungalow summer €42-56, winter €29-38; sleeps 4.) While in Armona, check out the international **Restaurante Santo António** ❷ (☎289 70 65 49), at the entrance to the beach 15min. from the dock. Try their specialty: grilled *chocos* (large squid) caught right off the island's coast. (Meals €7-11. Open Apr. 15-Sept. 15 9am-11pm.)

ALENTEJO

The Alentejo, a sharp contrast to the commotion of Lisboa or the wilds of the Algarve, graces travelers with a historic Portuguese setting. Évora, Elvas, and other towns preserve their pristine state in the Alto Alentejo, while Beja remains the only major town on the seemingly endless Baixo Alentejo plain. The region is known for its cork—more than two-thirds of the world's supply comes from here. The Alentejo is best in the spring; be prepared for fiery temperatures in summer.

ÉVORA ☎266

Évora (pop. 55,000) is the capital and largest city of the Alentejo region. The historic center houses palaces, churches, and Roman ruins as well as an innovative medieval approach to recycling (see the *Capela dos Ossos*, below). University of Évora (UÉ) students liven up the town, especially during the *Queima das Fitas*, a week-long graduation celebration with live music, dancing, and drunkenness. The festivities take place during the last week of May and culminate with the burning of little ribbons with messages from friends and family.

▐ TRANSPORTATION

Trains: Lg. da Estação de CP, at Av. dos Combatentes de Grande Guerra (☎/fax 266 74 23 36). To: **Beja** (1½hr., 6 per day 5:30am-7:15pm, €5.80); **Faro** (5hr., 2 per day 7:47am and 7:47pm, €12.50); **Lisboa** (2½hr., 5 per day 5:30am-7:15pm, €8.15).

Buses: Av. São Sebastião (☎266 76 94 10), 300m outside the town wall. More convenient schedules than trains. Normal buses often stop in several smaller towns and serve as local transportation while in bigger ones. Express buses stop only in major cities, are faster, and cost twice as much. To: **Beja** (1½hr., 6-8 per day 8:45am-12:45am, €4.40-7.40); **Braga** (7¾-9¾hr., 4-6 per day 6am-8pm, €17) via **Porto** (6-8½hr., 5 per day, €15.50-€16); **Elvas** (1½-2hr., 5 per day 8am-9:05pm, €4.80-€8.50); **Faro** (5hr., 4 per day 8:45am-6pm, €11.80); **Lisboa** (3hr., every 1-1½hr. 6:30am-8pm, €5.05-€8.80); **Portalegre** (1¾-3hr., 3-5 per day 10:25am-5:40pm, €5.55-9.80); **Setúbal** (1¾hr., 8 per day 6:30am-6pm, €5.05-€8.50).

Taxis: ☎266 73 47 34 or 73 47 35. Taxis hang out 24hr. in Pr. do Giraldo.

▉ ▐ ORIENTATION AND PRACTICAL INFORMATION

To reach **Praça do Giraldo** from the **bus station** (15min. walk), turn right up Av. São Sebastião, and continue straight when it turns into R. Serpa Pinto at the city wall; follow this curving road into Pr. do Giraldo. No direct bus connects the **train station** to the center of town. To walk, go up Av. Dr. Baronha and continue straight as it turns into R. da República at the city wall, until you reach Pr. do Giraldo. To avoid either hike, hail a taxi (€3).

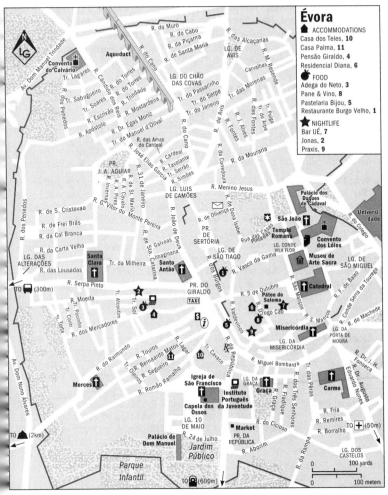

Évora

🏠 ACCOMMODATIONS
Casa dos Teles, 10
Casa Palma, 11
Pensão Giraldo, 4
Residencial Diana, 6

🍴 FOOD
Adega do Neto, 3
Pane & Vino, 8
Pastelaria Bijou, 5
Restaurante Burgo Velho, 1

⭐ NIGHTLIFE
Bar UÉ, 7
Jonas, 2
Praxis, 9

Tourist Office: Pr. do Giraldo, 73 (☎266 73 00 33). Attendants speak and conduct tours in a variety of languages. Consult the desk for a list of guides. Wheelchair-accessible. Open Apr.-Oct. M-F 9am-7pm, Sa-Su 9am-5:30pm; Nov.-Mar. M-F 9am-6pm.

Currency Exchange: 24hr. **ATM** outside the tourist office. Several banks line Pr. do Giraldo, all open M-F 8:30am-3pm.

Police: R. Francisco Soares Lusitano (☎266 70 20 22).

Pharmacy: Farmacia Galeno, R. da República, 34 (☎266 70 32 77). Open M-F 9am-1pm and 3-7pm.

Hospital: Hospital do Espírito Santo, Lg. Senhor Jesus da Pobreza (☎266 74 01 00), near the city wall and the intersection with R. Dr. Augusto Eduardo Nunes.

Internet Access: Instituto Português da Juventude, R. da República, 105; often a long wait in the afternoon. Free. Open M-F 9am-10pm. **Bar Oficin@,** R. Moeda, 27 (☎266 70 73 12). €0.50 per 10min., €2.50 per hr. Open Tu-F 8pm-2am, Sa 9pm-2am.

Post Office: R. de Olivença (☎266 74 54 80; fax 74 54 86). **Posta Restante** and **fax.** Open M-F 8:30am-6pm. **Postal Code:** 7999.

🏠 🏕 ACCOMMODATIONS AND CAMPING

Most hostels cluster on side streets off Pr. do Giraldo and are well-advertised; just follow signs when in doubt. They're crowded in the summer, especially during graduation in May and the *Feira de São João*, the celebration of Evora's patron saint, which runs June 18-30. Private *quartos*, €20-25 per double, are pleasant summer alternatives to crowded *pensões;* check with the tourist office for listings.

🏠 Casa Palma, R. Bernardo Matos, 29A (☎266 70 35 60). Located right off Pr. da República. Offers clean, well-kept rooms with TVs at unbeatable prices. You would never guess that the house is actually over 100 years old, given the excellent shape in which its grandmotherly owner has kept it. Singles €20-25; doubles €30-35. ❷

Casa dos Teles, R. Romão Ramalho, 27 (☎266 70 24 53). It's not labeled, so look for signs pointing in its direction. Family-run, and often less crowded than other accommodations in Évora. Reservations suggested during Easter and summer. June-Sept. singles without bath €25; doubles €35, with bath €40; triples €37/€40. Oct.-May €5 less. ❷

Pensão Residencial Giraldo, R. dos Mercadores, 27 (☎266 70 58 33). With TVs and A/C in every room, your stay is sure to be comfortable. A little bargaining may get you a better deal. Reservations recommended in the summer. Summer singles €29, with bath €45; doubles €35/€50. Winter singles €25/€35; doubles €30/€35. AmEx/MC/V. ❸

Residencial Diana, R. Diogo Cão, 2-3 (☎266 70 20 08; www.softline.pt/Residencial-Diana). A more upscale alternative to hostels and private residences, as evidenced by the elegant foyer and marble bathrooms. Rooms come with cable TV, A/C, hardwood floors, and minibars. Buffet breakfast included. Singles €40, with bath €53; doubles €50/€60. In winter €5-10 less. AmEx/MC/V. ❹

Camping: Orbitur's Parque de Campismo de Évora, Estrada das Alcáçovas (☎266 70 51 90; fax 70 98 30). A 3-star campground which branches off at the bottom of R. Raimundo. A 30min. walk to town, but 2 buses (€1.50) run to the nearby Vila Lusitano stop from Pr. do Giraldo: #5 (10-20min.; M-F 10 per day 7:45am-7:15pm, Sa 3 per day 8:25am-12:35pm) and #8 (15min.; M-F 6 per day 9:40am-5:45pm, Sa 9:25am, Su 2:50, 7:05pm). Taxi €3.50. Laundry service, market, tennis court, and bank on grounds. Reception 8am-10pm. Prices vary with season. €2.50-3.80 per person, €1-1.70 per child, €2-5 per tent, €3.50 per car. AmEx/MC/V. ❶

🍴 FOOD

Restaurants are scattered near Pr. do Giraldo, especially along **Rua dos Mercadores,** but many are tourist-oriented; to find local favorites, wander a bit away from the center. The **market,** near Pr. da República, sells crafts and other regional goods as well as cheese and produce (open Tu-Su 6am-1pm).

🍴 Restaurante Burgo Velho, R. de Burgos, 10 (☎266 22 58 58). A couple of blocks off Pr. Giraldo lies this true gem of *alentejano* cuisine. Cozy and quiet, it offers an intimate dining experience where the excellent service and well-presented large portions take top billing. Entrees €5-8.50. Open M-Sa noon-3pm and 7-10pm. AmEx/MC/V. ❷

Pane & Vino, Páteo do Salema (☎266 74 69 60). It may seem strange eating Italian food here, but this popular spot's classic, thin-crust pizzas are too good to be missed. Students, families, and travelers rendezvous in the spacious dining room and bar where the rustic decor evokes the Tuscan countryside. Pizzas and pasta (€5-8) are accompanied by pricier meat entrees. Open Tu-Su noon-3pm and 6:30-11pm. AmEx/MC/V. ❷

Adega do Neto, R. dos Mercadores, 46 (☎963 94 73 19). Locals flock here for typical *alentejano* dishes under €6, such as the house specialty, *feijoada*, a pork, bean, and sausage stew. Entrees €5-6. Open M-Sa noon-3pm and 7-9:30pm. ❶

Pastelaria Bijou, R. da República, 15. A variety of excellent pastries displayed beneath the long, marble countertop can be enjoyed in air-conditioned comfort. Ask for a *bolo de berlim* (sugar-coated cake with delicious cream) or a *romana* (flaky pastry with sweet potato and almond spread) for a taste of their baking expertise. Pastries €0.65-1.40. Coffee €0.40-0.60. Open daily 7am-7pm. ❶

🔆 SIGHTS

🦴 **CAPELA DOS OSSOS.** The Capela dos Ossos (Chapel of Bones) warmly welcomes visitors: *"Nós ossos que aqui estamos, pelos vossos esperamos"* (We bones that are here are waiting for yours). In order to provide a hallowed space to reflect on the profundity of life and death, three Franciscan monks built this chapel from the remains of over 5000 people. The hip bone's connected to the thigh bone all over the walls and ceiling, while the three founders lie enclosed in stone sarcophagi to the right of the altar. For thrills and chills, read the sign below the one undecomposed corpse in the chapel (then go give mom a call): legend has it that it is a son cursed by his mother for disobedience and cruelty. *(Pr. 1 de Mayo. Follow R. da República from Pr. do Giraldo, then take a right into Pr. 1 de Mayo; enter the chapel through the door of the Convento de São Francisco to the right of the church steps. ☎266 70 45 21. Open May-Sept. M-Sa 9am-1pm and 2:30-6pm, Su 10am-1pm; Oct.-Apr. M-Sa 9am-1pm and 2:30-5:30pm, Su 10am-1pm. Tours in several languages. €1.)*

BASÍLICA CATEDRAL. Built during the 12th century, the Basílica Cathedral, also known as the Sé, looms over Évora like a mad scientist's castle; inside, however, its ornate carvings and splendid architecture are similar to those of other European cathedrals, though its darkness does contribute to the spooky motif. Climb the **cloister's** stairs to see the view of Évora from the cathedral's terrace or tour the **Muse de Arte Sacra,** which features a 13th-century Virgin of paradise, the tunics worn by bishops of the Sé (including those worn by Vasco da Gama's grandson), and the precious jewel-encrusted Relicário do Santo Lenho, a relic made from a piece of the cross that Jesus was crucified on. *(From the center of Pr. do Giraldo, head to the end of R. 5 de Outubro. Cathedral open daily 9am-noon and 2-5pm. Free. Cloisters open daily 9am-noon and 2-4:30pm. Museum open Tu-Su 9am-12:30pm and 2-4:30pm. Cloisters and museum €3, students €1.50. July to mid Sept. ticket includes visit to the tower. Visits to just the cloister on M €1.50.)*

TEMPLO ROMANO. Columns still stand in Largo Conde do Vila Flor as a reminder of Évora's long history as a central city of several empires. The small temple dates back to the time of Roman occupation in the 2nd and 3rd centuries and was allegedly built in honor of the goddess Diana. *(Open 24hr.)*

IGREJA DE SÃO JOÃO DE EVANGELISTA AND PALÁCIO DE DUQUES DE CADAVAL. Also known as the Igreja de Loíos, immediately facing the Templo Romano is the Igreja de São João de Evangelista (1485). The church and ducal palace are owned by the Cadaval family, descendants of the original dukes, who restored the buildings with their personal fortunes in 1957-8. The interior of the church is covered with dazzling azulejos (tiles); a beautiful cloister with an outdoor cafe is open to tourists. *(Lg. Conde do Vila Flor. Open Tu-Su 10am-12:30pm and 2-6pm. €2.50 for church, €4.20 for church and next door exhibition hall.)*

NIGHTLIFE

Évora's nightlife is fueled largely by the students from the university who fill the bars after midnight and then move on to the clubs. Even so, families and non-students also find plenty of evening excitement in and around Pr. do Giraldo, where people stay and socialize until well past midnight. Wednesday nights are student nights at most establishments, so expect considerably larger crowds.

Praxis, R. Valdevinos (☎933 35 57 82). Though it's the only nightclub in town, Praxis does not disappoint, with 4 different bars for hard dancing, quiet socializing, and weekly live music. Beer €1.50. Mixed drinks €4-6. Minimum consumption €5 for men, €3 for women. Open daily 11pm-4am.

Bar UÉ, R. Diogo Cão, 19 (☎266 74 39 24). Packed to capacity with university students, Bar UÉ appeals to a younger crowd as an early stop before serious clubbing later. Its terrace is perfect for conversation, and at €1, the beer is sinfully cheap. Open Tu-Su noon-2am; serves food 1-3pm and 7:30-9:30pm.

Jonas, R. Serpa Pinto, 115 (☎964 82 16 47). Wooden walls and dim lighting give this bar a cavernous feel, while the blue-lit room upstairs is made for chilling. Down-to-earth staff and different nightly drink specials keep the 20- and 30-somethings coming. Crowd starts filtering in around 1am to dance to everything from the Smashing Pumpkins to techno. Popular Brazilian *caipirinhas* €3, beer €1.50. Open M-Sa 11pm-4am.

ELVAS   ☎268

Elvas (pop. 25,000), a quiet and hilly town, is located 13km from the Spanish border. The town has an inviting main square and narrow, steep cobblestone streets that lead to fortified city walls. The old portion of town is quite picturesque, boasting traditional European architecture, which gives it the feel of a 19th-century town that has been frozen in time.

TRANSPORTATION. The nearest **train station** (☎268 62 28 16) is 3km away in **Fontaínhas** and runs to **Badajoz,** Spain (17min., 12:08pm, €1.10). A **taxi** (☎268 62 22 87) is always waiting there, however, providing the only transport from the train station to town (€5). The **bus station** (☎268 62 28 75), located at the entrance of the city, affords the best transportation option, with buses going to: **Albufeira** (6hrs., 6:40am, €13); **Beja** (3½hr., 6:40am, €9.90); **Évora** (1½hr.; 4 per day 6:40am-4:25pm; at 6:40am and 8:05am, €8.50, 1 and 6:30pm, €4.80.); **Faro** (6½hr., 6:40am, €13); **Lisboa** (3hr., 10 per day 5:40am-6pm, €8.50); **Portalegre** (1½hr., 4 per day M-F 7am-6:45pm, €4).

ORIENTATION AND PRACTICAL INFORMATION. Buses stop at the entrance to the city walls. The **tourist office** *(posto de turismo)* is in **Praça da República.** (☎268 62 22 36. Open Apr.-Oct. M-F 9am-6pm, Sa-Su 10am-12:30pm and 2-5:30pm; Nov.-Mar. daily 9am-5:30pm.) To get to the tourist office from the bus station (5min. walk), take a right and go through Lg. da Misericórdia; continue up to R. da Cadeia, and after a series of fountains take a left into Pr. da República—the *posto de turismo* will be on the right. The **Banco Espírito Santo** (☎268 63 92 40; open M-F 8:30am-4:30pm) is conveniently located in Pr. da República, right in front of the tourist office, with a 24hr. **ATM.** Other local services include: **Lavandaria Ecológica,** Lg. da Misericórdia, 4a (☎268 62 03 20; open M-F 9am-1pm and 3pm-

7pm, Sa 9:30am-1pm); **Farmácia Moutta,** directly behind the tourist office (☎62 21 50; open daily 9am-1pm and 3-7pm); **police,** R. André Gonçalves (☎268 63 94 70); **Hospital de Santa Luzia,** Estrada Nacional, 4 (☎268 62 22 25). For **Internet access,** the tourist office has free access for those in a hurry: one computer available with a 5min. limit. Otherwise, check out **O Livreiro de Elvas,** R. de Olivença, 4a, a little bookstore with two computers in the back room. (☎268 62 08 82. €0.80 for 15min., €1.40 for 30min. Open M-F 9:30am-1pm and 3:15-7:15pm, Sa 9:30am-1pm.) The **post office,** Lg. da Misericórdia 1, is one block behind the tourist office. (☎268 63 90 33. Open M-F 9am-6pm.) **Postal Code:** 7350.

█ █ ACCOMMODATIONS AND FOOD. António Mocisso e Garcia Coelho ❶, R. Aires Varela, 15, is one of the most reasonably priced options in town. From the tourist office, take a right out of the *praça* and then your first left; go left at the end of the street and the reception will be on the right. The large rooms have small TVs and private baths. Reservations are recommended from June to September. A breakfast of bread and jam, coffee, and juice is included with the room; new arrivals should check in after noon. (☎62 21 26. Singles €20; doubles €30; triples €40; quads €50.) If you don't mind staying less than 1km outside of Elvas (roughly a €3.20 taxi ride) and want to avoid the crowds, the **Carrascal Residencial ❸,** Av. de Badajoz, is an excellent choice, with spotless rooms complete with TVs and large private bathrooms with faux-marble floors. The hostel owners provide toiletries and towels if needed. (☎62 84 68. Breakfast included. Singles €27.50; doubles €50). For a more expensive but very comfortable stay, consider **Hotel Dom Luis ❹** on Av. de Badajoz. Located approximately 100m outside of the city itself, it's right in front of the aqueduct and closer than the Carrascal Residencial. The hotel's 88 rooms feature A/C, TVs and large, clean bathrooms; it also boasts a nice restaurant (entrees €7.50-9.50), as well as a conference room and nicely appointed common room. Large fireplaces and depictions of Portuguese conquistadors give the place a dignified look. (☎62 27 56. Singles €49; doubles €59. AmEx/MC/V.) **Parque de Campismo ❷** is ideal for a small group willing to rough it for a night. From the bus station, follow the road that leads toward the aqueduct until the *parque*'s sign. (☎62 89 97. €2.50 per car or tent).

For fresh fish, fruit, and vegetables, try the **mercado municipal** on Av. de São Domingos (open M-Sa 6am-1pm). The traveler with a penchant for Portuguese cuisine will appreciate **O Lagar ❷,** R. Nova da Vedoria, 7. Leaving Pr. da República on the opposite side of the castle, turn right on R. da Cadeia, take the second left on R. do Tabolado next to the fountain, and finally right onto R. Nova da Vedoria. Locals consider O Lagar the best restaurant in Elvas (with a bar to match), and its entrees, including tiger shrimp (€9.50), grilled veal (€9.50), and *gaspacho* (€1.25), live up to that reputation. (☎268 62 47 93. Entrees €7.50-15. Open Su-W and F-Sa noon-4pm and 7pm-midnight.) *Frango assado* (rotisserie chicken) is Portugal's white meat, and Elvas does it up right. Fans get their fill of it at **Canal 7 ❶,** R. dos Sapateiros, 16. Exit Pr. da República on R. dos Sapateiros next to Banco Espírito Santo, and follow the curving road to the left. Take your *frango assado* outside; €2 gets you a half chicken to go (dine-in €4). The *leitão* (grilled suckling pork; €6.50) is another specialty. (☎268 62 35 93. Entrees €3.50-7. Open Su-M and W-Sa 11am-3pm and 6-10pm; Su take-out only.)

◙ SIGHTS. Elvas's main sight, the ▨**Aqueduto da Amoreira,** clearly visible from kilometers away, marks the entrance to the city. Begun in 1529 and finished in 1622, the colossal structure is Europe's largest aqueduct—its 843 arches extend almost 8000m. The **castelo,** above Pr. da República, has a pleasant view of the aqueduct and the infinite rows of olive trees on the horizon; a stairwell to the right of the entrance leads up to the castle walls. (Castle open daily 9:30am-5:30pm.

€1.30; seniors and 14-25 €0.70, under 14 free.) The **Igreja de Nossa Senhora da Assunção**, better known as the **antiga Sé**, in Pr. da República, has *azulejos* and a beautiful ribbed ceiling. (☎ 268 62 59 97. The hours are tricky and change regularly; call ahead. Mass Su 6pm.) Behind the cathedral and uphill to the right is the **Igreja de Nossa Senhora da Consolação dos Aflitos.** Its octagonal interior has beautiful geometric tiles, and the view bests even that of the *castelo*. Informal tours given in Portuguese upon request. (Open Tu-Su 9:30am-noon and 2:30-5pm.)

▶ DAYTRIP FROM ELVAS

MARVÃO

From Elvas, take the train to Portalegre (1½hr., 4 per day M-F 7am-6:45pm, €4) and from there catch a bus to Marvão (50min., M-F 7:05am and 1:10pm, €1.60-5). Arriving by bus, you'll be dropped just outside the town wall. Enter through a gate and proceed up R. Cima until you see the stone whipping post in Pr. Pelourinho. From here, R. Espírito Santo leads toward the castelo and the tourist office. (☎ 245 99 38 86. Open Aug.-Sept. M-F 9am-7pm, Sa-Su 10am-12:30pm and 2-7pm; Oct.-July daily 9am-12:30pm and 2-5:30pm.)

This Portuguese candidate for UNESCO World Heritage status is one of the Alentejo's best kept secrets. The ancient walled town (pop. 185) sits almost as if on an island overlooking the ocean of the Alentejo plains; in fact, it's the highest town in Portugal. The hills and meadows of the **Parque Natural de São Mamede** make the view even more worthwhile. Almost all of the town's whitewashed houses are inside the 17th-century walls. Marvão's 13th-century ▧**castelo,** atop the ridge at the west end of town, hasn't been seized in 700 years; the 360° views of the Alentejo's arid plains are among the most breathtaking in all of Portugal. Prior to the castle's construction, however, Marvão passed through several different owners; founded by Ibn Maruán, a 9th-century Moorish knight, the town was also ruled by the Romans and the Visigoths before being captured by Christians in the 1200s. Remnants of these days, some dating as far back as the Paleolithic era, are on display at the **Museu Municipal,** near the castle in the **Igreja de Santa Maria.** (☎ 245 90 91 32. Open daily 9am-12:30pm and 2-5:30pm. €1, students €0.75.)

BEJA ☎ 284

A far cry from touristy Évora, Beja (pop. 38,000) provides a tranquil, small-town atmosphere combined with a rich historical tradition that includes Celtic, Roman, Visigothic, Moorish, and Christian elements. Originally called Pax Juliato, Beja is the site at which Julius Caesar signed a peace treaty with the Lusitanian tribes; from that point on, the city switched hands several times, with each conquering tribe adding different aspects to Beja's diverse cultural make-up. Since Dom Sancho II claimed it for Christianity in 1232, the last time the city was conquered, Beja has grown into a small yet modern town relatively untouched by tourism despite its prairie beauty and undeniable charm.

■ **TRANSPORTATION. Trains** run from the **station** (☎ 284 32 50 56), 1km outside of town, to: **Évora** (1½hr., 5 per day 5:22am-8:40pm, €6.50); **Faro** (3½hr.; 2 per day 9:30am, 9:13pm; €8) via **Funcheira; Ficalho,** a border town with connections to most major destinations in Spain (1½hr., noon, €6.70); **Lisboa** (2½-3hr., 4 per day 5:30am-7:20pm, €8.50). The **bus station** (☎ 284 31 36 20) is on R. Cidade de São Paulo, near the corner of Av. do Brasil. **Buses** to: **Évora** (1½hr., 6 per day 7:10am-7:15pm, €7.50); **Faro** (3½hr., 4 per day 10:10am-7:20pm, €12); **Lisboa** (3¼hr., 5 per day 7:45am-7:05pm, €10.50); **Portalegre** (3-4hr., 2 per day, €10).

⚧ PRACTICAL INFORMATION. The **tourist office,** R. Capitão J. F. de Sousa, 25, provides luggage storage, free Internet access, and walking tour maps. To get to the tourist office from the bus station, take a left onto Av. do Brasil. Make the third right onto Av. Vasco da Gama; when it ends, turn left and follow the road until you come upon Praça Diogo Fernandes de Beja on your right, where you will see an abstract metal structure, marking the beginning of R. Capitão J. F. de Sousa, a pedestrian avenue. (☎/fax 284 31 19 13. Open M-Sa 10am-1pm and 2-6pm.) Other local services include: **banks** (open M-F 8am-3pm); **ATMs** near the station and on R. de Sousa around the tourist office; **luggage storage** at the bus station on weekdays (€1.75 per day); **Lavandaria Baldeira,** R. Dr. Brito Camacho, 11 (☎284 32 99 57; open M-F 9:30am-1pm and 3-7pm, Sa 9:30am-1pm); **police** on R. D. Nuno Álvares Pereira (☎284 32 20 22 or 32 20 23), one block downhill from the tourist office; **Farmácia Oliveira,** R. 91, 1 (☎284 32 38 90; open M-F 9am-1pm and 3-7pm); **Internet access** at **Só Café,** R. João Hogan (☎284 32 75 41), in the Centro Comercial Pax Julia (€1.20 per hr.; open daily 9am-midnight), and at the **Instituto Português da Juventude,** next to the Pousada de Juventude de Beja on R. Professor Janeiro Acabado, with free but crowded terminals. To get to the **post office,** Lg. dos Correios, take a left from the tourist office and a right onto R. Infantaria. **Posta Restante** and **fax** (€2.20 per page) are available. (☎284 31 12 70. Open M-F 9am-6pm.) **Postal Code:** 7800.

⚧⚧ ACCOMMODATIONS AND CAMPING. Beja is a pleasant place to stay for the night, and it offers several satisfying accommodations options. Most are located within a few blocks of the tourist office. ▨**Pousada de Juventude de Beja (HI) ❶,** R. Professor Janeiro Acabado, is one such option. From the front of the bus station, turn left, and then left again on R. Cidade de São Paulo, then right on R. Professor Janeiro Acabado; the hostel is on the left. The squeaky clean inn has everything you need: a living room with TV and foosball, a laundry room, and a kitchen. Each guest has a personal cabinet with lock, but it is only accessible during reception hours. (☎284 32 54 58; fax 32 54 68. Breakfast included. Reception 8am-noon and 6pm-midnight. Check out 10:30am. Lockout noon-6pm. June 16-Sept. 15 dorms €11; doubles with bath €28. Sept. 16-June 15 €8.50/€22. €2 more without HI card.) The recently renovated three-star **Residencial Bejense ❸,** R. Capitão J. F. de Sousa, 57, offers 24 spotless rooms as well as tiled hallways, marble bathrooms, TVs, phones, and A/C. The lounge is cozy with a big screen TV, plush leather couches and a bar. Barbara, the friendly owner, gives this place a homey feel—if only your mom were as nice. (☎284 31 15 70; fax 31 15 79. Breakfast included. Singles €28; doubles €40, with 3rd bed €50. AmEx/MC/V.) The **Parque de Campismo Municipal de Beja ❶,** Av. Vasco da Gama, offers the security of a municipally run enclosed campground with modern amenities such as free showers, a bar, bathrooms, and cheap electricity (low season €0.81, high season €1.62). It is also conveniently located a short walk away from 2 major supermarkets. (☎/fax 284 31 19 11. Reception 8am-11pm. Oct.-May €1.07 per person, €0.79 per tent; May-Oct. €2.13/€1.57. 10% discount with student ID.)

⚧⚧ FOOD AND NIGHTLIFE. Beja is one of the best places to taste authentic (and affordable) cuisine *à l'Alentejana,* such as *biftoque* (pork steak with special spices) and *bacalhau à bras* (grilled cod with egg and caramelized onions). Restaurants are everywhere, and most have similar menus within the range of €6-9. A **market** next to the castle at the end of town has fresh produce and fish at great prices. (Open M-Sa 6am-1:30pm.) Many consider **Casa de Pasto Imperial ❶,** R. Santo Antonio, 14, the paragon of unadulterated *Alentejano* cooking. Leaving the tourist office, turn right and walk the rest of the block, turning right again on R. Dr. Brito Camacho. Walk up the hill two blocks to Lg. de S. João, then bear right on R. Tomás Vieira. Offering succulent *biftoques* at low prices, the restaurant attracts flocks of locals at mealtimes. Try the *bolo de bolacha* (cookie cake) for dessert. (Entrees €4-6. Open M-Sa 10am-9:30pm.) For a quick bite, pop by **Restaurante O Frangote ❶**, R. Cidade de São Paulo, 7, which offers quality *alentejano* cuisine for take out or dine-in at extremely affordable prices. (☎284 31 04 20. Sandwiches from €1.75, entrees €4-6. Open M-F 9:30am-10pm, Sa 9:30am-3pm.) At night, head for the mother ship at **UFO's** in the Centro Comercial do Carmo. Follow R. de Sousa from the tourist office, taking your first left onto R. dos Reis. Turn left after 2 blocks. Popular in the early evening (particularly with student crowds), it features karaoke on Tuesdays and live music twice a week. Pool tables and a projection TV keep guests entertained. (Beer €1.25. Open Tu-Sa 9:30pm-4am. Ages 16+.)

◙ SIGHTS. Beja's sights are scattered but can be seen easily in a day. Walking tour maps from the tourist office lead you at a leisurely pace to each historic area. The **Convento de Nossa Senhora da Conceição,** Lg. de Conceição, is a convenient starting point. Take a right from the tourist office and walk into Pr. Diogo Fernandes de Beja. Go right on R. Dr. Brito Camacho, through Lg. de São João to Lg. da Conceição; the museum is on the right. The convent is the scene of the passionate romance between Portuguese nun Mariana Alcoforado and the French Count of Chamilly Noel Bouton, which was immortalized in the *Cartas Portuguesas (Portuguese Letters)*. The interior dazzles with its ornate *talha dourada* (golden carvings) and 18th-century *azulejo* (tiles) panels that portray scenes of the lives of Mary and St. John the Baptist. (☎284 32 33 51. Open Tu-Su 9:30am-12:30pm and 2-5:15pm. €2, €1 for students, Su free. Ticket includes the **Museu Regional de Beja,** on the 2nd fl. of the convent, which displays intriguing artifacts from Beja's Roman and Moorish periods.)

One block downhill from the Convento-Museu is the 13th-century **Igreja de Santa Maria da Feira,** Lg. de Santa Maria, transformed into a mosque during the Moorish invasion and back into a church when the city reverted to Portuguese control. The elaborate *talha dourada* carvings on the side of the Igreja combine with the Moorish pillars and domed ceiling in a hybrid architectural style that meshes Christian and Islamic culture. (Open daily for mass 6-6:30pm and Su noon. Free.) After leaving the Igreja, turn left and take R. Dr. Aresta Branco until you see the looming **◙Castelo de Beja.** Epitomizing Beja's rich cultural heritage, the *Castelo* has switched hands several times; originally a Celtic fortified village founded approximately 40 B.C., the *Castelo* then became a Roman fortress; from that point on, it was taken over by the Visigoths, the Moors (who transformed the fortress into the castle that you see today) and finally the Christians, who, under Dom Dines, added the **Torre de Menagem** to it during the early 14th century. Its neo-Gothic architecture, enormous marble keep, and marvelous view of the Alentejano plains make the tower a worthwhile stop. (Castle open May-Sept. Tu-Su 10am-1pm and 2-6pm; Oct.-Apr. 9-11:30am and 1-3:30pm. Tower closes at 5:30pm. Free.) On the other side of town lies a beautiful garden, the **Jardim Gago Coutinho e Sacadura Cabral.** Named for Portuguese aviators, the garden is lined with orange trees and benches—a shady end for your trek through Beja. To get there from the castle, go straight back up R. Dr. Aresta Branco, past Lg. Santa Maria, straight as it turns into R. Dr. Manuel D. Arriaga and R. Almeida Garrett; then take a left on R. D. Nuno Alvares Pereira, followed by a right onto R. Afonso Henriques. The garden will be on your right. (Open daily sunrise-sunset.)

SINES
☎**269**

The birthplace of Vasco da Gama in 1469, Sines (pop. 13,000) was for centuries a small fishing town, until the construction of an industrial complex and a port in the 1970s pushed it into modernity. Though today its inhabitants live far more modern lives than their ancestors, Sines maintains the small town charm that has been a staple of its existence for nearly 2000 years. Having been a settling ground for Romans, Visigoths and Moors throughout the ages, Sines was finally captured for Christendom from the Moors in the late 12th-early 13th centuries, and its charter was granted by King Pedro in 1362. Sines differs from other Alentejano towns in its proximity to the Atlantic; the ocean has left a deeper mark on its culture than the traditionally fertile fields of this region.

TRANSPORTATION. The **bus station** (☎269 63 22 62) is located on R. Julio Gomes da Silva; it's an easily missed green booth with "Rodoviaria Alentejo" written on it. **Buses** are the only way in and out of town and go to: **Beja** (2½hr., 8:20am, €3.15); **Lisboa** (2¾hr., 13 per day 5am-7:30pm, €13); **Setúbal** (2hr., 12 per day 5am-7:30pm, €9). Station open M-F 7am-1:30pm and 3-6:30pm, Sa-Su 7:45-11:45am and 1:45-6pm.

ORIENTATION AND PRACTICAL INFORMATION. Everything in Sines is centered around the castle and its surroundings. A few shops line R. Serpa Pinto and R. Francisco Luís Lopes, both pedestrian walkways a block away from the castle. Sines's commercial hub is **Praça da República**. The **tourist office** is located within the castle itself and offers pamphlets, maps, and other essential information in Portuguese, French, and English. From the bus station, go through Pr. da República, take R. Marquês de Pombal, and go straight until you reach Lg. Afonso Albuquerque, where you take a left; go straight until you reach the castle. (☎269 63 44 72. Open daily 10am-1pm and 2-6pm.) Other local services include: **banks** and **ATMs** around Pr. da República; **police,** Av. General Humberto Delgado (☎269 63 64 95); **Health center** (Centro de Saúde), R. Julio Gomes da Silva, across from the bus station; **Lavandaria Varanda,** R. Francisco Luís Lopes, 47 (☎269 63 23 88; open M-F 9am-1pm and 3-9pm, Sa 9am-1pm); **Farmácia Atlântico** (☎269 63 00 10), on Pr. da República (open M-F 9am-1pm and 3-7pm). The **post office** is in Pr. Tomás Ribeiro and offers **Internet** access. (Open M-F 9am-6pm.) **Postal Code:** 7520.

ACCOMMODATIONS AND FOOD. Although Sines is a small town, it has plenty of good hostels that fill up during the summer months; as with almost everything in Sines, most hostels tend to be located near the castle. **Pensão Fredemar ❶,** R. Candido dos Reis, 31, is the cheapest option in town. The small, no-frills rooms all come with bathrooms. (☎63 21 22. Singles €15-20; doubles €30-40. Prices €5 lower in winter.) A few blocks from the bus station lies the **Habimar Residencial ❹,** Av. Domingos Rodrigues Pablo, 2, a three-star hostel whose cozy rooms all come with bathrooms, showers, and cable TV. The bar in the lounge area is run by a friendly staff. (☎63 54 77; fax 08 43 89. In summer singles €45-50; doubles €55. In winter singles €25; doubles €40.) Less than a block away from the castle, **Pensão Carvalho ❷,** R. Gago Coutinho, 27, has very clean rooms for decent prices. (☎63 20 19. Singles €15, with bath €25; doubles €25/€35. Prices about €10 lower in winter.)

Sines offers both typical *alentejano* meat-based dishes as well as an excellent variety of freshly caught seafood. Most seafood restaurants can be found around the castle, with beautiful views of the *praia* (beach) and port, while the Alentejano restaurants are scattered throughout the rest of the town. **Churrasqueira Regional ❶,** Av. General Humberto Delgado, serves excellent grilled cuisine, *churrasco* style. Affordable (and large) entrees run €5-9. Try the delicious *frango assado* (roast chicken, €5) or the succulent *leitao assado na brasa* (flame-grilled pork; €7.50). Take-out is also available. (☎ 00 70 95. Open only for lunch M-Sa noon-3pm). No visit to Sines would be complete without a night at **Restaurante Varanda do Oceano ❸**, Lg. Nossa Senhora Salvas, widely acknowledged by locals as the town's finest restaurant. Although it's a bit expensive (entrees run €8-20), the variety of seafood available will blow your mind. Perched on a cliff, the restaurant also offers a magnificent view of the ocean. (☎ 63 23 03; fax 63 31 35. Open M-Sa noon-4pm and 7pm-midnight. AmEx/MC/V.)

◙ SIGHTS. The highlight of any visit to Sines is clearly the **Castelo de Sines.** Although it's of medieval origin, the castle underwent a profound reconstruction under King Manuel during the 17th century. The famous Portuguese navigator Vasco da Gama was born in the castle's keep in 1469, although tourists are only granted access to the large courtyard and the castle's walls. (Open daily 10am-1pm and 2-6pm. Free.) Right next door is the **Igreja Matriz,** a 14th-century church that was rebuilt during the 18th century. As a testament to Sines's previous inhabitants, several Visigothic stones remain from a primitive chapel previously built on the same site. The choir displays some fine 17th- and 18th-century paintings. (Open daily 9am-6pm. Free.) Outside of Sines's historic center, you can find the **Ermida de Nossa Senhora de Salas.** Although it was rebuilt under the commission of Vasco da Gama himself in 1529, the origins of this chapel are unknown. It is believed that the Byzantine Princess D. Vetácia, granddaughter of Theodore Laskaris the Younger, emperor of Nicaea, founded the chapel after falling in love with Sines in 1336. To get there from the castle, walk straight until Av. General Humberto Delgado. Take a left and follow the road until R. 25 de Abril; then take a right and follow the road out of town to the chapel. Also known as Praia Vasco da Gama, **Praia Sines** stretches along Av. Vasco da Gama, its sparkling white sands and transparent water reminiscent of the Caribbean (that is, until you notice the lack of palm trees and the frigidity of the water).

RIBATEJO AND ESTREMADURA

The fertile region of the Ribatejo ("Above the Tejo") is perhaps the gentlest and greenest in the entire country. Known as the "Heart of Portugal," the Ribatejo is famous for lush wetlands and pastures that sharply contrast with the arid plains of the Alentejo to the west. The beauty is not limited to the area's landscapes, however. With ornate monasteries in Alcobaça and Batalha, the spooky medieval town of Óbidos, and the hallowed sanctuary at Fátima, the Ribatejo boasts some of the country's finest sights. Nearby, serrated cliffs and whitewashed fishing villages

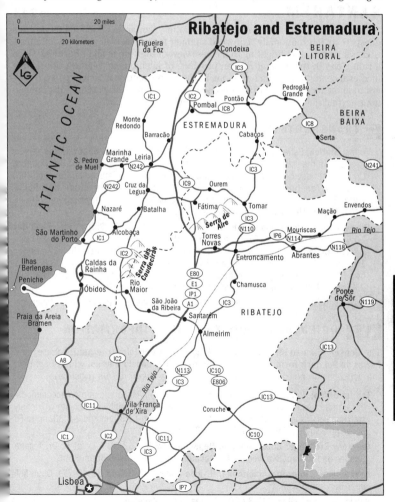

Ribatejo and Estremadura

line Estremadura's Costa de Prata (Silver Coast), whose beaches rival even those of the Algarve. Throngs of tourists and summer residents storm seafront Nazaré and Peniche, but smaller, less-touristed towns with sparkling beaches line the coast and the ruggedly beautiful Ilhas Berlengas lie just offshore.

HIGHLIGHTS OF RIBATEJO AND ESTREMADURA

CATCH the best view of the Rio Tejo in all of Portugal from **Santarém** (below).

RISK bodily injury surfing **Super-Tubos,** a famously unforgiving beachbreak (p. 752).

WORSHIP the mysterious ways of the Virgin Mary at **Fátima** (p. 761).

INVENT stories about the Knights Templar at Tomar's **Convento de Cristo** (p. 766).

SANTARÉM ☎243

Perhaps the most versatile of Ribatejo's cities, Santarém (pop. 30,000) invites guests to an internationally renowned summer festival as well as a slew of attractions ranging from bullfighting to the best view of the Tejo in all of Portugal. Once a ruling city in the ancient Roman province of Lusitania and later a flourishing medieval center, Santarém has a long history of prosperity. A visit exposes travelers to an attractive mix of picturesque churches and rolling green hills, only an hour beyond the commotion of metropolitan Lisboa.

▛ TRANSPORTATION

Trains: Station, Estrada da Estação (☎243 32 11 99), 2km outside town. **Bus** service to and from the station (10min., every 30min.-1hr. 7:30am-7pm, €1.30). To: **Coimbra** (2hr., 17 per day 6:25am-8:40pm, €8.50); **Faro** via Lisboa's Estação do Barreiro (4hr., 6 per day 7am-6pm, €14.50); **Lisboa** (1hr., 48 per day 4:30am-11pm, €5); **Portalegre** (3hr., 4 per day 8:30am-6pm, €8.50); **Porto** (4hr., 16 per day 6:25am-8:40pm, €13); **Tomar** (1hr., 18 per day 6:20am-11:30pm, €4).

Buses: Rodoviária do Tejo, Av. do Brasil (☎243 33 32 00). To: **Braga** (5hr., 5 per day 10:45am-7:45pm, €13.80); **Caldas da Rainha** (1½hr., 6 per day 7:20am-7:15pm, €4.10); **Coimbra** (2hr., 4 per day 10:45am-8:45pm, €9.90); **Faro** (7hr., 12 per day 10:30am-4:30pm, €15.50); **Leiria** (1½hr., 3 per day 10:45am-6:45pm, €8.80); **Lisboa** (1¼hr., 9 per day 7am-6:45pm, €3.70); **Óbidos** (1½hr., 4 per day 6:30am-2:45pm, €4.30); **Porto** (4hr., 7 per day 10:45am-7:45pm, €12.70).

Taxis: Scaltaxis (☎243 33 29 19) has a stand across the park from the bus station.

▛ ◪ ORIENTATION AND PRACTICAL INFORMATION

The densely packed streets between **Praça Sá da Bandeira** (the main square) and **Portas do Sol** park form the core of Santarém. **Rua Capelo e Ivens,** which begins at the *praça*, is home to the tourist office and many *residencials* (hostels).

Tourist Office: R. Capelo e Ivens, 63 (☎243 30 44 37). Maps and info on accommodations and transportation. Informative brochure on festivals, sights, and history. Friendly staff speaks English, Spanish, and French. Open M 9am-12:30pm and 2-5:30pm, Tu-Fri 9am-7pm, Sa-Su 10am-12:30pm and 2:30-5:30pm.

Currency Exchange: Caixa Geral de Depósitos, (☎243 33 30 07), at R. Dr. Texeira Guedes and R. Capelo e Ivens. €7.50 commission. Open M-F 8:30am-3pm.

Laundromat: Tintoreria Americana, R. João Afonso, 15 (☎243 32 45 77). Open M-F 9am-1pm and 3-7pm.

Police: Av. do Brasil (☎243 32 20 22), near the bus station.

Santarém

▲ **ACCOMMODATIONS**
Pensão José Rodrigues, **6**
Pousada da Juventude, **8**
Residencial Beirante, **2**
Residencial Muralha, **3**

● **FOOD**
O Saloio, **4**
Pastelaria Eureka, **3**
Restaurante Quintal do
  Beco, **7**

★ **NIGHTLIFE**
Cervejão, **1**

Pharmacy: Farmácia Veríssimo, R. Capelo e Ivens, 72 (☎243 33 02 30). Open M-F 9am-7pm, Sa 9am-1pm.

Hospital: Av. Bernardo Santareno (☎243 30 02 00). Take R. Alexandre Herculano until it becomes Av. Bernardo Santareno. English spoken.

Internet Access: Instituto Português da Juventude, downstairs from the youth hostel. 30min. limit. Free. Open M-F 9am-8pm.

Post Office: (☎243 30 97 00), on the corner of Lg. Cândido dos Reis and R. Dr. Teixeira Guedes. Open M-F 8:30am-6:30pm, Sa 9am-12:30pm. **Postal Code:** 2000.

▌ ACCOMMODATIONS

Prices are fairly high year-round, increasing during the Ribatejo Fair (10 days starting in early June). The tourist office can help find a room in a private house.

Pousada da Juventude de Santarém (HI), Av. Grp. Forcados Amadores de Santarém, 1 (☎/fax 243 39 19 14). Follow Av. Dom Afonso Henriques as it curves past the stadium-style bullring; the hostel is upstairs from the Instituto Português da Juventude. Rooms are clean and comfortable. Breakfast included (8:30-10am). Reception 8am-noon and 6pm-midnight. Check-in after 6pm. Check-out before 11am. Lockout 11am-6pm. HI card required, available at front desk (€2). Mid-June to mid-Sept. dorms €9.50; doubles with bath €23. Mid-Sept. to mid-June €7.50/€19. ❶

RIBATEJO AND ESTREMADURA

THE LOCAL STORY

G-RATED

The story of Santarém's founding could have been a fairy tale read to children at night: all the elements are there, including a beautiful girl, frustrated love, bitter jealousy, a little bit of magic, and no sex whatsoever. The daughter of two 7th-century nobles, Iria was sent to a convent at an early age to live a life of purity and devotion. She soon fell in love with a nobleman named Britaldo. The two contented themselves with innocent hand-holding and tried to live happily ever after. Enter Remígio, a former teacher of Iria's, now madly in love with her as well. Cue the jealous rage. Remígio decided that if he couldn't have Iria no one should, and slipped a potion into her soup that made her appear pregnant. Needless to say, sex is a convent no-no, and medieval moral codes were merciless, so the townspeople cast Iria into the river. Her spiritual sisters formed a search party and eventually discovered her body washed up on the shore. Before anyone could give her a proper burial, however, the river rose, leaving the girl with a watery grave. Santarém was founded on this tragic site, and it's name derived from "Santa Iria." A statue of Iria by the river marks the spot where she is said to lie even today.

Pensão José Rodrigues, Tr. do Froes, 14 (☎243 32 30 88). An elderly woman rents cheap, clean rooms in a central location. Popular during the summer, so call ahead. Singles €15; doubles €25. Prices drop €5 in winter. ●

Residencial Muralha, R. Pedro Canavarro, 12 (☎243 32 23 99; fax 32 94 77). Comfortable rooms, all with TV and large private bath. Reserve a week ahead in summer. Singles €30; doubles €35-40. ●

Residencial Beirante, R. Alexandre Herculano, 5 (☎243 32 25 47; fax 33 38 45). Clean rooms with all the perks, including phone, A/C, TV, breakfast, and even a blow-dryer in the tiled bathrooms. Call ahead in summer. Singles €30; doubles €40-45. ●

◖ FOOD

Eateries cluster around the parallel **Rua Capelo e Ivens** and **Rua Serpa Pinto.** The **municipal market** in the pagoda on Lg. Infante Santo near Jardim da República, sells fresh produce. (Open M-Sa 8am-2pm.) **Supermercado Minipreço,** R. Pedro Canavarro, 31, is on the street leading from the bus station to R. Capelo e Ivens. (Open M-Sa 9am-8pm.) **Restaurante Quintal do Beco** ●, Beco dos Fieis de Deus, 17, is hidden in an alley. This unique establishment serves tasty seafood, buffet-style; you are charged by weight, with each 100 grams costing €1.40 during lunchtime. Dinner specials for €5-10 are also available. (☎243 32 39 99. Open M-Sa 9am-11pm. AmEx/MC/V.) **Pastelaria Eureka** ●, R. Capelo e Ivens, 12, makes a wide variety of pastries (€0.60), not to mention some of the best bread in town. It is located conveniently right next to the main square. (☎243 32 23 16. Open M-F 8am-7pm, Sa 8am-1:30pm.) The local favorite for meals is **O Saloio** ●, Tr. do Montalvo, 11, off R. Capelo e Ivens, where they serve a variety of meat (duck, salmon, lamb, beef) and a mean *caldeirada*. (☎243 32 76 56. Entrees €5-8. Open M-Sa 10am-9pm.)

◉ SIGHTS

PORTAS DO SOL. This paradise of flowers and fountains surrounded by Moorish walls is best visited on a clear day, when they offer a striking view of the Alentejo plains and the river below. A great place for a family outing; leave the kids at the playground and sit on the walls while soaking in the romance. *(Take R. São Martinho and bear right on Av. 5 de Outubro after the closed art deco theater. Open daily 8am-11pm. Free.)*

PRAÇA VISCONDE DE SERRA PILAR. Centuries ago, Christians, Moors, and Jews gathered for social and business affairs in this *praça*. *(Take R. Serpa Pinto from Pr. Sá da Bandeira.)* The 12th-century **Igreja de Marvila**, off the *praça*, was revamped in the late 17th century with traditional ornamentation of the era. Don't be fooled, then, by the white-washed simplicity outside; the *azulejo*-covered interior is dazzling, as is the Manueline entrance. *(Open Tu-Su 9:30am-12:30pm and 2-5:30pm. Free.)* The early Gothic purity of nearby **Igreja da Graça** contrasts sharply with Marvila's over-flowing exuberance; construction began in 1380 on the orders of the first Earls of Ourém, and the cloister dates back to the 16th century. Within the church, in the **Capela de São João Evangelista**, lies Pedro Cabral, the explorer who "discovered" Brazil and one of the few to live long enough to return to his homeland. *(Open Tu-W and Sa-Su 9:30am-12:30pm and 2-5:30pm, Th-F 10am-12:30pm and 2-5:30pm. Free.)*

TORRE DAS CABAÇAS. The medieval **Torre das Cabaças** (Tower of the Gourds) was named after the eight earthen bowls installed in the 16th century to amplify the bell's ring. Inside the tower is the **Museu de Tempo** (Time Museum), with clocks and sundials from various times and civilizations. *(Take R. São Martinho from Pr. Visconde de Serra Pilar. Open Tu-Su 9:30am-12:30pm and 2-5:30pm. €1.)*

🎭 ENTERTAINMENT

Around the corner and two blocks down from the bus station is **Cervejão**, Av. António Maria Baptista, 10. The name means "big beer," and lots of it can be found here. (☎243 26 43 33. Beer €0.70. Whiskey shots €2. Open M-Sa 11am-midnight.) For unrestrained daytime partying, try the **Feira Nacional de Agricultura** (also known as the Feira do Ribatejo). Thousands of people come for a ten-day orgy of markets, bullfighting, and farmers racing tiny horses for personal glory. The party starts on June 4, running until the 11th or 13th.

ÓBIDOS   ☎262

A charismatic town of 200 hidden behind the walls of a massive 12th-century castle, Óbidos's charm is matched only by the friendliness of its residents, almost all of whom rent rooms to tourists or work in souvenir shops. Though the town's persona is inextricably tied to the castle and the tourist attention that it draws, that is not to say that Óbidos has lost its true identity; a walk through the narrow, cobblestone streets parallel to R. Direita reveals locals converging around cafes and children playing in the streets, oblivious to the presence of visitors. The **castelo** on the coast, originally a Moorish fortress rebuilt in the 12th century, gradually lost its importance as the ocean receded. Although the castle itself—now a luxury *pousada*—is open only to guests, everyone is free to walk the 1.5km of its **walls**. The **Igreja de Santa Maria**, to the right of the post office in the central *praça*, displays Josefa de Óbidos's vivid canvases off the main altar. Built in 1148 under the orders of Portugal's first king, Dom Afonso Henriques, the church was also the site of the 1441 wedding of 10-year-old Dom Afonso V to his 8-year-old cousin, Isabel. (Open daily Apr.-Sept. 9:30am-12:30pm and 2:30-7pm; Oct.-Mar. 9:30am-12:30pm and 2:30-5pm. Mass Su at noon. Free.)

There are several private rooms for rent in Óbidos, as advertised by the signs on and around R. Direita, but it may be difficult to find a good price. **Casa dos Castros** ❶, R. Direita, 83-85, has the cheapest rooms in town. Run by an elderly couple, rooms are simple yet clean; watch out for the low ceilings. (☎262 95 93 28. Doubles €25, with bath €30.) **ÓbidoSol** ❷, R. Direita, 40, is a charming 17th-century home that has three rooms with window seats, clean wood floors, an *azulejo*-covered common bath, and a large living room. Reservations recommended, especially during the summer. (☎262 95 97 35. June-Sept. singles €30; doubles €35; triples €50. Oct.-May €25/€35/€40. Request a €5 discount if you are traveling alone.) **Restaurants** (most with tourist prices) and several **markets** cluster on and around R. Direita. Eat light and save your euros for Óbidos's signature *ginja*, a delicious cherry liqueur; stores on R. Direita sell bottles for €5-8.50.

The **tourist office** is a small, green cottage near the entrance to the *castelo*; from the bus stop, go up the steps and turn left. The office is right next to the Porta da Vila restaurant. The staff speaks English, Spanish, and French, and provides basic information, luggage storage, and bus schedules. (☎262 95 92 31; fax 95 50 01. Open May-Sept. M-F 9:30am-6:30pm, Sa-Su 9:30am-7:30pm; Oct.-Apr. daily 9:30am-6pm.) **Buses** stop at the town gate and are more convenient than trains. Connections to: **Caldas da Rainha** (20min., 23 per day 7:30am-9:20pm, €1.30); **Lisboa** (1¼hr.; M-F 7 per day 7:05am-6pm, Sa-Su 5-7 per day via Caldas da Rainha; €6.20); **Peniche** (40min.; M-F 10 per day 8:10am-7:40pm, Sa 7 per day 8:10am-7:40pm, Su 5 per day 9:40am-7:40pm; €2.20). No bus schedules are posted here; ask at the tourist office.

PENICHE ☎262

Endowed with beautiful beaches and delicious seafood, Peniche's personality is clearly defined by its interaction with the ocean; here, beach towel-clutching sunbathers pass leather-skinned fishermen on the way to the town's most popular sunsoaking spots. Whether you come to relax on its beaches or learn about its history, Peniche is an excellent weekend rest spot.

▐▀ TRANSPORTATION

Buses: Peniche is accessible only by bus. The station is on R. Dr. Ernesto Moureira (☎262 78 21 33), on an isthmus outside the town walls. Buses run to: **Alcobaça** (1¾hr., 2:45pm, €7.20) via **Caldas da Rainha** (1hr., 3 per day 7am-6pm, €5.20); **Leiria** (2hr., 7 per day 7am-6:30pm, €8.90) via Caldas da Rainha; **Lisboa** (2hr., 13 per day 6am-10:30pm, €6.20); **Nazaré** (1½hr., 3 per day 7am-6pm, €6.70); **Porto** (6½hr., 12 per day 6am-6pm, €12.70); **Santarém** (1½hr., 7 per day 6am-5pm, €9.90) via Caldas da Rainha.

Taxis: (☎262 78 44 24 or 78 29 10) in Pr. J. Rodrigues Pereira and Lg. Bispo Mariana.

✳⃣ ▐▚ ORIENTATION AND PRACTICAL INFORMATION

Most of Peniche's services are situated in or around the grid of streets between **Largo Bispo Mariana** and the **fortaleza** on the coast. **Praça Jacob Rodrigues Pereira** marks the center of town, near the tourist office and the start of **Avenida do Mar,** which runs along the river to the docks and fishing port; at night, the streets along **Rua José Estévão** swarm with barhoppers, as several small local bars blast music until the wee hours.

Tourist Office: R. Alexandre Herculano (☎/fax 262 78 95 71). From the bus station, go left and cross the river over Ponte Velha to the right. Turn left on R. Alexandre Herculano, walk alongside the public garden, and follow signs to the office. English, Spanish, French, and Italian spoken. **Luggage storage** (for a few hours) available. Open daily July-Sept. 9am-8pm; June 9am-1pm and 2-6pm; Oct.-May 10am-1pm and 2-5pm.

Bank: Caixa Geral de Depósitos, on R. Alexandre Herculano. Open M-F 8:30am-3pm. 24hr. **ATMs** line R. Alexandre Herculano and Av. do Mar.

Police: R. Heróis Ultramar (☎262 78 95 55).

Hospital: R. Gen. Humberto Delgado (☎262 78 09 00). From the tourist office, turn right and take the 1st left onto R. Arquitecto Paulino Montez; walk past the post office, then take a right onto R. Gen. Humberto Delgado. English spoken.

Internet Access: PlayZone, R. Ramiro Matos Bilhau, 5 (☎/fax 262 78 48 53). Turn right from the tourist office onto R. Alexandre Herculano, left onto R. Arquitecto Paulino Montez, right onto R. Dr. Luís de Ataide, and then left. €1.20 for 30min., €2 per hr. Open M-F 10am-10pm, Sa 2:30-10pm, Su 3-7:30pm.

Post Office: R. Arquitecto Paulino Montez (☎262 78 00 60). From the tourist office, turn right on R. Alexandre Herculano, left on R. Arquitecto Paulino Montez, and walk 3 blocks. **Posta Restante** and **fax.** Open M-F 9am-6pm. **Postal Code:** 2520.

▐ ACCOMMODATIONS

Peniche's budget accommodations are located above restaurants of the same name; look for signs to find a *residencial* on or behind Av. do Mar. They fill quickly, though, especially from June to August, so try to arrive early in the day. Persistent elderly matrons renting rooms in their private houses gather in Pr. Jacob Rodrigues Pereira and meet the buses as they arrive. Rooms in private homes may be the best budget options, but insist on seeing them first and inquire about amenities. Learn the sport of bargaining: rarely accept their first offer.

Residencial Marítimo, R. José Estêvão, 109 (☎262 78 28 50), off the *praça* in front of the fortress. Newly renovated rooms, all with 42-channel TVs, hardwood floors, and private, beautifully tiled bathrooms. Buffet breakfast included. Reserve ahead. Aug. singles €25; doubles €45. July €20/€30. Sept.-June €15/€25. ❷

Residencial Maciel, R. José Estêvão, 38 (☎262 78 46 85), just off the *praça*, behind the church. 10 elegant, spacious rooms with complimentary bottled water and cable TV. Quite chic for Peniche. Buffet breakfast included. June-Sept. singles €40; doubles €50. Oct.-May €20/€30. MC/V. ❹

Peniche Praia Municipal Campground, Estrada Marginal Norte (☎262 78 34 60; www.penichepraia.pt). 2km outside town, at least a 30min. walk from the center. From the bus station, turn left onto Av. Porto de Pesca to reach EN 114, following it through the traffic circle and past the waterpark; the campsite is on the left. Or take a taxi (approx. €3 from downtown). About a 15min. walk from the beautiful rock formations of Peniche and decorated with old fishing boats. Free hot showers and swimming pool. Open year-round. €3.10 per person, €1.55 per child ages 5-10, under 5 free, €3.10-3.90 per tent, €2.80 per car. ❶

◖ FOOD

Restaurants lining **Avenida do Mar** serve excellent fresh grilled seafood. Despite the multilingual menus, the prices are reasonable and there are plenty of locals mixed in among tourists. Peniche's *sardinhas* (sardines) are exceptional, as are the seafood *espetadas* (skewers). The outdoor cafes on **Praça Jacob Rodrigues Pereira** are lively, particularly on Sundays when the rest of town is quiet. The **market,** on R. António da Conceição Bento, stocks fresh produce (open Tu-Su 7am-1pm).

Ristorante Il Boccone, Av. do Mar, 4 (☎262 78 24 12). Fantastic pizza (€5-8) and enormous pasta dishes (€5-8.50) provide a welcome reprieve from seafood. Open Tu-Su noon-4pm and 6:30pm-midnight. ❷

Restaurante Mira Mar, Av. do Mar, 42 (☎/fax 262 78 16 66). One of the best of the string of nearby restaurants, this place is decorated tastefully with an ocean motif; admire the seashells and pictures of life under the sea. Fish entrees €5.50-9.50, meat entrees €5.50-8. Excellent *crème de marisco* (shellfish chowder; €2). Open daily noon-3:30pm and 7-11pm. AmEx/MC/V. ❷

RIBATEJO AND ESTREMADURA

Café Oceano, Pr. Jacob Rodrigues Pereira, 12-13 (☎262 78 23 15). Popular local hangout. Polish off a sandwich (€2-3.50) followed by coffee (€0.40-0.85) or a scoop of gourmet ice cream (€1) inside the cafe or out on the terrace. Specialty *pasteis de Peniche* (almond pastries; €0.70). Open daily 8am-midnight. ❶

🔘 SIGHTS

FORTALEZA. António Salazar, Portugal's longtime dictator, chose Peniche's formidable 16th-century fortress as one of his four high-security political prisons. Today it houses the **Museu de Peniche,** the highlight of which is a chilling walk through the cells of Salazar's prison, including replicas of the torture room, interrogation chamber, and descriptions of the horrors inmates faced. In an annex outside the museum, a small anti-Fascist exhibition traces the dictatorship and underground resistance from the seizure of power in 1926 to the coup that toppled the regime on April 25, 1974. *(Campo da República, near the dock where boats leave for the Ilhas Berlengas. Fortaleza open Tu-Su 10:30am-12:30pm and 2-6pm. Free. Museum ☎/fax 262 78 01 16. Same hours as Fortaleza. €1.30, under 16 free.)*

BEACHES. For sun and surf, head to any of the town's three beaches. The windy **Praia de Peniche de Cima,** along the north crescent, is the highlight of the three, with beautiful white sand and warm water. It merges with another beach at **Baleal,** a small fishing village popular with tourists. The southern **Praia do Molho Leste** marks the entrance to **Super-tubos;** also known as the "Portuguese Pipeline" (after the famous Hawaiian beach with huge waves), Super-tubos is perfect for watching daring surfers risk bodily injury on the unforgiving beachbreak. Beyond it is crowded **Praia da Consolação,** a favorite of Portuguese families on weekend getaways. The strange humidity at this beach and its hot rocks supposedly cure bone diseases. Watch out for elderly visitors seeking relief from their afflictions, often wearing nothing but expectation on their faces. *(Buses to the beaches 7am-7pm, €1.10. Check with the tourist office for changes.)*

🌸 🔘 FESTIVALS AND NIGHTLIFE

Peniche may seem sleepy during the day, but the town's nightlife heats up from the after-dinner hours until late, especially during the summer. For daytime party-seekers, Peniche's biggest festival starts on August 6, when boats bedecked in wreaths of flags and flowers sail into the harbor to launch the two-day **Festa de Nossa Senhora da Boa Viagem,** celebrating the protector of sailors and fishermen. The town lets loose with carnival rides, live entertainment, wine, and seafood, continuing the festivities that begin two weeks before the launch. September brings the **Sabores do Mar** festival, and with it a celebration of all things seaworthy, including discounts at restaurants; look for festivities to begin on September 2.

■ **Adego do Becas,** Lg. da Ribeira, 24 (☎262 18 91 14), at the end of Av. do Mar, behind the last restaurant on the right. Hugely popular with locals, it famously combines 2 favorites: €1 beers and €6 steaks, prepared in a variety of ways. Come after 1am, which is when it really gets going, although it may be hard to get a table by that time. The basement dance floor and rooftop terrace attract those looking for versatile party space. Open daily 1pm-3am.

Bar No. 1, R. Afonso Albuquerque, 14 (☎262 78 45 41), close to the intersection with R. José Estévão. Popular with both tourists and locals, the owner mans the DJ booth from midnight-2am. Lively crowds turn the tiny space into a miniature dance floor while he plays an interesting mix of Portuguese pop and Brazilian samba. The bar hosts exhibits of local art. Beer and shots €1-1.50. Mixed drinks €3. Open daily noon-2am.

HIKING

To truly enjoy the ocean air, hike around the peninsula (8km, 2hr.). Start at **Papôa,** just north of Peniche. From Pr. Jacob Rodrigues Pereira, take R. Alexandre Herculano and then Av. 25 de Abril and follow the signs along the coast. Stopping occasionally along the wall at the edge of the road, you can observe the hundreds of playful fish. At Papôa, stroll out to the tip, where majestic orange cliffs rise from a swirling blue sea. Nearby lie the sparse ruins of an old fortress, **Forte da Luz.** As you pass the campsite (20-30min. later), the pancake-shaped rocks piled atop one another inspire interesting stories about their origin. The endpoint of the peninsula, **Cabo Carvoeiro,** is the most popular of Peniche's natural sights, as the view of the Ilhas Berlengas below is unparalleled.

◤ DAYTRIP FROM PENICHE

ILHAS BERLENGAS

Several companies operate boats from Peniche's public dock. The largest is Viamar ferry (☎262 78 56 46; fax 78 38 47. Ticket booth open 8:30am-5:30pm), which offers 2 crossings per day. (40min.; July-Aug. 2 per day 9:30am and 4:30pm; return trips at 11:30am and 6:30pm. Sept. 1-15 10am, returns 4:30pm. Same-day round-trip ticket €17, children 5-12 €10, under 5 free.) To stay overnight, buy a €11 ticket each way. Reserve 3-4 days in advance. Arrive 1hr. in advance, 2½hr. in Aug. The crossing from Peniche to the island is notoriously rough; expect to witness or experience sea sickness. Trips with Berlenga Turpesca (☎262 78 99 60) include visits to the caves, although scheduling can be difficult. €17.

The rugged Ilhas Berlengas rise out of the Atlantic Ocean 12km northwest of Peniche. The main island of Berlenga and archipelago of several smaller islands (the Farilhões, Estelas, and Forcados) are inhabited by thousands of screeching seagulls. The **Reserva Natural da Berlenga** is home to wild black rabbits, lizards, and a very small fishing community. Unfortunately for visitors, the *reserva* is off-limits to non-researchers. Nevertheless, the islands' real prize is the rock formations that compose them. Deep gorges, natural tunnels, and rocky caves carve through Berlenga, and the main path (2km) allows for some scrambling and exploration. The only beach accessible by foot lies in a small cove by the landing dock. For beachgoers willing to brave the cold, dips in the calm water bring abrupt respite from the heat. Hikers can trek to the island's highest point for a gorgeous view of the 17th-century **Forte de São João Batista,** now a luxury hostel run by the Associação Amigos da Berlenga (AAB). The entire hike lasts no more than an hour.

NAZARÉ   ☎262

Home to a beautiful three kilometer stretch of golden sand and calm turquoise water, it's no surprise that Nazaré (pop. 16,000) has become one of the Ribatejo's main tourist attractions, and the townsfolk have responded en masse. As you walk through the beachside Av. da República, you can't help but encounter persistent old ladies in black shawls offering you rooms, charming restaurants with beautiful views of the beach and tantalizing seafood, and scores of artisans hawking seashell necklaces. Mostly frequented by the urban Portuguese, Nazaré is a pleasant alternative to the nonstop partying of the Algarve.

▭ TRANSPORTATION

Buses: Av. Vieira Guimarães (☎808 20 03 70), perpendicular to Av. da República. More convenient than trains (6km away). To: **Alcobaça** (20min., 6 per day 7:10am-6:45pm, €1.40); **Batalha** (50min., 4 per day 7:10am-8pm, €2.70); **Caldas da Rainha** (1¼hr.,

10 per day 6:30am-7:15pm, €2.50); **Coimbra** (2hr., 6 per day 6:25am-7:25pm, €8.90); **Fátima** (1½hr., 4 per day 7:10am-8pm, €3.50); **Leiria** (1¼hr., 9 per day 6:25am-7:25pm, €2.80); **Lisboa** (2hr., 10 per day 6:50am-8pm, €7.30); **Peniche** (1½hr., 5 per day 11:15am-8pm, €6.70); **Porto** (3½hr., 5 per day 6:25am-7:25pm, €11.20); **São Martinho do Porto** (20min., 10 per day 6:30am-7:15pm, €1.50); **Tomar** (1½hr., 4 per day 7:10am-8pm, €5).

Taxis: Praça de Taxi, ☎ 262 55 13 63.

■✚ 🔑 ORIENTATION AND PRACTICAL INFORMATION

All of the action in Nazaré takes place along the beach. The two main squares, **Praça Sousa Oliveira** and **Praça Dr. Manuel de Arriaga,** are near the cliffside away from the fishing port. The cliffside funicular and a winding road lead up to the **Sítio,** the old town, which preserves a sense of calm and tradition less prevalent in the crowded resort below. To get to the tourist office from the bus station, take a right toward the beach and then another onto Av. da República; the office is a five minute walk along the shore between the two *praças.*

Tourist Office: (☎ 262 56 11 94), beachside on Av. da República. Provides maps and information on entertainment and transportation. English, Spanish, and French spoken. Open daily July-Aug. 10am-10pm; Sept. 10am-8pm; Oct.-March 9:30am-1pm and 2:30-6pm; Apr.-June 15 10am-1pm and 3-7pm; June 15-30 10am-1pm and 3-8pm.

Bank: Major banks lie on and around Av. da República. **Millennium BCP,** Av. Manuel Remigio (☎ 262 56 90 02), right on the beach. Open M-F 8:30am-3:30pm.

Laundromat: Pelfatima, R. Banco Martins, 3. Right off Av. da República. Open M-F 9:30am-1pm and 3-7pm, Sa 9:30am-1pm.

Police (☎ 262 55 12 68), 1 block from the bus station at Av. Vieira Guimarães and R. Sub-Vila.

Hospital: Hospital da Confraria da Nossa Senhora de Nazaré (☎ 262 55 01 00), in the Sítio district on the cliffs above the town center. **Centro de Saúde** (☎ 262 56 91 20), Urbanizacão Caixins, in the new part of town.

Pharmacy: Farmácia Silvéria, R. Adrião Batalha, 41-43 (☎ 262 55 23 94). Between the two main *praças.* Open M-F 9am-1pm and 3-7pm, Sa 9am-1pm.

Internet Access: Centro Cultural, Av. Manuel Remigio (☎ 262 56 19 44), the extension of Av. da República by the port. Free. Open M-F 9:30am-1pm and 2-7pm, Sa-Su 3-7pm.

Post Office: Av. da Independência Nacional, 2 (☎ 262 56 91 06). From Pr. Sousa Oliveira, walk up R. Mouzinho de Albuquerque. 1 block past Pensão Central. **Posta Restante** and **fax.** Open M-F 9:30am-12:30pm and 2:30-6pm. **Postal Code:** 2450.

🏠 🛏 ACCOMMODATIONS AND CAMPING

Nazaré is inhabited by the most aggressive room-renters in Portugal; they swarm arriving buses at the station and line Av. da República proffering their homes to sleepy tourists; make sure that they are certified by the municipality before even beginning to bargain with them. Use the buyer's market to your advantage, and bargain with the same aggressive attention with which they court you. Agree on a price before seeing the room, but don't settle the deal until afterward. In summer, take nothing over €25. For less stressful lodging, look above the restaurants in Pr. Dr. Manuel de Arriaga and Pr. Sousa Oliveira.

▨ **Pensão Ideal,** R. Adrião Batalha, 98 (☎262 55 13 79), between the 2 main *praças*. 5 rooms with high ceilings, mirrors, and comfortable beds share a clean bath with retro linoleum. See if they are offering *pensão completa:* a double room and 3 meals in the restaurant for 2 people (€70-75). Reception 10am-10pm in the restaurant downstairs. July-Sept. doubles €25; triples €35-40. Sept.-May €15-20/€30-35. ❶

Vila Turística Conde Fidalgo, Av. da Independência Nacional, 21-A (☎262 55 23 61), 3 blocks uphill from Pr. Sousa Oliveira. The best option for families and groups, and a favorite of windsurfers. Private apartments come with TV, kitchen, refrigerator, microwave, bathrooms, and more. Large, comfortable rooms have flowered curtains and white metal beds. Reception 9am-1am. Reservations are absolutely necessary; 50% pre-payment required if far in advance. Aug. singles €40; doubles €45, with kitchen €70. July €30/€35/€60. Sept.-June €15-20/€25-30/€25. ❷

Camping: Vale Paraíso, Estrada Nacional, 242 (☎262 56 18 00), 2½km out of town in a wooded area. Take the buses to Alcobaça or Leiria (10min., 12 per day 7am-7pm). Swimming pools, restaurant-bar, supermarket, occasional Internet access (€2 per 30min., €3 per hr.), and laundry (€7 per load). Pool open Apr.-Oct.; June-Sept. €2; Apr.-May and Oct. free. Free showers. June-Sept. €3.80 per person, €3-4.70 per tent, €3 per car. Oct.-May €2.90/€2.50-3.70/€2.50. AmEx/MC/V. ❶

◗ FOOD

For groceries, check out the **market** across from the bus station. (Open July-Sept. daily 8am-1pm; Oct.-June Tu-Su 8am-1pm.) **Supermarkets,** such as **Supermercado Ecoloja,** line R. Sub-Vila, parallel to Av. da República. (☎262 56 18 87. Open daily June-Aug. 9am-10pm; Sept.-May 9am-8pm.)

▨ **Casa Marquês,** R. Gil Vicente (☎262 55 16 80), directly behind Pr. Dr. Manuel Arriaga. Slightly hidden yet overwhelmingly popular, Marquês is packed with locals and tourists. The cook has prepared *caldeirada* (fish stew; €7) for over 25 years, making it one of the best recipes in a town known for the best *caldeirada* in Portugal. Other dishes €5-8; good seafood *especialidades*. Open daily 11am-midnight, but often closed 5-7pm. ❷

0 Borgas, R. Mouzinho de Albuquerque, 4 (☎262 57 91 03), near Pr. Sousa Oliveira. Bright and roomy, this upscale restaurant serves fish, but specializes in steak. *Bife na lage,* seasoned steak grilled on a heated rock at the diner's table, is their specialty (€10). Other entrees €8-12. Open daily 1pm-midnight. MC/V. ❸

Pastelaria Batel, R. Mouzinho de Albuquerque, 2 (☎262 55 11 47). The best-known pastry shop in Nazaré, with a 34-year history. The place to try sweet local specialties. All pastries €0.70. Try the *tamares* (little boats with custard filling capped with chocolate), *sardinhas* (flaky pastry, not fish), and *Nazarenos* (almond pastry). Open June-Aug. daily 8am-2am; Sept.-May M-Tu and Th-Su 8am-2am. MC/V. ❶

◖ ◗ BEACHES AND ENTERTAINMENT

Nazaré's main attraction is the expansive and windy **beach.** With grainy, golden sand and water that's a pretty shade of green, this is where the action takes place during the day, with several volleyball, racquetball and soccer games going on constantly. After catching some rays, take the **funicular** (3min.; every 15min. 7:15am-9:30pm, every 30min. 9:30pm-midnight; 1-way €0.70), which runs from R. Elevador off Av. da República to the **Sítio,** the clifftop area of Nazaré. For centuries, the Sítio constituted the whole of Nazaré; the tide below could not be trusted. Now, uneven cobbled streets, weathered buildings, and staggering views provide the perfect ambience for a picnic.

THE LOCAL STORY

EAT YOUR HEART OUT, DON JUAN

There's love and then there's *love*. While a prince, Dom Pedro I fell head over heels for Inês de Castro, the daughter of a Spanish nobleman and lady-in-waiting to his first wife. Pedro's father, Afonso IV, steadfastly opposed the romance, afraid that such an alliance would open the Portuguese throne to Spanish domination. True to the fashion of a disobedient son, Pedro fled with Inês to Bragança, where they were secretly wed. Afonso's vengeance was cruel; he had Inês killed, plunging Pedro headfirst into depression.

Upon ascending to the throne two years later, Pedro personally ripped out the hearts of the men who had slit his wife's throat and proceeded to eat them, earning himself the nickname "Pedro the Cruel." In a macabre ceremony, he had Inês's body exhumed and officially deemed her his queen; legend has it that he even made his court kiss her rotting hand. Thankfully, he had her reinterred in a beautifully carved tomb in his favorite monastery, the Mosteiro de Santa Maria de Alcobaça. Pedro's remains soon joined his beloved Inês, in an equally exquisite tomb next to hers. The inscription on their tombs reads, *"Até ao fim do mundo"* (until the end of the world).

Cafes in Pr. Sousa Oliveira teem with people past midnight. The intimate **Ta Bar Es,** R. de Rio Maior, 20-22, off R. Mouzinho de Albuquerque near Pr. Dr. Manuel de Arriaga, is a mellow haven from the sun by day, but livens up with *bossa nova* and traditional Portuguese music most summer evenings after 11pm. Ta Bar Es also serves a variety of pizzas for €5-7. (☎262 56 23 19. Coffee €0.50. Before 7pm beer €1.50, mixed drinks €3-4. After 7pm beer €1.50-2.50, mixed drinks €3.50-4.50. Open daily 2pm-4am. Closed Nov. 1-15.)

On Saturday afternoons in May and June, locals dress in traditional outfits and haul the fishing nets out of the water, enacting the old-fashioned technique in an event known as **Arte Xávega,** followed by an exciting fish auction open to the public. During the summer, look out for late-night **folk music** gatherings on the beach. **Bullfights** are also popular; Nazaré is on the schedule that brings *corridas* to a different city in the province each summer weekend (usually Sa 10pm; tickets from €27). Bullfights occur the first three Saturdays in June, July, and August.

⬛ DAYTRIPS FROM NAZARÉ

ALCOBAÇA

Buses are the best way to reach Alcobaça. The bus station on Av. Manuel da Silva Carolino (☎262 58 22 21) offers service to: Batalha (30min., 8 per day 7:30am-7:10pm, €2.20); Coimbra (2hr., 4:25pm, €8.80); Leiria (1hr., 7 per day 7:30am-7:10pm, €2.70); Lisboa (2hr.; M-F 5 per day, Sa-Su 3 per day 6:30am-6pm; €7.80); Nazaré (25min., 12-15 per day 7:30am-8:20pm, €1.40); Porto (3½hr., 4:25pm, €10.80).

A sleepy town in the hills not too far from the coast, Alcobaça welcomes thousands of visitors each year for one reason: its dominating ◪**Mosteiro de Santa Maria de Alcobaça,** the oldest church in Portugal. The town was founded in 1153, following Dom Afonso Henriques's expulsion of the Moors. The king granted the land to Cistercian monks for a monastery, an attempt to secure Christianity in the region. Slaves and monks began construction in 1178, with additions continuing over the course of several centuries. Today it is the largest building of the Cistercian order in Europe. In the smaller naves adjacent to the towering central one, the **tombs** of Dom Pedro I and his wife, Inês de Castro, display sophisticated carvings, immortalizing one of Portugal's great, twisted royal love stories (see **Eat Your Heart Out, Don Juan,** left). Surrounding the monastery's cloisters are numerous Gothic rooms, most notably the **Sala dos Monges** (Monks' Hall), and the immense **kitchen** and **refectory,** where the monks could roast more than six oxen at a time. Also check out the neo-Gothic **Royal Pantheon,** where queens Urraca and Beatriz are buried along with young princes Fernando, Sancho, and Vicente, as well as the **Hall of Kings,** where statues of several past monarchs line the walls. (☎262 50 51 20. Monastery and cloisters open daily Apr.-Sept. 9am-7pm; Oct.-Mar. 9am-5pm. €4.50, students ages 14-25 and seniors €2.30, under 14 free. Su before 2pm free.)

The **Museu da Vinha e do Vinho,** five minutes from the bus station on Estrada de Leiria (which branches off Av. dos Combatentes de Grande Guerra on the way out of town), houses a comprehensive exhibit about the history and methods of Portugal's wine industry; particularly interesting is their display on the history of port wine. The best exhibit, however, is participatory and involves free samples. (☎262 58 22 22. Open M-F 9am-12:30pm and 2-5:30pm. €1.50, students €0.75. Weekend visits for large groups available with reservation.)

The **tourist office** sits on the corner of Pr. 25 de Abril. Turn right out of the bus station and right onto Av. dos Combatentes de Grande Guerra, following the road towards the monastery, keeping the main garden to your left; the office is one block up and on the right. The staff hands out accommodation lists, maps, and guides to Alcobaça and surrounding areas. (☎262 58 23 77. English and French spoken. Free Internet access for 15min. Open daily Aug. 10am-7pm; May-July and Sept. 10am-1pm and 3-7pm; Oct.-Apr. 10am-1pm and 2-6pm.) Alcobaça can easily be appreciated as a daytrip, but should you have to spend the night, **Pensão Corações Unidos ❷,** R. Frei António Brandão, 39, off Pr. 25 de Abril, has 20 rooms with flower bedspreads, all with newly renovated bathrooms. (☎/fax 262 58 21 42. Breakfast included. Reception 8am-midnight. July-Sept. singles €20; doubles €40. Oct.-June €15/€30.) Their **restaurant ❶** serves typical yet touristy Portuguese food, including *frango na púcara* (chicken in sauce with vegetables; €6.50).

SÃO MARTINHO DO PORTO

Buses run to Nazaré (20min., 7 per day 9:30am-7:30pm, €1.35) and other towns. Schedules are posted in the tourist office. The bus stops on the main road leading into town.

Countless millennia of crashing surf hollowed out the surrounding coast to create the bay of São Martinho do Porto. Nearly enclosed on all sides by rolling hills and steep cliffs, the town lies at the base of the inlet, while its windless **beach,** populated with swim-

THE HIDDEN DEAL

SING IT, CISTER

Although the Cistercian order of monks is best known for the impressive Mosteiro de Santa Maria de Alcobaça, residents of Alcobaça know that these holy men have an appreciation of the arts that goes beyond elaborate marble coffins and gothic spires.

Every year, the Cistercian order sponsors the arts festival Cistermúsica, offering a series of free concerts and operas in the colossal Mosteiro. Last year's 12th such festival featured renowned Portuguese and international classical musicians and opera singers, bringing in several thousand spectators. The festival celebrates the town of Alcobaça and its rich history, also offering discussions and conferences on the importance of the lurid romance between Inês de Castro and Dom Pedro I (see **Eat Your Heart Out, Don Juan,** p. 756).

Taking place every Saturday and Sunday between May 15 and June 4, Cistermúsica offers one the opportunity to experience world class entertainment for free, as professional musicians perform pieces by Bach, Couperin, and Scarlatti among others.

For more information and for exact dates in 2005, ask the tourist office in Alcobaça (☎262 58 23 77, on the corner of Pr. 25 de Abril, in front of the Mosteiro).

mers, sweeps 3km along and around the bay, forming an almost perfect semicircle. Its red-roofed houses and palm-studded hillside give São Martinho do Porto an almost Mediterranean charm; it's an ideal escape from crowded Nazaré and Peniche. Vacationers disturb the peace somewhat in July and August, but not enough to make a visit here at that time unpleasant.

The **tourist office**, on Lg. Frederico Ulrich at the end of Av. 25 de Abril, provides a list of private rooms, which are generally the cheapest accommodation options. (☎262 98 91 10. Open June-Sept. Tu-Su 10am-1pm and 3-7pm; Oct.-May Tu-Su 10am-1pm and 2-7pm.) If a day at the beach calls for a night of quality relaxation, then **Pensão Atlântica ❹**, R. Miguel Bombarda, 6, just behind the tourist office, is the town's best bet. Newly decorated rooms come complete with cable TV, throw rugs, enormous bathrooms, and a varying buffet breakfast. Avoid staying here in August, and you'll get a steal. (☎262 98 01 51. Reserve ahead for July and Aug. July 15-Aug. 31 singles €50; doubles €75. May-June €30/€50; Sept.-Apr. €20/€30.)

LEIRIA ☎244

With 120,000 inhabitants, Leiria is one of Portugal's biggest cities; unlike most big cities, however, its accommodations are among the very best in quality and price that Portgual has to offer. An ancient castle overlooks the city from a hill, and a brand new soccer stadium, the Estádio Doutor Magalhães Pessoa, built especially for two Euro 2004 soccer games, sparkles below. Situated between Lisboa and Coimbra, Leiria was a strategic point during D. Afonso Henriques's campaign against the Moors; since its recapture in 1135, it has become one of the country's most charming cities. Leiria makes a practical base for exploring the region, with buses to nearby cities and the beaches of the Costa da Prata.

▐ TRANSPORTATION

Trains: The train station is 3km outside town (☎244 88 20 27). Buses run between the station and the tourist office (15min., every hr. 7:05am-7:20pm, €1). To: **Coimbra** (2hr., 7 per day 7am-9:20pm, €3.60); **Figueira da Foz** (1hr., 7 per day 7am-9:20pm, €4); **Lisboa** (1¾hr., 10 per day 7am-10pm, €7.60-8.50).

Buses (☎244 81 15 07), off Pr. Paulo VI, next to the main park and near the tourist office. Ticket office down the steps in back. Most convenient transport out of Leiria. Express buses are twice the price of regional buses. To: **Alcobaça** (50min., 6 per day 7:10am-6:30pm, €2.60); **Batalha** (20min., 9 per day 7:10am-7:10pm, €1.30); **Coimbra** (1hr., 11 per day 7:15am-2am, €6.50); **Fátima** (1hr., 20 per day 6:40am-7:05pm, €2.40); **Figueira da Foz** (1½hr., M-F 8 per day 7:55am-8:30pm, €3.90-6.50); **Lisboa** (2hr., 13 per day 6am-11pm, €7.80); **Nazaré** (1hr., 6-9 per day 7:20am-7:20pm, €2.60-6); **Porto** (3½hr., 10 per day 7:15am-2am, €10.20); **Santarém** (2hr., 5 per day 7:10am-7:15pm, €4.50-8.80); **Tomar** (1½hr., 8 per day 6:45am-6pm, €3.10-6.70).

Taxis: Many gather at the Jardim Luís de Camões (☎244 81 59 00 or 88 15 50).

✱ ▐ ORIENTATION AND PRACTICAL INFORMATION

The **Jardim Luís de Camões** is at the center of Leiria, while the castle is a 10min. climb from town.

Tourist Office: (☎244 84 87 70; fax 83 35 33), in the Jardim Luís de Camões, across the park from the bus station. Maps, accommodations lists, and a ▐ **precise model of Batalha's monastery** made entirely of sugar. Free short-term **luggage storage** and Internet access (15min. limit). English, French, and Spanish spoken. Open daily May-Sept. 10am-1pm and 3-7pm; Oct.-Apr. 10am-1pm and 2-6pm.

Laundromat: Ecosec Lavanderia, R. Capitão Mouzinho Albuquerque, 7 (☎244 83 36 38), behind Centro Comercial Maringá. €2.50 per kg, shirts and pants €2.80.

Police: Lg. São Pedro (☎244 85 98 30), next to the castle.

Hospital: Hospital de Santo André (☎244 81 70 00), on R. Olhalvas, on the way to Fátima. For non-emergencies, go to the closer **Serviço Atendimento Permanente** (☎244 81 13 90), Av. General Norton de Maxos. 30min. walk from the tourist office.

Internet Access: The city offers a convenient (and free) service at **Leiria Digital,** Lg. de Santana (☎244 81 50 91), in the pedestrian mall. 12 computers with fast connections. 1hr. time limit enforced only when people are waiting; gets crowded in the afternoon, so come early. Open M-F 10:30am-9:30pm, Sa 3-8pm.

Post Office: Downtown office (☎244 82 04 60), in Lg. Santana on Av. dos Combatentes da Grande Guerra, between the tourist office and the youth hostel. Label **Posta Restante** mail "Estação Santana." Open M-F 8:30am-12:30pm and 2-6pm. **Main office,** Av. Heróis de Angola, 99 (☎244 84 94 00), a bit farther away, past the bus station toward the mall. Open M-F 8:30am-12:30pm and 2-6:30pm, Sa 9am-12:30pm. **Postal Code:** 2400.

⚑ ACCOMMODATIONS

Staying in Leiria, even during high season, is a chance to score big with amenities without spending your week's lunch money. The list below includes the best options, although services and prices are fairly consistent throughout the town.

▨ Residencial Dom Dinis, Tr. Tomar, 2 (☎244 81 53 42; fax 82 35 52). Turn left after exiting the tourist office, cross the bridge over Rio Lis, walk 2 blocks, and turn left again. 24 comfortable rooms with huge bathtubs, telephone, and cable TV. Buffet breakfast included. Singles €21; doubles €33; triples €42. AmEx/MC/V. ❷

Pousada da Juventude de Leiria (HI), Lg. Cândido dos Reis, 9 (☎/fax 244 83 18 68). From the bus station, walk to the cathedral and exit Lg. da Sé onto R. Barão de Viamonte. Lg. Cândido dos Reis is 6 blocks ahead. Large guest kitchen, TV room, and game room with pool table (€2 per hr.). Elegant garden courtyard. Breakfast included. Reception daily June 16-Sept. 15 8am-midnight; Sept. 16-June 15 8am-noon and 6pm-midnight. Lockout noon-6pm (bag drop-off still available). June 16-Sept. 15 dorms €11; doubles €27. Sept. 16-June 15 €8.50/€21. AmEx/MC/V. ❶

Pensão Alcôa, R. Rodrigues Cordeiro, 24 (☎244 83 26 90), off Pr. Rodrigues Lobo and next to the restaurant of the same name. All 16 rooms come with wood floors, small tile bathrooms, windows overlooking the pedestrian street, and cable TV. Breakfast included. June 16-Sept. singles €20; doubles €30; triples €45. Oct.-June 15 €15/ €25/€30. AmEx/MC/V. ❷

Hotel São Luís, R. Henrique Sommer (☎244 84 83 70; fax 84 83 79). From the tourist office, take a left onto R. João de Deus; bear left on R. António da Costa Santos, and at Lg. Rainha Santa Isabel take a left onto R. Henrique Sommer. Chic, even by Leiria's high standards; all rooms elegantly decorated and equipped with A/C, cable TV, and private bath. Singles €40; doubles €50; triples €65. AmEx/MC/V. ❹

◗ FOOD

The **mercado,** on Av. Cidade de Maringá, sells fresh produce. (Open M-F 8am-4pm, Sa 8am-1pm.) Groceries and fresh baked bread are at **Supermercado Ulmar,** Av. Heróis de Angola, 56, just past the bus station. (☎244 83 30 42. Open M-Sa 8am-9pm, Su 10am-1pm and 3-8pm.) Budget restaurants line side streets between the park and the castle; other quality finds are near Pr. Lobo and the youth hostel.

RIBATEJO AND ESTREMADURA

Restaurante Alcôa, R. Rodrigues Cordeiro, 24 (☎244 83 26 90), off Pr. Rodrigues Lobo and below the *pensão* of the same name. Besides a host of traditional Portuguese options, Alcôa offers one of the best deals in town, with a full meal (appetizer, salad, potatoes, main dish, and dessert) all for €5. Other entrees €5-8. Open June-Sept. daily noon-3pm and 7-10pm; Oct.-May M-Sa noon-3pm and 7-10pm. AmEx/MC/V. ❶

Restaurante O Rocha, R. Dr. Correria Mateus, 54-58 (☎244 83 31 03). Conveniently located in a corner of the pedestrian mall. Offers huge portions of quality grilled entrees at moderate prices. Comfortable outdoor seating. Entrees €7-7.50. Large half portions €4.80-5.50. Open M-Sa 9am-11:30pm. ❷

🔵🔴 SIGHTS AND BEACHES

From the main square, follow the signs past the austere **Sé** (cathedral) to the city's most significant monument, the **Castelo de Leiria.** Built by Dom Afonso Henriques after he snatched the town from the Moors, this granite fort presides atop the crest of a volcanic hill on the north edge of town. The passing centuries have been good to it, leaving the remains in an adventurous state of disrepair. The preserved **Torre de Menagem** (Homage Tower) houses rusty swords, old armor, and artifacts found on-site. Before discos and clubs took over the nightlife, the **Sala dos Namorados** (Lovers' Hall) set the stage for medieval courting. Old habits die hard, and local couples still come to the garden for cuddling and smooching. From the Sala dos Namorados, the terrace opens to a view of the town and river. (*☎244 81 39 82. Castle open Tu-Su 10am-6pm, Torre 10am-5pm. €2.20; students, children, and seniors €1.10.*)

Nearby beaches are accessible via buses running from the station July-Sept. 14 to **Praia de Viera** (45min.; 9 per day 7am-6:35pm, last return 7:25pm; €2.30); **Praia Pedrógão,** popular with locals and lined with stately residences (1hr.; 6 per day 8:25am-6:35pm, last return 6:15pm; €2.40); and the more secluded **São Pedro de Muel** (45min.; M-F 8 per day 7:55am-6:30pm, Sa 7 per day 6:55am-5:30pm, Su 7 per day 7:55am-5:30pm, last return 7:15pm; €2).

BATALHA ☎244

There are two reasons to visit Batalha (pop. 7500): the gigantic **Mosteiro de Santa Maria da Vitória,** which rivals Belém's Mosteiro dos Jerónimos in its righteous splendor, and the impressive caves in the nearby natural park.

⬛ TRANSPORTATION. Buses stop in Lg. 14 de Agosto de 1385 across the street from the monastery. Inquire at the tourist office for info or call the bus station in Leiria (☎244 81 15 07). Buses to: **Leiria** (20min., 16 per day 7:15am-7:45pm, €1.50); **Lisboa** (2hr., 5 per day 7:25am-6:10pm, €6.60); **Nazaré** (1hr., 8 per day 7:35am-6:50pm, €2.90) via **Alcobaça** (45min., €2.30); **Tomar** (1½hr., 3 per day 8:05am-6pm, €2.90) via **Fátima** (40min., €1.60).

📑🔢 ORIENTATION AND PRACTICAL INFORMATION. The tourist office is on Pr. Mouzinho de Albuquerque along R. Nossa Senhora do Caminho, just across from the monastery. Its friendly, English- and French-speaking staff offers maps and bus information as well as accommodations lists, free short-term **luggage storage,** and 15min. of free Internet. (☎244 76 51 80. Open daily May-Sept. 10am-1pm and 3-7pm; Oct.-Apr. 10am-1pm and 2-6pm.) The **police** (☎244 76 51 34) are on R. Mouzinho de Albuquerque, across the street from the bus stop. The **Centro de Saúde** (medical center; ☎244 76 99 20) is on Estrada da Freiria. **Internet** access is available at **Cafeteria Online,** R. Nossa Senhora do Caminho, down the pedestrian path from the tourist office, in the opposite direction from the rotary. (1 computer; €2 per 30min., €2.50 per hr.) The **post office,** in Lg. Papa Paulo VI near the freeway entrance, has **fax** (€2.20 per page) and **Posta Restante.** (☎244 76 91 00; fax 76 91 06. Open M-F 9:30am-1pm and 2:30-6:30pm.) **Postal Code:** 2440.

⌐ ⌐ ACCOMMODATIONS AND FOOD. Pensão Vitória ❷, on Lg. da Misericórdia next to the bus stop, has three rooms, each with one double bed; solo travelers can ask for a discount. (☎244 76 56 78. Reception 9am-11:30pm. Rooms €20.) **Pensão Residencial Gládius ❷,** Pr. Mouzinho de Albuquerque, 7, has seven comfortable rooms, all with TV and bath. Two rooms have a view of the plaza. (☎244 76 57 60. Reception 9am-11:30pm. June-Sept. doubles €30; triples €40. Oct.-May €25/€35.) The **restaurant** below Pensão Vitória offers daily specials for €5-8 and *frango assado na brasa* (roasted half-chicken with rice, potatoes, and salad; €4.50). Meals are served daily noon-3pm and 7-11pm. Several inexpensive *churrasquei-ras* (barbecue houses) line the squares flanking the monastery.

◙ SIGHTS. Batalha's ▨**Mosteiro Santa Maria da Vitória** puts it on the map, and for good reason. Its flamboyant facade soars upward in Gothic and Manueline style, opulently decorated and topped by dozens of spires. Construction began in 1386 under Dom João I to thank the Virgin Mary for the Portuguese victory at the Battle of Aljubarrota a year earlier. The **Capela do Fundador,** the pantheon of João I and the Avis dynasty, lies immediately to the right of the church, housing the elaborate sarcophagi of Dom João I, his English-born queen Philippa of Lancaster, and their more famous son Prince Henry the Navigator. The rest of the complex is accessible via a door in the nave of the church; enter through the broad Gothic arches of the **Claustro de Dom João I,** the delicate columns of which initiated the Manueline style. Adjacent to the cloister lies the **Tomb of the Unknown Soldier,** always guarded by two silent and oppressed-looking men in uniform. Through the 15th-century **Claustro de Dom Afonso V** are the **Capelas Imperfeitas** (Unfinished Chapels). Jealous of his predecessor's impressive pantheon, Dom Duarte commissioned the con-struction of an equally impressive pantheon to house his remains and those of his progeny; however, construction of the Mosteiro dos Jerónimos drained resources and interest, leaving the elegant Renaissance chapel roofless. (Open daily Apr.-Sept. 9am-6pm; Oct.-Mar. 9am-5pm. €4.50, under 25 and seniors €2.30, under 14 and Su before 2pm free. Church free.)

◪ CAVES. A 20min. drive outside town brings you to a spelunker's paradise: a series of spectacular underground *grutas* (caves) in Estremadura's natural park. The **Grutas de Mira de Aire** are the deepest, though **Grutas de Santo António** and **Alva-dos** are equally impressive. Although exploration of the caves takes only an hour or two, set aside a whole day, as the bus schedules from Batalha are tricky and require careful planning. From Batalha, take a bus to **Porto do Mós** (20min.; 3 per day 8:35am-6:40pm, last return 6:30pm; €2.70). If a 16km hike from Porto do Mós doesn't sound like a good time, then wait a couple hours for the bus to **Alvados** (10min., 6 per day 7:35am-6:40pm), which is still 5km from the caves. When plan-ning, check with the tourist office to confirm schedules. (Caves open daily July-Aug. 9:30am-8:30pm; June and Sept. 9:30am-7pm; Apr.-May 9:30am-6pm; Oct.-Mar. 9:30am-5:30pm. €3.50, students and seniors €2.50.)

FÁTIMA ☎249

Until May 13, 1917, when the Virgin Mary appeared to three peasant children, Fátima was a quiet sheep pasture. Today, the town of 15,000 is known for its stun-ning Santuário, as well as the 4 million Catholic pilgrims who visit it yearly. A sign at the entrance of the town's holy Santuário complex states, "Fátima is a place for adoration; enter as a pilgrim." Only Lourdes rivals this site in popularity with Catholic pilgrims; the miracles believed to have occurred here attract an endless international procession of religious groups. The plaza in front of the church, larger than St. Peter's Square in the Vatican, floods with pilgrims on the 12th and 13th of each month and stays busier than any other monument throughout the year.

▄ TRANSPORTATION

Trains: The **Caxarias** station (☎249 72 07 01), 10km out of town, is closer than the Fátima station (☎249 56 61 22), 22km away. Caxarias to: **Coimbra** (1hr., 11 per day 7:15am-8:45pm, €4.10); **Lisboa** (2½hr., 12 per day 7am-3:45am, €5.70); **Porto** (4hr., 13 per day 7:15am-8:40pm, €9.50); **Santarém** (1½hr., 8 per day 7am-3:45am, €3.30). **Buses** run between Caxarias and Fátima (30min., 7 per day 7:50am-7:50pm, €2) and between the Fátima train and bus stations (45min., 5 per day 6:10am-6:35pm, €2.40).

Buses: Av. D. José Alves Correia da Silva (☎249 53 16 11). To: **Batalha** (30min., 3 per day 9am-6:35pm, €1.50); **Coimbra** (1½hr., 10 per day 7:45am-7:40pm, €8.50); **Leiria** (1hr., 13 per day 7:45am-8pm, €4.80); **Lisboa** (1½-2½hr., 11-17 per day 7am-5pm, €8); **Nazaré** (1½hr., 3 per day 9am-6:25pm, €3.50); **Porto** (3-3½hr.; 11 per day 7:45am-9:30pm, Sa last bus 5:30pm; €11.20); **Santarém** (1hr., 11 per day 7:15am-7:40pm, €6.50); **Tomar** (1¼hr., 3 per day 8:30am-6:35pm, €2.70).

Taxis: Next to the bus station (☎249 53 16 22).

▄✴ ▄ ORIENTATION AND PRACTICAL INFORMATION

Fátima is essentially a religious monument with a series of souvenir shops surrounding it; all activity centers around the basilica complex. The **Santuário de Fátima** is the huge, open *praça* that fills with visitors on special occasions and the 12th and 13th of each month. On **Avenida Dom José Alves Correia da Silva,** below the Santuário, are the bus station and tourist office, in a lovely stone building with a wooden roof. From the bus station, take a right and walk approximately 10min. They offer free Internet access (15min. limit) and speak English and French. (☎249 53 11 39. Open daily Aug. 10am-7pm; June-July and Sept. 10am-1pm and 3-7pm; Oct.-May 10am-1pm and 2-6pm.) The Santuário has its own information office, on the left side when facing the basilica. (☎249 53 96 00. English, French and Spanish spoken. Open M-Sa 9am-6pm, Su 9am-5pm.) Several major **banks** have branches along the commercial center of R. Jacinta Marto (most open 8:30am-3pm). Local services include: **police,** Av. D. José Alves Correia da Silva (☎249 53 97 30); **Centro de Saúde,** on R. Jacinta Marto (☎249 53 18 36); **Internet access** at **X-Medi@,** R. S. João de Deus, 13, in the Edificio Varandas de Fátima, a few blocks behind and to the right of the basilica (☎249 53 22 60; €2 per hr.). The **post office** is on R. Cónego Formigão. (☎249 53 18 10. Open M-F 8:30am-6pm.) **Postal Code:** 2495.

▄▄ ACCOMMODATIONS AND FOOD

Scores of *residenciales* surround the basilica complex; prices vary little. During the grand pilgrimages on the 12th and 13th of every month, population and prices rise; the crowds are so big that they fill the entire plaza, an amazing feat given its mammoth size. It's always best to reserve a week ahead, and a month ahead on summer weekends and holidays. The plain but comfortable rooms of ▨**Residencial São Francisco ❶,** R. Francisco Marto, 100, near the Santuário, all come with

TV, phone, and private bath; half have private balconies. (☎249 53 30 17; fax 53 20 28. Reception 7:30am-midnight. Singles €20; doubles €30; triples €40.) **Residêncial São Jorge ❷**, R. Santa Cruz, 4, off R. Jacinta Marto near the wax museum, has hotel-like rooms with TV, private bath, and flower-lined balconies. During the day, enter through the religious souvenir shop next door on the left. (☎/fax 249 53 14 64. Light breakfast included. Reception 7:30am-12:30am. Lockout 12:30am. Summer singles €25; doubles €35; triples €50. Winter €20/€30/€45. AmEx/MC/V.) If *residenciales* are not your thing, try **Hotel Coração de Fátima ❸**, R. Cónego Formigão, 14, parallel to the Santuário on its right side. Forty-four well-appointed rooms include satellite TV, phones, nice private bathrooms with brand new tiles, and continental breakfast. (☎249 53 14 33; fax 53 11 57. Reservations required, particularly in Aug. Summer singles €35; doubles €55; triples €75. 30% cheaper in winter. AmEx/MC/V.)

Restaurants and snack bars cluster in commercial centers along R. Francisco Marto, R. Santa Isabela, and R. Jacinta Marto. Close to the wax museum, **O Terminal ❷**, R. Jacinta Marto, 24, offers some of the biggest portions for the best prices in town. Local favorites, such as grilled lamb, run €7-9, while the *pratos do dia* can be €5-7. (☎249 53 19 77. Open daily 9am-midnight; meals served 11:30am-3:30pm and 7-10pm.) On the other side of the Santuário, well-established **Restaurant Alfredo ❷**, R. Francisco Marto, 159 CV, serves huge plates and is filled with locals. Don't miss their *bacalhau no forno* (oven-broiled cod), a specialty. (☎249 53 12 49. Entrees €6-9. Open daily noon-3pm and 7-10pm.)

🄶 SIGHTS

🄢 SANTUÁRIO DE FÁTIMA. The modern holy sanctuary is a visually overwhelming site. Many of the devout travel the length of the plaza on their knees, all the way from the cross to the *capelinha*, praying for divine assistance or giving thanks to the Virgin Mary. After decades of fervent speculation, the Vatican disclosed the closely guarded "third secret" of Fátima in 2000, ending fears that it revealed the apocalypse: the Virgin is said to have prophesied the 1981 assassination attempt on Pope John Paul II in St. Peter's Square as well as the fall of the Soviet Union. The Pope now credits the Virgin with saving his life and had the bullet placed in her crown here.

At the end of the plaza rises the **Basílica do Rosário** (erected in 1928), featuring a crystal cruciform beacon atop the tower's seven-ton bronze crown. Inside

THE LOCAL STORY

FROM PASTURES TO PILGRIMAGE

Ten-year-old Lúcia de Jesus and her younger cousins Francisco and Jacinta Marto were tending their flock and playing in what is now Fátima on May 13, 1917, when suddenly a flash lit up the sky and they saw "a lady more brilliant than the sun"—the Virgin Mary. The Virgin's message to the children was to pray often and return to the same spot on the 13th of every month for the next 5 months.

The devout children kept the Virgin Mary's apparition a secret and followed her request. The day of the last apparition, in October, she asked the children to gather the villagers; she revealed to the crowd of 70,000 that she was the "Lady of the Rosary," and that a chapel should be built on that spot in her honor. Then, the villagers witnessed a miracle: the sun took on the shape of a silver disc, whirling on itself like a wheel of fire, and then seemed to fall upon the earth.

Since then, Fátima has become one of Catholicism's most important centers; the Santuário at Fátima receives more than 4 million Catholic pilgrims per year from all over the world. Today, the Capelinha das Apariçoes is built on the exact spot where the 3 children first saw the Virgin Mary; daily mass is held there in several different languages so that many others may hear her message as well.

are the tombs of two of the children who witnessed the apparitions; Francisco lies in the right nave, while Jacinta is in the left. Lúcia, the third and oldest child and a devout nun, still lives in Coimbra. *(Open daily 7:30am-10:30pm. Mass daily at 7:30, 9, 11am, 3, 4:30, and 6:30pm. Free.)* To the left is the **Capelinha das Aparições,** where the miracles are said to have taken place. Sheltered beneath a metal and glass canopy, the *capelinha* was built in 1919 and continues to house "Perpetual Adoration," which consists of mass during the day and a fire that never dies. The faithful from all over the world make pilgrimages to the site and perform mass at the chapel; an international mass is held there every Thursday at 9am, and a candlelight procession occurs every evening at 9:30pm from April to October.

MUSEUMS. The **Museu de Arte Sacra e Etnologia** exhibits Catholic icons from various centuries and cultures, showcasing the interplay between local people and the Catholic religion. The museum also exhibits religious icons from several different religions and the clothing worn by the three children who witnessed the apparition of the Virgin Mary. *(R. Francisco Marto, 5. ☎ 249 53 94 70; fax 53 94 79. Open Apr.-Oct. Tu-Su 10am-7pm; Nov.-Mar. noon-5pm. €3.50, seniors and students €1.80.)* The **Museu Fátima 1917 Aparições** uses light, sound, and special effects to re-create the apparition and is one of the only places in town where the message of the Virgin is readily accessible to the public in Portuguese, Spanish, English, French, Italian, and German. *(R. Jacinta Marto. To the left of the basilica, through the park, in the complex beneath Hotel Fátima. ☎ 249 53 28 58; www.museuaparicoes.com. Open daily Apr.-Oct. 9am-7pm; Nov.-Mar. 9am-6pm. €2.50, under 12 €1.50.)*

TOMAR ☎ 249

Visitors come to Tomar (pop. 20,000) mainly to walk quietly and wide-eyed through the Convento de Cristo, which includes a castle, a fortress, a convent, and several beautiful gardens. Around the year 1160 Dom Afonso Henriques enlisted the Knights Templar (a kind of sanctified swat team) to build a fortified castle at Tomar, then the weak spot between Lisboa and Coimbra. When the Knights fell out of favor with the Pope two hundred years later, sheepish Portuguese royalty quickly founded a new religous order and gave them the Templar's property, resulting in today's unique collage of menacing medieval walls and piously ornate architecture. The rest of the town lazes beside the Rio Nabão, stirring only for the legendary **Festival dos Tabuleiros** every four years (due again in 2007).

▛ TRANSPORTATION

Trains: Av. dos Combatentes da Grande Guerra (☎ 249 72 07 55). Tomar is the northern end of a minor line, so most destinations require a transfer at Entroncamento or Lamarosa; ask about this when purchasing your ticket and pay attention to the stops. Ticket office open Su-F 5:30am-8:30pm and 9:30-10:30pm, Sa 5:30am-8:30pm. To: **Coimbra** (2½hr., 15 per day 6:05am-8pm, €5.60-6.40); **Lisboa** (2hr., 20 per day 5am-10pm, €6.50); **Porto** (4½hr., 14 per day 6am-8pm, €12-17.50); **Santarém** (1hr., 19 per day 5am-10pm, €4).

Buses: Rodoviária Tejo, Av. dos Combatentes da Grande Guerra (☎ 968 94 35 50). Express buses are twice the price of regular buses. To: **Coimbra** (2½hr., 7am, €9.20); **Fátima** (30min., 4 per day 7:50am-7:20pm, €5.20); **Figueira da Foz** (4½hr., 7am, €9.40); **Lagos** (9hr.; M-Sa 9:15am via Santarém and Évora, daily 10:15am via Lisboa; €19); **Leiria** (1hr.; M-F 7:15am and 5:45pm, Sa 7am; €3.10); **Lisboa** (2hr., 4 per day 9:15am-6pm, €6.50); **Nazaré** (1½hr., 3 per day 6:30am-5:20pm, €5.50); **Porto** (4hr., 7am, €11.60); **Santarém** (1hr., 12:30pm, €4.70).

Taxis: Vitorino e Marguerita, Ltd. (☎963 04 23 06). **Autotáxi Capítulo** (☎917 20 14 35). Taxis cluster near the bus and train stations and across the river on R. Santa Iria.

ORIENTATION AND PRACTICAL INFORMATION

The **Rio Nabão** divides Tomar, but almost everything travelers need—the train and bus stations, accommodations, and sights—is on the western bank. The lush **Parque Mouchão** straddles the two banks, while the ancient **Ponte Velha** (Old Bridge) connects them. From the **Ponte Nova** (New Bridge), **Avenida Dr. Cândido Madureira** leads to **Praça Infante Dom Henrique,** behind which lie the trails of the **Parque da Mata Nacional dos Sete Montes.** (Park open daily 10am-6pm.) The bus and train stations sit side by side on **Avenida dos Combatentes da Grande Guerra** at the edge of town. The pedestrian-only **Rua Serpa Pinto** cuts across town from the river to the castle and connects Ponte Velha to **Praça da República,** the main square.

Tourist Office: Av. Dr. Cândido Madureira (☎249 32 24 27). From the bus/train station, head down Av. General Bernardo Faria toward the city past several municipal buildings. Turn left 3 blocks later onto Av. Cândido Madureira. Short-term **luggage storage** available. English and French spoken. Open M-F 10am-7pm, Sa-Su 10am-noon and 2-6pm.

Laundromat: 5 á Sec (☎249 32 35 31), inside Supermercado Modelo. From Pr. da República, take R. Serpa Pinto and go straight for about 1.5km; the Supermercado will be on your right after passing the McDonald's. Open daily 9am-9pm.

Police: R. Dr. Sousa (☎249 31 34 44).

Pharmacy: Farmácia Central, R. Marquês de Pombal, 18 (☎249 31 23 29). From Pr. da República, take R. Serpa Pinto and cross the bridge; it will be on your left. Open M-F 9am-1pm and 3-7pm, Sa 24hr.

Hospital: Hospital Nossa Senhora da Graça, Av. Dona Maria de Lourdes Melo e Castelo (☎249 32 01 00), on the other side of the river (25min. walk).

Internet Access: Espaço Internet, R. Antorim Rosa, between R. Marquês de Pombal and Av. Norton de Matos, on the other side of the river. Free. 30min. limit only enforced if people are waiting. Open daily 10am-10pm.

Post Office: Av. Marquês de Tomar (☎249 31 04 00; fax 31 04 06), across from Parque Mouchão. **Posta Restante** and **fax** available. Open M-F 8:30am-6pm, Sa 9am-12:30pm. **Postal Code:** 2300.

ACCOMMODATIONS

Finding accommodations is a problem only during the **Festival dos Tabuleiros.** R. Serpa Pinto is lined with quality lodging, while cheaper options lie closer to the bus and train stations.

Residencial União, R. Serpa Pinto, 94 (☎249 32 31 61; fax 32 12 99), halfway between Pr. da República and the bridge. The nicest budget accommodation in Tomar, in a central location. 28 rooms all have satellite TV, phone, regal red carpet, and private bath. Well-stocked bar and large, comfortable TV room. Continental breakfast included. Reception 8am-midnight. Reservations recommended July and Aug. Apr.-Sept. singles €25; doubles €37.50; triples €42.30. Oct.-Mar. €20/€30/€35. ❷

Residencial Luz, R. Serpa Pinto, 144 (☎249 31 23 17; www.residencialluz.com). 14 clean, comfy rooms, most with private bath, TV, and phone. Antique aficionados can request the room with the 1973 big screen TV. May 16-Sept. singles €19; doubles €32.50; triples €35; quads €60. Oct.-May 15 €17.50/€30/€35/€45. ❷

Pensão Residencial Cavaleiros de Cristo, R. Alexandre Herculano, 7 (☎249 32 12 03; fax 32 11 92). Located 1 street off Pr. da República and boasting beautiful new rooms with A/C, cable TV, mini-bar, and tile bathrooms, this place is a steal during the winter (and reasonably priced in summer, given its amenities). Breakfast included. Summer singles €35; doubles €49; triples €64. Winter €20.50/€41/€51. AmEx/MC/V. ❸

Casa de Dormidas, R. de D. Aurora de Macedo, 46 (☎249 31 19 03). Go to the Casa Costa shop on Av. Dr. Cândido Madureira, 18, near the traffic circle, and speak with owner José Costa. The older rooms are ideal for those who like big spaces and aren't particular about how they look. Singles €15; doubles €20. For the absolute rock bottom deal in town, ask about his rooms without bath at **Casa de Dormidas Convento,** Av. dos Combatentes da Grande Guerra, 7. Singles €10; doubles €15. ❶

🍴 FOOD

Parque Mouchão, across from Av. Marquês de Tomar, is the perfect spot for a picnic. The **market**, across the river on the corner of Av. Norton de Matos and R. Santa Iria, provides all but the red-checked blanket. (Open Tu and Th-F 8am-2pm. Flea market on F.) Several inexpensive **mini-markets** line the side streets between the tourist office and Pr. da República.

▧ Ristorante/Pizzeria Bella Italia, R. Everard, 91 (☎249 32 29 96), near the river, between the bridges. Family owners serve delicious pastas (€4-7) and pizzas (€4-9) in stuff-yourself portions. Ambience is the real treat, with rapid fire Italian and delicious aromas wafting in from the kitchen. Specialties include *pasta mista* (€12; serves 2). The tiramisu (€2.50) is quite popular. Open M and W-Su noon-3pm and 7-11pm. ❶

Salsinha Verde, Pr. da República, 19 (☎249 32 32 29), in the corner, to the left when facing the town hall. Students pop *petingas* (small fish; €0.15) at the bar. Local cuisine served in the dining room. Meat entrees €4.25-7, fish €5-7.50. Cheaper *pratos do dia* (€3), but the real steal is the *ementa económica*, a full meal consisting of soup, an entree, dessert, and coffee for only €5.50. Pray that your trip lands you here on a Tuesday, when the cook makes his legendary *bacalhau com natas* (creamy codfish). It tastes much better than it sounds. Open daily 8am-midnight. ❶

⊙ ▧ SIGHTS AND FESTIVALS

The reason to come to Tomar is the **▧Convento de Cristo,** which displays an intriguing range of architecture and landscaping. From the tourist office, take a right and bear left on the dirt path, following its 10min. leisurely ascent. A UNESCO World Heritage site, the convent's first structure was built by the Moors during the 9th century to defend themselves from pesky invaders; that clearly failed, and the Knights Templar fortified it in 1160 after the defeat of the Moors. Successive architectural enterprises really deserve the credit for its beauty, adding an eclectic collection of cloisters, convents, and buildings. The most impressive aspect of the convent is the grounds that surround its entrance; *azulejo*-covered benches beckon visitors to sit among the orange trees and admire the views of the nearby national forest. Upon entering, an ornate octagonal canopy protects the high altar of the **Templo dos Templares,** modeled after the Holy Sepulchre in Jerusalem. Below stands the **Janela do Capítulo** (chapter window), an exuberant tribute to the Age of Discovery. One of Europe's masterpieces of Renaissance architecture, the **Claustro dos Felipes** honors Felipe II of Castilla, who was crowned here as Felipe I of Portugal during Iberia's unification (1580-1640). Stairs spiral upward to sweeping views of the **Terraço da Cera.** Tucked behind the Palladian main cloister and the nave is the **Claustro da Santa Bárbara,** where gargoyle rain spouts writhe in pain as they cough up a fountain. The **Charola** (oratory) was inspired by the Temple of Jerusalem, which explains its peculiar shape: eight pillars descending from a domed top to surround the altar in the middle. On the northeast side of the church is the Gothic **Claustro do Cemitério.** (☎249 31 34 81; fax 32 27 36. Open daily June-Sept. 9am-6:30pm; Oct.-May 9am-5:30pm. Last visit 30min. before closing. €4.50, under 25 and seniors €2.30.)

The **Museu Luso-Hebraico Abraáo Zacuto** is Portugal's most significant reminder of its historical importance to the European Jewish community. This synagogue, built between 1430 and 1460 and lost in 1496 when the Jews faced exile or conversion to Christianity, is the oldest Hebrew temple in Portugal; it became the town prison in 1516 and now houses a small museum of international Jewish history, with a collection of tombstones, inscriptions, and pieces from around the world. (R. Dr. Joaquim Jaquinto, 73. Open daily 10am-1pm and 2-6pm. Free.) During October 19-23, handicrafts, folklore, *fado*, and raisins storm the city during the **Feira de Santa Iria,** which includes the **Feira das Passas** (Raisin Fair). The **Feira de Artesanato** has taken place during the first half of July every year since 1984. The biggest party in Tomar, however, is the **Festival dos Tabuleiros,** which takes place once every four years as an act of thanks for good harvests. Six thousand people swarm the town for a week to watch young girls walk in a 4km procession bearing the traditional *tabuleiro* (tray) stacked on their heads. The *tabuleiro* itself must be as tall as its bearer and is composed of bread, paper flowers, ribbons, and shafts of wheat. Tomar also hosts four summer **bullfights;** look for large, brightly colored posters advertising the *corridas.*

THE NORTH

Plenty of Europeans lament the loss of the "old country," as if the big cities and big governments of the last century squashed the soul of the continent. Be that as it may, the march of progress must have lost its beat when it neared the north of Portugal. The picturesque villages and laid-back cities of the region force the traveler to forget the teeming beaches and bustle of the south. Just like the rest of the country, the history of the area goes back to the Neolithic period—but only the very eccentric come to poke around old museums. Instead, the region brings salvation to nature lovers. The mountain ranges that enclose the country are diverse

enough for hiking, camping, or just strolling. Although many come to get goofy with the *vinho do porto* and other local wines, the natural environment is not to be missed. Wine can be shipped—the north of Portugal cannot.

HIGHLIGHTS OF THE NORTH

TASTE the famed wine of **Porto** for free by visiting its numerous port lodges (p. 772).

CRAWL through Celtic ruins on Monte de Santa Luzia in **Viana do Castelo** (p. 784).

ENVISION your favorite childhood fairy tale in the enchanting **Buçaco Forest** (p. 793).

SEE the sinking Convento de Santa Clara in **Coimbra** while you still can (p. 791).

HIKE from village to village in the **Parque Natural de Montesinho** (p. 805).

DOURO AND MINHO

The region around the Douro and Minho rivers is defined by the land they irrigate. The purples, blues, and greens of the fruit orchards, vineyards, and olive trees that grow in its soil are worthy of the most melodramatic romantic poetry. The city of Porto is worthy of odes as well—it presents an interesting alternative to Lisboa's take on Portuguese city life, and its muted palette evokes a strange sense of nostalgia, even in those who've never visited before.

PORTO (OPORTO)   ☎ 22

Magnificently situated on a gorge cut by the Douro River just 6km from the sea, Portugal's second-largest city is characterized by an elegance reminiscent of Paris or Prague. The wine cellars that dot the banks of the Rio Douro are easily its most popular attractions, with free tours and samples. But Porto has more to offer than fine wine. It's a city with personality, totally distinct from heart-wrenching, *fado*-wailing Lisboa. A visit to Porto may call up the past, but it also offers a comfortable stroll through the present: clever museums, beautiful vistas, and the wide variety of produce form a package that locals prize and tourists relish.

▐▀ TRANSPORTATION

Flights: Aeroporto Francisco de Sá Carneiro (☎ 229 41 25 34), 13km from downtown. City bus #56 goes to the airport from R. do Carmo, but makes multiple stops. The **aerobus** from Av. dos Aliados near Pr. da Liberdade is more efficient (40min., every 30min. 7am-6:30pm, €2.60). Buy tickets on board. **Taxis** are even quicker (15-20min., €18-20). **TAP Air Portugal,** Pr. Mouzinho de Albuquerque, 105 (☎226 08 02 31), flies to most major European cities, with 6 daily shuttles to Lisboa (35min., €100-150).

Trains: Estação de Campanhã (☎225 36 41 41), on R. da Estação. To: **Aveiro** (1¼hr., 14 per day 6:15am-12:30am, €4.50-9.50); **Braga** (1½-1¾hr., 3 per day 11am-10pm, €9.50); **Coimbra** (2hr., 14 per day 6:15am-12:50am, €7.50-12); **Lisboa** (3½-4½hr., 14 per day 6:15am-12:50am, €14.50-22.50); **Madrid,** Spain (13-14hr., 6:10pm, €60; transfer at Entroncamento); **Viana do Castelo** (1½-2hr., 9 per day 6am-7pm, €5.50); **Vigo,** Spain (2½hr., 7:40am and 6:55pm, €12.80). Buses #34 and 35 connect Campanhã to downtown (every 30min., €0.90). **Estação de São Bento** (☎222 00 27 22), Pr. Almeida Garrett, serves mostly local and regional trains. Frequent connections to **Estação São Campanhã** (5-10min., every 20-30min. 5:55am-11:10pm, €0.90).

Buses: Several companies operate out of garages through the downtown area.

Internorte, Pr. Galiza, 96 (☎226 05 24 20) has service to **Madrid,** Spain (10½hr.; Tu, Th, and Sa-Su 9am; €34), as well as other international cities. Book 3 days ahead. Open M-F 9am-12:30pm and 2-6:30pm, Sa 9am-12:30pm and 2-4pm, Su 9am-12:30pm and 2-5:30pm.

Rede Expressos, R. Alexandre Herculano, 366 (☎222 05 24 59), sends buses to: **Braga** (1¼hr., 8 per day 9:25am-12:15am, €4.70); **Bragança** (5hr., 7 per day 7:15am-8:15pm, €8.20); **Coimbra** (1½hr., 11 per day 7:15am-12:45am, €7.50); **Lisboa** (4hr., 12 per day 7:15am-12:45am, €14); **Viana do Castelo** (1¾hr., 10:55am and 6:40pm, €8.20).

REDM, R. Dr. Alfredo Magalhães, 94 (☎222 00 31 52), 2 blocks from Pr. da República, has buses to **Braga** (1hr.; M-F 26 per day 6:45am-8pm, Sa-Su 9-12 per day 7:15am-8pm; €3.30).

Renex, Campo Mártires da Pátria (☎222 00 33 95), has express service to **Lagos** (8½hr., 6 per day 9am-1:15am, €18) via **Lisboa** (3½hr., 7-8 per day, €3.50) and **Vila Real de Santo António** (9½hr., 5 per day 9am-1:15am, €20).

Rodonorte, R. Ateneu Comercial do Porto (☎222 00 43 98), goes to **Vila Real** (1¾hr.; M-F 16 per day 6:50am-10:30pm, Sa 7 per day 6:50am-9:20pm, Su 7 per day 6:50am-10:30pm; €5.50) via **Amarante** (1hr., €4.30).

Public Transportation: STCP (☎808 20 01 66) operates **tram** and **bus** lines throughout the city (both €0.55). Tickets purchased on the bus cost twice as much. Buy bus tickets beforehand at small kiosks around the city or at the **STCP** office, Pr. Almeida Garrett, 27 (open M-F 8am-7:30pm, Sa 8am-1pm). Buy 1-day unlimited tickets (€2.10) onboard.

Taxis: Av. dos Aliados and along the river in Ribeira. Ask for a quote before getting in, and make sure the taxi has an electronic meter. **Radiotáxis,** R. de Alegria, 1802 (☎225 07 39 00).

■ 🔼 ORIENTATION AND PRACTICAL INFORMATION

Porto's heavy traffic and chaotic maze of one-way streets fluster travelers who come by car; if that's you, ditch the car in a safe parking lot and make the trek by foot. The city center is easy to navigate: hillside **Praça da Liberdade** is joined to **Praça General Humberto Delgado** by **Avenida dos Aliados,** and the rest of the city radiates from these two squares. Between the Rio Douro and the city center lies the **Ribeira** district, where much of Porto's sights and nightlife are located on steep, narrow sidestreets. Directly across from Ribeira, the two-level **Ponte de Dom Luís I** spans the river to **Vila Nova de Gaia,** where the port wine cellars are located. Back on the other side of the river, 5km west of the center, is the **Foz** district, where beaches and nightclubs are the main attraction.

Tourist Office: Main office, R. Clube dos Fenianos, 25 (☎223 39 34 72). Short-term luggage storage, maps, and info about Porto provided by the English- and French-speaking staff. Open July-Sept. M-F 9am-7pm, Sa-Su 9:30am-6:30pm; Oct.-May M-F 9am-5:30pm, Sa-Su 9:30am-4:30pm. **Ribeira branch,** R. Infante Dom Henrique, 63 (☎222 00 97 70); same services, same hours. **ICEP (National Tourism) office,** Pr. Dom João I, 43 (☎222 05 75 14). Open July-Aug. daily 9am-7:30pm; Apr.-June and Sept.-Oct. M-F 9am-7:30pm, Sa-Su 9:30am-3:30pm; Nov.-Mar. M-F 9am-7pm, Sa-Su 9:30am-3:30pm. **Airport branch** (☎229 41 25 34). Open daily 8am-11:30pm. 24hr. multilingual **computer info stands** in the main shopping centers and the larger squares; one in front of McDonald's in Pr. da Liberdade.

Budget Travel: Tagus, R. Campo Alegre, 261 (☎226 09 41 46). English-speaking staff offers advice and student rates. Open M-F 9am-6pm, Sa 10am-1pm.

Currency Exchange: Portocâmbios, R. Rodrigues Sampaio, 193 (☎222 00 02 38). Open M-F 9am-6pm, Sa 9am-noon. **Automatic exchange machine** up Av. dos Aliados.

American Express: Top Tours, R. Alferes Malheiro, 96 (☎222 07 40 20). Handles all AmEx functions. Open M-F 9:30am-1:30pm and 2:30-6:30pm.

Luggage Storage: Free in the **tourist office** during the day.

Laundromat: Lavanderia Tropical, R. Bragas, 329 (☎222 05 13 97). Wash and dry €3 per kg. Open M-F 8:30am-6:30pm, Sa 9:30am-1pm. Closed 1st 2 weeks of Aug.

Porto

▲ **ACCOMMODATIONS**
Grande Hotel de Paris
Residencial, **6**
Hospedaria Luar, **2**
Hotel Internacional, **7**
Pensão Douro, **13**
Pensão Duas Nações, **4**

♦ **FOOD**
A Grade, **14**
Café Guarany, **8**
Churrasqueria Central dos
Clérigos, **5**
Confeitaria Império, **9**
Majestic Café, **10**
Mercado de Bolhão, **3**
Restaurante Tripeiro, **11**

★ **NIGHTLIFE**
Discoteca Swing, **1**
O Muro, **16**
Petrus Bar/Wine Café, **15**
Solar do Vinho do Porto, **12**

THE NORTH

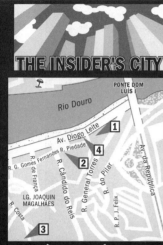

À SUA SAÚDE!

You haven't really been to Porto unless you cross the Ponte de Dom Luís I into the Vila Nova da Gaia district and immerse yourself in the city's namesake. Be careful though: excessive tasting along the beautiful Douro may make you want to stay in Porto forever. À sua saúde (Cheers)!

1 **Cálem,** Av. Diogo Leite, 26 (☎223 74 66 60). The house of Cálem has been a major player in the port industry for 200 years, since it began shipping its precious product to Brazil in 1859. Today, its knowledgeable guides offer tours in several languages, explaining the port-making process and history of the powerful Cálem family. Tours every 15-20min. €2. Open daily summer 10am-7pm; winter 10am-6pm. AmEx/MC/V.

2 **Sandeman,** Lg. Miguel Bombarda, 3 (☎223 74 05 33), just off Av. Diogo Leite. Founded by a Scottish merchant two centuries ago, Sandeman now offers a very tourist-

Police: R. Clube dos Fenianos, 11 (☎222 08 18 33).

Late-Night Pharmacy: Rotation list posted on the door of every pharmacy (and printed in many newspapers) with address and phone number of 24hr. pharmacy.

Hospital: Hospital de Santo António (☎222 07 75 00), on R. Alberto Aires Gouveia.

Internet Access: Portweb, Pr. Gen. Humberto Delgado, 291 (☎222 00 59 22). €1.20 per hr. Coffee €0.50. Plays classic MTV. Open M-Sa 10am-2am, Su 3pm-2am.

Post Office: Pr. Gen. Humberto Delgado (☎223 40 02 00). **Fax,** phone, and **Posta Restante.** Most services closed after 6pm. Open M-F 8:30am-9pm, Sa-Su 9am-6pm. **Postal Code:** 4000.

ACCOMMODATIONS AND CAMPING

Hostels in Porto are rarely charming and often over-priced. For the best deals, look west of Av. dos Aliados, or on R. de Fernandes Tomás and R. Formosa, perpendicular to Av. dos Aliados. Prices usually dip in the low season.

☒ **Pensão Duas Nações,** Pr. Guilherme Gomes Fernandes, 59 (☎222 08 96 21; fax 08 16 16). The best combination of low price and comfortable rooms. To "keep the youngsters upbeat," the owner paints the walls in bright colors. Rooms have large windows with small terraces and TVs (some with satellite). Laundry €7 per load. Internet €0.50 per 15min. Reserve ahead. Singles €13.50, with bath €22.50; doubles €22.50/€30; triples €33/€40; quads €44/€48; 1 room with 6 beds and bath €11 per person. ❶

☒ **Hospedaria Luar,** R. Alferes Malheiro, 133 (☎222 08 78 45). Recently built rooms offer huge spaces, cable TV, and private bath for excellent prices. Ask the friendly owner about doing a load of laundry for €5. Singles €20-25; doubles €25-30; inquire about discounts for extended stays. ❷

Grande Hotel de Paris Residencial, R. da Fábrica, 27-29 (☎222 07 31 40; www.ghparis.pt). The place to sleep in historical Porto. In business since 1888, it's the 2nd oldest hotel in Portugal. The charming, well-maintained building with marble staircases houses an upright piano and luxury breakfast room. All rooms have bath, cable TV, and phone; half have balconies. Apr.-Sept. singles €36; doubles €46-48. Oct. €40/€50-52. Nov.-Mar. €32/€42-44. ❹

Pensão Douro, R. do Loureiro, 54 (☎222 05 32 14), closer to the river than many of the other *pensões*. Old-fashioned rooms come with couches and lots of space; for those who want to spend little, stay close to the action, and bypass amenities (though most rooms now have TVs). Singles €15-20, with bath €25-30; doubles €25/€30. ❶

Hotel Internacional, R. do Almada, 131 (☎222 00 50 32; fax 00 90 63). Classy rooms right off Pr. da Liberdade. A stay here immerses you in elegance; rooms have large, beautiful baths, cable TV, A/C, and phone. Reservations recommended in summer. Summer singles €75; doubles €85; triples €103. Winter €60/€70/€87.50. AmEx/MC/V. ❺

Camping Prelada (☎228 31 26 16), on R. Monte dos Burgos, in Quinta da Prelada, 4km from the town center and 5km from the beach. Bus #6, 50, 54, or 87 from Pr. da Liberdade (only #50 and 54 run at night). Amenities include free hot showers, electricity and baths. Reception 8am-1am. €3 per person, €3-3.50 per tent, €2.60 per car. ❶

Camping Salgueiros, R. do Campismo (☎227 81 05 00; fax 81 01 36), near Praia Salgueiros in Vila Nova de Gaia. A less accessible and less equipped campsite, but also less expensive and closer to the beach. To get there, catch the green Espírito Santo bus from Pr. da Batalha in front of the Teatro Nacional de São João (€1.10). €1.50 per person, €1.50-2 per tent, €0.75 per car. ❶

◪ FOOD

Quality budget meals can be found near Pr. da Batalha on **Rua Cimo de Vila** and **Rua Cativo.** Places selling *bifanas* (small pork sandwiches) line R. Bomjardim. Ribeira is the place to go for a high-quality, affordable dinner, particularly on **Cais da Ribeira, Rua Reboleira,** and **Rua Cima do Muro.** Local *azeitarias* (olive houses) offer a fantastic selection of olives tucked between the tourist traps. Adventurous eaters can try the city's specialty, *tripas à moda do Porto* (tripe and beans), if chewy and greasy cow innards sound appealing. The ◪**Mercado de Bolhão** has an enormous selection, including fresh bread, cheese, meat, and olives. The upper level has fresh produce. (Open M-F 8:30am-5pm, Sa 8:30am-1pm.)

◪ **Majestic Café,** R. de Santa Catarina, 112 (☎222 00 38 87). One of the best snapshots of 19th-century bourgeois opulence—it's no surprise that it was originally called Elite Café—this cafe is the oldest and best-known in the city. The management knows it, so expect overpriced sandwiches, cigars, and pastries. Best for a coffee and a look around at the chandeliers and sculptures of cherubim grinning like they know something you don't. Entrees €13-15. Sandwiches €4-10. Elaborate pastries €4-6. Cigars €6-23. Open M-Sa 9:30am-midnight. AmEx/MC/V. ❷

friendly dive into the world of port, with costumed guides, a souvenir shop, and a museum. Tours every 20min. €3. Open Apr.-Oct. daily 10am-12:30pm and 2-6pm; Nov.-Mar. M-F 9:30am-12:30pm and 2-5pm. AmEx/MC/V.

3 **Taylor's,** R. do Choupelo, 250 (☎223 74 28 00). Perhaps the most prestigious name in the industry, Taylor's expert staff will amaze you with their knowledge; the beautiful outdoor gardens, complete with peacocks, are the perfect environment in which to enjoy the delicious wine. Free tours (every 20-30min.) and tasting. Open Aug. M-Sa 10am-6pm; Sept.-July M-F 10am-6pm; last visit starts 5pm. AmEx/MC/V.

4 **Quinta do Noval,** Av. Diogo Leite, 256 (☎223 77 02 82; www.quintadonoval.com). One of the more well-known brands of port worldwide, Quinta do Noval has long focused on the foreign markets, particularly the United States and the United Kingdom. Founded in 1715, the makers of one of the finest ports on the market got their start when the almighty Marquês de Pombal gave a vineyard to a noble family. Free tours June-Sept. 10am-7pm; Oct.-May M-F 9am-5pm.

▨ Churrasquería Central dos Clérigos, R. da Fábrica, 69 (☎222 00 80 77). A lively and cheerful restaurant lined with *azulejos,* this *churrasquería* offers assorted grilled fish and meat dishes accompanied by generous portions of salad and other extras. *Pratos do dia* (€3) are perfect for experimenting cheaply with local cuisine. Entrees €3-14. Open M-Sa noon-3:30pm and 7:30-10:30pm. ❶

Restaurante Tripeiro, R. de Passos Manuel, 195 (☎222 00 58 86). Well-prepared dishes, including regional specialties such as *bacalhau a braz* (cod with fried potatoes and eggs; €12.50) and *filete de polvo* (octopus; €13). Perfect for a night of classy dining without the touristy atmosphere. Entrees €8-15. Open M-Sa noon-3pm and 7-10pm. AmEx/MC/V. ❸

Café Guarany, Av. dos Aliados, 85 (☎223 32 12 72; www.cafeguarany.com). An elegant café right on Pr. da Liberdade; diners listen to classical piano while being served by tuxedoed waiters. Best for a coffee and a dessert (€2-3). Sandwiches €3.50-9.30. Entrees €9.50-13.50. Open daily 9am-midnight. AmEx/MC/V. ❸

Confeitaria Império, R. de Santa Catarina, 149-151 (☎222 00 55 95). Founded in 1941, this *pastelaría* has a huge selection of excellent pastries and inexpensive lunch specials (€3) served in the back dining room. Try the *especialidade Império* pastry (€0.60). Open M-Sa 7:30am-8:30pm. A new **branch** at R. de Fernandes Tomás, 755, is the largest self-service cafe in the city, offering a variety of meals and snacks. ❶

A Grade, R. de São Nicolau, 9 (☎223 32 11 30), in Ribeira. A welcoming restaurant furnished with old-fashioned wooden tables, benches, and wine bottles. Tasty lunch *menú* €6-7. Entrees €6-9. Specialties including *polvo assado no forno* (baked octopus) and *cabrito assado no forno* (baked baby goat) €10-11. Open daily M-Sa 9am-midnight. ❷

◉ SIGHTS

Your first brush with Porto's rich stock of fine artwork may be, of all places, at Estação de São Bento, home to a celebrated collection of *azulejos.* Up Av. dos Aliados in Pr. General Humberto Delgado, the formidable **Câmara do Porto** (City Hall) is a monument to Porto's late 19th-century greatness.

▨ PALÁCIO DA BOLSA. The elegant Palácio da Bolsa (Stock Exchange) was built from 1842 to 1910 over the ruins of the Convento de São Francisco, after it was destroyed by fire in 1832. At the entrance is the **Pátio das Nações** (Hall of Nations), which served as the trading floor of the stock exchange until 1991 when the building was given to the Commerce Society of Oporto. The domed ceiling is decorated with the coats of arms of 20 countries friendly with Portugal. Leading up to the top floor is the **Escadaria Nobre** (Noble Staircase), decorated with carved granite, topped with two giant bronze chandeliers, each weighing over one metric ton, and adorned with busts by Soares dos Reis, one of Portugal's greatest artists. Among the exquisitely decorated rooms is the **Sala dos Retratos** (Portrait Room), which features a wooden table that took a man and his pocket knife three painstaking years to carve. Perhaps the most curious room is the **Sala das Asambleas Gerais** (Room of the General Assembly), where nothing is as it seems; the "wooden" walls and "bronze" emblem are actually painted plaster, made to resemble wood and bronze to showcase the skill of the artists. The most striking room of the Palácio is the opulent **Sala Árabe** (Arabian Hall). The green crests on the ceiling proclaim "Allah above all," and its gold and silver walls are covered with the oddly juxtaposed inscriptions "Glory to Allah" and "Glory to Dona Maria II." Note that the door to the hall is set slightly off-center—an intentional alteration to symbolize that only Allah is perfect. Interestingly enough, the artists responsible for this elaborate room were all

Portuguese and had never even visited the Middle East; at the time, the Arabic style was considered the most beautiful, and the room was commissioned to demonstrate the power of Porto's magnanimous merchants. The various rooms of the Palácio are now used for occasional ceremonies and official receptions. *(R. Ferreira Borges. ☎ 223 39 90 00. Open daily Apr.-Oct. 9am-7pm, Nov.-Mar. 9am-1pm and 2-6pm. Multilingual tours every 30min. €5, students €3.)*

IGREJA DE SÃO FRANCISCO. The Gothic and Baroque eras of ecclesiastical architecture favored gilded wood, no question. But they outdid themselves with this church. In all of Portugal, few, if any, chapels approach the detail and sheer quantity of glittering handiwork; the opulence of the Rococo carvings will leave you awestruck upon entry. At one point, there were between 400-600kg. of gold on the chapel's walls and altar, all donated by rich families trying to buy their way into paradise. Next door to the chapel, a museum showcases religious art and artifacts from the 16th-18th centuries; in the basement of the museum lies the *Ossário*, a creepy cemetery with several individual graves and countless mass ones over which visitors tread. *(R. Infante Dom Henrique. ☎ 222 06 21 00. Open daily 9am-6pm. €3, students €1.50.)*

MUSEU NACIONAL DE SOARES DOS REIS. A former royal residence, this 18th-century museum houses an exhaustive collection of 19th-century Portuguese painting and sculpture, much of it by Soares dos Reis, often called Portugal's Michelangelo. It also features works by other great Portuguese artists including Marques de Oliveira. *(R. Dom Manuel II, 44. ☎ 223 39 37 70. Open Tu 2-6pm, W-Su 10am-6pm. €3, seniors and students €1.50. Su until 2pm free.)*

SÉ. Fortified on the hilltop slightly south of the train station is Porto's imposing Romanesque *Sé* (cathedral). Built in the 12th and 13th centuries, the Gothic, *azulejo*-covered cloister was added in the 14th century. The **Capela do Santíssimo Sacramento,** to the left of the high altar, shines with solid silver and plated gold and is used as the bishop's study. During the Napoleonic invasion, crafty townspeople whitewashed the altar to prevent vandalism. Climb the staircase to the Renaissance house for a splendid view of the old quarter. *(Terreiro da Sé. ☎ 222 05 90 28. Open M-Sa 9am-12:30pm and 2:30-6pm, Su 2:30-6pm. Cloister €1.25.)*

MUSEU DE ARTE CONTEMPORÂNEA. This museum houses rotating exhibits of contemporary Portuguese art and architecture, as well as international photography and sculpture. Its 44 colossal acres of manicured gardens, fountains, and old farmland tumbling down toward the Douro River are also easy on the eyes. *(R. D. João de Castro, 210. Several km out of town, on the way to the beach. Bus #78 leaves from Av. dos Aliados; ask the driver to stop at the museum; 30min., return buses run until midnight. ☎ 226 15 65 00. Museum open Tu-W, F-Sa 10am-7pm, Th 10am-10pm. Park closes daily 7pm. Museum and park €5, park only €2.50. Su before 2pm free.)*

IGREJA E TORRE DOS CLÉRIGOS. The 18th-century **Igreja dos Clérigos** is decorated with Baroque and Rococo carvings. Its **Torre dos Clérigos** is the city's tallest landmark and the tallest tower in Portugal, reaching a height of 75.6m. Atop the 200 steps await spectacular views of Porto and the Rio Douro valley. *(R. dos Clérigos. ☎/fax 222 00 17 29. Church open M-Th 10am-noon and 2-5pm, Sa 10am-noon and 2-8pm, Su 10am-1pm. Tower open daily July-Aug. 9:30am-1pm and 2:30-7pm; Sept.-July 10am-noon and 2-5pm. Church free, tower €1.50.)*

JARDIMS DO PALÁCIO DE CRISTAL. Beautiful gardens lie outside the Palácio do Cristal (Glass Palace). Take a gander at the geese, swans, ducks, peacocks, and fountains, while enjoying a pleasant stroll through the lush vegetation. *(R. Dom Manuel II. ☎ 226 05 70 80. Open daily until dark.)*

NIGHTLIFE

For whatever reason, Porto is not a party city after hours. Most people congregate around the bar-restaurants of **Ribeira,** where spicy Brazilian music plays until 2am. The narrow streets and poor lighting, however, can be spooky; don't go alone. Pr. da Ribeira, Muro dos Bacalhoeiros, and R. Nova da Alfândega harbor most of the bars and pubs. Be cautious, as Pr. da Ribeira and Cais da Ribeira can be unsafe at night. Most clubs are located along the river in **Foz** and in the new industrial zones; nightlife in Porto is hard to follow without a car. Bus #1 runs all night from Pr. da Liberdade to the beach at Matosinhos, passing Foz along the way. A taxi to Foz from downtown costs about €4.

Solar do Vinho do Porto, R. Entre Quintas, 220 (☎226 09 47 49). What could be better than enjoying a fine glass of port while sitting on the outdoor terrace of a former manor house and gazing across the river at port cellars as the sun sets? Twin sister of the Solar in Lisboa and an excellent place to spend an afternoon or evening savoring the fruits of the Douro's fertile lands. Port €1.20-€15. Open M-Sa 2pm-midnight. AmEx/MC/V.

Discoteca Swing, Pr. Engenheiro Amaro Costa, 766 (☎226 09 00 19). Guest DJs rock the weekends, while regular house, new wave, and Latin go strong during the week. Mostly frequented by early 20-somethings. Th is ladies' night with 3 free drinks. Beer €3. Mixed drinks €7.50. M-W no cover, Th-Su €7.50-€12.50. Open daily midnight-7am, but the fun starts around 1am. AmEx/MC/V.

O Muro, Muro dos Bacalhoeiros, 87-88 (☎222 08 34 26), a pedestrian street in Ribeira. A tiny yet remarkable restaurant during the day, O Muro attracts night owls with a great view of the river and the complimentary olives and *tremoço,* a local edible seed, that come with each beer (€1-4). Open Tu-Su noon-2am.

Petrus Bar/Wine Café, R. Fonte Taurina, 97 (☎919 86 77 80). During the day, Petrus is a cool escape from the sun. At night, jazz, soul, and blues stream from the lounge. The patio is a perfect spot to enjoy the view of the port lodges across the river. Beer €2-3.50. Mixed drinks €3.50. Open daily 10:30am-5am.

FESTIVALS

Porto hosts the **Fantasporto Film Festival** (2 weeks during February), screening international fantasy, sci-fi, and horror flicks for crowds of film enthusiasts. Early June brings the **Festival Internacional de Teatro de Expressão Ibérica,** which stages free performances of Portuguese and Spanish drama. Porto's biggest party, however, is the **Festa de São João** (June 23-24), when locals storm the streets for free concerts, folklore, *fado,* and (of course) wine. Although not as big a production as in Lisboa, the northern version is still a guaranteed party.

BRAGA   ☎253

In Braga (pop. 166,000), a fountain graces every plaza, loudspeakers channel music to the streets, and gardens breathe freshness into urban air. A city impressive enough on its own, it's a shame that Braga's nickname, "Portuguese Rome," relegates it to mere reference. The 1926 coup that paved Salazar's path to power was launched from here, and the city retains conservative tendencies to this day with somber religious processions crossing flower-carpeted streets during Holy Week. However, Braga has its own wild side, with vibrant nightlife and crowds constantly flowing through the central Pr. da República. Those who come to Braga expecting just to pass through often end up staying for several days, as the city makes a convenient base for worthwhile daytrips.

Braga

▲ ACCOMMODATIONS
Pensão Grande Residência
Avenida, **7**
Pensão Residencial Francfort, **4**
Pousada da Juventude (HI), **3**
Residencial Dona Sofia, **11**

● FOOD
Abade de Priscos, **2**
Churrasqueria da Sé, **9**
Cozinha da Sé, **10**
Restaurante Cruz Sobral, **8**

★ NIGHTLIFE
Café Astória, **6**
Insólito Bar, **5**
Populum, **1**

THE NORTH

📳 TRANSPORTATION

Trains: The recently renovated train station, **Estaçaõ da Braga** (☎808 20 82 08), is 1km from Pr. da República. Take R. do Souto and pass through the town gate; the station is 400m to the left. Trains run to: **Lisboa** (4hr., 3 per day 7:25am-6:30pm, €25), **Porto** (45-60min.; M-F 26 per day 5:07am-5:07pm, Sa-Su 13-14 per day 6:07am-9:07pm; €9.50), and **Vigo**, Spain (4hr., 7:53am and 7:07pm, €12.30).

Buses: The bus station is the **Central de Camionagem** (☎253 61 60 80; offices open M-Sa 6am-8:30pm, Su 9am-9pm), a few blocks north of the city center. **Rodoviária** runs to: **Guimarães** (1hr.; every 30min. M-F 7:15am-8:35pm, Sa-Su 8am-8:35pm; €2.20) and **Porto** (1¼hr.; M-F every 30min. 6:45am-8:05pm, Sa 7 per day 7am-7pm, Su 5 per day 11am-10pm; €3.60). **Rede Expressos** runs to: **Coimbra** (3hr., 6-9 per day 6am-11:30pm, €10); **Faro** (12-15hr.; June-Sept. 6 per day 7am-11:30pm, Oct.-May 3 per day 11am-7pm; €20); **Lisboa** (5¼hr., 10-11 per day 6am-11:30pm, €14.50). **Hoteleira do Gerês** runs to **Caldas de Gerês** (1½hr.; M-F 11 per day 7:05am-8pm, Sa 8 per day 8am-8pm, Su 6 per day 8am-7:10pm; €8).

Taxis: ☎253 68 32 28. About €0.80 per km.

⚊🔃 ORIENTATION AND PRACTICAL INFORMATION

Braga's focal point is the **Praça da República,** the large central square full of fountains and cafes, and the start of **Avenida da Liberdade.** Pedestrian thoroughfare **Rua do Souto** begins at the tourist office corner of Pr. da República, eventually becoming R. Dom Diogo de Sousa and then R. Andrade Corvo, before leading to the train station. To get to Pr. da República from the bus station, take a right onto the commercial street with your back to the station. Continue straight under the modern building's overpass onto Pr. Alexandre Herculano, then take R. dos Cháos straight ahead into the square.

Tourist Office: Av. da Liberdade, 1 (☎253 26 25 50; www.cm-braga.pt), in Pr. da República. Open June-Sept. M-F 9am-7pm, Sa-Su 9am-12:30pm and 2-5:30pm; Oct.-May M-Sa 9am-12:30pm and 2-5:30pm.

Budget Travel: Tagus, Pr. Municipal, 7 (☎253 21 51 44). Open June-Sept. M-F 9am-1pm and 2:30-6pm, Sa 10am-1pm; Oct.-May M-F 9am-12:30pm and 2:30-6pm.

Currency Exchange: Caixa Geral de Depósitos, Pr. da República (☎253 60 01 00), next to Café Astória. Open M-F 8:30am-3pm. **ATM** outside.

English-Language Bookstore: Livraria Central, Av. da Liberdade, 728 (☎253 26 23 83). Small selection of books and travel guides in English. Open M-Sa 10am-7pm.

Police: R. dos Falcões, 12 (☎253 20 04 20).

Hospital: Hospital de São Marcos, Lg. Carlos Amarante, 6e (☎253 20 90 00).

Internet Access: Espaço Internet Braga, Pr. Conde de Agrolongo, 177 (☎254 26 74 84). 10 computers. Free. 1hr. limit if people are waiting; go in the early morning to avoid a crowd. Open M-F 9am-7:30pm, Sa 9am-1pm. **Videoteca Municipal,** R. do Raio, 2 (☎253 26 77 93). Free. 1hr. limit. Open M-Sa 10am-12:30pm and 2-6:30pm.

Post Office: Av. da Liberdade (☎253 20 03 64). For **Posta Restante,** indicate "Estação Avenida." Phone, fax, and other services. Open M-F 8:30am-6pm. **Postal Code:** 4700.

🏠🏕 ACCOMMODATIONS AND CAMPING

🏨 **Pensão Grande Residência Avenida,** Av. da Liberdade, 738, 2nd fl. (☎253 60 90 20). Handsome, well-lit rooms with phone and TV overlook the avenue or a backyard garden. Breakfast €3. July-Aug. singles €25, with bath €40; doubles €35/€45; triples €45/€52. Sept.-June singles €20/€22; doubles €25/€30; triples €30/€37.50. MC/V. ❷

Pousada da Juventude de Braga (HI), R. Santa Margarida, 6 (☎/fax 253 61 61 63). Taxi from the train station €4. Crowded dorm rooms, with 8-10 beds each, are offset by a friendly atmosphere and a convenient location. Reception 8am-midnight. Mid-June to mid-Sept. dorms €10; doubles with bath €27. Mid-Sept. to mid-June €7.50/€21. ❶

Pensão Residencial Francfort, Av. Central, 7 (☎253 26 26 48). A large red-tiled building in a premium location; some of the small rooms overlook Pr. da República. Reception 8am-midnight. Curfew midnight. May-Sept. singles €20, with bath €25; doubles €20/€35; triples €35. Oct.-Apr. singles €13/€20; doubles €18/€25; triples €30. ❷

Residencial Dona Sofía, Lg. S. João do Souto, 131 (☎253 26 31 60; hotel.d.sofia@oninet.pt). The comfortable rooms in this 3-star hotel come with bar, TV, A/C, phone, bath, and large windows. An excellent break from budget rooms. Breakfast included. Singles €45-50; doubles €65-70; suites €80. ❹

Camping: Camping Parque da Ponte (☎253 27 33 55), 2km down Av. da Liberdade from the center, next to the stadium and municipal pool. Buses every 20min. 6:30am-11pm. €2 per person, €1.60-2.40 per tent, €1.70 per car. Electricity €1.50. ❶

🔲 FOOD

Braga has many crowded cafes perfect for a small meal and an afternoon of people-watching on Pr. da República. For fast meals, head to the food court of the **BragaShopping** mall, facing the plaza (☎253 20 80 10). Supermarket **Pingo Doce** is in the basement. (Open daily 10am-11pm.) The **market** is in Pr. do Comércio. (Open M-Sa 7am-3pm.)

Churrasquería da Sé, R. D. Paio Mendes, 25 (☎253 26 33 87). Efficiently serves delicious, generous half-portions of meat and fish entrees to lunch crowds (€4.50-6.50). *Prato do dia* €4-7.80. Open M-Tu and Th-Su 9:30am-3pm and 6:30-9:30pm. ❶

Abade de Priscos, Pr. Mouzinho de Albuquerque, 7, 2nd fl. (☎253 27 66 50). Named after a priest from the early 1900s who is still widely considered to have been Portugal's best chef, this restaurant serves traditional Portuguese cuisine; specialties include *galinha morisca* and *bacalao gratinado* (€7.80). Open M 7:30-10pm, Tu-Sa noon-2:30pm and 7:30-10pm. Closed last 2 weeks of June and 1st week of July. ❷

Restaurante Cruz Sobral, Campo das Hortas, 5 (☎253 61 66 48). From Pr. da República, walk down R. do Souto to Campo das Hortas. Quiet, more upscale restaurant serving delicious fish and veal dishes; half-portions available. Entrees €13.50-19, half-portions €9.50-11.50. Open daily 12:20-3pm and 7:30-10pm. AmEx/MC/V. ❸

Cozinha da Sé, R. D. Frei Caetano Brandão, 95 (☎253 27 73 43). This spot boasts excellent service and some of the most affordable and well-prepared fish dishes in Braga, including salmon, bass, and squid. Entrees €6.50-10. Open Tu-Su 12:30-3pm and 7:30-10pm. AmEx/MC/V. ❷

🔄 SIGHTS

IGREJA DO BOM JESUS. Braga's most famous landmark crowns a hillside 5km outside of town. This 18th-century church was built in an effort to recreate Jerusalem in Braga, providing Iberian Christians with a pilgrimage site closer to home. To visit, you can take the 285m ride on the antique cable car (8am-8pm, €1). However, the 20-25min. walk up the zig-zagging staircase passes by several spots that you can't see from the cable car, including stations of the cross, fountains representing the five senses ("smell" spouts water through a boy's nose), and stony prophets. The church, a few small cafes, and stunning sunset views await at the top. If your legs can handle it, you can continue uphill around the church to a small lake and more chapels with scenes from Jesus's life. **Café Esplanada** (sandwiches €1.60-3.30, beautiful ice cream sundaes €2.50-5; open daily 8am-2am.) is a popular place to wait for the sunset with a drink or sandwich. *(Buses labeled "#02 Bom Jesus" depart at 10 and 40min. past the hr. in front of Farmácia Cristal, Av. da Liberdade, 571. Buses stop at the bottom of the stairway; the last bus from Bom Jesus leaves at 9pm. €1.10.)*

CATHEDRAL. Braga's **Sé**, Portugal's oldest cathedral, has undergone a series of renovations since its construction in the 11th to 12th centuries. Guided tours (in Portuguese, French, or English) of its treasury, choir, and chapels run frequently. The treasury showcases the archdiocese's most precious paintings and relics. On display is the *Cruz do Brasil*, an iron cross from the ship Pedro Cabral captained when he discovered Brazil on April 22, 1500. Perhaps most curious is the cathedral's collection of *cofres cranianos* (brain boxes), one of which contains the 6th-century cortex of São Martinho Dume, Braga's first bishop. The notable **Capela dos Reis** (Chapel of the Kings) guards the 12th-century stone sarcophagi of Dom Afonso Henriques's parents and the mummified remains of a 14th-century archbishop. The tour also takes you upstairs to the heavily adorned choir overlooking the nave; you can practically reach out and touch the two 18th-century organs with their 2400 fully functioning pipes. *(☎ 253 26 33 17. Mass daily 5pm. Open daily June-Aug. 8:30am-6:30pm; Sept.-May 8:30am-5pm. Cathedral free. Treasury and chapels €2.)*

◨ NIGHTLIFE

Locals and travelers of all ages head to ▨**Populum,** off of Pr. Conde de Agrolongo. The cavernous bar and discoteca always has at least two dance floors going at full force, where you can listen to the top 40 or practice your merengue and salsa. (☎ 253 61 09 66. Beer €2, mixed drinks €5. Minimum consumption for men €5, after 12:30am €10; for women €5, Th free. Open Th-Sa 10pm-5am. Closed Aug.) The cafes in Pr. da República fill with people after midnight. The upstairs bar of **Café Astória,** Pr. da República, 5, next door to Café Vianna, is a popular student hangout after midnight. The bar has red velvet curtains and couches and a large balcony overlooking the plaza. (☎ 966 08 36 97. Beer €1. Open M-Sa 8am-6am, Su 10am-6am.) Nearby is the **Insólito Bar,** Av. Central, 47, between Pr. da República and the youth hostel. Student artwork on the walls inside and live music twice a week in the yard out back attracts a university crowd. (☎ 968 01 62 40. Beer €1. Mixed drinks €3.50. Minimum consumption M-Th €1, F-Sa €2.50. Open M-Sa 10pm-6am. Closed Aug.) The area around Pr. do Comércio between Tr. do Carmo and R. Alferes Ferreira is quite dangerous at night; be cautious after dark.

◈ FESTIVALS

Braga's biggest festival of the year is the **Festa de São João,** a week-long celebration beginning on June 19 and peaking the night of June 23. The bash in Porto is supposedly better, but the *bracarenses* still know how to party. Traditional folk music, good food, colorful lights and decorations, concerts, and general revelry take over Av. da Liberdade and Lg. São João da Ponte. Don't be surprised to see locals running around beating each other on the head with toy hammers; few seem to remember the bizarre ritual's origin, but older folks relate that it's a tribute to São João, Protector of the Head.

⚡ DAYTRIPS FROM BRAGA

MOSTEIRO DE TIBÃES

City bus #3 labeled "Ruães" heads 6km from Braga to the monastery. Buses leave from the stop across from the bus station on Av. General Norton de Matos (25min.; M-F 7 per day 9:15am-8:20pm, Sa-Su 6 per day 9:15am-8:15pm; €1.40). From the bus stop, walk to the rotary and turn left; the monastery is a 15-20min. walk uphill.

Surrounded by unspoiled forest, this 11th-century Benedictine monastery provided a haven for its monks until 1864, functioning as both a religious sanctuary and a school of aesthetics. Unfortunately, it has suffered from centuries of neglect; stones rattle underfoot in the weathered cloister and the monastery is undergoing much-needed restoration expected to continue through 2006. Check with the tourist office in Braga or the monastery office to find out which areas are open for visits. Adjoining the cloister is an exceptionally well-preserved church with an ornate gilded altar. (☎253 62 26 70. Open Apr.-Oct. Tu-Su 10am-6:30pm; Nov.-Mar. Tu-Su 9:30am-5:30pm. €4, ages 14-25 €2, under 14 free.)

GUIMARÃES

REDM buses (☎253 51 62 29) run from Braga to Guimarães (40min.; M-F 19 per day 7:15am-8:35pm, Sa-Su 13-15 per day 8am-8:35pm; €2.20), and return (40min.; M-F 19 per day 6:30am-8:30pm, Sa-Su 13-15 per day 6:55am-8:30pm; €2.20).

Ask any native about Guimarães (pop. 60,000), and they will tell you that it was the birthplace of the nation. Guimarães was the hometown of the first king of Portugal, Dom Afonso Henriques, and the site of his initial court in the 12th century. It was also where Henriques began the reconquest of Portugal from the Moors. One of the country's most gorgeous palatial estates, the ⚡**Paço dos Duques de Bragança** (Ducal Palace), is modeled after the manors of northern Europe. The museum inside includes furniture, silverware, tapestries, and weapons once used at the palace. Don't miss the elaborate Pastrana tapestries in the **Sala dos Pasos Perdidos** (Hall of Lost Footsteps), depicting scenes from the 15th-century North African campaigns of Dom Alfonso V, or the interesting display of archaic weaponry in the **Sala das Armas** (Arms Room). (☎253 41 22 73. Palace open daily 9:30am-12:30pm and 2-5:30pm; last entrance noon and 5pm. €3, ages 15-25 and seniors €1.50. Su morning free.) Overlooking the city is the **Monte da Penha,** home to an excellent campsite as well as picnic areas, mini-golf, and cafes. To get there, take the **teleférico** (tram) which runs from Lg. das Hortas to the mountaintop. Walkways lined by massive boulders greet you at the top; be sure to visit the Miradouro lookout point and the chapels that have been built into the rocks. (☎253 51 50 85. Open Aug. daily 10:30am-8pm; Apr.-July and Sept. M-F 10:30am-7pm, Sa-Su 10:30am-8pm. €1.50, round-trip €2.50.)

The **train station** (☎253 41 23 51) is a 10min. walk down Av. Afonso Henriques from the tourist office. The **bus station** (☎253 51 62 29) is in the **GuimarãeShopping** complex, on Alameda Mariano Felgueiras. To get there, follow Av. Conde Margaride downhill. The main **tourist office** is on Alameda de São Dâmaso, 83, facing Lg. do Toural. From the bus station, take Av. Conde Margaride to the right, walk uphill, and turn right at the fork onto R. Paio Galvão; the tourist office is two streets across from the far corner of Lg. do Toural. The English-speaking staff distributes maps and brochures and offers short-term **luggage storage.** (☎253 41 24 50. Open M-F 9:30am-12:30pm and 2-6:30pm.) A second tourist office on Pr. de Santiago has longer hours. (☎253 51 87 90. Open M-F 9:30am-6:30pm, Sa 10am-6pm, Su 10am-1pm.) Local services include: **police** on

Alameda Alfredo Pimenta (☎253 51 33 34); **hospital** on R. dos Cutileiros (☎253 51 26 12). Follow the crowds for lunch at the family-run **Restaurante O Pinguim ❷**, Tr. do Picoto, off R. Picoto. From Lg. Navarros de Andrade, go up Av. Humberto Delgado (across the square from the post office) and take a left onto R. Picoto up the hill, then another left off the street as it curves to the right. Their specialty is *bacalhau à pinguimu*, a salted cod dish (€14.50, serves 2). Other entrees run €5.50-9.50. (☎253 41 81 82. Open Tu-Su 8am-10:30pm; serves meals 11:30am-3:30pm and 7-10:30pm. MC/V, debit only.)

BARCELOS

REDM buses (☎253 80 83 00) run from Braga to Barcelos (40-50min.; M-F 23 per day 6:35am-7:10pm, Sa 14 per day 7:15am-7:10pm, Su 6 per day 8am-7:10pm; €1.80) and return from Av. Dr. Sidónio Pais, 245, across from Campo da República (M-F 23 per day 6:30am-7:20pm, Sa 13 per day 7:40am-7:20pm, Su 6 per day 7:40am-7:20pm).

Though Barcelos is known throughout Portugal for its famous rooster, the town also hosts one of the largest weekly markets in Europe—vendors from the entire region come on Thursdays to sell everything from produce to local ceramics. This market, the **Feira de Barcelos,** was inaugurated in 1412 by Dom João I. Vendors begin arriving at the huge **Campo da República** late Wednesday night to set up, and by 8am on Thursday the market is going at full force. Old ladies carry live roosters by the feet, artisans display traditional ceramics, and aggressive pastry sellers work from trucks on the square's edge along Av. da Liberdade until 5pm, or 7:30pm in summer. Even if you miss market day, Barcelos is still worth a trip. The **Templo do Bom Jesus** in Lg. da Porta Nova is an octagonal Baroque church dating from 1704, with blue and white glazed tiles and a golden altar. In Lg. do Município is the 12th-century **Igreja Matriz,** a Romanic-Gothic church with a magnificent organ. Behind the church and overlooking the river is the 14th-century **Paço Condal,** site of the famous monument to the Barcelos cock, and the open-air **Museu Arqueológico.** (All sights open daily 9am-noon and 2-5pm. Free.)

The **tourist office** is in the Torre da Porta Nova, part of the town's original 15th-century wall and the only remaining of three towers that once marked the entrance to the ancient city. The office provides short-term **luggage storage.** (☎/fax 253 81 18 82; www.camaramunicipal.bcl.pt. Open Mar.-Oct. M-F 10am-6pm, Sa 10am-12:30pm and 2:30-5:30pm, Su 2:30-5:30pm; Nov.-Feb. M-F 9:30am-5:30pm, Sa 9:30am-5pm.) Local services include the **police** (☎253 80 25 70) on Av. Dr. Sidónio Pais and the **hospital** (☎253 80 92 00) on Lg. Campo da República.

PARQUE NACIONAL DE PENEDA-GERÊS

A crescent-shaped nature reserve along the Spanish border, the Parque Nacional de Peneda-Gerês became Portugal's first protected area in 1971, consisting of the northern Serra da Peneda and the southern Serra do Gerês. The main base is Vila do Gerês, a spa town that draws hordes of Portuguese vacationers in July and August, from where you can venture any time of year throughout the park's many relaxing villages. The park's turquoise waters, tree-covered mountains, and archaeological remnants from the Iron Age leave little to be desired, and activities range from simple hikes by abandoned monasteries and water sports to relaxation in thermal waters and pampering in spas.

🖿 🈂 TRANSPORTATION AND PRACTICAL INFORMATION. Empresa Hoteleira do Gerês (☎253 61 58 96) runs **buses** between Gerês and **Braga** (1½hr.; M-F 11 per day 6:30am-6:30pm, Sa-Su 6 per day 7:15am-6:30pm; €3.20). To get to the

tourist office from the bus stop, walk uphill along Av. Manuel Francisco da Costa; the office is surrounded by a semicircle of shops. The English-speaking staff provides info on activities in the national park as well as **luggage storage.** (☎253 39 11 33; fax 39 12 82. Open Apr.-Aug. M-Sa 9:30am-12:30pm and 2:30-6pm, Su 9:30am-12:30pm; Sept.-Mar. M-W and F-Sa 9am-12:30pm and 2:30-5:30pm.) The **police** (☎253 39 11 37) are off Av. Manuel Francisco da Costa, and the **Red Cross** (☎253 39 16 60) is on Cha de Ermida. The **Biblioteca Municipal** on Av. Manuel Francisco da Costa, across from the spa, has free **Internet.** (☎253 39 17 97. Open M-F 9:30am-9:30pm, Sa 9:30am-1:30pm.) The **post office** is located off the rotary that leads uphill into the center. (☎253 39 00 10; fax 39 00 16. Open M-F 9am-12:30pm and 2-5:30pm.)

⌂☐ ACCOMMODATIONS AND FOOD. There are plenty of *pensões* in Gerês. One option is **Casa de Ponte ❷**, on Av. D. João V. From the bus stop, head downhill until you see the hostel on the left corner where the road splits, next to the Escola Primaria. The English-speaking owner offers rooms with bath and TV; most also have porches overlooking the garden. (☎253 39 11 25. Breakfast included. Midnight curfew. Aug.-Oct. singles €25; doubles €40; triples €45. May-July €20/€30/€35. Nov.-Apr. €15/€20/€35.) For camping, try **⬛Camping Vidoeiro ❶**, 1km out of town by the river. Facing the tourist office, take the uphill road to the left. The campground is another 400m up the gravel road, past the park information office. On the river's edge under the shade of giant sequoia trees, this quiet, well-maintained campground provides a gateway into the park. (☎253 39 12 89. Reception 8am-7pm. Open May 15-Oct. 15. €2.05 per person, €1.80-2.30 per tent, €2.30 per car.) Meals are available at the *pensões* throughout town. **Restaurants** and **cafes** line Av. Manuel Francisco da Costa, around the corner from the bus stop.

☒⛰ HIKING AND OUTDOOR ACTIVITIES. The main **park information office** is located in **Braga**, on Av. António Macedo. (☎253 20 34 80; fax 61 31 69. Open M-F 9:30am-12:30pm and 2:30-5:30pm.) The Gerês **branch office**, on Av. Manuel Francisco da Costa, 1km uphill from the tourist office, can assist with hike planning. (☎253 39 01 10. Open M-F 9am-noon and 2-5:30pm.) More casual visitors tend to stay south, where the few trails provide scenic and manageable journeys, while dedicated hikers head to the northern trails. In both areas, numerous hamlets and villages offer accommodations, campsites, and food. The most popular hike is the easily accessible, 5km **Trilho da Preguiça**. It begins just north of Gerês proper and follows the Rio Gerês. Another hike follows the road 10km farther toward **Portela do Homem**, a small town on the Portuguese-Spanish border with a river pool at the bottom of the **Minas dos Carris** valley.

South of Gerês, the **Miradouro do Gerês** overlooks the **Caniçada** reservoir—beware the en masse migration of weekend picnickers. The village of **Rio Caldo,** at the base of Caniçada reservoir just 8km south of Gerês, offers canoeing and water-skiing, which visitors can arrange through **Agua Montanha Lazer.** (☎253 39 17 79; www.aguamontanha.com. Single canoe €4 per hr., €13 per half day, €19 per day. Waterskiing €35 per 20min., €80 per hr.) The main attraction in Gerês proper is **Empresa das Aguas do Gerês**, on Av. Manuel Francisco da Costa. Along with famed therapeutic waters, the spa complex includes a pool, tennis courts, horseback riding, hiking, and canoeing. (☎253 39 11 13. Open May-Oct.) Next door, **Parque das Termas** has fluorine mineral waters. (☎253 39 11 13; fax 39 11 84. Entrance €1, under 12 €0.50. Pool open daily Aug. 10am-8pm; Apr.-July and Sept. 10am-6pm. M-F €4, Sa-Su €6, under 12 €2/€4. Tennis and canoeing €3 per hr. 30min. full-body massage €16. Whirlpool €5.)

THE NORTH

VIANA DO CASTELO
☎**258**

Although it is visited mainly as a beach resort, Viana do Castelo (pop. 37,000) also has a lively historic district centered around the Praça da República, excellent and unique culinary specialties, and intriguing architecture that includes a bridge designed by Gustave Eiffel. The surrounding hilltops and the nearby Monte de Santa Luzia offer excellent views of the fertile landscape and the sea. Those passing through en route to Galicia soon discover the town's charm.

▐▀ TRANSPORTATION

Trains: The station (☎258 82 13 15) is at the top of Av. dos Combatentes da Grande Guerra, under the Santa Luzia hill. Trains to: **Porto** (2hr., 13-14 per day 5:12am-10:07pm, €5.50); **Valença do Minho** (1hr., 7-8 per day 7:39am-8:35pm, €2.40); **Vigo,** Spain (2½hr., 9:28am and 8:35pm, €8.20).

Buses: The station is the **Central de Camionagem** (☎258 82 50 47), on the eastern edge of town and a 20min. walk from the center. **REDM** runs to **Braga** (1½hr.; M-F 9 per day 6:50am-7:05pm, Sa 6 per day 6:50am-6:35pm, Su 4 per day 8:15am-6:35pm; €3.20). **AVIC** (☎258 82 97 05) and **A.V. Minho** (☎258 80 03 41) go to: **Lisboa** (5½hr.; M-F and Su 3 per day 8am-11:45pm, Sa 12:30pm and 7pm; €14); **Porto** (2hr.; M-F 11 per day 6:45am-11:45pm, Sa 9 per day 7:30am-7pm, Su 11 per day 7:30am-9pm; €5); **Valença do Minho** (1hr.; M-F 6 per day 11:30am-8:15pm, Sa 3 per day 10:30am-5:20pm, Su 5:30pm; €3).

Taxis: Táxis Vianenses (☎258 82 66 41). About €0.75 per km.

✚▐ ORIENTATION AND PRACTICAL INFORMATION

Wide **Avenida dos Combatentes da Grande Guerra** runs from the train station to the port. Most accommodations and restaurants are on or near the Avenida. The **historic center** stretches east of the Avenida around **Praça da República,** while the fortress and sea are to the west and **Templo de Santa Luzia** to the north. Beaches, sights, and stations are all within a 20min. walk from Pr. da República.

Tourist Office: Tr. do Hospital Velho, 8 (☎258 82 26 20), on the corner of Pr. da Erva. From the train station, take the 4th left onto R. da Picota and then a right. Open M-F 9am-12:30pm and 2:30-6pm, Sa 9:30am-1pm and 2:30-6pm, Su 9:30am-1pm.

Currency Exchange: Montepio Geral, Av. dos Combatentes da Grande Guerra, 332 (☎258 82 88 97), near the train station. 24hr. **ATM.** Open M-F 8:30am-3pm.

Police: R. de Aveiro (☎258 82 20 22).

Hospital: Hospital de Santa Luzia, Estrada Sta. Luzia (☎258 82 90 81).

Internet Access: Free at the **Biblioteca Municipal** on R. Cândido dos Reis (☎258 80 93 02), up from Pr. da República. 5 computers. ID required. Strict 30min. limit. Open M-F 9:30am-12:30pm and 2-7pm, Sa 9:30am-12:30pm. Also available at the **post office.** A €5 card lasts about 3hr.

Post Office: Av. dos Combatentes da Grande Guerra (☎258 80 00 82). **Posta Restante** and **fax.** Open M-F 8:30am-6pm, Sa 9am-12:30pm. **Postal Code:** 4900.

▐▐▀ ACCOMMODATIONS AND CAMPING

Accommodations in Viana do Castelo are easy to find. Check the side streets off Av. dos Combatentes da Grande Guerra if you have trouble finding a place.

▨ **Pousada de Juventude de Viana do Castelo (HI),** R. de Límia (☎258 80 02 60; fax 80 02 61), right on the marina, off R. da Argaçosa and Pr. da Galiza. Rooms with balconies and great views make this welcoming, well-equipped hostel worth the 15min. walk from the town center. Lounge with pool, ping-pong tables, and a bar. Internet access €1.50 per 30min., €2.50 per hr. Breakfast included. Laundry €5 per load. Reception 8am-midnight. Check-out 10:30am. Reservations recommended. June 16-Sept. 15 dorms €12.50; doubles with bath €35. Sept. 16-June 15 €10/€28. ❶

Pensão Dolce Vita, R. Poço, 44 (☎258 82 48 60), across from the tourist office. In an excellent location. Sleek, newly renovated rooms with 2 twin beds, TV, bath, A/C, and plenty of light. Aug. for 1 person €40, €60 per room; June-July €30/€50; Sept.-May reduced prices. MC/V. ❸

Residencial Viana Mar, Av. dos Combatentes da Grande Guerra, 215 (☎/fax 258 82 89 62), 2min. from the train station. Large, convenient *residencial*-restaurant combo with TV and A/C. Mid-July to Aug. singles €30, with shower €40, with bath €40; doubles €35/€45/€50. May to mid-July and Sept. singles €15/€20/€25, doubles €30/€35/€40. Oct.-Apr. reduced prices. AmEx/MC/V. ❷

Residencial Jardim, Lg. 5 de Outubro, 68 (☎258 82 89 15; fax 82 89 17). Considering the elegance, river view, and convenience of this *residencial*, the rooms come at a bargain with private bath, TV, radio, and phone. Breakfast included. June-Aug. singles €42.50; doubles €50; triples €60. Sept.-May €35/€45/€50. AmEx/MC/V. ❹

Pousada de Viana do Castelo, Monte Santa Luzia (☎258 80 03 70; fax 82 88 92). Built in 1918 atop a mountain, this gorgeous hotel features amazing views from its vast balcony, restaurant, and bar. A €5 cab ride from the center of town, but there's no hurry to stray from the swimming pool, tennis courts, mountain bikes, and billiards anyway. Apr.-Oct. Su-Th doubles €143, with view €153; F-Sa €157/€175. Nov.-Mar. Su-Th €97/€107; F-Sa €107/€118. Under 30 and over 60 discounts. AmEx/MC/V. ❺

Camping: Orbitur (☎258 32 21 67; fax 32 19 46), at Praia do Cabedelo. Catch a Trans-Cunha "Cabedelo" bus (M-F 6 per day 7:35am-6:45pm, €0.80) from Lg. 5 de Outubro. A well-equipped campsite with free showers. June-Sept. €4.10-4.30 per person, €3.30-5.30 per tent, €3.40-3.80 per car. Oct.-Apr. €2.40/€2.10-2.80/€2.80. ❶

🍴 FOOD

People eat well in Viana do Castelo. The local specialties are *arroz de sarabulho* (rice cooked with blood and served alongside sausages and potatoes) and *bacalhau à Gil Eanes* (cod cooked with milk, potato, onion, garlic, and oil). Most budget restaurants lie on the small streets off Av. dos Combatentes da Grande Guerra. The **municipal market** is on Av. Rocha Páris, in front of Pr. Dona Maria II. (☎258 82 26 57. Open M-Sa 8am-3pm.) A weekly **market,** attracting many of the same vendors as the one in Barcelos, is held Fridays from dawn to sunset off Av. Capitão Gaspar de Castro, on the same road as the bus station. For groceries, go to **Estacão Supermercado** in the mall next to the train station. (☎288 10 08 10. Open daily 9am-11pm.)

▧ Restaurante Dolce Vita, R. Poço, 44 (☎258 82 48 60), at the corner of Pr. da Erva, across the square from the tourist office. Brick-oven pizzas with fresh toppings (€4.50-5.80) are served to a bustling crowd of locals and travelers. Portuguese dishes and pastas €4.50-13. Open daily noon-3pm and 7:30-10:30pm. MC/V. ❶

A Matriz, R. do Tourinho, 5 (☎258 82 60 69), on the corner with R. Sacadura Cabral. Enjoy the quiet setting with excellent fish and meat dishes, including meat fondue for 2 (€11-12.30). Entrees €6.50-10.80. Open M-Sa noon-3:30pm and 7-10pm. ❷

Confeitaria Natário, R. Manuel Espregueira, 37 (☎258 82 23 76), just off Av. dos Combatentes da Grande Guerra. People line up at 10:30am to catch the meat and fish pastries hot out of the oven (€0.60-2.80). Their delicious specialty is *bolos de berlim* (€0.75), a sweet pastry filled with fresh egg cream. Open M and W-Su 9am-10pm. ❶

Restaurante Glamour, R. da Bandera, 185 (☎258 82 29 63). Choose from a small menu of fish and meat entrees and an extensive wine selection in this sleek, contemporary restaurant upstairs from the bar. Try the *magret de pato,* sliced duck breast with a secret-recipe salsa. Entrees €9-12. Open daily 7:30pm-2am. V. ❷

Ruela Bar, Av. Campo do Castelo, 11 (☎258 81 10 72), on the street below the castle, across from the square. Popular with students for its *prato do dia* (€3.20) and burgers (€2.80-3.80). Open M-Sa 11:30am-3pm and 6pm-midnight. ❶

⚫ SIGHTS

The ⚑**Monte de Santa Luzia,** overlooking the city, is crowned by magnificent Celtic ruins and the **Templo de Santa Luzia,** an early-20th-century neo-Byzantine church. Though the cable car no longer runs, you can huff your way up the hundreds of stairs that begin behind the train station (20-30min.) or take a taxi to the hilltop (€5). The view of Viana is fantastic, especially from the top of the church; take the elevator (€0.50) up the tower, or climb the narrow stairway that leads to the **Zimbório** at the very top. (Templo open daily summer 8am-7pm; winter 8am-5pm. Mass daily at 4pm. Free.) Right in the town center, Viana do Castelo's **Praça da República,** marked by an elaborate 16th-century fountain, is a stately representative of Portugal's impressive squares. Here, the **Museu de Traje** provides a glimpse into the region's distinctive attire, from festive costumes to work clothes. (☎258 80 01 71. Open Tu-Su 10am-1pm and 3-7pm. €2, students €1.) Diagonally across the plaza, granite columns support the playful and flowery facade of the **Igreja da Misericórdia** (1598, rebuilt in 1714), which is known for its *azulejo* interior. (Open daily 9:30am-12:30pm and 2-5:30pm. Free.)

⚫ BEACHES

Sunbathers, swimmers, and windsurfers alike fill the beaches of Viana do Castelo and its neighboring towns. **Praia Norte,** at the end of Av. do Atlântico at the west edge of town, is an easy 15min. walk from the town center and has two natural swimming pools. **Praia da Argaçosa,** a small beach on Rio Lima next to the youth hostel and marina, is popular with sunbathers in summer. The ferry to **Praia do Cabedelo,** a great beach for surfing and windsurfing, is indefinitely out of service; take the bus on Av. dos Combatentes da Grande Guerra, across from the Caixa Geral de Depositos (M-F 6 per day 7:35am-6:45pm, return M-F 4 per day 8am-5:10pm; €0.75). A 10min. train ride north of Viana leads to Afife's **Praia do Bico,** frequented by surfers, where the acclaimed surfing school **Escola Zurf** offers lessons and has equipment rentals. (☎966 22 10 92; www.surfingviana.nortenet.pt. Lessons June to mid-Sept. €30 private, €15 group. Surfboards, bodyboards, wetsuits, and bikes €10 per 3hr., €15 per day; fins €5/€10). The larger **Praias de Âncora, Moledo,** and **Caminha** are farther north.

⚫ ⚘ NIGHTLIFE AND FESTIVALS

The cafes and bars around Pr. da República fill up in the evening. The most popular place in Viana is **Bar Glamour,** R. da Bandeira, 183, down the street from the plaza and away from the main avenue. The immaculate, mirror-lined interior dance floor features mainstream dance music, and the garden hosts live music, karaoke, and summer fashion shows. (☎258 82 29 63. Minimum consumption Su-Th 1 drink; F-Sa women €3, men €5. Open daily 10pm-4am.) Another bar popular with a similar crowd is the nearby **Casting Bar,** R. Nova San Bento, 120-124. (☎258 82 73 96. Beer €1.50. Ladies free W. Minimum consumption €3. Open W and F-Sa

11pm-4am.) Viana's biggest festival of the year is the **Festa de Nossa Senhora da Agonia,** celebrated with processions, parties, and performances in the plaza on August 20 and the following weekend.

⚡ DAYTRIP FROM VIANA DO CASTELO

VALENÇA DO MINHO
Valença do Minho is a 1hr. bus ride from Viana do Castelo. A.V. Minho (☎ 258 80 03 41) runs buses back to Viana do Castelo (1hr.; M-F 5 per day 6:50am-10:35pm, Sa 3 per day 5:50am-11:50am, Su 3 per day 6:50am-10:35pm; €1.90). There's also a train (☎ 808 20 82 08) back to town (1hr., 5 per day 5:20am-8:15pm, €2.20). To get to the fortaleza, exit the bus station and take a right past the rotary and modern sculpture. Take the first left uphill until you reach another rotary. Cross this rotary and veer left uphill toward the fortaleza. To get to the fortaleza from the train station, walk through the rotary in front and take a right at the end of the street. Up this hill is another rotary. Cross the rotary and from here make your way uphill. You should be able to see the fortaleza.

Valença's sizeable **fortaleza,** whose 13th century walls were once used as a barrier to outsiders, is now the town's main attraction. Wide-eyed tourists, busy locals, vibrant merchandise, and patient cars jumble together in the *fortaleza's* streets, infusing the tiny walled-in town with uninterrupted movement and dynamism. Despite the prevalence of polyester outfits and cheap souvenirs overflowing from shops, walking through the bustling streets of this town on the border with Spain gives a feel of the crowds of years past. The hilltop location also offers panoramic views of the neighboring countryside and Rio Minho. Just outside the walls is **El Puente Internacional,** built in 1886. Walk across into Spain's **Túy** (p. 616), whose *casco viejo* also makes a worthwhile trip.

THE THREE BEIRAS
The Three Beiras region offers a versatile sampling of the best of Portugal: the pristine beaches of the coast, the rich greenery of the interior, and the ragged peaks of the Serra da Estrela. The Costa da Prata (Silver Coast) encompasses the wild nightlife of Figueira da Foz and passes through Aveiro on the way to Porto. The countryside is dotted with red-roofed farmhouses surrounded by expanses of corn, sunflowers, and wheat. A mecca for youth since the days in which it boasted the only university in Portugal, Coimbra hosts an opinionated and vibrant population; its nightlife and gorgeous architecture continue to attract young people. Still undisturbed by tourists, the region has retained a wealth of Portuguese traditions.

COIMBRA   ☎ 239
The crown jewel of the three Beiras, Coimbra is a vibrant city of 200,000, although it possesses the cosmopolitan charm of a metropolis ten times its size. Backpackers and local college students roam its streets and provide a youthful exuberance that cannot be found anywhere else in the Portuguese interior. For centuries, the Universidade de Coimbra was the only university in Portugal, attracting young men from the country's elite; though now universities abound throughout Portugal, Coimbra's university district maintains its historical appeal.

⬛ TRANSPORTATION

Trains: (Info ☎ 808 208 208). **Estação Coimbra-A (Nova)** is 2 blocks from the lower town center. **Estação Coimbra-B (Velha)** is 3km northwest of town. Regional trains stop first in Coimbra-B, then continue to Coimbra-A, departing in reverse order. Long-

THE NORTH

distance trains stop in Coimbra-B only; take a connecting train to Coimbra-A to reach the city (4min., immediately after trains arrive, €0.70 or free if transfer). To: **Braga** (3hr., 25 per day 5:45am-8:40pm, €7-8); **Figueira da Foz** (1¼hr., 18 per day 5:20am-12:15am, €1.60); **Lisboa** (3hr., 22 per day 5:40am-12:15am, €8.50-9.50); **Porto** (2hr., 30 per day 5:45am-10pm, €5.60-6.40).

Buses: AVIC, R. João de Ruão, 18 (☎239 82 01 41). To **Condeixa** (25min., 14 per day 7:35am-7:35pm, €1.50) and **Conímbriga** (30min.; departs 9:35am, returns 6pm; €1.80). **RBL** (☎239 82 70 81), near the end of Av. Fernão de Magalhães and 15min. past Coimbra-A. To: **Évora** (4hr., 14 per day 8:45am-2:15am, €12.40); **Faro** (8hr., 9 per day 9:25am-2:10am, €17); **Lisboa** (2½hr., 25 per day 6:15am-2:15am, €9.40); **Luso** and **Buçaco** (45min.; M-F 5 per day 7:35am-7:20pm, Sa 9am; €2.50); **Porto** (1½hr., 17 per day 6:45am-12:45am, €8.90).

Public Transportation: SMTUC buses and street cars. Three-trip ticket €1.40 at kiosks and vending machines; one-way on the bus €1.20. Book of 11 €4.80; 3-day pass (€6.20) sold at vending machines in Lg. da Portagem, Pr. da República, and elsewhere.

Taxis: Politaxis, outside Coimbra-A and the bus station (☎239 49 90 90).

Car Rental: Avis (☎/fax 239 83 47 86, reservations toll-free 800 20 10 02), in Coimbra-A. 21+. From €75 per day. Open M-F 8:30am-12:30pm and 3-7pm. AmEx/MC/V.

■✴🛈 ORIENTATION AND PRACTICAL INFORMATION

Coimbra's steep cobbled streets rise in tiers above the **Rio Mondego.** Of the three major parts of town, the most central is **Baixa,** site of the tourist office and the Coimbra-A train station, and set within the triangle formed by the river, **Largo da Portagem,** and **Praça 8 de Maio.** The historic **university district** looms atop the steep hill overlooking Baixa. On the other side of the university, the area around **Praça da República** is home to cafes, a shopping district, and the youth hostel.

Tourist Office: Regional office, Lg. da Portagem (☎239 85 59 30; fax 82 55 76). English-, French-, and Spanish-speaking staff distributes maps and provides short-term **luggage storage.** Open June-Sept. M-F 9am-7pm, Sa-Su 10am-1pm and 2:30-5:30pm; Oct.-May M-F 9am-6pm, Sa-Su 10am-1pm and 2:30-5:30pm. **Municipal offices,** Lg. Dom Dinis (☎239 83 25 91). Open M-F 9am-6pm, Sa-Su 9am-12:30pm and 2-5:30pm. Also at Pr. da República (☎239 83 32 02). Open M-F 10am-6:30pm.

Budget Travel: Tagus (☎239 83 49 99; coimbra@viagenstagus.pt) inside the A.A.C. building on R. Padre António Vieira. Sells ISICs. Open M-F 9:30am-6pm.

Currency Exchange: Montepio Geral, Lg. da Portagem (☎239 85 17 00). €5 commission above €50. Open M-F 8:30am-3pm.

Laundromat: Lavandaria Lucira, Av. Sá da Bandeira, 86 (☎239 82 57 01). Wash and dry €2 per kg. Open M-F 9am-1pm and 3-7pm, Sa 9am-1pm.

Police: Local police, R. Olímpio Nicolau Rui Fernandes (☎239 82 20 22). **Serviço de Estrangeiros** (tourist police), R. Venâncio Rodrigues, 25 (☎239 82 81 34).

Hospital: Hospital da Universidade de Coimbra (☎239 40 04 00), at Pr. Professor Mota Pinto and Av. Dr. Bissaya Barreto. Take bus #7 or #29.

Internet Access: Espaço Internet, Pr. 8 de Maio. This city-run, free service is popular and requires advance same-day sign up. Open M-F 10am-8pm, Sa-Su 10am-10pm. **Central Modem,** on R. Quebra-Costas. €0.55 per 15min. Open M-F 11am-11pm. **Sp@cenet,** Av. Sá da Bandeira, 67 (☎239 83 68 44). €2 per hr. Open M-Sa 10am-midnight, Su 2pm-midnight.

Post Office: Estação Santa Cruz, Av. Fernão de Magalhães, 223 (☎239 85 07 70). **Posta Restante** and fax. Open M-F 8:30am-6:30pm. **Branch office,** Pr. da República (☎239 85 18 20). Open M-F 9am-6pm. **Postal Code:** 3000.

Coimbra

♣ FOOD
Café Santa Cruz, **9**
Pastelaria Arco Iris, **2**
Restaurante Barca Serrana, **7**

▲ ACCOMMODATIONS
Hotel Bragança, **3**
Pensão Santa Cruz, **8**
Pousada da Juventude de Coimbra (HI), **17**
Residência Lusa Atenas, **1**
Residência Solar Navarro, **12**
Residencial Domus, **5**
Residencial Vitória, **4**

★ NIGHTLIFE
Cartola, **14**
Centro de Convívio Académico Dom Dinis, **13**
Diligência Bar, **6**
English Bar, **16**
Pitchclub, **11**
Quebra Costas, **10**
Via Latina, **15**

THE NORTH

ACCOMMODATIONS

Pensão Santa Cruz, Pr. 8 de Maio, 21, 3rd fl. (☎/fax 239 82 61 97; www.pensaosantacruz.com). A family-owned *pensão* with comfortable rooms, most with cable TV and some with bath; the friendly owners will gladly provide maps and suggestions for what to see and do in Coimbra. 2 rooms share a balcony overlooking the plaza, ideal for viewing free summer concerts. July-Sept. singles or doubles €20, with bath €30; triples €25/€40. Oct.-June €20/€35/€25/€40. Ask about discounts for extended stays. ❷

Pousada da Juventude de Coimbra (HI), R. Henrique Seco, 14 (☎239 82 29 55; fax 82 17 30). From R. Lourenço Azevedo, to the left of Parque de Santa Cruz, take the 2nd right. Kitchen, TV room (with pool table and foosball), and impeccable bathrooms. Breakfast included. Laundry €5 per load. Reception 8am-noon and 6pm-midnight. Lockout noon-6pm, but bag drop-off is possible. June 16-Sept. 15 dorms €11; doubles with bath €30. Sept. 16-June €8.50/€24. AmEx/MC/V. ❶

Residência Solar Navarro, Av. Emídio Navarro, 60-A, 2nd fl. (☎239 82 79 99). All rooms with bath and TV, some with balconies and views of the park; though the rooms are relatively simple, the view of the park, the rock-bottom prices, and the very friendly owner make this place worth your money. Singles €12.50; doubles €25; triples €37.50; enormous quints €60. ❶

Residencial Vitória, R. da Sota, 11-19 (☎239 82 40 49; fax 84 28 97). Many rooms newly renovated with bath, phone, cable TV, and A/C. Summer singles €45; doubles €60; triples €70. Winter €30/€40/€50. Older rooms, which lack the slick modernity of the rest, are still spacious and calm. Singles €15; doubles €25. AmEx/MC/V. ❶

Residência Lusa Atenas, Av. Fernão de Magalhães, 68, upstairs (☎239 82 64 12; fax 82 01 33). Rooms with bath, phone, A/C, and cable TV in a classic, aristocratic building. TV room with cushy brown couches. Reception 8am-midnight. July-Aug. singles €20-25; doubles €30-40; triples €45-50; quads €50-60. May-June €20/€30/€38/€50. Sept.-Apr. €18-20/€25-30/€38-40/€40-50. ❸

Residencial Domus, R. Adelino Veiga, 62 (☎239 82 85 84; residencialdomus@sapo.pt.). A 3-star *residencial* with a more economical annex across the street. Ask for the rooms with retro green or yellow carpet on the walls. Main rooms all have bath, phone, A/C, and cable TV; annex rooms lack bath. Breakfast included. July-Sept. main rooms: singles €35; doubles €40-50; triple €60. Annex: singles €30; doubles €35. Oct.-June main rooms €25/€33-35/€40; annex €20/€30. Annex also serves as an apartment for €50-60 per night. Discounts for stays beyond 3 nights. ❸

Hotel Bragança, Lg. das Ameias, 10 (☎239 822 171; hbraganza@mail.telepac.pt). This hotel is luxurious, complete with room service and complimentary mints; all rooms with satellite TV, A/C, and phones. A great deal during the low season. May-Sept. singles with shower €33, with full bath €50; doubles €57.50/€67.50; triples with full bath €85. Oct.-Apr. singles €35-40; doubles €50. AmEx/MC/V. ❹

FOOD

Check out the areas around R. Direita off Pr. 8 de Maio, the side streets between the river and Lg. da Portagem, and the university side of Pr. da República. Restaurants offer steamy portions of *arroz de lampreia*. The cheapest meals around are at **UC Cantina** (under €3), the university student cafeteria, on the right side of R. Oliveiro Matos, but you'll need an ISIC. Get fruits and veggies at the enormous **Mercado Dom Pedro V** on R. Olímpio Nicolau Rui Fernandes. (Open M-Sa 8am-1pm.) Discount fiends will appreciate **Supermercado Minipreço,** R. António Granjo, 6C, in the town center. (☎239 82 77 57. Open M-Sa 8:30am-8pm, Su 9am-1pm and 3-7pm.)

🍽 **Restaurante Barca Serrana,** R. Direita, 46 (☎239 82 06 16). A popular and inexpensive lunch spot. Be sure to try the house specialty, *leitão* (roasted pork; €7.50) or a sandwich (€2). The 2 daily specials are a steal (€3.50), though the half-portions are also great deals (€2.80-5.50). Open M-F 9:30am-10:30pm, Sa 9:30am-3:30pm. ❷

🍽 **Pastelaria Arco Iris,** Av. Fernão de Magalhães, 22 (☎239 83 33 04). A veritable rainbow of pastries (€0.60-0.95) is displayed. Locals swarm this place all day. Travelers can live off the *bolos de passa* (raisin buns, €0.70), which are as big as your forearm. Sandwiches (€0.95-1.80) and coffee (€0.50-0.90). Open M-Sa 7am-8:30pm. ❶

Café Santa Cruz, Pr. 8 de Maio, 5 (☎239 83 36 17). Formerly part of the cathedral, this is the city's most famous cafe. Vaulted ceiling with birds holding lamps in their beaks. Best on summer eves, when the weather is cool and people gather outside. Sandwiches €1.25-2.50. Open May-Sept. M-Sa 7am-2am; Oct.-Apr. M-Sa 7am-midnight. ❶

🔆 SIGHTS

OLD TOWN. Take in Coimbra's old town sights by making the steep 15min. climb from the river up to the university. Begin at Pr. 8 de Maio and the **Igreja de Santa Cruz.** The 16th-century church boasts an enormous and ornate center dome and *azulejo*-lined walls, although its real centerpiece is the tomb of Dom Afonso Henriques, Portugal's first king. *(Open M-Sa 9am-12:30pm and 2-6pm, Su 4-6pm. Check the schedule at the main door for Mass times.)* The ascent continues to the ancient **Arco de Almedina,** a remnant of the Moorish town wall, one block uphill from Lg. da Portagem. The gate leads past several university bookstores to the aptly named R. Quebra-Costas (Back-Breaker Street). Up a narrow stone stairway looms the 12th-century Romanesque **Sé Velha** (Old Cathedral). Although the gilded altar is certainly impressive, the sheer enormity of the interior is more so. Don't miss the peaceful cloister upstairs from the main nave. *(Open M-Th 10am-1pm and 2-6pm, F-Su 10am-1pm. Cathedral free. Cloister €1, students €0.75.)* Follow the signs to the nearby 16th-century **Sé Nova** (New Cathedral), whose exterior was completed by architects for the resident Jesuit community. Bring sunglasses; the opulently gilded main altar can be blinding. *(Open Tu-Sa 9am-noon and 2-6:30pm. Free.)*

UNIVERSIDADE DE COIMBRA. Though many buildings have since been constructed from reinforced concrete, the original law school retains its spot on the architectural Dean's List. Enter the old university through the **Porta Férrea** (Iron Gate), off R. São Pedro, to the **Pátio das Escolas,** which sports an excellent view of the rural outskirts of Coimbra as well as the river and the city's new suspension bridge. *(Uphill from the new cathedral. Open daily May-Sept. 9am-7:30pm; Oct.-Apr. 9:30am-12:30pm and 2-5:30pm.)* The staircase at right leads up to the **Sala Grande dos Actos** or **Sala dos Capelos** (Graduates' Hall), where portraits of Portugal's kings (6 of whom were born in Coimbra) hang below a 17th-century ceiling; this is the room where grateful students finally receive their diplomas. *(Open daily 9:30am-12:30pm and 2-5pm. €2.50.)* The **Capela de São Miguel** smells funny, but gives an idea of the religious life of the students; adorned with magnificent *talha dourada* carvings (especially the organ), it is a sight to behold. At the end of the row of buildings, the mind-boggling, gilded 18th-century **Biblioteca Joanina** surprises visitors with its ostentation. *(☎239 85 98 00. Open daily May-Sept. 9am-7:30pm; Oct.-Apr. 9:30am-noon and 2-5:30pm. Only 20 people allowed at a time every 20min., so there is generally a wait of up to 1hr. €2.50, teachers and students free. A ticket for all university sights can be purchased for €4 from the office in the main quad.)*

ACROSS THE RIVER. Cross Ponte de Santa Clara to discover the 14th-century **Convento de Santa Clara-a-Velha.** Don't be surprised to see huge cranes trying to lift it inch by inch; more than half of it is submerged in the morass. The multi-million dollar attempt at rescue will continue indefinitely. Before this round of repairs, another renovation revealed an ancient church founded in 1330 by Dona Isabel, wife of Dom Dinis. Isabel's tomb was relocated uphill to the ornate **Convento de Santa Clara-a-Nova.** (☎ 239 44 16 74. Interior closed for massive renovation; call ahead to see if it has reopened. Church open M-Sa 9am-noon and 2-6pm. Cloisters and sacristy €1.)

⚑ NIGHTLIFE

After dinner, outdoor cafes surrounding **Praça da República** buzz with animated conversation from midnight to 2am, after which crowds move on to the bars and clubs farther afield. The scene is best October through July, when the students are in town. **Figueira da Foz** (p. 794) offers more nightlife options an hour's drive away and makes a popular "night trip."

⌘ Quebra Costas, R. Quebra-Costas, 45 (☎ 239 821 661). Specializing in 12 different salads during the day, this artistic joint blasts jazz and funk to an eager crowd in their 20s and 30s. Admire the modern art on the wall, or wonder about the half-car in the main room. Beer €1-3, mixed drinks €4-5. Open daily midnight-4am. AmEx/MC/V.

Via Latina, R. Almeida Garrett, 1 (☎ 239 83 30 34). Large club popular with students on weekends and older crowds M-Th. Latin music Sa-Th, house F. 2 1100L tanks of Super Bock fuel the whole operation. Best place for dancing. Tu ladies' night (3 drinks with entrance). Beer €1.50, mixed drinks €3.50-5. Minimum consumption M-Th €2.50 for men, €1.50 for women; F-Sa €5/€3.50. Open M-Sa 11pm-7am. AmEx/MC/V.

Pitchclub, Lg. da Sé Velha, 4-8 (☎ 239 83 81 64). This recently renovated club is one of Coimbra's newest dance spots. Stone, wood, and metal walls reverberate with house, Brazilian, African, and pop. Serves vegetarian options during the day. Salads €2-5. Beer €1, mixed drinks €2.50. 1 drink minimum after 11pm. Open June-Sept. 15 M-Sa 11am-4am; Sept. 16-May M-Sa 9pm-4am. AmEx/MC/V.

Cartola, Pr. da República (☎ 239 836 236). Good luck finding a seat; this place brims with young folk after 9pm. A great place to get together, chat, and have a beer before heading off to the clubs. Coffee €0.50. Beer €1. Open M-Sa 7am-2am, Su 8am-1am.

Centro de Convívio Acadêmico Dom Dinis, Lg. Dom Dinis (☎ 239 83 85 38). A conference center by day, the university-owned Centro converts to a student hangout with a DJ M-Th and live music F-Sa 1-3am. ISIC or college ID required. Beer €1. Best Oct.-July after midnight, especially Th. Open Sept.-July M-Sa 10:30pm-3am.

English Bar, R. Lourenço de Almeida Azevedo, 24 (☎ 919 50 94 39). The bottom-floor restaurant serves traditional English pub grub and plays Latin music, while a DJ spins classic rock to a bar-side crowd of all ages upstairs. Huge backyard patio. Beer €1.50-2, mixed drinks €4-5. Best F-Sa at midnight. Bar-restaurant open daily 2pm-4am; dance floor upstairs open 11pm-4am.

Diligência Bar, R. Nova, 30 (☎ 239 82 76 67). Shamelessly touristy during the summer, yet still intimate and pleasant. Local fado performed nightly after 10pm. Although not as professional as its Lisboa counterparts, it gives an idea of the traditional music. Dinner is expensive, but people come for more than food. Entrees €8-15. Sangria €9.50 per jug. Open daily 6pm-2am. AmEx/MC/V.

❀ FESTIVALS

Students run wild during the **Queima das Fitas** (Burning of the Ribbons), Coimbra's infamous week-long festival in the first or second week of May. The festivities begin when graduating seniors set fire to narrow ribbons received from friends and family to commemorate their graduation and receive wide, ornamental replacements. Live choral music echoes in the streets and the city's largest fireworks display lights up the sky during the **Festas da Rainha Santa,** held the first week of July. During even-numbered years, two processions of the statue of Rainha Santa (one at the beginning, one at the end) more visibly reflect the festival's religious roots. The firework-punctuated **Feira Popular** in the second week of July offers carnival rides and games across the river.

 DAYTRIPS FROM COIMBRA

CONÍMBRIGA

AVIC buses (☎ 239 82 37 69) run each morning from Coimbra (30min.; M-F 9:05 and 9:35am, Sa-Su 9:35am; €1.75) and return in the afternoon (M-Sa 1 and 6pm, Su 6pm). Buses run more frequently to Condeixa, 2km away from Conímbriga (25min.; 6-30 per day M-F 6:35am-10pm, Sa-Su 7:05am-6:05pm; €1.50). Come in the morning and leave at 1pm; if that doesn't work, heading to Condeixa is mildly complicated but still doable. Follow the signs and walk along the highway for approx. 10min., then turn left onto the street heading toward Condeixa. Follow it for another 25min. until the bus stop. Taxis (☎ 239 94 12 43) are a more expensive but secure bet.

The **Ruínas de Conímbriga** is Portugal's largest preserved Roman site. Highlights include a 3rd-century town wall, an ancient, luxurious villa, and baths complete with sauna and furnace room. Stunningly well-preserved mosaics are visible under the shelter of a glass canopy. (Open daily Mar. 16-Sept. 15 9am-8pm; Sept. 16-Mar. 15 9am-6pm. Ticket office closes 30min. before the ruins. €3, under 25 and seniors €2, under 14 free.) The ticket for the ruins includes the nearby **Museu Monográfico de Conímbriga,** with displays of regional artifacts. (☎ 239 94 11 77. Open Tu-Su same hours as the ruins.) The **tourist office** is inside the museum. (☎ 239 94 47 64; fax 94 14 74. Open daily 9am-12:30pm and 2-5:30pm.)

BUÇACO FOREST AND LUSO

Buses run from Coimbra to Luso (45min.; M-F 5 per day 7:35am-7:20pm, Sa 9am; €2.50) before continuing on to Viseu. Buses back to Coimbra depart a few blocks from the Luso tourist office, across from the natural springs (35min.; M-F 4 per day 7:35am-6:35pm, Sa 10:35am; €2.50).

Home to Portugal's most revered forest, Buçaco (Bussaco) is a favorite weekend retreat for many residents of Coimbra. The forest has drawn wanderers escaping from the city for centuries. Benedictine monks settled the Buçaco area in the 6th century, established a monastery, and remained in control until the 1834 disestablishment of all religious orders. The forest owes its fame, however, to the Carmelites, who arrived here barefoot and set on a life of seclusion nearly 400 years ago. Selecting the forest for their *desertos* (isolated dwellings for penitence), the Carmelites planted over 700 types of trees and plants brought from around the world by missionaries. In the center of the forest, adjoining the old Carmelite convent, is Dom Carlos's exuberant **Palácio de Buçaco.** Now a luxury hotel, the building is a flamboyant display of neo-Manueline architecture. The *azulejos* on the outer walls depict scenes from Camões' *Os Lusíadas*, the great Portuguese epic about the Age of Discovery (see **Literature,** p. 669). In the forest itself, landmarks include the lovely **Fonte Fria** (Cold Fountain), the **Vale dos Fetos** (Fern Valley), and the **Porta de Rainha** (Queen's Gate). A 1hr. hike along the Via Sacra leads past 17th-century chapels to a sweeping panorama of the countryside from the **Cruz Alta** viewpoint. Before visiting the forest, make sure to stop at Luso's **tourist office,** R. Emidio Navarro, 136, to pick up detailed maps outlining the different hikes and routes, ranging from 1hr. nature walks to a 3hr. historic hike. (☎ 231 93 91 33. Open M-F 9am-7pm, Sa-Su 10am-1pm and 3-5pm.)

FIGUEIRA DA FOZ

Two words: bars and beaches. Figueira da Foz (pop. 62,000) appeals to young pilgrims in search of the vacation Holy Land. When Pedro Santana Lopes, the current Portuguese Prime Minister, was mayor of Figueira da Foz, he set out to transform it into a major tourist destination, building modern highways to facilitate access to Coimbra and other urban centers. The plan was successful, and the town now plays host to a bevy of sun-seekers from Portugal and abroad. The expansive 3km stretch of coast, covered with recreational distractions from a bike track to beach soccer, is within spitting distance of a stretch of bars that keep crowds rocking until those with day jobs start waking up. As if that weren't enough, Figueira's infamous casino makes losing money an art.

TRANSPORTATION. Trains run from **Coimbra** (1½hr.; M-Sa 20-24 per day 5:20am-12:20am, Su 17 per day 6:19am-12:20am; €1.60). Most trains from the Figueira station go through **Coimbra** (1½hr., 11 per day 6am-7:20pm, €2.20) en route to: **Aveiro** (1½-2½hr., 21 per day 7:30am-7:40pm, €6); **Lisboa** (3-4¼hr., 4 and 7:45pm, €12); **Porto** (2¼-3½hr., 11 per day 7:45am-7:45pm, €11.50). From the Figueira station, it's an easy 25min. walk to the tourist office and beach. With the river on your left, follow Av. de Saraiva de Carvalho as it becomes R. 5 de Outubro at the fountain and then curves into Av. 25 de Abril. For those who want to save their energy for the waves, the local **AVIC bus** goes to the center (7min., every 30min. until midnight, €0.80).

ORIENTATION AND PRACTICAL INFORMATION. Packed with hotels, beachfront **Avenida 25 de Abril** runs the length of Figueira, turning into **Avenida Foz do Mondego** after the fortress, before becoming **Avenida de Saraiva de Carvalho** as it nears the train station. Four blocks inland and parallel to Av. 25 de Abril, **Rua Bernardo Lopes** is lined with semi-affordable hostels and restaurants, and is the heart of the city's nightlife.

The **tourist office,** Av. 25 de Abril, 24, is next to Hotel Mecure, facing the beach. Its friendly English-, Spanish-, and French-speaking staff hand out maps, recommend accommodations, and provide info on bus and train schedules. (☎233 40 28 27; fax 40 28 28. Open June-Sept. daily 9am-midnight; Oct.-May M-F 9am-5:30pm, Sa-Su 10am-12:30pm and 2:30-6:30pm.) For a **Laundromat,** follow R. Candido dos Reis in the direction opposite the beach, pass the casino, and on the left will be **Tinturaria Figueirense,** R. Candido dos Reis, 15. (Open M-F 9am-1pm and 3-7pm, Sa 9am-1pm.) The **police** are on R. Joaquim Carvalho, by the bus station (☎233 42 88 81). Take the "Gala" or "Hospital" bus (from in front of the market on R. 5 de Outubro; €0.85) or catch a cab (approx. €5) to the **Hospital Distrital de Figueira da Foz,** across the river in the Gala district (☎233 40 20 00). **Pharmacies** abound near R. Bernardo Lopes and the casino; one block over from R. Bernardo Lopes, you will find **Farmácia Praia,** R. da Liberdade, 100. (☎233 42 21 83. Open M-F 9am-1pm and 2:30-7pm, Sa 9am-1pm.) Near the top of Av. 25 de Abril is the **Internet** cafe **Webgest,** Av. 25 de Abril, 74. (☎/fax 233 42 03 28. €2 per hr. Open daily 3:30pm-midnight.)

ACCOMMODATIONS AND FOOD. Several *pensões* line R. Bernardo Lopes and R. Miguel Bombarda; prices are steep, and unless you win at the casino, Coimbra is a much better bet. Partying all night and taking the morning train is not unusual. Located in the midst of Figueira's nightlife, **Pensão Central ❸,** R. Bernardo Lopes, 36, features simple rooms with old wooden floors, private baths and cable TV. (☎233 42 23 08; http://figueira.net/pensaocentral. Breakfast included. Summer singles €25-30; doubles €40; triples €50-55. Winter €20/€30/€35-40.) Comfortable **Pensão Residencial Bela Figueira ❸,** R. Miguel Bombarda, 13, is two blocks from the tourist office. The modern rooms are spacious with beautiful hardwood floors; most importantly, they're only a couple of blocks from the beach. (☎233 42 27 28. Doubles €30, with bath €35. AmEx/MC/V.) To reach the **Parque Municipal de Campismo da Figueira da Foz Municipal ❶,** on Estrada Buarcos, walk up Av. 25 de Abril with the beach on the left, turn right at the rotary onto R. Alexandre Herculano, then left onto Av. Manuel Gaspar de Lemos. A taxi from the bus or train station runs €3. The well-kept grounds have an Olympic-size pool (€1.75 per day), tennis courts (€2 per hr.), market, and currency exchange. (☎233 40 28 18. 2-person min. Reception June-Sept. 8am-8pm; Oct.-May 8am-7pm. Quiet hours midnight-7am. €1 per person, €2-2.50 per tent, €1.50 per car. Showers €0.55 per 7min.)

Eating in Figueira da Foz is not cheap; bring a picnic basket and save your dough for the nightlife. Several restaurants and snack bars are scattered along **Rua Bernardo Lopes** and the beach. A local **market** offering fruit, bread, and beach gear sets up beside the public garden between Av. Foz do Mondego and R. Dr. Francisco A. Dinis. (Open June-Sept. 15 daily 7am-7pm; Sept. 16-May M-Sa 7am-4pm.) Fill your picnic basket at **Supermercado Ovo,** on the corner of R. Francisco António Dinis and R. Bernardo Lopes. (☎233 42 00 52. Open M-Sa 8:30am-8pm, Su 9am-2pm.) At **Restaurante Andaluz ❷,** R. Maestro David de Sousa, 91, the dark, rustic wood interior creates a striking contrast to the sunny beach outside. Excellent, generous meals are served at some of the most reasonable prices in town. (☎233 42 04 54. *Pratos de dia* €6-10. Meat entrees €6.50-7, fish €6-8.80. Beer €0.70. Open M and W-Su noon-3pm and 7-10pm. Bar open until midnight. AmEx/MC/V.) One block off R. Bernardo Lopes is **Taberna Típica Cristal ❸,** R. Académico Zagalo, 28, a quaint restaurant specializing in typical Portuguese cuisine. The esplanade is perfect for people-watching in the late afternoon while enjoying *arroz de frutos do mar* (rice with shellfish; €8.60) or *feijoada de marisco* (seafood stew; €8.90). (☎/fax 233 42 24 39. Entrees €8-9. Open daily noon-3:30pm and 7pm-3am; winter closed W. AmEx/MC/V.)

◙ ▣ SIGHTS AND FESTIVALS. The popular **casino complex,** on R. Dr. Calado, at the corner of R. Bernardo Lopes, houses a nightclub, huge showroom, and arcade. For non-gamblers, the daily variety shows in the Salão Nobre still make this a worthwhile stop. (☎233 40 84 00; www.casinofigueira.com. 18+ with ID. No shorts or sneakers. Casino open daily 3pm-3am. Game room open daily 3pm-4am. Day pass Su-F €5.50, Sa €11. Slot machines and bingo free.) Just up from the public gardens on R. 5 de Outubro, the **Museu Municipal Dr. Santos Rocha,** R. Calouste Gulbenkian, in Parque Abadias, displays ancient coins, medieval weapons, and the fashions of Portuguese nobility, along with a large collection of Portuguese sculpture. (☎233 40 28 40. Open June-Sept. 15 Tu-Su 9:30am-5:15pm; Sept. 16-May M-F 9:30am-5:15pm, Sa-Su 2:15-5:15pm. €1.20, seniors €0.70.) On R. Joaquim Sotto Mayor, the continuation of R. da Liberdade parallel to the beach, the modest exterior of **Palácio Sotto Mayor** conceals a shameless extravagance within; Sotto Mayor made his fortune as a banker in the volatile markets of 19th-century Brazil. Lavish green marble columns line the main hallway, works by important Portuguese artists like António Ramalho adorn the palace, and gold leaf covers the ceiling. (☎233 42 20 41. Open June-Aug. Tu-Su 2-6pm; Sept.-May Sa-Su 2-6pm. €1.)

The drinking shenanigans that normally characterize Figueira's party life take on a more religious tone with the **Festa de São João,** usually starting in mid-June and continuing through the first week of July. The party includes the biggest display of fireworks in the area, as well as a somber procession where the sea receives the official blessing of the Catholic Church for the good of the community. On the night of June 23, the eve of the **◙Dia de São João,** crowds of locals dance in the streets and on the beach, gleefully bonking each other on the head with plastic noisemakers. After a spectacular fireworks display at 1am, crowds congregate around bonfires along the beach until the 5am *banho santo* (holy bath), when the brave take a dip in the ocean, and the not-so-brave take pictures and applaud.

▨ NIGHTLIFE. The quality of bars and clubs is not on par with Lisboa, but that matters little to the hordes of beachgoers. Easy socializing makes Figueira da Foz a nighttime hot spot. Summer crowds get thick between 10pm and 2am and persist until dawn. However, many bars and clubs open all week in summer have more limited hours during the rest of the year, and on winter weekdays, nightlife is best back in Coimbra. Crowds fill several nearby bars before hitting the small but up-and-coming club scene. **▨Rolls Bar**, R. Poeta Acácio Antunes, 1E, is an Irish pub with a twist. The clever owners allow patrons to set the price, Wall Street style: a screen shows the price of drinks, like the price of stocks, and popularity makes them rise or fall. (☎233 42 61 57. 1 drink min. Beer €1.50-2.50; mixed drinks €3-4. Open July-Aug. daily 5pm-6am; Sept.-June M-Sa 5pm-6am.) Grab a Bacardi (€4) at Cuban bar **Havana**, R. Cândido dos Reis, 86. It's best around 11pm, although crowds filter in from 8pm on. Come on a Saturday for the huge discounted drink parties, during which a specific drink is honored and consumed by the liter. (☎233 43 48 99. Beer €1. Mixed drinks €3-5. Open Tu-Su 8pm-4am.) End the night and welcome the morning at **Discoteca Bergantim**, R. Dr. A. Lopes Guimarães, 28, a block from the beach. Crowds groove to pop and rock (5-7am); don't bother coming before 4am. (☎233 42 38 85. Beer €1.50. Mixed drinks €4. Min. consumption women €4, men €5. Open July-Aug. daily 2-8am; Sept.-June F-Sa 2-8am.) The **Beach Club**, Esplanada Silva Guimarães, 3, on the terrace above the tourist office, features a dance floor downstairs and a chill bar and sandwich menu upstairs. Enter through the door to the left of the downstairs bar. (☎233 42 08 82. Beer €1. Popular martinis €2. Open daily 11am-4am.)

AVEIRO   ☎234

Through the old center of Aveiro winds a network of canals, along which traditional *moliceiros* (seaweed-coated fishing boats reminiscent of gondolas) drift out to sea. Home to 80,000 residents, Aveiro is also close to a series of beautiful beaches; however, unlike Figueira da Foz, Aveiro's personality isn't defined entirely by its relationship with the ocean. Instead, this city's charm emanates from its canals, modern shops, and classic architecture. Aveiro is also home to the convent where the canonized princess Santa Joana once lived (p. 798). The "Venice of Portugal" is also known for its numerous beaches, all of which are easily accessible from town by bus or ferry.

▉ TRANSPORTATION

Trains: Lg. Estação (☎234 38 16 32), at the end of Av. Dr. Lourenço Peixinho. To: **Braga** (2hr., 3 per day 10:25am-9:15pm, €10-14); **Coimbra** (1hr., 21 per day 6:15am-1:45am, €4.50); **Lisboa** (5hr., 14 per day 6:45am-1:45am, €12-16); **Ovar** (20min., 26 per day 5:45am-11:30pm, €1.45); **Porto** (45min., 15 per day 9:10am-10:45pm, €6.50-9.50).

Ferries: TransRia (☎234 33 10 95; fax 33 15 61) ferries depart for the beach at **São Jacinto** from the Vera Cruz docks, site of the old fish auction (16 per day 7:05am-12:40am, last return midnight; €2.50). From the tourist office follow R. João Mendonça as it winds around the park, turn left onto R. João Afonso, and then right onto R. B. Machado; the ferry dock is on a continuation of this street.

Taxis: Near the train station on Av. Lourenço Peixinho and along the canal in Pr. Humberto Delgado (☎234 42 29 43).

ORIENTATION AND PRACTICAL INFORMATION

Aveiro is split by a central canal and its parallel street, **Avenida Dr. Lourenço Peixinho,** running from the train station to **Praça Humberto Delgado.** The fishermen's quarter, **Beira Mar,** is north of the canal (the side with the train station). The residential district and Aveiro's monuments lie in the southern end of the city. To reach the **tourist office** from the train station, walk straight up Av. Dr. Lourenço Peixinho until you reach the bridge (15min.); the office is on the next block.

Tourist Office: R. João Mendonça, 8 (☎234 42 07 60; fax 42 83 26), off Pr. Humberto Delgado, on the street to the right of the canal facing the lagoon. English-, Spanish-, and French-speaking staff provide information and maps, bus, ferry and train schedules, and short-term luggage storage. Open July-Sept. daily 9am-8pm; Oct.-June M-F 9am-7pm, Sa 9:30am-1pm and 2-5:30pm.

Currency Exchange: Banks lining Av. Dr. Lourenço Peixinho are generally open M-F 8:30am-3pm. **ATMs** can be found on Av. Dr. Lourenço Peixinho, Pr. Humberto Delgado and Pr. Marquês de Pombal.

Laundromat: Lavandaria Popular, Pr. 14 de Julho (☎234 42 39 53). Open M-F 9am-12:30pm and 2:30-7pm, Sa 9am-1pm.

Police: Pr. Marquês de Pombal (☎234 42 20 22).

Pharmacy: Farmácia Aveirense, R. de Coimbra, 13 (☎234 42 48 33). Open M-F 9am-1pm and 3-7pm, Sa 9am-1pm.

Hospital: Av. Dr. Artur Ravara (☎234 37 83 00), near the park across the canal.

Internet Access: Cidade Digital, in Pr. da República across from the statue of José Estevão. Free. There is usually a short wait; sign up and hang around until your name is called. 30min. limit enforced when there is a line. Open M-Sa 10am-8:30pm.

Post Office: Main office, Pr. Marquês de Pombal (☎234 38 08 40), across the canal and up R. Coimbra. Open M-F 8:30am-6:30pm, Sa 9am-12:30pm. **Branch,** Av. Dr. Lourenço Peixinho, 169B (☎234 38 04 90), 2 blocks from the train station. Open M-F 8:30am-6:30pm. **Postal Code:** north of the canal 3800, south 3810.

ACCOMMODATIONS AND CAMPING

Inexpensive hostels line the streets of the old town, north of Pr. Humberto Delgado, and on the side of the canal with the tourist office; look for signs advertising *quartos* or *dormidas*. Hostel prices generally fall in winter. Those lining Av. Dr. Lourenço Peixinho and the streets around Pr. Marquês de Pombal are somewhat expensive, but serve as good backups.

Residencial Palmeira, R. de Palmeira, 7-11 (☎234 42 25 21). Take a left out of the tourist office, left again onto the 1st street, and once more onto R. Sargento C. Morais, across from the post office; follow the sign to the hostel. Newly renovated rooms, all with cable TV, sparkling hardwood floors, and bath. Reserve 2 weeks ahead in summer. June-Sept. singles €30; doubles €40; 1 triple €50. Oct.-May €20/€30/€35. MC/V. ❸

Residencial Estrela, R. José Estêvão, 4 (☎234 42 38 18), off Pr. Humberto Delgado, on the right 1 block before the tourist office. All but 2 rooms have baths, TVs, and decorated ceilings reminiscent of French baroque palaces. June-Aug. singles €25, with bath €30-35; doubles €30/€40; triples €45/€60; 1 quad with bath €80. Sept.-May €17.50/€20/€25/€30/€30/€35/€50. ❷

Pensão Beira, R. José Estêvão, 18 (☎234 42 42 97), off Pr. Humberto Delgado just past Residencial Estrela. Large rooms, all with cable TV and most with bath; some also have balconies. Apr.-Sept. singles €25, with bath €30; doubles €30/€35; triples with bath €40-50. Oct.-Mar. €18/€20/€22/€25/€37.50-40. ❷

Hotel Moliceiro, R. Dr. Barbosa de Magalhães, 15-17 (☎234 37 74 00; www.hotelmoliceiro.com.), a block from the tourist office. One of the most comfortable, and pricey, stays in town. Fully loaded rooms with cable TV, baths, safes, minibars, A/C, and phones. Summer singles €87.50; doubles €97.50. Winter €65/€85. AmEx/MC/V. ❺

Camping Municipal de Aveiro (☎/fax 234 33 12 20), in São Jacinto. Take the ferry to São Jacinto (16 per day 7:05am-12:40am, €2.50). Owned by the city. Provides basic amenities, including free hot showers, baths, and electricity. Reception 8am-7pm. Open Jan.-Nov. €1.80 per person, €0.80 per tent, €0.60-1.80 per car.

◪ FOOD

Seafood restaurants cluster around the fish market off Pr. do Peixe ("fish square") in the old town, a few blocks behind the tourist office. Aveiro's specialty pastry, called *ovos moles* (sweetened egg yolks), can be sampled at most of the *pastelarias* (pastry shops) along Av. Dr. Loureço Peixinho and R. J. Mendonça. **Supermercado Pingo Doce,** R. Batalhão Caçadores, 10, is across the canal from the tourist office. (☎234 38 60 42. Open daily 9am-10pm.)

Restaurante Zico, R. José Estêvão, 52 (☎234 42 96 49), off Pr. Humberto Delgado. Typical Portuguese food, including *bife ao churrasco* (grilled beef; €8.30), at decent prices. Nightly mix of local families and tourists seeking authentic Portuguese cuisine. Entrees €4.80-11. Open M-Sa 8am-2am; serves food noon-4pm and 7-11:30pm. ❷

Casa Necas, R. Tenente Resende, 51-53 (☎234 42 37 81), just off Pr. do Peixe. A small and solid Portuguese menu attracts flocks of locals. Friendly staff and friendlier prices. Large half-portions €4-5, full portions €8-9. Try the special *vitela assada* (roast veal; half-portion €3.50). Open M-Sa noon-2:30pm and 7-9:30pm. ❶

◉ SIGHTS

The old town's main attraction is the ◪**Museu de Aveiro,** R. Sta. Joana Princesa. King Afonso and his daughter Infanta Joana, who wanted to become a nun despite her father's objections, fought it out here in 1472. Luckily for the poor and sick of Aveiro, she won. In the Sala do Túmulo de Santa Joana, beneath the magnificent gilded Baroque ceiling and *azulejo* panels depicting the story of her life, lies one of the most famous works of art in Portugal—Santa Joana's Renaissance tomb, supported by the heads of four angels. Also noteworthy is the Sala de Lavor, where Santa Joana spent the days before her death on May 12, 1490; the elaborate gold carvings adorn a room that had previously served as a place for the nuns to work. (☎234 42 32 97. Open Tu-Su 10am-5:30pm. €2, students and seniors €1, under 14 free. Su before 2pm free.) Simple but strikingly blue *azulejos* cover the walls of the **Igreja da Misericórdia** in Pr. República, across the canal and a block uphill from the tourist office. (☎234 42 67 32. Open M-F 10am-12:30pm and 2:30-5pm.) In the same square, the **Câmara Municipal** (city hall), with a regal French design, displays its exceptional bell tower.

◪ ◪ BEACHES AND ENTERTAINMENT

Some of the beach towns near Aveiro boast beautiful sand dunes worth a short trip. The beaches of **Barra** and **Costa Nova** can be reached by bus from the *canal central* or train station stops (15min., July-Aug. 19 per day 7:10am-12:45am,

€1.80). Be sure to check out the lighthouse. More distant beaches, like the natural reserve at the **Dunas de São Jacinto** (10km away), are accessible by ferry (see **Ferries,** p.796).

At night, the bars around **Praça do Peixe** fill to overflowing capacities. Other popular places line R. Canal de São Roque. Check out **Salpoente,** on Cais de São Roque, or neighboring **Estrondo Bar** and **Urgência,** on R. São Roque.

◤ DAYTRIP FROM AVEIRO

OVAR

Buses stop in front of the train station, near the tourist office, and to the right of the garden (30-45min.; M-F 21 per day 7:10am-8:10pm, Sa 11 per day 7:10am-7:10pm, Su 5 per day 9:30am-8:10pm; last return M-F 7:20pm, Sa-Su 6pm; €0.70). The train station (☎ 256 58 59 76), on Lg. Serpa Pinto, off R. António Coentro Pinho, has quicker service to Aveiro, as buses tend to make several stops along the way (20min., 26 per day 5:45am-11:30pm, €1.50).

This *azulejo*-filled town, bounded on two sides by pine forest and on another side by an isolated beach, is a relaxing stopover on the way to Porto. While there's not much to do here except hang out at the beach, **Praia do Furadouro,** no one seems to mind (to get there, catch a bus in front of the cinema on R. Ferreira de Castro; 5min., every 30min. 6:30am-7:45pm, €1).

Pousada da Juventude de Ovar (HI), on Av. Dom Manuel I (EN 327), is difficult to reach from the center of town, but within convenient walking distance of Furadouro beach. Take the bus toward the beach and get off at the Carregal stop, just before the traffic circle, then turn right onto Av. Dom Manuel I (follow the signs to Porto), and walk for about 10min. (☎/fax 256 59 18 32. Reception 8am-midnight. Reservations recommended 3 days ahead in summer. June 16-Sept. 15 dorms €11; doubles with bath €30. Sept. 16-June 15 €8.50/€24.) For food, shop at the **mercado municipal** on R. Gomes Freire (open Th and Sa 8am-3pm).

The **tourist office,** on R. Elias Garcia, has maps as well as info about accommodations and transport. From the train station, head straight up the street, through the traffic circle on Pr. São Cristóvão, and take Av. Bom Reitor (the 2nd left; not the sharp left, but the one across the rotary), following it as it becomes R. Elias Garcia. (☎ 256 57 22 15; fax 58 31 92. Open July-Aug. M-F 9am-1pm and 2-6pm, Sa 10am-12:30pm and 2-6pm, Su 10am-12:30pm and 2-5:30pm; Sept.-June M-F 2-6pm.)

GUARDA ☎ 271

Although barely distinguishable from other towns in the region, Guarda (pop. 27,000) has become a popular vacation spot for Spanish and Portuguese travelers hoping to escape into its quietly enduring historic district or venture into the mountains of the nearby Parque Natural da Serra da Estrela. Living at the highest altitude of mainland Portugal, Guarda's residents have survived centuries of physical isolation and notoriously harsh winters. Two of the town's epithets—*fria* (cold), *fuerte* (strong)—allude to this legacy; however, Guarda's self-proclaimed titles also include *fiel* (faithful) and *formosa* (beautiful). Despite the town's challenges, from unending steep hills to erratic weather even in the short summer, Guarda provides yet another glimpse into forgotten centuries and serves as a convenient base for exploring the park.

▐ TRANSPORTATION. Buses depart Guarda from Centro Coordenador de Transportes, R. António Sérgio (☎ 271 22 15 15), a 10min. walk downhill from the town center. **Joalto** runs to: **Braga** (4-5hr.; M-Th 3 per day 8:05am-6:40pm, F

6 per day 8:05am-6:40pm, Sa 8:05am and 2:20pm, Su 5 per day 10:45am-6:40pm; €10.80); **Coimbra** (3hr.; M-F 6:05am and 2:15pm, Sa 8:05am, Su 2:15pm; €9.20); **Lisboa** (4½hr.; M-F 5 per day 7am-5pm, Sa 8:30am and 2:15pm, Su 4 per day 8:30am-7:30pm; €11.40). **Rede Expressos** runs to **Faro** (9-10hr.; daily 11:40am, Su also 7:30pm; €17.50). **Taxis** (☎271 21 32 22) to the town center cost about €3.

■▪ ▪ **ORIENTATION AND PRACTICAL INFORMATION.** The town center at **Praça Luis de Camões** is home to the cathedral, tourist office, and several restaurants and cafes. To get there from the bus station, exit from the upper level and turn right onto R. do Nuno Alvares Pereira, walking up a steep hill for several blocks. At the large rotary, Jardim José de Lemos, bear right and walk another block to Lg. General Humberto Delgado. From there, take the second right up R. Alves Roçadas and a left onto R. do Comércio, just past the white church. Pr. Luis de Camões is one block uphill. The **tourist office** in the corner has free **Internet** and city and regional maps. (☎271 20 55 30; www.rt-serradaestrla.pt. Open daily 9am-12:30pm and 2-5:30pm.) The bank **Millennium BCP** is next-door and has a 24hr. **ATM** outside. (☎271 20 51 60. Open M-F 10am-5pm.) Local services include: **Hospital Distrital**, Av. Rainha D. Amelia (☎271 20 02 00); **police**, Lg. Frei Pedro (☎271 22 20 22). The **post office**, Lg. São João de Dios, 24, can send and receive faxes. (☎271 20 00 30. Open M-F 8:30am-6pm, Sa 9am-12:30pm.) **Postal Code:** 6300.

▪▪ **ACCOMMODATIONS AND FOOD.** Inexpensive *pensões* and *residenciales* aren't hard to come by around Pr. Luis de Camões, but they fill up quickly, especially on weekends. **Pensão Aliança ❷**, R. Vasco da Gama, 8, upstairs from the restaurant, greets guests with a warm welcome and has rooms with cable TV and private baths. (☎271 22 22 35; fax 271 22 14 51. Breakfast included. Singles €15-20; doubles €23-35; triples €30-45.) Another option is **Residencial Filipe ❷**, R. Vasco da Gama, 9, with small but comfortable rooms, all equipped with TV and shower, only a block from Pr. Luis de Camões. (☎271 22 14 02. Breakfast included. Singles €17.50. AmEx/MC/V.) Those intent on camping can go to the less pleasant **campsite ❶** next to the stadium at the town's edge. From Jardim José de Lemos, take R. Vasco Borges, which becomes Av. Alexandre Herculano. Walk right around the rotary by the park entrance and take the second street; the campground is 200m to the left. (☎271 21 12 00. Reception 8:30am-11:30pm. €1.75 per person, €1.75-2.25 per tent, €1.75 per car. Electricity is €1.50.) Traditional restaurants abound in the historic district; a local favorite is **Restaurante A Floresta ❷**, R. Francisco de Passos, 40, where you can try Guarda's *morcelas torradas* (barbecued black pudding) in the pleasant stone-walled interior. (☎271 21 23 14. Entrees €4.50-9. Open daily noon-3:30pm and 7pm-12:30am. AmEx/MC/V.)

▣ **SIGHTS.** Hopefully you haven't gotten sick of cathedrals and museums yet, because the town has little to offer its visitors beyond the remnants of centuries past. The **Sé** (cathedral) is an amusingly confused smorgasbord of architectural styles, which is hardly surprising since it took 150 years to complete. (Open Tu-Su 9am-noon and 2-5pm. Free.) The nearby **Museu da Guarda**, in the 17th-century Episcopal Seminary, has an archaeological and ethnographic collection as well as regional painting and sculpture. (☎271 21 34 60; www.ipmuseus.pt. Open Tu-Su 10am-12:30pm and 2-5:30pm. €2, students €1. Su mornings free.) It's also worth visiting the **castle ruins** to scramble up the rocks for a view of the countryside; from Pr. Luis de Camões take R. Miguel Alarcão and turn right at Lg. João Soares.

📑 DAYTRIP FROM GUARDA

PARQUE NATURAL DA SERRA DA ESTRELA

Buses from platform 1 of the Guarda bus station to the gas station in Manteigas run infrequently and only on weekdays (1½hr.; M-F 11:30am and 5pm, return to Guarda M-F 7am and 12:50pm; €3). If you are planning to hike into the park from Guarda, the Parque Natural da Serra da Estrela information office, Rua D. Sancho, 1 (☎271 22 54 54), has books and detailed topographic maps of the park, with clearly illustrated trails and points of interest. Alternatively, the first place to get information in Manteigas is the information center across the street from the gas station where the bus arrives and departs. Both offices sell the invaluable book Discovering the Region of the Serra da Estrela *(€4.30), which includes maps and detailed descriptions of all trails, including altitude changes, walking times, and landmarks along the way. (☎275 98 00 60; fax 98 00 69. Both offices open M-F 9am-12:30pm and 2-5pm.)*

From craggy, barren mountains lazily dotting the horizon to rivers flowing through timeworn glacial valleys, **Parque Natural da Serra da Estrela** has attracted visitors since its designation in 1976. Quiet communities of stone cottages within the park have grown into industrialized towns producing wool, cheese, and other local specialties. Hiking through the serene landscape of the park is the most popular activity, and there are several trails running north and south through the length of the park. The three main **trails** are T1 (indicated with a solid red line), T2, and T3 (both marked with solid yellow lines). These three trails pass through the mountain ranges, rivers, and villages of the park, and each covers a distance of about 80-90km, suitable for several days of hiking. Six shorter trails—T11, T12, T13, T14, T31, and T32—marked with dotted lines, branch off of the main routes. Manteigas provides an opportunity to do several **day hikes** on portions of the trails that pass through the town. These include walking up a gradual incline along the **Rio Zezere** towards **Albergaria,** 14km south of Manteigas, as well as a more challenging 12km hike to the stunning **Poço de Inferno** waterfall. The weather in the park is erratic at best; snowfall often obscures the trail markers in winter, summer heat can be scorching, and the frequent presence of mist on the horizon indicates imminent rainfall. Check with the offices about weather conditions and be sure to bring extra waterproof layers.

In recent years, the park has also been home to several other adventure sports such as **skiing, kayaking, mountain climbing, rappelling,** and **mountain biking.** Near Manteigas, **SkiParque** leads excursions into the mountains or through the Rio Zezere, and fills its slopes between December and March. (☎275 98 28 70; www.skiparque.pt. Guided hikes €20-40 per day, kayaking €6 per hr. and €17.50 per half-day, mountain biking €7/€15.) **UniversoTT** operates directly out of Guarda and provides similar services (☎967 94 91 96; www.universott.com). The most popular spot for skiing is **Torre,** a €15-20 cab ride from Manteigas. (☎275 31 47 08. Slopes open Nov. to mid-Apr.)

For those planning to hike by day and return to town at night, the cheapest **accommodations** in Manteigas are at **Pensão Serradalto,** R. 1 de Maio, upstairs from the **restaurant** about 50m from the gas station. They have bright rooms overlooking the valley with impeccable private baths. (☎/fax 275 98 11 51. Breakfast included. Singles €25; doubles €30. Restaurant open daily noon-3pm and 7-11pm. Entrees €6.50-13.) **Camping** in the park is prohibited, except at designated sites. If you plan to hike the entirety of the park, consult with the information offices in Guarda or Manteigas about campsites or cabins along the way. You can also camp at SkiParque, located off the main road 6km from Manteigas. (Taxis from Manteigas €5-6. €1.50 per person, €1.50-2 per tent, €1.25 per car.)

TRÁS-OS-MONTES

The country's roughest and most isolated region, Trás-Os-Montes ("beyond the mountains") is a land of extremes. Its inhabitants describe their seasons as "nine months of winter and three months of hell." Still, residents have cared for the land intimately, leaving vast expanses of wilderness that visitors can enjoy. Rocky hilltops give way to fields of corn, followed by arid stretches good for olives.

Trás-Os-Montes has long been home to Portugal's political and religious exiles. Dom Sancho I practically had to beg people to settle here after he incorporated it into Portugal in the 12th century, and it was here that the Jews chose to hide during the Inquisition. Despite the tough conditions in their region, *trasmontanos* themselves are quite possibly the friendliest people in the country. Today, Trás-Os-Montes is one of the last outposts of traditional Portugal.

BRAGANÇA   ☎273

Wedged in a narrow valley between two steep slopes, Bragança (pop. 37,000) is a steadfast wilderness outpost. While most visitors come for clean air, blue skies, and olive-covered hillsides—or the massive 12th-century castle—the people of Bragança make the town unique. Its substantial distance from the rest of Portuguese civilization has preserved an older sense of hospitality and festivity even amidst the city's extensive revitalization projects. Bragança is also the perfect base for exploring the Parque Natural de Montesinho, which extends into Spain.

⌐ TRANSPORTATION

Trains: No train service. Nearest station is **Mirandela,** 1hr. away and accessible by bus.

Buses: The bus station is at the top of Av. João da Cruz. **Rodonorte** (☎273 30 01 83) runs to **Braga** via **Mirandela** and **Vila Real** (4-5hr.; M-F 4 per day 6am-3:10pm, Sa 7:25am, Su 2 and 3:10pm; €10.70). **Rede Expressos** (☎273 33 18 26; www.rede-expressos.pt) runs to: **Coimbra** (6hr.; M-F 5 per day 6am-7pm, Sa 4 per day 8:30am-7pm, Su 5 and 9:30pm; €10.20); **Lisboa** (8hr.; M-F 7 per day 6am-7pm, Sa 6 per day 8am-7pm, Su 7 per day 8am-9:30pm; €14); **Porto** (5hr.; M-F 7 per day 6am-7pm, Sa 5 per day 8am-7pm, Su 7 per day 8am-9:30pm; €8.80); **Vila Real** (2hr.; M-F 6 per day, Sa 4 per day 8am-7pm, Su 7 per day noon-9:30pm; €7.50). **Santos** (☎279 65 21 88) goes to **Lisboa** via **Vila Real** and **Porto** (8hr; M-F 3 per day 6am-2pm, Sa 2pm, Su 2 and 5pm; €14, students €12). **Autocares F. Ledesma** (☎980 52 83 71) runs to **Madrid** via **Zamora, Spain** (5hr.; Tu and F 12:30pm, Su 5:45pm; €37).

Taxis: (☎273 32 21 38). Av. João da Cruz, near the post office and bus station.

▲▎ ORIENTATION AND PRACTICAL INFORMATION

The bus station is located only blocks from the center of town. From the corner of the station, take a left onto R. Santo António and a quick right onto hostel-lined **Avenida João da Cruz.** Continue straight, merging onto downward-sloping R. Almirante dos Reis, which leads to more budget *pensões* and the **Praça da Sé** at the heart of the old town. To reach the **fortress,** on the hill west of Pr. da Sé, take R. dos Combatentes da Grande Guerra uphill and enter through the opening in the walls.

Tourist Office: Av. Cidade de Zamora (☎273 38 12 73). From Pr. da Sé, take R. Abilio Beca and take the 2nd left onto R. Marqués. Turn right onto Av. Cidade de Zamora. Short-term **luggage storage.** Open M-F 9am-12:30pm and 2-5pm, Sa 10am-12:30pm.

Currency Exchange: Millennium BCP, R. Almirante dos Reis, 53 (☎273 30 01 60). Also has Western Union services. Open M-F 10am-5pm. 24hr. **ATM** at **Crédito Predial Português,** R. Almirante dos Reis, 30.

Library: Biblioteca Municipal, Pr. Mercado, just off Pr. da Sé. Has a cultural center and **Internet** access. Open M-F 9am-12:30pm and 2-5:30pm.

Police: R. Dr. Manuel Bento (☎273 30 34 00).

Hospital: Hospital Distrital de Bragança, Av. Abade de Baçal (☎273 31 08 00), before the stadium on the road to Vinhais.

Internet Access: CyberCentro (☎273 33 12 80), 2nd fl. of the *mercado municipal.* From Pr. da Sé, walk up R. Almirante dos Reis, go left onto Av. General Humberto Delgado, past the *Forum Theatrum* and through the rotary. It will be uphill on your left. €1 per hr., students €0.80 per hr. Open M-Sa 10am-11pm, Su 10am-8pm.

Post Office: (☎273 31 09 40), on the corner of R. Almirante dos Reis and R. 5 de Outubro. Open M-F 8:30am-5:30pm, Sa 9am-noon. **Postal Code:** 5300.

ACCOMMODATIONS AND CAMPING

Lots of cheap *pensões* and *residenciales* line Pr. da Sé and R. Almirante dos Reis.

Pensão Poças, R. Combatentes da Grande Guerra, 200 (☎273 33 14 28). From Pr. da Sé, walk toward the castle and bear right. Spacious rooms with high ceilings and clean common baths. Ask for a room that does not overlook the noisy street below. Reception in restaurant. Singles, some with bath, €10; doubles €20; triples €30. AmEx/MC/V. ❶

Pousada de Juventude–Bragança (HI), Forte de São João de Deus (☎273 30 46 00; fax 32 61 36), off Av. 22 de Maio. From the rotary next to the bus station, take Av. Eng. Amaro da Costa past the modern church and up the hill; the hostel will be on the right (10min.). The 24 4-bed dorms each have a kitchen, sitting room, and terrace. Laundry €3. Check-in 6pm-midnight. Mid-June to mid-Sept. dorms €12.50; doubles with bath €35. Mid-Sept. to mid-June €10/€28. AmEx/MC/V. ❶

Residencial Tic-Tac, R. Emídio Navarro, 85 (☎273 33 13 73; fax 22 16 73). From Pr. da Sé, take R. Almirante Reis, turn right onto R. Nova Cemiterio, and take an immediate right onto R. Emídio Navarro. Comfortable rooms with TV, A/C, and bath. Breakfast included. Aug.-Sept. singles €35; doubles €40. Oct.-July singles €30/€35. MC/V. ❸

IN RECENT NEWS

BRAGANÇA BORN AGAIN

While it has preserved centuries of history in its narrow alleys, Bragança has recently taken a forward-looking turn with an extensive, ambitious urban revitalization project that has changed the nature of the city without sacrificing its deeply embedded medieval aura. Still protected by the imposing 13th-century castle and dotted with long-standing churches, Bragança has introduced a modern twist to the city in the hope of "stimulating economic opportunity and strengthening social and territorial cohesion," according to Mayor Antonio Jorge Nuñes. Now, alongside its ancient structures, Bragança offers residents and visitors the comforts of more industrialized cities, from its shopping centers to its sunlit library.

Work begun in 2000 has made consistent progress, with the construction of two remarkable public spaces in 2004. Perhaps the most impressive new structure is the Teatro Municipal in Pr. Cavaleiro de Ferreira, which serves as a forum for plays, concerts, and art exhibits throughout the year. The elegant Biblioteca Municipal is a pleasant spot to learn about regional history. Bragança also enjoys a new *mercado municipal* and *centro comercial.* With support from the national government and the EU, Bragança has managed to transition into the new millennium gracefully, remembering its past without overlooking its present and future.

Camping: Parque de Campismo Municipal do Sabor, 6km from town on the edge of the Parque Natural de Montesinho, on the road to Portelo (☎273 33 15 35). The #7 yellow STUB bus toward Meixedo passes nearby, leaving from the Caixa Geral de Depósitos on Av. João da Cruz (10min.; M-F 12:43, 2:09, 6pm; return to Bragança 1:34, 2:36, 6:26pm; €1.10). Surrounded by trees and mountains, the campground has a playground, cafe, and swimming lagoon. Reception 8am-midnight. Open May-Oct. €2 per person, €1.50-2 per tent, €1.50 per car. 6-person cabin €50. Electricity €2. ❶

◖ FOOD

The region is celebrated for its *presunto* (cured ham) and *salsichão* (sausages), as well as the local delicacy, *alheiradas*, sausages made with bread and various meats. You can find these and fresh produce at the stores that surround the *mercado municipal*, two blocks down from Pr. da Sé.

◪ Solar Bragançano, Pr. da Sé (☎273 32 38 75). A Victorian setting with crystal chandeliers and a beautiful garden on the back patio of a renovated mansion. Entrees (€7.50-19.50) include wild game and excellent vegetarian soups (€2) and omelettes (€5). Open daily 11:30am-3:30pm and 5:30pm-midnight. AmEx/MC/V. ❸

Restaurante Dom Fernando, R. Rainha D. Maria II, 197 (☎273 32 62 73), inside the castle walls, above the bar. After entering the castle walls, turn right onto the 1st street. Surprisingly untouristed for its location, this small restaurant has vegetarian options and endless meat dishes. Entrees €5-10. *Menú* €9. Open M-W and F-Su 9am-10pm. ❷

Restaurante Poças, R. Combatentes da Grande Guerra, 200 (☎273 33 14 28), off Pr. da Sé. Share seating with both locals and fellow travelers. Meals include appetizers of bread, pâté, and black olives (€2-3). Entrees €5-9. Open 8am-midnight; full menu served noon-3pm and 7-10:30pm. AmEx/MC/V. ❷

◉ SIGHTS

The majestic 12th-century ▧**castelo,** uphill from Pr. da Sé, watches quietly over the town. The castle is encircled by massive restored walls that provide phenomenal views of Bragança and Spain. Inside the walls, the castle's **Museu Militar** has a wide range of military paraphernalia that trace Portugal's war history, from the medieval treaties with Spain to the Portuguese efforts in WWI and the African campaigns. (Open M-W and F-Su 9-11:45am and 2-4:45pm. €1.50, Su mornings free.) The venerable **pelourinho** (pillory) in the square behind the castle has a granite pig at its base, a vestige of pagan ideology; sinners and criminals were bound there in the Middle Ages. The **Domus Municipalis,** behind the church across the square from the castle, once served as the city's municipal meeting house. Today, it is the only remaining example of Roman civil architecture on the Iberian Peninsula.

Museu do Abade de Baçal, R. Abilio Beca, 27, just downhill from Pr. da Sé, occupies the former *Paço Episcopal de Bragança* (Bishop's Palace). It contains a small but eclectic collection, from baroque sculpture and archaeological finds to festive masks and religious paintings. (☎273 33 15 95; www.ipmuseus.pt. Open Tu-F 10am-5pm, Sa-Su 10am-6pm. €2, students €1, free Su until 2pm.)

▣ ▧ NIGHTLIFE AND FESTIVALS

Students from the polytechnic institute liven up the nightlife in the city. A popular hangout, especially after 1am on weekends, is **Zona+,** Av. Sá Carneiro, 2A, below Confeitaria Veneza through the door to the right. (☎933 37 63 95. Beer €1 before 1:30am, €1.30 after. Open M-Sa 10pm-3am.) Even more convenient is **Klaustrus Cafe,** Pr. da Sé, 16, a feel-good bar with karaoke and live music once per week. (☎273 33 34 59. Beer €1. Open daily 8:30pm-3am.)

The most important festival in Bragança is the **Festa de Nossa Senhora das Graças,** which includes concerts, art exhibits, and ceramics fairs in mid-August. It culminates in fireworks the night of the 21st and religious processions the following day. During the **Festa do Estudante** for a week in mid-May, *tunas* (student musical groups) gather to play for the entire town.

🎿 DAYTRIP FROM BRAGANÇA

PARQUE NATURAL DE MONTESINHO

Getting to the park can be complicated. STUB bus #5 to the border village of Rio de Onor leaves Bragança from the stop near the fountain, going downhill on Av. João da Cruz. (June-Sept. M-F 2:09pm; return bus runs year-round Su-F 6:50pm.) Taxis to the park run €18 one-way; arrange ahead for pick-up in the park. Information center in Bragança, R. Cónego Albano Falcão, 5. Walk downhill from the tourist office on Av. Cidade de Zamora, take the 1st left onto a paved street and the 1st left again; it's at the end of the street on the right. Park trails are unmarked, but the office has maps and can help plan hikes. (☎273 38 14 44; fax 38 11 79. Open M-F 9am-12:30pm and 2-5:30pm.) The office rents Casas Abrigos (traditional houses. Call ☎273 38 12 34. Doubles €25-38; quads €50.)

One of the largest protected areas in Portugal, the **Parque Natural de Montesinho** covers 290 square miles between Bragança and the Spanish border. The park consists of 92 traditional aldeias (villages). Rich in tradition, these villages preserve age-old communal customs and enact ancient rituals, from the carving of pigs to lively festivals such as the **Festa dos Rapazes** (see **On the Prowl,** right). Some of the villages can be reached in a day's hike or bike ride, but visitors with more time often design multi-day hikes between villages.

Old mountain paths lead through rolling woodlands of oak, chestnut, pine, and cherry trees. *Pombais pombales* (pigeon lofts) dot the landscape, and the park is home to many rare and endangered species—the Iberian wolf, royal eagle, and black stork, among others. Trout fishing, hiking, and horseback riding are popular, and the riverbanks are ideal for picnics. **França,** a village in the eastern central region of the park, has a horseback riding center (☎273 91 91 41). If you have only one day to visit the park, the most worthwhile trip is to **Rio de Onor,** a village near the northeast corner, on the Spanish border. Here the Portuguese and Spanish have lived together for centuries, intermarrying and even speaking their own hybrid dialect, *rionorés*. A subtle stone post, with a "P" for "Portugal" on one side and an "E" for

ON THE PROWL

The *Festa dos Rapazes,* a ritual enacted in the villages of the eastern Lombada region of Parque Natural de Montesinho, is certainly not lacking in erotic innuendo. The festival, which supposedly dates back to the Saturnalia rites of Roman times, has regional variations, but the general idea is the same everywhere. On December 26th or January 6th, the single young men of the villages dress up as *caretos,* wearing shaggy colored suits, diabolic painted masks, and cowbells, prowling around in groups in search of lone females. Upon finding a *rapariga,* they surround her and one of the *caretos* grabs and shakes her, knocking the bells attached to his belt against her hips (the verb is *chocalhar*). The *festa* continues today, as shy young men use the event to meet and flirt with local girls.

Fortunately for all involved, festivals and ritual gatherings are thought to be times when the natural order of things is suspended. According to anthropologist Ernesto Veiga de Oliveira, the festival "is a time of great licentious freedom where all excesses are authorized." Caro Baroja asserts that "the inversion of the normal order of things has a predominant role." All scholarly theory aside, this makes for one hell of an excuse to get wild. So loose your inhibitions, defy the norm, and, go ahead, find your inner animal. You know you want to.

"España" on the other, marks the border. Villagers cross into Spain for groceries and back into Portugal for coffee at **Cervejaria Preto**, a bar that's not hard to find, as it's the only one in town. You can eat on the stone tables overlooking the river (sandwiches €1.50, beer €0.60; open daily 8am-12:30pm and 1-8pm). Several short hikes on exposed gravel paths off the main road head toward neighboring towns and offer good views of the mountains. The village is in the process of constructing a campsite; inquire at the office in Bragança for more info.

MIRANDA DO DOURO   ☎273

Perched precariously atop a cliff overlooking the Rio Douro, the delightful town of Miranda do Douro (pop. 4500) attracts visitors primarily for its convenient access to the natural park. Intriguing sites within the town include its 16th-century cathedral, castle ruins, and narrow cobblestone streets, which display the town's rich history from the Roman occupation and Muslim conquest to the present. Proximity to Spain, just across the river, has led to the development of Mirandés, a hybrid dialect and Portugal's second official language, which can be heard in the streets. Miranda do Douro provides a refreshing respite from surrounding urban centers, as well as an opportunity to explore the villages and trails of the natural park.

◪▨ TRANSPORTATION AND PRACTICAL INFORMATION. The Miranda do Douro **bus stop** is located just off of the central rotary, Lg. de Moagem. The ticket office is open daily 8am-7:30pm. **Rodonorte** buses travel from **Bragança** (1½hr., M-F 11am and 5pm) and back (M-F 6:40am and 1:30pm, €5.20). The **tourist office,** across the street from the bus stop, offers a map of the town and information about accommodations. (☎273 43 11 32; mirdouro@mail.telepac.pt. Open July-Aug. M-Sa 9am-12:30pm and 2-7pm; Sept.-June M-Sa 10am-12:30pm and 2-5:30pm.) Other services include: **Guarda Nacional Republicana** (police), R. do Convento (☎273 43 01 10), and **Hospital de Miranda do Douro** (☎273 43 11 33). The **post office** is at R. do Paso, 3. (☎273 43 14 54. Open M-F 8:30am-3pm.) **Postal Code:** 5210.

▨◖ ACCOMMODATIONS AND FOOD. For luxury accommodations at a bargain, head to ▨**Hospedaria Flor do Douro** ❷, R. do Mercado, 7. From the tourist office, approach the rotary from the left and turn left onto R. do Mercado. The spacious rooms come complete with TV, full bath, and elegant furniture; several overlook the river. (☎273 43 11 86. Breakfast included. Singles €15; doubles €30.) The quiet **campsite** ❶ is a 25min. walk from town and has trails leading to several neighboring villages. From the rotary, walk downhill on R. D. Dinia, keeping the castle ruins on your left as you walk around the town. Take a sharp right downhill just before the next rotary, cross the stone bridge, veer left at the fork in the road, and turn right as the road becomes a dirt path. (☎273 43 12 73. Open June-Sept. Reception 8am-10pm. €1.50 per person, under 10 €0.80, €2-3 per tent, €2 per car. Electricity €2.) For a taste of Miranda's cuisine outside of the pricier restaurants in the historic district, head to the popular **Restaurante Miradouro** ❷, R. do Mercado, 53, whose specialty is *posta à mirandesa* (€12), a regionally famous roast beef dish that draws many visitors. (☎273 43 12 59. *Menu do dia* €10, entrees €6.50-9. Open daily noon-3pm and 6:30-10:30pm.)

◙ SIGHTS. The town's main attraction is its 16th-century **cathedral,** which boasts chapels laden with Baroque art and an altar painted by Gregorio Fernández and Francisco Velázquez from 1610 to 1614. (Open Tu-Su 10am-12:30pm and 2-6pm. Free.) Behind the cathedral are the outdoor **Ruinas do Paço Episcopal** (ruins of the Bishop's Palace), where remnants of stone walls overlook the tranquil river.

PARQUE NATURAL DE DOURO INTERNACIONAL. While its name may be a mouthful, the phenomenal views offered by the Parque Natural de Douro Internacional will leave you speechless. Established in May 1998, the park covers 85,150 hectares on the border between Portugal and Spain and is home to several endangered species, including the Egyptian vulture, golden eagle, and black stork. Flowering almond trees soften the rough terrain, and favorite pastimes among locals include hunting partridge and hare and trout fishing. Situated in the northern corner of the park, Miranda do Douro provides an excellent base for exploring the undisturbed beauty of eastern Portugal's mountains, cliffs, flora, and fauna. Several **hikes** leave from there to neighboring *pueblos* that dot the landscape. One long but manageable day hike comprises a 19km loop to **São João das Arribas,** a village to the northeast that also overlooks the river. Along the way, you will pass old stone cottages, quiet farmlands, and the villages of Vale de Aguia and Aldeia Nova. You can also head out the trail about 2.5km and turn right on a dirt path that will lead to a stunning view of the tranquil fjord-like waters below. Those with more time can try the **Linha do Sabor,** a 62km 2-day hike that heads south through the park and ends at the village Freixo de Espada a Cinta. The hike passes through antiquated railroad stations that have become points of interest in recent years.

Before heading out, consult the park's **information office,** R. do Convento, which sells topographic maps (€0.50) outlining the trails and offers advice about hiking in the park. From the tourist office, take Av. Aranda del Duero, which becomes R. da Alfandega and R. da Trinidade. Turn left when you reach the *Biblioteca Municipal;* the office will be immediately on your left. (☎ 273 43 14 57; www.pndi.pt. Open M-F 9am-12:30pm and 2-5:30pm.) Trails are well-maintained and well-marked by signs with two horizontal yellow and red lines. To begin a day hike, take R. 25 de Abril from the tourist office and follow the trail when you reach the end of the road after 5-10min.

VILA REAL ☎259

Vila Real (pop. 25,000) presides over the edge of the gorges of the Corgo and Cabril Rivers in the foothills of the Serra do Marão. The small, historic town center is surrounded by new neighborhoods reaching up into the hills, a lively main street, and a few caves. As the principal commercial center for the southern farms and villages of Trás-Os-Montes, Vila Real is a good point of departure for excursions into the fields and slopes of the Serra do Alvão and Serra do Marão.

TRANSPORTATION. Trains (☎ 259 32 21 93) run from Av. 5 de Outubro to **Porto** (4½hr., 6 per day 7am-8pm, €6.50). From the train station, it's a simple 5min. walk to the town center: head up Av. 5 de Outubro, cross the bridge onto R. Miguel Bombarda, take a left onto R. Roque da Silveira, and then bear left until you hit Av. 1 de Maio. **Buses** are a better option, since they are quicker and don't require transfers at Paso da Régua. **Rede Expressos buses,** R. D. António Valente da Fonseca, are located right off the city center; to reach the tourist office from here, go right onto R. D. António Valente da Fonseca and then take a left onto Av. Carvalho Araújo. Buses run to: **Bragança** (2hr., 5-9 per day 8:45am-12:30am, €7.50); **Coimbra** (4hr., 5-7 per day 7:45am-9pm, €7.50); **Lisboa** (6½hr., 3-8 per day 7:45am-9pm, €13.50); **Porto** (1¾hr., 3-8 per day 7:45am-9pm, €5.70). **Taxis,** including **Rádiotáxi** (☎ 259 37 31 38), gather along Av. Carvalho Araújo.

ORIENTATION AND PRACTICAL INFORMATION. All activity in Vila Real centers around **Av. Carvalho Araújo,** a charming boulevard in the middle of town lined with trees, cafes, shops, and the **tourist office,** Av. Carvalho Araújo, 94. Its English-, Spanish-, and French-speaking staff will provide you with maps

THE BIG SPLURGE

WILD ON THE ALVÃO

Maybe you don't dig hiking. Maybe you're one of those adrenaline junkies who needs something a little different in order to be satisfied. If you fit this profile, Glaciar Aventura's "alternative" tours of the Parque Natural do Alvão will probably appeal to you.

Glaciar Aventura allows you to put together extreme sports packages in the natural park, with activities ranging from rafting, 4-wheel drive excursions in Land Rovers, hot air ballooning, bungee jumping and yes, even hiking. Not only does this group of professionals give you the opportunity to obtain that much-needed adrenaline rush, but their packages are also one of the only ways to truly experience the natural beauty of the mountainous park, seeing as it's quite difficult to get there in the first place.

Though these packages are quite pricey (prices range from €80-150, depending on the number and type of activities included), the gorgeous mountain vistas, unspoiled beauty, and the sensation that you'll get in the pit of your stomach as you jump off a bridge, hurtle towards the earth at breakneck speed, and scream for your life, make this an excellent "alternative" to your simple day-long hike.

For more information, contact Glaciar Aventura, Av. Cidade de Orense, Lote 2 - Loja 2, Vila Real (☎ 259 32 31 26; www.glaciar-aventura.com).

and information in addition to **short-term luggage storage.** (☎ 289 32 28 19; fax 32 17 12. Open daily summer 9:30am-7pm; winter 9:30am-12:30pm and 2-6pm.) The **currency exchange** is at **Realvitur,** Lg. Pioledo, 2, four blocks uphill and to the right from the tourist office. (☎ 259 34 08 00. Open M-F 9am-7pm, Sa 9am-1pm.) You can find **Lavandaria Miracorgo,** R. Camilo Castelo Branco, 33-33A, a small, family-run **laundromat,** on a street parallel to the main drag. (Open M-F 9am-1pm and 2:30-7pm, Sa 9am-1pm). Conveniently located, **Farmácia Almeida,** Av. Carvalho de Araújo, 41-43, offers excellent service. (Open M-F 9am-1pm and 2:30-7pm, Sa 9am-1pm.) The **Centro de Saúde** is on R. Dr. Manuel Cardona. (☎ 259 32 40 95, emergencies 32 81 05). The city provides free **Internet access** at **Espaço Internet,** Av. 1 de Maio. (Open M-Sa 10am-7pm, Su 2-7pm.) The **post office,** Av. Carvalho Araújo, is across the street from the tourist office. (☎ 259 33 03 00. Open M-F 8:30am-6pm, Sa 9am-12:30pm.) **Postal Code:** 5657.

⌘⌘ ACCOMMODATIONS AND FOOD. Staying in Vila Real, as in the rest of Northern Portugal, is inexpensive. A good bet is to walk down Av. Carvalho de Araújo and explore the rooms that several cafes advertise above their shops. ■**Residencial S. Domingos ❶,** Tr. de S. Domingos, 33, offers comfortable yet old rooms, all with private bath, cable TV, and phone. (☎ 259 32 20 39; fax 32 20 39. Singles €15; doubles €25; triples €35). For cheaper rooms without amenities, try the **Pousada de Juventude de Vila Real (HI) ❶,** R. Dr. Manuel Cardona, on top of the Instituto Português da Juventude, which provides free Internet access. Rooms are typical youth hostel fare. (☎ 259 37 31 93. Breakfast 8:30-10am. Reception 8am-midnight. Summer dorms €11; doubles with bath €27. Winter €8/€21. AmEx/MC/V.) For a more central stay, try **Hotel Tocaio ❷,** Av. Carvalho Araújo. Though somewhat old, rooms have big baths and TVs. (☎ 259 37 16 75. Singles €20; doubles €35; triples €45. AmEx/MC/V.) Camp at **Parque de Campismo Municipal de Vila Real ❶,** R. Dr. Manuel Cardona, beside the river and past the youth hostel, at the end of the street on the right. It has free showers and space to pitch a tent or park a car, but little else. (☎ 259 32 47 24. Reception June-Aug. 8am-10pm; Sept.-May 8:30am-5pm. Open Jan.16-Dec. 15. €2.75 per person, €1.75 per tent and per car.)

Eating well on a budget is no challenge here. **Avenida Carvalho Araújo** and the parallel **Rua Antonio de Azevedo** are good places to look; restaurants on **Rua Teixeira de Sousa** tend to be more touristy, but there are some cheaper ones there as well. The cafes along Av. Carvalho Araújo and in the square at its end offer what humble nightlife options the town has. ▓**Churrasquería Real ❶**, R. Teixeira de Sousa, 14, is a well-decorated locale that serves up quality grilled meat. Try the house specialty, *frango ao churrasco* (€4.50), served with heaping piles of french fries, salad, and rice. (☎259 32 20 78. Entrees €4-9.50. Open Tu-Su 9am-11pm.) The local favorite **Museu dos Presuntos ❷**, Av. Cidade de Orense, 43, at R. D. Afonso III and R. Morgado de Mateus, is a bit of a hike from the town center, but worth it for the *presunto* combinations; *presunto* is essentially what results from hanging a full pig in a vat of salt for a month. From the tourist office, cross Av. Carvalho Araújo, take a right, and continue up R. Dom Pedro de Castro. Past the Rodonorte bus station, bear right onto R. Dom Pedro de Menzes and take a right onto R. D. Afonso III. The restaurant is at the end of the street across the intersection. (☎259 32 60 17. Entrees €8-13, half portions €7-9. Open Su-M and W-Sa 12:30-2:30pm and 7:30-9:30pm; closed lunch F. AmEx/MC/V.) A staple in Vila Real for over 30 years, the classy **O Espadeiro ❸**, Av. Almeida Lucena, serves up quality food in an elegant dining room with tuxedoed waiters. Clearly the nicest restaurant in town, the prices are nonetheless manageable, making this an excellent opportunity to try some of the best Portuguese food in Trás-Os-Montes without breaking the bank; the *cabrito assado* (roast goat; €14.20) is excellent. (☎259 32 23 02. Entrees €10-14. Open M-Sa 10am-10pm.)

◧◪ **SIGHTS AND EXCURSIONS.** The **Parque Natural de Alvão** is Portugal's smallest natural park; nonetheless, this pine-covered paradise offers excellent hiking routes and the chance to spend a day amongst the beauty of Trás-Os-Montes's mountains, only 15km north of Vila Real. Among other very unique flora and fauna the endangered Iberian wolf (usually harmless and fairly rare) lives in the Serra. The expanse includes a remote community that has maintained its rural appeal, including impressive homes representative of the designs and building materials used several centuries ago. Getting to the park without a car is problematic, to say the least; bus schedules are extremely erratic and offer no regular service to the park (though the municipality of Vila Real's local bus line should improve service by Sept. 2005). Perhaps the best option for those truly intent on exploring this mountainous expanse would be to take a taxi from Vila Real (€5-7); travelers can spend a few hours on the trails, and then hike 15km downhill on the major road or simply call another taxi to pick them up (the park information office provides detailed maps with specific hikes ranging from 4-18km). Unfortunately, camping is not an option, as the municipality has prohibited it to prevent forest fires. For those with a sense of adventure (and just a touch of insanity), **Glaciar Aventura** offers a series of extreme sports within the park (see **Wild on the Alvão,** p. 808). Prior to setting out, a stop at the **park information office,** Lg. dos Freitas, is absolutely essential; the office is located at the bottom of Av. Carvalho de Araújo, behind the Câmara Municipal. (☎259 30 28 30; fax 30 28 31. Open daily 9am-12:30pm and 2-5:30pm.)

APPENDIX

CLIMATE

In the following charts, the first two columns for each month list the average daily minimum and maximum temperatures in degrees Celsius and Fahrenheit. The rain column lists the average number of days of rain that month.

SPAIN	JANUARY			APRIL			JULY			OCTOBER		
	°C	°F	Rain	°C	°F	Rain	°C	°F	Rain	°C	°F	Rain
Barcelona	4-13	40-55	5	8-17	47-62	9	19-27	66-81	4	12-21	54-70	9
Bilbao	6-13	42-55	8	8-17	46-62	8	16-25	60-77	5	12-21	53-69	8
Madrid	0-11	32-51	8	6-17	42-63	9	16-32	61-90	2	8-20	47-68	8
Santiago de Compostela	5-10	41-50	21	8-18	46-64	7	13-24	55-75	1	11-21	52-70	10
Sevilla	6-16	42-61	8	10-22	50-71	7	19-35	66-95	0	13-26	56-78	6

PORTUGAL	JANUARY			APRIL			JULY			OCTOBER		
	°C	°F	Rain	°C	°F	Rain	°C	°F	Rain	°C	°F	Rain
Faro	7-16	45-61	9	10-19	50-67	9	18-28	64-83	0	14-23	61-72	6
Lisboa	8-14	46-58	15	8-17	46-63	15	15-24	63-81	2	14-22	58-72	9
Porto	5-13	41-56	18	9-18	48-64	18	15-25	59-76	5	11-21	52-69	15

TIME DIFFERENCES

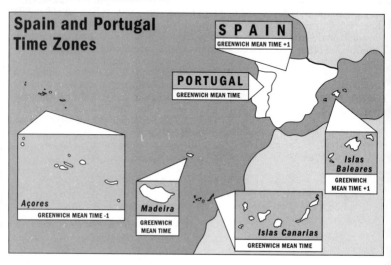

Spain and Portugal Time Zones

SPAIN
GREENWICH MEAN TIME +1

PORTUGAL
GREENWICH MEAN TIME

Islas Baleares
GREENWICH MEAN TIME +1

Açores
GREENWICH MEAN TIME -1

Madeira
GREENWICH MEAN TIME

Islas Canarias
GREENWICH MEAN TIME

ADDRESSES

"Av.," "C.," "R.," and "Tr." are abbreviations for street; "Po.," "Pg.," and "Rmbla." for promenade; "Pl.," "Pr.," and "Lg." for plaza; and "Ctra." for highway. A building's number follows the street name.

SPANISH PHRASEBOOK

Each vowel has only one pronunciation: a ("ah" in "father"); e ("eh" in "pet"); i ("ee" in "eat"); o ("oh" in "oat"); u ("oo" in "boot"); y, by itself, is pronounced the same as Spanish i ("ee"). Most consonants are the same as in English. Important exceptions are: j ("h" in "hello"); ll ("y" in "yes"); $ñ$ ("ny" in "canyon"); and r at the beginning of a word or rr anywhere in a word is trilled. H is always silent. G before e or i is pronounced like the "h" in "hen;" elsewhere it is pronounced like the "g" in "gate."X has a bewildering variety of pronunciations; depending on dialect and word position, it can sound like English "h," "s," "sh," or "x." Spanish words receive stress on the syllable marked with an accent. In the absence of an accent mark, words that end in vowels, n, or s receive stress on the second to last syllable. For words ending in all other consonants, stress falls on the last syllable. The Spanish language has masculine and feminine nouns, and gives a gender to all adjectives. Masculine words generally end with an o: *él es un tonto* (he is a fool). Feminine words generally end with an a: *ella es graciosa* (she is funny). Pay close attention—slight changes in word ending can have drastic changes in meaning. For instance, when receiving directions, mind the distinction between *derecho* (straight; more commonly *recto*) and *derecha* (right).

ENGLISH	SPANISH	ENGLISH	SPANISH
	The Bare Minimum		
Yes/No/OK	Sí/No/Vale	**Do you speak English?**	¿Habla (usted) inglés?
Hello	Hola (Sí on the phone)	**I don't understand**	No entiendo
Good morning	Buenos días	**I don't speak Spanish**	No hablo español
Good afternoon	Buenas tardes	**I don't know**	No sé
Good evening/night	Buenas noches	**What/When**	¿Qué?/¿Cuándo?
Goodbye	Adiós/Hasta luego	**Where/How**	¿Dónde?/¿Cómo?
Please/Thank you	Por favor/Gracias	**Who/Why**	¿Quién?/¿Por qué?
Excuse me	Perdón/Perdóname	**How are you?**	¿Cómo está (usted)?
Help	Socorro/Ayuda	**good/bad/so-so**	bien/mal/así así
No smoking/Got a lighter (cigarette)?	No fumar/¿Tiene fuego (un cigarillo)?	**What time is it?**	¿Qué hora es?
here/there/left/ right/straight	aquí/allí/izquierda/ derecha/recto	**How much does it cost?**	¿Cuánto cuesta?
open/closed	abierto/cerrado	**Can you drop me off here?**	¿Usted me puede dejar aquí?
hot/cold	caliente/frío	**My name is...**	Me llamo...
I am hot/cold	Tengo calor/frío	**What is your name?**	¿Cómo se llama?
Where is a late-night pharmacy?	¿Dónde está una farma-cia de guardia?	**Is there a telephone that I could use?**	¿Hay un teléfono que podría usar?
Where is the toilet?	¿Dónde está el baño?	**I'm sick.**	Estoy enfermo/a.
Can you repeat that?	¿Podría repetirlo?	**Can you write it down?**	¿Podría escribirlo?
	Accommodations and Transportation		
I want/I would like	Quiero/Quisiera	**How do I reach...?**	¿Cómo llego a...?
I would like a room.	Quisiera un cuarto.	**One ticket to...**	Un billete para...

ENGLISH	SPANISH	ENGLISH	SPANISH
Do you have any rooms?	¿Tiene cuartos libres?	bus (train) station/airport	estación de autobús (tren)/aeropuerto
I would like to reserve a room, please.	Quisiera reservar una habitación, por favor.	How much is the fare to...?	¿Cuánto cuesta un billete a...?
bath/shower/water	baño/ducha/agua	train/plane/bus	tren/avión/autobús
key/sheets	llave/sábanas	round-trip	ida y vuelta
air conditioning	aire acondicionado	How long is the trip?	¿Cuánto dura el viaje?
hotel/hostel/campgrounds/inn	hotel/hostal or albergue/camping/posada	At what time does it leave/arrive?	¿A qué hora sale/llega?
Food and Dining (also see Glossary, p. 811)			
breakfast	desayuno	the check, please	la cuenta, por favor
lunch	almuerzo	drink	bebida
dinner	cena	dessert	postre
Can I get this without the meat?	¿Me puede preparar este plato sin carne?	Can you please bring me...?	¿Me puede traer...por favor?
Days			
Sunday	domingo	today	hoy
Monday	lunes	tomorrow	mañana
Tuesday	martes	day after tomorrow	pasado mañana
Wednesday	miércoles	yesterday	ayer
Thursday	jueves	day before yesterday	anteayer
Friday	viernes	week	semana
Saturday	sábado	weekend	fin de semana

PORTUGUESE PHRASEBOOK

Portuguese words are often spelled like their Spanish equivalents, although the pronunciation is quite different. In additional to regular vowels, Portuguese has nasal vowels as in French; vowels with a *til* (*ã*, *õ*, etc.) or before an *m* or *n* are pronounced with a nasal twang. At the end of most words, *o* is pronounced "oo" as in "room," and *e* is sometimes silent (usually after a *t* or *d*). The consonant *s* is pronounced "sh" or "zh" when it occurs before another consonant. The consonants *ch* and *x* are pronounced "sh," although the latter is sometimes pronounced as in English; *j* and *g* (before an *e* or *i*) are pronounced "zh." The combinations *nh* and *lh* are pronounced "ny" as in "canyon" and "ly" as in "billion."

ENGLISH	PORTUGUESE	PRONUNCIATION
Yes/No	Sim/Não	seem/nowm
Hello	Olá	oh-LAH
Good day, afternoon/night	Bom dia, Boa tarde/noite	bom DEE-ah, BO-ah tard/noyt
Goodbye	Adeus	ah-DAY-oosh
Please	Por favor	poor fer-VOR
Thank you	Obrigado (male)/Obrigada (female)	oh-bree-GAH-doo/dah
Sorry/Excuse me, please	Desculpe	dish-KOOLP
Do you speak English?	Fala inglês?	FAH-lah EEN-glaysh?
I don't understand.	Não entendo.	now ayn-TAYN-doa
Where is...?	Onde é...?	OHN-deh eh...?
How much does this cost?	Quanto custa?	KWAHN-too KOOSH-tah?
Do you have a single/double room?	Tem um quarto individual/duplo?	tem oom KWAR-too EEN-dee-vee-du-ahl/DOO-ploo?
Help!	Socorro!	soo-KOA-roo!

GLOSSARY

In the following glossary we have tried to include the most useful shortlist of common terms possible, particularly words we use in the text and those that you will encounter frequently in menus. Non-Castilian words are specified as **C** (Catalan), **B** (Basque), or **G** (Galician), respectively.

SPAIN: TRAVELING

abadía: abbey
abierto: open
ayuntamiento/ajuntament (C): city hall
albergue: youth hostel
alcazaba: Muslim citadel
alcázar: Muslim palace
arena: sand
autobús/autocar: bus
avenida/avinguda (C): avenue
bahía: bay
bakalao: Spanish techno
bandera azul: blue flag, EU award for clean beaches
baños: baths
barcelonés: of Barcelona
barrio viejo: old quarter
biblioteca: library
billete: ticket
buceo: scuba diving
cabo: cape
cajero automático: ATM
calle/carrer (C): street
cambio: currency exchange
capilla: chapel
casa particular: lodging in a private home
caseta: party tent for Sevilla's *Feria de Abril*
castillo/castell (C): castle
catedral: cathedral
cerrado: closed
carretera: highway
casco antiguo/viejo: old city, old district
chocolate: chocolate or hash
churrigueresco: ornate Baroque architecture style
ciudad vieja/ciutat vella (C): old city
colegio: high school
consigna: luggage storage
Correos: post office
corrida: bullfight
cripta: crypt
cuarto: room
encierro: running of the bulls
entrada: entrance
ermita/ermida (C): hermitage
escuela: (elementary) school
estación: station
estanco: tobacco shop
estanque: pond
estany (C): lake
extremeño: of Extremadura
fachada: facade
feria: outdoor market or fair

ferrocarriles: trains
fiesta: holiday or festival
fuente/font (C): fountain
gallego: of Galicia
gitano: gypsy
glorieta: rotary
iglesia/església (C)/igrexa (G): church
IVA: value-added tax
jardín público: public garden
judería: Jewish quarter
librería: bookstore
lista de correos: poste restante
litera: sleeping car (in trains)
llegada: arrival
madrileño: Madrid resident
madrugada: early morning
manchego: from La Mancha
mercado/mercat (C): market
mezquita: mosque
mirador: lookout point
monestir (C): monastery
monte: mountain
mosteiro (G): monastery
mozárabe: Christian art style
mudéjar: Muslim architectural style
muelle/moll (C): wharf, pier
murallas: walls
museo/museu (C): museum
oficina: office
palau (C): palace
parador nacional: state-owned luxury hotel
parte viejo: old town
paseo, Po.: promenade, stroll
passeig, Pg. (C): promenade
pico: peak
plateresque: architectural style noted for its facades
playa/platja (C): beach
plaza/plaça, Pl. (C), praza, Pr. (G): square, plaza
puente: bridge
quiosco: newsstand
rastro: flea market
real: royal
REAJ: the Spanish HI youth hostel network
Reconquista: the Christian reconquest of the Iberian peninsula from the Muslims
refugio: shelter, refuge
reina/rey: queen/king
retablo: altarpiece
ría (G): estuary
río/riu (C): river
rua (G): street

sacristía: part of the church where sacred objects are kept
sala: room or hall
salida: exit, departure
selva: forest
Semana Santa: Holy Week, leading up to Easter Sunday;
sepulcro: tomb
seu (C): cathedral
sevillanas: type of flamenco
SIDA: AIDS
sierra, serra (C): mountain range
Siglo de Oro: Golden Age
sillería: choir stalls
tienda: shop or tent
tesoro: treasury
torre: tower
universidad: university
v.o.: *versión original*, a foreign-language film subtitled in Spanish
valle: valley
zarzuela: Spanish light opera

SPAIN: FOOD AND DRINK

a la plancha/a brasa: grilled
aceite: oil
aceituna: olive
adabo: battered
agua: water
aguacate: avocado
aguardiente: firewater
ahumado/a: smoked
ajo: garlic
al horno: baked
albóndigas: meatballs
alioli: Catalan garlic sauce
almejas: clams
almendras: almonds
almuerzo: midday meal
alubias: kidney beans
anchoas: anchovies
anguila: eel
arroz: rice
arroz con leche: rice pudding
asado: roasted
atún: tuna
bacalao: salted cod
bacón: (American) bacon
bistec: steak
bocadillo: sandwich
bodega: wine cellar
bollo: bread roll
boquerones: anchovies
brasa: chargrilled
cacahuete: peanut
café con leche: coffee w/milk

café solo: black coffee
calabacín: zucchini
calamares: calamari, squid
caldereta: stew
caldo gallego: white bean and potato soup
calimocho: red wine and coke
callos: tripe
camarones: shrimp
caña: small beer in a glass
canelones: cannelloni
cangrejo: crab
caracoles: snails
carne: meat
cava (C): champagne
cebolla: onion
cena: dinner
cerdo: pig, pork
cereza: cherry
cervecería: beer bar
cerveza: beer
champiñones: mushrooms
choco: cuttlefish
chorizo: spicy red sausage
chuleta: chop, cutlet
chupito: shot
churros: fried dough sticks
cocido: cooked; stew
conejo: rabbit
coñac: brandy
copas: drinks
cordero: lamb
cortado: coffee with little milk
croquetas: fried croquettes
crudo: raw
cuba libre: rum w/Coca-Cola
cuchara: spoon
cuchillo: knife
cuenta: the bill
desayuno: breakfast
dorada: sea bass
empanada: meat/fish pastry
ensaladilla rusa: vegetable salad with mayonnaise
entremeses: hors d'oeuvres
escabeche: pickled fish
espagueti: spaghetti
espárragos: asparagus
espinacas: spinach
fabada asturiana: bean soup with sausage and ham
flan: crème caramel
frambuesa: raspberry
fresa: strawberry
frito/a: fried
galleta: cookie
gambas: prawns
garbanzos: chickpeas
gazpacho: cold tomato soup with garlic and cucumber
ginebra: gin
guindilla: hot chili pepper
guisantes: peas
helado: ice cream
hielo: ice
horchata: sweet almond drink
horneado: baked
huevo: egg

jamón dulce: cooked ham
jamón ibérico: Iberia ham
jamón serrano: cured ham
jatetxea (B): restaurant
jerez: sherry
langosta: lobster
langostino: large prawn
leche: milk
lechuga: lettuce
lenguado: sole
lomo: pork loin
manzana: apple
manzanilla: dry, light sherry
mayonesa: mayonnaise
mejillones: mussels
melocotón: peach
menestra de verduras: vegetable mix/pottage
menú: full meal with bread, drink, and side dish
merienda: tea/snack
merluza: hake
migas: fried breadcrumb dish
mojito: white rum and club soda with mint and sugar
morcilla: blood sausage (black pudding)
mostaza: mustard
muy hecho: well-done (steak)
naranja: orange
natillas: creamy milk dessert
navajas: razor clams
paella: rice and seafood dish
pan: bread
pasa: raisin
pastas: small sweet cakes
pastel: pastry
patatas bravas: potatoes w/ spicy tomato sauce and mayo
patatas fritas: French fries
pato: duck
pavo: turkey
pechuga: chicken breast
pepino: cucumber
picante: spicy
pimienta (negra): (black) pepper
pimiento (rojo): (red) pepper
piña: pineapple
pintxo (B): Basque for tapa
plancha: grill
plátano: banana
plato del día: daily special
plato combinado: entree and side dish
poco hecho: rare (steak)
pollo: chicken
pulpo: octopus
queso: cheese
rabo de toro: bull's tail
ración: small dish
rebozado: battered and fried
refrescos: soft drinks
relleno/a: stuffed
sal: salt
salchicha: pork sausage
sangria: red wine punch
seco: dried
servilleta: napkin

sesos: brains
setas: wild mushrooms
sidra: (alcoholic) cider
solomillo: sirloin
sopa: soup
taberna: tapas bar
tapa: bite-sized snack
tenedor: fork
ternera: beef, veal
terraza: patio seating
tinto: red (wine)
tocino: (Canadian) bacon
tomate: tomato
tortilla española: potato fritatta
tortilla francesa: omelette
tostada: toast
trucha: trout
trufas: truffles
tubo: tall glass of beer
txakoli (B): fizzy white wine
uva: grape
vaca, carne de: beef
vaso: glass
verduras: green vegetables
vino: wine
vino blanco: white wine
vino tinto: red wine
xampanyería (C): champagne bar
yema: candied egg yolk
zanahoria: carrot
zarzuela de marisco: shellfish stew
zumo: fruit juice

PORTUGAL: TRAVELING

alto/a: upper
autocarro: bus
bairro: neighborhood, district
baixo/a: lower
berrões: stone pigs found in Trás-Os-Montes
bicicleta de montanha: mountain bike
bilhete: ticket
bilheteria: ticket office
câmara municipal: town hall
camioneta: long distance bus
capela: chapel
casa de abrigo: shelter-house, usually in parks
castelo: castle
centro de saúde: state-run medical center
chegadas: arrivals
cidade: city
claustro: cloister
conta: bill
coro alto: choir stalls
Correios: post office
cruzeiro: cross
Dom, Dona: courtesy titles, usually for kings and queens
domingo: Sunday
entrada: entrance
esquerda: left (abbr. E, Esqa)
estação rodoviária: bus station

estrada: road
feriado: holiday
floresta: forest
fortaleza: fort
grutas: caves
horario: timetable
igreja: church
ilha: island
intercidade: inter-city train
lago: lake
largo: small square
ligação: connecting bus/train
livraria: bookstore
miradouro: lookout
mosteiro: monastery
mouraria: Moorish quarter
mudança: switch/change
obras: construction
paço: palace
paragem: stop
partidas: departures
pelourinho: stone pillory
pensão (s.), pensões (pl.):
pension(s)/guesthouse(s)
ponte: bridge
porta: gate/door
pousada da juventude: youth
hostel
pousada: guest house
praça: square
praça de touros: bullring
praia: beach
PSP: Polícia de Seguranca
Pública, the local police force
quarta-feira: Wednesday
quarto de casal: room with
double bed
quinta-feira: Thursday
quiosque: kiosk; newsstand
rés do chão: ground floor,
abbr. R/C
residencial: guesthouse,
more expensive than *pensões*
retábulo: altarpiece
ribeira: stream
ria: narrow lagoon
rio: river
romaria: pilgrimage-festival
rossio: rotary
rua: street
sábado: Saturday
saída: exit
sé: cathedral
segunda-feira: Monday
selos: stamps
sexta-feira: Friday
terça-feira: Tuesday
termas: spa
tesouraria: treasury
tourada: bullfight
turismo: tourist office
velha: old
vila: town

PORTUGAL: FOOD AND DRINK

açorda: thick soup with bread
adega: wine cellar, bar

aguardente: firewater
alface: lettuce
alho: garlic
almoço: lunch
ameijoas: clams
Antiqua: aged grape brandy
arroz: rice
arrufada de Coimbra: raised
dough cake with cinnamon
assado: baked
azeitonas: olives
bacalhau: cod
bacalhau à Gomes de Sá:
cod with olives and eggs
bacalhau à transmontana:
cod braised with cured pork
balcão: counter in bar or café
batata: potato
batido: milkshake
bem passado: well done
bica: espresso
bifinhos de vitela: veal filet
with wine sauce
bitoque de porco: pork chops
bitoque de vaca: steak
bolachas: cookies
branco: white (wine)
cabrito: kid
café com leite: coffee with
milk, in a mug
café da manhã: breakfast
caldeirada: shellfish stew
caldo: broth/soup
caldo verde: kale soup
camarões: shrimp
caneca: pint-size beer mug
caracóis: snails
carioca: coffee with hot
water; like American coffee
carne: meat
carne de vaca: beef
cebola: onion
cerveja: beer
chocos: cuttlefish
chouriço: sausage
churrasqueira: BBQ house
cogumelos: mushrooms
conta: bill
couvert: cover charge added
to bill for bread
cozido: boiled
doce: sweet
ementa: menu
ervilhas: green peas
esacalfado: poached
espadarte: swordfish
espetadas: skewered meat
served with melted butter
esturjão: sturgeon
fatia: slice
feijao: bean
frango: chicken
frito: fried
galão: coffee with hot milk
garrafa: bottle
gasosa: lemonade
gelado: ice cream
grão: chickpeas
grelhado: grilled

guisado: stewed
hambúrguer no prato: ham-
burger patty with fried egg
imperial: draft beer
jantar: dinner
lagosta: lobster
lampreia: lamprey
laranja: orange
legumes: vegetables
leitão: roasted pork
linguado: sole
linguiça: very thin sausage
lula: squid
maca: apple
manteiga: butter
mariscos: shellfish
massapão: marzipan
mexilhões: mussels
no churrasco: barbecued
no forno: baked
ovos: eggs
padaria: bakery
panado: breaded
pão: bread
passas: raisins
pastelaria: pastry shop
peru: turkey
pimentos: peppers
polvo: octopus
porco: pork
posta: slice of fish or meat
prato do dia: dish of the day
presunto: ham
queijo: cheese
recheado: stuffed
salmão: salmon
sande: sandwich
seco: dry
sobremesa: dessert
sopa juliana: soup with
shredded vegetables
sumo: juice
tasca: bistro/cafe
tigelada: sweet egg dessert
tinto: red (wine)
tomatada: rich tomato sauce
tosta: grilled cheese
tosta mista: grilled ham and
cheese sandwich
toucinho do ceu: kind of
marzipan pudding
vinho de casa: house wine
vinho verde: white wine
vitela: veal

AVERAGE TRAVEL TIMES IN SPAIN AND PORTUGAL

	Algeciras	Badajoz	Barcelona	Bilbao	Córdoba	Granada	León	Málaga	Madrid	Pamplona	Salamanca	San Sebastián	Santiago	Sevilla	Toledo	Valencia	Zaragoza
Algeciras																	
Badajoz	10hr.																
Barcelona	19½hr.	13½hr.															
Bilbao	11-13hr.	10-11½hr.	8-11hr.														
Córdoba	5-6hr.	6hr.	11hr.	9-11hr.													
Granada	5-7hr.	7½-9½hr.	12-13hr.	10-12hr.	3hr.												
León	11hr.	8½hr.	11½hr.	7hr.	7-9hr.	10hr.											
Málaga	5½hr.	7-8hr.	13hr.	11-13hr.	2½-3hr.	2hr.	9-11½hr.										
Madrid	6hr.	4½hr.	7hr.	5-7hr.	2-6hr.	5hr.	4½-5½hr.	4-6hr.									
Pamplona	11hr.	9½hr.	6-8hr.	2hr.	9hr.	10hr.	4hr.	9-11hr.	5hr.								
Salamanca	9hr.	5½hr	11½hr.	5½-6½hr.	6-8hr.	8hr.	3hr.	7-9hr.	3hr.	6-7hr.							
San Sebastián	12-14hr.	10-12hr.	7-10hr.	11hr.	10-12hr.	11-13hr.	5¼hr.	12-14hr.	6-8hr.	1-2hr.	5½-6½hr.						
Santiago	14hr.	12-13hr.	15hr.	11hr.	11-13hr.	13hr.	5½hr.	12-14hr.	7½-8hr.	12hr.	7-8hr.	12hr.					
Sevilla	4-5hr.	4½hr.	13-16hr.	8-11hr.	1½hr.	3-5hr.	7-9hr.	2½-3hr.	2½-3½hr.	8hr.	8hr.	9-11hr.	11hr.				
Toledo	6hr.	5hr.	7hr.	6-8hr.	3-5hr.	14hr.	6hr.	5-6hr.	1½hr.	9hr.	4hr.	7-9hr.	12hr.	3hr.			
Valencia	13-15hr.	10hr.	4-6hr.	12hr.	7hr.	8hr.	10-13hr.	11hr.	5-7½hr.	10hr.	8-10½hr.	10hr.	11hr.	9hr.	5-7½hr.		
Zaragoza	9hr.	8hr.	4hr.	4hr.	6-8hr.	8hr.	5½-6hr.	7-9hr.	3hr.	2hr.	7hr.	4hr.	11-12hr.	8½hr.	4hr.	6hr.	

Braga	Coimbra	Évora	Faro	Fátima	Lisboa	Porto	
	4hr.	9-10hr.	12-15hr.	5½hr.	8½hr.	2hr.	Braga
		6hr.	12hr.	1½hr.	3hr.	3hr.	Coimbra
			6hr.	5½hr.	3hr.	7hr.	Évora
				7½hr.	5hr.	8½hr.	Faro
					2½hr.	3½hr.	Fátima
						6hr.	Lisboa
							Porto

MOROCCO ESSENTIALS

On a clear day, you can stand on a hill in southernmost Andalucía and gaze across the Strait of Gibraltar, where the faint ridges of the Atlas Mountains—and North Africa—beckon along the horizon. The North African influence permeating Andalucía often piques the curiosity of travelers, who take advantage of the proximity of the two continents to travel to Morocco. This path is well-trodden, having served for centuries as a trade route for language, religion, and culture. Fortunately for the modern traveler, the trek has only become easier.

Northern Morocco, the part most easily accessible from Spain, is intriguing for its exoticism but frightening for how it caters to tourists, both in the sterility of interactions with Moroccan culture and in the adeptness of natives at conning less-than-wily tourists. If you're heading for Tangier or other Mediterranean towns, keep your wits about you. If you have the time, be certain to head down to bewildering Fez, medieval Meknes, and even vibrant Marrakesh, farther to the south. Information about places within Morocco was last updated in August 2002.

PRACTICAL INFORMATION

DIAL AWAY	The **country code** for Morocco is ☎212. For the **police**, dial ☎19. For **information**, call ☎16.

Ferries: *Embarcaciones rápidas* (fast ferries) depart from **Algeciras** (p. 273) to **Ceuta,** a Spanish enclave in North Africa; normal and fast ferries leave for the Moroccan port of **Tangier.** Only **Trasmediterránea** (☎902 45 46 45), at the entrance to the port, offers Eurail discounts. Open daily 9am-7pm. MC/V. All ferry companies sell tickets for all departures at the same price, regardless of whose boat it is. Allow 30min. to clear customs and board, 90min. with a car. Summer ferries to **Ceuta** (35min.; depart 16 per day 6am-9:45pm, return 7:30am-11pm Moroccan time; €22.80, under 12 €11, small car €60.70, motorcycle €19.60) and **Tangier** (2½hr.; depart every hr. 7am-11pm, return 6am-9pm Moroccan time; €25.30, with Eurail pass €20, under 12 €11.70, small car €71.90, motorcycle €22.20). Fast ferries also go to **Tangier** (1hr., 9am and 1:45pm, €25). Limited service in winter. MC/V. Ferries also depart from **Gibraltar** (p. 275) to **Tangier** (1¼hr.; F 6pm, return Sa 5:30pm Moroccan time; £18/€32, under 12 £9/€16.20).

Visas: To enter Morocco for less than 90 days, citizens of **Australia, Canada, Ireland, New Zealand, the UK,** and **the US** need a passport.

EMBASSIES AND CONSULATES

MOROCCAN EMBASSIES

Australia and New Zealand: Morocco has no embassies in Australia or New Zealand. The embassy in **Tokyo,** Japan handles all inquiries; Silva Kingdom Building 3-16-3, Sendagaya - Shibuya Ku, Tokyo 151 (☎813 34 78 32 71; fax 34 02 08 98).

Canada: 38 Range Rd., Ottawa, ON K1N 8J4 (☎613-236-7391 or 236-7392; www.ambassade-maroc.ottawa.on.ca). **Consulate:** 1010 Sherbrooke West, Suite 1510, Montreal, QU H3A 2R7 (☎514-288-8750; www.consulatdumaroc.ca).

Ireland: 39 Raglan Rd., Ballsbridge, Dublin 4 (☎353 1 660 9449; fax 1 660 9468).

United Kingdom: 49 Queens Gate Gardens, London SW7 5NE (☎0207 581 5001; fax 225 3862).

United States: 1601 21st St. NW, Washington, D.C. 20009 (☎202-462-7979; fax 462 7643). **Consulates:** 10 East 40th. St., 23rd fl., New York, NY 10016 (☎212-758-2625; www.moroccanconsulate.com); 1821 Jefferson Pl. NW, Washington, D.C. 20036 (☎202-462-7979; fax 452-0106).

FOREIGN EMBASSIES IN MOROCCO

Australia: The Canadian embassy in Morocco provides all services for Australians.

Canada: 13 Bis, Jaafar As-Saddik, B.P.709, Agdal, Rabat (☎037 68 74 00).

Ireland: Contact the Irish embassy in Portugal (p. 672).

New Zealand: Contact the embassy of New Zealand in Madrid (p. 78).

United Kingdom: 17 bd. de la Tour Hassan, B.P. 45, Rabat (☎037 72 96 96; www.britain.org.ma). **Consulates:** 43 bd. d'Anfa, B.P. 13.762, Casablanca (☎022 43 77 00); 41 Av. Mohammed V, B.P. 2122, Tangier (☎039 94 15 57; fax 94 22 84).

United States: 2 Av. de Mohammed El Fassi, Rabat (☎037 76 22 65, after-hours 76 96 39; rabat.usembassy.gov). **Consulate:** 8 bd. Moulay Youssef, Casablanca (☎022 26 45 50; fax 20 41 27).

TANGIER طنجة

For travelers venturing out of Europe for the first time, Tangier can be stressful. Many make the city out to be a living nightmare, but despite the very real difficulties, it remains the best way to enter from Spain. Once in Tangier, however, the best thing you could do is leave it.

Trains leave from **Mghagha Station** (☎039 95 25 55), 6km from the port. *Petit taxi* to the station 15dh. To: **Casablanca** (6hr., 4 per day 8am-11pm, 117dh); **Fez** (5½hr., 4 per day 8am-11pm, 96dh); **Meknes** (5hr., 4 per day 8am-11pm, 80dh).

Private buses run from Av. Yacoub al-Mansour at pl. Jamia al-Arabia, 2km from the port. Ask blue-coated personnel or check boards for ticket info. Luggage 5dh. *Petit taxi* from the port to the terminal 8dh. To: **Casablanca** (6hr., every hr. 5am-1am, 69dh); **Chefchaouen** (4hr., 7am and 2:45pm); **Ceuta** (40min., 7 per day 6:15am-5:45pm, 10dh); **Fez** (6hr., 11 per day 11:30am-9:30pm, 63dh); **Marrakesh** (10hr.; 3 per day 6:45am-8:30pm; 115dh); **Meknes** (5hr., 8 per day 6am-5:45pm, 57dh). **CTM buses** (☎039 93 11 72) to: **Agadir** (3 per day 11am-9pm); **Casablanca** (6 per day 11am-midnight); **Chefchaouen** (12:30pm); **Fez** (3 per day 3, 7, 9pm); **Marrakesh** (11am and 4:30pm); **Meknes** (3 per day 3-9pm).

Tourist Office, 29 bd. Pasteur (☎039 94 80 50). Some English, French, and Spanish spoken. List of accommodations available. Open M-F 8:30am-7:30pm.

CEUTA (SEBTA) سبتة

Travelers hoping to avoid Tangier altogether may opt to ferry to the Spanish enclave of Ceuta and from there cross the Moroccan border, only 5km away. Most visitors don't stay in Ceuta, moving on immediately to Tetouan (35min. away) or Chefchaouen (allow 4hr.). If you're trapped in Ceuta, try the helpful **tourist booth** (☎956 50 62 75) in the ferry terminal, which has a map. If you need to spend the night, accommodation options do exist.

INDEX

A

accommodations 39–43
   in Portugal 674
   in Spain 83
adventure tourism 46
   Aínsa 499
   Arenas de Cabrales 583
   Cangas de Onís 581
   Corralejo 651
   Jaca 492
   Parque Nacional de Ordesa 497
   Parque Natural da Serra da
      Estrela 802
   Picos de Europa 572, 583
   Potes 590
   Ribadesella 577
   Val d'Aran 484
   Vila Real 808
Águilas 352
Aínsa (L'Ainsa) 499
airmail 34
airplanes. See flights.
Albufeira 727
Alcalá de Henares 144
Alcobaça 756
alcohol 16
Alcúdia 366
Alentejo 734–742
Alfonso X el Sabio 143, 154,
   233, 261, 352
Alfonso XIII 67, 139, 597, 598
Algarve 719–734
Algarve and Alentejo 719–
   744
Algeciras 273
Alhambra 306
Alicante (Alacant) 334–340
Almada 709
Almagro 200
Almería 288
Almodóvar, Pedro 75
Altamira. See caves.
Alternatives to Tourism 53–
   62
American Express 12, 13
American Red Cross 19
Andalucía 245–318
Andorra 486–490
   Andorra la Vella 487
Ansó 495
Antequera 298
Appendix 810–818
aquariums
   Aquarium de San Sebastián 550
   Aquarium Finisterrae 626

Casa del Campo 135
L'Aquàrium de Barcelona 428
L'Oceanogràfic 325
Oceanário 703
Arab baths 232, 251, 261,
   307, 309, 461
Aragón 508–521
**Aragón, La Rioja, and
   Navarra** 507–542
Aragonese Pyrenees 491–502
Aranjuez 146
architecture
   best of 2
   Churrigueresque 72
   Gothic 72
      in Portugal 668
      in Spain 72
   Manueline 668, 793
   Modernista 72, 437
   Neoclassicism 136
   Plateresque 72, 164
   Renaissance 72
   Roman 72
   Romanesque 165, 517
Arcos de la Frontera 263
Arenas de Cabrales 581
Armona 733
Arrecife 653
Arucas 639
Astorga 175
Asturias 568–591
Asturias and Cantabria
   567–600
ATM cards 13
Aveiro 796–799
Ávila 156–160
Aznar, José María 68, 115

B

backpacks 45
Badajoz 217
Baeza 317
Balearic Islands. See Las Islas
   Baleares.
Baquiera-Beret 482
Barcelona 390–433
   accommodations 400
   Barri Gòtic and Las Ramblas
      408
   daytrips 432
   El Raval 417
   entertainment 403
   festivals 407
   food 401
   intercity transportation 390
   l'Eixample 420

La Ribera 414
local transportation 396
Montjuïc 425
Montserrat 432
nightlife 407
practical information 397
shopping 406
sights 402
Waterfront 427
Zona Alta 429
Barcelos 782
bargaining 14
   in Portugal 674
   in Spain 81
Basílica (Évora) 737
Basque
   country. See País Vasco.
   identity 566
   language 69
   separatist movement 67, 544
Batalha 760
Bayona (Baiona) 617
beaches 292
Beja 740
Benasque 501
Benidorm 341–344
Bilbao 553–559
birds 159, 262, 263, 329
Blanes 452
Boabdil 301, 308
bodegas
   Cambados 621
   Haro 524
   Jerez de la Frontera 260
   Logroño 521
   Sanlúcar de Barrameda 262
Boí 481
bone chapels
   Évora 737
   Faro 731
Bosch, Hieronymus 124, 137,
   142
Braga 776–781
Bragança 802
Bubión 314
Buçaco Forest 793
bullfighting
   abolition of 55, 405
   Barcelona 405
   Córdoba 253
   Lisboa 688
   Madrid 108
   Murcia 351
   Pamplona 533
   Portugal 732
   Ronda 296
   Sevilla 229

Spain 76
Buñuel, Luis 75
Burgos 181–185
Burguete 503
buses 29
  in Portugal 673
  in Spain 80

C

Cabo Finisterre 609
Cabral, Pedro 664, 749, 780
Cáceres 207–211
Cadaqués 465
Cádiz 265–270
Caesar, Augustus 213, 440, 508
Caesar, Julius 221, 242, 677
Calatrava, Santiago 73, 325, 643, 703
Callela 455
calling cards 35
Calpe (Calp) 344
Camabdos 620
Cambrils del Mar 445
camel rides 654
Camino de Santiago 73, 166, 175, 186, 471, 491, 502, 521, 524, 536, 540, 606
Camões, Luis de 704
Camões, Luís de 669, 704
camping 43
  equipment 45
  in Portugal 675
  in Spain 83
Camprodon 474
Canary Islands. See Las Islas Canarias.
Cangas 615
Cangas de Onís 579
Cantabria 592–600
Cap de Formentor 369, 370
Capileira 314
Carlos I. See Carlos V.
Carlos V 138, 154, 252, 307, 309, 553
Carmona 243
Carrión de los Condes 186
cars. See driving.
Cartagena 353
casas colgadas 204
Cascais 706
Castellón (Castelló) 330
Castilla La Mancha 193–207
Castilla La Mancha and Extremadura 193–220
Castilla y León 150–192
Castillo de Javier 535
Castillo de Loarre 493
Catalan (català) 435

Catalan Pyrenees 471–486
Cataluña (Catalunya) 434–470
cathedrals
  Basílica de Nuestra Señora del Pilar (Zaragoza) 514
  Cádiz 268
  Ciudad Rodrigo 168
  Iglesia Catedral de Santa María (León) 173
  La Seu (Palma) 361
  Magistral (Alcalá de Henares) 145
  Nuestra Señora de la Almudena (Madrid) 117
  Nueva (Salamanca) 165
  Santa Iglesia (Burgos) 184
  Santa María (Jaén) 316
  Santa María de Mediavilla (Teruel) 520
  Santiago de Compostela 606
  Sé (Braga) 780
  Seu Vella (Lleida) 469
  Sevilla 232
  Sigüenza 206
  Tarragona 443
  Toledo 197
  Túy 617
  Valencia 326
  Vieja (Salamanca) 165
caves
  casas cuevas 310, 312
  Covas d'en Xoroi 379
  Coves del Drac 370
  Cueva de los Verdes 656
  Cueva de Tito Bustillo 576
  Cuevas de Altamira 599
  Cuevas de la Pileta 297
  Ermita de San Saturio 191
  Grutas de Mira de Aire, Santo António, and Alvados 761
  in Antequera 299
  in Berlenga 753
  in Lagos 724
  lava caves 656
  St. Michael's Cave 278
Cedeira 628
Celts
  artifacts 191, 210, 580
  history 662
  in Andalucía 313
  in Galicia 601
  music festival 628
  mythology 576
  resistance against Rome 192
  ruins 610, 616, 742, 786
Centers for Disease Control (CDC) 19
Cercedilla 147
Cervantes, Miguel de 74, 121, 144, 145, 176, 178, 193, 201, 234, 237, 240

Ceuta (Sebta) 818
changing money 12
Charlemagne 486
Chillida, Eduardo 141, 205, 549, 550, 561
Churriguera, Alberto 165
Cibeles 139
Ciudad de las Artes y Las Ciencias 325
Ciudad Rodrigo 168
Ciutadella (Ciudadela) 376–378
Civil War. See Spanish Civil War.
climate 810
cloistered nuns 210, 237
Coimbra 787–793
Colón, Cristóbal. See Christopher Columbus.
Columbus, Christopher 138, 211, 233, 252, 308, 617, 664
  death of 176
  letters to Fernando and Isabel 234
  tomb 233
Comillas 598
communications. See keeping in touch.
Comunidad de Madrid 144–147
Conil de la Frontera 271
Conímbriga 793
Consuegra 199
Córdoba 245–256
Corralejo 650
Cortés, Hernán 193
Costa Blanca 333–349
Costa Brava 448–467
Costa de la Luz 256–278
Costa del Sol 278–300
Costa Dorada 435–448
Covadonga 587
credit cards 13
Cubism 74
Cuenca 202–205
Culatra 733
currency exchange 12
current events
  in Portugal 666
  in Spain 68
customs 11

D

Dalí, Salvador 74, 448
  film works 75
  in Cadaqués 467
  in Figueres 462
  Teatre-Museu Dalí 464
Deià 365, 369
Dénia 345

DHL 35
Dias, Bartolomeu 664
dietary concerns 50
Dinis I 664, 669
dinosaurs 539
disabled travelers 49
Discover Spain and
  Portugal 1–7
  what to do 2
  when to go 1
diseases
  food- and water-borne 20
dolphin watching 717
Domènech i Montaner, Lluís
  72, 402, 416, 423, 424
Don Quixote 167, 193, 254
Douro and Minho 769–787
driving
  car rental 31
  in Portugal 673
  in Spain 81
  insurance 32
  permits 32
drugs 16
dunes
  Corralejo 651
  Maspalomas 638
  s'Albufera des Grau 367
  São Jacinto 799

E

Earthquake of 1755 188, 648,
  664, 677
Echo. See Hecho.
Eivissa 380–387
El Call 413, 460
El Cid 74, 184, 187, 319
El Cotillo 649
El Escorial. See San Lorenzo de
  El Escorial.
El Greco 73, 124, 125, 135,
  142, 187, 197, 198, 211, 236,
  326, 437, 464, 558, 565
El Grove (O Grove) 621
El Palmar 271
El Rastro 109
El Torcal de Antequera 300
Elche (Elx) 340
Elvas 738
email. See Internet.
embassies and consulates
  abroad 8, 817
  in Morocco 818
  in Portugal 672
  in Spain 78
emergency medical services 21
emergency numbers
  in Portugal 674
  in Spain 81
environmental conservation 54

Ericeira 708
Espot 480
Essentials 8–52
  in Portugal 672
  Spain 78
Estany de Sant Maurici 480
Estella 540
Estoril 705
ETA 67
Eurailpass 25
European Union (EU)
  Portugal's entry 665
  Spain's entry 68
Évora 734–738
exchange rates 12
Extremadura 207–220

F

fado 670, 687, 688, 702
Faro 729–731
Farol 733
Fátima 761–764
FC Barcelona 404, 406, 431
Federal Express 34
Felipe el Hermoso 66, 180, 310
Felipe II 66, 73, 85, 114, 115,
  147, 234, 508, 531, 664, 766
Felipe IV 66, 73, 116, 137
Felipe V 66, 116, 156, 434
female travelers 47
Fernando and Isabel 66, 85,
  150, 160, 175, 211, 233, 252,
  308, 309, 362
Fernando III 184, 233, 234
festivals
  Batalla del Vino (Haro) 525
  Carnaval (Sitges) 438, 439
  Carnaval (Tenerife) 642
  Concurs de Castells (Tarragona)
    444
  Corpus Cristi (Granada) 311
  Dia de São João (Figueira da Foz)
    795
  Feria de Abril (Sevilla) 230
  Festa de Sant Joan (Barcelona)
    420
  Festa do Percebe (Cedeira) 629
  Festa dos Rapazes (Parque
    Natural de Montesinho) 805
  Festa Major (Dénia) 347
  Festival de Sant Joan (Alicante)
    337, 340
  Festival dos Tabuleiros (Tomar)
    767
  Fiesta de la Virgen Santa del Pilar
    (Zaragoza) 516
  Fiesta de San Juan (Ciutadella)
    377
  Fiesta de San Xuan (Vigo) 615
  Fiesta del Pastor (Picos de
    Europa) 588

Fiestas del Ángel (Teruel) 520
  International Theater Festival
    (Almagro) 201
  Las Fallas (Valencia) 328
  Queima das Fitas (Coimbra) 792
  San Fermín (Pamplona) 532
  San Sebastián Film Festival 549
  Semana Santa (Sevilla) 230
  Veranos de la Villa (Madrid)
    135
Figueira da Foz 794–796
Figueras (Figueres) 462–465
financial matters 12
flamenco
  Granada 311
  history of 75
  Madrid 106
  Sevilla 228
flights
  Air Europa 79
  courier 23
  fares 21
  Iberia 79
  in Portugal 673
  in Spain 79
  Ryanair 23
  standby 24
food and drink
  Canarian cuisine 637
  cheese 582
  garlic 169
  in Portugal 667
  in Spain 69
  jamón 315
  paella 320, 324
  pastries 713
  peppers 625
  pintxos 548
  truffles 332
Formentera 389
Franco, Francisco 67, 74, 85,
  143, 211, 273, 275, 525
Fuente Dé 591
Fuerteventura 649–653
fútbol (futebol). See soccer.

G

Galicia (Galiza) 601–629
Galician (gallego) 69, 601
Gama, Vasco da 664
Gandía 348
Gaudí, Antoni 72, 174, 175,
  361, 402, 419, 422, 445, 447,
  599
gay and lesbian services
  Barcelona 398
  Granada 303
  Madrid 98
  Sevilla 226
gay and lesbian travelers 47

Gay Pride. See Orgullo Gay.
Gehry, Frank 557
Gibraltar 275–278
Gijón 573
Girona 456–462
GLBT travelers 47
Golden Age (*Siglo de Oro*) 74, 201
  painting 73
  Sevilla 240
González, Felipe 68
Goya, Francisco 73, 78, 85, 110, 117, 123, 135, 138, 156, 287, 296, 514, 517, 626
Gran Canaria 634–640
Granada 300–311
Gregorian chant 185
Gris, Juan 362
Guadalupe 211
Guadix 311
Guanche history 643
Guarda 799
Guernica (Gernika) 74, 124, 559, 560
guesthouses 40
Guimarães 781

H

Haro 524
health 18–21
  AIDS 20
  dehydration 19
  diarrhea 20
  environmental hazards 19
  food- and water-borne diseases 20
  heat exhaustion 19
  hepatitis B 20
  hypothermia 20
  immunizations 18
  in Portugal 674
  in Spain 82
  insect-borne diseases 20
  insurance 18
  STDs 20
  sunburn 19
  women's health 21
Hecho 494
helicopter rides 490
Hemingway, Ernest 78, 113, 121, 363, 503, 526, 530
Hendaye 553
Henriques, Afonso 662, 699, 756, 781
Herrera, Juan de 114, 116, 142, 147, 178
hiking
  Alcúdia 367
  Andorra 490
  Arenas de Cabrales 583

Camprodon 474
Cangas de Onís 581
Castillo de Loarre 493
Cercedilla 148
El Teide 647
equipment 45
Garajonay 660
Jaca 492
L'Albufera 329
Las Alpujarras 312
Menorca 378, 379
Monte Jaizkibel 553
Montserrat 432
Núria 476
Ochagavía 504
Parc Nacional d'Aigüestortes 480
Parque Nacional de Ordesa 497
Parque Nacional de Timanfaya 654
Parque Natural da Serra da Estrela 801
Parque Natural de Alvão 809
Parque Natural de Montesinho 805
Parque Natural de Peneda-Gerês 782
Peniche 753
Picos de Europa 572, 583
Puerto de Navacerrada 149
Puigcerdà 476
Sierra de Guadarrama 147
Tossa de Mar 450
Valle de Ansó 495
Valle de Benasque 501, 502
Valle de Hecho 494
Valle de Roncal 505
Zamora 170
Zuriza 496
history
  of Portugal 662
  of Spain 63
hitchhiking 33
  in Portugal 674
  in Spain 81
holidays, national
  Portugal 671
  Spain 77
Holy Grail 493
home exchange 40
Hondarribia 551
hostels 39
  Hostelling International (HI) 39
  in Portugal 675
  in Spain 83
hotels 40
Huelva 256

I

Ibiza 380–389
Ibiza City. See Eivissa.

identification 11
Ilhas Berlengas 753
immigration issues 54
immunizations 18
Inquisition 66, 160, 252, 600
insurance 18, 32
International Driving Permit (IDP) 32
Internet 36
  in Portugal 676
  in Spain 84
Iruña. See Pamplona.
Irving, Washington 77, 306, 308
Isaba 505
Isla Tabarca 341
Islas Cíes (Illas Cíes) 615
Iso 535
Itálica 243
itineraries, suggested 5–7

J

Jaca 491
Jaén 315
jai alai 66, 77
Játiva (Xàtiva) 329
Jávea 347
Javier 535
Jerez de la Frontera 257–262
jerez. See sherry.
Jews 66, 198, 234, 308, 398, 413, 425, 456, 460, 518, 666, 731, 767, 802
  synagogues 50, 197, 198, 252
João I 664, 693, 714
Juan Carlos I 67
Juana la Loca 66, 180, 310

K

keeping in touch 34–39
  from Portugal 675
  from Spain 84
Knights Templar 193, 664, 764
kosher 50

L

L'Ainsa. See Aínsa.
La Coruña (A Coruña) 622–627
La Giralda 233
La Gomera 657–661
La Granja de San Ildefonso 156
La Guardia (A Guarda) 616
La Isla Graciosa 655
La Manga del Mar Menor 352
La Movida 85, 130
La Orotava 648
La Rioja 521–525
La Seu d'Urgell 485

La Toja (A Toxa) 621
Lagos 719–725
Lagos de Enol y Ercina 588
language schools 57
languages
  Aranese 484
  Basque (*euskera*) 69
  Catalan (*català*) 69, 435
  Galician (*gallego*) 69, 601
  in Portugal 666
  in Spain 69
  Silbo 659
La Lanzada 622
Lanzarote 653–657
Las Alpujarras 312–315
Las Islas Baleares 355–389
  Formentera 389
  Ibiza 380
  Mallorca 357
  Menorca 371
Las Islas Canarias 630–661
  Fuerteventura 649
  Gran Canaria 634
  La Gomera 657
  Lanzarote 653
  Tenerife 640
Las Palmas de Gran Canaria
  634–638
Leiria 758–760
León 170–174
Lérida (Lleida) 467–470
Lisboa 677–718
  accommodations 684
  Alfama 699
  Bairro Alto 693
  Baixa 690
  Belém 704
  daytrips 705
  entertainment 687
  food 686
  Graça 702
  intercity transportation 680
  local transportation 682
  nightlife 687
  orientation 682
  Parque das Nações 703
  practical information 683
  São Sebastião 699
  shopping 696
Lista de Correos 34
literature
  in Portugal 669
  in Spain 74
Llafranc 455
Llanes 577
Lleida. See Lérida.
Lloret de Mar 452
Logroño 521–524
López García, Antonio 74
Lorca 351

Los Cotos 149
Los Cristianos 644
Louro 611
Lumbier Gorges 535
Luna, Bigas 76
Lusitania 213
Luso 793

M

Machado, Antonio 74, 126,
  155, 190, 317
Madinat Al-Zahra 255
Madrid
  Lavapiés 118
Madrid 85–149
  accommodations 100
  Argüelles and Moncloa 133
  Bilbao 136
  daytrips 141
  El Centro 111
  El Rastro 109
  entertainment 105
  festivals 110
  food 101
  Gran Vía 127
  Huertas 119
  intercity transportation 85
  local transportation 94
  Malasaña and Chueca 129
  museums 122
  nightlife 109
  practical information 96
  shopping 108
  sights 105
  The Paseos 138
Mafra 708
Mahón (Maó) 371–376
mail. See keeping in touch.
Málaga 279–283
Mallorca 357–370
Manuel I 664, 714
Marbella 284–288
Marín 620
Marquês de Pombal 664, 677,
  693
Marvão 740
Maspalomas 638
media
  in Portugal 670
  in Spain 76
Medina del Campo 179
Las Meninas 73, 123
Menorca 371–380
Mérida 213–217
La Mezquita 251
minority travelers 50
Miranda do Douro 806
Miró, Joan 74, 124, 141, 287,
  361, 362, 411, 426, 565
Modernisme 435

Mojácar 290–293
Monasterio de San Juan de la
  Peña 493
Moneo, Rafael 73, 140
money 12
  in Portugal 674
  in Spain 81
Montserrat 432
mopeds 33
Morella 330, 332
Morocco
  Ceuta (Sebta) 818
  essentials 817
  Tangier 818
Morro Jable 652
mosques. See Muslims.
Mosteiro de Tibães 781
motorcycles 33
Mozárabes 245
Mudéjares 245
Mulhacén 314
Murcia 349
Murillo, Bartoloméo 73, 117,
  124, 233, 234, 236
Muros 611
museums
  Artium 565
  Casa de Colón 637
  Casa Lis Museo Art Nouveau y Art
    Deco 166
  Casa Museo de Unamuno 166
  Casa Museo del Greco 198
  Casa-Museo de Antonio Machado
    155
  Casa-Museu Salvador Dalí 467
  Es Baluard 361
  Fundació Miró 426
  Guernica Peace Museum 561
  Museo Canario 637
  Museo Chillida-Leku 549
  Museo de Arte Abstracto Español
    205
  Museo de Chocolate 175
  Museo de la Tortura y de la
    Inquisición 600
  Museo de Semana Santa 170
  Museo del Prado 122
  Museo Domus 626
  Museo Guggenheim Bilbao 557
  Museo Internacional de Arte
    Contemporáneo 656
  Museo Nacional Centro de Arte
    Reina Sofía 124
  Museo Nacional de Arte Romano
    216
  Museo Nacional del Teatro 201
  Museo Pablo Gargallo 515
  Museo Picasso (Málaga) 282
  Museo Provincial de Bellas Artes
    (Sevilla) 236
  Museo Sefardí 198
  Museo Sorolla 137

Museo Taurino 296
Museo y Centro Didáctico del Encaje 180
Museo-Monasterio de la Huelgas Reales 184
Museu d'Història de la Ciutat 413
Museu da Vinha e do Vinho 757
Museu de Aveiro 798
Museu de l'Eròtica 412
Museu del Fútbol Club Barcelona 431
Museu Picasso 416
Teatre-Museu Dalí 464
Thyssen-Bornemisza Museum 125
music
  in Portugal 670
  in Spain 75
Muslims 66, 193, 198, 202, 245, 300, 301, 309, 517, 518, 520, 662, 666, 714
  mosques 72, 116, 194, 219, 233, 251, 261, 278, 309, 310, 398
  racism 50

N

Napoleon 73, 531, 664
national parks 44
  Aigüestortes (Catalunya) 478
  Alvão (Trás-Os-Montes) 809
  Arrábida (Lisboa) 717
  Corralejo y Lobos (Fuerteventura) 651
  Coto de Doñana (Andalucía) 262, 263
  El Teide (Tenerife) 647
  Garajonay (La Gomera) 660
  L'Albufera (Valencia) 329
  Monasterio de Piedra (Aragón) 517
  Montesinho (Trás-Os-Montes) 805
  Ordesa (Aragón) 497
  Peneda-Gerês (Douro and Minho) 782
  Picos de Europa (Asturias and Cantabria) 583
  Ria Formosa (Algarve) 731
  s'Albufera des Grau (Mallorca) 367
  São Mamede (Alentejo) 740
  Serra da Estrela (Trás-Os-Montes) 801
  Timanfaya (Lanzarote) 654
Navarra (Navarre) 525–542
Navarran Pyrenees 502–506
Nazaré 753–756
The North 768–809
Numancia 192

O

O Castro de Baroña 610
Óbidos 749
Ochagavía 504
Olhão 732
Olite 537
Orgullo Gay 110
Os Lusíadas 669, 793
Osuna 242
Otsagabia. See Ochagavía.
outdoors 43
Ovar 799
Oviedo 568–572

P

painting
  in Portugal 669
  in Spain 73
País Vasco (Euskadi) 543–565
Palafrugell 453–455
Palencia 186–188
Palma 357–364
Pampaneira 313
Pamplona (Iruña) 526–535
Parc Nacional d'Aigüestortes 478
Parque del Monasterio de Piedra 517
Parque Natural da Peneda-Gerês 782
Pas de la Casa 487
passports 9
Pedro the Cruel 237, 756
Peniche 750–753
pensiones 40
Pessoa, Fernando 670
phone cards 35
phones 35
Picasso, Pablo 73, 411, 437, 561
  Guernica 74, 124, 559
Picos de Europa 583–591
Pizarro, Francisco 193, 211, 213
planes. See flights.
Playa Blanca 655
Playa de las Américas 644
political activism 55
Poncebos 589
Pontevedra 617–620
Popular Front 67
Poqueira Gorge 313
Port d'Alcúdia 366
Port de Pollença 369
Port de Sóller 366
Port Lligat 465
port lodges 772

Port Pollença 367
Porto (Oporto) 769–776
Portugal 662–676
  accommodations 674
  architecture 668
  current events 666
  customs and etiquette 668
  essentials 672
  food and drink 667
  history 662
  keeping in touch 675
  language 666
  literature 669
  media 670
  music 670
  painting and sculpture 669
  religion 666
  sports 671
  tipping and bargaining 674
  transportation 672
post. See keeping in touch.
Posta Restante 34
Potes 590
Prado, Museo del 122
Praia da Rocha 725
Praia de Figueirinha 718
Primo de Rivera, General Miguel 166
Primo de Rivera, José Antonio 143
Prince Felipe 114
Prince Henry the Navigator 664, 705, 726, 761
Puerto de la Cruz 645
Puerto de Navacerrada 149
Puerto del Carmen 653
Puerto del Rosario 649
Puigcerdà 476
The Pyrenees 471–506

Q

Queluz 707
Quevedo, Francisco de 121, 144, 240

R

railpasses 25
Real Academía de Bellas Artes de San Fernando 117
Real Madrid 76, 107, 141
Red Cross 19
religion
  in Portugal 666
  in Spain 69
Reus 445
Revolution of the Carnations 665
Rías Altas 622–629
Rías Bajas 611–622

Ribadeo 628
Ribadesella 575
Ribatejo and Estremadura 745–767
Ribera, José de 233, 239
Ripoll 471
Rock of Gibraltar 278
Roman ruins 72
  Arcos de la Frontera 265
  Carmona 244
  Cartagena 353
  Ciudad Rodrigo 168
  Conímbriga 793
  Évora 734
  Itálica 243
  Mérida 216
  Numancia 192
  Port de Alcúdia 367
  Segovia 154
  Tarragona 442
  Tossa de Mar 451
  Trujillo 212
Roncal 505
Roncesvalles 502
Ronda 293–297
running of the bulls. See San Fermín. 532

S

Sa Calobra 366
safety
  in Portugal 674
  in Spain 81
Sagres 725
Sagunto (Sagunt) 329
Salamanca 160–168
Salazar, António de Oliveira 665, 752, 776
Salou 444
Sampaio, Jorge 665
San Antonio de Portmany (Sant Antoni) 387
San Fermín 532
San Lorenzo de El Escorial 73, 141
San Sebastián (Donostia) 544–551
San Sebastián de la Gomera 657–660
Sangüesa 536
Sanlúcar de Barrameda 262
Sant Antoni. See San Antonio de Portmany.
Sant Joan de les Abadesses 474
Santa Cruz de Tenerife 640–644
Santander 592–598
Santarém 746–749
Santiago de Compostela 602–

608
Santillana del Mar 600
Santiponce 243
Santo Domingo de Silos 185
São Martinho do Porto 757
Saramago, José 670, 672
scenic drives 368
scuba diving
  Corralejo 651
  Los Cristianos 645
  Morro Jable 653
  Playa Blanca 655
  Playa de Las Canteras 638
  Playa del Inglés 638
  Puerto del Carmen 653
  Tarifa 272
  Tossa de Mar 451
  Valle Gran Rey 661
Segovia 150–155
self defense 17
Semana Santa 1, 230, 271
Sert, Josep Lluís 73, 361, 426
Sesimbra 709
Setúbal 715–717
Sevilla 221–244
  accommodations 226
  daytrips 242
  El Arenal and Triana 240
  El Centro 235
  entertainment 228
  festivals 230
  food 227
  intercity transportation 221
  La Macarena 238
  local transportation 225
  nightlife 228
  Outer Neighborhoods 241
  practical information 225
  Santa Cruz 230
  shopping 236
  sights 227
sherry 71
  Jerez de la Frontera 260
  Sanlúcar de Barrameda 262
  sherry triangle 262
  types 260
sidra 70, 71, 571, 574
Sierra de Guadarrama 147, 147–149
Sierra de Peña Sagra 590
Sierra de Torcal 300
Sierra de Tramontana 357
Sigüenza 206
Sines 743
Sintra 710–714
Sitges 435–439
skiing
  Andorra 490
  Baqueira-Beret 482
  Camprodon 474
  Isaba 505

Ochagavía 504
Parque Natural da Serra da Estrela 802
Puigcerdà 478
Sierra de Guadarrama 147
Soares, Mario 665
soccer
  Barcelona 404
  in Portugal 671
  in Spain 76
  Lisboa 688
  Madrid 107
  Sevilla 229
social welfare 55
Sóller 366
solo travelers 47
Soria 188–192
Spain 63–84
  accommodations 83
  architecture 72
  current events 68
  customs and etiquette 71
  essentials 78
  film 75
  food and drink 69
  history 63
  keeping in touch 84
  language 69
  literature 74
  media 76
  music 75
  painting 73
  religion 69
  sports 76
  tipping and bargaining 81
  transportation 79
Spanish Civil War 67, 514, 525, 544, 567, 640
Spanish-American War 67, 74
specific concerns
  dietary concerns 50
  disabled travelers 49
  GLBT travelers 47
  minority travelers 50
  solo travel 47
  sustainable travel 46
  women travelers 47
sports
  in Portugal 671
  in Spain 76
STA Travel 22
standby flights 24
study abroad 55–59
  American programs 56
  foreign programs 57
  language schools 57
  other 58
  universities 56
surfing
  Cedeira 629
  El Cotillo 650

INDEX

Ericeira 708
Lagos 724
Lanzarote 650
Maspalomas 638
San Sebastián 551
Santander 598
Viana do Castelo 786
Surrealism 74
sustainable travel 46
synagogues. See Jews.

T

Tangier 818
tapas 103
Tápies, Antonio 74, 205, 362, 424
Tarazona 517
Tarifa 271–273
Tarragona 440–444
taxes 14
teaching English 60
telephones 35
in Portugal 676
in Spain 84
Tenerife 640–648
Teror 639
terrorism 16
al-Qaeda 16, 82
ETA (Basque) 16, 82, 544
March 11 attacks 16, 82
Teruel 518–521
theme parks 444
The Three Beiras 787–802
time differences 810
tipping 14
in Portugal 674
in Spain 81
Toledo 194–199
Tomar 764–767
Tordesillas 180
Torremolinos 283
Tossa de Mar 448–452
trains 25–29
in Portugal 673
in Spain 79
transportation
bicycles 33
boats 30
cars 31
in Portugal 672
in Spain 79
mopeds 33
motorcycles 33
trains 25
Trás-Os-Montes 802–809
travel agencies 22
traveler's checks 12
Tresviso 590
Trevélez 314
Trujillo 211–213

Tudela 534
tunas 167, 606
Túy (Tui) 616

U

Unamuno, Miguel de 74, 165, 166, 559
universities 56
Urdón 590
US State Department 14

V

vaccinations 18
Val d'Aran 482
Valdoviño 628
Valença do Minho 787
Valencia 320–328
Valencia and Murcia 319–354
Valladolid 175–179
Valldemossa 364, 368
Valle de Ansó 495
Valle de Benasque 501
Valle de Hecho 494
Valle de los Caídos 143
Valle de Núria 475
Valle de Roncal 505
Valle Gran Rey 660
Valls 448
Vega, Lope de 144, 201, 240
vegetarian travelers 50, 219
Vejer de la Frontera 270–271
Velázquez, Diego 66, 73, 117, 123, 168, 326
Viana do Castelo 784–787
Vielha 483
Vigo 611–614
Vila Real 807
Vilanova i la Geltrù 439
Visa 13
visas 10
student 56
work 10, 59
Vitoria-Gasteiz 562–565
Viveiro 627
volunteering 53–55
environmental conservation 54
immigration issues 54
political activism 55
social welfare 55

W

War of the Spanish Succession 66, 116, 434
water parks 444
Western Union 13
wilderness 45
windsurfing

Corralejo 651
El Cotillo 650
Manga del Mar Menor 352
Morro Jable 653
Playa de las Américas 644
Sagres 726
Tossa de Mar 451
wine routes
Cambados 621
Oviedo 572
Zaragoza 517
wines
Albariño 610
in Portugal 668
in Spain 71
port 772
Rioja 521
sangria 71
women travelers 47
women's health 21
work permits 10, 59
working abroad 59–61
au pair 61
long-term 59
short-term 61
teaching English 60

X

Xàbia. See Jávea.
Xàtiva. See Játiva.

Y

youth hostels. See hostels.

Z

Zamora 169
Zaragoza 508–516
zarzuela 106
zoos
Casa del Campo 135
Jardines del Real 327
La Grandera 581
La Magdalena 597
Los Cabos 597
Parc Zoològic 416
Zurbarán, Francisco de 73, 115, 117, 124, 236
Zuriza 496

LONG ON WEEKEND. SHORT ON CASH.

The fastest way to the best fare.

AND GO!™

MAP INDEX

A Coruña 623
Alfama 700
Algarve and Alentejo 720
Alhambra, The 307
Alicante 335
Andalucía 246
Andorra La Vella 488
Aragón, La Rioja, and
  Navarra 507
Asturias and Cantabria 567
Ávila 157
Bairro Alto 694
Baixa 691
Barcelona 392-393
Bilbao 554
Braga 777
Burgos 182
Cáceres 208
Cádiz 266
Castilla La Mancha and
  Extremadura 193
Castilla y León 151
Catalunya 434
Ciutat Vella 394-395
Coimbra 789
Comunidad de Madrid 145
Córdoba 248

Cuenca 203
Eivissa (Ibiza) 382
Évora 735
Galicia 601
Gibraltar 277
Girona 458
Granada 302
Islas Baleares 355
Islas Canarias 631
Jerez 258
Lagos 723
Las Palmas 635
León 171
Lisboa 678-679
Lisboa and Vicinity 680
Lisboa Metro 683
La Macarena 238
Madrid 88-89
Madrid Overview 86-87
Mahón 372
Málaga 280
Marbella 285
Mérida 214
Northern Portugal 768
Oviedo 569
País Vasco 543
Palma 358

Pamplona 527
Picos de Europa 585
Porto 771
Portugal 663
Pyrenees, The 472
Ribatejo and Estremadu
  745
Salamanca 162
San Sebastián 546
Santa Cruz 231
Santander 592
Santarém 747
Santiago de Compostel
  603
Segovia 153
Sevilla 222-223
Sintra and Vila 711
Spain 64-65
Spain and Portugal Cha
  ters x-xi
Spain and Portugal
  Transportation xii-xiii
Toledo 195
Valencia 321
Valencia and Murcia 31
Valencia Metro 323
Vitoria-Gasteiz 563
Zaragoza 510

MAP LEGEND

■ Point of Interest	✈ Airport	⚑ Convent/Monastery	🎿 Ski Area
🏠 Accommodation	⌂ Arch/Gate	⚓ Ferry Landing	℞ Pharmacy
▲ Camping	$ Bank	N-I Highway Sign	Police
Food	☂ Beach	✚ Hospital	Post Office
Shopping	Bus Station/Stop	Internet Café	Synagogue
🏛 Museum	Castle	Library/Bookstore	Theater
● Sight	Church	M Metro Station	ℹ Tourist Office
★ Nightlife	Consulate/Embassy	Mountain	Train Station
Park	Water	Beach	Pedestrian Zone / Stairs	The Let's Go compass always points NORTH.